Cases and Materials on
Employment Law

Tenth edition

Richard W. Painter

LLB (Hons.), MA (Industrial Relations: Warwick), FHEA

*Emeritus Professor of Law, Staffordshire University and Senior Teaching Fellow in
Employment Law, Keele Management School, Keele University, Staffordshire*

Ann E. M. Holmes

BA, M.Phil, Pg.D (Occupational Health and Safety), FRSA, FHEA

*Emeritus Professor of Law, formerly Deputy Vice-Chancellor, University of
Wolverhampton*

OXFORD
UNIVERSITY PRESS

OXFORD
UNIVERSITY PRESS

Great Clarendon Street, Oxford, OX2 6DP,
United Kingdom

Oxford University Press is a department of the University of Oxford.
It furthers the University's objective of excellence in research, scholarship,
and education by publishing worldwide. Oxford is a registered trade mark of
Oxford University Press in the UK and in certain other countries

Seventh Edition published 2008
Eighth Edition published 2010
Ninth Edition published 2012
Impression: 1

Public sector information reproduced under Open Government Licence v2.0
(http://www.nationalarchives.gov.uk/doc/open-government-licence/
open-government-licence.htm)

Published in the United States of America by Oxford University Press
198 Madison Avenue, New York, NY 10016, United States of America

British Library Cataloguing in Publication Data
Data available

Library of Congress Control Number: 2015936022

ISBN 978-0-19-967909-6

Printed in Great Britain by
Ashford Colour Press Ltd, Gosport, Hampshire

PREFACE

The need for a 10th edition of this collection of cases and materials, 19 years after the publication of the first edition, is yet a further illustration of the dynamic and controversial nature of employment law. Such is the constantly changing content of the subject matter, we have now determined to maintain a website—the Online Resource Centre (ORC)—in order to provide an online update service for the reader. Two additional chapters on Health and Safety and Family Rights are also to be found on the ORC.

The 10th edition will fully update the reader in relation to developments in both European and domestic legislation and case law. The significant changes introduced by the Enterprise and Regulatory Reform Act 2013, the Growth and Infrastructure Act 2013, and the Small Business, Enterprise and Employment Act 2015 are fully documented and discussed. In relation to the latest developments in case law, these include a trio of important Supreme Court judgments relating to termination and breach of contract (*Société Générale (London Branch)* v *Geys* (2012); *Edwards v Chesterfield Royal Hospital NHS Trust* (2012); *Chhabra v W. London Mental Health NHS Trust* (2014)). In addition, two highly significant and well-publicised decisions of the Court of Justice of the European Union in the areas of holiday pay (*Lock v British Gas Trading Ltd* (2013)) and disability discrimination and obesity (*Kaltoft v Kommunernes Landsforening* (2014)) are highlighted. In the area of human rights, the judgment of the European Court of Human Rights in *Eweida v UK* (2013) has important implications for the law relating to indirect discrimination on the grounds of religious belief.

The new edition contains the most recent statistics on trade union membership; levels of industrial action; the work of ACAS; and employment tribunal claims. With regard to the latter, the impact of the recent introduction of tribunal fees is analysed.

As with the first edition, our intention has been to provide students with a 'laptop labour law library': a collection of statutory and case law extracts linked by questions and commentary. We have attempted to state the law as at 1 April 2015.

We would like to thank our editor at OUP, Felicity Boughton, for her patience, support, and encouragement.

This new edition is again dedicated to our children—Adam, Daniel, and James—as well as Port Vale and West Bromwich Albion football clubs. A final dedication must go to Ann's mum (now deceased) and dad, aged 96, who acted as 'child minders' throughout the early editions of the text.

Richard W. Painter
Ann E. M. Holmes
Eccleshall, Staffordshire
April 2015

ACKNOWLEDGEMENTS

The authors and publishers would like to thank the following for permission to reproduce copyright material:

Employment Tribunal Service

The Controller of Her Majesty's Stationery Office

Extracts from *The Law Reports, The Weekly Law Reports* and *The Industrial Cases Reports* are reproduced with the permission of the Incorporated Council of Law Reporting for England and Wales.

Extracts from the *All England Reports* are reproduced with the permission of Butterworths Tolley.

Extracts from the *Industrial Relations Law Reports* are reproduced with the permission of Butterworths Tolley.

ABBREVIATIONS

ACAS	Advisory, Conciliation and Arbitration Service
ASHE	Annual Survey of Hours and Earnings
CA	Court of Appeal
CAB	Citizens Advice Bureau
CAC	Central Arbitration Committee
CBI	Confederation of British Industry
CEEP	European Centre of Enterprises with Public Participation
CEHR	Commission for Equality and Human Rights
CIPD	Chartered Institute of Personnel and Development
CJEU	Court of Justice of the European Union
CO	Certification Officer
CPAUIA	Commissioner for the Protection Against Unlawful Industrial Action
CPI	Consumer Price Index
CRE	Commission for Racial Equality
CRTUM	Commissioner for the Rights of Trade Union Members
DDA	Disability Discrimination Act
DDP	Dismissal and Disciplinary Procedures
DEFRA	Department for Environment, Food & Rural Affairs
DRA	Default Retirement Age
DRC	Disability Rights Commission
DTI	Department of Trade and Industry
EA	Employment Acts (1980–2002)
EAT	Employment Appeal Tribunal
EC	Early Conciliation
ECHR	European Convention on Human Rights
ECJ	European Court of Justice
ECtHR	European Court of Human Rights
EDT	Effective Date of Termination
EFTA Court	Court of Justice of the European Free Trade Association States
EHRC	Equality and Human Rights Commission
EOC	Equal Opportunities Commission
EPA	Equal Pay Act 1970
EPCA	Employment Protection (Consolidation) Act 1978
EqA	Equality Act 2010
ERA	Employment Rights Act
ERRA 2013	Enterprise and Regulatory Reform Act 2013
ET	Employment Tribunal
ETA	Employment Tribunals Act
ETO	Economic, Technical, or Organisational
ETUC	European Trade Union Confederation
EWC	European Works Council
FfW	Fit for Work
GOQ	Genuine Occupational Qualification
GOR	Genuine Occupational Requirement
HASAWA	Health and Safety at Work etc. Act 1974
HL	House of Lords
HR	Human Resources

HRA	Human Rights Act 1998
HSE	Health and Safety Executive
ICFTD	In Contemplation and Furtherance of a Trade Dispute
IJDL	International Journal of Discrimination Law
ILJ	Industrial Law Journal
ILO	International Labour Organization
IRLB	Industrial Relations Law Bulletin
IT	Industrial Tribunal
MoD	Ministry of Defence
MPLR	Maternity and Parental Leave Regulations 1999
NICA	Northern Ireland Court of Appeal
NIRC	National Industrial Relations Court
NMW	national minimum wage
NMWA	National Minimum Wage Act 1988
NMWR	National Minimum Wage Regulations 1999
ONS	Office for National Statistics
PAL	Paternity and Adoption Leave Regulations 2002
PCP	Provision, Criterion, or Practice
PILON	Payment in Lieu of Notice
PRP	Pay Reference Period
QMV	Qualified Majority Voting
RPI	Retail Price Index
RRA	Race Relations Act 1976 (as amended)
SDA	Sex Discrimination Act 1975 (as amended)
SPA	Social Policy Agreement
SPP	Social Policy Protocol
TFEU	Treaty on the Functioning of European Union
TUC	Trades Union Congress
TULRA	Trade Union and Labour Relations Act 1974
TULR(C)A	Trade Union and Labour Relations (Consolidation) Act 1992
TUPE	Transfer of Undertakings (Protection of Employment) Regulations 2006
TURERA	Trade Union Reform and Employment Rights Act 1993
UN	United Nations
UNICE	Union of Industrial and Employers' Confederations of Europe
WFA	Work and Families Act 2006
WTD	Working Time Directive
WTR	Working Time Regulations
ZHC	'Zero Hours' Contract

OUTLINE CONTENTS

DETAILED CONTENTS

10   Trade Unions and their Members   559

11   Industrial Conflict (1)   629

TABLE OF CASES

Case names and page numbers in bold indicate verbatim quotations from case reports.

TABLE OF STATUTES

Page references in bold indicate that the section is reproduced in full.

TABLE OF SECONDARY LEGISLATION

Page references in bold indicate that the provision is reproduced in the text.

TABLE OF TREATIES AND CONVENTIONS

Page references in bold indicate that the Article is reproduced in full.

1

Introduction to Employment Law

A: The traditional approach

O. Kahn Freund, in Flanders and Clegg (eds.), *The System of Industrial Relations in Great Britain*
(Oxford: Blackwell, 1954), p. 44

There exists something like an inverse correlation between the practical significance of legal sanctions and the degree to which industrial relations have reached a state of maturity. The legal aspect of those obligations on which labour-management relations rests is, from a practical point of view, least developed where industrial relations are developed most satisfactorily. There is, perhaps, no major country in the world in which the law has played a less significant role in the shaping of these relations than in Great Britain and in which today the law and the legal profession have less to do with labour relations. In the writer's opinion this is an indication that these relations are fundamentally healthy.

NOTE: This description of the State's traditional approach to the conduct of British industrial relations, known variously as legal abstentionism, voluntarism, or collective *laissez-faire*, was by the 1970s in need of considerable modification. The droplets of legal intervention discernible in the 1960s assumed torrential proportions during the following decade.

The Labour Government of 1974–9, as part of the 'Social Contract' between the Government and the Trades Union Congress (TUC), enacted a 'statutory floor' of employment rights, originally brought together by the Employment Protection (Consolidation) Act 1978, and now contained in the Employment Rights Act (ERA) 1996; legislation on sex and race discrimination (Sex Discrimination Act (SDA) 1975; Equal Pay Act (EPA) 1970; Race Relations Act (RRA) 1976); and a statutory regime regulating occupational safety (Health and Safety at Work etc. Act 1974).

While the enactment of a range of minimum individual employment rights was perceived as a way of protecting those workers not covered by collective bargaining, the Labour Administration still retained the traditional policy of legal abstentionism in relation to collective labour law. Collective bargaining was perceived to be the best way of conducting labour relations and the 'Social Contract' legislation, while providing a degree of support for union organisation and collective bargaining, eschewed intervention in strikes and other forms of industrial conflict. It was felt that the dangers of departing from the traditional abstentionist model were evident from the brief currency of the Industrial Relations Act (1971–4), which was a failed attempt to introduce a comprehensive legal regulation of employment relations in line with the North American model.

B: The alternative approach

F. A. Hayek, *1980s Unemployment and the Unions*
(London: Institute of Economic Affairs, 1980), p. 58 and p. 52

There can be no salvation for Britain until the special privileges granted to the trade unions three-quarters of a century ago are revoked. Average real wages of British workers would undoubtedly be higher and their chances of finding employment better, if the wages paid in different occupations were again determined by the market, and if *all limitations* on the work an individual is allowed to do were removed . . . [The] legalised powers of the unions have become the biggest obstacle to raising the living standards of the working class as a whole . . . They are the prime source of unemployment. They are the main reason for the decline of the British economy in general.

NOTES

1. The writings of F. A. Hayek appear to have had a significant effect on the direction of Conservative Government policy post-1979. For arguments in favour of this link, see Lord Wedderburn, 'Freedom of association and philosophies of labour law' (1989) 18 ILJ 1; McCarthy, W., 'The rise and fall of collective laissez faire' in McCarthy, W. (ed.), *Legal Intervention in Industrial Relations: Gains and losses* (Oxford: Basil Blackwell, 1992), Ch. 1; and Fosh, P. et al., 'Politics, pragmatism and ideology: The "wellsprings" of Conservative Union legislation (1979–92)' (1992) 22 ILJ 14. By contrast, Simon Auerbach is critical of the thesis that the theories of the 'new right' were so influential on Government policy, arguing that the content of legislation had less to do with the ideological thinking of Hayek and others than the reaction of the Government to particular political and industrial events in the 1970s and 1980s (Auerbach, S., *Legislating for Conflict* (Oxford: Clarendon Press, 1990)). But, as Wedderburn observes, 'Hayek did not of course write the "step-by-step" programme of labour law for 1980–1988; but one would need to be juridically tone deaf not to pick up the echoes of his philosophy in recent policies and pronouncements' (*ibid.*, p. 15).

2. In radical contrast to the 1974–9 period, the legislation of the 1980s and 1990s—the Employment Acts (EA) 1980 to 1990, the Trade Union Act 1984, the Wages Act 1986, the Trade Union Reform and Employment Rights Act (TURERA) 1993—aimed to deregulate so far as employment protection and collective bargaining are concerned, but imposed major legal restrictions on trade unions.

   This legislation aimed to place major obstacles in the way of the organisation of industrial action. Strike organisers and trade unions were exposed to court orders and damages by the narrowing of the statutory immunities from judge-made liabilities. In this way, secondary industrial action, solidarity and political strikes, picketing away from the pickets' own workplaces, and official action not preceded by ballot were, in effect, made unlawful. In addition, the reduction of strikers' dependants' entitlement to supplementary benefit and the widening of the employer's freedom to sack strikers without incurring the risk of liability for unfair dismissal were put in place in order to make individual workers think twice before withdrawing their labour.

3. In addition to the civil law, the Public Order Act 1986 redefined and expanded some of the criminal law offences which were extensively used against pickets in the 1984–5 miners' dispute. (For an excellent discussion of this area see Lewis, R., 'The role of law in employment relations' in Lewis, R. (ed.), *Labour Law in Britain* (Oxford: Basil Blackwell, 1986) and Lewis, R., 'Reforming labour law: Choices and constraints' (1987) 9(4) *Employee Relations* 28–31.)

4. While the logic of the 'free market' points to the legal restriction of trade unions, it requires that most of the burdens of State intervention are lifted from employers. According to free market theory, such legal and bureaucratic controls deter employers, especially small employers, from recruiting labour. Landmarks in the deregulatory process included:

   (a) the abolition of the procedure under the Employment Protection Act 1975 and the Fair Wages resolution, measures designed to establish the 'going rate' of pay and other conditions in particular industries and fair wages in companies awarded government contracts

   (b) the removal of persons under the age of 21 from the protection of the Wages Council system, followed by abolition of the Wages Council system altogether in 1993

   (c) the repeal of the Truck Acts 1831–1940, a series of statutes which, albeit in a somewhat complicated, anachronistic, and piecemeal manner, offered groups of workers a measure of legal protection against arbitrary deductions from pay and the right to payment in cash

   (d) the removal of restrictions on working hours and conditions of women (the SDA 1986, s. 7 removed all major restrictions on women working shifts and at night, overtime restrictions, and maximum hours limitations)

   (e) the quadrupling of the qualification period for workers before they could claim unfair dismissal—from 26 weeks in 1979 to two years in 1985

   (f) a weakening of maternity rights (in particular, firms employing five or fewer employees being given complete exclusion from employees having a right to return to work after maternity leave).

5. The Conservative Administration claimed that the employment protection legislation had a negative employment effect. However, surveys of management attitudes and responses suggest that the legislation has had only a minor impact in discouraging recruitment. It has induced, however, a greater care in selection in order to ensure the right quality of recruits rather than reducing quantity (see Daniel, W. W. and Stilgoe, E., *The Impact of the Employment Protection Laws* (London: PSI, 1978); Clifton, A. and Tatton-Brown, C., *The Impact of Employment Protection on Small Firms*, Department of Employment Research Paper 7 (London: HMSO, 1979)). Later research found that only 8% of firms surveyed expressed reluctance to recruit additional staff on account of the law of unfair dismissal (Evans, S., Goodman, J., and Hargreaves, L., *Unfair Dismissal Law and Employment Practice in the 1980s*, DES Research Paper 53 (London: HMSO, 1985)). The most recent survey does no more than confirm the previous findings (Wood, D. and Smith, P., *Employers' Labour Use Strategies: First report on the 1987 survey*, Department of Employment Research Paper 63 (London: HMSO, 1989)).

6. The policy of deregulation, though significant, was subject to certain constraints or countervailing pressures.

   The curtailment of statutory rights did not prevent, and may have even encouraged, resort to alternative remedies provided by the common law. For example, recent developments have seen the courts display a greater willingness to grant injunctions in order to halt dismissals which take place in breach of a contractually incorporated disciplinary procedure, or to prevent a breach of the employer's other obligations under the contract (see *Irani* v *Southampton & SW Hampshire HA* [1985] ICR 590, discussed in Chapter 7). Other cases have seen courts upholding claims for breach of contract against employers based on terms incorporated into the contract of employment from a collective agreement (see *Rigby* v *Ferodo Ltd* [1987] IRLR 516, also discussed in Chapter 7).

   Furthermore, Conservative Governments of the 1980s and 1990s were forced, mainly on account of pressures from Europe, actually to introduce new measures such as the Transfer of Undertakings Regulations 1981, Equal Pay (Amendment) Regulations 1983, the Data Protection Act 1984, the SDA 1986, and the pregnancy and employment documentation provisions of TURERA 1993. EC membership means that UK law is subordinate to the provisions of the Treaty of Rome, the Single European Act, and the regulations and directives made under the Treaty. This conflict between the Conservative Governments' policies of deregulation and the interventionist stance adopted by the European Commission is discussed in more detail later in this chapter.

C: A conclusion on the Conservative Government's employment relations strategy (1979–1997)

P. Fosh, H. Morris, R. Martin, P. Smith, and R. Undy, 'Politics, pragmatism and ideology: The "wellsprings" of Conservative Union legislation (1979–92)'
(1993) 22 ILJ 14

The Conservatives appear to have had twin aims in their legislative activity for the reform of industrial relations and the reshaping of the labour market. These were the deregulation of the labour market (regulation of terms conditions by statute or by collective bargaining must be reduced as a 'burden on business') and individual freedom (the individual must be free to enter into those contracts which seem to him/her appropriate or necessary), often summarised as 'ideological individualism'.

There are, however, a number of apparent contradictions contained within the Conservative Government's twin aims: (i) if the individual is free, then he/she is free to form unions with others and organise them how they wish, and the operations of these unions, if efficient, can prevent the deregulation of the labour market; (ii) the massive legislative programme mounted by the Conservatives since 1979 seems as much focused on regulating unions' internal affairs as on restricting unions' activities in collective bargaining. In introducing so much legislation, the Conservatives have now *reregulated* the labour market.

■ QUESTION

Do you accept that there is a contradiction here?

D: A third way?

Foreword by the Prime Minister, *Fairness at Work*
(Cm. 3968), May 1998

This White Paper is part of the Government's programme to replace the notion of conflict between employers and employees with the promotion of partnership. It goes along with our emphasis on education and skills—not overburdensome regulation—in the labour market, as the best means of equipping business and people for a modern economy. It complements our prudent economic management and our proposals for encouraging small businesses and stimulating long-term investment.

The White Paper steers a way between the absence of minimum standards of protection at the workplace, and a return to the laws of the past. It is based on the rights of the individual, whether exercised on their own or with others, as a matter of their choice. It matches rights and responsibilities. It seeks to draw a line under the issue of industrial relations law.

There will be no going back. The days of strikes without ballots, mass picketing, closed shops and secondary action are over. Even after the changes we propose, Britain will have the most lightly regulated labour market of any leading economy in the world. But it cannot be just to deny British citizens basic canons of fairness—rights to claim unfair dismissal, rights against discrimination for making a free choice of being a union member, rights to unpaid parental leave—that are a matter of course elsewhere.

These proposals, together with the introduction of a minimum wage—set sensibly, implemented sensibly—put a very minimum infrastructure of decency and fairness around people in the workplace. They have been extensively consulted upon with business and industry. They offer the right way forward for the future.

NOTE: Following the election of the new Labour Government in May 1997, there was a flurry of legislative activity in the field of employment law. Legislation was introduced for a national minimum wage below which pay would not fall. The Government also supported Richard Shepherd's Private Member's Bill on public interest disclosure, or 'whistleblowing'. The Public Interest Disclosure Act 1998 provides protection against dismissal or victimisation for employees who responsibly raise concerns about criminal offences, failures to meet legal obligations, miscarriages of justice, health, safety, and environmental dangers, and 'cover up' of these matters. The Government also supported the Employment Rights (Dispute Resolution) Act 1998, introduced by Lord Archer of Sandwell. This Act aimed to improve and streamline the procedures of employment tribunals, encourages the use of internal procedures, and promotes a new voluntary arbitration scheme, developed by ACAS, to settle unfair dismissal claims.

However, the most significant package of reforms to employment and trade union law were outlined in the Government's White Paper, *Fairness at Work*, published in May 1998 (Cm. 3968) and developed in the light of consultation. The three main elements of the *Fairness at Work* framework are:

(a) provisions for the basic fair treatment of employees

(b) new procedures for collective representation at work

(c) policies that enhance family life while making it easier for people—both men and women—to go to work.

Fairness at Work
(Cm. 3968), May 1998

NEW RIGHTS FOR INDIVIDUALS

The government *proposes* to:

1. reduce the qualifying period for unfair dismissal claims to one year
2. abolish the maximum limit on awards for unfair dismissal
3. introduce a legislation to index-link limits on statutory awards and payments 'subject to a maximum rate'.

The government *invites views* on:

4. whether the limits on 'additional' and 'special' awards should be retained; and whether tribunals should be able to award 'aggravated' damages

5. possible options for changing the law allowing employees with fixed-term contracts to waive their right to claim unfair dismissal, and receive statutory redundancy payments

6. whether further action should be taken to address the potential abuse of 'zero hours' contracts and, if so, how to take this forward without undermining labour market flexibility

7. whether legislation is needed to extend the coverage of some or all existing employment rights by regulation to all those who work for another person.

COLLECTIVE RIGHTS

The government *proposes* to:

8. enable employees to have a trade union recognised by their employer, but only where the majority of the relevant workforce wishes it. Statutory procedures for both recognition and derecognition, where currently there are few rules (or limitations on employers), will be introduced.

9. change the law so that, in general, those dismissed for taking part in lawfully organised official action should have the right to complain to a tribunal of unfair dismissal

10. make it unlawful to discriminate by omission on grounds of trade union membership, non-membership or union-related activities

11. prohibit blacklisting of trade unionists

12. amend the law on ballots before industrial action and notice to make clear that, while the union's notice to the employer should still identify as accurately as reasonably practicable the group or category of employees concerned, it need not give names

13. create a legal right to be accompanied by a fellow employee or trade union representative of their choice during grievance and disciplinary procedures

14. abolish the Commissioner for the Rights of Trade Union Members (CRTUM) and Commissioner for the Protection Against Unlawful Industrial Action (CPAUIA), and give new powers to the Certification Officer, to hear complaints involving most aspects of the law where CRTUM is currently empowered to provide assistance

15. make funds available which would contribute to the training of managers and employee representatives in order to assist and develop partnerships at work;

and the government *invites views* on:

16. whether training should be among the matters automatically covered by an award of trade union recognition

17. how procedures for derecognition should work

18. how protection against dismissal for those taking part in lawfully organised industrial action should be implemented

19. simplifying the law, and Code of Practice, on industrial action ballots and notice.

FAMILY-FRIENDLY POLICIES

The government proposes to:

20. extend the right to maternity leave to 18 weeks and to align it with maternity pay

21. give employees rights to extended maternity leave; and parental leave, but only after one year's service

22. provide for the contract of employment to continue during the whole period of maternity or parental leave (unless it is expressly determined by either party, by dismissal, or resignation)

23. provide similar rights to employees to return to their jobs after parental leave, as apply under present arrangements after maternity absence

24. provide three months' parental leave for adoptive parents

25. provide a right to 'reasonable time off' for family emergencies, applicable to all employees regardless of length of service

26. ensure that employees are protected against dismissal (or 'detriment') if they exercise rights to parental leave and time off for 'urgent family reasons';

and invites views on:

27. simplifying notice requirements relating to maternity leave

28. its options for framing legislation to comply with the Parental Leave Directive

29. the difficulties small firms could face in complying with the Directive on parental leave.

NOTES

1. Following the publication of *Fairness at Work*, the Government consulted on a number of proposals. In some instances, the consultation process resulted in legislation not being pursued ('zero hours' contracts, for example). In others, it led to the proposals being modified. On 17 December 1998, for example, the Secretary of State for Trade and Industry announced that there would be a

limit on the compensatory award (£50,000 from the then current £12,000 rather than abolition of the limit). The Government also diluted its original proposal that a union should be automatically recognised where it had at least 50% membership within a particular bargaining unit. The revised proposal allowed the Central Arbitration Committee (CAC) to conduct a ballot in such circumstances where it was satisfied that it was 'in the interests of good industrial relations' or there was evidence that a significant number of the union members with the bargaining unit did not want the union to conduct collective bargaining on their behalf. The *Fairness at Work* package, as revised, was implemented by the Employment Relations Act 1999.

2. These legislative changes did not mean that we saw a complete return to the voluntary policies of the post-war years. In *Fairness at Work*, the Labour Government confirmed that it did not intend radically to change the highly restrictive laws governing lawful industrial action introduced by the previous Conservative Administration. Also, the Government distanced itself from a clear commitment given by its former party leader, John Smith, to give all workers basic employment rights 'on the first day of employment'.

3. A notable feature of the *Fairness at Work* legislation was that it left a substantial amount of the detail to regulations. In practical terms this meant that consultation will undoubtedly continue behind the scenes in the lead-up to specific regulations being made. By subjecting large areas of employment law to a new enabling system under which modifications can readily (and at short notice) be made by regulations (rather than keeping basic entitlements and responsibilities in primary legislation), there is obviously scope in the future for developing them further. Equally, there is increased scope for rolling back entitlements, and with the minimum of parliamentary debate and prior consultation, under such a system.

4. After the re-election of the Labour Government in 2001, the Employment Act 2002 contained two main policy thrusts: first, the extension of 'family-friendly' policies (covering longer maternity leave, paternity and adoption leave, and the right to request flexible working arrangements); second, the provision of a set of 'standard procedures' designed to resolve grievance and disciplinary procedures 'in-house' in order to take the pressure off an already overloaded employment tribunal system.

5. In the midst of this welter of employment legislation, the Government introduced the Employment Act 2008. The Act aimed to 'simplify' and 'clarify' key aspects of employment law with a view to achieving significant administrative, cost and time savings, and greater clarity for employers, trade unions, and employees.
   The main provisions in the Act included:
   • implementation of the Gibbons Review, including the repeal of the statutory dispute resolution procedures;
   • clarification and strengthening of the enforcement framework for the National Minimum Wage with penalties for non-compliant employers;
   • strengthening employment agency standards;
   • amending the law on trade union membership in the light of the ECHR judgment in *ASLEF v UK*, which held that trade unions can expel members on the basis of their membership of a political party.

6. For a critique of the Labour Government's employment relations policies, see Smith, P., 'New Labour and the commonsense of neoliberalism: Trade unionism, collective bargaining and workers' rights' (2009) 40(3) *Industrial Relations Journal* 337–55. The central argument of the paper is that Labour's policies owed much to the neoliberal approaches of its Conservative predecessors, albeit tempered to a degree by its social democratic heritage. See also Davies, P. and Freedland, M., *Towards a Flexible Labour Market: Labour legislation since the 1990s* (Oxford: OUP, 2007).

E: Plus ça change, plus c'est la même chose: a return to deregulation of the individual contractual relationship (and further restrictions on industrial action?)

The Government believes that a flexible labour market is not simply about making life easy for employers. (<http://www.bis.gov.uk/news/topstories/2011/May/employment-law-review>)

Following the election of the Coalition Government in May 2010, it produced a pro-gramme for government to be considered over the life of the 2010–15 Parliament, including the pledge to 'review employment and workplace laws, for employers and employees, to ensure they maximize flexibility for both parties while providing fair-ness and providing the competitive environment for enterprise to thrive.' As part of this programme, the Coalition committed to cutting 'red tape' by introducing a 'one-in, one-out' rule whereby no new regulation is brought in without another regulation being cut by a greater amount. In addition, the Government would impose 'sunset clauses' on regulations to ensure that they are regularly reviewed (*The Coalition: Our programme for government*, HM Government, May 2010). While light on detail, the doc-ument was undoubtedly deregulatory in tone. On the implicit review agenda were, *inter alia*, the qualifying period to claim unfair dismissal, unfair dismissal exemp-tions for small businesses, the paid annual leave entitlement under the Working Time Regulations, and the removal of service provision changes from specific protection under the Transfer of Undertakings (Protection of Employment) Regulations (both of the latter two regulations offer greater rights than is required by the respective EU directives).

The Employment Law Review—2010 to 2015
(<http://www.bis.gov.uk/policies/employment-matters/employment-law-review>)

BIS [the Department of Business Innovation and Skills] is leading a review of employment laws across Government to make it as easy as possible for businesses to take people on.

…

The Government set out in the Coalition Agreement that it will review employment and workplace laws, for employers and employees, to ensure they maximize flexibility for both parties while protecting fairness and providing the competitive environment required for enterprise to thrive.

SCOPE OF THE EMPLOYMENT LAW REVIEW
The Employment Law Review is looking at all BIS Employment Laws. In addition, all employment laws which are the policy responsibility of other government departments are within the scope of the Review.

ACHIEVEMENTS TO DATE
Since the Employment Law Review was announced, the Government has:
- Consulted on a package of reforms to the employment tribunal system, aimed at encouraging earlier resolution of disputes in the workplace and reducing the number of tribunal cases (which are costly for employers, employees and Government)—(Resolving Workplace Disputes)
- launched an Employer's Charter that reassures employers about what they can already do to deal with staff issues in the workplace (Employer's Charter)
- launched a review of the compliance and enforcement arrangements for those employment rights enforced by Government. (Review of Government's workplace rights compliance and enforcement arrangements—Terms of reference)
- Removed the Default Retirement Age, thus removing significant paperwork obligations for employers and bringing wider benefits to the economy, making it easier for older people to continue working (ending employment relationship)
- Announced the proposed abolition of the Agricultural Wages Board and Agricultural Minimum Wage
- Commissioned an independent review jointly with DWP (from David Frost and Dame Carol Black) of the system for managing sickness absence
- As part of the Growth Review, we announced:
1. a moratorium on all new domestic regulation for micro businesses (employing less than ten staff) and startups for a period of three years that began on 1st April 2011, as part of the Government's Plan for Growth, which also applies to employment law.
2. repealed the planned extension of the right to request flexible working to parents of 17 year olds (managing people)
3. decided not to bring forward the dual discrimination provision in the Equality Act (ending employment relationships)

4. decided not to extend the right to request time to train to companies with fewer than 250 staff (managing people)

The Red Tape Challenge

The Government launched The Red Tape Challenge in April 2011 and it will run for two years until 2013.

The challenge aims to look at the stock of over 21,000 statutory rules and regulations that are active in the UK today. Everyone is invited to give their views whether as an individual, as a business, or as a representative body. The priority will be to focus on regulations that we know place the biggest burdens on businesses and society. Employment is a theme in the Red Tape Challenge and we are considering comments through the employment law review.

...

We have published a discussion paper setting out the principles that are guiding our approach to the labour market framework and a number of thematic questions.

Discussion paper—Flexible, effective, fair: promoting economic growth through a strong and efficient labour market (PDF, 171 Kb).

Medium Term Plans for the Review

In May 2011, we announced new areas to be reviewed:
- Collective redundancy consultation periods
- Transfer Undertakings (Protection of Employment) Regulations (TUPE)
- Compensation for discrimination awarded by employment tribunals (all ending employment relationships)
- Paperwork simplification

NOTES

1. More radically, in October 2011, a leaked draft of a government-commissioned report by Adam Beecroft, a Conservative party donor and venture capitalist ('The Beecroft Report') proposed that the right to claim unfair dismissal should be entirely removed.

   'The rules make it difficult to prove that someone deserves to be dismissed, and demand a process for doing so which is so lengthy and complex that it is hard to implement', the leaked report reads. 'This makes it too easy for employees to claim they have been unfairly treated and to gain significant compensation.'

   The Beecroft Report also claimed that workers 'coast along' owing to the difficulty employers face because of the laws on unfair dismissal, and that a change would boost the economy. The report stated that current employment protection laws addressed yesterday's problems and that even if it meant employers could sack staff simply because they did not like them, it was a price worth paying.

   It is understood that the report recommends the introduction of a 'compensated no-fault dismissal' where employers must pay a fixed amount of compensation (akin to a redundancy payment) and notice pay when dismissing an employee, but the employee then has no right of redress.

   Although the report was commissioned by the Prime Minister and its findings were to be considered by the Government, it was believed that the measures will be unlikely to be adopted because they would be unacceptable to some ministers, especially those who are Liberal Democrats. Indeed, the Business Secretary, Vince Cable, was quoted as saying that the proposed measures were 'unnecessary, based on no evidence and unlikely to improve labour market flexibility'. Cable's aides said the proposals would do nothing to promote growth as 25 million consumers would face job insecurity and find it more difficult to get a mortgage, hitting government efforts to boost growth (see *Daily Telegraph*, 27 October 2011; *Guardian*, 27 October 2011). In March 2012, the Coalition Government launched a call for evidence, 'Dealing with dismissal and "Compensated no fault dismissal" for microbusinesses'. Part of this consultation relates to whether the concept of compensated no fault dismissal should be introduced for businesses employing fewer than ten staff.

   While none of these specific proposals saw the legislative light of day to date, a series of other changes have severely weakened the protection against unfair dismissal.

   First, the much-vaunted increase in the unfair dismissal qualification period from one to two years came into force with effect from 6 April 2012.

   Second, the Enterprise and Regulatory Reform Act 2013 (ERRA 2013) provides a power to vary the unfair dismissal compensatory award limit. As a result, with effect from 29 July 2013, the compensatory award is limited to 52 weeks' pay or the statutory cap (currently £76,574 with effect from 6 April 2014), whichever is the lower (see The Unfair Dismissal (Variation of the Limit of Compensatory Award) Order 2013, SI 2013/1949).

Third, the Growth and Infrastructure Act 2013 creates a new shareholder employment status under which an existing employee or new recruit can agree to trade certain employment rights, including unfair dismissal, for shares in the company. This represents a major inroad into the fundamental principle that employees should not be able to waive their employment protection rights.

Finally, and perhaps most significantly, the Employment Tribunals and Employment Appeal Tribunal Fees Order 2013, SI 2013/1893, with effect from 29 July 2013, introduces fees for lodging claims to an employment tribunal and the Employment Appeal Tribunal. For claims such as unfair dismissal and discrimination, there is currently an issue fee of £250 and a hearing fee of £950. Unsurprisingly, there was a 79% drop in all tribunal applications between October and December 2013 compared to the same quarter in 2012 (45,240 claims in 2012 down to 9,801 in 2013) (source: *Tribunal Quarterly Statistics October to December 2013*, MoJ, 13 March 2014). More specifically, unfair dismissal claims fell by 65% and sex discrimination claims by 77%. This prompted the Enterprise Minister, Matthew Hancock, to hail the 79% drop as demonstrating the ending of the tribunal system being 'ruthlessly exploited by people seeking to make a fast buck' ('Minister hails the 80% fall in employment tribunals', *Daily Telegraph*, 26 April 2014). Speaking at the TUC Congress on 8 September 2014, Shadow Business Secretary Chuka Umunna stated that the next Labour Government would scrap the Government's employment tribunal system and replace it with a fairer system to ensure that affordability is not a barrier to employees seeking redress in the workplace.

2. If all of the above does not find a resonance with the free market principles of the 'Thatcher years', then the 'clincher' must be the Coalition Government's veiled threats to further restrict lawful industrial action. In June 2011, in response to strikes by a number of public sector unions over pension reform, and threats of more strike action in the near future, the UK's main employers' organisation, the Confederation of British Industry (CBI), renewed its call for the tighter regulation of industrial action. Two leading government ministers indicated that the UK's Coalition Government is considering possible amendments to legislation on strikes but at present does not believe there is a 'compelling case' for change.

The CBI wants the 30-year-old strike laws to be changed. It believes at least 40% of the balloted workforce and a simple majority of those voting should support strike action before it happens.

> Workers must also be made aware of the consequences of going on strike...Ballot papers should include a clear warning that pay and other benefits can be withdrawn if an employee goes on strike. (CBI news release, 17 June 2011)

This statement finds an echo in proposals put forward by the CBI in a *Report on the legal framework of industrial relations* published in 2010. This too called for the introduction of a requirement that, to be lawful, strikes must have the support of 40% of balloted members, as well as a majority of those voting.

On 6 June 2011, in an address to the annual conference of the GMB union, Business Secretary, Vince Cable, said that UK strike levels 'remain historically low' and that the right to strike is a 'fundamental principle...On that basis, and assuming this pattern continues, the case for changing strike law is not a compelling one.' However, he emphasised that 'should the position change and should strikes impose serious damage to our economic and social fabric, the pressure on us to act will ratchet up'.

On 15 June 2011, a report in the *Guardian* quoted the Cabinet Office minister Francis Maude as saying that legislation to alter existing strike laws had 'not been ruled out'. The newspaper reported that ministers had taken part in discussions with the Mayor of London on how to change strike laws should an upsurge in industrial action threaten to disrupt the economy and future international events such as the 2012 Olympic Games (see Hall, M., 'Uncertainty over calls for further restrictions on strikes', EIROnline, 18 August 2011).

As a reaction to further public sector strikes over pay and pensions in July 2014, the Conservative Party announced that its 2015 general election manifesto would include proposed reforms to the law governing industrial action. The changes included: the requirement for a minimum 50% strike ballot threshold (of the number of eligible voting union members, in contrast to the current simple majority of those who actually vote); a three-month time limit after the ballot for the action to be conducted; curbs on picketing; and requirements for unions to provide longer notice and greater details of proposed industrial action ('Tories outline strike law manifesto pledge',

18 July 2014, <http://www.bbc.co.uk/news/uk-politics-28360636>). Such reforms may be incompatible with the right to freedom of association under Article 11 of the European Convention on Human Rights (ECHR).

In this context, it is pertinent to note that a further Conservative-proposed manifesto pledge was that rulings of the ECHR could be vetoed by the UK Parliament. If this change were to be rejected by the Council of Europe, a future Conservative Government would be prepared to withdraw from the Convention and introduce a British Bill of Rights (*Protecting Human Rights in the UK: The Conservatives' Proposals For Changing Britain's Human Rights Law*, Conservative Party, 2014).

SECTION 2: THE INSTITUTIONAL FRAMEWORK OF EMPLOYMENT LAW

A: The Advisory, Conciliation and Arbitration Service

The Advisory, Conciliation and Arbitration Service (ACAS) was established in 1974 and put on a statutory basis by the Employment Protection Act 1975. The constitution of ACAS is now to be found in the Trade Union and Labour Relations (Consolidation) Act (TULR(C)A) 1992, ss. 247–53. Its functions are set out in ss. 209–14 of the Act.

TRADE UNION AND LABOUR RELATIONS (CONSOLIDATION) ACT 1992

209. General duty to promote improvement of industrial relations

It is the general duty of ACAS to promote the improvement of industrial relations...

210. Conciliation

(1) Where a trade dispute exists or is apprehended ACAS may, at the request of one or more parties to the dispute or otherwise, offer the parties to the dispute its assistance with a view to bringing about a settlement.

(2) The assistance may be by way of conciliation or by other means, and may include the appointment of a person other than an officer or servant of ACAS to offer assistance to the parties to the dispute with a view to bringing about a settlement.

(3) In exercising its functions under this section ACAS shall have regard to the desirability of encouraging the parties to a dispute to use any appropriate agreed procedures for negotiation or the settlement of disputes.

211. Conciliation officers

(1) ACAS shall designate some of its officers to perform the functions of conciliation officers under any enactment (whenever passed) relating to matters which are or could be the subject of proceedings before an industrial tribunal.

(2) References in any such enactment to a conciliation officer are to an officer designated under this section.

212. Arbitration

(1) Where a trade dispute exists or is apprehended ACAS may, at the request of one or more of the parties to the dispute and with the consent of all the parties to the dispute, refer all or any of the matters to which the dispute relates for settlement to the arbitration of—

    (a) one or more persons appointed by ACAS for that purpose (not being officers or employees of ACAS), or

    (b) the Central Arbitration Committee.

(2) In exercising its functions under this section ACAS shall consider the likelihood of the dispute being settled by conciliation.

(3) Where there exist appropriate agreed procedures for negotiation or the settlement of disputes, ACAS shall not refer a matter for settlement to arbitration under this section unless—

    (a) those procedures have been used and have failed to result in a settlement, or

    (b) there is, in ACAS's opinion, a special reason which justifies arbitration under this section as an alternative to those procedures.

(4) Where a matter is referred to arbitration under subsection (1)(a)—

(a) if more than one arbitrator or arbiter is appointed, ACAS shall appoint one of them to act as chairman; and

(b) the award may be published if ACAS so decides and all the parties consent.

(5) Part I of the Arbitration Act 1950 (general provisions as to arbitration) does not apply to an arbitration under this section.

212A. Arbitration scheme for unfair dismissal cases etc

(1) ACAS may prepare a scheme providing for arbitration in the case of disputes involving proceedings, or claims which could be the subject of proceedings, before an employment tribunal arising out of a contravention or alleged contravention of—

(a) Part X of the Employment Rights Act 1996 (unfair dismissal), or

(b) any enactment specified in an order made by the Secretary of State.

(2) When ACAS has prepared such a scheme it shall submit a draft of the scheme to the Secretary of State who, if he approves it, shall make an order—

(a) setting out the scheme, and

(b) making provision for it to come into effect.

…

(5) Where the parties to any dispute within subsection (1) agree in writing to submit the dispute to arbitration in accordance with a scheme having effect by virtue of an order under this section, ACAS shall refer the dispute to the arbitration of a person appointed by ACAS for the purpose (not being an officer or employee of ACAS).

…

213. Advice

(1) ACAS may, on request or otherwise, give employers, employers' associations, workers and trade unions such advice as it thinks appropriate on matters concerned with or affecting or likely to affect industrial relations.

(2) ACAS may also publish general advice on matters concerned with or affecting or likely to affect industrial relations.

214. Inquiry

(1) ACAS may, if it thinks fit, inquire into any question relating to industrial relations generally or to industrial relations in any particular industry or in any particular undertaking or part of an undertaking.

(2) The findings of an inquiry under this section, together with any advice given by ACAS in connection with those findings, may be published by ACAS if—

(a) it appears to ACAS that publication is desirable for the improvement of industrial relations, either generally or in relation to the specific question inquired into, and

(b) after sending a draft of the findings to all parties appearing to be concerned and taking account of their views, it thinks fit.

NOTES

1. Prior to its amendment by TURERA 1993, s. 209 read as follows:

   It is the general duty of ACAS to promote the improvement of industrial relations, and in particular to encourage the extension of collective bargaining and the development and, where necessary, reform of collective bargaining machinery.

   This ostensibly minor change perfectly encapsulated the Conservative Government's policy of disestablishing collectivism. It is also significant that the new Labour Government did not see fit to reinstate ACAS's original duty as part of *Fairness at Work* reforms.

2. Settling complaints about employee rights (i.e. individual conciliation) is by far the biggest area of ACAS's work. In the year 2013/14, the number of cases received for conciliation was 40,938 compared to 67,825 in 2012/13. This drop is almost wholly explicable by the introduction of employment tribunal fees in July 2013.

3. Of the potential tribunal hearing days arising from all cases received for individual conciliation, 74.8% were saved, with an overall resolution rate of 67.8%.

4. The cost of an individual conciliation case settled or withdrawn was £219 in 2013/14 (£195 in 2012/13).

5. The ERRA 2013 contains provisions setting out the ACAS early conciliation (EC) system, including providing for an extension to tribunal time limits to allow for conciliation. The EC system requires most prospective claimants to contact ACAS before they can lodge tribunal proceedings. A conciliation officer will then endeavour to promote a settlement between the parties. Both

parties remain at liberty to decline EC and the claimant may proceed to lodge a claim, providing they have a certificate from ACAS confirming that settlement was not possible. EC became mandatory w.e.f. 6 May 2014. ACAS has produced a Code of Practice on Settlement Agreements (2013).

6. In the area of collective dispute resolution, ACAS received 858 requests for conciliation and was able to resolve matters or help the parties move towards a resolution in 93% of cases. The matters were headed by pay-related issues (52%), followed by recognition and changes to working practices, which accounted for 14% of cases and 12% respectively (ACAS, Annual Report and Accounts 2013/14).

B: The Central Arbitration Committee

The Central Arbitration Committee (CAC) is a permanent arbitral body which was established by the Employment Protection Act 1975 and replaced the Industrial Arbitration Board. Rules governing its composition etc are set out in TULR(C)A 1992, ss. 259–65, as amended.

Under the 1975 Act, the CAC had a wide-ranging jurisdiction which included recognition disputes, and also where it was claimed that an employer was not observing 'the going rate' established by collective bargaining for that trade or industry. Both functions were repealed by the EA 1980 as the CAC became one of the first victims of the new Conservative Government's industrial relations reforms.

Until the passage of the Employment Relations Act 1999, the only statutory functions which CAC retained were in relation to disputes over disclosure of information to recognised trade unions for the purposes of collective bargaining (TULR(C)A 1992, ss. 181–5; discussed in Chapter 10). Section 1 of and Sch. 1 to the 1999 Act confer new functions on the CAC to administer the statutory recognition and derecognition scheme and determine cases brought under it (see Chapter 10 for a detailed discussion).

C: The Certification Officer

TRADE UNION AND LABOUR RELATIONS (CONSOLIDATION) ACT 1992

254. The Certification Officer

(1) There shall continue to be an officer called the Certification Officer.

(2) The Certification Officer shall be appointed by the Secretary of State after consultation with ACAS.

...

(5) ACAS shall provide for the Certification Officer the requisite staff (from among the officers and servants of ACAS) and the requisite accommodation, equipment and other facilities.

...

258. Annual report and accounts

(1) The Certification Officer shall, as soon as reasonably practicable after the end of each calendar year, make a report of his activities during the year to ACAS and to the Secretary of State.

The Secretary of State shall lay a copy of the report before each House of Parliament and arrange for it to be published.

(2) The accounts prepared by ACAS in respect of any financial year shall show separately any sums disbursed to or on behalf of the Certification Officer in consequence of the provisions of this Part.

NOTES

1. The Certification Officer (CO) is an independent statutory officer originally appointed under the Employment Protection Act 1975. He has taken over the powers of the Chief Registrar of Friendly Societies. Although finance and staff are provided by ACAS, the CO is formally independent of the Service and of the Government.

2. Under TULR(C)A 1992, the CO must maintain a list of all organisations which fall within the statutory definition of 'trade union' and which apply for listing. In addition, the CO has the power to determine whether a trade union should be granted a certificate of independence. As we shall see in Chapter 10, achieving the status of independence has important legal implications for trade unions as it is a precondition for claiming a number of statutory rights. The decisions of the CO in respect of listing and independence are subject to appeal to the Employment Appeal Tribunal (EAT) on both law and fact.

3. The other jurisdictions of the CO include: monitoring the annual returns which unions are legally obliged to provide; hearing complaints of union members regarding the conduct of ballots to set up a political fund, to elect members of the union executive or to approve trade union amalgamations; determining whether there has been a breach of the rules relating to the operation of a union's political fund; and hearing applications from members that the union has failed to compile or maintain a register of members' names and addresses.

4. Section 29 of the Employment Relations Act 1999 gives effect to Sch. 6, which amends the statutory powers of the CO, as set out in the 1992 Act. The overall effect is to widen the scope for trade union members to make complaints to the CO of alleged breaches of trade union law or trade union rules, thereby enlarging the CO's role as an alternative to the courts as a means to resolve disputes. It achieves this by giving the CO order-making powers in areas of trade union law where previously he could only make declarations, and by extending his powers to make declarations and orders into areas where previously he had no competence to hear complaints and issue such orders.

D: The Commission for Equality and Human Rights

The Sex Discrimination Act 1975 and the Race Relations Act 1976 established two distinct commissions to work towards the elimination of discrimination within their respective areas—the Equal Opportunities Commission (EOC) and the Commission for Racial Equality (CRE). A third commission, the Disability Rights Commission, was founded in 1999.

With the extension of protection against discrimination to grounds of religion, sexual orientation, and age by the Framework Employment Directive (2000/78/EC), there was a strong case for creating a single commission to promote equality and human rights. Following a consultation, it was agreed that a single integrated body dealing with equality and human rights should be established. The enactment which brings this merger about is the Equality Act 2006.

On 1 October 2007, the three equality commissions merged into the Commission for Equality and Human Rights (CEHR).

The CEHR is established by Part 1 of the Equality Act 2006. The Commission has the responsibility for promoting equality of opportunities and awareness of good practice in relation to equality, diversity and human rights. In addition to taking over the duties and powers of the previous three commissions, the CEHR's remit also extends to equal treatment in relation to sexual orientation, religion or belief, and age.

EQUALITY ACT 2006

PART 1 THE COMMISSION FOR EQUALITY AND HUMAN RIGHTS
The Commission

3. General duty

The Commission shall exercise its functions under this Part with a view to encouraging and supporting the development of a society in which—

(a) people's ability to achieve their potential is not limited by prejudice or discrimination,

(b) there is respect for and protection of each individual's human rights,

    (c) there is respect for the dignity and worth of each individual,

    (d) each individual has an equal opportunity to participate in society, and

    (e) there is mutual respect between groups based on understanding and valuing of diversity and on shared respect for equality and human rights.

Duties

8. Equality and diversity

(1) The Commission shall, by exercising the powers conferred by this Part—

    (a) promote understanding of the importance of equality and diversity,

    (b) encourage good practice in relation to equality and diversity,

    (c) promote equality of opportunity,

    (d) promote awareness and understanding of rights under the equality enactments,

    (e) enforce the equality enactments,

    (f) work towards the elimination of unlawful discrimination, and

    (g) work towards the elimination of unlawful harassment.

(2) In subsection (1)—

'diversity' means the fact that individuals are different,

'equality' means equality between individuals, and

'unlawful' is to be construed in accordance with section 34.

(3) In promoting equality of opportunity between disabled persons and others, the Commission may, in particular, promote the favourable treatment of disabled persons.

(4) In this Part 'disabled person' means a person who—

    (a) is a disabled person within the meaning of the Disability Discrimination Act 1995 (c. 50), or

    (b) has been a disabled person within that meaning (whether or not at a time when that Act had effect).

9. Human rights

(1) The Commission shall, by exercising the powers conferred by this Part—

    (a) promote understanding of the importance of human rights,

    (b) encourage good practice in relation to human rights,

    (c) promote awareness, understanding and protection of human rights, and

    (d) encourage public authorities to comply with section 6 of the Human Rights Act 1998 (c. 42) (compliance with Convention rights).

(2) In this Part 'human rights' means—

    (a) the Convention rights within the meaning given by section 1 of the Human Rights Act 1998, and

    (b) other human rights.

(3) In determining what action to take in pursuance of this section the Commission shall have particular regard to the importance of exercising the powers conferred by this Part in relation to the Convention rights.

(4) In fulfilling a duty under section 8 or 10 the Commission shall take account of any relevant human rights.

(5) A reference in this Part (including this section) to human rights does not exclude any matter by reason only of its being a matter to which section 8 or 10 relates.

10. Groups

(1) The Commission shall, by exercising the powers conferred by this Part—

    (a) promote understanding of the importance of good relations—

        (i) between members of different groups, and

        (ii) between members of groups and others,

    (b) encourage good practice in relation to relations—

        (i) between members of different groups, and

        (ii) between members of groups and others,

    (c) work towards the elimination of prejudice against, hatred of and hostility towards members of groups, and

    (d) work towards enabling members of groups to participate in society.

(2) In this Part 'group' means a group or class of persons who share a common attribute in respect of any of the following matters—

    (a) age,

    (b) disability,

(c) gender,

(d) proposed, commenced or completed reassignment of gender (within the meaning given by section 82(1) of the Sex Discrimination Act 1975 (c. 65)),

(e) race,

(f) religion or belief, and

(g) sexual orientation.

(3) For the purposes of this Part a reference to a group (as defined in subsection (2)) includes a reference to a smaller group or smaller class, within a group, of persons who share a common attribute (in addition to the attribute by reference to which the group is defined) in respect of any of the matters specified in subsection (2)(a) to (g).

(4) In determining what action to take in pursuance of this section the Commission shall have particular regard to the importance of exercising the powers conferred by this Part in relation to groups defined by reference to race, religion or belief.

(5) The Commission may, in taking action in pursuance of subsection (1) in respect of groups defined by reference to disability and others, promote or encourage the favourable treatment of disabled persons.

(6) The [Minister] may by order amend the list in subsection (2) so as to—

(a) add an entry, or

(b) vary an entry.

(7) This section is without prejudice to the generality of section 8.

11. Monitoring the law

(1) The Commission shall monitor the effectiveness of the equality and human rights enactments.

(2) The Commission may—

(a) advise central government about the effectiveness of any of the equality and human rights enactments;

(b) recommend to central government the amendment, repeal, consolidation (with or without amendments) or replication (with or without amendments) of any of the equality and human rights enactments;

(c) advise central or devolved government about the effect of an enactment (including an enactment in or under an Act of the Scottish Parliament);

(d) advise central or devolved government about the likely effect of a proposed change of law.

(3) In this section—

(a) 'central government' means Her Majesty's Government,

(b) 'devolved government' means—

(i) the Scottish Ministers, and

(ii) the [Welsh Ministers, the First Minister for Wales and the Counsel General to the Welsh Assembly Government], and

(c) a reference to the equality enactments shall be treated as including a reference to any provision of this Act.

12. Monitoring progress

(1) The Commission shall from time to time identify—

(a) changes in society that have occurred or are expected to occur and are relevant to the aim specified in section 3,

(b) results at which to aim for the purpose of encouraging and supporting the development of the society described in section 3 ('outcomes'), and

(c) factors by reference to which progress towards those results may be measured ('indicators').

(2) In identifying outcomes and indicators the Commission shall—

(a) consult such persons having knowledge or experience relevant to the Commission's functions as the Commission thinks appropriate,

(b) consult such other persons as the Commission thinks appropriate,

(c) issue a general invitation to make representations, in a manner likely in the Commission's opinion to bring the invitation to the attention of as large a class of persons who may wish to make representations as is reasonably practicable, and

(d) take account of any representations made.

(3) The Commission shall from time to time monitor progress towards each identified outcome by reference to any relevant identified indicator.

(4) The Commission shall publish a report on progress towards the identified outcomes by reference to the identified indicators—

    (a) within the period of three years beginning with the date on which this section comes into force, and

    (b) within each period of three years beginning with the date on which a report is published under this subsection.

(5) The Commission shall send each report to the [Minister], who shall lay a copy before Parliament.

NOTE: The Commission may issue information and advice, undertake research and provide education and training (s. 13). It may also issue Codes of Practice on matters within its remit, subject to ministerial and parliamentary approval (s. 14).

16. Inquiries

(1) The Commission may conduct an inquiry into a matter relating to any of the Commission's duties under sections 8, 9 and 10.

(2) If in the course of an inquiry the Commission begins to suspect that a person may have committed an unlawful act—

    (a) in continuing the inquiry the Commission shall, so far as possible, avoid further consideration of whether or not the person has committed an unlawful act,

    (b) the Commission may commence an investigation into that question under section 20,

    (c) the Commission may use information or evidence acquired in the course of the inquiry for the purpose of the investigation, and

    (d) the Commission shall so far as possible ensure (whether by aborting or suspending the inquiry or otherwise) that any aspects of the inquiry which concern the person investigated, or may require his involvement, are not pursued while the investigation is in progress.

(3) The report of an inquiry—

    (a) may not state (whether expressly or by necessary implication) that a specified or identifiable person has committed an unlawful act, and

    (b) shall not otherwise refer to the activities of a specified or identifiable person unless the Commission thinks that the reference—

        (i)   will not harm the person, or

        (ii) is necessary in order for the report adequately to reflect the results of the inquiry.

(4) Subsections (2) and (3) shall not prevent an inquiry from considering or reporting a matter relating to human rights (whether or not a necessary implication arises in relation to the equality enactments).

(5) Before settling a report of an inquiry which records findings which in the Commission's opinion are of an adverse nature and relate (whether expressly or by necessary implication) to a specified or identifiable person the Commission shall—

    (a) send a draft of the report to the person,

    (b) specify a period of at least 28 days during which he may make written representations about the draft, and

    (c) consider any representations made.

(6) Schedule 2 makes supplemental provision about inquiries.

20. Investigations

(1) The Commission may investigate whether or not a person—

    (a) has committed an unlawful act,

    (b) has complied with a requirement imposed by an unlawful act notice under section 21, or

    (c) has complied with an undertaking given under section 23.

(2) The Commission may conduct an investigation under subsection (1)(a) only if it suspects that the person concerned may have committed an unlawful act.

(3) A suspicion for the purposes of subsection (2) may (but need not) be based on the results of, or a matter arising during the course of, an inquiry under section 16.

(4) Before settling a report of an investigation recording a finding that a person has committed an unlawful act or has failed to comply with a requirement or undertaking the Commission shall—

    (a) send a draft of the report to the person,

    (b) specify a period of at least 28 days during which he may make written representations about the draft, and

    (c) consider any representations made.

(5) Schedule 2 makes supplemental provision about investigations.

21. Unlawful act notice

(1) The Commission may give a person a notice under this section (an 'unlawful act notice') if—
   (a) he is or has been the subject of an investigation under section 20(1)(a), and
   (b) the Commission is satisfied that he has committed an unlawful act.
(2) A notice must specify—
   (a) the unlawful act, and
   (b) the provision of the equality enactments by virtue of which the act is unlawful.
(3) A notice must inform the recipient of the effect of—
   (a) subsections (5) to (7),
   (b) section 20(1)(b), and
   (c) section 24(1).
(4) A notice may—
   (a) require the person to whom the notice is given to prepare an action plan for the purpose of avoiding repetition or continuation of the unlawful act;
   (b) recommend action to be taken by the person for that purpose.
(5) A person who is given a notice may, within the period of six weeks beginning with the day on which the notice is given, appeal to the appropriate court or tribunal on the grounds—
   (a) that he has not committed the unlawful act specified in the notice, or
   (b) that a requirement for the preparation of an action plan imposed under subsection (4)(a) is unreasonable.
(6) On an appeal under subsection (5) the court or tribunal may—
   (a) affirm a notice;
   (b) annul a notice;
   (c) vary a notice;
   (d) affirm a requirement;
   (e) annul a requirement;
   (f) vary a requirement;
   (g) make an order for costs or expenses.
(7) In subsection (5) 'the appropriate court or tribunal' means—
   (a) an employment tribunal, if a claim in respect of the alleged unlawful act could be made to it, or
   (b) a county court (in England and Wales) or the sheriff (in Scotland), if a claim in respect of the alleged unlawful act could be made to it or to him.

22. Action plans

(1) This section applies where a person has been given a notice under section 21 which requires him (under section 21(4)(a)) to prepare an action plan.
(2) The notice must specify a time by which the person must give the Commission a first draft plan.
(3) After receiving a first draft plan from a person the Commission shall—
   (a) approve it, or
   (b) give the person a notice which—
      (i) states that the draft is not adequate,
      (ii) requires the person to give the Commission a revised draft by a specified time, and
      (iii) may make recommendations about the content of the revised draft.
(4) Subsection (3) shall apply in relation to a revised draft plan as it applies in relation to a first draft plan.
(5) An action plan comes into force—
   (a) if the period of six weeks beginning with the date on which a first draft or revised draft is given to the Commission expires without the Commission—
      (i) giving a notice under subsection (3)(b), or
      (ii) applying for an order under subsection (6)(b), or
   (b) upon a court's declining to make an order under subsection (6)(b) in relation to a revised draft of the plan.
(6) The Commission may apply to a county court (in England and Wales) or to the sheriff (in Scotland)—
   (a) for an order requiring a person to give the Commission a first draft plan by a time specified in the order,
   (b) for an order requiring a person who has given the Commission a revised draft plan to prepare and give to the Commission a further revised draft plan—
      (i) by a time specified in the order, and
      (ii) in accordance with any directions about the plan's content specified in the order, or

(c)   during the period of five years beginning with the date on which an action plan prepared by a person comes into force, for an order requiring the person—

(i)   to act in accordance with the action plan, or

(ii)   to take specified action for a similar purpose.

(7)   An action plan may be varied by agreement between the Commission and the person who prepared it.

(8)   Paragraphs 10 to 14 of Schedule 2 apply (but omitting references to oral evidence) in relation to consideration by the Commission of the adequacy of a draft action plan as they apply in relation to the conduct of an inquiry.

(9)   A person commits an offence if without reasonable excuse he fails to comply with an order under subsection (6); and a person guilty of an offence under this subsection shall be liable on summary conviction to a fine not exceeding level 5 on the standard scale.

23. Agreements

(1)   The Commission may enter into an agreement with a person under which—

(a)   the person undertakes—

(i)   not to commit an unlawful act of a specified kind, and

(ii)   to take, or refrain from taking, other specified action (which may include the preparation of a plan for the purpose of avoiding an unlawful act), and

(b)   the Commission undertakes not to proceed against the person under section 20 or 21 in respect of any unlawful act of the kind specified under paragraph (a)(i).

(2)   The Commission may enter into an agreement with a person under this section only if it thinks that the person has committed an unlawful act.

(3)   But a person shall not be taken to admit to the commission of an unlawful act by reason only of entering into an agreement under this section.

(4)   An agreement under this section—

(a)   may be entered into whether or not the person is or has been the subject of an investigation under section 20,

(b)   may include incidental or supplemental provision (which may include provision for termination in specified circumstances), and

(c)   may be varied or terminated by agreement of the parties.

(5)   This section shall apply in relation to the breach of a duty specified in section 34(2) as it applies in relation to the commission of an unlawful act; and for that purpose the reference in subsection (1)(b) above to section 20 or 21 shall be taken as a reference to section 32.

24. Applications to court

(1)   If the Commission thinks that a person is likely to commit an unlawful act, it may apply—

(a)   in England and Wales, to a county court for an injunction restraining the person from committing the act, or

(b)   in Scotland, to the sheriff for an interdict prohibiting the person from committing the act.

(2)   Subsection (3) applies if the Commission thinks that a party to an agreement under section 23 has failed to comply, or is likely not to comply, with an undertaking under the agreement.

(3)   The Commission may apply to a county court (in England and Wales) or to the sheriff (in Scotland) for an order requiring the person—

(a)   to comply with his undertaking, and

(b)   to take such other action as the court or the sheriff may specify.

NOTES

1. The Commission may apply for an injunction to restrain discriminatory advertising, and instructions and pressure to discriminate (s. 25).

2. The Commission may make arrangements for the provision of conciliation services in respect of proceedings which have been brought or could have been brought under the discrimination legislation (s. 27).

3. The Commission may assist an individual who is or may become party to legal proceedings if:

(a)   the proceedings relate or may relate (wholly or partly) to a provision of the equality enactments and

(b)   the individual alleges that he has been the victim of behaviour contrary to a provision of the equality enactments (s. 28).

E: Employment tribunals

EMPLOYMENT TRIBUNALS ACT 1996

PART I EMPLOYMENT TRIBUNALS

Introductory

1. Employment tribunals

(1) The Secretary of State may by regulations make provision for the establishment of tribunals to be known as employment tribunals.

(2) Regulations made wholly or partly under section 128(1) of the Employment Protection (Consolidation) Act 1978 and in force immediately before this Act comes into force shall, so far as made under that provision, continue to have effect (until revoked) as if made under subsection (1)…

Jurisdiction

2. Enactments conferring jurisdiction on employment tribunals

Employment tribunals shall exercise the jurisdiction conferred on them by or by virtue of this Act or any other Act, whether passed before or after this Act.

NOTES

1. Employment tribunals were formerly known as industrial tribunals. The change of title was made by the Employment Rights (Dispute Resolution) Act 1998, s. 1(1), with effect from 1 August 1998. According to Lord Archer of Sandwell, the bill's sponsor, the term 'employment tribunals', as opposed to 'industrial tribunals', 'conveys more clearly what the function of these tribunals is intended to be' (Hansard HL 25 July 1997, col. 1583). The 1998 Act was also renamed the Industrial Tribunals Act 1996 accordingly.

2. Employment tribunals were created in 1964 in order to resolve disputes regarding training levies on employers under the Industrial Training Act of that year. From this very limited beginning, their jurisdiction has expanded to embrace virtually every statutory employment right. Until recently, they had no jurisdiction over breach of contract claims. However, the ministerial power, now contained in the Employment Tribunals Act (ETA) 1996, s. 3, to transfer jurisdiction in order to give employment tribunals the right to determine contract claims was eventually exercised in 1994. As a result, an employee presenting an unfair dismissal claim to an employment tribunal is also able to sue under common law for arrears of wages or damages for wrongful dismissal, provided that the value of the claim is less than £25,000.

EMPLOYMENT TRIBUNALS ACT 1996

3. Power to confer further jurisdiction on employment tribunals

(1) The appropriate Minister may by order provide that proceedings in respect of—

(a) any claim to which this section applies, or

(b) any claim to which this section applies and which is of a description specified in the order,

may, subject to such exceptions (if any) as may be so specified, be brought before an employment tribunal.

(2) Subject to subsection (3), this section applies to—

(a) a claim for damages for breach of a contract of employment or other contract connected with employment,

(b) a claim for a sum due under such a contract, and

(c) a claim for the recovery of a sum in pursuance of any enactment relating to the terms or performance of such a contract,

if the claim is such that a court in England and Wales or Scotland would under the law for the time being in force have jurisdiction to hear and determine an action in respect of the claim.

(3) This section does not apply to a claim for damages, or for a sum due, in respect of personal injuries.

THE EMPLOYMENT TRIBUNALS EXTENSION OF JURISDICTION (ENGLAND AND WALES) ORDER 1994

Extension of jurisdiction

3. Proceedings may be brought before an employment tribunal in respect of a claim of an employee for the recovery of damages or any other sum (other than a claim for damages, or for a sum due, in respect of personal injuries) if—

    (a) the claim is one to which [ETA 1996, s. 3(2)] applies and which a court in England and Wales would under the law for the time being in force have jurisdiction to hear and determine;

    (b) the claim is not one to which article 5 applies; and

    (c) the claim arises or is outstanding on the termination of the employee's employment.

4. Proceedings may be brought before an employment tribunal in respect of a claim of an employer for the recovery of damages or any other sum (other than a claim for damages, or for a sum due, in respect of personal injuries) if—

    (a) the claim is one to which [ETA 1996, s. 3(2)] applies and which a court in England and Wales would under the law for the time being in force have jurisdiction to hear and determine;

    (b) the claim is not one to which article 5 applies;

    (c) the claim arises or is outstanding on the termination of the employment of the employee against whom it is made; and

    (d) proceedings in respect of a claim of that employee have been brought before an employment tribunal by virtue of this Order.

5. This article applies to a claim for breach of a contractual term of any of the following descriptions—

    (a) a term requiring the employer to provide living accommodation for the employee;

    (b) a term imposing an obligation on the employer or the employee in connection with the provision of living accommodation;

    (c) a term relating to intellectual property;

    (d) a term imposing an obligation of confidence;

    (e) a term which is a covenant in restraint of trade.

In this article, 'intellectual property' includes copyright, rights in performances, moral rights, design right, registered designs, patents and trade marks.

Manner in which proceedings may be brought

6. Proceedings on a contract claim may be brought before an employment tribunal by presenting a complaint to an employment tribunal.

Time within which proceedings may be brought

7. An employment tribunal shall not entertain a complaint in respect of an employee's contract claim unless it is presented—

    (a) within the period of three months beginning with the effective date of termination of the contract giving rise to the claim, or

    (b) where there is no effective date of termination, within the period of three months beginning with the last day upon which the employee worked in the employment which has terminated, or

    (c) where the tribunal is satisfied that it was not reasonably practicable for the complaint to be presented within whichever of those periods is applicable, within such further period as the tribunal considers reasonable.

8. An employment tribunal shall not entertain a complaint in respect of an employer's contract claim unless—

    (a) it is presented at a time when there is before the tribunal a complaint in respect of a contract claim of a particular employee which has not been settled or withdrawn;

    (b) it arises out of a contract with that employee; and

    (c) it is presented—

        (i) within the period of six weeks beginning with the day, or if more than one the last of the days, on which the employer (or other person who is the respondent party to the employee's contract claim) received from the tribunal a copy of an originating application in respect of a contract claim of that employee; or

        (ii) where the tribunal is satisfied that it was not reasonably practicable for the complaint to be presented within that period, within such further period as the tribunal considers reasonable.

■ **QUESTION**

Which claims are excluded by the Order?

NOTES

1. Tribunals sit in most local centres of population in Great Britain. An employment tribunal is composed of three members: a legally qualified chair (now known as an employment judge, who is a barrister or solicitor of seven years' standing) and two lay members, drawn from both sides of industry. The lay members are full members of the tribunal and can outvote the employment judge, though over 90% of decisions are reached unanimously. As a result of amendments introduced under TURERA 1993 and now embodied in the ETA 1996, s. 4, as amended by the Employment Rights (Dispute Resolution) Act 1998, s. 3, chairs may sit alone in certain cases, including claims relating to unauthorised wage deductions; unauthorised deduction of union subscriptions; interim relief for trade union and health and safety representative dismissals; redundancy payments; breach of contract claims; and uncontested claims and those where the parties have consented in writing. The most significant extension came in 2012 when regulations permitted tribunal judges to sit alone in unfair dismissal cases (The Employment Tribunals Act 1996 (Tribunal Composition) Order 2012 SI 2012/988). Appeals in these cases, and appeals from interlocutory tribunal decisions, will usually be heard by an Employment Appeal judge sitting alone (ETA 1996, s. 28(4)).

2. The aim of conferring jurisdiction on tribunals was to provide a decision-making forum which was less formal, more accessible, quicker, and less expensive than the ordinary courts. However, the law the tribunals have to apply has become increasingly more complex, and therefore it is not surprising that around one-third of applicants and over one-half of respondent employers were legally represented at tribunal hearings during the 1970s and early 1980s (see Hawes, W. R. and Smith, G., 'Patterns of representation of the parties in unfair dismissal cases: A review of the evidence', D.E. Research Paper No. 22 (London: Department of Employment, 1981); Genn, H. and Genn, Y., *The Effectiveness of Representation at Tribunals* (London: Lord Chancellor's Department, 1989)).

3. The fact that the procedure is adversarial means that the onus is on the parties to present their own evidence. This can result in major injustice if one party can afford legal representation and the other cannot. A survey found that it was only the employer's side which had some form of representation in about one-quarter of all cases, and unrepresented applicants faced legally represented employers in about 12% of cases surveyed (see Genn, *ibid.*). Furthermore, a series of studies has shown that there is a clear causal relation between legal and other forms of representation and a successful outcome of the case (see Kumar, V. C., *Industrial Tribunal Applicants under the Race Relations Act 1976* (London: CRE, 1986); Leonard, A., *The First Eight Years: A profile of applicants to the industrial tribunals under the Sex Discrimination Act 1975 and the Equal Pay Act 1970* (Manchester: EOC, 1986) and Dickens, L., et al., *Dismissed: A study of unfair dismissal and the industrial tribunal system* (Oxford: Blackwell, 1985). This situation has brought forward calls for legal aid to be extended to cover representation before industrial tribunals. It is testimony to the growing legalism surrounding employment tribunals that the latest figures record that 65% of claimants were legally represented (source: *Employment Tribunals and EAT Statistics, 1st April 2010 to 31st March 2011*, Ministry of Justice/HM Courts and Tribunals Service, 1 September 2011).

4. A review of the employment tribunal system by a committee appointed by JUSTICE concluded that in 90% of all unfair dismissal and redundancy payment cases an investigative (or inquisitorial) approach by the tribunal is the most suitable, offering the optimum in terms of accessibility, informality, and speed, and the most efficient return on costs to both litigants and the public purse (*Industrial Tribunals: A report by JUSTICE* (Chairman of Committee: Bob Hepple) (London: JUSTICE, 1987)). Other commentators have argued that a system of voluntary private arbitration would be cheaper, quicker, and generally much less formal and legalistic (see Dickens et al., *Dismissed*; Lewis, R. and Clark, J., *The Case for Alternate Dispute Resolution* (London: Institute of Employment Rights, 1993)).

5. *Tribunal Applications.* Over the last decade or so there has been a significant increase in applications to employment tribunals. In 1993/4 there were around 70,000 applications while in 2009/10, at the height of the economic crisis, there were 236,103. By 2012/13, as the UK economy started to improve, the number had dropped back to 191,541. The effect of a range of measures, most notably fees but also including the extension of liability for costs, the increase in the maximum amount of deposit orders (see Note 6), the lengthening of the unfair dismissal qualification period, the reduction of the cap on the compensatory award, and ACAS EC, have clearly had a major impact, with applications for 2013/14 recording a 45% drop at 105,803 applications.

Comparing the first quarter of 2014 with the same period of 2013, the number of claims, at 5,619, was 56% fewer than in the same period of 2013 (*Tribunal Statistics Quarterly: January to March 2014*, MoJ, 12 June 2014).

6. Employment tribunals are now constituted by the ETA 1996, ss. 4–5 and their procedure is now regulated primarily by the Employment Tribunals (Constitution and Rules of Procedure) Regulations 2013 (SI 2013/1237).

Since the inception of the right to claim unfair dismissal, there has been political pressure exerted by employers' groups to 'weed out' those claims portrayed as lacking merit and/or time wasting. Such so-called 'nuisance value' claims, it was said, caused many employers to settle rather than face the time and expense of defending the claim at tribunal. Combined with this, in recent years, successive governments have attempted to control the burgeoning number of tribunal applications. A series of procedural measures have been adopted in order to deal with these dual sources of pressure:

Striking Out. Rules 26–28 of the Rules of Procedure provide that after the claim and employer's response have been presented to the tribunal, it will be considered by an employment judge. At what is called the 'sift stage', the employment judge will determine whether the claim should be struck out. A claim may be struck out at any stage of the proceedings, by the judge or on the application of either party, on grounds which include that it is scandalous, vexatious, or has no reasonable prospect of success, or because the manner in which the proceedings have been conducted by or on behalf of the claimant or respondent has been scandalous, unreasonable, or vexatious (rule 37).

Deposit Orders. A preliminary hearing may be held on the discretion of the tribunal itself or on the application of one of the parties. The purpose of this is to consider both case management and substantive preliminary issues (rules 53–56). The latter issues include whether a claim or response, or any part of it, should be struck out under rule 37 or to make a deposit order under rule 39. Where a tribunal considers that any specific allegation or argument in a claim or response has 'little reasonable prospect of success', it may make an order requiring a party to pay a deposit not exceeding £1,000 as a condition of continuing to advance that allegation or argument (rule 39(1)). The deposit will be forfeited and paid to the other party if, subsequently in the proceedings, the tribunal decides that the allegation or argument was unreasonable for substantially the reasons given in the deposit order (rule 39(5)).

Costs. Conventionally, it is relatively rare for the tribunal to require the losing party to pay the legal costs of the other side. This is in line with the original aim of ensuring, as far as possible, that tribunal proceedings were not trammelled by legalism and retained a degree of informality. However, tribunals have always retained a residual power to award costs. Initially, this power was only exercisable where there was frivolous or vexatious conduct by a party. In 1980, this was extended to embrace cases brought 'otherwise unreasonably'. The further extended and current power is now governed by rule 76, as follows:

WHEN A COSTS ORDER OR A PREPARATION TIME ORDER MAY OR
SHALL BE MADE

76.-(1) A Tribunal may make a costs order or a preparation time order, and shall consider whether to do so, where it considers that—
   (a) a party (or that party's representative) has acted vexatiously, abusively, disruptively or otherwise unreasonably in either the bringing of the proceedings (or part) or the way that the proceedings (or part) have been conducted; or
   (b) any claim or response had no reasonable prospect of success.
   ...

It should be noted that the rule also allows for the making of a 'preparation time order' designed to compensate the other party for the time spent working on the case while not legally represented. The maximum amount of costs a tribunal may award without a detailed assessment of costs currently stands at £20,000. There is also a power to make a 'wasted costs order'. Such an order may be made against a party's paid representative where, 'as a result of any improper, unreasonable or negligent act or omission' on their part, time has been wasted (rule 80).

7. *Fees*. The Employment Tribunals and the Employment Appeal Tribunal Fees Order 2013 introduces fees for claims made to an employment tribunal and appeals to the Employment Appeal Tribunal. The Order came into force on 29 July 2013.

There are two fee levels in the employment tribunal. In broad terms, discrimination, detriment and unfair dismissal claims are allocated to the higher type 'B' fees, with wage deductions, refusals to allow time off, and other 'simpler' claims attracting the lower type 'A' fee. For single claimants, a type B claim has an issue fee of £250 and a hearing fee of £950, with type A attracting a £160 issue and £230 hearing fee.

In the EAT the fees are £400 to lodge an appeal and £1,200 for a full hearing.

As stated in Section 1, the introduction of fees has resulted in a major drop in tribunal applications. Research had already identified that the tribunal system created obstacles to justice for workers who are not unionised and cannot afford legal advice and representation (see Busby, N., McDermott, M., 'Workers, marginalised voices and the employment tribunal system: Some preliminary findings' (2012) 41 *Industrial Law Journal* 166). The introduction of fees can only have exacerbated this problem.

8. Reflecting on the cumulative effect of the changes to tribunal procedure outlined earlier, Smith and Wood observe:

> If one adds together the demise of side members in so many cases, the consequent emphasis on the position of the judge alone (no longer simply the tribunal 'chairman'), the attempt to extend the costs regime, the charging of fees and the inexorable lengthening of hearings with arguably a significant decrease over the years of the original inquisitorial nature of tribunals, the question might well be asked-are these really still tribunals as originally understood, or simply courts by another name? (Smith, I., and Baker, A., *Smith & Wood's Employment Law*, 11th edn (Oxford: OUP, 2013) p. 30)

This phenomenon has been termed 'isomorphism', i.e. the tendency of the tribunals to evolve and become assimilated with the mainstream court system (see Corby, S., Latreille, P., 'Employment Tribunals and the Civil Courts: Isomorphism Exemplified' (2012) 42 *Industrial Law Journal* 387).

9. *Financial penalties for employers*. One of the least popular changes for employers, introduced by ERRA 2013, s. 16, was the introduction, from 6 April 2014, of financial penalties for those found to have breached employment rights. The penalty is payable to the Secretary of State, on top of any compensation due to the employee. The starting point for determining the penalty is 50% of the compensation awarded, subject to a minimum sum of £100 and maximum of £5,000, with reductions applying for early payment.

Importantly, not all unsuccessful respondents will find themselves liable to a penalty; in addition to finding a breach of employment rights, the tribunal must identify one or more 'aggravating features'. What these features might be are not elaborated upon, although the Government has suggested that negligence or malice are possible examples.

10. An award made by an employment tribunal attracts interest the day after the relevant decision day but no interest is payable if the full amount of the award is paid within 14 days after the relevant decision day. Interest is not payable on any costs awarded. Interest remains payable if the tribunal's decision is subject to appeal or review (Employment Tribunals Act 1996, s. 14; Employment Tribunals (Interest) Order 1990 (SI 1990/479); Employment Tribunals (Interest) Order (Amendment) Order 2013 (SI 2013/1671)). A tribunal does not have the power to enforce its own order and so, in the last resort, the claimant has to apply to the county court in order to enforce the award. Research conducted on behalf of the Department for Business, Innovation and Skills on the payment of tribunal awards in 2013 found that fewer than half of tribunal awards (49%) were paid in full (*Payment of Tribunal Awards: 2013 Study*, IFF Research, Department for Business, Innovation and Skills, 2013 (<http://www.gov.uk/bis>)). In order to help address this problem, the Small Business, Enterprise and Employment Act 2015 amends the ETA 1996 so as to allow the imposition of a financial penalty on non-compliant respondents. The new provisions also cover non-payment of sums owed in settlement agreements reached following ACAS conciliation. The financial penalty is, generally, 50% of the unpaid amount (ETA 1996, ss. 37A–Q).

11. *The ACAS Arbitration Scheme*. In May 2001 a voluntary arbitration scheme was introduced as an alternative to going to tribunal for dealing with simple unfair dismissal disputes. This scheme, which came into force in England and Wales in 2001 (in Scotland in 2004), was designed to relieve some of the workload of the employment tribunals. In April 2003, it was extended to cover claims under the flexible working legislation. It has been very little used and from its inception in 2001 until 2009, only 61 cases were lodged (*ACAS Annual Report 2008–09*). The reasons for the lack of take up may lie in the fact that, under the ACAS scheme, there is an absence of an obligation on the arbitrator to apply strict law in reaching a decision. This, together with the lack of a right of appeal against the arbitrator's decision, could lead to decision-making on the basis of 'unfettered pragmatism' and a two-tier system of unfair dismissal justice (see

MacMillan, J., 'Employment tribunals: Philosophies and practicalities' (1999) 28 ILJ 33–56; and Earnshaw, J., Hardy, S., 'Assessing an arbitral route for unfair dismissal' (2001) 30 ILJ 289–304).

F: The Employment Appeal Tribunal

EMPLOYMENT TRIBUNALS ACT 1996

Jurisdiction

21. Jurisdiction of Appeal Tribunal

(1) An appeal lies to the Appeal Tribunal on any question of law arising from any decision of, or arising in any proceedings before, an employment tribunal under or by virtue of—

(a)–(c) [repealed]
(d) the Trade Union and Labour Relations (Consolidation) Act 1992,
(e) [repealed]
(f) the Employment Rights Act 1996,
(g) this Act,
(ga) the National Minimum Wage Act 1998,
(gb) the Employment Relations Act 1999,
(gc) the Equality Act 2006,
(gd) the Pensions Act 2008,
(ge) the Equality Act 2010,
(h) the Working Time Regulations 1998,
(i) the Transnational Information and Consultation of Employee Regulations 1999,
(j) the Part-time Workers (Prevention of Less Favourable Treatment) Regulations 2000,
(k) the Fixed-term (Prevention of Less Favourable Treatment) Regulations 2002,
(l)–(m) [repealed]
(n) the Merchant Shipping (Working Time: Inland Waterways) Regulations 2003,
(o) the European Public Limited-Liability Company Regulations 2004,
(p) the Fishing Vessels (Working Time: Sea Fishermen) Regulations 2004,
(q) the Information and Consultation of Employees Regulations 2004,
(r) under paragraph 4 or 8 of the Schedule to the Occupational and Personal Pension Schemes (Consultation by Employers and Miscellaneous Amendment) Regulations 2006,
(s) [repealed]
(t) the European Cooperative Society (Involvement of Employees) Regulations 2006,
(u) the Companies (Cross-Border Mergers) Regulations 2007,
(v) the Cross-border Railway Services (Working Time) Regulations 2008,
(w) the European Public Limited-Liability Company (Employee Involvement) (Great Britain) Regulations 2009 (S.I. 2009/2401),
(x) the Employment Relations Act 1999 (Blacklists) Regulations, or
(y) the Agency Workers Regulations 2010.

(2) No appeal shall lie except to the Appeal Tribunal from any decision of an employment tribunal under or by virtue of the Acts listed in subsection (1).

(3) Subsection (1) does not affect any provision contained in, or made under, any Act which provides for an appeal to lie to the Appeal Tribunal (whether from an employment tribunal, the Certification Officer or any other person or body) otherwise than on a question to which that subsection applies.

NOTE: Appeal from a tribunal decision lies to the EAT. The EAT was originally constituted by the Employment Protection Act 1975 and is now governed by the ETA 1996, ss. 22–8, as amended. Hitherto, the majority of EAT cases were determined by a panel comprising a judge and lay members. The ERRA 2013, s.12 now requires all EAT cases to be heard by a judge alone, unless a judge directs otherwise or where the Lord Chancellor orders that certain proceedings should be heard by a panel (see the Employment Tribunals Act 1996, s. 28, as amended). By reducing the role of lay members in the EAT, the Government is looking to cut costs; however, critics fear that the quality of decision-making will deteriorate in their absence and tribunals will become more legalistic.

The EAT is a superior court of record and its decisions are binding on employment tribunals. The EAT hears all appeals from the employment tribunals in England and Wales and in Scotland. In general, appeal lies to the EAT on *a point of law only*. The only exceptions to this are an appeal from the decision of the CO on the question of registration or certification as an independent trade union, or on an appeal in a claim for unreasonable exclusion or expulsion from a union where appeal may be on law or fact.

Neale v Hereford and Worcester County Council
[1986] IRLR 168, Court of Appeal

Mr Neale was head of the music department at one of the appellant county council's schools. He was dismissed following an incident which occurred while he was invigilating pupils sitting an 'A' level examination. An industrial tribunal dismissed Mr Neale's complaint of unfair dismissal. While critical of some procedural aspects of the case, the industrial tribunal concluded that such procedural defects could not lead to the conclusion that, in the circumstances, the dismissal was outside the band of reasonable responses open to a reasonable employer.

The EAT allowed Mr Neale's appeal against that finding and ruled that this was one of the exceptional cases where the industrial tribunal's decision fell to be reversed, because it was one which no reasonable tribunal could have reached. The Court of Appeal allowed the county council's appeal and restored the decision of the industrial tribunal.

MAY LJ: ... An industrial tribunal has been described as an 'industrial jury', and so in many ways it is. It knows its area; it comprises a lawyer, a representative of employees and a representative of employers within that district; each has substantial experience of industrial relations problems and they are hearing this type of case regularly. Their job is to find the facts, to apply the relevant law and to reach the conclusion to which their findings and experience lead them. It will not, in my opinion, be often that when an industrial tribunal has done just that, and with the care, clarity and thoroughness which the Industrial Tribunal in the present case displayed, that one can legitimately say that their conclusion 'offends reason', or that their conclusion was one to which no reasonable industrial tribunal could have come. Deciding these cases is the job of industrial tribunals and when they have not erred in law neither the EAT nor this Court should disturb their decision unless one can say in effect: 'My goodness, that was certainly wrong'.

NOTE See also *Yeboah* v *Crofton* [2002] IRLR 634, CA.

Piggott Brothers & Co. Ltd v Jackson
[1991] IRLR 309, Court of Appeal

LORD DONALDSON MR: The EAT, in unanimously allowing the employers' appeal, reminded itself of the limitations upon its own jurisdiction in the following passage in the judgment delivered by Knox J.:

> We were very properly reminded by Miss Warren that the jurisdiction of this tribunal is limited to questions of law by [what is now ETA 1996, s. 21], that it is not right that questions of fact should be dressed up as points of law so as to encourage appeals or to go through the reasoning of Industrial Tribunals with a fine-tooth comb to see if some error can be found here or there. See *Hollister* v *NFU* [1979] IRLR 238 at 241, 17 per Lord Denning MR. In that judgment there is also a quotation from Lord Russell of Killowen's judgment in *Retarded Children's Aid Society Ltd* v *Day* [1978] IRLR 128 at p. 130, 9 where he said:
>
>> The function of the Employment Appeal Tribunal is to correct errors of law where one is established and identified. I think care must be taken to avoid concluding that an experienced Industrial Tribunal by not expressly mentioning some point or breach has overlooked it, and care must be taken to avoid, in a case where the Employment Appeal Tribunal members would on the basis of the merits and the oral evidence have taken a different view from that of the Industrial Tribunal, searching around with a fine-tooth comb for some point of law.

In short, it is not for us on a question of reasonableness to substitute our view for that of the Industrial Tribunal.

There are, however, three categories of case where it is the duty of the EAT to interfere. They are stated by Lord Donaldson MR in *British Telecommunications* v *Sheridan* [1990] IRLR 27 at p. 30 as follows:

> The Employment Appeal Tribunal can indeed interfere if it is satisfied that the Tribunal has misdirected itself as to the applicable law, or if there is no evidence to support a finding of fact, since the absence of evidence to support a finding of fact has always been regarded as a pure question of law. It can also interfere if the decision is perverse, as has been explained by May LJ in *Neale* v *Hereford & Worcester CC* [1986] IRLR 168 at p. 173, 44.

This last is an allusion to the now very familiar sentence at p. 173, 45:

> Deciding these cases is the job of Industrial Tribunals and when they have not erred in law neither the appeal tribunal nor this Court should disturb their decision unless one can say in effect. 'My goodness, that was certainly wrong'.

I accept, as I must, the exposition of May LJ. Indeed, it has the added authority of, I think, being derived, albeit expressed in more homely terms, from the speech of Lord Diplock in *R* v *Secretary of State for Foreign and Commonwealth Affairs ex parte Council of Civil Service Unions* [1985] IRLR 28 at p. 36, 49 where he said that a decision which was plainly wrong could found an application for judicial review and that it was no longer necessary to resort to Viscount Radcliffe's explanation in *Edwards* v *Bairstow* [1956] AC 14 of irrationality as raising an inference of an unidentifiable mistake of law.

Nevertheless, it is an approach which is not without its perils. A finding of fact which is unsupported by *any* evidence clearly involves an error of law. The Tribunal cannot have directed itself, as it should, that findings of fact need *some* evidence to support them. The danger in the approach of May LJ is that an appellate court can very easily persuade itself that, as it would certainly not have reached the same conclusion, the Tribunal which did so was 'certainly wrong'. Furthermore, the more dogmatic the temperament of the judges concerned, the more likely they are to take this view. However, this is a classic non sequitur. It does not matter whether, with whatever degree of certainty, the appellate court considers that it would have reached a different conclusion. What matters is whether the decision under appeal was a permissible option. To answer that question in the negative in the context of employment law, the EAT will almost always have to be able to identify a finding of fact which was unsupported by *any* evidence or a clear self-misdirection in law by the Industrial Tribunal. If it cannot do this, it should re-examine with the greatest care its preliminary conclusion that the decision under appeal was not a permissible option and has to be characterised as 'perverse'.

NOTE: These decisions reflect the Court of Appeal's concern relating to excessive legalism and the proliferation of appeals from employment tribunals. In a series of rulings, the court has adopted a two-pronged strategy designed to reverse the trend and reduce the number of cases coming through on appeal from employment tribunals to the EAT.

First, it has ruled that many issues in employment law are ultimately questions of fact and not questions of law. Given that appeal to the EAT *must* involve a claim that the employment tribunal misdirected itself in law, this is clearly an attempt to return decision-making to the tribunals. The following are examples of this policy of classifying issues as question of fact and thus limiting the possibility of appeals: whether a worker is an 'employee'; whether a 'constructive dismissal' has taken place; whether an employee resigned or was forced to do so; whether it was reasonably practicable to present an unfair dismissal claim on time.

The second element of the strategy against legalism has been the Court of Appeal's rejection of the EAT's practice of laying down guidelines for tribunals to follow when confronted with major problem areas of unfair dismissal law, for example redundancy procedure, suspected dishonesty, and long-term sickness absence. The nature of the Court of Appeal's attack on what was seen as the EAT's unduly interventionist role is clearly illustrated by the following statement of Lawton LJ in *Bailey* v *BP Oil (Kent Refinery) Ltd* [1980] IRLR 287:

> Each case must depend on its own facts. In our judgement it is unwise for this court or the Employment Appeal Tribunal to set out guidelines, and wrong to make rules and establish presumptions for industrial tribunals to follow or take into account.

While the concern of the Court of Appeal to rid the law of unfair dismissal of excessive legal technicality is understandable, it may be that the court has taken matters too far and that the attack on legalism and the proliferation of appeals may be achieved at the cost of certainty and consistency. In the absence of established guidelines and precedent, it becomes extremely difficult for legal or personnel practitioners to offer advice on any particular case. For example, if the question of 'employee' status is classified a question of fact, there is every prospect that employment tribunals in different parts of the country can come to diametrically opposed conclusions in cases involving identical facts, and with little or no prospect of the EAT resolving the matter on appeal.

Concern about the restricted role of the EAT is clearly evident in the next extract.

East Berkshire Health Authority v Matadeen

[1992] IRLR 336, Employment Appeal Tribunal

WOOD J (PRESIDENT): The law as it stands seems to me to indicate that the EAT can only interfere with a decision of the 'industrial jury', i.e. the Industrial Tribunal if, first, there is ex facie an error of law, a misdirection or a misapplication of the law. Secondly, that there is a material finding of fact relied upon by the Tribunal in the decision, which was unsupported by any evidence or contrary to the evidence before them. Thirdly, and as a free-standing basis in law, there is a finding of perversity. It is likely to be a very rare occasion upon which the Employment Appeal Tribunal can interfere on this ground and it should caution itself against so doing and in particular to be careful not merely to substitute its own view for that of the Industrial Tribunal.

The fact that perversity, properly understood, is a free-standing basis in law is also supported by a passage in the speech of Lord Fraser of Tullybelton in *Melon* v *Hector Powe Ltd* [1980] IRLR 477 where at p. 479, 12 he says:

> It is common ground that the appeal from the Industrial Tribunal to the Employment Appeal Tribunal and thence to the courts is open only on a question of law. The appellate tribunals are therefore only entitled to interfere with the decision of the Industrial Tribunal if the appellants can succeed in showing, as they seek to do, that it has either misdirected itself in law or reached a decision which no reasonable Tribunal, directing itself properly on the law, could have reached (or it has gone fundamentally wrong in certain other respects, none of which is here alleged). The fact that the appellate tribunal would have reached a different conclusion on the facts is not a sufficient ground for allowing an appeal.

Thus, even on factual findings of an Industrial Tribunal, the EAT can interfere if the members are completely satisfied in the light of their own experience and of the sound practices in the industrial field that the decision is 'not a permissible option' per Lord Donaldson of Lymington MR: 'a conclusion which offends reason or is one to which no reasonable Industrial Tribunal could come' or 'so very clearly wrong that it just cannot stand' per May LJ, or to paraphrase Lord Diplock in the *GCHQ* case, the decision was 'so outrageous in its defiance of logic or of accepted standards of industrial relations that no sensible person who had applied his mind to the question and with the necessary experience could have arrived at it.' It is also interesting to note that Lord Diplock continues at p. 36, 49:

> Whether a decision falls within this category is a question that judges by their training and experience should be well equipped to answer or else there would be something badly wrong with our judicial system.

I would respectfully add that there is something wrong with our system and with this Appeal Tribunal if those industrial members who are appointed to it, with their vast experience of industry, were not able to recognise a decision which fell within this category.

I have cautioned the members against interfering with decisions of Industrial Tribunals. They cannot interfere merely because they disagree. They cannot interfere even if they feel strongly that the result is unjust, though in this latter case it may be that on a careful analysis of the true reason lying behind such a view the decision flies in the face of properly informed logic.

SECTION 3: THE INTERNATIONAL LABOUR ORGANISATION

The International Labour Organization (ILO) was established in 1919. It is based in Geneva and, as an agency of the United Nations (UN), is charged with setting universal labour standards. It is a tripartite body composed of representatives of governments, employers and workers. As of 2013, 185 of the 193 member states of the UN were members of the ILO.

ILO standards are set by the International Labour Conference—convened annually—in the form of Conventions and Recommendations. There are now some 189

Conventions, of which the most significant include Convention No. 87 on Freedom of Association and Protection of the Right to Organise (1949) and Convention No. 98 on the Right to Organise and Collective Bargaining (1949). If a State ratifies a Convention, it undertakes to ensure that its domestic law conforms with the Convention's standards. Since 1979, the UK Government has denounced four of the Conventions which it had previously ratified. Those include Convention No. 94 Labour Clauses (Public Contracts) (1949), allowing the Government to rescind the Fair Wages Resolution of 1946, and Convention No. 95 (Protection of Wages Convention) (1949), enabling the Government to enact the Wages Act 1986 and to repeal the Truck Act which required wages to be paid in cash rather than in kind.

For further discussions of these issues see Ewing, K. D., *Britain and the ILO* (London: Institute of Employment Rights, 1989); Brown, D. and McColgan, A., 'UK employment law and the International Labour Organisation: The spirit of co-operation?' (1989) 21 ILJ 265.

SECTION 4: THE EUROPEAN CONVENTION ON HUMAN RIGHTS AND THE HUMAN RIGHTS ACT 1998

The European Convention for the Protection of Human Rights and Fundamental Freedoms (the Convention) was adopted by the Council of Europe in 1950, and came into force in 1953, for the purpose of protecting individuals' rights against infringement by States. It seeks to protect certain rights and freedoms, such as freedom from torture; the prohibition of slavery and forced labour; freedom of thought, conscience, and religion; freedom of association; the right to liberty and security; the right to a fair trial; a right to privacy; and a right not to be subjected to degrading and inhuman treatment. The Convention only unreservedly prohibits torture; inhuman and degrading treatment; slavery and forced labour. The other rights and freedoms set out in the Convention are qualified to varying degrees.

Prior to the passage of the Human Rights Act (HRA) 1998, the Convention was not generally regarded as a source of law by UK courts, although it has been used as a guide when interpreting ambiguous statutory provisions (see *R v Secretary of State for the Home Department, ex p. Brind* [1991] AC 696). The HRA 1998 incorporates Convention rights into UK law, but on a restricted basis only. The Act, which came into force on 2 October 2000, has three main elements:

(a) a requirement that courts and tribunals should interpret legislation in accordance with the Convention;

(b) giving courts the right to make declarations on incompatibility;

(c) making it unlawful for a public body to act in way which is incompatible with Convention rights.

A: Interpreting legislation in accordance with the Convention

Under s. 3 of the HRA 1998, there is a requirement that all primary and subordinate legislation, '[so] far as it is possible to do so...must be read and given effect in a way which is compatible with the Convention rights' (s. 3(1)). However, if domestic legislation is unambiguous, and it is not possible to interpret it in accordance with the Convention, the domestic statute takes precedence over Convention rights. A statutory instrument will be struck down if inconsistent with Convention rights unless the primary legislation prevents the removal of the incompatibility.

B: Declarations on incompatibility

If UK legislation is incompatible with Convention rights, the higher courts have the discretion (not the duty) to make a 'declaration of incompatibility' (s. 4). Employment tribunals and the EAT cannot make a declaration of incompatibility. Employment claims will have to wait until they reach the Court of Appeal (unless started in the High Court). Even when a declaration of incompatibility is made, this will have no effect on the parties before the court. A litigant who succeeds in persuading a court to issue a declaration of incompatibility will still be able to take his or her case to Strasbourg.

Under s. 19 of the Act, all legislation introduced by the Government must be coupled with a Statement of Compatibility with the Convention. This Statement (which must be in writing) must be provided by the minister in charge of the passage of the bill prior to its second reading. If the minister is unable to make a Statement of Compatibility, the minister must state (in writing) that he or she is unable to do so but the Government nevertheless wishes to proceed with the bill. Accordingly, the real effect of this section is to require ministers to alert Parliament to the fact that a bill is potentially incompatible with Convention rights. There is no analogous requirement in respect of private members' bills.

C: Public authorities must act in compliance with the Convention

Under ss. 6–8, all public authorities must act in compliance with the Convention. It is a defence, however, to show that the public authority was prevented from acting in accordance with the Convention as the result of UK legislation (which takes precedence). Sections 6–8 of the HRA 1998 provide:

6(1) It is unlawful for a public authority to act in a way which is incompatible with a Convention right.
6(2) Subsection (1) does not apply to an act if—
   (a) as the result of one or more provisions of primary legislation, the authority could not have acted differently; or,
   (b) in the case of one or more provisions of, or made under, primary legislation which cannot be read or given effect in a way which is compatible with the Convention rights, the authority was acting so as to give effect to or enforce these provisions.
6(3) In this section 'public authority' includes—
   (a) a court or tribunal, and
   (b) any person certain of whose functions are functions of a public nature but does not include either House of Parliament or a person exercising functions in connection with proceedings in Parliament.
   ...
6(5) In relation to a particular act, a person is not a public authority by virtue only of subsection 3(b) if the nature of the act is private.
6(6) An 'act' includes a failure to act but does not include a failure to—
   (a) introduce in, or lay before, Parliament a proposal for legislation; or,
   (b) make any primary legislation or remedial order.
7(1) A person who claims that a public authority has acted (or proposes to act) in a way which is made unlawful by section 6(1) may—
   (a) bring proceedings against the authority under this Act in the appropriate court or tribunal, or
   (b) rely on the Convention right or rights concerned in any legal proceedings, but only if he is (or would be) a victim of the unlawful act.
   ...

8(1) In relation to any act (or proposed act) of a public authority which the court finds is (or would be) unlawful, it may grant such relief or remedy, or make such order, within its powers as it considers just and appropriate.

8(2) But damages may be awarded only by a court which has power to award damages, or to order the payment of compensation, in civil proceedings.

NOTE: It is only a 'public authority' which is required to act in a way that is compatible with Convention rights. The courts are likely to follow a similar approach to that taken in judicial review cases to determine who is a 'public authority'. If a public authority acts in a way which is inconsistent with Convention rights, then a claim for damages or an injunction will lie against it. It is a defence for the public authority to demonstrate that it acted in the way that it did because it was required to do so by UK legislation (s. 6(2)). Courts and tribunals are deemed by s. 6(3) to be public authorities for the purpose of the Act. Thus courts act unlawfully if they breach Convention rights. This carries the implication that the courts can impose articles of the Convention in disputes between private individuals, thus achieving an indirect horizontal effect (see *X* v *Y* [2004] IRLR 625, CA).

In addition, a distinction is made between bodies with mixed public and private functions. When exercising public functions, such bodies must apply Convention rights. When exercising private functions, no such obligations exist. Since entering into an employment contract is viewed by the law as a function of a private nature (*ex p. Walsh* [1984] ICR 743, *McLaren* v *Home Office* [1990] ICR 824, 836), employers who are mixed bodies will argue that the obligation to comply with the Convention does not arise in employment disputes.

D: The Human Rights Act and the implications for employment law

A number of the Convention articles will be relevant to employment law. Rights provided for by the HRA 1998, which are commonly raised in an employment context, are:

- the right to a fair trial (Article 6)
- the right to respect for private and family life (Article 8)
- the right to freedom of thought, conscience and religion (Article 9)
- the right to freedom of expression (Article 10)
- the right of freedom of association and assembly (Article 11).

Article 6—Right to a fair trial

In the determination of his civil rights and obligations or of any criminal charge against him, everyone is entitled to a fair and public hearing within a reasonable time by an independent and impartial tribunal established by law…

This is likely to have the following employment law implications. First, employees of public bodies may be able to argue that an unfair disciplinary procedure infringes Article 6, and is therefore rendered unlawful by s. 6(1) of the HRA 1998. Second, it may be contended that the employment tribunal system itself is in breach of Article 6. In *Smith* v *Secretary for State for Trade and Industry* [2000] IRLR 6, the issue was raised whether the employment tribunals can satisfy the Article in cases where the Secretary of State for Trade and Industry is a party to the proceedings, as where claims are made against the Secretary of State because the employer is insolvent. The issue is not only that the lay members of the tribunals are appointed and subject to periodic reappointment by the Secretary of State, but also that the funding of the tribunals derives from the Department of Trade and Industry (DTI).

The EAT offered the view that employment tribunals may not be independent when it came to determining matters relating to redundancy payments from the DTI fund. Although the EAT gave permission to appeal, that option was not taken up.

This question was revisited by the EAT in *Scanfuture UK Ltd* v *Secretary of State for Trade and Industry* [2001] IRLR 416. The procedures for the appointment of lay members had been changed from those in place in 1999 when the employment tribunal first heard the *Scanfuture* case. The EAT found that the new procedures complied with the Convention. However, as to the position in 1999, the EAT took the view that the procedures for the appointment of lay members breached Article 6(1) of the Convention.

Article 8—Right to respect for private and family life

8(1) Everyone has the right to respect for his private and family life, his home and his correspondence.

  8(2) There shall be no interference by a public authority with the exercise of this right except such as in accordance with the law and is necessary in a democratic society in the interests of national security, public safety or the economic well-being of the country, for the prevention of disorder or crime, for the protection of health and morals, or for the protection of the rights and freedom of others.

There is a *general* right to privacy within the office—thus a search of a lawyer's office was held to be in breach of Article 8 (*Niemitz* v *Germany* (1993) 16 EHRR 97). The Court stated that 'to interpret the words "private life" and "home" as excluding certain professional or business activities or premises would not be consonant with the essential object and purpose of Article 8.'

In *Halford* v *United Kingdom* [1997] IRLR 471, it was held that the absence of domestic legislation dealing with an employer's right or otherwise to 'tap' telephone calls at work was a breach of Article 8. In that case, the applicant, an Assistant Chief Police Constable, had alleged that her office telephone was being tapped by her employers to obtain evidence to use in a sex discrimination claim she had brought. The European Court of Human Rights (ECtHR) held that such recording, without the knowledge of the employee, was a breach of the right to private life and correspondence. The applicant was awarded £10,000 for non-pecuniary loss.

In *Leander* v *Sweden* (1987) 9 EHRR 433, the European Court held that storing information about a job applicant in a secret police register and releasing it to a prospective employer breached his right to privacy. However, the Court held that this interference could be justified as 'necessary in a democratic society'. The use of such information for vetting candidates for posts which are not of importance for national security may be more difficult to defend.

In *Smith and Grady* v *United Kingdom* [1999] IRLR 734, the ECtHR held that a ban on homosexuals in employment in the UK armed forces contravened the right to respect for private life.

Emerging issues under Article 8 include monitoring email and telephone communications, CCTV surveillance, employee searches, and random drug/alcohol testing. Recent case law on such issues includes the following:

* Drug testing—an employee was unsuccessful in arguing that random drug testing by her employer was an infringement of her right to respect for private life (*O'Flynn* v *Airlinks the Airport Coach Company Ltd* [2002] All ER (D) 05 (Jul)).

* Video surveillance—video footage of a claimant which had been secretly obtained was considered relevant and admissible evidence in court although the court expressed its disapproval of the manner in which the evidence was obtained by making a costs award against the respondent (*Jones* v *Warwick University*; see also *McGowan* v *Scottish Water* [2003] 1 WLR 954).

* Email—although not yet determined in the UK, the French Supreme Court has ruled that an employee's right to private life under the Convention extended to private emails received at work, even where the employer had prohibited personal use of the facilities (*Onof* v *Nikon France*, Decision no. 4164, 2 October 2001 (99.42.942)).

* The covert collection of video evidence to support a sexual harassment claim (*XXX* v *YYY* [2004] IRLR 471, CA).

Article 10—Freedom of expression

10(1) Everyone has a right to freedom of expression. This right shall include freedom to hold opinions and to receive and impart information and ideas without interference by public authority and regardless of frontiers. This article shall not prevent States from requiring the licensing of broadcasting, television or cinema enterprises.

10(2) The exercise of these freedoms, since it carries with it duties and responsibilities, may be subject to such formalities, conditions, restrictions or penalties as are prescribed by law and are necessary in a democratic society, for the prevention of disorder or crime, for the protection of health and morals, for the protection of the reputation or rights of others, for preventing the disclosure of information received in confidence, or for maintaining the authority and impartiality of the judiciary.

NOTES

1. It is possible to envisage a number of challenges under this Article:
   * With regard to recruitment, it may now be unlawful for public bodies to refuse to recruit (or promote) people on the basis of their political views (*Vogt* v *Germany* (1996) 24 EHRR 205).
   * There may be challenges to the compatibility of the Public Interest Disclosure Act 1998. Only a limited number of disclosures are protected under the Act, and those disclosures must either be to designated persons or comply with the strict requirements of ERA, ss. 43G and 43H. The ECtHR held that the dismissal of a geriatric nurse after having brought a criminal complaint against her employer alleging deficiencies in the care provided amounted to a violation of the right to freedom of expression contrary to Article 10 of the European Convention. In *Heinisch* v *Germany* [2011] IRLR 922, the applicant repeatedly complained to management about shortcomings in the care provided in the nursing home in which she worked. When nothing was done, she brought a criminal complaint against the company alleging that it was putting patients at risk and that it had tried to cover up the problems. Following this, she was dismissed. The national court held that the criminal complaint meant that continuation of the employment relationship was unacceptable. The ECtHR confirmed that whistleblowing in the workplace falls within the ambit of Article 10, and that the State has a positive obligation to protect freedom of expression even between an employee and a private employer. The Court went on to hold, contrary to the argument of the German Government, that the interference with the applicant's rights was not justified as being a proportionate means of protecting the reputation and rights of her employer. It accepted that an employee owes a duty of loyalty and discretion to the employer and that therefore disclosure should be made in the first instance to the person's superior or other competent authority. Disclosing to the public, it said, should be a last resort. 'In assessing whether the restriction on freedom of expression was proportionate, therefore, the Court must take into account whether the applicant had any other effective means of remedying the wrongdoing which he intended to uncover.' This emphasises the importance of employers having whistleblowing procedures in place, albeit that it is not currently compulsory in the UK (cf. Australia and New Zealand, for example).
2. 'Freedom of expression' is guaranteed under the Convention but is qualified by such 'restrictions…as are…necessary in a democratic society…for the protection of health or morals, for the protection of the reputation or rights of others'. *Palomo Sanchez* v *Spain* [2011] IRLR 934 was a case which arose out of an industrial dispute between a group of deliverymen in Barcelona and the company in which they were employed. The deliverymen founded a trade union, which published a newsletter which was displayed on the company's notice board. The cover of the newsletter caricatured the human resources manager sitting at his desk being sexually serviced, and two employees who had testified against the workers in tribunal proceedings were shown waiting to take their turn. An article in the newsletter criticising those employees was entitled 'when you've rented out your arse you can't shit when you please'. Six employees who were members of the union's executive were dismissed on grounds of serious misconduct. The Spanish courts found that the dismissals were justified and that they were on grounds of the content of the newsletter rather than the employees' trade union membership. The applicants claimed that their dismissal contravened Article 10, read together with the right to freedom of association conferred by Article 11. Although the claim was unsuccessful because the applicants were held to have overstepped the mark, the judgment of the Grand Chamber of the ECtHR is important in emphasising the right of trade union representatives, and employees generally, to exercise their right to freedom of expression in respect of employment-related issues, even where this involves a dispute with a private employer. The Court acknowledges that 'for the purpose of guaranteeing the meaningful and effective nature of trade union rights, the national authorities must

ensure that disproportionate penalties do not dissuade trade union representatives from seeking to express and defend their members' interests'. Moreover, 'in certain cases the State has a positive obligation to protect the right to freedom of expression, even against interference by private persons...The applicants' dismissal was not the result of direct intervention by the national authorities. The responsibility of the authorities would nevertheless be engaged if the facts complained of stemmed from a failure on their part to secure to the applicants the enjoyment of the right enshrined in Article 10 of the Convention.' This means that domestic employment law must protect the right of employees to speak out. However, there are limits: 'a clear distinction must be made between criticism and insult'. According to the majority of the Court, 'Article 10 of the Convention does not guarantee an unlimited freedom of expression and the protection of the reputation or rights of others, in the present case the reputation of the persons targeted in the drawings and texts at issue, constitutes a legitimate aim permitting a restriction of that freedom of expression.' Furthermore, 'the extent of acceptable criticism is narrower as regards private individuals than as regards politicians or civil servants acting in the exercise of their duties.' This led the majority of the Court, by a vote of 12 to 5, to hold that dismissal 'was not a manifestly disproportionate or excessive sanction capable of requiring the State to afford redress by annulling it or by replacing it with a more lenient measure'.

Article 11—Freedom of assembly and association

11(1) Everyone has the right to freedom of peaceful assembly and to freedom of association with others, including the right to form and to join trade unions for the protection of his interests.

11(2) No restrictions shall be placed on the exercise of these rights other than such as are prescribed by law and are necessary in a democratic society in the interests of national security or public safety, for the prevention of disorder or crime, for the protection of health and morals or for the protection of the rights and freedoms of others. This article shall not prevent the imposition of lawful restrictions on the exercise of these rights by members of the armed forces, of the police or of the administration of the State.

NOTES

1. The very notion of freedom of association implies 'some measure of freedom of choice as to its exercise'. To put it another way, the freedom to associate included, to some extent, the freedom not to associate (*Young, James and Webster* v *United Kingdom* (1981) 4 EHRR 38; cf. *Sibson* v *United Kingdom* (1993) 17 EHRR 193).
2. The right to join a trade union does not override reasonable union rules about membership—*Cheall* v *United Kingdom* (1986) 8 EHRR 74. See also *Associated Society of Locomotive Engineers & Firemen (ASLEF)* v *United Kingdom* [2007] IRLR 361 (an extract appears at p. 617 (Chapter 10, Section 4.B)).
3. Article 11 sets out no obligation on an employer to recognise trades union or to engage in collective bargaining (*Swedish Engine Driver's Union* v *Sweden (1979–80)* 1 EHRR 617: although the Employment Relations Act 1999 does contain obligations relating to compulsory recognition).
4. *National Union of Rail, Maritime and Transport Workers* v *United Kingdom* [2014] IRLR 467, involved a challenge by RMT alleging that its ability to protect its members' interests was subject to excessive statutory restriction, in violation of its right to freedom of association under Article 11. The application raised two specific issues: the complex strike-balloting provisions in British legislation and the prohibition on all secondary strike action. Both claims were unsuccessful. In relation to the ban on secondary action, the ECtHR stated that:

   by its nature secondary action may well have much broader ramifications than primary action. It has the potential to impinge upon the rights of persons not party to the industrial dispute, to cause broad disruption within the economy and to affect the delivery of services to the public. Accordingly, the Court is satisfied that in banning secondary action, Parliament pursued the legitimate aim of protecting the rights and freedoms of others, not limited to the employer side in an industrial dispute.' This left the question whether the statutory ban on secondary industrial action is 'necessary in a democratic society.

The Court observed that this meant that it must be shown that the interference 'corresponds to a "pressing social need", that the reasons given by the national authorities to justify it are relevant and sufficient and that it is proportionate to the legitimate aim pursued'. In holding that this was satisfied, the ECtHR accepted that 'strike action is clearly protected by Article 11'. However, Contracting States have a margin of appreciation as to how trade union freedom is to be protected. If a legislative restriction strikes at the core of trade union activity, a lesser margin of appreciation is to be accorded, but the Court took the view that 'it cannot be said that the effect of the ban on secondary action struck at the very substance of the applicant's freedom of association'. Therefore, the margin of appreciation was a wider one. This led the ECtHR to conclude that there was not 'an unjustified interference with the applicant's right to freedom of association, the essential elements of which the applicant was able to exercise, in representing its members, in negotiating with the employer on behalf of its members who were in dispute with the employer and in organising a strike of those members at their place of work'.

(For a more detailed analysis of the HRA 1998 and the implications for Employment Law see: Ewing, K. D. (ed.), *Human Rights At Work* (London: Institute of Employment Rights, 2000); Ewing, K. D., 'The Human Rights Act and labour law' (1998) 27 ILJ 275; Honeyball, S., *Honeyball & Bowers' Textbook on Employment Law*, 13th edn (Oxford: OUP, 2014), Ch. 16; Allen, R. and Crasnow, R., *Employment Law and Human Rights* (Oxford: OUP, 2002).)

4. In 2014, the Conservative Party pledged that, if re-elected, it would legislate to ensure that rulings of the ECtHR could be vetoed by the UK Parliament. If this change were to be rejected by the Council of Europe, a future Conservative Government would be prepared to withdraw from the Convention and introduce a British Bill of Rights (*Protecting Human Rights in the UK: The Conservatives' proposals for changing Britain's human rights law*, Conservative Party, 2014).

SECTION 5: EUROPEAN COMMUNITY LAW

A: Historical background

When the Treaty of Rome was signed by the UK in 1972, the prospects for using it as a vehicle for improvements in labour law protections were not readily apparent. The primary idea behind the Treaty was the benefits which would flow from liberalisation of trade and the expansion of the market for goods and services. With the exceptions of Article 119 (now 157) (dealing with equal pay) and Articles 48–51 (now 45–48) (requiring free movement of workers), the references to social policy issues were extremely vague with little indication as to how improvements would be achieved. Indeed, the articles on equal pay and free movement were inserted primarily on the basis of an economic—as opposed to a social—rationale (see Davies, P. L., 'The emergence of European labour law' in William McCarthy (ed.), *Legal Intervention in Industrial Relations: Gains and losses* (Oxford: Basil Blackwell, 1992), Ch. 10).

By 1972, there was an emerging view amongst the heads of government of the Member States that the Community should adopt a policy of more rigorous action in the social field. This led to the Social Action Programme which was adopted by the Council of Ministers in 1974. However, 'the argument for a social policy was still one that made social policy subordinate to economic goals, but it was now accepted that economic growth through closer European economic integration would require the support of a *Community* social policy, both to ensure that the benefits of growth were adequately diffused throughout Europe and to help socialise the costs of economic growth' (Davies, 'The emergence of European labour law', at p. 326).

The Social Action Programme produced a series of directives which were adopted between 1974–9 and which constitute the main body of Community labour law. These are as follows:

- The Equal Pay Directive 75/117/EEC.
- The Directive on Collective Redundancies 75/129/EEC.
- The Equal Treatment Directive 76/207/EEC.
- The Transfer of Undertakings Directive 77/187/EEC.
- The Social Security Directive 79/7/EEC.
- The Directive on Insolvency 80/987/EEC.

The 'legal base' for these measures was generally Article 100 (now 94), though, on occasion, Article 235 (now 308) was employed. Both Articles require a unanimous vote in the Council of Ministers. Following this flurry of activity, little else was achieved until the late 1980s. The election of a Conservative Government in 1979, determined to free the labour market from control imposed by legislation or collective bargaining, meant that all but the most innocuous measures, generally concerned with health and safety, were vetoed. Among the measures which were blocked by the UK were draft directives on parental leave and temporary and part-time work. Also moves by the EEC to finalise draft directives on company law and on information and consultation procedures (the 'Vredling' Directive) were strongly opposed, and this left the process of introducing EC legislation on worker rights of participation temporarily in limbo.

During the 1980s, it was accepted that the completion of the single internal market required amendments to the Treaty of Rome. This was achieved by the passage of the Single European Act, which came into force in July 1987. Under the Act, certain Community legislation can be adopted by qualified majority voting (QMV) rather than by requiring the agreement of all Member States. This included measures relating to the establishment or functioning of the internal market but, significantly, specifically excluded provisions 'relating to the rights and interests of employed persons' (Article 100a (now 114) of the Treaty of Rome). On the other hand, provisions on 'improvements, especially in the working environment, as regards the health and safety of workers' were covered by QMV (Article 118a (now 153). Under the QMV procedure, Council members' votes are weighted according to the size of their State's population.

While the UK Government was pursuing its policy of deregulation during the 1980s, the EC was following a different path. In 1989 the European Commission published its Charter of Fundamental Social Rights. The Charter represented principles on the future of European workplace policy, and proposed a number of social and employment rights for EC citizens. These included, for example, a right to 'fair remuneration' and annual paid leave, the right to belong to a trade union, and rights in relation to working time.

Other aspects of the Charter, for example those establishing rights to 'equal treatment' and 'participation' in decision-making processes and in redundancy situations, were, of course, anathema to the then UK Government.

The Commission's hope was that the Charter would be unanimously adopted by the Council of Ministers. It would then form the basis of an 'action programme' which would be binding on Member States if adopted.

The then UK Government strongly opposed the Charter, and continued to resist much of the detailed legislation designed to implement it, on the ground that it would lead to excessive regulation and would impede rather than foster the creation of jobs. Indeed, Mrs Thatcher described the Charter as 'inspired by the values of Karl Marx and the class struggle'. It was, therefore, unsurprising when, at the meeting of the European Council in Strasbourg in December 1989, the UK was the only dissenting voice amongst 'the twelve' on the question of the adoption of the Charter.

At the Maastricht summit in December 1991, the UK strongly resisted the expansion of EC legislative activity in the area of social policy. The Treaty on European Union which resulted from the negotiations was signed by the Heads of the Member States at Maastricht on 7 February 1992. However, the accompanying protocol and agreement which extended the scope of the qualified voting procedure into new areas of social policy covered only 14 of the then 15 Member States—the UK being in a minority of one. In July 1993, after a bitter and prolonged parliamentary struggle culminating in a vote of confidence in the Major Government, the Social Protocol was not incorporated in the Act approving the Maastricht Treaty.

The Social Policy Agreement (SPA) extended the areas in which directives can be enacted by qualified majority to include health and safety; working conditions; the information and consultation of workers; equality of treatment with regard to labour market opportunities and treatment at work; and the 'integration' of people excluded from the labour market. It continues to require unanimity for social security and social welfare; representation and collective defence of workers; conditions of employment for non-EU nationals; and financing job promotion and creation. The basis of the protocol was that all Member States apart from the UK 'wish to continue along the path laid down in the 1989 Social Charter'.

The UK's situation was further complicated by the fact that the Commission retained its powers within the framework of the EC of 15 to propose and press for directives in the social field on the basis of the EC Treaty, i.e. Articles 118a (now 153 of the Treaty on the Functioning of the European Union), 100a (now 114) and 100 (now 115). This caused immediate problems in relation to measures the EC was keen to enact using those provisions. Not least of these was the Directive on Working Hours and Holidays (Directive 93/104/EC concerning the organisation of working time), which had been adopted by the EC Commission in 1990 and was based on Article 118a (now 153). This was not unreasonable given the co-relation between excessive hours of work and accidents, and the recognised effects of stress at work. It was not, however, how the UK Government saw things, and in a belated attempt to block progress on the measure it launched an unsuccessful action in the European Court of Justice against the directive (see *Council of the European Union* [1997] IRLR 30).

During the five years of the British opt-out from the Social Policy Protocol (SPP) only two pieces of legislation were adopted—the European Works Council (EWC) Directive 94/95, and the Directive on Parental Leave (96/34/EC). As Barnard wryly observes: 'It seems that despite the avowed intention in the SPP "to continue along the path laid down in the 1989 Social Chapter" they have done so with little enthusiasm in the absence of their recalcitrant brother' (Barnard, C., 'The United Kingdom, the "Social Chapter" and the Amsterdam Treaty' (1997) 26 ILJ 275, at p. 279).

With the election of the new Labour Government in May 1997 came a marked change of policy in the UK towards the social dimension of the European Union. Within days of its election, the Government formally announced its commitment to 'sign up' to the Social Chapter. The new, more positive UK approach towards the European Union was underlined with the signing of the Treaty of Amsterdam in October 1997.

The Treaty of Lisbon was signed on 13 December 2007 by representatives of the then 27 Member States. It came into force on 1 December 2009, after being ratified by the Member States. The Treaty amends the EU's two core treaties, the Treaty of European Union and the Treaty Establishing the European Union. The latter is renamed the Treaty on the Functioning of European Union (TFEU).

CONSOLIDATED VERSIONS OF THE TREATY ON EUROPEAN UNION AND THE TREATY ON THE FUNCTIONING OF THE EUROPEAN UNION (OJ 2008,C115/01)

TITLE X SOCIAL POLICY

Article 151 (ex Article 136)

The Union and the Member States, having in mind fundamental social rights such as those set out in the European Social Charter signed at Turin on 18 October 1961 and in the 1989 Community Charter of the Fundamental Social Rights of Workers, shall have as their objectives the promotion of employment, improved living and working conditions, so as to make possible their harmonisation while the improvement is being maintained, proper social protection, dialogue between management and labour, the development of human resources with a view to lasting high employment and the combating of exclusion.

To this end the Union and the Member States shall implement measures which take account of the diverse forms of national practices, in particular in the field of contractual relations, and the need to maintain the competitiveness of the Union economy.

They believe that such a development will ensue not only from the functioning of the internal market, which will favour the harmonisation of social systems, but also from the procedures provided for in this Treaty and from the approximation of provisions laid down by law, regulation or administrative action.

Article 153 (ex Article 137)

1. With a view to achieving the objectives of Article 151, the Union shall support and complement the activities of the Member States in the following fields:
   (a) improvement in particular of the working environment to protect workers' health and safety;
   (b) working conditions;
   (c) social security and social protection of workers;
   (d) protection of workers where their employment contract is terminated;
   (e) the information and consultation of workers;
   (f) representation and collective defence of the interests of workers and employers, including co-determination…
   (g) conditions of employment for third-country nationals legally residing in Union territory;
   (h) the integration of persons excluded from the labour market…
   (j) the combating of social exclusion;
   (k) the modernisation of social protection systems without prejudice to point (c).

NOTES: Certain significant issues of social policy are specifically excluded from the remit of the EU. These are pay, the right of association, the right to strike, or the right to impose lock-outs (Article 153(5)). The major exception to the exclusion of EU competence in relation to pay relates to equal pay between the sexes (see Article 157).

The social policy objectives set out in Article 153(1)(c), (d), (f), and (g) must be passed unanimously by the European Council of Ministers (Article 153(2)). As a result, any Member State has an effective veto over legislative initiatives aimed at harmonising social security regulation, laws protecting workers where their employment contract is terminated, trade union representation, and worker participation. On the other hand, the policy objectives set out in Article 153(1)(a), (b), (e), (h), (i), and (j) can be passed by a majority vote.

Article 154 (ex Article 138)

1. The Commission shall have the task of promoting the consultation of management and labour at Union level and shall take any relevant measure to facilitate their dialogue by ensuring balanced support for the parties.

2. To this end, before submitting proposals in the social policy field, the Commission shall consult management and labour on the possible direction of Union action.

3. If, after such consultation, the Commission considers Union action advisable, it shall consult management and labour on the content of the envisaged proposal. Management and labour shall forward to the Commission an opinion or, where appropriate, a recommendation.

4. On the occasion of such consultation referred to in paragraphs 2 and 3, management and labour may inform the Commission of their wish to initiate the process provided for in Article 155. The duration of the procedure shall not exceed nine months, unless the management and labour concerned and the Commission decide jointly to extend it.

Article 155 (ex Article 139)

1. Should management and labour so desire, the dialogue between them at Community level may lead to contractual relations, including agreements.

2. Agreements concluded at Community level shall be implemented either in accordance with the procedures and practices specific to management and labour and the Member States or, in matters covered by Article 153, at the joint request of the signatory parties, by a Council decision on a proposal from the Commission. The European Parliament shall be informed.

The Council shall act unanimously where the agreement in question contains one or more provisions relating to one of the areas for which unanimity is required pursuant to Article 153(2).

Article 156 (ex Article 140)

With a view to achieving the objectives of Article 151 and without prejudice to the other provisions of the Treaties, the Commission shall encourage cooperation between the Member States and facilitate the coordination of their action in all social policy fields under this Chapter, particularly in matters relating to:
• employment;
• labour law and working conditions;
• basic and advanced vocational training;
• social security;
• prevention of occupational accidents and diseases;

- occupational hygiene;
- the right of association and collective bargaining between employers and workers.

To this end, the Commission shall act in close contact with Member States by making studies, delivering opinions and arranging consultations both on problems arising at national level and on those of concern to international organisations . . .

Before delivering the opinions provided for in this Article, the Commission shall consult the Economic and Social Committee.

Article 157 (ex Article 141)

1. Each Member State shall ensure that the principle of equal pay for male and female workers for equal work or work of equal value is applied.

2. For the purpose of this Article, 'pay' means the ordinary basic or minimum wage or salary and any other consideration, whether in cash or in kind, which the worker receives directly or indirectly, in respect of his employment, from his employer.

Equal pay without discrimination based on sex means:

(a) that pay for the same work at piece rates shall be calculated on the basis of the same unit of measurement;

(b) that pay for work at time rates shall be the same for the same job.

3. The European Parliament and the Council, acting in accordance with the procedure referred to in Article 251, and after consulting the Economic and Social Committee, shall adopt measures to ensure the application of the principle of equal opportunities and equal treatment of men and women in matters of employment and occupation, including the principle of equal pay for equal work or work of equal value.

4. With a view to ensuring full equality in practice between men and women in working life, the principle of equal treatment shall not prevent any Member State from maintaining or adopting measures providing for specific advantages in order to make it easier for the under-represented sex to pursue a vocational activity or to prevent or compensate for disadvantages in professional careers.

Article 158 (ex Article 142

Member States shall endeavour to maintain the existing equivalence between paid holiday schemes.

NOTE: There are also extensive references to employment rights in the European Union's Charter of Fundamental Rights, which was signed in Nice in 2000. These include: freedom of assembly and association (Article 12); freedom to choose an occupation and the right to engage in work (Article 15); non-discrimination 'based on any ground such as sex, race, colour, ethnic, or social origin, genetic features, language, religion or belief, political or other opinion, membership of a national minority, property, birth, disability, age or sexual orientation' (Article 21); equality between men and women (Article 23); integration of persons with disabilities (Article 26); workers' rights to information and consultation within the undertaking (Article 27); rights of collective bargaining and action (Article 28); protection in the event of unjustified dismissal (Article 30); the right to fair and just working conditions (Article 31); prohibition of child labour and the protection of young people at work (Article 32); the right to protection from dismissal for a reason connected with maternity and the right to paid maternity leave and to paternity leave (Article 33).

Article 6 of the Treaty on European Union (as amended by Article 1(8) of the Treaty of Lisbon) provides that 'The Union recognises the rights, freedoms and principles set out in the Charter of Fundamental Rights of the European Union of 7 December 2000, as adapted at Strasbourg, on 12 December 2007, which shall have the same legal value of the Treaties'. Previously, the Charter had no more than advisory status in relation to Member States.

B: Recent examples of the impact of EU employment legislation

- **Posting of Workers Directive 96/71/EC (adopted 24 September 1996)** This seeks to give workers temporarily sent to work in another Member State (posted workers) the right to receive the minimum pay and conditions applicable to that State's own nationals. Implementation date: 24 September 1999. In Britain, most existing legislation relevant to the directive already applies to all employees or workers whether or not working permanently here. However, minor changes to legislation have been made to implement the directive. First, the Employment Relations Act 1999, s. 32 has removed territorial provisions in the Employment Rights Act 1996, so that the rights affected apply to all employees in Britain, including those temporarily posted here. Second, the legislation to counter discrimination on the grounds of sex, race, and disability has been amended so that those employed mainly outside Britain are no longer excluded from its scope. These changes have been made by the Equal Opportunities (Employment Legislation) (Territorial Limits) Regulations 1999 (SI 1999/3163).

- **Parental Leave Directive 96/34/EC (adopted June 1996)** This allows parents the right to take at least three months' unpaid parental leave. The Employment Relations Act 1999 provides the Secretary of State with the power to make regulations designed to regulate parental leave. The Maternity and Parental Leave etc. Regulations 1999 (SI 1999/3312) came into force on 15 December 1999. The Employment Act 2002 provided for extended maternity and parental rights, including two weeks' paid paternity leave and 26 weeks' paid adoption leave, to be introduced from 2003.

- **Part-time Work Directive 97/81/EC (adopted May 1997)** This provides for 'the removal of discrimination against part-time workers and to improve the quality of part-time work' and 'to facilitate the development of part-time work'. The Employment Relations Act 1999, s. 19 provides the Secretary of State with the power to make regulations designed to implement the directive. The Part-time Workers (Prevention of Less Favourable Treatment) Regulations (SI 2000/1551) came into force on 1 July 2000.

- **European Works Councils Directive 94/45/EEC (adopted 22 September 1994)** This envisages the setting up of bodies for the informing and consulting of employees within Community-scale undertakings above a certain size. The UK had to give effect to this law by December 1999. This directive is implemented in the UK by the Transnational Information and Consultation of Employees Regulations 1999 (SI 1999/3323), which came into force on 15 January 2000. They set out the procedures for negotiating a European Works Council agreement (or other European-level information and consultation procedure), the enforcement mechanisms, provisions on confidential information, transitional provisions and exemptions, and statutory protection for employees.

- **Burden of Proof in Sex Discrimination Cases Directive 97/80/EC (adopted 15 December 1997, extended to the UK by Directive 98/52)** This requires Member States to take measures to ensure that the burden of disproving discrimination shifts to the employer when facts from which it may be presumed that there has been direct or indirect discrimination have been established. The directive also contains a definition of indirect discrimination and defines the justification which is needed to defeat a claim of indirect discrimination. The directive was implemented in the UK by the Sex Discrimination (Indirect Discrimination and Burden of Proof) Regulations 2001 (SI 2001/2660) which came into force on 12 October 2001 (see now Equality Act (EqA) 2010, s. 136).

- **Framework Directive establishing a general framework for equal treatment in employment and occupation 2000/78/EC (adopted 27 November 2000); Race Directive, implementing the principle of equal treatment between persons irrespective of racial or ethnic origins 2000/43/EC (adopted 29 June 2000)** The directives require Member States to outlaw discrimination on the grounds of race, sexual orientation, religion or belief, disability, and age in the fields of employment and training. Member States had until 2 December 2003 to implement measures combating discrimination on grounds of sexual orientation, religion, or belief and until 2 December 2006 to implement measures on age and disability discrimination. The Employment Equality (Sexual Orientation) Regulations 2003 and the Employment Equality (Religion or Belief) Regulations 2003 implement the major strands of Council Directive 2000/78/EC. They came into force on 1 and 2 December 2003 respectively. Amendments to the Disability Discrimination Act 1995 came into force in October 2004 and the new regulations oblige service providers (e.g. businesses and organisations) to make reasonable adjustments to the physical features of their premises to overcome physical barriers to access—(see the Disability Discrimination (Providers of Services) (Adjustment of Premises) Regulations 2001 (SI 2001/3253). Changes to the RRA 1976 came into force in July 2003. The Race Relations Act 1976 (Amendment) Regulations 2003 implement Article 13 of the Race Directive. The regulations enhance the RRA by, for example, amending the definition of indirect discrimination and changing the way in which the burden of proof applies, as well as removing a number of exceptions from the legislation. In relation to age discrimination, in July 2005 the Government launched a consultation on the draft Employment Equality (Age) Regulations 2006. The legislation came into force on 1 October 2006.

- **The Revised Acquired Rights Directive 98/50/EC** The Government published a consultation paper on how it proposed to revise the Transfer of Undertakings (Protection of Employment) Regulations to bring them into line with the revised directive (see *Transfer of Undertakings (Protection of Employment) Regulations 1981, Government Proposals for Reform*, Employment Relations Directorate, DTI, September 2001). After much delay, the Government laid the revising regulations before Parliament on 7 February 2006, bringing them into force on 6 April 2006. The reason given for the delay was the large volume of responses to the consultation document (URN 05/926) and the many issues raised by the respondents.

- **Young Workers Directive 94/33/EC (adopted 22 June 1994)** This was implemented by 22 June 1996. Certain provisions were implemented in Britain on 1 October 1998 when the Working Time Regulations 1998 (SI 1998/1833) came into force. But the Government took advantage of a time-limited opt-out allowing it not to adopt other provisions. The opt-outs ended on 22 June 2000. The Working Time (Amendment) Regulations 2000 (SI 2000/3128) seek to implement the remaining parts of the directive. The regulations came into force with effect from 6 April 2003.

- **Council Directive 1999/70/EC of 28 June 1999 concerning the framework agreement concluded by the European Trade Union Confederation (ETUC), the Union of Industrial and Employers' Confederations of Europe (UNICE), and the European Centre of Enterprises with Public Participation (CEEP) on fixed-term work** The directive aimed to prevent workers on fixed-term contracts being treated less favourably than similar workers on permanent contracts, and to limit the use of successive fixed-term contracts. The Government announced on 8 November 2001 that it would be using the Employment Act 2002 to prevent pay and pensions discrimination against fixed-term workers and to transpose the Fixed Term Work Directive. The Government was due to transpose the directive into UK regulations via the Fixed-term Employees (Prevention of Less Favourable Treatment) Regulations 2002 (SI 2002/2034), which came into force on 10 October 2002.

- **Directive 2000/34/EC** This directive extended the original directive on the organisation of working time to cover previously excluded sectors and activities. (Adopted on 22 June 2000; to be implemented by Member States by 1 August 2003; with regard to junior doctors the date was 1 August 2004.) The Working Time Regulations were amended with effect from 1 August 2003 to extend working time measures in full to all non-mobile workers in road, sea, inland waterways, and lake transport; to all workers on the railway; and to offshore workers. Mobile workers in road transport have more limited protection. The regulations would apply to junior doctors from 1 August 2004 (see the Working Time (Amendment) Regulations 2003 (SI 2003/1684)).

- **Council Directive 2001/86/EC** This supplements the Statute for a European Company with regard to employee involvement (adopted 8 October 2001; to be implemented by Member States by 8 October 2004).

- **Directive 2002/14/EC establishing a general framework for informing and consulting employees in the EC** Adopted in February 2002, the directive requires Member States to introduce new legislation requiring all undertakings with at least 50 employees to inform and consult employee representatives on a range of key business, employment, and restructuring issues. The UK had three years to commence the implementation of the directive (i.e. until March 2005). In the first instance, it applied to businesses with 150 or more employees. In 2007, it applied to businesses with 100 or more employees and after a further one year (w.e.f. 1 April 2008) to ones with 50 or more employees.

- **Directive 2008/104/EC on conditions for temporary (agency) workers—more usually known as the 'Agency Workers Directive'** Member States had until 5 December 2011 to implement the directive. It provides agency workers in the UK who have worked in the end-user organisation for 12 weeks with the right to equal treatment in basic working and employment conditions with employees of the end-user. The directive is implemented in the UK by the Agency Workers Regulations 2010 (SI 2010/93). The regulations came into force on 1 October 2011.

C: The relationship between Community law and domestic law

The general rule is that the articles of the Treaty of Rome cannot be enforced directly by the individual citizen against a Member State. The citizen must wait for the Government to legislate and transform its international treaty obligation into domestic law. In relation to the Treaty of Rome, this was accomplished by the European Communities Act 1972.

EUROPEAN COMMUNITIES ACT 1972

2. (1) All such rights, powers, liabilities and restrictions from time to time created or arising by or under the Treaties, and all such remedies and procedures from time to time provided for by or under the Treaties, as in accordance with the Treaties are without further enactment to be given legal effect or used in the United Kingdom shall be recognised and available in law, and be enforced, allowed and followed accordingly; and the expression 'enforceable Community right' and similar expressions shall be read as referring to one to which this subsection applies.

NOTE: Where Community legislation has been enacted, there are limits to the extent to which any Member State has the freedom to avoid its obligations. Under Article 226 (ex 169), if the Commission considers that a Member State has failed to fulfil an obligation under Community law, it may bring infringement proceedings against the State before the European Court of Justice (ECJ) and obtain a declaration obliging the Member State to end that violation. Moreover, the UK is subject to the interpretation given to EC law by the ECJ, particularly in response to references from the courts of Member States under Article 234 (ex 177).

(i) Supremacy

R v *Secretary of State for Transport, ex p. Factortame Ltd (No. 2)*
(Case C–213/89) [1991] 1 All ER 70, European Court of Justice

DECISION: 17. It is clear from the information before the court, and in particular from the judgment making the reference and, as described above, the course taken by the proceedings in the national courts before which the case came at first and second instance, that the preliminary question raised by the House of Lords seeks essentially to ascertain whether a national court which, in a case before it concerning Community law, considers that the sole obstacle which precludes it from granting interim relief is a rule of national law must disapply that rule.

18. For the purpose of replying to that question, it is necessary to point out that in its judgment in *Amministrazione delle Finanze dello Stato* v *Simmenthal SpA* Case 106/77 [1978] ECR 629 at 643 (paras 14, 17) the court held that directly applicable rules of Community law—

> must be fully and uniformly applied in all the Member States from the date of their entry into force and for so long as they continue in force [and that] in accordance with the principle of the precedence of Community law, the relationship between provisions of the Treaty and directly applicable measures of the institutions on the one hand and the national law of the Member States on the other is such that those provisions and measures…by their entry into force render automatically inapplicable any conflicting provision of…national law…

19. In accordance with the case law of the court, it is for the national courts, in application of the principle of co-operation laid down in art 5 of the EEC Treaty, to ensure the legal protection which persons derive from the direct effect of provisions of Community law (see, most recently, the judgments in *Amministrazione delle Finanze dello Stato* v *Ariete SpA* Case 811/79 [1980] ECR 2545 and *Amministrazione delle Finanze dello Stato* v *Sas Mediterranea Importazione Rappresentanze Esportazione Commercio (MIRECO)* Case 826/79 [1980] ECR 2559).

20. The court has also held that any provision of a national legal system and any legislative, administrative or judicial practice which might impair the effectiveness of Community law by withholding from the national court having jurisdiction to apply such law the power to do everything necessary at the moment of its application to set aside national legislative provisions which might prevent, even temporarily, Community rules from having full force and effect are incompatible with those requirements, which are the very essence of Community law (see the *Simmenthal* case, Case 106/77 [1978] ECR 629 at 644 at (paras 22–23)).

21. It must be added that the full effectiveness of Community law would be just as much impaired if a rule of national law could prevent a court seised of a dispute governed by Community law from granting interim relief in order to ensure the full effectiveness of the judgment to be given on the existence of the rights claimed under Community law. It follows that a court which in those circumstances would grant interim relief, if it were not for a rule of national law, is obliged to set aside that rule.

22. That interpretation is reinforced by the system established by art 177 [now 234] of the EEC Treaty, whose effectiveness would be impaired if a national court, having stayed proceedings pending the reply by the Court of Justice to the question referred to it for a preliminary ruling, were not able to grant interim relief until it delivered its judgment following the reply given by the Court of Justice.

23. Consequently, the reply to the question raised should be that Community law must be interpreted as meaning that a national court which, in a case before it concerning Community law, considers that the sole obstacle which precludes it from granting interim relief is a rule of national law must set aside that rule.

(ii) Direct effect

Kowalska v *Freie und Hansestadt Hamburg*
[1990] IRLR 447, European Court of Justice

…Article 119 [now 141] of the EEC Treaty is sufficiently precise to be relied upon by an individual before a National Court in order to have any national provision set aside, which may include a collective agreement, which is contrary to that Article.

NOTE: The Treaty of Rome is supplemented by directives made by the Council of Ministers. Under Article 249 (ex 189) of the Treaty, a directive is 'binding as to the result to be achieved' but the form and method of achieving the result is left to the individual Member State.

In certain circumstances, however, a directive may be held to be directly enforceable. In *Van Duyn* v *Home Office* [1975] 3 All ER 190, it was held that a directive *could* be enforceable by an individual, and this depended on whether the directive was 'clear, precise, admitted of no exceptions, and therefore of its nature needed no intervention by the national authorities'.

Unlike provisions of the Treaty which may be enforceable against private individuals and organisations and have, therefore, a 'horizontal direct effect', directives can only have a direct effect against the Member State itself as an employer (i.e. a vertical direct effect); they are not enforceable against a private sector employer.

Marshall v Southampton and South-West Hampshire Area Health Authority (Teaching)
[1986] IRLR 140; [1986] ECR 723, European Court of Justice

The facts of this case are set out at p. 230 (Chapter 5, Section 2).

DECISION: It is necessary to recall that, according to a long line of decisions of the Court (in particular its judgment of 19.1.82 in Case 8/81, *Becker* v *Finanzamt Munster-Innenstadt* [1982] ECR 53), wherever the provisions of a Directive appear, as far as their subject-matter is concerned, to be unconditional and sufficiently precise, those provisions may be relied upon by an individual against the State where that State fails to implement the Directive in national law by the end of the period prescribed or where it fails to implement the Directive correctly.

That view is based on the consideration that it would be incompatible with the binding nature which Article 189 [now 249] confers on the Directive to hold as a matter of principle that the obligation imposed thereby cannot be relied on by those concerned. From that the Court deduced that a Member State which has not adopted the implementing measures required by the Directive within the prescribed period may not plead, as against individuals, its own failure to perform the obligations which the Directive entails...

With regard to the argument that a directive may not be relied upon by an individual, it must be emphasised that according to Article 189 [now 249] of the EEC Treaty the binding nature of a directive, which constitutes the basis for the possibility of relying on the directive before a national court, exists only in relation to 'each Member State to which it is addressed'. It follows that a directive may not of itself impose obligations on an individual and that a provision of a directive may not be relied upon as against such a person.

NOTES
1. While it is clear that directives can be enforced only against bodies which are 'organs or emanations of the State', there was, until recently, some doubt as to the scope of this phrase. In *Foster* v *British Gas* [1990] IRLR 354, the House of Lords referred the matter to the European Court for a ruling. The ECJ was prepared to give a wide definition to these terms. It held that a directive which has direct effect may be relied upon in a claim against a body, whatever its legal form, which has been made responsible for providing a public service under the control of the State and has for that purpose special powers beyond those which result from the normal rules applicable in relations between private individuals. This broad approach means that local government, universities and colleges, and nationalised industries all clearly now fall within the potential scope of direct effect.
2. The limitation on the enforceability of directives is perhaps less important than it would be given the ruling of the ECJ in *Francovich* v *Italian Republic* [1992] IRLR 84. In *Francovich* the ECJ ruled that when an individual suffers damage as a result of a Member State's failure correctly to implement a directive which confers rights for the benefit of the individual, the individual can sue the State directly under European law for the damage suffered by the State's failure. This ruling considerably strengthens the position of private sector workers.
3. In more recent judgments, the ECJ has elaborated upon the criteria for State liability. In *R* v *HM Treasury, ex p. British Telecommunications plc* [1996] IRLR 300, the ECJ held that where a Member State incorrectly transposes a Community directive into national law the following conditions apply: the rule of law infringed must be intended to confer rights on individuals; the breach must be sufficiently serious; and there must be a direct causal link between the breach of the obligation resting on the State and the damage sustained by the injured parties.

4. A breach is 'sufficiently serious' where, in the exercise of its legislative powers, an institution or a Member State has manifestly and gravely disregarded the limit on the exercise of its powers. Factors which the competent court may take into account include the clarity and precision of the rule breached (see also (1) *Brasserie du Pêcheur SA* v *Federal Republic of Germany* and (2) *R* v *Secretary of State for Transport, ex p. Factortame Ltd and others (No. 3)* [1996] IRLR 267, ECJ).

(iii) Indirect effect

Litster v Forth Dry Dock Engineering Co. Ltd
[1989] 1 All ER 1134, House of Lords

This case is concerned with the interpretation of the Transfer of Undertakings (Protection of Employment) Regulations 1981 in the light of the EC Employee Rights on Transfer of Business Directive 77/187. This aspect of the case is discussed at p. 530 (Chapter 9, Section 5.B(iii)).

LORD TEMPLEMAN: In *von Colson and Kamann* v *Land Nordrhein-Westfalen* (Case 14/83) [1984] ECR 1891, 1909 the European Court of Justice dealing with Directive (76/207/EEC), forbidding discrimination on grounds of sex regarding access to employment, ruled that:

the Member States' obligation arising from a Directive to achieve the result envisaged by the Directive and their duty under Article 5 [now 10] of the Treaty to take all appropriate measures, whether general or particular, to ensure the fulfilment of that obligation, is binding on all the authorities of Member States including, for matters within their jurisdiction, the courts. It follows that, in applying the national law and in particular the provisions of a national law specifically introduced in order to implement Directive [(76/207/EEC)], national courts are required to interpret their national law in the light of the wording and purpose of the Directive in order to achieve the result referred to in the third paragraph of Article 189 [now 249].

Thus the courts of the United Kingdom are under a duty to follow the practice of the European Court in giving a purposive construction to directives and regulations issued for the purpose of complying with directives. In *Pickstone* v *Freemans plc* [1988] IRLR 357, this House implied words in a regulation designed to give effect to Directive (75/117/EEC) dealing with equal pay for women doing work of equal value. If this House had not been able to make the necessary implication, the Equal Pay (Amendment) Regulations 1983 would have failed their object and the United Kingdom would have been in breach of its treaty obligations to give effect to Directives.

Duke v GEC Reliance Ltd
[1988] IRLR 118, House of Lords

The complainant alleged sex discrimination when she had been required to retire at the age of 60, while men could work on to 65. Because she was not a State employee, she could not rely on EC law as interpreted in *Marshall* (in Section (ii)). Further, her case was brought before changes introduced by the SDA 1986 took effect. Her argument was based on interpreting the SDA 1975, s. 6(4) (a provision which allowed for differential retirement ages based on gender) in accordance with the Equal Treatment Directive. The argument was rejected by the House of Lords.

LORD TEMPLEMAN: Section 2(4) of the European Communities Act 1972 does not in my opinion enable or constrain a British court to distort the meaning of a British statute in order to enforce against an individual a Community directive which has no direct effect between individuals...It would be most unfair to the respondent to distort the construction of the 1975 Sex Discrimination Act in order to accommodate the Equal Treatment Directive as construed by the European Court in the 1986 *Marshall* case. As between the appellant and respondent the Equal Treatment Directive did not have direct effect and the respondent could not be reasonably expected to appreciate the logic of Community legislators in permitting differential retirement ages. The respondent is not liable to the appellant under Community law. I decline to hold that liability under British law attaches to the respondent or any other private employer to pay damages based on wages which women over 60 and under 65 did not earn before the amending Sex Discrimination Act 1986 for the first time and without retrospective effect introduced the statutory tort of operating differential retirement ages.

NOTES

1. The correctness of this approach was acknowledged by the House of Lords in *Webb* v *EMO Air Cargo (UK) Ltd* [1993] IRLR 27, HL. However, there is a strong argument that the House of Lords' view that it cannot construe a national Act purposively, where it was enacted prior to the relevant directive, flies in the face of EC law. In *Marleasing SA* v *La Commercial Internacional di Alimentacion* Case 106/89 (13 November 1990), the ECJ stated:

   > It followed from the obligation on Member States to take all measures appropriate to ensure the performance of their obligations to achieve the results provided for in Directives, that in applying national law, whether it was a case of provisions prior to or subsequent to the Directive, the national court called on to interpret it was required to do so as far as possible in the light of the wording and purpose of the Directive in order to achieve the result sought by the Directive.

2. Other Community measures include:
   (a) Recommendations: in *Grimaldi* v *Fonds des Maladies Professionelles* [1990] IRLR 400, the ECJ ruled that national courts must take such non-binding measures into account, in particular to clarify the interpretation of other provisions of national and Community law.
   (b) Regulations: under Article 288 (ex 249) of the TFEU, a regulation is stated to be of general application, binding in its entirety and directly applicable in all Member States.

FURTHER READING

Cabrelli, D., *Employment Law in Context: Text and Materials* (Oxford: OUP, 2014), Ch. 2.

Honeyball, S., *Honeyball and Bowers' Textbook on Employment Law*, 13th edn (Oxford: OUP, 2014), Ch. 1.

2

Defining the Contract of Employment and its Continuity

SECTION 1: GENERAL INTRODUCTION: THE RESIDUAL IMPORTANCE OF THE LAW OF CONTRACT

As we saw in Chapter 1, the individual employment relationship was altered quite radically by the legislation of the 1970s which created the statutory floor of employment rights and a specialised system of industrial tribunals through which disputes over these rights are adjudicated. Does this mean that the law of contract no longer provides the foundation of employment law? Is possession of the status of 'employee' the all-important issue, given that it is that status and not contract which attracts the rights bestowed by statute? To accept this view would be going too far, however, for a number of reasons.

First, today there are still many situations for which statute has not legislated, and it is then up to the law of contract to fill the gap and supply the answers to questions such as whether there is a right to receive wages when absent through sickness (see *Mears* v *Safecar Security Ltd* [1982] 2 All ER 865).

Second, even when it comes to adjudicating statutory rights, the courts and tribunals will often look to the guidance of contractual theories in reaching a decision, for example in the context of unfair dismissal, whether an employee's repudiation of the contract requires acceptance by the employer in the form of a dismissal or whether the repudiation automatically brings the contract to an end.

Third, the law of industrial action and possible immunity from the economic torts is often influenced by whether or not a breach of contract has occurred.

Last, as was seen in the introduction, the perceived weakness of the 'statutory floor of employment rights' has caused workers to look towards contractual remedies as a more effective form of job protection.

As Anderman observes, 'a thorough understanding of the characteristics of the contract of employment is a virtual precondition to an understanding of the subject of labour law' (Anderman, S. D., *Labour Law: Management decisions and workers' rights*, 4th edn (Oxford: OUP, 2000), at p. 36).

SECTION 2: EMPLOYEE STATUS

The distinction between contracts of employment and self-employment is of fundamental importance, because only 'employees' qualify for employment protection rights such as unfair dismissal, redundancy payments, minimum notice on termination, etc. Wider protection is provided under the Health and Safety at Work etc. Act 1974, and the discrimination and equal pay legislation which applies to those both under a contract of service and a contract 'personally to execute any work or labour' includes the self-employed.

Given the fundamental importance of the distinction, it is unfortunate that the formulation of the test of employee status has come from the courts and tribunals rather than from statute. The only guidance on the question in the legislation is so completely circular as to be absolutely useless.

EMPLOYMENT RIGHTS ACT 1996

230. Employees, workers, etc.

(1) In this Act 'employee' means an individual who has entered into or works under (or, where the employment has ceased, worked under) a contract of employment.

(2) In this Act 'contract of employment' means a contract of service or apprenticeship, whether express or implied, and (if it is express) whether oral or in writing.

NOTE: The case law on this subject is confusing and contradictory. Historically, the leading approach was to apply the test of 'control', i.e. could the employer control how, when and where the worker was to work? If he could, that worker was his employee. However, as nowadays many employees possess skills not held by their employer, control as the sole determinant of status had been rejected. Along the way the test of 'integration' was floated, i.e. whether the worker was fully integrated into the employing organisation, but the test was never widely adopted. The modern approach has been to abandon the search for a single test and adopt a multifactorial test, weighing up all the factors for and against the existence of a contract of employment to determine whether the worker is 'in business on his own account'.

Ready Mixed Concrete (South East) Ltd v *Minister of Pensions and National Insurance*
[1968] 2 QB 497, Queen's Bench Division

The minister claimed that the plaintiff company was liable to pay national insurance contributions in respect of a driver employed by it to transport concrete. The contract between the driver and the company stated that he was an independent contractor (self-employed) and provided that, for a fixed period, he would carry nothing but the company's concrete in a vehicle which he would hire purchase from the company. He was to wear the company's uniform and the vehicle was to be painted with the company's colours and insignia. Repairs to the vehicle could be required by the company, the driver being responsible for all running and repair costs. If, at any time, the driver was unable to carry out the company's requirements because of illness, he could hire another driver for the vehicle.

MACKENNA J: A contract of employment exists if these three conditions are fulfilled. (i) The servant agrees that, in consideration of a wage or other remuneration, he will provide his own work and skill in the performance of some service for his master. (ii) He agrees, expressly or impliedly, that in the performance of that service he will be subject to the other's control in a sufficient degree to make that other master. (iii) The other provisions of the contract are consistent with its being a contract of service…I have shown that [the driver] must make the vehicle available throughout the contract period. He must maintain it…in working order, repairing and replacing worn parts when necessary. He must hire a competent driver to take his place if he should be for any reason unable to drive at any time when the company requires the service of the vehicle. He must do whatever is needed to make the vehicle (with a driver) available throughout the contract period. He must do all this, at his own expense, being paid a rate per mile for the quantity which he delivers. These obligations are more consistent, I think, with a contract of carriage than with one of service. The ownership of the assets, the chance of profit and the risk of loss in the business of carriage are his and not the company's.

NOTE: As can be seen from the above extract, control is still an important factor in the employee status test. In *Troutbeck SA* v *White* [2013] IRLR 949, the Court of Appeal (CA) held that the key question is not whether in practice the worker has day-to-day control of his own work, but whether there was a right to control as a matter of contract.

A: A checklist

Market Investigations v Minister of Social Security
[1969] 2 QB 173, Queen's Bench Division

COOKE J: No exhaustive list can be compiled of the considerations which are relevant to [the] question, nor can strict rules be laid down as to the relevant weight which the various considerations should carry in particular cases. The most that can be said is that control will no doubt always have to be considered, although it can no longer be regarded as the sole determining factor; and that factors which may be of importance are such matters as whether the man performing the services provides his own equipment, whether he hires his own helpers, what degree of financial risk he takes, what degree of responsibility for investment and management he has, and whether and how far he has an opportunity of profiting from the sound management of his task.

NOTES
1. The business test, together with the checklist set out above, received the approval of the Privy Council in *Lee* v *Chung and Shun Sing Construction and Engineering Co. Ltd* [1990] IRLR 236. However, the Court of Appeal has warned against a mechanistic application of Cooke J's checklist (see *Hall (HM Inspector of Taxes)* v *Lorimer* [1994] IRLR 171). While the checklist should not be regarded as laying down an all-purpose definition, it does offer valuable guidance in many cases.
2. In the next case, the Court of Appeal utilised the traditional tests to provide a liberal interpretation of the concept of 'employee' on policy grounds.

Lane v Shire Roofing Co. Ltd
[1995] IRLR 493, Court of Appeal

The plaintiff was a roofer who traded as a one-man firm and was categorised as self-employed for tax purposes. In 1986, he was hired by the defendants, a newly established roofing business which had not wanted to take on direct labour, and so had taken on the plaintiff on a 'payment-by-job' basis. While re-roofing the porch of a house, he fell off a ladder, suffering serious injuries. The central question in the case was whether the defendants owed the plaintiff a duty of care. In the High Court, Judge Hutton held the defendants were not liable for the injuries sustained because Mr Lane was doing the work as an independent contractor, not as an employee, and that accordingly the defendants owed him no duty of care.

The Court of Appeal allowed the appeal and awarded damages of £102,500.

HENRY LJ: We were taken through the standard authorities on this matter: *Ready Mixed Concrete (South-East) Ltd* v *Minister of Pensions and National Insurance* [1968] 2 QB 497; *Market Investigations* v *Minister of Social Security* [1969] 2 QB 173; and *Ferguson* v *Dawson & Partners (Contractors) Ltd* [1976] IRLR 346, to name the principal ones. Two general remarks should be made. The overall employment background is very different today (and was, though less so, in 1986) than it had been when those cases were first decided. First, for a variety of reasons there are more self-employed and fewer in employment. There is a greater flexibility in employment, with more temporary and shared employment. Second, there are perceived advantages for both workman and employer in the relationship between them being that of independent contractor. From the workman's point of view, being self-employed brings him into a more benevolent and less prompt taxation regime. From the employer's point of view, the protection of employees' rights contained in the employment protection legislation of the 1970s brought certain perceived disincentives to the employer to take on full-time long-term employees. So even in 1986 there were reasons on both sides to avoid the employee label. But, as I have already said, there were, and are, good policy reasons in the safety at work field to ensure that the law properly categorises between employees and independent contractors.

That line of authority shows that there are many factors to be taken into account in answering this question, and, with different priority being given to those factors in different cases, all depends on the facts of each particular case. Certain principles relevant to this case, however, emerge.

First, the element of control will be important: who lays down what is to be done, the way in which it is to be done, and the time when it is done? Who provides (i.e. hires and fires) the team by which it is done, and who provides the materials, plant and machinery and tools used?

But it is recognised that the control test may not be decisive—for instance, in the case of skilled employees, with discretion to decide how their work should be done. In such cases the question is broadened to whose business was it? Was the workman carrying on his own business, or was he carrying on that of his employers? The American Supreme Court, in *United States of America* v *Silk* [1946] 331 US 704, asks the question whether the men were employees 'as a matter of economic reality'. The answer to this question may cover the same ground as the control test (such as whether he provides his own equipment and hires his own helpers) but may involve looking to see where the financial risk lies, and whether and how far he has an opportunity of profiting from sound management in the performance of his task (see *Market Investigations* v *Minister of Social Security*, supra).

And these questions must be asked in the context of who is responsible for the overall safety of the men doing the work in question. Mr Whittaker, of the respondents, was cross-examined on these and he agreed that he was so responsible. Such an answer is not decisive (though it may be indicative) because ultimately the question is one of law and he could be wrong where the legal responsibility lies (see *Ferguson* v *Dawson*, supra, at 1219G).

NOTE: The policy-orientated approach adopted in this case is to be welcomed (see the case note by McKendrick in (1996) 25 ILJ 136). However, the question arises whether it would have been decided in the same way if it had been an unfair dismissal claim, where the courts have a tendency to focus on whether there was a *general* long-term employment relationship involving mutuality of obligation. The following two cases illustrate this point.

B: Mutuality of obligation

O'Kelly and others v Trusthouse Forte plc
[1983] IRLR 369, Court of Appeal

Messrs O'Kelly, Pearman and Florent all worked as 'regular casuals' for Trusthouse Forte in the Banqueting Department at the Grosvenor House Hotel. They complained to an industrial tribunal that they had been unfairly dismissed by the company for being members of a trade union and for taking part in the activities of that union. They applied to the tribunal for interim relief under what is now the Trade Union and Labour Relations (Consolidation) Act (TULR(C)A) 1992, s. 161.

As a preliminary point, the industrial tribunal considered whether or not the claimants were 'employees' of the company within the meaning of what is now the Employment Rights Act (ERA) 1996, s. 230(1), which is a prerequisite for a claim under the interim relief provisions. In determining this question, the industrial tribunal directed itself in accordance with the following test: 'What we derive from the authorities is that the tribunal should consider all aspects of the relationship, no single feature being in itself decisive and each of which may vary in weight and direction, and having given such balance to the factors as seems appropriate, to determine whether the person was carrying out business on his own account.'

On the facts of the case, the industrial tribunal found the following factors to be consistent with the regular casuals being employed under a contract of employment as opposed to a contract for services:

(a) The applicants provided their services in return for remuneration for work actually performed. They did not invest their own capital or stand to gain or lose from the commercial success of the functions organised by the Banqueting Department.

(b) They performed their work under the direction and control of the respondents.

(c) When the casual workers attended at functions they were part of the respondents' organisation and for the purpose of ensuring the smooth running of the business they were represented in the staff consultation process.

(d) When working they were carrying on the business of the respondents.

(e) Clothing and equipment were provided by the respondents.

(f) The applicants were paid weekly in arrears and were paid under deduction of income tax and social security contribution.

(g) Their work was organised on the basis of a weekly rota and they required permission to take time off from rostered duties.

(h) There was a disciplinary and grievance procedure.

(i) There was holiday pay or an incentive bonus calculated by reference to past service.

The tribunal then found that the following additional factors in the relationship were not inconsistent with a contract of employment:

(j) The applicants were paid for work actually performed and did not receive a regular wage or retainer. The method of calculating entitlement to remuneration is not an essential aspect of the employment relationship.

(k) Casual workers were not remunerated on the same basis as permanent employees and did not receive sick pay and were not included in the respondents' staff pension scheme and did not receive the fringe benefits accorded to established employees. There is, however, no objection to employers adopting different terms and conditions of employment for different categories of employee (e.g. different terms for manual and managerial staff).

(l) There were no regular or assured working hours. It is not a requirement of employment that there should be 'normal working hours'.

(m) Casual workers were not provided with written particulars of employment. If it is established that casual workers are employees there is a statutory obligation to furnish written particulars.

Five factors, however, were found to be inconsistent with the relationship being that of employer and employee. These were:

(n) The engagement was terminable without notice on either side.

(o) The applicants had the right to decide whether or not to accept work, although whether or not it would be in their interest to exercise the right to refuse work is another matter.

(p) The respondents had no obligation to provide any work.

(q) During the subsistence of the relationship it was the parties' view that casual workers were independent contractors engaged under successive contracts for services.

(r) It is the recognised custom and practice of the industry that casual workers are engaged under a contract for services.

The majority of the industrial tribunal then went on to say that while the relationship did have many of the characteristics of a contract of employment, there was one important ingredient missing—mutuality of obligation.

On this basis, together with the finding that the intention of the parties in the light of the known custom and practice in the industry was not to create an employment relationship, the industrial tribunal dismissed the claim. This view was ultimately upheld by the Court of Appeal.

ACKNER LJ: It was submitted that the industrial tribunal, having found that in practice 'regular' casuals on the list had priority in the offer of available work and a reciprocal practical requirement to do the work once rostered (because failure to do the work could lead to possible suspension and subsequent removal from the list) the right conclusion to draw was that there was a contractual obligation on Trusthouse Forte to offer work to 'regulars' in priority and on 'regulars' to do the work when offered. It was therefore contended that factors (o) and (p) in paragraph 23 of the industrial tribunal's reasons should not have been placed in the balance against there being a contract of employment. On the contrary, 'the one important ingredient' (namely, mutuality of obligation) which the industrial tribunal found to be missing was indeed present...I do not think this is right. The 'assurance of preference in the allocation of any available work' which the 'regulars' enjoyed was no more than a firm expectation in practice. It was not a contractual promise. The appellants, of course, expected the respondents to accept engagements rostered, but to suggest that a failure to accept amounted to a breach of contract is going too far. They were entitled to choose whether or not to attend, and however irritating it might have been to Trusthouse Forte if faced with a refusal it would have been quite unreal to conclude that either party would have thought it was a breach of contract.

NOTES

1. The implications of the 'mutuality of obligation' test for workers with irregular working patterns are highly disadvantageous—at least if it is applied in a strict sense. The sort of narrow reasoning seen in *O'Kelly* is also to be found in the judgment of the Employment Appeals Tribunal (EAT) in *Wickens* v *Champion Employment* [1984] ICR 365, where 'temps' engaged by a private employment agency were not accorded employment status because of the lack of binding obligation on the part of the agency to make bookings for work and the absence of any obligation by the worker to accept them. (Cf. *McMeechan* v *Secretary of State for Employment* [1997] IRLR 353, where the Court of Appeal held that a temporary worker can have the status of employee of an employment agency in respect of each assignment actually worked, notwithstanding that the same worker may not be entitled to employee status under his general terms of engagement.) A return to the *Wickens* approach is again in evidence in *Montgomery* v *Johnson Underwood Ltd* [2001] IRLR 275, CA. Mrs Montgomery was registered with an agency and was sent to work as a receptionist for the same client company for more than two years. Following her dismissal, she named both the agency and the client as respondents. The employment tribunal (ET) and the EAT both held that she was an employee of the agency, but this view was rejected by the Court of Appeal. Buckley J stated that 'mutuality of obligation' and 'control' are the 'irreducible minimum legal require-ment for a contract of employment to exist'. According to Buckley J, 'a contractual relationship concerning work to be carried out in which one party has no control over the other could not possibly be called a contract of employment'. In Mrs Montgomery's case, there may have been sufficient mutuality, but a finding of fact that there was no control by the agency was fatal to the argument that she was an employee of the agency.

2. Yet more confusion relating to the status of agency work was introduced by the decision of the Scottish EAT in *Motorola* v *Davidson and Melville Craig* [2001] IRLR 4. Davidson worked for Motorola as a mobile telephone repairer. His contract was with Melville Craig, who assigned him to work for Motorola. Motorola paid Melville Craig for his services, and Melville Craig paid Davidson. Davidson was largely subject to Motorola's control. They gave him instructions, pro-vided tools, and he arranged holidays with them. He wore their uniform and badges, and obeyed their rules. If Davidson chose not to work for Motorola, that might have breached his contract with Melville Craig, but not a contract with Motorola. The agreement between Motorola and Melville Craig gave Motorola the right to return Davidson to them if they found him 'unac-ceptable'. His assignment was terminated by Motorola following a disciplinary hearing held by one of their managers. Mr Davidson claimed unfair dismissal against Motorola who maintained that he was an employee of Melville Craig. However, the ET concluded that there was sufficient control to make Motorola the employer and the EAT agreed. In the view of the EAT, in determin-ing whether there is a sufficient degree of control to establish a relationship of employer and employee, there is no good reason to ignore practical aspects of control that fall short of legal rights. Nor is it a necessary component of the type of control exercised by an employer over an employee that it should be exercised only directly between them and not by way of a third party acting upon the directions, or at the request of the third party.

3. In *Wilson* v *Circular Distributors Ltd* [2006] IRLR 38, the claimant was a relief area manager whose contract provided that he was 'required' to carry out the duties of an area manager during periods

of holiday and sickness absence. However, the contract expressly stated that 'there will be occasions when no work is available'. The EAT, finding employee status, held that 'it is the absence of *mutual* obligations that is crucial. It is not sufficient for there to be an absence of an obligation of the employer to provide work. There has to be an absence of an obligation of the employer to provide work and an absence on the part of the employee when work is offered to accept that work.'

4. The Employment Relations Act 1999, s. 23 gives the Secretary of State power to confer employment rights on non-employees. Unless and until this is done, a typical worker's rights are dependent on this catalogue of contradictory and confusing case law.

5. Most recently, in *Dacas v Brook Street Bureau (UK) Ltd* [2004] IRLR 358, the Court of Appeal, by a majority, held that the client end-user can be the employer of an agency worker provided mutuality of obligation and control are present (see also *Franks v Reuters* [2003] IRLR 423, CA).

Dacas v *Brook Street Bureau (UK) Ltd*
[2004] IRLR 358, Court of Appeal

Mrs Dacas had worked regularly and continuously for four years as a cleaner in a hostel (West Drive) for Wandsworth Borough Council ('the Council'), which was a client of Brook Street ('the agency'). No contract existed between Mrs Dacas and the Council. Mrs Dacas' work was done for the Council on its premises and under its supervision and control. Mrs Dacas was paid, not by the Council that derived the benefit from her work, but by the agency that supplied her; and her contract with the agency provided that its provisions 'shall not give rise to a contract of employment between Brook Street and the temporary worker, or the temporary worker and the client.'

She was dismissed following an incident in which she swore at a visitor to the hostel. Mrs Dacas claimed unfair dismissal, arguing that she had either been an employee of the Council or of the agency.

The ET first considered whether she was an employee of the Council. They concluded that there was no employment relationship because there was no direct contract between Mrs Dacas and the Council. They then went on to consider whether she was employed by the agency. They took the view that, although a contract existed between Mrs Dacas and the agency, they could not be employers here because they had no direct control over her daily work. Consequently, it was held that she could not bring a claim of unfair dismissal.

Mrs Dacas appealed to the EAT (but, crucially, only against the decision that she was not an employee of the agency). The EAT upheld her appeal. They held that the agency exercised control over Mrs Dacas, because they paid her wages, had the right to exercise disciplinary action, and had the right to terminate her contract. They also agreed that mutuality of obligation was present between Mrs Dacas and the agency.

The agency then appealed successfully to the Court of Appeal.

MUMMERY LJ: ... [I]n ascertaining the overall legal effect of the triangular arrangements on the status of Mrs Dacas the employment tribunal should not focus so intently on the express terms of the written contracts entered into by Brook Street with Mrs Dacas and the council that it is deflected from considering finding facts relevant to a possible implied contract of service between Mrs Dacas and the council in respect of the work actually done by her exclusively for the council at its premises and under its control, until it took the initiative in terminating that arrangement. The formal written contracts between Mrs Dacas and Brook Street and between Brook Street and the council relating to the work to be done by her for the council may not tell the whole of the story about the legal relationships affecting the work situation. They do not, as a matter of law, necessarily preclude the implication of a contract of service between Mrs Dacas and the council. There may be evidence of a pattern of regular mutual contact of a transactional character between Mrs Dacas and the council, from which a contract of service may be implied by the tribunal. I see no insuperable objection in law to a combination of transactions in the triangular arrangements, embracing an express contract for services between Mrs Dacas and Brook Street, an express contract between Brook Street and the council and an implied contract of service between Mrs Dacas and the council, with Brook Street acting in certain respects as an agent for Mrs Dacas and as an agent for the council under the terms of the express written agreements.

I approach the question posed by this kind of case on the basis that the outcome, which would accord with practical reality and common sense, would be that, if it is legally and factually permissible to do so, the applicant has a contract, which is not a contract of service, with the employment agency, and that the applicant works under an implied contract, which is a contract of service, with the end-user with a right not to be unfairly dismissed. The objective fact and degree of control over the work done by Mrs Dacas at West Drive over the years is crucial. The council in fact exercised the relevant control over her work and over her. As for mutuality of obligation, (a) the council was under an obligation to pay for the work that she did for it and she received payment in respect of such work from Brook Street, and (b) Mrs Dacas, while at West Drive, was under an obligation to do what she was told and to attend punctually at stated times. As for dismissal, it was the council which was entitled to take and in fact took the initiative in bringing to an end work done by her at West Drive. But for the council's action she would have continued to work there as previously. It is true that the obligations and the power to dismiss were not contained in an express contract between Mrs Dacas and the council. The fact that the obligations were contained in express contracts made between Mrs Dacas and Brook Street and between Brook Street and the council does not prevent them from being read across the triangular arrangements into an implied contract and taking effect as implied mutual obligations as between Mrs Dacas and the council.

NOTES

1. This decision could have signalled a significant shift in the status of temporary agency workers. As can be seen above, Lord Justice Mummery found that the tribunal should have considered whether there was an implied contract of service between Mrs Dacas and the Council. Lord Justice Sedley concluded that the evidence indicated that the Council was the employer but he would have remitted the case to the tribunal to make further findings of fact. Unfortunately, his judgment did not give Mrs Dacas the right to pursue her claim because she did not join the Council as a party to her appeal.

   Mr Justice Munby concluded that the tribunal was right to find that Mrs Dacas was employed by neither the agency nor the Council. Mr Justice Munby pointed out that the judgments of Lord Justices Mummery and Sedley 'put in question the most basic assumptions upon which the whole of [the employment agency] industry has hitherto conducted its business': that 'if the obligation to remunerate the worker is imposed on the agency, there cannot be a contract of employment between the worker and the end-user.' Having said that, he nevertheless found the present situation to be 'most unsatisfactory'.

2. The significant issue for employment law practitioners is that, if there are grounds to appeal a decision of an ET in a case such as this, both respondents should be joined in the appeal so as to avoid what happened in the instant case; Mrs Dacas had a case that, at the very least, required further consideration by the ET but she could not pursue it because she had effectively abandoned the case against the Council.

3. In *Dacas*, the Court of Appeal held that the agency worker was not an employee of the employment agency. This was the same approach adopted by the Court of Appeal in *Bunce* v *Postworth Ltd t/a Sky Blue* [2005] IRLR 557, CA. In that case, a welder sought to claim unfair dismissal on the basis that a contract of employment with the agency was entered into each time he was sent on an assignment. It was acknowledged that the necessary element of control rested with the client company, but it was contended that this did not negate a contract of service with the agency because control had been delegated to the client under the contract between worker and the agency, which contained a standard term requiring the worker to accept the directions and instructions of the client. The Court of Appeal rejected this argument. According to Keane LJ, 'The law has always been concerned with who *in reality* has the power to control what the worker does and how he does it. In the present case, during the periods when the appellant was working on an assignment, it was the client, the end-user, who had the power to direct and control what he did and how he did it.'

   Rubenstein proffers the view that: 'In *McMeechan* v *Secretary of State for Employment*, the Court of Appeal managed to find that a temporary worker in much the same position as Mr Bunce was employed by the agency under a series of short-term contracts. The Court of Appeal here distinguishes *McMeechan* because the contract in that case referred to the worker accepting instructions either from the agency or the client. This difference of wording of a boilerplate clause seems a somewhat flimsy hook on which to hang such a fundamental difference in outcome' ('Highlights' [2005] IRLR 502).

4. In *Cairns* v *Visteon UK Ltd* [2007] IRLR 175, the EAT held that, although it was clear from the judgments of the majority in *Dacas* v *Brook Street Bureau (UK) Ltd* that where there is no contract of employment between worker and agency, a contract of service may be implied between worker and end-user as a matter of necessity, the possibility of dual contracts of service in respect of the same work done by the worker remained problematic. Where the worker is employed by the agency and thus is protected for unfair dismissal purposes, there is no good policy reason for extending that protection to a second and parallel employer.

5. In *Cable & Wireless plc* v *Muscat* [2006] IRLR 354, CA, Mr Muscat had been directly employed by his employers before his work was supplied to them by an agency. Subsequently, Mr Muscat was informed by Cable & Wireless that his services were no longer required. On a claim for unfair dismissal, Cable & Wireless argued that Mr Muscat was not their employee.

   The Court of Appeal dismissed Cable & Wireless's appeal. The Court of Appeal held that the claimant was an employee of the appellant company throughout the period that he worked for them, notwithstanding that, some time into his employment, he had entered into a contract for services with an employment agency and it was the agency which paid him. In finding that there was an implied contract of employment between the claimant and the appellants, as the end-user, the ET had properly applied the guidance of the majority of the Court of Appeal in *Dacas* v *Brook Street Bureau (UK) Ltd*.

   Nevertheless, the law relating to the employment status of agency workers continues to be in a confused state, as the next case illustrates.

James v London Borough of Greenwich
[2008] IRLR 302, CA

In 1997, Merana James worked for the council on a full-time basis as a support worker. Later that same year, she ceased working for the council. From 2001, she began working for the council again through an employment agency, Greenwich Social and Care Staff Agency. In 2003, she left that agency and joined BS Project Services Ltd, which paid her a better hourly wage. She had a contract with the agency, and the agency had a contract with the council, as end-user, but there was no express contract directly between Ms James and the end-user.

Ms James was absent from work through sickness in August 2004 and for most of September. Another worker was provided by the agency to the council in her absence. When she returned to work, she was told that she was no longer required and that the agency had sent a replacement.

Ms James sought to bring a claim of unfair dismissal against the council. An ET dismissed her claim on the ground that she did not have a contract of employment with the council. The tribunal found as a fact that various terms which would be found in the contracts of employment of those working directly for the council did not apply to Ms James. These included the disciplinary and grievance procedures, and terms relating to sick pay and holiday pay.

The tribunal rejected a contention on behalf of Ms James that once a year had elapsed, it was necessary to imply a contract of employment with the end-user to give business efficacy to the relationship. Instead, it held that there was no mutuality of obligation between Ms James and the council: 'there was no obligation upon the claimant to provide her services for Greenwich Council and there was no obligation on the part of Greenwich Council to provide the claimant with work.'

On appeal to the EAT, it was argued on behalf of the claimant that there were certain features of the relationship which clearly demonstrated an implied contract. Ms James had virtually no contract with the agency at all. She had only worked for one employer. She acted at all times under the direction of the council without any intervention from the agency, and she was treated in all respects as a full-time member of staff on the permanent rota. The claimant relied on Lord Justice Sedley's observations in *Dacas* v *Brook Street Bureau (UK) Ltd* that once arrangements like these had been in place for a year or more there was an inexorable inference that there was a contract of employment.

The EAT ([2007] IRLR 168) dismissed the appeal. It held that the ET had been fully entitled to find that the circumstances did not exist which could justify the inference of an implied contract. It stated that although the ET had focused on mutuality of obligations, it might more pertinently have said simply that there was no necessity to imply a contract in the present case. It held that the mere passage of time was not sufficient to require any such implication. Ms James appealed to the Court of Appeal.

It fell to be determined, amongst other things, whether there was a conflict in the relevant authorities, and if so how the conflict should be resolved.

The Court of Appeal (Lord Justice Mummery, Lord Justice Thomas and Lord Justice Lloyd) on 5 February 2008 dismissed the appeal.

MUMMERY LJ: *Dacas* was the first case in this court to confront head on the question whether a contract of service with the end user could be implied in the tripartite setting of an agency worker under contract with an agency, which also has a contract with the end user. I agree with Mr Cohen that there was no appeal before the Court of Appeal in that case against the decision of the ET that the claimant was not an employee of the end user. I also agree with him that the majority judgments raised the possibility, which had not been considered by the ET in that case when holding that the claimant was not an employee of the agency or of the end user, whether a contract of service might by necessary inference be found to exist with the end user. I did not expand on the possibilities, let alone decide the implied contract issue, in the absence of the relevant findings of fact. *Dacas* is not authority for the proposition that the implication of a contract of service between the end user and the worker in a tripartite agency situation is inevitable in a long-term agency worker situation. It only pointed to it as a possibility, the outcome depending on the facts found by the ET in the particular case. I would add that, having regard to the nature and constitution of the proceedings before the Court of Appeal in that case, it was not the most suitable occasion for offering more detailed guidance on the circumstances in which a contract of service could be implied.

Muscat (Cable & Wireless plc v Muscat [2006] IRLR 354, CA) was a case in which a contract of service was implied, but it was not a tripartite agency case. Its importance is in the extent of approval given to the legal analysis in the majority judgments in *Dacas* and in the guidance given on the applicable legal principles, in particular emphasis on the requirement that the implication of a contract of service must be necessary to give effect to the business reality of a relationship between the worker and the end user.

The decision of the House of Lords in *Carmichael* v *National Power* [2000] IRLR 43 was cited by Mr Cohen for the proposition that, for a contract of service to exist, mutuality of obligation must be found. The ET found that there was no such mutuality of obligation between Ms James, who was under no obligation to the council to do work for it, and the council, which was under no obligation to Ms James to provide her with work and therefore no employment relationship between them. Mr Cohen accepted that in *Carmichael* the issue was different from the tripartite agency worker cases. No employment agency was involved. There was a direct express contract between the workers and the user of their services and the dispute was whether or not it was a contract of service or whether they were casual workers working under a contract of another kind, there being periods in the relationship when no work was being performed or paid for. In the agency worker cases the issue is whether a third contract exists at all between the worker and the end user. The relevant question in such cases is whether it is necessary, in the tripartite setting, to imply mutual contractual obligations between the end user to provide the worker with work and the worker to perform the work for the end user.

The EAT added observations (paragraphs 53–61) which are intended to assist tribunals in the task of deciding whether a contract of employment with the end user should be implied. ETs would be well advised to follow the guidance given by the EAT, which I would expressly approve.

In conclusion, the question whether an 'agency worker' is an employee of an end user must be decided in accordance with common law principles of implied contract and, in some very extreme cases, by exposing sham arrangements. Just as it is wrong to regard all 'agency workers' as self-employed temporary workers outside the protection of the 1996 Act, the recent authorities do not entitle all 'agency workers' to argue successfully that they should all be treated as employees in disguise. As illustrated in the authorities there is a wide spectrum of factual situations. Labels are not a substitute for legal analysis of the evidence. In many cases agency workers will fall outside the scope of the protection of the 1996 Act because neither the workers nor the end users were in any kind of express contractual relationship with each other and it is not necessary to imply one in order to explain the work undertaken by the worker for the end user.

I have already expressed my agreement with the EAT that, in this case, the mutuality of obligation approach in the *Carmichael* case and adopted by the ET in this case is not particularly helpful. As I have explained the issue in *Carmichael*, which was not a tripartite situation, was whether there was an overarching employment contract or a series of contracts that were not contracts of employment. This case presents a tripartite situation with two express contracts, which are not contracts of employment, (1) between Ms James and the agency and (2) between the agency and the council. The issue here is whether, having regard to the way in which the parties have conducted themselves, it is necessary to imply (3) a contract of employment between Ms James as worker and the council as the end user.

I would dismiss the appeal. It is impossible to say that the decision of the ET that Ms James was not an employee of the council was arrived at by applying the wrong legal test or that the conclusion reached, on applying the correct test, was perverse.

NOTES

1. The Court of Appeal held that no implied contract was 'necessary' in this case, as the relationship was fully explained by the contracts between the worker and the agency, and between the agency and the end-user. According to Lord Justice Mummery, 'there is no significant difference between the law stated and applied in the decisions of this court and in those of the EAT.' Consequently, a contract will only be implied between an agency worker and the end-user in the most exceptional of circumstances—only where it is necessary to do so in order to explain the work undertaken by the worker for the end-user. This does not depend on the length of service with the end-user (*pace* Sedley LJ in *Dacas*) or on the degree to which they have been integrated into the workforce, but instead is likely to be relevant mainly in cases where the agency relationship itself can be regarded as a sham, or where there have been direct negotiations on terms and conditions between the end-user and the agency worker. This means that few agency workers will have unfair dismissal rights against the end-user unless and until Parliament legislates otherwise (see also *Muschett* v *HM Prison Service* [2010] IRLR 451; *Smith* v *Carillion Ltd* [2015] EWCA Civ 209).

2. In *Tilson* v *Alstrom Transport* [2011] IRLR 169, the Court of Appeal held that even if there is a significant degree of integration of an agency worker into an organisation (the 'end-user') that is not inconsistent with an agency relationship in which there is no contract between worker and end-user. The Court of Appeal also held that the need to apply to a line manager before taking annual leave is not sufficient to justify the implication of a contract of employment between worker and end-user.

   Lord Justice Elias also stated: 'Even where employers are seeking to avoid liabilities with respect to workers who would prefer to enter into an employment relationship, if as a matter of law the arrangements have in fact achieved the objective for which they were designed, tribunals cannot find otherwise simply because they disapprove of the employer's motives.' This view provides employers and their legal advisers considerable scope for drafting their way out of employment status. However, the decision is out of kilter with the *Protectacoat/Autoclenz* approach on sham contracts. Hopefully, the issue will be resolved by the Supreme Court in the near future.

3. In 2009, the UK finally agreed to the Directive on Conditions for Temporary (Agency) Workers—Directive 2008/104/EC—more usually known as the 'Agency Workers Directive'. Member States had until 5 December 2011 to implement the directive. The directive provides agency workers in the UK who have worked in the end-user organisation for 12 weeks with the right to equal treatment in basic working and employment conditions with employees of the end-user. However, the directive does not affect the employment status of temporary workers and so we will still lack authoritative guidance in this area. The directive is implemented in the UK by the Agency Workers Regulations 2010 (SI 2010/93). In line with the directive, the regulations do not provide for employment status for agency workers, nor do they give redundancy pay rights. The regulations came into force on 1 October 2011 (see regs. 5, 7).

4. Guidance on whether volunteer workers fall within the definition of 'employee' was provided in *South East Sheffield Citizens Advice Bureau* v *Grayson* [2004] IRLR 353, EAT. It was held that a provision in a CAB volunteer agreement that there was a 'usual minimum commitment' of six hours a week did not impose a contractual obligation on the volunteer to do work, 'such that were the volunteer to give notice immediately terminating his relationship with the Bureau, the latter would have a remedy for breach of contract against him'. Subsequently, the case of *Melhuish* v *Redbridge CAB* [2005] IRLR 419, EAT concerned the case of a volunteer working two days a week, who claimed unfair dismissal. The claimant received no pay or other remuneration other than reimbursement of expenses. He was under no obligation to attend work and the CAB was not obliged to offer him work. The EAT held that the lack of consideration in terms of remuneration and the lack of mutuality of obligation was inconsistent with the existence of a contract of employment or, indeed, any contract.

Nethermere (St Neots) Ltd v *Taverna and Gardiner*
[1984] IRLR 240, Court of Appeal

Mrs Taverna and Mrs Gardiner were at one time both employed at the appellants' garment factory but later became 'home workers'. Mrs Taverna began working at home at the beginning of 1978. The sewing machine that she used for the work was provided by the appellants. She had no fixed hours for doing the work and for a number of weeks she did no work at all. She was paid weekly according to the number of garments she did. Mrs Gardiner ceased working at the factory in 1976. In September 1979, the appellants asked if she would do work at home and she agreed. At first she used her own machine but was then supplied with one by the appellants. She normally put 200 pockets onto trousers each day. If she wanted less work she would tell the driver who delivered the materials to her. The only stipulation was that it had to be sufficient to make it worthwhile for the driver to call.

When these arrangements came to an end in 1981 following a dispute about holiday pay, Mrs Taverna and Mrs Gardiner complained that they had been unfairly dismissed. As a preliminary issue, the industrial tribunal were asked to decide whether the two women were employees of the company within the meaning of what is now the ERA 1996, s. 230(1)—i.e. that they were employed under a contract of service—or whether they were self-employed under a contract for services. The tribunal held that the women were employed under a contract of service and were eligible therefore to complain of unfair dismissal.

Both the EAT and the Court of Appeal dismissed the employer's appeal against the industrial tribunal's decision.

DILLON LJ: For my part I would accept that an arrangement under which there was never any obligation on the outworkers to do work or on the company to provide work could not be a contract of service. But the mere facts that the outworkers could fix their own hours of work, could take holidays and time off when they wished and could vary how many garments they were willing to take on any day or even to take none on a particular day, while undoubtedly factors for the industrial tribunal to consider in deciding whether or not there was a contract of service, do not as a matter of law negative the existence of such a contract.

I see no reason in law why the existence of a contract of service may not be inferred from a course of dealing, continued between the parties over several years, as in *Airfix*. This is indeed a line with the decision in *Brogden* v *Metropolitan Railway Company*, (1877) 2 AC 666. The fact that machines were supplied by the company to each of the applicants indicates at the least an expectation on both sides that the applicants would be doing work for the company which was provided for them by the company, and I find it unreal to suppose that the work in fact done by the applicants for the company over the not inconsiderable periods which I have mentioned was done merely as a result of the pressures of market forces on the applicants and the company and under no contract at all.

Mr Weisfeld's evidence that it was up to the home workers to decide how much work they did subject to making it worthwhile for van drivers to call, is capable of being read as importing an obligation on the outworkers to take a reasonable amount of work once they have agreed to act as outworkers for the company. Conversely the statement of Mr Weisfeld that it was the van driver's duty to be as fair as he could is capable of being read as importing an obligation on the company to provide a reasonable share of work for each outworker whenever the company had more work available than could be handled by the factory.

There was a regular course of dealing between the parties for years under which garments were supplied daily to the outworkers, worked on, collected and paid for. If it is permissible on the evidence to find that by such conduct a contract had been established between each applicant and the company, I see no necessity to conclude that that contract must have been a contract for services and not a contract of service.

In my judgment there was material to support the view of the industrial tribunal in paragraph 11 and it was entitled to reach the conclusion that a contract of employment had been created between the parties and both the applicants were employees. Thus the court is not entitled to interfere with that conclusion and so I would dismiss this appeal.

STEPHENSON LJ: ...I cannot see why well founded expectations of continuing homework should not be hardened or refined into enforceable contracts by regular giving and taking of work over periods of a year or more and why outworkers should not thereby become employees under contracts of service like those doing similar work at the same rate in the factory.

KERR LJ [dissenting]: ...A course of dealing can be used as a basis for implying terms into individual contracts which are concluded pursuant thereto, but I can find no authority for the proposition that even a lengthy course of dealing can somehow convert itself into a contractually binding obligation—subject only to reasonable notice—to continue to enter into individual contracts, or to be subject to some 'umbrella' contract. The nearest analogy appears to be *Brogden* v *Metropolitan Railway*, (1877) 2 AC 666. But the parties in that case had concluded a contract in principle which only lacked formal signature, and their course of dealing within its terms was treated as an acceptance of its terms by conduct. There is nothing of a similar nature in the present case.

NOTES

1. In *Cornwall County Council* v *Prater* [2006] IRLR 362, CA, a home tutor worked for a local authority for some ten years. The council was not under any contractual obligation to offer pupils to her and she was under no obligation to accept. Once she had agreed to take on the work, however, she was obliged to continue to provide work until the particular engagement ceased. The local authority argued that none of the individual teaching assignments amounted to a contract of employment because they lacked the necessary mutuality of obligation. According to them, in order for there to be a contract of employment, there had to be a continuing obligation on the local authority to provide work and on the worker to do that work. The Court of Appeal rejected this contention. It held that the fact that the contract was not of indefinite duration is no barrier to the establishment of mutuality of obligation. During each work assignment, there was an obligation on the claimant to teach and on the council to pay. Since it was accepted that the times between each contract were 'temporary cessations of work' within the meaning of the ERA 1996, s. 212, continuity of employment was preserved.

2. In *Cotswold Developments Construction Ltd* v *Williams* [2006] IRLR 181, we see the EAT offering a liberal approach to the issue of mutuality of obligation. Langstaff J was of the view that 'a contract under which there is no obligation to work could not be a contract of employment'. However, the fact that an employee has a right to refuse work, and that the employer may exercise a choice to withhold work, does not deprive the contract of mutuality of obligation. 'The focus must be upon whether or not there is *some* obligation upon an individual to work, and some obligation upon the other party to provide or pay for it.'

Express and Echo Publications Ltd v *Tanton*

[1999] IRLR 367, Court of Appeal

Mr Tanton worked for the appellants as an employee until he was made redundant. He was then re-engaged as a driver on an ostensibly self-employed basis. Clause 3.3 of his contract provided that: 'In the event that the contractor is unable or unwilling to perform the services personally, he shall arrange at his own expense entirely for another suitable person to perform the service.' Mr Tanton found the agreement unacceptable and refused to sign it. However, he continued to work in accordance with its terms and, on the odd occasion, utilised the right to provide a substitute driver. He later brought a claim to an ET complaining that he had not been provided with a written statement of particulars—effectively asking for his status as an employee to be confirmed. The ET chairman approached the case on the basis of what actually had occurred, rather than what the document recorded as being the obligations of the parties. Having carried out a balancing exercise, he concluded that the factors pointing to Mr Tanton being an employee outweighed the factors which pointed to contractor status. Mr Tanton was required to follow a set route, wear a uniform provided by the company and drive a vehicle from the company's pool. The chairman regarded those requirements and the degree of control exercised by the company as suggesting a contract of employment. According to the chairman, the provision enabling Mr Tanton to provide a substitute driver which, on his own evidence, he had used from time to time, was only one factor of many; and though there might come a point at which the provision of a substitute was so frequent as to change the whole nature of the arrangement, there was no evidence that that point had been approached. The EAT (Judge Clark presiding) dismissed an appeal against this decision at a preliminary hearing on the ground that it raised no arguable point of law. Both the tribunal chair and the EAT considered that the substitution clause was not fatal to there being a contract of employment, either in law or in fact. However, the Court of Appeal ruled that the right to provide a substitute is 'inherently inconsistent' with employment status. A contract of employment must necessarily contain an obligation on the part of the employee to provide services personally. Without such an 'irreducible minimum' of obligation, it cannot be said that there is a contract of employment, according to the Court of Appeal.

PETER GIBSON LJ: …Clause 3.3, to my mind vividly illustrates the difficulty in approaching the identification of the terms of the agreement by concentrating on what actually occurred rather than looking at the obligations by which the parties were bound. Of course, it is important that the industrial tribunal should be alert in this area of the law to look at the reality of any obligations. If the obligation is a sham, it will want to say so. But to concentrate on what actually occurred may not elucidate the full terms of the contract. If a term is not enforced, that does not justify a conclusion that such a term is not part of the agreement. The obligation could be temporarily waived. If there is a term that is inherently inconsistent with the existence of a contract of employment, what actually happened from time to time may not be decisive, given the existence of that term. For example, if, under an agreement, there is a provision enabling, but not requiring, the worker to work, and enabling, but not requiring, the person for whom he works to provide that work, the fact that work is from time to time provided would not mean that the contract was a contract of service, consider *Clark v Oxfordshire Health Authority* [1998] IRLR 125. For my part, therefore, I think that the chairman went wrong at that point in concentrating on what occurred rather than seeking to determine what were the mutual obligations…

In these circumstances, it is, in my judgment, established on the authorities that where, as here, a person who works for another is not required to perform his services personally, then as a matter of law the relationship between the worker and the person for whom he works is not that of employee and employer. Mr Tanton has submitted to us that, though the personal service to the appellant was a highly material consideration, it was not conclusive. I am afraid that the proposition cannot stand in the light of the authorities.

In my judgment, on the facts this is a plain case. One starts with the common intention of the parties that Mr Tanton should not be an employee but should be a self-employed contractor. The terms which the chairman found to be pointers to a contract of service are in no way inconsistent with a contract for services, and, as the chairman himself recognised, some of the facts which he found are pointers to the relationship being one of contractor and client, for example the absence of holiday pay and sickness pay. But, for the reasons which I have given, clause 3.3 entitling Mr Tanton not to perform any service personally, is a provision wholly inconsistent with the contract of service which the chairman found the contract to be. In my judgment, therefore, the chairman and the Employment Appeal Tribunal erred in law.

NOTES
1. Rubenstein offers the following criticism of the above decision:

> A number of points can be made, but the most important of them is that this decision carries with it the real danger of abuse. It opens the possibility for employers and their advisers to draft contracts which will negate employment status for certain workers by including a substitution clause in their contracts (Rubenstein, M., 'Highlights' [1999] IRLR 337). (Cf. *Byrne Brothers (Formwork) Ltd* v *Baird* [2002] IRLR 96 EAT.)

A similar anxiety was expressed by Mr Justice Elias in *Consistent Group Ltd* v *Kalwak* [2007] IRLR 367: 'The concern to which tribunals must be alive is that armies of lawyers will simply place substitution clauses or clauses denying any obligation to accept or provide work in employment contracts, as a matter of form, even where such terms do not begin to reflect the real relationship.' So the issue for the EAT was whether the 'agreed' terms were, in reality, a sham.

However, when *Kalwak* went to the Court of Appeal, it overruled the EAT and controversially held that in order for a contract excluding employment status to be held to be a sham, it must be found that *both* parties intended it to paint an inaccurate picture as to the true nature of their respective obligations. The matter was reconsidered in *Protectacoat Firthglow Ltd* v *Szilagyi* [2009] IRLR 365, a case in which the employers took advice as to the wording they should use in order to avoid employment status. On this occasion, the Court of Appeal re-emphasised the importance of looking at the reality of the relationship. Lady Justice Smith stated that 'the court must look at the substance not the label'. Where it is asserted that the written contract is a sham, the court or tribunal has to determine 'what the true legal relationship is between the parties'. It will 'ordinarily regard the documents as the starting point and will ask itself what legal rights and obligations the written agreement creates. But it may then have to ask whether parties ever realistically intended or envisaged that its terms, particularly the essential terms, would be carried out as written.' 'Essential terms' in this context means mutuality of obligation and the obligation of personal performance of the work. Lady Justice Smith recognised that unlike in a commercial agreement, 'in the field of work...the reality may be that the principal/employer dictates what the written agreement will say and the contractor/employee must take it or leave it'. Moreover, whether or not the words of the written contract represent the true expectations of the parties has to be considered 'not only at the inception of the contract but, if appropriate, as time goes by'. This means that even though the documents remain the same, whether there is or is not an employment relationship can change over time. In this case, the employment tribunal was entitled to find that the claimant installer was an employee rather than an independent contractor, and therefore entitled to claim unfair dismissal, notwithstanding that he had signed an agreement entering into a partnership with the respondents. That agreement was a sham. As Lady Justice Smith puts it, 'Protectacoat wanted the ha'penny of treating their installers as employees when it came to attendance and control and also wanted the bun of not having to give them the rights they would enjoy as employees...' The approach in *Protectacoat* was applied by the EAT in *Archer-Holbin Contractors Ltd* v *MacGettigan* [2009] UKEAT 0037 09 0307. The *Protectacoat* position was advanced by the Supreme Court in *Autoclenz Ltd* v *Belcher* [2011] UKSC 41. Here the Court confirmed that an employment tribunal should consider whether the terms of a written contract represent what was actually agreed between the parties, not only at the beginning of the relationship but at any later stage, where the relationship and the terms governing it may have changed. Crucially, the Court held that there does not need to be evidence of an intention to deceive a third party for the ET to look beyond the terms of the written agreement.

Autoclenz Ltd v Belcher

[2011] IRLR 820, Supreme Court

Autoclenz described the car valeters it 'employed' as 'sub-contractors', and required them to sign a contract specifying that they were 'a self-employed independent contractor' and not an employee. The contract also stated that 'as an independent contractor, you are entitled to engage one or more individuals to carry out the valeting on your behalf' and that 'you will not be obliged to provide your services on any particular occasion'. The claimants brought proceedings seeking a declaration that they were 'workers' as defined under the National Minimum Wage Regulations and the Working Time Regulations and were therefore entitled to holiday pay. The ET found that the written contractual terms did not reflect the true agreement between the parties. In reality, the valeters could not send a substitute and had to carry out the work that was offered to them. Ultimately, the Supreme Court granted a declaration that the claimants were working under a contract of employment.

LORD CLARKE: In my judgment the true position, consistent with *Tanton, Kalwak* and *Szilagyi*, is that where there is a dispute as to the genuineness of a written term in a contract, the focus of the enquiry must be to discover the actual legal obligations of the parties. To carry out that exercise, the tribunal will have to examine all the relevant evidence. That will, of course, include the written term itself, read in the context of the whole agreement. It will also include evidence of how the parties conducted themselves in practice and what their expectations of each other were. Evidence of how the parties conducted themselves in practice may be so persuasive that the tribunal can draw an inference that that practice represents the true obligations of the parties. But the mere fact that the parties conducted themselves in a particular way does not of itself mean that the conduct accurately reflects the legal rights and obligations. For example, there could well be a right to provide a substitute worker and the fact that right was never exercised in practice does not mean that it was not a genuine right.

...

[T]he relative bargaining power of the parties must be taken into account in deciding whether the terms of any written agreement in truth represent what was agreed and the true agreement will often have to be gleaned from all the circumstances of the case, of which the written agreement is only a part. This may be described as a purposive approach to the problem. If so, I am content with that description.

NOTES

1. The lesson of *Belcher* is that employers, and their advisers, cannot draft their way out of employment status if that does not accord with the reality of the relationship.

2. In *Staffordshire Sentinel Newspapers Ltd v Potter* [2004] IRLR 752, EAT, a contract for work as a home delivery agent provided that an agent was not required to discharge his or her responsibilities personally, but in the event that they did not do so, they would provide an appropriate substitute. An ET held that there was a contract of employment in the instant case because, in practice, the right to substitute was not unfettered since the substitute had to meet with the company's approval, which had not always been given, and, on one occasion, they had provided their own substitute. Allowing an appeal, Clark J emphasised that a written contractual term is determinative. 'Where there is no clear express term in writing then it may be necessary to look at the overall factual matrix in order to discern that term...However, where the term is clear from the contractual document that course is unnecessary, subject to variation of the term or where it can be said to be a sham.'

3. A growing subcategory of temporary workers is those on a 'zero hours' contract (ZHC), i.e. a contract in which the employer does not guarantee the individual any work. The employment status of such workers is cloaked with uncertainty. In their pure form, ZHCs require workers to be on call but specify no hours of work, and no work is guaranteed. A variant arrangement is the 'min-max' contract where minimum hours are specified. Such arrangements have gained prevalence in recent years and are most likely to be found in sectors such as public services (notably health and social work) and in distribution, accommodation, and food services industries. According to the Office for National Statistics (ONS) estimates, there were 583,000 people self-identified as being on ZHCs in the fourth quarter of 2013 (*Zero Hours Analysis*, ONS, February 2014). The ONS also estimated that there were a total of 1.4 million contracts that did not guarantee a minimum number of hours which provided work in January 2014 (this figure includes individuals who have more than one ZHC) (*Analysis of Employee Contracts that Do Not Guarantee a Minimum Number of hours*, ONS, April 2014). A survey by the Chartered Institute of Personnel and Development (CIPD) found that 9% of individuals on ZHCs are never allowed to work for another employer when their primary employer has no work for them (*Zero Hours Contracts: myth and reality*, CIPD, November 2013). On the basis of these figures the Department of Business, Innovation and Skills estimates that as many as 125,000 workers could be covered by exclusivity clauses (*Zero Hours Employment Contracts. Banning exclusivity clauses: Tackling avoidance*, Department of Business, Innovation and Skills, August 2014, at p. 8.)

   A survey of selected organisations conducted in the mid-1990s found that just over one-fifth used 'something which could be described as zero-hours contracts'. Almost all the employers surveyed (80%) said that their zero-hours workers were employees and the authors concluded that this was probably the case given the evidence relating to the employees' limited right to refuse work and the degree of control and integration (see Cave, K. E., *Zero Hours Contracts: A report into the incidence and implications of such contracts* (Huddersfield: University of Huddersfield, 1997)). In the light of subsequent developments in the case law, this might be regarded as an overly optimistic conclusion. The report (p. 23) discussed two then-unreported cases (*Clark v Oxfordshire Health Authority* (1996); *Carmichael and Leese v National Power plc* (1996)), where employee status was found in one (a bank nurse) but not the other (a 'casual as required' tourist guide). Subsequently, the Court of Appeal overruled both decisions, thus underlining the uncertainties and inconsistencies pervading this area (see [1998] IRLR 125 and [1998] IRLR 301 respectively).

   In *Carmichael*, the Court of Appeal held that a 'casual as required' contract had the requisite mutuality of obligations between the parties to be regarded as an umbrella contract of employment because there was an implied term in the contract that the applicants would take on a reasonable amount of work and a corresponding implied term that the employers would provide a reasonable share of guiding work as it became available. However, no such implied term was found to exist between the parties in *Clark*. Sir Christopher Slade cited *Nethermere (St Neots) Ltd v Gardiner* [1984] IRLR 240, CA and *McLeod v Hellyer Brothers Ltd* [1987] IRLR 232, CA as authority 'for the proposition that "no contract of employment" within the definition contained in [what is now ERA, s. 230(1)] (whether it be given the extra-statutory name "global" or "umbrella" or any other name) can exist in the absence of mutual obligations subsisting over the entire duration of the relevant period'. While accepting that the mutual obligations required to found a global contract need not necessarily and in every case consist of obligations to provide and perform work, the example he gave—the obligation to accept work, on the one hand, and the obligation, on the other hand, to pay a retainer—would be of little relevance or help to most workers with intermittent working patterns. It is indeed ironic that the Lord Chancellor should call in aid to his argument the decision in *Nethermere*. Whilst the case is clearly authority for the need for there to be a minimum mutuality of obligation in order to found employee status, the Court of Appeal then went on to find that minimum requirement to be present in the working arrangements of the home workers.

The judicial approach adopted by the *Carmichael* decision in the Court of Appeal was welcomed by some commentators, not least because the preponderance of women in these marginal and intermittent areas of work has led to their further disadvantage in terms of employment protection rights (see Ross, J., 'Marginal notes? Gender and the contract of employment' in Morris, M. and O'Donnell, T. (eds.), *Feminist Perspectives on Employment Law* (London: Cavendish, 1999)). However, while the Court of Appeal's reasoning offered the prospect of enhanced protection for casual workers, it would not be difficult for employers to avoid a similar outcome by drafting terms which expressly exclude a requirement to undertake specified levels of work (or on the employer to provide work when available). The availability of this avoidance tool is underlined by the approach adopted by the Court of Appeal in *Express and Echo Publications Ltd* v *Tanton* [1999] IRLR 367, CA (extracted earlier).

Commentators hoped that when *Carmichael* was heard by the House of Lords the opportunity would be taken for a general review of the case law. In this respect, the Lords' decision is disappointing, demonstrating a continued judicial suspicion of the concept of umbrella contracts as a means of extending the scope of employment protection to so-called flexible workers.

Carmichael and Leese v National Power plc
[1999] IRLR 43, House of Lords

Mrs Carmichael and Mrs Leese worked as power-station tour guides. When they were offered the work in March 1989 they were requested to sign a letter that stated: 'I am pleased to accept your offer of employment as a station guide on a casual as required basis.' The guides were paid an hourly rate as determined by the relevant National Joint Council and they were paid after deduction of income tax and national insurance at an employed person's rate. They received training, a uniform, and, when necessary, a company vehicle. In 1989, when they started the job, they only worked an average of three or four hours a week, but by 1995 they were working as many as 25 hours in a week. On these facts, the House of Lords, overruling the Court of Appeal, upheld the decision of the industrial tribunal that the guides were not entitled to a written statement of particulars of employment as they were not employees.

LORD IRVINE OF LAIRG LC: The industrial tribunal held that their [the Applicants'] case 'founders on the rock of absence of mutuality', that is that, when not working as guides, they were in no contractual relationship of any kind with CEGB.

The tribunal made this finding on the basis of (a) the language of the March 1989 documentation; (b) the way in which it had been operated; and (c) the evidence of the parties as to how it had been understood. For reasons I will amplify later, this was in my judgment the correct approach. In substance, it held that the documents did no more than provide a framework for a series of ad hoc contracts of service or for services which the parties might subsequently make; and that when they were not working as guides they were not in any contractual relationship with the CEGB. The parties incurred no obligations to provide or accept work, but at best assumed moral obligations of loyalty in a context where both recognised that the best interests of each lay in being accommodating to the other. The contrary, however, was argued by Mr Langstaff QC. He maintained that, once appointed, they became employees under contracts of employment which obliged the CEGB to provide them with such guide work as might become available in the future, which they in turn were obliged to undertake when made available.

This submission construes the words, 'Employment will be on a casual as required basis', as empowering the CEGB to require Mrs Leese and Mrs Carmichael to undertake guide work as need for it arose.

If the issue were to be determined solely by reference to the documentation, I would, as a matter of construction, reject it. The words imposed no obligation on Mrs Leese and Mrs Carmichael, but intimated that casual employment on the pay terms stated could ensue as and when the CEGB's requirements for the services of the guides arose. Thus, the documents provided no more than a framework for ad hoc contracts of service or services which Mrs Leese and Mrs Carmichael might make with CEGB in the future...

If this appeal turned exclusively—and in my judgment it does not—on the true meaning and effect of the documentation of March 1989, then I would hold as a matter of construction that no obligation on the CEGB to provide casual work, nor on Mrs Lease and Mrs Carmichael to undertake it, was imposed. There would therefore be an absence of that irreducible minimum of mutual obligation necessary to create a contract of service (*Nethermere (St Neots) Ltd* v *Gardiner* [1984] IRLR 240 *per* Stephenson LJ, and *Clark* v *Oxfordshire Health Authority* [1998] IRLR 125, 128 *per* Sir Christopher Slade, at paragraph 22).

In my judgment, it would only be appropriate to determine the issue in these cases solely by reference to the documents in March 1989, if it appeared from their own terms and/or what the parties said or did then, or subsequently, that they intended them to constitute an exclusive memorial of their relationship. The industrial tribunal must be taken to have decided that they were not so intended but constituted one, albeit important, relevant source of material from which they were intended to infer the parties' true intention, along with the other objective inferences which could reasonably be drawn from what the parties said and did in March 1989 and subsequently...

Appeal allowed.

NOTES

1. The House of Lords in *Carmichael*, whilst producing a rather disappointing and perfunctory judgment holding that the relationship on its facts did not have the minimum mutuality of obligations necessary to create an employment relationship, did at least offer refreshing guidance as to the approach to be taken in determining the terms of the contract of employment. Both the Lord Chancellor and Lord Hoffmann adopt a modern view that this should only be regarded as a question to be determined solely by reference to documents where the parties intended all the terms of the contract to be contained in the documents. Otherwise, the court can look beyond the written documentation to the evidence of the parties as to what they understood their respective obligations to be, and to their subsequent conduct, as evidence as to the terms of the contract. This approach did not help Carmichael but it is argued it would have helped Tanton and many other marginal workers to combat slick employment-documentation drafting. In *Pulse Healthcare Ltd* v *Carewatch Care Services Ltd* (UKEAT/0123/12/BA, 6 August 2012), it was held that the written contract—labelled the 'Zero Hours Contract Agreement'—did not reflect the true agreement between the parties and mutuality of obligation was present.

2. A number of wider implications flow from *Carmichael*. The decision has erected significant obstacles in the way of any attempts to extend employment status to casual workers. Furthermore, it could be used by employers to try to question the employment status of other workers on the margins of employment protection, for example agency workers and home workers. Finally, 'highly evolved' HR practitioners have always faced an uphill struggle in trying to convince line managers that it was not sufficient to label a worker as 'casual' and then assume that they possessed no employment rights. The *Carmichael* decision does not aid the HR manager's cause (see Leighton, P. and Painter, R. W., 'Casual workers: Still marginal after all these years?' (2001) 23(1/2) Employee Relations 75–93).

   In the light of this confusion, the Government considered it desirable to clarify the coverage of employment protection legislation and to better reflect the diversity of working relationships in the modern labour market. Consequently, s. 23 of the Employment Relations Act 1999 gives the Secretary of State the power, by order subject to the affirmative resolution procedure, to extend to individuals who do not at present enjoy them the employment rights under TULR(C)A 1992, the ERA 1996, and the 1999 Act itself. The Government envisages using this power to ensure that workers other than the genuinely self-employed enjoy the minimum standard of protection that the legislation is intended to provide, and that none is excluded simply because of the technicalities relating to the type of contract or other arrangement under which they are engaged.

   Indeed, a recent trend has been to extend the scope of the newer employment protection rights to a broader category of 'workers': this definition has been adopted by the Public Interest Disclosure Act 1998, the Working Time Regulations 1998, and the National Minimum Wage Act 1998. Broadening this approach to all employment protection rights, including unfair dismissal, would avoid the illiberal implications of the *Carmichael* judgment. This definition includes not only those working under a contract of employment but also people working under other contracts for personal services.

3. The legal protection available to part-time and temporary workers was significantly increased as a result of the judgment of the House of Lords in *R* v *Secretary of State for Employment, ex p. EOC* [1995] 1 AC 1, HL (discussed at p. 71 (Section 3.A); see also *R* v *Secretary of State for Employment, ex p. Seymour-Smith and Perez* C–167/97 [1999] IRLR 253, ECJ (discussed at p. 71 (Section 3.A)).

The EC has been concerned for some while to ensure that part-time workers receive no less favourable treatment than full-time workers. There are a number of policy considerations for this, including recent rapid increases in part-time and 'atypical' working within Member States and the need to promote labour market objectives of 'employability', and conditions generally in which workers are going to remain in employment rather than leave work to take up out-of-work State benefits. The principles of equal treatment in respect of terms and conditions of employment and the application of statutory employment protection are recognised in most other European Member States (see, for example, the French *Code du Travail*, Article L212–4–2). However, the translation of this principle into an EC directive was, for many years, opposed by the UK's Conservative Government on the ground of the negative employment effect it would allegedly create.

The Directive on Part-time Work (EC Directive 97/81) was the result of an earlier framework agreement between the 'social partners' (employers, unions, and public sector employers). The directive itself is open to criticism in that it allows governments to exclude casual workers from the definition of part-time worker entirely (clause 2), while the equal treatment of part-time workers is subject to the possible justification of special conditions on objective grounds. The range of objective grounds envisaged includes time worked and an earnings qualification. Such qualifications have proved to be an effective means of excluding part-time workers from employment rights. (See Rose, J., 'Marginal notes? Gender and the contract of employment' in Morris, A. and O'Donnell, T. (eds.), *Feminist Perspectives on Employment Law* (London: Cavendish, 1999); Jeffrey, M., 'Not really going to work? "Atypical work" and attempts to regulate it' (1998) ILJ 27, pp. 193–213.)

On 1 July 2000 the Government brought into force the Part-time Workers (Prevention of Less Favourable Treatment) Regulations 2000 (SI 2000/1551) in order to implement the directive. The regulations define a full-time worker as a person who is 'paid wholly or in part by reference to the time he works and, having regard to the custom and practice of the employer in relation to workers employed by the worker's employer under the same type of contract, is identifiable as a full-time worker' (reg. 2(1)).

PART-TIME WORKERS (PREVENTION OF LESS FAVOURABLE TREATMENT) REGULATIONS 2000 (SI 2000/1551)

5(1) A part-time worker has the right not to be treated by his employer less favourably than the employer treats a comparable full-time worker—

(a) as regards the terms of his contract; or

(b) by being subjected to any other detriment by any act, or deliberate failure to act, of his employer.

(2) The right conferred by paragraph (1) applies only if—

(a) the treatment is on the ground that the worker is a part-time worker, and

(b) the treatment is not justified on objective grounds.

(3) In determining whether a part-time worker has been treated less favourably than a comparable full-time worker the pro rata principle shall be applied unless it is inappropriate.

(4) A part-time worker paid at a lower rate for overtime worked by him in a period than a comparable full-time worker is or would be paid for overtime worked for him in the same period shall not, for that reason, be regarded as treated less favourably than the comparable full-time worker where, or to the extent that, the total number of hours worked by the part-time worker in the period, including overtime, does not exceed the number of hours the comparable full-time worker is required to work in the period, disregarding absences from work and overtime.

NOTES

1. This means part-timers are entitled to:

(a) the same hourly rate of pay (subject to reg. 5(4) on overtime);

(b) the same access to company pension schemes;

(c) the same entitlements to annual leave and maternity/parental leave on a pro rata basis;
(d) the same entitlement to contractual sick pay;
(e) no less favourable treatment in access to training.

2. In the draft form of the regulations, the Government proposed to confine their coverage to 'employees' not 'workers' (draft reg. 1(2)). As a consequence, many economically dependent workers—such as Mrs Carmichael—would have been disenfranchised from significant parts of the framework of employment protection. Ultimately, the Government responded to the threat of legal action from the TUC and broadened the coverage of the regulations.

2(4) A full-time worker is a comparable full-time worker in relation to a part-time worker if, at the time when the treatment is alleged to be less favourable to the part-time worker takes place—
  (a) both workers are—
    (i) employed by the same employer under the same type of contract, and
    (ii) engaged in the same or broadly similar work having regard, where relevant, to whether they have a similar level of qualifications, skills and experience; and
  (b) the full-time worker works or is based at the same establishment as the part-time worker or, where there is no full-time worker working or based at that establishment who satisfies the requirements of sub-paragraph (a), works or is based at different establishments and satisfies those requirements.

NOTES

1. Despite the broadening of the coverage of the regulations to 'workers'—as opposed to 'employees'—the regulations retained the potential to disenfranchise many economically dependent workers from the scope of their protection. This was because comparisons under the regulations could only be employed under the regulations between an actual comparator (cf. the Sex Discrimination Act and Race Relations Act) employed under the same contract. Thus, for example, a part-time worker employed on a fixed-term contract could not compare his or her treatment with that of a full-time worker employed on a permanent contract. Similarly, workers employed under contracts for services ('workers') cannot compare their treatment with full-time workers employed under contracts of employment ('employees')—see reg. 2(3). In other words, the *Carmichael* problem is not resolved. The only cases in which a claim may be made without reference to an actual full-time comparator are set out in the regulations. Broadly, these exceptions cover (a) a full-time worker who becomes part-time (reg. 3); and (b) full-time workers returning to work part time for the same employer within a period of less than 12 months (reg. 4).

    In February 2002 the Government issued draft amendments to the Part-time Workers (Prevention of Less Favourable Treatment) Regulations 2000. These cover comparators (reg. 2) and access to occupational pension schemes (reg. 8). The regulations came into force on 1 October 2002 as the Part-time Workers (Prevention of Less Favourable Treatment) Regulations 2000 (Amendment) Regulations 2002 (SI 2002/2035).

    The Government recognised that regulations needed to be amended to comply with the Fixed-term Work Directive, 1999/70/EC. The Amendment Regulations seek to ensure that fixed-term and permanent workers will be regarded as 'employed under the same contract', although the fact that a worker is on a particular type of contract may be justification for less favourable treatment. Also, the Amendment Regulations do not address the issue, referred to earlier, where individuals employed under a contract of employment cannot compare themselves with workers who are engaged on a contract for services.

    The Amendment Regulations also remove the limitation on remedies following a complaint relating to access to, or treatment under, an occupational pension scheme. Under reg. 8(8), where an ET has upheld a complaint from a part-timer for equal access to an occupational pension scheme, the remedies which it orders may not go back further than two years. This time limit was originally inserted to ensure consistency with existing equal pay and pensions legislation, which provides that employer contributions to a pension scheme may not be backdated by more than two years. In *Preston* v *Wolverhampton Healthcare Trust* [2001] IRLR 237, the House of Lords ruled that the two-year time limit on backdating contravened EC law and could no longer be maintained. As a consequence, the Amendment Regulations remove the two-year limit.

2. Even the DTI's Regulatory Impact Assessment, which accompanied the draft regulations, evidences their likely limited effect when it states:

    There are approximately 6 million part-time employees in Great Britain—all of whom will benefit from added security. We estimate that 1 million have a comparable full-time employee.

Equal treatment could directly benefit 400,000 part-time workers through increases in pay and non-wage benefits.

In other words, less than 17 per cent of all part-time workers work alongside a potential full-time comparator and less than 7 per cent stand directly to benefit through increase in pay and non-wage benefits.

3. The right of part-timers not to be treated less favourably than a comparable full-timer applies only if the treatment is not justified on objective grounds (see reg. 5(4), extracted earlier). The Explanatory Note accompanying the regulations states that:

Less favourable treatment will only be justified on objective grounds if it can be shown that the less favourable treatment:
  (i)   is to achieve a legitimate objective, for example, a genuine business objective;
  (ii) is necessary to achieve that objective; and
  (iii) is an appropriate way to achieve the objective.

4. In *Mathews* v *Kent & Medway Towns Fire Authority* [2006] IRLR 367, the House of Lords, by a majority, held that, in determining whether full-time or part-time workers are doing the 'same or broadly similar' work, the focus should be on the similarities and not the differences, since it is almost inevitable that there will be some differences. The focus should be on the core activities of the workers. The fact that full-timers do some extra tasks would not prevent their work being held to be the same or broadly similar.

5. In *McMenemy* v *Capital Business Services Ltd* [2007] IRLR 400, the Court of Session, like the EAT, held that a part-time employee, who did not work on Mondays, was not entitled to rely on the Part-time Workers Regulations to claim additional time off pro rata for the public holidays which fell on a Monday. The claimant, who worked only on Wednesday, Thursday, and Friday, was held to have not been treated less favourably, contrary to reg. 5, than a comparable full-time worker. The Court of Session took the view that a full-time worker who did not work on Mondays would have been treated in the same way.

Unfair dismissal and the right not to be subjected to detriment

7.—(1) An employee who is dismissed shall be regarded as unfairly dismissed for the purposes of Part X of the 1996 Act if the reason (or, if more than one, the principal reason) for the dismissal is a reason specified in paragraph (3).

(2) A worker has the right not to be subjected to any detriment by any act, or any deliberate failure to act, by his employer done on a ground specified in paragraph (3).

(3) The reasons or, as the case may be, grounds are—
  (a) that the worker has—
    (i)   brought proceedings against the employer under these Regulations;
    (ii) requested from his employer a written statement of reasons under regulation 6;
    (iii) given evidence or information in connection with such proceedings brought by any worker;
    (iv) otherwise done anything under these Regulations in relation to the employer or any other person;
    (v)   alleged that the employer has infringed these Regulations; or
    (vi) refused (or proposed to refuse) to forgo a right conferred on him by these Regulations, or
  (b) that the employer believes or suspects that the worker has done or intends to do any of the things mentioned in sub-paragraph (a).

(4) Where the reason or principal reason for dismissal or, as the case may be, ground for subjection to any act or deliberate failure to act, is that mentioned in paragraph (3)(a)(v), or (b) so far as it relates thereto, neither paragraph (1) nor paragraph (2) applies if the allegation made by the worker is false and not made in good faith.

(5) Paragraph (2) does not apply where the detriment in question amounts to a dismissal within the meaning of Part X of the 1996 Act.

NOTES

1. An unfair dismissal claim is generally only exercisable after the employee has completed at least one year's service. Until that service threshold is attained, the part-time worker remains vulnerable.

2. The rights set out in the regulations are exercisable by the complaint to an employment tribunal. Regulation 6 provides a right for the employee to receive a written statement of reasons for less favourable treatment within 21 days of the request.

3. Where a tribunal finds that a complaint of less favourable treatment presented to it under the regulations is well founded, it may, *inter alia*, order the employer to pay such compensation which is just and equitable in all the circumstances (reg. 8(7), (9)). The calculation will not include injury to feelings (reg. 8(11)).

4. In *Sharma* v *Manchester City Council* [2008] IRLR 336, the EAT held that it was not a legitimate construction of the regulations to read into them the requirement that the part-time nature of the worker's status had to be the *sole* reason for the discriminatory treatment. Once it is found that the part-timer is treated less favourably than a comparator full-timer and being part time is one of the reasons for that less favourable treatment, that will suffice to trigger the regulations. This approach was followed by the EAT in *Carl* v *University of Sheffield* [2009] IRLR 616. More controversially, the EAT held that, under the regulations, claimants could not compare themselves to a 'hypothetical'—as opposed to an actual—comparator.

C: Employee status: a question of law or fact?

1. Chung and 2. Shun Shing Lee v Construction & Engineering Co. Ltd
[1990] IRLR 236, Privy Council

LORD GRIFFITHS: Whether or not a person is employed under a contract of service is often said in the authorities to be a mixed question of fact and law. Exceptionally, if the relationship is dependent solely upon the true construction of a written document it is regarded as a question of law: see *Davies* v *Presbyterian Church of Wales* [1986] IRLR 194. But where, as in the present case, the relationship has to be determined by an investigation and evaluation of the factual circumstances in which the work is performed, it must now be taken to be firmly established that the question of whether or not the work was performed in the capacity of an employee or as an independent contractor is to be regarded by an appellate court as a question of fact to be determined by the trial court. At first sight it seems rather strange that this should be so, for whether or not a certain set of facts should be classified under one legal head rather than another would appear to be a question of law. However, no doubt because of the difficulty of devising a conclusive test to resolve the question and the threat of the appellate courts being crushed by the weight of appeals if the many borderline cases were considered to be questions of law, it was held in a series of decisions in the Court of Appeal and in the House of Lords under the English Workmen's Compensation Acts that a finding by a county court judge that a workman was, or was not, employed under a contract of service was a question of fact with which an appellate court could only interfere if there was no evidence to support his finding: see *Smith* v *General Motor Cab Company* [1911] AC 188, *Bobbey* v *Crosbie* [1915] 114 LT 244 and *Easdown* v *Cobb* [1940] 1 All ER 49. More recently, in *O'Kelly* v *Trusthouse Forte* [1983] IRLR 369 the Court of Appeal, despite a powerful dissenting judgment by Ackner LJ, held that whether or not a waiter was employed under a contract of employment within the meaning of the Employment Protection (Consolidation) Act 1978 was a question of mixed fact and law, and that the finding of an industrial tribunal on this issue, from which an appeal lay on a point of law only, could only be impugned if it could be shown that the tribunal correctly directing itself on the law could not reasonably have reached the conclusion under appeal. Lord Donaldson pointed out that this was a heavy burden on an appellant and concluded by saying: 'I would have thought that all this was trite law, but if it is not, it is set out with the greatest possible clarity in *Edwards* v *Bairstow* [1956] AC 14'.

In *Edwards* v *Bairstow* the question that fell to be decided was whether the General Commissioners were right in their finding that the respondents had not entered into 'an adventure in the nature of trade'. Whether or not persons have entered into 'an adventure in the nature of trade' is a decision of a like nature to whether or not a person is employed under a contract of service or, to state the question in modern language, under a contract of employment. The decision will depend upon the evaluation of many facts and there will be many borderline cases in which similarly instructed minds may come to different conclusions. It is in such situations that an appeal court must not interfere and it is in this sense that the decision is said to be one of fact. But an appellate court must not abdicate its responsibility and it is worth bearing in mind the works with which Lord Radcliffe concluded his speech in *Edwards* v *Bairstow* at pp. 38 and 39:

I think it possible that the English courts have been led to be rather over-ready to treat these questions as 'pure questions of fact' by some observations of Warrington and Atkin LJJ in *Cooper* v *Stubbs* [1925] 2 KB 753. If so, I would say, with very great respect, that I think it a pity that such a tendency should persist. As I see it, the reason why the courts do not interfere with commissioners' findings or determinations when they really do involve nothing but questions of fact is not any supposed advantage in the commissioners of greater experience in matters of business or any other matters. The reason is simply that by the system that has been set up the commissioners are the first tribunal to try an appeal, and in the interest of the efficient administration of justice their decisions can only be upset on appeal if they have been positively wrong in law. The court is not a second opinion, where there is reasonable ground for the first. But there is no reason to make a mystery about the subjects that commissioners deal with or to invite the courts to impose any exceptional restraints upon themselves because they are dealing with cases that arise out of facts found by commissioners. Their duty is no more than to examine those facts with a decent respect for the tribunal appealed from and if they think that the only reasonable conclusion on the facts found is inconsistent with the determination come to, to say so without more ado.

NOTES

1. See also *Clifford* v *Union of Democratic Mineworkers* [1991] IRLR 518, CA.

■ QUESTION

If the question of employee status is held to be largely a question of fact, is there not a risk of inconsistency in outcome in cases involving similar facts?

2. In the course of his opinion in *Chung*, Lord Griffiths refers to *Davies* v *Presbyterian Church of Wales* [1986] IRLR 194, HL. That case involved the employment status of a church minister and the decision found no employment status. For a more recent and liberal judgment relating to the employment status of the clergy, see *Percy* v *Church of Scotland Board of National Mission* [2006] IRLR 195, HL. According to Lord Nicholls in *Percy*: 'holding an office and being an employee are not inconsistent. A person may hold an "office" in the terms of, and pursuant to, a contract of employment.' In *New Testament Church of God* v *Stewart* [2007] IRLR 178, the EAT applied the principles as formulated in *Percy* and held that a minister of religion could be entitled to bring a claim of unfair dismissal because he or she is employed under a contract of employment. Ansell J stated: 'if the relationship between church and minister has many of the characteristics of a contract of employment in terms of rights and obligations, these cannot be ignored simply because the duties are of a religious or pastoral nature.' (c.f. *The President of the Methodist Conference* v *Preston* [2013] IRLR 646, SC, where the Supreme Court, by a majority, overruled the EAT and CA which had taken the view that the claimant, an ordained Minister, was entitled to bring an unfair dismissal claim after she resigned.)

D: Self-description

Young and Woods Ltd v *West*
[1980] IRLR 201, Court of Appeal

West, a sheet metal worker, requested that he be treated as self-employed. This was accepted by his employer and, although there was no difference between his working conditions and the 'employees' he worked alongside, doing the same job and under the same level of supervision, he was paid gross of tax. When West's job was terminated, he claimed that he was an employee after all and therefore entitled to claim unfair dismissal. The Court of Appeal held that, despite West's arrangement with his employer, he was really an employee and the industrial tribunal had jurisdiction to hear the complaint.

STEPHENSON LJ: Mr Clifford [counsel for the employer] has submitted that, though a party cannot alter the true relationship, if the parties genuinely and expressly intend to establish a person (on the employer's books) to do a job as a self-employed person, then he cannot make a claim as an employee for the purpose of getting compensation for unfair dismissal. Either, he says, the parties cannot resile from the position which they have deliberately and openly taken up in any circumstances or, if that is putting the matter too high, the presumption created by their deliberately and openly chosen relationship is rebuttable, but not easily rebuttable.

I am satisfied that the parties can resile from the position which they have deliberately and openly chosen to take up and that to reach any other conclusion would be, in effect, to permit the parties to contract out of the [Employment Rights] Act [1996] and to deprive, in particular, a person who works as an employee within the definition of the Act under a contract of service of the benefits which this statute confers upon him. If I consider the policy of the Act I can see the dangers, pointed out by Lord Justice Ackner in the course of the argument, of employers anxious to escape from their statutory liabilities under this legislation or the Factories Acts offering this choice to persons whom they intend to employ, as Mr West was employed, as employees within the definition of the Act and pressing them to take that employment—it may be even insisting upon their taking that employment—on the terms that it shall not be called that employment at all, but shall be called a contract for services with a self-employed person. I, therefore, reject Mr Clifford's submission in its extreme form.

NOTE: In *Quashie* v *Stringfellow Restaurants Ltd* [2013] IRLR 99, the Court of Appeal had to determine whether a lap dancer was an employee or self-employed. On the facts, there was a relatively high level of control in that there were rules relating to shifts and penalties for non-attendance or lateness, On the other hand, she was not paid by the company but by fees negotiated with the customer; she had a degree of financial risk, provided her own equipment, and did not receive sick pay, holiday pay, or other benefits. In addition, her work documentation described her as self-employed and provided that she was responsible for her own tax and national insurance. The Court of Appeal found that the employment tribunal's decision that she was self-employed was not perverse. In the course of his judgment, Elias LJ observed:

> It is trite law that the parties cannot by agreement fix the status of their relationship: that is an objective matter to be determined by an assessment of all the relevant facts. But it is legitimate for a court to have regard to the way in which the parties have chosen to categorise their relationship, and in a case where the position is uncertain, it can be decisive . . . (at para. 52)

Stevedoring & Haulage Services Ltd v *Fuller and others*
[2001] IRLR 627, Court of Appeal

Mr Fuller and his fellow applicants were employed by the company as permanent dockworkers between 1989 and 1995, when they accepted voluntary redundancy terms. In January 1996, however, they were taken on as casual workers.

A letter offering that work made it clear that they would not be employees of the company but would provide their services on 'an ad hoc and casual basis' with 'no obligation on the part of the company to provide such work for you nor for you to accept any work so offered'. The applicants signed and returned copies of that letter together with another document headed 'Temporary terminal operatives' terms and conditions of engagement', which included the following statement: 'You are not an employee of the company; your services being utilised only when mutually agreed, with no obligation by either party other than to honour a specific pre-agreed period of engagement.'

From January 1996, the applicants worked for the company on many more days than not. They did not work for any other employer. They were engaged directly by the company and were offered work before any casual labour which was engaged through an agency. A rota system ensured that those who said that they were available for work but were not offered it were rewarded and that those who were offered work for which they were not available were penalised.

After working on this basis for three years, the applicants applied to an employment tribunal for written statements of their particulars of employment. The ERA 1996, s. 1 requires such statements to be provided to 'employees'. The tribunal concluded that the applicants were 'employees'. They were not simply working under a series of individual engagements, but under an 'overarching' contract of employment. The tribunal found that although the documents containing the terms upon which casual work was offered and accepted 'expressly negative mutuality of obligation' terms providing for an 'irreducible minimum of obligation on each side' could be implied from the way in which the parties had conducted themselves. Those implied terms were that the company would offer the applicants a reasonable amount of work as and when the work was available, and do so in priority to other casual workers, and that, in return, the applicants would make themselves available for work on at least a reasonable number of occasions when work was offered to them.

The EAT dismissed the company's appeal. The EAT concluded that the implied terms reflected the reality of the agreement between the parties. It was open to the employment tribunal to find that those terms were not inconsistent with the express terms of the agreement and that it was necessary to imply them to give the agreement business efficacy. The company's appeal to the Court of Appeal was successful.

TUCKEY LJ: ...If there was a contract, we cannot see any way in which the ET's implied terms could be incorporated into it. The implied terms flatly contradict the express terms contained in the documents: a positive implied obligation to offer and accept a *reasonable amount* of casual work (whatever that means) cannot be reconciled with express terms that neither party is obliged to offer or accept any casual work. None of the conventional routes for the implication of contractual implied terms will work. Neither business efficacy nor necessity require the implication of implied terms which are entirely inconsistent with a supposed contract's express terms.

NOTE: This case does not sit easily with the approach in *Young and Woods Ltd* v *West* and opens up the possibility that employers will be able to avoid legal responsibilities by including express terms denying 'employee' status to their workers (see also *Express and Echo Publications Ltd* v *Tanton* [1999] IRLR 367, CA—an extract is to be found at p. 58 (Section B)). This, in turn, raises the question as to whether the extent and express term denying employee status should be permitted to override statutory employment rights without falling foul of restrictions against contracting out. Compare, for example, *Hanson* v *Fashion Industries (Hartlepool) Ltd* [1980] IRLR 393, in which the EAT regarded a term in a re-engagement agreement that no previous employment 'counts as part of your continuous service' as being void as an attempt to exclude the statutory continuity provisions.

■ QUESTION

The Court of Appeal's reliance on the express term in *Fuller* in preference to the economic reality has been described by Rubenstein ('Highlights' [2001] IRLR 586) as 'a triumph of form over substance'. Would you agree?

A NOTE ON RECENT DEVELOPMENTS: *Zero hours contracts:* In June 2014, following a consultation exercise, the Government announced plans to ban exclusivity clauses in ZHCs. As a result, the Small Business, Enterprise and Employment Act 2015 inserts a new s. 27A into the ERA 1996 rendering exclusivity clauses in zero hours contracts unenforceable.

ZHCs are defined in the Act as:
- a contract of employment or a worker's contract under which the undertaking to do or perform work or services is an undertaking to do so conditionally on the employer making the work or services available to the worker; and
- where there is no certainty that any such work or services will be made available to the worker (s. 27A(1)).

Discussions with stakeholders, however, indicated that any such ban would be straightforward for employers to circumvent, e.g. by offering contracts that guarantee just one hour of work. As a result, the 2015 Act inserts a new s. 27B into the ERA 1996. This section provides the Secretary of State with an order-making power that will allow avoidance of the ban to be dealt with by secondary legislation.

In August 2014, a further consultation was launched, seeking views on whether, how, and when the power in s. 27B should be used—the best mechanism for tackling avoidance of the exclusivity ban if felt necessary—as well as routes for redress.

Further guidance could be provided by 'industry-led, industry-owned, sector specific' codes of practice on the use of zero hours contracts, drawn up jointly by employers and unions with the support of government (*Zero Hours Employment Contracts. Banning exclusivity clauses: Tackling avoidance*, Department of Business, Innovation and Skills, August 2014).

The consultation closed on 3 November 2014.

Employment status: In October 2014, the Government announced a wide-ranging review to help clarify and potentially strengthen the employment status of workers. According to Government estimates, there may be up to a million people on 'worker' contracts; the review aimed to seek to offer further clarity on numbers by working with statistical experts, think tanks, and employment lawyers. Announcing the review, the Business Secretary, Vince Cable, said:

> Workers should not be finding out that they are not protected by law once they get to employment tribunal. We need a system that is fair, simple and transparent—an environment where businesses feel more confident knowing what type of contracts to hire staff on and where individuals know their rights and have the security they deserve.'

The announcement states:

> Without prejudging the review...it could be that after further analysis, an extension of all employment rights to 'workers' is not overly costly or bureaucratic (especially if the analysis shows the current group to be small).

BIS civil servants aimed to submit recommendations to ministers by March 2015 ('Employment review launched to improve clarity and status of British workforce', Department of Business, Innovation and Skills Press Release, 6 October 2014).

SECTION 3: CONTINUITY OF EMPLOYMENT

Even where part-time or casual workers could establish their status as employees, many were excluded from employment law protections either because they did not work sufficient hours per week, or because their employment was intermittent or of a short duration. Generally, the law required employees to have worked for the employer for at least 16 hours per week for a minimum of two calendar years before they could mount a claim for unfair dismissal or redundancy payments. Those who worked between 8 and 16 hours per week had to have five years' service in order to bring a complaint. Only in exceptional cases was no period of qualification required, for example dismissals relating to union membership and activities or to non-unionism and sex and race discrimination. However, EC-inspired case law in 1994 and 2000 brought about a dramatic change to the situation.

A: Continuity: hours of work/length of service

First, the House of Lords held in *R* v *Secretary of State for Employment, ex p. EOC* [1994] 1 AC 1 that the hours thresholds were in breach of Article 141 (ex 119) of the Treaty of Rome and the EEC Equal Treatment Directive in that they were discriminatory against women, the majority of whom worked part time.

As a consequence of that judgment, the Government was forced to introduce the Employment Protection (Part-time Employees) Regulations 1995, which came into force on 6 February 1995. The regulations repealed various provisions of what was Sch. 13 to the Employment Protection (Consolidation) Act 1978 so that periods of part-time service now count in computing the employee's continuous employment under the legislation. This ensured that employees working fewer than 16 hours per week had only to complete two years' service with their employer before they qualified for the right to claim unfair dismissal and redundancy pay.

The next development was a challenge to the two-year continuity rule for unfair dismissal and redundancy claims in *R* v *Secretary of State for Employment, ex p. Seymour-Smith and Perez (No. 2)* [2000] IRLR 263, HL. Here the proposition on the part of the claimants was that to require a two-year period indirectly discriminated against women (because a smaller proportion of women could comply with this condition than men), thereby contravening EU sex discrimination law.

In finding the 1985 increase not discriminatory, three Lords (Lords Goff, Jauncey, and Nicholls) held that any adverse effect was justified and two (Lords Slynn and Steyn) held that there was no significant adverse effect in the first place.

By the time the above case was decided, the discriminatory effect of the service quali-fication was reduced with the introduction of the requirement for one year's continuous service for unfair dismissal applicants—though it remains at two years for redundancy payment claims (Unfair Dismissal and Statement for Reasons for Dismissal (Variation of Qualifying Period) Order 1999 (SI 1999/1436)). The period of continuous employment is relevant not only for determining whether an employee is *qualified* to make a claim for unfair dismissal, redundancy payments, etc., but also for calculating the *amount* of compensation. The statutory provisions attempt to ensure that 'continuity' is preserved despite certain changes of employer and certain periods where the employee is away from work.

B: Continuity: periods away from work

EMPLOYMENT RIGHTS ACT 1996

212. Weeks counting in computing period

(1) Any week during the whole or part of which an employee's relations with his employer are governed by a contract of employment counts in computing the employee's period of employment.

(2) Any week (not within subsection (1)) during an employee's period of absence from work occasioned wholly or partly by pregnancy or childbirth after which the employee returns to work in accordance with section 79, or in pursuance of an offer described in section 96(3), counts in computing the employee's period of employment.

(3) Subject to subsection (4), any week (not within subsection (1)) during the whole or part of which an employee is—

   (a) incapable of work in consequence of sickness or injury,
   (b) absent from work on account of a temporary cessation of work,
   (c) absent from work in circumstances such that, by arrangement or custom, he is regarded as continuing in the employment of his employer for any purpose, or
   (d) absent from work wholly or partly because of pregnancy or childbirth, counts in computing the employee's period of employment.

(4) Not more than twenty-six weeks count under subsection (3)(a) or (subject to subsection (2)) subsection (3) (d) between any periods falling under subsection (1).

Ford v *Warwickshire County Council*
[1983] IRLR 126, House of Lords

Mrs Ford was a teacher who had been employed by the County Council under a series of consecutive short-term contracts, each for an academic year, for a total of eight years. There was, therefore, a break between the end of one contract and the beginning of the next. The House of Lords held that (what is now) the ERA 1996, s. 212(3)(b) could apply in order to preserve the continuity of her employment and allow her claim for unfair dismissal and a redundancy payment to be heard.

LORD DIPLOCK: My Lords since [s. 212(3)] only applies to an interval of time between the coming to an end of one contract of employment and the beginning of a fresh contract of employment, the expression 'absent from work', where it appears in [ERA 1996, s. 212(3)(b), (c) and (d)], must mean not only that the employee is not doing any actual work for his employer but that there is no contract of employment subsisting between him and his employer that would entitle the latter to require him to do any work. So in this context the phrase 'the employee is absent from work on account of a temporary cessation of work' as descriptive of a period of time, as it would seem to me must refer to the interval between (1) the date on which the employee who would otherwise be continuing to work under an existing contract of employment is dismissed because for the time being his employer has no work for him to do, and (2) the date on which work for him to do having become again available, he is re-engaged under a fresh contract of employment to do it; and the words 'on account of a temporary cessation of work' refer to the reason why the employer dismissed the employee, and make it necessary to inquire what the reason for the dismissal was. The fact that the unavailability of work had been foreseen by the employer sufficiently far in advance to enable him to anticipate it by giving to the employee a notice to terminate his contract of employment that is of sufficient length to satisfy the requirements of [ERA 1996, s. 86] (which may be as long as 12 weeks), cannot alter the reason for the dismissal or prevent the absence from work following upon the expiry of the notice from being 'on account of a temporary cessation of work'.

...

My Lords, I am quite unable to be persuaded that [s. 212(3)] is *not* applicable to cases where a contract of employment for a fixed term has expired and upon expiry has not been renewed by the employer, in exactly the same way as it is applicable to contracts of employment of indefinite duration which are terminated by the employer by notice. One looks to see what was the reason for the employer's failure to renew the contract on the expiry of its fixed term and asks oneself the question: was that reason 'a temporary cessation of work', within the meaning of that phrase in [s. 212(3)(b)]?

...

From the fact that there is no work available for the employee to do for the employer during the whole of the interval between the end of one fixed-term contract of employment and the beginning of the next, and that this was the reason for his non-employment during that interval, it does not necessarily follow that the interval constitutes a '*temporary* cessation of work'. In harmony with what this House held in *Fitzgerald* v *Hall, Russell & Co. Ltd* [1970] AC 984, [s. 212(3)(b)], in cases of employment under a succession of fixed-term contracts of employment with intervals in between, requires one to look back from the date of the expiry of the fixed-term contract in respect of the non-renewal of which the employee's claim is made over the whole period during which the employee has been intermittently employed by the same employer, in order to see whether the interval between one fixed-term contract and the fixed-term contract that next preceded it was short in duration relative to the combined duration of those two fixed-term contracts during which work had continued; for the whole scheme of the Act appears to me to show that it is in the sense of 'transient', i.e. lasting only for a relatively short time, that the word 'temporary' is used in [ERA 1996, s. 212(3)(b)]. So, the continuity of employment for the purposes of the Act in relation to unfair dismissal and redundancy payments is not broken unless and until, looking backwards from the date of the expiry of the fixed term contract on which the employee's claim is based, there is to be found between one fixed-term contract and its immediate predecessor an interval that cannot be characterised as short relatively to the combined duration of the two fixed-term contracts. Whether it can be so characterised is a question of fact and degree and so is for decision by an Industrial Tribunal rather than by the Employment Appeal Tribunal or an appellate court of law.

...

In the instant case, however, it is conceded by the Council that each of the intervals between Mrs Ford's successive fixed-term contracts could properly be characterised as 'temporary'. I would therefore allow the appeal and remit Mrs Ford's claims to the Industrial Tribunal to decide such other matters, if any, as may remain in dispute between her and the Council.

My Lords, as I indicated at the outset, the length of successive fixed-term contracts on which part-time lecturers are employed and the intervals between them vary considerably with the particular course that the part-time lecturer is engaged to teach: so it by no means follows that a similar concession would be made or would be appropriate in each of their cases. It also follows from what I have said that successive periods of seasonal employment of other kinds under fixed-term contracts, such as employment in agriculture during harvest-time or in hotel work during the summer season will only qualify as continuous employment if the length of the period between two successive seasonal contracts is so short in comparison with the length of the season during which the employee is employed as properly to be regarded by the Industrial Tribunal as no more than a *temporary* cessation of work in the sense that I have indicated.

NOTE: This approach is undoubtedly of benefit to many workers, such as part-time or temporary teachers, and makes it much more difficult for employers to avoid the employment protection laws by offering a succession of fixed-term contracts. However, it may not be appropriate where patterns of employment are not regular, as they were in Ford's case, but are subject to fluctuation. To look only at a particular period of unemployment and to compare that period with the combination of the periods either side could lead to some unjust results. This issue was addressed by the Court of Appeal in the next case.

Flack v Kodak Ltd

[1986] IRLR 258, Court of Appeal

Mrs Flack had been employed by Kodak in their photo-finishing department over a number of years for periods which fluctuated markedly. Following her final dismissal, she and the other 'seasonal employees' claimed redundancy payments. An industrial tribunal, purporting to follow what Lord Diplock had said in *Ford* with regard to temporary cessation, rejected their claim. In coming to this conclusion, the tribunal confined itself to a purely mathematical comparison of the gap in employment falling within the two years preceding the final dismissal with the period of employment immediately before and after that gap. Both the EAT and the Court of Appeal thought that this was the wrong approach in the context of this particular case. They were of the view that the correct approach was to take into account all the relevant circumstances and, in particular, consider the length of the period of employment as a whole.

WOOLF LJ: Where the pattern of employment is a regular pattern of the type that existed in the *Ford* case, then it may be of little assistance to look at more than one period of dismissal. However, where the periods of dismissal are irregular, to look only at a particular period of dismissal and to compare that period with the combination of the periods either side, in the manner which was adopted by the Industrial Tribunal in this case, could lead to a wrong result.

The word 'temporary' in [s. 212(3)(b)] is not being used in the sense of something which is not permanent, since otherwise in every case where employment is resumed where there has been a dismissal on account of cessation of work, para. 9(1)(b) would apply. It is, as stated by Lord Diplock, being used in the sense of 'lasting only for a relatively short time'. (I myself would not use the word 'transient', however, I would stress the word *relatively*.)

What is a short time in one employment is not necessarily a short time in another employment. In deciding what is relatively a short time in a particular employment, it is now clearly established that it is necessary to look at the period of dismissal with hindsight—looking backwards as to the circumstances from the date of the final dismissal. In doing this, the period of dismissal relative to the period of employment is of the greatest importance. However, it is the whole period of employment which is relevant. In the case of irregular employment, if the periods of employment either side of the dismissal are only looked at, a most misleading comparison would be drawn.

NOTES

1. It has been suggested that the 'mathematical approach' used in *Ford* should apply where the gaps in employment are regular, whereas the 'broad-brush' approach seen in *Flack* should be adopted where the pattern of employment is irregular (see *Sillars* v *Charrington Fuels Ltd* [1989] IRLR 152, CA).

2. Absence from work 'in circumstances such that, by arrangement or custom...' (ERA 1996, s. 212(3)(c)). It would appear that in order to fall within this provision, the arrangement or understanding must be established before or at the time the absence commences (see, e.g., *Murphy* v *A. Birrell & Sons* [1978] IRLR 458; *Booth* v *United States of America* [1999] IRLR 16, EAT, cf. *London Probation Board* v *Kirkpatrick* [2005] IRLR 443, in note 4). The absences that might be encompassed could be leave-of-absence arrangements, employees placed upon a 'reserve list' to be called upon as necessary, and employees on secondment. A number of commentators argue that the EAT's broad application of the subparagraph in *Lloyds Bank Ltd* v *Secretary of State for Employment* [1979] IRLR 41 is no longer good law following the judgments of their Lordships in *Ford*. In the *Lloyds* case, the EAT held that where an employee works on a one-week-on and one-week-off basis, the weeks which she does not work count towards continuity by virtue of what is now s. 212(3)(c). In the *Lloyds* case a contract did exist throughout the period of employment. In the *Ford* case, the House of Lords placed considerable emphasis on the requirement that there be no subsisting contract before what is now s. 212(3) could operate. On that basis, the authority of the *Lloyds* case looks extremely suspect.

3. *Curr* v *Marks & Spencer plc* [2003] IRLR 74, CA, involved the question of the continuity of employment on a career break. The EAT had held that even though the company's four-year child break scheme required the employee to resign from her employment, the continuing relationship was an 'arrangement' by which she was 'absent from work in circumstances such that... [she was]

regarded as continuing in the employment of [her] employer' within the terms of the ERA 1996, s. 212(3)(c), so that her contract of employment was preserved during the career break.

The Court of Appeal reversed the EAT's decision. According to the court, for s. 212(3)(c) to apply, the ex-employee must, by arrangement (which can, but need not, be a contract) or custom be 'regarded' by each of the parties as continuing in the employment of the employer for any purpose during that period. There must be *mutual recognition* by the arrangement that the ex-employee, though absent from work, nevertheless continues in the employment of the employer. Without there being a meeting of minds by the arrangement that both parties regard the ex-employee as continuing in employment for some purpose, s. 212(3)(c) will not be satisfied. The parties might, for example, agree that for pension purposes, the ex-employee is to be treated during the period of absence as continuing in the employment of the employer.

In the present case, the applicant was not mutually regarded as continuing in employment for any purpose during the period of her absence under the child break scheme. The emphasis of the arrangement was on bringing her previous employment to an end. She was required to resign, given her P45, and required to pay her house purchase loan. All her staff benefits ceased and her pension was frozen. She was given an option to take up a post at the end of her child break that was similar to the one she held before she resigned. The quid pro quo was that she met certain conditions such as keeping in contact with the employers during her absence, keeping her hand in by working for a minimum of two weeks each year at mutually agreed times, and not working for anyone else without prior consultation. None of those features showed that she was mutually regarded as continuing in the employers' employment.

■ QUESTION

The employer in this case was maintaining contact with an able management employee taking a career break. If s. 212(3)(c) does not cover the career break arrangements in *Curr*, what is the point of the provision?

4. As seen earlier, continuity of employment is preserved where the employee is 'absent from work in circumstances such that, by arrangement or custom, he is regarded as continuing in the employment of his employer for any purpose.' The key element in *London Probation Board* v *Kirkpatrick* [2005] IRLR 443, EAT, is whether such an arrangement can be made retrospectively. The employee was dismissed with pay in lieu of notice and exercised his contractual right to appeal. Two months later, the appeal panel determined that he should be reinstated, but before he returned to work, the employers decided that the dismissal should stand. The EAT held that the gap between the date of the original dismissal and the date of the appeal panel's decision constituted an 'arrangement' to preserve continuity of employment. According to the EAT, there is no reason why an 'arrangement' to preserve continuity within the meaning of s. 212(3) cannot be made retrospectively. As a matter of construction, there is no temporal qualification to the 'arrangement'. An arrangement can be in place without ever being put into operation in a specific case. Although logically a 'custom' should exist prior to the gap, there was no reason to add words to the statute so as to limit arrangements to those made in advance of the gap.

   In the present case, therefore, the agreement to reinstate the claimant was an 'arrangement' within the meaning of s. 212(3)(c), notwithstanding that it was made after the gap. Alternatively, the discipline and appeal procedure which gave the claimant a contractual right to have an appeal heard by an independent body, with the power to put right a wrong or unfair decision, could aptly be described as an 'arrangement' which was in place prior to the gap in the claimant's employment and under which he was regarded as being in the employment of the employers for at least the purpose of the appeal.

5. The *Booth* case is a prime example of the vulnerability of workers on fixed-term contracts. The case concerned a US airbase in the UK, where maintenance workers were employed under a series of fixed-term contracts for a total period in excess of two years but with a gap of about two weeks between each contract. Despite the fact that the aim of this arrangement was to evade the employment protection legislation, the EAT declined to adopt a purposive approach and to find continuity. As Mr Justice Morrison put it:

   > ...[W]hilst it is generally desirable that employees should enjoy statutory protection during their employment, Parliament has laid down the conditions under which that protection is afforded. If, by so arranging their affairs, an employer is lawfully able to employ people in such a manner that the employees cannot complain of unfair dismissal or seek a redundancy

payment, that is a matter for him. The courts simply try and apply the law as it stands. It is for the legislators to close any loopholes that might be perceived to exist.

THE FIXED-TERM EMPLOYEES (PREVENTION OF LESS FAVOURABLE TREATMENT) REGULATIONS 2002

NOTE: The position of workers in cases such as *Booth* has improved with the coming into force of the Fixed-term Employees (Prevention of Less Favourable Treatment) Regulations 2002. The regulations came into force on 1 October 2002. They make certain changes to the way fixed-term employees are treated by the law and should be treated by their employers.

The overall aim of the regulations is to seek to ensure that fixed-term employees should not be treated less favourably than comparable permanent employees on the ground that they are fixed-term employees, unless this is objectively justified.

The regulations apply to employees on contracts that last for a specified period of time or will end when a specified task has been completed or a specified event does or does not happen. Examples include employees covering for maternity leave and peaks in demand and employees on task contracts such as setting up a database.

It will be interesting to observe whether the Government will be forced to review and modify the existing legislation in order to comply with the terms of EC Directive 99/70/EC which refers to the wider category of 'workers'. It is arguable that by restricting the scope of the regulations to employees, the Government has excluded those individuals, such as casual or freelance workers, who are most likely to suffer detriment in the first place because of their loose working relationships.

The regulations define 'permanent' employees as those who are not on fixed-term contracts. These employees may more generally be referred to as employees on contracts for an indefinite or indeterminate term.

Less favourable treatment of fixed-term employees

3.—(1) A fixed-term employee has the right not to be treated by his employer less favourably than the employer treats a comparable permanent employee—
   (a) as regards the terms of his contract; or
   (b) by being subjected to any other detriment by any act, or deliberate failure to act, of his employer.

(2) Subject to paragraphs (3) and (4), the right conferred by paragraph (1) includes in particular the right of the right of the fixed-term employee in question not to be treated less favourably than the employer treats a comparable permanent employee in relation to—
   (a) any period of service qualification relating to any particular condition of service,
   (b) the opportunity to receive training, or
   (c) the opportunity to secure any permanent position in the establishment.

(3) The right conferred by paragraph (1) applies only if—
   (a) the treatment is on the ground that the employee is a fixed-term employee, and
   (b) the treatment is not justified on objective grounds.

(4) Paragraph (3)(b) is subject to regulation 4.

(5) In determining whether a fixed-term employee has been treated less favourably than a comparable permanent employee, the pro rata principle shall be applied unless it is inappropriate.

(6) In order to ensure that an employee is able to exercise the right conferred by paragraph (1) as described in paragraph (2)(c) the employee has the right to be informed by his employer of available vacancies in the establishment.

(7) For the purposes of paragraph (6) an employee is 'informed by his employer' only if the vacancy is contained in advertisement which the employee has a reasonable opportunity of reading in the course of his employment or the employee is given reasonable notification of the vacancy in some other way.

4.—(1) Where a fixed-term employee is treated by his employer less favourably than the employer treats a comparable permanent employee as regards any term of his contract, the treatment in question shall be regarded for the purposes of regulation 3(3)(b) as justified on objective grounds if the terms of the fixed-term employee's contract of employment, taken as a whole, are at least as favourable as the terms of the comparable permanent employee's contract of employment.

NOTES
1. Fixed-term employees can compare their conditions to employees who are not on fixed-term contracts and are employed by the same employer to do the same or broadly similar work. Where relevant, the comparator should have similar skills and qualifications to the fixed-term employee. If there is no comparator in the establishment, a comparison can be made with a similar permanent employee working for the same employer in a different establishment.
2. The guidance notes accompanying the Regulations offer the following advice on the scope of the objective justification defence:

OBJECTIVE JUSTIFICATION
The key question employers must ask themselves: 'is there a reason for treating this employee less favourably?' Employers should give due regard to the needs and rights of individual employees and try to balance those against business objectives.
Less favourable treatment will be justified on objective grounds if it can be shown that the less favourable treatment:
- is to achieve a legitimate and necessary business objective
- is an appropriate way to achieve that objective.
Objective justification may be a matter of degree. Employers should therefore consider whether it is possible to offer fixed-term employees certain benefits, such as annual subscriptions, loans, clothing allowances, and insurance policies, on a pro-rata basis. Sometimes, the cost to the employer of offering a particular benefit to an employee may be disproportionate when compared to the benefit the employee would receive, and this may objectively justify different treatment. An example of this may be where a fixed-term employee is on a contract of three months and a comparator has a company car. The employer may decide not to offer the car if the cost of doing so is high and the need of the business for the employee to travel can be met in some other way.

HOW DO EMPLOYERS OBJECTIVELY JUSTIFY DIFFERENT CONDITIONS FOR FIXED-TERM EMPLOYEES?
When applying the equal treatment requirement, employers can objectively justify different terms and conditions for fixed-term employees in two different ways:
  (i) By showing that there is an objective justification for not giving the fixed-term employee a particular benefit or for giving him or her the benefit on less good terms. This approach is used in other discrimination law, including sex discrimination and race relations law and the regulations preventing part-time workers from being treated less favourably than comparable full-time ones.
  (ii) By showing that the value of the fixed-term employee's total package of terms and conditions is at least equal to the value of the comparable permanent employee's total package of terms and conditions.
  A comparison needs to be made, either on a term-by-term basis or on a package basis.
Employers and employees may take what may be called a 'term-by-term' approach to equal treatment. This means that every individual term of a fixed-term employee's employment package should be completely the same, or if appropriate the same on a pro rata basis, as the equivalent term of the comparable permanent employee, unless a difference in the term is objectively justified. For example, if a permanent employee is paid £450 per week, has 30 days' annual leave per year, and receives an annual clothing allowance of £250, the same conditions should apply to a fixed-term employee (on a pro rata basis if appropriate), unless objectively justified.

HOW MIGHT THE PACKAGE APPROACH WORK?
The regulations provide in particular that less favourable treatment in relation to particular contractual terms is justified where the fixed-term employee's overall package of terms and conditions is no less favourable than the comparable permanent employee's overall package.
  Employers will be able to balance a less favourable condition against a more favourable one, provided they ensure a fixed-term employee's overall employment package is not less favourable than that of a comparable permanent employee. Employers will not be prevented from paying higher up-front rewards in return for reduced benefits elsewhere if the overall package is not less favourable. This is what is meant by a 'package approach'.
  The value of benefits should be assessed on the basis of their objective monetary worth, rather than the value the employer or employee perceives them to have.

Employers can still objectively justify not giving a particular benefit if they choose to use a package approach. Employers do not have to make up for the value of a missing benefit if they can objectively justify not giving it. If a package approach is used, it will be objectively justified for a fixed-term employee to have a less favourable overall package than a comparable permanent employee, if the difference consists in one or more terms that it is objectively justified not to give the fixed-term employee.

Example of using the package approach: a fixed-term employee is paid £20,800 per year (£400 per week), which is the same as a comparable permanent employee, but gets three days' fewer paid holiday per year than comparable permanent employees. To ensure that the fixed-term employee's overall employment package is not less favourable, their annual salary is increased to £20,970 (£170 is added on, since this is the value of three days' holiday pay. A day's holiday pay is worked out as annual salary divided by 365) (*Fixed-term Work—Guidance*, Department of Business, Enterprise and Regulatory Reform, URN No. 06/535).

3. A fixed-term employee has a right to ask their employer for a written statement setting out the reasons for less favourable treatment if they believe that this may have occurred. The employer must provide this statement within 21 days (reg. 5).

4. See also *Adneler v Ellinikas Organismos Galaktos* [2006] IRLR 716, where the European Court of Justice expressed the view that the concept of 'objective reasons' requires the use of fixed-term contracts 'to be justified by the presence of specific factors relating in particular to the activity in question and the conditions under which it is carried out'.

Successive fixed-term contracts

8.—(1) This regulation applies where—

(a) an employee is employed under a contract purporting to be a fixed-term contract, and

(b) the contract mentioned in sub-paragraph (a) has previously been renewed, or the employee has previously been employed on a fixed-term before the start of the contract mentioned in sub-paragraph (a).

(2) Where this regulation applies then, with effect from the date specified in paragraph (3), the provision of the contract mentioned in paragraph (1)(a) that restricts the duration of the contract shall be of no effect, and the employee shall be a permanent employee, if—

(a) the employee has been continuously employed under the contract mentioned in paragraph 1(a), or under that contract taken with a previous fixed-term contract, for a period of four years or more, and

(b) the employment of the employee under a fixed-term contract was not justified on objective grounds—

(i) where the contract mentioned in paragraph (1)(a) has been renewed, at the time when it was last renewed;

(ii) where that contract has not been renewed, at the time when it was entered into.

(3) the date referred to in paragraph (2) is whichever is the later of—

(a) the date on which the contract mentioned in paragraph (1)(a) was entered into or last renewed, and

(b) the date on which the employee acquired four years' continuous employment.

NOTE:

1. The use of successive fixed-term contracts will be limited to four years, unless the use of further fixed-term contracts is justified on objective grounds. However, it will be possible for employers and employees to increase or decrease this period or agree a different way to limit the use of successive fixed-term contracts via collective or workforce agreements. For the purposes of this part of the regulations, service accumulated from 10 July 2002 count towards the four-year limit. There is no limit on the duration of the first fixed-term contract, although if a contract of four years or more is renewed, it will be treated from then as permanent unless the use of a fixed-term contract is objectively justified.

2. Guidance on the meaning of what are 'objective' reasons was laid down by the Court of Justice of the European Union in *Márquez Samohano v Universitat Pompeu Fabra* [2014] IRLR 459. Under Spanish law, universities are allowed to renew successive fixed-term contracts with part-time associate lecturers, with no limitation as to the maximum duration and the number of renewals of those contracts. Associate lecturers are specialists in their field who are otherwise employed outside the university. The Court holds that the practice of using fixed-term contracts with associate lecturers is 'justified by the need to entrust "specialists with recognised competence" who exercise a professional activity otherwise than in a university with the performance, in a part-time basis, of

specific teaching tasks, so that those specialists can bring their knowledge and professional experience to the university, thus establishing a partnership between university teaching circles and professional circles'. The CJEU emphasises that the renewal of fixed-term employment contracts 'in order to cover needs which are, in fact, not temporary in nature but, on the contrary, fixed and permanent, is not justified' under the Framework Agreement. However, 'whilst fixed-term employment contracts concluded with associate lecturers cover a permanent need of the universities, in that the associate lecturer performs, under such a fixed-term employment contract, specifically defined tasks which are part of the universities' usual activities, the fact remains that the need in terms of employment of associate lecturers remains temporary in so far as that lecturer is supposed to resume his professional activity on a full-time basis at the end of his contract.'

3. If a fixed-term contract is renewed after the four-year period, it will be treated as a contract for an indefinite period (unless the use of a fixed-term contract is objectively justified). A fixed-term employee has a right to ask their employer for a written statement confirming that their contract is permanent or setting out objective reasons for the use of a fixed-term contract beyond the four-year period. The employer must provide this statement within 21 days.

4. Any redundancy waiver that is included in a fixed-term contract which is agreed, extended, or renewed after 1 October 2002 is invalid.

5. Fixed-term employees should receive information on permanent vacancies in their organisation.

6. From 1 October 2002, the end of a task contract that expires when a specific task has been completed or a specific event does or does not happen will be a dismissal in law. The non-renewal of a fixed-term contract concluded for a specified period of time is already a dismissal in law. Employees on these task contracts of one year or more now have a right to a written statement of reasons for this dismissal and the right not to be unfairly dismissed. If the contract lasts two years or more and the contract is not renewed by reason of redundancy, the employee now has a right to a statutory redundancy payment.

7. From 1 October 2002, employees on fixed-term contracts of three months or less have a right to statutory sick pay and to payments on medical suspension, guarantee payments, and the right to receive and duty to give a week's notice after one month's continuous service. These new notice requirements only apply to a termination of the contract before it is due to expire. This will put these fixed-term employees on the same footing as permanent and fixed-term employees on longer contracts.

8. If fixed-term employees believe they are being less favourably treated than a comparable permanent employee because they are fixed-term or that their employer has infringed their rights under the regulations, then they may present their case to an employment tribunal.

Complaints to employment tribunals etc.

...

(7) Where an employment tribunal finds that a complaint presented to it under this regulation is well founded, it shall take such of the following steps as it considers just and equitable—

   (a) making a declaration as to the rights of the complainant and the employer in relation to the matters to which the complaint relates;

   (b) ordering the employer to pay compensation to the complainant;

   (c) recommending that the employer take, within a specified period, action appearing to the tribunal to be reasonable, in all the circumstances of the case, for the purpose of obviating or reducing the adverse effect on the complainant of any matter to which the complaint relates.

...

(10) Compensation in respect of treating an employee in a manner which infringes the right conferred on him by regulation 3 shall not include compensation for injury to feelings.

C: Strikes and lockouts

EMPLOYMENT RIGHTS ACT 1996

216. Industrial disputes

(1) A week does not count under section 212 if during the week, or any part of the week, the employee takes part in a strike.

(2) The continuity of an employee's period of employment is not broken by a week which does not count under this Chapter (whether or not by virtue only of subsection (1)) if during the week, or any part of the week, the employee takes part in a strike; and the number of days which, for the purposes of section 211(3), fall within the intervening period is the number of days between the last working day before the strike and the day on which work was resumed.

(3) The continuity of an employee's period of employment is not broken by a week if during the week, or any part of the week, the employee is absent from work because of a lock-out by the employer; and the number of days which, for the purposes of section 211(3), fall within the intervening period is the number of days between the last working day before the lock-out and the day on which work was resumed.

NOTES

1. The effect of s. 216 is that the period of the industrial dispute does not count towards continuity, but it does not break it.
2. For the rules governing continuity of employment on a change of employer, see Chapter 9.

FURTHER READING

Bell, M., 'Achieving the objectives of the Part-Time Work Directive? Revisiting the Part-Time Workers Regulations' (2011) 40(3) ILJ 254.

Bogg, A., 'Sham self-employment in the Supreme Court' (2012) 41 ILJ 328.

Cabrelli, D., *Employment Law in Context: Text and Materials* (Oxford: OUP, 2014), Ch. 3.

Honeyball, S., *Honeyball and Bowers' Textbook on Employment Law*, 13th edn (Oxford: OUP, 2014), Ch. 2.

Leighton, P., Wynn, M., 'Classifying employment relationships—More sliding doors or a better regulatory framework?' (2011) 40(1) ILJ 5.

McClelland, J., 'A purposive approach to employment protection or a missed opportunity?' (2012) 75 *Modern Law Review* 427.

Prassl, J., 'The notion of the employer' (2013) 129 *Law Quarterly Review* 380.

3

Constructing the Contract of Employment

In this chapter the sources of the contract of employment will be examined. The various possible component parts of the contract are illustrated in Figure 3.1.

SECTION 1: EXPRESS TERMS

Only in exceptional cases must the contract be in writing, for example contracts under the Merchant Shipping Act 1970 or contracts of apprenticeship. However, since 1963 most employees have possessed the right to receive a written statement of some of the most important terms.

EMPLOYMENT RIGHTS ACT 1996

PART I EMPLOYMENT PARTICULARS

Right to statements of employment particulars

1. Statement of initial employment particulars

(1) Where an employee begins employment with an employer, the employer shall give to the employee a written statement of particulars of employment.

(2) The statement may (subject to section 2(4)) be given in instalments and (whether or not given in instalments) shall be given not later than two months after the beginning of the employment.

(3) The statement shall contain particulars of—

    (a) the names of the employer and employee,

    (b) the date when the employment began, and

    (c) the date on which the employee's period of continuous employment began (taking into account any employment with a previous employer which counts towards that period).

(4) The statement shall also contain particulars, as at a specified date not more than seven days before the statement (or the instalment containing them) is given, of—

    (a) the scale or rate of remuneration or the method of calculating remuneration,

    (b) the intervals at which remuneration is paid (that is, weekly, monthly or other specified intervals),

    (c) any terms and conditions relating to hours of work (including any terms and conditions relating to normal working hours),

    (d) any terms and conditions relating to any of the following—

        (i) entitlement to holidays, including public holidays, and holiday pay (the particulars given being sufficient to enable the employee's entitlement, including any entitlement to accrued holiday pay on the termination of employment, to be precisely calculated),

        (ii) incapacity for work due to sickness or injury, including any provision for sick pay, and

        (iii) pensions and pension schemes,

    (e) the length of notice which the employee is obliged to give and entitled to receive to terminate his contract of employment,

    (f) the title of the job which the employee is employed to do or a brief description of the work for which he is employed,

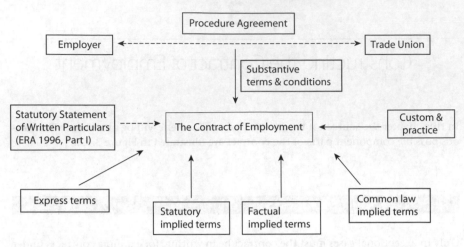

Figure 3.1 The sources of the Contract of Employment

(g) where the employment is not intended to be permanent, the period for which it is expected to continue or, if it is for a fixed term, the date when it is to end,

(h) either the place of work or, where the employee is required or permitted to work at various places, an indication of that and of the address of the employer,

(i) any collective agreements which directly affect the terms and conditions of the employment including, where the employer is not a party, the persons by whom they were made, and

(j) where the employee is required to work outside the United Kingdom for a period of more than one month—

    (i) the period for which he is to work outside the United Kingdom,

    (ii) the currency in which remuneration is to be paid while he is working outside the United Kingdom,

    (iii) any additional remuneration payable to him, and any benefits to be provided to or in respect of him, by reason of his being required to work outside the United Kingdom, and

    (iv) any terms and conditions relating to his return to the United Kingdom.

(5) Subsection (4)(d)(iii) does not apply to an employee of a body or authority if—

(a) the employee's pension rights depend on the terms of a pension scheme established under any provision contained in or having effect under any Act, and

(b) any such provision requires the body or authority to give to a new employee information concerning the employee's pension rights or the determination of questions affecting those rights.

2. Statement of initial particulars: supplementary

(1) If, in the case of a statement under section 1, there are no particulars to be entered under any of the heads of paragraph (d) or (k) of subsection (4) of that section, or under any of the other paragraphs of subsection (3) or (4) of that section, that fact shall be stated.

(2) A statement under section 1 may refer the employee for particulars of any of the matters specified in subsection (4)(d)(ii) and (iii) of that section to the provisions of some other document which is reasonably accessible to the employee.

(3) A statement under section 1 may refer the employee for particulars of either of the matters specified in subsection (4)(e) of that section to the law or to the provisions of any collective agreement directly affecting the terms and conditions of the employment which is reasonably accessible to the employee.

(4) The particulars required by section 1(3) and (4)(a) to (c), (d)(i), (f) and (h) shall be included in a single document.

(5) Where before the end of the period of two months after the beginning of an employee's employment the employee is to begin to work outside the United Kingdom for a period of more than one month, the statement under section 1 shall be given to him not later than the time when he leaves the United Kingdom in order to begin so to work.

(6) A statement shall be given to a person under section 1 even if his employment ends before the end of the period within which the statement is required to be given.

3. Note about disciplinary procedures and pensions

(1) A statement under section 1 shall include a note—

    (a) specifying any disciplinary rules applicable to the employee or referring the employee to the provisions of a document specifying such rules which is reasonably accessible to the employee,

    (aa) specifying any procedure applicable to the taking of disciplinary decisions relating to the employee, or to a decision to dismiss the employee, or referring the employee to the provisions of a document specifying such a procedure which is reasonably accessible to the employee,

    (b) specifying (by description or otherwise)—

        (i) a person to whom the employee can apply if dissatisfied with any disciplinary decision relating to him, and

        (ii) a person to whom the employee can apply for the purpose of seeking redress of any grievance relating to his employment,

        (iii) and the manner in which any such application should be made, and

    (c) where there are further steps consequent on any such application, explaining those steps or referring to the provisions of a document explaining them which is reasonably accessible to the employee.

(2) Subsection (1) does not apply to rules, disciplinary decisions, decisions to dismiss, grievances or procedures relating to health or safety at work.

(3) and (4) [*repealed*]

(5) The note shall also state whether there is in force a contracting-out certificate (issued in accordance with Chapter I of Part III of the Pension Schemes Act 1993) stating that the employment is contracted-out employment (for the purposes of that Part of that Act).

NOTES

1. Prior to the passage of the Trade Union Reform and Employment Rights Act (TURERA) 1993, the statement had to be provided within 13 weeks of entering employment. An employee had to work for 16 hours or more a week in order to qualify unless he or she had been continuously employed for five years under a contract of employment requiring him or her to work eight hours or more per week. The adoption of the EC directive on proof of an employment relationship (1991/533) requires that 'essential aspects of the contract or employment relationship should be given to all employees, except where the Member State is able to justify excluding those working less than eight hours a week, or those who have been employed for less than a month, or those whose work is of a casual and/or specific nature'. The necessary information must be provided within two months of the beginning of the employment. In terms of the type of information which is required, in many areas UK law already went further than the directive. But there were certain aspects where our law was lacking. TURERA 1993 was designed to comply with the directive (see now the Employment Rights Act (ERA) 1996, Pt I).

2. Under TURERA 1993 amendments, employers have now to give the following information in addition to that already required:

    (a) the place of work;

    (b) where the employee is required (or permitted) to work in various places, an indication of that fact and the address of the employer;

    (c) any collective agreement which directly affects the terms and conditions of employment of the individual employee (including the identity of the parties by whom such collective agreements were made);

    (d) where the employment is not intended to be permanent, the period of the expected duration of the contract;

    (e) where the employee is to work outside the UK for a period of one month, certain additional information.

The employers have to give this written statement no later than two calendar months after the beginning of employment. In addition, all employees are entitled to this as of right, unless their contract involves fewer than eight hours a week.

3. Under the previous law, instead of giving a written statement of particulars in statutory form to each employee, the statement could merely refer the employee to some other document which the employee had reasonable opportunities of reading in the course of employment, or which was made reasonably accessible to the employee. Second, while any changes in terms had to be

communicated to the employee within one month of the alteration, the employer could indicate that any future changes in the document to which the employee was referred would be made in that document within the permissible period.

TURERA 1993 tightened up the law in a number of important respects. It is no longer sufficient to refer employees to another document (e.g. a collective agreement) for details of their hours of work, pay, or holiday entitlement. These must be given in the statement of terms itself. However, it is still permissible to refer the employee to other reasonably accessible documents for sickness and pension provisions, and to the law or a collective agreement for details regarding notice rights. It is also still possible to cross-refer in relation to disciplinary rules and procedures.

With these exceptions, all the other required particulars now have to be supplied directly to the employee. Previously, it was not necessary for a written statement to be given if an employer gave a written contract or made a copy reasonably accessible, and the written contract might be scattered across a number of documents.

Some particulars must be set out in one document, known as the 'principal statement'. These particulars are the ones listed by the following provisions: s. 1(3); s. 1(4)(a)–(c), (d)(i), (f) and (h). The remaining particulars set out in s. 1 must be given to the employee, but can be given in instalments so long as this is done no later than two months after the start of the employment.

If there is a change to any of the terms about which particulars must be provided or referred to in the document, the employer now has to notify employees individually in writing. This notice must be given at the earliest opportunity, and, in any event, no later than one month after the change. Where the change results from the employee being required to work outside the UK for a period of more than one month, the change must be notified no later than the time the employee leaves the UK, if that is earlier. The statement of change may refer the employee to other reasonably accessible documents, or to the law or a collective agreement as appropriate, *but only in respect of changes to sickness, pension, notice and disciplinary provisions*.

4. By virtue of the ERA 1996, s. 11, the employee can complain to an employment tribunal (ET) if he or she is provided with no statement at all, or an incomplete statement or a complete but inaccurate statement. The tribunal is empowered to determine what particulars ought to have been provided, or to amend inaccurate particulars (see *Mears* v *Safecar Security Ltd* [1982] IRLR 183, CA).

5. Given the weakness of the remedy it is not surprising that research has shown that many employers do not keep their employees informed in writing of their principal terms of employment (see Leighton, P. and Dumville, S., 'From statement to contract' (1977) 6 ILJ 133). Any new employee who successfully complained to an ET that he or she had not received the statutory statement may well have achieved a 'Pyrrhic' victory. The employer's response may have been to dismiss what he saw as an 'employment protection rip-off artist' who will have insufficient continuity to claim unfair dismissal. Fortunately, as a result of amendments introduced by TURERA 1993, it is automatically unfair to dismiss an employee for asserting a statutory right, including failure to supply written particulars (see the ERA 1996, s. 104; discussed at p. 396 (Chapter 8, Section 2.C)).

6. The Employment Act 2002, ss. 35–8 made a number of positive changes in relation to the supply of written statements and conditions. These are as follows:

   (a) Section 35 provides for part of the written statement dealing with disciplinary and grievance matters to cover the procedure which applies when the employee is dismissed or disciplined, whereas at present it must only describe what he must do if he or she is dissatisfied with disciplinary action taken against him or her. This ensures that all stages of the new minimum statutory disciplinary and dismissal procedures must be set out in a written statement. The ERA 1996, s. 3(1) has been amended accordingly.

   (b) Section 36 removes the current exemption relating to the need for details of disciplinary rules and procedures for employers with fewer than 20 employees. This means that all employers of whatever size will have to mention their disciplinary rules and the new minimum procedures in the written statement. This is a long-overdue reform.

   (c) Section 37 provides flexibility for employers by allowing particulars included in a copy of the contract of employment or letter of engagement given to the employee to form, or to form part of the written statement. This reduces the need to duplicate existing documents. It also enables such documents to be given to the employee before his or her employment begins (see the ERA 1996, ss. 7A, 7B).

   (d) Section 38 provides for ETs to award compensation to an employee where the lack, incompleteness, or inaccuracy of the written statement becomes evident upon a claim being made under specified tribunal jurisdictions (which cover the main areas such as unfair dismissal, and all types of discrimination—Sch. 5). This is done by requiring the tribunal to increase any award made against the employer in respect of the complaint under the other jurisdiction by two or four weeks' pay, or to award two or four weeks' pay where compensation is not a remedy available for the particular complaint or where it is not a remedy that the tribunal chooses. Whether to award two or four weeks' pay is a matter for the tribunal's discretion. No award needs to be made or increased if the tribunal considers that to do so would be unjust or inequitable.

7. The statement is not a contract itself but it provides strong prima facie evidence of the express terms of the contract of employment.

Gascol Conversions Ltd v *Mercer*
[1974] IRLR 155, Court of Appeal

Mr Mercer was employed as a gas inspector. He worked a 54-hour week, calculated on the basis of 40 hours basic and 14 hours overtime. He was then asked to sign a document which was entitled 'Non-Staff Employees' Contract of Employment', which stated his normal working week to be 40 hours. When he was dismissed for redundancy, he claimed that his normal working week should have been 54 hours as opposed to the 40 hours which was used to calculate his compensation. The industrial tribunal and the National Industrial Relations Court (NIRC) supported Mercer's claim but the Court of Appeal allowed the employer's appeal.

LORD DENNING MR: ... In February 1972 the Industrial Relations Act 1971 came into operation. By Schedule 2, Part II, the employer was bound to give to the employee a written statement specifying among other things 'any terms and conditions relating to hours of work (including any terms and conditions relating to normal working hours)'. In pursuance of that statutory obligation, the employers, Gascol Conversions Ltd, on 25.2.72 sent a new contract of employment to each of their men. One was sent to Mr Mercer. He sent it back signed on 21.3.72. He was given a copy of it for himself to keep. He agreed to it by a document in these terms which he signed himself:

I confirm receipt of a new Contract of Employment dated 25.2.72 which sets out, as required under the Industrial Relations Act (1971), the terms and conditions of my employment.
Signed JW Mercer Date 21.3.72.

That was clearly a binding contract. Being reduced into writing, it is the sole evidence that is permissible of the contract and its terms. Turning to the terms themselves, the opening words are clear. They follow the very words of the national agreement:

The normal working week consists of 40 hours which shall be worked Monday to Friday, five days of eight hours, at times specified by the Department concerned.

Overtime: Employees will be expected to work overtime where necessary for completion of the conversion work. You will be paid at the rate of 1½ times the basic hourly rate on week days, and at double time on Sundays.

That agreement seems to me to be conclusive. There is no possible ground for setting it aside. There was no mistake, misrepresentation or misunderstanding of any kind. It shows that the normal working week was 40 hours and the employers were not bound to provide any more. Even the employees were not bound to work more. They were only 'expected' to work extra hours when necessary.

...

In the Industrial Court, Sir Hugh Griffiths was more concerned about the written contract of March 1972. He spoke of it as 'a most formidable point'. But in the end, that Court held that 'the Tribunal was entitled to look, as it did, at the reality of the situation and to conclude that it was not intended by either party that the mutual obligation to provide and work 54 hours a week should be altered by the written contract of employment'. I am afraid that observation goes against the general law. It is well settled that where there is a written contract of employment, as there was here, and the parties have reduced it to writing, it is the writing which governs their relations. It is not permissible to say they intended something different.

I would only add this: it is a very great advantage to the men to have short working hours of 40 hours a week—on basic rates—with considerable overtime work—on overtime rates. It means a great increase in the take-home pay. It means also that they can take industrial action—by banning overtime—without thereby being in breach of their contracts of employment. Those conditions can carry however with them this disadvantage: when a man is made redundant, his redundancy payment is less because his normal working hours are only 40 hours. No doubt the union feel that the advantages outweigh the disadvantage. The men cannot have it both ways. Having committed themselves by written agreement to normal working hours of 40, they cannot go back on it.

Systems Floors (UK) Ltd v Daniel
[1982] ICR 54, Employment Appeal Tribunal

Mr Daniel commenced work for the employers in September 1979 as an agency worker. In November he requested to work directly for the employers and was told to start on 26 November. When he was provided with his statutory statement, this stated that his employment had commenced on 19 November. Mr Daniel signed for this, to acknowledge receipt. He was dismissed on 14 November 1980 and, when he made a claim for unfair dismissal, the question arose as to whether he had the requisite length of continuous service (at that time 52 weeks). The Employment Appeal Tribunal (EAT) held that the employer could adduce evidence to show that the commencement date expressed in the statutory statement was not the actual starting date.

BROWNE-WILKINSON J: The first issue is whether the industrial tribunal was right in holding the statement was a contract and fell within *Gascol Conversions Ltd* v *Mercer* [1974] ICR 420. The statement was served under the statutory provisions now included in [ERA 1996, Part I]. Under section [1(3)(b)], an employer is required, in a statement which must be served under that section, to specify the date when the employment began.

There is some authority as to the effect of the statutory particulars of the terms of employment. In *Turriff Construction Ltd* v *Bryant* [1967] 2 KIR 659, the Divisional Court had to consider for the purposes of redundancy payment what effect was to be given to the number of hours worked specified in a statutory statement. Speaking of the statutory predecessor of section 1 of the Act of 1978, Lord Parker CJ, giving the decision of the court, said, at p. 662:

It is, of course, quite clear that the statement made pursuant to section 4 of the Act of 1963 is not the contract; it is not even conclusive evidence of the terms of a contract.

Again, the Divisional Court in *Parkes Classic Confectionery Ltd* v *Ashcroft* (1971) 8 ITR 43 overruled the decision of an industrial tribunal which had held that where the terms of the contract of employment had been varied, but the employers had failed to serve particulars of the changes in the terms in accordance with what is now section 4 of the [Act of 1996], the employers were not entitled to rely on the varied contract. The Divisional Court held that notwithstanding the failure to serve the necessary statutory statement and notwithstanding that that might be a criminal offence, there was nothing in the Act to provide that a change of contractual terms should be ineffectual between the parties merely because the employer had failed to give written notice of the change.

It seems to us, therefore, that in general the status of the statutory statement is this. It provides very strong prima facie evidence of what were the terms of the contract between the parties, but does not constitute a written contract between the parties. Nor are the statements of the terms finally conclusive: at most, they place a heavy burden on the employer to show that the actual terms of contract are different from those which he has set out in the statutory statement.

Against that background we turn to consider the decision of the Court of Appeal in *Gascol Conversions Ltd* v *Mercer* [1974] ICR 420, which was the basis of the industrial tribunal's decision in this case. In that case there was an agreed variation in the terms on which the employees were engaged. When the Industrial Relations Act 1971 came into operation the employers became bound to give a written statement of particulars, and in pursuance of that obligation the employers sent a new contract of employment to each of their men. Each man was given a copy to keep, and he was required to sign a document in these terms: 'I confirm receipt of a new contract of employment dated February 25, 1972, which sets out, as required under the Industrial Relations Act 1971, the terms and conditions of my employment.' Mr Mercer signed such a document. The Court of Appeal held that in those circumstances the document constituted a binding written contract and that accordingly no evidence was admissible to show that the terms of the contract were otherwise.

In our view that case does not cover the present case. In that case Mr Mercer had signed a document which he confirmed was a new contract of employment and that it set out the terms and conditions of his employment. The Court of Appeal treated that as being a contract in writing, as indeed it was, having been signed by both parties. But in the case of an ordinary statutory statement served pursuant to the statutory obligation, the document is a unilateral one merely stating the employer's view of what those terms are. In the absence of an acknowledgment by the parties that the statement is itself a contract and that the terms are correct, such as that contained in the *Mercer* case, the statutory statement does not itself constitute a contract in writing.

In the present case, all that the employee did was to sign an acknowledgment that he had received the statement. In no sense did he sign it as a contract or acknowledge the accuracy of the terms in it. We, therefore, think that the industrial tribunal erred in law in treating the date of commencement mentioned in the statement as decisive because it was a contractual term. In our view the statement is no more than persuasive, though not conclusive, evidence of the date of commencement.

NOTES

1. In *Gascol Conversions Ltd* v *Mercer* the written statement was actually described as the 'new contract of employment', so it was not simply a case of signing a receipt to say that the document had been received by the employee. If the latter was the case, it would not be so easy to construe it as a written contract.

   This was the view taken by the EAT in *System Floors (UK) Ltd* v *Daniel*, which distinguished *Gascol* on the basis that it involved a signed contract of employment, whereas in the instant case Daniel was merely signing to acknowledge he had received the statement. The approach adopted by the EAT was subsequently adopted by the Court of Appeal in *Robertson* v *British Gas Corporation* [1983] ICR 351 (see Section 2.A(i)).

2. As stated earlier, the statutory provisions are based on the European Directive 91/533/EC and it is unsurprising, therefore, that under European law it has also been held that the written statement of terms is of probative value only of what constitute the terms of the contract. So, in *Hardarson* v *Askar Capital hf* [2013] IRLR 475, the Court of Justice of the European Free Trade Association States (EFTA Court) held that an employer's failure to update changes in the particulars relating to monthly remuneration did not mean that the reduction in the employee's salary was ineffective as a matter of contract.

3. While a statutory statement on its own cannot bring about a contractual variation, where the employee continues to work without protest under the changed terms, this may be held to amount to an implied agreement to the change. However, where the alleged variation is not one which has an immediate impact, like a change in pay or hours, it is asking too much of the 'ordinary employee to require him either to object to an erroneous statement of his terms of employment...or be taken to have assented to the variation' (per Browne-Wilkinson J in *Jones* v *Associated Tunnelling Co. Ltd* [1981] IRLR 477). (See also *Aparau* v *Iceland Frozen Foods plc* [1996] IRLR 119; an extract appears at p. 360 (Chapter 7, Section 3.C(iii)) In *Harlow* v *Artemis International Corporation Ltd* [2008] IRLR 629, the High Court held that the employer's unilateral variation of an enhanced redundancy payments scheme could not be taken to be accepted just because the employee had not objected. On the other hand, in *Wess* v *Science Museum Group* [2014] UKEAT 0120_14_0610, the EAT held that an employee had impliedly accepted a variation of her contract of employment—a reduction in her notice period from 6 months to 12 weeks—by continuing to work, without expressly objecting to it, for nine years.

SECTION 2: COLLECTIVE BARGAINING

TRADE UNION AND LABOUR RELATIONS (CONSOLIDATION) ACT 1992

ENFORCEABILITY OF COLLECTIVE AGREEMENTS

179. Whether agreement intended to be a legally enforceable contract

(1) A collective agreement shall be conclusively presumed not to have been intended by the parties to be a legally enforceable contract unless the agreement—

    (a) is in writing, and

    (b) contains a provision which (however expressed) states that the parties intend that the agreement shall be a legally enforceable contract.

(2) A collective agreement which does satisfy those conditions shall be conclusively presumed to have been intended by the parties to be a legally enforceable contract.

(3) If a collective agreement is in writing and contains a provision which (however expressed) states that the parties intend that one or more parts of the agreement specified in that provision, but not the whole of the agreement, shall be a legally enforceable contract, then—

(a) the specified part or parts shall be conclusively presumed to have been intended by the parties to be a legally enforceable contract, and

(b) the remainder of the agreement shall be conclusively presumed not to have been intended by the parties to be such a contract.

(4) A part of a collective agreement which by virtue of subsection (3)(b) is not a legally enforceable contract may be referred to for the purpose of interpreting a party of the agreement which is such a contract.

A: Methods of incorporation

(i) Agency

Burton Group Ltd v Smith
[1977] IRLR 361, Employment Appeal Tribunal

Mr Smith volunteered for redundancy under a scheme negotiated by his union and was due to leave sometime between October and December. On 24 October, the union and employer agreed that the terminations would take place on 26 December. Mr Smith died before he could be informed of the agreed date. His right to a redundancy payment depended on him being under notice of dismissal when he died. It was argued, on behalf of Mr Smith's personal representative, that the union received notice of his dismissal on his behalf as agent by agreeing the date with the employer. This contention was rejected by the EAT.

ARNOLD J: There is no reason at all why, in a particular case, union representatives should not be the agents of an employee to make a contract, or to receive a notice, or otherwise effect a binding transaction on his behalf. But that agency so to do does not stem from the mere fact that they are union representatives and that he is a member of the union; it must be supported in the particular case by the creation of some specific agency, and that can arise only if the evidence supports the conclusion that there was such an agency. It is sufficient to say that in this case there was no evidence before the tribunal of the existence of such an agency.

NOTE: For two cases which seem to approve the agency argument see *Singh* v *British Steel Corporation* [1974] IRLR 131 and *Land* v *West Yorkshire Metropolitan County Council* [1979] ICR 452. The decision in both cases is based on the premise that a worker who has resigned from union membership cannot be bound by a variation in terms which was collectively agreed subsequent to his or her resignation.

■ QUESTION

What is the main disadvantage of basing incorporation of collective agreements on the concept of agency?

(ii) Express incorporation

National Coal Board v Galley
[1958] 1 WLR 16, Court of Appeal

In 1949, the defendant, a pit deputy, entered into a written contract of employment with the Board which provided that his wages should be 'regulated by such national agreement and county wages agreement for the time being in force and that this contract of service shall be subject to those agreements and to any other agreements relating to or in connection with or subsidiary to the wages agreement and to statutory provisions for the time being in force affecting the same'.

In 1952 revised national terms were agreed between the Board and the union. This agreement contained a clause that required pit deputies to work 'such days or part days in each week as may reasonably be required'.

In June 1956, Galley and other pit deputies at his colliery gave notice that they intended to ban Saturday working. The Court of Appeal held that Galley had broken his contract.

PEARCE LJ: The judge thought that, since one of the objects of NACODS [the union] was to negotiate the wages and conditions of all members and the defendant was a member of the local trade union which was itself a member of NACODS the defendant was individually bound by the NACODS agreement. But in any event, by the defendant's personal contract his wages were to be regulated by national agreements for the time being in force and the contract was to be subject to those agreements; and therefore, since the NACODS agreement was a national agreement, the defendant was bound by it. 'He has' continued the judge 'in fact accepted it and worked under it. He has taken the advantages of it and accepted the responsibilities of it for a period of some four years before this particular trouble arose. On the point that the agreement itself was not properly made, I think the complete answer would be that it is expressly admitted in the defence that the Coal Board, the plaintiffs, and the union did enter into an agreement which in fact contains the vital matters which are in dispute here'.

[Defendant's counsel] contends that the judge was wrong in holding that the defendant was personally bound by the NACODS agreement. If that point fell to be decided it might well be a matter of some difficulty. But, as the judge said, it is clear that the defendant's personal contract of service is regulated by the NACODS agreement, and the defendant by working on the terms of the NACODS agreement has entered into an agreement which contains the term now in dispute.

Robertson v British Gas Corporation
[1983] IRLR 302, Court of Appeal

In 1970, the offer letter to men appointed as meter readers/collectors stated: 'Incentive bonus scheme conditions will apply to meter reading and collecting work.'

At this time, there was in existence a collective agreement made between the employers and the union which regulated the amounts payable under the bonus scheme. In 1977, the men received a s. 1 statement, which stated:

The provisions of the agreement of the National Joint Council for Gas Staffs relating to remuneration will apply to you. Any payment which may, from time to time, become due in respect of incentive bonuses will be calculated in accordance with the rules of the scheme in force at the time.

In 1981, the employers gave the union notice that they were terminating the bonus aspect of the agreement at the end of the year. Robertson and another successfully sued British Gas in the county court for the loss of what amounted to a third of their wages.

Before the Court of Appeal the employers argued that the men's contracts were to be found in the 1977 s. 1 statement, which on their understanding was to be interpreted as meaning that if there was no bonus scheme in force then no bonus was payable.

The Court of Appeal disagreed with the employers' interpretation of the 1977 statement but was of the view that, even if it were correct, the s. 1 statement could not be used as an interpretation of the 1970 letter which was the contract itself (approving the view of the status of the statement adopted in *System Floors (UK) Ltd* v *Daniel*—see Section 1).

KERR LJ: It is true that collective agreements such as those in the present case create no legally enforceable obligation between the trade union and the employers. Either side can withdraw. But their terms are in this case incorporated into the individual contracts of employment, and it is only if and when those terms are varied collectively by agreement that the individual contracts of employment will also be varied. If the collective scheme is not varied by agreement, but by some unilateral abrogation or withdrawal or variation to which the other side does not agree, then it seems to me that the individual contracts of employment remain unaffected. This is another way of saying that the terms of the individual contracts are in part to be found in the agreed collective agreements as they exist from time to time, and, if these cease to exist as collective agreements, then the terms, unless expressly varied between the individual and the employer, will remain as they were by reference to the last agreed collective agreement incorporated into the individual contracts.

NOTES

1. For a similar approach, see *Gibbons* v *Associated British Ports* [1985] IRLR 376 and *Whent* v *T. Cartledge Ltd* [1997] IRLR 153, EAT; cf *Kaur* v *MG Rover Group Ltd* [2005] IRLR 40, CA.
2. Provisions from other documents, such as staff handbooks, may be expressly incorporated into employment contracts and thus become legally binding (see *Briscoe* v *Lubrizol Ltd.* [2002] IRLR 607, CA; *Keeley* v *Fosroc International Ltd* [2006] IRLR 961, CA; *Harlow* v *Artemis International Corporation Ltd* [2008] IRLR 629, EAT.
3. The question of incorporation is not always so straightforward and, as Wedderburn has observed, 'if a term of a collective agreement is incorporated into the employment contract with legal effect, it may still profit the worker nothing if, on its proper construction, the employer is entitled unilaterally to deprive him of its benefit' (*The Worker and The Law*, 3rd edn (Harmondsworth: Penguin, 1986), p. 336). This observation was prompted by the next case.

Cadoux v Central Regional Council
[1986] IRLR 131, Court of Session

Mr Cadoux's letter of appointment stated: 'The post is subject to the Conditions of service laid down by the National Joint Council for Local Authorities' Administrative, Professional, Technical and Clerical Services (Scottish Council) and as supplemented by the Authorities' Rules and as amended from time to time.' These rules provided Mr Cadoux with a non-contributory life assurance scheme. Subsequently, however, the employers unilaterally withdrew the scheme.

The Scottish Court of Session dismissed Mr Cadoux's claim for breach of contract.

LORD ROSS: In my opinion, the reference to the authorities' rules as amended from time to time shows that it was in the contemplation of the parties that the defenders' rules might be altered. The rules contain no express provision regarding amendment, and the clear inference from the fact that they are the defenders' rules is that the defenders have power to alter them, the only obligation being to enter the amendments in the rules or otherwise record them for the pursuer to refer to within a stipulated period.

NOTES

1. *Robertson* was distinguished on the basis that, in that case, a collective agreement had been made between an employer and a trade union, whereas in *Cadoux* there was no agreement but merely 'local arrangements entered into after consultation'.
2. The *Cadoux* decision has been subject to the following criticisms by Napier.

B. Napier, 'Incorporation of Collective Agreements'
(1986) 15 ILJ 52, at p. 53

Two comments can be made about this disposal of the issue. In the first place it would appear to run quite contrary to the general position in contract law, which does not allow there to be departure by unilateral act from an entitlement which has acquired contractual status. An employer cannot, for example, alter rates of pay once these have acquired contractual status—even if these rates of pay were introduced by his unilateral act in the first place. It is, with respect, not convincing to reply to this point by stating that here it was within the contemplation of the parties that the defender's rules might be changed at his will. Such a finding is inherently incompatible with the earlier determination that there was a contractual right to receive non-contributory life assurance. It is a strange variety of contractual obligation under which one party remains free to alter or cancel altogether any part of his indebtedness to another. The very idea of obligation is opposed to the notion that one party has complete licence to behave as he likes, and any assertion to the contrary is open to the charge of empty conceptualism.

The second comment relates to the reason used by Lord Ross to support his conclusion on this point. The fact that the life assurance scheme was not founded in any 'agreement' between the employer and the trade union, but only in consultations, meant that no collective agreement could be identified here, and decisions such as *Robertson* v *British Gas Corporation* [1982] ICR 351, taking a restrictive view of the employer's power to alter the contract by unilateral declaration, distinguished. By pursuing this line of argument, however, Lord Ross has arguably taken the same approach as Lord Denning did in *Gascol* v *Mercer* [1974] IRLR 155 in that he too has made a link between questions of substantive rights within the employment relationship and the legal nature of the source from which incorporation is alleged to proceed. Why should it make any difference to the employee's position in law that the contractual entitlement to life assurance arose following consultation and not agreement with the trade union? Yet such is the substance of Lord Ross's reasoning. It is respectfully submitted that, whether or not this reasoning is properly classified as a restatement of the heresies to be found in *Gascol Ltd* v *Mercer*, it is unwelcome on policy grounds and should not be followed.

NOTES

1. See *Airlie* v *City of Edinburgh District Council* [1996] IRLR 516, where the Scottish EAT adopted similar reasoning to that utilised in *Cadoux*. In *Wetherill* v *Birmingham City Council* [2007] IRLR 781, the Court of Appeal allowed an appeal against a finding that a local authority was liable to pay damages for breach of contract because it unilaterally changed the terms of a car allowance scheme from a rate related to the engine capacity of the car actually used to a rate appropriate to the duties which were to be performed. According to the Court of Appeal, the Council had the right to vary the allowance unilaterally, on proper notice, so long as it did not exercise that right 'for an improper purpose, capriciously or arbitrarily, or in a way in which no reasonable employer, acting reasonably, would exercise it'. See also *Bateman* v *Asda Stores Ltd* [2010] IRLR 370, where the EAT held that a broad contractual right to alter terms and conditions of employment in line with business needs, even if contained in a company handbook, permitted an employer to make unilateral changes to contractual terms, including rates of pay and hours of work, without the need for the express consent of the employee, provided that the changes are properly implemented and the employer acts in line with the duty to maintain trust and confidence.

2. The Court of Appeal's reasoning in the next case is in line with the approach advocated by Napier.

Marley v *Forward Trust Ltd*

[1986] IRLR 369, Court of Appeal

Marley's contract of employment with Forward Trust Group Ltd expressly incorporated the terms of a collective agreement which had been negotiated with the trade union, ASTMS, and was subject to modifications to that agreement. There had always been a 'mobility clause' in his contract of employment which obliged him to work in any department of the company to which he might be posted.

Early in 1983, the union negotiated an amendment to the collective agreement which introduced certain provisions as to redundancy. These provided that, in the event of redundancy, employees who were offered significant changes to the terms of their employment such as location would have the right to a six-month trial period. If at the end of this trial period, they rejected the job, their right to an agreed scheme of redundancy payments would be preserved.

At the end of 1983, the employer, faced with redundancies, closed the Bristol office where Marley was employed and he was transferred to London. Marley, having tried the job, was unhappy and decided to leave and claim under the redundancy agreement. The company resisted his claim because in their view he had been transferred under the mobility clause and not under the redundancy agreement. Further, the redundancy clause did not have the force of law because the collective agreement was expressed to be 'binding in honour only'. This argument was accepted by both the industrial tribunal and EAT.

The Court of Appeal allowed Marley's appeal and remitted the case to the industrial tribunal.

LAWTON LJ: There has been a long judicial history to the problem of incorporation of the terms of collective agreements into contracts of personal service. The judicial history goes back to the days when there were arguments as to whether collective agreements were enforceable in law. All that line of argument has now been rendered otiose by the provisions of s. 18 of the Trade Union and Labour Relations Act 1974 as amended by subsequent Acts [see now TULR(C)A 1992, s. 179]. No collective agreement now is enforceable as between the parties to it save in special circumstances and in ways specifically agreed by the parties. So there was not much point, as Mr McMullen has pointed out, in the union putting in clause 11 when they negotiated this collective agreement with the respondents. But, since 1974, the courts on a number of occasions have had to consider whether, when there is an unenforceable collective agreement incorporated into a contract of personal service, the terms of it, or some of them, can be incorporated into that contract of personal service. We found it unnecessary to go into all the cases because, as recently as 1983, this Court considered the problem in *Robertson v British Gas Corporation* [1983] IRLR 302. This Court decided that such terms can be incorporated into contracts of personal service and, when they are so incorporated, they are enforceable.

(iii) Incorporation by conduct

This is sometimes called implied incorporation or, in the words of Kahn-Freund, 'crystallised custom', and will operate where, in the absence of express agreement, collectively bargained terms and conditions are uniformly observed for a group of workers of which the employer is a member.

B: Inappropriateness of collective terms

On occasion, the question arises as to whether certain terms of a collective agreement are appropriate for inclusion in the individual contract of employment. This is very much a 'grey' area, compounded by the fact that the courts have never developed a test for what makes a particular clause 'appropriate'. The most that can be said is that much will depend on whether the particular clause is seen as relating to collective rather than individual relationships, such as union recognition (*Gallagher* v *The Post Office* [1970] 3 All ER 712), or redundancy planning (*British Leyland (UK) Ltd* v *McQuilken* [1978] IRLR 245), or dispute resolution (*National Coal Board* v *National Union of Mineworkers* [1986] IRLR 439).

Alexander v *Standard Telephone & Cables Ltd (No. 2)*
[1991] IRLR 286, Queen's Bench Division

The plaintiff employees were seeking to rely on seniority provisions in the redundancy procedure of the relevant collective agreement, which they said had been breached by their employers when dismissing them. On an application for an interim injunction, the High Court—assuming a breach of contract—had refused to grant the order on the basis that trust and confidence had broken down. Subsequently, the plaintiffs brought an action for damages for breach of contract. Their actions failed because Hobhouse J held that the redundancy procedure was not incorporated into their individual contracts of employment. Their statement of terms and conditions clearly referred to the collective agreement, but it was held that this particular part of the agreement was inappropriate for incorporation, thus remaining in the collective sphere and therefore unenforceable.

HOBHOUSE J: In the case *National Coal Board* v *National Union of Mineworkers* [1986] IRLR 439, to which some individual employees were also parties, Mr Justice Scott reviewed the authorities on incorporation at pp. 453 and following. In that case there was an express provision in the individual contracts of employment that the employees' 'wages and conditions of service shall be regulated by and subject to such national, district and pit agreements as are for the time being in force'. The question was the application of that clear contractual intent: the question in the action therefore was: what was the extent of the resultant incorporation? He drew a distinction which was derived from the argument of Mr Dehn before him, at p. 454 (151).

> He seeks, however, to draw a distinction between the terms of a collective agreement which are of their nature apt to become enforceable terms of an individual's contract of employment and terms which are of their nature inapt to become enforceable by individuals. Terms of collective agreements fixing rates of pay, or hours of work, would obviously fall into the first category. Terms…dismissing an employee also would fall into the first category. But conciliation agreements setting up machinery designed to resolve by discussions between employers' representatives and union representatives, or by arbitral proceedings, questions arising within the industry, fall, submitted Mr Dehn, firmly in the second category. The terms of conciliation schemes are not intended to become contractually enforceable by individual workers whether or not referred into the individual contracts of employment.
>
> …
>
> A collective agreement between an employer and a union providing machinery for collective bargaining and for resolving industrial disputes may be of very great importance to each and every worker in the industry. But it is not likely to be an agreement intended to be legally enforceable as between employer and union, and it is almost inconceivable to my mind that it could have been intended to become legally enforceable at the suit of an individual worker. In the procedures laid down by the 1946 Scheme, for instance, no part is played by an individual mineworker. The machinery is designed to be invoked and operated either by the NCB or by the NUM with the co-operation of the other. It simply does not lend itself at all to enforceability at the suit of an individual mineworker.

Therefore, even in a case which involved wide express words of incorporation the court considered it necessary to look at the content and character of the relevant parts of the collective agreement in order to decide whether or not they were incorporated into the individual contracts of employment.

The principles to be applied can therefore be summarised. The relevant contract is that between the individual employee and his employer; it is the contractual intention of those two parties which must be ascertained. In so far as that intention is to be found in a written document, that document must be construed on ordinary contractual principles. In so far as there is no such document or that document is not complete or conclusive, their contractual intention has to be ascertained by inference from the other available material including collective agreements. The fact that another document is not itself contractual does not prevent it from being incorporated into the contract if that intention is shown as between the employer and the individual employee. Where a document is expressly incorporated by general words it is still necessary to consider, in conjunction with the words of incorporation, whether any particular part of that document is apt to be a term of the contract; if it is inapt, the correct construction of the contract may be that it is not a term of the contract. Where it is not a case of express incorporation, but a matter of inferring the contractual intent, the character of the document and the relevant part of it and whether it is apt to form part of the individual contract is central to the decision whether or not the inference should be drawn.

In the present cases I have concluded that the wording of the only document directly applicable to the individual plaintiffs, the statutory statements, is not sufficient to effect an express incorporation of the provisions relating to redundancy in the collective agreements: accordingly it is a matter of considering whether or not to *infer* that the selection procedures and the principle of seniority have been incorporated into the individual contracts of employment and this has to be decided having regard to the evidence given and an evaluation of the character of the relevant provisions in the collective agreements.

NOTES

1. The judge went on to hold that there could be no inference that the redundancy selection clause was intended to form part of the individual contract because the clause happened to be situated in an agreement containing other provisions incapable of incorporation, i.e. statements of policy.

   Do you agree with the judge's reasoning? As Rubenstein observes:

   > It requires no great expertise to appreciate that some terms of collective agreements are suitable for incorporation and others are not. That much of a given collective agreement is not apt to be incorporated into individual contracts is the starting point for legal analysis, we would submit, not the finish line. I doubt whether there are many labour lawyers reading this

commentary who, if called upon to advise the firm, would not have recommended that the wording of the redundancy selection clause should be qualified by reference to additional criteria if avoiding enforceability was intended (and that is just what the employers subsequently did). ('Highlights' [1991] IRLR 282.)

(Cf. *Anderson* v *Pringle of Scotland* [1997] IRLR 208; and *Kaur* v *MG Rover Group Ltd* [2005] IRLR 40, CA.)

2. *Malone* v *British Airways plc* [2011] IRLR 32 was an appeal against the High Court's finding that BA was not in breach of the claimants' contracts of employment in unilaterally imposing revised and reduced crew complements for flights based at Heathrow Airport below the levels which had been agreed through collective bargaining with Unite. The revised crew complements were still in excess of the legal minimum. In line with the High Court, the Court of Appeal concluded that there was insufficient evidence of a mutual intention to give the provisions of the collective agreement relating to worldwide scheduling legal enforceability by any individual crew member. Lady Justice Smith stated that it was not clear from the language whether the relevant clause was intended to be enforceable by an individual employee. 'Although crew complements do impact to some extent upon the working conditions of individual employees' and in that respect were apt for incorporation, 'set against that are the disastrous consequences for BA which could ensue if this term were to be individually enforceable. It seems to me that they are so serious as to be unthinkable'. It could not have been intended by the parties that the clause would enable 'an individual or a small group of cabin crew members to bring a flight to a halt by refusing to work under complement'. Accordingly, the parties 'did not mean this term to be individually enforceable'. Lady Justice Smith concluded that 'it was intended to be binding only in honour, although it created a danger that, if breached, industrial action would follow'.

C: 'No-strike clauses'

TRADE UNION AND LABOUR RELATIONS (CONSOLIDATION) ACT 1992

180. Effect of provisions restricting right to take industrial action

(1) Any terms of a collective agreement which prohibit or restrict the right of workers to engage in a strike or other industrial action, or have the effect of prohibiting or restricting that right, shall not form part of any contract between a worker and the person for whom he works unless the following conditions are met.

(2) The conditions are that the collective agreement—
  (a) is in writing,
  (b) contains a provision expressly stating that those terms shall or may be incorporated in such a contract,
  (c) is reasonably accessible at his place of work to the worker to whom it applies and is available for him to consult during working hours, and
  (d) is one where each trade union which is a party to the agreement is an independent trade union; and that the contract with the worker expressly or impliedly incorporates those terms in the contract.

(3) The above provisions have effect notwithstanding anything in section 179 and notwithstanding any provision to the contrary in any agreement (including a collective agreement or a contract with any worker).

SECTION 3: CONSTRUCTING THE CONTRACT OF EMPLOYMENT: IMPLIED TERMS

A: Subjective or objective tests

Although an increasing role has been played by statutory obligations which cannot be contracted out of by the employer, the common law implied terms of employment are still of considerable importance.

The judges of the common law laid down two, or probably one combined, test(s) to determine whether a term should be implied into the contract. These tests allow the court to imply a term 'of which it can be predicated that "it goes without saying", some term not expressed but necessary to give to the transaction such business efficacy as the parties must have intended' (per Lord Wright in *Luxor (Eastbourne) Ltd* v *Cooper* [1941] AC 108, at p. 137).

This subjective basis for implication always had an air of unreality about it, given, as Kahn-Freund has observed. 'It is...sheer utopia to postulate a common interest in the substance of labour relations' (*Labour and the Law*, 3rd edn (London: Stevens & Sons, 1983), p. 28). Also, as we shall see, the courts have long been willing to hold that at common law there are certain terms which will be implied to most if not all employments, not on the basis of the intention of the parties but because they were a 'necessary condition of the relation of master and man' (per Viscount Simonds in *Lister* v *Romford Ice Co.* [1957] AC 555, at p. 576). Last, in recent years we have witnessed a distinct shift away from a subjective test as the basis for incorporation towards an objective test which questions whether it is 'necessary' to imply a term.

Mears v *Safecar Security Ltd*
[1982] 2 All ER 865, Court of Appeal

Other aspects of this case are discussed at p. 124 (Section 8).

STEPHENSON LJ: I am of the opinion that when, in exercising its statutory jurisdiction under [ERA 1996, s. 12] an industrial tribunal has to imply and insert missing terms, it is not tied to the requirements of the test propounded by Lord Justice Scrutton, a test for commercial contracts which goes back to *The Moorcock* (1889) 14 Probate Division 64 but can and should consider all the facts and circumstances of the relationship between the employer and employee concerned, including the way in which they had worked the particular contract of employment since it was made in order to imply and determine the missing term which ought to have been particularised by the employer and so to complete the contract.

...We can treat as an agreed term a term which would not have been at once assented to by both parties at the time when they made the contract, e.g. where one party would at once have assented to it and the other would have done so after it had been made clear to him that unless he did so there would be no contract—which is, I think, this case.

B: Factual implied terms: some examples

Jones v *Associated Tunnelling Co. Ltd*
[1981] IRLR 477, Employment Appeal Tribunal

The respondent firm were contractors. For many years, part of their work consisted of doing specialist tunnelling and bunkering work at National Coal Board collieries. Mr Jones was first employed by the respondents in December 1964 to work on a contract at Chatterley Whitfield Colliery, which was about two miles from his home. He was sent a statement of the terms and conditions of employment. The only reference to his place of employment was the word 'Chatterley'. In 1969, Mr Jones ceased working at Chatterley and started to work at Hem Heath Colliery, some 12 to 13 miles from his home. In October 1973, he was issued with a fresh statement of terms and conditions. This stated that he was to work 'at Hem Heath Colliery or such place or places in the UK the employers may decide from time to time'. A further statement was issued in April 1976. This stipulated: 'You may be required to transfer from one site to another on the instruction of the Employer.'

In March 1980, the respondents' contract with the National Coal Board at Hem Heath Colliery came to an end. The employers told Mr Jones that they had work available for him on the construction of a bunker at Florence Colliery. This colliery was very close to Hem Heath Colliery and equally accessible to Mr Jones's home. Mr Jones, however, did not accept this work. Instead he obtained employment with the NCB and claimed a redundancy payment from the respondents.

An industrial tribunal held that the employers were entitled under the contract to require Mr Jones to work at the Florence Colliery and to do bunkering work. Accordingly, there had been no breach of contract by the employers and Mr Jones had not been dismissed in law.

Jones's appeal to the EAT was unsuccessful, although the EAT's grounds for rejection were not the same as the tribunal's.

BROWNE-WILKINSON J: The starting point must be that a contract of employment cannot simply be silent on the place of work: if there is no express term, there must be either some rule of law that in *all* contracts of employment the employer is (or alternatively is not) entitled to transfer the employee from his original place of work or some term regulating the matter must be implied into each contract. We know of no rule of law laying down the position in relation to all contracts of employment, nor do we think it either desirable or possible to lay down a single rule. It is impossible to conceive of any fixed rule which will be equally appropriate to the case of, say, an employee of a touring repertory theatre and the librarian of the British Museum. Therefore, the position must be regulated by the express or implied agreement of the parties in each case. In order to give the contract business efficacy, it is necessary to imply *some* term into each contract of employment.

The term to be implied must depend on the circumstances of each case. The authorities show that it may be relevant to consider the nature of the employer's business, whether or not the employee has in fact been moved during the employment, what the employee was told when he was employed, and whether there is any provision made to cover the employee's expenses when working away from daily reach of his home. These are only examples; all the circumstances of each case have to be considered: see *O'Brien* v *Associated Fire Alarms Ltd* [1969] 1 All ER 93; *Stevenson* v *Teesside Bridge and Engineering Ltd* [1971] 1 All ER 296; *Times Newspapers* v *Bartlett* (1976) 11 ITR 106.

Looking at the circumstances of this case, what would the parties have said had an officious bystander asked them 'At what sites can Mr Jones be asked to work?' The employers might have replied 'Anywhere in the United Kingdom'. But the industrial tribunal's findings indicate that Mr Jones, as one would expect, would have objected to being transferred anywhere outside daily reach of his home. The employers were in business as contractors working at different sites; so the parties must have envisaged a degree of mobility. In 1969, Mr Jones himself was moved from his original place of work to Hem Heath Colliery without objection. All the statements of terms and conditions subsequently issued contain mobility clauses, albeit in varying terms. From these factors we think that the plain inference is that the employers were to have *some* power to move Mr Jones's place of work and that the reasonable term to imply (as the lowest common denominator of what the parties would have agreed if asked) is a power to direct Mr Jones to work at any place within reasonable daily reach of Mr Jones's home. Such a term would permit Mr Jones to be required to work at Florence Colliery...

...[I]t is essential to imply *some* term into the contract in order to give the contract business efficacy: there must be some term laying down the place of work. In such a case, it seems to us that there is no alternative but for the tribunal or court to imply a term which the parties, if reasonable, would probably have agreed if they had directed their minds to the problem. Such a term will not vary the express contractual terms. This view is supported by the very many cases in which the courts have decided what terms as to mobility ought to be included in a contract of employment...

NOTE: The EAT had reservations regarding the industrial tribunal's alternative conclusion that, by failing to object to the new statement of terms and conditions in 1973 and 1976 (which both provided for mobility between sites), Jones had assented to a variation in the terms of his employment. (For further reference to this aspect of the case, see p. 97, note 2.)

Courtaulds Northern Spinning Ltd v Sibson
[1988] IRLR 276, Court of Appeal

There was no express term in the contract as to the employee's place of work or the employer's right of transfer. The employee, an HGV driver, resigned and claimed constructive dismissal after he was required to move to another depot following a union membership dispute. An industrial tribunal held that any right to require the employee to move was subject to the limitations that the transfer was reasonable and made for operational reasons. The Court of Appeal, however, allowed the employer's appeal.

SLADE LJ: The most salient factors seem to me to be these. Mr Sibson was employed as a heavy goods vehicle driver. The very nature of his employment, therefore, meant that he would spend by far the greater part of his working hours *on the road*. Though constant reference has been made in the course of argument to Greengate as Mr Sibson's 'place of work', it was in truth no more than a starting and finishing place for his work shifts—just as the bus depot will ordinarily be no more than a starting and finishing place for the work shifts of a bus driver. (The present case is quite different, for example, from that of a shop assistant whose place of work will ordinarily be a particular shop in a particular locality throughout the working day.) Mr Sibson was initially asked to report to the Greengate depot and to work with that as his base, and had in fact worked from that base since the start of his employment. The employer had other depots at Bolton, Mansfield, Worksop and Chadderton, which was only about a mile away. There was no union membership agreement.

Against this background, in asking myself the question 'What term with regard to mobility would the parties, if reasonable, have agreed (in 1973) if they had directed their minds to the problem?' I find little difficulty in supplying the answer.

Mr Philipson based his argument on the modest submission that parties, if reasonable, would have at least agreed that Courtaulds should have the right to transfer Mr Sibson to Chadderton if it saw fit. I do not disagree with this submission, so far as it goes, but would go further. If reasonable, the parties would, in my judgment, have been likely to agree the term which Browne-Wilkinson J in *Jones* (at p. 480, para. 16) described as the 'lowest common denominator', namely a power in the employer to direct the employee to work at any place within reasonable daily reach of Mr Jones' home—and I would add *for any reason*. I cannot see how Mr Sibson could reasonably have objected to a term giving the contract this limited degree of flexibility when he entered the employment in 1973. If the evidence had disclosed any special circumstances which, as at that time, made it a matter of importance to him that he should continue to be based at Courtaulds' Greengate depot rather than at (say) Chadderton, the Industrial Tribunal would no doubt have said so.

Lord Denning MR was prepared to imply essentially the same term in the *O'Brien* case [1969] 1 All ER 93 at p. 96, where he expressed it as a term that 'they should be employed within daily travelling distance of their homes or if you please within a reasonable distance of their homes.'

In my judgment there was no need or justification for the Industrial Tribunal to import into the implied term a requirement that the employer's request to the employee to work at another place must itself be 'reasonable'— still less that a request could only be reasonable if made 'for genuine operational reasons'. Any such fetter on the employer's right to request the employee to move would have been potentially uncertain and difficult in operation and the employer could, I think, reasonably have objected to it. On the other hand, so far as I can see, all the protection which the employee could reasonably have demanded would have been conferred by the requirement of reasonable daily travelling distance.

NOTES

1. Holland and Chandler ((1988) 17 ILJ 253) expose the strange logic employed in this judgment:

   ...Slade LJ (delivering the only judgment) argued that post-contractual conduct provided evidence of the *reasonable* intentions of the parties at the time of the contract's formation. His conclusion was that the parties would have been likely to agree that the employer had the power to direct the employee to work at any place within reasonable daily commuting distance; and that that requirement need not be reasonable, nor result from any genuine operational reasons, but *could be for any reason*. This assumes that the parties, as reasonable men, would have accepted the inclusion of a term which allowed one party absolute discretion over its operation; a discretion that need bear no relation to reasonableness or even managerial necessity. Indeed, Slade LJ felt that the employer could reasonably object to any such fetter on his rights. But what of Sibson's reasonable objections to the exercise of any unrestricted managerial prerogative?

2. Following *Sibson*'s case, it would appear that in the absence of an express mobility clause in the contract, there is a strong presumption that the courts will be prepared to imply a term to the effect that the employee's place of work covers all sites within reasonable daily travelling distance of his home (see also *O'Brien* v *Associated Fire Alarms Ltd* [1969] 1 All ER 93 and *Jones* v *Associated Tunnelling Co. Ltd* [1981] IRLR 477).

3. Where a contract of employment did not specify payment for overtime, the employee was implied under the contract to be entitled to be paid a reasonable sum (*Driver* v *Air India* [2011] IRLR 992, CA).

SECTION 4: CONSTRUCTING THE CONTRACT OF EMPLOYMENT: CHARACTERISTIC OR IMPOSED TERMS

I. Smith, 'The creation of the contract of employment' in *Butterworths Employment Law Guide*, 2nd edn
(London: Butterworths, 1996), p. 15

One important aspect of the wide, reasonableness test for implied terms is that it can be used by a court or tribunal for a purpose other than that of giving effect to what may (or may not) have been the basis of the agreement between that particular employer and that particular employee. It may be used instead as a device to *regulate* contracts of employment by the imposition of implied terms based on the nature of the employment itself. Such terms might be considered to be characteristic or 'imposed' terms which will normally be implied into employment contracts (either generally, or into contracts of a particular type) unless there is clear evidence that the parties did not intend them to apply. Such terms have little or nothing to do with any supposed intention of the parties themselves. The implied term is here simply used as a device with which to apply what are really just free-standing rules and concepts of the law of employment.

The scope and content of these characteristic or imposed terms is illustrated in Section 8 of this chapter.

SECTION 5: CONSTRUCTING THE CONTRACT OF EMPLOYMENT: WORK RULES

Secretary of State for Employment* v *ASLEF (No. 2)
[1972] 2 QB 455, Court of Appeal

The Court of Appeal had to determine whether the respondent union's 'work to rule' was in breach of contract. In disputing this, the union claimed that it was merely following the employer's rule book to the letter. (For other aspects of this case see p. 166 (Section 8 (xiv).))

LORD DENNING MR: Each man signs a form saying that he will abide by the rules, but these rules are in no way terms of the contract of employment. They are only instructions to the man as to how he is to do the work.

■ QUESTION

What are the implications of this approach for the scope of managerial prerogative unilaterally to alter rules?

NOTE: It is probable, however, that those sections of rule books which cover matters of which written notice must be given by statute will provide strong prima facie evidence of contractual terms.

Sagar v *Ridehalgh & Son Ltd*
[1931] 1 Ch 310, Court of Appeal

The plaintiff, a weaver, was employed by the defendant under an oral contract of employment. His wages were determined by reference to a collective agreement between the employers and the workers' unions. Evidence showed a custom observed by most mills in Lancashire for deductions to be made for work which was not done with reasonable care and skill. Sagar challenged the lawfulness of this practice but was unsuccessful.

LAWRENCE LJ: …[T]he practice of making reasonable deductions for bad work has continually prevailed at the defendant's mill for upwards of thirty years, and during the whole of that time all weavers employed by the defendants have been treated alike in that respect. The practice was therefore firmly established at the defendant's mill when the plaintiff entered upon his employment there. Further, I think it is clear that the plaintiff accepted employment in the defendant's mill on the same terms as others employed at that mill…Although I entirely agree with the learned judge in finding it difficult to believe that the plaintiff did not know of the existence of the practice at the mill, I think it is immaterial whether he knew it or not, as I am satisfied that he accepted his employment on the same terms as to deductions for bad work as other workers at the mill.

NOTES
1. If a custom is to have legal effect, it must be 'reasonable, certain and notorious'. There is some confusion as to whether there is an additional requirement that the individual worker must be aware of the practice. This was not required in *Sagar* but in *Meek* v *Port of London* [1918] 1 Ch 415, the long-established deduction of income tax was not incorporated into the employee's contract because employees were unaware of it.
2. For an example of a relatively recent, unsuccessful attempt to imply a term via custom and practice, see *Quinn* v *Calder Industrial Materials Ltd* [1996] IRLR 126, EAT. The attempt, however, succeeded in the next case.

Henry v *London General Transport Services Ltd*
[2001] IRLR 132, Employment Appeal Tribunal

The case arose out of a framework agreement negotiated on behalf of bus staff by the T&GWU prior to a management buy-out. The agreement reduced pay rates, but it was accepted by the majority of the staff affected. However, a number of staff at the Stockwell Garage expressed their dissatisfaction, and ultimately brought proceedings claiming unlawful deduction of wages. The ET acknowledged that there had been a tradition of collective bargaining between the employers and the union, but it held that this was insufficient to establish that there was a custom and practice that fundamental changes, such as those in the framework agreement, were incorporated into a contract of employment by virtue of the collective bargaining. The EAT allowed an appeal against the tribunal's finding.

MR JUSTICE LINDSAY (PRESIDENT):...

Custom and practice
The tribunal held that, whilst there had been a tradition of collective negotiation between the company and the T&GWU, the framework agreement proposed fundamental changes and it was not satisfied that the tradition was sufficient to establish that such fundamental changes were incorporated into individuals' contracts by virtue of the collective bargaining. The burden was on the company to establish but that burden had not been satisfied.

As to the law relating to the role of custom and practice in employment law, the tribunal made, as it seems to us, four potentially significant holdings, namely that:

(i)   in relation to the incorporation into a contract of employment of a term by way of a custom and practice, the custom and practice so relied on must be reasonable, certain and notorious;

(ii)   that where what is shown in relation to the custom and practice, the term thus supported is incorporated on the assumption that represents the wishes of the parties;

(iii) that strict proof is required of the custom and practice and that the burden of such proof is upon the party seeking to rely upon the consequential incorporation of the term into the contract;

and, as it would seem:

(iv)   that there is some relevant distinction generally to be made between a custom and practice enabling changes to be made and one enabling 'fundamental' changes to be made in a man's terms and conditions of employment.

As for the certainty of the custom and practice alleged by the employer, the terms so alleged thereby to be incorporated in the case in hand, if fully spelled-out, would…have been something on these lines, namely that a term or condition of employment representing a change in the staff's terms and conditions in respect of which the T&GWU had reached agreement with the employer, which had been notified to the staff and which the union bona fide believed (and so informed the employer) had attracted the support of the majority of staff affected, would, without more, thereafter become a term or condition of all the staff so affected, whether members of the union or not. Such a term seems to us certain enough and the employment tribunal does not appear to have declined its incorporation on the grounds of uncertainty.

As for reasonableness, given the large number of staff concerned, the occasional need for a speedy decision on changes in employment rights and practices and the consequential difficulty in conducting individual negotiations and given also the settled history of the union's negotiating role over a number of years, it would be hard to describe such a term as unreasonable and the employment tribunal did not do so.

As for notoriety, the employees' chief witness Mr Ibekwe said (as recorded in the chairman's notes):

'respondent always negotiated terms and conditions with T&GWU as long as I can remember.'

which seems to have been a reference to as far back as 1988…Mr Elms, the company's operations director, in his written evidence-in-chief had said that it had been the company's practice over many years to negotiate changes to terms and conditions (both beneficial and detrimental to staff) with the T&GWU…In cross-examination he said that there was one major negotiation each year and some years several more and that he had not believed that there was a period when workers were not informed of union agreements.…There was plainly material on which the employment tribunal could have found that the custom and practice asserted by the employer was notorious…

As for a term incorporated by way of custom and practice being taken to represent the wishes of the parties or the presumed intention of the parties, that may be the notion on which such an incorporation rests but, if the required general notoriety is proven, then one does not undermine that foundation (and hence the incorporation of the term) by showing that some individuals sought to be charged with the term did not know of the practice or that he or she did not intend or wish it—see e.g. *Chitty on Contracts* vol. 2 para. 13–018. Once the reasonableness, certainty and notoriety is sufficiently proven, the tribunal has to presume that all relevant parties had so wished and intended.

Moreover, on the related third point, it is hard to see why the required reasonableness, certainty and notoriety have to be proved 'strictly', if by that was meant to some standard higher than that of the balance of probabilities. *Chitty on Contracts* cites no such requirement, nor any authority for it. The only authority which the tribunal relied on to that end was *Singh* v *British Steel Corporation* [1974] IRLR 131, where, in one line at p. 135 (and without supporting authority) it is said:

'Custom requires strict proof by those seeking to set it up'.

It is plain that courts and tribunals should not lightly find a custom to exist, but a requirement that the three ingredients of reasonableness, certainty and notoriety are proved on the conventional balance of probabilities is in our judgment a sufficient bar to ensure that customs will not too lightly be taken to be present. We have found no reason to require 'strict proof'…

As for the idea that changes or proposed changes are fundamental and others not and that there may be a custom and practice sufficient so as to be able to effect one but not the other, it is not to be rejected out of hand as, despite the vagueness or variability of the term 'fundamental', the law is familiar enough with the question of whether, for example, a breach is or is not 'fundamental'. But the context in which that is usually asked is as between two or few more parties. The notion of what is 'fundamental' when one is dealing with 1,500 individuals is more difficult to grasp…

In our judgment, the tribunal erred in law by distinguishing in the very general manner in which it did between a practice sufficient to effect changes and a practice sufficient to effect fundamental changes.

NOTES

1. The EAT also held that presentation of a petition to management protesting against the introduction of the new terms was insufficient to justify a finding that the applicants had kept alive their ability to insist on employment under their old terms, in circumstances in which they worked and were paid in accordance with the new terms for almost two years without further protest before making their tribunal application.

2. In *Garratt* v *Mirror Group Newspapers Ltd* [2011] IRLR 591, the Court of Appeal held that a custom and practice (applied since 1993) that employees would not be entitled to the contractual enhanced redundancy scheme unless they signed a compromise agreement constituted an implied and overriding term.

3. In *Shumba & others* v *Park Cakes Ltd* [2013] IRLR 800, the Court of Appeal provided the following helpful guidance on when contractual rights concerning enhanced redundancy benefits may arise through custom and practice:

    (a) On how many occasions, and over how long a period, the benefits in question have been paid.

    (b) Whether the benefits are always the same.

    (c) The extent to which the enhanced benefits are publicised generally.

    (d) *How the terms are described*: 'ex gratia' versus 'entitlement' or 'paid as a matter of policy'.

    (e) *What is said in the express contract*, i.e. does an express term contradict the implied term by custom argument?

    (f) *Equivocalness*. Is the practice, viewed objectively, equally explicable on the basis that it is pursued as a matter of discretion rather than legal obligation? The burden of proof is on the employee (see also *Albion Automotive Ltd* v *Walker* [2002] EWCA 946).

SECTION 7: CONSTRUCTING THE CONTRACT OF EMPLOYMENT: STATUTORY IMPLIED TERMS

A: Some examples

(i) Equality Act 2010

66. Sex equality clause

(1) If the terms of A's work do not (by whatever means) include a sex equality clause, they are to be treated as including one.

(2) A sex equality clause is a provision that has the following effect—

    (a) if a term of A's is less favourable to A than a corresponding term of B's is to B, A's term is modified so as not to be less favourable;

    (b) if A does not have a term which corresponds to a term of B's that benefits B, A's terms are modified so as to include such a term.

NOTE: See Chapter 4 for a detailed discussion.

(ii) Employment Rights Act 1996

PART III GUARANTEE PAYMENTS

28. Right to guarantee payment

(1) Where throughout a day during any part of which an employee would normally be required to work in accordance with his contract of employment the employee is not provided with work by his employer by reason of—

    (a) a diminution in the requirements of the employer's business for work of the kind which the employee is employed to do, or

    (b) any other occurrence affecting the normal working of the employer's business in relation to work of the kind which the employee is employed to do, the employee is entitled to be paid by his employer an amount in respect of that day.

(2) In this Act a payment to which an employee is entitled under subsection (1) is referred to as a guarantee payment.

(3) In this Part—

(a) a day falling within subsection (1) is referred to as a 'workless day', and

(b) 'workless period' has a corresponding meaning.

NOTE: With effect from 1 April 2014 the statutory guarantee payment is £26 per day (with effect from 6 April 2015).

(iii) National Minimum Wage Act 1998 (as amended)

1. Workers to be paid at least the minimum wage

(1) A person who qualifies for the national minimum wage shall be remunerated by his employer in respect of his work in any pay reference period at a rate which is not less than the national minimum wage.

(2) A person qualifies for the national minimum wage if he is an individual who—

(a) is a worker;

(b) is working, or ordinarily works, in the United Kingdom under his contract; and

(c) has ceased to be of compulsory school age.

(3) The national minimum wage shall be such single hourly rate as the Secretary of State may from time to time prescribe.

(4) For the purposes of this Act 'a pay reference period' is such period as the Secretary of State may prescribe for the purpose.

...

NOTES

1. With effect from 1 April 1999, all relevant workers became entitled to the national minimum wage (NMW). The statutory provisions relating to the national minimum wage are contained in the National Minimum Wage Act (NMWA) 1998 as augmented by the National Minimum Wage Regulations (NMWR) 1999 (SI 1999/584) as amended. The NMWA 1998 contains the basic framework of the statutory scheme, and the NMWR contain the detail on the applicable rate and the methods of calculation to be applied in order to assess whether the rate has been complied with in any particular case.

2. The introduction of a NMW was one of the first measures announced by the new Labour Government when it came into office. The adoption of this measure does clearly represent an important step back to intervention and the re-establishment of a framework of minimum workplace standards. In the wages field it also marks a return to compulsory wage-setting as a feature of the employment scene which has been missing since the abolition of the Wages Councils in 1993. The new provisions do, however, go further than that legislation, given that they establish a *national* minimum wage applicable to most eligible workers aged 26 or above. In contrast, the Wages Councils were limited to specific areas of the labour market in which low pay was particularly prevalent, and where collective bargaining as a means of negotiating wage minima and other wage-related entitlements, and of maintaining pay levels by periodic revision, did not operate effectively.

    In dealing with wages, the Act represents a significant extension of the 'floor of rights' concept. Until the arrival of the 1998 Act, matters of pay had largely remained unregulated other than by statutory restrictions on pay rises during periods of wage controls and by protective legislation (now mostly in Pts I and II of the ERA 1996 dealing with such matters as the provision of pay particulars in the written statement, deductions of wages, itemised pay statements, and so forth).

3. The involvement of the State, and State agencies, in measures for raising low wages does, in fact, go back a long way. In 1797, for example, the Speenhamland system in Berkshire entailed a system of poor relief which included wages 'top-ups' for labourers at times when wage levels fell. By 1909, and following the Fair Wages Resolutions system, Winston Churchill's Trade Boards Act 1909 laid the foundations for minimum wage schemes in some industries. Part of the rationale for the Act was that the 'sweated trades', in which employers paid abnormally low wages, placed a burden on the rest of society and were seen as 'subsidised' by the poor relief system and the

charities. They were also, to some extent, regarded as engaging in unfair competition by other employers who paid higher wages to their workers. The Act was primarily designed to improve the protection given by the Fair Wages Resolution of 1891. Other precedents for the 1998 statute can be found in legislation like the Holidays with Pay Act 1938 and the Wages Councils Act 1945.

In introducing the 1998 Act, the Government has also had some regard to the position in other EC Member States. In all cases these countries have some form of minimum wage system, although they vary considerably in form and operation. In adopting the new measures a similar approach has been taken to that in countries like France and the Netherlands, where minimum wage levels are generally set by reference to a minimum hourly rate (and in some instances a monthly minimum level of income for groups working above a set level of weekly hours).

4. The Government's policy on the minimum wage has been driven by a number of policy objectives. First and foremost has been its concern, since its Commission on Social Justice reported, about the problems generated by low wages. But a separate, and perhaps equally important, agenda has resulted from the Government's declared objective of reducing the 'burden' placed on the State benefits system by low pay. The link between falling average pay—particularly in sectors formerly covered by the Wages Councils and in public sector pay (aggravated by a number of factors, including compulsory competitive tendering)—and the on-costs to the State (in the form of State benefits expenditure and increased NHS costs) has convinced the Government that it was right to proceed with its minimum wage proposal. By putting responsibility back onto employers (at least in part, given the on-going importance of benefits support) it believes that there will, in time, be a slow-down in the escalating demands placed on the welfare system. (For further discussion of the policies behind the Act, see Simpson, B., 'A milestone in the legal regulation of pay: The National Minimum Wage Act 1988' (1999) 28 ILJ 1; and Sayers Bain, G., 'The national minimum wage: Further reflections' (1999) 21(1/2) *Employee Relations* 15–25.)

NATIONAL MINIMUM WAGE ACT 1998 (as amended)

3. Exclusion of, and modifications for, certain classes of person

(1) This section applies to persons who have not attained the age of 26.

(1A) This section also applies to persons who have attained the age of 26 who are—

(a) within the first six months after the commencement of their employment with an employer by whom they have not been previously employed;

(b) participating in a scheme under which shelter is provided in return for work;

(c) participating in a scheme designed to provide training, work experience or temporary work;

(d) participating in a scheme to assist in the seeking or obtaining of work;

(e) undertaking a course of higher education requiring attendance for a period of work experience; or

(f) undertaking a course of further education requiring attendance for a period of work experience.

(2) The Secretary of State may by regulations make provision in relation to any of the persons to whom this section applies—

(a) preventing them being persons who qualify for the national minimum wage; or

(b) prescribing an hourly rate for the national minimum wage other than the single hourly rate for the time being prescribed under section 1(3) above.

(3) No provision shall be made under subsection (2) above which treats persons differently in relation to—

(a) different areas;

(b) different sectors of employment;

(c) undertakings of different sizes; or

(d) different occupations.

(4) If any description of persons who have attained the age of 26 is added by the regulations under section 4 below to the descriptions of persons to whom this section applies, no provision shall be made under subsection (2) above which treats persons of that description differently in relation to different ages over 26.

4. Power to add to the persons to whom section 3 applies

(1) The Secretary of State may by regulations amend section 3 above by adding descriptions of persons who have attained the age of 26 to the descriptions of persons to whom the section applies.

(2) No amendment shall be made under subsection (1) above which treats persons differently in relation to—

(a) different areas;

(b) different sectors of employment;

(c) undertakings of different sizes;
(d) different ages over 26; or
(e) different occupations.

NOTES

1. The Act provides for the establishment of a minimum basic hourly rate of pay for workers over the age of 26. Provision exists (in s. 3) for preventing those under 26 qualifying for the NMW at all, or for prescribing differentiated rates within that group according to age. Subsection (1A) was added to s. 3 by the National Minimum Wage Act 1998 (Amendment) Regulations 1999 (SI 1999/583). There is also power to extend those restrictions to people who are aged 26 or over; but this does not explain on what basis this can be done, or provide limitations on the power (s. 4). Both those sections do, however, make it clear that the Secretary of State may not, when setting lower rates, differentiate between different areas, sectors of employment, undertakings of different sizes or different occupations.

2. The provisions relating to the rate of the NMW are contained in Pt II of NMWR 1999, regs. 11–13 (as amended). The rates are currently (with effect from 1 October 2014) £6.50 per hour for those aged 21 and over (the adult rate) and £5.13 per hour for those aged 18–20 (the Development Rate). From 1 October 2004, a new NMW was introduced for 16- and 17-year-olds. This currently stands at £3.79 (with effect from 1 October 2014). There is a rate for apprentices aged 16–18 and those aged 19 or over in the first year of their apprenticeship. This currently stands at £2.73 (w.e.f. 1 October 2014). All other apprentices are entitled to the NMW for their age.

   From 1 October 2015:

   * the adult rate increases to £6.70 per hour;
   * the rate for 18- to 20-year-olds increases to £5.30 per hour;
   * the rate for 16- to 17-year-olds increases to £3.87 per hour;
   * the apprentice rate increases to £3.30 per hour;
   * the accommodation offset increases to £5.35.

   Before making the first regulations under s. 1(3) setting the initial rate, or under s. 1(4) fixing the 'pay reference period', the Secretary of State was required to refer a number of key matters to the Low Pay Commission for their consideration. These included the level of the single hourly rate; the method or methods for determining the hourly rate at which a person is to be treated as remunerated; and the question of possible exclusions of those under 26 (s. 5). Following receipt of the Low Pay Commission's recommendations (by the Prime Minister and the Employment Secretary), if the Secretary of State decided to make regulations differing from those recommendations (or adding to them) then a report was required to be laid before Parliament explaining the reasons for the decision.

   After the 'first' regulations were made (the NMWR 1999), which followed the procedures required for involving the Low Pay Commission and informing Parliament of the actions taken, the Secretary of State was thereafter no longer obliged to refer matters to the Low Pay Commission for its views before making revising regulations, for example when changing the minimum wage or related regulations setting out entitlements. Basically, he now has discretion as to whether or not to refer proposed changes; and he will also have a general power to refer 'such matters' as he 'thinks fit' to them for their consideration (s. 6). Having said that, the Government has chosen to adopt the reports of the Commission since the inception of the legislation.

3. In contrast with social security benefits, which are uprated at the start of each tax and benefits year by an uprating order, there is no requirement stipulating that there *must* be an annual uprating or even a 'review'. Nor is there any indexation procedure (as there is for awards and payments made under the ERA 1996).

4. As well as paying the required wage, employers are required to keep adequate records to show that the wage has been paid, and to produce such records on request (by workers, the enforcement agency, tribunals, and courts). In proceedings the onus is generally on the employer to show that the wage has been paid correctly. It is a criminal offence to refuse to pay the minimum wage, or to fail to keep proper records. There is no provision for agreements between an employer and workers to 'opt out' of the requirements.

5. The Low Pay Commission reported:

   > Based on revised ONS (Office for National Statistics) data, the latest estimate suggests that 1.3 million people were entitled to the higher wages as a result of the introduction of the minimum wage. Around 70 per cent of beneficiaries were women, and around two-thirds of

jobs affected were part-time. In a tight labour market wages have risen ahead of the minimum wage, the numbers set to benefit from the upratings in 2000 was significantly lower than the introduction of the minimum wage in April 1999. Our latest estimate of the initial impact of the minimum wage on the national wage bill is 0.35 per cent.

We were especially concerned about the possible negative employment effects of the minimum wage. Employment has continued to grow strongly since the introduction of the minimum wage, and there were no discernible adverse effects at the aggregate level. In particular, employment among groups that were particularly vulnerable—women, young people, part-time workers, most ethnic minority groups, and disabled people continued to increase. We realise that this did not, of course, tell us what employment would have been in the absence of a minimum wage; but our research showed that even after controlling for this and other factors the impact of the minimum wage was broadly neutral.' ('The National Minimum Wage: Making a difference', Third Report of the Low Pay Commission, vol. 1 (Cm. 5075), March 2001.)

In its 2014 report, the Low Pay Commission reviewed the impact of the NMW in the following way: 'The adult rate of the NMW has increased by around 75% since its introduction at £3.60 an hour in April 1999. This is greater than the increase in average earnings or prices over the same period. However, in recent years the real value of the NMW has been lower than the increase in both CPI [Consumer Price Index] and Retail Price Index (RPI) inflation' (*National Minimum Wage*, Low Pay Commission Report 2014, March 2014, Cm. 8816, para.7).

(a) Individuals qualifying for the minimum wage

As we have seen, s. 1(2) of the NMWA 1998 states that a person qualifies for the NMW if he or she is an individual who is a worker; is working, or ordinarily works, in the UK under his or her contract; and has ceased to be of compulsory school age. 'Worker' for the purposes of the 1998 Act is widely defined.

NATIONAL MINIMUM WAGE ACT 1998

54. Meaning of 'worker', 'employee' etc.

. . .

(3) In this Act 'worker' (except in the phrases 'agency worker' and 'home worker') means an individual who has entered into or works under (or, where the employment has ceased, worked under)—

    (a) a contract of employment; or

    (b) any other contract, whether express or implied and (if it is express) whether oral or in writing, whereby the individual undertakes to do or perform personally any work or services for another party to the contract whose status is not by virtue of the contract that of a client or customer of any profession or business undertaking carried on by the individual;

and any reference to a worker's contract shall be construed accordingly.

NOTES

1. This wide definition is intended as an anti-avoidance measure. It seeks to exclude only the genuinely self-employed from its ambit and makes it extremely difficult for any employer to restructure its working relationships in order to avoid paying the NMW and gaining an unfair competitive advantage in relation to market rivals.

2. However, the Court of Appeal gave the term a restrictive interpretation in *Edmunds v Lawson QC* [2000] IRLR 391. The applicant was a pupil in the defendant's chambers and was over the age of 26. Accordingly, she did not fall within reg. 12(2) which excludes workers under the age of 26 on the first 12 months of a contract of apprenticeship from the NMW. At first instance Sullivan J held that the applicant was entitled to the NMW on the basis that during the pupillage there was a contract of apprenticeship between the applicant and the barristers' chambers. On appeal, the Court of Appeal held that the pupillage arrangement between the applicant and the chambers had the essential characteristics of an intention to create legal relations and, accordingly, there was a legally binding contract between the applicant and the chambers. The Court of Appeal held, however, allowing the appeal, that the contract was not a contract of apprenticeship and did not fall within the definition of a contract of employment within s. 54(3) of the NMWA 1998. A contract of apprenticeship contains mutual covenants under which the master undertakes to educate and train the apprentice or pupil in the practical or other skills needed to practise a skilled trade or learned profession, and the apprentice or pupil binds himself to service and

work for the master and to comply with all reasonable directions. In contrast, according to the Court of Appeal, there is no duty on a pupil barrister to do anything not conducive to the pupil's own training and development. In relation to s. 54(3)(b) (which relates to any other contract whereby the individual undertakes to do or perform any work or services for another party) the Court of Appeal held that the pupil did not undertake to perform work or services for members of the chambers and in the event that the pupil did any work for which she was paid, the person for whom the work was done was the pupil's professional client. Accordingly, the pupil was not entitled to the benefit of the NMW.

3. The definition of 'worker' in the 1998 Act is effectively widened to include agency workers (s. 34) and home workers (s. 35).

NATIONAL MINIMUM WAGE ACT 1998

SPECIAL CLASSES OF PERSONS

34. Agency workers who are not otherwise 'workers'

(1) This section applies in any case where an individual ('the agency worker')—

  (a) is supplied by a person ('the agent') to do work for another ('the principal') under a contract or other arrangements made between the agent and the principal; but

  (b) is not, as respects that work, a worker, because of the absence of a worker's contract between the individual and the agent or the principal; and

  (c) is not a party to the contract under which he undertakes to do the work for another party to the contract whose status is, by virtue of the contract, that of a client or customer of any profession or business undertaking carried on by the individual.

(2) In a case where this section applies, the other provisions of this Act shall have effect as if there were a worker's contract for the doing of the work by the agency worker made between the agency worker and—

  (a) whichever of the agent and the principal is responsible for paying the agency worker in respect of the work; or

  (b) if neither the agent nor the principal is responsible, whichever of them pays the agency worker in respect of the work.

35. HOME WORKERS WHO ARE NOT OTHERWISE 'WORKERS'

(1) In determining for the purposes of this Act whether a home worker is or is not a worker, section 54(3)(b) . . . shall have effect as if for the word 'personally' were substituted '(whether personally or otherwise)'.

(2) In this section 'home worker' means an individual who contracts with a person, for the purposes of that person's business, for the execution of work to be done in a place not under the control or management of that person.

NOTES

1. By virtue of s. 35(1), home workers are covered even where they sub-contract work to family or friends. The minimum wage also applies to workers from outside the UK working in the UK (however long their stay is). British workers who normally work in the UK, and who are temporarily working abroad, are also subject to the minimum wage requirement.

   It may be noted that the Secretary of State may, by regulations made under s. 41, apply the Act, with or without modifications, to any *other* individuals of a prescribed description who would not otherwise be classed as a 'worker'. By s. 42, the Act can also be applied to 'offshore employment'. In the latter case, an Order in Council made under s. 42 can apply the Act (or some of it) to individuals who are not necessarily British subjects, and to bodies corporate whether or not they are incorporated under UK law. In doing so, the Order could confer jurisdiction on courts or tribunals outside the UK.

2. Initially, the NMW did not extend to 16- and 17-year-olds. However, in March 2004 the Low Pay Commission recommended that a minimum wage for 16- and 17-year-olds of £3.00 should be introduced in October 2004 and the Government accepted the recommendation (see *The National Minimum Wage: Protecting young workers*, Low Pay Commission's Report (London: The Stationery Office, March 2004)). The rate currently stands at £3.79 (w.e.f. 1 October 2014). The Chairman of the Low Pay Commission, Adair Turner, said:

   > We have concluded that a minimum wage for 16–17 year olds will tackle the worst cases of jobs which pay very low wages and provide minimal training, without encouraging young people

out of education and training or pricing them out of the jobs market. (Low Pay Commission Press Release, 15 March 2004)

The NMW was extended to apprentices with effect from 1 October 2010. The apprentices' rate, for apprentices aged 16 to 18 or those aged 19 or over and in the first year of their apprenticeship currently stands at £2.73 (w.e.f. 1 October 2014). Trainees on government-funded training schemes are outside the minimum wage scheme unless they are employed by the employer. In this case they will normally have to be aged 18 and over, and paid their wages by the employer, to qualify. The following groups are also excluded:

(a) *share fishermen* (including fishing vessels' master and crew who are remunerated in respect of that employment only by a share in the profits or gross earnings of the vessel) (s. 43);

(b) certain *voluntary workers*, including those employed by charities, voluntary organisations, associated fund-raising bodies or statutory bodies, who in respect of their employment do not receive, and are not entitled to receive, monetary payments of any description or payments for expenses, and have no benefits in kind other than for subsistence or accommodation which is 'reasonable in the circumstances of the employment' (s. 44, and the detailed provisions which amplify these points in s. 44(2)–(4));

(c) *prisoners* (including those detained or on temporary release) in respect of work done in pursuance of prison rules (s. 45).

Also excluded from the minimum wage requirements are friends and neighbours working under informal arrangements, and people living and working within the family (au pairs, nannies, companions, etc.). Nor do they apply to family members who live at home and work in the family business (NMWR 1999, reg. 2(2)).

3. There are provisions in the Act for 'harmonising' it with requirements in the Agricultural Wages Act 1948 (and equivalent legislation in Scotland and Northern Ireland) and the other legislation on remuneration which will still apply (with modifications) to agricultural workers. Accordingly, wages set by the Agricultural Wages Boards can continue to apply to such workers. There are mechanisms for ensuring that wage minima set by that legislation are consistent with the Act (and for amending the agricultural workers legislation): see s. 47 of and Sch. 2 to the 1998 Act. As well as ensuring that agricultural workers get the NMW (and in some cases more than the minimum wage) there is also provision in s. 46 for ensuring that underpaying employers are not prosecuted twice. It is also made clear (by s. 46(2)) that workers cannot recover unpaid amounts under both sets of legislation in respect of the same work.

4. To deal with potential problems in determining who is a worker's immediate 'employer', the Act says in s. 48 that where the immediate employer of a worker is himself in the employment of some other person, and the worker is employed on the premises of that other person, that other 'person' will be 'deemed for the purposes of this Act to be the employer of the worker jointly with the immediate employer'. In practical terms this means that if the immediate employer defaulted in meeting the requirements to pay the minimum wage, then the other employer could be responsible in default.

(b) Operation of the wage provisions

Section 1(3) of the NMWA 1998 requires the national minimum wage to be expressed as a single hourly rate. However, the variety and complexity of payment systems necessitated regulatory guidance in order to determine whether any particular worker is being paid at the NMW rate. Three questions must be answered: the period over which a worker's pay is calculated (the 'pay reference period'); the payments which count for calculating a worker's pay; and the hours during which the worker is deemed to be working for the purposes of the NMW.

The pay reference period A worker does not have to be paid the NMW for each and every hour worked, but he or she must be paid the NMW *on average* in each 'pay reference period' (PRP). This is defined as a calendar month or, where the worker is paid by reference to a shorter period, that period (NMWR 1999, reg. 10(1)).

Payments made by an employer to a worker in any PRP include:

(a) all payments received by the worker in that period (reg. 30(a));

(b) any payments earned by the worker in that period but not received by him or her until the following PRP (reg. 30(b));

(c) if the worker does not get paid until he or she submits a completed timesheet or other similar record to the employer, and he or she submits that less than four working days before the end of the PRP following the one in which the work was done, payments made in either the PRP in which the completed record was submitted or the one after that.

Where payments are 'transferred' from the PRP in which they were received to the period when they were earned, they cannot also be allocated to the former period. In other words, double-counting is not permitted.

What is 'pay' for minimum wage purposes? In determining whether the NMW is being complied with, it is necessary to exclude certain items from gross pay and to include others. Clearly, the inclusion of items that should be excluded is likely to be a major cause of 'underpayment' for minimum wage purposes. Particular care will therefore be needed with this aspect of the scheme.

NMW pay is gross pay less any items that should be excluded. The following do *not* count towards NMW pay:

- any loans or advances of wages made to workers (reg. 8(a));
- pension payments, lump sums paid at retirement, and compensation for losing a job (reg. 8(b));
- court or tribunal awards, or payments to settle actual or potential court or tribunal proceedings, other than payment of an amount due under the workers' contract (reg. 8(c));
- redundancy payments (reg. 8(d));
- awards under suggestion schemes (reg. 8(e));
- payments during absences from work (such as sick pay, holiday pay, maternity pay and guarantee payments) and payments for rest breaks or during industrial action (reg. 31(1)(b));
- the actual or notional monetary value of all benefits in kind, whether or not they are taxable, other than living accommodation (reg. 9(a)), for which there is currently a maximum permitted off-set of £5.08 per day (£5.35 with effect from 1 October 2015);
- the monetary value of vouchers, stamps, or similar documents that are exchangeable for money, goods, and/or services (reg. 9(b));
- premium payments for overtime and shift working to the extent that they exceed the lowest hourly rate payable for that work (reg. 31(1)(c)(i));
- premium payments for output work so far as they exceed the rate normally applicable to that work (reg. 31(1)(c)(ii));
- allowances attributable to a particular aspect of a worker's working arrangements or to his or her working or personal circumstances that are not consolidated into his or her basic pay, e.g. unsocial hours payments, on-call or standby payments, payments for performing additional duties, payments for working in unpleasant or dangerous conditions or in a particular area (e.g. London weighting), and being available for work when no work is provided) (regs. 2(1) and 31(1)(d));
- service charges, tips, gratuities, or cover charges whether paid directly in cash to the worker or through the payroll (reg. 31(1)(e), as amended by the National Minimum Wage Regulations 1999 (Amendment) Regulations 2009, reg. 31(1)(e) (SI 2009/1902));
- deductions made by the employer from the worker's pay, or payments made by the worker to the employer, in respect of the worker's expenditure in connection

with his or her job (regs. 32(1)(a) and 34(1)(a)), e.g. cost of a uniform, tools, or other equipment;

- payments made by a worker to a third party on account of such expenditure, or refunds of such payments made by the employer (regs. 34(1)(b) and 31(1)(f)), e.g. travelling expenses, overnight accommodation;

- deductions made by the employer from the worker's pay, or payments made by the worker to the employer, for the employer's 'own use and benefit' (regs. 32(1)(b) and 34(1)(c)) with the exception of those made: (i) in respect of the worker's conduct or any other event for which he or she, either alone or with other workers, is contractually liable (e.g. disciplinary deductions or fines); (ii) to repay a loan or an advance of wages made to the worker; (iii) to recover or refund an accidental overpayment of wages made to the worker; or (iv) in respect of a worker's purchase of shares (regs. 33 and 35(a)–(d)).

Hours: calculating the hours for which the national minimum wage must be paid Broadly, the rules of the scheme may depend on the type of work being done. The four main types of working dealt with are time working, salaried hours working, 'output' work, and unmeasured work:

(a) Timeworking For the purposes of the scheme this refers to systems where a worker is paid according to the number of hours he or she is at work, even if this may vary. The majority of workers in the UK work under this type of arrangement. In addition, for the purposes of the scheme, people paid on piecework systems (i.e. according to how much they produce) are treated as timeworkers to the extent that they work within identifiable hours of work. For example, a worker who is paid according to the number of toys he or she produces, but who works a six-hour day, will need to be paid at a level of at least the NMW for each hour he or she works in his or her pay period.

A 'timeworker' for the scheme's purposes excludes those paid an annual salary, but includes someone who works to agreed hours or time periods. Those undertaking piecework within set hours are also treated in accordance with timeworking rules.

The times when the worker is expected to be working, and is at the workplace and working, must be within the NMW calculation. The times spent during meal or rest breaks are, however, excluded (reg. 15(7)). If the worker is at work, and *available* for work, that time must be included, even if work is not provided (reg. 15(1); see *British Nursing Association* v *IRC* [2003] ICR 19, CA; *Scottbridge Construction Ltd* v *Wright* [2003] IRLR 21, CS). Being 'on call' at home does not count, however.

Although travel time between home and work is not to be included for NMW purposes, travel in connection with the worker's job *is* included. This includes travel between work assignments, and any time in which travel during a work period and for work purposes is required (reg. 15(2)(a)). This extends to travel for training purposes (other than travel from home to a training centre). Absences from work, and pay during those absences, are ignored. The time spent on holidays, maternity leave, and sick leave does not count for NMW purposes. Time during which a worker is engaged in industrial action does not count as time when the NMW is payable, and any pay actually received during such periods is disregarded when calculating minimum wage payments (reg. 15(6)).

(b) Salaried workers This includes people who are paid an annual salary; paid under their contract of employment for a set number of hours, or minimum hours each year; or paid for set periods referable to a year (e.g. for 52 weeks, at 52 equal instalments). It extends to people whose work may vary, either in terms of pay following increases, or because of additional payments over and above their basic pay. The basic rules are similar to those described for timeworkers. The key difference is that most time during

the salary period is counted, so that rest periods and other periods when the person is not working are not taken away from the time that counts for pay purposes. For some workers this can, of course, make a significant difference for NMW purposes. That said, there may be periods when under the contract pay is not paid, or it is paid at reduced amounts, e.g. during a period of sickness or recovery from injury. Such periods must be taken away from the total hourage for which the NMW is payable in the PRP. Unpaid leave, industrial action and other periods in which pay does not have to continue under the contract do not count towards the time when the NMW is payable.

It is, of course, helpful if the basic hours which the worker is expected to work have been agreed (and this can be done on an annualised basis, or by reference to a weekly or monthly norm). This will facilitate calculation of the salaried hours worked in the worker's PRP. Once it is clear what the hours are, and the salary is known, calculation of an hourly rate is usually straightforward.

(c) 'Output' work Output work can be defined for the purposes of the scheme as work which is remunerated according to work performance, whether measured by reference to 'pieces' produced, business transacted, work results achieved, etc. As discussed earlier, piecework is one form of output work. If such work is done within set hours then it comes within the time working arrangements already explained. If it is not, then there are two options available under the scheme. The worker's hours can be assessed according to either:

(i) a 'fair estimate agreement'; or

(ii) paying on the basis of the hours *actually worked*.

Fair estimate agreements must be agreed between the employer and the worker concerned before the PRP commences. Such an agreement must be in writing and identify the hours likely to be worked during the PRP. In addition, it must be fair to the extent that the number of hours mutually agreed must be at least four-fifths of the number of hours which an average worker would take to do the same job and in the same working conditions (reg. 25(2)). The worker must record the actual hours of output work undertaken in the PRP, and then give that record to the employer to form part of the employer's records. Finally, there must be a contract giving the worker the right to be paid an agreed rate for each 'piece', sale, etc. in the PRP. A single agreement can be used for more than just the initial PRP as long as the worker undertakes the same work in each of the later periods. In the absence of a valid fair estimate agreement the worker must be paid at or above the NMW for each hour actually worked. In February 2003, the Government entered into a consultation with employers and trade unions on replacing fair estimate agreements with a system of fair piece rates. Responses from all sides supported a move to fair piece rates and the removal of the 'four-fifths' rule which was not working well. From October 2004, the Government proposed that employers would have to pay their workers the minimum wage for every hour they work or a fair piece rate set at 100% of the minimum wage. The rate increased to 120% of the minimum wage in April 2005, at which point most home workers received the minimum wage (*Draft Guidance on Proposals to Introduce Fair Piece Rate for Output Workers, including Homeworkers* (DTI: December 2003)).

(d) 'Unmeasured' work This is work which is not within one of the types already discussed, and in which employment or tasks are undertaken but there are no agreed hours or times within which work is completed. It would apply, for example, in situations in which staff are 'on call' or work 'when required'. To calculate the hours worked, and at which the NMW is payable, there are two options available:

(i) the worker and employer agree a 'daily average agreement' which records the average hours that the worker is likely to be working on jobs, tasks, etc.;

(ii) the employer pays the hours actually worked at or above the NMW.

If the first method is adopted, daily average hours must be a realistic average in terms of the work that is likely (the onus of showing this being on the employer for enforcement purposes). As with fair estimate arrangements (see point (c)), a single agreement can be used for later pay reference periods if there is no change in the average number of hours.

Walton v Independent Living Organisation Ltd
[2003] IRLR 469, Court of Appeal

Julie Walton, a live-in carer who was required to be in the client's home for a continuous period of 72 hours per week, was held not to be entitled to be paid the NMW for all the hours she was present in the client's home, but only in respect of the time when she was carrying out her duties.

She was assigned to a client with epilepsy who had fits on a regular basis but could attend to her own personal needs and required a minimum of supervision. Ms Walton was responsible for her washing, ironing, shopping, preparation of meals, and medication. When not performing services for the client, she could do what she wanted. However, she was required to remain on the premises 24 hours a day in case the client needed assistance, which she occasionally did, sometimes during the night.

In August 1999, in connection with a visit from the National Minimum Wage Compliance Team, assessment was made of the time Ms Walton required for each of the tasks that she carried out for the client. At the end of the exercise, she signed a form which recorded that on average it took 6 hours 50 minutes each day to carry out the required tasks.

Ms Walton made an application to an ET claiming that she was not being paid the NMW (which was then £3.60 per hour). She claimed that the relevant legislation required her hourly rate to be ascertained by dividing her daily rate of pay of £31.40 by 24, on the basis that her hours of work consisted of all the time she was required to be at the client's home and to be mentally alert to her needs. The employers argued that the relevant hours were the 6 hours 50 minutes that had been agreed as the time taken to perform the required tasks for the client and, on that basis, her wage exceeded the national minimum.

The issue before the tribunal was whether for the purposes of the NMWR, Ms Walton was employed on 'time work' or whether she carried out 'unmeasured work'.

The ET concluded that Ms Walton was not paid by reference to the time for which she worked and that she therefore carried out 'unmeasured work', not 'time work'. The tribunal went on to find that there was a written agreement in terms of reg. 28(1) and that the hours specified in that agreement was a realistic assessment of the time taken to carry out the required duties. Accordingly, the tribunal concluded that the regulations required that her hourly rate should be ascertained by dividing her daily rate of £31.40 by the agreed 6 hours 50 minutes, giving a wage of £4.60 per hour. Since that exceeded the then NMW of £3.60 per hour, the tribunal dismissed Ms Walton's claim. Both the EAT and the Court of Appeal dismissed Ms Walton's appeal.

LADY JUSTICE ARDEN: As I see it, the appellants' approach in this case confuses time as a convenient unit for the quantification of a payment of remuneration with time as the yardstick by reference to which the rate of pay is determined. There is a distinction between paying remuneration by reference to time periods where time is used as a unit of account and paying remuneration at a rate determined by the amount of time spent on the work (or deemed work...)

...

This case is distinguishable on its facts from *British Nursing Association* v *IRC* [2002] IRLR 480 and *Scottbridge Construction Ltd* v *Wright* [2003] IRLR 21. In those cases, the rate of pay was determined by applying the agreed hourly rate only to the number of hours worked. Remuneration was paid solely by reference to time.

In the definition of 'unmeasured work' (reg. 6), the 1999 Regulations contemplate that the number of hours may not be specified. Regulation 27 enables the number of hours to be ascertained for minimum wage purposes.

But this regulation is subject to reg. 28, which permits arrangements to be made to predetermine the 'average daily number of hours the worker is likely to spend in carrying out the duties required of him under his contract'.

There is, as we see it, a clear distinction in the 1999 Regulations between 'working' and being 'available for work'; see, for example, regs. 3 and 15. However, that antithesis is not drawn in the context of unmeasured work.

The tribunal's finding was that, when not performing her specified tasks, Miss Walton was not required to give Miss Jones her full attention (tribunal's extended reasons, paragraph 12). In view of this finding, in my judgment it cannot be said that Miss Walton was continuously performing her contractual duties for 24 hours each day for the purposes of reg. 28. Not every worker who 'only stands and waits' carries out contractual duties: it is a question of fact.

■ QUESTION

If the entire social care workforce were entitled to the NMW for the whole time that they were on call, there would be some significant economic implications for the public sector. How much are policy considerations at work here?

(c) Record-keeping, minimum wage 'statements', and enforcement

Record-keeping Employers are required by ss. 9–12 of the NMWA 1998 to keep and preserve records in accordance with the regulations made under s. 9. As well as facilitating enforcement, these records may, of course, be important in the event of proceedings in tribunals and the courts.

NATIONAL MINIMUM WAGE ACT 1998

10. Worker's right of access to records

(1) A worker may, in accordance with the following provisions of this section—
  (a) require his employer to produce any relevant records; and
  (b) inspect and examine those records and copy any part of them.
(2) The rights conferred by subsection (1) above are exercisable only if the worker believes on reasonable grounds that he is or may be being, or has or may have been, remunerated for any pay reference period by his employer at a rate which is less than the national minimum wage.

NOTES
1. There is no formal requirement on employers to specify NMW entitlements on pay slips. But as the Government has advised, it is prudent for employers to try to ensure that workers know how their pay has been calculated, and how the NMW scheme operates in relation to their pay. This will assist in avoiding complaints and time spent on answering inquiries from employees who think their pay may be incorrect.
2. The inspection must be for the *purpose* of establishing that the worker has been underpaid in that way (s. 10(3)). In other words, inspections cannot be carried out for any *other* or *wider* purposes. An employer who is given a 'production notice' by the worker (which must request production and identify the period the worker is concerned about) could at that stage object, particularly if he thinks that these requirements are *not* satisfied. There is nothing in the legislation to that effect, however, so an employer would need to be cautious in rejecting requests for access, and be sure that he has good grounds for objection. An employer's right to object seems to be implicit given that s. 11 sets up an appeal mechanism by which a complaint can be made to an ET that there has been a failure to produce records or allow the worker to exercise the other rights associated with a production notice (such as the right to be 'accompanied by such other person as the worker may think fit': s. 10(4)(b)).
   Following receipt of a production notice, the employer is required:
   (a) to give the worker reasonable notice of the place and time at which the relevant records will be produced (namely the worker's place of work, or other place at which it is reasonable for him to attend, or which may be agreed);
   (b) to produce the records before the end of 14 days following the date of receipt of the notice (or a later time if this is agreed during that 14-day period).

3. Complaints to the tribunal that the employer has failed to produce some or all of the records required, or otherwise failed to allow the rights referred to above to be exercised, can be made under s. 11(1). If the tribunal finds the complaint to be well-founded it shall:
   (a) make a declaration to that effect;
   (b) make an award that the employer pay to the worker a sum equal to 80 times the hourly amount of the NMW in force when the award is made.
   Minimum wage statements Regulations may make provision for the details of the minimum wage statement which is to be given to workers 'at or before the time at which any payment of remuneration is made to the worker'. Basically this would be an extension of existing requirements as to itemised pay statements; and for this purpose the jurisdiction of tribunals to deal with references under the ERA 1996, ss. 11–12 would be extended. It would enable tribunals to hear complaints and thereupon determine what workers should be receiving, and what should be included in pay statements regarding entitlements under the 1998 Act.

It is interesting to note that no regulations have been made under NMWA, s. 12 as a result of consultations on the draft regulations. A number of employer respondents saw the costs involved in providing such a statement as disproportionate given the numbers involved. Simpson has observed:

> Workers who are employees still will have the right to an itemised pay statement under section 8 of the Employment Rights Act 1996. If they are aware of the NMW rate applicable to them, and the government said that it intended to spend some £2 million on publicising the introduction of the NMW, they may be able to calculate whether or not they are being paid less than their NMW entitlement. Many workers who do not have employee status will have nothing to go on. The desire to be seen to respond to pressure from business not to impose what employers perceive to be unacceptable and unnecessary cost would appear to have blinded the government to what was earlier seen to be the desirability if not the necessity of putting in place a range of linked enforcement mechanisms. [Simpson, R., 'Implementing the National Minimum Wage: The 1999 Regulations' (1999) 28 ILJ 171, at p. 180.]

Enforcement Officers can be appointed for the purposes of monitoring the operation of the Act—these are currently drawn from HM Revenue & Customs (HMRC).

Sections 17–19E of the 1998 Act contain a variety of important enforcement measures. These measures have been strengthened as a result of changes made by the Employment Act 2008, subsequent regulations and the Small Business, Enterprise and Employment Act 2015. The revised enforcement powers are as follows:

- *Penalty where employers fail to pay the minimum wage* If HMRC find that there has been an underpayment of the NMW in an investigation that is ongoing from 6 April 2009, they may issue a notice of underpayment requiring the employer to repay arrears to the workers and to pay a financial penalty to the Secretary of State. Employers are able to appeal against the notice of underpayment to the ET (an industrial tribunal in Northern Ireland).

- The penalty will only be charged in respect of underpayments of the NMW occurring in pay reference periods starting on or after 6 April 2009 (i.e. there will be no penalty in respect of underpayments occurring before this date).

- Prior to 7 March 2014, the penalty was set at 50% of the total underpayment (for periods starting on or after 6 April 2009) but there was a minimum penalty of £100 and a maximum penalty of £5,000. But this was changed by the National Minimum Wage (Variation of Financial Penalty) Regulations 2014 (SI 2014/547). As a result, with effect from 7 March 2014, the maximum penalty for those who flout the NMW has been 100% of the total underpayment, subject to a maximum of £20,000. The maximum penalty currently applies per notice, irrespective of the number of underpaid workers. This position will change as a result of the Small Business, Enterprise and Employment Act 2015. The Act amends s. 19A of the NMWA so that the financial penalty in the notice of underpayment would be set at 100% of the arrears of *each* worker to whom the notice relates, subject to a maximum of £20,000 per worker (new s. 19A(5) NMWA 1998). These amendments only apply to pay reference periods commencing on or after the date on which the new provisions come into force. Employers who comply fully with the notice of underpayment within 14 days of service will receive a discount of 50% on the penalty (see the NMWA 1998, s. 19A(10)).

- *A new method of calculating NMW arrears* Workers who are owed arrears of the NMW for pay reference periods starting on or after 6 April 2009 are entitled to have their arrears repaid at current rates where these are higher than the rate or rates that applied when the arrears arose. The increase to current NMW rates takes account of the length of time that the arrears have been outstanding (i.e. it compensates workers who have had to wait for their arrears).

  The arrears must be calculated according to a formula which is set out in the Act and this change applies retrospectively (i.e. from 6 April 2009, workers will be entitled to have their arrears repaid at current rates for all periods that they have been underpaid, including periods prior to 6 April 2009). The formula only applies if the current rate is higher than the rate or rates that applied at the time the worker was underpaid (see the NMWA 1998, s. 17).

- *New powers of inspection for HMRC compliance officers* Compliance officers are now able to remove NMW records from an employer's premises for photocopying. The compliance officer will be entitled to remove complete records but must return them within a reasonable period.

- *New criminal regime for NMW offences* The 2008 Act gives HMRC the power to use the search and seize powers in the Police and Criminal Evidence Act 1984 when investigating criminal offences under the NMWA 1998.

  The Act also makes changes to the way that criminal offences under the NMWA 1998 are investigated and enforced: in particular, with effect from 6 April 2009, the most serious cases will be triable in the Crown Court. This means that employers who deliberately fail to pay the minimum wage may face more stringent penalties (see the NMWA 1998, s. 31).

(d) Non-compliance: tribunal and civil proceedings

Having identified what the worker's legal entitlement is, the Act provides several ways in which it may be *secured*. Section 18 makes it clear that for the purposes of s. 17 the worker and the employer will be regarded as having that relationship for the purposes of the application of Pt II of the ERA 1996. This contains the 'protection of wages' provisions which enable workers to make complaints to an ET in respect of unauthorised 'deductions'. To facilitate proceedings, either before a tribunal under Pt II or a court in a claim in contract, in relation to any 'additional remuneration' due, s. 18 *deems* a worker to have a contract in relation to that amount. This may, of course, not be necessary in many cases. But in cases where this might prove to be a procedural obstacle, s. 18 supplies the necessary contractual relationship.

In its 2014 report, the Low Pay Commission had the following observations to make on compliance and operation of the NMW:

> Over the past year there has been progress in improving the compliance and enforcement regime. This includes the revision of the naming scheme, which should lead to the public naming of more employers who flout the requirement to pay the minimum wage, and an increase in the penalties where employers failed to pay at least the NMW. We will continue to monitor the operation of these arrangements.
>
> Other areas of the compliance and enforcement framework still require improvement, namely the depth of official guidance, awareness of the NMW among employers and workers, and a need to increase the use of prosecutions for the most serious infringers. The Government has indicated what further information was required to improve the NMW guidance and is undertaking to review its prosecutions policy. It remains important to maintain sufficient resource for HMRC and BIS to support and deliver the compliance systems. (*National Minimum Wage*, Low Pay Commission Report 2014, March 2014, Cm. 8816, paras. 16, 17.)

Non-compliance notices and penalties Section 19 sets out a system for dealing with non-compliance with enforcement notices. This can involve either a complaint under s. 23(1)(a) of the ERA 1996 (deductions from wages in contravention of s. 13 of the 1996 Act) by an officer on behalf of the worker to an ET, or commencement of other civil proceedings for recovery of sums due under s. 17, based on a claim in contract.

(e) Unfair dismissal and right not to suffer 'detriment'

Linked to the enforcement measures described, the NMWA 1998 gives workers several important rights in relation to the minimum wage.

NATIONAL MINIMUM WAGE ACT 1998

23. The right not to suffer detriment

(1) A worker has the right not to be subjected to any detriment by any act, or any deliberate failure to act, by his employer, done on the ground that—

(a) any action was taken, or was proposed to be taken, by or on behalf of the worker with a view to enforcing, or otherwise securing the benefit of, a right of the worker's to which this section applies; or

(b) the employer was prosecuted for an offence under section 31...as a result of action taken by or on behalf of the worker for the purpose of enforcing, or otherwise securing the benefit of, a right of the worker's to which this section applies; or

(c) the worker qualifies, or will or might qualify, for the national minimum wage or for a particular rate of national minimum wage.

NOTES

1. Section 23(2) makes it clear that it is immaterial for the purposes of s. 23(1)(a) or (b) whether or not the worker actually *has* the right concerned, or whether it has been infringed or not. It will, however, be necessary to show that the claim to the right and, if applicable, the claim that it has been infringed are made in good faith. The section applies to rights to bring complaints before the tribunals, and rights to additional remuneration.

2. Complaints may be made to an ET by a worker that he has been subjected to a detriment in contravention of s. 23. Limits are placed on the compensation that may be made; details are as set out in s. 24(3)–(5).

3. A new s. 104A is inserted in the ERA 1996 providing for dismissal to be treated as unfair if it was for any of the reasons specified in that section. The grounds mirror the provisions referred to earlier in relation to detrimental action.

4. The National Minimum Wage Regulations 2015 (SI 2015/621) consolidate the existing 28 separate statutory instruments dealing with the NMW. The regulations came into force on 6 April 2015.

(iv) Working Time Regulations 1998

The statutory implied right

4. Maximum weekly working time

(1) Unless his employer has first obtained the worker's agreement in writing to perform such work, a worker's working time, including overtime, in any reference period which is applicable in his case shall not exceed an average of 48 hours for each seven days.

NOTE: The Working Time Regulations 1998 (SI 1998/1833) (WTR) implement the Working Time Directive (93/104) (WTD). However, the 1998 Regulations have since been amended by the Working Time Regulations 1999 (SI 1999/3372) which are intended to 'relieve some of the administrative burdens imposed on employers'. This has resulted in the record-keeping requirements being reduced. The main purpose of the regulations is to prevent people working excessively long hours without adequate rest periods. The regulations are enforced by the Health and Safety Executive. However, many of the provisions can be contracted out of by written agreement.

The UK Government originally challenged the adoption of this directive as a health and safety measure on the basis of Article 118a (now 153). In the UK's view, the WTD was not a measure the essential purpose of which was to put in place minimum health and safety requirements. As a result, it should not have been adopted under Article 118a (now 153), which required a qualified majority but on the basis of a unanimous vote within the Council. (See *United Kingdom of Great Britain and Northern Ireland* v *Council of the European Union* [1997] IRLR 30.) The European Court of Justice (ECJ) concluded that the directive had been adopted correctly as a health and safety measure on the basis of Article 118a (now 153) and that, as a result, the qualified majority procedure applied. The impact of this decision not only resulted in the WTR 1998 but also provided a foundation for claims for damages from private sector workers who suffered a loss as a result of the failure to transpose the directive into UK law (as per *Francovich* v *Italian Republic* [1992] IRLR 84). However, it should be noted that the directive does not have direct effect and therefore could not be relied on by an individual employee in respect of claims before the 1992 Regulations—*Gibson* v *East Riding of Yorkshire Council* [2002] IRLR 598.

(a) Who is covered?

WORKING TIME REGULATIONS 1998

2(1) In these Regulations—

...

'worker' means an individual who has entered into or works under (or, where the employment has ceased, worked under)—

    (a) a contract of employment; *or*

    (b) any other contract, whether express or implied and (if it is express) whether oral or in writing, whereby the individual undertakes to do or perform personally any work or services for another party to the contract whose status is not by virtue of the contract that of a client or customer of any profession or business undertaking carried on by the individual;

and any reference to a worker's contract shall be construed accordingly...

NOTE: The key elements of the regulations are as follows:

(a) *48-hour week* This is to be averaged over a 17-week period; records must be kept for each employee. In *Barber* v *RJB Mining (UK) Ltd* [1999] IRLR 308, the High Court held that reg. 4(1) imposed a contractual obligation on an employer not to require an employee to work more than an average 48 hours per week during the reference period. All contracts of employment should be read so as to provide that an employee should work no more than the permitted number of hours. As reg. 4(1) imposes the contractual obligation, the civil courts have jurisdiction to consider such cases. Employees may therefore seek a declaration of rights and/or an injunction barring the employer from requiring them to work additional hours.

For an evaluation of the full potential of the *Barber* case on health and safety law, see Edwards, A., '*Barber* v *RJB Mining* in the wider context of health and safety legislation' (2000) 29 ILJ 280.

(b) *Daily rest breaks* Every worker is entitled to a break of at least 11 consecutive hours between finishing work one day and starting work the next day.

(c) *Weekly rest periods* Every worker is entitled to an uninterrupted weekly rest period of not less than 24 hours in each seven-day period, in addition to the 11-hour daily rest entitlement. This rest period may be averaged over seven or 14 days.

(d) *Rest breaks* Where the daily working time exceeds six hours, workers are entitled to a rest break away from the work station. This break must be not less than 20 minutes. The Advocate General has advised that the DTI guidance is misleading in that it advises that employers must make sure that workers can take their rest but does not require the employer to ensure that they do. The responsibility on the employer is to make sure that rest periods are observed (2006) C-484/04.

(e) *Monotonous work* Where work is monotonous or the work rate predetermined, the employer is required to provide the worker with adequate rest breaks where there is a health and safety risk to the worker.

(f) *Night work* There are special provisions for night workers. 'Night worker' is defined as anyone who works at least three hours of their working time during night-time as a normal course, or anyone who is likely, during night-time, to work a certain proportion of their working time as defined by a collective or workforce agreement. In *R* v *Attorney-General for Northern Ireland, ex p. Burns* [1999] IRLR 315, the Northern Ireland Court of Appeal held that a 'normal course' simply means that night work should be a regular feature of employment. A worker who spent one week in three of a rotating shift, working at least three hours during the night, was a night worker for the purposes of the directive. As the case was brought before the WTD had been transposed into UK law, it was also concluded that the Member State would be liable for an injury sustained by an individual who suffered loss and damage in consequence of the failure to transpose (see also *Dillen Kofer* v *Federal Republic of Germany* [1997] IRLR 60). The normal working hours for night workers shall not exceed an average of eight in each 24-hour period (averaged over a 17-week period). Where the work involves special hazards, the normal working hours must not exceed eight in any particular 24-hour period with no averaging out. Night-time is defined as a period of not less than seven hours, including the period between midnight and 5.00 a.m. and, by default, 11.00 p.m. to 6.00 a.m. Before workers are assigned to night work, they must be given the opportunity of a free health assessment, which must then be carried out at appropriate regular intervals.

(g) *Collective or workforce agreements* Provisions relating to rest breaks and the length of night work may be modified or excluded either by a collective agreement or by a workforce agreement. However, an equivalent period of rest should be allowed wherever possible (WTR 1998, regs. 23(a), 24). Such agreements may also extend the reference period for averaging the 48-hour week from 17 weeks up to a maximum of 52 weeks (WTR 1998, reg. 23(b)).

(h) *Annual leave*

    (i)   Article 7 of the WTD guarantees that every worker is entitled to paid annual leave of at least four weeks and this right is transposed into UK law by the WTR 1998, reg. 13. When the Regulations were first introduced, the four-week entitlement was *not* in addition to bank holidays and so an employer could choose to count them towards the entitlement. Following a lengthy trade union campaign, the Government increased the leave entitlement to 5.6 weeks (28 days) with effect from April 2009 (see Working Time (Amendment) Regulations 2007 and WTR 1998, reg.13(A)). In *Gibson* v *East Riding of Yorkshire Council* [1999] IRLR 359, the EAT held that Article 7 had direct effect and, as a result, an employee of an 'emanation of the State' was able to take direct action against his employer. However, this was subsequently reversed by the Court of Appeal ([2000] IRLR 598).

    (ii)   In the UK, the right of workers to paid annual leave is given effect by reg. 13 of the WTR 1998. However, under reg. 13(7), entitlement to such leave was made conditional upon the worker having been continuously employed for 13 weeks by the same employer. The 13-week condition on the entitlement in reg. 13 was challenged in *R* v *Secretary of State for Trade and Industry, ex p. Broadcasting Entertainment, Cinematographic and Theatre Union* [2001] IRLR 559. The ECJ held that the directive precludes Member States from unilaterally limiting the entitlement to paid annual leave conferred on all workers under Article 7(1) by applying a precondition to such entitlement which has the effect of preventing certain workers from benefiting from it. The Working Time (Amendment) Regulations 2002 removed the qualifying period for paid annual leave entitlement so as to bring short-term contract workers within the scope of the regulations and ensure compliance with the directive.

        This decision provided a challenge to employers as to how to deal with paid leave for part-time, casual and temporary workers on short-term contracts. The response by many employers was to include an element of holiday pay in the hourly rate of pay (a so-called 'rolled-up' rate). The issue of whether holiday pay can be 'rolled-up' to form part of the basic rate is a contentious one and may contravene the WTR, as it lacks transparency and does not ensure that four weeks' annual leave is taken. In *Robinson-Steele* v *R D Retail Services Ltd; Clarke* v *Frank Staddon Ltd; Caulfield and others* v *Hanson Clay Products* [2006] IRLR 386, the ECJ held that the practice of rolling up holiday pay is unlawful as it might lead to situations where the minimum period of paid annual leave is replaced by an allowance in lieu of leave. This was principle was reiterated by the ECJ in *Federatie Nederlandse Vakbeweging* v *Staat der Nederlanden* [2006] IRLR 561.

    (iii)   Reg. 15 allows the employer considerable discretion in determining the dates on which leave is to be taken. The scope of this discretion is clearly illustrated by the decision of the Supreme Court in *Russell* v *Transocean International Resources Ltd* [2012] ICR 185, where it was held that oil and gas rig workers, whose pattern of work involved an alternating shift pattern of two or three weeks' work offshore, followed by two or three weeks' onshore leave, could be required by their employer to take their annual leave during the 'field break' onshore periods.

        Taking this decision to its logical conclusion could mean that the employer could require workers to take their leave on weekends or in blocks of less than one week. However, Lord Hope offered the following *obiter* opinion that workers could insist on taking their leave in weekly blocks:

There seems to be much to be said for the view that, when article 7 of the [WTD] is read together with the purposes with the purposes identified in the preamble and in light of what was said in [*Merino Gomez* v *Continental Industrias del Caucho SA*] [2005] ICR 1040, para 30, the entitlement is to periods of annual leave measured in weeks, not days. The worker can opt to take all or part of it in days, if he chooses to do so. But the employer cannot force him to do so. *But I do not need to reach a concluded view on this point, and I have not done so* [authors' emphasis].

Despite this *obiter* statement, the authors of *Smith and Wood* still harbour major concerns:

This troubling decision leaves open, for example, the possibility that it would be lawful for an employer to operate for only eleven months out of each year and then require that workers all take their leave during the twelfth month. Indeed, it appears that it would be acceptable for a business to shut down for five weeks distributed throughout the year and oblige employees to take their leave during these weeks. If such an arrangement resulted in, say, an eight month period without any possibility of annual leave it could be argued that the health and safety objectives of the WTR were thus successfully circumvented. In short, some serious questions around this issue remain in need of clarification. (Smith, I.T., Baker, A., *Smith & Wood's Employment Law*, 11th edn (Oxford: OUP, 2013) p. 248)

(iv)   In *Stringer* v *HM Revenue & Customs* [2009] IRLR 214, the ECJ ruled that a worker who is on sickness absence does not lose their entitlement to statutory paid annual holiday leave under the WTD. What *Stringer* left open was whether an employer can insist that a worker takes their statutory leave while they are on sick leave, or whether instead the worker is entitled to postpone taking their holiday entitlement until they return to work. This issue was resolved by the ECJ in *Pereda* v *Madrid Movilidad SA* [2009] IRLR 959. The case concerned the holiday entitlement of a wheel clamper in Madrid, who was off work sick for almost all of the annual leave period to which he was entitled. When he returned to work, he sought to take the holiday that he had missed. In its judgment, the European Court set out the principle that, although a worker may choose to take their annual leave during the time they are off work sick, where 'that worker does not wish to take annual leave during a period of sick leave, annual leave must be granted to him for a different period'. As a result, it is now clear that an employer cannot require a worker to take their annual leave when they are off work sick. According to *Pereda*, they must be allowed to carry over their holiday, even if that is to a different leave year. However, since the WTR currently prohibit carrying over more than eight days of statutory holiday to another year (and then only where there is a relevant agreement), this means that the UK is in partial breach of the requirements of EU law in this respect. As Rubenstein observes: 'There is a further complication arising out of *Pereda*: what happens when a worker who is taking their annual holiday falls sick? On the ECJ's reasoning, they should be able to treat the day as one of sick leave and reclaim their annual leave subsequently. Will employers require a more stringent standard of evidence to allow this than mere self-certification via a phone call as currently suffices to claim statutory sick pay?' ('Highlights' [2009] IRLR 881).

   In line with the *Pereda* approach, the ECJ, in *Zentralbetriebsrat der Landeskrankhauser Tirols* v *Land Tirol* [2010] 3 CMLR 30, ruled that a worker's entitlement to paid annual leave is not lost as a result of the worker having taken a period of parental leave. Similarly, in *Merino Gomez* v *Continental Industries del Caucho SA* [2005] ICR 1040, the ECJ decided that where a worker is on maternity leave, she cannot lose her entitlement to paid annual leave.

   In *NHS Leeds* v *Larner* [2011] IRLR 894, EAT, the NHS rules only allowed employees to carry over holidays accrued during sick leave if they applied in writing before the pay year elapsed. The claimant failed to do this and the employers treated her entitlement to leave as having been lost. Dismissing an appeal by the employer, the EAT held that the entitlement to paid annual leave of a worker absent for the whole of a pay year through sickness does not depend on the worker submitting a request for that annual leave before the pay year ends. Applying the ECJ decisions in *Stringer* and *Pereda*, Mr Justice Bean stated that, since Mrs Larner did not have the opportunity during the leave year to take her annual leave, she had the right to have her leave entitlement carried over to the following year, and she had that right without having to make a formal request for the leave to be carried over. As a consequence, the claimant had the right to payment in respect of unused statutory holiday entitlement when she was dismissed on grounds of her ill health. The judge stated that 'the position might be different in the case of a fit employee who fails to make any request for leave during the whole of a pay year. He or she might then lose the right to take annual leave, certainly if the contract so provides, because that worker, unlike Mrs Larner, has in the words of the Court in *Pereda* "had the opportunity" to exercise the right to leave.'

(v) *Williams* v *British Airways plc* [2011] IRLR 948 involved a claim by BA pilots that they were entitled under EU working time law to holiday pay calculated on the basis of flight supplements,
in addition to their basic salary. The general principle set out by the Court of Justice of the
European Union (CJEU) is that 'paid annual leave' means that workers must receive their 'normal remuneration'. Consequently, the Court held that a pilot was entitled during annual leave
'not only to the maintenance of his basic salary, but also, first, to all the components intrinsically linked to the performance of the tasks which he is required to carry out under his contract
of employment and in respect of which a monetary amount, included in the calculation of
his total remuneration, is provided and, second, to all the elements relating to his personal
and professional status as an airline pilot'. The case was referred back to the Supreme Court to
determine what elements of a pilot's pay constitute part of normal remuneration so defined,
and in particular whether BA was entitled to exclude 'flying supplements' and 'time away from
base allowances' from pilots' holiday pay. In arriving at its conclusion, the CJEU distinguished
between aspects of remuneration which are 'linked intrinsically to the performance of the
tasks which the worker is required to carry out under his contract of employment', such as the
time spent flying, and 'the components of the worker's total remuneration which are intended
exclusively to cover occasional or ancillary costs arising at the time of performance of the tasks
which the worker is required to carry out under his contract of employment', such as payment
for being away from home. The distinction drawn by *Williams* would seem to call into question
the treatment of overtime in calculating holiday pay, where the employee is regularly required
to work it. As Rubenstein states: 'The distinction drawn by *Williams* would seem to call into
question the treatment of overtime in calculating holiday pay, where the employee is regularly
required to work it. Under UK law at present, as interpreted by the Court of Appeal in *Bamsey*
v *Albon Engineering and Manufacturing* [2004] IRLR 457, CA, compulsory overtime is excluded
from the calculation of holiday pay unless it is guaranteed by the employer. In contrast, the
Court of Justice focuses on tasks which the worker is required to carry out under his contract of
employment' ('Highlights' [2011] IRLR 881).

The *Williams* approach was followed by the CJEU in *Lock* v *British Gas Trading Ltd* [2014]
IRLR 648. This case concerned a salesman whose remuneration consisted of two main components: basic salary and commission. Commission was payable on a monthly basis, calculated by reference to sales achieved, and represented 60% of his pay. During periods of
annual leave, there was no opportunity for commission to be earned. The CJEU held that
article 7(1) of the WTD:

> must be interpreted as precluding national legislation and practice under which a worker whose
> remuneration consists of a basic salary and commission, the amount of which is fixed by refer-
> ence to the contracts entered into by the employer as a result of sales achieved by that worker,
> is entitled, in respect of his pay to annual leave, to remuneration composed exclusively of his
> basic salary.

In the light of the above decisions, the EAT in *Bear Scotland Ltd* v *Fulton* (and conjoined cases)
[2015] IRLR 15 made the following key findings:
- that non-guaranteed overtime which the employee is required to work and allowances
  which the employee normally receives must be included in holiday pay in respect of the
  four weeks' leave provided for by the Directive;
- that applies only to the basic four weeks' leave granted under the WTD, not the additional
  1.6 weeks under reg. 13A of the WTR;
- it was possible to interpret the WTR as compatible with the Directive;
- claims for arrears of holiday pay will be out of time if there has been a break of more
  than three months between successive underpayments (subject to the reasonable
  practicability test);
- payment for 'additional' (1.6 weeks) leave would be the last to be agreed during the course
  of a leave year and cannot form part of a series of deductions which the worker claims, so
  reducing the likelihood of employment awards going back years;
- that, as time spent travelling was directly linked to work and was remunerated, it formed
  part of the worker's normal remuneration and, as such, should also be reflected when
  calculating holiday pay.

The EAT refused to grant a reference to the CJEU, but gave leave to appeal to the Court of
Appeal.

The EAT's decision will place significant limitations on retrospective claims but, of course
it is subject to appeal. Therefore, following the *Bear* judgment, the Government announced

that it was setting up a taskforce to assess the implications of the decision and to discuss how the impact on business could be limited (Depatment of Business, Innovation and Skills, Press Release, 4 November 2014). The taskforce included a selection of government departments and business representative groups but did not include representation from the trade unions. The upshot of these deliberations was the introduction of the Deduction from Wages (Limitation) Regulations 2014 (SI 2014/3322) which came into force on 8 January 2015.

The Regulations seek to limit how far back employees can go in making claims for holiday pay. However, the Regulations are drafted in very broad terms and cover almost all types of claims for unauthorised deductions from wages.

Regulation 2 amends ERA 1996, s. 23, to insert a limitation on how far back in time an ET is able to consider when determining whether a worker has suffered unauthorised deductions from their wages. The effect of this amendment is that the ET can only consider deductions from wages where the wages from which the deduction was made were paid within the previous two years before the worker brought their complaint to an ET. In particular, these changes relate to complaints in respect of deductions from wages which arise as a result of the employer failing to pay appropriate levels of holiday pay in accordance with the WTR.

Regulation 3 explicitly states that the right to payment in respect of annual leave provided by reg. 16 of the WTR is not intended to be incorporated as a term in employment contracts. It is a separate statutory right. The aim of this provision is to prevent workers seeking to recover holiday pay via contractual claims in the civil courts, taking advantage of the six-year limitation period for breach of contract claims.

Regulation 4 provides for a transitional period before the changes made by reg. 2 take place. Those new provisions will only apply to complaints presented to an ET on or after 1 July 2015.

(b) What constitutes 'working time'?

WORKING TIME DIRECTIVE (2003/88/EC)

ARTICLE 2

For the purposes of this Directive, the following definitions shall apply:

(1) 'working time' means any period during which the worker is working, at the employer's disposal and carrying out his activity or duties, in accordance with national laws and/or practice;...

Sindicato de Médicos de Asistencia Pública (SIMAP) v Conselleria de Sanidad y Consumo de La Generalidad Valenciana
[2000] IRLR 845

This case concerning the working hours of doctors in Spain raised issues as to the treatment of time on call for the purposes of the EC Working Time Directive.

The case was brought by SIMAP, the Union of Doctors in the Public Health Service, against the Ministry of Health of the Valencia Region. Under the Spanish regulations implementing the Working Time Directive, doctors who work in primary care teams in the public health sector are required to work 40 hours a week plus any time as may be required as a result of being on call. For example, one group of doctors work from 8.00 a.m. to 3.00 p.m., to which period is added, every 11 days, a period of duty on call extending from the end of the working day until 8.00 a.m. the following morning. Where a doctor is on call, only time actually worked is taken into account in determining the maximum working time.

SIMAP claimed that this meant that the Working Time Directive was not correctly transposed into Spanish law. Article 2 of the directive defines 'working time' as 'any period during which the worker is working, at the employer's disposal and carrying out his activity or duties, in accordance with national laws and/or practice.' Article 6(2) of the directive provides that Member States shall take the measures necessary to ensure that 'the average working time for each seven-day period, including overtime, does not exceed 48 hours'.

DECISION: Time spent on call by doctors in primary healthcare teams must be regarded as 'working time' within the meaning of the EC Working Time Directive, where their presence at the health centre is required.

In the scheme of the directive, working time, which is defined as any period during which the worker is working, at the employer's disposal and carrying out his activity or duties in accordance with national laws and/or practice, is placed in opposition to rest periods, the two being mutually exclusive.

In the present case, the fact that doctors are obliged to be present and available at the workplace with a view to providing their professional services means that they are carrying out their duties.

However, where doctors are on call by being contactable without having to be at the health centre, only time linked to the actual provision of primary care services must be regarded as 'working time' within the meaning of the directive. In that situation, even if they are at the disposal of their employer, in that it must be possible to contact them, they may manage their time with fewer constraints and pursue their own interests.

JUDGMENT: ...the national court seeks essentially to determine whether time spent on call by doctors in primary care teams, whether they are required to be present in the health centre or merely contactable, must be regarded as working time or as overtime within the meaning of Directive 93/104.

It must be borne in mind that that Directive defines working time as any period during which the worker is working, at the employer's disposal and carrying out his activity or duties, in accordance with national laws and/or practice. Moreover, in the scheme of the Directive, it is placed in opposition to rest periods, the two being mutually exclusive.

In the main proceedings the characteristic features of working time are present in the case of time spent on call by doctors in primary care teams where their presence at the health centre is required. It is not disputed that during periods of duty on call under those rules, the first two conditions are fulfilled. Moreover, even if the activity actually performed varies according to the circumstances, the fact that such doctors are obliged to be present and available at the workplace with a view to providing their professional services means that they are carrying out their duties in that instance.

That interpretation is also in conformity with the objective of Directive 93/104, which is to ensure the safety and health of workers by granting them minimum periods of rest and adequate breaks (eighth recital in the preamble to the Directive). It is clear, as the Advocate General emphasises in point 35 of his Opinion, that to exclude duty on call from working time if physical presence is required would seriously undermine that objective.

As the Advocate General also states in point 37 of his Opinion, the situation is different where doctors in primary care teams are on call by being contactable at all times without having to be at the health centre. Even if they are at the disposal of their employer, in that it must be possible to contact them, in that situation doctors may manage their time with fewer constraints and pursue their own interests. In those circumstances, only time linked to the actual provision of primary care services must be regarded as working time within the meaning of Directive 93/104.

As regards the question whether time spent on call may be regarded as overtime, although Directive 93/104 does not define overtime, which is mentioned only in Article 6, relating to the maximum length of the working week, the fact remains that overtime falls within the concept of working time for the purposes of the Directive, which draws no distinction according to whether or not such time is spent within normal hours of work.

The answer to questions 2(a) to 2(c), 3(a), 3(b) and 4(c) is therefore that time spent on call by doctors in primary healthcare teams must be regarded in its entirety as working time, and where appropriate as overtime, within the meaning of Directive 93/104 if they are required to be present at the health centre. If they must merely be contactable at all times when on call, only time linked to the actual provision of primary care services must be regarded as working time.

NOTES
1. Certain sectors of activity were specifically exempted from reg. 13 by virtue of reg. 18. Regulation 18 is in accordance with Article 1(3) of the directive. As a result, the following sectors of activity were exempted: air, rail, road, sea, inland waterways, and lake transport. In *Bowden v Tuffnells Parcels Express Ltd* [2001] IRLR 839, the ECJ was asked to consider the extent to which reg. 18 applied to all road transport workers, irrespective of the type of activity in which they were engaged. Mrs Bowden and her fellow applicants were employed as part-time clerical workers.

The ECJ held that the exclusion of the road transport sector from the WTDf5 93/104 applied to all workers in that sector, including office staff. This interpretation was indicated by the Community legislature as the list was without qualification; for example, in other parts of the directive it refers to 'other work at sea' and 'the activities of doctors in training', which are far more precise.

The position has now been modified as a result of the Working Time (Amendment) Regulations 2003 (SI 2003/1684) which distinguish between mobile workers and others. A mobile worker is defined as 'any worker employed as a member of the travelling or flying personnel by an undertaking which operates transport services for passengers or goods by rail or air' (see reg. 2, Working Time Regulations 1998, as amended). It is these mobile workers who are excluded from the Working Time Regulations and for whom special arrangements are made to cope with the special nature of their work.

2. There was originally an exception, which was introduced under pressure from the UK Government, for doctors in training. This exception was phased out by the Working Time Regulations 2003, reg. 25A. Under the regulations, junior doctors' maximum working hours were progressively reduced and were set at 48 hours from 1 August 2009, although a 26-week reference period is used to calculate this.

3. Protection under the regulations is offered to 'workers' and there is likely to be continued debate about who is a 'worker'. For example in *Bryne Brothers Ltd* v *Baird* [2002] IRLR 96, 'self-employed labour-only subcontractors' were held to be workers within the meaning of reg. 2 as they personally performed work or services for the company (cf. *Bacica* v *Muir* [2006] IRLR 35). The regulations distinguish between young workers, which covers someone between 15 and 18 and who 'is over compulsory school age', and a child. Children are not covered by the Working Time Regulations (as yet). In *Addison and another t/a Brayton New* v *Ashby* [2003] IRLR 211, the EAT concluded that a 15-year-old paper boy was not a 'worker' within the regulations as there is no specific reference to a child in the regulations and there was no intention for a child to be included within the definition 'worker'. Children in employment are covered by the Children and Young Persons Act 1933 (as amended). Regulation 36 of the Working Time Regulations covers agency workers who are not otherwise workers, by deeming the agency or principal to be the employer depending upon who is responsible for paying the worker.

4. The significance of the *SIMAP* case is that workers who are on call (in this case doctors) and are required to be physically present at work can expect this time to be counted as 'working time'. However, where such staff are merely required to be contactable, the time on call is not 'working time' until they are actually called upon to work, as in this situation they are able to manage their time more flexibly. The controversial issue raised but not concluded in *SIMAP* regarding whether a person on call is within the regulations has been resolved by the ECJ in *Landeshauptstadt Kiel* v *Jaeger* [2003] IRLR 804. The ECJ ruled that there is a distinction between being on call at one's place of work, which is within the regulations, and being on call where a worker is permitted to be away from the work place and is free to do leisure activities—such a period is not within the regulations. The former is the case even where, as in the *Jaeger* case, the doctors in question who were on call on hospital premises were permitted to rest at their place of work. In this respect the decision in *SIMAP* was applied.

The key points in determining whether someone who is on call falls within the WTR are if the place at which the worker is on call is determined by the employer and whether the worker has to be available to the employer in order to provide their services immediately should the need arise (see *MacCartney* v *Oversley House Management* [2006] IRLR 514, EAT).

5. The following cases consider the right to daily rest breaks under the WTR 1998. In *Gallagher* v *Alpha Catering Services Ltd* [2005] IRLR 102, the applicants were employed to deliver food and drink to airlines operating out of Gatwick Airport. They claimed they had been denied a rest break, which under reg. 12(3) must be an uninterrupted period of not less than 20 minutes. The employers contested the claim on the ground that the applicants were within categories of workers to whom the right to rest breaks did not apply, by virtue of reg. 21(C): 'Where the worker's activities involve the need for continuity of service or production as may be the case in relation to...(2) Work at Docks or Airports.' The Court of Appeal held that the activities referred to in reg. 21(C) as 'involving the need for continuity of service or production' are those of the worker, not the employer. As was pointed out by Lord Justice Peter Gibson, to allow any other interpretation would permit the employer to avoid the duty to provide rest breaks by not employing enough staff to cover such periods. Further support for the approach taken in respect of reg. 21 can be seen in the case of *Pfeiffer* v *Deutsches Rotes Kreuz* [2005] IRLR 137, in which the ECJ held

that emergency workers employed by the German Red Cross were covered by the Working Time Directive and therefore were not obliged to work more than 48 hours per week.

In calculating the 48 hours, periods of duty time should also be included. Workers may opt out, but consent must be given by the individual and must be expressly and freely given.

The EAT in *Sumsion* v *BBC Scotland* [2007] IRLR 678 held that to require an employee to take Saturdays as annual leave did not contravene the Working Time Regulations. It could not be assumed that non-Saturday working is the norm in the UK and therefore to require a worker to take leave on a Saturday was not 'real leave'. The EAT concluded that 'it is open to an employer to give notice that specified single days will be leave days. Further there is nothing in the regulations to restrict the days which an employer can nominate as leave days.' The Working Time (Amendment) Regulations 2006 removes the 'unmeasured times' exemption. As a result employers of workers who choose to do additional work, such as taking work home, will be required to 'take all reasonable steps' to ensure that the total duration of their working time does not exceed an average of 48 hours a week.

6. Enforcement.

- The primary responsibility for enforcement is placed on the Health and Safety Executive (reg. 28(2)). An employer who fails to comply with the 'relevant requirements' relating to the 48-hour maximum working week, night working, and patterns of work may face fines of up to the statutory maximum on summary conviction or unlimited fines on conviction on indictment (reg. 29).

- Employers are obliged to maintain records that are adequate to show whether time limits for maximum working time, night working, and assignment to night work are being complied with, and to keep them for two years (reg. 9).

- A worker may lodge a complaint to an ET if it is alleged that the Regulations relating to rest breaks and paid annual leave have been breached (reg. 30). The tribunal or employment judge may make a declaration, award (uncapped) compensation for refusal to allow one of these rights to be exercised, or, where the complaint is of failure to pay holiday pay, order the employer to pay the amount due (reg. 30(3)–(5)). The time limit for lodging the claim is the usual three-month period, subject to the 'not reasonably practicable' discretionary extension power.

- The individual worker cannot complain of breach of the maximum working week or night-work provisions, but breach of these obligations may constitute evidence of unreasonable conduct in order to found other claims, such as personal injury, constructive dismissal, or breach of contract (see *Barber* v *RJB Mining (UK) Ltd* [1999] IRLR 308).

- Any dismissal for refusal to comply with a breach of the Regulations, to waive a right, to sign a workforce agreement, or because of being or seeking to be a worker representative, is automatically unfair (reg. 32; ERA 1996, s. 101A).

- A worker has a right not to suffer detriment (short of dismissal) for asserting a right under the Regulations (reg. 31; ERA 1996, s.45A).

7. For a review of the Working Time Regulations 1998, see Barnard, C., 'The Working Time Regulations 1998' (1999) 28 ILJ 61; and for a review of the 1999 Regulations, see Barnard, C., 'The Working Time Regulations 1999' (2000) 29 ILJ 167. For an in-depth survey of the impact on employees, see 'A survey of workers' experiences of the Working Time Regulations' (BMRB Social Research, Nov. 2004 (<http://webarchive.nationalarchives.gov.uk/20090609003228/http://www.berr.gov.uk/files/file11485.pdf>)); *Slaying the Working Time Myths* (Trade Union Congress, April 2009) (<https://www.tuc.org.uk/sites/default/files/extras/workingtimemyths.pdf>); Barnard, C., Deakin, S., and Hobbs, R., 'Opting out of the 48 hour week: Employer necessity or individual choice' (2003) 32 ILJ 223. See also Honeyball, S., *Honeyball & Bowers' Textbook on Employment Law*, 13th edn (Oxford: OUP, 2014), Ch. 12, pp. 305–310.

SECTION 8: THE CHARACTERISTIC RIGHTS AND OBLIGATIONS OF THE EMPLOYER AND EMPLOYEE

Duties of employer

(a) to pay wages;

(b) to provide work;

(c) to exercise care;

(d) to cooperate;

(e) to provide access to a grievance procedure.

Duties of employee:

(a) to obey reasonable orders;

(b) to exercise reasonable care and competence;

(c) to maintain fidelity (which may be broken down into the following sub-headings):

(i) honesty;

(ii) not to compete;

(iii) not to misuse confidential information;

(iv) not to impede the employers' business;

(v) the duty to account.

(i) The obligation to pay wages

What effect does sickness absence have on the obligation to pay wages?

Mears v Safecar Security Ltd
[1982] IRLR 183, Court of Appeal

For other aspects of this case, see p. 95 (Section 3).

Mr Mears, a security guard, received a s. 1 statement which did not indicate whether or not he was entitled to sick pay. He applied to an industrial tribunal for a declaration as to what particulars should have been included. The tribunal—applying *Orman* v *Saville Sportswear Ltd* [1960] 3 All ER 105—held that a term that wages would be paid during sickness must be implied, unless the employers could show otherwise, which they had failed to do. The tribunal also concluded that the implied sick pay term would provide for the deduction of social security benefits received by Mr Mears.

STEPHENSON LJ: In *Orman's* case Mr Justice Pilcher said that the authorities which had been cited to him establish the following proposition. Where the written terms of the contract of service are silent as to what is to happen in regard to the employee's right to be paid whilst he is absent from work due to sickness, the employer remains liable to continue paying so long as the contract is not determined by proper notice, except where a condition to the contrary can properly be inferred from all the facts and the evidence in the case. If the employer seeks to establish an implied condition that no wages are payable, it is for him to make it out, and the court, in construing the written contract, will not accept any implied term which will not pass the test laid down by Lord Justice Scrutton in *Reigate* v *Union Manufacturing Co.* [[1916] 1 KB 592].

Mr Clark has submitted that that proposition correctly stated the law and the effect of the earlier authorities. Alternatively he preferred to adopt the somewhat narrower submission made by Mr Bridge in *Orman's* case (at page 1060 of the report) that:

When the contract contains no express term and no unexpressed term can properly be implied as to the remuneration during periods of illness, the presumption is that the contractual remuneration remains payable until the contract of service is determined.

As, however, that presumption must prevail unless rebutted and the employer is the party who will want to rebut it, it appears in fact to place the onus of rebutting it on the employer, as Mr Justice Pilcher said.

In the Employment Appeal Tribunal's judgment, now reported in [1981] IRLR 99, Mr Justice Slynn reviewed those authorities, which were the decisions of this court in *Marrison* v *Bell* [1939] 2 KB 187, *Petrie* v *MacFisheries Ltd* [1940] 1 KB 265, and *O'Grady* v *M. Saper Ltd* [1940] 2 KB, 469 to which he added *Hancock* v *BSA Tools Ltd* [1939] 4 All ER 538, a decision of Mr Justice Atkinson given between the decision of the Court of Appeal, of which he had been a member, in *Petrie's* case, and the decision in *O'Grady's* case. Mr Justice Slynn ended his review of those cases with the following citation from the judgment of Lord Justice MacKinnon in *O'Grady's* case, at page 529:

The whole question in such a case as this is what the terms of the contract between the employer and the servant were and what those terms provided in regard to payment of wages to him during his absence from the service by reason of illness…Was it agreed that the man should be paid when he was ready and willing to work, or that he should be paid only when he was actually working?…In this case, as it seems to me, there was abundant evidence that the terms, not expressed but no doubt implied, upon which this man was employed were that he should not be paid wages whilst he was sick. Conclusive evidence of that is furnished by the fact that on at least three occasions during the time he had been employed he was not paid wages when he was away sick, and he acquiesced in that position.

…

[THE EAT's] decision disapproves the conclusion of Mr Justice Pilcher as expressed in the proposition cited from *Orman's* case and substitutes an approach to the facts and evidence in each case with an open mind unprejudiced by any preconception, presumption or assumption. With this I respectfully agree.

…For this court to affirm the Employment Appeal Tribunal's decision involves preferring, or as I think being bound by the latest of conflicting decisions of this court at least when that decision has considered earlier conflicting decisions and resolved the conflict. *Barrington* v *Lee* [1972] 1 QB 326. If *Marrison* v *Bell* had stood alone I think I would have felt bound by it to follow the *Orman* case. In justice to the reporter of the *Marrison* case, I have to say that I regard his headnote as correctly stating the main point there argued and decided, in spite of the criticism diverted in *Petrie* case from the decision to the report of it. But we are bound to follow *O'Grady's* case…

Here the facts and circumstances all pointed, as I have said against the term of which Mr Mears wanted the Tribunal to include particulars and in favour of a term that there was to be no sick pay. If there had been no factors pointing either way, nothing for or against sick pay, then the statutory duty to determine particulars of a term or condition to comply with [ERA 1996, s. 1(4)(d)(ii)] could have been discharged only by resorting to the presumption that the wage is to be paid till the employment is ended, whether the employee works or is absent from work. That was, I think, rightly recognised by the Employment Appeal Tribunal in the conclusion of the passage which I have already referred to in the judgment of Mr Justice Slynn. Those sentences reflect and follow what Lord Justice du Parcq who had been a party to the decision in *Marrison's* case said in *Petrie's* [1940] 1 KB at page 265, echoed by Mr Justice Atkinson in the same case at page 270.

That is what is left of the presumption attributed to *Marrison* v *Bell* and it does not apply to this case. To apply it, as if there were 'nothing more', would be manifestly unjust for it would require the Industrial Tribunal to compel an employer, who though in breach of his statutory duty to give the required particulars would never have agreed to pay any employee wages when absent sick, to pay them to an employee who never expected to get them. The Employment Appeal Tribunal was right in holding that they were not driven by law to uphold a conclusion so repugnant to common sense and the justice of the case.

To sum up the guidance which I would give to Industrial Tribunals in every reference under s. 11 in which an employee asks the Industrial Tribunal to determine the particulars required by s. 1 of a term (or terms) of which no written particulars have been given by his employer, the Tribunal must act under [s. 12(1)], and their first duty is to determine whether that term has been agreed expressly by word of mouth or by necessary implication. If it has, the Tribunal determines that particulars of it ought to be included in the employee's statement of terms. If it has not, the Tribunal has to find and imply the term which all the facts and circumstances, including the subsequent actions of the employer and employee, show were agreed or must have been agreed and to determine that particulars of that term ought to be included. Where, as here, the Tribunal is searching for the right term to imply relating to the payment of wages during absence through sickness and are left by lack of material in doubt about that particular term, the doubt will be resolved in favour of the employee by *Marrison* v *Bell* as interpreted in the authorities ending with this case. When the missing term relates to payment of wages during periods of absence through sickness, the Tribunal must approach the search for the missing term by considering all the facts and circumstances, including the subsequent conduct of the parties, and only if they do not indicate what that term is or must be, should the Tribunal assume that it is a term that wages should be paid during those periods and determine that that is the term of which particulars ought to be included.

In most cases the Tribunal will have enough material, as had this Tribunal, to determine what has, or would have been agreed between employer and employee and so ought to have been particularised by the employer. By the end of the 13 weeks [now two months] allowed by s. 1 of the Act, or by the time the employee's complaint is heard by the Tribunal the problem of what was agreed generally 'solvitur ambulando', and the way in which the employment has worked in practice will supply the missing term on one or other of the common law principles of necessary implication. But there may be cases in which the Tribunal are left in doubt as to what has been agreed and what particulars ought to have been included. What then? Is the Tribunal to decide what term should have been agreed? Is the statutory duty to determine particulars as being those which ought to have been given in a statement, a duty to decide what the Tribunal think the parties ought to have agreed? Can the employer shelter behind s. 2(1) by stating that there are no particulars to be entered under the statutory head on which the employee relies?

If the employer has stated that there are no particulars to be entered thereunder, but the Tribunal find that there are because the term has been agreed, then they can act probably by amendment or substitution under [s. 12(2)] rather than under [s. 12(1)]. But what if no particulars have been entered because the relevant term has not been agreed? Is the Tribunal stopped by s. 2(1) from going behind the employer's negative statement and inserting particulars which he shall be deemed to have given?

It may be that we are here considering cases which Parliament never considered and questions to which only Parliament can supply answers. But I am inclined to think that when any of the terms specified in the statute has not been agreed, the Tribunal have nevertheless to state it for them. This they can only do by deciding which term fits in best with all the circumstances of the case, which may be getting near to deciding what is a reasonable term, or a term which, to quote the Industrial Tribunal's decision, would be sensible if the parties had in fact agreed it.

[Section 12] would seem to impose on the Tribunal the statutory duty to find the specified terms, and in the last resort invent them for the purpose of literally writing them into the contract. In discharging that duty, the Tribunal can and must go into all the facts and circumstances of the case and, when those fail to provide a basis for implying a specified term, to justice, and the implication of a reasonable term. If the Tribunal have not enough material in the facts and circumstance to determine what *would* have been agreed, they must determine what *should* have been agreed, bearing in mind that it is the employer's breach of *his* statutory duty which has made the employee's application for a reference necessary and that in consequence they would generally be right to resolve any doubt about what particulars ought to be included in favour of the employee.

But this is not a case of that kind, and we have not been asked to consider it on the basis that there was insufficient material for the implication of the relevant term without resorting to considering what would be reasonable or just. Not having heard argument on that aspect of the statutory duty, I express no concluded opinion upon it. No authoritative guidance can be given on it until Tribunals are faced with a decision which requires it. But I have ventured to raise questions which the sections we have had to consider, including in particular s. 2(1), inevitably raise, in the hope that Parliament may find time to consider whether some amendment of those sections might not clarify the statutory duty thereby intended to be imposed on Industrial Tribunals…

If the first issue is decided in the company's favour, it is unnecessary to consider the second issue. I would only comment that on the facts of this case two Tribunals widely experienced in such matters, have unanimously concluded that if Mr Mears was entitled to sick pay it would be paid nett after deduction of Social Security benefits, and it would have taken cogent argument, possibly exceeding even Mr Clark's powers of persuasion to convince me that there was any error of law in the decision of either Tribunal on the point.

NOTE: In the course of his judgment, Stephenson LJ suggested (*obiter*) that where the parties have failed to agree on a relevant term specified in what is now the ERA 1996, Pt I '[s. 12] would seem to impose on the tribunal the statutory duty to find the specified terms, and in the last resort invent them for the purpose of literally writing them into the contract'. This view has received considerable criticism and has now been rejected by the Court of Appeal in *Eagland* v *British Telecommunications plc* [1992] IRLR 323. Parker LJ thought it 'undesirable' that the guidance given in Mears 'should remain in the authorities'. Leggatt LJ stated:

> For my part I too am unable to envisage circumstances in which it might become appropriate for an Industrial Tribunal to invent a term. I use the word 'invent' as it was used by Lord Justice Stephenson … in the sense of determining either what term should have been agreed or what term would have been reasonable. If an essential term, such as a written statement must contain, has not been agreed, there will be no agreement. If it has, it is the duty of the employment tribunal, where necessary, to identify the term as having been agreed, whether expressly, by necessary implication, or by inference from all the circumstances, including in particular the conduct of the parties, without recourse to invention.

■ QUESTION

Is there likely to be a difference in outcome depending on whether the approach is 'identification' or 'invention' of the missing term?

NOTE: The following cases consider the question of lay-offs and the obligation to pay.

Hanley v Pease & Partners Ltd

[1915] 1 KB 698, King's Bench Division

Mr Hanley, a cokeman, was required to work on Sundays. On one Sunday, he overslept and failed to turn up for work. The following day he arrived for work but was suspended without pay for one day. He claimed damages for the loss of one day's pay on the Monday. At first instance his claim was rejected, but was successful on appeal.

LUSH J: Whether the right of a master to dismiss a servant for misconduct or breach of duty or anything else of the kind is treated as a right arising out of the ordinary right of a contracting party to put an end to the contract when there has been a repudiation by the other party, or whether it is treated as a right which the master has on the ground that obedience to lawful orders must be treated as a condition of the contract, is wholly immaterial. I do not think it is necessary to say which is the proper way to regard it, because in either view the right of the master is merely an option. The contract has become a voidable contract. The master can determine it if he pleases. Assuming that there has been a breach on the part of the servant entitling the master to dismiss him, he may if he pleases terminate the contract, but he is not bound to do it, and if he chooses not to exercise that right but to treat the contract as a continuing contract notwithstanding the misconduct or breach of duty of the servant, then the contract is for all purposes a continuing contract subject to the master's right in that case to claim damages against the servant for his breach of contract. But in the present case after declining to dismiss the workman—after electing to treat the contract as a continuous one—the employers took upon themselves to suspend him for one day; in other words to deprive the workman of his wages for one day, thereby assessing their own damages for the servant's misconduct at the sum which would be represented by one day's wages. They have no possible right to do that. Having elected to treat the contract as continuing it was continuing. They might have had a right to claim damages against the servant, but they could not justify their act in suspending the workman for the one day and refusing to let him work and earn wages.

NOTE: As a result of this decision, it is clear that employers cannot suspend without pay where there is no express or contractual right to do so—see *Marshall* v *Midland Electric* [1945] 1 All ER 653.

Devonald v Rosser & Sons

[1906] 2 KB 728, Court of Appeal

Devonald was a pieceworker employed at a tinplate works. His contract of employment gave him an entitlement to one month's notice of termination of employment. Devonald's employers found they could not run at a profit because of depressed market conditions. They gave Devonald a month's notice but closed down the works immediately. Devonald claimed damages for the wages he lost during this period, arguing that there was an implied term that he would be provided with work during the notice period.

LORD ALVERSTONE CJ: …In my opinion the necessary implication to be drawn from this contract is at least that the master will find a reasonable amount of work up to the expiration of a notice given in accordance with the contract. I am not prepared to say that that obligation is an absolute one to find work at all events, for the evidence showed that it was subject to certain contingencies, such as breakdown of machinery and want of water and materials. But I am clearly of opinion that it would be no excuse to the master, for non-performance of his implied obligation to provide the workman with work, that he could no longer make his plates at a profit either for orders or for stock…

Browning v Crumlin Valley Collieries Ltd

[1926] 1 KB 522, King's Bench Division

Browning and others were miners who refused to work in the defendant's mine because it had become unsafe. It was found as a fact that this was not due to the fault of the employer, but was caused by natural forces. The miners sought to recover compensation for the wages they lost during the period when the mine was closed to allow the essential repair work to be done.

GREER J: The consideration for work is wages, and the consideration for wages is work. Is it to be implied in the engagement that the wages are to be paid when through no fault of the employer the work cannot be done? The principle that ought to guide the Court when asked to say whether any term should be read by implication into a written contract was stated by Bowen LJ, in *The Moorcock* [(1889) 16 Probate Division 64], and his words have ever since been accepted as the guiding principle. In any case in which it is necessary to ascertain whether any and what term should be implied in a written contract the correct application of this guiding principle has to be determined. Bowen LJ, said: 'Now, an implied warranty, or, as it is called, a covenant in law, as distinguished from an express contract or express warranty, really is in all cases founded on the presumed intention of the parties, and upon reason. The implication which the law draws from what must obviously have been the intention of the parties, the law draws with the object of giving efficacy to the transaction and preventing such a failure of consideration as cannot have been within the contemplation of either side'...

It seems to me that there must in the circumstances of the present case be some implied term. The men did not work, they were not ready and willing to work in the state the mine was in, and the agreement is silent on the question whether they are in these circumstances entitled to be paid wages. Were the mineowners to bear 'all the chances of failure' due to the operation of natural forces without any fault on their part? Were the perils of the transaction in that event to be all on one side, or must the consequences be divided between the two parties, the employers losing the advantages of continuing to have their coal gotten and being compelled to undertake expensive repairs, and the men on their part losing their wages for such time as was reasonably required to put the mine into a safe condition? The latter, I think, must be presumed to have been the intention of both parties. I am satisfied that no employer would have consented to agree that the workmen should be free to withhold their work if the mine became dangerous through no fault on his part and yet should be entitled to be paid their wages. I think the employer would only have agreed to the workmen's right to withhold their labour under these circumstances, subject to the condition that they should not be entitled to their wages. Further, it seems to me clear from the way in which the present case was conducted, and from the evidence given by several witnesses, that this was the usual understanding of the effect of the men's contract of employment...

Great reliance was placed by Mr Matthews on the decision in *Devonald* v *Rosser & Son*, but in that case the defendant's failure to provide work for the plaintiff so as to enable him to earn his piecework pay was due to the employer deciding that owing to bad trade it would pay him better to close down. It was not due to a cause over which he had no control, it was neither illegal nor impossible for him to continue to find work for the plaintiff, and the Court expressly left open the question whether the plaintiff could have succeeded if the stoppage had been due to such a cause, indicating, I think, that they inclined to the opinion that he could not: see per Lord Alverstone CJ, and per Sir Gorell Barnes, President, where the learned President uses these words: 'I can quite understand that, having regard to a certain set of circumstances, such as breakage of machinery, it may be reasonable to hold that it was the intention of the parties that those risks should be shared, that risks of that character which are known to both parties, and which prevent both from doing what was contemplated, should excuse from the obligation to maintain the continuance of the work.' I think these observations apply *a fortiori* to contracts between mineowners and their workpeople.

NOTE: Freedland has criticised the Browning decision as comparable 'to a hypothetical finding that the owner of a factory was not responsible to his employees for the shut-down of a building where the roof collapsed as a result of the gradual and perceptible erosion of the fabric by wind and rain' (*The Contract of Employment* (Oxford: Clarendon Press, 1976), p. 59). Wedderburn wonders, given that the judges were saying the intention of the parties must have been to share the loss of this natural event, 'would they have said the same if a crop of diamonds had appeared?' (*The Worker and the Law*, 3rd edn (Harmondsworth: Penguin, 1986), p. 231).

■ QUESTION

Do you think that the decision in *Browning* accords with contemporary views as to the extent of an employer's responsibilities?

NOTES
1. An express term or custom may permit lay-off without pay. From the Second World War there have developed many collectively bargained provisions for guaranteed minimum weekly wages in the event of lay-off or short-term working, though these payments are generally subject to suspension in the event of industrial action. In the absence of collectively agreed arrangements

there is a restricted right to guarantee payments in every contract of employment (see now the ERA 1996, ss. 28–35).

2. Part I of the Wages Act 1986 came into force at the beginning of 1987. It replaced the protection, formerly provided by the Truck Acts, from arbitrary deductions from wages. The relevant provisions are now contained in Pt II of the ERA 1996. Section 13 of the 1996 Act allows deductions to be made only if they are authorised or required by a written term of the contract of employment or of some other agreement, or by a term (whether oral or written) whose existence has been explained in writing. The meaning of 'wages' is given in s. 27.

EMPLOYMENT RIGHTS ACT 1996

27. Meaning of 'wages' etc.

(1) In this Part 'wages', in relation to a worker, means any sums payable to the worker in connection with his employment, including—

  (a) any fee, bonus, commission, holiday pay or other emolument referable to his employment, whether payable under his contract or otherwise,

  (b) statutory sick pay under Part XI of the Social Security Contributions and Benefits Act 1992,

  (c) statutory maternity pay under Part XII of that Act,

  (d) a guarantee payment (under section 28 of this Act),

  (e) any payment for time off under Part VI of this Act or section 169 of the Trade Union and Labour Relations (Consolidation) Act 1992 (payment for time off for carrying out trade union duties etc.),

  (f) remuneration on suspension on medical grounds under section 64 of this Act and remuneration on suspension on maternity grounds under section 68 of this Act,

  (g) any sum payable in pursuance of an order for reinstatement or re-engagement under section 113 of this Act,

  (h) any sum payable in pursuance of an order for the continuation of a contract of employment under section 130 of this Act or section 164 of the Trade Union and Labour Relations (Consolidation) Act 1992, and

  (i) remuneration under a protective award under section 189 of that Act, but excluding any payments within subsection (2).

(2) Those payments are—

  (a) any payment by way of an advance under an agreement for a loan or by way of an advance of wages (but without prejudice to the application of section 13 to any deduction made from the worker's wages in respect of any such advance),

  (b) any payment in respect of expenses incurred by the worker in carrying out his employment,

  (c) any payment by way of a pension, allowance or gratuity in connection with the worker's retirement or as compensation for loss of office,

  (d) any payment referable to the worker's redundancy, and

  (e) any payment to the worker otherwise than in his capacity as a worker.

(3) Where any payment in the nature of a non-contractual bonus is (for any reason) made to a worker by his employer, the amount of the payment shall for the purposes of this Part—

  (a) be treated as wages of the worker, and

  (b) be treated as payable to him as such on the day on which the payment is made.

(4) In this Part 'gross amount', in relation to any wages payable to a worker, means the total amount of those wages before deductions of whatever nature.

(5) For the purposes of this Part any monetary value attaching to any payment or benefit in kind furnished to a worker by his employer shall not be treated as wages of the worker except in the case of any voucher, stamp or similar document which is—

  (a) of a fixed value expressed in monetary terms, and

  (b) capable of being exchanged (whether on its own or together with other vouchers, stamps or documents, and whether immediately or only after a time) for money, goods or services (or for any combination of two or more of those things).

13. Right not to suffer unauthorised deductions

(3) Where the total amount of wages paid on any occasion by an employer to a worker employed by him is less than the total amount of the wages properly payable by him to the worker on that occasion (after deductions), the amount of the deficiency shall be treated for the purposes of this Part as a deduction made by the employer from the worker's wages on that occasion.

Delaney v Staples (t/a De Montfort Recruitment)

[1992] IRLR 191, House of Lords

Miss Delaney was summarily dismissed by her employer and given a cheque for £82 as payment in lieu of notice. Subsequently, the employer stopped the cheque, alleging that Delaney had taken away confidential information and that, therefore, he was entitled to dismiss her without notice.

Miss Delaney complained to an industrial tribunal under the Wages Act 1986 with regard to a number of matters, including the failure to pay her the £82 in lieu of notice. The tribunal rejected this aspect of her claim, holding that payment in lieu did not fall within the definition of 'wages' as set out in what is now the ERA 1996, s. 27. Her appeal on this issue was rejected by the EAT, the Court of Appeal, and the House of Lords.

LORD BROWNE-WILKINSON: … The proper answer to this case turns on the special definition of 'wages' in [s. 27] of the Act. But it is important to approach such definition bearing in mind the normal meaning of that word. I agree with the Court of Appeal that the essential characteristic of wages is that they are consideration for work done or to be done under a contract of employment. If a payment is not referable to an obligation on the employee under a subsisting contract of employment to render his services it does not in my judgment fall within the ordinary meaning of the word 'wages'. It follows that if an employer terminates the employment (whether lawfully or not), any payment in respect of the period after the date of such termination is not a payment of wages (in the ordinary meaning of that word) since the employee is not under obligation to render services during that period.

The phrase 'payment in lieu of notice' is not a term of art. It is commonly used to describe many types of payment, the legal analysis of which differs. Without attempting to give an exhaustive list, the following are the principal categories:

1. An employer gives proper notice of termination to his employee, tells the employee that he need not work until the termination date, and gives him the wages attributable to the notice period in a lump sum. In this case (commonly called 'garden leave') there is no breach of contract by the employer. The employment continues until the expiry of notice: the lump sum payment is simply advance payment of wages.

2. The contract of employment provides expressly that the employment may be terminated either by notice or, on payment of a sum in lieu of notice, summarily. In such a case if the employer summarily dismisses the employee he is not in breach of contract provided that he makes the payment in lieu. But the payment in lieu is not a payment of wages in the ordinary sense since it is not a payment for work to be done under the contract of employment.

3. At the end of the employment, the employer and the employee agree that the employment is to terminate forthwith on payment of a sum in lieu of notice. Again, the employer is not in breach of contract by dismissing summarily and the payment in lieu is not strictly wages since it is not remuneration for work done during the continuance of the employment.

4. Without the agreement of the employee, the employer summarily dismisses the employee and tenders a payment in lieu of proper notice. This is by far the most common type of payment in lieu and the present case falls into this category. The employer is in breach of contract by dismissing the employee without proper notice. However, the summary dismissal is effective to put an end to the employment relationship, whether or not it unilaterally discharges the contract of employment. Since the employment relationship has ended, no further services are to be rendered by the employee under the contract. It follows that the payment in lieu is not a payment of wages in the ordinary sense since it is not a payment for work done under the contract of employment.

The nature of a payment in lieu falling within the fourth category has been analysed as a payment by the employer on account of the employee's claim for damages for breach of contract. In *Gothard* v *Mirror Group Newspapers Ltd* [1988] IRLR 396, 14, Lord Donaldson Lymington MR stated the position to be as follows:

> If a man is dismissed without notice, but with money in lieu, what he receives is, as a matter of law, payment which falls to be set against, and will usually be designed by the employer to extinguish, any claim for damages for breach of contract, i.e. wrongful dismissal. During the period to which the money in lieu relates he is not employed by his employer.

In my view that statement is the only possible legal analysis of a payment in lieu of the fourth category. But it is not, and was not meant to be, an analysis of a payment in lieu of the first three categories, in none of which is the dismissal a breach of contract by the employer. In the first three categories, the employee is entitled to the payment in lieu not as damages for breach of contract but under a contractual obligation on the employer to make the payment.

Against that background, I turn to the relevant provisions of the Act. Section 1(1) prohibits an employer from making 'any deduction from any wages of any worker employed by him' unless such deduction is of a kind authorised by s. 1 of the Act. Therefore, to fall within the prohibition contained in s. 1 two things have to be demonstrated: first, that there has been a 'deduction': second that the deduction was made from 'wages'.

[His Lordship then set out what is now ERA 1996, s. 13(3) and continued:]

The Court of Appeal in this case held that a total failure to make any payment of a sum due could be a 'deduction' within this definition. There is no appeal against that decision, nor has there been any submission that it was wrong. I must therefore proceed on the basis that it is correct, without expressing any view of my own one way or the other.

[His Lordship set out the definition of 'wages' now found in ERA 1996, s. 27 and continued:]

The critical question is whether a payment in lieu falls within this wide definition as being a sum payable to an employee 'in connection with his employment'.

...

... The first inquiry must be whether the language of the Act throws any light on the problem. The words 'in connection with his employment' are very wide, in my judgment quite wide enough to include a payment in lieu. I do not agree with the Court of Appeal that prima facie the words are not wide enough to include a payment in lieu because such payments are payments of damages for breach of contract. First, not all payments in lieu (other than garden leave) are payments of damages. Even in the fourth category of case where payments in lieu are properly analysed as being payment of damages, that does not in my judgment mean that they are not payments 'in connection with' the employment. Apart from a context indicating the contrary view, payments connected with the termination of employment (whether or not characterised as damages) are quite capable of being described as made 'in connection with that employment.'

Nor do I get any help from the items expressly included and excluded by [ERA 1996, s. 27(1) and (2)]. Given the presence of express inclusions as well as express exclusions, there is no room for an argument that by expressly excluding certain items that draftsman was indicating that such items would otherwise be payments 'in connection with' the employment. Nor can I detect a rough division between the express inclusions as being payments arising from services rendered under the contract and the express exclusions as payments arising from events on or after the termination of the employment. For example, the advances of wages and expenses incurred in carrying out the employment (both of which are excluded items under [ERA 1996, s. 27(2)(a) and (b)] both relate to acts occurring during the subsistence of the contract of employment.

...

Therefore on the language of the Act, I find neither anything which cuts down the wide meaning of the words 'in connection with his employment' nor anything which demonstrates that Parliament intended payments in lieu to fall within the definition of 'wages'. I turn therefore to the way in which the Act would operate if payments in lieu were included in the word 'wages'. Like the Court of Appeal I find that the provisions of the Act cannot be made to work if payments in lieu are included in the meaning of wages. I will demonstrate the difficulties by reference to the fourth and most common category of payment in lieu, i.e. where the worker is summarily dismissed in breach of contract and the employer makes no payment in lieu or a payment in lieu of a sum less than the full amount of the wages for the notice period.

First, in order to demonstrate that such payment in lieu is a 'deduction' the worker will have to satisfy the requirements of [ERA 1996, s. 13(3)]. He will have to show that there was an occasion on which 'wages' were payable to him and the amount of the wages which should properly have been paid to him on that occasion. These requirements cannot be satisfied in relation to a payment in lieu. There is no 'occasion' on which the payment in lieu was 'properly' payable. The worker has no contractual or other right to the lump sum of liquidated damages at any time prior to the judgment. Even assuming that the occasion for such payment in lieu was the date of summary dismissal, what was the sum 'properly' then payable? If the worker obtains alternative employment during the notice period, the damages for wrongful dismissal on account of loss of wages which would be payable by the employer falls to be reduced by the wages received by the worker from the alternative employment during the notice period. It is therefore impossible at the time of dismissal to quantify the correct amount of the payment in lieu. Accordingly there is no way in which the amount of the 'deduction' can be calculated under [s. 13(3)].

Next, under [ERA 1996, s. 23(2)(a)] a complaint to an Industrial Tribunal in relation to an improper deduction has to be made within three months of 'the date of payment of the wages from which the deduction was made'. As I have said, it is impossible to identify the date on which the payment in lieu should have been made. Therefore the time limit in [s. 23(2)] cannot be calculated.

Next, under the general law an employer, in paying damages for wrongful dismissal or a payment in lieu by way of liquidated damages, is entitled to set off any cross-claim he may have against his employee. For example, in the present case the employer, Mr Staples, was asserting a cross-claim against Miss Delaney for an alleged breach of her duty of confidentiality. If a payment in lieu constitutes 'wages' for the purposes of the Act, no such deduction of cross-claims is permissible since it would not be authorised by [s. 13]. Moreover, if the employer were to exercise his right of set-off under the general law by deducting the amount of his cross-claim from a payment in lieu, if the payment in lieu is 'wages' the worker could apply to the Industrial Tribunal for an order that the employer repay the unauthorised deduction even if it was a legitimate cross-claim. The Industrial Tribunal would be bound to order such repayment [s. 24] and in consequence the employer would lose his right to enforce his cross-claim in any proceedings to the extent of the sum wrongly deducted: [s. 25(4)]. I find it impossible to believe that Parliament in passing this legislation intended, by a side wind, to alter the common law rights of employers and workers on the termination of employment.

For these reasons, I am forced to the conclusion that payments in lieu of the fourth category do not fall within the statutory definition of 'wages'. Where then is the dividing line to be drawn? In my judgment one is thrown back to the basic concept of wages as being payments in respect of the rendering of services during the employment, so as to exclude all payments in respect of the termination of the contract, save to the extent that such latter payments are expressly included in the definition in [s. 27(1)]. It follows that payments in respect of 'garden leave' (my category 1) are 'wages' within the meaning of the Act since they are advance payments of wages falling due under a subsisting contract of employment. But all other payments in lieu, whether or not contractually payable (my categories 2, 3 and 4), are not wages within the meaning of the Act since they are payments relating to the termination of the employment, not to the provision of services under the employment. To draw a distinction between those cases where the payment in lieu is contractually based and the normal payment in lieu which consists of liquidated damages would be to invite numerous disputes as to the jurisdiction of the Industrial Tribunal, which cannot have been Parliament's intention. For these reasons, I agree with the decision of the Court of Appeal.

This conclusion produces an untidy and unsatisfactory result. On any dismissal, the summary procedure of the Industrial Tribunal under the Act will be exercisable in relation to unpaid wages (in the ordinary sense), holiday pay, commission, maternity leave etc, but claims relating to the failure to give proper notice will continue to have to be brought in the County Court. The employee is therefore forced either to bring two sets of proceedings or to proceed wholly in the County Court on a claim for damages. To be forced to bring two sets of proceedings for small sums of money in relation to one dismissal is wasteful of time and money. It brings the law into disrepute and is not calculated to ensure that employees recover their full legal entitlement when wrongfully dismissed. The position is capable of remedy by an order under s. 131 of the Employment Protection (Consolidation) Act 1978 [now ETA 1996, s. 3(1)] which enables the Minister to confer jurisdiction on Industrial Tribunals to deal with claims for breach of contract. As the judgment of Lord Donaldson of Lymington MR in the present case shows, the courts have been suggesting that this power be exercised for nearly 20 years, so far without success [1991] IRLR 112, 31–8. I believe that all your Lordships are of the view that the present unsatisfactory position calls for fresh consideration by the Minister.

My Lords, for these reasons I would dismiss the appeal.

NOTE: In *Delaney v Staples (t/a De Montfort Recruitment)* [1991] IRLR 112, the Court of Appeal held that the Act can apply to a simple non-payment. This conclusion was not the subject of an appeal to the House of Lords. One division of the EAT had consistently held that the Act only applied to a 'deduction', not a failure to pay altogether (which therefore remained a matter for the county court). However, the Court of Appeal approved the view of other EAT decisions that the statutory definition of a deduction in what is now the ERA 1996, s. 13(3) has to be applied literally, thus ignoring any common law distinction between non-payment and deduction:

> The Act was concerned with unauthorised deduction. But [s. 13(3)] made it plain that, leaving aside errors of computation, any shortfall in the amount of wages properly payable was to be treated as a deduction. That being so, a dispute on whatever grounds as to the amount of wages properly payable could not have the effect of taking the case outside [s. 13(3)]. [*Per* Nicholls LJ.]

Thus, Miss Delaney could bring industrial tribunal proceedings to recover £55.50 unpaid commission and holiday pay outstanding on her dismissal, as an unauthorised deduction. From a policy standpoint this must be correct. The distinction made by Wood J in *Alsop v Star Vehicle Contracts Ltd* [1990] ICR 378 and *Barlow v Whittle* [1990] ICR 270 would have had the result that an underpaid employee would be able to go to the industrial tribunal, whereas an employee not paid at all would be forced to go to the ordinary courts. As Mr Justice Nicholls put it, 'This hardly seems sensible'.

■ QUESTION

The House of Lords' conclusion in *Delaney* is recognised by Lord Browne-Wilkinson as producing 'an untidy and unsatisfactory result'. What prompts this conclusion, and how far will the orders made under the Employment Protection (Consolidation) Act (EPCA) 1978, s. 131 (now the ETA 1996, s. 3(1))—set out at p. 19 (Chapter 1, Section 2.E)—help matters?

NOTES

1. The assumption behind the legislation is that freedom of contract is a sufficient general protection against the level and purpose of deductions. However, there is a degree of recognition of the need to give an additional element of protection to workers in retail employment, where the deduction from wages for cash shortages or stock deficiencies is a relatively common practice.

   The workers covered are those whose employment involves them in the sale or supply of goods or services (including financial services) directly to members of the public, fellow workers, or other individuals in their personal capacities (the ERA 1996, s. 17). This definition would encompass those employed as petrol station cashiers, shop assistants, waiters, and bank cashiers, but would leave other equally vulnerable groups without special protection, e.g. warehouse and stockroom staff, kitchen staff, etc. For those who do fall within the protected category, s. 18 limits the amount that may be deducted in respect of cash and stock shortages on any one pay day to one-tenth of the gross wages due on that day.

   The limitations on the amount deducted or demanded at any one time are not aimed at limiting the overall size of the worker's liability to the employer; the provisions merely serve to allow liability to be discharged by 'easy payments'. There seems no reason why an employer cannot recover for cash shortages or stock deficiencies far in excess of the 10% figure by spreading the deductions or payments over several pay days.

   Section 22 makes it clear that the 10% limit does not apply to the 'final payment of wages', i.e. wages for the last period the worker is employed before termination or, if paid later, wages in lieu of notice. Therefore, an employer who has not been able to recover the total liability during the currency of the contract may do so without limit at its termination. Indeed, it may be argued that some employers will be tempted to dismiss workers responsible for cash shortages and stock deficiencies in order to avoid the 10% deduction/payment threshold and to recover their losses immediately. This would result in an onerous double indemnity for workers in retail employment, particularly those who lack the requisite length of employment to qualify for unfair dismissal rights.

2. Section 23 of the Act allows the worker the right to complain to an ET, within three months, of any alleged infringement of the restrictions imposed by ss. 13, 15, and 18.

   Where the tribunal finds the complaint well founded, it must make a declaration to that effect and either:

   (a) order the employer to repay to the worker the amount of deduction or payment if made in contravention of general restrictions under s. 1;

   (b) in the case of breach of the 10% deduction/payment threshold for retail workers, order repayment of the amount which exceeded the limit.

   It appears the tribunal order can relate to all such deductions/payments which have been made in breach of the provisions. In this regard the remedy is more effective than the one offered by statute for unnotified deductions under the ERA 1996, s. 12(4), the latter allowing only for the recoupment of deductions which have taken place in the preceding 13 weeks.

3. Section 11 of the Wages Act 1986 repealed the Truck Acts 1831–1940 and any other statutes connected with the payment of wages, including the Payment of Wages Act 1960. The last statute allowed an employer to arrange for wages to be paid into an individual's bank account, by money order, postal order, or by cheque, where that individual consented in writing. Either party could terminate such an agreement by giving four weeks' notice. The effect of these repeals is to remove the manual worker's right to be paid in the 'coin of the realm'.

4. The ERA, s. 14 provides that an employee's right to complain to an ET about an unauthorised deduction from wages does not apply to certain situations. These include 'where the purpose of the deduction is the reimbursement of the employer in respect of an overpayment of wages' and 'where the worker has taken part in a strike or other industrial action and the deduction is made by the employer on account of the worker's having taken part in that strike or other action.' Where s. 14 is applicable, an ET does not have jurisdiction to determine the legality of the deduction and the claimant must bring an action in the civil courts for breach of contract. However, in the joint decision of *Gill* v *Ford Motor Co. Ltd; Wong* v *BAE Systems Operations Ltd* [2004] IRLR 840, the EAT held that this does not mean that the tribunal should determine the jurisdictional issue

without first hearing evidence and making a finding of fact as to whether there was an overpayment, or that the worker concerned had taken part in industrial action.

5. As stated above, deductions from the wages of those taking industrial action are exempted from the requirement of the ERA 1996 by s. 14(5). The subsection does not provide any positive authority to the employer to make deductions from salary. Whether such a right exists remains a question governed by the common law.

Miles v Wakefield Metropolitan District Council

[1987] IRLR 193, House of Lords

Mr Miles was a superintendent registrar of births, marriages and deaths. He normally worked 37 hours per week, three of which were on Saturday mornings.

Between August 1981 and October 1982, as part of industrial action, Mr Miles refused to carry out marriages on Saturday mornings. The council made it clear that if he was not prepared to undertake the full range of his duties on Saturdays, he would not be required to attend for work and would not be paid. Accordingly, although Mr Miles performed other work on Saturday mornings, the council withheld 3/37ths of his pay for the relevant period, effectively not paying him for Saturday mornings.

Mr Miles brought an action claiming the sums withheld, but his claim was ultimately dismissed by the House of Lords.

LORD TEMPLEMAN: …In a contract of employment wages and work go together. The employer pays for work and the worker works for his wages. If the employer declines to pay, the worker need not work. If the worker declines to work, the employer need not pay. In an action by a worker to recover his pay he must allege and be ready to prove that he worked or was willing to work. Different considerations apply to a failure to work by sickness or other circumstances which may be governed by express or implied terms or by custom. In the present case the plaintiff disentitled himself for his salary for Saturday morning because he declined to work on Saturday morning in accordance with his duty.

Where industrial action takes the form of working inefficiently, the employer may decline to accept any work and the worker will not then be entitled to wages.

I agree with my noble and learned friend Lord Bridge of Harwich that industrial action can take many forms and that the legal consequences of industrial action will depend on the rights and obligations of the worker, the effect of the industrial action on the employer and the response of the employer. For my part, however, I take the provisional view that on principle a worker who, in conjunction with his fellow workers, declines to work efficiently with the object of harming his employer, is no more entitled to his wages under the contract than if he declined to work at all. The worker whose industrial action takes the form of 'going slow' inflicts intended damage which may be incalculable and non-apportionable but the employer, in order to avoid greater damage, is obliged to accept the reduced work the worker is willing to perform. In those circumstances, the worker cannot claim that he is entitled to his wages under the contract because he is deliberately working in a manner designed to harm the employer. But the worker will be entitled to be paid on a quantum meruit basis for the amount and value of the reduced work performed and accepted. In the present case, the council, by their letter dated 18.10.81, refused to accept any work from the plaintiff unless he worked normally and discharged all his duties. The plaintiff offered to work inefficiently on Saturday but could not compel the council to accept that offer, and upon their refusal to accept that offer, he ceased to be entitled to be paid for Saturday. My present view is that a worker who embarks on any form of industrial action designed to harm his employer gives up his right to wages under his contract of employment, in the hope that the industrial action will be successful in procuring higher wages in the future, and possibly in the hope that negotiations which end the industrial dispute will provide for some payment for the period of the industrial action.

LORD BRIGHTMAN: If an employee offers partial performance, as he does in some types of industrial conflict falling short of a strike, the employer has a choice. He may decline to accept the partial performance that is offered, in which case the employee is entitled to no remuneration for his unwanted services, even if they are performed. That is the instant case. Or the employer may accept the partial performance. If he accepts the partial performance as if it were performance which satisfied the terms of the contract, the employer must pay the full wage for the period of the partial performance because he will have precluded or estopped himself from asserting that the performance was not that which the contract required. But what is the position if the employee offers partial performance and the employer, usually of necessity, accepts such partial performance, the deficient work being understood by the employer and intended by the employee to fall short of the contractual requirements and being accepted by the employer as such? There are, as it seems to me, two possible answers. One possible answer is that the employer must pay the full wage but may recover by action or counterclaim or set-off damages for breach of contract. The other possible answer is that the employee is only entitled to so much remuneration as represents the value of the work he has done, i.e. quantum meruit. My noble and learned friend, Lord Templeman, prefers the latter solution, and so do I. My reason is this. One has to start with the assumption that the employee sues for his pay; the employer is only bound to pay the employee that which the employee can recover by action. The employee cannot recover his contractual wages because he cannot prove that he has performed or ever intended to perform his contractual obligations. If wages and work are interdependent, it is difficult to suppose that an employee who has voluntarily declined to perform his contractual work can claim his contractual wages. The employee offers partial performance with the object of inflicting the maximum damage on the employer at the minimum inconvenience to himself. If, in breach of his contract, an employee works with the object of harming his employer, he can hardly claim that he is working under his contract and is therefore entitled to his contractual wages. But nevertheless in the case supposed the employee has provided *some* services, albeit less than the contract required, and the employer has received those (non-contractual) services; therefore the employer must clearly pay something—not the contractual wages because the contractual work has deliberately not been performed. What can he recover? Surely the value of the services which he gave and which the employer received, i.e. quantum meruit.

LORD BRIDGE OF HARWICH:…Industrial action can take many different forms and there are a variety of options open to an employer confronted by such action. In particular I should, for my part, have preferred to express no opinion on questions arising in the case of an employee who deliberately 'goes slow' or otherwise does his work in a less than satisfactory way, when the employer nevertheless acquiesces in his continuing to work the full number of hours required under his contract. There may be no single, simple principle which can be applied in such cases irrespective of differences in circumstances. But I find it difficult to understand the basis on which, in such a case, the employee in place of remuneration at the contractual rate would become entitled to a quantum meruit. This would presuppose that the original contract of employment had in some way been superseded by a new agreement by which the employee undertook to work as requested by the employer for remuneration in a reasonable sum. This seems to me to be contrary to the realities of the situation.

NOTE: The House of Lords does not definitely answer the question of what the position would be where the employee goes slow or works to rule in breach of contract and the employer accepts (albeit reluctantly) the reduced work as partial performance of the contract (this was not a problem on the facts of the *Miles* case because his employers had refused his offer to attend on Saturday mornings to perform other duties). As will be seen from the extract, this is a difference of judicial view.

■ QUESTION

Can you explain the competing views?

Wiluszynski v *Tower Hamlets London Borough Council*
[1989] IRLR 259, Court of Appeal

On the facts, the employee was informed that he should not attend work if he was not prepared to carry out his full duties and that if he carried out work it would be regarded as unauthorised and undertaken in a voluntary capacity. However, throughout the month-long industrial dispute, Mr W (an estate officer in the housing department) continued to report for work and carried out his duties normally and conscientiously—except for a limited form of industrial action which involved refusing to deal with enquiries from councillors about their constituents' housing problems. Estate officers normally received only a handful of such queries per week. Indeed, once the dispute was over, Mr W dealt with all the outstanding councillor enquiries in less than three hours. Nevertheless, the council saw the answering of councillor queries as a significant part of officers' duties and refused to pay Mr W and the other officers any salary for the whole month of the dispute. The Court of Appeal upheld the employer's right to take that course of action.

NICHOLLS LJ: The defendant did not wish to take any steps, and it did not take any steps, physically to prevent the plaintiff and the other estate officers concerned from remaining at their desks. For instance, the defendant did not attempt to call in the police or security staff, or apply to the court for an injunction. For its part, the union did not wish to call its members out on strike, with all the ensuing dislocation to the defendant's numerous tenants, and it did not do so. Accordingly, the plaintiff and his colleagues insisted on continuing to work. The upshot was that, although the defendant had said it would not accept services which amounted to no more than partial performance of the employees' duties, in fact it did accept such services. On analysis, the plaintiff's case is that the defendant thereby resiled from its attitude as stated in the letter of 14 August. By accepting the services proffered, it waived its rights not to pay for those services. The defendant must therefore pay the plaintiff his salary, less a deduction for his failure to carry out one part of his duties: answering Members' Enquiries.

I cannot accept this argument. Implicit in this argument, with its reliance on the defendant's 'acceptance' of the plaintiff's services is the notion that in the event the defendant acted inconsistently with the attitude expressed in its warning letter, and that having chosen or elected so to act, it could not subsequently rely on the terms of the letter. But a person is not treated by the law as having chosen to accept that which is forced down his throat despite his objections. The rationale underlying the principle of waiver is that a person cannot have it both ways: he cannot blow hot and cold; he cannot eat his cake and have it; he cannot approbate and reprobate. But this does not mean that an employer of a large workforce is required physically to eject a defaulting employee from his office, or prevent him from going round the estate of houses for which he is responsible, on penalty that if he, the employer, does not do so he must pay the employee for the work which the employee insists on carrying out contrary to the employer's known wishes.

■ QUESTION

The interesting feature of this case was the rather narrow view of what constitutes 'acceptance' of the part performance. Indeed, would you agree that Lord Justice Nicholls does appear to be allowing the employer to 'have his cake and eat it'?

NOTES
1. See also *Ticehurst* v *British Telecommunications plc* [1992] IRLR 219, CA, set out at p. 639 (Chapter 11, Section 3.A).
2. For an illustration of the 'no work, no pay' principle in a case not involving industrial action, see *Luke* v *Stoke-on-Trent City Council* [2007] IRLR 777, CA.

(ii) An obligation to provide work?

Turner v *Sawdon & Co.*
[1901] 2 KB 653, Court of Appeal

Turner was a salesman who was paid a fixed salary and was not entitled to commission. He brought an action for breach of contract because, although his salary continued to be paid, he was given no work to do.

A. L. SMITH MR: The real question which the plaintiff thought to raise, and which was raised, was whether beyond the question of remuneration there was a further obligation on the masters that, during the period over which the contract was to extend, they should find continuous, or at least some, employment for the plaintiff. In my opinion such an action is unique—that is an action in which it is shown that the master is willing to pay the wages of his servant, but is sued for damages because the servant is not given employment. In *Turner* v *Goldsmith* [1891] 1 QB 544 the wages were to be paid in the form of commission, and that impliedly created a contract to find employment for the servant. This contract is different, being to employ for wages which are to be paid at a certain rate per year. I do not think this can be read otherwise than as a contract by the master to retain the servant, and during the time covered by the retainer to pay him wages under such a contract. It is within the province of the master to say that he will go on paying the wages, but that he is under no obligation to provide work. The obligation suggested is said to arise out of the undertaking to engage and employ the plaintiff as their representative salesman. It is said that if the salesman is not given employment which allows him to go on the market his hand is not kept in practice, and he will not be so efficient a salesman at the end of the term. To read in an obligation of that sort would be to convert the retainer at fixed wages into a contract to keep the servant in the service of his employer in such a manner as to enable the former to become *au fait* at his work. In my opinion, no such obligation arose under this contract, and it is a mistake to stretch the words of the contract so as to include in what is a mere retainer an obligation to employ the plaintiff continuously for the term of his service.

Collier v *Sunday Referee Publishing Co. Ltd*
[1940] 2 KB 647, King's Bench Division

Collier was employed as the chief sub-editor of the *Sunday Referee* newspaper. His employers sold the newspaper and the new owners did not wish to employ Collier, and so his employers retained him. They continued to pay his wages but gave him no work to do. He claimed damages arising from his employer's breach of contract in not providing him with work. The High Court upheld his claim.

ASQUITH J: It is true that a contract of employment does not necessarily, or perhaps normally, oblige the master to provide the servant with work. Provided I pay my cook her wages regularly she cannot complain if I choose to take any or all of my meals out. In some exceptional cases there is an obligation to provide work. For instance, where the servant is remunerated by commission, or where (as in the case of an actor or singer) the servant bargains, among other things, for publicity, and the master, by withholding work, also withholds the stipulated publicity: *Marbe* v *George Edwardes (Daly's Theatre) Ltd* [1928] 1 KB 269; but such cases are anomalous, and the normal rule is illustrated by authorities such as *Lagerwall* v *Wilkinson, Henderson & Clarke Ltd* [80 LT 55] and *Turner* v *Sawdon & Co.* [1901 2 KB 653] where the plaintiffs (a commercial traveller and a salesman respectively, retained for a fixed period and remunerated by salary) were held to have no legal complaint so long as the salary continued to be paid, notwithstanding that owing to their employers' action they were left with nothing to do. The employers were not bound to supply work to enable the employee, as the phrase goes, to 'keep his hand in', or to avoid the reproach of idleness, or even to make a profit out of a travelling allowance. In such a case there is no breach of contract, but the result is much the same as if there had been, because in either event the plaintiff is entitled to a sum or sums which are measured prima facie by the amount of salary in respect of the unexpired period of service.

   I do not hold that in the present case there was in the contract of employment an implied stipulation for publicity and an obligation to provide work for the purpose of providing publicity. But I do hold that the very foundation of the contract was the appointment of the plaintiff, during the contract period to a specific office. The defendants engaged the plaintiff, not to perform at large the sort of work commonly performed by any chief sub-editor. They engaged him to fill the office of chief sub-editor of a specific Sunday newspaper. By selling that newspaper they destroyed the office to which they had appointed him. That this is a breach of contract, I cannot doubt.

Breach v *Epsylon Industries Ltd*
[1976] IRLR 180, Employment Appeal Tribunal

Breach worked as the employer's chief engineer. The contracts on which he was employed were transferred to an overseas office and he was left with no work to do. He claimed that the failure to provide him with work amounted to a constructive dismissal and that he was entitled to a redundancy payment. The industrial tribunal rejected his claim and he appealed to the EAT.

PHILLIPS J: The difficulty that we find in the case is this: *Turner* v *Sawdon & Co* [1901] 2 KB 653 is a decision in the Court of Appeal. It is binding upon us as it was binding upon the industrial tribunal. However, it appears from the judgments in that case, and in particular from the observations of Stirling LJ, that there may well be cases which are exceptions to the general rule and where it can be said that from the nature of the employment, the circumstances in which it has to be served, and so on, there is indeed an obligation on the part of the employer to provide work. The line is a difficult one to draw. It may be said that the underlying thought in *Turner* v *Sawdon* is somewhat out of date and old fashioned now; that fact, if it be a fact, cannot invalidate the binding effect of that decision, but it may within limits lead to the consequence that a consideration of the facts will more easily lead to the conclusion that the case is one where there is such an obligation to provide work.

   ...It seems to us at least possible that the tribunal was saying to themselves that *Turner* v *Sawdon & Co* lays down a principle of law of the effect that employers are under no obligation to provide their employees with work to do. If that is so, then, with respect, there was a misdirection because it was necessary to look at the background to the contract to see how it should be construed, and whether a term ought not to be implied that in the circumstances of this case there was an obligation on the employers to provide work suitable for a chief engineer. If the tribunal did consider that, and if in fact, after considering all the material factors, they reached the view that there was no such implied term in the present case, then again with respect the decision is faulty, because it does not set out as it should do the reasoning by which that conclusion was reached.

NOTE: The EAT concluded that the industrial tribunal had made an error of law and remitted the case for rehearing.

Langston v Amalgamated Union of Engineering Workers
[1974] IRLR 182, National Industrial Relations Court

Langston objected on principle to the 'closed shop' and had refused to join the union. Following industrial action in protest against Langston's continued employment, the employers suspended him from work on full pay. In the course of legal action taken against the union under the now repealed Industrial Relations Act 1971, it was contended that, by inducing Langston's employers to suspend him, the union had induced a breach of contract.

SIR JOHN DONALDSON: The crucial question to be asked is, 'What is the consideration moving from the employers under the contract of employment?' In the case of theatrical performers it is a salary plus the opportunity of becoming better known. Thus a failure to pay the salary produces a partial failure of the consideration, and thus a breach of contract. But so does the cancellation of the performance even if the salary is paid: see *Herbert Clayton and Jack Waller Ltd* v *Oliver* ([1930] AC 209). Similarly the consideration in a commission or piece work contract of employment is the express obligation to pay an agreed rate for work done plus the implied obligation to provide a reasonable amount of work: see *Devonald* v *Rosser & Son* ([1906] 2 KB 728). In a contract for the employment of one who needs practice to maintain or develop his skills, the consideration will include an obligation to pay the salary or wage, but it may also extend to an obligation to provide a reasonable amount of work. The complainant's work as a spot welder may have been in the 'skilled' category, but we do not think that he needs practice in order to maintain his skills. There are, however, other cases in which the sole consideration moving from the employer is the obligation to pay a wage. An example is provided by *Turner* v *Sawdon & Co.* ([1901] 2 KB 653).

The complainant told us: 'I have always worked for my money. I have my pride. I would not be content to get my money for nothing.' We entirely accept what he says, but it does not follow that this was known to his employers when he was engaged. Still less does it follow that his contract of employment was made on the basis that his employers agreed to provide sufficient work to give the complainant a measure of job satisfaction. However, on the facts of this case we think that he comes into the piece worker category. The consideration moving from the employers was to pay him his basic wage for the normal working week, plus premium payments for hours actually worked on night shift or on overtime. The complainant, in common with other employees, was obliged to work days or nights and in such shop as the employers might require. But this right to require him to work a particular shift or in a particular place was not unfettered. Both night shifts and overtime had advantages and disadvantages. It was not only the employers' right but also their duty, forming part of the consideration, to allocate days, nights, overtime and place of work in such a way as to give all a fair opportunity of enjoying the rough as well as the smooth and, in particular, of earning premium payments. Once the employers suspended the complainant, they deprived him of his opportunity of earning premium payments. This was a breach of his contract of employment.

It is perfectly true, and greatly to the employers' credit, that they have sought to calculate what he would have earned if he had not been suspended. They paid him his basic wage week by week and later paid him a further sum in respect of lost premium payments. The calculation was long and difficult and during the hearing they agreed that an error had been made. They then agreed to pay him a further sum. No one can be quite sure that the sums are right now, but they have done their best. But this does not matter. These additional sums are not wages or premium payments. They are damages for breach of contract by failing to allow him the opportunity of earning a like amount.

NOTE: In *Langston* v *AUEW (No. 1)* [1974] 1 All ER 980, Lord Denning had attempted to completely sweep away the 'no right to work' rule. Commenting on the rule as set out in the dictum of Asquith J in *Collier*, Lord Denning stated:

> That was said 33 years ago. Things have altered much since then. We have repeatedly said in this court that a man has a right to work, which the courts will protect...I would not wish to express any decided view, but simply state the argument which could be put forward for Mr Langston. In these days an employer, when employing a skilled man, is bound to provide him with work. By which I mean that the man should be given the opportunity of doing his work when it is available and when he is ready and willing to do it.

As we have seen, when the *Langston* case came up for full consideration by the NIRC, Sir John Donaldson was not so expansive in approaching the right to work and preferred to fit the case within one of the established exceptions. Nevertheless after the *Breach* case, the exceptions are very wide, allowing plenty of room for judicial discretion in what is perceived to be a deserving case.

William Hill Organisation Ltd v Tucker
[1998] IRLR 313, Court of Appeal

Mr Tucker joined the William Hill organisation in 1987 and initially worked in the fixed-odds compiling department in Leeds. In April 1995, he moved to London and was appointed the senior dealer at William Hill Index and, as such, was the person who conducted the new and specialised business of spread betting. On appointment to that position, he entered into a new contract of employment.

The contract included details of Mr Tucker's salary and normal hours of work. It also emphasised that he must be prepared to work those hours necessary to carry out his duties in a proper and professional manner, and underlined the employer's commitment to their staff and readiness to ensure that they had every opportunity to develop their skills.

There was also a clause dealing with conflicts of interest which provided that 'Whilst in employment, you must not undertake any other employment or hold office, which creates a conflict of interest with the company.' A further clause prohibited the employee, for a period of 12 months following the termination of employment, from endeavouring to entice away the company's employees or customers with whom he had had dealings.

Under the terms of a new contract, the employers were required to give three months' notice of termination and Mr Tucker had to give one month's notice. However, in September 1996, that provision was varied. In return for a salary increase and entitlement to a company car, Mr Tucker agreed to increase the period of notice which he was required to give from one to six months.

Notwithstanding that agreed variation, on 2 February 1998, Mr Tucker purported to give one month's notice to leave William Hill Index. In his letter of resignation, he made it clear that he had received a more challenging and lucrative job offer from City Index Ltd, the company which had pioneered spread betting. He also explained his reasons for not giving six months' notice.

The employers responded by indicating that six months' notice was required and that his employment would continue until 1 August. However, he would not be required to attend for work for the remainder of his notice but would continue to receive his salary and all other contractual benefits. In other words, he would be required to take 'garden leave'.

Subsequently, the employers applied for an injunction restraining Mr Tucker until 1 August or further order from entering into employment with City Index or doing or omitting to do anything else which would amount to a breach of his obligation to the employers of good faith and fidelity. In dismissing that application, the High Court held that, in the absence of a contractual term entitling the employers to require Mr Tucker to take 'garden leave', they had a duty to provide him with work during the notice period, so as to enable him to exercise his skills. Their failure to do so amounted to a breach of contract which Mr Tucker was entitled to accept as terminating the contract and, accordingly, there was no basis for granting the injunction.

The Court of Appeal dismissed the employer's appeal.

MORRITT LJ: It is important to appreciate the limits to the obligation for which Mr Tucker contends. It is not suggested that there is an obligation to find work if there is none to be done or none which can be done with profit to the employer. Nor does he contend that the employer is bound to allocate work to him in preference to another employee if there is not enough work for both of them. He submits that if the job is there to be done and the employee was appointed to do it and is ready and willing to do so, then the employer must permit him to do so. He submits, by reference to the analogy of the cook given by Asquith J, in *Collier* v *Sunday Referee Publishing Co Ltd* [1940] 2 KB 647, that though the judge was not bound to eat the food his cook provided he was not entitled to put another cook in her kitchen. So, likewise in this case, he submits, the employer is not entitled to exclude Mr Tucker from the post to which they appointed him; the work is there to be done and it is the obligation of the employer to permit Mr Tucker to do it unless, which there is not, there is a provision in the contract absolving the employer from that obligation.

For my part, I accept that the contract of employment in this case can and should be construed as giving rise to such an obligation on the part of the employer. First, the post of senior dealer was a specific and unique post. It is not in dispute that Mr Tucker was asked by the employer in August 1994 to investigate what was involved in setting up a spread betting business. After considering the product of his researches, the employer decided to extend its operations into that field. Mr Tucker was the only senior dealer. There were juniors below him and a manager above him but he was the person appointed to conduct this new and specialised business. No doubt every employment nowadays has a title and job description which make it sound specific and unique but I have no doubt that the post to which Mr Tucker was appointed merited that description both in substance as well as form. Secondly, the skills necessary to the proper discharge of such duties did require their frequent exercise. Though it is not a case comparable to a skilled musician who requires regular practice to stay at concert pitch I have little doubt that frequent and continuing experience of the spread betting market, what it will bear and the subtle changes it goes through, is necessary to the enhancement and preservation of the skills of those who work in it.

NOTE: Although the Court of Appeal rejected the idea of a general right to work during notice, it did hold that there are cases where an employer is under an obligation to provide work, as well as pay, such as this case in which the employee's skills required frequent exercise. Where the circumstances are such that the employer has a contractual obligation to provide work, garden leave will only be lawful if it is expressly provided for in the contract of employment. If there is no express provision entitling the employer to send the employee on garden leave, employers may find the court refusing to grant an injunction restraining the employee from taking other employment during the notice period.

On the other hand, even if there is no contractual right to impose garden leave, the court may be willing to grant an injunction where the employee is guilty of a serious breach of infidelity (see *SG&R Valuation Services Co* v *Boudrais* [2008] IRLR 770, HC and *Standard Life Health Care Ltd* v *Gorman* [2010] IRLR 233, CA).

(iii) Care

Lister v *Romford Ice and Cold Storage Co. Ltd*
[1957] AC 555, House of Lords

L was a lorry driver employed by R Ltd, who negligently injured a fellow employee—who happened also to be his father—while packing his lorry in the course of his employment. L's father sued the company and obtained damages in respect of their vicarious liability. The company's insurers, exercising their rights of subrogation, then brought an action against L in the company's name. They claimed: (1) contribution from L as a joint tortfeasor under the provisions of the Law Reform (Married Women and Tortfeasors) Act 1935, s. 6; and (2) damages for breach of an implied term in his employment contract that he would use reasonable skill and care in his driving.

In the High Court, Ormrod J gave judgment for the company, holding that they were entitled under the 1935 Act to a contribution that would amount to a complete indemnity. L's appeal was dismissed by the Court of Appeal, Denning LJ dissenting; and L unsuccessfully appealed to the House of Lords.

VISCOUNT SIMONDS: ...It is, in my opinion, clear that it was an implied term of the contract that the appellant would perform his duties with proper care. The proposition of law stated by Willes J in *Harmer* v *Cornelius* [(1858) 5 CBNS 236 at 246] has never been questioned: 'When a skilled labourer,' he said, 'artizan, or artist is employed, there is on his part an implied warranty that he is of skill reasonably competent to the task he undertakes—Spondes peritiam artis. Thus, if an apothecary, a watch-maker, or an attorney be employed for reward, they each impliedly undertake to possess and exercise reasonable skill in their several arts...An express promise or express representation in the particular case is not necessary.' I see no ground for excluding from, and every ground for including in, this category a servant who is employed to drive a lorry which, driven without care, may become an engine of destruction and involve his master in very grave liability. Nor can I see any valid reason for saying that a distinction is to be made between possessing skill and exercising it. No such distinction is made in the cited case: on the contrary, 'possess' and 'exercise' are there conjoined. Of what advantage to the employer is his servant's undertaking that he possesses skill unless he undertakes also to use it? I have spoken of using skill rather than using care, for 'skill' is the word used in the cited case, but this embraces care. For even in so-called unskilled operations an exercise of care is necessary to the proper performance of duty.

I have already said that it does not appear to me to make any difference to the determination of any substantive issue in this case whether the respondents' cause of action lay in tort or breach of contract. But, in deference to Denning LJ, I think it right to say that I concur in what I understand to be the unanimous opinion of your Lordships that the servant owes a contractual duty of care to his master, and that the breach of that duty founds an action for damages for breach of contract, and that this (apart from any defence) is such a case. It is trite law that a single act of negligence may give rise to a claim either in tort or for breach of a term express or implied in a contract. Of this the negligence of a servant in performance of his duty is a clear example.

I conclude, then, the first stage of the argument by saying that the appellant was under a contractual obligation of care in the performance of his duty, that he committed a breach of it, that the respondents thereby suffered damage and they are entitled to recover that damage from him, unless it is shown either that the damage is too remote or that there is some other intervening factor which precludes the recovery.

[His Lordship turned to the question of indemnity, and discussed the various ways in which the alleged term had been formulated. In the course of concluding that no such term could be implied into the contract, his Lordship said:]

[It was not] suggested that in the present case there were any features which distinguished the relation of the appellant and the respondents from that of any other driver and his employer. That is why at the outset of this opinion I said that this appeal raises a question of general importance. For the real question becomes, not what terms can be implied in a contract between two individuals who are assumed to be making a bargain in regard to a particular transaction or course of business; we have to take a wider view, for we are concerned with a general question, which, if not correctly described as a question of status, yet can only be answered by considering the relation in which the drivers of motor-vehicles and their employers generally stand to each other. Just as the duty of care, rightly regarded as a contractual obligation, is imposed on the servant, or the duty not to disclose confidential information (see *Robb* v *Green* [1895] 2 QB 315), or the duty not to betray secret processes (see *Amber Size and Chemical Co Ltd* v *Menzel* [1913] 2 Ch 239), just as the duty is imposed on the master not to require his servant to do any illegal act, just so the question must be asked and answered whether in the world in which we live today it is a necessary condition of the relation of master and man that the master should, to use a broad colloquialism, look after the whole matter of insurance. If I were to try to apply the familiar tests where the question is whether a term should be implied in a particular contract in order to give it what is called business efficacy, I should lose myself in the attempt to formulate it with the necessary precision. The necessarily vague evidence given by the parties and the fact that the action is brought without the assent of the employers shows at least ex post facto how they regarded the position. But this is not conclusive; for, as I have said, the solution of the problem does not rest on the implication of a term in a particular contract of service but upon more general considerations.

LORD RADCLIFFE [dissenting]: ...On the first point [i.e. what liability did the appellant incur as a result of his negligent driving?] I think it plain that the law does impute to an employee a duty to exercise reasonable care in his handling of his employer's property. It is the fact of such employment that places the property within his control; and if, as must be the case, he owes a general duty to all concerned not to be negligent in his exercise of that control, it would be a surprising anomaly that, merely because there was also a contractual relationship between himself and his employer, the standard of his obligation to his employer were to be somehow lower than the standard of his obligation to the outside world.

I cannot see any good reason why we should uphold the existence of such an anomaly. If the contract of employment is viewed as a general legal relationship in which the law imputes certain rights and responsibilities to each side, it would assign a very undignified position to the employee to suppose that the employer takes him 'with all faults' and that the employee does not by virtue of his engagement impliedly undertake to use all reasonable care in the conduct of his employer's affairs. To say this is to say nothing new in the law. I am satisfied that from early times the law has consistently recognised the existence of this duty. I need not lengthen my opinion by reciting the authorities, some of which are noticed by others of your Lordships.

It was much canvassed in argument before your Lordships whether, if there was some such duty on the appellant, it was anything more than the general duty he owed the world to avoid the tort of negligence...

It is perhaps sufficient if I say that, in my view, this question is a somewhat artificial one. The existence of the duty arising out of the relationship between employer and employed was recognised by the law without the institution of an analytical inquiry whether the duty was in essence contractual or tortious. What mattered was that the duty was there. A duty may exist by contract, express or implied. Since, in any event, the duty in question is one which exists by imputation or implication of law and not by virtue of any express negotiation between the parties, I should be inclined to say that there is no real distinction between the two possible sources of obligation. But it is certainly, I think, as much contractual as tortious. Since in modern times the relationship between master and servant, between employer and employed, is inherently one of contract, it seems to me entirely correct to attribute the duties which arise from that relationship to implied contract. It is a familiar position in our law that the same wrongful act may be made the subject of an action either in contract or in tort at the election of the claimant, and, although the course chosen may produce certain incidental consequences which would not have followed had the other course been adopted, it is a mistake to regard the two kinds of liability as themselves necessarily exclusive of each other.

[His Lordship went on to hold, contrary to Viscount Simonds, that there was also an implied term in the contract to the effect that the employer would not seek to be indemnified by the employee in the event of third party liability.]

[Lord Morton and Lord Tucker delivered judgments concurring with Viscount Simonds; Lord Somervell agreed with Lord Radcliffe.]

Appeal dismissed.

NOTES
1. Since 1957, there has been a 'gentlemen's agreement' among insurance companies not to bring such actions against workers.
2. The Health and Safety at Work etc. Act 1974 places a duty on every employer 'to ensure, so far as is reasonably practicable, the health, safety and welfare at work of all his [*sic*] employees' (s. 2). Breach of the Act's provisions may lead to criminal prosecution or a civil action for breach of statutory duty. In addition, under the contract of employment there is a general implied duty on employers to exercise care. This is primarily a duty to take reasonable care for the safety of employees. This duty extends to acting reasonably in dealing with complaints about lack of safety which are drawn to their notice by employees (see *Waters* v *Commissioner of Police of the Metropolis* [2000] IRLR 720—failing to deal with a complaint of sexual assault by a colleague; *British Aircraft Corporation Ltd* v *Austin* [1978] IRLR 332—failing to respond to an employee's complaint about lack of adequate safety equipment; and *Waltons & Morse* v *Dorrington* [1997] IRLR 448—failure to deal adequately with an employee's complaints about exposure to the cigarette smoke of her fellow employees).

In addition to the duty to deal adequately with complaints, the duty of care includes an obligation to maintain a safe working environment so as not to expose the employee in a position of exposure to excessive physical danger (see *Graham Oxley Tool Steels Ltd* v *Firth* [1980] IRLR 135—employees left working for several months in intolerable working conditions), or stress owing to workload (*Walker* v *Northumberland County Council* [1995] IRLR 35—extracted later in this section), or excessive workload (*Johnstone* v *Bloomsbury Health Authority* [1991] IRLR 118, CA). Breach of the duty of care can lead to an action for damages in tort or contract and applies to psychiatric as well as physical injuries (*Gogay* v *Hertfordshire County Council* [2000] IRLR 703). Breach of the implied term can also constitute constructive dismissal for unfair dismissal claims. The duty of care is an implied term which is capable of overriding the employer's exercise of discretion based upon express contractual powers (*Johnstone* v *Bloomsbury Health Authority* [1991] IRLR 118, CA).

(a) Stress

Walker v Northumberland County Council
[1995] IRLR 35, Queen's Bench Division

Mr Walker was employed by the council as an area social services officer, with responsibility for four teams of field workers. His immediate superior was Mr Davison.

The volume of work to be undertaken by Mr Walker and his team gradually increased, but there was no corresponding increase in staffing levels. From 1985 onwards, Mr Walker and others produced reports and memoranda concerning the urgent need to alleviate the work pressures and calling for redistribution of staff or reorganisation. In 1986, Mr Walker suffered a nervous breakdown. Before returning to work in March 1987 he discussed his position with Mr Davison who agreed to provide him with assistance. However, within a month of his return to work, assistance was withdrawn. In September 1987 he suffered a second mental breakdown, and in February 1988 he was dismissed on grounds of permanent ill health.

It was held that the defendants were in breach of the duty of care owed to the plaintiff as his employer in respect of the second mental breakdown which he suffered as a result of stress and anxiety occasioned by his job.

COLEMAN J: ... There has been little judicial authority on the extent to which an employer owes to his employees a duty not to cause them psychiatric damage by the volume or character of the work which the employees are required to perform. It is clear law that an employer has a duty to provide his employee with a reasonably safe system of work and to take reasonable steps to protect him from risks which are reasonably foreseeable. Whereas the law on the extent of this duty has developed almost exclusively in cases involving physical injury to the employee as distinct from injury to his mental health, there is no logical reason why risk of psychiatric damage should be excluded from the scope of an employer's duty of care or from the co-extensive implied term in the contract of employment. That said, there can be no doubt that the circumstances in which claims based on such damage are likely to arise will often give rise to extremely difficult evidential problems of foreseeability and causation. This is particularly so in the environment of the professions where the plaintiff may be ambitious and dedicated, determined to succeed in his career in which he knows the work to be demanding, and may have a measure of discretion as to how and when and for how long he works, but where the character or volume of the work given to him eventually drives him to breaking point. Given that the professional work is intrinsically demanding and stressful, at what point is the employer's duty to take protective steps engaged? What assumption is he entitled to make about the employee's resilience, mental toughness and stability of character, given that people of clinically normal personality may have a widely differing ability to absorb stress attributable to their work?

...

In the result, it is established that by April 1987 Mr Walker was exposed in his job to a reasonably foreseeable risk to his mental health which materially exceeded the risk to be anticipated in the ordinary course of an area officer's job. Was it in those circumstances reasonable for the council to take action to alleviate or remove that risk? In my view, the only course which would have had a reasonable probability of preventing another mental breakdown was the provision of continuous or at least substantial backup for Mr Walker in the Blyth office from Mr Robinson or somebody of equal experience who could in effect have acted as Mr Walker's deputy. However, in deciding what was reasonable conduct I must have regard to the acute staffing problems which at the relevant time confronted the council.

...

In my judgment the policy decision/operational decision dichotomy has no more part to play in the context of the duty of care to an employee with whom a statutory body has a contract of employment than it would have in the context of any other contract made by such a body. Just as it would be no defence to a claim for non-performance of a contract for the sale of goods that the local authority had resolved as a matter of policy that the use of its scarce resources for the performance of the contract was inexpedient, so it would be no defence to a claim for breach of the implied term in a contract of employment that the employer would exercise reasonable care for the safety of his employee that its failure to do so was the result of a policy decision on the exercise of its statutory powers. Since the scope of the duty of care owed to an employee to take reasonable steps to provide a safe system of work is co-extensive with the scope of the implied term as to the employee's safety in the contract of employment, see for example, *Johnstone* v *Bloomsbury Health Authority* [1991] IRLR

118, to introduce a ring fence round policy decisions giving rise to unsafe systems of work for the purposes of claims in tort which was not available to the defendant statutory body in defences to claims in contract would be to implant into employment law a disparity which, in my judgment, would be wholly wrong in principle. Whereas the mutual intention to be imputed to the parties to a contract of employment with a public body could be expected to qualify the employer's duty of safety by requiring the employer to do no more than take reasonable steps to procure the employee's safety at work, it is inconceivable that such mutual intention would require the employer to take only such steps for the employee's safety as political expediency from time to time permitted if the exercise of statutory powers were involved. In the absence of authority to the contrary or of compelling common law principle, there can be no sustainable basis for subjecting the duty of care in tort to such a qualification.

That said, the duty of an employer public body, whether in contract or tort, to provide a safe system of work is, as I have said, a duty only to do what is reasonable, and in many cases it may be necessary to take into account decisions which are within the policy-making area and the reasons for those decisions in order to test whether the body's conduct has been reasonable. In that exercise there can be no basis for treating the public body differently in *principle* from any other commercial employer, although there would have to be taken into account considerations such as budgetary constraints and perhaps lack of flexibility of decision-taking which might not arise with a commercial employer.

Having regard to the reasonably foreseeable size of the risk of repetition of Mr Walker's illness if his duties were not alleviated by effective additional assistance and to the reasonably foreseeable gravity of the mental breakdown which might result if nothing were done, I have come to the conclusion that the standard of care to be expected of a reasonable local authority required that in March 1987 such additional assistance should be provided, if not on a permanent basis, at least until restructuring of the social services had been effected and the workload on Mr Walker thereby permanently reduced. That measure of additional assistance ought to have been provided, notwithstanding that it could be expected to have some disruptive effect on the council's provision of services to the public. When Mr Walker returned from his first illness the council had to decide whether it was prepared to go on employing him in spite of the fact that he had made it sufficiently clear that he must have effective additional help if he was to continue at Blyth Valley. It chose to continue to employ him, but provided no effective help. In so doing it was, in my judgment, acting unreasonably and therefore in breach of its duty of care.

I understand it to be accepted that if there was breach of duty, damage was caused by that breach. However, in view of the fact that I have decided this case on the second breakdown alone, it is right to add that I am satisfied on the evidence that had the further assistance been provided to Mr Walker, his second breakdown would probably not have occurred.

NOTE: In *Sutherland* v *Hatton* [2002] IRLR 263, the Court of Appeal laid down important new guidelines for determining employer liability for psychiatric illness caused by workplace stress. The overall result of the decision is likely to make it more difficult for employees to win stress at work claims. The case holds that to trigger the duty on an employer to take steps to safeguard an employee, the indications must be plain enough for any reasonable employer to realise that he or she should do something about it.

'Foreseeability' depends upon what the employer knows, or ought reasonably to know, about the individual employee. The question is not whether psychiatric injury is foreseeable in a person of 'ordinary fortitude'. The employer's duty is owed to each individual employee, not to some unidentified outsider. The test, therefore, is whether a harmful reaction to the pressures of the workplace is reasonably foreseeable to the individual concerned. Such a reaction will have two components: (1) an injury to health; which (2) is attributable to stress at work.

The answer to the foreseeability question will thus depend on the interrelationship between the particular characteristics of the employee concerned and the particular demands which the employer casts upon him. The test is the same whatever the employment. There are no occupations which should be regarded as intrinsically dangerous to mental health. It is not the job but the interaction between the individual and the job which causes harm. Factors likely to be relevant in answering the threshold question include, first, the nature and extent of the work done by the employee. Is the workload more than is normal for the particular job? Is the work particularly intellectually or emotionally demanding for this employee? Are demands being made of this employee unreasonable when compared with the demands made of others in the same or comparable jobs? Or are there signs that others doing this job are suffering harmful levels of stress? Is there an abnormal level of sickness or absenteeism in the same job or department? Second, and more important, are there signs of impending harm to health from the employee himself? Has he a particular problem or vulnerability? Has he already suffered from illness attributable to stress at work? Have there recently been frequent or prolonged absences which are uncharacteristic of him or others? If the employee or his doctor makes it plain that unless something is done to help there is a clear risk of a breakdown in physical or mental health, then the employer will have to think what can be done about it.

Once the risk of harm to health from stresses in the workplace is foreseeable, it is essential to consider whether and in what respect the employer has broken that duty. Before finding an employer in breach of his duty of care, it is necessary in every case to consider whether and in what respect the employer has broken that duty. Before finding an employer in breach of his duty of care, it is necessary in every case to consider not only what the employer could have done but what he should have done. The employer is only in breach of duty if he has failed to take the steps which are reasonable in the circumstances, bearing in mind the magnitude of the risk of harm occurring, the gravity of harm which may occur, the costs and practicability of preventing it, and the justifications for running the risk.

Steps which might be suggested include giving the employee a sabbatical; transferring him to other work; redistributing the work; giving him some extra help for a while; arranging treatment or counselling; or providing 'buddying' or mentoring schemes to encourage confidence. Whether it is reasonable to expect the employer to take such steps depends upon factors such as the size and scope of the employer's operation, its resources, whether it is in the public or private sector, and other demands placed upon it, such as the interests of other employees at the workplace. It may not be reasonable to expect the employer to rearrange the work for the sake of one employee which prejudices the work of others. An employer who tries to balance all these interests by offering a confidential advice service, with referral to appropriate counselling or treatment services, to employees who fear that they may be suffering harmful levels of stress is unlikely to be found in breach of duty, except where he has been placing totally unreasonable demands upon an individual in circumstances where the risk of harm was clear. (But see *Dickins* v *O2 plc* [2009] IRLR 58 discussed later in this note.)

An employer can only reasonably be expected to take steps which are likely to do some good and this is a matter on which the court is likely to require expert evidence. If the only reasonable and effective way of safeguarding the employee would be to demote or dismiss him, the employer will not be in breach of duty in allowing a willing employee to continue in the job. In principle, the law should not be saying to the employer that it is his duty to dismiss an employee who wants to go on working for him. If there is no alternative solution, it has to be for the employee to decide whether or not to carry on in the same employment and take the risk of a breakdown in his health, or whether to leave that employment and look for work elsewhere before he becomes unemployable.

Where a breach of duty has been shown, it is then necessary to show that particular breach of duty caused the harm. It is not enough to show that occupational stress caused the harm. However, the employee does not have to show that the breach of duty was the sole cause of his ill-health; it was enough to show that it made a material contribution.

Where the harm suffered had more than one cause, the employer should only pay for that proportion of the harm suffered which is attributable to his wrongdoing, unless the harm is truly indivisible. It is for the defendant to raise the question of apportionment. Where the breach of duty has exacerbated a pre-existing disorder or accelerated the effect of a pre-existing vulnerability, that will be reflected in the assessment of damages, as will the chance that the employee would have succumbed to a stress-related disorder in any event.

In *Young* v *Post Office* [2002] IRLR 660, the Court of Appeal in considering *Sutherland* concluded that where an employee has already suffered from psychiatric illness resulting from occupational stress, it is plainly foreseeable that there might be a recurrence if appropriate steps are not taken when the employee returns to work. *Sutherland* does not require an employee who is known to be vulnerable to tell his employer that the job is again becoming too much for him.

In *Intel Corporation (UK) Ltd* v *Daw* [2007] IRLR 355, the Court of Appeal held that the fact that the employer had a counselling service, which the employee could have used, did not discharge the employer's duty of care. The guidance provided in *Hatton* does not have to be applied *in toto*.

As the impact of the decision in *Sutherland* takes effect, issues as to foreseeability of psychiatric illness continue to involve the courts. In *Pratley* v *Surrey County Council* [2003] IRLR 794, the Court of Appeal drew a distinction between the risk of psychiatric injury arising in the future through continuing work overload and a risk of collapse in the short term. Even though there was a causative link between the breakdown and the failure to implement a new system of work, the immediate collapse was not reasonably foreseeable. As a result the employers were not negligent. The Court of Appeal in *Hartman* v *South Essex Mental Health & Community Care NHS Trust* [2005] IRLR 293 confirms the general principles to be applied in cases involving psychiatric injury arising out of stress at work, as laid down in *Sutherland* v *Hatton*. Furthermore, where an employee is referred to the employer's occupational health department, such information is to be treated as confidential and cannot be attributed to an employer's knowledge of either a disability or psychiatric problems. If an employee therefore wants to take advantage of any recommendations made in such a confidential report, they will have to waive their right to confidentiality. This decision has been followed in *Harding* v *The Pub Estate Company Ltd* [2005] EWCA (Civ) 553, which held that to succeed in a claim for stress at work, such harm must have been reasonably foreseeable and therefore the employer must have had some indication of possible harm to his employee. As a result the employee cannot rely on information confidential to him in establishing the extent of reasonable foreseeability.

However, the decision in *Sutherland* has been qualified by the decision in *Barber* v *Somerset County Council* [2004] IRLR 475, in which the House of Lords held that the practical guidance in *Sutherland* should not be read as having anything like statutory force. The Court of Appeal judgment in *Dickins* v *O2 plc* [2009] IRLR 58 is in line with this approach. The court held that a reasonable employer may need more than a confidential counselling service to deal with work-related stress. Active intervention may be necessary in order to avoid liability for an employee's subsequent illness.

It should be noted that the HSE has recently produced new guidelines on work-related stress: *Managing the Causes of Work-related Stress: A step by step approach using the management standards* (HSE, 2007).

See also *Connor* v *Surrey County Council* [2010] EWCA Civ 286.

(b) A duty of care in supplying references

In *Spring* v *Guardian Assurance plc* [1993] IRLR 122, CA, the House of Lords held that in certain circumstances there was an implied duty of care on employers not to be negligent in preparation and presentation of references.

Spring v Guardian Assurance plc
[1994] IRLR 460, House of Lords

Mr Spring claimed damages for economic loss from his former employers. He claimed that, in supplying a reference containing allegedly inaccurate information to a prospective employer, they had broken a duty of care to Mr Spring and were liable in the tort of negligent misstatement. In the High Court, the judge allowed the claim. The Court of Appeal allowed the appeal of Mr Spring's former employers and set aside the judgment in the plaintiff's favour. The House of Lords, by a majority of four to one, allowed Mr Spring's appeal.

LORD SLYNN OF HADLEY: ...two questions therefore arise. The first is whether the nature of the tort of defamation and the tort of injurious falsehood is such that it would be wrong to recognise the possibility of a duty of care in negligence for a false statement. The second question is whether, independently of the existence of the other two torts, and taking the tests adopted by Lord Bridge of Harwich in *Caparo Industries plc* v *Dickman* [1990] 2 AC 605, a duty of care can in any event arise in relation to the giving of a reference. If the answer to the first is no, and to the second yes, then it remains to consider whether in all the circumstances such a duty of care was owed in this case by an employer to an ex-employee.

As to the first question, the starting point in my view is that the suggested claim in negligence and the torts of defamation and injurious and malicious falsehood do not cover the same ground, as Mr Tony Weir shows in his note in (1993) CLJ 376. They are separate torts, defamation not requiring a proof by the plaintiff that the statement was untrue (though justification may be a defence) or that he suffered economic damage, but being subject to defences quite different from those in negligence, such as the defence of qualified privilege which makes it necessary to prove malice. Malicious falsehood requires proof that the statement is false, that harm has resulted and that there was express malice. Neither of these involves the concept of a duty of care. The essence of a claim in defamation is that a person's reputation has been damaged; it may or not involve the loss of a job or economic loss. A claim that a reference has been given negligently is essentially based on the fact, not so much that reputation has been damaged, as that a job, or an opportunity, has been lost. A statement carelessly made may not be defamatory—a statement that a labourer is 'lame', a secretary 'very arthritic', when neither statement is true, though they were true of some other employee mistakenly confused with the person named.

I do not consider that the existence of either of these two heads of claim, defamation and injurious falsehood, a priori prevents the recognition of a duty of care where, but for the existence of the other two torts, it would be fair, just and reasonable to recognise it in a situation where the giver of a reference has said or written what is untrue and where he has acted unreasonably and carelessly in what he has said.

The policy reasons underlying the requirement that the defence of qualified privilege is only dislodged if express malice is established do not necessarily apply in regard to a claim in negligence. There may be other policy reasons in particular situations which should prevail. Thus, in relation to a reference given by an employer in respect of a former employee or a departing employee (and assuming no contractual obligation to take care in giving a reference) it is relevant to consider the changes which have taken place in the employer/employee relationship, with far greater duties imposed on the employer than in the past, whether by statute or by judicial decision, to care for the physical, financial and even psychological welfare of the employee.

As to the second question, it is a relevant circumstance that in many cases an employee will stand no chance of getting another job, let alone a better job, unless he is given a reference. There is at least a moral obligation on the employer to give it. This is not necessarily true when the claim is laid in defamation, even if on an occasion of qualified privilege. In the case of an employee or ex-employee the damage is clearly foreseeable if a careless reference is given; there is as obvious a proximity of relationship in this context as can be imagined. The sole question therefore, in my view, is whether balancing all the factors (Lord Bridge in *Caparo*) as to whether 'the situation should be one in which the court considers it fair, just and reasonable that the law should impose a duty of a given scope upon the one party for the benefit of the other'.

Hedley Byrne & Co. Ltd. v *Heller & Partners Ltd.* [1964] AC 465 does not decide the present case, but I find it unacceptable that the person to whom a reference is given about an employee X should be able to sue for negligence if he relies on the statement (and, for example, employs X who proves to be inadequate for the job) as it appears to be assumed that he can; but that X who is refused employment because the recipient relies on a reference negligently given should have no recourse unless he can prove express malice as defined by Lord Diplock in *Horrocks* v *Lowe* [1975] AC 135 at pp. 149–151.

I do not accept the in terrorem arguments that to allow a claim in negligence will constitute a restriction on freedom of speech or that in the employment sphere employers will refuse to give references or will only give such bland or adulatory ones as is forecast. They should be and are capable of being sufficiently robust as to express frank and honest views after taking reasonable care both as to the factual content and as to the opinion expressed. They will not shrink from the duty of taking reasonable care when they realise the importance of the reference both to the recipient (to whom it is assumed that a duty of care exists) and to the employee (to whom it is contended on existing authority there is no such duty). They are not being asked to warrant absolutely the accuracy of the facts or the incontrovertible validity of the opinions expressed, but to take reasonable care in compiling or giving the reference and in verifying the information on which it is based. The courts can be trusted to set a standard which is not higher than the law of negligence demands. Even if it is right that the number of references given will be reduced, the quality and value will be greater and it is by no means certain that to have more references is more in the public interest than to have more careful references.

Those giving such references can make it clear what are the parameters within which the reference is given, such as stating their limited acquaintance with the individual either as to time or as to situation. This issue does not arise in the present case but it may be that employers can make it clear to the subject of the reference that they will only give one if he accepts that there will be a disclaimer of liability to him and to the recipient of the reference.

Nor does it follow that if a duty of care is recognised in some situations it must exist in all situations. It seems to me that for the purposes of deciding whether the law recognises the duty as being fair, just and reasonable, there may be a difference between the situation where it is an employer or ex-employer who gives a reference and the situation where a reference is given by someone who has only a social acquaintance with the person who is the subject of the reference. There may be difficult situations in between but these will, as is the common practice, have to be worked out in particular situations.

I do not for my part consider that to recognise the existence of a duty of care in some situations when a reference is given necessarily means that the law of defamation has to be changed or that a substantial section of the law relating to defamation and malicious falsehood is 'emasculated' (Court of Appeal [1993] IRLR 122 at p. 131, 100). They remain distinct torts. It may be that there will be less resort to these torts because a more realistic approach on the basis of a duty of care is adopted. If to recognise that such a duty of care exists means that there have to be such changes—either by excluding the defence of qualified privilege from the master/servant situation or by withdrawing the privilege where negligence as opposed to express malice is shown—then I would in the interests of recognising a fair, just and reasonable result in the master/servant situation accept such change.

NOTES
1. Lords Goff, Slynn, and Woolf held that there was also an implied term in the contract of employment which places a duty on the employer to take due care and skill in preparation of references.

2. According to Lord Slynn and Lord Woolf, there are circumstances in which it is necessary to imply a term into the contract of employment that the employer will provide the employee with a reference at the request of a prospective employer. Such circumstances might arise where the contract relates to an engagement of a class where it is normal practice to require a reference from a previous employer and that the employee cannot be expected to enter that class unless and until a reference is supplied.

3. In *Cox v Sun Alliance Life Ltd* [2001] IRLR 48, the Court of Appeal found employers liable in negligence for failing to take reasonable care to be accurate and fair when they provided a reference which suggested that they had a reasonable basis for dismissing the claimant on the ground of dishonesty amounting to corruption. In fact, the charges of dishonesty had never been put to him, had not been made the subject of proper investigation, and were shelved pending negotiation of an agreed resignation settlement.

   According to Mummery LJ, discharge of the duty of care to provide an accurate and fair reference will usually involve making a reasonable inquiry into the factual basis of the statement in the reference. A similar approach to that set out in *British Home Stores Ltd* v *Burchell* [1978] IRLR 379, EAT, in relation to dismissal on grounds of misconduct is appropriate. In order to take reasonable care to give a fair and accurate reference, an employer should confine unfavourable statements about the employee to those matters into which they had made reasonable investigation and had reasonable grounds for believing to be true—although, in order to discharge the duty of care, an employer is not obliged to carry on with an inquiry into an employee's conduct after the employee has resigned. If an investigation is discontinued, unfavourable comments should be confined to matters which had been investigated before the investigation.

   In a helpful *obiter*, Mummery LJ advised that where the terms of an agreed resignation or the compromise of an unfair dismissal claim make provision for the supply of a reference, the parties should ensure, as far as possible, that the exact wording of a fair and accurate reference is fully discussed, clearly agreed, and carefully recorded in writing on the COT3 at the same time as other severance terms.

(iv) The duty to cooperate

Isle of Wight Tourist Board v *Coombes*

[1976] IRLR 413, Employment Appeal Tribunal

Mrs Coombes was personal secretary to the Director of the Board. She resigned when, in her hearing and after an altercation, the Director said to a fellow employee, 'she is an intolerable bitch on a Monday morning'. Her unfair dismissal claim was upheld by an industrial tribunal and the EAT rejected the employer's appeal.

BRISTOW J: ... [T]he relationship between somebody in the position of the director of this board and his personal secretary must be one of complete confidence. They must trust each other; they must respect each other. I suspect one should go further and say that, if the work is to be done properly, they must like each other.

Malik v *BCCI SA (in liq.)*

[1997] IRLR 462, House of Lords

In litigation arising out of the collapse of BCCI, the House of Lords decided that the employees' contracts contained an implied term that the bank would not, without reasonable and proper cause, conduct itself in a manner likely to destroy or seriously damage the relationship of confidence and trust between employer and employee.

LORD STEYN: ...

THE IMPLIED TERM OF MUTUAL TRUST AND CONFIDENCE

The employees do not rely on a term implied in fact. They do not therefore rely on an individualised term to be implied from the particular provisions of their employment contracts considered against their specific contextual setting. Instead they rely on a standardised term implied by law, that is, on a term which is said to be an incident of all contracts of employment: *Scally* v *Southern Health and Social Services Board* [1991] IRLR 522, at 525, 12. Such implied terms operate as default rules. The parties are free to exclude or modify them. But it is common ground that in the present case the particular terms of the contracts of employment of the two employees could not affect an implied obligation of mutual trust and confidence.

The employees' primary case is based on a formulation of the implied term that has been applied at first instance and in the Court of Appeal. It imposes reciprocal duties on the employer and employee. Given that this case is concerned with alleged obligations of an employer I will concentrate on its effect on the position of employers. For convenience I will set out the term again. It is expressed to impose an obligation that the employer shall not:

> …without reasonable and proper cause, conduct itself in a manner calculated and likely to destroy or seriously damage the relationship of confidence and trust between employer and employee.

See *Woods* v *WM Car Services (Peterborough) Ltd* [1981] IRLR 347 (Browne-Wilkinson J), approved in *Lewis* v *Motorworld Garages Ltd* [1985] IRLR 465 and *Imperial Group Pension Trust Ltd* v *Imperial Tobacco Ltd* [1991] IRLR 66. A useful anthology of the cases applying this term, or something like it, is given in Sweet and Maxwell's *Encyclopedia of Employment Law* (loose leaf edn), vol. 1, paragraph 1.507, pp. 1467–1470. The evolution of the term is a comparatively recent development. The obligation probably has its origin in the general duty of cooperation between contracting parties: B.A. Hepple, *Employment Law*, 4th edn (1981), paragraphs 291–292, pp. 134–135. The reason for this development is part of the history of the development of employment law in this century. The notion of a 'master and servant' relationship became obsolete. Lord Slynn of Hadley recently noted 'the changes which have taken place in the employer and employee relationship, with far greater duties imposed on the employer than in the past, whether by statute or judicial decision, to care for the physical, financial and even psychological welfare of the employee': *Spring* v *Guardian Assurance plc* [1994] IRLR 460 at 474, 86. A striking illustration of this change is *Scally*, to which I have already referred, where the House of Lords implied a term that all employees in a certain category had to be notified by an employer of their entitlement to certain benefits. It was the change in legal culture which made possible the evolution of the implied term of trust and confidence.

There was some debate at the hearing about the possible interaction of the implied obligation of confidence and trust with other more specific terms implied by law. It is true that the implied term adds little to the employee's implied obligations to serve his employer loyally and not to act contrary to his employer's interests. The major importance of the implied duty of trust and confidence lies in its impact on the obligations of the employer: Douglas Brodie, 'Recent Cases, Commentary, The Heart of the Matter: Mutual Trust and Confidence' (1996) 25 ILJ 121. And the implied obligation as formulated is apt to cover the great diversity of situations in which a balance has to be struck between an employer's interest in managing his business as he sees fit and the employee's interest in not being unfairly and improperly exploited.

The evolution of the implied term of trust and confidence is a fact. It has not yet been endorsed by your Lordships' House. It has proved a workable principle in practice. It has not been the subject of adverse criticism in any decided cases and it has been welcomed in academic writings. I regard the emergence of the implied obligation of mutual trust and confidence as a sound development.

Given the shape of the appeal, my preceding observations may appear unnecessary. But I have felt it necessary to deal briefly with the existence of the implied term for two reasons. First, the implied obligation involves a question of pure law and your Lordships' House is not bound by any agreement of the parties on it or by the acceptance of the obligation by the judge or the Court of Appeal. Secondly, in response to a question, counsel for the bank said that his acceptance of the implied obligation is subject to three limitations:

(1) That the conduct complained of must be conduct involving the treatment of the employee in question;

(2) That the employee must be aware of such conduct while he is an employee;

(3) That such conduct must be calculated to destroy or seriously damage the trust between the employer and employee.

In order to place these suggested limitations in context it seemed necessary to explain briefly the origin, nature and scope of the implied obligation. But subject to examining the merits of the suggested limitations, I am content to accept the implied obligation of trust and confidences as established.

BREACH OF THE IMPLIED OBLIGATION

Two preliminary observations must be made. First, the sustainability of the employees' claims must be approached as if an application to strike out was under consideration. That is how the judge and the Court of Appeal approached the matter. And the same approach must now govern. Secondly, given the existence of an obligation of trust and confidence, it is important to approach the question of a breach of that obligation correctly. Mr Douglas Brodie of Edinburgh University, in his helpful article to which I have already referred, put the matter succinctly (pp. 121–122):

In assessing whether there has been a breach, it seems clear that what is significant is the impact of the employer's behaviour on the employee rather than what the employer intended. Moreover, the impact will be assessed objectively.

Both limbs of Mr Brodie's observations seem to me to reflect classic contract law principles and I would gratefully adopt his statement.

NOTES

1. The impact of the decision on the scope of damages for wrongful dismissal is considered following a further extract from the case at p. 367 (Chapter 7, Section 5.A).
2. We shall see in Chapter 7 on termination of employment that, in the context of unfair dismissal, the courts have been prepared to make expansive use of the implied term that the employer must not seriously damage the relationship of trust and confidence between employer and employee.
3. Failure to investigate grievances in certain specific instances has in the past been regarded as a breach of the obligation of trust and confidence on the part of the employer. More recently, the EAT has held that there is a *general* implied term that an employer will reasonably and promptly afford a reasonable opportunity to its employee to obtain redress of any grievance he or she may have (*W. A. Goold (Pearmak) Ltd* v *McConnell and another* [1995] IRLR 516; an extract appears at p. 363 (Chapter 7, Section 3.C(v))).
4. In *BG plc* v *O'Brien* [2001] IRLR 296, EAT, Mr O'Brien was singled out by not being offered a revised contract of employment providing for an enhanced redundancy payment because the employers mistakenly regarded him as not employed as a permanent employee. Both the ET and the EAT held that by failing to offer the applicant the opportunity of a new contract, the employers were in breach of the implied term of trust and confidence.
5. The duty of cooperation is not merely one way and, as we shall see, is placed equally on the employee.

(v) Obedience to reasonable orders

Ottoman Bank v *Chakarian*
[1930] AC 277, Privy Council

Chakarian worked for the bank in Turkish Asia Minor. In 1919 he had narrowly escaped execution at the hands of the Turkish forces. He requested a transfer outside Turkey but this was refused by his employer. Chakarian fled from Constantinople to Athens and was summarily dismissed by the bank. The Privy Council upheld his claim for wrongful dismissal.

LORD THANKERTON: ...[T]he risk of personal danger which caused the respondent's flight from Constantinople, in disregard of the appellants' repeated refusals to allow him to leave, was real and justified from the point of view of his personal safety...It was not seriously maintained by the appellants that their order to the respondent to remain in Constantinople was a lawful order which the respondent was bound to obey at the grave risk to his person. In their Lordships' opinion, the risk to the respondent was such that he was not bound to obey the order, which was therefore not a lawful one.

NOTE: In a case heard by the same court on the same day, *Bouzouru* v *Ottoman Bank* [1930] AC 271, PC, the appellant refused to accept a transfer to a branch in Turkey on the grounds of his lack of knowledge of Turkish and the hostile attitude of the civil authorities he would have to deal with. His claim was dismissed, there being no evidence that the transfer would have put him in personal danger.

Morrish v *Henlys (Folkestone) Ltd*
[1973] 2 All ER 137, National Industrial Relations Court

SIR HUGH GRIFFITHS: This is an appeal from an industrial tribunal which, on 26 October 1972, awarded the appellant the sum of £100 on the ground that he had been unfairly dismissed by the respondents on 3 August

1972. The appellant appeals against the amount of the award. The respondents cross-appeal on the ground that he was not unfairly dismissed.

The facts are in a small compass and are not in dispute. For nearly four years the appellant had been employed by the respondents as a stores driver, and he drove one vehicle all the time. It was his duty to draw diesel oil for the vehicle as and when it was required. On the morning of 2 August 1972 he drew five gallons of diesel oil from one of his employers' forecourt pumps and recorded this on a document called a monthly fuel invoice. He entered in this document the date, the number of the vehicle, the amount and grade of fuel, and he signed it. Next day he drew another five gallons, but when he went to record it on the invoice he discovered that the figure of five gallons he had entered on the previous day had been altered to seven. He changed it back to five. Later that day he found that the entry had again been altered to seven, and again he changed it to five. Still later, he saw that a further entry had been made which showed that on 2nd August two gallons of diesel had been drawn by the vehicle he was driving on that day, and this entry was signed by the manager, Mr Wilkes. The appellant had by this time learned that the manager had made the previous alterations to his figure of five, and so, after crossing out the number of his vehicle against the entry of two gallons, he went to see the manager. A heated interview ensued. Mr Wilkes explained that there was no suggestion that the appellant had in fact drawn seven gallons and not five gallons, but that there was a deficiency of two gallons in the forecourt pumps and the alteration was merely to cover this deficiency and the forecourt staff. The appellant was not willing to have an entry recorded which showed that two gallons of diesel had been put into the vehicle which he was driving, when this was not in fact the case, even if it was against the signature of the manager. The manager told the appellant that as he would not accept his instructions to leave the record showing two gallons attributed to that vehicle, he had no alternative but to give him notice; and this he did. On these facts the tribunal held that the appellant had been unfairly dismissed.

The respondents contended that as there was evidence before the tribunal that it was a common practice to alter the records in this way to cover deficiencies, it was unreasonable of the appellant to object, and he should have accepted the manager's instructions. Accordingly his refusal to do so was an unreasonable refusal to obey an order, which justified dismissal. We cannot accept this submission. It involves the proposition that it is an implied term of an employee's contract of service that he should accept an order to connive at the falsification of one of his employers' records. The proposition only has to be stated to be seen to be untenable. In our view, the appellant was fully entitled to refuse to be in any way party to a falsification of this record and the tribunal was manifestly right in holding that he had been unfairly dismissed. The cross-appeal therefore fails.

[Appeal allowed on other grounds.]

Cresswell v Board of Inland Revenue
[1984] ICR 508, Chancery Division

The Inland Revenue Board introduced a new computerised system (COP 1) which replaced the traditional manual method of tax coding. The employees unsuccessfully sought a declaration that the employers were acting in breach of contract in requiring them to operate the computerised system.

WALTON J: The description of the job of a Tax Officer is like the description of the job of any other grade, namely 'the general duties appropriate to the grade concerned.' Bearing this in mind, it will be convenient, as a form of shorthand, to refer to the jobs as those of Clerical Assistant [CA], [Tax Officer] TO or [Tax Officer Higher Grade] TOHG as the case may be.

Granted that down to the present the work of each of these three grades has been done manually, with pen, paper and pocket calculator, if the employer changes this so as largely to remove the necessity to use pen and paper but requires the person concerned to use a computer instead, or in some cases in addition, is the nature of the job thereby fundamentally changed? I do not think that the drawing of parallels with other situations really assists because, at the end of the day, it is the precise impact which is made by the computerisation programme on the day-to-day work of these three grades which is in question…

…there can really be no doubt as to the fact that an employee is expected to adapt himself to new methods and techniques introduced in the course of his employment (cf. *North Riding Garages Ltd* v *Butterwick* [1967] 2 QB 56). Of course, in a proper case the employer must provide any necessary training or re-training…it will, in all cases, be a question of pure fact as to whether the re-training involved the acquisition of such esoteric skills that it would not be reasonable to expect the employee to acquire them. In an age when the computer has forced its way into the school room and where electronic games are played by schoolchildren in their own homes as a matter of everyday occurrence, it can hardly be considered that to ask an employee to acquire basic skills as to retrieving information from a computer or feeding such information into a computer is something in the slightest esoteric or, even nowadays, unusual...

Of course the changes in working methods and practices which COP brings in its train are great—although I think that the evidence has tended to exaggerate them. But that, as it seems to me, is not the point. COP merely introduces up to date modern methods for dealing with bulk problems: it leaves the jobs done by those who operate the new methodology precisely the same as before, although the content of some of the jobs, most notably that of the grade CA, will have been considerably altered, but in no case altered anything like sufficiently to fall outside the original description of the proper functions of the grade concerned.

Moreover, the contrary conclusion would fly in the face of common sense. Although doubtless, all of us, being conservative (with a small 'c') by nature desire nothing better than to be left to deepen out accustomed ruts, and hate change, a TO has no right to remain in perpetuity doing one defined type of work in one particular way.

(vi) The duty of fidelity

A variety of employee obligations fall within this broad heading. The common thread is that a breach of each of the obligations will destroy the employer's trust and confidence in the employee.

(vii) The obligation to account

Reading v Attorney-General
[1951] AC 507, House of Lords

The appellant was a sergeant in the Royal Army Medical Corps stationed in Egypt. While wearing uniform, he accompanied a number of civilian lorries carrying illicit brandy and whisky in and about Cairo. He earned £20,000 in this way. Having been court-martialled and sent to prison for two years, he claimed the return of the money. The House of Lords rejected his claim.

LORD PORTER: ... [I]t is a principle of law that if a servant, in violation of his duty of honesty and good faith, takes advantage of his service to make a profit for himself, in this sense, that the assets of which he has control, or the facilities which he enjoys, or the position which he occupies, are the real cause of his obtaining the money...i.e. if they play a predominant part in his obtaining the money, then he is accountable for it to the master. It matters not that the master has not lost any profit, nor suffered any damage.

(viii) A duty to disclose misdeeds?

Bell v Lever Brothers Ltd
[1932] AC 161, House of Lords

Bell was employed as chairman of a subsidiary of Lever Brothers Ltd. Bell's fixed-term contract was terminated and he received £30,000 in compensation. Subsequently, the company discovered that Bell had committed breaches of contract for which he could have been dismissed without compensation. The company's claim for repayment was rejected by the House of Lords.

LORD ATKIN: It is said that there is a contractual duty of the servant to disclose his past faults. I agree that the duty in the servant to protect his master's property may involve the duty to report a fellow servant whom he knows to be wrongfully dealing with that property. The servant owes a duty not to steal, but having stolen, is there a superadded duty to confess that he has stolen? I am satisfied that to imply such a duty would be a departure from the well established usage of mankind and would be to create obligations entirely outside the normal contemplation of the parties concerned.

Sybron Corporation v Rochem

[1983] IRLR 253, Court of Appeal

Mr Wilfred Roques was the Director of Operations, European Zone, for Gamblen UK, a company owned by the Sybron Corporation. During his employment, payments were made on his behalf by the company into a pension scheme. When he retired in 1973 he was given a lump sum payment.

Subsequently, it was discovered that Roques, together with his main subordinates, had been conspiring to set up in direct competition with Gamblen. The company sought restitution of the pension payments, claiming that, under the rules of the pension scheme, Roques could have been dismissed for gross misconduct and the payments would not have been made. The Court of Appeal held that the company was entitled to recover the payments it had made.

STEPHENSON LJ: In *Bell* v *Lever Bros* nothing was said about a duty to disclose the misconduct of fellow servants, except by Lord Justice Scrutton in the Court of Appeal and Lord Atkin in the House of Lords. Beginning at the bottom of p. 586 of the report in the Court of Appeal, Lord Justice Scrutton said:

> I do not propose to lay down any general rule for disclosure by servants: I only desire to say that I notice that Wright J held himself bound by the remark of Avory J in *Healey* v *Societé Anonyme Française Rubastic* [1917] 1 KB 946: 'I cannot accept the view that an omission to confess or disclose his own misdoing was, in itself a breach of the contract on the part of the plaintiff'. This statement was also accepted, though I think it was not material to his decision, by Lord Warrington in *Ramsden* v *David Sharratt & Sons Ltd* 30 CC 314, (1930) 35 CC 314. I must reserve myself liberty to reconsider this as a general rule if it becomes relevant in any subsequent case. I cannot think that a servant who knows his fellow servant is stealing the goods of his employer is under no obligation to disclose this to his employer. If the servant himself has stolen goods, and his employer, finding out the theft, accuses an innocent fellow servant of having committed it, is not the real thief bound to inform his employer of his delinquency? His theft is a vital breach of his contract of employment; is he not bound by his contract of service to inform his employer of acts detrimental to his employer? However, it is not in the present case necessary to lay down any general rule: it is enough to deal with the present case.

There, as Mr Munby rightly pointed out, Lord Justice Scrutton is, as it were, talking on what he says about a duty, which he plainly accepted, to disclose a theft by a fellow servant to his duty to disclose his own theft, which was also accepted by Lord Justice Scrutton and the other Lords Justices but has been negatived by the House of Lords.

At p. 228 of the report in the House of Lords, Lord Atkin said this:

> It is said that there is a contractual duty of the servant to disclose his past faults. I agree that the duty in the servant to protect his master's property may involve the duty to report a fellow servant whom he knows to be wrongfully dealing with that property. The servant owes a duty not to steal, but, having stolen, is there superadded a duty to confess that he has stolen? I am satisfied that to imply such a duty would be a departure from the well established usage of mankind and would be to create obligations entirely outside the normal contemplation of the parties concerned.

So there again, what that judge is saying about the duty to report a fellow servant is linked to the question of a duty to report his own wrongdoing, but it is I think significant that Lord Atkin is agreeing that the duty of a servant to protect his master's property 'may involve the duty to report a fellow servant whom he knows to be wrongfully dealing with that property', although the learned Lord was of the firm view that he had no such duty to report his own wrongful conduct. It is, as I have already indicated, puzzling that it never seems to have occurred to counsel or to any of the many judges who dealt with the case of *Bell* v *Lever Bros*, that they might have to consider the duty of Bell to report Snelling's misconduct, or Snelling's duty to report Bell's.

But the question was not there considered, let alone decided, and there is the direct authority of a decision of this court, in a case in which *Bell* v *Lever Bros* was considered, that there is in certain circumstances a duty to report the misconduct of fellow servants. That case is *Swain* v *West (Butchers) Ltd*, reported at first instance in [1936] 1 AER 224 and in this court in [1936] 3 All ER 261. There the plaintiff was employed for a term of five years as a general manager of the defendant company. His contract of service provided, *inter alia*, that he would do all in his power to promote, extend and develop the interests of the company. The managing director gave the plaintiff certain unlawful orders, which orders the plaintiff carried out. The matter came to the notice of the chairman of the board of directors who, in an interview with the plaintiff, told the plaintiff that if he gave conclusive proof of the managing director's dishonesty he would not be dismissed. The plaintiff duly supplied the information required and was then dismissed, the defendants alleging fraud and dishonesty. The plaintiff did not deny the allegations, but he brought an action for breach of contract and wrongful dismissal on the grounds that under the terms of a verbal agreement between the plaintiff and the chairman it was not open to the defendants to rely upon information given by the plaintiff relating to his own fraud and dishonesty. It was held that it was the plaintiff's duty, as part of his contract of service, to report to the board of directors any acts which were not in the interests of the company; that there was therefore no consideration for the alleged verbal agreement and the defendant company was not prevented from relying upon the information received from the plaintiff.

...

It follows from that decision, which is consistent with *Bell's* case and is binding upon us, that there is no general duty to report a fellow-servant's misconduct or breach of contract; whether there is such a duty depends on the contract and on the terms of employment of the particular servant. He may be so placed in the hierarchy as to have a duty to report either the misconduct of his superior, as in *Swain's* case, or the misconduct of his inferiors, as in this case. Mr Munby will not have it that Mr Roques' No. 2 was subordinate to Mr Roques, or that the other managers involved in the conspiracy were his subordinates or inferiors; but on this point I agree with the judge and I refer, again without apology and with approval, to the way in which he put the matter, this time at p. 234 of the transcript of his judgment:

> 'I do not think', said the judge, 'that there is any general duty resting upon an employee to inform his master of the breaches of duty of other employees; the law would do industrial relations generally no great service if it held that such a duty did in fact exist in all cases. The duty must, in my view, depend upon all the circumstances of the case, and the relationship of the parties to their employer and *inter se*. I think it would be very difficult to have submitted, with any hope of success, that Messrs Bell and Snelling, having been appointed to rescue the affairs of their employers' African subsidiary in effect jointly, ought to have denounced each other'—

that is a reference to the finding that Messrs Bell and Snelling were, according to the report of the case in the House of Lords, in joint management and therefore one was not subordinate to the other.

The learned judge goes on:

> However, where there is an hierarchical system, particularly where the person in the hierarchy whose conduct is called into question is a person near the top who is responsible to his employers for the whole of the operation of a complete sector of the employers' business—here the European Zone—then in my view entirely different considerations apply.

That the principle of disclosure extends at least as far as I think it extends (and perhaps further, but that is of no consequence for present purposes) has been decided once and for all, so far as this court is concerned, by the case of *Swain v West (Butchers) Limited*, a decision of the Court of Appeal. The case of *Bell v Lever Bros* was very much in the forefront of everybody's mind in that case, but none of the Lords Justices thought it had any bearing on the case before them.

NOTE: In *Item Software (UK) Ltd v Fassihi and others* [2004] IRLR 928, CA, the issue related to a director's duty to disclose his own wrongdoing. The company sued the defendant, their sales and marketing director, for breach of his duty of good faith in seeking to divert their main contract to a new company of his own. The Court of Appeal held that the duty of a director to disclose his own misconduct is not a separate and independent duty. It is part of a director's fundamental duty to act in what he considers in good faith to be the best interests of the company. This duty of loyalty is the 'time-honoured' rule. A director is not simply a senior manager of the company. He is a fiduciary and with his fellow directors he is responsible for the success of the company's business. The very general terms in which a director's duty of loyalty is expressed is one of its strengths. It reflects the flexible quality of the doctrines of equity and makes it capable of application in cases where it has not previously been applied but the principle or rationale of the rule applies. Thus, the fact that the duty of loyalty has never before been applied so as to require a fiduciary to disclose his own misconduct was not a good objection to the application of the fiduciary principle in such a situation.

(ix) Competition while in employment

The courts are very reluctant to accept that what workers do in their spare time should be of any concern of the employer (see *Nova Plastics Ltd v Froggett* [1982] IRLR 146). However, sometimes they are bound to do so. An employer's interests would clearly be harmed by an employee's spare-time work if this involved direct competition with the employer's business.

Hivac Ltd v Park Royal Scientific Instruments Ltd
[1946] 1 Ch 169, Court of Appeal

Hivac manufactured midget valves for hearing aids. Two of its employees worked in their spare time for Park Royal, a competitor, and also encouraged certain of their fellow employees to do the same. There was, however, no evidence that the employees had passed on confidential information to Park Royal. Hivac applied for an injunction to restrain Park Royal from employing or procuring to be employed certain of Hivac's employees in such a way as to cause a breach of such employees' contracts. The Court of Appeal granted the injunction.

LORD GREENE MR: It has been said on many occasions that an employee owes a duty of fidelity to his employer. As a general proposition that is indisputable. The practical difficulty in any given case is to find exactly how far that rather vague duty of fidelity extends. Prima facie it seems to me on considering the authorities and the arguments that it must be a question on the facts of each particular case. I can very well understand that the obligation of fidelity, which is an implied term of the contract, may extend very much further in the case of one class of employee than it does in others. For instance, when you are dealing, as we are dealing here, with mere manual workers whose job is to work five and a half days for their employer at a specific type of work and stop their work when the hour strikes, the obligation of fidelity may be one the operation of which will have a comparatively limited scope. The law would, I think, be jealous of attempting to impose on a manual worker restrictions, the real effect of which would be to prevent him utilising his spare time. He is paid for five and a half days in the week. The rest of the week is his own, and to impose upon a man, in relation to the rest of the week, some kind of obligation which really would unreasonably tie his hands and prevent him adding to his weekly money during that time would, I think, be very undesirable. On the other hand, if one has employees of a different character, one may very well find that the obligation is of a different nature. A manual worker might say: 'You pay me for five and a half days work. I do five and a half days work for you. What greater obligation have I taken upon myself? If you want in some way to limit my activities during the other day and a half of the week, you must pay me for it.' In many cases that may be a very good answer. In other cases it may not be a good answer because the very nature of the work may be such as to make it quite clear that the duties of the employee to his employer cannot properly be performed if in his spare time the employee engages in certain classes of activity. One example was discussed in argument, that of a solicitor's clerk who on Sundays it was assumed went and worked for another firm in the same town. He might find himself embarrassed because the very client for whom he had done work while working for the other firm on the Sunday might be a client against whom clients of his main employer were conducting litigation, or something of that kind. Obviously in a case of that kind, by working for another firm he is in effect, or may be, disabling himself from performing his duties to his real employer and placing himself in an embarrassing position. I can well understand it being said: 'That is a breach of the duty of fidelity to your employer because as a result of what you have done you have disabled yourself from giving to your employer that undivided attention to his business which it is your duty to give.' I merely put that forward, not for the purpose of laying down the law or expressing any concluded opinion, but merely as illustrating the danger of laying down any general proposition and the necessity of considering each case on its facts.

The authorities which have been cited are few, and the facts with which they were concerned differed from the facts of this particular case. For instance, the authority on which reliance was principally placed was *Wessex Dairies Ltd v Smith* [1935] 2 KB 80 in this court. There the defendant, who was a dairy roundsman, in his master's time proceeded to solicit customers of his master for the purpose of obtaining their custom in a business which he was shortly about to set up for himself. That is, I should have thought, a clear case, because he was doing it first of all in his master's time; and in his master's time he was making use of the information which his master had placed at his disposal, namely, the identity of the various customers and their particular requirements. Greer LJ, in the course of his judgment, placed some emphasis on the fact that the case was one in which the servant was using his master's time for the purpose of furthering his own interest...

Maugham LJ started his judgment with the following words: 'The claim in this case raises a question of some interest in relation to the duty of a servant to his master during the period of his employment.' He goes on and examines the earlier case of *Nichol v Martyn* [(1799), 2 Esp 732], which is not satisfactorily reported, and *Robb v Green* [1895] 2 QB 315, and he then said this, after looking at Hawkins J's judgment in that case: 'That appears to show that Hawkins J did not take the view, which the other passage I read seems to indicate, that a servant can properly canvass his master's customers for himself as from a near approaching day. The question to be determined essentially depends upon the term to be implied in the ordinary case of a contract of employment in the absence of express agreement.' Then he refers to the fact that there was a reference to the duty of fidelity in the contract, but he said that he wished to decide the case on a wider ground. He quotes a passage from A. L. Smith LJ in *Robb* v *Green*, where he said: ' "I think that it is a necessary implication which must be engrafted on such a contract that the servant undertakes to serve his master with good faith and fidelity".' Then he says: 'On the other hand, it has been held that while the servant is in the employment of the master he is not justified in making a list of the master's customers.' That is what had been done in *Robb* v *Green* and that immediately introduces a quite different set of ideas because if a servant took copies of his master's list of customers; he would be quite obviously committing a breach of duty in making use of something which is the master's property, namely, the list of customers, for an improper purpose, other than that for which he was employed…

Talbot J appears to have agreed with both the judgments pronounced, and we have to consider to what extent the judgments assist us in deciding on an interlocutory application the proper course for this court to pursue.

Anything that I say on this matter stands, of course, to be varied and corrected when the full facts are known, but prima facie it appears to me the question we have to consider resolves itself into these elements. First of all, what was done here was done in the spare time of the employees. That leads to this: we have to consider what implication, if any, needs to be read into the contract of service with regard to the employee's use of his spare time. Does that implication in any way restrict him, or, rather (which is the practical question here) did that implication make it a breach of duty on his part to do what he did, with the consequential result that the defendants, in persuading the employees to do what they did, procured a breach of contract? I think the judgment of Maugham LJ in *Wessex Dairies Ltd* v *Smith*, which is quite deliberately placed by him on a broad ground, does lead to this. Although the case before him was concerned with an employee who had done certain things in his employer's time, I cannot find that in his reasoning that was regarded as an essential part of the offence. I cannot read the judgment as meaning that if the roundsman had on a Saturday afternoon, when his work was over, gone round to all these customers and canvassed them, he would have been doing something he was entitled to do. It would be a curious result if, quite apart from making use of the list of customers or his special knowledge or anything of that kind, he could set himself during his spare time deliberately to injure the goodwill of his master's business by trying to get his customers to leave him. Then again the question here is not a question of getting the customers to leave the business but a question of building up a rival in business to the prejudice of the goodwill of the employer's business.

I am not ashamed to confess that in the course of the argument my mind has fluctuated considerably on this question. As I see it, the court stands in a sense between Scylla and Charybdis, because it would be most unfortunate if anything we said, or any other court said, should place an undue restriction on the right of the workman, particularly a manual workman, to make use of his leisure for his profit. On the other hand, it would be deplorable if it were laid down that a workman could, consistently with his duty to his employer, knowingly, deliberately and secretly set himself to do in his spare time something which would inflict great harm on his employer's business. I have endeavoured to raise the questions in the way that they appeal to me and, on the best consideration I can give to the matter, I think that the plaintiffs are prima facie right in this case.

NOTES

1. Working in competition or disclosing confidential information may provide a fair reason for dismissal. In *Smith* v *Du Pont (UK) Ltd* [1976] IRLR 107, Mrs Smith worked as a secretary and on two previous occasions had been warned about dealing with a former employee of the company who now worked for a rival concern. She was dismissed when the company learned that she had given information of a contact—'the name of the buyer at Sainsbury's'—to the former employee. The industrial tribunal took the view that, although the information was of no great weight which would in fact damage the company, in view of the earlier warnings, Mrs Smith 'seemed to be setting up her judgement against that of the company'. In the circumstances, there was no obligation on the company to wait 'until she passed on information of significance'. The dismissal was held to be fair.

2. One exception to the duty not to misuse confidential information arises where disclosure by the employee or ex-employee is in the public interest. In *Initial Services Ltd* v *Putterill* [1968] 1 QB 396, Lord Denning stated that the exception against disclosure went beyond disclosure of crime or fraud on the part of the employer: 'it extends to any misconduct of such a nature that it ought in the public interest to be disclosed to others.' Moreover, disclosure in the public interest may be

particularly justified where the disclosure is to the proper authorities, e.g. a regulatory body, as in *Re a Company's Application* [1989] ICR 449, ChD. For a detailed discussion of this area see Vickers, L., *Protecting Whistleblowers at Work* (London: Institute of Employment Rights, 1995).

3. In 1998, the Government supported Richard Shepherd's private member's bill on public-interest disclosure or 'whistleblowing'. The Public Interest Disclosure Act 1998 came into force on 1 January 1999 and its aim is to protect individuals against dismissal or victimisation where they make disclosures to their employer, to another responsible person, or to a 'person prescribed' about criminal offences, failure to meet legal obligations, miscarriages of justice, health, safety and environmental dangers, and deliberate concealment of information relating to these matters. (For a more detailed discussion of the Act and its impact on the law of unfair dismissal, see Chapter 8, Section 2.C(ii) at pp. 409–410; see also the note by Lewis, D. (1998) 27 ILJ 325; and Hobby, C., *Whistleblowing and the Public Interest Disclosure Act 1988* (London: Institute of Employment Rights, 2001).)

(x) Competition by ex-employees

As a general rule, ex-employees are free to go into competition with their former employer. However, in certain restricted circumstances, the duty of fidelity survives the termination of the employment relationship.

Wessex Dairies Ltd v *Smith*

[1935] 2 KB 80, Court of Appeal

MAUGHAN LJ: In this case the question is whether the defendant acted with fidelity when, on the Saturday in question and perhaps on the previous days of the week, in going his round he informed the customers that he would cease on Saturday to be in the employment of the plaintiffs, that he was going to set up business for himself, and would be in a position to supply them with milk. He was plainly soliciting their custom as from Saturday evening. In my opinion that was deliberate as it was a successful canvassing at a time when the defendant was under an obligation to serve the plaintiff with fidelity. I am of opinion therefore that he committed a breach of his implied contract...

Robb v *Green*

[1895] 2 QB 315, Court of Appeal

The defendant, an employee of the plaintiff who was a tradesman, left his service and set up a similar business on his own. Before he left, he copied out lists of the plaintiff's customers and tried to persuade them to transfer their custom to him.

LORD ESHER MR: The question arises whether such conduct is a breach of contract. That depends upon the question whether in a contract of service the Court can imply a stipulation that the servant will act in good faith towards his master. I think that in a contract of service the Court must imply such a stipulation as I have mentioned, because it is a thing which must necessarily have been in the view of both parties when they entered into the contract. It is impossible to suppose that a master would have put a servant into a confidential position of this kind, unless he thought that the servant would be bound to use good faith towards him; or that the servant would not know, when he entered into that position, that the master would rely on his observance of good faith in the confidential relation between them.

NOTE: The above cases show that an employee may not do anything while still employed which is in breach of the duty of fidelity (see also *Sanders* v *Parry* [1967] 2 All ER 803; *Roger Bullivant Ltd* v *Ellis* [1987] IRLR 491; *Johnson & Bloy (Holdings) Ltd* v *Wolstenholme* [1987] IRLR 499; *Adamson* v *B & L Cleaning Services Ltd* [1995] IRLR 193, EAT; *Crowson Fabrics Ltd* v *Rider* [2008] IRLR 288; cf. *Helmet Integrated Systems Ltd* v *Tunnard* [2007] IRLR 126, CA). However, in the absence of an express covenant, there is no general restriction on ex-employees canvassing or doing business with customers of their former employers. This rule applies to solicitors as much as to any other trade or profession (see *Wallace Brogan & Co.* v *Cove and others* [1997] IRLR 453, CA).

Nevertheless, as the next case extract clearly indicates, ex-employees are entitled to make use of their knowledge and skill acquired while in their employer's business and, in this sense, the implied duty of fidelity is narrower than in the case of existing employees.

Faccenda Chicken Ltd v *Fowler*

[1986] IRLR 69, Court of Appeal

Fowler had been employed as a sales manager of Faccenda Chicken Ltd's chicken marketing business until he resigned, along with eight other employees, in order to establish a rival operation selling fresh chickens from refrigerated vehicles. Neither Fowler nor any of the other former employees were subject to any express agreement restricting activities after leaving Faccenda's employ. Faccenda claimed that Fowler and his colleagues had broken their contracts by using confidential sales information, relating to the requirements of their customers and the prices they paid, to the detriment of the company. The High Court, Chancery Division (Goulding J) dismissed the claims for damages. Faccenda appealed to the Court of Appeal.

NEILL LJ: …Having considered the cases to which we were referred, we would venture to state these principles as follows:

(1) Where the parties are, or have been, linked by a contract of employment, the obligations of the employee are to be determined by the contract between him and his employer: cf *Vokes Ltd* v *Heather* [1945] 62 RPC 131, 141.

(2) In the absence of any express term, the obligations of the employee in respect of the use and disclosure of information are the subject of implied terms.

(3) While the employee remains in the employment of the employer the obligations are included in the implied term which imposes a duty of good faith or fidelity on the employee. For the purpose of the present appeal it is not necessary to consider the precise limits of this implied term, but it may be noted:

    (a) that the extent of the duty of good faith will vary according to the nature of the contract (see *Vokes Ltd* v *Heather* (ibid));

    (b) that the duty of good faith will be broken if an employee makes or copies a list of the customers of the employer for use after his employment ends or deliberately memorises such a list, even though, except in special circumstances, there is no general restriction on an ex-employee canvassing or doing business with customers of his former employer (see *Robb* v *Green* [1895] 2 QB 315 and *Wessex Dairies Ltd* v *Smith* [1935] 2 KB 80).

(4) The implied term which imposes an obligation on the employee as to his conduct after the determination of the employment is more restricted in its scope than that which imposes a general duty of good faith. It is clear that the obligation not to use or disclose information may cover secret processes of manufacture such as chemical formulae (*Amber Size & Chemical Co.* v *Menzel* [1913] 2 Ch 239)), or designs or special methods of construction (*Reid and Sigrist Ltd* v *Moss and Mechanism Ltd* [1932] 49 RPC 461), and other information which is of a sufficiently high degree of confidentiality as to amount to a trade secret.

The obligation does not extend, however, to cover all information which is given to or acquired by the employee while in his employment, and in particular may not cover information which is only 'confidential' in the sense that an unauthorised disclosure of such information to a third party while the employment subsisted would be a clear breach of the duty of good faith.

This distinction is clearly set out in the judgment of Mr Justice Cross (as he then was) in *Printers & Finishers Ltd* v *Holloway* [1965] RPC 239, where he had to consider whether an ex-employee should be restrained by injunction from making use of his recollection of the contents of certain written printing instructions which had been made available to him when he was working in his former employers' flock printing factory. In his judgment, delivered on 29.4.64 (not reported on this point in [1965] 1 WLR 1, 3), he said this ([1965] RPC 253):

In this connection one must bear in mind that not all information which is given to a servant in confidence and which it would be a breach of his duty for him to disclose to another person during his employment is a trade secret which he can be prevented from using for his own advantage after the employment is over, even though he has entered into no express covenant with regard to the matter in hand.

For example, the printing instructions were handed to Holloway to be used by him during his employment exclusively for the plaintiffs' benefit. It would have been a breach of duty on his part to divulge any of the contents to a stranger while he was employed, but many of these instructions are not really 'trade secrets' at all. Holloway was not, indeed, entitled to take a copy of the instructions away with him; but in so far as the instructions cannot be called 'trade secrets' and he carried them in his head, he is entitled to use them for his own benefit or the benefit of any future employer.

The same distinction is to be found in *E Worsley & Co. Ltd* v *Cooper* [1939] 1 All ER 290 where it was held that the defendant was entitled, after he had ceased to be employed, to make use of his knowledge of the source of the paper supplied to his previous employer. In our view it is quite plain that this knowledge was nevertheless 'confidential' in the same sense that it would have been a breach of the duty of good faith for the employee, while the employment subsisted, to have used it for his own purposes or to have disclosed it to a competitor of his employer.

(5) In order to determine whether any particular item of information falls within the implied term so as to prevent its use or disclosure by an employee after his employment has ceased, it is necessary to consider all the circumstances of the case. We are satisfied that the following matters are among those to which attention must be paid:

(a) The nature of the employment. Thus employment in a capacity where 'confidential' material is habitually handled may impose a high obligation of confidentiality because the employee can be expected to realise its sensitive nature to a greater extent than if he were employed in a capacity where such material reaches him only occasionally or incidentally.

(b) The nature of the information itself. In our judgment the information will only be protected if it can properly be classed as a trade secret or as material which, while not properly to be described as a trade secret, is in all the circumstances of such a highly confidential nature as to require the same protection as a trade secret *eo nomine*. The restrictive covenant cases demonstrate that a covenant will not be upheld on the basis of the status of the information which might be disclosed by the former employee if he is not restrained, unless it can be regarded as a trade secret or the equivalent of a trade secret: see, for example, *Herbert Morris Ltd* v *Saxelby* [1916] 1 AC 688, 710 by Lord Parker of Waddington; *Littlewoods Organisation Ltd* v *Harris* [1977] 1 WLR 1472, 1484 per Megaw LJ.

We must therefore express our respectful disagreement with the passage in Goulding J's judgment where he suggested that an employer can protect the use of information in his second category, even though it does not include either a trade secret or its equivalent by means of a restrictive covenant. As Lord Parker of Waddington made clear in *Herbert Morris Ltd* v *Saxelby* [1916] 1 AC 688, 709, in a passage to which Mr Dehn drew our attention, a restrictive covenant will not be enforced unless the protection sought is reasonably necessary to protect a trade secret or to prevent some personal influence over customers being abused in order to entice them away.

In our view the circumstances in which a restrictive covenant would be appropriate and could be successfully invoked emerge very clearly from the words used by Cross J in *Printers & Finishers Ltd* v *Holloway*…(in a passage quoted later in his judgment by Goulding J [1984] IRLR 61, 66):

If [the managing director] is right in thinking that there are features in his process which can fairly be regarded as trade secrets and which his employers will inevitably carry away with them in their heads, then the proper way for the plaintiffs to protect themselves would be by exacting covenants from their employees restricting their field of activity after they have left their employment, not by asking the court to extend the general equitable doctrine to prevent breaking confidence beyond all reasonable bounds.

It is clearly impossible to provide a list of matters which will qualify as trade secrets or their equivalent. Secret processes of manufacture provide obvious examples, but innumerable other pieces of information are *capable* of being trade secrets, though the secrecy of some information may be only short-lived. In addition, the fact that the circulation of certain information is restricted to a limited number of individuals may throw light on the status of the information and its degree of confidentiality.

(c) Whether the employer impressed on the employee the confidentiality of the information. Thus, though an employer cannot prevent the use or disclosure *merely* by telling the employee that certain information is confidential, the attitude of the employer towards the information provides evidence which may assist in determining whether or not the information can properly be regarded as a trade secret. It is to be observed that in *E. Worsley & Co. Ltd* v *Cooper* [1939] 1 All ER 290 Morton J at page 307 attached significance to the fact that no warning had been given to the defendant that 'the source from which the paper came was to be treated as confidential'.

(d) Whether the relevant information can be easily isolated from other information which the employee is free to use or disclose. In *Printers & Finishers Ltd* v *Holloway* [1965] RPC 239, Cross J at page 256 considered the protection which might be afforded to information which had been memorised by an ex-employee. He put on one side the memorising of a formula or a list of customers or what had been said (obviously in confidence) at a particular meeting, and continued:

The employee might well not realise that the feature or expedient in question was in fact peculiar to his late employer's process and factory; but even if he did, such knowledge is not readily separable from his general knowledge of the flock printing process and his acquired skill in manipulating a flock printing plant, and I do not think that any man of average intelligence and honesty would think that there was anything improper in his putting his memory of particular features of his late employer's plant at the disposal of his new employer.

(e) For our part we would not regard the separability of the information in question as being conclusive, but the fact that the alleged 'confidential' information is part of a package and that the remainder of the package is not confidential is likely to throw light on whether the information in question is really a trade secret.

...

Information about the price to be charged for a new model of a car or some other product or about the prices negotiated, for example, for various grades of oil in a highly competitive market in which it is known that prices are to be kept secret from competitors occur to us as providing possible further instances of information which is entitled to protection as having the requisite degree of confidentiality.

But in the present case the following factors appear to us to lead to the clear conclusion that neither the information about prices nor the sales information as a whole had the degree of confidentiality necessary to support Faccenda's case. We would list these factors as follows:

1. The sales information contained some material which Faccenda conceded was not confidential if looked at in isolation.

2. The information about the prices was not clearly severable from the rest of the sales information.

3. Neither the sales information in general, nor the information about the prices in particular, though of some value to a competitor, could reasonably be regarded as plainly secret or sensitive.

4. The sales information, including the information about prices, was necessarily acquired by the respondents in order that they could do their work. Moreover, as the judge observed in the course of his judgment, each salesman could quickly commit the whole of the sales information relating to his own area to memory.

5. The sales information was generally known among the van drivers who were employees, as were the secretaries, at quite a junior level. This was not a case where the relevant information was restricted to senior management or to confidential staff.

6. There was no evidence that Faccenda had ever given any express instructions that the sales information or the information about prices was to be treated as confidential.

We are satisfied that, in the light of all the matters set out by the judge in his judgment, neither the sales information as a whole nor the information about prices looked at by itself fell within the class of confidential information which an employee is bound by an implied term of his contract of employment or otherwise not to use or disclose after his employment has come to an end.

Accordingly these appeals must be dismissed.

NOTES

1. This is an important decision and, indeed, Professor R. W. Rideout has stated 'that there is no question but that this decision rewrites the duty of confidentiality contained in the law of employment' (15 ILJ 183, at p. 187).

■ QUESTION

What prompted Professor Rideout to make such a statement?

2. *Helmet Integrated Systems Ltd* v *Tunnard* [2007] IRLR 126, CA concerned a senior salesman for a protective equipment company, who took preparatory steps while still employed to market his own safety helmet. The employers brought forward proceedings claiming that he had acted in breach of his duty of confidentiality by developing a helmet which would be in competition with their own, and had acted in breach of his fiduciary duties in failing to report his activities while still being an employee. The Court of Appeal rejected the claim, refusing to imply a term that an employee cannot prepare to compete. (The question of what preparatory acts in establishing a competing business be considered illegitimate will revolve on the facts of each case: *Shepherd Investments Ltd* v *Walters* [2007] IRLR 110, HC.)

(xi) Restraint of trade clauses

The second exception to ex-employees' freedom to go into competition with their former employer may be a restraint of trade clause in the contract of employment. Given the weakness of the implied term of confidentiality once employment has ended, many employers would be well advised to protect themselves against the divulgence of trade secrets or loss of customers by the insertion of such clauses in the contract. Note, however, that in *Faccenda* (Section (x)), the Court of Appeal expressly disagreed with the statement of Goulding J, at first instance, that confidential information which became part of the employee's skill and knowledge could be protected by an express restraint of trade clause. Therefore, only trade secrets (as defined in *Faccenda*) or customer connections may be protected by such a clause. Furthermore, the restrictive covenant must be shown to go no further, in terms of time and area of restraint, than is reasonable for the protection of the employer's proprietary interests and must be generally in the public interest.

Littlewoods Organisation Ltd v *Harris*
[1977] 1 WLR 1472, Court of Appeal

The plaintiff ran a retail chain-store business and mail order business in the UK. The main rival in the field was Great Universal Stores Ltd (GUS) which had some 200 subsidiary companies carrying on business throughout the world. Between them the plaintiff and GUS conducted two-thirds of all mail order business in the UK. The defendant was executive director of the plaintiff's mail order business.

Clause 8 of his service agreement provided:

> In the event of the determination of this agreement...the [defendant] shall not at any time within 12 months after such determination:—(i) Enter into a Contract of Service or other Agreement of a like nature with Great Universal Stores Ltd or any company subsidiary thereto or be directly or indirectly engaged concerned or interested in the trading or business of the said Great Universal Stores Ltd or any such company aforesaid.

On 4 January 1977, the defendant resigned and refused to give an assurance that he would not work with GUS within the 12-month period as set out in the clause. The plaintiff sought an injunction restraining entry into employment with GUS. At first instance, Caulfield J refused to grant the injunction on the ground that the plaintiff had not demonstrated that it had confidential information or trade secrets which could be properly protected by the restraint. The plaintiff's appeal to the Court of Appeal was successful.

> MEGAW LJ: Counsel for the defendant in this context of construction has relied strongly on the decision of this court in *Commercial Plastics Ltd* v *Vincent* [1965] 1 QB 623. That was a case in which the court, having held that there were confidential matters which could have been protected by a properly drawn covenant, refused, though with obvious regret, to uphold the covenant on the ground that it was too widely drawn. There were two respects in which it was held that it was too widely drawn. First, the business, including the secrets which it was sought to protect, was limited to trading in the United Kingdom, whereas the words in the letter in which the restrictive provision was contained did not express such a limitation. The words of the letter were:
>
>> In view of the highly technical and confidential nature of this appointment you have agreed not to seek employment with any of our competitors in the PVC calendering field, for at least one year after leaving our employ.
>
> The second respect in which the covenant was held to be too wide was that it was not restricted to the particular, rather specialised, type of technological information with which the defendant had been concerned while he was in the plaintiff's employment.
>
> Counsel for the defendant submits that that case is an authority binding on this court showing that it is not permissible to construe the clause in this case in any way which is limited beyond the terms which it actually contains. I have felt very much impressed by that submission; and if, in the end, I had thought that the ratio decidendi of that case was relevant to the present case, I should without hesitation have followed it. Counsel for the defendant says that one of the elements in respect of which the present covenant is too wide is that it is expressed perfectly generally so far as geography is concerned, it is not limited to the UK, and the plaintiffs cannot properly claim any protection in respect of any operations which may be conducted outside the UK by any company to which the defendant hereafter may be employed in the Great Universal Stores group.

It seems to me on full consideration of *Commercial Plastics Ltd* v *Vincent* that it was there accepted and assumed that the agreement there in question was properly to be construed as being universal in its operation and was properly to be construed as applying over the whole area of the business concerned. It was not argued, on the basis of the authorities such as those which I have recently cited, that the court could and should as a matter of construction treat the covenant as being less wide than its literal words appeared to make it, having regard to all the surrounding circumstances which existed at the time when the covenant was entered into. For that reason I have reached the conclusion that *Commercial Plastics Ltd* v *Vincent* is not an authority which precludes us from putting on cl.8 of the agreement a construction which in my judgment is, on the basis of the authorities which I have cited, and on the circumstances appearing in the evidence, the proper construction.

Counsel for the defendant was disposed to stress the point that the covenant does not purport to relate in any way to confidential information, much less to indicate what the sphere of that confidential information is. I do not regard that as being a fatal objection to it. The difficulty which I regard as most serious as against the enforceability of the covenant is the width of the phrase 'any companies subsidiary thereto'. Let me just read the subclause again:

> …the Divisional Director shall not…(i) Enter into a Contract of Service or other Agreement of a like nature with Great Universal Stores Limited or any company subsidiary thereto or be directly or indirectly engaged concerned or interested in the trading or business of the said Great Universal Stores Limited or any such company aforesaid.

Great Universal Stores Ltd have many such companies. Many of them on the evidence which was accepted by Caulfield J have no connection with mail order trade. Many of them, I think, are concerned with business outside the UK. So far as they are concerned, if they are on the true construction to be included in this clause then it would be too wide and, regrettable though it might be, it would be the duty of this court to hold that the covenant could not stand and it would not be enforceable. But, applying the principles of construction which I derive from the cases which I have cited, in my judgment the words 'any company subsidiary thereto' are properly to be read by reference to the circumstances existing at the time when the contract was made. Just as in *Moenich* v *Fenestre* (1892) 67 LT 602, CA when Lindley LJ and the other members of the court were able to interpret the phrase in that case as meaning something different from its literal words because of the nature of the business with reference to which it was made, so here I think that 'any company subsidiary thereto' ought to be treated in this way. 'Any company subsidiary thereto' means any subsidiary which at any relevant moment of time during the period covered by the covenant is concerned wholly or partly in the mail order business carried on in the UK. That would include, for example, a subsidiary which was concerned with the buying of goods which were going to be used by some other company in the group in the mail order business in the UK. It would include any subsidiary in which it was sought to employ the defendant, whatever the function of that subsidiary and whether or not there might be any reference thereto in his contract of service, to deal in any way with, or advise in any way, or give anyone information relating to the mail order business in the UK. It will, I hope, be clear from what I have said that I am not suggesting that the covenant requires to be rewritten. I am interpreting the covenant as I understand it ought to be interpreted in the circumstances which exist in this case, as I conceive to have been done in the cases which I have cited.

Greer v Sketchley Ltd
[1979] IRLR 445, Court of Appeal

Mr Greer was employed by Sketchleys for some 20 years. In 1974 he was made director of their dry-cleaning business, with special responsibility for the Midlands area. The activities of the company covered all the Midlands and London area but they did not include the North of England, Scotland, Devon and Cornwall, Northern Ireland and the greater part of Wales.

Mr Greer's contract stated:

> In view of the access to trade secrets and secret processes which the Employee may have during the course of his employment hereunder he shall not within a period of 12 months from the termination thereof either directly or indirectly and either alone or in association with any other person firm or company engage in any part of the United Kingdom in any business which is similar to any business involving such trade secrets and/ or secret processes carried on by the Company or any of its subsidiaries during the course of his employment hereunder.

In 1977, Mr Greer decided to leave and was offered a job with another firm in the dry-cleaning business. Mr Greer sought a declaration that the restraint clause was invalid. The High Court declared it to be invalid and this finding was upheld by the Court of Appeal.

LORD DENNING MR: In a way, as the *Littlewoods* case illustrated, it is often difficult to sort out what is confidential and what is not. Sometimes it is permissible to make an agreement, as in that particular case, saying that the man is not to go to a rival concern for 12 months. That is what happened in the *Littlewoods* case. The Great Universal Stores in effect approached Mr Harris and offered him all sorts of better terms and induced him to go to them. That was a breach of the restrictive covenant which Littlewoods had expressly made saying that Mr Harris was not to go to their rival the Great Universal Stores for 12 months. That clause was held valid because it was the one way of protecting the position. But in this particular case it seems to me, for all Mr Buckley's admirable arguments, this is a much wider clause which says that he shall not engage in any part of the United Kingdom in any similar business. If Sketchleys operated all over England, Scotland and Wales, it might be reasonable to have such a covenant, but Sketchleys do not operate as widely. In 1974 their operations were confined to the Midlands and the South of England, excluding Wales, Cornwall and Devon and Lancashire right up to the north. Sketchleys did not cover any of that area. Was it reasonable for them to have a covenant restraining Mr Greer from going to any of these other parts of England, Scotland and Wales? Suppose for instance, there had been a group of dry cleaning shops in the Tyne and Wear conurbation or in the Lancashire conurbation or Glasgow and Edinburgh or down in Devon, Sketchleys had not any kind of operation in those areas then. Was it reasonable to restrain him from engaging in any of those businesses or with any of those groups which were in those areas in which Sketchleys did not operate at all? It is said by Mr Buckley that they might expand into those areas in the future. Now over three years later they have not expanded into Devon and Cornwall or into Yorkshire or Lancashire or into the North of England or into Scotland. It seems to me that that problematical and possible expansion into all these other areas is much too vague and much too wide to justify restraint over every part of the United Kingdom.

NOTES
1. Even if the restraint is reasonable as between the parties, it may still be struck down as unlawful and void if it is regarded by the court as being contrary to public policy. In *Bull* v *Pitney-Bowes* [1966] 3 All ER 384, the plaintiff had been employed by the defendants for 25 years. It was a condition of his employment that he should become a member of a non-contributory pension scheme. Rule 16 of this scheme provided that a retired member should be liable to forfeit his pension rights if he was 'engaged or employed in any activity or occupation which is in competition with or detrimental to the interests of [the defendants]'. On his retirement, the plaintiff entered the employment of a competing company. On being warned that he might lose his pension rights unless he left his new employment, he sued for a declaration that rule 16 was an unreasonable restraint of trade and therefore void. Thesiger J held that rule 16 was a restraint of trade, and further that it was unenforceable because it was against public policy. It was contrary to public policy that the community should be deprived of the services of a man skilled in a particular trade or technique. (See also *Greig* v *Insole* [1978] 1 WLR 302.)
2. The employer's main remedy for breach of a restraint of trade clause is an injunction, although it is also possible to seek damages. It has been held that an injunction to restrain the use of trade secrets should not last longer than is necessary to prevent the defendant from taking unfair advantage of the springboard gained by use of the information obtained (see *Roger Bullivant Ltd* v *Ellis* [1987] IRLR 491).

(xii) Inventions by employees

Prior to the passing of the Patents Act 1977, the common law implied a term into every contract of employment that inventions produced in the course of employment became the property of the employer (see *British Syphon Co. Ltd* v *Homewood* [1956] 1 WLR 1190). This position prompted one commentator to remark that: '...in few areas of British law can the effect of the imbalance of bargaining power between employer and employee have led so clearly to injustice as in the distribution of the fruits of inventions made by an employee while in his employer's services' (Phillips, J., 'Employee inventions and the new Patents Act' (1978) 7 ILJ 30).

The Patents Act 1977 replaces the earlier law in respect of the ownership of inventions, the right of the employee to be rewarded, the amount of the reward, and the exclusion of statutory rights.

(xiii) Right to employees' inventions

PATENTS ACT 1977

39. Right to employees' inventions

(1) Notwithstanding anything in any rule of law, an invention made by an employee shall, as between him and his employer, be taken to belong to his employer for the purposes of this Act and all other purposes if—

(a) it was made in the course of the normal duties of the employee or in the course of duties falling outside his normal duties, but specifically assigned to him, and the circumstances in either case were such that an invention might reasonably be expected to result from the carrying out of his duties; or

(b) the invention was made in the course of the duties of the employee and, at the time of making the invention, because of the nature of his duties and the particular responsibilities arising from the nature of his duties he had a special obligation to further the interests of the employer's undertaking.

(2) Any other invention made by an employee shall, as between him and his employer, be taken for those purposes to belong to the employee.

...

40. Compensation of employees for certain inventions

(1) Where it appears to the court or the comptroller on an application made by an employee within the prescribed period that the employee has made an invention belonging to the employer for which a patent has been granted, that the patent is (having regard among other things to the size and nature of the employer's undertaking) of outstanding benefit to the employer and that by reason of those facts it is just that the employee should be awarded compensation to be paid by the employer, the court or the comptroller may award him such compensation of an amount determined under section 41 below.

(2) Where it appears to the court or the comptroller on an application made by an employee within the prescribed period that—

(a) a patent has been granted for an invention made by and belonging to the employee;

(b) his rights in the invention, or in any patent or application for a patent for the invention, have since the appointed day been assigned to the employer or an exclusive licence under the patent or application has since the appointed day been granted to the employer;

(c) the benefit derived by the employee from the contract of assignment, assignation or grant or any ancillary contract ('the relevant contract') is inadequate in relation to the benefit derived by the employer from the patent; and

(d) by reason of those facts it is just that the employee should be awarded compensation to be paid by the employer in addition to the benefit derived from the relevant contract;

the court or the comptroller may award him such compensation of an amount determined under section 41 below.

(3) Subsections (1) and (2) above shall not apply to the invention of an employee where a relevant collective agreement provides for the payment of compensation in respect of inventions of the same description as that invention to employees of the same description as that employee.

(4) Subsection (2) above shall have effect notwithstanding anything in the relevant contract or any agreement applicable to the invention (other than any such collective agreement).

(5) If it appears to the comptroller on an application under this section that the application involves matters which would more properly be determined by the court, he may decline to deal with it.

(6) In this section—

'the prescribed period', in relation to proceedings before the court, means the period prescribed by rules of court, and 'relevant collective agreement' means a collective agreement within the meaning of the Trade Union and Labour Relations Act 1974, made by or on behalf of a trade union to which the employee belongs, and by the employer or an employers' association to which the employer belongs which is in force at the time of the making of the invention.

(7) References in this section to an invention belonging to an employer or employee are references to it so belonging as between the employer and the employee.

41. Amount of compensation

(1) An award of compensation to an employee under section 40(1) or (2) above in relation to a patent for an invention shall be such as will secure for the employee a fair share (having regard to all the circumstances) of the benefit which the employer has derived, or may reasonably be expected to derive, from the patent or from the assignment, assignation or grant to a person connected with the employer of the property or any right in the invention or the property in, or any right in or under, an application for that patent.

(2) For the purposes of subsection (1) above the amount of any benefit derived or expected to be derived by an employer from the assignment, assignation or grant of—

(a) the property in, or any right in or under, a patent for the invention or an application for such a patent; or

(b) the property or any right in the invention;

to a person connected with him shall be taken to be the amount which could reasonably be expected to be so derived by the employer if that person had not been connected with him.

(3) Where the Crown or a Research Council in its capacity as employer assigns or grants the property in, or any right in or under, an invention, patent or application for a patent to a body having among its functions that of developing or exploiting inventions resulting from public research and does so for no consideration or only a nominal consideration, any benefit derived from the invention, patent or application by that body shall be treated for the purposes of the foregoing provisions of this section as so derived by the Crown or, as the case may be, Research Council.

In this subsection 'Research Council' means a body which is a Research Council for the purposes of the Science and Technology Act 1965.

(4) In determining the fair share of the benefit to be secured for an employee in respect of a patent for an invention which has always belonged to an employer, the court or the comptroller shall, among other things, take the following matters into account, that is to say—

(a) the nature of the employee's duties, his remuneration and the other advantages he derives or has derived from his employment or has derived in relation to the invention under this Act;

(b) the effort and skill which the employee has devoted to making the invention;

(c) the effort and skill which any other person has devoted to making the invention jointly with the employee concerned, and the advice and other assistance contributed by any other employee who is not a joint inventor of the invention; and

(d) the contribution made by the employer to the making, developing and working of the invention by the provision of advice, facilities and other assistance, by the provision of opportunities and by his managerial and commercial skill and activities.

(5) In determining the fair share of the benefit to be secured for an employee in respect of a patent for an invention which originally belonged to him, the court or the comptroller shall, among other things, take the following matters into account, that is to say—

(a) any conditions in a licence or licences granted under this Act or otherwise in respect of the invention or the patent;

(b) the extent to which the invention was made jointly by the employee with any other person; and

(c) the contribution made by the employer to the making, developing and working of the invention as mentioned in subsection (4)(d) above.

(6) Any order for the payment of compensation under section 40 above may be an order for the payment of a lump sum or for periodical payment, or both.

...

42. Enforceability of contracts relating to employees' inventions

(1) This section applies to any contract (whenever made) relating to inventions made by an employee, being a contract entered into by him—

(a) with the employer (alone or with another); or

(b) with some other person at the request of the employer or in pursuance of the employee's contract of employment.

(2) Any term in a contract to which this section applies which diminishes the employee's rights in inventions of any description made by him after the appointed day and the date of the contract, or in or under patents for those inventions or applications for such patents, shall be unenforceable against him to the extent that it diminishes his rights in an invention of that description so made, or in or under a patent for such an invention or an application for any such patent.

(3) Subsection (2) above shall not be construed as derogating from any duty of confidentiality owed to his employer by an employee by virtue of any rule of law or otherwise.

...

(xiv) The duty of fidelity: impeding the employer's business

**Secretary of State for Employment v Associated Society
of Railway Engineers & Firemen (No. 2)**
[1972] 2 QB 455, Court of Appeal

This case concerned an application by the Secretary of State for a ballot of railwaymen under the provisions of the Industrial Relations Act 1971. The railwaymen were engaged in industrial action in support of a pay claim. The action consisted of an overtime ban and a work to rule. In order to gain a ballot order, the Secretary of State had to establish, *inter alia*, that the railwaymen were in breach of their contracts of employment. The Court of Appeal held that the work to rule was a breach of contract and overturned previous assumptions that a strict work to rule did not amount to a breach.

LORD DENNING MR: ... Now I quite agree that a man is not bound positively to do more for the employer than his contract requires. He can withdraw his goodwill if he pleases. But what he must not do is wilfully to obstruct his employer as he goes about his business ... If he, with the others takes steps wilfully to disrupt the undertaking, to produce chaos so that it will not run as it should, then each one who is a party to those steps is guilty of a breach of contract. It is no answer for any of them to say 'I am only obeying the rule book or that I am not bound to do more than a 40 hour week'. That would be all very well if done in good faith without any wilful disruption of services; but what makes it wrong is the object with which it is done.

BUCKLEY LJ: ... [I]n my judgment, in the case of a contract of a commercial character the wilful act of one party which, although not, maybe, departing from the literal letter of the agreement, nevertheless defeats the commercial intention of the parties in entering into the contract, constitutes a breach of an implied term of the contract to perform the contract in such a way as not to frustrate that commercial objective.

(xv) A 'new' implied term: the employer's obligation to bring contingent rights to the attention of employees

Scally and others v Southern Health & Social Services Board
[1991] IRLR 522, House of Lords

The plaintiffs were medical practitioners employed in the Northern Ireland health service. They sought to sue their employers for loss sustained by them by reason of their employers' failure to bring to their notice their right to purchase added years of pension entitlement before that right lapsed.

LORD BRIDGE OF HARWICH: ... Will the law then imply a term in the contract of employment imposing such an obligation on the employer? The implication cannot, of course, be justified as necessary to give business efficacy to the contract of employment as a whole. I think there is force in the submission that, since the employee's entitlement to enhance his pension rights by the purchase of added years is of no effect unless he is aware of it, and since he cannot be expected to become aware of it unless it is drawn to his attention, it is necessary to imply an obligation on the employer to bring it to his attention to render efficacious the very benefit which the contractual right to purchase added years was intended to confer. But this may be stretching the doctrine of implication for the sake of business efficacy beyond its proper reach. A clear distinction is drawn in the speeches of Viscount Simonds in *Lister* v *Romford Ice and Cold Storage Co Ltd* [1957] AC 555, 576 and Lord Wilberforce in *Liverpool City Council* v *Irwin* [1977] AC 239, 255 between the search for an implied term necessary to give business efficacy to a particular contract and the search, based on wider considerations, for a term which the law will imply as a necessary incident of a definable category of contractual relationship. If any implication is appropriate here, it is, I think, of this latter type. Carswell J accepted the submission that any formulation of an implied term of this kind which would be effective to sustain the plaintiffs' claims in this case must necessarily be too wide in its ambit to be acceptable as of general application. I believe, however, that this difficulty is surmounted if the category of contractual relationship in which the implication will arise is defined with sufficient precision. I would define it as the relationship of employer and employee where the following circumstances obtain: (1) the terms of the contract of employment have not been negotiated with the individual employee but result from negotiation with a representative body or are otherwise incorporated by reference; (2) a particular term of the contract makes available to the employee a valuable right contingent upon action being taken by him to avail himself of its benefit; (3) the employee cannot, in all the circumstances, reasonably be expected to be aware of the term unless it is drawn to his attention. I fully appreciate that the criterion to justify an implication of this kind is necessity, not reasonableness. But I take the view that it is not merely reasonable, but necessary, in the circumstances postulated, to imply an obligation on the employer to take reasonable steps to bring the term of the contract in question to the employee's attention, so that he may be in a position to enjoy its benefit. Accordingly I would hold that there was an implied term in each of the plaintiff's contracts of employment of which the Boards were in each case in breach.

NOTES

1. In *University of Nottingham* v *(1) Eyett (2) The Pensions Ombudsman* [1999] IRLR 87, the High Court held that the implied duty of trust and confidence does not include a positive obligation on the employer to warn an employee who is proposing to exercise important rights in connection with the contract of employment that the way he is proposing to exercise them may not be the most financially advantageous. Thus, the pensions ombudsman erred in holding that the employers were in breach of their implied duty in failing to alert the employee that, in view of the way his pension was calculated, he was making a financial mistake by not delaying his proposed date of retirement for a few days. *Scally* was distinguished on the basis that Mr Eyett:

   > . . . undoubtedly knew of the existence of his early retirement rights. He was also able, *pace* the ombudsman, to have worked out for himself how best to avail himself of those rights by care-fully studying the information set out in the explanatory booklet. There is no suggestion that he ever asked for advice as to whether the choice he was making was a suitable one, nor, as I have already indicated, was there any finding that the university knew that he was making a decision under the influence of a mistake. [*Per* Hart J]

2. Two more recent contrasting cases illustrate the scope of the implied term as identified in *Scally*. In *Crossley* v *Faithful Gould Holdings Ltd* [2004] IRLR 377, CA, a senior executive claimed dam-ages on the ground that the employers had failed to warn him of the consequences that resign-ing would have as regards obtaining benefits under a long-term disability scheme. The Court of Appeal held that there is no general implied duty on an employer to protect an employee's economic well-being. According to Dyson LJ: '[Such an implied term] would impose an unfair and unreasonable burden on employers. It is one thing to say that, if an employer assumes the responsibility for giving financial advice to his employees, he is under a duty to take reasonable care in the giving of that advice . . . It is quite a different matter to impose on an employer the duty to give his employee financial advice in relation to benefits accruing from his employment, or generally to safeguard the employee's economic well-being.' Lord Bridge's third criterion in *Scally*, that the employee cannot, in all the circumstances, reasonably be expected to be aware of the term unless it was brought to his attention, was not met. In reaching this conclusion, it was appropriate to take into account the fact that the claimant was a director and senior employee of the company. In particular, the fact that the claimant had access to the advice of an insurance broker who had arranged the scheme was of critical importance to that question. Compare this decision with *Lennon* v *Commissioner of Police of the Metropolis* [2004] IRLR 385, CA, where the employer expressly assumed responsibility for the advice. A police officer in London wished to transfer to Northern Ireland and to retain his housing allowance. His transfer arrangements were dealt with by a personnel executive, who assured him that the allowance would not be affected by a short break before he joined the Northern Ireland force. That advice was erroneous, and he broke his continuity of service and lost his continuing right to housing allowance. The Court of Appeal upheld a finding that the Commissioner was liable for the resultant economic loss sus-tained as a result of the negligent advice on which the claimant had relied.

FURTHER READING

Brodie, D., 'How relational is the employment contract?' (2011) 40(3) ILJ 232.

Cabrelli, D., *Employment Law in Context: Text and materials* (Oxford: OUP, 2014), Chs. 5, 6, 7.

Honeyball S., *Honeyball and Bowers' Textbook on Employment Law*, 13th edn (Oxford: OUP, 2014), Ch. 3.

4

Equality Law (1): Equal Pay

Preamble to equality law

There is no *general* principle of equality in English law…capable of…enforcement…The common law, based as it is in the primordial ideas of freedom of contract and the right to own property, means that in essence employers can contract with whomsoever they like and on whatever terms they choose, no matter how capriciously such a right is exercised. [Barnard, C., Deakin, S. and Kirkpatrick, C., 'Equality, non-discrimination and the labour market in the UK' (2002) 18(2) *International Journal of Comparative Labour Law and Industrial Relations*–47]

[T]he 'liberal' conception of equality which] abstracts persons from their unequal positions and puts them in a competition in which their prior inequality and its effects are ignored. [O'Donovan, K. and Szyszczak, E., *Equality and Sex Discrimination Law* (Oxford: Blackwell, 1988), p. 4]

In this and the next two chapters, the law relating to discrimination at work will be considered.

As can be seen from the above quotations, the common law does not recognise inequality in employment relations. To remedy this deficiency, statutory intervention was required. UK discrimination laws have developed over more than 40 years since the first Race Relations Act in 1965. Subsequently, other personal characteristics besides race have been protected from discrimination and similar conduct, sometimes as a result of domestic initiatives and sometimes through implementing European directives.

Domestic law relating to discrimination was, until 2010, mainly contained in the following legislation (where applicable, as amended):

- the Equal Pay Act 1970;
- the Sex Discrimination Act 1975;
- the Race Relations Act 1976;
- the Disability Discrimination Act 1995;
- the Employment Equality (Religion or Belief) Regulations 2003;
- the Employment Equality (Sexual Orientation) Regulations 2003;
- the Employment Equality (Age) Regulations 2006;
- the Equality Act 2006, Part 2;
- the Equality Act (Sexual Orientation) Regulations 2007.

The main European directives affecting domestic legislation relating to discrimination at work are:

- Council Directive 75/117/EEC on the approximation of the laws of the Member States relating to the application of the principle of equal pay for men and women;
- Council Directive 76/207/EEC on the implementation of the principle of equal treatment for men and women as regards access to employment, vocational training and promotion, and working conditions, as amended by the European Parliament and Council Directive 2002/73/EC;

- Council Directive 2000/43/EC implementing the principle of equal treatment between persons irrespective of racial or ethnic origin;
- Council Directive 2000/78/EC establishing a general framework for equal treatment in employment and occupation;
- European Parliament and Council Directive 2006/54/EC (as recast) on the implementation of the principle of equal opportunities and equal treatment of men and women in matters of employment and occupation. Also relevant in this context is Article 141 of the Treaty Establishing the European Community (Official Journal C 325/33 of 24 December 2002).

As early as 1998, the Equal Opportunities Commission (EOC) published a paper advocating a single equality statute (*Equality in the 21st Century: A new approach (1998)*). In February 2005, the Government set up the Discrimination Law Review to address long-term concerns about inconsistencies in the current discrimination law framework. The Review was tasked with considering the fundamental principles of discrimination legislation and its underlying concepts, and the opportunities for creating a clearer and more streamlined framework of equality legislation which produces better outcomes for those who experience disadvantage. As noted in the Review's terms of reference: 'Any proposals will have due regard to better regulation principles and take into account the need to minimise bureaucratic burdens on business and public services. A key priority will be seeking to achieve greater consistency in the protection afforded to different groups while taking into account evidence that different legal approaches may be appropriate for different groups.'

In June 2007 the Department for Communities and Local Government published a consultation paper, *A Framework for Fairness: Proposals for a Single Equality Bill for Great Britain*. This was followed in June and July 2008 by two Command Papers published by the Government Equalities Office: *Framework for a Fairer Future: The Equality Bill* (Cm. 7431); and *The Equality Bill: Government response to the consultation* (Cm. 7454). In January 2009, the Government published the New Opportunities White Paper (Cm. 7533) which, amongst other things, committed the Government to considering legislation to address disadvantage associated with socio-economic inequality.

On 24 April 2009, the Equality Bill was introduced in the House of Commons. After a protracted journey, it was approved by Parliament on 6 April 2010 and received Royal Assent on 8 April 2010. The majority of its provisions came into force in October 2010 with the implementation of some provisions being delayed until 2011 to allow public and private sector organisations to prepare. In the event, while some of the remaining provisions were brought into force on 5 April 2011, others were controversially dropped completely by the Coalition Government.

The position is as follows:

Equality Act provisions which came into force on 5 April 2011

Summary

The Equality Act (EqA) 2010 has two main purposes: to harmonise discrimination law, and to strengthen the law to support progress on equality.

The EqA 2010 brings together and restates all the enactments listed above and a number of other related provisions. It harmonises existing provisions to give a single approach where appropriate. Most of the pre-existing legislation is repealed. The EqA 2006 remains in force (as amended by the Act 1) so far as it relates to the constitution and operation of the Equality and Human Rights Commission (EHRC)—and the Disability Discrimination Act 1995 so far as it relates to Northern Ireland.

The EqA 2010 also aimed to strengthen workplace equality law in a number of areas by:

- placing a new duty on certain public bodies to consider socio-economic disadvantage when making strategic decisions about how to exercise their functions;
- requiring both public and private sector employers of 250 or more to regularly publish information relating to the gender pay gap in their organisation;
- extending the circumstances in which a person is protected against discrimination, harassment, or victimisation because of a protected characteristic;
- extending the circumstances in which a person is protected against discrimination by allowing people to make a claim if they are directly discriminated against because of a combination of two relevant protected characteristics ('dual discrimination');
- creating a duty on listed public bodies, when carrying out their functions, and on other persons, when carrying out public functions, to have due regard when carrying out their functions to: the need to eliminate conduct which the Act prohibits; the need to advance equality of opportunity between persons who share a relevant protected characteristic and those who do not; and the need to foster good relations between people who share a relevant protected characteristic and people who do not. (The practical effect is that listed public bodies will have to consider how their policies, programmes and service delivery will affect people with the protected characteristics);
- allowing an employer to take 'positive action' to appoint someone from an under-represented group where there are two equally qualified candidates;
- enabling an employment tribunal to make a recommendation to a respondent who has lost a discrimination claim to take certain steps to remedy matters not just for the benefit of the individual claimant (who may have already left the organisation concerned) but also the wider workforce.

Commencement

As stated above, the 'core' of the Act's provisions came into force on 1 October 2010, with the implementation of some provisions being delayed until 2011 to allow the Government to embark upon a consultation exercise. In the event, while some of the remaining provisions were brought into force on 5 April 2011, others were controversially dropped completely by the Coalition Government.

The current position is as follows:

Equality Act provisions which came into force on 5 April 2011

- positive action in recruitment and promotion;
- the public sector equality duty.

Equality Act provisions that the Government decided not to take forward

- the public sector duty regarding socio-economic equalities;
- mandatory gender pay gap reporting;
- combined discrimination: combined characteristics.

The EHRC has produced two Codes of Practice, one relating to employment and the other to equal pay, to support the provisions of the Equality Act. Both codes came into operation on 6 April 2011. They can be downloaded from the EHRC website.

NOTE: EqA 2010, s. 78 contains a power for the government to make regulations requiring employers with at least 250 employees to publish information about their gender pay gap. As noted above, no regulations have been made.

To date, the government has only introduced gender pay reporting on a voluntary basis under the *'Think, Act, Report'* scheme. However, despite more than 275 companies signing up to the scheme, in August 2014 it was reported that only four companies had published their gender pay information.

Following pressure from the Liberal Democrats, the Government tabled an amendment to what is now the Small Business, Enterprise and Employment Act 2015 requiring regulations under s. 78 to be made within 12 months of the Act coming into force.

SECTION 1: INTRODUCTION TO EQUAL PAY LAW

The Equal Pay Act (EPA) 1970 required the equal treatment of men and women in the same employment. The Act was passed with the intention of bringing about equality in respect of pay and other terms and conditions within a person's existing contract of employment. To this extent an equality clause is implied into every contract of employment. The relevant provision is now contained in s. 66 of the EqA 2010.

EQUALITY ACT 2010

66 Sex equality clause

(1) If the terms of A's work do not (by whatever means) include a sex equality clause, they are to be treated as including one.

(2) A sex equality clause is a provision that has the following effect—

(a) if a term of A's is less favourable to A than a corresponding term of B's is to B, A's term is modified so as not to be less favourable;

(b) if A does not have a term which corresponds to a term of B's that benefits B, A's terms are modified so as to include such a term.

NOTES

1. Section 67 contains the sex equality rule. This section requires that every occupational pension scheme is to have a sex equality rule read into it. The rule requires that men and women are treated equally to comparable members of the opposite sex in relation both to the terms on which they are permitted to join the scheme, and to the terms on which they are treated once they have become scheme members.

   The rule, insofar as it applies to the terms on which a person is treated once they have become a member of the scheme, does not apply to pensionable service before 17 May 1990. This was the date of the European Court's decision in *Barber* v *Guardian Royal Exchange Insurance Group* [1990] IRLR 240, which established that occupational pensions were equal pay for the purposes of Article 119 of the Treaty of Rome. Where the application of the rule relates to the terms on which a person becomes a member of the scheme, it has effect from 8 April 1976. This was the date of the judgment in *Defrenne* v *Sabena*, where the Court, in holding that the principle of equal pay was directly effective, indicated that Article 157 (formerly 119) of the EU Treaty should not be applied to periods of service prior to the judgment.

2. Whilst the EPA 1970 used the word 'woman' throughout to describe the potential victim of pay disparity, men had and continue to have exactly the same rights under the legislation (as seen earlier, the EqA 2010 uses the gender neutral terms of 'A' and 'B'). Realistically, however, equality is a woman's problem. This is borne out by the number of female applicants, particularly in respect of the equal value provisions. In theory the equality clause should operate automatically, but the reality is that in the most needy cases, it does not and a claim to an employment tribunal is required.

   Both HM Courts and Tribunal Service and ACAS no longer produce statistics on the volume and outcome of equal pay clams, which is regrettable. Earlier annual employment tribunal and Employment Appeal Tribunal (EAT) statistics produced by the Employment Tribunals Service indicated that the success rate in equal pay claims is low, with a high percentage of cases being withdrawn. This would suggest that the equal pay legislation itself may be a significant obstacle to a successful outcome, particularly, as we shall see, the need to have a comparator of the opposite sex. Also in reality the legislation does not address the underlying causes, such as the persistent undervaluing of women in the workplace—see Horrell, S., Rubery, J., and Burchell, B., 'Unequal Jobs or Unequal Pay?' (1990) 20 *Industrial Relations Journal* 176.

The 2014 Annual Survey of Hours and Earnings (ASHE) shows that the gender pay difference, based on median gross hourly earnings (excluding overtime), for full-time workers had narrowed to 9.6%, compared to 10% in 2013. This is the lowest since records began in 1997, and despite a relatively large increase between 2012 and 2013, there is an overall downward trend, from 17.3% in 1997.

The gap for all employees (full-time and part-time) was also the lowest on record at 19.1%, down from 19.8% in 2013. The gap has also decreased long-term, from 25.7% in 1997 (*Annual Survey of Hours and Earnings, 2014, provisional results*, Office for National Statistics, 19 November 2014). See also *An Anatomy of Inequality in the UK: Report of the National Equality Panel* (Government Equalities Office, January 2010, <http://www.equalities.gov.uk>).

The Gender Agenda: The unfinished revolution
(EOC, 2007), p. 5

Closing the income gap

Women who work full-time earn, on average, 17 per cent less per hour than men working full-time. For women who work part-time, the gap in pay relative to full-time men is a huge 38 per cent per hour. The causes of the pay gap are complex—in part to do with discrimination; in part because women are more likely than men to work in low paid sectors; and in part because women often have to 'trade down' or face other work and pay penalties once they become mothers. The average woman working full-time could lose out on £330,000 over the course of her working life. These aren't figures from the 1970s before equal pay laws came into force—they're current and show the shocking income gap that persists between men and women. The problem affects us throughout our lives because lower pay means that women face a pensions gap too—their retirement income is 40 per cent less than men's. And some groups of women face an even bigger income gap—for example, Pakistani women are paid less on average for full-time work than white British women and substantially less than white British men.

Until we close these glaring income gaps and fundamentally change Britain's workplaces, our choices will remain limited. Men and women will not be able to organise family life in a way that works for them, older women will continue to be less independent than men and with the under-use of women's skills our country will become less productive in a tougher global economy.

D. Grimshaw and J. Rubery, *Undervaluing Women's Work*
(EOC Working Paper Series No. 53, 2007), pp. xiii–xv

POLICY OPTIONS TO REDUCE UNDERVALUATION

This report has found diverse, but strong, evidence that women's work is undervalued. Policies to reduce undervaluation and to protect against the emergence of new forms of undervaluation need to address the status and pay attached to work done by women; and the position of women within the current job and pay structure. Both these elements of undervaluation need to be addressed at a number of different levels: the labour market; the occupation; the organisation; and the workplace or job level.

Improving the pay and status of work done by women

The labour market level

Policies are needed to reduce the penalties attached to being placed at a low position within the pay and job hierarchy. These may include policies to raise the floor to the labour market, by for example establishing a living wage as the minimum pay level, or taking action to counter trends towards widening inequality at the top end of the labour market. Promoting greater transparency and accountability in remuneration decisions could help to turn the tide.

The integration of payment systems between organisations and sectors should provide mechanisms to link pay in female-dominated jobs to pay in male-dominated jobs. Current policies of outsourcing should not be allowed to fragment the systems of wage-fixing in the public sector. Change to equal pay laws to allow comparisons across employers could also promote greater integration of pay systems.

The occupational level

Promoting and professionalising the general status of an occupation through skill and career development may help to change perceptions of its value and the pay it commands. Failure to do so may result in costs for employers, employees and society through high turnover and loss of valuable skills.

The organisational level

Policies to reduce undervaluation associated with low ability to pay depend on where the problem lies. Where, for example, it is powerful clients who are pushing down wages in subcontracted sectors, living wage campaigns may be effective. Trade unions are currently trying to protect pay for outsourced services in the public sector, for example by agreeing a minimum wage for all contractors in the NHS. Where it is not possible to increase productivity, but the service provided is essential and valuable, the removal of undervaluation depends on society's willingness to pay, through taxation of both enterprises and individuals.

If equal pay laws are to be effective, they must begin to allow for comparisons across organisational borders to reduce incentives to outsource in order to pay low wages in gender segregated areas. Another strategy could be to require all large organisations, that is including those organised around chains of small workplaces, to conduct and publish equal pay reviews.

The workplace and job level

Equal pay legislation currently applies only within the workplace of a single employer. Even here, the equal value element to the legislation only applies if the jobs are of equal value, so that a woman's job that is 'worth' 80% of a man's job, may be legally paid at 50% of the wage. The adoption of a general and proportionate equal pay for work of equal value principle would be a first step to tackle undervaluation at the workplace.

In addition, organisations should adopt the policies to counter the problems of lack of visibility of skills, low valuation of skills, low pay on grounds of vocation, exclusion from high value-added employment and pay penalties because of variance in work patterns.

Improving the position of women within the current job and pay structure

The labour market level

Policies to reduce women's vulnerability to undervaluation need to extend women's career choices at the point of childbirth and re-entry to the labour market.

The right to work flexibly should be both strengthened and extended to include other carers, not just parents of young children. More positive incentives for men to participate in care on an equal basis with women are required. And consideration should be given to establishing a parallel right to request a return to full-time work when care responsibilities change to prevent the crowding of women on to 'mommy tracks' at work.

Perhaps most importantly, there needs to be a move away from the long hours culture that often leaves mothers with few options other than to go down the part-time route. This culture change has to be effected at the organisation and workplace level, but the change could be assisted symbolically and in practice, by the abolition of the opt out from the maximum 48 hour week.

Finally, there should be policies to recognise that becoming a parent is a positive contribution to society. This could include giving rights to reduce hours, with earnings compensation during periods of responsibility for young children.

The occupational level

Promoting women's position within occupational structures may involve two quite separate strategies. In male-dominated occupations, policies are needed to ensure that women are able to move off the lowest rungs of the ladder, that they are not so discouraged by the dominant male culture that they leave the occupation, and that they avoid being confined to a specific and low paid job segment. In female-dominated occupations, the main tasks may be to create more promotion opportunities and to ensure those opportunities do not become monopolised by a minority of male employees.

The organisational level

Women need to gain access to higher paying organisations that provide better career opportunities. Organisations can be encouraged or required to report on their equal opportunity policies and practices through specific equality or equal pay reviews, as required in many Nordic countries, or to include information on equality within a general reporting framework such as an addendum to a company report.

The workplace and job level

Countering undervaluation requires attention to be paid to where men and women are placed initially within a pay and grading structure and how their pay progresses over time. A set of principles that may help ensure that the pay system promotes gender equality include commitments to:

- equal pay for work of equal value for all staff, not just between men and women;
- transparency of pay and reward structures;
- the reward of actual performance *at* work, not presumed commitment *to* work, such as willingness to work extra and long hours; and
- the reward of contribution/performance in the job and not the market power of the employee.

5. *Equal pay and transparency* The right to serve an equal pay questionnaire on an employer was introduced into the EPA 1970 (s. 7B) by the Employment Act 2002. This brought the EPA 1975 in line with the Sex Discrimination Act 1975 and the Race Relations Act 1976. The questionnaire made it easier for individuals to discover key information from their employer in order to enable them to decide whether to proceed with an equal pay claim. For example, it allowed them to discover what their fellow employees earn. However, the completion of the questionnaire by the employer was not compulsory and employers had a defence of 'confidentiality', although a failure to comply permitted an ET to draw an inference which it believes to be 'just and equitable' (see EqA 2010, s. 138).

The Government had received claims from employer lobby groups that the questionnaires were often used as a 'fishing expedition' by individuals who did not have any real or reasonable cause for complaint. The Government estimated that between 9,000 and 10,000 businesses complete questionnaires each year with each questionnaire taking about 5 to 6 hours to complete, totalling somewhere between 45,000 to 60,000 employee hours. Following a consultation exercise, the Government decided to abolish the procedure despite the fact that 83% of rspondents to the consultation were in favour of its retention. As such, the proposals formed part of the Coalition's commitment to cut red tape. The repeal of s. 138 was effected by the Enterprise and Regulatory Reform Act 2013, s. 66 and came into force on 6 April 2014.

In the absence of s. 138, employees will still be able to ask questions of their employer, albeit without the structure provided by the standard form questionnaire and the time limits for the employer's response, which was eight weeks.

ACAS has produced guidance entitled *Asking and Responding to Questions of Discrimination in the Workplace*, which explains how the new, non-statutory approach should operate. The ACAS document includes a six-step guide for individuals when asking questions and a three-step guide for employers to follow when responding.

There is no direct penalty for failure to comply with the guidance, but any failure to respond or offering evasive replies to questions could be taken into account by tribunals hearing a subsequent discrimination claim against the employer. Also, the abolition of s. 138 may, where the parties are already involved in litigation, result in an increase in applications to tribunals for further information and disclosure under the existing Employment Tribunal Rules of Procedure.

The EqA 2010 has introduced two new provisions designed to further transparency in the reward process.

First, s. 77 is designed to protect people who discuss their pay with colleagues (as defined in s. 79) with a view to finding out if differences exist that are related to a protected characteristic. Any action taken against them by the employer as a result of doing so is treated as victimisation, as defined in s. 27.

Terms of employment or appointment that prevent or restrict people from disclosing their pay to their colleagues are made unenforceable to the extent that they would prevent or restrict such a discussion. As a result of an amendment in the Lords, protection is afforded not only for such discussions between colleagues who are in the same employment, but also for any disclosure of information about pay which the employee can show had the purpose of finding out whether there was a connection between pay and a protected characteristic, e.g. disclosures to trade union officials who are not fellow employees.

Second, s. 78 enables a minister of the Crown to make regulations requiring employers with at least 250 employees in Great Britain to publish information about the differences in pay between their male and female employees. However, the Coalition Government determined not to bring this mandatory requirement into force, preferring instead to encourage a voluntary approach. It is interesting to note that EHRC's Code of Practice regards the process of reviewing or auditing pay as good practice (*Equality Act 2010 Statutory Code of Practice on Equal Pay, 2011, Part 2 Good Equal Pay Practice*).

6. *Work and families* One of the most dynamic areas of development in recent years has been in the area of maternity, paternity, and adoption rights. There have been additional rights for parents at work in terms of flexible working, paternity, and adoption leave, as well as an increase to statutory maternity pay and entitlement to maternity pay and maternity allowance. Given the rapidly evolving picture, often affected by regulatory change, it has been decided to include the chapter on 'Family Rights' as part of the Online Resource Centre which supports this book (see <http://www.oxfordtextbooks.co.uk/orc/painter/>). In this way we can keep the reader as up to date as possible.

SECTION 2: EUROPEAN COMMUNITY LAW

Article 157 of the Treaty on the Functioning of the European Union (TFEU) (ex 119 of the Treaty of Rome) establishes the principle of equal pay for equal work. The Article is directly enforceable in the Member States and takes precedence over domestic law. It has to be read subject to Directive 75/117, the Equal Pay Directive. While the directive is not directly enforceable against individual employers, Article 157 (ex 119) must be interpreted in accordance with the directive; consequently, in effect it is applied directly.

Treaty on the Functioning of the European Union (EX TREATY OF ROME)

Article 157 (ex Article 119)

1. Each Member State shall ensure that the principle of equal pay for male and female workers for equal work or work of equal value is applied.

2. For the purpose of this Article, 'pay' means the ordinary basic or minimum wage or salary and any other consideration, whether in cash or in kind, which the worker receives directly or indirectly, in respect of his employment, from his employer.

Equal pay without discrimination based on sex means:

    (a) that pay for the same work at piece rates shall be calculated on the basis of the same unit of measurement;

    (b) that pay for work at time rates shall be the same for the same job.

3. The Council, acting in accordance with the procedure referred to in Article 251, and after consulting the Economic and Social Committee, shall adopt measures to ensure the application of the principle of equal opportunities and equal treatment of men and women in matters of employment and occupation, including the principle of equal pay for equal work or work of equal value.

4. With a view to ensuring full equality in practice between men and women in working life, the principle of equal treatment shall not prevent any Member State from maintaining or adopting measures providing for specific advantages in order to make it easier for the under-represented sex to pursue a vocational activity or to prevent or compensate for disadvantages in professional careers.

DIRECTIVE 2006/54, ARTICLE 4

SPECIFIC PROVISIONS

CHAPTER 1   EQUAL PAY

Article 4 Prohibition of discrimination

For the same work or for work to which equal value is attributed, direct and indirect discrimination on grounds of sex with regard to all aspects and conditions of remuneration shall be eliminated.

In particular, where a job classification system is used for determining pay, it shall be based on the same criteria for both men and women and so drawn up as to exclude any discrimination on grounds of sex.

Jenkins v Kingsgate (Clothing Productions) Ltd

[1981] IRLR 228, European Court of Justice

Mrs Jenkins was employed as a machinist by a manufacturer of ladies' clothing. She worked on a part-time basis of 30 hours per week. All male machinists except one were employed on a full-time basis. The hourly rate for full-time workers was 9½ pence higher than that paid to part-time employees. Mrs Jenkins based her claim under the EPA 1970 on the fact that she was doing 'like work' to that of a full-time male employee. The industrial tribunal dismissed her claim on the basis that there was a valid general material difference defence (the EPA 1970, s. 1(3)). The EAT accepted that she could not succeed under the EPA 1970 but agreed to refer the matter to the European Court

of Justice (ECJ) to determine whether the employer's practice contravened Article 119 (now 157).

It was held that Article 119 (now 157) is directly applicable in the national courts to a situation where the payment of lower hourly rates of remuneration for part-time work than for full-time work represents discrimination based on the difference of sex.

DECISION: In the fourth and last question, the national court asks whether the provisions of Article 119 [now 141] of the Treaty are directly applicable in the circumstances of this case.

As the Court has stated in previous decisions (judgment of 8.4.76 in Case 43/75, Defrenne [1976] ECR 455; judgment of 27.3.80 in Case 129/79, *Wendy Smith* [1980] ECR 1275 ([1980] IRLR 210) and judgment of 11.3.81 in Case 69/80, *Worringham* ([1981] IRLR 178)), Article 119 [now 157] of the Treaty applies directly to all forms of discrimination which may be identified solely with the aid of criteria of equal work and equal pay referred to by the article in question, without national or Community measures being required to define them with greater precision in order to permit of their application. Among the forms of discrimination which may be thus judicially identified, the Court mentioned in particular cases where men and women receive unequal pay for equal work carried out in the same establishment or service, public or private.

Where the national court is able, using the criteria of equal work and equal pay, without the operation of Community or national measures, to establish that the payment of lower hourly rates of remuneration for part-time work than for full-time work represents discrimination based on difference of sex the provisions of Article 119 [now 157] of the Treaty apply directly to such a situation.

Article 1 of Council Directive No. 75/117 of 10.2.75.

The national court also raises with regard to Article 1 of Council Directive No. 75/117 of 10.2.75 the same questions of interpretation as those examined above in relation to Article 119 [now 157] of the Treaty.

As may be seen from the first recital in the preamble the primary objective of the above-mentioned Directive is to implement the principle that men and women should receive equal pay which is 'contained in Article 119 [now 157] of the Treaty'. For that purpose the fourth recital states that 'it is desirable to reinforce the basic laws by standards aimed at facilitating the practical application of the principle of equality'.

The provisions of Article 1 of that Directive are confined, in the first paragraph, to re-stating the principle of equal pay set out in Article 119 [now 157] of the Treaty and specify, in the second paragraph, the conditions for applying that principle where a job classification system is used for determining pay.

It follows, therefore, that Article 1 of Council Directive No. 75/117 which is principally designed to facilitate the practical application of the principle of equal pay outlined in Article 119 [now 157] of the Treaty in no way alters the content or scope of that principle as defined in the Treaty.

NOTES
1. Directive 75/117 has been consolidated into Directive 2006/54, which consolidates the equal pay and equal treatment directives.
2. With respect to the difference in pay between full-time and part-time workers in *Jenkins'* case, the ECJ concluded that this did not amount to discrimination prohibited by 'Article 119 [now 157] unless it is in reality merely an indirect way of reducing the level of pay of part-time workers on the ground that the group of workers is composed exclusively or predominantly of women'.

    The issue of qualifying periods denying part-time employees access to employment rights and therefore discriminating against females was considered in *R v Secretary of State for Employment, ex p. EOC* [1994] 2 WLR 409 and *R v Secretary of State for Employment, ex p. Seymour-Smith & Perez (No. 2)* [2000] IRLR 263 (see Chapter 2). While it was held that a two-year qualifying period for unfair dismissal complaints had a disparately adverse impact on women so as to amount to indirect discrimination contrary to Article 157 (ex 119), the House of Lords concluded that the Secretary of State had objectively justified the require-ment by providing evidence that to reduce the requirement might inhibit the recruitment of employees and show that it was unrelated to any discrimination based on sex. For a critique of *Seymour-Smith* see Townsend-Smith, R., 'Seymour-Smith: The closing stages' (2000) 29 ILJ 297. The potential impact of these decisions has been somewhat diminished by the Employment Protection (Part-time Employees) Regulations 1995 (SI 1995/31) and the Employment Relations Act 1999, the latter reducing the qualifying period for unfair dismissal claims from two years to one year (1 June 1999).

3. Following *Jenkins'* case it was thought that Article 119 (now 1157) was not applicable in cases of unintentional indirect discrimination, i.e. it would apply only to overt intentional acts, although it could be implied into the EPA 1970. This point was clarified in *Bilka-Kaufhaus* v *Weber von Hartz* [1986] IRLR 317, where the ECJ ruled that such discrimination was within Article 119 (now 157).

4. Where part-time female employees claim that a difference in pay impacts on part-time staff, it is still a requirement that the claimant produce statistical evidence concerning the disadvantaged group. This is particularly the case where not all of the part-time staff are treated less favourably. In *Barry* v *Midland Bank plc*, a female part-time employee claimed that the severance pay awarded to part-time staff was less favourable than for full-time staff but could not produce statistics for her disadvantaged group. In any event, the severance scheme was objectively justifiable in this case, as its primary aim was to cushion the effects of unemployment and to compensate employees for the loss of their jobs—legitimate non-discriminatory aims *per* Peter Gibson LJ, at p. 145.

   The decision in *Barry* v *Midland Bank plc* suggests that indirect discrimination cannot be established under Article 141 (ex 119) where there is no relevant difference in treatment, even though there is a disparate impact. The Part-time Workers (Prevention of Less Favourable Treatment) Regulations 2000 (SI 2000/1551) now make it unlawful to discriminate against part-time workers in respect of pay and conditions. It also addresses the issue of indirect discrimination between full and part-time employees (see Chapter 2). Also in *Elsner-Lakeberg* v *Land Nordrhein-Westfalen* [2005] IRLR 209, ECJ, a regulation which provided that both part-time and full-time teachers should not receive any remuneration for additional hours worked, when the additional work does not exceed three hours per calendar month, was found to be contrary to Article 141 and the Equal Pay Directive as it affected considerably more women than men. Although in this case the requirement was applied to both full- and part-time staff, 'the three additional hours was in fact a greater burden for part-time teachers than it was for full-time teachers'.

5. The ECJ found in *Angestelltenbetriebsstrat der Wiener Gebietskrankenkasse* v *Wiener Gebietskrankenkasse* [1999] IRLR 804 that psychotherapists with a degree in psychology, most of whom were women, did not do 'the same work within the meaning of Article 157 (ex 119) as higher paid and predominantly male doctors employed as psychotherapists'. While the two groups performed for the most part identical work, they had received different professional training and, because of the different scope of the qualifications resulting from that training, were called upon to perform different tasks. It transpired that in treating patients, the two groups drew upon knowledge and skills acquired from their different disciplines. While one may conclude that this is a questionable decision, particularly as they were carrying out identical tasks, it may have been more appropriate for the female psychologists to claim work of equal value.

6. Directive 75/117 (now Directive 2006/54) is binding insofar as the EqA 2010 should be interpreted so as to avoid conflict with EC law. Directives require the Member State to amend their domestic legislation accordingly. The European Commission challenged the UK for failing to implement in its own legislation the principle of equal pay for work of equal value as laid down in Directive 75/117—see *Commission of the European Communities* v *United Kingdom of Great Britain and Northern Ireland* [1982] IRLR 333, ECJ.

   The following case highlights the importance of taking a 'purposive' approach when interpreting UK law in the light of Community law.

Pickstone & others (respondents) v *Freemans plc (appellants)*
[1988] IRLR 357, House of Lords

In the present case the respondent, Mrs Pickstone, who is employed by the appellant employers as a 'warehouse operative', claims that her work as such is of equal value with that of a man, Mr Phillips, who is employed in the same establishment as a 'checker warehouse operative', and who is paid £4.22 per week more than she is paid. However, it happens to be the fact that one man is employed in the establishment as a warehouse operative doing the same work as Mrs Pickstone. The employers maintain that the existence of this fact precludes Mrs Pickstone from claiming equal pay with Mr Phillips under s. 1(2)(c) of the Act of 1970 as amended, notwithstanding that she may be performing work of equal value with his and notwithstanding that the difference in pay may be the result of discrimination on grounds of sex.

This argument is based on the words in paragraph (c) 'not being work in relation to which para. (a) or (b) above applies'. The employers say that the work on which Mrs Pickstone is employed is work to which paragraph (a) applies because it is like work with a man in the same employment, namely the one male warehouse operative. So Mrs Pickstone's work does not qualify under paragraph (c).

The EAT [1986] IRLR 335 dismissed the appeal against this decision. The EAT concluded that the 'words in para. (c) mean what they appear to say—namely, that "equal value" only falls to be considered where the work of the comparator is neither "like work" nor "equivalent work" to which paras. (a) and (b) apply'. The EAT did not purport to construe EEC law, because it held that the issue could be determined under domestic law.

The Court of Appeal [1987] IRLR 218 held that the words of s. 1(2)(c) were unambiguous and had the effect that a woman employed on work which is the same as that of one man but which is also of equal value with the work of another man could not claim equal pay with that other man where she was already being paid as much as the man engaged on the same work as herself.

However, it concluded her claim was not barred under Article 119 (now 141), which must prevail. The employers appealed to the House of Lords.

It was held, dismissing the appeal, that the EPA 1970, s. 1(2)(c) should be construed in such a way that it is consistent with the objects of the EC Treaty, the provisions of the Equal Pay Directive and the rulings of the European Court.

LORD KEITH OF KINKEL: The question is whether the exclusionary words in para. (c) are intended to have effect whenever the employers are able to point to some man who is employed by them on like work with the woman claimant within the meaning of para. (a) or work rated as equivalent with hers within the meaning of para. (b), or whether they are intended to have effect only where the particular man with whom she seeks comparison is employed on such work. In my opinion the latter is the correct answer. The opposite result would leave a large gap in the equal work provision, enabling an employer to evade it by employing one token man on the same work as a group of potential women claimants who were deliberately paid less than a group of men employed on work of equal value with that of the women. This would mean that the United Kingdom had failed yet again fully to implement its obligations under Article 119 (now 141) of the Treaty and the Equal Pay Directive, and had not given full effect to the decision of the European Court in *Commission of the European Communities* v *United Kingdom* [1982] IRLR 333. It is plain that Parliament cannot possibly have intended such a failure. The draft Regulations of 1983 were presented to Parliament as giving full effect to the decision in question. The draft Regulations were not subject to the Parliamentary process of consideration and amendment in Committee, as a Bill would have been. In these circumstances and in the context of s. 2 of the European Communities Act 1972 I consider it to be entirely legitimate for the purpose of ascertaining the intention of Parliament to take into account the terms in which the draft was presented by the responsible Minister and which formed the basis of its acceptance. The terms in which it was presented to the House of Commons are set out in the speech of my noble and learned friend, Lord Templeman. Much the same was said before the House of Lords. There was no suggestion that the exclusionary works in para. (c) were intended to apply in any other situation than where the man selected by a woman complainant for comparison was one in relation to whose work para. (a) or para. (b) applied. It may be that, in order to confine the words in question to that situation, some necessary implication falls to be made into their literal meaning. The precise terms of that implication do not seem to me to matter. It is sufficient to say that the words must be construed purposively in order to give effect to the manifest broad intention of the maker of the Regulations and of Parliament. I would therefore reject the appellant's argument.

LORD TEMPLEMAN: According to the employers in the present appeal, the Regulations of 1983 had the additional effect of depriving some women of the right to pursue their claims by judicial process or otherwise although they considered themselves wronged by failure to apply the principle of equal pay. The respondents may have a valid complaint in that they are not receiving equal pay with Mr Phillips for work of equal value. But if the respondents seek to remedy that discrimination under s. 1(2)(c) of the act of 1970 as amended by the Regulations, they will be debarred because they are employed on 'work in relation to which para. (a) or (b) above applies'. It is said that para. (a) operates, not because the respondents are employed on like work with Mr Phillips but because the respondents are employed on like work with some other man. Since para. (c) is expressed to apply only when a woman is employed on work which is not 'work in relation to which para. (a) or

(b) above applies,' it follows, so it is said, that where a woman is employed on like work with any man or where a woman is employed on work rated as equivalent with any man, no claim can be made under para. (c) in respect of some other man who is engaged on work of equal value. In my opinion para. (a) or (b) only debars a claim under para. (c) where para. (a) or (b) applies to the man who is the subject of the complaint made by the woman. If the Tribunal decide that the respondents are engaged 'on like work' with Mr Phillips then para. (a) applies and the respondents are not entitled to proceed under para. (c) and to obtain the report of an ACAS expert. If there is a job evaluation study which covers the work of the respondents and the work of Mr Phillips then the respondents are debarred from proceeding under para. (c) unless the job evaluation study itself was discriminatory.

Whenever there is a claim for equal pay, the complainant, or the complainant's trade union representative supporting the claimant, may wish to obtain a report from an ACAS expert under para. (c) to use for the purpose of general pay bargaining and in the hope of finding ammunition which will lead to a general increase in wage levels irrespective of discrimination. For this purpose the more ACAS reports there are the better. It may be significant that in the present case a claim is made under para. (c) and not under para. (a) as well, or, in the alternative, although it is obvious that work of equal value in terms of the demands made on a woman under such headings as effort, skill and decision which may amount to discrimination under para. (c) may also be work of a broadly similar nature with differences of no practical importance which found a complaint under para. (a). If there is discrimination in pay the Industrial Tribunal must be able to grant a remedy. But the remedy available under para. (c) is not to be applied if the complainant has a remedy in respect of the male employee with whom she demands parity under para. (a) or if para. (b) applies to the woman and to that male employee. To prevent exploitation of para. (c) the Tribunal must decide in the first instance whether the complainant and the man with whom she seeks parity are engaged on 'like work' under para. (a). If para. (a) applies, no ACAS report is required. If para. (a) does not apply, then the Tribunal considers whether para. (b) applies to the complainant and the man with whom she seeks parity; if so, the Tribunal can only proceed under para. (c) if the job evaluation study obtained for the purposes of para. (b) is itself discriminatory. If para. (b) applies then, again, no ACAS report is necessary. If paras. (a) and (b) do not apply, the Tribunal must next consider whether there are reasonable grounds for determining that the work of the complainant and the work of the man with whom she seeks parity is of equal value. If the Tribunal are not so satisfied, then no ACAS report is required. The words in para. (c) on which the employers rely were not intended to create a new form of permitted discrimination. Para. (c) enables a claim to equal pay as against a specified man to be made without injustice to an employer. When a woman claims equal pay for work of equal value, she specifies the man with whom she demands parity. If the work of the woman is work in relation to which para. (a) or (b) applies in relation to that man, then the woman cannot proceed under para. (c) and cannot obtain a report from an ACAS expert. In my opinion there must be implied in para. (c) after the word 'applies' the words 'as between the woman and the man with whom she claims equality.' This construction is consistent with Community law. The employers' construction is inconsistent with Community law and creates a permitted form of discrimination without rhyme or reason.

Macarthys Ltd v Smith
[1980] ICR 672, European Court of Justice

M, a man, was employed as the manager of one of the stockrooms of the employers' warehouses, at a remuneration of about £60 a week. On 20 October 1975, he left. For four months the post was not filled and then the employee was appointed, her duties differing slightly from M's. She was paid £50 a week. On 9 March 1977, she left her employment. She brought proceedings before an industrial tribunal claiming that, by virtue of s. 1(1) and (2)(a) of the EPA 1970, her contract of employment should be treated as modified with regard to her remuneration so as to entitle her to pay equal to M's pay at the termination of his employment. The tribunal upheld her claim and decided that the employee was entitled to compare the work done by her with M's work and that her services and those of M were broadly comparable so as to justify calculating her remuneration on the same basis as his.

The EAT dismissed the employers' appeal. The Court of Appeal (Lord Denning MR dissenting) held that the words in s. 1(2) of the Act of 1970, as amended, by the use of the present tense looked to the present and the future and thus, giving them the grammatical construction, they were consistent with a comparison between a man and a woman contemporaneously in the same employment, but, bearing in mind that construction of the section, the application of Article 119 (now 157) of the EEC Treaty to the circumstances of the section was not easy to discern and that a reference should be made to the European Court of Justice.

On the reference to the European Court of the questions, *inter alia*, whether the principle of equal pay for equal work contained in Article 119 (now 157) of the Treaty and Article 1 of the EEC Council Directive of 10 February 1975 (75/117/EEC) was confined to situations in which men and women were contemporaneously doing equal work for their employer, it was held that the principle in Article 119 (now 157) of the EEC Treaty that men and women should receive equal pay for equal work was not confined to situations in which men and women were contemporaneously doing equal work for the same employer, and that the principle applied to a case where, having regard to the nature of her services, a woman had received less pay than a man who was employed prior to the woman and did equal work for the employer.

DECISION: ...The employers contended that, according to its natural and ordinary meaning, the Equal Pay Act 1970 makes it impermissible for a woman to compare her situation with that of a man formerly in the employment of the same employer. In their submission, such an interpretation would not be inconsistent with the principle of equal pay for men and women laid down in Article 119 [now 157] of the EEC Treaty.

6. For her part, the employee contended that the employers' interpretation was contrary to Article 119 [now 157] and to article 1 of Directive No. 75/117/EEC in that the principle of equal pay for equal work is not confined to situations in which men and women are contemporaneously doing equal work for their employer but that, on the contrary, that principle also applies where a worker can show that she receives less pay in respect of her employment than she would have received if she were a man doing equal work for the employer or than had been received by a male worker who had been employed prior to her period of employment and had been doing equal work for her employer.

7. In order to decide the dispute the Court of Appeal formulated four questions worded as follows:
1. Is the principle of equal pay for equal work, contained in Article 119 [now 157] of the EEC Treaty and Article 1 of the EEC Council Directive of February 10, 1975 (75/117/EEC), confined to situations in which men and women are contemporaneously doing equal work for their employer?
2. If the answer to question (1) is in the negative, does the said principle apply where a worker can show that she receives less pay in respect of her employment from her employer: (a) than she would have received if she were a man doing equal work for the employer; or (b) than had been received by a male worker who had been employed prior to her period of employment and who had been doing equal work for the employer?
3. If the answer to question (2)(a) or (b) is in the affirmative, is that answer dependent upon the provisions of Article 1 of the Directive?
4. If the answer to question (3) is in the affirmative, is Article 1 of the Directive directly applicable in member States?

8. It follows from the wording of these questions, as much as from the reasons given in the order making the reference, that the questions relating to the effect of the Directive and to the interpretation of Article 1 thereof only arise if the application of Article 119 [now 157] of the Treaty should not permit the issue raised in the proceedings to be resolved. It is therefore appropriate to consider first how Article 119 [now 157] is to be interpreted having regard to the legal situation in which the dispute has its origin.

The interpretation of Article 141 [ex 119] of the EEC Treaty

9. According to the first paragraph of Article 119 [now 157] the member states are obliged to ensure and maintain 'the application of the principle that men and women should receive equal pay for equal work.'

10. As the court indicated in *Defrenne* v *Sabena* [1976] ICR 547, that provision applies directly, and without the need for more detailed implementing measures on the part of the Community or the member states, to all forms of direct and overt discrimination which may be identified solely with the aid of the criteria of equal work and equal pay referred to by the article in question. Among the forms of discrimination which may be thus judicially identified, the court mentioned in particular cases where men and women receive unequal pay for equal work carried out in the same establishment or service.

11. In such a situation the decisive test lies in establishing whether there is a difference in treatment between a man and a woman performing 'equal work' within the meaning of Article 119 [now 157]. The scope of that

concept, which is entirely qualitative in character in that it is exclusively concerned with the nature of the services in question, may not be restricted by the introduction of a requirement of contemporaneity.

12. It must be acknowledged, however, that, as the Employment Appeal Tribunal properly recognised, it cannot be ruled out that a difference in pay between two workers occupying the same post but at different periods in time may be explained by the operation of factors which are unconnected with any discrimination on grounds of sex. That is a question of fact which it is for the court or tribunal to decide.

13. Thus the answer to the first question should be that the principle that men and women should receive equal pay for equal work, enshrined in Article 119 [now 157] of the EC Treaty, is not confined to situations in which men and women are contemporaneously doing equal work for the same employer.

14. The second question put by the Court of Appeal and expressed in terms of alternatives concerns the framework within which the existence of possible discrimination in pay may be established. This question is intended to enable the court to rule upon a submission made by the employee and developed by her before the European Court of Justice to the effect that a woman may claim not only the salary received by a man who previously did the same work for her employer but also, more generally, the salary to which she would be entitled were she a man, even in the absence of any man who was concurrently performing, or had previously performed, similar work. The employee defined this term of comparison by reference to the concept of what she described as 'a hypothetical male worker.'

15. It is clear that the latter proposition, which is the subject of question 2(a), is to be classed as indirect and disguised discrimination, the identification of which, as the court explained in *Defrenne* v *Sabena* [1976] ICR 547, implies comparative studies of entire branches of industry and therefore requires, as a prerequisite, the elaboration by the Community and national legislative bodies of criteria of assessment. From that it follows that, in cases of actual discrimination falling within the scope of the direct application of Article 119 [now 157], comparisons are confined to parallels which may be drawn on the basis of concrete appraisals of the work actually performed by employees of different sex within the same establishment or service.

16. The answer to the second question should therefore be that the principle of equal pay enshrined in Article 119 [now 157] applies to the case where it is established that, having regard to the nature of her services, a woman has received less pay than a man who was employed prior to the woman's period of employment and who did equal work for the employer.

17. From the foregoing it appears that the dispute brought before the national court may be decided within the framework of an interpretation of Article 119 [now 157] of the Treaty alone. In those circumstances it is unnecessary to answer the questions submitted in so far as they relate to the effect and to the interpretation of EEC Council Directive (75/117/EEC).

NOTES

1. The decision in *Pickstone* does not provide an automatic right to claim work of equal value; it is subject to an assessment by the employment tribunal of whether this is the correct head of claim, first after considering 'like work' and secondly 'work rated equivalent'. However, the decision is important not only for showing the effect of EC law on domestic law, but also for ensuring that employers do not avoid their obligations under the equal pay legislation by employing a token man to work alongside women.

2. The impact of Article 157 (ex 119) and Directive 75/117 can be seen in *Macarthys Ltd* v *Smith*. The equal pay legislation must be interpreted in the light of this decision, thereby allowing any applicant the right of comparison with a predecessor. The *Macarthys* approach has now been given statutory recognition (see the EqA 2010, s. 64(2), extracted in Section 3). Furthermore, in *Murphy* v *Bord Telecom Eireann* [1988] IRLR 267, where a female employee was doing work of a higher value than her male comparator, the ECJ held that the words 'equal value' should include higher or greater value. In fact, to conclude otherwise would have created an anomaly, allowing an employer to assign additional or more onerous duties to workers of a particular sex, who could then be paid at a lower wage. The Court of Appeal in *Redcar & Cleveland Borough Council* v *Bainbridge (No. 1)* [2007] IRLR 984, applying the decision in *Murphy*, held that claimants were entitled to make claims under s. 2(1)(b) (work rated equivalent) in respect of comparators who were placed in a lower band but received more pay. As in *Murphy*, adopting a purposive approach to interpreting the legislation was key to ensuring it achieved its intended outcomes.

3. An analysis of the decisions in *Pickstone, Murphy*, and *Hayward* v *Cammell Laird Shipbuilders Ltd* [1988] IRLR 257, in respect of the permitted comparisons which can be made by a complainant, was undertaken by Schofield, P. (1988) 17 ILJ, at pp. 241–4.

4. For a discussion of the impact of EC law, see Ellis, E., *EU Anti-Discrimination Law* (Oxford: Oxford EC Law Library, 2005); Bell, M., *Anti-Discrimination Law and the European Union* (Oxford: OUP, 2002).

5. The importance of Article 157 (ex 119) is well illustrated by case law interpreting the word 'pay'.

6. One of the most significant decisions regarding the definition of 'pay' was *Barber* v *Guardian Royal Exchange Assurance Group* [1990] IRLR 240, in which the meaning of 'pay' was extended to include 'contracted-out' pension schemes. The judgment of the ECJ in *Barber* placed a limitation on the retrospective impact of their decision by restricting claims for equality in pensions under Article 119 (now 157) to claims made after the date of the judgment, except for those who had before that date initiated legal proceedings or raised an equivalent claim under the applicable national law. This restriction was placed to reduce the financial consequences of the decision. The decision in *Ten Oever* v *Stichting Bedrijfspensioenfonds voor het Glazenwassers- en Schoonmaakbedrijf* [1992] IRLR 601 confirms that there cannot be retrospective claims where the claim relates to the level of benefit as opposed to access to benefits—see also the decision of the Court of Appeal in *Quirk* v *Burton Hospitals NHS Trust* [2002] IRLR 353.

7. See Ward, S., 'The *Barber* judgment: Implications for employers' (1990) 32 *Equal Opportunities Review*, at p. 40 for an analysis of the impact of the *Barber* decision.

8. The issue of what is included in the word 'pay' in Article 157 (ex 119) has been considered in cases other than *Barber* but not with the same legal and financial implications. In *Rinner-Kuhn* v *FWW Spezial-Gebaudereinigung GmbH* [1989] IRLR 493, wages continued to be paid to employees who fell ill. To qualify for this continuing payment an employee's normal working hours had to exceed ten hours a week or 45 hours a month. German national legislation permitted employers to operate such an exclusion. The ECJ held that such payments amounted to 'pay' within the meaning of Article 157 (ex 119) and that Article 157 (ex 119) prevails over national legislation where the provision affects a considerably greater number of women than men, unless the Member State can show that the legislation is justified by objective factors unrelated to any discrimination on grounds of sex. This decision throws considerable doubt on the legality of excluding employees from the receipt of or access to pay-related benefits based on hours or even length of service where it has a disparate impact on one particular sex. See also *Arbeiterwohlfahrt der Stadt Berlin ev* v *Botel* [1992] IRLR 423, in which the ECJ held that paid leave, in this particular case to attend training courses, amounted to 'pay' within the meaning of Article 119 (now 157) and Directive 75/117. To fail to pay part-time employees 'who were generally women' the same as full-time employees in these circumstances amounted to indirect discrimination contrary to Article 119 (now 157). Furthermore, while bridging pensions amount to 'pay', it is not contrary to Article 157 (ex 119) for an employer to reduce the amount of bridging pension to take into account the state pension which the employee will receive, even though in the case of men and women aged between 60 and 65 the result is that the female ex-employee receives a smaller bridging pension (*Roberts* v *Birds Eye Walls Ltd* [1994] IRLR 29). Interestingly the ECJ, in *Stadt Lengerich* v *Angelika Helming* [1995] IRLR 216, held that payment of overtime rates only where normal working hours for full-time workers were exceeded did not discriminate against part-time female employees, as in effect full-time and part-time employees were being treated equally. However, it could be argued that this ignores the fact that part-time employees are predominantly female and as a result subject to indirect discrimination, as the rule clearly disadvantaged them since part-time employees would in this case have had to work 38 hours per week to obtain overtime pay.

The categories of 'pay' as interpreted by the courts continue to grow; for example, in *Lewen* v *Denda* [2000] IRLR 67 a Christmas bonus was held by the ECJ to constitute 'pay' as it was a benefit granted in connection with employment. However, it was not a 'payment' within the Pregnant Workers Directive (92/85), since it was not intended to ensure a minimum level of income during a worker's maternity leave.

In *Gillespie* v *Northern Health and Social Services Board* [1996] IRLR 214, the ECJ ruled that women on maternity leave are not entitled to full pay. This ruling was based on the special position of such women who are not therefore in a comparable position to men or other women. Reference should also be made to *Webb* v *EMO Air Cargo (UK) (No. 2)* [1995] IRLR 645, as a clear distinction has developed between the treatment of the pregnant woman and the woman on maternity leave. Furthermore, the 'sick man' remains a legitimate comparison.

In *Todd* v *Eastern Health and Social Services Board* [1997] IRLR 410, in which maternity pay provisions were less generous than sick pay provisions, it was held by the Northern Ireland Court of Appeal (NICA) that maternity pay and sick pay could not be treated the same, i.e. as a 'disability' in that a healthy pregnancy could not be treated as either a disability or equivalent to an illness (see Conaghan, J., 'Pregnancy, equality and the ECJ: Interrogating Colette Gillespie' (1998) 3 *International Journal on Discrimination Law*, 115–33). However, the decision in *Todd* must now be read in the light of the decision of the ECJ in *Handels- og Kontorfunktionaererernes Forbund i Danmark Acting on behalf of Pedersen* v *Faellsforeningen vor Danmarks Brugsforeninger Acting on behalf of Kvickly Skive* [1999] IRLR 55 (see p. 274 (Chapter 5, Section 4.C)). Ruling on Danish employment law, which provided that pregnant employees who are ill before the beginning of the maternity leave period are entitled to pay only if the illness is unconnected with pregnancy, the ECJ concluded that it was contrary to Article 119 (now 157) and the Equal Pay Directive to deprive a woman of her full pay when she is unfit for work before the beginning of her maternity leave as a result of a pregnancy-related condition, when a worker is in principle entitled to receive full pay in the event of incapacity for work on grounds of illness. Such treatment was based essentially on pregnancy and thus was discriminatory. However, Article 119 (now 157) and the Equal Pay Directive do not preclude national legislation, which provides that a pregnant woman is not entitled to be paid where, before the beginning of maternity leave, she is absent from work not because of any incapacity for work but by reason either of routine pregnancy-related inconveniences or because of a medical recommendation intended to protect the unborn child. Loss of pay in such circumstances is not treatment based essentially on the pregnancy, but rather is based on the choice made by the employee not to work.

The distinction between these two scenarios in *Pedersen* is, it is suggested, extremely subtle. Both appear to be pregnancy-related; however, the former is an incapacity to work by reason of the pregnancy and the latter is apparently not!

It should be noted that in *North Western Health Board* v *McKenna* [2005] IRLR 895, the ECJ held that a sick leave scheme which treats female workers suffering from a pregnancy-related illness in the same way as other workers suffering from an illness that is unrelated to pregnancy amounts to 'pay' within the meaning of Article 157 and the Equal Pay Directive. A reduction in sick pay where an absence exceeds a certain duration is not discriminatory *per se*, provided that the amount of payment is not so low as to undermine the objective of protecting pregnant workers, and as long as a male worker who is absent on grounds of illness is treated the same way. It is suggested by Rubenstein ('Highlights' (2005) IRLR 285) that this decision results in an inconsistent approach between the treatment of pregnancy-related illness for dismissal purposes and treatment of the pregnant woman for pay purposes—the latter being justified by the ECJ on the basis that the special nature of a pregnancy-related illness may be accommodated in respect of pay by other means.

9. The ECJ continues to be asked to rule on issues which may have pecuniary consequences but which do not necessarily fall within Article 157 and Directive 75/117. Where working conditions have pecuniary consequences for the worker, it is a matter to be considered under the Equal Treatment Directive not Article 157 or the Equal Pay Directive—*Steinicke* v *Bundesanstalt Fur Arbeit* [2003] IRLR 892 and *Lommers* v *Minister van Landbouw, Natuubeheer en Visserij* [2002] IRLR 430—see Chapter 5.

10. Lastly, in *Garland* v *British Rail Engineering Ltd* [1982] IRLR 111, the ECJ held that concessionary rail travel given to employees after retirement amounted to 'pay' and thereby fell within the scope of Article 119 (now 157). As a result the provision of such facilities which had only been accorded to former male employees discriminated against former female employees.

■ **QUESTIONS**

1. Following the decision in *Barry* v *Midland Bank plc*, when is the most appropriate time to consider 'justification'?

2. How can the effect of the decision in *Pickstone* be by-passed?

3. What is the current position on the relationship between the three heads of claim under the EPA 1970? Is this affected by EC law?

4. Would there still be inequality in piecework payments if the women carried out particularly dextrous work, or the men used greater physical strength?

SECTION 3: EQUALITY ACT 2010 (PART 5, CHAPTER 3)

EQUALITY OF TERMS

SEX EQUALITY

64 Relevant Types of Work

(1) Sections 66 to 70 apply where—

    (a) a person (A) is employed on work that is equal to the work that a comparator of the opposite sex (B) does;

    ...

(2) The references in subsection (1) to the work that B does are not restricted to work done contemporaneously with work done by A.

    ...

65 Equal work

(1) For the purposes of this Chapter, A's work is equal to that of B if it is—

    (a) like B's work,

    (b) rated as equivalent to B's work, or

    (c) of equal value to B's work.

(2) A's work is like B's work if—

    (a) A's work and B's work are the same or broadly similar, and

    (b) such differences as there are between their work are not of practical importance in relation to the terms of their work.

(3) So on a comparison of one person's work with another's for the purposes of subsection (2), it is necessary to have regard to—

    (a) the frequency with which differences between their work occur in practice, and

    (b) the nature and extent of the differences.

(4) A's work is rated as equivalent to B's work if a job evaluation study—

    (a) gives an equal value to A's job and B's job in terms of the demands made on a worker, or

    (b) would give an equal value to A's job and B's job in those terms were the evaluation not made on a sex-specific system.

(5) A system is sex-specific if, for the purposes of one or more of the demands made on a worker, it sets values for men different from those it sets for women.

(6) A's work is of equal value to B's work if it is—

    (a) neither like B's work nor rated as equivalent to B's work, but

    (b) nevertheless equal to B's work in terms of the demands made on A by reference to factors such as effort, skill and decision-making.

    ...

131 Assessment of whether work is of equal value

(1) This section applies to proceedings before an employment tribunal on—

    (a) a complaint relating to a breach of an equality clause or rule, or

    (b) a question referred to the tribunal by virtue of section 127(2).

(2) Where a question arises in the proceedings as to whether one person's work is of equal value to another's, the tribunal may, before determining the question, require a member of the panel of independent experts to prepare a report on the question.

(3) The tribunal may withdraw a requirement that it makes under subsection (2); And, if it does so, it may—

    (a) request the panel member to provide it with specified documentation;

    (b) make such other requests to that member as are connected with the withdrawal of the requirement.

(4) If the tribunal requires the preparation of a report under subsection (2) (and does not withdraw the requirement), it must not determine the question unless it has received the report.

(5) Subsection (6) applies where—

    (a) a question arises in the proceedings as to whether the work of one person (A) is of equal value to the work of another (B), and

    (b) A's work and B's work have been given different values by a job evaluation study.

(6) The tribunal must determine that A's work is not of equal value to B's work unless it has reasonable grounds for suspecting that the evaluation contained in the study—

    (a) was based on a system that discriminates because of sex, or

(b) is otherwise unreliable.

(7) For the purposes of subsection (6)(a), a system discriminates because of sex if a difference (or coincidence) between values that the system sets on different demands is not justifiable regardless of the sex of the person on whom the demands are made.

(8) A reference to a member of the panel of independent experts is to a person—

(a) who is for the time being designated as such by the Advisory, Conciliation and Arbitration Service (ACAS) for the purposes of this section, and

(b) who is neither a member of the Council of ACAS nor one of its officers or members of staff.

(9) 'Job evaluation study' has the meaning given in section 80(5).

NOTE: As noted in the introduction to this chapter, the EqA 2010 (formerly the EPA 1970) introduces an equality clause into all contracts of employment. This clause operates automatically to bring about equality between a male's and female's terms of employment. In reality most claims relate to rate of pay. Where the employer fails to put the equality clause into effect, the EqA 2010 provides three heads of claim for an applicant; these are known as 'like work', 'work rated as equivalent', and 'work of equal value'. Any applicant must have a comparator of the opposite sex with whom a comparison can be made. The comparator may be employed by the same or an associated employer, at the same establishment or at an establishment where common terms and conditions are observed.

A: What amounts to 'pay'?

Hayward v Cammell Laird Shipbuilders Ltd
[1988] IRLR 257, House of Lords

Hayward was employed as a canteen cook. She claimed equal pay for work of equal value with the tradesmen in the shipyard who were paid a higher basic and overtime rate. The industrial tribunal referred the case to the independent expert who found that her work was of equal value to that of her male comparators. The employer did not raise a s. 1(3) defence and the industrial tribunal found in her favour.

At a further hearing, the employers contended that they did not have to pay Miss Hayward the same basic wage and overtime rates as her male comparators because, considered as a whole, her terms and conditions were not less favourable. Although Miss Hayward received lower basic pay and overtime rates, she had a paid meal break, additional holidays, and better sickness benefits. On the employers' valuation of these benefits, when they were taken into account, she was better off on the whole than her comparators.

The industrial tribunal, and subsequently the EAT, ruled that the EPA 1970, s. 1(2)(c) should be interpreted as meaning that, when implementing an equal value award, equal pay means terms relating to pay which, considered as a whole, are not less favourable. The EAT also emphasised that if each term relating to pay had to be looked at individually, it would produce 'leap-frogging' which would result in widespread chaos. The Court of Appeal also dismissed Hayward's appeal, stating it was artificial to look merely at one part of the overall remuneration package.

The House of Lords held, allowing her appeal, that a woman who can point to a term of her contract which is less favourable than a term of a similar kind in the man's contract is entitled to have that term made not less favourable irrespective of whether she is treated as favourably as the man when the whole of her contract and the whole of his contract are considered.

LORD GOFF OF CHIEVELEY: Section (2) is subdivided into three subsubsections—the first, (a), being concerned with like work, the second, (b), with work rated as equivalent, and the third, (c), with work of equal value. Each of these subsubsections makes provisions for two alternative situations—(i) where any term of the woman's contract is (or becomes) less favourable to her than a term of a similar kind in the male comparator's contract, and (ii) where the woman's contract does not include a term corresponding to a term benefiting the male comparator included in his contract. I will call the first situation the case of the less favourable term, and the second situation the case of the absent term.

In considering the question of construction, it is plain that we have to consider it in relation both to the case of the less favourable term, and the case of the absent term, for the same policy considerations must underlie each. Furthermore, I find it easier to approach the problem by considering first the case of the absent term, because the provisions of subsubsection (ii) of each subsection are in simpler terms than those of subsubsection (i), and are therefore easier to construe.

What does subsubsection (ii) in each case provide? It provides that if the woman's contract does not include a term corresponding to a term benefiting the male comparator included in his contract, her contract shall be treated as including such a term. Next, what does such a provision mean? If I look at the words used, and give them their natural and ordinary meaning, they mean quite simply that one looks at the man's contract and at the woman's contract, and if one finds in the man's contract a term benefiting him which is not included in the woman's contract, then that term is treated as included in hers. On this simple and literal approach, the words 'benefiting that man' mean precisely what they say—that the term must be one which is beneficial to him, as opposed to being burdensome. So if, for example, the man's contract contains a term that he is to be provided with the use of a car, and the woman's contract does not include such a term, then her contract is to be treated as including such a term.

It is obvious that this approach cannot be reconciled with the approach favoured by the Court of Appeal, because it does not require, or indeed permit, the court to look at the overall contractual position of each party, or even to look at their overall position as regards one particular matter, for example, 'pay' in the wide sense adopted by the Court of Appeal. To achieve that result, it would be necessary, in subsubsection (ii), to construe the word 'term' as referring to the totality of the relevant contractual provisions relating to a particular subject matter, for example 'pay' or alternatively to construe the words 'benefiting that man' as importing the necessity of a comparison in relation to the totality of the relevant contractual provisions concerning a particular subject matter and then for a conclusion to be reached that, on balance, the man has thereby benefited. The latter construction I find impossible to derive from the words of the statute; and, to be fair, I do not think that there is any evidence that it would have found favour with the Court of Appeal. But what of the former, which is consistent with the judgment of the Court of Appeal? Again, I find myself unable to accept it. First, it would mean that the situation of the absent term must be confined only to those cases where there was *no* provision relating, for example, to pay—or, I suppose, to overtime, or to some other wholly distinct topic. I cannot think that that was the intention of the legislature. In commonsense terms, it means that subsubsection (ii) would hardly ever be relevant at all; certainly, since every contract of employment makes some provision for 'pay' in the broad sense adopted by the Court of Appeal, subsubsection (ii) would never be relevant in relation to pay or any other form of remuneration in cash or in kind or in the form of other benefits. I find this proposition to be startling.

Second, it imposes upon the word 'term' a meaning which I myself do not regard as its natural or ordinary meaning. If a contract contains provisions relating to (1) basic pay, (2) benefits in kind such as the use of a car, (3) cash bonuses, and (4) sickness benefits, it would never occur to me to lump all these together as one 'term' of the contract, simply because they can all together be considered as providing for the total 'remuneration' for the services to be performed under the contract. In truth, these would include a number of different terms; and in my opinion it does unacceptable violence to the words of the statute to construe the word 'term' in subsubsection (ii) as embracing collectively all these different terms.

It is against the background of this reasoning in relation to the case of the absent term, that I turn to subsubsection (i) and the case of the less favourable term. Here the Court of Appeal was able to build their construction upon the basis of a reference, in the subsubsection, to 'a term of a similar kind' in the male comparator's contract. They considered that these words referred necessarily to a term relating to the same overall subject matter, in particular pay; and that the question whether the relevant term in the woman's contract was less favourable than that in the man's contract could only sensibly be considered by comparing all the provisions relating to this subject matter in the contracts of each. From this they derived the broad meaning of the word 'term' which I have described.

For my part, I cannot accept this reasoning. Suppose that there is a term in a woman's contract which provides that she is to be paid £x per hour, and that there is a term in the male comparator's contract that he is to be paid £y per hour, y being greater than x. On the natural and ordinary meaning of the words in the statute, there is, in my opinion, in such a case, a term of the woman's contract which is less favourable to her than a term of a similar kind in the male comparator's contract; and that would be so even if there was some other provision in her contract which conferred upon her a benefit (which fell within her overall 'remuneration') which the man was not entitled to receive under his contract, such as, for example, the use of a car. I do not consider that the words 'a term of a similar kind' are capable of constituting a basis for building the construction of the word 'term' favoured by the Court of Appeal. Again, in my opinion, the words mean precisely what they say. You look at the two contracts: you ask yourself the commonsense question—is there in each contract a term of a similar kind, i.e. a term making a comparable provision for the same subject matter; if there is, then you compare the two, and if, on that comparison, the term of the woman's contract proves to be less favourable than the term of the man's contract, then the term in the woman's contract is to be treated as modified so as to make it not less favourable. I am, of course, much fortified in this approach in that it appears to me to be consistent with the only construction of subsubsection (ii), concerned with the case of the absent term, which I find to be acceptable. But, in addition, I feel that the Court of Appeal's attempt to introduce the element of overall comparison placed them firmly, or rather infirmly, upon a slippery slope; because, once they departed from the natural and ordinary meaning of the word 'term,' they in reality found it impossible to control the ambit of the comparison which they considered to be required. For almost any, indeed perhaps any, benefit will fall within 'pay' in the very wide sense favoured by them, in which event it is difficult to segregate any sensible meaning of the word 'term'.

NOTES

1. There is little doubt that had the Court of Appeal's approach been adopted regarding the meaning of 'pay', i.e. the whole remuneration package, a woman whose contract lacked a particular term would have been prevented from bringing an action because all contracts of employment contain a term relating to or equivalent to remuneration. However, the decision in *Degnan* v *Redcar & Cleveland Borough Council* [2005] IRLR 615 may have muddied the waters (see later). Interestingly, the ECJ in *Jamstalldhetsombudsmannen* v *Orebro Lans Landsting* [2000] IRLR 421 concluded that in comparing the pay of midwives and a clinical technician, the appropriate comparison was between the monthly basic salary of the two groups. No account was to be taken of a supplement paid to the midwives for working inconvenient hours. The rationale for this was that 'the effectiveness of Article 119 would be diminished if the national courts were under an obligation to make a comparison of all of the various types of consideration granted to men and women. It followed that genuine transparency, permitting effective review is assured only if the principle of equal pay applies to each of the elements of remuneration.'

   The ECJ went on to affirm that if there is a difference in pay between the two groups and there is a substantially higher proportion of women than men in the disadvantaged group, the burden moves to the employer to objectively justify the difference in pay.

   This was applied in *Brunhoffer* v *Bank der Österreichischen Postsparkasse* [2001] IRLR 571, where the ECJ not only concluded that each aspect of remuneration should be compared, but that a collective agreement may be only one aspect in adducing evidence of remuneration.

   In *St Helens & Knowsley Hospitals NHS Trust* v *Brownbill* [2011] IRLR 815, the Court of Appeal confirmed that equal pay claimants were entitled to compare the distinct contractual terms in their contracts governing the rate of pay for working unsocial hours to a similar term in the contracts of their male comparators, even though the women, overall, received higher pay than the men. This approach is in line with that adopted by the House of Lords in *Hayward* v *Cammell Laird Shipbuilders Ltd*. As stated earlier, doubt seemed to be cast on this fundamental principle, however, by the Court of Appeal's decision in *Degnan* v *Redcar and Cleveland Borough Council*, in which bonuses and allowances were held to form part of the same contractual term as basic pay. In *Brownbill*, however, the Court of Appeal emphasised that *Degnan* turned on its own special facts. Lord Justice Maurice Kay stated, 'it did not, and was not intended to, give rise to an exception to the principle in *Hayward*'. The principle that equal pay claims are based on a term-by-term comparison is supported by the decision of the ECJ in *Barber* v *Guardian Royal Exchange Assurance Group*, which emphasised the importance of transparency and the ability of the courts to review pay systems to prevent sex discrimination. As Michael Rubenstein observes: 'If different parts of the contractual remuneration package are lumped together for comparison purposes, a precise value would have to be placed on each term. While it may seem strange that a higher paid employee can use equal pay legislation, it remains open to the employer in such a case to use the material factor defence, where appropriate, to explain that the higher overall pay package received by the claimant explains the difference in respect of the particular term under scrutiny' ('Highlights' [2011] IRLR 799).

2. The ECJ's interpretation of the word 'pay' is extremely wide and has had a significant impact on the EPA 1970—see the *Barber* case and *McKechnie* v *UBM Building Supplies (Southern) Ltd* [1991] IRLR 283, in which it was decided that a scheme which made *ex gratia* redundancy payments to women up to the age of 60 years and men up to the age of 65 years was covered by Article 119 (now 141) of the Treaty of Rome.

3. The genuine material factor defence (the EPA 1970, s. 1(3)—see now EqA 2010, s. 69) was not pleaded in *Hayward*'s case, although Lord Mackay stated *obiter* at p. 261:

s. 1(3) would not provide a defence to an employer against whom it was shown that a term in the woman's contract was less favourable to her than a corresponding term in the man's contract on the basis that there was another term in the woman's contract which was more favourable to her than the corresponding term in the man's contract. At the very least for s. 1(3) to operate it would have to be shown that the unfavourable character of the term in the woman's contract was in fact due to the difference in the opposite sense in the other term and that the difference was not due to the reason of sex. I consider that counsel for the appellant succeeds on the natural reading of the words of s. 1(2) which are in issue and that your Lordships do not require to reach any final conclusion in this case on the meaning and effect of s. 1(3).

■ QUESTION

Is the issue of mutual enhancement/leap-frogging a problem?

B: Who are 'comparators'?

EQUALITY ACT 2010

79 Comparators

(1) This section applies for the purposes of this Chapter.

(2) If A is employed, B is a comparator of A's only if subsection (3) or (4) applies.

(3) This subsection applies if—

    (a) B is employed by A's employer or by an associate of A's employer, and

    (b) A and B work at the same establishment.

(4) This subsection applies if—

    (a) B is employed by A's employer or an associate of A's employer,

    (b) B works at an establishment other than the one at which A works, and

    (c) common terms apply at the establishments (either generally or as between A and B).

NOTE: The EPA 1970, s. 1(6) defined a worker in the 'same employment' as the comparator in order for an equal pay/equal value claim to be made. The EqA 2010, s. 79 has not changed the definition of a relevant comparator. As a result, the case law developed under the EPA 1970, s. 1(6) should still be relevant.

Leverton v *Clwyd County Council*

[1989] IRLR 28, House of Lords

Mrs Leverton was employed by the council as a nursery nurse in an infants' school. She brought an equal value claim comparing herself with male clerical staff employed in different establishments. At the time of the industrial tribunal hearing, Mrs Leverton's annual salary was £5,058 and that of her comparators ranged from £6,081 to £8,532. Both Mrs Leverton and her comparators were employed pursuant to the Scheme of Conditions of Service of the NJC for Local Authorities' Administrative, Professional, Technical and Clerical Services. Under the terms of that agreement, nursery nurses are paid under scale 1. The comparators were at different points on scales 3 and 4.

The right to equal pay is restricted to men and women 'in the same employment'. Section (6) of the EPA stipulates that 'men shall be treated as in the same employment with a woman if they are men employed by her employer...at the same establishment or at establishments in Great Britain which include that one and at which common terms and conditions of employment are observed either generally or for employees of the relevant classes'.

The employers contended that common terms and conditions were not observed for the relevant employees, notwithstanding that they were covered by the same collective agreement and there were many common terms of employment, because the nurses worked 32½ hours per week and had 70 days' annual holiday as against the comparators' 37-hour week and 20 days' basic annual holiday entitlement.

The Court of Appeal dismissed Leverton's appeal in respect of the EPA 1970, s. 1(6) and supported the view of the industrial tribunal that a s. 1(3) defence was applicable.

On appeal, the House of Lords held that s. 1(6) calls for a comparison between the terms and conditions of employment observed at the establishment at which the woman is employed and the establishment at which the men are employed, and applicable either generally, i.e. to all the employees at the relevant establishments, or to a particular class or classes of employees to which both the woman and the men belong.

LORD BRIDGE: On the question of whether the appellant was in the same employment as the comparators working at different establishments, the view which prevailed with the majority of the Industrial Tribunal, the Employment Appeal Tribunal, and the majority of the Court of Appeal was that the comparison called for by s. 1(6) was between the terms and conditions of employment of the appellant on the one hand and of the comparators on the other and that it was only if this comparison showed their terms and conditions of employment to be 'broadly similar' that the test applied by the phrase 'common terms and conditions of employment' in s. 1(6) was satisfied. The majority of the Industrial Tribunal affirmed by the Employment Appeal Tribunal and the majority of the Court of Appeal, held that the difference in this case in working hours and holidays was a radical difference in the 'core terms' of the respective contracts of employment which prevented the comparison from satisfying the statutory test. The contrary view embraced by the dissenting member of the Industrial Tribunal and by May LJ in the Court of Appeal was that the comparison called for was much broader, viz a comparison between the terms and conditions of employment observed at two or more establishments, embracing both the establishment at which the woman is employed and the establishment at which the men are employed, and applicable either generally, i.e. to all the employees at the relevant establishments, or to a particular class or classes of employees to which both the woman and the men belong. Basing himself implicitly on this view, the dissenting member of the Industrial Tribunal expressed his conclusion in the matter tersely. Having referred to the purple book, he said:

> 3. Within that agreement there are nine sections and numerous clauses. They do not apply, with few exceptions, to any particular grade. It is clearly a general agreement and not specific to any particular group or class of employee. 4. It is, in my opinion, beyond doubt that the applicant and the comparators are employed on common terms and conditions, i.e. the APT & C agreement, and clearly it is within the provisions of s. 1(6).

My Lords, this is an important difference in principle which depends on the true construction of s. 1(6). I have no hesitation in preferring the minority to the majority view expressed in the courts below. It seems to me, first, that the language of the subsection is clear and unambiguous. It poses the question whether the terms and conditions of employment 'observed' at two or more establishments (at which the relevant woman and the relevant men are employed) are 'common', being terms and conditions of employment observed 'either generally or for employees of the relevant classes.' The concept of common terms and conditions of employment observed generally at different establishments necessarily contemplates terms and conditions applicable to a wide range of employees whose individual terms will vary greatly inter se. On the construction of the subsection adopted by the majority below the phrase 'observed either generally or for employees of the relevant classes' is given no content. Terms and conditions of employment governed by the same collective agreement seem to me to represent the paradigm, though not necessarily the only example, of the common terms and conditions of employment contemplated by the subsection.

But if, contrary to my view, there is any such ambiguity in the language of s. 1(6) as to permit the question whether a woman and men employed by the same employer in different establishments are in the same employment to depend on a direct comparison establishing a 'broad similarity' between the woman's terms and conditions of employment and those of her claimed comparators, I should reject a construction of the subsection in this sense on the ground that it frustrates rather than serves the manifest purpose of the legislation. That purpose is to enable a woman to eliminate discriminatory differences between the terms of her contract and those of any male fellow employee doing like work, work rated as equivalent or work of equal value, whether he works in the same establishment as her or in another establishment where terms and conditions of employment common to both establishments are observed. With all respect to the majority view which prevailed below, it cannot, in my opinion, possibly have been the intention of Parliament to require a woman claiming equality with a man in another establishment to prove an undefined substratum of similarity between the particular terms of her contract and his as the basis of her entitlement to eliminate any discriminatory differences between those terms.

On the construction of s. 1(6) which I would adopt there is a sensible and rational explanation for the limitation of equality claims as between men and women employed at different establishments to establishments at which common terms and conditions of employment are observed. There may be perfectly good geographical or historical reasons why a single employer should operate essentially different employment regimes at different establishments. In such cases the limitation imposed by s. 1(6) will operate to defeat claims under s. 1 as between men and women at the different establishments. I take two examples by way of illustration. A single employer has two establishments, one in London and one in Newcastle. The rates of pay earned by persons of both sexes for the same work are substantially higher in London than in Newcastle. Looking at either the London establishment or the Newcastle establishment in isolation there is no sex discrimination. If the women in Newcastle could invoke s. 1 of the Act of 1970 to achieve equality with the men in London this would eliminate a differential in earnings which is due not to sex but to geography. Section. 1(6) prevents them from doing so. An employer operates factory A where he has a long standing collective agreement with the ABC union. The same employer takes over a company operating factory X and becomes an 'associated employer' of the persons working there. The previous owner of factory X had a long standing collective agreement with the XYZ union which the new employer continues to operate. The two collective agreements have produced quite different structures governing pay and other terms and conditions of employment at the two factories. Here again s. 1(6) will operate to prevent women in factory A claiming equality with men in factory X and vice versa. These examples are not, of course, intended to be exhaustive. So long as Industrial Tribunals direct themselves correctly in law to make the appropriate broad comparison, it will always be a question of fact for them, in any particular case, to decide whether, as between two different establishments, 'common terms and conditions of employment are observed either generally or for employees of the relevant classes.' Here the majority of the Industrial Tribunal misdirected themselves in law and their conclusion on this point cannot be supported.

NOTE: While the difference in hours and holiday entitlement did not prevent there being common terms and conditions in Leverton's case, the House of Lords concluded that the employment tribunal had not erred in finding that there was a genuine material factor defence provided by this difference in hours and holidays which justified the difference in pay (the EPA 1970, s. 1(3)). Basically the men had to work much longer hours and had shorter holidays to earn their salaries.

British Coal Corporation v Smith

[1996] IRLR 404, House of Lords

Some 1,286 women employed by British Coal as canteen workers or cleaners submitted applications between December 1986 and April 1988 claiming equal pay for work of equal value and comparing their work with that of 150 comparators employed either as surface mineworkers or clerical workers. Canteen workers employed by British Coal were predominantly women, cleaners were mainly women, clerical workers were approximately half men and half women, and surface mineworkers were men. The claimants were employed at 47 different establishments, and the comparators were employed at 14 different establishments.

In the Court of Appeal [1994] IRLR 342, the case was heard consecutively with *North Yorkshire County Council* v *Ratcliffe*. The Court of Appeal allowed the employers' appeal in respect of s. 1(6) and the appeal by canteen workers and cleaners in respect of s. 1(3). The Court of Appeal held that 'common terms and conditions' within the meaning of s. 1(6) of the EPA are 'the same' terms and conditions rather than terms and conditions which are 'broadly similar' or 'to the same overall effect'. Accordingly, s. 1(6) permits the choice of a male comparator from a separate establishment, if the terms and conditions of employment for men of the relevant class at his establishment are common with, meaning the same as, those of men of the relevant class employed at the woman's establishment, or which would be available for male employees for that work at her establishment. In this case, the Court of Appeal held the terms and conditions on which the male comparator class of surface mineworkers were employed were not the same, regardless of the establishments at which they worked, since the terms entitling them to an incentive bonus and to concessionary coal were agreed and implemented at local level with widely varying results. Therefore, the claimants were limited in their choice of male comparators who were surface workers to the district or other area in respect of which the same terms of employment as regards the payment of an incentive bonus and the concessionary coal allowance were agreed. Thus, the industrial tribunal had erred in finding that all the comparators named by every applicant, other than those employed at the same establishment as the applicant, were in 'the same employment' as the applicant for the purposes of s. 1(6).

It was held that the applicant canteen workers and cleaners were in the 'same employment' (within the meaning of s. 1(6) of the EPA 1970) as their male comparators in different establishments employed as surface mineworkers because there were 'common terms and conditions of employment' observed as between the establishments.

LORD SLYNN: ...It is plain that from the beginning, although the woman had to show that her comparator or comparators ('men') was or were employed by her employer or by an associated employer of her employer, and that she could not point to higher wages being paid by other employers, yet she was not limited to selecting male workers from the place where she herself worked. The reason for this is obvious, since otherwise an employer could so arrange things as to ensure that only women worked at a particular establishment or that no man who could reasonably be considered as a possible comparator should work there. A woman can thus point to men employed in her own establishment or in other establishments of her employer in Great Britain. But the other establishments which include her establishment must be ones at which common terms and conditions of employment are observed generally or for employees of the relevant classes. The words 'which include that one' may at first sight be puzzling since she can under the earlier words point to men employed at the same establishment as hers. The words are, however, to be read with the following words: 'at which common terms...are observed'. Those common terms must thus be observed not only at other establishments but also at the establishment at which the woman works if employees of the relevant classes are employed there.

Common terms and conditions of employment must be observed either generally (i.e. for all or perhaps for most workers) or for employees of the relevant classes. Subject to a misdirection in law, it is for the industrial tribunal to decide on the evidence what is or are the relevant class or relevant classes. It has been said by the corporation that the relevant class here is 'ancillary workers' so that all the claimants must be treated as one relevant class. The effect of that would be that not all ancillary workers in the relevant class would be women, even though a majority might still be. In my view, having regard to the nature of the work and the different ways in which their pay structures were established, the industrial tribunal was perfectly entitled to take the various categories of worker separately. Thus canteen workers and cleaners are separate groups largely composed of women.

The real question, however, is what is meant by 'common terms of conditions of employment' and between whom do such terms and conditions have to be common?

It is plain and it is agreed between the parties that the woman does not have to show that she shares common terms and conditions with her comparator, either in the sense that all the terms are the same, since necessarily his terms must be different in some respect if she is to show a breach of the equality clause, or in regard to terms other than that said to constitute the discrimination.

It is accepted by the corporation that for the purposes of this appeal as between the different establishments common terms and conditions do in any event apply to the two classes of applicants, canteen workers and cleaners. What therefore has to be shown is that the male comparators at other establishments and at her establishment share common terms and conditions. If there are no such men at the applicant's place of work then it has to be shown that like terms and conditions would apply if men were employed there in the particular jobs concerned.

The corporation contends that the applicants can only succeed if they can show that common terms and conditions were observed at the two establishments for the relevant classes in the sense that they apply 'across the board'; in other words the terms and conditions of the comparators (e.g. surface mineworkers) are 'common in substantially all respects' for such workers at her pit and at the places of employment of the comparators. This in effect means that all the terms and conditions must be common, i.e. the same, subject only to de minimis differences.

The applicants reject this and contend that it is sufficient if there is a broad similarity of terms rather than that they are strictly coterminous.

Your Lordships have been referred to a number of dictionary definitions of 'common', but I do not think that they help. The real question is what the legislation was seeking to achieve. Was it seeking to exclude a woman's claim unless, subject to de minimis exceptions, there was complete identity of terms and conditions for the comparator at his establishment and those which applied or would apply to a similar male worker at her establishment? Or was the legislation seeking to establish that the terms and conditions of the relevant class were sufficiently similar for a fair comparison to be made, subject always to the employer's right to establish a 'material difference' defence under s. 1(3) of the Act?

If it was the former then the woman would fail at the first hurdle if there was any difference (other than a de minimis one) between the terms and conditions of the men at the various establishments, since she could not then show that the men were in the same employment as she was. The issue as to whether the differences were material so as to justify different treatment would then never arise.

I do not consider that this can have been intended. The purpose of requiring common terms and conditions was to avoid it being said simply: 'a gardener does work of equal value to mine and my comparator at another establishment is a gardener.' It was necessary for the applicant to go further and to show that gardeners at other establishments and at her establishment were or would be employed on broadly similar terms. It was necessary but it was also sufficient.

Whether any differences between the woman and the man selected as the comparator were justified would depend on the next stage of the examination under s. 1(3). I do not consider that the s. 1(3) enquiry, where the onus is on the employer, was intended to be excluded unless the terms and conditions of the men at the relevant establishments were common in the sense of identical. This seems to me to be far too restrictive a test.

NOTE: In *North v Dumfries and Galloway Council* [2013] IRLR 737, SC, the claimants were women employed in schools whose comparators employed at different premises include groundsmen, road workers, and refuse workers. The employment tribunal held that it was sufficient to ask whether, if the comparators had been employed at the claimants' establishment, they would have continued to have been employed under broadly similar terms. The key question before the Supreme Court was whether it also had to be shown that there was a possibility that the comparators would work at the claimants' establishments, i.e. would a road worker be employed at the school, in order for the comparison to be made? Giving the Supreme Court's decision, Lady Hale acknowledges that the proposed male comparators would never be employed to do their current jobs in the same place as the women, but to adopt such a test, she says, 'would be to defeat the object of the exercise'. Instead, the correct test 'sets a low threshold'. The correct test is *if* the comparators were transferred to do their present jobs in a different location, would they would remain employed on the same or broadly similar terms to those applicable in their current place of work? Lady Hale observed that the employer has various opportunities to defeat an equal pay claim, including by establishing that a difference in treatment is due to a material factor, but stated that the 'same employment' test 'should not be used as a proxy for those tests or as a way of avoiding the often difficult and complex issues which they raise...Its function is to establish the terms and conditions with which the comparison is to be made. The object is simply to weed out those cases in which geography plays a significant part in determining what those terms and conditions are' (see also *Edinburgh City Council v Wilkinson* [2012] IRLR 202).

Allonby v Accrington & Rossendale College
[2004] IRLR 224, European Court of Justice

Debra Allonby was employed by Accrington & Rossendale College as a part-time hourly paid lecturer in office technology from 1990 to 1996 on a succession of one-year contracts. In 1996, in order to reduce the financial impact of new rights for part-time workers, the college decided to terminate or not renew the contracts of employment of part-time lecturers and instead to retain their services as subcontractors.

This was done through an arrangement with Education Lecturing Services (ELS), the second respondents, who are an agency holding a database of available college lecturers. Ms Allonby's employment was terminated with effect from 29 August 1996 and, like other lecturers, she was told that if she wanted to continue to work, she had to register with ELS and thereby become self-employed. The pay of part-time lecturers in Ms Allonby's position became a proportion of the fee agreed between ELS and the college. Their income fell and they lost a series of benefits, ranging from sick pay to career structure, which went with employment. ELS did not contribute to the Teachers' Superannuation Scheme (TSS). It is a condition of the TSS that the member be an employee and no lecturer engaged by ELS is an employee.

Ms Allonby brought test-case proceedings against the college for indirect sex discrimination by reason of the dismissal. She also brought a claim against the college on the grounds that it was discriminating against her as a contract worker contrary to s. 9 of the Sex Discrimination Act, an equal pay claim against ELS contending that it was obliged to pay her pro rata with a male full-time lecturer (a Mr R. Johnson) at the college, and a claim against the Department for Education contending that it was unlawful to deny her access, as a self-employed worker, to the TSS.

HELD (European Court of Justice): A woman whose contract of employment has not been renewed and who is immediately made available to her previous employer through another undertaking to provide the same services is not entitled to rely on the principle of equal pay in Article 141 (now 157) of the EC Treaty in a claim against the new employer, using as a basis for comparison the remuneration received for equal work or work of the same value by a man employed by the woman's previous employers.

Although Article 141(now 157) is not limited to situations in which men and women work for the same employer and may be invoked in cases of discrimination arising directly from legislative provisions or collective agreements, as well as in cases in which work is carried out in the same establishment or service, where the differences identified in the pay conditions of workers performing equal work or work of equal value cannot be attributed to a single source, there is no body which is responsible for the inequality and which could restore equal treatment. Such a situation does not come within the scope of Article 141(157).

JUDGMENT: The national court submitted the first question to enable it to rule on Ms Allonby's claim for entitlement to remuneration from ELS equal to that of a male lecturer employed by the College.

Accordingly, this question must be construed as seeking to ascertain whether, in circumstances such as those of the main proceedings, Article 141(1) EC must be interpreted as meaning that a woman whose contract of employment with an undertaking has not been renewed and who is immediately made available to her previous employer through another undertaking to provide the same services is entitled to rely, vis-à-vis the intermediary undertaking, on the principle of equal pay, using as a basis for comparison the remuneration received for equal work or work of the same value by a man employed by the women's previous employer.

It must be borne in mind at the outset that Article 141(1) EC can be relied on only by workers within the meaning of that provision.

However, even if that condition is satisfied, the first question cannot be answered in the affirmative.

Admittedly, there is nothing in the wording of Article 141(1) EC to suggest that the applicability of that provision is limited to situations in which men and women work for the same employer. The principle established by that article may be invoked before national courts, in particular in cases of discrimination arising directly from legislative provisions or collective labour agreements, as well as in cases in which work is carried out in the same establishment or service, whether private or public (see, *inter alia*, Case 43/75 *Defrenne II* [1976] ECR 455, paragraph 40, and Case C–320/00 *Lawrence and Others* [2002] IRLR 822, paragraph 17).

However, where the differences identified in the pay conditions of workers performing equal work or work of equal value cannot be attributed to a single source, there is no body which is responsible for the inequality and which could restore equal treatment. Such a situation does not come within the scope of Article 141(1) EC. The work and the pay of those workers cannot therefore be compared on the basis of that provision (*Lawrence*, paragraph 18).

It is clear from the order for reference that the male worker referred to by Ms Allonby is paid by the College under conditions determined by the College, whereas ELS agreed with Ms Allonby on the pay which she would receive for each assignment.

The fact that the level of pay received by Ms Allonby is influenced by the amount which the College pays ELS is not a sufficient basis for concluding that the College and ELS constitute a single source to which can be attributed the differences identified in Ms Allonby's conditions of pay and those of the male worker paid by the College.

Moreover, it is clear from the order for reference that ELS and the College are not associated employers within the meaning of s. 1(6)(c) of the Equal Pay Act 1970.

Therefore, the answer to the first question must be that, in circumstances such as those of the main proceedings, Article 141(1) EC must be interpreted as meaning that a woman whose contract of employment with an undertaking has not been renewed and who is immediately made available to her previous employer through another undertaking to provide the same services is not entitled to rely, vis-à-vis the intermediary undertaking, on the principle of equal pay, using as a basis for comparison the remuneration received for equal work or work of the same value by a man employed by the woman's previous employer.

NOTES
1. The decision in *British Coal Corporation* v *Smith* has been applied by the Court of Appeal in *South Tyneside Metropolitan Borough Council* v *Anderson* [2007] IRLR 715 in holding that a female learning support assistant was in the same employment as a road sweeper employed on the same point of a grade set out in a collective agreement. ' "Common" as applied to terms and conditions of employment, means sufficiently similar for a broad comparison to be made.'
2. In *Lawson* v *Britfish Ltd* [1988] IRLR 53, the EAT, in considering the application of s. 1(6)(c) and the words 'common terms and conditions', concluded that these words do not relate to employment at the same establishment. Once it is established that the applicant and her comparator are employed at the same establishment, the issue of whether there are common terms and conditions does not arise. The decision of the EAT in *Scullard* v *Knowles* [1996] IRLR 344 moves away from the more restrictive aspects of the interpretation of s. 1(6) which confine comparison to associated companies. It is suggested that s. 1(6) should be displaced by the wider interpretation to be found in Article 157 (ex 119) which encompasses comparators employed 'in the same establishment or service', thereby increasing the scope for public sector employees to make equal pay claims.

   Applying the decision in *Scullard*, the EAT in *South Ayrshire Council* v *Morton* [2001] IRLR 28 held that a teacher employed by a local education authority in Scotland was entitled to bring an equal pay claim comparing herself with a teacher employed by a different education authority in Scotland. The decision of the EAT has been confirmed by the Court of Session [2002] IRLR 256.

   However, the decision of the ECJ in *Lawrence* v *Regent Office Care Ltd* [2002] IRLR 822 appears to limit the application of *Morton*, as, while it does not preclude cross-employer comparisons, it limits them to situations where the differences identified can be attributed to a single source for which there is an identifiable body/person that is responsible.

   The decision in *Allonby* confirms that claims under Article 157 are not confined to situations where men and women work for the same employer. The ECJ in *Allonby* defined the term 'worker' under Article 157 as the person who, for a certain period of time, performed services for and under the direction of another person in return for remuneration. It suggests that mutuality of obligation is not required. The key factor in this case was the extent of any limitation on Miss Allonby's freedom to choose her timetable and the place and content of her work. Finally the ECJ concluded that where State legislation is the cause of the inequality, there is no need for a worker to identify a named comparator. This would allow Miss Allonby to invoke Article 157 against her employer as a public authority to enforce her rights. Further support for the decision in *Lawrence* v *Regent Office Care Ltd* [2002] can be found in *Robertson & others* v *Department for Environment, Food & Rural Affairs* [2005] IRLR 363. In this case six male civil servants working for DEFRA brought an equal pay claim comparing themselves with Personal Secretaries in the Department of the Environment, Transport and the Regions. The Court of Appeal held that although all civil servants are employed by the Crown, Article 141 requires pay and conditions to be attributed to a 'single source'. As pay and conditions of civil servants are not negotiated or agreed centrally on a civil service-wide basis there was no single source responsible, even though there was common employment by the Crown.
3. The Court of Session, upholding the decision of the ET in *South Ayrshire Council* v *Milligan* [2003] IRLR 153, has recognised the validity of contingency claims. In this case a male primary school teacher was allowed to claim equal pay with a male secondary school head teacher by naming as his comparator a female colleague on the same or less pay than himself who in her own equal pay claim had cited as comparator the male secondary head teacher. The court in this case adopted a purposive approach in interpreting the legislation to ensure compliance with Article 157 and the Equal Pay Directive. Failure to allow a claim on a contingent basis to proceed could result in the applicant suffering prejudice in relation to back pay since he or she could lodge a claim only after the comparative claim had succeeded.
4. The word 'employed' in the EPA 1970, s. 1(6) has a wider meaning than is ordinarily provided by employment protection legislation. It includes not only persons in the master–servant relationship but also those who are self-employed yet are engaged in an activity to execute personally work or labour—see *Quinnen* v *Hovells* [1984] IRLR 227, a sex discrimination case, the Sex Discrimination Act (SDA) 1975 providing a similar definition of the word 'employment'. In *Mirror Group Newspapers Ltd* v *Gunning* [1986] IRLR 27 (another sex discrimination case), the Court of Appeal considered the words 'a contract personally to execute any work or labour'. It held that it includes any contract where the dominant purpose is that the person contracting to provide

services under it performs personally the work which forms the subject matter of the contract. It is a qualitative rather than a quantitative test and requires consideration of the type of work or labour to be performed.

As the right to protection is given to those 'employed', it will not necessarily be defeated even where the contract of employment is tainted by illegality (*Leighton* v *Michael & Charalambous* [1996] IRLR 67).

The decision of the NICA in *Perceval-Price* v *Department of Economic Development* [2000] IRLR 380 recognises the shift in rights being accorded to 'workers' as opposed to those in employment by allowing a person holding 'statutory office' to claim equal pay under Article 119 (now 157); a claim which was barred under the EPA and SDA.

■ QUESTIONS

1. Did Mrs Leverton 'cast her net too widely' in respect of her comparators (*obiter* Lord Bridge)?

2. Following *Leverton's* case, would Miss Hayward's claim have been defeated?

3. What is there to prevent a female employee based at the employer's Cardiff factory comparing herself with a male employee at his London factory?

4. Following the decision in *Scullard*, what options are available for the applicant in selecting s. 79 comparators?

C: 'Like work'

To succeed in a claim based on 'like work' under the Equality Act, s. 65(1) (formerly the EPA 1970, s. 1(2)(a)), it must be shown that the applicant is employed on the same work or work of a broadly similar nature to the comparator. As a result of the EqA 2010, s. 65(2)(3) (formerly s. 1(4) of the EPA 1970), any differences between their jobs which are not of practical importance can be disregarded, but regard should be had to the frequency with which such differences occur in practice and the nature and extent of the differences.

E. Coomes (Holdings) Ltd v *Shields*
[1978] IRLR 263, Court of Appeal

Miss Shields was employed as a counter-hand in the appellants' bookmakers' shop in Sussex Street, London, on an hourly rate of 92p. A male counter-hand, Mr Rolls, was also employed at this shop on the higher rate of £1.06 an hour. The shop was one of nine operated by the company that it considered to be vulnerable to trouble, both from risk of attack on the premises by robbers, particularly when the shop was opened in the morning, and from the risk of disturbance from customers in the shop.

To guard against these potential dangers, it was the policy of the company to employ male counter-hands at these nine shops. The main work of these men was the same as that of the women counter-hands but, in addition, they were required to be around when the manager opened up in the morning, as a reinforcement in case of trouble; they were required, simply by their presence, to act as a deterrent to potential rowdy or violent customers and to deal with these if the need arose; and they were also used in the transporting of cash between branches.

The industrial tribunal held that Miss Shields was not employed on 'like work' to her male comparator because his duties of deterring trouble amounted to differences of practical importance for the purposes of the EPA 1970, s. 1(4). The EAT allowed Miss Shields' appeal.

The Court of Appeal, dismissing the employer's appeal, held that s. 1(4) requires a comparison to be made not between the contractual obligations of the man on the one hand and the woman on the other, but between the things that each actually does and the frequency with which they are done. The industrial tribunal had erred in paying too much attention to the contractual obligations and too little to the fact that the man had never, on the evidence, had to deal with any disturbance or attempted violence.

> LORD DENNING MR: The only thing that is clear to me is that, when men and women are engaged on like work in the same establishment, the women are to be paid the same 'rate for the job' as the men. That is, usually an hourly rate. But an exception can be made where a man deserves more than the woman because he has special personal claims to a higher rate because of his superior skill or responsibility or merit, so long as it is not based on the difference in sex. I turn to the sections which bear this out.

Section 1(4)—'LIKE WORK'

When a woman claims equal pay with a man in the same employment, she has first to show that she is employed on 'like work' with him. This is defined in s. 1(4), which proceeds in this fashion:

First, her work and that of the men must be 'of the same or a broadly similar nature'. Instances of the 'same nature' are men and women bank cashiers at the same counter; or men and women serving meals in the same restaurant. Instances of a 'broadly similar nature' are men and women shop assistants in different sections of the same department store; or a woman cook who prepares lunches for the directors and the men chefs who cook breakfast, lunch and teas for the employees in the canteen—see *Capper Pass Ltd* v *Lawton* [1976] IRLR 366.

Second, there must be an inquiry into (i) the 'differences between the things that the woman does and the things that the men do'; and (ii) a comparison of them so as to see 'the nature and extent of the differences' and the 'frequency or otherwise with which such differences occur in practice': and (iii) a decision as to whether those differences are, or are not 'of practical importance in regard to terms and conditions of employment'.

This involves a comparison of the two jobs—the woman's job and the man's job—and making an evaluation of each job as a job irrespective of the sex of the worker and of any special personal skill or merit that he or she may have. This evaluation should be made in terms of the 'rate for the job' usually a payment of so much per hour. The rate should represent the value of each job in terms of the demand made on a worker under such headings as effort, skill, responsibility, or decision. If the value of the man's job is worth more than the value of the woman's job, it is legitimate that the man should receive a higher 'rate for the job' than the woman. For instance, a man who is dealing with production schedules may deal with far more important items than the woman—entailing far more serious consequences from a wrong decision. So his job should be rated higher than hers, see *Eaton* v *Nuttall* [1977] IRLR 71. But, if the value of the woman's job is equal to the man's job, each should receive the same rate for the job. This principle of 'equal value' is so important that you should ignore differences between the two jobs which are 'not of practical importance'. The employer should not be able to avoid the principle by introducing comparatively small differences in 'job content' between men and women: nor by giving the work a different 'job description'. Thus where a woman driver in a catering department drives vans within the factory premises to and from the kitchens and a man driver in a transport section drives vans on the public highway, it could properly be held that the differences were 'not of practical importance' and she should receive the same 'rate for the job' an hour rate as he, see *British Leyland* v *Powell* [1978] IRLR 57. Again in a hospital, the attendance on patients may be done by women called 'nurses' and men called 'orderlies': and there may be differences in 'job content' in that, while both do many similar things, the men 'orderlies' deal with the special needs of men patients, but these differences are not such as to warrant a 'wage differential' between the nurses and the orderlies—see *Brennan* v *Prince William Hospital* (1974) 503 Fed Rep 2nd, page 282.

Nor should the employer be able to avoid the principle of 'equal value' by having the work (at the same job) done by night or for longer hours. The only legitimate way of dealing with night work or for longer hours is by paying a night shift premium or overtime rate assessed at a reasonable figure. Article 119 of the Treaty says specifically that the 'pay for work at time rates shall be the same for the same job'. The decided cases are to the same effect—see *Schulz* v American Can Company (1970) 424 Fed Rep 2nd 358; *Dugdale* v *Kraft Foods* [1976] IRLR 204; *Electrolux Ltd* v *Hutchinson* [1977] IRLR 410.

If it is found that the differences are 'not of practical importance' then the woman is employed on 'like work' with the men: and her contract is deemed to include an equality clause giving her the same 'rate for the job' as the men, see s. 1(2).

Section 1(3)—PERSONAL DIFFERENCES

Section 1(3) says that a variation in pay is justifiable 'if the employer proves that the variation is genuinely due to a material difference (other than the difference of sex) between her case and his'.

This sub-section deals with cases where the woman and the man are doing 'like work', but the personal equation of the man is such that he deserves to be paid at a higher rate than the woman. Even though the two jobs, viewed as jobs, are evaluated equally, nevertheless there may quite genuinely, be 'material differences' between the two people who are doing them—which merit a variation in pay—irrespective of whether it is a man or woman doing the job. One instance is length of service. In many occupations, a worker, be he man or woman, gets an increment from time to time, according to his seniority or length of service. Another instance is special personal skill or qualifications. In many occupations a degree or diploma is a qualification for higher pay, irrespective of sex. So is a higher grading for skill or capacity within the firm itself, see *National Vulcan Insurance v Wade* [1978] IRLR 225. Likewise, a bigger output or productivity may warrant a 'wage differential' so long as it is not based on sex. So may the place of work, see *NAAFI v Varley* [1976] IRLR 408. In all these cases the two jobs are evaluated equally as jobs, but, nevertheless, there are material differences (other than sex) which warrant a 'wage differential' between the two persons doing them.

But the escape route offered by s. 1(3) is so open to abuse that the section requires that the variation should be 'genuinely due' to the difference and that the employer should 'prove' it—not by an excessively high standard of proof, but by the ordinary standard of the balance of probabilities—'see *National Vulcan Insurance v Wade*'.

NOTES

1. Lord Denning spent some time in *Shields*'s case considering the applicability of EC law, and while he was content to conclude that Miss Shields and her comparator were employed on 'like work', he had wondered whether her comparator deserved a higher rate of pay for his 'protective role'. However, in considering the supremacy of EC law he stated:

   > Under that law it is imperative that 'pay for work at time rates shall be the same for the same job'; and that 'all discrimination on the ground of sex shall be eliminated with regard to all aspects and conditions of remuneration'. The differences found by the majority of the industrial tribunal are all based on sex. They are because he is a man. He only gets the higher hourly rate because he is a man. In order to eliminate all discrimination, there should be an equality clause written into the woman's contract.

2. The issue of what amounts to 'like work' within the EPA 1970, s. 1(4) (now the EqA 2010, s. 65) has arisen in numerous cases. What the student must not forget is that although 'like work' may be established, the employer may yet be able to justify the difference in pay under s. 1(3) of the Act (now the EqA 2010, s. 69).

3. The decision in *Capper Pass v Lawton* [1976] IRLR 366 proposed a two-stage test for establishing 'like work' within the EPA 1970, s. 1(4) (now EqA 2010, s. 65). First, is the work which the woman does and the work which the man does of the same or a broadly similar nature? Second, if it is work of a broadly similar nature, are the differences in the work of practical importance in relation to terms and conditions of employment?

4. Other cases have concluded in respect of the EPA 1970, s. 1(4) (now the EqA 2010, s. 65) that the time at which work is done is irrelevant—see *Dugdale v Kraft Foods Ltd* [1976] IRLR 368 and *Sherwin v National Coal Board* [1978] IRLR 122; although if, for example, night work brings with it additional responsibilities, then this may amount to a difference of practical importance in relation to terms and conditions; at the very least this may allow the payment of shift premiums (*Calder & Cizakowsky v Rowntree Mackintosh Confectionery Ltd* [1993] IRLR 212). In *Thomas v National Coal Board* [1987] IRLR 451, the EAT held that a canteen assistant on permanent night work was not employed on 'like work' with canteen assistants employed to work during the day, as the former worked alone and without supervision, which amounted to a 'difference of practical importance'.

   It is clear that the work done in practice is the nub of the comparison and cannot be ignored. Where, therefore, the comparator is paid more for some aspect of the job which he personally does, this aspect cannot be disregarded in deciding whether he and the applicant are employed on 'like work' (*Maidment v Cooper & Co. (Birmingham) Ltd* [1978] IRLR 462). A key factor may be the degree of responsibility between the man's job and woman's job (*Eaton Ltd v Nuttall* [1977] IRLR 71).

■ **QUESTION**

How can an employer pay employees on night work more pay than those doing the same work during the day without contravening the EqA 2010? See *Calder & Cizakowsky v Rowntree Mackintosh Confectionery Ltd* [1993] IRLR 212.

D: Work rated as equivalent

This head of claim under the EqA 2010, s. 65(1)(b) (formerly the EPA 1970, s. 1(2)(b)), is dependent upon the existence of a valid job evaluation scheme, i.e. analytical and non-discriminatory. There is no obligation on employers to carry out such schemes. However, where a job evaluation scheme has been carried out, the applicant may claim that his or her work has been rated as equivalent under such a scheme. Where the job evaluation scheme does not meet the requirements of the EqA 2010, s. 65(4), in that it contains elements that are 'sex-specific', i.e. it sets values for men different from those it sets for women (s. 64(5)), the claimant may challenge the scheme using the equal value provisions. (The equivalent but not identical provision to s. 65(4) was EPA, s. 1(5).)

Bromley and others v H. & J. Quick Ltd
[1988] IRLR 249, Court of Appeal

The respondents employed the 11 appellant women as clerical workers. The women brought an equal value claim comparing their work to that of male managers. The employer challenged this claim on the basis that a job evaluation study within s. 1(5) of the Act had been carried out and this had given different values to the women's jobs and those of their comparators. The job evaluation scheme carried out by consultants on the part of the employer involved job ranking and paired comparisons. Some representative jobs produced descriptions based on selected factors: skill/training/experiences; mental demand; responsibility; physical environment; external contacts. Benchmark jobs were selected from the representative jobs and the necessary paired comparisons and ranking made. The jobs of the appellants and three out of the four comparators were not assessed by using factor values but were merely slotted into the job ranking order by management.

The Court of Appeal (allowing the appeal) held that s. 1(5) requires an evaluation to be made of the demands of the job under various headings (for example effort, skill, decision making). If s. 2A(2)(a) of the Act is to be successfully pleaded the employer must show that both the work of the woman and the work of the man have been valued in terms of the demands made on them under the various headings.

DILLON LJ: It may be noted that s. 1(5) serves two different functions under the Act. On the one hand, if a woman wants to claim that she is within subheading (b) of s. 1(2) as a woman employed on work rated as equivalent with that of a man she has to point to a job evaluation study such as is mentioned in s. 1(5) which has so rated the work of her job. On the other hand, if an application is made by the woman employee to an industrial tribunal and the employer wishes to avoid a reference to a member of the panel of independent experts for report, it is for the employer to show if he can, under s. 2A(2),

(a) that the work of the woman and the work of the man in question have been given different values on a job evaluation study such as is mentioned in s. 1(5), and

(b) that there are no reasonable grounds for determining that the evaluation contained in that study was, within the meaning of s. 2A(3), made on a system which discriminated on grounds of sex.

It is in this latter context that the questions have arisen in the present case, since the respondent company sought to have the appellants' claims dismissed by the industrial tribunal under s. 2A(1) because of the job evaluation study that there had been. The onus was therefore initially, in my judgment, on the respondent company to show, to put it briefly

(a) that there had been a job evaluation study which satisfied the requirements of s. 1(5) and thus was 'a study such as is mentioned in s. 1(5)', and

(b) that there are no reasonable grounds for determining that the evaluation contained in that study was tainted by sex discrimination.

...

What s. 1(5) does require is, however, a study undertaken with a view to evaluating jobs in terms of the demand made on a worker under various headings (for instance effort, skill, decision). To apply that to s. 2A(2)(a) it is necessary, in my judgment, that both the work of the woman who has made application to the industrial tribunal and the work of the man who is her chosen comparator should have been valued in such terms of demand made on the worker under various headings. Mr Lester submitted that the method used on undertaking a study within s. 1(5) must necessarily be 'analytical', a word he used in the sense of describing the process of dividing a physical or abstract whole into its constituent parts to determine their relationship or value. Sir Ralph Kilner-Brown criticised the use of the word 'analytical' as a gloss on the section. In my judgment, the word is not a gloss, but indicates conveniently the general nature of what is required by the section, viz that the jobs of each worker covered by the study must have been valued in terms of the demand made on the worker under various headings. The original application of s. 1(5) to women within subheading (b) in s. 1(2) of the Act (women employed on work rated equivalent to that of a man) necessarily required that the woman's work and the man's should each have been valued in terms of the demand made on the worker under appropriate headings; the wording of s. 2A(2)(a), read with that of s. 1(5), necessarily shows that the same applies to the present appellants who claim to be within subheading (c), and their male comparators. It is not enough, in my judgment, that the 23 benchmark jobs were valued—if indeed they were (and on this I do not go so far as Woolf LJ as I do not find it necessary to do so)—on the factor demand basis required by s. 1(5), if the jobs of the appellants and their comparators were not.

But on the facts it is clear that none of the comparators' jobs and none of the appellants' jobs, save those of Mrs Bromley and Mrs Owen at the appeal stage, were ever valued according to the demands made on the worker under the five or six selected headings. The relative weightings of the selected factors had indeed been worked out by reference to the 23 benchmark jobs as I have indicated. But short of the appeal stage those weightings were not used in evaluating any of the other jobs, nor were those other jobs, including those of the appellants and their comparators, broken down under the factor headings. What happened at the appeal stage in relation to Mrs Bromley and Mrs Owen makes no difference to the outcome in their cases, since there was never any appeal by their comparator.

NOTES

1. The decision of the Court of Appeal in *Bromley* relied on that of the ECJ in *Rummler* v *Dato-Druck GmbH* [1987] IRLR 32, which considered the validity of a pay grading scheme which took into account degrees of muscular effort. The ECJ concluded that such a criterion is not *per se* discriminatory as long as it is objectively required for the job and does not result in female employees being disadvantaged because they are unable to undertake such jobs. An analytical evaluation scheme will therefore recognise the skills and aptitudes on the part of employees of both sexes.

2. If a woman's job is ranked as equal to that of a man under a valid scheme, she may use s. 1(2)(b) (now EqA, s. 65(1)(b)) to pursue her claim, even if the scheme has not been implemented, as long as it is complete and the parties have accepted its validity (*Arnold* v *Beecham Group Ltd* [1982] IRLR 307). A person will be deemed to be on 'work rated as equivalent' even though the same points may not have been awarded under the job evaluation scheme where conversion from points to grades puts the respective jobs on the same grade (*Springboard Sunderland Trust* v *Robson* [1992] IRLR 261).

3. In *Eaton* v *Nuttall Ltd*, the EAT concluded that a valid job evaluation scheme required an objective assessment of the nature of the work. In an appendix to the case the principal methods of job evaluation are reproduced from the ACAS Guide No. 1.

Eaton v *Nuttall Ltd*

[1977] IRLR 71, Employment Appeal Tribunal

APPENDIX

As not all concerned are familiar with Job Evaluation, we set out below a note on the principal methods (*see*: ACAS Guide No. 1).

Job ranking

This is commonly thought to be the simplest method. Each job is considered as a whole and is then given a ranking in relation to all other jobs. A ranking table is then drawn up and the ranked jobs grouped into grades. Pay levels can then be fixed for each grade.

Paired comparisons

This is also a simple method. Each job is compared as a whole with each other job in turn and points (0, 1 or 2) awarded according to whether its overall importance is judged to be less than, equal to or more than the other. Points awarded for each job are then totalled and a ranking order produced.

Job classification

This is similar to ranking except that it starts from the opposite end; the grading structure is established first and individual jobs fitted into it.

A broad description of each grade is drawn up and individual jobs considered typical of each grade are selected as 'benchmarks'. The other jobs are then compared with these benchmarks and the general description is placed in their appropriate grade.

Points assessment

This is the most common system in use. It is an analytical method, which, instead of comparing whole jobs, breaks down each job into a number of factors—for example, skills, responsibility, physical and mental requirements and working conditions. Each of these factors may be analysed further.

Points are awarded for each factor according to a predetermined scale and the total points decide a job's place in the ranking order. Usually, the factors are weighted so that, for example, more or less weight may be given to hard physical conditions or to a high degree of skill.

Factor comparison

This is also an analytical method, employing the same principles as points assessment but using only a limited number of factors, such as skill, responsibility and working conditions.

A number of 'key' jobs are selected because their wage rates are generally agreed to be 'fair'. The proportion of the total wage attributable to each factor is then decided and a scale produced showing the rate for each factor of each key job. The other jobs are then compared with this scale, factor by factor, so that a rate is finally obtained for each factor of each job. The total pay for each job is reached by adding together the rates for its individual factors.

4. Discriminatory job evaluation schemes can be challenged not only under the EPA 1970 and the SDA 1975, but also under Article 1(2) of the Equal Pay Directive, which provides that a 'job classification system must be based on the same criteria for both men and women and so drawn up as to exclude any discrimination on grounds of sex'.

■ QUESTION

Would s. 1(5) have been satisfied had the jobs of the appellants in Bromley's case been given factor values under a job evaluation scheme?

E: 'Equal value'

The provisions under the EqA 2010, s. 65(1)(c) (formerly the EPA 1970, s. 1(2)(c)) relating to equal value were introduced in 1983. The applicant may claim the same pay as a man if she is doing work of the same value in terms of the demands made on her. An equal value claim may be pursued even though there is a man employed in the same job as the woman (see *Pickstone* v *Freemans plc* [1988] IRLR 357). Readers should refer to the decision in *Hayward* v *Cammell Laird Shipbuilders* (extracted earlier in Section A) which was the groundbreaking equal value case. The following case also considers whether monetary terms should be aggregated or—if a woman is deemed to be undertaking work of equal value to a man—whether each term should be deemed to be a single term.

Degnan v Redcar & Cleveland Borough Council
[2005] IRLR 615, Court of Appeal

Female cleaners, supervisory assistants in schools, and home helps in social services brought equal pay claims comparing their work to gardeners, refuse workers, drivers, and road workers. The council conceded that the women were employed on work rated equivalent to their comparators. However, the comparators, whilst receiving the same hourly rate as each other, were paid variable bonuses and attendance allowances. The women wished to equalise their 'pay' with different comparators depending on which would be the most financially beneficial. However, the issue was whether the attendance allowance should be treated as a separate term or not.

HELD: The Court of Appeal upheld the decision of the EAT in concluding that all monetary terms received for normal working hours should be aggregated and divided by the number of hours in the working week, to give an hourly rate; the women's pay would then be equalised to that rate. The women were not entitled to select the most advantageous comparator for each element.

KAY LJ: First, Miss Gill submits that, far from being consonant with *Hayward* v *Cammell Laird*, the approach of the Employment Appeal Tribunal is inconsistent with it. I do not accept this submission. The Employment Appeal Tribunal did not (to use Lord Goff's words) 'lump together' or engage in 'overall comparison' of different terms. Rather it applied its collective mind to the reality of the contractual provisions in the circumstances of the particular case and analysed them. I do not understand Lord Goff to have considered that, for example, basic pay and cash bonuses are always and forever dissimilar provisions. Indeed, it is common ground in the present case that the bonus payments are to be treated as part of basic pay. What the Employment Appeal Tribunal decided was that the employment tribunal had fallen into error when finding functional and conceptual differences between basic pay and the attendance allowance. As I have indicated, I am at one with the Employment Appeal Tribunal on this issue. Secondly, Miss Gill submits that the reasoning of the Employment Appeal Tribunal is flawed because it is founded upon a 'manufactured' classification, namely 'provision for monetary payment for the performance of the contract by employers during normal working hours'. However, s. 1 of the Act and *Hayward* v *Cammell Laird* necessitate classification. If the submission is that the classification deployed by the Employment Appeal Tribunal is 'manufactured' in the sense of 'artificial', I disagree. In my judgment it is a realistic classification based on careful analysis. Thirdly, it is suggested that the council has chosen to fight the wrong battle. Instead of engaging in a dispute of this kind, it ought to have conceded the differences and sought to justify them under s. 1(3). However, whether or not differences would be so justifiable, the structure of s. 1 requires the prior process of analysis and classification of the respective contractual provisions.

Fourthly, Miss Gill seeks to rely on decisions of the European Court of Justice of support a submission that the approach of the Employment Appeal Tribunal in the present case ignores the transparency which is necessary in the formulation and subsequent analysis of contractual terms. She cites *Danfoss* [1989] IRLR 532 and *Barber* v *Guardian Royal Exchange Assurance* [1990] IRLR 240 in which the Court said (at para. 28):

> It follows that genuine transparency, permitting an effective review, is assured only if the principle of equal pay applies to each of the elements of remuneration granted to man or woman.

All this informed the decision of the House of Lords in *Hayward* v *Cammell Laird*. In particular it explains the rejection of the totality of 'swings and roundabouts' approach. It requires the analysis to which I have referred but, as the Employment Appeal Tribunal pointed out (at para. 26), its approach to the present case

> …satisfies the principle of transparency; it is no more difficult to analyse and compare than the more limited terms for which [the appellants] contend.

I agree, just as I have already indicated my agreement with the analysis of the Employment Appeal Tribunal in the long extract set out in paragraph 34 of its judgment.

Thus, whilst acknowledging the ingenuity of Miss Gill's submissions, I am satisfied that the approach of the Employment Appeal Tribunal was rigorous and correct. I consider it to be entirely consistent with the principles propounded in *Hayward* v *Cammell Laird* and the European authorities. Moreover, it has the desirable result that it will facilitate what was intended by the Equal Pay Act, namely equalisation, rather than the upward movement of the women's rate of monetary pay to a level higher than that of any single male comparator. The result is, as the Employment Appeal Tribunal put it (at para. 30):

> All monetary payments received by male comparators for normal working hours should be aggregated and divided by the number of hours in the working week, to give an hourly rate; if it is greater, the woman's hourly rate should be increased to eliminate the difference.

NOTES
1. The procedure and role of the independent expert in equal value claims has become a dominant issue because of the burden on the employment tribunal to avoid unnecessary expense and delay

which may be incurred if a referral is made to the independent expert. The procedure is now set out in the EqA 2010, s. 130. Where an employment tribunal has to decide if the work of a claimant and comparator are of equal value, this provision gives it the power to require an independent expert, designated by the Advisory, Conciliation and Arbitration Service to prepare a report on the matter. Unless the tribunal withdraws its request for a report (in which case it can ask the expert to give it any documents or other information the expert has to help it make a decision) it must wait for the expert's report before deciding whether the work is of equal value.

If there has been a job evaluation study in relation to the work involved and the study finds that the claimant's work is not of equal value to the work of the comparator, the tribunal is required to come to the same decision unless it has a good reason to suspect that the study is discriminatory or unreliable.

There are still issues in respect of what amounts to equal value. Early decisions of the tribunals arrived at conflicting conclusions: see, e.g., *Wells v F. Smales & Son (Fish Merchants)* (1985) COIT 1643/113 and *Brown & Royle v Cearns & Brown* (1985) COIT 1614/215. In the former, while some of the applicants scored a higher score than their comparator in the independent expert's report and were therefore found to be on work of equal value, some of the applicants scored between 79% and 95% of the comparator's score. These too were found to be on work of equal value by the tribunal, although not by the expert, on the grounds that the scores were so close and the differences between them and the comparator were not relevant or real material differences. However, in the latter case, the applicant's score was 95% of her comparator's, yet the tribunal found that her work was not of equal value as precise equality or greater value was required. The application of a 'broad brush' approach was confirmed in *Pickstone v Freemans plc* (1993) COIT 28811/84.

2. See Szyszczak, E., 'Pay inequalities and equal value claims' (1985) 48 *Modern Law Review* 139–55, which considers the impact of the 1983 amendment and suggests that the equal value amendment will have a very limited effect on the earnings differential between men and women. At the same time, however, the scope and potential of EC law as a means of challenging the EPA 1970 is recognised.

F: Genuine material factor

EQUALITY ACT 2010

69 Defence of Material Factor

(1) The sex equality clause in A's terms has no effect in relation to a difference between A's terms and B's terms if the responsible person shows that the difference is because of a material factor reliance on which—

(a) does not involve treating A less favourably because of A's sex than the responsible person treats B, and

(b) if the factor is within subsection (2), is a proportionate means of achieving a legitimate aim.

(2) A factor is within this subsection if A shows that, as a result of the factor, A and persons of the same sex doing work equal to A's are put at a particular disadvantage when compared with persons of the opposite sex doing work equal to A's.

(3) For the purposes of subsection (1), the long-term objective of reducing inequality between men's and women's terms of work is always regarded as a legitimate aim.

The EqA 2010, s. 69 (formerly the EPA 1970, s. 1(3)) provides a defence for the employer. The burden of proof is on the employer to show not only that the variation in pay is genuinely due to a material factor, but also to prove that this is not due to a difference of sex (*The Financial Times Ltd v Byrne and others (No. 2)* [1992] IRLR 163).

Bilka-Kaufhaus v *Weber von Hartz*

[1986] IRLR 317, European Court of Justice

Bilka-Kaufhaus is a department store in the Federal Republic of Germany. It has an occupational pension scheme for its employees, which supplements the state pension scheme. Under the rules of the occupational scheme, part-time employees are eligible for pensions only if they have worked full time for at least 15 years over a total period of 20 years.

Mrs Weber von Hartz was employed as a sales assistant for 15 years, but over the last few years of her employment she chose to work part time. Since she had not worked full time for the minimum period of 15 years, the employers refused to pay her an occupational pension under the scheme.

In proceedings before the German labour courts, Mrs Weber argued that the occupational pension scheme was contrary to the principle of equal pay for men and women laid down in Article 119 (now 157) of the EEC Treaty. She contended that the requirement of a minimum period of full-time employment placed women at a disadvantage, since they were more likely than their male colleagues to take part-time work so as to be able to care for their family and children. The employers argued that there were objectively justified economic grounds for the exclusion of part-time workers, emphasising that the employment of full-time workers entails lower ancillary costs and permits the use of staff throughout opening hours.

The ECJ held that an occupational scheme which excludes part-time employees infringed Article 119 (now 157), where that exclusion affected a far greater number of women than men, unless the undertaking could show that the exclusion was based on objectively justified factors unrelated to any discrimination on the ground of sex; this may include economic grounds.

LORD MACKENZIE STUART: ... In the first of its questions the national court asks whether a staff policy pursued by a department store company excluding part-time employees from an occupational pension scheme constitutes discrimination contrary to Article 119 [now 141] where that exclusion affects a far greater number of women than men.

In order to reply to that question reference must be made to the judgment of 31.3.81 (Case 96/80, *Jenkins v Kingsgate* [1981] IRLR 228).

In that judgment the Court considered the question whether the payment of a lower hourly rate for part-time work than for full-time work was compatible with Article 119 [now 157].

Such a practice is comparable to that at issue before the national court in this case: Bilka does not pay different hourly rates to part-time and full-time workers, but it grants only full-time workers an occupational pension. Since, as was stated above, such a pension falls within the concept of pay for the purposes of the second paragraph of Article 119 [now 157] it follows that, hour for hour, the total remuneration paid by Bilka to full-time workers is higher than that paid to part-time workers.

The conclusion reached by the Court in its judgment of 31.3.81 is therefore equally valid in the context of this case.

If, therefore, it should be found that a much lower proportion of women than of men work full time, the exclusion of part-time workers from the occupational pension scheme would be contrary to Article 119 [now 157] of the Treaty where, taking into account the difficulties encountered by women workers in working full time, that measure could not be explained by factors which exclude any discrimination on grounds of sex.

However, if the undertaking is able to show that its pay practice may be explained by objectively justified factors unrelated to any discrimination on grounds of sex there is no breach of Article 119 [now 157].

The answer to the first question referred by the national court must therefore be that Article 119 [now 157] of the EEC Treaty is infringed by a department store company which excludes part-time employees from its occupational pension scheme, where that exclusion affects a far greater number of women than men, unless the undertaking shows that the exclusion is based on objectively justified factors unrelated to any discrimination on grounds of sex.

Question 2(a)

In its second question the national court seeks in essence to know whether the reasons put forward by Bilka to explain its pay policy may be regarded as 'objectively justified economic grounds', as referred to in the judgment of 31.3.81, where the interests of undertakings in the department store sector do not require such a policy.

In its observations Bilka argues that the exclusion of part-time workers from the occupational pension scheme is intended solely to discourage part-time work, since in general part-time workers refuse to work in the late afternoon and on Saturdays. In order to ensure the presence of an adequate workforce during those periods it was therefore necessary to make full-time work more attractive than part-time work, by making the occupational pension scheme open only to full-time workers. Bilka concludes that on the basis of the judgment of 31.3.81 it cannot be accused of having infringed Article 119 [now 157].

In reply to the reasons put forward to justify the exclusion of part-time workers Mrs Weber von Hartz points out that Bilka is in no way obliged to employ part-time workers and that if it decides to do so it may not subsequently restrict the pension rights of such workers, which are already reduced by reason of the fact that they work fewer hours.

According to the Commission, in order to establish that there has been no breach of Article 119 [now 141] it is not sufficient to show that in adopting a pay practice which in fact discriminates against women workers the employer sought to achieve objectives other than discrimination against women. The Commission considers that in order to justify such a pay practice from the point of view of Article 119 [now 157] the employer must, as the Court held in its judgment of 31.3.81, put forward objective economic grounds relating to the management of the undertaking. It is also necessary to ascertain whether the pay practice in question is necessary and in proportion to the objectives pursued by the employer.

It is for the national court, which has sole jurisdiction to make findings of fact, to determine whether and to what extent the grounds put forward by an employer to explain the adoption of a pay practice which applies independently of a worker's sex but in fact affects more women than men may be regarded as objectively justified economic grounds. If the national court finds that the measures chosen by Bilka correspond to a real need on the part of the undertaking, are appropriate with a view to achieving the objectives pursued and are necessary to that end, the fact that the measures affect a far greater number of women than men is not sufficient to show that they constitute an infringement of Article 119 [now 157].

The answer to question 2(a) must therefore be that under Article 119 [now 157] a department store company may justify the adoption of a pay policy excluding part-time workers, irrespective of their sex, from its occupational pension scheme on the ground that it seeks to employ as few part-time workers as possible, where it is found that the means chosen for achieving that objective correspond to a real need on the part of the undertaking, are appropriate with a view to achieving the objective in question and are necessary to that end.

■ **QUESTION**

Bilka is noted for introducing the concept of indirect discrimination into Article 141 (ex 157). How far has this concept been imported into the EPA 1970 (now the EqA 2010)? See *Enderby* v *Frenchay Area Health Authority* [1993] IRLR 591; IRLR 234 and *Ratcliffe* v *North Yorkshire County Council* [1995] IRLR 439; *Jamstalldhetsombudsmannen* v *Orebro Lans Landsting* [2000] IRLR 421.

Rainey v Greater Glasgow Health Board
[1987] IRLR 26, House of Lords

Mrs Rainey and her male comparator, Mr Crumlin, were employed at Belvidere Hospital, Glasgow as prosthetists. At the time of the industrial tribunal hearing, Mrs Rainey earned £7,295 p.a. and Mr Crumlin was paid £10,085. It was conceded that they were employed on like work, but the employers contended that the variation in pay was 'genuinely due to a material difference other than the difference of sex' between the two cases.

In 1980, it had been decided to set up a prosthetic fitting service within the National Health Service in Scotland. Until then, all qualified prosthetists were employed by private contractors. It was decided that the remuneration of employees in the new prosthetic service should be related to the NHS Whitley Council scale and that the appropriate pay scale for them would be that for medical physics technicians. However, in order to attract a sufficient number of experienced prosthetists, it was regarded as advantageous to obtain the transfer of prosthetists employed by private contractors into the NHS and it was considered that it would be necessary to offer them the same level of pay as they enjoyed in the private sector. It was therefore agreed that all employees who were willing to transfer from private contractors would have the option of remaining on their existing rates of pay and conditions of service, subject to future changes as negotiated by their trade union, ASTMS, for the prosthetists employed by contractors.

Mr Crumlin transferred to the NHS on these terms. He commenced employment on 1 July 1980 at a salary of £6,680. Mrs Rainey went straight into the NHS after her training was completed. She commenced employment on 1 October 1980 at a starting salary of £4,773.

After the block transfer in 1980, no transfers on special terms were permitted, and all new entrants were engaged on the NHS scale of remuneration.

The House of Lords held, dismissing Mrs Rainey's appeal, that the difference in pay was due to a genuine material difference within the EPA 1970, s. 1(3). The onus is on the employer to establish objectively justified grounds for the difference in pay between the woman and the man. Such grounds may be economic or for administrative efficiency in a concern not engaged in commerce or business.

LORD KEITH OF KINKEL: The facts found by the industrial tribunal make it clear that the Secretary of State for Scotland decided, as a matter of general policy, that the Whitley Council scale of remuneration and negotiating machinery, which applied throughout the National Health Service in Scotland, was appropriate for employees in the prosthetic service. It was also decided that the appropriate part of the scale for such employees was that applicable to medical physics technicians, presumably because the nature of their work was considered comparable to that of the prosthetists. So all direct entrants to the service, whether male or female, were to be placed on that part of the scale and made subject to Whitley Council negotiations. But it was apparent that the new service would not get off the ground unless a sufficient number of the prosthetists in the employment of the private contractors could be attracted into it. So the further policy decision was taken to offer these prosthetists the option of entering the service at their existing salaries and subject to the ASTMS negotiating machinery. As it happened, all the prosthetists privately employed were male. In the result, Mr Crumlin had the benefit of the offer and so emerged with a higher salary and better prospects for an increase than did the appellant, who did not have that benefit.

The main question at issue in the appeal is whether those circumstances are capable in law of constituting, within the meaning of s.1(3) of the Act of 1970, 'a material difference (other than the difference of sex) between her case and his'.

...

In my opinion these statements (per Lord Denning and Lawton LJ in *Clay Cross (Quarry Services) Ltd* v *Fletcher* [1978] IRLR 361 at pp. 363 and 364 respectively) are unduly restrictive of the proper interpretation of s.1(3). The difference must be 'material', which I would construe as meaning 'significant and relevant', and it must be between 'her case and his'. Consideration of a person's case must necessarily involve consideration of all the circumstances of that case. These may well go beyond what is not very happily described as 'the personal equation', i.e. the personal qualities by way of skill, experience or training which the individual brings to the job. Some circumstances may on examination prove to be not significant or not relevant, but others may do so, though not relating to the personal qualities of the employer. In particular, where there is no question of intentional sex discrimination whether direct or indirect (and there is none here) a difference which is connected with economic factors affecting the efficient carrying on of the employer's business or other activity may well be relevant.

The European Court had occasion to consider the question afresh in *Bilka-Kaufhaus GmbH* v *Weber von Hartz* (Case 170/84) [1986] IRLR 317. A German department store operated an occupational pension scheme for its employees, under which part-time employees were eligible for pensions only if they had worked full time for at least 15 years over a total period of 20 years. That provision affected disproportionately more women than men. A female part-time employee claimed that the provision contravened Article 119 [now 157] of the Treaty. The employers contended that it was based upon objectively justified economic grounds, in that it encouraged full-time work which resulted in lower ancillary costs and the utilisation of staff throughout opening hours. The European Court by its decision made it clear that it was not sufficient for the employers merely to show absence of any intention to discriminate, saying, at pp. 320–321:

It is for the national court, which has sole jurisdiction to make findings of fact, to determine whether and to what extent the grounds put forward by an employer to explain the adoption of a pay practice which applies independently of a worker's sex but in fact affects more women than men may be regarded as objectively justified economic grounds. If the national court finds that the measures chosen by Bilka correspond to a real need on the part of the undertaking, are appropriate with a view to achieving the objectives pursued and are necessary to that end, the fact that the measures affect a far greater number of women than men is not sufficient to show that they constitute an infringement of Article 119 [now 157]. The answer to question 2(a) must therefore be that under Article 119 [now 157] a department store company may justify the adoption of a pay policy excluding part-time workers, irrespective of their sex, from its occupational pension scheme on the ground that it seeks to employ as few part-time workers as possible, where it is found that the means chosen for achieving that objective correspond to a real need on the part of the undertaking, are appropriate with a view to achieving the objective in question and are necessary to that end.

It therefore appears that the European Court has resolved the doubts expressed by Browne-Wilkinson J in *Jenkins* v *Kingsgate (Clothing Productions) Ltd* [1981] IRLR 228 and established that the true meaning and effect of Article 119 [now 157] in this particular context is the same as that there attributed to s. 1(3) of the Act of 1970 by the Employment Appeal Tribunal. Although the European Court at one point refers to 'economic' grounds objectively justified, whereas Browne-Wilkinson J speaks of 'economic or other reasons', I consider that read as a whole the ruling of the European Court would not exclude objectively justified grounds which are other than economic, such as administrative efficiency in a concern not engaged in commerce or business.

The decision of the European Court on Article 119 [now 157] must be accepted as authoritative and the judgment of the Employment Appeal Tribunal on s. 1(3) of the Act of 1970, which in my opinion is correct, is in harmony with it. There is now no reason to construe s. 1(3) as conferring greater rights on a worker in this context than does Article 119 [now 157] of the Treaty. It follows that a relevant difference for purposes of s. 1(3) may relate to circumstances other than the personal qualifications or merits of the male and female workers who are the subject of comparison.

In the present case the difference between the case of the appellant and that of Mr Crumlin is that the former is a person who entered the National Health Service at Belvidere Hospital directly while the latter is a person who entered it from employment with a private contractor. The fact that one is a woman and the other a man is an accident. The findings of the industrial tribunal make it clear that the new prosthetic service could never have been established within a reasonable time if Mr Crumlin and others like him had not been offered a scale of remuneration no less favourable than that which they were then enjoying. That was undoubtedly a good and objectively justified ground for offering him that scale of remuneration. But it was argued for the appellant that it did not constitute a good and objectively justified reason for paying the appellant and other direct entrants a lower scale of remuneration. This aspect does not appear to have been specifically considered by either of the tribunals or by their Lordships of the First Division, apart from Lord Grieve who said [1985] IRLR 414, 425:

> I accept that the facts which provided the evidence before both tribunals were sufficient to explain why Mr Crumlin (and his colleagues) were paid on a scale equivalent to that which they had been receiving while employed in the private sector, but in my opinion that evidence is not sufficient to explain why, when the National [Health] Service door was opened to the appellant (and other prosthetists not previously employed in the private sector) the appellant (and her fellow prosthetists) were paid on a lower scale. In the absence of a reasonable explanation as to why the appellant was paid on a lower scale than Mr Crumlin I am of opinion that the respondents have not discharged the onus placed upon them by s. 1(3) of the Act of 1970, and that the majority of the Employment Appeal Tribunal were not entitled on the facts before them to conclude that they had.

The position in 1980 was that all National Health Service employees were paid on the Whitley Council scale, and that the Whitley Council negotiating machinery applied to them. The prosthetic service was intended to be a branch of the National Health Service. It is therefore easy to see that from the administrative point of view it would have been highly anomalous and inconvenient if prosthetists alone, over the whole tract of future time for which the prosthetic service would endure, were to have been subject to a different salary scale and different negotiating machinery. It is significant that a large part of the difference which has opened up between the appellant's salary and Mr Crumlin's is due to the different negotiating machinery. Accordingly, there were sound objectively justified administrative reasons, in my view, for placing prosthetists in general, men and women alike, on the Whitley Council scale and subjecting them to its negotiating machinery. There is no suggestion that it was unreasonable to place them on the particular point on the Whitley Council scale which was in fact selected, ascertained by reference to the position of medical physics technicians and entirely regardless of sex. It is in any event the fact that the general scale of remuneration for prosthetists was laid down accordingly by the Secretary of State. It was not a question of the appellant being paid less than the norm but of Mr Crumlin being paid more. He was paid more because of the necessity to attract him and other privately employed prosthetists into forming the nucleus of the new service.

I am therefore of the opinion that the grounds founded on by the board as constituting the material difference between the appellant's case and that of Mr Crumlin were capable in law of constituting a relevant difference for purposes of s. 1(3) of the Act of 1970, and that on the facts found by the industrial tribunal they were objectively justified.

Enderby v Frenchay Health Authority
[1993] IRLR 591, European Court of Justice

Dr Pamela Enderby, a senior speech therapist, claimed that she was employed on work of equal value with male principal grade pharmacists and clinical psychologists employed in the National Health Service. At the relevant time, her annual pay as a chief III grade speech therapist was £10,106, while that of a principal clinical psychologist was £12,527 and that of a grade III principal pharmacist was £14,106. The pay of speech therapists generally was up to 60% less than that of pharmacists.

The industrial tribunal dismissed the complaints. It held that the employers had established a material factor defence within the meaning of s. 1(3) by showing that the variation in pay 'arose because of the bargaining structure and its history which was non-discriminatory, and from the structures within their own professions which were also non-discriminatory'.

The industrial tribunal found in the alternative, however, that the employers had not shown that the difference in pay with respect to pharmacists was due to market forces because market forces could not explain the whole of the difference.

Dr Enderby did not appeal against the finding that there was no direct discrimination in the wage-setting process. Her appeal was based on the contention that under EEC law she had established a prima facie case of indirect sex discrimination in pay by showing that she was a member of a predominantly female group doing work of presumed equal value with her male comparator employed in a group which was predominantly male and that she was paid less than him. The employer cross-appealed against the industrial tribunal's failure to find that the difference in pay between the speech therapists and pharmacists was due to market forces and was permissible under s. 1(3) of the EPA.

The EAT [1991] IRLR 44 dismissed Dr Enderby's appeal. It held that the mere fact of a difference in pay is not sufficient to found an allegation of unintentional indirect discrimination, without the identification of a barrier, requirement or condition causing disparate impact. The EAT took the view that if the factor causing the disparate impact has no taint of gender, there is nothing which requires justification. It is the cause which requires justification, not simply the result. It is only if a woman is paid less because she is a woman that she has suffered discrimination and without such discrimination a woman is not entitled to equal pay for work of equal value.

The EAT also allowed the cross-appeal against the industrial tribunal's decision, holding that once it had been found by the tribunal that market forces played *a* part in the difference of pay between speech therapists and pharmacists, that was sufficient. It was not necessary for the employers to establish that the factor of market forces justified the whole of the difference.

The Court of Appeal [1992] IRLR 15 referred the following questions for consideration by the European Court of Justice:

■ QUESTION 1

Does the principle of equal pay enshrined in Article 119 (now 157) of the Treaty of Rome require the employer to justify objectively the difference in pay between job A and job B?

■ QUESTION 2

If the answer to question 1 is in the affirmative can the employer rely as sufficient justification for the difference in pay upon the fact that the pay of jobs A and B respectively have been determined by different collective bargaining processes which (considered separately) do not discriminate on grounds of sex and do not operate so as to disadvantage women because of their sex?

■ QUESTION 3

If the employer is able to establish that at times there are serious shortages of suitable candidates for job B and that he pays the higher remuneration to holders of job B so as to attract them to job B, but it can also be established that only part of the difference in pay between job B and job A is due to the need to attract suitable candidates to job B:

(a) is the whole of the difference of pay objectively justified; or

(b) is that part but only that part of the difference which is due to the need to attract suitable candidates to job B objectively justified; or

(c) must the employer equalise the pay of jobs A and B on the ground that he has failed to show that the whole of the difference is objectively justified?

The first question

…It is normally for the person alleging facts in support of a claim to adduce proof of such facts. Thus, in principle, the burden of proving the existence of sex discrimination as to pay lies with the worker who, believing himself to be the victim of such discrimination, brings legal proceedings against his employer with a view to removing the discrimination.

However, it is clear from the case law of the Court that the onus may shift when that is necessary to avoid depriving workers who appear to be the victims of discrimination of any effective means of enforcing the principle of equal pay. Accordingly, when a measure distinguishing between employees on the basis of their hours of work has in practice an adverse impact on substantially more members of one or other sex, that measure must be regarded as contrary to the objective pursued by Article 119 [now 157] of the Treaty, unless the employer shows that it is based on objectively justified factors unrelated to any discrimination on grounds of sex (judgments in Case 170/84 *Bilka-Kaufhaus* [1986] IRLR 317; Case C–33/89 *Kowalska* [1990] IRLR 447, at paragraph 16; and Case C–184/89 *Nimz* [1991] IRLR 222)…

However, if the pay of speech therapists is significantly lower than that of pharmacists and if the former are almost exclusively women while the latter are predominantly men, there is a prima facie case of sex discrimination, at least where the two jobs in question are of equal value and the statistics describing that situation are valid.

It is for the national court to assess whether it may take into account those statistics, that is to say, whether they cover enough individuals, whether they illustrate purely fortuitous or short-term phenomena, and whether, in general, they appear to be significant.

Where there is a prima facie case of discrimination, it is for the employer to show that there are objective reasons for the difference in pay. Workers would be unable to enforce the principle of equal pay before national courts if evidence of a prima facie case of discrimination did not shift to the employer the onus of showing that the pay differential is not in fact discriminatory (see, by analogy, the judgment in Danfoss [1989] IRLR 532).

In these circumstances, the answer to the first question is that, where significant statistics disclose an appreciable difference in pay between two jobs of equal value, one of which is carried out almost exclusively by women and the other predominantly by men, Article 119 [now 157] of the Treaty requires the employer to show that that difference is based on objectively justified factors unrelated to any discrimination on grounds of sex.

The second question

…As is clear from Article 4 of Council Directive 75/117/EEC of 10 February 1975 on the approximation of the laws of the Member States relating to the application of the principle of equal pay for men and women (Official Journal 1975 L.45, p. 19), collective agreements, like laws, regulations or administrative provisions, must observe the principle enshrined in Article 119 [now 157] of the Treaty.

The fact that the rates of pay at issue are decided by collective bargaining processes conducted separately for each of the two professional groups concerned, without any discriminatory effect within each group, does not preclude a finding of prima facie discrimination where the results of those processes show that two groups with the same employer and the same trade union are treated differently. If the employer could rely on the absence of discrimination within each of the collective bargaining processes taken separately as sufficient justification for the difference in pay, he could, as the German Government pointed out, easily circumvent the principle of equal pay by using separate bargaining processes.

Accordingly, the answer to the second question is that the fact that the respective rates of pay of two jobs of equal value, one carried out almost exclusively by women and the other predominantly by men, were arrived at by collective bargaining processes which, although carried out by the same parties, are distinct, and, taken separately, have in themselves no discriminatory effect, is not sufficient objective justification for the difference in pay between those two jobs.

The third question

The Court has consistently held that it is for the national court, which has sole jurisdiction to make findings of fact, to determine whether and to what extent the grounds put forward by an employer to explain the adoption of a pay practice which applies independently of a worker's sex but in fact affects more women than men may be regarded as objectively justified economic grounds (judgments in Case 170/84 *Bilka-Kaufhaus*, cited above, at paragraph 36 and Case C–184/89 *Nimz*…). Those grounds may include, if they can be attributed to the needs and objectives of the undertaking, different criteria such as the worker's flexibility or adaptability to hours and places of work, his training or his length of service (judgment in Case 109/88 *Danfoss*…).

The state of the employment market, which may lead an employer to increase the pay of a particular job in order to attract candidates, may constitute an objectively justified economic ground within the meaning of the case law cited above. How it is to be applied in the circumstances of each case depends on the facts and so falls within the jurisdiction of the national court.

If, as the question referred seems to suggest, the national court has been able to determine precisely what proportion of the increase in pay is attributable to market forces, it must necessarily accept that the pay differential is objectively justified to the extent of that proportion. When national authorities have to apply Community law, they must apply the principle of proportionality.

If that is not the case, it is for the national court to assess whether the role of market forces in determining the rate of pay was sufficiently significant to provide objective justification for part or all of the difference.

The answer to the third question, therefore, is that it is for the national court to determine, if necessary by applying the principle of proportionality, whether and to what extent the shortage of candidates for a job and the need to attract them by higher pay constitutes an objectively justified economic ground for the difference in pay between the jobs in question.

■ QUESTIONS

1. What impact has the decision in *Enderby* had on the criteria for justifying inequalities as propounded in *Rainey*?

2. Can an 'understandable error' amount to a genuine material difference/factor?

3. How far is a non-sex based reason a complete defence to both direct and indirect discrimination?

NOTES

1. The hurdles raised by the EAT in *Enderby* have been removed by the decision of the ECJ. The applicant need not identify a requirement or condition, or show gender-based disparate impact in alleging indirect discrimination relating to pay. Indirect discrimination will be presumed whenever there is significant statistical evidence to show that a predominantly female group of workers is doing work of equal value but is being paid less than a male group of workers. The onus then moves to the employer to show that the difference is objectively justified. This should have a considerable impact on equal value claims based on job segregation. It should also impact upon the interpretation of the SDA 1975 and the Race Relations Act (RRA) 1976. The Court of Appeal in *Bailey and others* v *Home Office* [2005] IRLR 369 has attempted to clarify the position further regarding the circumstances when an employer must establish a genuine material factor defence. The Court of Appeal held that the employer is required to establish such a defence in all situations, where a prima facie case of sex discrimination is established. The requirement is not confined, as had been previously decided, to cases where there was a gender neutral requirement or condition which was found to have an adverse impact on a greater proportion of women than men. A prima facie case can be established where the statistics show that the proportion of disadvantaged men compared with disadvantaged women when expressed as a ratio is significant enough to establish the case, even where there are a significant number of the 'non-disadvantaged' sex in the disadvantaged group. The disparity in favour of men in this particular case required justification by the employer.

2. The decision of the Court of Appeal in *Armstrong* v *Newcastle-upon-Tyne NHS Hospital Trust* [2006] IRLR 124 appears to be out of line with orthodox legal reasoning in that it suggests that even where the pay criterion in question indirectly discriminates against women, in that it has an adverse impact, the employer does not have to provide an objective justification if it can show that the difference in treatment was attributable to a difference other than gender. This issue resurfaced in *Gibson* v *Sheffield City Council* [2010] IRLR 331. In *Gibson*, productivity bonuses had been awarded for male-dominated jobs (street cleaners and gardeners) but not for female-dominated work (carers and cleaners). A majority of the Court of Appeal (Lady Justice Smith and Lord Justice Maurice Kay) concluded that *Armstrong* was correctly decided. According to Smith LJ, an employer can refute a finding of disparate impact by showing that the impact was not causally linked to the claimant's gender. In this case, however, where the jobs were sex-segregated and the pay differential was around 35%, the Court of Appeal was unanimous in holding that there was a 'sexual taint', so that the employer was required to justify the pay differential.

3. *Enderby* also makes inroads into the market forces defence. This is no longer a blanket defence to a claim of indirect discrimination. The ECJ felt that, where market forces is pleaded, the tribunals must assess what proportion of the pay differential can be attributed to market forces as objectively justified by the employer. This may, indeed, result in applicants being awarded proportional equal pay rather than nothing where the market forces defence is successful.

4. Non-discriminatory collective bargaining will no longer objectively justify an act of discrimination. The employer must now, in establishing a defence under s. 1(3), justify the discriminatory result not just the cause. In *British Road Services* v *Loughran* [1997] IRLR 1992, the Northern Ireland Court of Appeal considered how far separate pay structures based on different collective agreements amounted to an objective justification for the purposes of s. 1(3). The Northern Ireland Court of Appeal decided that 'where a significant number of the claimant's group are women, an employer cannot rely merely on the existence of a separate collective agreement. Nor does the decision in *Enderby* require the group to be exclusively women before the [material factor] defence is to be used.'

Handels- og Kontorfunktionaerernes Forbund i Danmark v Dansk Arbejdsgiverforening (acting for Danfoss)

[1989] IRLR 532, European Court of Justice

In accordance with a collective agreement between HK, the Danish Union of Commercial and Clerical Staff (hereafter the staff union), and DA, the Danish Association of Employers (hereafter the employers' association), Danfoss pays the same basic minimum pay to workers in the same pay grade. Grading is determined by job classification. Article 9 of the collective agreement, however, allows the company to make additional payments to individuals within a grade on the basis of the employee's 'flexibility', defined as including an assessment of their capacity, quality of work, autonomy and responsibilities. In addition, pay is increased on the basis of the employee's vocational training and seniority.

The union pointed out that within a pay grade the average pay of women was less than that of men and it contended that the employer's pay system discriminated on the ground of sex contrary to the provisions of Danish law implementing the EEC Equal Pay Directive.

Under Danish law, when two parties to a collective agreement are in dispute on whether pay in an undertaking is discriminatory, in the event of a failure to agree, the case is referred to an industrial arbitration tribunal. Before the arbitration tribunal, the staff union submitted the results of a statistical survey covering the pay of 157 Danfoss employees which showed a difference of 6.85% between the average pay of male and female workers within the relevant pay grades. The union contended that this difference in itself showed pay discrimination. It argued that because of the way in which pay is determined in Denmark, a woman would not be able to avail herself of the right to equal pay if she could not base her claim on statistical data.

The industrial arbitration tribunal decided to stay the proceedings and submitted a number of questions to the ECJ for a preliminary ruling on the interpretation of the Equal Pay Directive.

The ECJ held that the effect of Directive 75/117 is that where the employer operates a pay structure which lacks transparency in respect of the criteria used for the payment of employees, the burden of proof is on the employer to show that his pay practice is not discriminatory where a female worker establishes by comparison with a relatively large number of employees, that the average pay of female employees is lower than that of male employees.

Concerning the burden of proof (questions 1(A) and 3(A))

The file shows that the main dispute between the parties originates in the fact that the mechanism of individual increases applied to the basic wage is operated in such a way that a female worker is incapable of identifying the causes of a difference in pay between her and a male worker carrying out the same work. The workers do not actually know which are the criteria for the increases which are applied to them and how they are applied. They are only informed of the amount of their increased wages, without being able to establish the effect each of the criteria for the increases has had. Those who fall into a particular pay grade are, therefore, unable to compare the different components of their pay with those of the pay of their fellow workers who are part of the same grade.

In those circumstances the questions submitted by the national court must be understood as seeking to establish whether the Equal Pay Directive must be interpreted as meaning that, where an undertaking applies a pay system which is characterised by a total lack of transparency, the burden of proof is on the employer to show that his pay practice is not discriminatory, if a female worker establishes that, by comparison with a relatively high number of employees, the average pay of female workers is lower than that of male workers.

In this respect it should be recalled, first of all, that in its decision of 30 June 1988 (*Commission of the European Communities* v *France*, 318/86, not yet published, point 27) the Court condemned a system of recruitment characterised by a lack of transparency as being contrary to the principle of equality of access to employment, on the grounds that such lack of transparency prevented any form of control on the part of the national courts.

It should be emphasised, moreover, that in a situation where a mechanism of individual pay increases characterised by a total lack of transparency is involved, female workers can only establish a difference between average pay. They would be deprived of any effective means of ensuring the respect of the principle of equal pay before the national court if the effect of furnishing such proof was not to impose the burden of proof on the employer to show that his pay practice is, in fact, not discriminatory.

In those conditions, the answer to questions 1(A) and 3(A) must be that the Equal Pay Directive must be interpreted as meaning that when an undertaking applies a system of pay which is characterised by a total lack of transparency, the burden of proof is on the employer to show that his pay practice is not discriminatory, where a female worker establishes, by comparison with a relatively large number of employees, that the average pay of female workers is lower than that of male workers.

Concerning the lawfulness of the incremental criteria concerned (questions 1(B) and 2(A) and (C))

These questions seek essentially to ascertain whether the Directive must be interpreted as meaning that, when it appears that the application of incremental criteria such as flexibility, vocational training or the seniority of the worker works systematically to the disadvantage of female workers, the employer may nevertheless justify their use, and, if so, under what conditions. In order to answer this question, each of the criteria must be examined separately.

First of all, concerning the criterion of flexibility the file does not show clearly the scope to be given to it. At the hearing the Employers' Association stated that the fact of being willing to work at different hours does not in itself justify a wage increase. In order to apply the criterion of flexibility the employer would make an overall assessment of the quality of the work carried out by his employees. For this purpose, he would take into account in particular their zeal at work, their sense of initiative and the amount of work done.

In those circumstances a distinction is to be made according to whether the criterion of flexibility is used in order to reward the quality of the work carried out by the employee or whether it is used to reward the adaptability of the employee to variable work schedules and places of work.

In the first case, the criterion of flexibility is indisputably totally neutral from the point of view of sex. Where it results in systematic unfairness to female workers, that can only be because the employer has applied it in an abusive manner. It is inconceivable that the work carried out by female workers would be generally of a lower quality. The employer may not therefore justify the use of the criterion of flexibility so defined where its application shows itself to be systematically unfavourable to women.

It would be different in the second case. If it were understood as referring to the adaptability of the worker to variable work schedules and places of work, the criterion of flexibility may also operate to the disadvantage of female workers who, as a result of household and family duties for which they are often responsible may have greater difficulty than male workers in organising their working time in a flexible manner.

In its judgment of 13 May 1986 (*Bilka-Kaufhaus GmbH* v *Weber von Hartz* [1986] IRLR 317), the Court took the view that the policy of an undertaking which results in workers, who are excluded from an occupational pension scheme, might affect a much higher number of women than men, taking into account the difficulties encountered by female workers in working full-time. The Court nevertheless held that the undertaking might establish that its pay practice was determined by objectively justified factors unrelated to any discrimination based on sex and that, if the undertaking succeeded, there was no infringement of Article 119 [now 141] of the Treaty. Those considerations also apply in the case of a pay practice which gives special rewards for the adaptability of workers to variable work schedules and places of work. The employer may, therefore, justify payment for such adaptability by showing that it is of importance in the performance of the specific duties entrusted to the worker concerned.

Second, as regards the criterion of vocational training, it cannot be ruled out that it may act to the detriment of female workers insofar as they have fewer opportunities to obtain vocational training which is as advanced as that of male workers, or that they use those opportunities to a lesser extent.

However, having regard to the considerations laid down in the aforementioned judgment of 13 May 1986, the employer may justify rewarding specific vocational training by demonstrating that that training is of importance for the performance of the specific duties entrusted to the worker.

Third, as regards the criterion of seniority, it cannot be ruled out either that, like that of vocational training, it may result in less favourable treatment of female workers than for male workers, insofar as women have entered the labour market more recently than men or are subject to more frequent interruptions of their careers. However, since seniority goes hand in hand with experience which generally places a worker in a better position to carry out his duties, it is permissible for the employer to reward it without the need to establish the importance which it takes on for the performance of the specific duties to be entrusted to the worker.

Strathclyde Regional Council v *Wallace*
[1998] IRLR 146, House of Lords

Each of the nine respondent women teachers performed the duties of a principal teacher. However, none of them were appointed to the position of a principal teacher and none of them received the salary appropriate for the holder of an appointment as a principal teacher. They were among a group of 134 unpromoted teachers who claimed to be carrying out principal teachers' duties, 81 of whom were men and 53 women.

The nine women brought equal pay claims, identifying at least one male comparator who had been appointed as a principal teacher and was receiving a salary appropriate to that responsibility. The industrial tribunal found that the applicants had been performing like work.

Given the gender composition of the unpromoted teachers, it was an agreed fact that the disparity in pay was not based on sex. The employers argued that the variation in pay between the applicants and their male comparators was due to a combination of material factors. These included that the promotion structure for teachers was established by statute and posts were filled only on merit after competition, and that financial constraints prevented the applicants from being appointed principal teachers when it might have been appropriate.

It was held that the industrial tribunal had erred in law in finding that the employers had failed to prove that the variation in pay between the applicants, who had acted as principal teachers but had not been paid the salary for that post and their male comparators appointed as principal teachers, was genuinely due to a material factor other than sex within the meaning of s. 1(3) of the EPA, in circumstances in which it was agreed that the disparity in pay had nothing to do with gender. The industrial tribunal erred in holding that in order for the employers to succeed in a s. 1(3) defence, they had to establish that the reasons for the difference in pay justified the disparity.

LORD BROWNE-WILKINSON: [Section 1(3)] provides a defence if the employer shows that the variation between the woman's contract and the man's contract is 'genuinely' due to a factor which is (a) material and (b) not the difference of sex. The requirement of genuineness would be satisfied if the industrial tribunal came to the conclusion that the reason put forward was not a sham or a pretence. For the matters relied upon by the employer to constitute 'material factors' it would have to be shown that the matters relied upon were in fact causally relevant to the difference in pay, i.e. that they were significant factors. Finally, the employer had to show that the difference of sex was not a factor relied upon. This final point is capable of presenting problems in other cases. But in the present case it presents none: there is no suggestion that the matters relied on were in any way linked to differences in sex.

If that approach had been adopted by the industrial tribunal, this case would have been straightforward. The five factors summarised by the industrial tribunal were undoubtedly genuine reasons for there being a difference between the pay of the appellants and that of principal teachers. They were also significant and causally relevant factors leading to that disparity. They did not relate to sex in any way. Therefore, on the straightforward application of the section the respondents have established a subsection (3) defence. There is nothing in the words of the subsection which requires the employer to 'justify' the factors giving rise to this disparity by showing that there was no way in which the employer could have avoided such disparity if he had adopted other measures.

How then did the industrial tribunal come to mislead itself by introducing into the case the concept of 'justification'?

The answer is that they wrongly thought that the authorities demanded such justification in every case where an employer seeks to establish a subsection (3) defence whereas, on a proper reading, the question of justification only arises where a factor relied upon is gender discriminatory. Although in the present case there is no question of gender discrimination, the authorities are in such a state of confusion that it is desirable for your Lordships to seek to establish the law on a clear and sound basis.

...

In my judgment, the law was correctly stated by Mummery J giving the judgment of the Employment Appeal Tribunal in *Tyldesley* v *TML Plastics Ltd* [1996] IRLR 395, in which he followed and applied the earlier EAT decisions in *Calder* v *Roundtree Mackintosh Confectionery Ltd* [1993] IRLR 212 and *Yorkshire Blood Transfusion Service* v *Plaskitt*

[1994] ICR 74. The purpose of s. 1 of the Equal Pay Act 1970 is to eliminate sex discrimination in pay not to achieve fair wages. Therefore, if a difference in pay is explained by genuine factors not tainted by discrimination that is sufficient to raise a valid defence under subsection (3); in such a case there is no further burden on the employer to 'justify' anything. However, if the factor explaining the disparity in pay is tainted by sex discrimination (whether direct or indirect) that will be fatal to a defence under subsection (3) unless such discrimination can be objectively justified in accordance with the tests laid down in the *Bilka* and *Rainey* cases.

NOTE: Women tend to have less continuous employment than men. In *Wilson* v *H&S Executive* [2010] IRLR 59, the Court of Appeal held that an employer can be required to objectively justify both the adoption and length of a service-related pay scale. In the instant case, there was a finding of fact by the employment tribunal that all the requisite skills to do the job were acquired after five years and so the Court of Appeal held that a ten-year incremental scale had not been shown to be objectively justified.

Snoxell v Vauxhall Motors

[1977] IRLR 123, Employment Appeal Tribunal

Miss Snoxell and Mrs Davis had been employed by the company for many years as inspectors of motor machine parts. They worked alongside male inspectors, including a group of men designated OX—the red-circle group. The men in this group were paid at a higher rate than the two women although it was common ground that they were all employed on the same work. The red-circle group was formed in 1970 as a result of a revision of the existing pay structure and arose as a result of the fact that at this revision, it was realised that male inspector jobs previously graded X2 should be regraded into a lower category under the new structure (H3). It was these former X2 male inspectors who were red-circled and ultimately received the special designation OX. Because the former grade X2 was a male grade, there were no women in it and thus no women fell to receive the protections accorded to the employees in this grade when the new structure was introduced. Thus there were no women in the red circle. In June 1975, Miss Snoxell and Mrs Davies took advantage of the company's offer to transfer women employed on like work with men to the appropriate male rate and were then regraded H3. Grade H3 thus currently consists of men who entered employment after 1970 to do quality control stores inspection work and women who were performing that work prior to 1970 and those who have joined the company since. The continuation of the OX category is not subject to a fixed time limit or any phasing out provisions.

It was held, allowing Miss Snoxell's and Mrs Davies's appeal, that the correct approach for an industrial tribunal, confronted with a claim by an employer under s. 1(3) of the EPA that a variation resulting from red-circling was genuinely due to a material difference other than the difference of sex, is to elicit and analyse *all* the circumstances of the particular case, including the situation prior to the formation of the red circle. It is necessary to examine the origin of the red-circling, to see whether in other respects the arrangements are unisex and non-discriminatory, and generally to look at all the facts in order to see whether the employers, upon whom lies a heavy burden of proof, have satisfied the requirements of s. 1(3). In this context, that there was no discriminatory motive or intent is irrelevant.

PHILLIPS J: Mr Lester submitted that s. 1(3) is not a general escape clause designed to enable employers to phase in equal pay gradually; that was provided for in the Equal Pay Act 1970 itself which did not come into operation until 29 December 1975, five years after it was enacted. Nor, he submitted, could reliance be placed on s. 1(3) where the facts said to constitute the difference other than sex could be shown to have their origin in sex discrimination. Thus in the present case, although the immediate cause of the discrimination lay in the fact that the male inspectors were 'red-circled' whereas Miss Snoxell and Mrs Davies were not, and although they were 'red-circled' in order to preserve their status for reasons unconnected with sex, it was necessary to look to see why Miss Snoxell and Mrs Davies were not also within the red circle. The answer was that, because they were women, they were not able to enter Grade X2, and so did not qualify. Thus at the root of the difference relied upon lay sex discrimination, and it would be contrary to the purpose and intent of the Equal Pay Act 1970 to allow such an answer to the claim.

Mr Grabiner submitted that the reason for the red-circling of the male inspectors had nothing to do with sex discrimination, but was intended merely to preserve their status, and that it was not brought into existence to discriminate against women. If there had been no circle, he submitted, all the men and women would have been paid the same. The difference for the purpose of s. 1(3) was the formation of the red circle. The substantive cause of the discrimination, he submitted, was the formation of the red circle, and it was the effective cause. Thus there was no discrimination, and a good answer to the claim was available to Vauxhall Motors Ltd under s. 1(3).

Putting these arguments side by side it can be seen that the solution depends upon whether, in analysing the history of the difference in treatment of Miss Snoxell and Mrs Davies on the one hand and the red circle male inspectors on the other, one stops at the moment of the formation of the circle or looks further back to see why Miss Snoxell and Mrs Davies were not within it. The arguments presented to us have, not surprisingly, considered questions of causation, and it has been said that the inability of Miss Snoxell and Mrs Davies to join the red circle was, or was not, the effective cause of the current variation in the terms of their contracts of employment. It seems to us that this earlier discrimination can be said to be an effective cause of the current variation. But we would put the matter more broadly. The onus of proof under s. 1(3) is on the employer and it is a heavy one. Intention, and motive, are irrelevant; and we would say that an employer can never establish in the terms of s. 1(3) that the variation between the woman's contract and the man's contract is genuinely due to a material difference (other than the difference of sex) between her case and his when it can be seen that past sex discrimination has contributed to the variation. To allow such an answer would, we think, be contrary to the spirit and intent of the Equal Pay Act 1970, construed and interpreted in the manner we have already explained. It is true that the original discrimination occurred before 29 December 1975 and accordingly was not then unlawful; nonetheless it cannot have been the intention of the Act to permit the perpetuation of the effects of earlier discrimination…

Nelson v Carillion Services Ltd
[2003] IRLR 428, Court of Appeal

Ms Nelson was employed by Carillion Services on 22 June 1998 as a steward on the Chelsea Wing of the Chelsea and Westminster Hospital. She was paid £5.00 per hour, in accordance with the respondents' standard terms and conditions.

Carillion had taken over an existing contract to provide services at the hospital on 1 April 1997. The Transfer of Undertakings Regulations 1981 applied to the change of contractor and, as a result, Carillion were obliged to maintain the pay and conditions of some 300 employees who were transferred. These included four men and two women employed as stewards on the Chelsea Wing. One of these was Mr d'Silva, whose pay on 22 June 1998 had increased through routine annual pay increases to £6.11 per hour. The transferred employees also received a food allowance and double time if they worked on bank holidays.

In July 1998, the respondents employed a man, Mr Sinarda, as a steward on the wing. His terms and conditions were identical to those of Ms Nelson. In 2000, Ms Nelson brought an equal pay claim, naming Mr d'Silva as her comparator. He was then receiving £6.38 per hour compared with her hourly rate of £5.22.

The applicant argued that the employer's arrangements were indirectly discriminatory against women because of the stewards working on the Chelsea Wing, 80% of the men (the four employees transferred) were protected by the Transfer of Undertakings (Protection of Employment) Regulations (TUPE) 1981 compared with 66.66% of women (the two women transferred). An employment tribunal took the view that a pool for comparison of only eight employees was not appropriate, given that the balance of the sexes over the whole hospital might be considerably different. It held that the burden was on the applicant to show, on the balance of probabilities, that there had been indirect discrimination and that no sufficient or appropriate evidence had been produced to show this. Accordingly, the tribunal concluded that the pay differential was not due to reasons of sex, either directly or indirectly.

The EAT dismissed an appeal against that decision on grounds that the employment tribunal was entitled to find that the statistical comparison, based on the pool selected by the applicant, was fortuitous rather than being significant.

HELD (Court of Appeal): The employment tribunal did not err in holding that the burden of proof under s. 1(3) of the EPA 1970 was on the applicant to establish that the employers' explanation for the variation between her pay and that of her male comparator, that they were required by TUPE to honour the terms and conditions under which the comparator was transferred, was indirectly discriminatory against women. The tribunal did not err, therefore, in finding that since the statistical comparisons made by the applicant were not appropriate, the pay differential could not be held to be due to reasons of sex.

SIMON BROWN LJ: Enderby establishes that the burden of proving sex discrimination lies initially on the employee (para. 13). To shift that burden to the employers, the employee (depending upon the particular nature of the case) must establish that the measure 'has in practice an adverse impact on substantially more members of one or other sex' (the first limb of para. 14) or, where the system lacks transparency, must 'establish…in relation to a relatively large number of employees, that the average pay for women is less than that for men' (the second limb of para. 14). Or, as is described in paragraphs 16–18, the complainant must establish 'a prima facie case of sex discrimination' (the phrase used in paras. 16 and 18), on statistics which are 'valid' (para. 16) and 'appear to be significant' (para. 17), at which point 'it is for the employer to show that there are objective reasons for the difference in pay' (para. 18). Or, as summarised in paragraph 19, it is for the employee to establish 'an appreciable difference in pay' by 'significant statistics', at which point the onus shifts to the employer to show that difference is justified.

63A. Burden of proof: employment tribunals [Sex Discrimination Act 1975]

(1) This section applies to any complaint presented under s. 63 to an employment tribunal.

(2) Where, on the hearing of the complaint, the complainant proves facts from which the tribunal could, apart from this section, conclude in the absence of an adequate explanation that the respondent—

   (a) has committed an act of discrimination against the complainant which is unlawful by virtue of Part 2, or

   (b) is by virtue of s. 41 or 42 to be treated as having committed such an act of discrimination against the complainant, the tribunal shall uphold the complaint unless the respondent proves that he did not commit, or as the case may be is not to be treated as having committed, that act.

It seems to me tolerably clear that the effect of s. 63A was to codify rather than alter the pre-existing position established by the case law. The burden of proving indirect discrimination under the 1975 Act was, as Mr Langstaff accepts, always on the complainant and there pursuant to s. 63A it remains, the complainant still having to prove facts from which the tribunal could conclude that he or she has been unlawfully discriminated against 'in the absence of an adequate explanation' from the employer. Unless and until the complainant establishes that the condition in question has had a disproportionate adverse impact on his/her sex the tribunal could not in my judgment, even without explanation from the employer, conclude that he or she has been unlawfully discriminated against.

This to my mind accurately reflects the position laid down by the ECJ in Enderby and that, indeed, is hardly surprising. True it is, as Mr Langstaff points out, that the Burden of Proof Directive expressly provides that, '[T]his Directive shall not prevent Member States from introducing rules of evidence which are more favourable to plaintiffs'. It is difficult to see, however, why the UK should have wished to introduce a rule more favourable to claimants (a) than had earlier been established by the domestic authorities, or (b) than the ECJ thought appropriate for a claim directly brought under Article 119.

All these considerations notwithstanding, it is the appellant's submission that when one comes to a claim brought under the 1970 Act the burden lies throughout on the respondent employer, the claimant in an indirect discrimination case having to advance no more than 'a credible suggestion' of disproportionate adverse impact.

This somewhat surprising conclusion, Mr Langstaff submits, is justified, indeed required, by the plain language of s. 1(3) itself, a provision differently framed from anything in the 1975 Act. Section 1(3) in terms puts the burden of proof on the employer. And support for this approach, he argues, is to be found in Lord Nicholls' speech in Glasgow Corporation v Marshall (see para. 9 above). He relies in particular upon Lord Nicholls' statement, in the second of the two paragraphs I have cited, that:

In order to fulfil the third requirement [that the reason for the less favourable treatment is not 'the difference of sex', a phrase 'apt to embrace any form of sex discrimination, whether direct or indirect'] he must prove the absence of sex discrimination, direct or indirect.

The argument is in my judgment unsustainable. In the first place, it overlooks the very next sentence in Lord Nicholls' speech:

If there is any evidence of sex discrimination, such as evidence that the difference in pay has a disparately adverse impact on women, the employer will be called upon to satisfy the tribunal that the difference in pay is objectively justifiable.

This seems to me to recognise that it is for the complainant initially to establish that the matter complained of has indeed had 'a disparately adverse impact on women'.

I have in short come to the clear conclusion that in an indirect discrimination case the burden of proving disproportionate adverse impact lies on the complainant, and that merely to raise 'a credible suggestion' that, were the relevant (valid and significant) statistics provided, these might establish disproportionate impact is not sufficient for the claimant's purposes and imposes no further burden of explanation upon the employer.

Cadman v Health & Safety Executive

[2006] IRLR 969, European Court of Justice

Bernadette Cadman was employed as a band 2 principal inspector. She was paid between £4,000 to £9,000 less, per annum, than her four identified male comparators in the same band who were employed on work which had been rated as equivalent under a job evaluation study. The principal reason for this differential was that the men had longer service. Until 1992, the employers operated a scale with annual increments. A performance-related element was then introduced. In 1995, a new pay system was introduced with bands enabling an employee to progress upwards over a period of time by reference to performance-related increases. Further changes were made in 2000. However, the previous differentials based on service were not eliminated.

Mrs Cadman brought a claim under the EPA. It was common ground before the tribunal that since women in the pay band, overall, had shorter service than men, length of service had a disproportionate impact as between male and female employees and was, therefore, indirectly discriminatory. Thus, the average length of service of the 17 female band 2 inspectors was 4.4 years, whereas the average length of service of 119 male band 2 inspectors was 16.3 years.

The European Court of Justice held: ...Where there is a disparity in pay between men and women employed on equal work or work of equal value as a result of using the criterion of length of service as a determinant of pay, the employer does not have to establish specifically that recourse to that criterion is appropriate as regards a particular job to attain the legitimate objective of rewarding experience acquired which enables the worker to perform his duties better, unless the worker provides evidence capable of raising serious doubts in that regard.

In accordance with Article 141 [now 157] of the EC Treaty, whenever there is evidence of discrimination, it is for the employer to prove that the practice at issue is justified by objective factors unrelated to any discrimination based on sex. The justification given must be based on a legitimate objective and the means chosen to achieve that objective must be appropriate and necessary for that purpose.

In paragraphs 24 and 25 of the judgment in *Danfoss*, the Court, after stating that it is not to be excluded that recourse to the criterion of length of service may involve less advantageous treatment of women than of men, held that the employer does not have to provide special justification for recourse to that criterion.

By adopting that position, the Court acknowledged that rewarding, in particular, experience acquired which enables the worker to perform his duties better constitutes a legitimate objective of pay policy.

As a general rule, recourse to the criterion of length of service is appropriate to attain that objective. Length of service goes hand in hand with experience, and experience generally enables the worker to perform his duties better.

The employer is therefore free to reward length of service without having to establish the importance it has in the performance of specific tasks entrusted to the employee.

In the same judgment, the Court did not, however, exclude the possibility that there may be situations in which recourse to the criterion of length of service must be justified by the employer in detail.

That is so, in particular, where the worker provides evidence capable of giving rise to serious doubts as to whether recourse to the criterion of length of service is, in the circumstances, appropriate to attain the objective. It is in such circumstances for the employer to prove that that which is true as a general rule, namely that length of service goes hand in hand with experience and that experience enables the worker to perform his duties better, is also true as regards the job in question.

It should be added that where a job classification system based on an evaluation of the work to be carried out is used in determining pay, it is not necessary for the justification for recourse to a certain criterion to relate on an individual basis to the situation of the workers concerned. Therefore, if the objective pursued by recourse to the criterion of length of service is to recognise experience acquired, there is no need to show in the context of such a system that an individual worker has acquired experience during the relevant period which has enabled him to perform his duties better. By contrast, the nature of the work to be carried out must be considered objectively (*Rummler*, para. 13).

It follows from all of the foregoing considerations that the answer to the first and second questions referred must be that Article 141 [now 157] EC is to be interpreted as meaning that, where recourse to the criterion of length of service as a determinant of pay leads to disparities in pay, in respect of equal work or work of equal value, between the men and women to be included in the comparison:

- since, as a general rule, recourse to the criterion of length of service is appropriate to attain the legitimate objective of rewarding experience acquired which enables the worker to perform his duties better, the employer does not have to establish specifically that recourse to that criterion is appropriate to attain that objective as regards a particular job, unless the worker provides evidence capable of raising serious doubts in that regard;

- where a job classification system based on an evaluation of the work to be carried out is used in determining pay, there is no need to show that an individual worker has acquired experience during the relevant period which has enabled him to perform his duties better.

NOTES
1. The onus is on the employer to establish a s. 1(3) (now EqA 2010, s. 69) defence.
2. In *Barton v Investec Henderson Crosswaite Securities Ltd* [2003] IRLR 332 (Chapter 5), the EAT not only confirmed that the burden of proof is on the claimant to establish a prima facie case, but also that the tribunal should take into account an employer's failure to deal properly with statutory questionnaire procedure; from this it may be possible to draw an inference regarding the employer's conduct or policies.

   The decision in *Nelson* sought to clarify the contentious issue of whether the burden of proof directive (Directive 97/80), as implemented by the Sex Discrimination (Indirect Discrimination and Burden of Proof) Regulations 2001 (SI 2001/2660) merely codifies the existing principle by shifting the burden of proof to the employer once the primary case has been established. Lord Justice Brown in *Nelson* is quite clearly of the opinion that the burden of proof in indirect discrimination cases relating to pay should be approached in the same way under Article 141[now 157], the SDA and the EPA. He concluded that the burden of proof remains on the complainant to show, on the balance of probabilities, that the matter complained of has a disproportionate adverse impact on their sex. However, this approach was questioned by the Court of Appeal in *Igen Ltd* v *Wong* [2005] IRLR 258, which approved the decision in *Barton* and also in *Bailey and others* v *Home Office* [2005] (mentioned earlier in note 1 of the *Ratcliffe* extract). See Hockney, C., 'Why *Bailey* should be preferred to *Nelson*' (2005) 142 EOR 18–20.

3. The current criteria for deciding whether a genuine material factor defence has been established is to be found from the decisions in *Bilka-Kaufhaus* and *Rainey*, i.e. that any difference is based on objectively justified factors unrelated to sex. It must be shown that there is a real need on the part of the undertaking and that the difference was an appropriate way of achieving the objective necessary to that end. This test acknowledges that there may be numerous grounds such as market forces, administrative efficiency, economics, merit, service, red-circling, etc. which can justify the difference in the terms of a woman's contract compared with a male's.

   The issue of the time at which work is done has generally been irrelevant to any decision regarding equality of pay. However, *Calder and Cizakowsky* v *Rowntree Mackintosh Confectionery Ltd* [1993] IRLR 212 adds further documented evidence that the courts are prepared to adopt a flexible approach to this issue when it arises as a genuine material defence. The application of *Danfoss* is also of interest, in that the Court took the view that 'transparency' does not require a precise explanation of how the premium was achieved. The long-awaited decision of the ECJ in *Cadman* v *Health & Safety Executive* [2006] has not in reality clarified the current position on the ruling in *Danfoss* and whether *Danfoss* is still a valid approach. Whilst indirectly discriminatory criteria must normally be objectively justified by the employer, the decision in *Cadman* reinforces the stance taken in *Danfoss* by allowing the employer to reward experience and service through the use of incremental pay scales without having to link it to improved performance. The argument in *Danfoss* and *Cadman* is that the benefit of experience on a business can be assumed. However, there is authority in *Nimz* v *Freie und Hansestadt Hamburg* [1991] IRLR 222 for the proposition that a link between seniority and performance must be demonstrated.

   Furthermore, as the EPA 1970 and the SDA 1975 are to be regarded as a single code, the criteria used to establish the justification defence under s. 1(1)(b) of the SDA 1975 should be the same as the criteria used for the EPA 1970, s. 1(3); it follows that this must be the case in respect of justification under s. 1(1)(b) of the RRA 1976 (see *Hampson* v *Department of Education and Science* [1989] IRLR 69).

4. Following *Strathclyde*, in justifying a difference in pay it need only be causally relevant to the difference in pay. The reason for the difference must be explained by the employer; arguably this is now a subjective rather than an objective test. The case goes on to reinforce the point that the right to equal pay is not the same as a right to fair pay.

   Further support for the decision in *Strathclyde* can be found in *Glasgow City Council* v *Marshall* [2000] IRLR 272 in which the House of Lords applies the reasoning in *Strathclyde*, concluding that 'an employer who proves the absence of sex discrimination, direct or indirect, is under no obligation to prove a "good" reason for the pay disparity.'

   However, Rubenstein argues ('Highlights' [2001] IRLR 493, at p. 495) that the decision of the ECJ in *Brunhoffer* v *Bank der Österreichischen Postsparkasse* [2001] IRLR 571 challenges the interpretation in *Marshall* in establishing that the need for objective justification where a difference in pay between men and women is established is not confined to indirect discrimination. The decision in *Strathclyde* has been confirmed in *Parliamentary Commissioner for Administration and another* v *Fernandez* [2004] IRLR 22, in which the EAT held that an employer was not required objectively to justify the difference in pay between the complainant and his fellow comparator in circumstances where there was no suggestion that the factor relied on by the employer in seeking to establish the 'material factor' defence to the pay claim was indirectly discriminatory. See also *Redcar and Cleveland Borough Council* v *Bainbridge (No. 1)* [2007] IRLR 984 (Section 2).

5. Under EPA 1975, s. 2(4), a claim had to be brought within six months of the end of employment. This blanket rule was held by the CJEU to infringe the effectiveness of a right conferred by Community law in certain circumstances, e.g. where the applicant delayed bringing proceedings as a result of a deliberate misrepresentation by the employer: *Levez* v *T H Jennings (Harlow Pools) Ltd* [1999] IRLR 36, ECJ (see also *Preston* v *Wolverhampton Healthcare NHS Trust* [2000] IRLR 506, ECJ). The six-month time limit was amended by The Equal Pay (Amendment) Regulations 2003 (SI 2003/1656). EqA 2010, s. 129 now sets out the qualifying period as normally six months after the last day of employment. But this date may be qualified in three situations:

   • where the employer and employee are in a 'stable employment relationship', the qualifying date is six months after the end of that relationship, regardless of the fact that there may have been more than one contract of that period (*Preston* v *Wolverhampton Healthcare NHS Trust* [2000]IRLR 506, ECJ);

- where the employee was under an incapacity, the qualifying date is six months after s/he ceased to be under that incapacity;
- where the employer deliberately concealed relevant facts from the employee, the qualifying date is six months after s/he discovered (or could with reasonable diligence have discovered) the information in question (EqA 2010, s. 129(3)).

6. Until 1999, it was not possible to claim more than two years' arrears of pay following a successful equal pay claim. A successful challenge to the two-year limitation on arrears of remuneration in EPA, s. 2(5) was made in *Levez v T.H. Jennings (Harlow Pools) Ltd (No. 2))* [1999] IRLR 764. The conclusion of the EAT being that such a limitation was in breach of EC law; the most appropriate limit being the six-year time limit to be found in the Limitation Act 1980. See also *Kells v Pilkington plc* [2002] IRLR 693. The Equal Pay (Amendment) Regulations 2003 (SI 2003/1656) enacted an extension of the limit on backdated claims to six years. However, in addition, if an employer has deliberately concealed information about inequality from their employee or in an incapacity case, arrears run from the date the first breach occurred (EQA 2010, s.132(4)). However, the six-year limit does not apply to work-rated equivalent claims based on job evaluation schemes where the back pay can only be awarded from the date of the scheme—see *Bainbridge v Redcar and Cleveland Borough Council (No. 2)* [2007] IRLR 494.

7. Since October 2014, employment tribunals have the power to order equal pay audits where an employer is found liable in respect of gender pay discrimination. This is a reform which has long been campaigned for by the EOC. The provision is to be found in EqA 2010, s. 139A (as amended by the Enterprise and Regulatory Reform Act 2013) and details are set out in the Equality Act 2010 (Equal Pay Audits) Regulations 2014 (SI 2014/2559).

   Audit is defined in EQA 210, s. 139A(3) as an audit designed to identify action to be taken to avoid equal pay breaches occurring or continuing.

   Regulation 11 provides that a tribunal may order the respondent to pay a penalty to the Secretary of State when the respondent fails to comply with the order or where the tribunal is not satisfied as to the content of the audit. The amount of any individual penalty may not exceed £5,000. However, a penalty may be imposed on more than one occasion where the failure to comply with the order continues.

8. See Gill, T., 'Making equal pay defences transparent' (1990) 33 *Equal Opportunities Review* 48, for an analysis of the impact of the *Danfoss* case and its relationship to the decision in *Bilka-Kaufhaus* and *Reed Packaging Ltd v Boozer*. See also Gay, V. (1989) 18 ILJ 63–6, for a discussion of the impact of *Reed's* case in respect of collective bargaining as a material factor defence; and Kilpatrick, C. (1994) 23 ILJ 311, for a critical evaluation of s. 1(3).

■ QUESTIONS

1. Can a job evaluation scheme ever be 'objectively justified'?

2. If a variation in pay is not based on sex, does the employer have to justify the difference under the EqA 2010, s. 69 (formerly the EPA 1970, s. 1(3))?

3. Was the applicant's argument in *Nelson* ever sustainable?

NOTES

1. There have been a number of works highlighting deficiencies in the current equal pay legislation. For example, note the recommendations of the EOC in *Equal Pay for Men and Women, Strengthening the Acts* (EOC, 1990). See also Scorer, C. and Sedley, A., *Amending the Equality Laws* (NCCL, 1983); and Honeyball, S., *Honeyball & Bowers' Textbook on Employment Law,* 13th edn (Oxford: OUP, 2014), Ch. 11.

   The Equal Pay Task Force has called for mandatory equal pay reviews to be carried out by employers. It also believes that the procedure in equal pay cases needs to be streamlined and that the absence of a comparator should not act as a bar to an equal pay claim. The study by the Equal Pay Task Force looks at the consequences of the gender pay gap. The Task Force state that:

   > the gender pay gap caused by discrimination in pay systems should be reduced by 50 per cent within the next 5 years and eliminated entirely within 8 years (*Just Pay: Report of the Equal Pay Task Force* (2001), EOC).

2. For a critical review of the problems faced by complainants, see Gregory, J., *Trial by Ordeal* (EOC, 1989), in which a study was made of those complainants who lost their tribunal hearings. This research highlights the problems of stress, lack of representation (only about 50% were

represented in some way) and victimisation (few of the applicants interviewed in the research remained with the same employer). Leonard, A., *Pyrrhic Victories: Winning sex discrimination and equal pay cases in the industrial tribunals* (EOC, 1987) examines whether those complainants who succeeded in their application before the employment tribunal were in the real sense victors. Again, the problems of victimisation and stress were highlighted.

FURTHER READING

Cabrelli, D., *Employment Law in Context: Text and materials* (Oxford: OUP, 2014), Ch. 14.

Honeyball, S., *Honeyball and Bowers' Textbook on Employment Law*, 13th edn (Oxford: OUP, 2014), Ch. 11.

5

Equality Law (2): Discrimination in the Workplace—Sex and Race

The Sex Discrimination Act (SDA) 1975 and the Race Relations Act (RRA) 1976 made certain types of discrimination unlawful. This was not, however, the sole purpose of this legislation, as both statutes intended to promote equality of opportunity for men and women and racial groups. The RRA 1976 had as its model the SDA 1975; accordingly the wording of the RRA 1976 corresponded for the most part with that of the SDA 1975. To these measures the Disability Discrimination Act (DDA) 1995 may be added, together with regulations outlawing discrimination on the grounds of religion or belief, sexual orientation and age. These areas will be covered in Chapter 6. As stated in the Preamble to Chapter 5, the Equality Act (EqA) 2010 has two main aims: to harmonise discrimination law, and to strengthen the law to support progress on equality.

The EqA 2010 brought together and restated all the enactments covering discrimination. The Act also attempted to strengthen equality law in a number of areas. It harmonises existing provisions to give a single approach where appropriate. Most of the pre-existing legislation is repealed. The EqA 2006 will remain in force (as amended by the bill) so far as it relates to the constitution and operation of the Equality and Human Rights Commission; and the DDA 1995 so far as it relates to Northern Ireland.

The Act also aimed to strengthen workplace equality law in a number of areas. It, *inter alia*:

- extends the circumstances in which a person is protected against discrimination, harassment or victimisation because of a protected characteristic;
- extended the circumstances in which a person is protected against discrimination by allowing people to make a claim if they are directly discriminated against because of a combination of two relevant protected characteristics (the Coalition Government has seen fit not to bring the provision into force);
- allows an employer to take 'positive action' to appoint someone from an under-represented group where there are two equally qualified candidates;
- enables an employment tribunal to make a recommendation to a respondent who has lost a discrimination claim to take certain steps to remedy matters not just for the benefit of the individual claimant (who may have already left the organisation concerned) but also the wider workforce.

EQUALITY ACT 2010

PART 2
EQUALITY: KEY CONCEPTS
CHAPTER 1
PROTECTED CHARACTERISTICS

4 The protected characteristics

The following characteristics are protected characteristics—
  age;
  disability;
  gender reassignment;
  marriage and civil partnership;
  pregnancy and maternity;
  race;
  religion or belief;
  sex;
  sexual orientation.

While this chapter and the following chapter concentrate on discrimination in employment, it should be noted that the EqA 2010 and its predecessor statutes are much wider in scope, covering discrimination in education; housing; the provision of goods, facilities, and services, etc.

As a result of the EqA 2006, the Commission for Equality and Human Rights (CEHR) came into operation in October 2007 (see <http://www.equalityhumanrights.com>). The CEHR is a single commission which takes over the work of the Equal Opportunities Commission (EOC), Commission for Racial Equality (CRE) and Disability Rights Commission (DRC). There was extensive equalities review chaired by Trevor Phillips, the then Head of the CEHR. *Fairness and Freedom: The final report of the Equalities Review* was published on 28 February 2007 and called for simplified legislation, a relaxation of the law on positive discrimination, greater use of procurement within the public sector as a means of achieving equality and the expansion of the public sector duties (see *Fairness and Freedom: The final report of the Equalities Review*, <http://communities.gov.uk/publications/corporate/fairnessfreedom>). The EqA 2010 seeks to implement these proposals.

The Commission for Equality and Human Rights: Vision & Mission

Our Mission

- The Commission for Equality and Human Rights will be the independent advocate for equality and human rights in Britain. The CEHR aims to reduce inequality, eliminate discrimination, strengthen good relations between people, and promote and protect human rights.
- The CEHR will challenge prejudice and disadvantage, and promote the importance of human rights.
- The CEHR will be a statutory body established under the Equality Act 2006.
- It will enforce quality legislation on age, disability and health, gender, race; religion or belief, sexual orientation or transgender status, and encourage compliance with the Human Rights Act 1998.
- The CEHR will work to bring about effective change, using its influence and authority to ensure that equality and human rights remain at the top of agendas for government, employers and society. It will campaign for social change and justice.
- The CEHR will act directly and by fostering partnerships at local, regional and national levels. It will stimulate debate on equality and human rights.
- It will give advice and guidance, including to businesses, to voluntary and public sectors, and also to individuals.

> • The CEHR will develop an evidence-based understanding of the causes and effects of inequality for people
> across Britain, and will be an authoritative voice for reform.
> [Source: <http://www.cehr.org.uk>]

A: The Human Rights Act 1998

It was thought that the Human Rights Act (HRA) 1998 would have a significant impact
on employment law and in particular on those areas of discrimination which were
either not protected or were inadequately protected. For example, the right to have
respect for one's private life (Article 8) is likely to encompass sexual orientation, sexual activity, dress codes, and family life—such as working hours. Article 9 embodies
the right to religious and political freedom. However, Article 14 does not provide a
freestanding right not to be discriminated against. It prohibits discrimination solely
in relation to the 'enjoyment' of the substantive Convention rights. As we shall see
in Chapter 6, there has been some consideration of the right not to be discriminated
against on grounds of sexual orientation in the light of the HRA 1998. The HRA has
not necessarily made a significant impact in the field of employment law, and to some
extent has been overtaken by the expansion of discrimination law to cover religion
or belief—see *Azmi* v *Kirklees Metropolitan Borough Council* [2007] IRLR 484. One possible drawback has been the way in which individuals are able to enforce the Human
Rights Act. Section 6 of the Act imposes a duty on public authorities to ensure that
their actions are compatible with Convention rights. This allows employees of such
authorities to enforce their rights directly against their employers. However, someone
employed by a private employer is not able to take such action. They therefore have to
rely on the general duty of the courts to interpret all legislation consistently with the
Convention so far as possible (s. 3). As a result, private sector employees have to rely on
indirect protection resulting from case law and statutory interpretation.

Article 14 Prohibition of Discrimination

The enjoyment of the rights and freedoms set forth in this Convention shall be secured without discrimination
on any ground such as sex, race, colour, language, religion, political or other opinion, national or social origin,
association with a national minority, property, birth or other status.

NOTE: For further reading, see 'Human rights in employment' in Honeyball, S., *Honeyball & Bowers'*
Textbook on Employment Law, 13th edn (Oxford: OUP, 2014), Ch. 16.

B: Stereotyping

Stereotyping of people by sex, race, and disability is one of the principal causes of discrimination, although clearly there are other factors which play a part, such as ignorance and self-interest. A study of the impact of gender and the family in the recruitment
process was undertaken by M. Curran in *Stereotypes and Selection* (EOC, 1985). While the
research was confined to clerical and retail posts, it revealed inherent discrimination in
the selection process, from advertisements to selection criteria, based on explicit gender preferences; many employers believed they had a legitimate right to base selection
for employment on gender and take into account family commitments. The research
also highlighted the fact that discrimination founded in stereotyping is not necessarily
against women but can work against men. Nevertheless, it should be recognised that the
stereotyping of women has far-reaching consequences, in that it can lead to job segregation, which in turn may prevent women obtaining equality in respect of their terms and
conditions of employment due to a lack of comparator.

M. Curran, *Stereotypes and Selection*

(London: HMSO, 1985), pp. 51, 52

Direct sex discrimination in recruitment is not confined to preferences for appointing a woman, or for appointing a man, and the survey also revealed substantial, *prima facie* unlawful, direct sex discrimination in employers' considerations of the family commitments of job applicants. Almost three-quarters of the employers in the survey said that they preferred not to employ the mothers of young children, but did not express any preference about the parental status of male job applicants. If these preferences were reflected in the actual selection decisions made by employers (and all the evidence suggests that they were), they would constitute unlawful direct sex discrimination since mothers were, on grounds of sex, treated less favourably than fathers.

The survey thus revealed a widespread intention, on the part of employers, to adopt selection criteria which would result in prima facie unlawful direct discrimination. In addition there was considerable potential for unlawful indirect discrimination in the adoption of arbitrary age requirements and the use of internal and informal methods of recruitment, which might inhibit applications from members of one sex. More generally, employers gave considerable emphasis to subjective factors such as 'personality', manner and appearance, assessments of which are both susceptible to gender stereotyping and sufficiently indeterminate to obscure the operation of more direct discrimination.

Most of the vacancies (86 per cent) yielded applications from women and from men and employers rarely made reference to gender as a factor in shortlisting applicants for interview, or in their selection decisions. However, these decision processes resulted in almost half of the employers interviewing one gender only, and in a clear tendency to select an employee of the 'preferred' or customary gender. The jobs which offered better pay and prospects tended to be offered to men. Family commitments were also rarely mentioned as shortlisting or selection criteria, but only one of the 82 women appointed to the jobs in the survey was known by her employer to have a child under school age.

In general there was a widespread acceptance, among the recruitment decision makers who participated in the survey, that gender and family commitments were attributes of job applicants on which it was legitimate for them to 'take a view'. This acceptance was reinforced by the routine collection of personal information on the application forms used by their own and other organisations. Although some employers clearly took account of the personal circumstances of individual job applicants, most interpreted information about applicants' gender, marital status and parenthood in terms of their generalised 'commonsense' stereotypes of male and female roles in society. The precedents in the Industrial Tribunal cases cited in this report suggest that interview questions and selection decisions based on these stereotypes are likely to constitute unlawful direct sex discrimination.

The picture of the recruitment process which emerges from the survey is one of complex, implicit and often subjective criteria being weighed in the balance by an employer who is often 'spoilt for choice'. In this context it is difficult for an 'outsider', be they researcher, job applicant or Industrial Tribunal, to identify the ultimate rationale for a particular selection decision.

In the recruitment exercises studied in the survey it seems unlikely that *any* of the job applicants would be aware of the preferences regarding gender and family which employers expressed in the survey interviews, since interviewers and recruiters did not feel any need to justify or explain their selection decisions to successful or to unsuccessful applicants. Indeed past tribunal cases suggest that job applicants are unlikely to challenge the actions of employers under the Sex Discrimination Act unless either a clear intention to discriminate has been revealed, or the unsuccessful applicant has some access to information about the person who was selected. Neither of these conditions would apply to the majority of the cases in the survey in which an intention to adopt *prima facie* unlawful discriminatory criteria was revealed. Since the legal remedy for unlawful discrimination in recruitment is dependent on an individual job applicant taking a case to an Industrial Tribunal, the opaque and complex nature of the processes of recruitment and selection thus serves to inhibit any challenge to unlawful direct discrimination. In the case of indirect discrimination these difficulties of enforcement are compounded both by the fact that certain issues, e.g., the discriminatory impact of internal and informal recruitment, have not yet been fully tested in law, and by the imprecise notion of the 'justifiability' of indirectly discriminatory criteria and recruitment practices.

NOTE: The EOC recognised that one way of eradicating stereotyping is through education. See *Sex Stereotyping: From school to work* (EOC, 2001). Practical guidance can be found in *Fair and Efficient Selection* (EOC, 1993), which highlights the following assumptions which may result in discrimination in the recruitment of staff.

Equal Opportunities Commission, *Fair and Efficient Selection*
(London: HMSO, 1993), pp. 2–6

There are two basic attitudes and beliefs which can, and do, influence decision and actions at every one of the steps involved in the recruitment and selection process. These merit consideration at the outset.

1 SEX DIFFERENCES IN ABILITIES, PHYSICAL AND TEMPERAMENTAL CHARACTERISTICS

There are many commonly-held beliefs about sex differences in abilities, physical characteristics and temperament. Some of these, such as alleged differences in intelligence, are not true. There are however some abilities, physical and temperamental characteristics, in which there are differences. But usually these are of little or no importance in selection. The differences which do exist are differences on the average and tell us nothing about individuals. The most obvious example is perhaps height. It is true that the average height of men is greater than the average height of women. But the range of heights of women and of men is far greater than the difference between the two averages. The ranges therefore overlap greatly. The fact is that there are a lot of women who are taller than many men. In making a selection decision for any job for which there is a justifiable minimum height, it would therefore be wrong to exclude all women. The only fair and efficient procedure is to assess each candidate, man or woman, as an individual and not to make any generalised assumptions. This particularly applies in respect of physical or mental abilities. It may well be true that one sex is better than the other on average in, say, verbal, mathematical or spatial ability. This may change with time but even now does not, and should not, mean that we exclude one sex entirely from consideration. To do so would amount to a breach of the Sex Discrimination Act.

To achieve fair assessment, selectors should forget all that they have ever believed or been told about sex differences in abilities, etc. and try to make assessments, as objectively as possible, about each person. The main exceptions arise when we select for one of the few jobs which fall within the Sex Discrimination Act's definition of a 'genuine occupational qualification'…

A special word is necessary regarding sex differences in temperamental characteristics because this is an area which is richest in generalisations, inaccuracies and myths. Research has revealed some differences, for example that men tend to be more aggressive than women. But this again is a difference between averages and tells us nothing about any individual. As can easily be observed, there are some women who are high up the scale for aggressiveness and some men near the bottom end. So general assumptions about men or women should not cause selectors to prejudge any individual because 'men are like this' or 'women are like that'.

This kind of generalisation (often called 'stereotyping') is not easy to overcome and anyone carrying out selection needs consciously to be aware of the danger and resist it at all times. This effort will not easily succeed because of the widespread, pervasive and continuous expression of uninformed and exaggerated beliefs, in everyday life, in the media and in literature. But the methods suggested below, for systematic selection procedures, should do much to help selectors avoid 'stereotyping'.

2 'MEN'S WORK' AND 'WOMEN'S WORK'

It is common to hear jobs referred to as 'men's work' or 'women's work'. Such distinctions are no more than acceptance of the existing conventions which are based upon nothing more than the customs of a bygone age. Women now do work which would have been regarded as utterly unsuitable for them before the first world war. No-one then would have accepted that women could do many of the jobs they are now doing, such as bus-driving or welding. Nor would they have accepted that men could be nurses and midwives, as they now are.

The convention that only women should use typewriters has no foundation in genuine sex differences in the abilities required. The irrational nature of the convention is shown by the fact that it is acceptable for journalists and authors to type. And it has been accepted for many years that men can operate keyboards (and be highly paid for it) provided they are setting type rather than typing on paper.

One other perspective in this matter comes from comparisons with other countries. In some eastern European countries women have, for many years, done engineering and other work which, with few exceptions, is regarded here as unusual for women. And there is no reason to believe that the physical and psychological characteristics of women in these other countries differ from those of women here.

In general, then, there is little or no rationale behind the idea of 'men's work' and 'women's work'. Whenever recruiting or promoting into any job which has in the past been done only by men or only by women, the selector should stop and question why this has been so and whether there are any rational reasons for it. Further he/she should question whether the existing practice is even lawful under the Sex Discrimination Act. Unless the previous single-sex recruitment proves to be both rational and lawful, it should cease.

There will quite often be difficulties to be overcome. There may, for example, be effects upon the wage structure and differentials, especially where only women have been employed on wages less than those paid to men for work of equal value—a situation which is still common but which should be changed as a result of the amendment to the Equal Pay Act introduced on January 1st 1984.

There may be industrial relations difficulties, but these should not be exaggerated. Most unions now have definite policies on securing equal opportunities for their members. In any case, such difficulties should not, and indeed must not, be allowed to prevent the ending of unfair, inefficient and unlawful practices.

A further difficulty may arise from the attitudes of women themselves. As both recent research and experience have shown, there are situations in which some women are unwilling to undertake jobs previously done only by men. The reasons can be complex. If, however, employers act in ways which are sensitive to the feelings of those concerned, but are nevertheless firm in their policies, the hesitation can be overcome. Usually, one or two individuals will be prepared to 'have a go', demonstrate that the fears were unjustified and so encourage movement towards a fairer and more efficient selection or promotion procedure.

Finally, it should not be assumed that people working part-time will be uninterested in full-time vacancies. Failure to consider part-timers (who are likely to be women) for full-time jobs may give rise to unlawful sex and/ or marriage discrimination. Conversely, it should not be assumed that no men will be interested in obtaining part-time work.

NOTES

1. The codes of practice are an effective way of promoting equality and eliminating discrimination, and are reviewed and updated as the legislation is amended: e.g. the CRE introduced a new Code of Practice on Racial Equality in April 2006. The alternatives include closing loopholes in the existing legislation, giving greater powers to the Commissions, increased penalties and such things as quotas, positive discrimination (see McCrudden, C., 'Rethinking positive action' (1986) 15 ILJ 219). Some concession to this may be found in Article 141(4) (ex 119, see Chapter 3) following the amendment of Article 119 by the Treaty of Amsterdam, which recognises that Member States may adopt measures provided for specific advantages in order to make it easier for the under-represented sex to pursue a vocational activity, or to prevent or compensate for disadvantages in professional careers. As we shall see, the Racial Equality Directive (2000/43) recognises that positive action may be a legitimate means of achieving equality.

2. It should be noted that Article 13 of the Amsterdam Treaty (OJ 2000 L303/16) extends anti-discrimination provisions to racial or ethnic origin, religion or belief, disability, age, and sexual orientation. It also prohibits both direct and indirect discrimination, and specifically recognises hypothetical comparisons in respect of direct discrimination. Member States will be subject to a series of deadlines by which each aspect must be legislated for.

3. See Ewing, K. D., 'The Human Rights Act and labour law' (1998) 27 ILJ 275.

4. The EqA 2006 created a 'gender duty' on public authorities which requires them to have due regard to the need to eliminate unlawful discrimination and to promote equality of opportunity between men and women—s. 76A of the SDA 1975 (see also the RRA 1976 and DDA 1995, s. 49A, which impose a similar public duty in these areas). The EqA 2010, s. 148 replaces this duty with a more expansive 'public sector equality duty' on the public bodies listed in Sch. 19 to the Act to have due regard to three specified matters when exercising their functions. The three matters are:
   - eliminating conduct that is prohibited by the Act, including breaches of non-discrimination rules in occupational pension schemes and equality clauses or rules which are read, respectively, into a person's terms of work and into occupational pension schemes;
   - advancing equality of opportunity between people who share a protected characteristic and people who do not share it;
   - fostering good relations between people who share a protected characteristic and people who do not share it.

The second and third matters apply to the protected characteristics of age, disability, gender reassignment, pregnancy and maternity, race, religion or belief, sex, and sexual orientation. They do not apply to the protected characteristic of marriage and civil partnership.

The section makes clear that complying with the duty might mean treating some people more favourably than others, where doing so is allowed by the Act. This includes treating disabled people more favourably than non-disabled people and making reasonable adjustments for them, making use of exceptions which permit different treatment, and using the positive action provisions in Chapter 2 of Pt 11 of the Act where they are available.

Section 148 replaces s. 71 of the RRA 1976, s. 49A of the DDA 1995, and s. 76A of the SDA 1975. These provisions impose similar public sector equality duties in relation to race, disability, and gender (including pregnancy and maternity as an implicit part of gender, and partly covering gender reassignment) respectively. There are no equivalent public sector equality duties for age, religion or belief, or sexual orientation in current legislation. The section extends the new public sector equality duty to cover gender reassignment in full, age, religion or belief, and sexual orientation.

SECTION 2: EUROPEAN COMMUNITY LAW

European Community law provides a range of anti-discrimination measures through Directive 2006/54 (previously Directive 76/207—the Equal Treatment Directive), which can be enforced directly in the UK national courts against the State or an organ of the State but not against a private employer and the Race Discrimination Directive (2000/43) which had to be implemented by Member States by July 2003. As can be seen, the Race Directive makes unlawful both direct and indirect discrimination on grounds of racial or ethnic origin. It also specifically recognises racial harassment as a distinct type of discrimination (Article 2(3)). Whilst it covers all aspects of employment, it also permits genuine occupational requirements as long as they are founded on legitimate objectives and are proportional (Article 4). Positive discrimination is also permissible (Article 5). (See Guild, E., 'EC Directive on Race Discrimination: Surprises, possibilities and limitations' (2000) 30 ILJ 416.).

It should be noted that EC law has generally extended anti-discrimination rights to 'workers' rather than employees. The term 'worker' includes not only employees but also independent contractors who personally undertake work (see *Edmunds* v *Lawson* [2000] IRLR 391). Directive 76/207/EC has been recast and replaced by Directive 2006/54. The effect of this directive is not to change the principles but to update and consolidate existing directives relating to equal opportunities and equal treatment of men and women. Pre-existing directives were repealed in 2009, with Member States expected to ensure compliance by August 2008.

DIRECTIVE 2006/54

TITLE I GENERAL PROVISIONS

Article 1   Purpose

The purpose of this Directive is to ensure the implementation of the principle of equal opportunities and equal treatment of men and women in matters of employment and occupation.

To that end, it contains provisions to implement the principle of equal treatment in relation to:

(a) access to employment, including promotion, and to vocational training;

(b) working conditions, including pay;

(c) occupational social security schemes.

It also contains provisions to ensure that such implementation is made more effective by the establishment of appropriate procedures.

Article 2   Definitions

1. For the purposes of this Directive, the following definitions shall apply:

(a) 'direct discrimination': where one person is treated less favourably on grounds of sex than another is, has been or would be treated in a comparable situation;

(b) 'indirect discrimination': where an apparently neutral provision, criterion or practice would put persons of one sex at a particular disadvantage compared with persons of the other sex, unless that provision, criterion or practice is objectively justified by a legitimate aim, and the means of achieving that aim are appropriate and necessary;

(c) 'harassment': where unwanted conduct related to the sex of a person occurs with the purpose or effect of violating the dignity of a person, and of creating an intimidating, hostile, degrading, humiliating or offensive environment;

(d) 'sexual harassment': where any form of unwanted verbal, non-verbal or physical conduct of a sexual nature occurs, with the purpose or effect of violating the dignity of a person, in particular when creating an intimidating, hostile, degrading, humiliating or offensive environment;

(e) 'pay': the ordinary basic or minimum wage or salary and any other consideration, whether in cash or in kind, which the worker receives directly or indirectly, in respect of his/her employment from his/her employer;

(f) 'occupational social security schemes': schemes not governed by Council Directive 79/7/EEC of 19 December 1978 on the progressive implementation of the principle of equal treatment for men and women in matters of social security whose purpose is to provide workers, whether employees or self-employed, in an undertaking or group of undertakings, area of economic activity, occupational sector or group of sectors with benefits intended to supplement the benefits provided by statutory social security schemes or to replace them, whether membership of such schemes is compulsory or optional.

2. For the purposes of this Directive, discrimination includes:

(a) harassment and sexual harassment, as well as any less favourable treatment based on a person's rejection of or submission to such conduct;

(b) instruction to discriminate against persons on grounds of sex;

(c) any less favourable treatment of a woman related to pregnancy or maternity leave within the meaning of Directive 92/85/EEC.

Article 3 Positive action

Member States may maintain or adopt measures within the meaning of Article 14(4) of the Treaty with a view to ensuring full equality in practice between men and women in working life.

CHAPTER 3

Equal treatment as regards access to employment, vocational training and promotion and working conditions

Article 14   Prohibition of discrimination

1. There shall be no direct or indirect discrimination on grounds of sex in the public or private sectors, including public bodies, in relation to:

(a) conditions for access to employment, to self-employment or to occupation, including selection criteria and recruitment conditions, whatever the branch of activity and at all levels of the professional hierarchy, including promotion;

(b) access to all types and to all levels of vocational guidance, vocational training, advanced vocational training and retraining, including practical work experience;

(c) employment and working conditions, including dismissals, as well as pay as provided for in Article 141 of the Treaty;

(d) membership of, and involvement in, an organisation of workers or employers, or any organisation whose members carry on a particular profession, including the benefits provided for by such organisations.

2. Member States may provide, as regards access to employment including the training leading thereto, that a difference of treatment which is based on a characteristic related to sex shall not constitute discrimination where, by reason of the nature of the particular occupational activities concerned or of the context in which they are carried out, such a characteristic constitutes a genuine and determining occupational requirement, provided that its objective is legitimate and the requirement is proportionate.

Article 15   Return from maternity leave

A woman on maternity leave shall be entitled, after the end of her period of maternity leave, to return to her job or to an equivalent post on terms and conditions which are no less favourable to her and to benefit from any improvement in working conditions to which she would have been entitled during her absence.

Article 16   Paternity and adoption leave

This Directive is without prejudice to the right of Member States to recognise distinct rights to paternity and/or adoption leave. Those Member States which recognise such rights shall take the necessary measures to protect working men and women against dismissal due to exercising those rights and ensure that, at the end of such leave, they are entitled to return to their jobs or to equivalent posts on terms and conditions which are no less favourable to them, and to benefit from any improvement in working conditions to which they would have been entitled during their absence.

RACIAL EQUALITY DIRECTIVE (DIRECTIVE 2000/43)

GENERAL PROVISIONS

Article 1   Purpose

The purpose of this Directive is to lay down a framework for combating discrimination on the grounds of racial or ethnic origin, with a view to putting into effect in the member states the principle of equal treatment.

Article 2   Concept of discrimination

1. For the purposes of this Directive, the principle of equal treatment shall mean that there shall be no direct or indirect discrimination based on racial or ethnic origin.

2. For the purposes of paragraph 1:
    (a) direct discrimination shall be taken to occur where one person is treated less favourably than another is, has been or would be treated in a comparable situation on grounds of racial or ethnic origin;
    (b) indirect discrimination shall be taken to occur where an apparently neutral provision, criterion or practice would put persons of a racial or ethnic origin at a particular disadvantage compared with other persons, unless that provision, criterion or practice is objectively justified by a legitimate aim and the means of achieving that aim are appropriate and necessary.

3. Harassment shall be deemed to be discrimination within the meaning of paragraph 1, when an unwanted conduct related to racial or ethnic origin takes place with the purpose or effect of violating the dignity of a person and of creating an intimidating, hostile, degrading, humiliating or offensive environment. In this context, the concept of harassment may be defined in accordance with the national laws and practice of the member states.

4. An instruction to discriminate against persons on grounds of racial or ethnic origin shall be deemed to be discrimination within the meaning of paragraph 1.

Article 3   Scope

1. Within the limits of the powers conferred upon the Community, this Directive shall apply to all persons, as regards both the public and private sectors, including public bodies, in relation to:
    (a) conditions for access to employment, to self-employment and to occupation, including selection criteria and recruitment conditions, whatever the branch of activity and at all levels of the professional hierarchy, including promotion;
    (b) access to all types and to all levels of vocational guidance, vocational training, advanced vocational training and retraining, including practical work experience;
    (c) employment and working conditions, including dismissals and pay;
    (d) membership of and involvement in an organisation of workers or employers, or any organisation whose members carry on a particular profession, including the benefits provided for by such organisations;
    (e) social protection, including social security and healthcare;
    (f) social advantages;
    (g) education;
    (h) access to and supply of goods and services which are available to the public, including housing.

2. This Directive does not cover difference of treatment based on nationality and is without prejudice to provisions and conditions relating to the entry into and residence of third-country nationals and stateless persons on the territory of member states, and to any treatment which arises from the legal status of the third-country nationals and stateless persons concerned.

Article 4   Genuine and determining occupational requirements

Notwithstanding Article 2(1) and (2), member states may provide that a difference of treatment which is based on a characteristic related to racial or ethnic origin shall not constitute discrimination where, by reason of the nature of the particular occupational activities concerned or of the context in which they are carried out, such a characteristic constitutes a genuine and determining occupational requirement, provided that the objective is legitimate and the requirement is proportionate.

Article 5   Positive action

With a view to ensuring full equality in practice, the principle of equal treatment shall not prevent any member state from maintaining or adopting specific measures to prevent or compensate for disadvantages linked to racial or ethnic origin.

Marshall v Southampton and South-West Hampshire Area Health Authority (Teaching)
[1986] IRLR 140, European Court of Justice

The retirement policy of the respondent health authority was that 'the normal retirement age will be the age at which social security pensions become payable', i.e. 60 for women and 65 for men. In certain circumstances retirement at the State pension age could be postponed by mutual agreement. Accordingly, Miss Marshall continued to work after 60 years of age. When she was dismissed at 62, the sole reason given for her dismissal was that she had passed the normal retirement age applied by the respondents to women. She would not have been dismissed when she was if she had been a man.

Miss Marshall complained to an industrial tribunal that her dismissal amounted to unlawful discrimination contrary to the SDA and the EEC Equal Treatment Directive. The tribunal dismissed her complaint under the SDA on the ground that the case fell within s. 6(4) which permits discrimination on the ground of sex arising from a provision in relation to retirement. Her claim under Community law was upheld. On appeal, however, the Employment Appeal Tribunal (EAT) held that although Miss Marshall's dismissal violated the principle of equal treatment laid down in EEC Directive 76/207, such violation could not be relied upon in proceedings before a UK court or tribunal ([1983] IRLR 237).

Miss Marshall appealed to the Court of Appeal which applied to the European Court of Justice (ECJ) for a ruling on the following questions:

1. whether the respondents' dismissal of the appellant, after she had passed her 60th birthday pursuant to their retirement age policy and on the ground only that she was a woman who had passed the normal retiring age applicable to women, was an act of discrimination prohibited by Directive 76/207;

2. If the answer to (1) above is in the affirmative, whether or not Directive 76/207 can be relied upon by the appellant in the circumstances of the present case in national courts or tribunals, notwithstanding the inconsistency (if any) between the directive and s. 6(4) of the SDA 1975.

The ECJ held that the dismissal of a woman solely because she has attained the State pension age, which is different for men and women, contravenes Article 5(1) of Directive 76/207. This matter did not fall within the exclusion provided by Article 7(1) of Directive 79/7—the Social Security Directive—which applies only to the determination of pensionable age for the purposes of granting old-age and retirement pensions. Article 5(1) may be relied upon against a State authority as employer in order to avoid the application of any national provision which does not conform with that Article.

DECISION: ...By the first question the Court of Appeal seeks to ascertain whether or not Article 5(1) of Directive no. 76/207 must be interpreted as meaning that a general policy concerning dismissal, followed by a State authority, involving the dismissal of a woman solely because she has attained or passed the qualifying age for a State pension, which age is different under national legislation for men and for women, constitutes discrimination on grounds of sex, contrary to that directive.

The appellant and the Commission consider that the first question must be answered in the affirmative.

According to the appellant, the said age limit falls within the term 'working conditions' within the meaning of Articles 1(1) and 5(1) of Directive no. 76/207. A wide interpretation of that term is, in her opinion, justified in view of the objective of the EEC Treaty to provide for 'the constant improving of the living and working conditions of [the Member States'] peoples' and in view of the wording of the prohibition of discrimination laid down in the above-mentioned articles of Directive no. 76/206 and in Article 7(1) of Regulation no. 1612/68 of the Council of 15.10.68 on freedom of movement of workers within the Community (Official Journal, English Special Edition 1968 (II), p. 475).

The appellant argues furthermore, that the elimination of discrimination on grounds of sex forms part of the corpus of fundamental human rights and therefore of the general principles of Community law. In accordance with the case law of the European Court of Human Rights, those fundamental principles must be given a wide interpretation and, conversely, any exception thereto, such as the reservation provided for in Article 1(2) of Directive no. 76/207 with regard to social security, must be interpreted strictly.

In addition, the appellant considers that the exception provided for in Article 7(1) of Directive no. 79/7 with regard to the determination of pensionable age for the purposes of granting old-age and retirement pensions, is not relevant since, unlike Case 19/81 (*Burton* v *British Railways Board* [1982] IRLR 116), this case does not relate to the determination of pensionable age. Moreover, in this case there is no link between the contractual retirement age and the qualifying age for a social security pension.

The Commission emphasises that neither the respondent's employment policy nor the State social security scheme makes retirement compulsory upon a person's reaching pensionable age. On the contrary, the provisions of national legislation take into account the case of continued employment beyond the normal pensionable age. In those circumstances, it would be difficult to justify the dismissal of a woman for reasons based on her sex and age.

The Commission also refers to the fact that the Court has recognised that equality of treatment for men and women constitutes a fundamental principle of Community law.

The respondent maintains, in contrast, that account must be taken, in accordance with the *Burton* case, of the link which it claims exists between the retirement ages imposed by it in the context of its dismissal policy, on the one hand, and the ages at which retirement and old-age pensions become payable under the State social security scheme in the United Kingdom, on the other. The laying down of different ages for the compulsory termination of a contract of employment merely reflects the minimum ages fixed by that scheme, since a male employee is permitted to continue in employment until the age of 65 precisely because he is not protected by the provision of a State pension before that age, whereas a female employee benefits from such protection from the age of 60.

The respondent considers that the provision of a State pension constitutes an aspect of social security and therefore falls within the scope not of Directive no. 76/207 but of Directive no. 79/7, which reserves to the Member States the right to impose different ages for the purpose of determining entitlement to State pensions. Since the situation is therefore the same as that in the *Burton* case, the fixing by the contract of employment of different retirement ages linked to the different minimum pensionable ages for men and women under national legislation does not constitute unlawful discrimination contrary to Community law.

The United Kingdom, which also takes that view, maintains, however, that treatment is capable of being discriminatory even in respect of a period after retirement in so far as the treatment in question arises out of employment or employment continues after the normal contractual retirement age.

The United Kingdom maintains, however, that in the circumstances of this case there is no discrimination in working conditions since the difference of treatment derives from the normal retirement age, which in turn is linked to the different minimum ages at which a State pension is payable.

The Court observes in the first place that the question of interpretation which has been referred to it does not concern access to a statutory or occupational retirement scheme, that is to say the conditions for payment of an old-age or retirement pension, but the fixing of an age limit with regard to the termination of employment pursuant to a general policy concerning dismissal. The question therefore relates to the conditions governing dismissal and falls to be considered under Directive no. 76/207.

Article 5(1) of Directive no. 76/207 provides that application of the principle of equal treatment with regard to working conditions, including the conditions governing dismissal, means that men and women are to be guaranteed the same conditions without discrimination on grounds of sex.

In its judgment in the *Burton* case the Court has already stated that the term 'dismissal' contained in that provision must be given a wide meaning. Consequently, an age limit for the compulsory dismissal of workers pursuant to an employer's general policy concerning retirement falls within the term 'dismissal' construed in that manner, even if the dismissal involves the grant of a retirement pension.

As the Court emphasised in its judgment in the *Burton* case, Article 7 of Directive no. 79/7 expressly provides that the Directive does not prejudice the right of Member States to exclude from its scope the determination of pensionable age for the purposes of granting old-age and retirement pensions and the possible consequences thereof for other benefits falling within the statutory social security schemes. The Court thus acknowledged that benefits tied to a national scheme which lays down a different minimum pensionable age for men and women may lie outside the ambit of the aforementioned obligation.

However, in view of the fundamental importance of the principle of equality of treatment, which the Court has reaffirmed on numerous occasions, Article 1(2) of Directive no. 76/207, which excludes social security matters from the scope of that Directive, must be interpreted strictly. Consequently, the exception to the prohibition of discrimination on grounds of sex provided for in Article 7(1)(a) of Directive no. 79/7 applies only to the determination of pensionable age for the purposes of granting old-age and retirement pensions and the possible consequences thereof for other benefits.

In that respect it must be emphasised that, whereas the exception contained in Article 7 of Directive no. 79/7 concerns the consequences which pensionable age has for social security benefits, this case is concerned with dismissal within the meaning of Article 5 of Directive no. 76/207.

Consequently, the answer to the first question referred to the Court by the Court of Appeal must be that Article 5(1) of Directive no. 76/207 must be interpreted as meaning that a general policy concerning dismissal involving the dismissal of a woman solely because she has attained the qualifying age for a State pension, which age is different under national legislation for men and for women, constitutes discrimination on grounds of sex, contrary to that Directive.

The second question

Since the first question has been answered in the affirmative, it is necessary to consider whether Article 5(1) of Directive no. 76/207 may be relied upon by an individual before national courts and tribunals.

The appellant and the Commission consider that that question must be answered in the affirmative. They contend in particular, with regard to Articles 2(1) and 5(1) of Directive no. 76/207, that those provisions are sufficiently clear to enable national courts to apply them without legislative intervention by the Member States, at least so far as overt discrimination is concerned.

In support of that view, the appellant points out that directives are capable of conferring rights on individuals which may be relied upon directly before the courts of the Member States; national courts are obliged by virtue of the binding nature of a directive, in conjunction with Article 5 [now 10] of the EEC Treaty, to give effect to the provisions of directives where possible, in particular when construing or applying relevant provisions of national law (judgment of 10.4.84 in Case 14/83, *Von Colson and Kamann* v *Land Nordrhein-Westfalen* [1984] ECR 1891). Where there is any inconsistency between national law and Community law which cannot be removed by means of such a construction, the appellant submits that a national court is obliged to declare that the provision of national law which is inconsistent with the directive is inapplicable.

The Commission is of the opinion that the provisions of Article 5(1) of Directive no. 76/207 are sufficiently clear and unconditional to be relied upon before a national court. They may therefore be set up against s. 6(4) of the Sex Discrimination Act, which, according to the decisions of the Court of Appeal, has been extended to the question of compulsory retirement and has therefore become ineffective to prevent dismissals based upon the difference in retirement ages for men and for women.

The respondent and the United Kingdom propose, conversely, that the second question should be answered in the negative. They admit that a directive may, in certain specific circumstances, have direct effect as against a Member State in so far as the latter may not rely on its failure to perform its obligations under the directive. However, they maintain that a directive can never impose obligations directly on individuals and that it can only have direct effect against a Member State *qua* public authority and not against a Member State *qua* employer. As an employer a State is no different from a private employer. It would not therefore be proper to put persons employed by the State in a better position than those who are employed by a private employer.

With regard to the legal position of the respondent's employees the United Kingdom states that they are in the same position as the employees of a private employer. Although according to United Kingdom constitutional law the health authorities, created by the National Health Service Act 1977, as amended by the Health Services Act 1980 and other legislation, are Crown bodies and their employees are Crown servants, nevertheless the administration of the National Health Service by the health authorities is regarded as being separate from the Government's central administration and its employees are not regarded as civil servants.

Finally, both the respondent and the United Kingdom take the view that the provisions of Directive no. 76/207 are neither unconditional nor sufficiently clear and precise to give rise to direct effect. The Directive provides for a number of possible exceptions, the details of which are to be laid down by the Member States. Furthermore, the wording of Article 5 is quite imprecise and requires the adoption of measures for its implementation.

It is necessary to recall that, according to a long line of decisions of the Court (in particular its judgment of 19.1.82 in Case 8/81, *Becker* v *Finanzamt Münster-Innenstadt* [1982] ECR 53), wherever the provisions of a directive appear, as far as their subject-matter is concerned, to be unconditional and sufficiently precise, those provisions may be relied upon by an individual against the State where that State fails to implement the Directive in national law by the end of the period prescribed or where it fails to implement the Directive correctly.

That view is based on the consideration that it would be incompatible with the binding nature which Article 189 [now 249] confers on the Directive to hold as a matter of principle that the obligation imposed thereby cannot be relied on by those concerned. From that the Court deduced that a Member State which has not adopted the implementing measures required by the Directive within the prescribed period may not plead, as against individuals, its own failure to perform the obligations which the Directive entails.

With regard to the argument that a directive may not be relied upon against an individual, it must be emphasised that according to Article 189 [now 249] of the EEC Treaty the binding nature of a directive, which constitutes the basis for the possibility of relying on the directive before a national court, exists only in relation to 'each Member State to which it is addressed'. It follows that a directive may not of itself impose obligations on an individual and that a provision of a directive may not be relied upon as such against such a person. It must therefore be examined whether, in this case, the respondent must be regarded as having acted as an individual.

In that respect it must be pointed out that where a person involved in legal proceedings is able to rely on a directive as against the State he may do so regardless of the capacity in which the latter is acting, whether employer or public authority. In either case it is necessary to prevent the State from taking advantage of its own failure to comply with Community law.

It is for the national court to apply those considerations to the circumstances of each case; the Court of Appeal has, however, stated in the order for reference that the respondent, Southampton and South-West Hampshire Area Health Authority (Teaching), is a public authority.

The argument submitted by the United Kingdom that the possibility of relying on provisions of the Directive against the respondent *qua* organ of the State would give rise to an arbitrary and unfair distinction between the rights of State employees and those of private employees does not justify any other conclusion. Such a distinction may easily be avoided if the Member State concerned has correctly implemented the Directive in national law.

Finally, with regard to the question whether the provision contained in Article 5(1) of Directive no. 76/207, which implements the principle of equality of treatment set out in Article 2(1) of the Directive, may be considered, as far as its contents are concerned, to be unconditional and sufficiently precise to be relied upon by an individual as against the State, it must be stated that the provision, taken by itself, prohibits any discrimination on grounds of sex with regard to working conditions, including the conditions governing dismissal, in a general manner and in unequivocal terms. The provision is therefore sufficiently precise to be relied on by an individual and to be applied by the national courts.

NOTES

1. The revised Equal Treatment Directive (2002/73) aligned the equal treatment provisions with the Race Directive (2000/43). This resulted in the Employment Equality (Sex Discrimination) Regulations (SI 2005/2467); changes included a new definition of direct discrimination, sexual harassment, and indirect discrimination; revised genuine occupational qualifications; explicit rights regarding pregnancy; promotion of equal treatment; and extension of the current legislation to pay discrimination. These are also reflected in the recast Directive 2006/54.

2. It is now firmly established that national law should be interpreted in accordance with the directives. Failure to do so may result in a challenge such as *Marshall*'s. The decision in *Marshall*'s case led to the SDA 1986, which made unlawful discrimination in retirement ages for all employees.

3. The issue of whether an employer is an organ or emanation of the State, thereby allowing an action based on Directive 76/207, was raised in *Doughty* v *Rolls Royce plc* [1992] IRLR 126 and *Foster* v *British Gas plc* [1990] IRLR 354. In the former the Court of Appeal held that Rolls Royce was not an 'organ or emanation of the State' as there was a lack of sufficient State control. In the latter, being a reference by the House of Lords, the ECJ attempted to give meaning to the words 'organ or emanation of the State' as follows:

   Unconditional and sufficiently precise provisions of a Directive can be relied on against an organisation, whatever its legal form, which is subject to the authority or control of the State or which has been made responsible, pursuant to a measure adopted by the State, for providing a public service under the control of the State and has for that purpose special powers beyond those which result from the normal rules applicable between individuals.

   The House of Lords, in applying this principle, concluded that British Gas was an organ or emanation of the State (see *Foster* v *British Gas* [1991] IRLR 268).

4. The SDA 1986 also put into effect the decision in *Commission of the European Communities* v *United Kingdom* [1984] ICR 192, in which the ECJ concluded that the SDA 1975 did not comply with Directive 76/207 as it specifically exempted small businesses and partnerships from the provisions of the Act, nor did it have within its remit non-contractual collective agreements and practices (ss. 1 and 6).

5. The relationship between EC law and domestic law has been reaffirmed in *Blaik* v *The Post Office* [1994] IRLR 280 in which the EAT held that 'if there is sufficient remedy given by domestic law, it is unnecessary and impermissible to explore the same complaint under the equivalent provisions in a Directive. It is only if there is a disparity between the two that it becomes necessary to consider whether the provisions in EC law are directly enforceable by the complainant...'

6. The overlap between the interpretation of the Equal Pay Directive (75/117) and the Equal Treatment Directive (76/207) can be seen in *Jorgensen* v *Foreningen Af Speciallaeger & Sygesikringens Fochandlingsudvalg* [2000] IRLR 726. In this case the ECJ was asked to determine whether a

collective agreement indirectly discriminated on grounds of sex contrary to Directive 76/207. The ECJ concluded that it was necessary to make a separate assessment of each of the key conditions as this was in line with the requirements when determining discriminatory pay structures under the Equal Pay Directive (75/117). The ECJ went on to conclude that:

> budgetary considerations cannot, in themselves, justify discrimination on grounds of sex. To permit this would allow member states to vary its applications and implementation of equal treatment provisions depending on the state of the public purse.

The decision in *Lommers* v *Minister Van Landbouw, Natuurbeheer en Visserij* [2002] IRLR 430 and *Steinicke* v *Bundesanstalt Fur Arbeit* [2003] IRLR 892 make it clear that where working conditions, such as the provision of nursery places, have pecuniary consequences for the worker, it is a matter for consideration under Directive 76/207 rather than Article 141.

7. In *Coote* v *Granada Hospitality Ltd* [1998] IRLR 656 the ECJ makes it clear that the Equal Treatment Directive requires Member States to provide protection from victimisation for those who make a complaint of discrimination, and that the remedies for victimisation must be effective and therefore appropriate to the nature of the complaint.

8. See Usher, J., 'European Community equality law: Legal instruments and judicial remedies' in McCrudden, C. (ed.), *Women Employment and European Equality Law* (London: Eclipse, 1987), at pp. 171–4, for a discussion of the direct effect of directives.

9. For further consideration of the effect of *Marshall* on cases such as *Burton* v *British Railways Board* [1982] QB 1080 and *Roberts* v *Tate and Lyle Industries Ltd* [1986] ICR 371, see Honeyball, S., *Honeyball & Bowers' Textbook on Employment Law*, 13th edn (Oxford: OUP, 2014), Ch. 10.

SECTION 3: POSITIVE DISCRIMINATION

EC TREATY

Article 141(4)

With a view to ensuring full equality in practice between men and women in working life, the principle of equal treatment shall not prevent any member state from maintaining or adopting measures providing for specific advantages in order to make it easier for the under-represented sex to pursue a vocational activity or to prevent or compensate for disadvantages in professional careers.

DIRECTIVE 2006/54

Article 19 Burden of proof

1. Member States shall take such measures as are necessary, in accordance with their national judicial systems, to ensure that, when persons who consider themselves wronged because the principle of equal treatment has not been applied to them establish, before a court or other competent authority, facts from which it may be presumed that there has been direct or indirect discrimination, it shall be for the respondent to prove that there has been no breach of the principle of equal treatment.

2. Paragraph 1 shall not prevent Member States from introducing rules of evidence which are more favourable to plaintiffs.

DIRECTIVE 2000/43

Article 5 Positive action

With a view to ensuring full equality in practice, the principle of equal treatment shall not prevent any member state from maintaining or adopting specific measures to prevent or compensate for disadvantages linked to racial or ethnic origin.

The following case recognises that positive discrimination in the public sector may provide a legitimate means of achieving equality.

Application by Badeck and others
[2000] IRLR 432, European Court of Justice

The German regional authority (Land) of Hesse enacted an equal rights law (HGlG) in 1993 to ensure equal access for men and women in public sector posts. The legislation requires departments adopt an 'advancement plan' to eliminate under-representation of women within the context of the general principle that 'women and men may not be discriminated against because of their sex or family status'.

Forty-six members of the Parliament of the Land of Hesse brought an application for judicial review of this legislation, seeking a declaration that it was incompatible with the Hesse constitution in that preference was given to candidates because of their sex rather than their merits, and on grounds that it was contrary to the principle of equal treatment and thus contrary to the Equal Treatment Directive as interpreted by the European Court in the *Kalanke* case. The prime minister of Hesse and the Attorney for the Land intervened in the case.

The State Constitutional Court of Hesse referred a series of questions to the ECJ.

JUDGMENT:

The first part of the question

By the first part of its question, the Staatsgerichtshof essentially asks whether Article 2(1) and (4) of the Directive precludes a national rule which, in sectors of the public service where women are underrepresented, gives priority, where male and female candidates for selection have equal qualifications, to female candidates where that proves necessary for complying with the binding targets in the women's advancement plan, if no reasons of greater legal weight are opposed.

The applicants in the main proceedings and the Land Attorney consider that Article 2(1) and (4) of the Directive precludes a national rule which gives priority to women where it is absolute and unconditional.

On this point, it appears from the order for reference that the legislature of the Land of Hesse opted for what is generally known as a 'flexible result quota' ('flexible Ergebnisquote'). The characteristics of that system are, first, that the HGlG does not determine quotas uniformly for all the sectors and departments concerned, but states that the characteristics of those sectors and departments are to be decisive for fixing the binding targets. Second, the HGlG does not necessarily determine from the outset automatically that the outcome of each selection procedure must in a 'stalemate situation' where the candidates have equal qualifications, necessarily favour the woman candidate.

According to the order for reference, the system introduced by the HGlG ensures that a candidate's sex is never decisive for the purposes of a selection procedure where that is not necessary in the particular case. That is so in particular where the initial evidence that a situation is unfavourable to women, based on the fact that they are underrepresented, is disproved.

To give a proper answer to the national court, it must be noted that, under para. 10(1)–(3) of the HGlG, the selection procedure for candidates starts by assessing the candidates' suitability, capability and professional performance (qualifications) with respect to the requirements of the post to be filled or the office to be conferred.

For the purposes of that assessment, certain positive and negative criteria are taken into account. Thus capabilities and experience which have been acquired by carrying out family work are to be taken into account in so far as they are of importance for the suitability, performance and capability of candidates, whereas seniority, age and the date of last promotion are to be taken into account only in so far as they are of importance in that respect. Similarly, the family status or income of the partner is immaterial, and part-time work, leave and delays in completing training as a result of looking after children or dependants in need of care must not have a negative effect.

Such criteria, although formulated in terms which are neutral as regards sex and thus capable of benefiting men too, in general favour women. They are manifestly intended to lead to an equality which is substantive rather than formal, by reducing the inequalities which may occur in practice in social life. Their legitimacy is not challenged in the main proceedings.

As the national court points out, it is only if a female candidate and a male candidate cannot be distinguished on the basis of their qualifications that the woman must be chosen where that proves necessary for complying with the objectives of the advancement plan in question and no reasons of greater legal weight are opposed.

It appears from the Prime Minister's answer to a written question put by the Court that those reasons of greater legal weight concern various rules of law, governed partly by statute and partly by decree, which make no reference to sex and are often described as 'social' aspects. These social factors are based, from a constitutional point of view, partly on the principle of the social State (Articles 20(1) and 28(1) of the Basic Law) and partly on the fundamental right of protection of marriage and the family (Article 6 of the Basic Law).

The Prime Minister observes that there are five groups of rules which justify overriding the rule of advancement of women. These are, first, the preferential treatment given to former employees in the public service who have left the service because of family work within the meaning of para. 10(1) of the HGlG, or who, for the same reason, have not been able to apply for definitive engagement in the public service after their preparatory service. Priority over new appointments is given, second, to persons who for reasons of family work worked on a part-time basis and now wish to resume full-time employment. The third group is former temporary soldiers, that is, those who voluntarily served for a limited period longer than compulsory military service (with a minimum of 12 years). Fourth, possibilities of advancement are more flexible for seriously disabled persons. The obligation to promote disabled persons takes precedence over that to promote women. Fifth, there is the possibility of ending a period of long-term unemployment by an appointment.

Contrary to the submissions of the applicants in the main proceedings and the Land Attorney, it follows that the priority rule introduced by the HGlG is not absolute and unconditional in the sense of paragraph 16 of *Kalanke*.

It is for the national court to assess, in the light of the above, whether the rule at issue in the main proceedings ensures that candidatures are the subject of an objective assessment which takes account of the specific personal situations of all candidates.

The answer must therefore be that Article 2(1) and (4) of the Directive does not preclude a national rule which, in sectors of the public service where women are underrepresented, gives priority, where male and female candidates have equal qualifications, to female candidates where that proves necessary for ensuring compliance with the objectives of the women's advancement plan, if no reasons of greater legal weight are opposed, provided that that rule guarantees that candidatures are the subject of an objective assessment which takes account of the specific personal situations of all candidates.

NOTE: Rather controversially, the ECJ ruled in *Kalanke* v *Freie Hansestadt Bremen* [1995] IRLR 660 that preferential treatment for women who are equally qualified with men is contrary to Directive 76/207, even where women are under-represented in the grade concerned. The decision in *Badeck* fails to clarify the position in *Kalanke*. It attempts to side-step the issue of when positive discrimination is acceptable by applying the reasoning in *Marshall* v *Land Nordrhein-Westfalen* [1998] IRLR 39—the key factors to positive discrimination being objectivity in the selection process and non-automatic priority to the under-represented sex. See Kuchhold, K., 'Badeck: The third German reference on positive action' (2001) 30 ILJ 116 for an analysis of the case.

This approach has further been upheld by the ECJ in *Abrahamsson* & *Anderson* v *Fogelqvist* [2000] IRLR 732, where automatic preference in the recruitment process to candidates belonging to the under-represented sex, so long as they are sufficiently qualified, was incompatible with Article 2(1) and (4) of the Equal Treatment Directive.

As a result the EC has amended Article 2 (Revised Equal Treatment Directive (Directive 2002/73)). The amendment allows positive measures to promote equal opportunities for women and men, in particular by removing existing factors of inequality which affect women's opportunities in the employment area. While positive action would encourage the appointment of women or men to posts where they are currently under-represented, such preferential treatment does not preclude assessment of the particular circumstances of an individual case (see (1996) 68 EOR 39). The EqA 2010, s. 158 takes a few more tentative steps towards legalising positive discrimination.

While previous legislation allowed employers to undertake a variety of positive action measures, for instance offering training and encouragement for certain forms of work, it did not allow employers to take any form of positive action at the actual point of recruitment or promotion. This section extends what is possible to the extent permitted by European law, and applies in relation to all protected characteristics.

EQUALITY ACT 2010

159 Positive action: recruitment and promotion

(1) This section applies if a person (P) reasonably thinks that—

(a) persons who share a protected characteristic suffer a disadvantage connected to the characteristic, or

(b) participation in an activity by persons who share a protected characteristic is disproportionately low.

(2) Part 5 (work) does not prohibit P from taking action within subsection (3) with the aim of enabling or encouraging persons who share the protected characteristic to—

(a) overcome or minimise that disadvantage, or

(b) participate in that activity.

(3) That action is treating a person (A) more favourably in connection with recruitment or promotion than another person (B) because A has the protected characteristic but B does not.

(4) But subsection (2) applies only if—

(a) A is as qualified as B to be recruited or promoted,

(b) P does not have a policy of treating persons who share the protected characteristic more favourably in connection with recruitment or promotion than persons who do not share it, and

(c) taking the action in question is a proportionate means of achieving the aim referred to in subsection (2).

(5) 'Recruitment' means a process for deciding whether to—

(a) offer employment to a person,

(b) make contract work available to a contract worker,

(c) offer a person a position as a partner in a firm or proposed firm,

(d) offer a person a position as a member of an LLP or proposed LLP,

(e) offer a person a pupillage or tenancy in barristers' chambers,

(f) take a person as an advocate's devil or offer a person membership of an

(g) advocate's stable,

(h) offer a person an appointment to a personal office,

(i) offer a person an appointment to a public office, recommend a person for such an appointment or approve a person's appointment to a public office, or

(j) offer a person a service for finding employment.

(6) This section does not enable P to do anything that is prohibited by or under an enactment other than this Act.

NOTE: This section is intended to allow the maximum extent of flexibility to address disadvantage and under-representation where candidates are as good as each other, within the confines of European law, as described earlier.

This section allows an employer to take a protected characteristic into consideration when deciding who to recruit or promote, where people having the protected characteristic are at a disadvantage or are under-represented. This can be only lawfully achieved where the candidates are equally qualified. The issue of whether one person is as qualified as another is not a matter only of academic qualification, but rather a judgement based on the criteria the employer uses to establish who is best for the job, which could include matters such as suitability, competence, and professional performance. The section does not permit employers to have a policy or practice of automatically treating people who share a protected characteristic more favourably than those who do not have it in these circumstances; each case must be considered on its merits. It is predictable that this section will keep the lawyers in employment for some time to come!

■ QUESTIONS

1. Can the decision in *Burton* v *British Railways Board* [1982] QB 1080 still be justified?

2. How far are EC resolutions and recommendations enforceable within a Member State, and what is the effect on the resolution on sexual harassment? See *Grimaldi* v *Fonds des Maladies Professionelles* [1990] IRLR 400.

3. What are the limitations on utilising positive discrimination to promote equality? How may they be overcome? Is EqA 2010, s. 159 the solution?

SECTION 4: SEX AND RACE DISCRIMINATION

The SDA 1975 and the RRA 1976 made discrimination on the grounds of sex, marital status, and race unlawful. Both statutes recognised two main types of discrimination—direct and indirect. Additionally there was victimisation and, under the RRA 1976, segregation. The SDA 1975 offered protection from discrimination to men and women alike, while the RRA 1976 protected members of a racial group against discrimination on racial grounds. Although the SDA 1975 offered protection against discrimination on the ground of marital status, i.e. because a person is married or has entered into a civil partnership, it did not offer the same protection to single people.

The EqA 2010 provides a standard definition of direct discrimination in relation to all the protected characteristic groups. Much of the pre-2010 case law will still be relevant.

A: Direct discrimination

EQUALITY ACT 2010

13 Direct discrimination

(1) A person (A) discriminates against another (B) if, because of a protected characteristic, A treats B less favourably than A treats or would treat others.

(2) If the protected characteristic is age, A does not discriminate against B if A can show A's treatment of B to be a proportionate means of achieving a legitimate aim.

(3) If the protected characteristic is disability, and B is not a disabled person, A does not discriminate against B only because A treats or would treat disabled persons more favourably than A treats B.

(4) If the protected characteristic is marriage and civil partnership, this section applies to a contravention of Part 5 (work) only if the treatment is because it is B who is married or a civil partner.

(5) If the protected characteristic is race, less favourable treatment includes segregating B from others.

(6) If the protected characteristic is sex—

    (a) less favourable treatment of a woman includes less favourable treatment of her because she is breast-feeding;

    (b) in a case where B is a man, no account is to be taken of special treatment afforded to a woman in connection with pregnancy or childbirth.

(7) Subsection (6)(a) does not apply for the purposes of Part 5 (work).

(8) This section is subject to sections 17(6) and 18(7).

14 Combined discrimination: dual characteristics

(1) A person (A) discriminates against another (B) if, because of a combination of two relevant protected characteristics, A treats B less favourably than A treats or would treat a person who does not share either of those characteristics.

(2) The relevant protected characteristics are—

    (a) age;

    (b) disability;

    (c) gender reassignment;

    (d) race;

    (e) religion or belief;

    (f) sex;

    (g) sexual orientation.

(3) For the purposes of establishing a contravention of this Act by virtue of subsection (1), B need not show that A's treatment of B is direct discrimination because of each of the characteristics in the combination (taken separately).

NOTE: Section 14 provides for the discrimination prohibited by the Act to include direct discrimination because of a combination of two protected characteristics ('dual discrimination'). The protected characteristics which may be combined are age, disability, gender reassignment, race, religion or belief, sex, and sexual orientation.

For a claimant to be successful, he or she must show that the less favourable treatment was because of the combination alleged, as compared with how a person who does not share either of the characteristics in the combination is or would be treated. A dual discrimination claim will not succeed where an exception or justification applies to the treatment in respect of either of the relevant protected characteristics—for example, where an occupational requirement in Sch. 9 (Work: exceptions) renders direct discrimination lawful.

The claimant does not have to show that a claim of direct discrimination in respect of each protected characteristic would have been successful if brought separately. A claimant is not prevented from bringing direct discrimination claims because of individual protected characteristics and a dual discrimination claim simultaneously (or more than one dual discrimination claim).

Pre-EqA legislation only allowed for claims alleging discrimination because of a single protected characteristic. This section allows those who have experienced less favourable treatment because of a combination of two relevant protected characteristics to bring a direct discrimination claim, such as where the single-strand approach may not succeed.

The explanatory notes accompanying the bill provide the following work context example:

> A black woman has been passed over for promotion to work on reception because her employer thinks black women do not perform well in customer service roles. Because the employer can point to a white woman of equivalent qualifications and experience who has been appointed to the role in question, as well as a black man of equivalent qualifications and experience in a similar role, the woman may need to be able to compare her treatment because of race and sex combined to demonstrate that she has been subjected to less favourable treatment because of her employer's prejudice against black women.

The Coalition Government has decided not to take this provision forward.

EQUALITY ACT 2010

9 Race

(1) Race includes—
   (a) colour;
   (b) nationality;
   (c) ethnic or national origins.
(2) In relation to the protected characteristic of race—
   (a) a reference to a person who has a particular protected characteristic is a reference to a person of a particular racial group;
   (b) a reference to persons who share a protected characteristic is a reference to persons of the same racial group.
(3) A racial group is a group of persons defined by reference to race; and a reference to a person's racial group is a reference to a racial group into which the person falls.
(4) The fact that a racial group comprises two or more distinct racial groups does not prevent it from constituting a particular racial group.
(5) A Minister of the Crown may by order—
   (a) amend this section to provide for caste to be an aspect of race;
   (b) amend this Act so as to provide for an exception to a provision of this Act to apply, or not apply, to caste in specified circumstances.

NOTES

1. In *R (on the application of E)* v *Governing Board of JFS* [2010] IRLR 136, the Supreme Court held by a majority that one of a Jewish faith school's admission requirements that a pupil's mother had to be Jewish amounted to discrimination on grounds of ethnic origin. Lord Mance stated: 'A test of membership of a religion that focuses on descent from a particular people is a test based on ethnic grounds.' As Rubenstein observes: 'Reading the concept of "descent" into the definition of racial grounds may mean that discrimination by reason of caste is covered by existing discrimination law, since a person's caste depends on who they are descended from' ('Highlights' [2010] IRLR 91).

2. *Caste discrimination* As a result of a Lords amendment, caste is now potentially a protected characteristic. For a discussion of caste discrimination in the UK, see Gopal, P., 'Dominating the diaspora' (Himal South Asian, April 2010) (<http://old.himalmag.com/component/magazine/tblcontent/2010/4.html>).

   The Enterprise and Regulatory Reform Act 2013 requires the definition of 'race' in the Equality Act 2010 to be extended to expressly cover caste. The term 'caste' itself is left undefined. This provision made its way into the Act despite Government opposition but it will only become effective when the Secretary of State makes an order; this is not expected to happen until 2015, following further evidence gathering and consultation.

   However, there is an argument that the definition of 'race' under s. 9(1) of the Equality Act 2010, which includes 'ethnic origins', is broad enough to already cover caste discrimination.

Indeed, in *Tirkey* v *Chandhok* [2015] All ER (D) 91 (Jan), the EAT held that, although 'caste' as an autonomous concept did not fall within the definition of 'race' in EqA 2010, s. 9, many of the facts relevant in considering caste in many of its forms might be capable of doing so, since 'ethnic origins' in s. 9(1)(c) had a wide and flexible ambit, including characteristics determined by descent.

Mandla v *Dowell Lee*

[1983] IRLR 209, House of Lords

The plaintiffs, father and son, were Sikhs. They alleged that the defendant school and its headmaster had committed an act of unlawful discrimination contrary to the RRA 1976 by refusing to offer the son a place in the school unless he removed his turban and cut his hair in conformity with the school rules so as to be able to wear the school uniform.

It was held that Sikhs were a racial group within the meaning of the RRA 1976, s. 3(1), as such a group can be defined by reference to its ethnic origins if it constitutes a separate and distinct community associated with common racial origin.

LORD FRASER OF TULLYBELTON: It is not suggested that Sikhs are a group defined by reference to colour, race, nationality or *national* origins. In none of these respects are they distinguishable from many other groups, especially those living, like most Sikhs, in the Punjab. The argument turns entirely upon whether they are a group defined by '*ethnic* origins'. It is therefore necessary to ascertain the sense in which the word 'ethnic' is used in the Act of 1976. We were referred to various dictionary definitions. The Oxford English Dictionary (1897 edition) gives two meanings of 'ethnic'. The first is 'pertaining to nations not Christian or Jewish; gentile, heathen, pagan'. That clearly cannot be its meaning in the 1976 Act, because it is inconceivable that Parliament would have legislated against racial discrimination intending that the protection should not apply either to Christians or (above all) to Jews. Neither party contended that that was the relevant meaning for the present purpose. The second meaning given in the Oxford English Dictionary (1897 edition) was 'pertaining to race; peculiar to a race or nation; ethnological'. A slighter shorter form of that meaning (omitting 'peculiar to a race or nation') was given by the Concise Oxford Dictionary in 1934 and was expressly accepted by Lord Denning MR as the correct meaning for the present purpose. Oliver and Kerr LJJ also accepted that meaning as being substantially correct, and Oliver LJ at [1983] IRLR 17 said that the word 'ethnic' in its popular meaning involved essentially a racial concept—the concept of something with which the members of the group are born; some fixed or inherited characteristic. The respondent, who appeared on his own behalf, submitted that that was the relevant meaning of 'ethnic' in the 1976 Act, and that it did not apply to Sikhs because they were essentially a religious group, and they shared their racial characteristics with other religious groups, including Hindus and Muslims, living in the Punjab.

My Lords, I recognise that 'ethnic' conveys a flavour of race but it cannot, in my opinion, have been used in the 1976 Act in a strictly racial or biological sense. For one thing, it would be absurd to suppose that Parliament can have intended that membership of a particular racial group should depend upon scientific proof that a person possessed the relevant distinctive biological characteristics (assuming that such characteristics exist). The practical difficulties of such proof would be prohibitive, and it is clear that Parliament must have used the word in some more popular sense. For another thing, the briefest glance at the evidence in this case is enough to show that, within the human race, there are very few, if any, distinctions which are scientifically recognised as racial. I respectfully agree with the view of Lord Simon of Glaisdale in *Ealing LBC* v *Race Relations Board* [1972] AC 342, 362, referring to the long title of the Race Relations Act 1968 (which was in terms identical with part of the long title of the 1976 Act) when he said:

> Moreover 'racial' is not a term of art, either legal or, I surmise, scientific. I apprehend that anthropologists would dispute how far the word 'race' is biologically at all relevant to the species amusingly called homo sapiens.

A few lines lower down, after quoting part of s. 1(1) of the Act, the noble and learned Lord said this:

> This is rubbery and elusive language—understandably when the draftsman is dealing with so unprecise a concept as 'race' in its popular sense and endeavouring to leave no loophole for evasion.

I turn, therefore, to the third and wider meaning which is given in the 1972 Supplement to the Oxford English Dictionary. It is as follows: 'pertaining to or having common racial, cultural, religious, or linguistic characteristics, esp. designating a racial or other group within a larger system'. Mr Irvine, for the appellant, while not accepting the third (1972) meaning as directly applicable for the present purpose, relied on it to this extent, that it introduces a reference to cultural and other characteristics, and is not limited to racial characteristics. The 1972 meaning is, in my opinion, too loose and vague to be accepted as it stands. It is capable of being read as implying that any one of the adjectives, 'racial, cultural, religious *or* linguistic' would be enough to constitute an ethnic group. That cannot be the sense in which 'ethnic' is used in the 1976 Act, as the Act is not concerned at all with discrimination on religious grounds. Similarly, it cannot have been used to mean simply any 'racial *or other* group'. If that were the meaning of 'ethnic', it would add nothing to the word group, and would lead to a result which would be unacceptably wide. But in seeking for the true meaning of 'ethnic' in the statute, we are not tied to the precise definition in any dictionary. The value of the 1972 definition is, in my view, that it shows that ethnic has come to be commonly used in a sense appreciably wider than the strictly racial or biological. That appears to me to be consistent with the ordinary experience of those who read newspapers at the present day. In my opinion, the word 'ethnic' still retains a racial flavour but it is used nowadays in an extended sense to include other characteristics which may be commonly thought of as being associated with common racial origin.

For a group to constitute an ethnic group in the sense of the 1976 Act, it must, in my opinion, regard itself, and be regarded by others, as a distinct community by virtue of certain characteristics. Some of these characteristics are essential; others are not essential but one or more of them will commonly be found and will help to distinguish the group from the surrounding community. The conditions which appear to me to be essential are these:–(1) a long shared history, of which the group is conscious as distinguishing it from other groups, and the memory of which it keeps alive; (2) a cultural tradition of its own, including family and social customs and manners, often but not necessarily associated with religious observance. In addition to those two essential characteristics the following characteristics are, in my opinion, relevant; (3) either a common geographical origin, or descent from a small number of common ancestors; (4) a common language, not necessarily peculiar to the group; (5) a common literature peculiar to the group; (6) a common religion different from that of neighbouring groups or from the general community surrounding it; (7) being a minority or being an oppressed or a dominant group within a larger community, for example a conquered people (say, the inhabitants of England shortly after the Norman conquest) and their conquerors might both be ethnic groups.

A group defined by reference to enough of these characteristics would be capable of including converts, for example, persons who marry into the group, and of excluding apostates. Provided a person who joins the group feels himself or herself to be a member of it, and is accepted by other members, then he is, for the purposes, of the Act, a member. That appears to be consistent with the words at the end of subsection (1) of s. 3:

> References to a person's racial group refer to any group into which he falls.

In my opinion, it is possible for a person to fall into a particular racial group either by birth or by adherence, and it makes no difference, so far as the 1976 Act is concerned, by which route he finds his way into the group. This view does not involve creating any inconsistency between direct discrimination under para. (a) and indirect discrimination under para. (b). A person may treat another relatively unfavourably 'on racial grounds' because he regards that other as being of a particular race, or belonging to a particular racial group, even if his belief is, from a scientific point of view, completely erroneous.

NOTES

1. The criteria laid down in *Mandla*'s case have been used successfully in *Commission for Racial Equality* v *Dutton* [1989] IRLR 8, to establish that gypsies are an ethnic group. However, in *Dawkins* v *Crown Suppliers* [1993] IRLR 284, the Court of Appeal concluded that Rastafarians did not fulfil the criteria because there was no group history, descent, or language; they were in effect a religious sect and therefore outside the scope of the Act.

   Muslims are not protected by the direct discrimination provisions in the RRA 1976, s. 1(1)(a) but may be able to show indirect discrimination (see p. 367 (Section B)) on the basis of ethnic group (see *Malik* v *Bertram Personnel Group* (1990) No. 4343/90).

2. Jews have posed something of a problem for the courts because religious discrimination is outside the scope of the RRA 1976. It has been concluded that Jews are a racial group as well as a religious group (see *Seide* v *Gillette Industries Ltd* [1980] IRLR 427 and *Simon* v *Brimham Associates* [1987] IRLR 307). It would appear that whether the act of discrimination falls within the statute is dependent upon the reasons for the discrimination.

3. The meaning of 'national origins' was considered in *Tejani* v *The Superintendent Registrar for the District of Peterborough* [1986] IRLR 502, CA, which concluded that 'national' must be equated with race, not 'citizenship'; but see *Ealing London Borough Council* v *Race Relations Board* [1972] AC 342, where it was concluded that unless the context otherwise requires, 'nationality' includes 'citizenship'.

   'National origins' was further defined in *Northern Joint Police Board* v *Power* [1997] IRLR 610 as having identifiable elements, both historically and geographically, which, at least at some point in time, reveal the existence of a nation. It was concluded that as England and Scotland were once separate nations, the complainant could base his claim that he was discriminated against because he was English on national origins. This has been confirmed in *BBC Scotland* v *Souster* [2001] IRLR 150 and *British Airways plc* v *Boyce* [2001] IRLR 157. It was made clear that such a case is based on 'national origins', not 'ethnic origins', as the English are not an ethnic group within the meaning of the RRA because a distinctive racial element is lacking. In *R* v *Secretary of State for Defence* [2006] IRLR 934, the Court of Appeal, upholding the decision of the High Court, found that 'place of birth' was not identical to 'national origins' and as a result, the former was not inextricably linked to a forbidden ground of discrimination. However, while there was no direct discrimination, the Court of Appeal found that there was indirect discrimination resulting from the place of birth test as a criteria to qualify for a compensation scheme for those who were interned by the Japanese during the Second World War. The Secretary of State failed to justify the proportionality of the eligibility criteria.

4. Discrimination on grounds of marital status is also covered by the SDA 1975 (and now by the EqA 2010). In *Hayle and Clunie* v *Wiltshire Healthcare NHS Trust* (1999) Case No. 140 1250/98, a requirement to work rotating shifts was found indirectly to discriminate against married people with childcare responsibilities. See also *Chief Constable of the Bedfordshire Constabulary* v *Graham* [2002] IRLR 239, in which a policy which restricted married officers or partners from working with each other amounted to indirect discrimination.

5. The significance of stereotypical assumptions and their resultant discrimination can be seen in *R (European Roma Rights Centre)* v *Immigration Officer at Prague Airport* [2005] 2 WLR 1, in which the House of Lords ruled that the use of such assumptions was unlawful. In this case the assumption was that Roma travelling to the UK were likely to be seeking asylum.

■ QUESTIONS

1. What differentiates 'national' from 'ethnic' origin?

2. Must the alleged discriminator know of the ethnic origins of the complainant to be guilty of discrimination?

3. Can language alone establish ethnic origin? See *Gwynedd County Council* v *Jones* [1986] ICR 833.

(i) What is direct discrimination?

This type of discrimination involves treating someone less favourably on racial grounds or because of their sex. It covers acts of overt discrimination. Comparison can be made with the hypothetical man or person. As discrimination has become more covert and subtle, direct discrimination has proved to be difficult to establish. However, developments in the case law have improved the position for the complainant.

Although the following case is not an employment case, it lays down the test for establishing direct discrimination.

R v *Birmingham City Council, ex p. Equal Opportunities Commission*

[1989] IRLR 173, House of Lords

Birmingham City Council makes provision for some 600 children to enter voluntary-aided grammar schools at age 11 each year. As a result of the selection policies of the schools, 390 places are allocated for boys and 210 for girls.

The EOC brought a suit seeking a declaration that the council was in breach of s. 23(1) of the SDA. This provides that: 'It is unlawful for a local education authority, in carrying out such of its functions under the Education Acts 1944 to 1981 as do not fall under section 22, to do any act which constitutes sex discrimination.'

On behalf of the EOC, it was argued that in providing selective secondary education, the council was carrying out a function under s. 8(1) of the Education Act 1944; that s. 23(1) of the SDA obliged the council not to discriminate on grounds of sex in carrying out that function; and that the council was discriminating against girls in the provision of grammar school education by treating girls less favourably on the ground of their sex.

It was held that girls had been treated less favourably 'on the ground of their sex' by the council's provision of fewer places in selective schools for girls, notwithstanding the fact that there was no intention or motive on the part of the council to discriminate. Such an intention is not a necessary condition of liability.

LORD GOFF OF CHIEVELEY: The first argument advanced by the council before your Lordships' House was that there had not been, in the present case, less favourable treatment of the girls on grounds of sex. Here two points were taken. It was submitted (1) that it could not be established that there was less favourable treatment of the girls by reason of their having been denied the same opportunities as the boys for selective education unless it was shown that selective education was better than non-selective education, and that no evidence to that effect was called before McCullough J; and (2) that, if that burden had been discharged, it still had to be shown that there was less favourable treatment on grounds of sex, and that involved establishing an intention or motive on the part of the council to discriminate against the girls. In my opinion, neither of these submissions is well founded.

As to the first it is not, in my opinion, necessary for the commission to show that selective education is 'better' than non-selective education. It is enough that, by denying the girls the same opportunity as the boys, the council is depriving them of a choice which (as the facts show) is valued by them, or at least by their parents, and which (even though others may take a different view) is a choice obviously valued, on reasonable grounds, by many others. This conclusion has been reached by all the judges involved in the present case; and it is consistent with previous authority (see, in particular, *Gill* v *El Vino Co. Ltd* [1983] IRLR 206 and *R* v *Secretary of State for Education and Science ex parte Keating* (1985) 84 LGR 469). I have no doubt that it is right. As to the second point, it is, in my opinion, contrary to the terms of the statute. There is discrimination under the statute if there is less favourable treatment on the ground of sex, in other words if the relevant girl or girls would have received the same treatment as the boys but for their sex. The intention or motive of the defendant to discriminate, though it may be relevant so far as remedies are concerned (see s. 66(3) of the Act of 1975), is not a necessary condition to liability; it is perfectly possible to envisage cases where the defendant had no such motive, and yet did in fact discriminate on the ground of sex. Indeed, as Mr Lester pointed out in the course of his argument, if the council's submission were correct it would be a good defence for an employer to show that he discriminated against women not because he intended to do so but, for example, because of customer preference, or to save money, or even to avoid controversy. In the present case, whatever may have been the intention or motive of the council, nevertheless it is because of their sex that the girls in question receive less favourable treatment than the boys, and so are the subject of discrimination under the Act of 1975. This is well established in a long line of authority: see, in particular, *Jenkins* v *Kingsgate (Clothing Productions) Ltd (No. 2)* [1981] IRLR 388, pp. 393, 394 per Browne-Wilkinson J and *ex parte Keating* per Taylor J at p. 475; see also *Ministry of Defence* v *Jeremiah* [1979] IRLR 436 per Lord Denning MR. I can see no reason to depart from this established view.

NOTES

1. This case establishes that the question is whether the woman would have been treated differently *but for* her sex—the motive for the differential treatment is irrelevant.

   In *Moyhing* v *Barts & London NHS Trust* [2006] IRLR 630, male nurses had to be chaperoned when performing intimate procedures on female patients; female nurses in the opposite situation did not have to be chaperoned. Mr Moyhing claimed this was sex discrimination. The EAT held that this was sex discrimination, even though there was a good reason for the less favourable treatment, i.e. the risk of assault on female patients or the risk of false accusations of assault by the female patients. The fact that the rule was not aimed at M personally and actually caused little inconvenience led to a small award of compensation.

   Similarly in *Amnesty International* v *Ahmed* [2009] IRLR 884, it was held by the EAT to be unlawful race discrimination to refuse to appoint a woman of Sudanese origin to the post of 'researcher' for Sudan, even though this was with good motives, (1) so as to avoid the possible appearance of bias and (2) also for the researcher's own safety if they had to visit Sudan.

2. The case law indicates that where an an employer adopts a gender-based, race-based, sexual orientatation-based etc. criterion, the employer's action amounts to inherent direct discrimination and motive is irrelevant (see *R (on the application of E)* v *Governing Board of JFS* [2010] IRLR 136; *Bull* v *Hall* [2013] UKSC 73).

3.2. If the less favourable treatment is for some other reason, it is not direct discrimination. In *B* v *A* [2007] IRLR 576, EAT, a jealous employer dismissed his PA who was in a relationship with him because she was going out with someone else.

She claimed direct sex discrimination on the basis that she had only been dismissed because she was a woman. The EAT held there was no discrimination. The secretary had not been dismissed because she was a woman but because of the breakdown of the relationship. The comparison had to be with a man in a similar situation. If the employer had been a gay man in a relationship with a male secretary, the male secretary would also have been dismissed.

Shamoon v Chief Constable of the Royal Ulster Constabulary
[2003] IRLR 286, House of Lords

Joan Shamoon was a chief inspector in the RUC and deputy head of the Urban Traffic Branch, one of three divisions in the Traffic Branch. One of her functions concerned staff appraisals. Although the RUC staff appraisal scheme provided that reports would 'normally be completed by a superintendent', it was the established custom and practice in the Traffic Branch for counselling in respect of staff appraisals for constables to be carried out by the chief inspectors.

In April 1997, a complaint was made to the head of the Traffic Branch, Superintendent Laird, by a Constable Lowens, about the manner in which Chief Inspector Shamoon had conducted his appraisal. The complaint was upheld. In September 1997, there was a complaint by a Constable Currie about the terms of Chief Inspector Shamoon's report on him. The constable took his complaint to the Police Federation, who met with Superintendent Laird to discuss staff appraisals. Superintendent Laird promised that thenceforth he would do the appraisals. Chief Inspector Shamoon did not carry out any further appraisals until the Force policy on appraisals changed in December 1997, although the two chief inspectors in the other two divisions of the Traffic Branch continued to perform these duties.

Chief Inspector Shamoon claimed that she had been discriminated against on grounds of sex in having the right to carry out appraisals removed from her.

HELD (House of Lords): The Northern Ireland Court of Appeal erred in law in holding that the applicant chief inspector had not suffered a 'detriment' within the meaning of article 8(2)(b) of the Sex Discrimination (Northern Ireland) Order (the equivalent of s. 6(2)(b) of the Sex Discrimination Act) when the right to carry out appraisals was removed from her, because in order to constitute a detriment there must be some physical or economic consequence which is material and substantial.

In order for a disadvantage to qualify as a 'detriment', it must arise in the employment field in that the court or tribunal must find that by reason of the act or acts complained of a reasonable worker would or might take the view that he had thereby been disadvantaged in the circumstances in which he had thereafter to work. An unjustified sense of grievance cannot amount to 'detriment'. However, contrary to the view expressed by the EAT in *Lord Chancellor* v *Coker*, on which the Court of Appeal relied in the present case, it is not necessary to demonstrate some physical or economic consequence.

LORD NICHOLLS: With this introduction, I turn to consider the application of these provisions in practice. In deciding a discrimination claim, one of the matters employment tribunals have to consider is whether the statutory definition of discrimination has been satisfied. When the claim is based on direct discrimination or victimisation, in practice tribunals in their decisions normally consider, first, whether the claimant received less favourable treatment than the appropriate comparator (the 'less favourable treatment' issue) and then, secondly, whether the less favourable treatment was on the relevant proscribed ground (the 'reason why' issue). Tribunals proceed to consider the reason why issue only if the less favourable treatment issue is resolved in favour of the claimant. Thus the less favourable treatment issue is treated as a threshold which the claimant must cross before the tribunal is called upon to decide why the claimant was afforded the treatment of which she is complaining.

No doubt there are cases where it is convenient and helpful to adopt this two-step approach to what is essentially a single question: did the claimant, on the proscribed ground, receive less favourable treatment than others? But, especially where the identity of the relevant comparator is matter of dispute, this sequential analysis may give rise to needless problems. Sometimes the less favourable treatment issue cannot be resolved without, at the same time, deciding the reason-why issue. The two issues are intertwined.

The present case is a good example. The relevant provisions in the Sex Discrimination (Northern Ireland) Order 1976 are in all material respects the same as those in the Sex Discrimination Act 1975 which, for case of discussion, I have so far referred to. Chief Inspector Shamoon claimed she was treated less favourably than two male chief inspectors. Unlike her, they retained their counselling responsibilities. Is this comparing like with like? Prima facie it is not. She had been the subject of complaints and of representations by Police Federation representatives, the male chief inspectors had not. This might be the reason why she was treated as she was. This might explain why she was relieved of her responsibilities and they were not. But whether this factual difference between their positions was in truth a material difference is an issue which cannot be resolved without determining why she was treated as she was. It might be that the reason why she was relieved of her counselling responsibilities had nothing to do with the complaints and representations. If that were so, then a comparison between her and the two male chief inspectors may well be comparing like with like, because in that event the difference between her and her two male colleagues would be an immaterial difference.

I must take this a step further. As I have said, prima facie the comparison with the two male chief inspectors is not apt. So be it. Let it be assumed that, this being so, the most sensible course in practice is to proceed on the footing that the appropriate comparator is a hypothetical comparator: a male chief inspector regarding whose conduct similar complaints and representations had been made. On this footing, the less favourable treatment issue is this: was Chief Inspector Shamoon treated less favourably than such a male chief inspector would have been treated? But here also the question is incapable of being answered without deciding why Chief Inspector Shamoon was treated as she was. It is impossible to decide whether Chief Inspector Shamoon was treated less favourably than a hypothetical male chief inspector without identifying the ground on which she was treated as she was. Was it grounds of sex? If yes, then she was treated less favourably than a male chief inspector in her position would have been treated. If not, not. Thus, on this footing also, the less-favourable-treatment issue is incapable of being decided without deciding the reason-why issue. And the decision on the reason-why issue will also provide the answer to the less-favourable-treatment issue.

This analysis seems to me to point to the conclusion that employment tribunals may sometimes be able to avoid arid and confusing disputes about the identification of the appropriate comparator by concentrating primarily on why the claimant was treated as she was. Was it on the proscribed ground which is the foundation of the application? That will call for an examination of all the facts of the case. Or was it for some other reason? If the latter, the application fails. If the former, there will be usually be no difficulty in deciding whether the treatment, afforded to the claimant on the proscribed ground, was less favourable than was or would have been afforded to others.

The most convenient and appropriate way to tackle the issues arising on any discrimination application must always depend upon the nature of the issues and all the circumstances of the case. There will be cases where it is convenient to decide the less-favourable-treatment issue first. But, for the reason set out above, when formulating their decisions employment tribunals may find it helpful to consider whether they should postpone determining the less-favourable-treatment issue until after they have decided why the treatment was afforded to the claimant. Adopting this course would have simplified the issues, and assisted in their resolution, in the present case.

NOTE: The burden is normally on the claimant to show less favourable treatment, as opposed to merely different treatment, compared with that of the opposite sex or a person of a different race. However, the burden of proof may shift to the employer under the SDA 1975, s. 63A (now covered by the EqA 2010, s. 136; see also the EU Burden of Proof Directive (97/80/EC)).

EQUALITY ACT 2010

136 Burden of proof

  (1) This section applies to any proceedings relating to a contravention of this Act.

  (2) If there are facts from which the court could decide, in the absence of any other explanation, that a person (A) contravened the provision concerned, the court must hold that the contravention occurred.

  (3) But subsection (2) does not apply if A shows that A did not contravene the provision.

  (4) The reference to a contravention of this Act includes a reference to a breach of an equality clause or rule.

NOTE: This section provides that, in any claim where a person alleges discrimination, harassment or victimisation under the Act, the burden of proving their case starts with the claimant. Once the claimant has established sufficient facts to point to a breach having occurred, in the absence of any other explanation the burden shifts onto the respondent to show that he or she did not breach the provisions of the Act.

In *Barton* v *Investec Henderson Crosthwaite Securities Ltd* [2003] IRLR 33, the EAT concluded that the respondent must show that sex or race etc. did not form part of the reasons for the discriminatory treatment. If the respondent does not discharge the burden of proof, the employment tribunal must find that there has been unlawful discrimination. This goes further than the decision in *King* v *The Great Britain-China Centre* [1991] IRLR 513, which gave the tribunal some flexibility before inferring discrimination had taken place. As a result of the decision in *Igen Ltd and others* v *Wong; Chamberlain Solicitors and another* v *Emokpae; Brunel University* v *Webster* ([2005] IRLR 258), the Court of Appeal has revised the guidelines on establishing the burden of proof laid down in *Barton* v *Investec Henderson Crosthwaite Securities Ltd.* In revising the guidelines it is clear that the tribunals must go through a two-stage process, which will involve considering the facts and determining whether discrimination can be inferred. If it can, the burden of proof then passes to the employer to offer a reasonable explanation for its actions and for the tribunal to determine whether the explanation is sufficient to discharge the burden of proof.

The claimant must also establish that not only has there been an unlawful act of discrimination, but that the employer committed the act. Finally, *Barton* requires the employer to establish that there was no discrimination whatsoever.

Igen Ltd and others v *Wong*

[2005] IRLR 258, Court of Appeal

The guidance issued by the EAT in *Barton* v *Investec Henderson Crosthwaite Securities Ltd* in respect of Sex Discrimination Act cases, which has been applied in relation to race and disability discrimination, would be approved in amended form, as set out below.

(1) Pursuant to s. 63A of the SDA, it is for the claimant who complains of sex discrimination to prove on the balance of probabilities facts from which the tribunal could conclude, in the absence of an adequate explanation, that the respondent has committed an act of discrimination against the claimant which is unlawful by virtue of Part II or which by virtue of s. 41 or s. 42 of the SDA is to be treated as having been committed against the claimant. These are referred to below as 'such facts'.

(2) If the claimant does not prove such facts he or she will fail.

(3) It is important to bear in mind in deciding whether the claimant has proved such facts that it is unusual to find direct evidence of sex discrimination. Few employers would be prepared to admit such discrimination, even to themselves. In some cases the discrimination will not be an intention but merely based on the assumption that 'he or she would not have fitted in'.

(4) In deciding whether the claimant has proved such facts, it is important to remember that the outcome at this stage of the analysis by the tribunal will therefore usually depend on what inferences it is proper to draw from the primary facts found by the tribunal.

(5) It is important to note the word 'could' in s. 63A(2). At this stage the tribunal does not have to reach a definitive determination that such facts would lead it to the conclusion that there was an act of unlawful discrimination. At this stage a tribunal is looking at the primary facts before it to see what inferences of secondary fact could be drawn from them.

(6) In considering what inferences or conclusions can be drawn from the primary facts, the tribunal must assume that there is no adequate explanation for those facts.

(7) These inferences can include, in appropriate cases, any inferences that it is just and equitable to draw in accordance with s. 74(2)(b) of the SDA from an evasive or equivocal reply to a questionnaire or any other questions that fall within s. 74(2) of the SDA.

(8) Likewise, the tribunal must decide whether any provision of any relevant code of practice is relevant and, if so, take it into account in determining, such facts pursuant to s. 56A(10) of the SDA. This means that inferences may also be drawn from any failure to comply with any relevant code of practice.

(9) Where the claimant has proved facts from which conclusions could be drawn that the respondent has treated the claimant less favourably on the ground of sex, then the burden of proof moves to the respondent.

(10) It is then for the respondent to prove that he did not commit, or as the case may be, is not to be treated as having committed, that act.

(11) To discharge that burden it is necessary for the respondent to prove, on the balance of probabilities, that the treatment was in no sense whatsoever on the grounds of sex, since 'no discrimination whatsoever' is compatible with the Burden of Proof Directive.

(12) That requires a tribunal to assess not merely whether the respondent has proved an explanation for the facts from which such inferences can be drawn, but further that it is adequate to discharge the burden of proof on the balance of probabilities that sex was not a ground for the treatment in question.

(13) Since the facts necessary to prove an explanation would normally be in the possession of the respondent, a tribunal would normally expect cogent evidence to discharge that burden of proof. In particular, the tribunal will need to examine carefully explanations for failure to deal with the questionnaire procedure and/or code of practice.

NOTE: The decision in *Igen* has been applied in *Laing* v *Manchester City Council* [2006] IRLR 748, in which the EAT held that (in deciding whether there is a prima facie case) the tribunal:

> should have regard to all the facts at the first stage to see what proper inferences can be drawn. The onus lies on the claimant to show potentially less favourable treatment from which an inference of discrimination could properly be drawn. Typically this will involve identifying an actual comparator treated differently or, in the absence of such a comparator, a hypothetical one who would have been treated more favourably. This involves a consideration of all material facts.

As a result, evidence that the manager in *Laing* treated all subordinates in an abrupt fashion was material.

The case of *Qureshi* v *London Borough of Newham* [1991] IRLR 264 considered when an inference of discrimination can be made by the employment tribunal. The Court of Appeal determined, applying *Noone*, that such an inference can be made only after an act of discrimination has been established. In this particular case the equal opportunities policy was so bad that every race was a victim. There was therefore no discrimination with regard to Mr Qureshi. The court went on to conclude that the Acts did not impose a duty to be a good employer (see also *Glasgow City Council* v *Zafar* [1998] IRLR 37; *Bahl* v *Law Society* [2004] IRLR 799).

James v *Eastleigh Borough Council*

[1990] IRLR 298, House of Lords

LORD LOWRY [dissenting]: My Lords, the facts of this appeal are simple, but I confess to having had some difficulty in deciding it. I can discern in your Lordships' speeches, which I have had the advantage of reading in draft, two logical and persuasive trains of thought which lead to opposite conclusion, and the question is how to choose between them.

The case has been presented by the plaintiff as an example of direct discrimination, an apt and by now customary description of a breach of s. 1(1)(a) of the Sex Discrimination Act 1975 which, as applied to men, provides:

> A person discriminates against a [man] in any circumstances relevant for the purposes of any provision of this Act if— (a) on the ground of [his] sex he treats [him] less favourably than he treats or would treat a [woman].

There are two questions for decision: (1) What, on its true construction, does this provision mean? (2) When the provision, properly construed, is applied to the facts, did the Council discriminate against the appellant contrary to s. 1(1)(a)?

With a view to construction, the crucial words are 'on the ground of his sex'. Mr Lester for the appellant, submits that this phrase means 'due to his sex' and does not involve any consideration of the reason which has led the alleged discriminator to treat the man less favourably than he treats or would treat a woman. I shall call this the causative construction and will presently advert to it. Mr Beloff, for the Council, contends for what I shall call the subjective construction, which involves considering the reason why the discriminator has treated the man unfavourably. He submits that this construction accords with the plain meaning of the words and the grammatical structure of the sentence in which they occur. I accept Mr Beloff's construction and I proceed to explain why I do so.

On reading s. 1(1)(a), it can be seen that the discriminator does something to the victim, that is, he treats him in a certain fashion, to wit, less favourably than he treats or would treat a woman. And he treats him in that fashion on a certain *ground*, namely, *on the ground of his sex*. These words, it is scarcely necessary for me to point out, constitute an adverbial phrase modifying the transitive verb 'treats' in a clause of which the discriminator is the subject and the victim is the object. While anxious not to weary your Lordships with a grammatical excursus, the point I wish to make is that the *ground* on which the alleged discriminator treats the victim less favourably is inescapably linked to the subject and the verb; it is the reason which has caused him to act. The meaning of the vital words, in the sentence where they occur, cannot be expressed by saying that the victim receives treatment which on the ground of (his) sex is less favourable to him than to a person of the opposite sex. The structure of that sentence makes the words 'on the ground of his sex' easily capable of meaning 'due to his sex' if the context so requires or permits.

...

I feel that I would have no difficulty in dealing with this argument, but for the fact that it has commended itself to the majority of your Lordships, including the author of the passage in question. It is therefore with even more than the usual measure of respect that I make the observations which follow. In their context both of the statements which I have extracted are perfectly correct statements of fact, but that does not mean that they are a guide to the proper construction of s. 1(1)(a), which I have considered above. The defence was not that the less favourable treatment was a purely undesigned and adventitious consequence of the Council's policy. It would have had to be admitted that the Council, however regretfully, knew it was treating the girls less favourably than the boys and that owing to the shortage of school places it had deliberately decided so to treat them because they were girls. The defence, based on absence of intention and motive, was rightly rejected and no other defence was made or could have been made. Whichever construction of s. 1(1)(a) had been applied, the Council would have lost, and no rival constructions of that provision were discussed. It is, I consider, worth noting that the examples and the cases which my noble and learned friend mentions are consistent with the subjective construction. If a men's hairdresser dismisses the only woman on his staff because the customers prefer to have their hair cut by a man, he may regret losing her but he treats her less favourably because she is a woman; that is, on the ground of her sex, having made a deliberate decision to do so. If the foreman dismisses an efficient and co-operative black road sweeper in order to avoid industrial action by the remaining (white) members of the squad, he treats him less favourably on racial grounds. If a decision is taken, for reasons which may seem in other respects valid and sensible, not to employ a girl in a group otherwise consisting entirely of men, the employer has treated that girl less favourably than he would treat a man and he has done so consciously on the ground (which *he considers* to be a proper ground) that she is a woman. In none of these cases is a defence provided by an excusable or even by a worthy motive.

It can thus be seen that the causative construction not only gets rid of unessential and often irrelevant mental ingredients, such as malice, prejudice, desire and motive, but also dispenses with an essential ingredient, namely, the ground on which the discriminator acts. The appellant's construction relieves the complainant of the need to prove anything except that A has done an act which results in less favourable treatment for B by reason of B's sex, which reduces to insignificance the words 'on the ground of'. Thus the causative test is too wide and is grammatically unsound, because it necessarily disregards the fact that the less favourable treatment is meted out to the victim *on the ground of* the victim's sex.

Redfearn v Serco Ltd (t/a West Yorkshire Transport)
[2006] IRLR 623, Court of Appeal

Arthur Redfearn, a white man, was employed by West Yorkshire Transport Service (WYTS) as a bus driver and escort for children and adults with special needs. His Asian supervisor, with whom he got on very well, nominated him for an award of first class employee status.

On 26 May 2004, a newspaper article identified Mr Redfearn as a candidate representing the British National Party (BNP) at the local election in June 2004 for Bradford city council. When this came to light, Unison wrote to the acting chief executive of Bradford council. The letter said that the 'continued presence within the workforce' of a BNP candidate was 'a significant cause for concern, bearing in mind the BNP's overt and racist/fascist agenda'. This was sent on to the general manager of WYTS, who also received a representation from the GMB. In the event, Mr Redfearn was elected as a councillor. Membership of the BNP, according to its constitution, is 'open to whites only'.

Bearing in mind that 70 to 80 per cent of WYTS's passengers were of Asian origin, as were 35 per cent of the workforce, the employers took the view that to continue to employ Mr Redfearn would raise significant difficulties. On 30 June, he was dismissed with immediate effect by the employers 'on the grounds of health and safety'. Although it was not said that Mr Redfearn had brought his political views into the workplace, the dismissal was said to be because of the fear of violence and/or anger by other employees; the feared reaction of Asians with whom Mr Redfearn might travel with or assist in the course of his work; and general annoyance or anger against the employers and/or Mr Redfearn by virtue of his BNP membership.

Mr Redfearn did not have sufficient service to bring a claim of unfair dismissal. However, he brought a claim of direct and indirect discrimination under the RRA. So far as direct discrimination is concerned, he sought to rely on the broad definition given to discrimination 'on racial grounds' based on the line of cases including *Showboat Entertainment Centre* v *Owens*. He alleged that Serco had dismissed him on the ground of the Asian race and ethnic origin of the people they transported.

HELD (Court of Appeal): The employment tribunal did not err in finding that the claimant bus driver had not been dismissed 'on racial grounds' within the meaning of s. 1(1)(a) of the RRA when the employers discovered his candidature as a BNP councillor, and that instead he had been dismissed on health and safety grounds having regard to the significant number of passengers and employees who were of Asian origin. In so finding, the employment tribunal did not take too narrow a view of the reasoning in *Showboat Entertainment Centre* v *Owens*. The EAT erred in allowing an appeal against the employment tribunal's judgment on that basis.

MUMMERY LJ: Mr Bowers submitted that Serco's decision to dismiss Mr Redfearn was based on considerations relating to the race of third parties, their perceived hostility to his views and his perceived attitude to the race of third parties. That was direct discrimination 'on racial grounds.' The employment tribunal had misapplied the law. Race considerations had significantly influenced the decision to dismiss on 'health and safety grounds' which could not be relied on as a justification for direct race discrimination. Mr Bowers argued that any concern on the part of a tribunal or court about the consequences of appearing to permit racist conduct, as might occur in allowing a claim like the present case, could be dealt with at the stage of remedy.

In my judgment, the ratio of *Showboat* advanced by Mr Bowers is far too wide. His citation of selected passages from the judgment must be read in the context of the judgment as a whole. His sweeping proposition is wrong in principle, is inconsistent with the purposes of the legislation and is unsupported by authority. His proposition covers cases that would produce consequences at odds with the legislative aim. Taken to its logical conclusion his interpretation of the 1976 Act would mean that it could be an act of direct race discrimination for an employer, who was trying to improve race relations in the workplace, to dismiss an employee, whom he discovered had committed an act of race discrimination, such as racist abuse, against a fellow employee or against a customer of the employer. I am confident that that is not the kind of case for which the anti-discrimination legislation was designed.

The essence of *Showboat* is that an employee who refuses to implement his employer's racially discriminatory policy is entitled to be protected from less favourable treatment under the 1976 Act. The use of the employee to implement the employer's racially discriminatory policy means that 'racial grounds' operate directly in the less favourable treatment of the employee, whether the race or colour in question be that of the employee or that of a third party. Mr Bowers' proposition goes far wider so as to embrace cases in which the employer, far from seeking to implement a racially discriminatory policy contrary to the policy of the 1976 Act, is acting to eliminate race discrimination in accordance with the policy of the 1976 Act. According to Mr Bowers (subject to his points on causation and remedy) the employee would be entitled to receive the same protection under the 1976 Act from unfavourable treatment, such as dismissal, however racially discriminatory he was towards third parties contrary to his employer's instructions.

Mr Bowers's proposition turns the ratio of *Showboat* and the policy of the race relations legislation upside down. It would mean that any less favourable treatment brought about because of concern about the racist views or conduct of a person in a multi-ethnic workplace would constitute race discrimination. The ratio of *Showboat* is that the racially discriminatory employer is liable 'on racial grounds' for the less favourable treatment of those who refuse to implement his policy or are affected by his policy. It does not apply so as to make the employer, who is not pursuing a policy of race discrimination or who is pursuing a policy of anti-race discrimination, liable for race discrimination.

In this case it is true that the circumstances in which the decision to dismiss Mr Redfearn was taken included racial considerations, namely the fact that Serco's customers were mainly Asian and that a significant percentage of the workforce was Asian. Racial considerations were relevant to Serco's decision to dismiss Mr Redfearn, but that does not mean that it is right to characterise Serco's dismissal of Mr Redfearn as being 'on racial grounds'. It is a non-sequitur to argue that he was dismissed 'on racial grounds' because the circumstances leading up to his dismissal included a relevant racial consideration, such as the race of fellow employees and customers and the policies of the BNP on racial matters. Mr Redfearn was no more dismissed 'on racial grounds' than an employee who is dismissed for racially abusing his employer, a fellow employee or a valued customer. Any other result would be incompatible with the purpose of the 1976 Act to promote equal treatment of persons irrespective of race by making it unlawful to discriminate against a person on the grounds of race.

In my judgment, the employment tribunal was correct in law in deciding that Mr Redfearn was not dismissed 'on racial grounds.' The grounds of dismissal were not racial. They did not become racial grounds because Serco dismissed him in circumstances in which it wished to avoid the perceived detrimental effects of Mr Redfearn's membership of, and election to office representing, the BNP, which propagated racially discriminatory policies concerning non-white races who formed part of Serco's workforce and customer base.

I would also reject the alternative argument advanced by Mr Bowers on the appeal (it was not raised in the employment tribunal) that this was a case of direct discrimination, because Serco adopted race-based criteria for dismissing him, i.e. his membership of the BNP, which is confined to white people.

…The BNP cannot make a non-racial criterion (party membership) a racial one by the terms of its constitution limiting membership to white people. Properly analysed Mr Redfearn's complaint is of discrimination on political grounds, which falls outside the anti-discrimination laws.

NOTES

1. For a discussion of the impact of the decisions in *R* v *Birmingham City Council, ex p. EOC and James* v *Eastleigh Borough Council*, see Holmes, A. and Migdal, S., 'James v Eastleigh Borough Council revisited' (1990) 11 *Business Law Review* 293.

2. Note the decision of the Court of Appeal in *Dhatt* v *McDonalds Hamburgers Ltd* [1991] IRLR 130, where, in applying the RRA 1976, s. 3(4), which requires comparison with persons whose circumstances are the same as or not materially different from those of the complainant, it was held that an Indian national who was requested by his employer to produce evidence of his right to work in the UK could not compare himself with British and EC nationals who were not requested to produce such evidence. As all other nationalities with whom he should have compared himself are required either to have a work permit or indefinite leave to enter (as the complainant had), he had not been treated less favourably. Such a restrictive interpretation of s. 3(4) in allowing nationality to be treated as a relevant ground will have the effect of preventing comparison with the indigenous nationality. For a critique of this case, see Anon, 'Nationality discrimination protection limited' (1991) 36 *Equal Opportunities Review* 35–6. See also Ross, J., 'Race discrimination and the importance of asking the right question' (1991) 20 ILJ 208.

3. The wording of the RRA 1976, s. 1(1)(a) was slightly different from that of the SDA 1975, s. 1(1(a), and was therefore wider in scope, allowing a complaint of direct discrimination where a person is treated less favourably because of another person's race. See *Zarczynska* v *Levy* [1979] 1 WLR 125 and *Weathershield Ltd (t/a Van and Truck Rentals)* v *Sargent* [1999] IRLR 94.

4. The SDA 1975, s. 5(3) and the RRA 1976, s. 3, required a 'like with like' comparison for the purposes of determining whether there has been an act of discrimination (see *Bain* v *Bowles* [1991] IRLR 356). Where there is no actual comparator the onus is on the employment tribunal to construct a hypothetical one, so held the Court of Appeal in *Balamoody* v *United Kingdom Central Council for Nursing, Midwifery and Health Visiting* [2002] IRLR 288. Failure to do so is an error in law. In *Shamoon*, the House of Lords emphasised that where there is no actual comparator whose circumstances are the same, statutory comparison should focus on how a hypothetical comparator in those same circumstances would be treated.

5. Whether an act of discrimination has taken place is a finding in fact; the jurisdiction of the employment tribunal on this matter being limited to acts which are the subject of the complaint in the originating application. It is not open to the employment tribunal to find another act of discrimination of which complaint has not been made (*Chapman* v *Simon* [1994] IRLR 124).

6. The contentious issues of dress codes and direct discrimination were raised again in *Smith* v *Safeway plc* [1996] IRLR 456. The Court of Appeal overturned the decision of the EAT, ruling that different dress codes for men and women are to be judged on what is 'conventional'. Such an approach, if even-handed, is not discriminatory, even if its content is different for men and women. In this case to dismiss a male employee because the length of his hair was unconventional, but to allow a female employee with long hair to continue in employment in a similar post did not amount to less favourable treatment. This approach is further supported by the decision in *Department for Work & Pensions* v *Thompson* [2004] IRLR 348, in which it was held that if a dress

code was part of an overarching requirement for all staff to look professional, it was not necessarily less favourable treatment.

■ QUESTIONS

1. Would the decision in *R v Birmingham City Council, ex p. EOC* be the same had the subjective construction proposed by Lord Lowry been adopted?

2. If all employees and prospective employees are asked the same question, can there be a complaint of discrimination?

3. Does the fact that an employer's policy results in potential discrimination against all races allow him to escape the provisions of the RRA 1976? (See *Qureshi* v *London Borough of Newham* [1991] IRLR 264.)

4. Is it discrimination to refuse a man entry to premises because he is wearing an earring when females wearing earrings are allowed to enter?

5. How far is the decision in *Redfearn* based on political correctness rather than objective reasoning?

(ii) Sexual and racial harassment

The concept of harassment was not directly encompassed in the initial discrimination legislation. Instead, and rather tentatively, it was recognised as a form of direct discrimination (see *Strathclyde Regional Council* v *Porcelli* [1986] IRLR 134; *De Souza* v *Automobile Association* [1986] IRLR 103). A major problem in attacking harassment via this route was that the claimant had to establish a 'detriment'—a formidable hurdle in cases like *De Souza*. However, the Equal Treatment Amendment Directive 2002/73/EC introduced a free-standing definition of harassment which avoided this problem. This found its way into the UK discrimination law regime via the SDA 1975, s. 4A; RRA 1976, s. 3A; DDA 1995, s. 3B; Employment Equality (Religion or Belief) Regulations 2003, reg. 5; Employment Equality (Sexual Orientation) Regulations 2003, reg. 5; Employment Equality (Age) Regulations 2006, reg. 6. It was given a general consolidation in the EqA 2010, s. 26.

EQUALITY ACT 2010

Other prohibited conduct

26 Harassment

(1) A person (A) harasses another (B) if—

    (a) A engages in unwanted conduct related to a relevant protected characteristic, and

    (b) the conduct has the purpose or effect of—

        (i) violating B's dignity, or

        (ii) creating an intimidating, hostile, degrading, humiliating or offensive environment for B.

(2) A also harasses B if—

    (a) A engages in unwanted conduct of a sexual nature, and

    (b) the conduct has the purpose or effect referred to in subsection (1)(b).

(3) A also harasses B if—

    (a) A or another person engages in unwanted conduct of a sexual nature or that is related to gender reassignment or sex,

    (b) the conduct has the purpose or effect referred to in subsection (1)(b), and

    (c) because of B's rejection of or submission to the conduct, A treats B less favourably than A would treat B if B had not rejected or submitted to the conduct.

(4) In deciding whether conduct has the effect referred to in subsection (1)(b), each of the following must be taken into account—

    (a) the perception of B;

    (b) the other circumstances of the case;

    (c) whether it is reasonable for the conduct to have that effect.

(5) The relevant protected characteristics are—
age;
disability;
gender reassignment;
race;
religion or belief;
sex;
sexual orientation.

Jones v Tower Boot Co. Ltd
[1997] IRLR 168, Court of Appeal

Raymondo Jones, whose mother was white and father black, worked for the employers as a machine operative from 16 April 1992, until he resigned a month later. During that time he was subjected to a number of incidents of racial harassment from work colleagues. One employee burnt his arm with a hot screwdriver, metal bolts were thrown at his head, his legs were whipped with a piece of welt, someone stuck a notice on his back bearing the words 'Chipmonks are go', and he was repeatedly called names such as 'chimp', 'monkey', and 'baboon'.

WAITE LJ: ...

The governing principles of statutory construction

Two principles are in my view involved. The first is that a statute is to be construed according to its legislative purpose, with due regard to the result which it is the stated or presumed intention of Parliament to achieve and the means provided for achieving it ('the purposive construction'); and the second is that words in a statute are to be given their normal meaning according to general use in the English language unless the context indicates that such words have to be given a special or technical meaning as a term of art ('the linguistic construction'). It will be convenient to deal with those separately.

The purposive construction

The legislation now represented by the Race and Sex Discrimination Act currently in force broke new ground in seeking to work upon the minds of men and women and thus affect their attitude to the social consequences of difference between the sexes or distinction of skin colour. Its general thrust was educative, persuasive, and (where necessary) coercive. The relief accorded to the victims (or potential victims) of discrimination went beyond the ordinary remedies of damages and an injunction—introducing, through declaratory powers in the court or tribunal and recommendatory powers in the relevant Commission, provisions with a proactive function, designed as much to eliminate the occasions for discrimination as to compensate its victims or punish its perpetrators. These were linked to a code of practice of which courts and tribunals were to take cognisance. Consistently with the broad front on which it operates, the legislation has traditionally been given a wide interpretation—see for example *Savjani* v *IRC* [1981] 1 QB 458 at p. 466 where Templeman LJ said of the Race Relations Act:

> ...the Act was brought in to remedy a very great evil. It is expressed in very wide terms, and I should be slow to find that the effect of something which is humiliatingly discriminatory in racial matters falls outside the ambit of the Act.

Since the getting and losing of work, and the daily functioning of the workplace, are prime areas for potential discrimination on grounds of race or sex, it is not surprising that both Acts contain specific provisions to govern the field of employment. Those provisions are themselves wide-ranging—as is evidenced, for example, by the inclusion of contract workers without employee status within the scheme of the legislation. There is no indication in the Act that by dealing specifically with the employment field Parliament intended in any way to limit the general thrust of the legislation.

A purposive construction accordingly requires s. 32 of the Race Relations Act (and the corresponding s. 41 of the Sex Discrimination Act) to be given a broad interpretation. It would be inconsistent with that requirement to allow the notion of the 'course of employment' to be construed in any sense more limited than the natural meaning of those everyday words would allow.

The linguistic construction

Mr Buckhaven's argument is attractively simple. Vicarious liability is a doctrine of tortious liability which has been applied by the common law to the employment context. Part Three of the Race Relations Act applies expressly to discrimination in the employment field. The two fields are the same. Words and phrases that have acquired a familiar and particular meaning through case law applied to employers' liability in the former context must therefore have been intended by Parliament to have the same meaning when applied to employers' liability in the latter context.

Mr Allen QC, while acknowledging that there is a broad conceptual similarity between the employers' responsibility that applies in both contexts, submits that substantial differences emerge when vicarious liability in tort is analysed and contrasted with the statutory scheme of which s. 32 forms part. The employer's authority, for example is a crucial element in vicarious liability in tort—as evidenced by the statement in *Salmond* (20th edition) in paragraph 21.5 that:

> A master is not responsible for a wrongful act done by his servant unless it is done in the course of his employment. It is deemed to be so done if it is either (1) a wrongful act authorised by the master, or (2) a wrongful and unauthorised way of doing some act authorised by the master.

That is to be contrasted with the position under s. 32(1) of the Race Relations Act, where all actions by a person in the course of employment are attributed to the employer 'whether or not…done with the employer's knowledge or approval'. Mr Allen points to other distinctions, such as the greater range of remedies available under the statute (including damages for injury to feelings) than those available in tort against an employer at common law, and the total absence from the concept of vicarious liability in tort of any provision corresponding to the reasonable steps defence under s. 32(3).

I am persuaded that Mr Allen's submission is to be preferred, and that there is here no sufficient similarity between the two contexts to justify, on a linguistic construction, the reading of the phrase 'course of employment' as subject to the gloss imposed on it in the common law context of vicarious liability.

The position apart from authority

Both approaches to statutory construction therefore lead to the same interpretation. But even more compelling, in my view, is the anomaly which would result (as the minority member Mr Blyghton pointed out) from adopting any other interpretation. Mr Buckhaven accepts (indeed in his written argument he relies upon) the fact that an inevitable result of construing 'course of employment' in the sense for which he contends will be that the more heinous the act of discrimination, the less likely it will be that the employer would be liable. That, he argues, is all to the good. Parliament must have intended the liability of employers to be kept within reasonable bounds.

I would reject that submission entirely. It cuts across the whole legislative scheme and underlying policy of s. 32 (and its counterpart in sex discrimination), which is to deter racial and sexual harassment in the workplace through a widening of the net of responsibility beyond the guilty employees themselves, by making all employers additionally liable for such harassment, and then supplying them with the reasonable steps defence under s. 32(3) which will exonerate the conscientious employer who has used his best endeavours to prevent such harassment, and will encourage all employers who have not yet undertaken such endeavours to take the steps necessary to make the same defence available in their own workplace…

NOTES
1. The definition of harassment is in line with the Code of Practice on Sexual Harassment, which bases harassment on the notion of 'unwanted conduct' on the part of the recipient and covers not only the 'violation of the recipient's dignity' but also the creation of an intimidating, hostile, degrading, humiliating, or offensive environment for the recipient. Sexual harassment extends sex-related harassment including verbal and non-verbal images such as pornography or sexually explicit emails.
2. In *Lindsay* v *London School of Economics and Political Science* [2014] IRLR 218, a black chef manager complained that her own manager used the word 'gollywog' during the course of a conversation. Did the use of the word in the presence of a black person *per se* amount to harassment? The Court of Appeal rejected the argument that there are some words which are inherently racial in nature so that, whatever the context in which they are used, they must be taken as having been uttered on the grounds of race. Lord Justice Floyd stated: 'I do not accept that submission. Context remains relevant.' He added that 'the term "gollywog" if used directly towards the appellant would be obviously racist and offensive. In the context accepted by the tribunal, however, its use may or may not have been on the grounds of race.' In this case, that meant that it was 'critically important for the employment tribunal to determine the reason why [the manager] used the words'.

3. It is clear that harassment does not have to involve physical contact; neither does it have to be a course of conduct (see *Bracebridge Engineering Ltd* v *Darby* [1990] IRLR 3, where it was concluded that a single serious incident will suffice). More controversially, it would appear that any lewd behaviour, even though not initially directed at the complainant, will amount to harassment in circumstances where, despite the complainant's objections, the behaviour continues. The industrial tribunal in *Johnstone* v *Fenton Barns (Scotland) Ltd* (1990) Case No. S/1688/89 concluded that this was evidence that the treatment had been 'meted out' to the complainant in accordance with the *ratio* of *Strathclyde Regional Council* v *Porcelli*.

   The employer is vicariously liable for *all* acts of discrimination carried out by his employees while acting within the course of their employment (the EqA 2010, s. 109). Harassment does not automatically take an employee outside the course of his employment. This is certainly the case with respect to supervisors, line managers, etc., but not always so with respect to employees on the same level or grade (compare *Strathclyde Regional Council* v *Porcelli* with *Irving* v *Post Office* [1987] IRLR 289 and *Bracebridge Engineering Ltd* v *Darby* (see Chapter 7). Furthermore, if the employer is not found to be vicariously liable for the alleged act of discrimination, an action based on victimisation is almost bound to fail; so ruled the Court of Appeal in *Waters* v *Commissioner of Police of the Metropolis* [1997] IRLR 589.

   The test for establishing vicarious liability in discrimination cases was finally clarified by the Court of Appeal in *Jones* v *Tower Boot Company Ltd* [1997] IRLR 168. In adopting a purposive approach to interpreting s. 32 of the RRA, it clearly distinguishes between the common law test for vicarious liability and that which had generally been applied to statutory vicarious liability. However, if the act is not within the course of employment, the fact that it is sexually or racially motivated will not sustain a claim of vicarious liability. In *Sidhu* v *Aerospace Composite Technology Ltd* [2000] IRLR 602, a family day out organised by the employer in which a racial assault took place was found by the Court of Appeal not to be in the course of employment. See Roberts, P. and Vickers, L., 'Harassment at work as discrimination: The current debate in England and Wales' (1998) 3 IJDL 91.

4. It is worth noting that liability for an act of discrimination passes to the transferee following the transfer of the undertaking under the Transfer of Undertakings (Protection of Employment) Regulations 1981, reg. 5(2)(b) (see *DJM International Ltd* v *Nicholas* [1996] IRLR 76).

5. Some clarification has been given to the term 'unwanted conduct' in the EC code of practice on sexual harassment. To amount to 'unwanted' it is not dependent upon rejection of the act by the complainant. This allows a single act to amount to harassment and prevents a situation arising whereby the harasser can argue that as this was the first time, he or she could not have known that the conduct was unwanted until it was actually rejected. In practical terms 'unwanted' is essentially the same as unwelcome or uninvited (*Insitu Cleaning Co. Ltd* v *Heads* [1995] IRLR 4).

6. The Court of Appeal dismissed the appeal in *Grant* v *HM Land Registry* [2011] IRLR 748 against a finding that a gay employee who disclosed his sexual orientation when he was employed at the Land Registry's Lytham office could not complain that he was discriminated against or harassed when he moved to Coventry and a new manager revealed his sexual orientation to work colleagues there against his wishes, in circumstances in which there was an express finding by the employment tribunal that the manager concerned did not have a harassive or discriminatory purpose. So long as there is no ill intent in disclosing the information, Lord Justice Elias stated that, 'having made his sexual orientation generally public, any grievance the claimant has about the information being disseminated to others is unreasonable and unjustified'. This is because 'by putting these facts into the public domain, the claimant takes the risk that he or she may become the focus of conversation and gossip'. Lord Justice Elias added that 'the claimant was no doubt upset that he could not release the information in his own way, but that is far from attracting the epithets required to constitute harassment. In my view, to describe this incident as the tribunal did as subjecting the claimant to a "humiliating environment" when he heard of it some months later is a distortion of language which brings discrimination law into disrepute.' As Michael Rubenstein observes: 'This is strong stuff, and arguably not entirely justified. Lord Justice Elias appears to accept that there could be unlawful discrimination if an employee is outed against their will, but says that this case is different because the claimant chose to reveal his sexual orientation elsewhere. It is hard to see why that ineluctably negates any humiliation he might feel at being outed in the new location and the effect that might have on his working environment. That having been said, the killer point on the facts of this case is that unless the Court of Appeal's reasoning is accepted, any of the employees at Lytham—and the employer—could have been legally liable for innocently mentioning the claimant's sexual orientation to a colleague at Coventry' ('Highlights' [2011] IRLR 713).

7. An employer may avoid liability if he can show that he acted as a reasonable employer in taking all reasonable steps to prevent the discrimination (the SDA 1975, s. 41 and the RRA 1976, s. 32 (now the EqA 2010, s. 109(4))).

EQUALITY ACT 2010

109 Liability of employers and principals

(1) Anything done by a person (A) in the course of A's employment must be treated as also done by the employer.

(2) Anything done by an agent for a principal, with the authority of the principal, must be treated as also done by the principal.

(3) It does not matter whether the thing is done with the employer's or principal's knowledge or approval.

(4) In proceedings against A's employer (B) in respect of anything alleged to have been done by A in the course of A's employment it is a defence for B to show that B took all reasonable steps to prevent A—

(a) from doing the thing, or

(b) from doing anything of that description.

Following *Balgobin* v *Tower Hamlets London Borough Council* [1987] IRLR 401, this section can be satisfied by the existence of an equal opportunities policy and evidence that complaints of discrimination are investigated, even though, as in this particular case, the employer takes no action against the alleged harasser because of the 'lack of evidence'. Townshend-Smith, R., *Sex Discrimination in Employment: Law, practice and policy* (London: Sweet & Maxwell, 1989), at p. 54, quite rightly takes the view that the EAT, in declaring that it was difficult to see what additional steps could have been taken by the employer, misinterpreted the SDA 1975, s. 41(3):

> Apart from showing unawareness of employer policies in respect of sexual harassment, this misinterprets s. 41(3) which places on the employer the burden of showing that all reasonable steps were taken. Employers should be required to show both that the policy was effectively implemented and made known to the employees, and that under it sexual harassment was a specific disciplinary offence. The danger is that tribunals may make decisions on the basis of how important *they* think it is to have effective antidiscrimination policies. It is certain that merely telling employees that they should not discriminate cannot be enough.

Employers are expected to take preventative action even though such action may not have prevented the act complained of from taking place—*Canniffe* v *East Riding of Yorkshire Council* [2000] IRLR 555. See Roberts, P., 'Employer's liability for sexual and racial harassment: Developing the reasonably practicable steps defence' (2001) 30 ILJ 388.

8. It was thought, following the decision in *Burton* v *DeVere Hotels* [1996] IRLR 596, that an employer could be liable for subjecting the employee to the detriment of harassment even where the conduct is outside the scope of the harasser's employment, or where the harasser is a third party, provided the employer could have prevented the harassment from taking place by applying the standards of good practice. However, the decision in *Burton* has now been overruled by the House of Lords in *Pearce* v *Governing Body of Mayfield Secondary School* [2003] IRLR 512, in which it was concluded that in the *Burton* case, while there was a failure on the part of the employer to prevent the act of discrimination, this failure had nothing to do with the sex or race of the employees. As a result, in the *Pearce* case, even if the homophobic abuse had amounted to sexual harassment, the failure to protect the employee on the part of the employer was not related to their sex. The decision in the *Pearce* case has been questioned by Michael Rubenstein in 'Bring back Bernard Manning' ((2003) 124 EOR 31). Rubenstein argues that the new free-standing definitions may also override the House of Lords' decision as it applies to discrimination by a third party.

9. There are two EAT cases to note. However, both pre-date the Employment Equality (Sex Discrimination) Regulations 2005, which implement the revised Equal Treatment Directive. In *Brumfitt* v *Ministry of Defence* [2005] IRLR 4, delegates attending a training course were subjected to numerous offensive and obscene remarks by the person conducting the course. The applicant brought an internal complaint and, when her grievance was not resolved satisfactorily, brought a claim of sex discrimination in respect of both harassment and the way in which her complaint was investigated. The EAT held that as the trainer's conduct was not directed towards the applicant or women generally, the reason for this treatment was not because of her sex and therefore her claim for sexual harassment failed. However, in *Moonsar* v *Five Ways Express Transport Ltd*

[2005] IRLR 9, the applicant was aware that male colleagues with whom she shared an office were downloading pornographic images onto their screens. She did not complain about it but, having been dismissed on grounds of redundancy, she brought complaints of sex and race discrimination. The EAT held that downloading pornography could clearly be regarded as degrading or offensive to a female employee working in close proximity to this action. There was evidence that the applicant found the behaviour unacceptable and the fact that she did not complain at the time did not provide a defence where the behaviour was so obvious as in this case. The employers had the opportunity to show that there was not less favourable treatment; however, they chose not to take part in the proceedings.

There is little doubt that the decision in *Moonsar* is the preferred approach. However, if the applicant's claim in *Moonsar* was to be lodged now, it would not be allowed to proceed as a result of the Dispute Resolution Regulations 2004, as she would have been required to make a complaint in writing to the employer before making a complaint to the employment tribunal.

10. See Rubenstein, M., *Dignity of Women at Work* (Commission of the European Communities, 1988) for a comprehensive comparative study of national laws relating to sexual harassment in Member States of the EC. The report by Rubenstein has led to the declaration and adoption of Recommendation 92/131/EEC on the protection of the dignity of men and women at work, and the publication of a code of practice to combat sexual harassment. Article 1 of the Recommendation on the Protection of the Dignity of Men and Women at Work (92/131/EEC) provides the following definition:

    > It is recommended that the member states take action to promote awareness that conduct of a sexual nature, or other conduct based on sex affecting the dignity of women and men at work, including conduct of superiors and colleagues, is unacceptable if:
    >
    > (a) such conduct is unwanted, unreasonable and offensive to the recipient;
    > (b) a person's rejection of, or submission to, such conduct on the part of employers or workers (including superiors or colleagues) is used explicitly or implicitly as a basis for a decision which affects that person's access to vocational training, access to employment, continued employment, promotion, salary or any other employment decisions; and/or
    > (c) such conduct creates an intimidating, hostile or humiliating work environment for the recipient; and that such conduct may, in certain circumstances, be contrary to the principle of equal treatment within the meaning of Articles 3, 4 and 5 of Directive 76/207/EEC.

    For a discussion of the legal impact of this development, see Rubenstein, M., 'Sexual harassment: European Commission Recommendation and Code of Practice' (1992) 21 ILJ 70. For a discussion of the inadequacies of the provisions relating to sexual harassment, see Bakirci, K., 'Sexual harassment in the workplace in relation to EC legislation' (1998) 3 IJDL 3. For an insight into the position in the USA, see Kelly, J. M., Kadue, D. D., and Mignin, R., 'Sexual harassment in the workplace: A US perspective' (2005) 7 IJDL 5–29.

11. The Protection from Harassment Act 1997 created a criminal offence of harassment (s. 2) as well as providing civil remedies (s. 3) in the form of damages and an injunction. It is unclear how far the Act covers harassment in the workplace; however, the Act refers to harassing a person including alarming the person or causing the person distress. It is clear that an act of harassment must have occurred on more than one occasion for there to be liability under the 1997 Act—see *Banks* v *Ablex Ltd* [2005] EWCA Civ 173.

    Although there is no specific provision regarding vicarious liability, it is possible for an employer to be vicariously liable for harassment of third parties where the act is committed by one of his employees and is in the course of employment. The House of Lords in *Majrowski* v *Guy's and St Thomas's NHS Trust* [2006] IRLR 695 held that an employer may be vicariously liable in damages under s. 3 of the Protection from Harassment Act 2006 for a course of conduct by one of its employees which amounts to harassment in breach of s. 1 of the Act. However, the decision of the Court of Appeal in *Sunderland City Council* v *Conn* [2007] IRLR 324 suggests that for the conduct to be 'unacceptable' it must be of an order which would sustain criminal liability. This limits the potential of the decision in *Majrowski*.

    The 1997 Act means that an employee suffering harassment now has an alternative cause of action. As the editors of *Smith & Wood's Employment Law* observe: 'Not only does an action under the 1997 Act have significant practical advantages (a six-year limitation, not three months; damages merely for "anxiety"; no "employer's defence" that it took all reasonable steps to avoid it) but is conceptually wider because "harassment" is not defined (and there are no signs at the time of writing of the discrimination law definition being read into it) and it applies to harassment for *any* reason (not just sex, race, disability, orientation, religion/belief or age)' (Smith, I. and Baker, A., *Smith & Wood's Employment Law*, 10th edn (Oxford: OUP, 2010), at p. 303).

Other statutory provisions which may assist the victim of harassment are: the Sexual Offences (Amendment) Act 2000, which creates an offence of breach of trust. It is now an offence for a person in a position of trust to engage in sexual activity with a person under the age of 18 years; and the HRA 1998, Article 3, which, it is argued, encompasses degrading treatment.

■ QUESTIONS

1. In what circumstances would an employer be vicariously liable for pornographic material being posted up on the walls of a factory workshop?

2. How far will an employer be liable for harassment of an employee carried out by third parties?

(iii) Segregation

Segregation of employees is a type of direct discrimination. It is only unlawful in the context of racial discrimination.

EQUALITY ACT 2010

13 Direct Discrimination

...

(5) If the protected characteristic is race, less favourable treatment included segregating B from others.

NOTE: To establish segregation the complainant must show that his employer had a policy to segregate workers of different races, or that it was a deliberate act on the part of the employer; this may be difficult to prove, hence the small number of cases pursued using RRA, s. 1(2) (now the EqA 2010, s.13).

Pel Ltd v Modgill
[1980] IRLR 142, Employment Appeal Tribunal

Mr Modgill and 15 other African Asians employed by Pel Ltd in their paint shop complained that they had been discriminated against contrary to the RRA by the company and by their union, the Furniture, Timber and Allied Trades Union (FTATU).

The company, it was claimed, discriminated in their acts and attitudes in relation to the appointment of a separate shop steward, in wage negotiations and transfers. There was also said to be a breakdown of communications. In addition, the complainants alleged that the company had segregated them from other persons on racial grounds within the meaning of s. 1(2) of the Act.

The EAT held that the tribunal had erred in concluding that segregation had taken place merely from the fact that only Asians were employed in the paint shop. This situation had arisen not from any intention on the part of the employer but from the acts of the Asian employees who worked in the paint shop.

SLYNN J: Apart from this question of communication, what really troubled the Tribunal most, in the case of the company, was the allegation that there had been segregation. It is this point which Mr Michael Howard has put in the forefront of his argument on behalf of the company. There is no doubt that if an employer does keep apart one person from others on the grounds of his race, that amounts to discrimination on the part of the employer. If it can be shown that it is the policy of the company to keep a man of one colour apart from others, and that it does in fact happen, then a Tribunal clearly is entitled to find that there has been discrimination contrary to the provisions of the Act...

Then it is said that if one turns to the facts it is plain that only Asians are employed in the paint spray shop; that they are sent there because it is a dirty job which others did not want. We have been told that at the time of the applications only Asian workers were employed in that shop...

The Tribunal had evidence which they appear to have accepted, in the body of their decision, that when vacancies arose in the paint shop they were filled by persons introduced by those who were already working there or those who were leaving. The Tribunal recite evidence that relatives had been introduced into this shop by those already working there. Indeed, the evidence was that, in a significant number of cases, people had applied for employment even before the company knew that there was either a vacancy or was about to be a vacancy because one of the Asian workers was to leave. The evidence even went further than that. Mr Barron, who was in charge of this shop, gave evidence, which the Tribunal appear to have accepted, that over the past 12 months or more, when a vacancy occurred in the department, someone came to him and asked about the job—on one occasion it was one of the existing personnel who came to ask; sometimes before he knew that a particular man was going to leave. Mr Barron agreed, so the Tribunal recite in their decision, that he had not had from the personnel department any applicants during the past two years, except in one instance when white persons were sent to him but they were persons who were not interested in the job. And so the facts appear to be that here, for a period of something like two years, the personnel department of the company had not had to select or interview persons for employment in this particular area. Those who worked there had produced candidates for appointment to Mr Barron and he had found men who were able and willing to take on the job. It seems to us that the Tribunal accepted that there arose a situation, really by the acts of those working in the paint shop itself, that all the workers were in fact Asian. This had not always been the position. A few years ago there had been a number of white men working there, and there had been some coloured, non-Asian workers there as well. But over a period the position had changed and, by the introduction of cousins and friends, Asians alone worked there.

The Tribunal, as we read their decision, really decided the case on the basis that there had been what they called 'indirect' or 'secondary' discrimination because the company had not had a more positive employment policy which would have removed any element of factual segregation, or suspicion of it, arising in the paint shop. This appears to suggest that it was the opinion of the Industrial Tribunal, not so much that the company had by its own acts segregated these men in this particular area away from others, but that it had not prevented the men themselves from coming together in this way. What appears to be suggested is that the company ought to have taken steps to ensure that for some of these jobs, white or non-Asian or coloured men were put in, and that Asians were not allowed to take on these jobs on the grounds of their colour, in order to prevent this segregation in fact arising. We repeat that had there been here evidence of a policy to segregate, and of the fact of segregation arising as a result of the company's acts, that might well have constituted a breach of the legislation; but it does not seem to us that there was evidence to support that position. We do not consider that the failure of the company to intervene and to insist on white or non-Asian workers going into the shop, contrary to the wishes of the men to introduce their friends, itself constituted the act of segregating persons on racial grounds within the meaning of s. 1(2) of the Act. A refusal to appoint other applicants because of their colour, or because they were Asians, might in itself indeed have amounted to discrimination within the meaning of the Act. Because of the view of the Tribunal in this case, in particular in regard to the company, we have considered this matter with some anxiety; but we are quite satisfied that what was relied upon by the Tribunal, namely the lack of communication, can only go to a question of efficiency and does not establish that there has been less favourable treatment of these applicants than others. Nor do we consider that, in law, the failure to have the policy referred to, on the facts of this case, is capable of constituting segregation of a person from others on racial grounds within the meaning of the Act.

B: Indirect discrimination

Indirect discrimination is a practice which has a disparate or an adverse impact on people with a protected characteristic. There does not have to be evidence of overt prejudice. Indeed, the practice will at least superficially appear to be gender, race, etc. neutral, in that it will apply equally to everyone. In effect, the issue is whether the practice in question adversely affects an individual who is a member of a group with a protected characteristic within the meaning of the EqA 2010. Where a particular group is disadvantaged in this way, a person in that group is indirectly discriminated against if he or she is put at that disadvantage, unless the person applying the policy can justify it.

EQUALITY ACT 2010

19 Indirect discrimination

(1) A person (A) discriminates against another (B) if A applies to B a provision, criterion or practice which is discriminatory in relation to a relevant protected characteristic of B's.

(2) For the purposes of subsection (1), a provision, criterion or practice is discriminatory in relation to a relevant protected characteristic of B's if—

    (a) A applies, or would apply, it to persons with whom B does not share the characteristic,

    (b) it puts, or would put, persons with whom B shares the characteristic at a particular disadvantage when compared with persons with whom B does not share it,

    (c) it puts, or would put, B at that disadvantage, and

    (d) A cannot show it to be a proportionate means of achieving a legitimate aim.

(3) The relevant protected characteristics are—

    age;

    disability;

    gender reassignment;

    marriage and civil partnership;

    race;

    religion or belief;

    sex;

    sexual orientation.

NOTE: Section 19 replaces similar provisions in the previous discrimination legislation. It applies the EU definition of indirect discrimination, replacing pre-existing domestic definitions in the SDA 1975 and the RRA 1976, to ensure uniformity of protection across all the protected characteristics in all areas where it applies.

(i) What amounts to a 'provision, criterion or practice'?

The claimant must isolate a 'provision, criterion or practice' (PCP) which the employer applies equally to persons of a different gender, marital status and race etc. Previously, the claimant in race and sex claims had to identify a 'requirement or condition' but this was changed by the Sex Discrimination (Indirect Discrimination and Burden of Proof) Regulations 2001 (SI 2001/2660) and the Race Relations Act (Amendment) Regulations 2003 (SI 2003/1626). There is a limited amount of case law which considers the new phraseology. Some of the earlier cases may also be instructive. The following case was the first to consider the 'PCP' test.

British Airways plc v Starmer

[2005] IRLR 863, Employment Appeal Tribunal

Jessica Starmer was employed as a pilot with British Airways. From May 2001, she was employed full time as a first officer, i.e. a co-pilot. In order to meet her needs for child-care, she requested to reduce her working hours to 50 per cent of full-time working. Her employer refused to let her work less than 75 per cent of full-time hours. Ms Starmer claimed that this decision amounted to indirect discrimination on the basis that it is more difficult for women than men to work full time.

THE EAT HELD: The employment tribunal did not err in finding that in rejecting the claimant pilot's application to change from full-time working to working 50% of the time, and requiring her to work at 75% of full-time, the employers had applied a 'provision, criterion or practice' within the meaning of s. 1(2)(b) of the Sex Discrimination Act.

The tribunal was entitled to find that the employers' decision was a 'provision', notwithstanding that it was a discretionary management decision not applying to others. The decision that if the claimant was to work part-time it must be at 75% and not 50% was a requirement or a condition or a provision. If it was a requirement or condition then, by virtue of Article 6 of the Burden of Proof Directive 97/80, it must also be a provision even if it was not a criterion or practice. Those alternatives are not cumulative. A provision does not have to be an absolute bar. It can allow for exceptions to be made.

Nor is there any necessity for the provision actually to apply to others. What is required in order to test whether the provision, criterion or practice is discriminatory is to extrapolate it to others. The reference in s. 1(2)(b) is not simply to a 'provision...which he applies equally to a man' but also to one which he 'would apply equally to a man'. The creation of a pool constitutes a similar test to the approach to a comparator in cases of direct discrimination. Similarly, the detriment to be considered under s. 1(2)(b)(i) is and can be that of the hypothetical comparator pool.

The employment tribunal did not err in finding that the provision that if the claimant was to work part-time, she was required to work 75% of full-time and not 50% was a provision which would be to the detriment of a considerably larger proportion of women than of men.

A tribunal is entitled to take into account, where appropriate, a more general picture than is specifically displayed by statistics put in evidence.

In the present case, there was evidence, over and above the limited statistics, upon which the tribunal was entitled to conclude that the one-off provision applied to the claimant was one which would be to the detriment of a considerably larger proportion of women than of men.

The employment tribunal did not err in finding that the employers had failed to show that the discriminatory provision, criterion or practice to work 75% of full-time was justifiable. The tribunal was entitled to reject the employers' arguments based on resource considerations.

Justification involves a weighing exercise, in which the detriment to the claimant and, in the present case, the hypothetical detriment to others, is put on the scales. The test is objective. The decision of the employer and its business reasons will be respected, but they must not be uncritically accepted.

In the present case, there was no basis for finding that the tribunal acted perversely in reaching its conclusion. Nor did the employment tribunal err in rejecting the employers' retrospective justification by reference to safety considerations. Whereas, in carrying out the critical evaluation, a tribunal is obliged to give respect to a business decision taken by the respondent at the time, that does not apply where, as here, safety did not form part of that decision at the time. In such a case, the test is entirely objective. In the present case, the tribunal did not err in finding that questions of safety, in the weighing exercise, did not override the detriment to the claimant. It was entitled to conclude that the employers had not given any cogent evidence as to why it would be unsafe or in any way unsuitable for the claimant to fly at 50% of full-time.

Price v Civil Service Commission
[1978] 1 All ER 1228, Employment Appeal Tribunal

The appellant, a woman, was born in 1940. She joined the Civil Service as a clerical officer at the age of 17 and served for two years. At the age of 20 she married and had two children. As well as looking after the children she did some work, mostly part time. In 1975 she saw an advertisement in a newspaper inviting applications for appointment in the Civil Service as an executive officer. No mention was made then of any age limits. She applied and was sent a booklet setting out in detail the conditions of the appointment; in particular it was stated that candidates 'should be at least 17½ years and under 28 years of age on the 31st December 1976', a condition with which she was unable to comply. She complained to an industrial tribunal that, under s. 1(1)(b) of the SDA 1975 the age range was discriminatory because the proportion of women who could comply with it, particularly the upper age limit of 28, was considerably smaller than the proportion of men who could do so, since many women in their 20s were engaged in bringing up and looking after young children and were thus prevented from applying.

It was held, allowing Price's appeal, that 'can comply' meant can comply in practice; this did not involve consideration of what was 'theoretically possible'. (See further Section (iii).)

PHILLIPS J: Experience shows that when considering s. 1(1)(b) it is necessary to define with some precision the requirement or condition which is called in question. Even when the facts are not in dispute it is possible to formulate the requirement or condition, usually at all events, in more than one way; the precise formulation is important when considering sub-paras (i), (ii) and (iii). A fair way of putting it in the present case seems to be that candidates for the post of executive officer must not be over 28 years of age. We do not accept the submission of counsel for the commission that the words 'can comply' must be construed narrowly, and we think that the industrial tribunal were wrong to accept this submission. In one sense it can be said that any female applicant can comply with the condition. She is not obliged to marry, or to have children, or to mind children; she may find somebody to look after them, and as a last resort she may put them into care. In this sense no doubt counsel for the commission is right in saying that any female applicant can comply with the condition. Such a construction appears to us to be wholly out of sympathy with the spirit and intent of the 1975 Act. Further, it should be repeated that compliance with sub-para. (i) is only a preliminary step, which does not lead to a finding that an act is one of discrimination unless the person acting fails to show that it is justifiable. 'Can' is defined (*Shorter Oxford English Dictionary*) as 'to be able: to have the power or capacity.' It is a word with many shades of meaning, and we are satisfied that it should not be too narrowly, or too broadly, construed in its context in s. 1(1)(b)(i). It should not be said that a person 'can' do something merely because it is theoretically possible for him to do so: it is necessary to see whether he can do so in practice. Applying this approach to the circumstances of this case, it is relevant in determining whether women can comply with the condition to take into account the current usual behaviour of women in this respect, as observed in practice, putting on one side behaviour and responses which are unusual or extreme.

Knowledge and experience suggest that a considerable number of women between the mid-twenties and the mid-thirties are engaged in bearing children and in minding children, and that while many find it possible to take up employment many others, while desiring to do so, find it impossible, and that many of the latter as their children get older find that they can follow their wish and seek employment. This knowledge and experience is confirmed by some of the statistical evidence produced to the industrial tribunal (and by certain additional statistical evidence put in by consent of the parties on the hearing of the appeal). This demonstrates clearly that the economic activity of women with at least one A level falls off markedly about the age of 23, reaching a bottom at about the age of 33 when it climbs gradually to a plateau at about 45.

Basing ourselves on this and other evidence, we should have no hesitation in concluding that our own knowledge and experience is confirmed, and that it is safe to say that the condition is one which it is in practice harder for women to comply with than it is for men. We should be inclined to go further and say that there are undoubtedly women of whom it may be properly said in the terms of s. 1(1)(b)(i) that they 'cannot' comply with the condition, because they are women; that is to say because of their involvement with their children. But this is not enough to enable Miss Price to satisfy the requirements of sub-para. (i). The difficulty we have is in saying whether the proportion of women who can comply with the condition is *considerably smaller* than the proportion of men who can comply with it...

NOTES

1. The decision in *Perera* v *Civil Service Commission* [1983] IRLR 166 has in effect been challenged by the EAT in *Falkirk Council* v *Whyte* [1997] IRLR 560. The EAT confirmed that a 'desirable' qualification could amount to a requirement or condition where 'it was clear that the qualification operated as the decisive factor in the selection process'. The EAT not only chose not to follow *Perera*, but also welcomed a more liberal approach to determining 'requirement or condition' and not having to establish an absolute bar.

   It is expected that the definition of indirect discrimination in s. 1(2) will provide greater flexibility and reflect the direction in which the employment tribunals were proceeding in such cases as *Falkirk Council* v *Whyte*. There may, for example, be less dependence on statistical evidence notwithstanding, in considering a possible act of indirect discrimination, the employment tribunal should focus on the discriminatory effect of the particular condition and determine whether the employer has objectively justified it. Although previous case law may still be relevant as an aid to interpretation it is likely that decisions such as that in *Perera* will not be regarded as good law.

2. There has been a series of cases considering the issue whether an obligation to work full time amounts to a requirement or condition for the purposes of s. 1(1)(b). As this affects many women who wish to return to work after maternity leave or while they have children at primary school, it has become an important issue. Initially, in *The Home Office* v *Holmes* [1984] IRLR 299, it was held that such a requirement fell within the meaning of s. 1(1)(b) in that it was an essential part of the employee's contract as, unless she went on working full time, she would not be allowed to continue her job. However, in *Clymo* v *London Borough of Wandsworth* [1989] IRLR 241, it was held (at p. 247) that where full-time working had been offered and accepted by the applicant and was part of the nature of the job, it could not be said that a requirement or condition had been applied to the applicant. The main problem with this case is that the EAT distinguished between jobs at management/supervisory level and lower grade jobs; in the former, full-time working would be part of the nature of the job, whereas in the latter it would amount to a requirement or condition. The matter has to some extent been settled by the decision in *Briggs* v *North Eastern Education and Library Board* [1990] IRLR 181, where it was held (*per* Hutton LCJ at p. 186) that the decision in *Holmes* was to be preferred to that in *Clymo*, and accordingly even though the nature of the job required full-time working this did not prevent there being a requirement or condition

being applied to the applicant. Lastly, where a person returns to part-time work having worked full time, the employer does not discriminate in dictating the days and hours worked in respect of the part-time employment (see *Greater Glasgow Health Board* v *Carey* [1987] IRLR 484), as this can be justified on the terms of administrative efficiency.

A contractual term which imposes an obligation on a party to the contract amounts to the application of a requirement or condition within the SDA 1975, s. 1(1)(b) notwithstanding that the term has not been invoked. A mobility clause in the present case was such a requirement/condition which had a disparate impact on women as the number of women who could comply with the clause was considerably smaller than the number of men (*Meade-Hill & National Union of Civil Servants* v *British Council* [1995] IRLR 478, CA). Naturally the employer has every right at the time of applying the clause to justify it objectively.

3. In the light of the decision in *Enderby* v *Frenchay Health Authority* [1993] IRLR 591, it was argued that it was no longer necessary to establish a requirement or condition under domestic law. This argument was, however, rejected in *Bhudi and others* v *IMI Refiners Ltd* [1994] IRLR 204, in which it was held that *Enderby* was solely concerned with the interpretation of Article 119 (now 141) of the EC Treaty and that there was no obligation to construe s. 1(1)(b) in such a way as to disregard the express provision relating to proof of a 'requirement or condition'.

(ii) What amounts to a particular disadvantage?

Once the complainant has established that a provision, criterion, or practice has been applied to him or her which is also applied equally to other persons, he or she must then show adverse impact. There is little doubt that this can be the most contentious part of his claim. The appropriate pool for comparison must be selected, preferably supported by statistical evidence. It is then a matter for the employment tribunal whether it will accept the pool selected by the complainant, for whom this area is full of pitfalls. The original formulation in the SDA 1975 and the RRA 1976 required proof that the proportion of women, or of people of the same racial group, who could comply with a condition or requirement was considerably smaller than the proportion of men, or people from other racial groups, who could comply with it. However, the amended wording of the SDA 1975, and the RRA 1976 (see Employment Equality (Sex Discrimination) Regulations 2005 (SI 2005/2467)—retained by the EqA 2010), means that a more theoretical comparison not based solely on statistical evidence may suffice. The case law highlighted below is still of relevance and offers guidance on the pool for comparison.

The selection of the correct pool and the proof of disparate impact are critical stages in establishing indirect discrimination. The decision of the Court of Appeal in *Jones* v *University of Manchester* [1993] IRLR 193 illustrates that any attempt by the applicant to manipulate the size of the pool for his or her own benefit will not be upheld. Following *Pearse* v *Bradford Metropolitan Council* [1988] IRLR 379, EAT, the pool should comprise those qualified for the job in question, excluding the requirement complained of. In Mrs Jones's case, this should have been all those graduates with the required experience. However, Mrs Jones as a mature graduate attempted to limit the pool to mature graduates. The court would not accept this further subdivision of the pool.

Jones v Chief Adjudication Officer

[1990] IRLR 533, Court of Appeal

Guidance is given in *Jones* v *Chief Adjudication Officer* (alleged discrimination regarding the receipt of social security benefits), where the criteria for establishing disparate impact were laid down (at p. 537):

MUSTILL LJ: What we must consider is whether, if one looks not at individuals but at the population of claimants as a whole, it can be seen that there is indirect discrimination. The parties agree that for this purpose it is the effect, not the intent, of the legislation which counts. They also agree that what was called the 'demographic' argument represents one way in which indirect discrimination can be established. As I understand it, the process for establishing discrimination on this basis takes the following shape. (For ease of illustration, I will assume that the complaint stems from the failure of a woman to satisfy a relevant positive qualification for selection, and that only one such qualification is in issue.)

1. Identify the criterion for selection;

2. Identify the relevant population, comprising all those who satisfy all the other criteria for selection. (I do not know to what extent this step in the process is articulated in the cases. To my mind it is vital to the intellectual soundness of the demographic argument);

3. Divide the relevant population into groups representing those who satisfy the criterion and those who do not;

4. Predict statistically what proportion of each group should consist of women;

5. Ascertain what are the actual male/female balances in the two groups;

6. Compare the actual with the predicted balances;

7. If women are found to be under-represented in the first group and over-represented in the second, it is proved that the criterion is discriminatory.

NOTES

1. This is a more complicated scheme which appears to work only where there is more than one requirement or condition. Also it ignores the fact that each individual has the right not to be discriminated against, not just the group to which he or she belongs.

2. Further guidance on establishing 'a considerably smaller proportion of a particular sex' can be found in *London Underground Ltd* v *Edwards (No. 2)* [1998] IRLR 364, *per* Potter LJ at p. 369. In the *Edwards* case, while 100 per cent (2,023) of male train operators could comply with the requirement or condition compared to 95.2 per cent of female train operators (20 out of 21), it was found to have a disproportionate effect on the women when the actual numbers involved were considered, i.e. not a single man was affected by the requirement or condition:

> ...In my view, there is a dual statutory purpose underlying the provisions of s. 1(1)(b) and in particular the necessity under subparagraph (i) to show that the proportion of women who can comply with a given requirement or condition is 'considerably smaller' than the proportion of men who can comply with it. The first is to prescribe as the threshold for intervention a situation in which there exists a substantial and not merely marginal discriminatory effect (disparate impact) as between men and women, so that it can be clearly demonstrated that a prima facie case of (indirect) discrimination exists, sufficient to require the employer to justify the application of the condition or requirement in question: see subparagraph (ii). The second is to ensure that a tribunal charged with deciding whether or not the requirement is discriminatory may be confident that its disparate impact is inherent in the application of the requirement or condition and is not simply the product of unreliable statistics or fortuitous circumstance. Since the disparate impact question will require to be resolved in an infinite number of different employment situations, well but by no means comprehensively exemplified in the arguments of Mr Allen, an area of flexibility (or margin of appreciation), is necessarily applicable to the question of whether a particular percentage is to be regarded as 'substantially smaller' in any given case.

3. A requirement that 'the successful candidate be personally known to...the employer does not necessarily have a disproportionate impact as between men and women. In effect, where such a requirement excludes almost the entirety of the pool, it cannot constitute indirect discrimination...It can only have a discriminatory effect if a significant proportion of the pool are able to satisfy the requirement': *Coker & Osamor* v *Lord Chancellor and Lord Chancellor's Department* [2002] IRLR 80, CA.

4. For a discussion of the American approach, which adopts a 'four-fifths rule' for determining disparate impact, see Townshend-Smith, R., *Sex Discrimination in Employment: Law, practice and policy* (London: Sweet & Maxwell, 1989), at p. 76.

5. For a critical examination of indirect discrimination, see the research paper undertaken by Byre, A., *Indirect Discrimination* (EOC, 1987).

Clarke v *Eley (IMI) Kynoch Ltd*
[1982] IRLR 482, Employment Appeal Tribunal

Mrs Clarke and Miss Powell were both employed part time at the company's munitions factory in Birmingham. They were among 60 part-time women to be made redundant on 23 October 1981. At the same time, 20 full-time men and 26 full-time women were also dismissed for reasons of redundancy. The dismissal of the part-timers was in accordance with the company's redundancy selection procedure of dismissing part-timers first before applying the last-in, first-out criterion to full-timers on a unit basis. That procedure was ratified by the union, the TGWU, after a mass meeting of employees had voted in its favour.

The circumstances of the two applicants are different. Miss Powell started work in 1975. She had a child in 1978. The industrial tribunal found that at no time did her domestic circumstances permit her to be a full-time worker. Mrs Clarke, on the other hand, started work in 1967. She had two adult children who had left school by 1975 or 1976. The tribunal found that once both her children had left school there was there-after no domestic reason why she should not have worked full time. The importance of the distinction between the domestic circumstances of the two ladies is that down to early 1980 there was nothing to prevent a part-time worker transferring so as to become a full-time worker. However, as from the middle of 1980 such transfer was not possible.

The EAT held, allowing Clarke's appeal, for the purposes of s. 1(1)(b), the relevant point of time at which the ability or inability of an applicant to comply with a require-ment or condition has to be shown is the date on which she alleges she has suffered detriment. This is the same point in time as that at which the requirement or condition has to be fulfilled. Therefore, the words 'can comply' in s. 1(1)(b)(i) and 'cannot comply' in s. 1(1)(b)(iii) do not include past opportunities to comply.

Consequently, the applicant Mrs Clarke had discharged the burden imposed on her since she had shown that she personally suffered the detriment of dismissal, the reason being that at the time she was dismissed she could not comply with the requirement that she should be a full-time worker. It was irrelevant that at some earlier date she could have avoided that detriment by becoming a full-time worker.

BROWNE-WILKINSON J: ...*Do the words 'can comply' in para. (1) and 'cannot comply' in para. (iii) include past opportunities to comply?*

The question is whether the applicant's inability to comply with a requirement or condition has to be judged as at the date of selection for redundancy or dismissal or as at some earlier date. The point has a dual importance in this case. First, if it is legitimate to have regard to the ability of part-time workers to become full-time workers before 1980, then for the purposes of para. (i) the proportion of women who 'can comply' at that earlier date will be different from the proportion who 'can comply' in 1981 when transfer from part-time to full-time workers had become impossible. Secondly, the Industrial Tribunal held that Mrs Clarke failed to satisfy the requirement of para. (iii) because at some earlier date she could have transferred to full-time work and if she had done so she would not have suffered the detriment.

On this issue we are unable to agree with the Industrial Tribunal. Counsel are agreed that the relevant point in time at which the ability to comply has to be assessed must be the same under both para. (i) and para. (iii). We will consider the case under para. (iii) first. The Industrial Tribunal, although accepting that both ladies had suffered a detriment, said that they had to show that they could not comply as individuals with the requirement to be full-time workers. No doubt this was a paraphrase of the statutory words, but we think that the paraphrase may have led the Industrial Tribunal astray. Para. (iii) does not in terms impose on the complainant the burden of showing that she cannot comply with the requirement: she has to show that the requirement 'is to her detriment *because* she cannot comply with it'. The paragraph imposes the burden of showing detriment to the individual applicant by reason of inability to comply. If one asked the question 'At what date is the detriment to be demonstrated?' there can only be one answer: namely, at the date the discriminatory conduct has operated so as to create the alleged detriment. In this case the detriment relied upon is the dismissal for redundancy. Therefore the relevant question under para. (iii) is 'did the applicant suffer the detriment of dismissal for redundancy because she could not comply with the requirement to be a full-time worker'? So analysed, it seems to us that under para. (iii) the only material question is whether *at the date of the detriment* she can or cannot comply with the requirement. If she can, para. (iii) is not satisfied; if she cannot, it is satisfied. The use of the present tense—'is' to her detriment because she 'cannot' comply—shows that only one point in time is being looked at.

If we are right in thinking that the date of detriment is the only relevant date under para. (iii), we think that counsel are right in conceding that the same date is the only relevant date under para. (i). If that is not the relevant date for the purposes of para. (i) what other date is to be taken? The proportion of men and women who can comply with any given requirement may well vary from time to time. In this case for example the company is arguing that the requirements of para. (i) have not been satisfied because there was no evidence before the Industrial Tribunal as to what proportion of women part-time workers could, like Mrs Clarke, in the past have become full time workers. If that line of inquiry is open, then the proportion of part-time workers whose domestic circumstances permitted them to take full time work will vary from time to time. At what point in time is the comparison between women and men to be made?

For these reasons we think that for all the purposes of s. 1(1)(b) the relevant point of time at which the ability or inability to comply has to be shown is the date on which the applicant alleges she has suffered detriment. This is in fact the same point in time as 'that at which the requirement or condition has to be fulfilled': see *Steel* v *Union of Post Office Workers* [[1977] IRLR 288].

NOTE: The date on which compliance with the requirement or condition is to be judged is the date on which it is applied, not at some future date (*Raval* v *DHSS* [1985] IRLR 370).

Shamoon v *Chief Constable of the Royal Ulster Constabulary*

[2003] IRLR 286, House of Lords

LORD HOPE OF CRAIGHEAD: The statutory cause of action which the appellant has invoked in this case is discrimination in the field of employment. So the first requirement, if the disadvantage is to qualify as a 'detriment' within the meaning of Article 8(2)(b), is that it has arisen in that field. The various acts and omissions mentioned in Article 8(2)(a) are all of that character and so are the words 'by dismissing her' in s. 8(2)(b). The word 'detriment' draws this limitation on its broad and ordinary meaning from its context and from the other words with which it is associated. Res noscitur a sociis. As May LJ put it in *De Souza* v *Automobile Association* [1986] IRLR 103, 107, the court or tribunal must find that by reason of the act or acts complained of a reasonable worker would or might take the view that he had thereby been disadvantaged in the circumstances in which he had thereafter to work.

But once this requirement is satisfied, the only other limitation that can be read into the word is that indicated by Lord Brightman. As he put it in *Ministry of Defence* v *Jeremiah* [1979] IRLR 436, 440, one must take all the circumstances into account. This is a test of materiality. Is the treatment of such a kind that a reasonable worker would or might take the view that in all the circumstances it was to his detriment? An unjustified sense of grievance cannot amount to 'detriment': *Barclays Bank plc* v *Kapur and others (No. 2)* [1995] IRLR 87. But, contrary to the view that was expressed in *Lord Chancellor* v *Coker and Osamor* [2001] IRLR 116, on which the Court of Appeal relied, it is not necessary to demonstrate some physical or economic consequence. As Lord Hoffmann pointed out in *Khan's* case, at p. 835, paragraph 52, the employment tribunal has jurisdiction to award compensation for injury to feelings whether or not compensation is to be awarded under any other head: Race Relations Act 1976, s. 57(4); 1976 Order, Article 66(4). Compensation for an injury to her feelings was the relief which the appellant was seeking in this case when she lodged her claim with the tribunal. Her complaint was that her role and position had been substantially undermined and that it was becoming increasingly marginalised.

The question, then, is whether there was a basis in the evidence which was before the tribunal for a finding that the treatment of which the appellant complained was to her detriment or, to put it more accurately, as the tribunal did not make any finding on this point, whether a finding that the appellant had been subjected to a detriment could reasonably have been withheld.

It is clear that the treatment of which the appellant complains was in the field of her employment. The practice by which she did the appraisals of constables as part of her job in the Urban Traffic Branch had been terminated. As for the question whether a reasonable person in her position might regard this as a detriment, the background is provided by the fact that not only was it the practice for the appraisals to be done by the chief inspectors but this was, as the tribunal put it, endemic in the Force. There was evidence that the appellant had carried out as many as 35 appraisals since she was promoted to the rank of chief inspector. Once it was known, as it was bound to be, that she had had this part of her normal duties taken away from her following a complaint to the Police Federation, the effect was likely to be to reduce her standing among her colleagues. A reasonable employee in her position might well feel that she was being demeaned in the eyes of those over whom she was in a position of authority. The tribunal did not make an express finding to that effect, but there was material in the evidence from which this conclusion could be reasonably be drawn. The respondent did not lead any evidence to the contrary, so he is in no position to resist the drawing of these inferences from the evidence. In my opinion, the appellant was entitled to a finding that she was subjected to a detriment within the meaning of Article 8(2)(b).

NOTE: The complainant must show that the requirement or condition is to his or her detriment or that the provision, criterion, or practice is to their disadvantage because he or she *cannot* comply with it, i.e. there must be *locus standi*. As can be seen from *Clarke*'s case (extracted earlier), the inability to comply must be judged at the date the requirement has to be fulfilled, which is also the same point in time at which the detriment is suffered. 'Detriment' is also used in the wording of SDA, s. 1(2) as amended.

The 'detriment' referred to in SDA 1975, s. 6(2)(b) does not have to be a detriment of a different kind to that which must be shown under s. 1(1)(b)(iii). It is entirely consistent with the scheme and language of the Act that the same disadvantage to the complainant may be relied on in both sections (see *Home Office* v *Holmes* (Section (i))).

Lord Wedderburn, *The Worker and the Law*, 3rd edn (Harmondsworth: Penguin Books, 1986), at pp. 466–8, considers the meaning of 'detriment' and criticises the attitude of, in particular, the appeal courts to ward such matters.

The decision in *Shamoon* confirms this approach and moves away from the decision in *Lord Chancellor* v *Coker* [2001] IRLR 116 in which it was felt that in order to establish a detriment there would have to be a physical or economic consequence. However, the earlier decision of the Court of Appeal in *Jiad* v *Byford* [2003] IRLR 232 placed a more onerous burden on the complainant by distinguishing transitory hurt feelings, which may not amount to a detriment, from a more enduring physical or mental hurt, which may. Clearly the decision of the House of Lords in *Shamoon* has redressed the balance in favour of the complainant.

(iii) Proportionate means of achieving a legitimate aim

The claimant may establish that the provision, criterion, or practice has put them at a particular disadvantage, but the employer can raise the defence that it was a 'proportionate means of achieving a legitimate aim'. The previous defence talked in terms of whether the requirement or condition was justifiable. The test for establishing justification is the same as the test for establishing a genuine material difference/factor under the EPA 1970, s. 1(3) (see *Rainey* v *Greater Glasgow Health Board* [1987] IRLR 26 and *Bilka-Kaufhaus GmbH* v *Weber von Hartz* [1986] IRLR 317). This was confirmed in the following case.

Hampson v Department of Education and Science
[1989] IRLR 69, Court of Appeal

This case was concerned with the RRA 1976, s. 41.

Mrs Hampson is a Hong Kong Chinese woman who was refused qualified teacher status in England. She claimed that this was the result of the application of indirectly discriminatory criteria by the Secretary of State for Education.

Mrs Hampson had taken a two-year initial teacher training course in Hong Kong, qualifying her to teach there. Eight years later, she took a third year full-time teaching course in Hong Kong. Subsequently, she came to England and sought qualified teacher status.

Section 27 of the Education Act 1980 provides that: 'The Secretary of State may by regulations make provision...for requiring teachers at schools...to possess such qualification as may be determined by or under the regulations.' Regulation 13(1) of the Education (Teachers) Regulations 1982 provides that 'no person shall be employed as a teacher at a school unless he is qualified...as mentioned in Schedule 5. Schedule 5 provides for the Secretary of State to determine who is a 'qualified teacher' and stipulates that the Secretary of State will approve as a qualified teacher a person who has completed an approved UK course for initial teacher training or a person who has successfully completed a course 'approved as comparable' to such a course.

Mrs Hampson's application was turned down on grounds that her training was not 'comparable' to that provided in the UK, as required by the 1982 Regulations. This was said to be because, unlike courses in the UK, her initial training was two rather than three years and because the content of courses in Hong Kong did not meet the Department of Education's standards.

It was held, on the meaning of 'justifiable' within s. 1(1)(b), that it requires an objective balance to be struck between the discriminatory effect of the requirement or condition and the reasonable needs of the person who applies it. The tests of justifiability in related fields should be consistent with each other.

BALCOMBE LJ: [Commenting on the meaning put forward in *Ojutiku* v *Manpower Services Commission* [1982] IRLR 418, *Steel* v *Union of Post Office Workers* [1977] IRLR 288 and *Singh* v *Rowntree Mackintosh Ltd* [1979] IRLR 199.]

However, I do derive considerable assistance from the judgment of Lord Justice Stephenson [in *Ojutiku*]. At p. 423 he referred to:

...the comments, which I regard as sound, made by Lord McDonald, giving the judgment of the Employment Appeal Tribunal in Scotland in the cases of *Singh* v *Rowntree Mackintosh Ltd* [1979] IRLR 199 upon the judgment of the Appeal Tribunal given by Phillips J in *Steel* v *Union of Post Office Workers* to which my Lords have referred.

What Phillips J there said is valuable as rejecting justification by convenience and requiring the party applying the discriminatory condition to prove it to be justifiable in all the circumstances on balancing its discriminatory effect against the discriminator's need for it. But that need is what is reasonably needed by the party who applies the condition...

In my judgment 'justifiable' requires an objective balance between the discriminatory effect of the condition and the reasonable needs of the party who applies the condition.

This construction is supported by the recent decision of the House of Lords in *Rainey* v *Greater Glasgow Health Board* [1987] IRLR 26, a case under the Equal Pay Act 1970, and turning on the provisions of s. 1(3) of that Act which at the material time was in the following terms:

An equality clause shall not operate in relation to a variation between the woman's contract and the man's contract if the employer proves that the variation is genuinely due to a material difference (other than the difference of sex) between her case and his.

The House of Lords held, applying the decision of the European Court in *Bilka-Kaufhaus GmbH* v *Weber von Hartz* [1986] IRLR 317, that to justify a material difference under s. 1(3) of the 1970 Act, the employer had to show a real need on the part of the undertaking, objectively justified, although that need was not confined to economic grounds; it might, for instance, include administrative efficiency in a concern not engaged in commerce or business. Clearly it may, as in the present case, be possible to justify by reference to grounds other than economic or administrative efficiency.

At p. 31 Lord Keith of Kinkel (who gave the leading speech, with which all the other law lords agreed) said, in reference to an argument based on s. 1(1)(b)(ii) of the Sex Discrimination Act 1975, which is identical, mutatis mutandis, to s. 1(1)(b)(ii) of the 1976 Act:

This provision has the effect of prohibiting indirect discrimination between women and men. In my opinion it does not, for present purposes, add anything to s. 1(3) of the Act of 1970, since, upon the view which I have taken as to the proper construction of the latter, a difference which demonstrated unjustified indirect discrimination would not discharge the onus placed on the employer. Further, there would not appear to be any material distinction in principle between the need to demonstrate objectively justified grounds of difference for purposes of s. 1(3) and the need to justify a requirement or condition under s. 1(1)(b)(ii) of the Act of 1975.

Mr Sedley constructed an elaborate argument designed to show that Ojutiku had been overruled by *Rainey*. (This argument will be found set out in detail in the judgment of the EAT in [1988] IRLR at pp. 93–95.) However, I do not find it necessary to consider this argument further here. For my part I can find no significant difference between the test adopted by Lord Justice Stephenson in *Ojutiku* and that adopted by the House of Lords in *Rainey*. Since neither Lords Justices Eveleigh nor Kerr in *Ojutiku* indicated what they considered the test to be—although Lord Justice Kerr said what it was not—I am content to adopt Lord Justice Stephenson's test as I have expressed it above, which I consider to be consistent with *Rainey*. It is obviously desirable that the tests of justifiability applied in all these closely related fields should be consistent with each other.

NOURSE LJ: I agree with Lord Justice Balcombe that the best interpretation which can be put on the authorities, in particular on the decisions of this court in *Ojutiku* v *Manpower Services Commission* [1982] IRLR 418 and of the House of Lords in *Rainey* v *Greater Glasgow Health Board* [1987] IRLR 26, is that the correct test is one which requires an objective balance to be struck between the discriminatory effect of the requirement or condition and the reasonable needs of the person who applies it. If, and only if, its discriminatory effect can be objectively justified by those needs will the requirement or condition be 'justifiable' within s. 1(1)(b)(ii) of the Race Relations Act.

> In attempting to justify an act of indirect discrimination, the 'range of reasonable responses' test as applied in unfair dismissal cases should not be used in discrimination cases which require objective justification.

Hardys & Hansons plc v Lax
[2005] IRLR 726, Court of Appeal

PILL LJ: Section 1(2)(b)(ii) requires the employer to show that the proposal is justifiable irrespective of the sex of the person to whom it is applied. It must be objectively justifiable (*Barry*) and I accept that the word 'necessary' used in *Bilka* is to be qualified by the word 'reasonably'. That qualification does not, however, permit the margin of discretion or range of reasonable responses for which the appellants contend. The presence of the word 'reasonably' reflects the presence and applicability of the principle of proportionality. The employer does not have to demonstrate that no other proposal is possible. The employer has to show that the proposal, in this case for a full-time appointment, is justified objectively notwithstanding its discriminatory effect. The principle of proportionality requires the tribunal to take into account the reasonable needs of the business. But it has to make its own judgment, upon a fair and detailed analysis of the working practices and business considerations involved, as to whether the proposal is reasonably necessary. I reject the appellants' submission (apparently accepted by the EAT) that, when reaching its conclusion, the employment tribunal needs to consider only whether or not it is satisfied that the employer's views are within the range of views reasonable in the particular circumstances.

The statute requires the employment tribunal to make judgments upon systems of work, their feasibility or otherwise, the practical problems which may or may not arise from job sharing in a particular business, and the economic impact, in a competitive world, which the restrictions impose upon the employer's freedom of action. The effect of the judgment of the employment tribunal may be profound both for the business and for the employees involved. This is an appraisal requiring considerable skill and insight. As this court has recognised in *Allonby* and in *Cadman*, a critical evaluation is required and is required to be demonstrated in the reasoning of the tribunal. In considering whether the employment tribunal has adequately performed its duty, appellate courts must keep in mind, as did this court in *Allonby* and in *Cadman*, the respect due to the conclusions of the fact finding tribunal and the importance of not overturning a sound decision because there are imperfections in presentation. Equally, the statutory task is such that, just as the employment tribunal must conduct a critical evaluation of the scheme in question, so must the appellate court consider critically whether the employment tribunal has understood and applied the evidence and has assessed fairly the employer's attempts at justification.

NOTES

1. *Hampson* went on appeal to the House of Lords ([1990] IRLR 302) where the argument was directed solely on the interpretation of the RRA 1976, s. 41.
2. There has been much criticism of the *Ojutiku* case, and although the decision in *Hampson* appears to confirm that it is not inconsistent with *Rainey* and *Bilka-Kaufhaus*, it has been considered that Rainey in fact supersedes it (see Townshend-Smith, R., *Sex Discrimination in Employment: Law, practice and policy* (London: Sweet & Maxwell, 1989), pp. 79–83).
3. Whether a requirement or condition can be justified is a question of fact for the tribunal applying the test in *Rainey*. In the past, a wide range of practices has been justified on the following grounds: safety (*Singh* v *Rowntree Mackintosh* [1979] IRLR 199; *Panesar* v *Nestlé Co.* [1980] ICR 144); qualifications (*Raval* v *DHSS* [1985] IRLR 370); part-time employment (*Greater Glasgow Health Board* v *Carey* [1987] IRLR 494; *Kidd* v *DRG (UK) Ltd* [1985] IRLR 190). See Vick, D., 'Disparate effects and objective justifications in sex discrimination law' (2001) 5 IJDL 3.
4. The fact that a requirement or condition is not inherently discriminatory does not amount to 'justification' within s. 1(1)(b). As the operation of s. 1(1)(b) is based on gender (or racially) neutral requirements which have a disparate impact on a particular sex (or race), it is not acceptable justification of the practice to argue that it may operate in a non-discriminatory manner—*Whiffen* v *Milham Ford Girls' School* [2001] IRLR 468.
5. It is worth noting the decision of the House of Lords in *Rutherford* v *Secretary of State for Trade and Industry (No. 2)* [2006] IRLR 551. This case involved a challenge to the upper age limit of 65 years for unfair dismissal claims and redundancy payments imposed by the Employment Rights Act (ERA) 1996. The key issue was whether this limit had a disparate impact on men. The House of Lords ruled that as the statutory bar applied to everyone aged 65 years and over, and applied to no one under that age, it could not disadvantage a higher proportion of one sex than the other, even though there was statistical evidence that relatively more women than men retired before

age 65 and were not therefore subject to the bar. The upper age limit for unfair dismissal claims has since been removed by the Age Discrimination Regulations.

6. In *GMB* v *Allen* [2007] IRLR 752, the EAT gave a narrow interpretation of whether the means to achieve the objective were proportionate to that objective: 'The issue is whether the difference in treatment can be justified as a proportionate response to a legitimate objective.' As a result, even though a criterion may have a disparate impact if its aim or objective is deemed to be legitimate, it is difficult to uphold the view that the means are inappropriate. It is suggested that the EAT has not applied the correct interpretation of 'proportionate'. 'Proportionate' should be interpreted in the light of the wording of the directive and should therefore consider whether the means used were 'appropriate and necessary'.

■ QUESTIONS

1. Does the test of 'putting a particular gender at a particular disadvantage' reduce the burden of proof for the claimant?

2. How far can budgetary considerations justify sex discrimination? (See *Jorgensen* in Section 2.)

3. Why should the 'reasonable response' test not be used in discrimination cases?

C: Pregnancy

Equality Act 2010

13 Direct discrimination

(6) If the protected characteristic is sex—
  (a) less favourable treatment of a woman includes less favourable treatment of her because she is breast-feeding;
  (b) in a case where B is a man, no account is to be taken of special treatment afforded to a woman in connection with pregnancy or childbirth.

18 Pregnancy and maternity discrimination: work cases

(1) This section has effect for the purposes of the application of Part 5 (work) to the protected characteristic of pregnancy and maternity.

(2) A person (A) discriminates against a woman if, in the protected period in relation to a pregnancy of hers, A treats her unfavourably—
  (a) because of the pregnancy, or
  (b) because of illness suffered by her as a result of it.

(3) A person (A) discriminates against a woman if A treats her unfavourably because she is on compulsory maternity leave.

(4) A person (A) discriminates against a woman if A treats her unfavourably because she is exercising or seeking to exercise, or has exercised or sought to exercise, the right to ordinary or additional maternity leave.

(5) For the purposes of subsection (2), if the treatment of a woman is in implementation of a decision taken in the protected period, the treatment is to be regarded as occurring in that period (even if the implementation is not until after the end of that period).

(6) The protected period, in relation to a woman's pregnancy, begins when the pregnancy begins, and ends—
  (a) if she has the right to ordinary and additional maternity leave, at the end of the additional maternity leave period or (if earlier) when she returns to work after the pregnancy;
  (b) if she does not have that right, at the end of the period of 2 weeks beginning with the end of the pregnancy.
  ...

The following cases illustrate how the law has developed to its current position. The appeal courts originally took a strong line on discrimination in respect of pregnancy by concluding that it was outside the SDA 1975, as a pregnant female complainant was not able to show that the less favourable treatment was on grounds of her sex as she had no one with whom she could compare herself, since men could not become pregnant (see *Turley* v *Allders Department Stores Ltd* [1980] ICR 66). This position was remedied to some extent by the decision in *Hayes* v *Malleable Working Men's Club* [1985] IRLR 367, which drew on the comparison between a pregnant woman and a sick man. While this analogy was originally followed in our national courts (see *Webb* v *Emo Air Cargo (UK) Ltd* [1993] IRLR 27, it has been superseded by the ruling of the ECJ.

Webb v EMO Air Cargo (UK) Ltd (No. 2)

[1995] IRLR 645, House of Lords

The respondent firm had 16 employees. It had an import department of four staff, including an import operations clerk, Mrs Stewart. In June 1987, it became known that Mrs Stewart was pregnant and would be taking maternity leave at the end of the year. Mrs Webb was taken on as an import operations clerk on 1 July. It was recognised that she would need six months' training from Mrs Stewart and would then be able to act as her temporary replacement. It was anticipated that Mrs Webb would probably stay in employment when Mrs Stewart returned.

Several weeks after starting work, however, Mrs Webb discovered that she was pregnant and so informed the employers. The employers took the view that they had no alternative but to dismiss her. She complained that she had been discriminated against on grounds of sex.

The House of Lords held that the appellant's dismissal did not constitute unlawful direct discrimination since a hypothetical man required for the same purpose who would also be unavailable at the material time would have been treated similarly. The case was remitted to the ECJ for them to determine whether a dismissal in these circumstances was discriminatory under EC law. The ECJ ([1994] IRLR 482) ruled that Directive 76/207 precluded dismissal of an employee who is recruited for an unlimited term with a view, initially, to replacing another employee during the latter's maternity leave and who cannot do so because, shortly after her recruitment, she is herself found to be pregnant. The case returned to the House of Lords.

LORD KEITH: …The ruling of the European Court of Justice was given on 14 July 1994 ([1994] IRLR 482). The paragraphs of the ruling principally relevant are these (p. 494):

24. First, in response to the House of Lords' inquiry, there can be no question of comparing the situation of a woman who finds herself incapable, by reason of pregnancy discovered very shortly after the conclusion of the employment contract, of performing the task for which she was recruited with that of a man similarly incapable for medical or other reasons.

25. As the applicant rightly argues, pregnancy is not in any way comparable with a pathological condition, and even less so with unavailability for work on non-medical grounds, both of which are situations that may justify the dismissal of a woman without discriminating on grounds of sex. Moreover, in *Handels- og Kontorfunktionaerernes Forbund i Danmark* v *Dansk Arbejdsgiverforening*, C–179/88 [1991] IRLR 31, the Court drew a clear distinction between pregnancy and illness, even where the illness is attributable to pregnancy but manifests itself after the maternity leave. As the Court pointed out, at paragraph 16, there is no reason to distinguish such an illness from any other illness.

26. Furthermore, contrary to the submission of the United Kingdom, dismissal of a pregnant woman recruited for an indefinite period cannot be justified on grounds relating to her inability to fulfil a fundamental condition of her employment contract. The availability of an employee is necessarily, for the employer, a precondition for the proper performance of the employment contract. However, the protection afforded by Community law to a woman during pregnancy and after childbirth cannot be dependent on whether her presence at work during maternity is essential to the proper functioning of the undertaking in which she is employed. Any contrary interpretation would render ineffective the provisions of the Directive.

27. In circumstances such as those of the applicant, termination of a contract for an indefinite period on grounds of the woman's pregnancy cannot be justified by the fact that she is prevented, on a purely temporary basis, from performing the work for which she has been engaged: see *Habermann-Beltermann* v *Arbeiterwohlfahrt, Bezirksverband Ndb/Opf eV*, C–421/92 [1994] IRLR 364 at p. 367, 25; and paragraphs 10 and 11 of the Advocate-General's Opinion in this case, ante, at [1994] IRLR 491.

> 28. The fact that the main proceedings concern a woman who was initially recruited to replace another employee during the latter's maternity leave but who was herself found to be pregnant shortly after her recruitment cannot affect the answer to be given to the national court.
>
> 29. Accordingly, the answer to the question submitted must be that Article 2(1) read with Article 5(1) of Directive (76/207/EEC) precludes dismissal of an employee who is recruited for an unlimited term with a view, initially, to replacing another employee during the latter's maternity leave and who cannot do so because, shortly after recruitment, she is herself found to be pregnant.

It is apparent from the ruling of the Court, and also from the Opinion of the Advocate-General, that it was considered to be a relevant circumstance that the appellant had been engaged for an indefinite or unlimited period.

...The ruling of the European Court proceeds on an interpretation of the broad principles dealt with in Articles 2(1) and 5(1) of the Directive 76/207/EEC. Sections 1(1)(a) and 5(3) of the Act of 1975 set out a more precise test of unlawful discrimination and the problem is how to fit the terms of that test into the ruling. It seems to me that the only way of doing so is to hold that, in a case where a woman is engaged for an indefinite period, the fact that the reason why she will be temporarily unavailable for work at a time when to her knowledge her services will be particularly required is pregnancy is a circumstance relevant to her case, being a circumstance which could not be present in the case of the hypothetical man. It does not necessarily follow that pregnancy would be a relevant circumstance in the situation where the woman is denied employment for a fixed period in the future during the whole of which her pregnancy would make her unavailable for work, nor in the situation where after engagement for such a period the discovery of her pregnancy leads to cancellation of the engagement.

NOTE: The impact of Directive 76/207, in particular Article 2(3), can be seen in the following cases.

Dekker v *Stichting Vormingscentrum Voor Jonge Volwassenen (VJV-Centrum) Plus*
[1991] IRLR 27, European Court of Justice

Elizabeth Dekker applied for a post of training instructor in a youth centre run by VJV. She was pregnant when she applied and so informed the selection committee. The committee recommended Mrs Dekker as the most suitable candidate, but the VJV Board decided that they could not take her on. The reason given to Mrs Dekker was that VJV were advised that their insurer, the Risk Fund for Special Education, would not reimburse the sickness benefits which VJV would have to pay to Mrs Dekker during her maternity leave because she was pregnant at the time of her application.

Under Dutch law covering the public sector, an employee who is unable to perform his or her duties as a result of illness is entitled to 100 per cent of their most recent monthly salary for the first year and 80 per cent for the next year. The relevant Royal decree provides that inability to work due to illness shall be treated in the same way as 'incapacity as a result of pregnancy and confinement'.

However, under the rules of the Risk Fund for Special Education, the fund's managers were entitled to refuse reimbursement of sickness benefit to the employer in the event of an insured person becoming unable to perform his or her duties within six months of the date on which the insurance cover was taken out, if the inability to work was foreseeable at the time when the cover commenced. In Mrs Dekker's case, the employers were concerned that pregnancy would be regarded as a foreseeable incapacity when the employment began. Accordingly, VJV contended that if they were not reimbursed, they would not be able to employ a replacement for Mrs Dekker during her absence, which would mean that they would lose some of their training places.

Mrs Dekker claimed damages, arguing that the refusal of employment was contrary to the provisions of the Dutch equal treatment law of 1 March 1980 implementing EEC Equal Treatment Directive 76/207. The Dutch courts held that the equal treatment law had been violated, but rejected the complaint on grounds that the employer had raised an acceptable ground for justification under Dutch law, which resulted in the violation of the law losing its unlawful character.

The ECJ held that refusing to employ a suitable female applicant on the ground of the possible adverse consequences arising from employing a woman who is pregnant at the time of the application is in contravention of Directive 76/207, Articles 2(1) and 3(1). If the principal reason for the act of discrimination is pregnancy then direct discrimination has occurred.

DECISION: As employment can only be refused because of pregnancy to a woman, such a refusal is direct discrimination on grounds of sex. A refusal to employ because of the financial consequences of absence connected with pregnancy must be deemed to be based principally on the fact of the pregnancy. Such discrimination cannot be justified by the financial detriment in the case of recruitment of a pregnant woman suffered by the employer during her maternity leave.

The fact that pregnancy is treated in the same way as illness and that the provisions of the Sick Act and the Sickness Benefit Regulations concerning payments of sickness benefit in connection with pregnancy are not identical, cannot be considered to result in discrimination on grounds of sex within the meaning of the Directive. Finally, where refusal to recruit by an employer because of the financial consequences of absence connected with pregnancy results in direct discrimination, there is no need to investigate whether national provisions like those referred to above are such that the employer is more or less compelled not to recruit pregnant women, which would result in discrimination within the meaning of the Directive.

It follows from the above considerations that the answer to the first question submitted for a preliminary ruling must be that an employer is acting in direct contravention of the principle of equal treatment referred to in Articles 2(1) and 3(1) of Council Directive 76/207 of 9 February 1976 on the implementation of the principle of equal treatment for men and women as regards access to employment, vocational training and promotion, and working conditions if he refuses to enter into a contract of employment with a female applicant found suitable by him for the post in question, where such refusal is on the ground of the possible adverse consequences for him arising from employing a woman who is pregnant at the time of the application, because of a Government Regulation concerning incapacity to work which treats inability to work because of pregnancy and confinement in the same way as inability to work because of illness.

Handels- og Kontorfunktionaerernes Forbund i Danmark v *Dansk Arbejdsgiverforening (acting for Aldi Marked K/S)*
[1991] IRLR 31, European Court of Justice

Mrs Hertz was employed by Aldi Marked in July 1982 as a part-time cashier and saleswoman. She gave birth to a child in June 1983 after a complicated pregnancy during which she was mainly on sick leave. After the expiry of her statutory entitlement to 24 weeks' maternity leave from the date of birth, she resumed work at the end of 1983 and had no health problems until June 1984. However, between June 1984 and June 1985, as a result of an illness arising out of her pregnancy and confinement, she was off work for 100 days. In June 1985, the employers dismissed Mrs Hertz on grounds of her repeated absences due to illness.

It was held that Directive 76/207, Articles 2 and 5 do not preclude dismissals resulting from absences due to an illness which originated in pregnancy or confinement. The dismissal of a female worker because of her pregnancy constitutes direct discrimination on grounds of her sex, in the same way as does the refusal to recruit a pregnant woman. However, in considering the treatment of a woman where an illness occurs after maternity leave, even though it is connected to the pregnancy or confinement, comparison must be made with the treatment of a sick man. If sickness absence would lead to dismissal of a male worker under the same conditions there is no direct discrimination on grounds of sex.

DECISION: Article 2(1) of the Directive provides that 'the principle of equal treatment shall mean that there shall be no discrimination whatsoever on grounds of sex, either directly or indirectly by reference in particular to marital or family status.' In the words of Article 5(1) 'the application of the principle of equal treatment with regard to working conditions, including the conditions governing dismissal, means that men and women shall be guaranteed the same conditions without discrimination on grounds of sex.'

Article 2(3) of the Directive provides that 'this Directive shall be without prejudice to provisions concerning the protection of women, particularly as regards pregnancy and maternity.'

It follows from the aforementioned provisions of the Directive that the dismissal of a female worker because of her pregnancy constitutes direct discrimination on grounds of sex, as does also the refusal to recruit a pregnant woman (see [*Dekker*] case 177/88, [1991] IRLR 27).

On the other hand, the dismissal of a female worker because of repeated sickness absence which does not have its origin in pregnancy or confinement does not constitute direct discrimination on grounds of sex, insofar as such sickness absence would lead to the dismissal of a male worker under the same conditions.

It should be pointed out that the Directive does not deal with the case of an illness which has its origin in pregnancy or confinement. It does, however, allow for national provisions which ensure specific rights for women in respect of pregnancy and maternity, such as maternity leave. It follows that during the maternity leave from which she benefits under national law, a woman is protected from dismissal because of her absence. It is a matter for each Member State to fix the period for maternity leave in such a way as to allow female workers to be absent during the period during which problems due to pregnancy and confinement may arise.

In regard to an illness which appears after maternity leave, there is not reason to distinguish an illness which has its origin in pregnancy or confinement from any other illness. Such a pathological condition therefore falls under the general scheme applicable to an illness.

Female and male workers are in fact equally exposed to illness. Although it is true that certain problems are specifically linked to one sex or another, the only question is whether a woman is dismissed for absence due to illness on the same conditions as a man: if that is the case, there is no direct discrimination on grounds of sex.

NOTES

1. The Sex Discrimination Act 1975 (Amendment) Regulations 2005 inserted s. 3B which provides protection from discrimination in the access to goods, facilities and services on grounds of pregnancy or maternity (see now EqA 2010, s. 17).

2. The impact of the decision in *Dekker* is reflected in the ECJ ruling in *Webb*. The latter case reaffirms the principle that discriminatory treatment on grounds of pregnancy or maternity amounts to sex discrimination as such treatment is gender-specific: the comparative approach is no longer necessary. However, see Rubenstein, M. ('Highlights' [1994] 23 IRLR) for further debate on the use of the comparative approach.

3. The restriction of the decision in *Webb* to contracts for an indefinite period has been qualified by the ruling of the EAT in *Caruana* v *Manchester Airport plc* [1996] IRLR 378. In this case it was held that protection should be afforded to women on fixed-term contracts, but this would be confined to situations where the woman was available for work.

   In *Mahlburg* v *Land Mecklenburg–Vorpommern* [2000] IRLR 265, the ECJ, in applying *Dekker* and *Habermann*, concluded that it was contrary to Article 2(1) of the Equal Treatment Directive for an employer to refuse to appoint a pregnant woman to a post of an unlimited duration on the ground that a statutory prohibition on employment arising on account of her pregnancy would prevent her from being employed in that post from the outset and for the duration of the pregnancy.

   To replace an employee on maternity leave with a permanent employee, knowing that the pregnant employee wanted to return to her post, amounted to less favourable treatment within the SDA—*(NICA) Patefield* v *Belfast City Council* [2000] IRLR 664. She was therefore disadvantaged in the circumstances in which she had to work.

   In *Busch* v *Klinikum Neustadt GmbH & Co. Betriebs-KG* [2003] IRLR 625 the ECJ held that a woman on parental leave who wishes to return to work before the end of the leave period does not have to give her employer notice that she is pregnant. A refusal to allow a person to return to work because she is pregnant and cannot therefore carry out all her duties is contrary to Article 2(1) of Directive 76/207 as amounting to direct discrimination.

   The ECJ has confirmed that protection of the pregnant woman under Article 5 of the Equal Treatment Directive and Article 10 of the Pregnant Workers Directive is not restricted to those employed for an indefinite period, but extends to those employed for a fixed term, even though, because of her pregnancy, she may be unable to work for a substantial part of the term of the contract. 'Dismissal' of a worker on account of pregnancy constitutes direct discrimination on grounds of sex, whatever the nature and extent of the economic loss incurred by the employer as a result of her absence because of pregnancy. Whether the contract was concluded for a fixed or an indefinite period has no bearing on the discriminating character of the dismissal. In either case, the employee's inability to perform her contract of employment is due to pregnancy—*Tele Danmark A/S* v *Handels- og Kontorfunktionaerernes Forbund i Danmark acting on behalf of Brandt-Nielsen* [2001] IRLR 853.

We can see the use of the purposive approach by the ECJ in considering whether the non-renewal of a fixed-term contract on grounds related to pregnancy fell within Article 10 of the Pregnant Workers Directive or Articles 2(1) and 3(1) of the Equal Treatment Directive.

While the ECJ concluded that non-renewal of a fixed contract when it comes to the end of its stipulated term cannot be regarded as dismissed within Article 10, it can be viewed as a refusal of employment which, if it relates to a worker's pregnancy, constitutes direct discrimination contrary to Articles 2(1) and 3(1) of Directive 76/207—*Jiménez Melgar* v *Ayuntamiento de los Barrios* [2001] IRLR 848.

4. The decisions in *Brown* v *Rentokil Ltd* [1998] IRLR 445, in which the ECJ ruled that sickness absence during and related to pregnancy should not be compared with absences of a male worker due to incapacity, and *Handels- og Kontorfunktionaerernes Forbund i Danmark (acting for Hoj Pedersen)* v *Faellesforeningen for Danmarks Brugsforeringer (acting for Kvickly Skive)* [1999] IRLR 55, in which the ECJ held that pregnant workers on pregnancy-related sick leave who were paid less than workers absent on non-pregnancy related illness were discriminated against contrary to Article 157 and Directive 76/207, highlight the difference in EC law between pregnant workers and those on maternity leave. Pregnancy is protected *per se* from discrimination under Article 157 (ex 119) and the Equal Treatment Directive. Those on maternity leave are provided with specific protection in the Pregnant Workers Directive but cannot claim discrimination in comparing themselves with the sick man. Nor can a woman on maternity leave bring an equal pay claim in respect of any alternative work performed during this period—*British Airways (European Operations at Gatwick) Ltd* v *Moore & Botterill* [2000] IRLR 296.

5. Protection against pregnancy discrimination does not extend to unfavourable treatment of an employee who is undergoing IVF treatment where, on the date of the discriminatory act, the employee's ova have been fertilised by her partner's sperm cells, but not yet transferred into her uterus (*Mayr* v *Bäckerei und Konditorei Gerhard Flöckner OHG* [2008] IRLR 387).

6. Where a woman has to delay actually taking up a post because she is on maternity leave, her continuous service for the purpose of calculating seniority commences on the date she was hired, not the date she was able to take up her duties. The fact that a man 'would have been treated in the same way has no bearing on an assessment of the position of the woman in this case since the deferment of the date on which her career was deemed to have started stemmed exclusively from the maternity leave to which she was entitled'—ECJ in *Sarkatzis Herrero* v *Insituto Madrileno de la Salud* [2006] IRLR 296. Rubenstein suggests that as a result of this decision, the fact that under UK law additional maternity leave does not count as service may contravene EC law ('Highlights' (2006) IRLR 246).

7. The difference between treatment of the pregnant woman during pregnancy and while on maternity leave and the limit to that protection once she has returned to work is highlighted in *Handels- og Kontorfunktionaerernes Forbund i Danmark (acting for Larson)* v *Dansk Handel and Service (acting for Fotex Supermarket)* [1997] IRLR 643. The ECJ confirmed that a woman is not automatically protected from dismissal due to an illness originating from her pregnancy where it occurs outside the maternity leave period. Dismissals occurring after the maternity leave period has ended should be compared to treatment of a sick man. Also there is no automatic right for women returning from maternity leave to job share (*British Telecommunications plc* v *Roberts and Longstaff* [1996] IRLR 60). The EAT concluded that where the employer turned down this request, it did not amount to direct discrimination. However, there is still a possibility that it amounts to indirect discrimination (although this is now subject to the Flexible Working Regulations (SI 2002/3207 and SI 2002/3236)). The ECJ in *Merino Gomez* v *Continental Industrias del Coucho SA* [2004] IRLR 407 decided that pregnant women have a separate entitlement to maternity leave and annual leave. They must therefore be allowed to take annual leave outside of and in addition to their maternity leave period.

Maternity leave periods do not interrupt the employment relationship nor should the maternity leave period be excluded from any qualifying period for other employment rights (ECJ in *Land Brandenburg* v *Sass* [2005] IRLR 147).

8. For a detailed discussion of Family Rights, see Ch. 14 on the Online Resource Centre.

■ QUESTIONS

1. Is the dismissal on moral grounds of an unmarried pregnant woman direct discrimination? See *Berrisford* v *Woodard Schools (Midland Division) Ltd* [1991] IRLR 247; *O'Neill* v *(1) Governors of St Thomas More RCVA Upper School* and *(2) Bedfordshire County Council* [1996] IRLR 372.

2. Does the dismissal of a woman who has had a hysterectomy amount to discrimination on the basis that it equates with pregnancy as being something only a woman can undergo?

3. Can pregnancy discrimination amount to indirect discrimination? See Wintemute, R., 'When is pregnancy discrimination indirect discrimination?' (1998) 27 ILJ 23–36.

SECTION 5: VICTIMISATION

Both the SDA 1975, s. 4 and the RRA 1976, s. 2 made unlawful victimisation by employers against those employees who have either brought proceedings under the respective statutes or have given evidence in proceedings taken against the employer. The EqA 2010, s. 27 introduces a generic civil wrong. Whether these provisions deter victimisation is open to question. There is evidence that action taken under the Acts has an adverse impact on the relationship between the employer and employee—see Leonard, A., *Pyrrhic Victories* (EOC, 1986).

EQUALITY ACT 2010

27 Victimisation

(1) A person (A) victimises another person (B) if A subjects B to a detriment because—
  (a) B does a protected act, or
  (b) A believes that B has done, or may do, a protected act.

(2) Each of the following is a protected act—
  (a) bringing proceedings under this Act;
  (b) giving evidence or information in connection with proceedings under this Act;
  (c) doing any other thing for the purposes of or in connection with this Act;
  (d) making an allegation (whether or not express) that A or another person has contravened this Act.

(3) Giving false evidence or information, or making a false allegation, is not a protected act if the evidence or information is given, or the allegation is made, in bad faith.

(4) This section applies only where the person subjected to a detriment is an individual.

(5) The reference to contravening this Act includes a reference to committing a breach of an equality clause or rule.

Nagarajan v *London Regional Transport*
[1999] IRLR 572, House of Lords

Gregory Nagarajan, who is of Indian racial origin, was employed by London Underground Ltd (LUL) as a station foreman between June 1979 and December 1988; from January 1989 for four months as a travel information assistant with London Regional Transport (LRT), the holding company for LUL; and from May 1989 until October 1989 as duty train manager with LUL.

Over the years, Mr Nagarajan brought a number of complaints of race discrimination and victimisation against LRT, LUL, and some of their employees. Some of these were settled on payment of compensation, some were successful before the industrial tribunal, and some were unsuccessful.

In 1989, Mr Nagarajan issued three originating applications alleging race discrimination by LUL. One of these was settled in September 1989 by payment to him of £20,000. After a period of unemployment, in September 1990, at the suggestion of his former manager, Mr Nagarajan again applied for a travel information post with LRT. (That application was rejected and led to the victimisation proceedings reported at ([1994] IRLR 61 EAT.)

In December 1992, he made another application for a travel information post. He was interviewed for this post in 1993 but was unsuccessful. He brought fresh proceedings, alleging that LRT's central personnel manager, Mr Swiggs, and LRT discriminated against him by victimisation.

Their Lordships held that the Court of Appeal had erred in holding that on a true construction of s. 2(1) of the RRA, a person alleged to have been victimised must establish that in treating him less favourably than he treats or would treat another, the alleged discriminator had a motive which was consciously connected with the race relations legislation. The decision of the employment tribunal, that the appellant had been victimised in respect of an unsuccessful application for a vacancy because the interviewers were 'consciously or subconsciously' influenced by the fact that he had brought proceedings against the employers, would be restored.

LORD STEYN: ...The focus of s. 1(1)(a) of the Act of 1976 is broad: it deals with the entire spectrum of direct discrimination. Section 2(1) is narrower in scope and targets cases where a specific protected act is the reason for the less favourable treatment. Nevertheless, there is no obvious explanation for not requiring proof of motive in s. 1(1)(a) but requiring a conscious motivation by the discriminator to treat the employee less favourably in s. 2(1). Counsel for LRT sought with the aid of the *Oxford English Dictionary* to argue that the difference in wording between 'on the ground of' ('on racial grounds') in s. 1(1)(a) and 'by reason that' in s. 2(1) indicate a legislative intention to make clear that in the latter provision a conscious motivation is required. It can readily be accepted that depending on the context the two expressions are capable of yielding different shades of meaning. But counsel put a weight on the difference of wording which it will not bear in the setting of the Act. The expressions appear in parallel provisions and are readily capable of parallel meanings. Counsel for LRT also relied on the marginal note to s. 2(1), viz 'Discrimination by way of victimisation'. At best this is a makeweight argument. In any event, s. 2(1) does not as counsel suggested define 'victimisation'. It uses the phraseology of 'the person victimised,' which carries no overtones of conscious motivation, as a useful shorthand expression in a provision containing language reminiscent of s. 1(1)(a). That is the origin of the marginal note. The fact that the words 'Discrimination by way of victimisation', divorced from the present context, would in ordinary speech usually import a conscious motive is of little weight. After all, it could be said that the marginal note to s. 1 ('Racial discrimination') conveys the idea of conscious discrimination. Yet it is settled that s. 1(1)(a) does not require proof of conscious motivation. The linguistic arguments put forward by LRT are transparently weak.

The question is whether there is any policy justification for the interpretation upheld by the Court of Appeal. The purpose of s. 2(1) is clear. Its primary purpose is to give to persons victimised on account of their reliance on rights under the Act effective civil remedies, thereby also creating a culture which may deter individuals from penalising those who seek to enforce their rights under the Act. Despite valiant efforts counsel for LRT was unable to point to any plausible policy reason for requiring conscious motivation under s. 2(1) but not under s. 1(1)(a). On the contrary, counsel for LRT accepted that victimisation is as serious a mischief as direct discrimination. In these circumstances policy considerations point towards similar interpretations.

For my part, it is not the logic of symmetry that requires the two provisions to be given parallel interpretations. It is rather a pragmatic consideration. Quite sensibly in s. 1(1)(a) cases the tribunal simply has to pose the question: why did the defendant treat the employee less favourably? They do not have to consider whether a defendant was consciously motivated in his unequal treatment of an employee. That is a straightforward way of carrying out its task in a s. 1(1)(a) case. Common sense suggests that the tribunal should also perform its functions in a s. 2(1) case by asking the equally straightforward question: did the defendant treat the employee less favourably because of his knowledge of a protected act? Given that it is unnecessary in s. 1(1)(a) cases to distinguish between conscious and subconscious motivation, there is no sensible reason for requiring it in s. 2(1) cases. Moreover, the threshold requirement laid down by the Court of Appeal in respect of s. 2(1) cases would tend to complicate the task of the tribunal. It would render the protection of the rights guaranteed by s. 2(1) less effective: see *Coote* v *Granada Hospitality Ltd* [1998] IRLR 656 ECJ at p. 666, paragraphs 22–24.

The Court of Appeal relied strongly on an observation by Slade LJ in *Aziz* [v *Trinity Street Taxis Ltd* [1988] IRLR 204] (at 211, 59). The passage in *Aziz* is in conclusionary form: it is to the effect that s. 2(1) contemplates 'a motive which is consciously connected with the race relations legislation'. But as the headnote of Aziz makes clear, the case was decided on a causative approach. In any event, the case pre-dates the decisions of the House of Lords in the *Equal Opportunities Commission* and *Jones* cases. A contemporary reviewer of *Aziz* argued convincingly that in the light of the decision in the House of Lords in the *Equal Opportunities Commission* case the observation of Slade LJ cannot stand: Jennifer Ross, *Reason, Ground, Intention, Motive and Purpose* (1990) 53 MLR 391. She said that the obiter dictum of Slade LJ 'wrongly emphasises the underlying motivation of the alleged discriminator rather than the immediate cause of the unfavourable treatment.' I agree.

St Helens Metropolitan Borough Council v Derbyshire
[2007] IRLR 540, House of Lords

The appellants, Mrs Derbyshire and 38 other women, along with some 470 other women employed by the respondent local education authority as catering staff in its school meal service, brought equal pay claims against the authority pursuant to s. 2 of the Equal Pay Act 1970. The authority compromised the claims of the other 470 women by paying an agreed lump sum. The 39 appellants, however, did not join in the settlement and proceeded with their claims before the employment tribunal. Those equal pay claims were all ultimately successful.

Some two months before the equal pay claims were due to be heard, the authority's acting head of environmental protection sent two letters. The first was addressed to and sent to all members of the catering staff. It stated, amongst other things, that 'the continuance of the current claims and a ruling against the council will have a severe impact on all staff', and explained in some detail why that would be so. The second letter was sent only to the 39 appellants (who had equal pay claims outstanding before the tribunal). It renewed an offer to settle proceedings and stated that the author was 'greatly concerned about the likely outcome of this matter as stated in the letter to all catering staff'.

HELD: The Court of Appeal had erred in finding that the employment tribunal had been wrong to find that the sending of the two letters amounted to victimisation under the 1975 Act. That the two letters amounted to victimisation was a conclusion to which the tribunal had been entitled to come.

LORD HOPE OF CRAIGHEAD:

Honest and reasonable

What is to be said then about the test of 'honest and reasonable' conduct? This is not a test which is set out in the statute, and there is a risk that it too may be taken out of context. It has a comfortable ring about it. But it should not be used as a substitute for the statutory test, which is whether the employer's conduct was 'by reason that' the employee was insisting on her equal pay claim. Properly understood, it is a convenient way of determining whether the statutory test is satisfied. But it may not fit every case, and in cases where it is used it must be used in the right way.

The context is provided by the judgment of the European Court of Justice in *Coote* v *Granada Hospitality Ltd* C–185/97 [1998] IRLR 656 which, as Lord Neuberger points out, was not cited in *Khan*. That was another case where the conduct did not relate directly to the proceedings. The case arose out of the employer's refusal to supply the employee with a reference after the employment had ended by mutual consent. The questions which were referred to the European Court were directed to the question whether, having regard to Council Directive (76/207/EEC), retaliatory measures after the employment relationship had ended were to be regarded as prohibited. But the Court took the opportunity to draw attention to the fact that Article 6 of the Directive requires Member States to introduce into their national legal systems such measures as are necessary to enable all persons who consider themselves the victims of discrimination 'to pursue their claims by judicial process.' In paragraph 24 the European Court said:

> The principle of effective judicial control laid down in Article 6 of the Directive would be deprived of an essential part of its effectiveness if the protection which it provides did not cover measures which, as in

the main proceedings in this case, an employer might take as a reaction to legal proceedings brought by an employee with the aim of enforcing compliance with the principle of equal treatment. Fear of such measures, where no legal remedy is available against them, might deter workers who considered themselves the victims of discrimination from pursuing their claims by judicial process, and would consequently be liable seriously to jeopardise implementation of the aim pursued by the Directive.

The European Court's reference to measures 'liable seriously to jeopardise implementation of the aim pursued by the Directive' provides the key to how the matter should be approached. It looks at the employer's conduct from the standpoint of the employee's interest, not that of the employer. What is 'honest and reasonable' is an objective test. It is designed to guide the tribunal after the event, not the employer who is trying to work out first what he can and cannot do. It carries with it the implication, which I would regard as sound, that the employer is entitled to take steps to protect his own interests. But he must not seriously jeopardise the employee's right to pursue her claim. It is the employee's interest in pursing [*sic.*] the claim that provides test of what is and what is not 'reasonable'.

But the employer who is looking for guidance needs a bit more than that. One can do no more than resort to generalities on such a fact-sensitive issue. However, I think that this much can be said. The employer should reflect on how the way he wishes to conduct himself will be seen through the eyes of the employee—how would she be likely to react if she were to be treated in that way? He is entitled to bear in mind that an unjustified sense of grievance cannot amount to 'detriment': *Barclays Bank plc* v *Kapur and others (No.2)* [1995] IRLR 87; *Shamoon* v *Chief Constable of the Royal Ulster Constabulary* [2003] IRLR 285, paragraphs 35 and 105. But he must also bear in mind that the right of the employee to enforce compliance with the principle of equal treatment is protected by the Directive. So he must avoid doing anything that might make a reasonable employee feel that she is being unduly pressurised to concede her claim. Indirect pressure of the kind that the tribunal found established in this case—fear of public odium, or the reproaches of colleagues—is just as likely to deter an employee from enforcing her claim as a direct threat. Sensitivity to the wider effects of what he plans to do will be crucial to the exercise of an informed judgment as to what is reasonable.

NOTES
1. The decision in *Nagarajan* finally overturns the restrictive approach adopted in *Aziz* v *Trinity Street Taxis Ltd* [1988] IRLR 204. The test for establishing direct discrimination and victimisation is now the same.

    The decision in *Coote* v *Granada Hospitality Ltd* [1998] IRLR 656 may allow a complainant to challenge the potential inadequacy of the SDA 1975 as it relates to victimisation using Article 6 of Directive 76/207. Additional redress is also provided under the Public Interest Disclosure Act 1998, which is designed to protect whistleblowers who may be victimised.
2. The House of Lords in *Chief Constable of West Yorkshire Police* v *Khan* [2001] IRLR 830 held that whilst failure to provide a reference may amount to victimisation, the withholding of the reference must be linked to a protected act on the part of the applicant. In the present case, the reason the reference was withheld was not because the applicant had brought discrimination proceedings, but rather because the employer temporarily needed to preserve his position in the outstanding proceedings. The evidence established that once the litigation was concluded, a reference would have been supplied. From this case it is clear that the reason for the alleged act of victimisation is relevant and must be identified.
3. The decision in *Bird* v *Sylvester* [2008] IRLR 232 upholds the right of an employer to enter into a compromise agreement and this in itself does not amount to victimisation.

SECTION 6: DISCRIMINATION IN EMPLOYMENT

EQUALITY ACT 2010

39 Employees and applicants

(1) An employer (A) must not discriminate against a person (B)—

    (a) in the arrangements A makes for deciding to whom to offer employment;

    (b) as to the terms on which A offers B employment;

    (c) by not offering B employment.

(2) An employer (A) must not discriminate against an employee of A's (B)—

    (a) as to B's terms of employment;

    (b) in the way A affords B access, or by not affording B access, to opportunities for promotion, transfer or training or for receiving any other benefit, facility or service;

    (c) by dismissing B;

    (d) by subjecting B to any other detriment.

(3) An employer (A) must not victimise a person (B)—

    (a) in the arrangements A makes for deciding to whom to offer employment;

    (b) as to the terms on which A offers B employment;

    (c) by not offering B employment.

(4) An employer (A) must not victimise an employee of A's (B)—

    (a) as to B's terms of employment;

    (b) in the way A affords B access, or by not affording B access, to opportunities for promotion, transfer or training or for any other benefit, facility or service;

    (c) by dismissing B;

    (d) by subjecting B to any other detriment.

(5) A duty to make reasonable adjustments applies to an employer.

(6) Subsection (1)(b), so far as relating to sex or pregnancy and maternity, does not apply to a term that relates to pay—

    (a) unless, were B to accept the offer, an equality clause or rule would have effect in relation to the term, or

    (b) if paragraph (a) does not apply, except in so far as making an offer on terms including that term amounts to a contravention of subsection (1)(b) by virtue of section 13, 14 or 18.

(7) In subsections (2)(c) and (4)(c), the reference to dismissing B includes a reference to the termination of B's employment—

    (a) by the expiry of a period (including a period expiring by reference to an event or circumstance);

    (b) by an act of B's (including giving notice) in circumstances such that B is entitled, because of A's conduct, to terminate the employment without notice.

(8) Subsection (7)(a) does not apply if, immediately after the termination, the employment is renewed on the same terms.

Saunders v Richmond-upon-Thames LBC

[1977] IRLR 362, Employment Appeal Tribunal

Miss Saunders applied for a job with Richmond Borough Council as a golf professional. She was one of seven candidates shortlisted and interviewed. However, she was not asked to attend for a second interview. She alleged that certain questions had been asked during her interview which were discriminatory.

It was held, dismissing Saunders' appeal, that the questions asked did not amount to discrimination within the SDA 1975, ss. 1(1)(a) and 6. The SDA 1975 did not make it automatically unlawful to ask a woman any questions which would not be asked of a man.

PHILLIPS J: During her interview Miss Saunders was asked about 19 questions, of which she claimed that seven were discriminatory in the sense summarised in the first contention. They were these (Reasons, para. 18):

    (1) Are there any women golf professionals in clubs?

    (2) So you'd be blazing the trail would you?

    (4) Do you think men respond as well to a woman golf professional as to a man?

    (8) If all this is true, you are obviously a lady of great experience, but don't you think this type of job is rather unglamorous?

    (9) Don't you think this is a job with rather long hours?

    (10) I can see that you could probably cope with the playing and teaching side of the job, but I am rather concerned as to whether you could cope with the management side.

    (12) If some of the men were causing trouble over the starting times on the tee, do you think you would be able to control this?

Mr Beloff's submission was that it was, as a matter of law, discriminatory within s. 1(1)(a) and 6(1)(a) to ask these questions. We do not agree. Assuming that the asking of questions may constitute 'arrangements' within s. 6(1)(a) the question whether they do must be one of fact in each case. The issue would be whether by asking the question she was, on the ground of her sex, treated less favourably than a man would be treated (s. 1(1)(a)). This would involve a consideration of the circumstances in which, and the purpose for which, the question was asked. In our judgment the Industrial Tribunal approached the matter correctly in this way in para. 18 of the Reasons for their Decision. They, having considered the matter, found as a fact that the questions of which complaint was made were not discriminatory. That is not a finding with which it is open to us to interfere.

Accordingly we reject the first contention.

However, it may be helpful to add a few words on the subject. Mr Beloff stressed the fact that since the enactment of the Sex Discrimination Act 1975 it is necessary for everyone, and in particular employers, to reconsider their approach to such matters and to rid themselves of (what are now) out-of-date ideas and prejudices. It is thus essential for an appointing committee to realise that (unless in exceptional cases) the sex of the applicant is totally irrelevant considered as a qualification or disqualification for a particular employment. If strength is a necessary qualification for appointment it is permissible to reject a woman because she is weak, but not because she is a woman. No doubt, this approach requires a difficult re-adjustment of mental attitudes among many people, and it is now entirely improper to regard a particular job as being 'suitable' or 'unsuitable' for a man or for a woman as the case may be. There is probably not much doubt that such questions as (1) 'Are there any women golf professionals in clubs?' or (4) 'Do you think men respond as well to a woman golf professional as to a man?' reflect, in part at least, what is now an out-of-date and proscribed attitude of mind. That such questions were asked may be very relevant when it comes to be determined (the second contention) whether there has been discrimination in not appointing a woman, and that is why we said earlier that the facts underlying the first contention are relevant upon a consideration of the second contention. But we do not think that it is unlawful to ask such questions, or that Mr Beloff is right when he says that it is now unlawful to ask a woman (or a man) any question which would not be asked of a man (or a woman). Indeed it may be desirable to do so. To take the example cited in the course of argument: suppose a man be considered as an applicant for the headship of a single sex girls' boarding school. If appointed it is obvious that in practice he might have problems with the girls which would be different from those which a female head would have. An appointing committee might well think it proper to enquire whether he had insight into this problem, and was prepared, and was the sort of man who would be able, to deal with it. For that reason they might well wish to enquire whether he had given consideration to his ability as a man to deal with pupils all of whom were girls. It would be absurd to regard such a question as in itself and by itself discriminatory. Indeed, so to rule would scarcely assist the cause of those who are active in the promotion of sex equality. If such questions were to be forbidden, they would not be asked; but not to ask them would not change the mental attitudes of those who would have asked them had they been allowed to do so. All that would be achieved would be that those of that cast of mind would continue to act in the same way as they would have acted had they been allowed to ask the question, but it will never be known, by examining the type of questions they do ask, the way in which they approached the problem. Assuming an employer who is in fact biased and prejudiced, this fact is much more likely to be revealed, and redress to be obtained, if he is free to ask what questions he likes, and thereby to show his true colours.

NOTES

1. While it may not be unlawful at present to ask questions about family or domestic circumstances if it is relevant to do so, employers should consider the answers objectively. The danger is that many employers have stereotyped assumptions about, for example, women with young children, and as a result such things are in effect considered subjectively. However, should the employer be challenged in the tribunals he will have to defend his reason for not employing the complainant as being the genuine reason as opposed to the existence of a covert reason (*Owen* v *Briggs & Jones* [1982] IRLR 502).

2. Any complaint of 'subjecting to a detriment' must now relate to treatment of the employee by the employer during the existence of the contract of employment. 'Detriment' for the purposes of the RRA 1976, s. 4(2)(c) and the SDA 1975, s. 6(2)(c) means disadvantaging the applicant in his/her employment. In *Garry* v *London Borough of Ealing* [2001] IRLR 681, the Court of Appeal concluded that an investigation by the employer into the activities of the appellant, which was continued for longer than an ordinary investigation would have been, amounted to a 'detriment' within the RRA 1976, s. 4(2)(c), even though the appellant was unaware that the investigation was continuing. As senior officers of the council were aware of this, it was held that this operated to her detriment.

3. In *Rhys Harper* v *Relaxion Group plc* [2001] IRLR 460, the Court of Appeal held that claims relating to acts occurring after termination of employment could not be brought under the SDA 1975, s. 6(2) (RRA 1976, s. 4). This was in line with the decision in *Adekeye* v *The Post Office (No.*

2) [1997] IRLR 105. The House of Lords in *Rhys Harper* [2003] IRLR 484 decided that the decision in *Adekeye* was wrong and would not be followed, concluding that post-employment discrimination could be considered within the provisions of the discrimination legislation including the SDA 1975. The exception was claims of victimisation occurring after the employment was terminated—*Coote* v *Granada Hospitality Ltd* (No. 2) [1999] IRLR 452.

4. The decision in Derby Specialist Fabrication Ltd v Burton [2002] IRLR 69 extends the term 'dismissal' to include constructive dismissal, even though it is not specifically included in the RRA 1976.

■ **QUESTION**

If the same question is asked of all applicants for a job, can there be a complaint of discrimination? (See *Dhatt* v *McDonalds Hamburgers Ltd* [1991] IRLR 130.)

NOTE: EqA 2010, s. 108 makes it unlawful to discriminate against or harass a worker after the termination of the employment relationship has ended. However, s. 108(7) states: 'But conduct is not a contravention of this section in so far as it amounts to victimisation of B by A.' The decision of the CA in *Jessemey* v *Rowstock* [2014] IRLR 368 resolved the conflict in earlier case law as to whether post-termination victimisation is unlawful under s. 108. The case is authority for saying that the failure to make express provision proscribing post-termination victimisation in the Act was a drafting error capable of being rectified by a purposive judicial construction. Lord Justice Underhill felt that there is a clear EU obligation to proscribe post-employment victimisation, and this can be given effect by implying into the statute at the end of s. 108(1) the sentence: 'In this sub-section discrimination includes victimisation.'

SECTION 7: GENUINE OCCUPATIONAL QUALIFICATIONS/ REQUIREMENTS

Both the SDA 1975 and the RRA 1976 provided specific defences for an employer against a claim of discrimination in the form of 'genuine occupational qualifications' (GOQs). As a result there are specific situations where it is permissible to select a person with a particular characteristic for a job or to provide access to promotion and training. The EqA 2010, Sch. 9 now provides a more wide-ranging exception.

EQUALITY ACT 2010

SCHEDULE 9
WORK: EXCEPTIONS
PART 1
OCCUPATIONAL REQUIREMENTS

General

(1) A person (A) does not contravene a provision mentioned in sub-paragraph (2) by applying in relation to work a requirement to have a particular protected characteristic, if A shows that, having regard to the nature or context of the work—

(a) it is an occupational requirement,

(b) the application of the requirement is a proportionate means of achieving a legitimate aim, and

(c) the person to whom A applies the requirement does not meet it (or A has reasonable grounds for not being satisfied that the person meets it).

This paragraph provides a general exception to what would otherwise be unlawful direct discrimination in relation to work. The exception applies where being of a particular sex, race, disability, religion or belief, sexual orientation, or age—or not being a transsexual person, married, or a civil partner—is a requirement for the work, and the person to whom it is applied does not meet it (or, except in the case of sex, does not meet it to the reasonable satisfaction of the person who applied it). The requirement must be crucial to the post, and not merely one of several important factors. It also must not be a sham or pretext. In addition, applying the requirement must be proportionate so as to achieve a legitimate aim.

This paragraph replicates the effect of exceptions for occupational requirements in the previous discrimination legislation, and creates new exceptions in relation to disability and replaces the existing exceptions for occupational qualifications in relation to sex, gender reassignment, colour, and nationality. It differs from the existing exceptions for occupational requirements in that it makes clear that the requirement must pursue a legitimate aim and that the burden of showing that the exception applies rests on those seeking to rely on it.

The Explanatory Notes accompanying the Equality Bill provide the following examples:

- The need for authenticity or realism might require someone of a particular race, sex, or age for acting roles (e.g. a black man to play the part of Othello) or modelling jobs.

- Considerations of privacy or decency might require a public changing room or lavatory attendant to be of the same sex as those using the facilities.

- An organisation for deaf people might legitimately employ a deaf person who uses British Sign Language to work as a counsellor to other deaf people whose first or preferred language is BSL.

- Unemployed Muslim women might not take advantage of the services of an outreach worker to help them find employment if they were provided by a man.

- A counsellor working with victims of rape might have to be a woman and not a transsexual person, even if she has a gender recognition certificate, in order to avoid causing them further distress.

Tottenham Green under Fives Centre v Marshall (No. 2)
[1991] IRLR 162, Employment Appeal Tribunal

The appellants run a day care centre in Tottenham. They are managed by a committee of parents and funded by the London Borough of Haringey. The Centre has a policy of maintaining a balance between those of different ethnic background both among the children taken and the staff.

When an Afro-Caribbean nursery worker left, it was decided to replace her with another person of Afro-Caribbean origin. At the relevant time, 84 per cent of the children were of Afro-Caribbean origin and the Centre had four white staff, one Greek Cypriot, and one other Afro-Caribbean. Accordingly, the advertisement stipulated that the post was for an 'Afro-Caribbean worker' and said that the applicant would need 'a personal awareness of Afro-Caribbean culture' and 'an understanding of the importance of anti-racist and anti-sexist child care'.

Mr Marshall, a white, did not see the advertisement, but heard about the vacancy and telephoned for an application form. He did not answer the question on the form about his ethnic origin. When this was drawn to his attention and he said that he was white, he was told that he would not be suitable for the job. He complained that he had been unlawfully discriminated against on grounds of race.

It was held, allowing the employer's appeal, the tribunal had erred in concluding that the applicants had failed to show that being Afro-Caribbean was a genuine occupational qualification within the RRA 1976, s. 5(2)(d). The exception in s. 5(2)(d) applied where the duty was genuine and not so trivial that it could be disregarded. Therefore the requirement that the post-holder should be Afro-Caribbean because such a person was more likely to be able to speak and read in dialect fell within this GOQ.

KNOX J: ... We are, however, bound by findings of fact unless there is no evidence upon which that finding could be based, or we come to the conclusion that the finding is a perverse one. We are not satisfied that from a factual point of view that particular finding is perverse. That, of course, does not conclude the question because there remains the issue whether, given that this particular service was in the nature of a desirable extra, it is something which can legitimately fall out of view in deciding whether or not the exception in s. 5(2)(d) applies.

Two other passages are to be found in the Industrial Tribunal's decision, which is under review, regarding the ability to speak a West Indian dialect. One is in paragraph 13 where they refer to the passage that I have alluded to about an African person qualifying and the Industrial Tribunal remarks that that confirms their view that the dialect-speaking requirement could be dispensed with and finally we find this in paragraph 17:

> As stated above, we do not consider that this was a requirement which was rated as fundamental to the post or an integral requirement with the other three.

That was appended to the general finding that the requirements listed by the respondents could most effectively be provided by any trained nursery assistant with the sole exception of the knowledge of West Indian dialect. In three different ways, therefore, the Industrial Tribunal has stated the way in which the ability to read and talk where necessary in dialect was viewed in contra-distinction to the other personal services. There is a perfectly clear finding that the other three could most effectively be provided by any trained nursery assistant, and no question therefore arises of our finding any error of law in that respect. With regard to the ability to read and talk where necessary in dialect, we have as we have explained above, a finding of fact which is binding upon us, that it is variously described, as a desirable extra; a requirement that could be dispensed with; and not a requirement that was rated as fundamental to the post; or an integral requirement with the other three.

The issue before us is within a small compass but nonetheless not entirely straightforward, and that is: whether it is open to an Industrial Tribunal to disregard a duty in coming to the conclusion that it does not figure for the purposes of deciding whether s. 5(2)(d) applies. One can set on one side two particular categories which it was common ground between the parties did not apply in this case but undoubtedly would be properly disregarded by an Industrial Tribunal which was looking at duties that had to be taken into account for the purposes of this exception. The first of those two categories is what lawyers call matters which are de minimis, that is to say, of such trivial nature as properly to be disregarded. Mr Meeran, who appeared for the applicant, Mr Gary Marshall, very properly disclaimed any reliance on the ability to read and talk when necessary in dialect as being something that was so trivial that it ought to be wholly disregarded.

The other category which would clearly very properly be disregarded in any case, is one where the duty in question is included as a sham or smokescreen to avoid the requirement that there should be no racial discrimination or indeed for any other purposes. It is common ground that this is not relevant in this particular case where as Mr Meeran was at pains to make clear to us, there is no suggestion at all that there was any desire to act otherwise than in a proper manner and there is no question of a sham duty being invented for the purpose of qualifying for the exception in s. 5(2)(d).

What remains is a relatively unimportant but not trivial duty and we have reached the conclusion that it is not the correct view of the meaning of this paragraph that the Industrial Tribunal can make an evaluation of the importance of the duty in question and disregard it although it is satisfied that it is something that is not so trivial that it can properly be disregarded altogether. It seems to us that subsection (3) indicates clearly that one of the duties of the job if it falls within any of the relevant paragraphs, in our case paragraph (d) of the preceding subsection, will operate to make the exception available. That is what one can discern that Parliament intended to provide.

There is no suggestion at all that one has to look to see whether some duties are more important than others, and once one reaches that conclusion, it seems to us, that as a matter of law it is not an answer to a reliance on s. 5(2)(d) that relevant duty is either only a desirable extra, or something that could be dispensed with, or something which is not fundamental to the post. It is still one of the duties of the job and in those circumstances, it not being trivial and it being genuine, it seems to us that the exception necessarily did apply.

SECTION 8: COMPENSATION

The upper limits on awards of compensation made under the SDA 1975 and the RRA 1976 have been removed. It is also clear that an award may include compensation for injury to feelings as well as aggravated damages, although exemplary damages cannot be awarded (see *Deane* v *London Borough of Ealing* [1993] IRLR 209 and *Ministry of Defence* v *Meredith* [1995] IRLR 539).

Marshall v Southampton and South-West Hampshire Area Health Authority (No. 2)
[1993] IRLR 445, European Court of Justice

Miss Marshall worked from July 1966 to March 1980 as a senior dietician for the Health Authority. At that time, the retirement policy of the Health Authority was that, in accordance with the State pension age, women should retire at age 60 and men at 65, but that retirement at those ages could be postponed by mutual agreement. Miss Marshall continued to work until she was dismissed with effect from 31 March 1980 upon reaching age 62. The sole reason given for her dismissal was that she had passed the employers' normal retirement age for women. She would not have been dismissed at that age if she had been a man.

Miss Marshall complained to an industrial tribunal that her dismissal amounted to unlawful discrimination contrary to the SDA and the EEC Equal Treatment Directive 76/207. The tribunal dismissed her complaint under the SDA on the ground that the case fell within s. 6(4), which at that time excluded complaints arising from a provision in relation to retirement. Her claim under Community law was upheld.

The EAT [1983] IRLR 237 held that although Miss Marshall's dismissal violated the principle of equal treatment laid down in the directive, such violation could not be relied upon in proceedings before a UK court or tribunal. Miss Marshall appealed to the Court of Appeal. It referred the matter to the European Court of Justice.

The European Court [1986] IRLR 140 ruled that Article 5(1) of the Equal Treatment Directive must be interpreted as meaning that a general policy concerning dismissal involving the dismissal of a woman solely because she has attained or passed the qualifying age for a State pension, in which age is different under national legislation for men and women, constitutes discrimination on grounds of sex contrary to the directive. The European Court went on to rule that Article 5(1) may be relied upon as against a State authority acting in its capacity as employer, in order to avoid the application of any national provision which does not conform to Article 5(1).

Upon receiving the European Court's decision, the Court of Appeal allowed Miss Marshall's appeal and remitted the application to the industrial tribunal to consider the question of remedy.

The industrial tribunal [1988] IRLR 325 assessed Miss Marshall's financial loss at £18,405, including £7,710 by way of interest calculated as from the date of dismissal to the date of the award. It awarded Miss Marshall £19,405 compensation (adding £1,000 compensation for injury to feelings), less £6,250 she had already received from the employers. The tribunal held that the statutory limit on compensation set by s. 65(2) of the SDA—then £6,250—did not provide an adequate remedy as required by Article 6 of the EEC Equal Treatment Directive, as interpreted by the European Court in *Von Colson* v *Land Nordrhein-Westfalen*, for somebody who is wronged by unlawful sex discrimination in the employment field. Accordingly, said the tribunal, the UK Government was in breach of Article 6 of the Equal Treatment Directive, which requires all Member States to introduce into their national legal systems 'such measures as are necessary to enable all persons who consider themselves wronged...to pursue their claims by judicial process.' As construed in *Von Colson*, that judicial process must include an adequate remedy. Therefore, Miss Marshall, as an employee of an emanation of the State, was entitled to rely upon Article 6 in a complaint before the industrial tribunal. The tribunal consequently ignored the limit on compensation under the SDA.

The employers appealed only against the award of interest. The EAT [1989] IRLR 459 allowed the appeal. The EAT held that Miss Marshall was not entitled to rely upon Article 6 of the Equal Treatment Directive. It took the view that EEC law established that where a State has provided access to the courts, the remedies are for the State, subject only to the principle of *de minimis*, and Article 6 has no direct effect.

The Court of Appeal [1990] IRLR 481, by a majority, dismissed Miss Marshall's appeal. The Court of Appeal also took the view that a sex discrimination complainant cannot rely on Article 6 of the directive to override the limit on compensation in the SDA. According to the majority of the Court of Appeal, the *Von Colson* decision was clear authority that the provisions as to compensation which the European Court held to be implicit in Article 6 are not 'unconditional and sufficiently precise' so as to have direct effect.

The House of Lords referred the following questions to the European Court of Justice for a preliminary ruling:

1. Where the national legislation of a Member State provides for the payment of compensation as one remedy available by judicial process to a person who has been subjected to unlawful discrimination of a kind prohibited by Council Directive 76/207/EEC of 9 February 1976 is the Member State guilty of a failure to implement Article 6 of the directive by reason of the imposition by the national legislation of an upper limit of £6,250 on the amount of compensation recoverable by such a person?

2. Where the national legislation provides for the payment of compensation as aforesaid, is it essential to the due implementation of Article 6 of the directive that the compensation to be awarded:

   (a) should not be less than the amount of the loss found to have been sustained by reason of the unlawful discrimination, and

   (b) should include an award of interest on the principal amount of the loss so found from the date of the unlawful discrimination to the date when the compensation is paid?

3. If the national legislation of a Member State has failed to implement Article 6 of the directive in any of the respects referred to in questions 1 and 2, is a person who has been subjected to unlawful discrimination as aforesaid entitled as against an authority which is an emanation of the Member State to rely on the provisions of Article 6 as overriding the limits imposed by the national legislation on the amount of compensation recoverable?

The ECJ held that it is contrary to Article 6 of EEC Equal Treatment Directive 76/207 for national provisions to lay down an upper limit on the amount of compensation recoverable by a victim of discrimination in respect of the loss and damage sustained.

Real equality of opportunity cannot be attained in the absence of measures appropriate to restore such equality when it has not been observed. In the event of a discriminatory dismissal, where financial compensation is the measure adopted in order to restore equality, it must be adequate, in that it must enable the loss and damage actually sustained as a result of the discriminatory dismissal to be made good in full in accordance with the applicable national rules. An upper limit, of the kind in the present case, on the amount of compensation recoverable by a victim of discrimination cannot, by definition, constitute proper implementation of Article 6, since it limits the amount of compensation *a priori* to a level which is not necessarily consistent with the requirement of ensuring real equality of opportunity through adequate reparation for the loss and damage sustained as a result of discriminatory dismissal.

Similarly, an award of interest, in accordance with applicable national rules, must be regarded as an essential component of compensation for the purposes of restoring full equality of treatment, since full compensation for the loss and damage sustained as a result of discriminatory dismissal cannot leave out of account factors, such as the effluxion of time, which may in fact reduce its value. Therefore, reparation for such loss and damage may not be limited by excluding an award of interest to compensate for the loss sustained by the recipient of the compensation as a result of the effluxion of time until the capital sum awarded is actually paid.

DECISION: Article 6 of the Directive puts Member States under a duty to take the necessary measures to enable all persons who consider themselves wronged by discrimination to pursue their claims by judicial process. Such obligation implies that the measures in question should be sufficiently effective to achieve the objective of the Directive and should be capable of being effectively relied upon by the persons concerned before national courts.

As the Court held in the judgment in Case 14/83 *Von Colson and Kamann* v *Land Nordrhein-Westfalen* [1984] ECR 1891, at paragraph 18, Article 6 does not prescribe a specific measure to be taken in the event of a breach of the prohibition of discrimination, but leaves Member States free to choose between the different solutions suitable for achieving the objective of the Directive, depending on the different situations which may arise.

However, the objective is to arrive at real equality of opportunity and cannot therefore be attained in the absence of measures appropriate to restore such equality when it has not been observed. As the Court stated in paragraph 23 of the judgment in *Von Colson and Kamann*, cited above, those measures must be such as to guarantee real and effective judicial protection and have a real deterrent effect on the employer.

Such requirements necessarily entail that the particular circumstances of each breach of the principle of equal treatment should be taken into account. In the event of discriminatory dismissal contrary to Article 5(1) of the Directive, a situation of equality could not be restored without either reinstating the victim of discrimination or, in the alternative, granting financial compensation for the loss and damage sustained.

Where financial compensation is the measure adopted in order to achieve the objective indicated above, it must be adequate, in that it must enable the loss and damage actually sustained as a result of the discriminatory dismissal to be made good in full in accordance with the applicable national rules.

The first and second questions

In its first question, the House of Lords seeks to establish whether it is contrary to Article 6 of the Directive for national provisions to lay down an upper limit on the amount of compensation recoverable by a victim of discrimination.

In its second question, the House of Lords asks whether Article 6 requires (a) that the compensation for the damage sustained as a result of the illegal discrimination should be full and (b) that it should include an award of interest on the principal amount from the date of the unlawful discrimination to the date when compensation is paid.

The Court's interpretation of Article 6 as set out above provides a direct reply to the first part of the second question relating to the level of compensation required by that provision.

It also follows from that interpretation that the fixing of an upper limit of the kind at issue in the main proceedings cannot, by definition, constitute proper implementation of Article 6 of the Directive, since it limits the amount of compensation a priori to a level which is not necessarily consistent with the requirement of ensuring real equality of opportunity through adequate reparation for the loss and damage sustained as a result of discriminatory dismissal.

With regard to the second part of the second question relating to the award of interest, suffice it to say that full compensation for the loss and damage sustained as a result of discriminatory dismissal cannot leave out of account factors, such as the effluxion of time, which may in fact reduce its value. The award of interest, in accordance with the applicable national rules, must therefore be regarded as an essential component of compensation for the purposes of restoring real equality of treatment.

Accordingly, the reply to be given to the first and second questions is that the interpretation of Article 6 of the Directive must be that reparation of the loss and damage sustained by a person injured as a result of discriminatory dismissal may not be limited to an upper limit fixed a priori or by excluding an award of interest to compensate for the loss sustained by the recipient of the compensation as a result of the effluxion of time until the capital sum awarded is actually paid.

The third question

In its third question, the House of Lords seeks to establish whether a person who has been injured as a result of discriminatory dismissal may rely, as against an authority of the State acting in its capacity as employer, on Article 6 of the Directive in order to contest the application of national rules which impose limits on the amount of compensation recoverable by way of reparation.

It follows from the considerations set out above as to the meaning and scope of Article 6 of the Directive, that that provision is an essential factor for attaining the fundamental objective of equal treatment for men and women, in particular as regards working conditions, including the conditions governing dismissal, referred to in Article 5(1) of the Directive, and that, where, in the event of discriminatory dismissal, financial compensation is the measure adopted in order to restore that equality, such compensation must be full and may not be limited a priori in terms of its amount.

Accordingly, the combined provisions of Article 6 and Article 5 of the Directive give rise, on the part of a person who has been injured as a result of discriminatory dismissal, to rights which that person must be able to rely upon before the national courts as against the State and authorities which are an emanation of the State.

The fact that Member States may choose among different solutions in order to achieve the objective pursued by the Directive depending on the situations which may arise, cannot result in an individual's being prevented from relying on Article 6 in a situation such as that in the main proceedings where the national authorities have no degree of discretion in applying the chosen solution.

It should be pointed out in that connection that, as appears in particular from the judgment in Joined Cases C–6/90 and C–9/90 *Francovich and others v Italian Republic* [1992] IRLR 84, at paragraph 17, the right of a State to choose among several possible means of achieving the objectives of a Directive does not exclude the possibility for individuals of enforcing before national courts rights whose content can be determined sufficiently precisely on the basis of the provisions of the Directive alone.

Accordingly, the reply to be given to the third question is that a person who has been injured as a result of discriminatory dismissal may rely on the provisions of Article 6 of the Directive as against an authority of the State acting in its capacity as an employer in order to set aside a national provision which imposes limits on the amount of compensation recoverable by way of reparation.

NOTES

1. In *Marshall*'s case it was made quite clear by the ECJ, in applying *Von Colson and Kamann v Land Nordrhein-Westfalen* (Case 14/83) [1984] ECR 1891, that UK domestic law and the interpretation by the national courts of both EC law and domestic law continued to contravene the Equal Treatment Directive. See the Sex Discrimination and Equal Pay (Remedies) Regulations 1993.

2. It is well established that injury to feelings is to be regarded as a fundamental element in awarding compensation (*Murray v Powertech* [1992] IRLR 257) and accordingly should be incorporated into the award (see *Sharifi v Strathclyde Regional Council* [1992] IRLR 259, where an award of £500 was deemed to be inadequate as being the minimum amount which should be awarded in any case). Injury to feelings may also lead to an award of aggravated damages—see *British Telecommunications plc v Reid* [2004] IRLR 327. Although it is now clear that they are two separate heads of claim, the Court of Appeal in *Scott v Commissioners of Inland Revenue* [2004] IRLR 213 held that aggravated damages are separate from damages for injury to feelings. Aggravated damages are intended to deal with cases where the injury was inflicted by conduct which was high-handed, malicious, insulting, or oppressive. Aggravated damages therefore should not be aggregated with and treated as part of damages for injury to feelings. In this particular case, Mr Scott had been subjected to an unfounded claim of sexual harassment, which whilst investigated by the employer resulted in him being disciplined on the basis of evidence which could not justify such action. As a result Mr Scott suffered from stress and depression and was dismissed by his employers on medical grounds.

3. The decision of the Court of Appeal in *Sheriff v Klyne Tugs (Lowestoft) Ltd* [1999] IRLR 481 provides a potential new head of damages for personal injury in discrimination cases. Where an applicant can show that the act of discrimination resulted in personal injury, the employment tribunal must award compensation for it. Compensation may be awarded for injury to feelings and psychiatric injury resulting from an act of discrimination. While they are distinct forms of injury, it is recognised that they are not always easily separable—*HM Prison Service v Salmon* [2001] IRLR 425.

4. In *Zaiwalla and Co. v Walia* [2002] IRLR 697, the EAT held that aggravated damages related to alleged misconduct in the defence of proceedings would be permitted. Furthermore where there has been an error in law resulting in the award of excessive damages, the Court of Appeal has the

power to substitute a new award—*Vento v Chief Constable of West Yorkshire Police (No. 2)* [2003] IRLR 103. In avoiding damages for non-pecuniary loss, the Court of Appeal advised tribunals to adhere to the general principles on compensation for such loss as laid down in *Armitage v Johnson* [1997] IRLR 162. If the applicant can show a direct causal link between the act of discrimination and their loss, they are entitled to compensation. Compensation is not limited to reasonably foreseeable harm—*Essa v Laing Ltd* [2004] IRLR 313. In this case the claimant could claim for the depression suffered as a result of racial abuse even though it was not reasonably foreseeable. The Court of Appeal in upholding the decision of the EAT, emphasised that all that was needed to be established is that the injury was caused by the discrimination.

5. Although compensation is the main remedy, there are other remedies such as declaration of rights and recommendations, but these have limited effect.

6. It should be noted that claims may also be brought against those who knowingly aid unlawful acts within the SDA 1975, s. 42 and the RRA 1976, s. 33. In *Yeboah v Crofton* [2002] IRLR 634, the Court of Appeal decided that even where an employer was not vicariously liable within s. 32 of the RRA 1976, the employee could be personally liable under s. 33(1) for 'knowingly' aiding the unlawful act by the employer. Following the decision of the Court of Appeal in *Gilbank v Miles* [2006] IRLR 538, a manager can be personally liable not only for personal acts of discrimination but also under s. 42 of the SDA for aiding acts of discrimination carried out by other employees. In order to aid an act of unlawful discrimination a person must have done more than merely create an environment in which discrimination can occur—*per* Lady Arden, at p. 543.

   In *Anyanwu v South Bank Students Union and South Bank University* [2001] IRLR 305, the House of Lords concluded that 'aids' amounts to help, assistance, cooperation or collaboration with another. It is irrelevant who initiates the relationship. 'Aids indicates the giving of some kind of assistance to the other person which helps him to do it. The amount or value of that help or assistance is of no importance'—Lord Craighead, at p. 311.

7. Further clarification is found in *Hallam v Cheltenham Borough Council* [2001] IRLR 312 in which the House of Lords held that s. 33(1) requires more than a general attitude of helpfulness and cooperation.

8. For a study of the effect of successful complaints, see Leonard, A., *Pyrrhic Victories: Winning sex discrimination and equal pay cases in the industrial tribunals* (EOC, 1987).

FURTHER READING

Cabrelli, D., *Employment Law in Context: Text and materials* (Oxford: OUP, 2014), Chs. 10, 11.

Honeyball, S., *Honeyball & Bowers' Textbook on Employment Law*, 13th edn (Oxford: OUP, 2014), Ch. 10.

6

Equality Law (3): Other Forms of Discrimination

SECTION 1: INTRODUCTION

In this chapter we shall be considering other prohibited forms of discrimination, in particular disability, sexual orientation, religion or belief, and age, although many aspects of the way in which the legislation has been interpreted in respect of sex and race discrimination will also be applicable in this chapter. It is also important to emphasise that the concepts of direct and indirect discrimination, harassment, and victimisation have generally been harmonised across all those groups holding protected characteristics by the Equality Act (EqA) 2010 (see the EqA 2010, ss. 13, 19, 26, 27, and Chapter 5).

As a result of the Framework Directive (2000/78) the breadth of the protection from discrimination was extended, resulting in not only new provisions for example on sexual orientation, but also amendments to existing provisions, e.g. the Disability Discrimination Act (DDA) 1995, to ensure parity of treatment. The implementation of the new provisions and amendments has been phased in as a result of the UK opting for the last possible period for implementation; for example, the age discrimination legislation was not implemented until October 2006.

SECTION 2: DISABILITY DISCRIMINATION: THE EQUALITY ACT 2010 (FORMERLY THE DISABILITY DISCRIMINATION ACT 1995)

This Act is intended to prevent discrimination on grounds of disability in employment, in relation to the provision of goods, facilities and services, premises, further and higher education, and public transport, including taxis, public service vehicles, and railways. It further requires employers to accommodate the needs of disabled persons to enable them to carry out their jobs. A complaint made under the Act may be heard by an employment tribunal. The DDA 1995 was subject to significant amendments by the DDA 2005.

The Framework Directive (2000/78) in implementing Article 13 pays particular attention to disability, age, and religion and belief. What is interesting is that these grounds are not all treated equally by the directive. Indeed, it has been suggested that the directive introduces a hierarchy amongst the discriminating grounds—see Waddington, L., 'Article 13 EC: Setting priorities in the proposal for a horizontal employment directive' (2000) 29 ILJ 176. For a discussion of discrimination based on social prejudices, such as sexuality, dress, criminal records, politics, and disability, see Lord Wedderburn, *The Worker and The Law* (Harmondsworth: Penguin, 1986), pp. 447–57. See also 'Facial discrimination: Extending handicap law to employment discrimination on the basis of physical appearance' (1987) 100 HLR 2035.

A number of significant changes were made to the DDA 1995 in order to ensure that it was consistent with the requirements of the Employment Framework Directive (2000/78). The Disability Discrimination Act 1995 (Amendment) Regulations 2003 (SI

2003/1673) introduced a new form of direct discrimination; a new definition of harassment; the widening of the employers' duty to make reasonable adjustments and the removal of the justification defence to a failure to comply with this duty; the removal of the small employer exemption and other currently excluded employment; the extension of the DDA 1995 to cover public bodies including the police, qualification bodies, partnerships, office and post-holders, and barristers; a prohibition on discriminatory advertisements; and changes to the burden of proof. There is also a revised code of practice. The Government issued revised guidance on the definition of 'disability' (May 2006).

In addition, the DDA 2005 introduced a positive duty on public bodies to promote equality of opportunity for disabled people; an extension of the DDA to cover all activities in the public sector; an extension of the meaning of disability to include HIV, multiple sclerosis, and cancer; an extension of the reasonable adjustment provisions to landlords which would include a requirement to provide auxiliary aids; and making Chief Officers of police vicariously liable for acts of discrimination committed by their officers in the performance of their duties (see now the EqA 2010, s. 149).

Many aspects of the DDA 1995 will be familiar to those with knowledge of the Sex Discrimination Act (SDA), although the DDA is not a mirror image of the existing legislation. The law relating to disability discrimination is now contained in the EqA 2010.

EQUALITY ACT 2010

6 Disability

(1) A person (P) has a disability if—
  (a) P has a physical or mental impairment, and
  (b) the impairment has a substantial and long-term adverse effect on P's ability to carry out normal day-to-day activities.
(2) A reference to a disabled person is a reference to a person who has a disability.
(3) In relation to the protected characteristic of disability—
  (a) a reference to a person who has a particular protected characteristic is a reference to a person who has a particular disability;
  (b) a reference to persons who share a protected characteristic is a reference to persons who have the same disability.
(4) This Act (except Part 12 and section 190) applies in relation to a person who has had a disability as it applies in relation to a person who has the disability; accordingly, except in that Part and that section—
  (a) a reference (however expressed) to a person who has a disability includes a reference to a person who has had the disability, and
  (b) a reference (however expressed) to a person who does not have a disability includes a reference to a person who has not had the disability.
(5) A Minister of the Crown may issue guidance about matters to be taken into account in deciding any question for the purposes of subsection (1).
(6) Schedule 1 (disability: supplementary provision) has effect.

A: Meaning of 'disability'

EQUALITY ACT 2010

SCHEDULE 1

DISABILITY: SUPPLEMENTARY PROVISION

PART 1

DETERMINATION OF DISABILITY

Impairment

1   Regulations may make provision for a condition of a prescribed description to be, or not to be, an impairment.

Long-term effects

2　(1)　The effect of an impairment is long-term if—

　　　　(a)　it has lasted for at least 12 months,

　　　　(b)　it is likely to last for at least 12 months, or

　　　　(c)　it is likely to last for the rest of the life of the person affected.

　　(2)　If an impairment ceases to have a substantial adverse effect on a person's ability to carry out normal day-to-day activities, it is to be treated as continuing to have that effect if that effect is likely to recur.

　　(3)　For the purposes of sub-paragraph (2), the likelihood of an effect recurring is to be disregarded in such circumstances as may be prescribed.

　　(4)　Regulations may prescribe circumstances in which, despite sub-paragraph (1), an effect is to be treated as being, or as not being, long-term.

Severe disfigurement

3　(1)　An impairment which consists of a severe disfigurement is to be treated as having a substantial adverse effect on the ability of the person concerned to carry out normal day-to-day activities.

　　(2)　Regulations may provide that in prescribed circumstances a severe disfigurement is not to be treated as having that effect.

　　(3)　The regulations may, in particular, make provision in relation to deliberately acquired disfigurement.

Substantial adverse effects

4　Regulations may make provision for an effect of a prescribed description on the ability of a person to carry out normal day-to-day activities to be treated as being, or as not being, a substantial adverse effect.

Effect of medical treatment

5　(1)　An impairment is to be treated as having a substantial adverse effect on the ability of the person concerned to carry out normal day-to-day activities if—

　　　　(a) measures are being taken to treat or correct it, and

　　　　(b) but for that, it would be likely to have that effect.

　　(2)　'Measures' includes, in particular, medical treatment and the use of a prosthesis or other aid.

　　(3)　Sub-paragraph (1) does not apply—

　　　　(a)　in relation to the impairment of a person's sight, to the extent that the impairment is, in the person's case, correctable by spectacles or contact lenses or in such other ways as may be prescribed;

　　　　(b)　in relation to such other impairments as may be prescribed, in such circumstances as are prescribed.

Certain medical conditions

6　(1)　Cancer, HIV infection and multiple sclerosis are each a disability.

　　(2)　HIV infection is infection by a virus capable of causing the Acquired Immune Deficiency Syndrome.

Deemed disability

7　(1)　Regulations may provide for persons of prescribed descriptions to be treated as having disabilities.

　　(2)　The regulations may prescribe circumstances in which a person who has a disability is to be treated as no longer having the disability.

　　(3)　This paragraph does not affect the other provisions of this Schedule.

Progressive conditions

8　(1)　This paragraph applies to a person (P) if—

　　　　(a)　P has a progressive condition,

　　　　(b)　as a result of that condition P has an impairment which has (or had) an effect on P's ability to carry out normal day-to-day activities, but

　　　　(c) the effect is not (or was not) a substantial adverse effect.

　　(2)　P is to be taken to have an impairment which has a substantial adverse effect if the condition is likely to result in P having such an impairment.

　　(3)　Regulations may make provision for a condition of a prescribed description to be treated as being, or as not being, progressive.

Past disabilities

9　(1)　A question as to whether a person had a disability at a particular time ('the relevant time') is to be determined, for the purposes of section 6, as if the provisions of, or made under, this Act were in force when the act complained of was done had been in force at the relevant time.

　　(2)　The relevant time may be a time before the coming into force of the provision of this Act to which the question relates.

NOTES
1. The legislation requires the tribunal to look at the evidence by reference to four different conditions:
   (i) Does the applicant have an impairment which is either mental or physical? The need to show that mental illness is 'clinically well recognised' was removed by the DDA 2005. This should make it easier for claimants to establish that they have a disability based on mental impairment. It should also alleviate some of the problems faced by the claimant in *Morgan* v *Staffordshire University* [2002] IRLR 129. In this case the evidence of stress, anxiety, and depression was found to be insufficient to establish that there was a clinically well-recognised condition.
   (ii) Does the impairment affect the applicant's ability to carry out normal day-to-day activities, and does it have an adverse effect? The Act is concerned with a person's ability to carry out activities. The fact that a person can carry out such activities does not mean that his ability to carry them out has not been impaired. The focus of the Act is on the things that the applicant either cannot do or can do only with difficulty, rather than on the things that the person can do.
   (iii) Is the adverse effect substantial? 'Substantial' means 'more than minor or trivial' rather than 'very large'. The tribunal may take into account how the applicant appears to the tribunal to 'manage', although it should be slow to regard a person's capabilities in the relatively strange adversarial environment as an entirely reliable guide to the level of ability to perform normal day-to-day activities. The tribunal should examine how an applicant's abilities have actually been affected whilst on medication and then consider the 'deduced effects'—the effects which it thinks there would have been but for the medication—and whether the actual and deduced effects on ability to carry out normal day-to-day activities are clearly more than trivial.
   (iv) Is the adverse effect long-term? The case of *Greenwood* v *British Airways plc* [1999] IRLR 600 considered the appropriate time for determining whether a disability has a long-term effect. While the EAT concluded that the relevant date was up to and including the employment tribunal hearing, interestingly Rubenstein ('Highlights' [1999] IRLR 597) suggests that this is incorrect and that the correct date is at the time of the alleged act of discrimination. Certainly, the latter is in line with other aspects of discrimination law. Rubenstein's view was vindicated in *Richmond Adult Community College* v *McDougall* [2008] IRLR 227. The claimant had her offer of a post withdrawn because she did not receive satisfactory medical clearance. The tribunal found that she had a mental illness, but that there was no evidence at the time the decision was taken that the illness was likely to recur, and therefore it did not have a long-term effect. In the event, subsequent to that but prior to the tribunal hearing, she was admitted to hospital under the Mental Health Act. The EAT held that the tribunal should have taken this into account. The Court of Appeal reversed the EAT's decision. According to Pill LJ: 'The central purpose of the Act is to prevent discriminatory decisions and to provide sanctions if such decisions are made. Whether an employer has committed a wrong must...be judged on the basis of the evidence available at the time of the decision complained of.' As Rubenstein observes: 'Undoubtedly, this was the correct decision on the language of the statute, but it does highlight one of the ironies of the DDA: the claimant lost her job presumably because the employers, subjectively, thought her mental illness was likely to recur, but the employers were able to defeat a disability discrimination claim by arguing that, objectively, there was insufficient evidence to establish that it was likely to recur' ('Highlights' [2008] IRLR 179).
2. The EAT in *Paterson* v *Commissioner of Police of the Metropolis* [2007] IRLR 763 held that a person suffering from dyslexia was 'disabled' within the meaning of s. 1 of the DDA 1995 as his condition resulted in a substantial and long-term adverse effect on his ability to carry out normal day-to-day activities. Applying the decision of the ECJ in *Chacón Navas* v *Eurest Colectividades SA* [2006] IRLR 706, in which it was held that 'day-to-day activities encompasses the activities which are relevant to participation in professional life', the EAT found that reading and comprehension are normal day-to-day activities which were affected by the dyslexia. It should be noted that the decision in *Chacón Navas* distinguishes between the concepts of 'disability' and 'sickness'; discriminatory treatment based on sickness rather than disability is outside the scope of Directive 2000/78.

Chacón Navas v Eurest Colectividades SA
[2006] IRLR 706, European Court of Justice

Sonia Chacón Navas was employed by the respondent catering firm. On 14 October 2003, she was certified as unfit to work due to sickness and thereafter received incapacity benefit. She remained off work and on 28 May 2004, the employers gave her notice of dismissal, without stating any reason. They acknowledged that the dismissal was unlawful under Spanish law and offered compensation.

Ms Chacón Navas brought proceedings seeking reinstatement. Spanish law distinguishes between unlawful dismissal and void dismissal. A dismissal which is on grounds of unlawful discrimination is rendered void. Ms Chacón Navas argued that the dismissal was on grounds of her absence from work due to sickness and that this was discriminatory.

DECISION: A person who has been dismissed by his employer solely on account of sickness is not protected by the prohibition against discrimination on grounds of disability in Framework Employment Directive 2000/78.

The concept of 'disability' for the purpose of Directive 2000/78 must be understood as referring to a limitation which results in particular from physical, mental or psychological impairments and which hinders the participation of the person concerned in professional life.

The concept of 'disability', however, differs from 'sickness' and the two concepts cannot simply be treated as being the same. In order for a limitation to fall within the concept of 'disability', it must be probable that it will last for a long time. There is nothing in Directive 2000/78 to suggest that workers are protected by the prohibition of discrimination on grounds of disability as soon as they develop any type of sickness.

JUDGMENT: Directive 2000/78 aims to combat certain types of discrimination as regards employment and occupation. In that context, the concept of 'disability' must be understood as referring to a limitation which results in particular from physical, mental or psychological impairments and which hinders the participation of the person concerned in professional life.

However, by using the concept of 'disability' in Article 1 of that Directive, the legislature deliberately chose a term which differs from 'sickness'. The two concepts cannot therefore simply be treated as being the same.

Recital 16 in the preamble to Directive 2000/78 states that the 'provision of measures to accommodate the needs of disabled people at the workplace plays an important role in combating discrimination on grounds of disability'. The importance which the Community legislature attaches to measures for adapting the workplace to the disability demonstrates that it envisaged situations in which participation in professional life is hindered over a long period of time. In order for the limitation to fall within the concept of 'disability', it must therefore be probable that it will last for a long time.

There is nothing in Directive 2000/78 to suggest that workers are protected by the prohibition of discrimination on grounds of disability as soon as they develop any type of sickness.

It follows from the above considerations that a person who has been dismissed by his employer solely on account of sickness does not fall within the general framework laid down for combating discrimination on grounds of disability by Directive 2000/78.

NOTE: This decision significantly alters the definition of a disabled person. The European Court of Justice (ECJ) stated that the concept of 'disability' must be understood as referring to 'a limitation which results in particular from physical, mental or psychological impairments and which hinders the participation of the person concerned in professional life.' So, does this mean professional life generally, or whether the person concerned is affected in respect of a particular job? *Chief Constable of Lothian and Borders Police* v *Cumming* [2010] IRLR 109 concerned an applicant for appointment as a regular constable, who failed the medical screening because she did not meet the requisite visual standard for recruitment as a police constable. Ms Cumming had reduced vision in her left eye, but excellent vision in her right eye and did not need to wear glasses or contact lenses. An employment tribunal found that she fell within the definition of a disabled person because her impairment substantially affected her participation in professional life—i.e. she didn't get the job for which she applied. However, the Employment Appeal Tribunal (EAT) held that the claimant's eye impairment could not be held to have had a substantial adverse effect on her ability to carry out normal day-to-day activities, even though it affected her entry into a profession. Lady Smith stated that the tribunal misunderstood the case law authorities. 'They are not authority for the broad proposition that being afforded general participation in or access to professional life is a day-to-day activity.' This, she said, is because 'the status of disability for the purposes of the DDA cannot be dependent on the decision of the employer as to how to react to the employee's impairment.'

McNicol v Balfour Beatty Rail Maintenance Ltd
[2002] IRLR 711, Court of Appeal

Daniel McNicol was employed as a trackman. He claimed that in October 1995, during the course of his work, a vehicle which he was driving went over a pothole, causing him to be jolted. From that time on, he was off work. He brought a claim under the DDA alleging that his employers had failed to make reasonable adjustments to his employment arrangements.

HELD: The employment tribunal did not err in law in finding that the applicant did not have a disability within the meaning of the DDA in that he had not established that his back pain resulted from either a physical or a mental impairment. There was no evidence before the tribunal of any organic physical pathology to establish the physical organic injury that formed the foundation of the applicant's claim, and no evidence was ever adduced by him to establish that his back pain was the result of, or consisted of, a clinically well-recognised mental illness or that it fitted the medical description of functional or psychological overlay.

MUMMERY LJ: In my judgment, only two general points are worth making. This appeal highlights the crucial importance (a) of applicants making clear the nature of the impairment on which the claim of discrimination is advanced and (b) of both parties obtaining relevant medical evidence on the issue of impairment. As happened in this case, a directions hearing should be held by the chairman of the tribunal to clarify the issues and to ascertain the nature of the evidence which the parties intend to adduce.

The approach of the tribunal should be that the term 'impairment' in this context bears its ordinary and natural meaning. It is clear from Schedule 1 to the 1995 Act that impairment may result from an illness or it may consist of an illness, provided that, in the case of mental impairment, it must be a 'clinically well-recognised illness'. Apart from this there is no statutory description or definition of physical or mental 'impairment'. The Guidance issued under s. 3 of the 1995 Act by the Department for Education and Employment on 25 July 1996 states in the introduction section in Part 1 that 'it is not necessary to consider how an impairment was caused' and some examples of physical and mental impairment are given (e.g. sensory impairments affecting sight or hearing), but no general definition or description of 'impairment' is attempted.

I agree with the recent observations of Lindsay J in *College of Ripon & York St John v Hobbs* [2002] IRLR 185 at paragraph 32:

> Nor does anything in the Act or the Guidance expressly require that the primary task of the ascertainment of the presence or absence of physical impairment has to, or is likely to, involve any distinctions, scrupulously to be observed, between an underlying fault, shortcoming or defect of or in the body on the one hand and evidence of the manifestations or effects thereof on the other. The Act contemplates (certainly in relation to mental impairment) that an impairment can be something that results from an illness as opposed to itself being the illness—Schedule 1 para. 1(1). It can thus be cause or effect. No rigid distinction seems to be insisted on and the blurring which occurs in ordinary usage would seem to be something the Act is prepared to tolerate. Nor is there anything there to be found to restrict the tribunal's ability, so familiar to tribunals in other parts of discrimination law, to draw inferences...

It is left to the good sense of the tribunal to make a decision in each case on whether the evidence available establishes that the applicant has a physical or mental impairment with the stated effects. Such a decision can and should be made without substituting for the statutory language a different word or form of words in an ambitious and unnecessary attempt to describe or to define the concept of 'impairment'. The essential question in each case is whether, on sensible interpretation of the relevant evidence, including the expert medical evidence and reasonable inferences which can be made from all the evidence, the applicant can fairly be described as having a physical or mental impairment. The ordinary meaning of the statutory language and of the Guidance issued by the Secretary of State under s. 3(1) is sufficiently clear to enable the tribunal to answer the question on the basis of the evidence. The decision of the employment tribunal in this case in consistent with that approach and does not contain any error of law.

As to the function of the tribunal, it was submitted that it should adopt an inquisitorial and more proactive role in disability discrimination cases, as they can be complex and involve applicants whose impairment leads them to minimise or to offer inaccurate diagnoses of their conditions and of the effects of their impairment. I do not think that it would be helpful to describe the role the employment tribunal as 'inquisitorial' or as 'proactive.' Its role is to adjudicate on disputes between the parties on issues of fact and law. I agree with the guidance recently given by Lindsay J in *Morgan v Staffordshire University* [2002] IRLR 190 in paragraph 20. The onus is on the applicant to prove the impairment on the conventional balance of probabilities. In many cases there will be no issue about impairment. If there is an issue on impairment, evidence will be needed to prove impairment. Some will be difficult borderline cases. It is not, however, the duty of the tribunal to obtain evidence or to ensure that adequate medical evidence is obtained by the parties. That is a matter for the parties and their advisers. Sensible and sensitive use of the tribunal's flexible and informal procedures and its case management powers enable it to do justice on this issue by reminding the parties at the directions hearing of the need in most cases for qualified and informed medical evidence, bearing in mind that an unrepresented person may need some explanation about what is involved and what is required and also bearing in mind the cost of obtaining such evidence, the need to keep costs down and the limited resources available to many parties in the employment tribunal. The tribunal may also grant an adjournment where it is appropriate for evidence to be obtained on the issue of impairment.

NOTES

1. The decision of the EAT in *Hospice of St Mary of Furness* v *Howard* [2007] IRLR 944 attempts to clarify the position where there is a dispute between the claimant and the employer as to whether the claimant is 'disabled'. As a general rule 'it is not necessary for the claimant to establish the cause of an alleged physical impairment, but where there is an issue as to the existence of a physical impairment it is open to the respondent to seek to disprove the existence of such impairment, including by seeking to prove that the claimed impairment is not genuine or is a mental not physical impairment'. In such circumstances it is open to the employer to seek their own medical report on the claimant's condition.

2. There continue to be issues regarding the meaning of 'disability' and whether therefore a person is 'disabled' within the meaning of the Act. The EAT has encouraged employment tribunals to adopt a purposive approach to the construction of the DDA 1995 with explicit reference being made to guidance issued by the Secretary of State and the codes of practice. The guidance provided by Morison J in *Goodwin* v *The Patent Office* [1999] IRLR 4 is still of relevance in determining whether the claimant is disabled.

Goodwin v Patent Office

[1999] IRLR 4, Employment Appeal Tribunal

MORISON J:

(1) The impairment condition

The applicant must have either a physical or mental impairment. Mental impairment includes an impairment which results from or consists of a mental illness provided that the mental illness is 'a clinically well-recognised illness'...

If there is doubt as to whether the impairment condition is fulfilled in an alleged mental illness case, it would be advisable to ascertain whether the illness described or referred to in the medical evidence is mentioned in the WHO's International Classification of Diseases. That Classification would very likely determine the issue one way or the other...

(2) The adverse effect condition

In many ways, this may be the most difficult of the four conditions to judge... The fact that a person can carry out such activities does not mean that his ability to carry them out has not been impaired... Furthermore, disabled persons are likely, habitually, to 'play down' the effect that their disabilities have on their daily lives. If asked whether they are able to cope at home, the answer may well be 'yes,' even though, on analysis, many of the ordinary day-to-day tasks were done with great difficulty due to the person's impaired ability to carry them out...

(3) The substantial condition

'Substantial' might mean 'very large' or it might mean 'more than minor or trivial.' Reference to the Guide shows that the word has been used in the latter sense…The tribunal will wish to examine how the applicant's abilities had actually been affected at the material time, whilst on medication, and then to address their minds to the difficult question as to the effects which they think there would have been but for the medication: the deduced effects. The question is then whether the actual and deduced effects on the applicant's abilities to carry out normal day-to-day activities is clearly more than trivial.

In many cases, the tribunal will be able to reach a conclusion on these matters without reference to the statutory Guidance (which is there to illuminate what is not reasonably clear)…Although Parliament has linked the effect of medication to the 'substantial condition,' as we have already said, splitting the statutory words into conditions should not divert attention from the definition as a whole, and in determining whether the adverse effect condition is fulfilled the tribunal will take into account deduced effects.

(4) The long-term condition

Paragraph 2 of Schedule 1 applies, as does paragraph B of the Guidance, where reference to it is necessary. The provisions appear to be straightforward and we have nothing useful to say about them.

One issue centres on the interpretation of 'substantial and long-term effect on his ability to carry out normal day-to-day activities'. In *Cruickshake* v *Vaw Motor Cast* Ltd [2002] IRLR 24, the EAT concluded that the material time at which to assess the disability is at the time of the alleged discriminatory act. Furthermore in assessing whether the applicant met the definition of disability where the effects of an impairment on an ability to carry out normal day-to-day activities fluctuates and may be exacerbated by conditions at work, the tribunal would consider the employee's ability to perform normal day-to-day activities, both while actually at work and while not at work.

In particular tribunals should avoid trying to find a cause for the disability, which can lead to inequitable decisions. For example in *Power* v *Panasonic UK Ltd* [2003] IRLR 151, an applicant with long-term depression was deemed not to have a disability within the DDA as the possible cause of the depression was an addiction to alcohol which fell within reg. 3 of the Meaning of Disability Regulations 1996 and therefore was not to be treated as amounting to an impairment for the purposes of the Act. However, the tribunal should have focused on whether her depression had a substantial and long-term adverse effect.

Tribunals should also consider whether the resultant condition is a direct result of a physical or mental impairment within the meaning of s. 1(1), DDA 1995. For example, in *Murray* v *Newham Citizens Advice Bureau Ltd* [2003] IRLR 340 the tribunal incorrectly concluded that a paranoid schizophrenic with a past history of violence was not disabled as the tendency to violence fell within reg. 4 of the Meaning of Disability Regulations whereas the tendency to violence was as a consequence of a recognised condition.

The focus for the employment tribunal should be what the applicant cannot do, or can do only with difficulty, not what he can do (see *Leonard* v *Southern Derbyshire Chamber of Commerce* [2001] IRLR 19). Also, the impairment and its effect should be considered holistically, e.g. an impairment to the hand should be considered in the light of an adverse effect on manual dexterity, ability to lift and carry everyday objects, instead of focusing on particular tasks or issues. Nor should tasks which are gender specific, e.g. applying make-up, be discounted as not being a normal day-to-day activity as they are carried out almost exclusively by women—see *Ekpe* v *Commissioner of Police of the Metropolis* [2001] IRLR 605.

In *College of Rippon and York Saint John* v *Hobbs* [2002] IRLR 185, the EAT held that as there was no statutory definition of 'impairment', it could be concluded that the Act contemplates that an impairment can be something that results from an illness as opposed to it being the illness itself, it can therefore be cause or effect. The physical manifestations, which the complainant suffered in this case, could therefore amount to a physical impairment without the tribunal knowing precisely what the underlying disease or trauma was. The reasoning of the Court of Appeal in *McNicol* overrules that of the EAT in attempting to clarify what amounts to 'impairment' as either '…resulting from an illness or consisting of an illness. It is not necessary to consider how an impairment is caused.' In *Miller* v *Inland Revenue Commissioners* [2006] IRLR 112, the Court of Session considered the standard of proof for establishing 'impairment'. It concluded that physical impairment can be established without reference to causation or any form of illness. There is therefore no need for the claimant to show how they came by the impairment.

The onus is on the employment tribunal to make its own assessment from the evidence before it, and avoid being over-influenced by medical opinion rather than fact. Also, where the applicant is receiving medical treatment for the condition, so that the final outcome cannot be determined or the removal of the treatment would result in a relapse, the medical treatment must be disregarded in determining whether there is a substantial adverse effect—see *Abadeh* v *British Telecommunications plc* [2001] IRLR 23.

Where the expert medical evidence demonstrates that the applicant has a disability which is controlled by medication, it still falls within the definition of disability—see DDA 1995, s. 1—*Kapadia* v *London Borough of*

Lambeth [2000] IRLR 699. However, in *Woodrup* v *London Borough of Southwark* [2003] IRLR 111, the Court of Appeal held that in establishing 'disability', the applicant must provide medical evidence that if the medical treatment were discontinued, the impairment would have a substantial adverse effect on her ability to carry out normal day-to-day activities within para. 6(1).

Progressive conditions have caused significant problems for the tribunal as we have seen in *Kirton* v *Tetrosyl Ltd* [2003] IRLR 353. In *Mowat-Brown* v *University of Surrey* [2002] IRLR 235, an applicant diagnosed with multiple sclerosis was found not to be disabled as the applicant's case did not fall within the definition of a 'progressive condition' within the meaning of para. 8(1) of Schedule 1 to the DDA 1995. The EAT concluded that it is not sufficient merely to show that one has a progressive condition that is likely to have a substantial adverse effect, the claimant must go on and show it is more likely than not that at some stage in the future he will have an impairment which will have a substantial adverse effect on his ability to carry out normal day-to-day activities.

Finally, a difficult area for the employment tribunals is where the alleged disability is actually due to a functional or psychological 'overlay', i.e. where a person claims to be suffering from a physical injury, which the doctor states is due to the individual's psychological state and is not related to any physical pathology. The problem for the employment tribunal is that the applicant is claiming a physical impairment (which does not in fact exist) whilst the employment tribunal must assess whether the mental impairment falls within the DDA 1995, s. 1, i.e. is a 'clinically well-recognised illness'. Interestingly, 'functional overlay' does not appear in the WHO's International Classification of Diseases or the American Psychiatric Association's Diagnostic and Statistical Manual of Mental Disorders—see *Rugamer* v *Sony Music Entertainment Ltd* [2001] IRLR 644.

It could be suggested that this places a further responsibility on the tribunal to consider not only whether the applicant has a disability, but why he has.

NOTE: The next, widely publicised, case is concerned with the question as to whether obesity can amount to a 'disability'.

FAG OG ARBEJDE, acting on behalf of Karsten Kaltoft v *KOMMUNERNES LANDSFORENING, acting on behalf of the Municipality of Billund*
Case C-354/13 [2015] IRLR 146, European Court of Justice

Karsten Kaltoft had been employed by a Danish public administrative authority as a child-minder for approximately 15 years. He was obese. He had made attempts over the years to lose weight and had received financial assistance from the Municipality of Billund to do so, but each time he had regained the weight which he had lost. In March 2010, he received several unexpected visits from the head of the childminders, who inquired into his weight loss and observed that his weight had remained virtually unchanged. He was authorised to care for four children and did so until later in 2010 when, owing to a decrease in the number of children in the municipality, he had only three children to care for. The education inspectors in the municipality were requested to nominate a childminder for dismissal; the head of the childminders decided that Mr Kaltoft would be that individual. Mr Kaltoft was informed that he was to be dismissed. During a meeting with the head of the child-minders, Mr Kaltoft asked why he was the only childminder to be dismissed. His obesity was mentioned during that meeting. His formal letter of dismissal stated that he was being dismissed due to a 'decline in the number of children'. Following his dismissal, proceed-ings were brought alleging that he had been discriminated against on the basis of obesity.

A Danish court referred questions to the Court of Justice of the European Union (CJEU). The first issue was whether EU law laid down a general principle of non-discrimination on grounds of obesity as regards employment and occupation. The second issue was whether the Equal Treatment Framework Directive 2000/78 meant that the obesity of a worker could constitute a 'disability' within the meaning of that Directive and, if so, what the criteria were which decided whether an obese worker could avail of any pro-tection afforded by the Directive.

The CJEU ruled:

1. EU law must be interpreted as not laying down a general principle of non-discrimination on grounds of obesity as such as regards employment and occupation.

2. Council Directive 2000/78/EC must be interpreted as meaning that the obesity of a worker constitutes a 'disability' within the meaning of that Directive where it entails a limitation resulting in particular from long-term physical, mental or psychological impairments which in interaction with various barriers may hinder the full and effective participation of the person concerned in professional life on an equal basis with other workers. That concept of 'disability' must be understood as referring not only to the impossibility of exercising a professional activity, but also to a hindrance to the exercise of such an activity. The concept of 'disability' within the meaning of the Directive does not depend on the extent to which the person may or may not have contributed to the onset of their disability. It should be noted that obesity does not in itself constitute a 'disability' within the meaning of the Directive, on the ground that, by its nature, it does not necessarily entail the existence of a limitation. However, in the event that, under given circumstances, the obesity of the worker concerned entails a limitation which results in particular from physical, mental or psychological impairments that in interaction with various barriers may hinder the full and effective participation of that person in professional life on an equal basis with other workers, and the limitation is a long-term one, obesity can be covered by the concept of 'disability' within the meaning of Directive 2000/78. Such would be the case, in particular, if the obesity of the worker hindered his full and effective participation in professional life on an equal basis with other workers on account of reduced mobility or the onset, in that person, of medical conditions preventing him from carrying out his work or causing discomfort when carrying out his professional activity. It is for the national court to determine whether, in the main proceedings, those conditions are met.

JUDGMENT

...

53 Following the ratification by the European Union of the United Nations Convention on the Rights of Persons with Disabilities, which was approved on behalf of the European Community by Council Decision 2010/48/EC of 26 November 2009 (OJ 2010 L 23, p.35), the Court held that the concept of 'disability' must be understood as referring to a limitation which results in particular from long-term physical, mental or psychological impairments which in interaction with various barriers may hinder the full and effective participation of the person concerned in professional life on an equal basis with other workers (see judgments in *HK Danmark* v *Dansk almennyttigt Boligselskab, C-335/11 and C-337/11* [2013] IRLR 571, paragraphs 37 to 39; *Z* v *A government department, C-363/12*, [2014] IRLR 563, paragraph 76; and *Glatzel* v *Freistaat Bayern*, C-356/12, [2014] 3 CMLR 1339, paragraph 45).

54 That concept of 'disability' must be understood as referring not only to the impossibility of exercising a professional activity, but also to a hindrance to the exercise of such an activity. Any other interpretation would be incompatible with the objective of that Directive, which aims in particular to enable a person with a disability to have access to or participate in employment (see judgment in *Z* v *A government department, C-363/12* [2014] IRLR 563, paragraph 77 and the case law cited).

55 Moreover, it would run counter to the very aim of the Directive, which is to implement equal treatment, to define its scope by reference to the origin of the disability (see judgment in *HK Danmark* v *Dansk almennyttigt Boligselskab, C-335/11 and C-337/11*, [2013] IRLR 571, paragraph 40).

56 The concept of 'disability' within the meaning of Directive 2000/78 does not depend on the extent to which the person may or may not have contributed to the onset of his disability.

57 In addition, the definition of the concept of 'disability' within the meaning of Article 1 of Directive 2000/78 comes before the determination and assessment of the appropriate accommodation measures referred to in Article 5 of the same Directive. According to recital 16 of Directive 2000/78, such measures are intended to accommodate the needs of disabled persons and they are therefore the consequence, not the constituent element, of the concept of 'disability' (see, to that effect, judgment in *HK Danmark* v *Dansk almennyttigt Boligselskab C-335/11 and C-337/11*, [2013] IRLR 571, paragraphs 45 and 46). Therefore, the mere fact that such accommodation measures may not have been taken in respect of Mr Kaltoft does not mean that he could not be a disabled person within the meaning of the Directive referred to.

58 It should be noted that obesity does not in itself constitute a 'disability' within the meaning of Directive 2000/78, on the ground that, by its nature, it does not necessarily entail the existence of a limitation as referred to in paragraph 53 of this judgment.

59 However, in the event that, under given circumstances, the obesity of the worker concerned entails a limitation which results in particular from physical, mental or psychological impairments that in interaction with various barriers may hinder the full and effective participation of that person in professional life on an equal basis with other workers, and the limitation is a long-term one, obesity can be covered by the concept of 'disability' within the meaning of Directive 2000/78 (see, to that effect, judgment in *HK Danmark* v *Dansk almennyttigt Boligselskab, C-335/11 and C-337/11,* [2013] IRLR 571, paragraph 41).

60 Such would be the case, in particular, if the obesity of the worker hindered his full and effective participation in professional life on an equal basis with other workers on account of reduced mobility or the onset, in that person, of medical conditions preventing him from carrying out his work or causing discomfort when carrying out his professional activity.

61 In the present case, as has been observed by the referring court, it is undisputed that Mr Kaltoft was obese for the entire period he was employed by the Municipality of Billund, thus for a long period.

62 It is for the referring court to ascertain whether, in the case in the main proceedings, irrespective of the fact that Mr Kaltoft, as has been noted in paragraph 17 of the present judgment, carried out his work for approximately 15 years, his obesity entailed a limitation which meets the conditions set out in paragraph 53 of this judgment.

NOTES:
1. The Court did not adopt the approach of the Advocate General that would have focused on whether there was a body mass index (BMI) of over 40 in order to constitute disability. According to the World Health Organisation, a BMI in excess of 40.00 are Obese Class III, which is sometimes referred to as severe, extreme, or morbid obesity. In the absence of such a threshold, there is plenty of room for argument as to whether lower levels of obesity can trigger a disability discrimination claim.
2. If an obese employee's condition constitutes a disability, the employer is under an obligation to make reasonable adjustments to their work or working environment (EqA 2010, s. 20). The law will penalise an employer who fails to be reasonably accommodating to employees with a disability they ought reasonably to know about.

■ QUESTION:

In making decisions about dismissal or redundancy, might the organisation's standard practice or procedure disadvantage those employees experiencing the effects of obesity?

EQUALITY ACT 2010

15 Discrimination arising from disability

(1) A person (A) discriminates against a disabled person (B) if—
  (a) A treats B unfavourably because of something arising in consequence of B's disability, and
  (b) A cannot show that the treatment is a proportionate means of achieving a legitimate aim.

(2) Subsection (1) does not apply if A shows that A did not know, and could not reasonably have been expected to know, that B had the disability.

NOTES
1. This section provides that it is unlawful to treat a disabled person unfavourably not because of the person's disability itself but because of something arising from, or in consequence of, his or her disability, e.g. the need to take a period of disability-related absence. However, such treatment may be justifiable if it can be shown to be a proportionate means of achieving a legitimate aim. An employer will only be liable for this form of discrimination if it knows, or could reasonably be expected to know, that the disabled person has a disability.

This section is a new provision. The DDA 1995 provided protection from disability-related discrimination but, following the judgment of the House of Lords in the case of *London Borough of Lewisham* v *Malcolm* [2008] IRLR 700, HL, those provisions no longer provided the degree of protection from disability-related discrimination that is intended for disabled people (cf. *Clark* v *TDG Ltd t/a Novacold* [1999] IRLR 318 and see Horton, R., 'The end of disability-related discrimination in employment' (2008) 37 ILJ 376–83). This section is aimed at re-establishing an acceptable balance between enabling a disabled person to establish a claim of experiencing a detriment which arises because of his or her disability, and providing an opportunity for an employer or other person to defend the treatment.

The explanatory notes accompanying the Equality Bill provide the following example:

> An employee with a visual impairment is dismissed because he cannot do as much work as a non-disabled colleague. If the employer sought to justify the dismissal, he would need to show that it was a proportionate means of achieving a legitimate aim.

2. In *Gallop* v *Newport City Council* [2014] IRLR 211, the question for the Court of Appeal (CA) was whether an employer could not reasonably have been expected to know that an employee with stress-reated symptoms was disabled. The employers had been informed by occupational health advisers that the employee was not disabled. However, the CA held that the statutory test for knowledge of disability does not permit an employer simply to adopt an occupational health adviser's opinion. When seeking outside advice from clinicians, the employer must not simply ask in general terms whether the employee is a disabled person within the meaning of the legislation, but pose specific *practical* questions directed to the particular circumstances of the putative disability. The answers to such questions will then provide real assistance to the employer in forming his judgment as to whether the criteria for disability are satisfied. In the present case, occupational health's expressed opinions as to whether Mr Gallop was or was not a disabled person had amounted to no more than assertions of their view that the DDA had not applied to Mr Gallop, or that he was not 'covered' by it or words to that effect. No supporting reasoning had been provided.

   The question is whether the employer had actual or constructive knowledge of the facts constituting the employee's disability.

3. The EqA 2010, ss. 26–7 make it unlawful to harass or victimise an individual with a protected characteristic.

4. In *EBR Attridge Law* v *Coleman (No. 2)* [2010] IRLR 10, the EAT held that the DDA could be interpreted, as required by the ECJ, so as to prohibit direct discrimination and harassment against an employee on the ground that they care for a disabled person. In other words, the DDA covers 'associative discrimination'. The EqA 2010 aims to prohibit associative discrimination in respect of all protected grounds (see EqA 2010, s. 13(1)).

B: Reasonable adjustments

EQUALITY ACT 2010

ADJUSTMENTS FOR DISABLED PERSONS

20 Duty to make adjustments

(1) Where this Act imposes a duty to make reasonable adjustments on a person, this section, sections 21 and 22, and the applicable Schedule apply; and for those purposes, a person on whom the duty is imposed is referred to as A.

(2) The duty comprises the following three requirements.

(3) The first requirement is a requirement, where a provision, criterion or practice of A's puts a disabled person at a substantial disadvantage in relation to a relevant matter in comparison with persons who are not disabled, to take such steps as it is reasonable to have to take to avoid the disadvantage.

(4) The second requirement is a requirement, where a physical feature puts a disabled person at a substantial disadvantage in relation to a relevant matter in comparison with persons who are not disabled, to take such steps as it is reasonable to have to take to avoid the disadvantage.

(5) The third requirement is a requirement, where a disabled person would, but for the provision of an auxiliary aid, be put at a substantial disadvantage in relation to a relevant matter in comparison with persons who are not disabled, to take such steps as it is reasonable to have to take to provide the auxiliary aid.

(6) Where the first or third requirement relates to the provision of information, the steps which it is reasonable for A to have to take include steps for ensuring that in the circumstances concerned the information is provided in an accessible format.

(7) A person (A) who is subject to a duty to make reasonable adjustments is not (subject to express provision to the contrary) entitled to require a disabled person, in relation to whom A is required to comply with the duty, to pay to any extent A's costs of complying with the duty.

21 Failure to comply with duty

(1) A failure to comply with the first, second or third requirement is a failure to comply with a duty to make reasonable adjustments.

(2) A discriminates against a disabled person if A fails to comply with that duty in relation to that person.

O'Hanlon v Commissions for HM Revenue & Customs

[2007] IRLR 404, Court of Appeal

Kathleen O'Hanlon was employed at material times by Revenue & Customs (or its predecessor). She suffered from clinical depression. It was accepted that she was suffering from a disability within the meaning of the DDA 1995. From 2001 onwards, she started to take long absences from work. In total, in the four years prior to 15 October 2002, she had a total absence of 365 days of sickness, of which 320 days related to her disability.

Revenue & Customs' sick pay policy provided that employees would normally be allowed to take paid sick absence on full pay for a maximum of six months in any period of 12 months, and on half pay for a further maximum period of six months, subject normally to an overriding maximum of 12 months' paid sick absence in any period of four years. After that, an employee would be paid his equivalent pension rate of pay, or half pay, whichever was less, subject to a requirement (which was not material in the present case) of having served two years' pensionable service. The policy also gave Revenue & Customs a discretion, in certain circumstances, to allow a limited number of additional days paid sick leave after an employee's usual entitlement was used up. The effect of those rules was, in Mrs O'Hanlon's case, that she was on pension rate for all further absences after 15 October 2002.

DECISION: The EAT had been entitled to reject both the full-pay argument and the non-aggregation argument as being necessary as reasonable adjustments for the reasons which it gave. The EAT had been entitled to reject the argument that an employer should have to determine whether to increase sick payments by assessing the financial hardship suffered by the employee, or the stress resulting from lack of money.

It would be wholly invidious for an employer to have to determine whether to increase sick payments by assessing financial hardship suffered by the employee, or the stress resulting from lack of money; stress which no doubt would be equally felt by a non-disabled person absent for a similar period.

HOPE LJ: ...

Discussion: is the claim for enhanced sick pay ever sustainable?

67. In our view, it will be a very rare case indeed where the adjustment said to be applicable here, that is merely giving higher sick pay than would be payable to a non-disabled person who in general does not suffer the same disability-related absences, would be considered necessary as a reasonable adjustment. We do not believe that the legislation has perceived this as an appropriate adjustment, although we do not rule out the possibility that it could be in exceptional circumstances. We say this for two reasons in particular.

68. First, the implications of this argument are that Tribunals would have to usurp the management function of the employer, deciding whether employers were financially able to meet the costs of modifying their policies by making these enhanced payments. Of course we recognise that tribunals will often have to have regard to financial factors and the financial standing of the employer, and indeed s. 18B(1) requires that they should. But there is a very significant difference between doing that with regard to a single claim, turning on its own facts, where the cost is perforce relatively limited, and a claim which if successful will inevitably apply to many others and will have very significant financial as well as policy implications for the employer. On what basis can the tribunal decide whether the claims of the disabled to receive more generous sick pay should override other

demands on the business which are difficult to compare and which perforce the tribunal will know precious little about? The tribunals would be entering into a form of wage fixing for the disabled sick.

69. Second, as the tribunal pointed out, the purpose of this legislation is to assist the disabled to obtain employment and to integrate them into the workforce. All the examples given in s. 18B(3) are of this nature. True, they are stated to be examples of reasonable adjustments only and are not to be taken as exhaustive of what might be reasonable in any particular case, but none of them suggests that it will ever be necessary simply to put more money into the wage packet of the disabled. The Act is designed to recognise the dignity of the disabled and to require modifications which will enable them to play a full part in the world of work, important and laudable aims. It is not to treat them as objects of charity which, as the tribunal pointed out, may in fact sometimes and for some people tend to act as a positive disincentive to return to work.

NOTES

1. A failure to comply with the duty imposed under the EqA 2010, s. 20 amounts to discrimination (see also EqA, Sch. 8). The duty to make reasonable adjustments extends not only to the physical features of the premises, but also to the working arrangements, including hours of work, duties, etc. In *Nottinghamshire County Council* v *Meikle* [2004] IRLR 703, the Court of Appeal held that the duty extended to the arrangements for the payment of contractual sick pay. The onus is not on the employee to suggest amendments but on the employer to assess the employee's needs. In *Mid-Staffordshire General Hospital NHS Trust* v *Cambridge* [2003] IRLR 566, the EAT held that a requisite part of the duty under what is now EqA 2010, s. 20 is a proper assessment of what is required to eliminate a disabled person's disadvantage. 'It is a necessary precondition to the fulfilment of that duty and therefore part of it.' The issue of 'reasonable adjustments' is also proving to be contentious. The test for determining whether there is a duty to make an adjustment, and whether the employer's failure to make an adjustment is justified, is an objective one.

   As we have seen, the decision in *Beart* encourages the tribunals to move away from a mechanistic approach in applying the law in disability cases. The Court of Appeal held that there was no need to apply all of the stages laid down by the EAT in *Morse* when considering whether an adjustment was reasonable as long as they 'properly applied themselves to considering whether the requirements of the statute were satisfied': Rubenstein, M., 'Highlights' [2003] IRLR 182.

   In *Rideout* v *TC Group* [1998] IRLR 628, the EAT concluded that there was no duty to make reasonable adjustments if the employer did not know or could not have reasonably been expected to know that the person had a disability and was likely to be placed at a substantial disadvantage in comparison with persons who were not disabled. The extent of the duty must therefore be measured against the actual or assumed knowledge of the employer, both as to the disability and to its likelihood of causing the individual a substantial disadvantage in comparison with persons who are not disabled.

2. In *Southampton City College* v *Randall* [2006] IRLR 18, the EAT made it clear that the tribunal should consider what a reasonable employer would have considered to be a reasonable adjustment. It also held that 'a proper assessment of what is required to eliminate the disabled person's disadvantage is a necessary part of the duty of reasonable adjustment, since that duty cannot be complied with unless the employer makes a proper assessment of what needs to be done.' It is therefore essential for the employer to be proactive in considering what reasonable adjustments can be made even if he feels that they will not work. However, the EAT in *HM Prison Service* v *Johnson* [2007] IRLR 951 held that the tribunal must identify with some particularity what step it is that the employers are said to have failed to take. 'Unless that is done the kind of assessment of reasonableness required by the Act . . . is not possible.' Both the *Randall* case and *Archibald* v *Fife Council* [2004] IRLR 651 considered whether there could be circumstances where the employer may need either to create a new post or to transfer the employee to an existing vacant post to meet the duty to make reasonable adjustments. In both cases it was concluded that while it would depend on the facts of the case, such adjustments were not precluded even though it may mean treating a disabled person more favourably than a non-disabled person.

3. An employer should also consider any adjustments proposed by the applicant, whether they were reasonable, and whether their implementation would have avoided the discriminatory act—*Fu* v *London Borough of Camden* [2001] IRLR 186; *Johnson and Johnson Medical Ltd* v *Filmer* (2002) 680 IRLB 7. The decision in *O'Hanlon* also highlights the point that it is not the responsibility of the claimant or her medical advisers to suggest 'reasonable adjustments'; the duty is on the employer.

4. The possible impact of the Human Rights Act (HRA) 1998 on establishing 'justification' was considered in *A* v *Hounslow* (2001) 679 IRLB 13. This involved the dismissal of a schizophrenic person from

his job as a laboratory technician in a school. The applicant took no medication for his condition and had entertained fantasies of mass murder. The applicant relied on the HRA 1998, s. 3, which, it was argued, would set a higher threshold for justification and would link to Article 1, Article 8, and Article 14 of the European Convention on Human Rights (ECHR). The EAT held that the application of the HRA 1998 made no difference to the construction of the relevant sections of the DDA 1995 or the code of practice in that it did not set a higher threshold of proof of justification than those set out in the DDA 1995.

5. If a tribunal reaches the conclusion that there is no connection between the disability and an applicant's work behaviour, it must give reasons. The employment tribunal must assess whether there is a disability and, if so, its impact on the applicant's ability to carry out his job—*Edwards v Mid Suffolk District Council* [2001] IRLR 190. As with all discrimination claims, there is a duty to mitigate one's loss. Failure to do so, e.g. by unreasonably refusing an offer of re-employment, will result in a reduction in damages—*Wilding v British Telecommunications plc* [2002] IRLR 524.

6. See Hamilton, J., 'Disability and discrimination in the context of disability discrimination legislation: The UK and Australian Acts compared' (2000) 4 IJDL 203. For a critique of the case law relating to constructive dismissal and discrimination see Rowland, D., 'Discrimination and constructive dismissal' (2001) 30 ILJ 381. For a critique of the DDA 1995, see Doyle, B., 'Disabled workers' rights, the Disability Discrimination Act and the UN Standard Rules' (1996) 25 ILJ 1, in which Doyle criticises the failure of the DDA 1995 to meet UN Standard Rules on disability, which, he feels, reflects the lack of commitment to the elimination of disability discrimination. For an assessment of the potential conflict between employers' responsibilities under the Health and Safety at Work etc. Act (HASAWA) 1974 and the DDA 1995, see Davies, J. and Davies, W., 'Rewarding risk and the employment of disabled persons in a reformed welfare state' (2000) 29 ILJ 347. The Institute for Employment Studies undertook research on behalf of the Disability Rights Commission to assess the impact of bringing small businesses within the DDA—'Impact on small businesses of lowering the DDA Part II threshold' (<http://www.equalityhumanrights.com>). See also Seymour, L. and Short, A., 'Still challenging disability discrimination at work' (Institute of Employment Rights, October 2005).

It has been suggested that the DDA and the way it is interpreted are failing to provide adequate protection for the mentally ill—James, G., 'An unquiet mind in the workplace: Mental illness and the Disability Discrimination Act 1995' (2004) 24 *Legal Studies* 516–39.

For an analysis of the impact of the Framework Directive on the disability legislation see Wells, K., 'The impact of the Framework Employment Directive on UK disability discrimination law' (2003) 32 ILJ 253.

SECTION 3: SEXUAL ORIENTATION AND GENDER REASSIGNMENT

There is a significant amount of case law relating to transsexuals and sexual orientation which pre-dates the Sex Discrimination (Gender Reassignment) Regulations 1999 (SI 1999/1102) and the Employment Equality (Sexual Orientation) Regulations 2003 (SI 2003/1661); the changes made by these regulations have now been consolidated into the EqA 2010, ss. 7 and 12. The sexual orientation regulations extended protection from discrimination to 1.3–1.9 million homosexuals in employment. They also covered discrimination on the basis of one's perceived sexual orientation. One important benefit is the protection from harassment on the grounds of homophobia. While a comparator is still needed and this is open to contention, the comparator needs to be a heterosexual of the same gender. Lack of knowledge of the applicant's sexuality will not remove liability from the employer. There are specific exceptions in the form of genuine occupational requirements.

The case law prior to the regulations and now the EqA 2010 demonstrates the challenge in attempting to use the SDA to provide protection. In *R* v *Ministry of Defence, ex p. Smith* [1996] IRLR 100, a challenge was made against dismissal from the armed forces of four people on grounds that they were homosexual and that this amounted to discrimination. The Court of Appeal ruled that in judging the Ministry of Defence's policy at the time of the dismissals in 1994, it was not irrational as it was supported by both Houses of Parliament: 'Furthermore there was nothing in the Equal Treatment Directive which suggests that the drafters were addressing their minds in any way whatever to problems of discrimination on grounds of sexual orientation. Indeed, *obiter*, it was concluded that a specific Directive was needed, not an extended construction of the Directive.'

This approach was further supported by the Court of Appeal in *Smith* v *Gardner Merchant Ltd* [1998] IRLR 510, in which it was held that discrimination on the grounds of sexual orientation was not discrimination on grounds of sex and was therefore outside the Act. However, in *P* v *S and Cornwall County Council* [1996] IRLR 347, the Directive was successfully used in a gender reassignment case where an employee undergoing gender reassignment was dismissed.

EQUALITY ACT 2010

7 Gender reassignment

(1) A person has the protected characteristic of gender reassignment if the person is proposing to undergo, is undergoing or has undergone a process (or part of a process) for the purpose of reassigning the person's sex by changing physiological or other attributes of sex.

(2) A reference to a transsexual person is a reference to a person who has the protected characteristic of gender reassignment.

(3) In relation to the protected characteristic of gender reassignment—

   (a) a reference to a person who has a particular protected characteristic is a reference to a transsexual person;

   (b) a reference to persons who share a protected characteristic is a reference to transsexual persons.

NOTE: The issue of discrimination of transsexuals, i.e. those who are undergoing or have undergone gender reassignment, has largely been addressed not only through the case law—see *Chessington World of Adventures Ltd* v *Reed* [1997] IRLR 556, which followed the decision in *P* v *S*—but also in the amendment to the SDA 1975 by the Sex Discrimination (Gender Reassignment) Regulations 1999 (SI 1999/1102) which brought this type of discrimination within the SDA 1975 (and consequently the EqA 2010). See also *Mills and the CPS* v *Marshall* [1998] IRLR 494. The case of *EB* v *BA* [2006] IRLR 471 raises issues about the burden of proof in discrimination cases, in particular at what point the burden of proof moves to the employer and how the burden of proof is then discharged. One possible interpretation of the decision by the Court of Appeal is that the employer must prove from the outset that there was no discrimination. However, this would in effect mean that the employer has to prove his innocence, which is outside all normal evidential requirements.

P v *S and Cornwall County Council*

[1996] IRLR 347, European Court of Justice

The applicant, P, was employed from 1 April 1991 as the general manager of a unit of an educational establishment, operated by the county council. The respondent, S, was the head of the establishment. The applicant was taken on as a male employee, but in April 1992 she informed S that she proposed to have a gender reassignment. She explained the background of her medical condition. She later wrote to S explaining that she was to embark on a 'life test', a one-year period during which a patient planning to undergo an operation for gender reassignment lives in the mode of the proposed gender.

The governors of the establishment were informed, and during the summer P took sick leave for initial surgical treatment. However, at the beginning of September 1992, she was given three months' notice of dismissal. She was not permitted to return from sick leave in her female gender role. The final surgical operation took place before the notice of dismissal expired.

P complained that she had been discriminated against on grounds of sex.

DECISION: The principle of equal treatment 'for men and women' to which the Directive refers in its title, preamble and provisions means, as Articles 2(1) and 3(1) in particular indicate, that there should be 'no discrimination whatsoever on grounds of sex'.

Thus, the Directive is simply the expression, in the relevant field, of the principle of equality, which is one of the fundamental principles of Community law.

Moreover, as the Court has repeatedly held, the right not to be discriminated against on grounds of sex is one of the fundamental human rights whose observance the Court has a duty to ensure (see, to that effect, case 149/77 *Defrenne* v *Sabena (No. 3)* [1978] ECR 1365, paragraphs 26 and 27, and joined cases 75/82 and 117/82 *Razzouk and Beydoun* v *Commission* [1984] ECR 1509, paragraph 16).

Accordingly, the scope of the Directive cannot be confined simply to discrimination based on the fact that a person is of one or other sex. In view of its purpose and the nature of the rights which it seeks to safeguard, the scope of the Directive is also such as to apply to discrimination arising, as in this case, from the gender reassignment of the person concerned.

Such discrimination is based, essentially if not exclusively, on the sex of the person concerned. Where a person is dismissed on the ground that he or she intends to undergo, or has undergone, gender reassignment, he or she is treated unfavourably by comparison with persons of the sex to which he or she was deemed to belong before undergoing gender reassignment.

To tolerate such discrimination would be tantamount, as regards such a person, to a failure to respect the dignity and freedom to which he or she is entitled, and which the Court has a duty to safeguard.

Dismissal of such a person must therefore be regarded as contrary to Article 5(1) of the Directive, unless the dismissal could be justified under Article 2(2). There is, however, no material before the Court to suggest that this was so here.

It follows from the foregoing that the reply to the questions referred by the industrial tribunal must be that, in view of the objective pursued by the Directive, Article 5(1) of the Directive precludes dismissal of a transsexual for a reason related to a gender reassignment.

NOTE: The amendments made to the SDA encompassed protection for those who are undergoing or have undergone a gender reassignment and provide protection for both direct discrimination and harassment. However, there are occupational requirements (see the EqA 2010, Sch. 9, Pt 1) which provide an employer with a defence to any claim. Whether the legislation affords protection in real terms remains to be seen; it is likely that there will still be contentious areas. Existing case law provides an insight into these. In *Croft* v *Consignia plc* [2003] IRLR 592, the Court of Appeal held that a pre-operative male to female was not discriminated against on grounds of sex when denied use of female communal toilets and changing facilities. The Court of Appeal concluded that to be treated as the new gender, surgery must be 'complete'. While this situation is subject to the Sex Discrimination (Gender Reassignment) Regulations 1999 (SI 1999/1102) as they cover the person intending to undergo gender reassignment, as well as those having undergone gender reassignment, it appears that the regulations are then subject to and overridden by such regulations as the Workplace (Health, Safety and Welfare) Regulations 1992. This decision is in line with *Goodwin* v *United Kingdom* [2002] IRLR 644. Furthermore, in *A* v *Chief Constable of West Yorkshire Police* [2002] IRLR 103, the Court of Appeal held that post-operative transsexuals are legally members of their chosen gender in the employment context except where there exist significant factors of public interest which outweigh the interests of the individual applicant in obtaining legal recognition of his or her gender reassignment. In this case the application for a post of police officer by a post-operative male to female transsexual was rejected on the basis that she could not carry out searches. It was held that the Chief Constable was bound to treat her as a female and could not invoke the genuine occupational qualifications in which he argued that searches had to be carried out by the same sex and that in this case this was a post-operative woman, who could not search men but legally was not a woman, and therefore could not search women. This decision was upheld on appeal by the House of Lords [2004] IRLR 573. How far the genuine occupational requirement provisions are compatible with the Framework Directive has been questioned in *R* v *Secretary of State for Trade and Industry and Christian Action Research Education and others* [2004] IRLR 430.

In *KB* v *National Health Service Pensions Agency* [2004] IRLR 240, KB, a female nurse with a female to male partner (R), was informed that R would not be able to receive a widows' pension if KB predeceased him. A reference was made to the ECJ on the following grounds: does the restriction of pension benefits under the NHS Pension Scheme to married persons contravene Article 141 and Directive 75/117? The ECJ held that it did not contravene Article 141 and Directive 75/117 as the restriction did not depend upon whether the claimant was male or female. The fact that UK law does not allow post-operative transsexuals to marry, however, is a breach of EC law and Article 12 of the ECHR (*Goodwin*). (See the Gender Recognition Act 2004, which has addressed this issue.)

EQUALITY ACT 2010

12 Sexual orientation

(1) Sexual orientation means a person's sexual orientation towards—
  (a) persons of the same sex,
  (b) persons of the opposite sex, or
  (c) persons of either sex.
(2) In relation to the protected characteristic of sexual orientation—
  (a) a reference to a person who has a particular protected characteristic is a reference to a person who is of a particular sexual orientation;
  (b) a reference to persons who share a protected characteristic is a reference to persons who are of the same sexual orientation.

Pearce v *Governing Body of Mayfield Secondary School*
[2003] IRLR 512, House of Lords

Shirley Pearce was employed as a science teacher from 1975 to 1996. She is a lesbian and from 1992 onwards she was subjected to homophobic abuse from the pupils. She suffered stress. Although she reported the abuse, when she returned to work the abuse continued. She took early retirement due to poor health and brought a claim for sex discrimination.

HELD (House of Lords): Gender does not include sexual orientation. Her sexual harassment was based on sexual orientation. She could not show that she was harassed because she was a woman, as she could not show that a male homosexual teacher would have been treated differently.

LORD NICHOLLS: For the like reason so also must Ms Pearce's principal ground of appeal fail. The disgraceful way she was treated by some of the pupils at the school was because of her sexual orientation, not her sex. Ms Pearce accepted that the children would have pursued a comparable campaign of harassment against a homosexual man.

The starting point here is to note that the expression 'sexual harassment' is ambiguous. The adjective 'sexual' may describe the *form* of the harassment; for instance, verbal abuse in explicitly sexual terms. Or it may be descriptive of the *reason* for the harassment; for instance, if a male employee makes office life difficult for a female employee because he does not wish to share his office with a woman. It is only in the latter sense that, although not as such prohibited by the Sex Discrimination Act, sexual harassment may nevertheless be within the scope of the Act as less favourable treatment accorded on the ground of sex. A claim under the Act cannot get off the ground unless the claimant can show she was harassed because she was a woman. A male employee may make office life difficult for a female employee, not because she is a woman, but because he objects to having anyone else in his office. He would be equally unwelcoming to a male employee. Harassment of a woman in these circumstances would not be sex discrimination.

In some cases there are suggestions of a different approach. It has been suggested that if the *form* of the harassment is sexual, that of itself constitutes less favourable treatment on the ground of sex. When the gender of the victim dictates the form of the harassment, that of itself, it is said, indicates the *reason* for the harassment, namely, it is on the ground of the sex of the victim. Degrading treatment of this nature differs materially from unpleasant treatment inflicted on an equally disliked male colleague, regardless of equality of overall unpleasantness: see Lord President Emslie in *Strathclyde Regional Council* v *Porcelli* [1986] IRLR 134, 136–8. Because the form of the harassment is gender-specific, there is no need to look for a male comparator. It would be no defence to a complaint of sexual harassment that a person of the opposite sex would have been similarly treated: see Morison J in *British Telecommunications plc* v *Williams* [1997] IRLR 668, 669.

In agreement with Ward LJ in *Smith* v *Gardner Merchant Ltd* [1998] IRLR 510, 516, I respectfully think some of these observations go too far. They cannot be reconciled with the language or the scheme of the statute. The fact that the harassment is gender-specific in form cannot be regarded as of itself establishing conclusively that the reason for the harassment is gender based: 'on the ground for her sex'. It will certainly point in that direction. But this does not dispense with the need for the tribunal of fact to be satisfied that the reason why the victim was being harassed was her sex. The gender-specific form of the harassment will be evidence, whose weight will depend on the circumstances, that the reason for the harassment was the sex of the victim. In some circumstances the inference may readily be drawn that the reason for the harassment was gender-based. A male employee who subjects a female colleague to persistent, unwelcome sexual overtures may readily be inferred to be doing so on the ground of her sex.

In the case of Ms Pearce the abuse was in homophobic terms: 'lezzie', 'lemon', 'lesbian shit' and the like. The natural inference to be drawn from this form of abuse is that the reason for this treatment was Ms Pearce's sexual orientation, not her sex. Further, as the employment tribunal noted, Ms Pearce did not put forward any evidence or argument that a male homosexual teacher would have been treated any differently either by the pupils or by the school. This being so, Ms Pearce did not establish that the harassment was on the ground of her sex. Her appeal on this second ground also must fail.

Grant v South-West Trains Ltd
[1998] IRLR 206, European Court of Justice

Lisa Grant was a clerical worker employed by South-West Trains (SWT). She was refused a travel pass for her female partner, with whom she had lived in a stable relationship. Her contract of employment with SWT provided that: 'You will be granted such free and reduced rate travel concessions as are applicable to a member of your grade. Your spouse and dependants will also be granted travel concessions.' SWT's staff travel facilities privilege ticket regulations provide that: 'Privilege tickets are granted to a married member of staff... for one legal spouse... Privilege tickets are granted for one common law spouse (of the opposite sex) subject to a statutory declaration being made that a meaningful relationship has existed for a period of two or more years.' Ms Grant's request for travel concessions for her partner was turned down because her partner was not of the opposite sex. She claimed that this was contrary to EC law. She pointed out that her male predecessor in her post, who cohabited with a woman, had received the benefit in respect of his partner.

HELD (European Court of Justice): A refusal by an employer to grant travel concessions to a person of the same sex with whom a worker has a stable relationship does not constitute discrimination based directly on the sex of the worker prohibited by Article 119 (now 141) of the EC Treaty or the Equal Pay Directive, even where such concessions are allowed to the person of the opposite sex with whom a worker has a stable relationship outside marriage.

DECISION: In the light of all the material in the case, the first question to answer is whether a condition in the regulations of an undertaking such as that in issue in the main proceedings constitutes discrimination based directly on the sex of the worker. If it does not, the next point to examine will be whether Community law requires that stable relationships between two persons of the same sex should be regarded by all employers as equivalent to marriages or stable relationships outside marriage between two persons of opposite sex. Finally, it will have to be considered whether discrimination based on sexual orientation constitutes discrimination based on the sex of the worker.

First, it should be observed that the regulations of the undertaking in which Ms Grant works provide for travel concessions for the worker, for the worker's 'spouse', that is, the person to whom he or she is married and from whom he or she is not legally separated, or the person of the opposite sex with whom he or she has had a 'meaningful' relationship for at least two years, and for the children, dependent members of the family, and surviving spouse of the worker.

The refusal to allow Ms Grant the concessions is based on the fact that she does not satisfy the conditions prescribed in those regulations, more particularly on the fact that she does not live with a 'spouse' or a person of the opposite sex with whom she has had a 'meaningful' relationship for at least two years.

That condition, the effect of which is that the worker must live in a stable relationship with a person of the opposite sex in order to benefit from the travel concessions, is, like the other alternative conditions prescribed in the undertaking's regulations, applied regardless of the sex of the worker concerned. Thus travel concessions are refused to a male worker if he is living with a person of the same sex, just as they are to a female worker if she is living with a person of the same sex.

Since the condition imposed by the undertaking's regulations applies in the same way to female and male workers, it cannot be regarded as constituting discrimination directly based on sex.

Second, the Court must consider whether, with respect to the application of a condition such as that in issue in the main proceedings, persons who have a stable relationship with a partner of the same sex are in the same situation as those who are married or have a stable relationship outside marriage with a partner of the opposite sex.

Ms Grant submits in particular that the laws of the Member States, as well as those of the Community and other international organisations, increasingly treat the two situations as equivalent.

While the European Parliament, as Ms Grant observes, has indeed declared that it deplores all forms of discrimination based on an individual's sexual orientation, it is nevertheless the case that the Community has not as yet adopted rules providing for such equivalence.

As for the laws of the Member States, while in some of them cohabitation by two persons of the same sex is treated as equivalent to marriage, although not completely, in most of them it is treated as equivalent to a stable heterosexual relationship outside marriage only with respect to a limited number of rights, or else is not recognised in any particular way.

The European Commission of Human rights for its part considers that despite the modern evolution towards homosexuality, stable homosexual relationships do not fall within the scope of the right to respect for family life under Article 8 of the Convention (see in particular the decisions in application No. 9369/81, *X and Y* v *the United Kingdom*, 3 May 1983, Decisions and Reports 32, p. 220; application No. 11716/85, *S* v *the United Kingdom*, 14 May 1986, DR 47 p. 274, paragraph 2; and application No. 15666/89, *Kerkhoven and Hinke* v *the Netherlands*, 19 May 1992, unpublished, paragraph 1), and that national provisions which, for the purpose of protecting the family, accord more favourable treatment to married persons and person of opposite sex living together as man and wife than to persons of the same sex in a stable relationship are not contrary to Article 14 of the Convention, which prohibits inter alia discrimination on the ground of sex (see the decisions in *S* v *the United Kingdom*, paragraph 7; application No. 14753/89, *C and L M* v *the United Kingdom* 9 October 1989, unpublished, paragraph 2; and application No. 16106/90, *B* v *the United Kingdom*, 10 February 1990, DR 64, p. 278, paragraph 2).

In another context, the European Court of Human Rights has interpreted Article 12 of the Convention as applying only to the traditional marriage between two persons of opposite biological sex (see the *Rees* judgment of 17 October 1986, Series A No. 106, p. 19, §49, and the *Cossey* judgment of 27 September 1990, Series A No. 184, p. 17, §43).

It follows that, in the present state of the law within the Community, stable relationships between two persons of the same sex are not regarded as equivalent to marriages or stable relationships outside marriage between persons of opposite sex. Consequently, an employer is not required by Community law to treat the situation of a person who has a stable relationship with a partner of the same sex as equivalent to that of a person who is married to or has a stable relationship outside marriage with a partner of the opposite sex.

In those circumstances, it is for the legislature alone to adopt, if appropriate, measures which may affect that position.

NOTES

1. Although the Employment Equality (Sexual Orientation) Regulations 2003 (SI 2003/1661) gave effect to the Framework Directive (Directive 2000/78), the EAT held in *English* v *Thomas Sanderson Blinds Ltd* [2008] IRLR 342 that UK law is narrower than the directive in that it introduces the element of causation. Mr English has been given leave to appeal to the Court of Appeal. Prior to the regulations *Smith* v *Gardner Merchant* provided a potential cause of action, particularly where there had been homophobic abuse. However, it became clear that discrimination on the grounds of sexual orientation was not, *per se*, unlawful, as it was not covered by Article 141 (ex 119) of the EC Treaty or the SDA 1975. This was confirmed in *R* v *Secretary of State for Defence, ex p. Perkins (No. 2)* [1998] IRLR 508, which applied the judgment of the ECJ in *Grant*. It was thought that there may be some redress under the HRA 1998. Indeed, the European Court of Human Rights (ECtHR) held that the Ministry of Defence (MoD) were in breach of Article 8 of the ECHR in banning homosexuals from the armed forces (see *Smith and Grady* v *United Kingdom* [1999] IRLR 734). As a result, the policy of barring homosexuals from the armed forces has been replaced with a code of sexual conduct which applies to all members of the armed forces.

2. Although considerable doubt was cast on the applicability of Article 14, ECHR by the decision in *Secretary of State for Defence* v *MacDonald* [2001] IRLR 43, the Court of Session confirmed that 'sex' within the meaning of the SDA, s. 1(1) did not include sexual orientation. This was supported by the decision of the ECtHR in *Salgueiro da Silva Mouta* v *Portugal* [2001] Fam LR 2, ECtHR.

As we have seen, the decision of the House of Lords in *MacDonald* v *Advocate General for Scotland; Pearce* v *Governing Body of Mayfield Secondary School* not only concludes that sex means gender and this does not include sexual orientation, but also that the appropriate comparator was a homosexual of the opposite sex. Clearly the Sexual Orientation Regulations address the contentious issue of the comparator by providing for comparison with a heterosexual person of the same sex.

3. For a critique of the Sexual Orientation Regulations see Oliver, H., 'Sexual orientation: Perceptions, definitions, and genuine occupational requirements' (2004) 33 ILJ 1. For an assessment of developments since the regulations became law, see Davies, C., 'Developments in the law on sexual orientation' (2005) 145 EOR 7–12.

4. The Civil Partnership Act 2004 provides for the legal recognition of same-sex partnerships. This will, once a partnership is registered, give civil partners the right to be treated in the same way in respect of certain legal benefits and obligations, e.g. paternity leave and pay and pension rights.

■ QUESTION

In determining whether harassment of a homosexual person amounts to sex discrimination, who is the comparator?

SECTION 4: RELIGION OR BELIEF

The Employment Equality (Religion or Belief) Regulations 2003 (SI 2003/1660) covered mainstream and minority religions as well as 'similar philosophical beliefs'. However, they did not extend to political opinion. It extended to protection on the grounds of perceived religious beliefs on the part of the discriminator. Under the regulations, employers were expected to audit and review their practices. The regulations mirrored the existing discrimination provisions in that they extended to direct and indirect discrimination. There was no defence to claims of direct discrimination. In addition, there were genuine occupational requirements which an employer had to justify. The EqA 2006 extended the definition of religion or belief to include 'lack of belief'. It also extended protection to the provision of goods, facilities, services, education, the use and disposal of premises, and the exercise of public functions. The relevant law is now contained in the EqA 2010, s. 10.

EQUALITY ACT 2010

10 Religion or belief

(1) Religion means any religion and a reference to religion includes a reference to a lack of religion.

(2) Belief means any religious or philosophical belief and a reference to belief includes a reference to a lack of belief.

(3) In relation to the protected characteristic of religion or belief—

(a) a reference to a person who has a particular protected characteristic is a reference to a person of a particular religion or belief;

(b) a reference to persons who share a protected characteristic is a reference to persons who are of the same religion or belief.

NOTES

1. At this stage there is relatively little case law in respect of this provision, although the momentum is increasing. In *Monaghan* v *Leicester Young Man's Christian Association* (2004) Case No. 1901830/2004, the employment tribunal dismissed a claim of religious discrimination. In this case, the applicant who held very strong Christian beliefs was a housing manager for the Association. He was instructed not to try to convert others to Christianity. The ET concluded that the grounds for the 'treatment' were not based on the applicant's religion but on the fact that he wished to convert others against the principles of the Association.

2. In *McClintock* v *Department of Constitutional Affairs* [2008] IRLR 29, a justice of the peace resigned from the family panel because he claimed that he could not in conscience, and compatibly with his philosophical and religious beliefs, agree to place children with same-sex couples. He said that he strongly believed that the question of allowing same-sex couples to adopt had not been sufficiently researched and tested and that 'to send a child to a same sex household is to make him/her the subject of an experiment in social science.' He asked to be relieved from the duty to officiate in such cases, and claimed that the Department had indirectly discriminated against him on grounds of religion or belief by not doing so. However, Mr McClintock could not show that he was disadvantaged as a consequence of holding a relevant 'belief' falling within the scope of the legislation. He had not put his objections on the basis of any religious or philosophical belief. The EAT held that to constitute a belief 'there must be a religious or philosophical viewpoint in which one actually believes'. Elias J emphasised that 'the kind of objection which Mr McClintock voiced here, depending as it did on the lack of evidence to justify the approach adopted in the legislation towards same sex parents, could not properly be described as a philosophical belief so as to fall within the scope of the Regulations, even after the amendment.'

3. In *Eweida* v *British Airways* [2010] EWCA Civ 80, the employer had adopted a dress code which forbade the wearing of a visible neck adornment and so prevented the appellant, Mrs Eweida, from wearing a small cross with her uniform.

   The Court of Appeal held that, by applying this rule, BA did not indirectly discriminate against Mrs Eweida on the grounds of her religion. 'The tribunal heard evidence from a number of practising Christians in addition to the claimant. None, including the claimant, gave evidence that they considered visible display of the cross to be a requirement of the Christian faith; on the contrary, leaders of the Christian Fellowship had stated that, "It is the way of the cross, not the wearing of it, that should determine our behaviour."' The court rejected the submission that one individual person could be the subject of indirect discrimination, observing that, if a solitary employee could be indirectly discriminated against, this could place an impossible burden on employers to anticipate and provide for what may be parochial or even facetious beliefs in society at large.

   The court upheld the view that, for a finding of indirect discrimination, some identifiable section of the workforce, albeit a small one, must be shown to suffer a particular disadvantage which the claimant shares.

   The court also found that, on the footing on which the claim had been advanced, namely disadvantage to a single individual arising out of her wish to manifest her faith in a particular way, the ET's findings of fact had shown that BA's staff dress code and the ban on a visible neck adornment was a proportionate means of achieving a legitimate aim.

   Eweida v *United Kingdom* [2013] IRLR 231 was a referral to the ECtHR relating to Article 9 of the European Convention, the right to freedom of religion and freedom to manifest religion. The European Court of Human Rights takes a different approach to the UK, holding that 'in order to count as a "manifestation" within the meaning of Article 9, the act in question must be intimately linked to the religion or belief.' It says that 'the existence of a sufficiently close and direct nexus between the act and the underlying belief must be determined on the facts of each case', but, contrary to the view of the UK courts, 'there is no requirement on the applicant to establish that he or she acted in fulfilment of a duty mandated by the religion in question.' In this case, applying those principles, the ECHR held that 'Ms Eweida's behaviour was a manifestation of her religious belief in the form of worship, practice and observance, and as such attracted the protection of Article 9.'

   As Rubenstein observes:

   > This emphasises the individual's belief and does not sit entirely easily with the statutory definition of indirect discrimination, which focuses on group disadvantage. However, it seems clear that because of the interpretative obligation in the Human Rights Act, the approach adopted by the Strasbourg court is likely to shape the way in which the relevant provisions of the Equality Act 2010 are construed in a claim of indirect discrimination because of religion or belief and that it will no longer be necessary to show group disadvantage; individual disadvantage resulting from the restriction will be sufficient. Until Eweida, the previous case law from Strasbourg was that in cases involving restrictions placed by employers on an employee's ability to observe religious practice, the possibility of resigning from the job and changing employment meant that there was no interference with the employee's religious freedom. Eweida resiles from this unsympathetic test. Instead, the ECHR now says: 'given the importance in a democratic society of freedom of religion in the workplace, rather than holding that the possibility of changing job would negate any interference with the right, the better

approach would be to weigh that possibility in the overall balance when considering whether or not the restriction was proportionate.' ('Highlights' [2013] IRLR, March 2013)

In terms of justification, the ECtHR upheld the claim of Ms Eweida. In weighing the proportionality of the measures taken by BA the domestic courts had not struck a fair balance. On one side of the scales was Ms Eweida's desire to manifest her religious belief—a fundamental right. On the other side of the scales was the employer's wish to project a certain corporate image. The ECtHR considered that, while this aim was undoubtedly legitimate, the domestic courts had accorded it too much weight. Ms Eweida's cross was discreet and could not have detracted from her professional appearance. There was no evidence that the wearing of other, previously authorised, items of religious clothing, such as turbans and hijabs, by other employees had any negative impact on British Airways' brand or image. Moreover, the fact that the company was able to amend the uniform code to allow for the visible wearing of religious symbolic jewellery demonstrated that the earlier prohibition was not of crucial importance. Therefore, in circumstances where there was no evidence of any real encroachment on the interests of others, the domestic authorities had failed sufficiently to protect her right to manifest her religion, in breach of the positive obligation under Article 9.

It would seem, therefore, that where there is no evidence that the rights of others will be infringed by allowing the religious manifestation, then it is likely to be unjustified not to allow it. Where, on the other hand, allowing the manifestation would conflict with the rights of others, or with health and safety obligations, or would undermine the employer's business objectives, it is likely to be justified.

4. The approach of the ECtHR in *Eweida* is evident in the decision of the Court of Appeal in *Mba v Merton LBC* [2014] IRLR 145. The Court found that an employer was justified in requiring a children's home care worker, who was a practising Christian, to work on Sundays. The majority considered that religious freedom under Article 9 of the ECHR was engaged. It was thus an error, when assessing justification, to take into account the suggestion that any group impact was limited because the belief that Sunday should be a day of rest was said not to be a core Christian belief. In judging proportionality, it was not necessary to establish whether an employee was disadvantaged with others sharing her belief, provided that there had been an interference with a personal right.

Although the tribunal should not have weighed in the employer's favour the fact that Mrs Mba's religious belief was not a core belief of her religion, that had been a peripheral part of the proportionality analysis of the tribunal which had not materially affected its conclusion. The tribunal's decision that the imposition of the PCP had been proportionate was 'plainly and unarguably right'. The council had established that there was really no viable or practicable alternative way of running the children's home effectively.

5. In *Grainger plc v Nicholson* [2010] IRLR 4, the EAT held that a belief in man-made climate change and the environment is capable of falling within the protection against discrimination on grounds of religion or belief. This decision suggests that these provisions potentially cover a wide range of philosophical beliefs, including belief in a political philosophy. Burton J adopted the view that it is not a bar to a philosophical belief being protected by the religion or belief provisions that it is a 'one-off' belief rather than being based on a philosophy of life. Whereas support for a political party would not meet the description of a philosophical belief, he held that the regulations are capable of embracing belief based on a political philosophy. The judge offered Marxism, communism, and free-market capitalism as examples. On the other hand, the judge said that 'there must be some limit placed upon the definition of "philosophical belief" for the purpose of the Regulations', and he suggested that these limits can be derived from the case law under the freedom of religion provisions of Article 9 of the European Convention. On that basis, he suggests that the law would not protect 'a racist or homophobic political philosophy' because it would offend against the Article 9 principle that the belief relied on must be 'worthy of respect in a democratic society and not incompatible with human dignity'.

Burton J held that the limitations placed upon the definition of 'philosophical belief' for the purpose of the 2003 Regulations were that: (1) the belief had to be genuinely held; (2) it had to be a belief and not an opinion or viewpoint based on the state of information available; (3) it had to be a belief as to a weighty and substantial aspect of human life and behaviour; (4) it had to attain a certain level of cogency, seriousness, cohesion and importance; and (5) it had to be worthy of respect in a democratic society, be compatible with human dignity, and not conflict with the fundamental rights of others.

5. Regulation 5(1) of the Religion or Belief Regulations prohibited harassment 'on grounds of religion or belief'. In *Saini v All Saints Haque Centre* [2009] IRLR 74, the EAT interpreted these words broadly to cover 'associative discrimination' on grounds of religion or belief. Citing the

judgment in *Coleman* v *Attridge Law* [2008] IRLR 722, ECJ, it held that reg. 5 'will be breached not only where an employee is harassed on the grounds that *he* holds certain religious or other relevant beliefs but also where he is harassed because someone else holds certain religious or other beliefs'. In this case, a Hindu advice worker claimed he had been bullied and harassed by managers who were of the Ravidassi faith, as part of their attempt to get rid of a Hindu colleague. Lady Smith stated that if an employee establishes that he has been subjected to harassive conduct 'because of his employer pursuing a discriminatory policy against the religious beliefs held by another employee that will be enough'. It is assumed that the EqA 2010, s. 13 will also encompass 'associative discrimination'.

SECTION 5: AGE

Following the Government's consultation document on age discrimination, regulations came into force in October 2006. The Employment Equality (Age) Regulations 2006 (SI 2006/1031) prohibited unjustified age discrimination in respect of recruitment, selection, promotion, and terms and conditions. The definitions of direct and indirect discrimination are similar to those found under the SDA 1975 and the Race Relations Act (RRA) 1976. One major difference was that, in relation to age, employers had a justification defence for direct as well as indirect discrimination. However, a significant exception existed for retirement. Schedule 9, paragraph 8 to the EqA 2010 provided: 'It is not an age contravention to dismiss a relevant worker at or over the age of 65 if the reason for dismissal is retirement' (the so-called Default Retirement Age (DRA)).

What was a retirement dismissal? This was defined in ss. 98ZA–ZF of the Employment Rights Act 1996, a highly complex set of provisions, but which, in essence, stated that if someone is 65 or over, and is retired, then it is a retirement dismissal. As long as the employer had given the employee six months' notice of its intention to retire the employee and informed the employee of his or her right to request working beyond retirement, the dismissal would be fair. The employer was not even obliged to offer reasons for its rejection of the request. Only if the employer failed to follow this procedure was there any chance of the employee mounting a successful unfair dismissal claim.

The regulations represented a significant dilution in relation to earlier proposals floated in the consultation process. First, the original proposals would have permitted an employee to challenge the legitimacy of a retirement dismissal, whereas reg. 30 stated that it is not unlawful discrimination to dismiss an employee 'at or over the age of 65 where the reason for dismissal is retirement' (this means that there was only a need to provide objective justification for retirement dismissals of employees under 65). Second, early proposals posited a model of age discrimination with no compulsory retirement age, but then a default age of 70 was proposed and eventually the Government settled on 65 (subject to review in 2011). In the light of these retreats, it is not surprising that the regulations attracted legal challenges from age campaign groups (see later in this section).

EQUALITY ACT 2010

5 Age

(1) In relation to the protected characteristic of age—

    (a) a reference to a person who has a particular protected characteristic is a reference to a person of a particular age group;

    (b) a reference to persons who share a protected characteristic is a reference to persons of the same age group.

(2) A reference to an age group is a reference to a group of persons defined by reference to age, whether by reference to a particular age or to a range of ages.

AGE DIVERSITY IN EMPLOYMENT: A CODE OF PRACTICE (2002)

The voluntary Code covers good practice in six aspects of the employment cycle: recruitment, selection, promotion, training, redundancy, and retirement. A key factor, though, in ensuring success in delivering good practice is a genuine commitment from top management to its implementation, which is communicated clearly throughout the organisation and beyond.

Recruitment

Recruit on the basis of the skills and abilities needed to do the job.

Selection

Select on merit by focusing on application form information about skills and abilities and on performance at interview.

Promotion

Base promotion on the ability, or demonstrated potential, to do the job.

Training and Development

Encourage all employees to take advantage of relevant and suitable training opportunities.

Redundancy

Base decisions on objective, job-related criteria to ensure the skills needed to help the business are retained.

Retirement

Ensure that retirement schemes are fairly applied, taking individual and business needs into account.

GOOD PRACTICE IN THE EMPLOYMENT CYCLE

Action to eradicate age discrimination should be taken as part of a wider personnel and equal opportunities strategy to create a flexible and motivated workforce. An effective strategy for implementing good practice will begin by reviewing the current position to clarify what needs to be done and how to monitor progress.

Recruitment

Recruit on the basis of the skills and abilities needed to do the job.

The aim of any sensible recruitment strategy is to find the right person for the job. To do that, companies need to identify the skills and abilities that are needed to carry out the work, and to make sure that the vacancy advertisement states these clearly.

To ensure the best candidates apply, employers should:
- not use age limits or age ranges in job adverts;
- place job adverts specifying the skills and abilities required for the post;
- think carefully about the language used in the advert and avoid using phrases which imply restrictions, such as 'young graduates' or 'mature person'; and
- think strategically about where jobs are advertised. Different magazines and periodicals are aimed at different sectors of the market.

Selection

To select the best candidate for the job, employers should:
- focus on skills, abilities and potential of the candidates when sifting applications;
- make sure that interviewers are aware of the need to ask job-related questions;
- use, where possible, a mixed-age interviewing panel;
- ensure all interviewers are trained to avoid basing decisions on prejudices and stereotypes; and
- avoid making age an integral part of the application form or process;
- select on merit, based on the application form information and the performance at interview.

Promotion

Base promotion on the ability, or demonstrated potential, to do the job.

The principles which apply to fair selection in recruitment apply equally to the promotion process. Consideration for promotion should be based on the ability of the candidates to do the job or whether they demonstrate the potential to do so after suitable training. Employers should:
- ensure that, wherever possible, the promotion opportunities are advertised through open competition;
- make sure that the promotion opportunities are made available to all staff who have demonstrated the ability or the potential to do the job;

- focus on the skills, abilities and potential of the candidates when sifting applications;
- make sure that interviewers are aware of the need to ask job-related questions;
- use, where possible, a mixed-age interviewing panel;
- ensure interviewers are trained to avoid basing decisions on prejudices and stereotypes; and
- select on merit.

Training and Development

Encourage all employees to take advantage of relevant and suitable training opportunities.

The business with the most skilled, flexible and committed workforce has a more competitive edge. Skilled and motivated people are more productive, produce higher quality work, reduce costs and wastage and increase profitability. It makes sense to ensure that all employees are encouraged to take advantage of relevant training and development opportunities throughout their employment. Employers should:

- ensure the training and development needs of all staff are regularly reviewed and that age is not a barrier to training;
- make sure that all employees are aware of the training and development opportunities that are available and are encouraged to use them;
- focus on the individual's and the company's need when providing training and development opportunities; and
- look at how training is delivered and ensure different learning styles and needs are addressed.

Redundancy

Base decisions on objective, job-related criteria to ensure the skills needed to help the business are retained.

Using age as the sole criterion when selecting people for redundancy can lead to the unnecessary loss of skills and abilities which are essential to the business. Employers should try to avoid this by:

- using objective, job-related criteria when considering candidates for redundancy;
- making sure the business retains the staff it needs to remain competitive;
- making sure age is not a criterion—and letting people know that; and
- looking at options such as part-time working, job-share or career breaks and short-term contracts when considering alternatives to redundancy.

Retirement

Ensure that retirement schemes are fairly applied, taking individual and business needs into account.

Employers can demonstrate their commitment to dealing fairly with employees, whilst looking to the best interests of the business by:

- basing retirement policy on business needs while also giving individuals as much choice as possible;
- making sure the loss to the company of skills and abilities is fully evaluated when operating early retirement schemes;
- considering alternatives to early retirement for those whose skills and abilities may be lost;
- not seeing age as the sole criterion when operating early retirement schemes (subject to pension rules);
- using flexible retirement schemes, where this is possible;
- using phased retirement, where possible, to allow employees to alter the balance of their working and personal lives and prepare for full retirement. This can also help the business to prepare for the loss of the employee's skills;
- making pre-retirement support available for employees; and applying mandatory company retirement age equally to all staff.

Palacios de la Villa v *Cortefiel Servicios SA*

[2007] IRLR 989, European Court of Justice

Félix Palacios de la Villa was born in 1940. He worked for Cortefiel Servicios SA as an organisational manager. In July 2005, Cortefiel notified him of the automatic termination of his contract of employment on the ground that he had reached the compulsory retirement age of 65, as provided for in a collective agreement which governed the terms and conditions of his employment.

Mr Palacios de la Villa took the view that that notification amounted to dismissal and commenced proceedings before the Spanish court. He requested that the measure that required him to retire be declared null and void on the ground that it was in breach of his fundamental rights and, in particular, his right not to be discriminated against on the ground of his age, as the measure was based solely on the fact that he had reached the age of 65.

HELD (European Court of Justice): Domestic legislation such as that at issue in the present case, according to which the fact that a worker has reached the retirement age laid down by that legislation leads to automatic termination of his employment contract, must be regarded as directly imposing less favourable treatment for workers who have reached that age as compared with all other persons in the labour force. Such legislation therefore establishes a difference in treatment directly based on age as referred to in Article 2 of Directive 2000/78.

Concerning differences of treatment on grounds of age, it is clear from Article 6(1) of the directive that such inequalities will not constitute discrimination prohibited under Article 2 if they were objectively and reasonably justified by a legitimate aim, such as one of those set out in Article 6(1).

In the present case, the single transitional provision, placed in context, was aimed at regulating the national labour market; in particular, for the purposes of checking unemployment. The legitimacy of such an aim could not reasonably be called into question.

JUDGMENT: As is already clear from the wording, 'specific provisions which may vary in accordance with the situation in Member States', in recital 25 in the preamble to Directive 2000/78, such is the case as regards the choice which the national authorities concerned may be led to make on the basis of political, economic, social, demographic and/or budgetary considerations and having regard to the actual situation in the labour market in a particular Member State, to prolong people's working life or, conversely, to provide for early retirement.

Furthermore, the competent authorities at national, regional or sectoral level must have the possibility available of altering the means used to attain a legitimate aim of public interest, for example by adapting them to changing circumstances in the employment situation in the Member State concerned. The fact that the compulsory retirement procedure was reintroduced in Spain after being repealed for several years is accordingly of no relevance.

It is, therefore, for the competent authorities of the Member States to find the right balance between the different interests involved. However, it is important to ensure that the national measures laid down in that context do not go beyond what is appropriate and necessary to achieve the aim pursued by the Member State concerned.

It does not appear unreasonable for the authorities of a Member State to take the view that a measure such as that at issue in the main proceedings may be appropriate and necessary in order to achieve a legitimate aim in the context of national employment policy, consisting in the promotion of full employment by facilitating access to the labour market.

Furthermore, the measure cannot be regarded as unduly prejudicing the legitimate claims of workers subject to compulsory retirement because they have reached the age limit provided for; the relevant legislation is not based only on a specific age, but also takes account of the fact that the persons concerned are entitled to financial compensation by way of a retirement pension at the end of their working life, such as that provided for by the national legislation at issue in the main proceedings, the level of which cannot be regarded as unreasonable.

Moreover, the relevant national legislation allows the social partners to opt, by way of collective agreements—and therefore with considerable flexibility—for application of the compulsory retirement mechanism so that due account may be taken not only of the overall situation in the labour market concerned, but also of the specific features of the jobs in question.

In the light of those factors, it cannot reasonably be maintained that national legislation such as that at issue in the main proceedings is incompatible with the requirements of Directive 2000/78.

R (on the application of the Incorporated Trustees of the National Council on Ageing (Age Concern England)) v Secretary of State for Business, Enterprise and Regulatory Reform
Case C–388/07 [2009] IRLR 373, European Court of Justice

Heyday, an organisation which was part of Age Concern, brought judicial review proceedings in the High Court challenging regs. 3(1), 7(4), and 30 of the Employment

Equality (Age) Regulations 2006 (SI 2006/1031), on the basis that they did not properly transpose the EC Equal Treatment Framework Directive 2000/78. In essence, it argued that by providing in reg. 30 for an exception to the principle of non-discrimination where the reason for the dismissal of an employee aged 65 or over was retirement, the regulations infringed Article 6(1) of the directive.

The Secretary of State relied on recital 14 in the preamble to the directive, which provides that the directive 'shall be without prejudice to national provisions laying down retirement ages'. He argued that the domestic provisions in issue did not fall within the scope of the directive. In the alternative, he submitted that the provisions were consistent with Article 6 of the directive.

Regulation 3(1) of the regulations, so far as material, provides:

> ...(b) A applies to B a provision, criterion or practice which he applies or would apply equally to persons not of the same age group as B, but—
> (i) which puts or would put persons of the same age group as B at a particular disadvantage when compared with other persons, and
> (ii) which puts B at that disadvantage, and A cannot show the treatment or, as the case may be, provision, criterion or practice to be a proportionate means of achieving a legitimate aim.

Regulation 7, so far as material, provides:

> (4) Subject to para. (5), para. (1)(a) and (c) does not apply in relation to a person—
> (a) whose age is greater than the employer's normal retirement age or, if the employer does not have a normal retirement age, the age of 65; or
> (b) who would, within a period of six months from the date of his application to the employer, reach the employer's normal retirement age or, if the employer does not have a normal retirement age, the age of 65.
> (5) Paragraph (4) only applies to a person to whom, if he was recruited by the employer, reg. 30 (exception for retirement) could apply.

Regulation 30, so far as material, provides:

> (2) Nothing in Part 2 or 3 shall render unlawful the dismissal of a person to whom this regulation applies at or over the age of 65 where the reason for the dismissal is retirement.

Article 2 of the directive, so far as material, provides:

> ...(b) indirect discrimination shall be taken to occur where an apparently neutral provision, criterion or practice would put persons having a particular religion or belief, a particular disability, a particular age, or a particular sexual orientation at a particular disadvantage compared with other persons unless:
> (i) that provision, criterion or practice is objectively justified by a legitimate aim and the means of achieving that aim are appropriate and necessary...

Article 6 of the directive, so far as material, provides:

> 1. Notwithstanding Article 2(2), member states may provide that differences of treatment on grounds of age shall not constitute discrimination, if, within the context of national law, they are objectively and reasonably justified by a legitimate aim, including legitimate employment policy, labour market and vocational training objectives, and if the means of achieving that aim are appropriate and necessary. Such differences of treatment may include, among others:
> (a) the setting of special conditions on access to employment and vocational training, employment and occupation, including dismissal and remuneration conditions, for young people, older workers and persons with caring responsibilities in order to promote their vocational integration or ensure their protection;
> (b) the fixing of minimum conditions of age, professional experience or seniority in service for access to employment or to certain advantages linked to employment;
> (c) the fixing of a maximum age for recruitment which is based on the training requirements of the post in question or the need for a reasonable period of employment before retirement.

The High Court stayed the proceedings and referred the following questions to the ECJ for preliminary ruling:

In relation to…Directive 2000/78…

[As regards] [n]ational retirement ages and the scope of the Directive[:]

(1) Does the scope of the Directive extend to national rules which permit employers to dismiss employees aged 65 or over by reason of retirement?

(2) Does the scope of the Directive extend to national rules which permit employers to dismiss employees aged 65 or over by reason of retirement where they were introduced after the Directive was made?

(3) In the light of the answers [to the preceding questions]

— were ss. 109 and/or 156 of the 1996 Act, and/or

— are regs. 30 and 7, when read with Schedules 8 and 6 to the Regulations, national provisions laying down retirement ages within the meaning of recital 14?

[As regards] [t]he definition of direct age discrimination: justification defence[:]

(4) Does Article 6(1) of the Directive permit member states to introduce legislation providing that a difference of treatment on grounds of age does not constitute discrimination if it is determined to be a proportionate means of achieving a legitimate aim, or does Article 6(1) require member states to define the kinds of differences of treatment which may be so justified, by a list or other measure which is similar in form and content to Article 6(1)?

[As regards] [t]he test for the justification of direct and indirect discrimination[:]

(5) Is there any, and if so what, significant practical difference between the test for justification set out in Article 2(2) of the Directive in relation to indirect discrimination, and the test for justification set out in relation to direct age discrimination at Article 6(1) of the Directive?

The ECJ on 5 March 2009 ruled as follows:

(1) National rules such as those set out in regs. 3, 7(4)–(5) and 30 of the Employment Equality (Age) Regulations 2006 fall within the scope of Council Directive 2000/78/EC of 27 November 2000 establishing a general framework for equal treatment in employment and occupation.

(2) Article 6(1) of Directive 2000/78 must be interpreted as meaning that it does not preclude a national measure which, like reg. 3 of the regulations at issue in the main proceedings, does not contain a precise list of the aims justifying derogation from the principle prohibiting discrimination on grounds of age. However, Article 6(1) offers the option to derogate from that principle only in respect of measures justified by legitimate social policy objectives, such as those related to employment policy, the labour market or vocational training. It is for the national court to ascertain whether the legislation at issue in the main proceedings is consonant with such a legitimate aim and whether the national legislative or regulatory authority could legitimately consider, taking account of the Member States' discretion in matters of social policy, that the means chosen were appropriate and necessary to achieve that aim.

(3) Article 6(1) of Directive 2000/78 gives Member States the option to provide, within the context of national law, for certain kinds of differences in treatment on grounds of age if they are 'objectively and reasonably' justified by a legitimate aim, such as employment policy, or labour market, or vocational training objectives, and if the means of achieving that aim are appropriate and necessary. It imposes on Member States the burden of establishing to a high standard of proof the legitimacy of the aim relied on as a justification. No particular significance should be attached to the fact that the word 'reasonably' used in Article 6(1) of the directive does not appear in Article 2(2)(b) thereof.

NOTES

1. The judgment of the ECJ referred the challenge to the Age Discrimination Regulations back to the Administrative Court to determine whether direct age discrimination such as the DRA can be justified in accordance with Article 6(1) of the Framework Employment Equality Directive as

being a proportionate means of achieving a legitimate aim. In *R (on the application of Age UK)* v *Secretary of Business and Skills* [2009] EWHC 2336 (Admin), the court held that reg. 30 (and a DRA in principle) was both legitimate and proportionate, although there were powerful reasons why an age over 65 should have been adopted. Two days before trial the Government announced it would review reg. 30 in early 2010. The court considered that if there had been no indication of this imminent review it would have granted the application. Likewise, if reg. 30 had been adopted for the first time in 2009, the application would have been granted.

The following extract from the judgment of Mr Justice Blake was instructive in offering a pointer for the future:

> I note that from the evidence of comparative EU practice that whilst Austria, Denmark, Ireland, Italy, Luxembourg, Netherlands, Poland and the European Commission appear to have retirement ages of 65 (at least for men). The age in Sweden is 67, in Finland 68, in Portugal where the employee has not requested retirement before 70 the contract is automatically changed to a short term one on achievement of this age. Six countries had no retirement age, and in the case of the European Commission employment could be extended for a further two years on application in the absence of countervailing factors.
>
> There may be no European consensus but in the light of changed economic circumstances and the generally recognised problems that a longer living population creates for the social security system the case for advancing the DRA beyond minimum age of 65 at least would seem to be compelling. I am conscious that very shortly before the hearing of this application, on the 13th July 2009 the government announced its intention to move forward the review of the regulations from 2011, its original planned date, to 2010. The Prime Minister is quoted as saying:
>
> > Evidence suggests that allowing older people to continue working, unfettered by negative views about ageing could be a big factor in the success of Britain's businesses and our future economic growth.
>
> That decision has been broadly welcomed by the claimants and the intervenor [the EHRC] as enabling the legislator to reconsider the balance of competing considerations in the light of contemporary conditions. Whether or not it will be decided that a DRA is still a valuable means of promoting the government's social policy aims is a matter entirely for the future, for the reasons I have sought to indicate. However, if a DRA is retained at all, the review must give particular consideration to whether the retention of 65 can conceivably now be justified.
>
> If Regulation 30 had been adopted for the first time in 2009, or there had been no indication of an imminent review, I would have concluded for all the above reasons that the selection of age 65 would not have been proportionate. It creates greater discriminatory effect than is necessary on a class of people who both are able to and want to continue in their employment. A higher age would not have any general detrimental labour market consequences or block access to high level jobs by future generations. If the selection of age 65 is not necessary it cannot therefore be justified. I would, accordingly, have granted relief requiring it to be reconsidered as a disproportionate measure and not capable of objective and reasonable justification in the light of all the information available to government.
>
> I have accepted Ms Rose's [Counsel for Defendant's] submission that this is a historic challenge to Regulations adopted in 2006 and the starting point must be the state of affairs then. I further recognise that:
>
> a) it is not for this court to identify when a particular age for a DRA is justified;
> b) age 65 had some support from past practice in the United Kingdom and the preponderance of consultees and continuing practice elsewhere in the European Union;
> c) no one was making a case for age 68 or so and age 70 commanded little popular support in the consultations;
> d) An appropriate margin of discretion must be afforded to government in the selection of the age for a DRA and in monitoring the impact of a DRA of 65.
>
> I do not consider that Regulation 30 as adopted in 2006 was beyond the competence of the government in applying the Directive or outside the discretionary area of judgment available in such matters. It was not a bold decision at the time but that is not the test. It was not a decision for the long term but that fact alone does not make it unlawful. Accordingly, despite the concerns I have identified in this part of the judgment, I conclude that it is not *ultra vires* to the Directive and I do not declare it to be void.
>
> The claim fails and I do not grant the claimant the relief sought. It will, however, be apparent from my observations at [128] above that the position might have been different if the government had not announced its timely review. I cannot presently see how 65 could remain as a DRA after the review.

2. The Employment Equality (Repeal of Retirement Age Provisions) Regulations 2011 (SI 2011/1069), which came into force on 6 April 2011, introduced transitional arrangements for the removal of the DRA. The Regulations also repealed sections of the equalities legislation and ERA 1996

relating to retirement. As a result, as from 1 October 2011 compulsory retirements constitute age discrimination unless the employer can justify the dismissal as a proportionate means of achieving a legitimate aim (see EqA 2010, s. 13(2)).

3. *Seldon* v *Clarkson Wright & Jakes* [2012] IRLR 590, SC, provides an example of some of the arguments employers might deploy in running the justification defence. The case involved an age discrimination claim by a partner in a law firm who was required to resign at age 65. The EAT upheld a finding that compulsory retirement was justified as a matter of principle and achieved certain legitimate objectives, including 'ensuring that associates are given the opportunity of partnership after a reasonable period as an associate thereby ensuring that associates do not leave the firm; facilitating the planning of the partnership and workforce across individual departments by having a realistic long-term expectation as to when vacancies will arise; and limiting the need to expel partners by way of performance management thus contributing to the congenial and supportive culture in the firm.' The EAT took the view, however, that the rule requiring retirement at age 65 involved stereotyping 'that partners will by the age of 65 be more likely to be under performing than partners of a younger age'. Mr Justice Elias commented: 'With respect to the tribunal, we think that reasoning of that kind is what the legislation is seeking to avoid. It is not self-evident that performance will dip in that way at that age, and there was no evidence to support that proposition before the tribunal.' However, a compulsory retirement age could be justified where there is 'a considered and reasoned explanation as to why the particular age had been chosen. Mere assertion would not be enough.' Tangible evidence must be presented.

The EAT's decision was approved by both the CA and SC.

The Court of Appeal held that although the term did directly discriminate, the employment tribunal had been entitled to find that there were three legitimate aims and that the term was a proportionate means of achieving a legitimate aim. The aims were:

(i)   ensuring associates (young solicitors) were given the opportunity of partnership after a reasonable period;

(ii) facilitating planning in the firm by having an expectation of when vacancies would arise; and

(iii) limiting the need to expel partners for declining performance.

These aims might involve mixed motives in that they served the self-interest of the firm as well as the interests of young would-be or actual employees, but as long as they were consistent with the social policy of providing employment prospects for young employees, the aims were legitimate.

The Supreme Court, in upholding the CA decision, held that the aims of the firm did not need to be the precise aims set out in Art. 6 of the Equality Framework Directive (2000/78/EC) (i.e. employment policy, labour market, and vocational training objectives). Instead, the employer's aims need only be consistent with those objectives.

> LADY HALE:
> [The firm] identified three aims for the compulsory retirement age, which the Court of Appeal summed up as 'dead men's shoes' and 'collegiality'. [Counsel] for the claimant has argued that these were individual aims of the business rather than the sort of social policy aims contemplated by the Directive. I do not think that that is fair. The first two identified aims were staff retention and workforce planning, both of which are directly related to the legitimate social policy aim of sharing out professional employment opportunities fairly between the generations (and were recognised as legitimate in *Fuchs* [2012] IRLR 785, CJEU). The third was limiting the need to expel partners by way of performance management, which is directly related to the dignity aims accepted in *Rosenbladt* [2012] All ER (EC)288, ECJ and Fuchs. It is also clear that the aims can be directly related to the type of business concerned...I would therefore accept that the identified aims were legitimate.

The Court also held that a general policy, as opposed to each retirement on its merits, could be justified, but the use of the general policy must be a proportionate means to the legitimate objectives, which in this case it was. Once the use of a general policy has been justified, each individual retirement under it is presumed justified.

The case was remitted to the employment tribunal to determine whether a retirement age of 65 was reasonably necessary to achieve the legitimate aims of workforce planning and retention of associate solicitors. The tribunal held that it was and the EAT, in *Seldon* v *Clarkson Wright & Jakes (No. 2)* [2014] IRLR 748, ruled that the tribunal was entitled to arrive at this conclusion. In particular, Mr Justice Langstaff held that the tribunal did not err in finding that the law firm was entitled to choose 65 as the retirement age rather than some other age that would achieve the legitimate aims with less discriminatory impact, such as 68 or 70. As Rubenstein observes:

It is difficult to reconcile this with the fundamental principle of discrimination law, reiterated by Lady Hale in the Supreme Court in this case, that a measure cannot be justified if there are other, less discriminatory measures that would equally meet the employer's legitimate objective. ('Highlights' [2014] IRLR, October)

4. *Petersen* v *Berufungsausschuss für Zahnärzte* [2010] IRLR 254 was a case concerned with the maximum age limit of 68 for practice as a dentist in the German public health service. Justification was alleged to be based on three grounds, the first of which was 'the need to protect patients insured under the statutory health insurance scheme against the risk presented by older panel dentists whose work is no longer the best...it being thought that the performance of dentists declines after a certain age.' The ECJ held that 'a member state may find it necessary to set an age limit for the practice of a medical profession such as that of a dentist in order to protect the health of patients.' In this case, however, that justification was held to be invalid, because the German legislation did not apply the same limit to dentists who practise in the private sector. However, the ECJ accepted the other two justifications: the financial balance of the German health system; and the distribution of employment opportunities between employees of different ages where jobs were limited.

5. In *Wolf* v *Stadt Frankfurt Am Main* [2010] IRLR 244, the case concerned a maximum recruitment age of 30 for a post in the Frankfurt fire service involving frontline firefighting duties. The ECJ referred to 'scientific data' from the German government 'which show that respiratory capacity, musculature and endurance diminish with age'. The Court accepted that 'very few officials over 45 years of age have sufficient physical capacity to perform the fire-fighting part of their activities.' On that basis, the Court concluded that physical fitness was a genuine and determining occupational requirement for the job within the meaning of Article 4(1) of the directive and that a maximum recruitment age of 30 was proportionate because 'the age at which an official is recruited determines the time during which he will be able to perform physically demanding tasks.' As Rubenstein observes:

> To UK eyes, it is contrary both to principles of discrimination law and good practice to set a maximum age for undertaking work on the basis of generalised data rather than individual assessment. Even more problematic, however, is the finding that the recruitment age was justified under EU law as a genuine occupational requirement. The claimant was aged 31 and presumably met all the fitness requirements for the job when he applied. To allow him to be discriminated against on the basis of a hypothesis about his physical condition 14 years hence represents a major expansion of the scope of an exception which has hitherto been interpreted strictly. ['Highlights' [2010] IRLR 181.]

In *Vital Pérez* v *Ayuntamiento de Oviedo* [2015] IRLR 158, the question for the CJEU was whether it was unlawful age discrimination for a Spanish municipality to fix a maximum age of 30 for recruitment to the post of local police officer. The Court accepted that possession of particular physical capabilities may be regarded as a 'genuine and determining occupational requirement' for the purposes of employment as a local police officer, and that the possession of particular physical capacities is one characteristic relating to age. In this case, however, the CJEU concluded that the age limit was disproportionate. It distinguished *Wolf* on the basis that whereas 'scientific data' before the Court in that case established that to be a front-line fire fighter requires 'exceptionally high' physical capacities and that very few individuals over the age of 45 have those capacities, this is not the case with all of the capacities which a police officer requires. Moreover, other Spanish municipalities operated a different, or no, maximum recruitment age for police officers, and the maximum age for recruitment to the Spanish national police force has been abolished. Furthermore, the advertised job qualifications stipulated that candidates would have to pass stringent physical tests, which would make it possible to ensure that local police officers possess the particular level of physical fitness required. Nor could the age limit be objectively justified under Article 6(1)(c) of the Directive in that it was based on the training requirements of the post and the need for a reasonable period of employment before retirement. The retirement age for police officers was 65 and there was no evidence linking the age limit to training requirements.

6. In *Pulham* v *London Borough of Barking and Dagenham* [2010] IRLR 184, EAT, the local authority had introduced a scheme for rewarding long service, which was based on length of service (minimum 25 years) and age (being at least 55). Because it was regarded as being potentially age discriminatory, the scheme was closed to new entrants with effect from 1 April 2007 as part of the council's single status agreement, but it was agreed that employees already in receipt of increments would have that part of their pay protected at their current rate, but without any

further increase for the remainder of their employment. The claimant, who satisfied the service criterion but not the age requirement when entry to the scheme was frozen, was one of a number of employees who brought a test case challenging the decision as age discriminatory, in that she was being treated less favourably than an employee with the same service who was aged 55 or over. An employment tribunal held that the pay protection arrangements were justified. The EAT held that transitional pay arrangements can be justified in principle, notwithstanding the Court of Appeal's decision in *Redcar and Cleveland Borough Council* v *Bainbridge* [2008] IRLR 776 that transitional pay protection arrangements maintaining differentials are impermissible where past direct sex discrimination has been 'recognised'. According to the EAT, this principle does not extend to direct age discrimination, which is a relatively new right. According to Mr Justice Underhill, 'We can see no reason why an employer faced with the coming into force of the Regulations should be absolutely disentitled to incorporate an element of pay protection into the adjustments necessary to conform to the new law, notwithstanding that that will of its nature involve a degree of continuing discrimination.' In this case, two of the key elements which led the tribunal to conclude that the pay protection arrangements were justified were that they represented the outcome of collective bargaining and that the local authority had no funds to extend the scheme by removing the age restriction. The EAT rules that the tribunal misdirected itself in its approach to both criteria. As to the role of collective bargaining, the EAT says this 'did no more than (potentially) constitute evidence that the proportionality test was satisfied. It could not be regarded as in itself conclusive.' It was for the tribunal to assess whether that outcome 'represented a fair balance between the reasonable needs of the Council and its undoubtedly discriminatory impact'. So far as cost is concerned, the EAT holds that 'employers cannot automatically justify a failure to eliminate discrimination by allocating the costs of doing so to a particular budget and then declaring that budget to be exhausted: any such allocation was their own choice, as was the size of the budget, and plainly they cannot be permitted definitively to limit the extent of their own obligations by the choices that they make.'

7. In Germany, service-related statutory minimum notice periods disregard periods of the employee's employment before the age of 25. The claimant in *Kücükdeveci* v *Swedex GmbH & Co KG* [2010] IRLR 346 maintained that this discriminated on grounds of age against younger people. The aim put forward in the reference was to afford employers greater flexibility by alleviating the burden on them in respect of dismissing young workers, from whom it is reasonable to expect a greater degree of personal or occupational mobility. The ECJ held that the legislation in question is contrary to the Framework Employment Equality Directive. It emphasised that 'the legislation is not appropriate for achieving that aim, since it applies to all employees who joined the undertaking before the age of 25, whatever their age at the time of dismissal.' As Rubenstein observes: 'This may call into question age-related elements in our own employment legislation, such as the age bands in calculating statutory redundancy pay and the unfair dismissal basic award' ('Highlights' [2010] IRLR 277).

8. In *Rosenbladt Oellerking Gebaudereinigungsges mBh* [2011] IRLR 51, the CJEU held that a compulsory retirement age of 65 in a contract of employment—whilst prima facie discriminatory on grounds of age—is justified if the following conditions are met:
   • the contract (i.e. the retirement age) has been collectively negotiated with a union;
   • the employee will receive a pension (on the facts, a State pension, but presumably an occupational pension will do when the State pension age rises) so that they have replacement income; and
   • compulsory retirement has been in widespread use in the relevant country for a long time without having had any effect on the levels of employment.

   Importantly, the DRA was intended (inter alia) to 'facilitate employment for young people, planning recruitment and allowing good management of a business's personnel, in a balanced manner according to age', which the CJEU accepted was a legitimate aim.

   This has significant implications for employers seeking to justify a compulsory retirement age after the default retirement age was abolished in October 2011.

9. An equally important case is *Prigge* v *Deutsche Lufthansa* [2011] IRLR 1052, CJEU. Mr Prigge, Mr Fromm, and Mr Lambach, the claimants, were employed for many years by Deutsche Lufthansa as pilots and then flight captains. The employment relationship was governed by a collective agreement that provided that the 'employment relationship shall terminate, without notice of termination, at the end of the month on which the 60th birthday falls'. Accordingly, their employment contracts terminated in 2006 and 2007 when they reached 60 years of age.

They brought proceedings in the German labour court, arguing that they were victims of discrimination on grounds of age and seeking an order that the airline continue their employment contracts.

International legislation in relation to pilots was developed by the Joint Aviation Authorities, an international institution, in which Germany participates. Part of that legislation (the 'joint aviation requirements') was adopted and officially published by the German Government. The joint aviation requirements provided for a compulsory retirement age of 65 for pilots of aircraft engaged in commercial air transport operations and that pilots aged over 60 could be employed so long as they were a member of a multi-pilot crew and were the only pilot in that crew who had attained the age of 60. Other collective agreements governing the pilots of other companies in Deutsche Lufthansa's group did not provide for an age limit of 60. The federal labour court referred the following question to the Court of Justice for a preliminary ruling: 'Must Article 2(5), Article 2(4) and/or Article 6(1), first sentence, of Directive 2000/78 and/or the general Community-law principle which prohibits discrimination on grounds of age be interpreted as precluding rules of national law which recognise an age-limit of 60 for pilots established by collective agreement for the purposes of air safety?'

Article 2(5) of Council Directive 2000/78/EC (the 'Equal Treatment Directive') states that the Directive 'shall be without prejudice to measures laid down by national law which, in a democratic society, are necessary for public security, for the maintenance of public order and the prevention of criminal offences, for the protection of health and for the protection of the rights and freedoms of others'.

Article 4 provides that 'Member States may provide that a difference of treatment...shall not constitute discrimination where, by reason of the nature of the particular occupational activities concerned or of the context in which they are carried out, such a characteristic constitutes a genuine and determining occupational requirement, provided that the objective is legitimate and the requirement is proportionate.' Article 6 of the Directive states that 'Member States may provide that differences of treatment on grounds of age shall not constitute discrimination, if, within the context of national law, they are objectively and reasonably justified by a legitimate aim, including legitimate employment policy, labour market and vocational training objectives, and if the means of achieving that aim are appropriate and necessary.' The national court submitted that the age limit for pilots guaranteed not only the proper performance of the work but, in addition, the protection of the life and health of crew members, passengers, and persons in the areas over which the aircraft flew. Age was objectively linked to the reduction of physical capabilities. The fact that international and national rules as well as other collective agreements did not totally prohibit, but limited, acting as a pilot after age 60 confirmed that the performance of that profession after that age presented a risk. The fact that other collective agreements governing the pilots of other companies in Deutsche Lufthansa's group did not provide for an age limit of 60 did not undermine the principle of equality, as those other agreements had been negotiated by different social partners and for other companies.

The CJEU (Grand Chamber) ruled as follows:

> Article 2(5) of Council Directive 2000/78/EC of 27 November 2000 establishing a general framework for equal treatment in employment and occupation must be interpreted as meaning that the Member States may authorise, through rules to that effect, the social partners to adopt measures within the meaning of Article 2(5) in the areas referred to in that provision that fall within collective agreements on condition that those rules of authorisation are sufficiently precise so as to ensure that those measures fulfil the requirements set out in Article 2(5). A measure such as that at issue in the main proceedings, which fixes the age limit from which pilots may no longer carry out their professional activities at 60 whereas national and international legislation fixes that age at 65, is not a measure that is necessary for public security and protection of health, within the meaning of the said Article 2(5). Article 4(1) of Directive 2000/78 must be interpreted as precluding a clause in a collective agreement, such as that at issue in the main proceedings, that fixes at 60 the age limit from which pilots are considered as no longer possessing the physical capabilities to carry out their professional activity while national and international legislation fix that age at 65.
>
> The first paragraph of Article 6(1) of Directive 2000/78 must be interpreted to the effect that air traffic safety does not constitute a legitimate aim within the meaning of that provision.

The CJEU held:

(a) Collective agreements must, the same as legislative, regulatory or administrative provisions, respect the principles implemented by the Equal Treatment Directive.

(b) Article 2(5) precluded the compulsory retirement age of 60 for pilots, as that measure was not necessary for public security and protection of health within the meaning of that provision.

In adopting Article 2(5), the EU legislature, in the area of employment and occupation, intended to prevent and arbitrate a conflict between, on the one hand, the principle of equal treatment and, on the other hand, the necessity of ensuring public order, security, and health, the prevention of criminal offences, and the protection of individual rights and freedoms, which are necessary for the functioning of a democratic society. As regards air traffic safety, it is apparent that measures that aim to avoid aeronautical accidents by monitoring pilots' aptitude and physical capabilities with the aim of ensuring that human failure does not cause accidents are undeniably measures of a nature to ensure public security within the meaning of Article 2(5). However, in the present case, national and international legislation considered that it was not necessary to prohibit pilots from acting as pilots after age 60 but merely to restrain those activities. Therefore, the prohibition on piloting after that age was not necessary for the achievement of the pursued objective.

A measure adopted by way of collective agreement can be a measure provided for by 'national law' within Article 2(5). Although the Court has already held that social partners are not bodies governed by public law, that ruling does not prevent Member States from authorising, through rules to that effect, social partners adopting measures that fall within collective agreements.

(c) Article 4(1) precluded the compulsory retirement age, as it was not a proportionate requirement within the meaning of that provision. It is essential that airline pilots possess particular physical capabilities insofar as physical defects in that profession may have significant consequences. It is also undeniable that those capabilities diminish with age. It follows that possessing particular physical capabilities may be considered as a 'genuine and determining occupational requirement' within the meaning of Article 4(1) for acting as an airline pilot and that the possession of such capabilities is related to age. Further, the aim of guaranteeing air traffic safety is a legitimate objective within the meaning of Article 4(1) of the Directive.

However, with regard to proportionality, the Directive states that it is in very limited circumstances that a difference of treatment may be justified where a characteristic related to age constitutes a genuine and determining occupational requirement. Moreover, insofar as it allows a derogation from the principle of non-discrimination, Article 4(1) of the Directive must be interpreted strictly. Given the different treatment by the national and international authorities and the lack of evidence that pilots no longer possessed the physical capabilities to perform over 60, the social partners had imposed a disproportionate requirement within the meaning of Article 4(1).

(d) Article 6(1) precluded the compulsory retirement age, as air traffic safety does not constitute a legitimate aim within the meaning of that provision. While the list is not exhaustive, the legitimate aims set out in Article 6(1) are related to employment policy, the labour market, and vocational training. The Court has also held that aims that may be considered 'legitimate' within the meaning of the Article 6(1) and, consequently, appropriate for the purposes of justifying derogation from the principle prohibiting discrimination on grounds of age, are social policy objectives, such as those related to employment policy, the labour market or vocational training. Air traffic safety does not fall within those objectives.

Implications of the Prigge *judgment* As the default retirement age of 65 in the UK is now abolished, cases such as *Prigge* will become increasingly important as employers decide whether to abolish the idea of compulsory retirement altogether or to try and justify a specific retirement age within their business. The CJEU has stressed that the defence of objective justification should be construed narrowly; and employers seeking to implement or retain DRAs should do so with caution. In particular, where the DRA is based on health and safety grounds, employers must ensure that they have credible evidence to justify their selection of a blanket cut-off point. In the absence of compelling medical or statistical evidence, the approach adopted by other employers within the relevant industry is likely to be a highly relevant and important consideration when assessing the necessity and proportionality of such measures.

10. EqA 2010, Sch. 9, Pt 2 provides exceptions from the age discrimination regime for the following:
    * benefits based on length of service (but benefits accruing beyond five years' service have to be reasonably based on achieving a business need) (para. 10);
    * the differential NMW rate for younger workers (para. 11);
    * enhanced redundancy payments for older workers (para. 13).

FURTHER READING

Cabrelli, D., *Employment Law in Context: Text and materials* (Oxford: OUP, 2014), Chs. 11, 12.

Hepple, B., *Equality: The new legal framework* (Oxford: Hart Publishing, 2011).

Honeyball, S., *Honeyball and Bowers' Textbook on Employment Law*, 13th edn (Oxford: OUP, 2014), Ch. 10.

For an excellent overview and critical analysis of the Equality Act 2010, see Deakin, S. (ed.), 'Equality Law and the Act of 2010' (2011) 40(4) ILJ 313.

7

Terminating the Contract

A variety of common law and statutory employment rights are dependent upon a dismissal taking place. But, as will be seen later, there are a number of instances where termination may take place without dismissal as such. In certain cases, statute seeks to ameliorate the harshness of the common law position by deeming a dismissal to have taken place, thus enhancing employment protection, e.g. Employment Rights Act (ERA) 1996, s. 136 (redundancy), and s. 95 (unfair dismissal) (referred to later). In other areas, however, the old common law rules remain unqualified by statute and it then becomes a question of judicial policy as to how far the common law doctrines, such as frustration, should be allowed to operate in a modern system of employment protection.

SECTION 1: TERMINATION INVOLVING DISMISSAL AT COMMON LAW

A: Dismissal with notice

The general principle is that either party to the contract of employment can bring it to an end by giving notice to the other. Once notice is given, it cannot be withdrawn unilaterally.

If the contract is for a fixed period, then the employment cannot lawfully be terminated before the end of that period unless, of course, the employee is in breach of contract or unless the contract provides for prior termination by notice.

The length of notice required to bring a contract to an end should be expressly agreed by the parties. If no notice is expressly agreed then the law requires that 'reasonable notice' should be given, with the length depending on such factors as the seniority and status of the employee. Apart from any contractual provision for notice, an employee is entitled to a statutory minimum period of notice, which statutory period takes precedence over any lesser contractual notice entitlement (the ERA 1996, s. 86(3)).

EMPLOYMENT RIGHTS ACT 1996

86. Rights of employer and employee to minimum notice

(1) The notice required to be given by an employer to terminate the contract of employment of a person who has been continuously employed for one month or more—

    (a) is not less than one week's notice if his period of continuous employment is less than two years,

    (b) is not less than one week's notice for each year of continuous employment if his period of continuous employment is two years or more but less than twelve years, and

    (c) is not less than twelve weeks' notice if his period of continuous employment is twelve years or more.

(2) The notice required to be given by an employee who has been continuously employed for one month or more to terminate his contract of employment is not less than one week.

NOTES

1. The minimum notice provision does not prevent either party from waiving the right to notice, affect the right of either party to terminate the contract without notice in response to a serious breach of contract by the other (see next section), or prevent the employee accepting a payment *in lieu of notice* (the ERA 1996, s. 86(3) and (6)).

2. Employers will often decide that it is in their interests not to require dismissed employees to work out their notice. At best such workers will lack motivation and at worst they may try to find a way of getting their own back! When such workers are given pay in lieu of notice, the law regards this as the payment of damages for wrongful dismissal (see Section 5).

3. Once a notice of termination is given, it will be hard for the employer to retract (see *C F Capital plc* v *Willoughby* [2011] IRLR 985, CA).

B: Summary dismissal for fundamental breach

(i) What conduct is sufficient to warrant termination?

The conduct of the employee may be viewed as sufficiently serious to justify immediate termination of employment without notice. In this event, the employee will lose entitlement to both contractual and statutory minimum notice.

Theft of or wilful damage to the employer's property, violence at work, dishonesty, and other criminal offences will normally justify instant dismissal. Disobedience to lawful and reasonable orders may justify instant dismissal, but not in every case—all the circumstances must be considered. Ordinarily, lesser misdemeanours would require the employer to give a warning as to future behaviour before dismissing. But a combination of lesser offences may justify instant termination.

Pepper* v *Webb

[1969] 2 All ER 216, Court of Appeal

HARMAN LJ: [T]he employee began (as they said) to lose interest; he did not give satisfaction. There were complaints of inefficiency and an insolent manner—what the judge described as 'dumb insolence'—at times. Things went on very uncomfortably during April, May and June. During part of that time he was very short of help; the promised second gardener did not turn up until May, though there was a third—jobbing—gardener from Monday to Friday.

The matter came to a head on Saturday 10th June, when the employer's wife went out between 9.00 a.m. and 10.00 a.m. and found that there were some fuchsia plants and geranium plants that had not yet been planted. She told the employee to put them in at once or they would die. There had been a good many plants—sweet peas in particular, and dahlias—that had died, according to her, from neglect previously, though it is fair to say that the employee denies it. Anyway on the morning of 10th June she said 'Put in these plants'. There were fuchsias, geraniums and some heath plants. The employee said: 'I am leaving at 12 o'clock; you can do what you like about them. If you don't like it you can give me notice'; and he walked off. The employer's wife was upset and went in and complained to the employer. He says that he went out to speak to the employee. The employee says he was ordered into the house but that is not accepted by the judge. I think that probably the critical interview occurred in the garden. Anyhow according to the employer, he went out, not with the idea of sacking the employee—because he could ill afford to do that in June—but in order to remonstrate with him, and he apparently said 'This job will only take you half an hour: why make all this trouble and fuss about it?' It was then fairly near 12 noon, which was shutting-up time for the employee. The employee, I think, must have lost his temper, for he said: 'I couldn't care less about your bloody greenhouse and your sodding garden'; and he walked off. The employer felt that he could not abide that degree of insolence and he gave him notice forthwith; and this action is for seven weeks' wages on the footing that that dismissal was not justified.

Now what will justify an instant dismissal?—something done by the employee which impliedly or expressly is a repudiation of the fundamental terms of the contract; and in my judgment if ever there was such a repudiation this is it. What is the gardener to do? He is to look after the garden and he is to look after the greenhouse. If he does not care a jot about either then he is repudiating his contract. That is what it seems to me the employee did, and I do not see, having done that, that he can complain if he is summarily dismissed. It is said on his behalf that one act of temper, one insolent outburst, does not merit so condign a punishment; but this, according to his employer, and I think rightly on the evidence, was the last straw. The employee had been acting in a very unsatisfactory way ever since April. He had that morning refused to obey the employer's wife's quite reasonable instructions, and when he in addition behaved in this way to the remonstrances of his employer I think he brought his dismissal upon himself and cannot complain of it. In my judgment, therefore, the appeal should be allowed and the claim dismissed.

KARMINSKI LJ: I agree that this appeal must be allowed. In my view the essential question here is whether the employer was justified in his summary dismissal of the employee on the ground of wilful disobedience of a lawful and reasonable order. Harman LJ, has set out the facts and I do not propose to add anything to what he has said. It has long been a part of our law that a servant repudiates the contract of service if he wilfully disobeys the lawful and reasonable orders of his master. There is no suggestion here that the order initiated by the employer's wife, and repeated by the employer a couple of hours later, was other than lawful. I see nothing on the facts before the learned deputy county court judge to suggest that that order was unreasonable; and there is ample evidence to show that the refusal by the employee was wilful. That being so, I have come to the conclusion that the employer was fully justified in dismissing the employee summarily.

Wilson v Racher

[1974] IRLR 114, Court of Appeal

Philip Wilson was the head gardener on Mr Racher's estate. He was dismissed following an incident in which Racher accused Wilson of shirking his work and in the course of the ensuing argument Wilson used obscene language.

EDMUND-DAVIES LJ: On Sunday 11.6.72, the defendant sacked the plaintiff. The plaintiff asserts that this constituted a wrongful dismissal and entitled him to the damages awarded by the learned judge. As to the quantum of those damages, no question arises. The sole issue here is whether the circumstances were such that the defendant acted wrongfully in prematurely terminating the plaintiff's employment.

There is no rule of thumb to determine what misconduct on the part of a servant justifies summary termination of his contract. For the purpose of the present case, the test is whether the plaintiff's conduct was insulting and insubordinate to such a degree as to be incompatible with the continuance of the relation of master and servant (per Hill, J, in *Edwards* v *Levy* (1860) 2 F and F p. 94, at p. 95). The application of such test will, of course, lead to varying results according to the nature of the employment and all the circumstances of the case. Reported decisions provide useful, but only general guides, each case turning upon its own facts. Many of the decisions which are customarily cited in these cases date from the last century and may be wholly out of accord with the current social conditions. What would today be regarded as almost an attitude of Czar-serf, which is to be found in some of the older cases where a dismissed employee failed to recover damages, would, I venture to think, be decided differently to-day. We have by now come to realise that a contract of service imposes upon the parties a duty of mutual respect.

What happened on Sunday the 11th June emerges from the learned judge's clear and helpful judgment, in which he reviews all the facts and sets out his findings. This Court lacks the advantage of seeing and hearing the witnesses which was enjoyed by the trial judge. It needs to be stressed that the appellant now challenges none of his findings of fact. The story began on the preceding Friday afternoon when the plaintiff had been trimming a new yew hedge with an electric cutter. It was a damp afternoon, but the plaintiff carried on, taking shelter when the rain became heavy and then resuming his work when conditions improved. But at about quarter to four the rain was so heavy that the plaintiff could not continue because there was danger of his being electrocuted by the cutter. He then proceeded to oil and clean his tools until his day's work was over. But he did make one mistake. He left a ladder leaning against a young yew hedge, which was an unfortunate thing to do. To that extent, the plaintiff was guilty of some dereliction of duty. But on the Sunday afternoon that was by no means the only topic discussed between the parties. It was after luncheon that the defendant and his wife and three young children were in the garden when the plaintiff passed and greeted them. The defendant asked where he was going, and the plaintiff replied that he was going to the garden shed to get his boots. Thereafter the defendant showered the plaintiff with questions. He shouted at him, and he was very aggressive. He accused the plaintiff of leaving his work prematurely on the Friday afternoon. The plaintiff explained that he had stopped cutting the hedge only because it would have been dangerous to continue, whereupon the defendant said, 'I am not bothered about you, Wilson, that's your lookout'. Though there was some reference to the ladder, the defendant did not make clear what his complaint was. But when the defendant accused the plaintiff of shirking his work on the Friday afternoon, there is no doubt that the plaintiff used most regrettable language, and it is part of my unpleasant duty to repeat it so as to make clear what happened. The plaintiff said: 'If you remember it was pissing with rain on Friday. Do you expect me to get fucking wet?' The learned judge, who found that Mrs Racher and the children did not hear those words, said: 'The plaintiff had a clear conscience, and he did reply somewhat robustly when he expressed the state of the weather. I think he felt under a certain amount of grievance at that remark.'

According to the learned judge, 'The defendant then moved to what he thought was stronger ground', thereby obviously referring to the defendant's determination to get rid of the plaintiff. The judge dealt with an allegation about a line of string having been left in the garden by the plaintiff, and commented: 'A more trivial complaint it would be difficult to imagine. It was an extremely trivial complaint, if indeed justified at all. I think it is clear from this and other evidence that Mr Racher sets very high standards and this seems to me to be an absurdly high standard of tidiness.' The learned judge continued: 'The defendant's second barrel is very odd and illustrates that the defendant was determined to get the plaintiff on something.' There was a dispute as to whether the string belonged to the plaintiff or to the defendant, and there was a complaint about leaving other things lying about. The judge accepted that the plaintiff moved away in an attempt to avoid any further altercation. But he was called back, and was then showered with questions. Mr Racher was pressing him and going on at him, and this was, indeed, confirmed to some extent by the evidence of the defendant himself. Finally, the plaintiff told the defendant, 'Get stuffed', and, 'Go and shit yourself'.

These last two expressions were used by the plaintiff immediately he was dismissed. He later apologised to Mrs Racher for using such language, as to which the learned judge said, 'One cannot condone them or commend them, but he said that when subjected to a number of petty criticisms and was not being allowed to go.' Despite the use of such language, the judge held that the plaintiff was entitled to say that he had been wrongly dismissed.

[His Lordship then examined and distinguished *Pepper* v *Webb* (extracted earlier) on the grounds it concerned a history of uncooperative behaviour on the part of the employee rather than one isolated outburst of bad temper. He continued:]

The present case, too, has to be looked at against the whole background. On the judge's findings, here was a competent, diligent and efficient gardener who, apart from one complaint of leaving a ladder against a yew tree, had done nothing which could be regarded as blameworthy by any reasonable employer, applying proper standards. Here, too, was an employer who was resolved to get rid of him; an employer who would use every barrel in the gun that he could find, or thought available; and an employer who was provocative from the outset and dealt with the plaintiff in an unseemly manner. The plaintiff lost his temper. He used obscene and deplorable language. He was therefore deserving of the severest reproof. But this was a solitary occasion. Unlike *Pepper* v *Webb*, there was no background either of inefficiency or of insolence. The plaintiff tried to avert the situation by walking away, but he was summoned back and the defendant continued his gadfly activity of goading him into intemperate language. Such are the findings of the county court judge.

In those circumstances, would it be just to say that the plaintiff's use of this extremely bad language on a solitary occasion made impossible the continuance of the master and servant relationship, and showed that the plaintiff was indeed resolved to follow a line of conduct which made the continuation of that relationship impossible? The learned judge thought the answer to that question was clear, and I cannot say that he was manifestly wrong. On the contrary, it seems to me that the parties could have made up their differences. The plaintiff apologised to Mrs Racher. There are no grounds for thinking that if the defendant had given him a warning that such language would not be tolerated, and further, if he had manifested recognition that he himself had acted provocatively, the damage done might well have been repaired and some degree of harmony restored. Perhaps there was such instinctive antipathy between the two men that the defendant would, nevertheless, have been glad to get rid of the plaintiff when 23.10.72 arrived.

In my judgment, in the light of the findings of fact the learned judge arrived at a just decision. That is not to say that language such as that employed by the plaintiff is to be tolerated. On the contrary, it requires very special circumstances to entitle a servant who expresses his feelings in such a grossly improper way to succeed in an action for wrongful dismissal. But there were special circumstances here, and they were of the defendant's own creation. The plaintiff, probably lacking the educational advantages of the defendant, and finding himself in a frustrating situation despite his efforts to escape from it, fell into the error of explosively using this language. To say that he ought to be kicked out because on this solitary occasion he fell into such grave error would, in my judgment, be wrong…

CAIRNS LJ: I agree that this appeal should be dismissed for the reasons which my Lord has given, and I only add, out of respect for the argument addressed to the Court by Mr Connell on behalf of the appellant, a few words about the other authority which he cited, namely, *Laws* v *London Chronicle (Indicator Newspapers) Ltd* ([1959] 1 WLR 698). That was a case where the plaintiff had been dismissed for disobedience. Lord Evershed, Master of the Rolls, in the course of a judgment with which the other members of the Court, Lords Justice Jenkins and Willmer, agreed, said at page 701: '… one act of disobedience or misconduct can justify dismissal only if it is of a nature which goes to show (in effect) that the servant is repudiating the contract, or one of its essential conditions; and for that reason, therefore, I think that you find in the passages I have read that the disobedience must at least have the quality that it is "wilful": it does (in other words) connote a deliberate flouting of the essential contractual conditions.'

There is certainly nothing more essential to the contractual relation between master and servant than the duty of obedience. Another duty on the part of the servant, particularly in the case of a man in such employment as this plaintiff had, a gardener in a domestic situation, is the duty of courtesy and respect towards the employer and his family. That is an important part of his obligations. But I would apply to that duty the same considerations as Lord Evershed applied in relation to the duty of obedience. In my view, this was not a case where it can be said with any justice to the plaintiff that the way in which he behaved, regrettable though it was, was such as to show 'deliberate flouting of the essential contractual conditions', having regard to the unjust accusation which had been made against him.

Denco Ltd v *Joinson*
[1991] IRLR 63, Employment Appeal Tribunal

The applicant was instantly dismissed for unauthorised access to computer information which the employer considered was done to assist the employee in his capacity as a union representative. The tribunal refused to accept that such conduct could justify dismissal without prior warning. The Employment Appeal Tribunal (EAT) allowed the employer's appeal.

WOOD J: The industrial members are clear in their view that in this modern industrial world if an employee deliberately uses an unauthorised password in order to enter or to attempt to enter a computer known to contain information to which he is not entitled, then that of itself is gross misconduct which prima facie will attract summary dismissal, although there may be some exceptional circumstances in which such a response might be held unreasonable. Basically, this is a question of 'absolutes' and can be compared with dishonesty. However, because of the importance of preserving the integrity of a computer with its information it is important that management should make it abundantly clear to its workforce that interfering with it will carry severe penalties.

Although it is not necessary to decide the practice in this case, cases may yet arise where evidence will show that the very tampering itself could produce malfunction with consequent damage and loss of information.

An analogy may be drawn with a situation where an employee enters the management offices of a company where he has no right to be, goes into an office, sees a key on the desk which he knows is the key to the filing cabinet which contains information to which he is not entitled and thereafter opens the filing cabinet and takes out a file.

If in the present case it had been material to consider whether there was evidence which in all the circumstances entitled management reasonably to have suspicion about the applicant's motive or purpose, then the present industrial members take the view that there was abundant such evidence. I agree with them.

When considering the issue of motive the Tribunal at one point say:

... Nor can we see on the menu anything to indicate that there was information which would have been the slightest use to Mr Joinson in his capacity as union negotiator.

With respect that does not seem to us to be the point. The issue is what did the applicant contemplate he might obtain by way of information by using the password of the wages department at Intek—a company by which he was not employed and the only connection with which would have been as a negotiator of pay.

(ii) Elective v automatic theories of termination
There has been a long-running judicial debate as to whether the breach automatically ends the contract, or whether it is only so effective once the innocent party elects to accept the breach. The view that 'an unaccepted repudiation is a thing writ in water and no value to anybody' (*per* Asquith LJ in *Howard* v *Pickford Tool Co. Ltd* [1951] 1 KB 417, at p. 421) has now been accepted by the House of Lords as applicable to contracts of employment just as it applies to the law of contract generally (see *Rigby* v *Ferodo Ltd* [1988] ICR 29, at p. 331 (later in this section)). If it were otherwise the guilty party could,

by his default, 'call the tune'. Note, however, the recent judicial support for the 'automatic theory' by Ralph Gibson LJ in *Boyo* v *London Borough of Lambeth* [1995] IRLR 50, considered below at p. 336 (later in this section).

Thomas Marshall (Exports) Ltd v Guinle and others

[1979] Ch 227, Chancery Division

In 1972, the defendant had been appointed to a ten-year fixed-term contract as managing director with the plaintiff company. There were various usual restrictions on competition and use of confidential information in his contract, effective both during and for five years after the end of the contract. During his employment, the defendant used, without his employer's knowledge, confidential information for the purposes of his own private companies and solicited the plaintiff's customers. The defendant resigned in 1977 with over four years of his contract to run. The plaintiff successfully sought injunctions against the defendant and his private companies, preventing solicitation of the plaintiff's customers and/or use of confidential information. Amongst other things, the defendant sought to argue that because he had broken the contract he was no longer bound by its terms.

MEGARRY V-C: I shall take first Mr Hutchison's submission that the defendant's service agreement was terminated by his unilateral repudiation of it on December 5, 1977, even though the company never accepted it as ending the agreement. This is a striking contention. It means that although the defendant and the company contractually bound themselves together for ten years from September 2, 1972, so that the agreement still has over 4½ years to run, the defendant, and also the company, was able at any time, without the consent of the other, to bring the contract to an end simply by saying so; and that is just what the defendant has done. Mr Hutchison accepted that the general rule was that a contract was not determined merely by the wrongful repudiation of it by one party, and that it was for the innocent party to decide whether to treat the contract as having determined or as continuing in existence. That rule, however, did not apply to contracts of employment, for they were subject to a special exception. Under the exception, any contract of employment could at any time be brought to an end by either party repudiating it. This exception, however, was itself subject to an exception, and that was where despite the repudiation the mutual confidence between the parties remained unimpaired. In that exceptional case the normal rule for contracts still applied, and the contract remained in being unless the innocent party elected to treat the repudiation as terminating it.

...

At least one thing is plain, and that is that the authorities on the point are in a far from satisfactory state. Let me say at the outset that I have great difficulty in accepting the view that contracts of employment are an exception to the general rule for repudiation, and that they are terminated forthwith by the repudiation, whether or not the innocent party elects to accept it as doing this. Indeed, Mr Hutchison was unable to contend that such a doctrine was right, and in order to make his proposition viable he had to narrow it to a substantial degree. Let me attempt to summarise the matter.

First, there will usually be a wide range of acts and omissions which will constitute a repudiation of a contract, whether for service or otherwise. In addition to an outright refusal to perform the contract, there are many other acts and omissions which can amount to a repudiation which will entitle the innocent party to treat the contract as being at an end. Such acts or omissions may consist either of a fundamental breach of the contract or the breach of a fundamental term of it: I adopt the distinction made by Lord Upjohn in *Suisse Atlantique Société d'Armement Maritime SA* v *NV Rotterdamsche Kolen Centrale* [1967] 1 AC 361, 421, 422. If cases of master and servant are an exception from the rule that an unaccepted repudiation works no determination of the contract, and instead are subject to what I have called the doctrine of automatic determination, the result would be that many a contract of employment would be determined forthwith upon the commission of a fundamental breach, or a breach of a fundamental term, even though the commission of this breach was unknown to the innocent party, and even if, had he known, he would have elected to keep the contract in being.

That would indeed be a remarkable result. I may take as an example a case that was not cited during argument, *Boston Deep Sea Fishing and Ice Co.* v *Ansell* (1888) 39 Ch D 339. That case, like this, concerned a managing director who was faithless to his company. He took a secret commission, but before he was discovered the company dismissed him: and this was before his five years' contract had run very long. It was held that when the company discovered his fraudulent conduct the company could sustain his dismissal on that ground. Bowen LJ pointed out, at p. 365, that the determination of the contract by the company could be looked at in two ways. One way was to regard it as the exercise by the company of its contractual right to dismiss a servant guilty of a breach of his implied condition to render faithful service. The other way was to treat the act as being a wrongful repudiation of the contract by the managing director which, being accepted by the company, determined the contract. This determination, it will be observed, occurs not on the date when the repudiatory act is done, but 'from the time the party who is sinned against elects to treat the wrongful act of the other as a breach of the contract.' It will be obvious how ill the views of Bowen LJ accord with the idea that 'the repudiation of a contract of employment… terminates the contract without the necessity for acceptance by the injured party.'

In order to avoid difficulties such as these, Mr Hutchison reformulated the doctrine of automatic determination. He said that in master and servant cases a breach of contract amounting to a repudiation did not forthwith determine the contract unless the party breaking the contract intended to bring the contract to an end. This, of course, is a very substantial narrowing of the doctrine as stated in the cases. It also emphasises the shift in intention. Whereas for contracts in general it is the innocent party who decides whether the contract continues or is at an end, for master and servant it is the guilty party who has the choice, or at least the initial choice; for presumably if the wrongdoer sought to keep the contract alive, the innocent party would then be able to elect nevertheless to treat it as having come to an end.

It is plain that some such narrowing and reformulation of the doctrine is necessary if absurd results are to be avoided. It is also plain that nothing in the cases which have been put before me point to such a reformulation. It also produces a result which seems to me to be far from just. Why should a person who makes a contract of service have the right at any moment to put an end to his contractual obligations? No doubt the court will not decree specific performance of the contract, nor will it grant an injunction which will have the effect of an order for specific performance: but why should the limitation of the range of remedies for the breach invade the substance of the contract? Why should it deprive the innocent party of any right to elect how to treat the breach, except, perhaps, in remainder and subject to the wrongdoer's prior right of election?

Second, it is difficult, if not impossible, to reconcile the doctrine of automatic determination with a number of authorities which, for the most part, do not appear to have been cited in any of the cases that I have mentioned. I need say no more about the *Boston* case, but I must refer to some others. Johanna Wagner contracted to sing for a period for Benjamin Lumley, and not to sing for anyone else. She then agreed to sing for someone else for a larger sum, but Lord St Leonards LC granted an injunction to restrain her from doing so: *Lumley* v *Wagner* (1852) 1 De GM & G 604. A company engaged a confidential clerk named Heuer for five years, the clerk agreeing to devote his whole time to the company's service and not during his engagement to engage as principal or servant in any business relating to goods of any description sold or made by the company. After some three years Heuer left and became employed by other manufacturers in the same line of business as the company. The Court of Appeal held that the company was entitled to an interlocutory injunction restraining Heuer from carrying on or being engaged in a business relating to goods of a description sold or made by the company: *William Robinson & Co. Ltd* v *Heuer* [1898] 2 Ch 451. Bette Davis, the film actress, entered into a contract with a film company for a period, agreeing to render her exclusive services as an actress to that company, and not during that period to render any services for any other stage or motion picture production or business. During the period of the contract the actress refused to be bound by it, and contracted with a third person to appear as a film artist. At the trial of the action Branson J granted an injunction which restrained the actress from rendering services in any motion picture or stage production for anyone save the film company: *Warner Brothers Pictures Incorporated* v *Nelson* [1937] 1 KB 209. Not surprisingly, Mr Hutchison was obliged to contend that the last two cases were both wrongly decided; and the same would seem to apply to the first of the three.

To these three cases I may add one where the injunction was refused: *Ehrman* v *Bartholomew* [1898] 1 Ch 671. That was a case of a traveller for a firm of wine merchants who was employed for 10 years under a contract to devote the whole of his time during usual business hours to the business of the firm, and not to employ himself in any other business or transact any business with or for any other person. Within a year the traveller had left the firm and had entered the service of other wine merchants. On motion, Romer J refused the firm an injunction which would restrain the traveller from engaging or employing himself in any other business. This was on the ground that the restriction was too wide, since it extended to all businesses and not merely to special services as in *Lumley* v *Wagner*, 1 De GM & G 604.

Apart from the citation of *Lumley* v *Wagner* in *Hill* v *C.A. Parsons & Co. Ltd* [1972] Ch 305 (see pp. 323, 324), none of these authorities seem to have been considered in any of the recent cases on automatic determination that I have mentioned. Yet if the doctrine of automatic determination is good law, all that Johanna Wagner, Heuer and Bette Davis had to do was to say that their contracts were at an end, and so they were free from the restrictions that they imposed while their employment continued. The claims to an injunction would thus have failed instead of succeeding. Sir William Jowitt KC and Mr J.D. Cassels KC, who appeared for Bette Davis, ought to have won instead of losing. Nor need the wine traveller have had to base his contentions on the width of the restrictions. I realise, of course, that in his dissenting judgment in *Hill* v *C.A. Parsons & Co. Ltd* at pp. 322, 323, 325, Stamp LJ referred to *Lumley* v *Wagner* as being 'a much criticised decision,' and spoke of the 'sure and safe guide' propounded by Lindley LJ in *Whitwood Chemical Co.* v *Hardman* [1891] 2 Ch 416, 426–428. At the same time I have to remember that at p. 427 Lindley LJ accepted *Lumley* v *Wagner* as having 'more or less definitely' laid down that where there was an express negative prohibition (which was lacking in the case before him) the court could enforce it by injunction. That, of course, was exactly what Sir Nathaniel Lindley—by then Master of the Rolls—did some seven years later in *William Robinson & Co. Ltd* v *Heuer* [1898] 2 Ch 451. As I have mentioned, Stamp LJ was considering a very different type of injunction; to restrain an employer from acting on a notice dismissing a servant is far removed from restraining the servant from acting in breach of his obligations to the employer.

There is one other case that I should refer to, although it was not mentioned in argument. That is *Howard* v *Pickford Tool Co. Ltd* [1951] 1 KB 417. This was cited in *Hill* v *C.A. Parsons & Co. Ltd* [1972] Ch 305 (though only in argument), but was not cited in any of the other automatic determination cases. There, a company contracted to employ the plaintiff as managing director for six years. Within six months the plaintiff, while continuing to act as managing director, brought proceedings against the company. In these, he claimed that the conduct of the chairman was such as to show that the company no longer intended to be bound by the contract; and he sought a declaration that the company had repudiated the contract, and that it no longer bound him. On the full doctrine of automatic determination, the chairman's conduct, if established, determined the contract. On the watered-down version, it determined the contract if the company intended it to do this. What happened in fact was that the Court of Appeal struck out the statement of claim. At p. 421 Sir Raymond Evershed MR said that as the plaintiff had not accepted the repudiation but had gone on performing his part of the contract, 'the alleged act of repudiation is wholly nugatory and ineffective in law.' On the same page Asquith LJ said that 'an unaccepted repudiation is a thing writ in water and of no value to anybody: it confers no legal rights of any sort or kind.' It seems to me to be quite impossible to add the gloss 'except in master and servant cases, where an unaccepted repudiation is etched in granite and is beautiful to the repudiator'; for the case was itself a master and servant case. Yet some gloss of this sort seems to be required if any doctrine of automatic determination is good law.

Quite apart from that case, there is the question whether I am required to treat the *Lumley* v *Wagner* line of authorities, which include a decision of the Court of Appeal, as having been overturned sub silentio in the automatic determination cases. I do not think that I can be. Those cases speak in a voice which is far from clear; and of the conflicting dicta, there seems to me to be great force in what was said in the *Decro-Wall* case, and by Sachs LJ in *Hill* v *C.A. Parsons & Co. Ltd*. I can see no ratio decidendi in any of the automatic determination cases which is necessarily inconsistent with the ratio decidendi in any of the *Lumley* v *Wagner* line of cases. Further, none of the automatic determination cases have had to deal with the question whether, by unilaterally refusing to serve, the servant can thereby release himself not merely from any further obligation to serve but also from any restrictions, whether imposed by his contract or implied by law, which apply only while the contract of service exists. Furthermore, I think the courts must beware of allowing a restriction of the range of remedies which it is proper to grant to destroy or unduly impair the rights of the parties.

Above all, I think the courts must be astute to prevent a wrongdoer from profiting too greatly from his wrong. If without just cause a servant who has contracted to serve for a term of years refuses to do so, it is easy to see that the court is powerless to make him do what he has contracted to do: neither by decreeing specific performance nor by granting an injunction can the court make the servant perform loyally what he is refusing to do, however wrongfully. If such an order were to be made, the ultimate sanction for disobedience is committal to prison; and this, far from forcing the servant to work for his master, would effectively stop him from doing this. But why should the court's inability to make a servant work for his employer mean that as soon as the servant refuses to do so the court is forthwith disabled from restraining him from committing any breach, however flagrant, of his other obligations during the period of his contract? I would wholly reject the doctrine of automatic determination, whether in its wide form or in its narrowed version.

I accept, of course, that there are difficulties in almost any view that one takes. To say that a contract of service remains in existence despite the servant's resolute refusal to do any work under it produces odd results. Here, however, I am concerned only with the issue whether the servant's wrongful refusal to serve has set him free of the obligations which bound him while his contract of service continued. Furthermore, since what is before me is a mere motion for an interlocutory injunction, strictly speaking all that I have to do before I turn to consider the balance of convenience is to see whether there is a serious question to be tried, and whether the company has any real prospect of succeeding at the trial: see *In re Lord Cable, decd.* [1977] 1 WLR 7, 19. To these questions I would answer with an unhesitating Yes. But, as I have mentioned, the interlocutory stage is so important to both parties that I have examined the authorities in some detail, and I think it right, for their assistance, to express my views more fully. I may summarise them as follows. First, in my judgment the service agreement between the parties has not been determined but remains still in force. Second, the defendant is subject to all the obligations that flow from his being bound by the service agreement. Third, as the service agreement is still in force, clause J2, which provides for the defendant to be free from restrictions when he ceases to be managing director, has not come into operation, and that is so whether or not the two provisos are satisfied. Fourth, there is ample jurisdiction in the court to grant an injunction to restrain the defendant from doing acts contrary to his obligations under the service agreement, subject always to the exercise of the court's discretion whether to grant an injunction at all, and, if so, in what width.

London Transport Executive v *Clarke*

[1981] ICR 355, Court of Appeal

LORD DENNING MR [dissenting]: [The facts] give rise to this question: when and by whom was this contract of employment 'terminated?' Was it terminated by the employee himself when he went off on February 28, 1979, without leave for a holiday in Jamaica? Or was it terminated by London Transport when they wrote the letter of March 26, 1979, taking his name off the books?

The common law

It is over 50 years ago now that I studied in depth the common law relating to the discharge of contract by breach or by incapacity or by repudiation. The result is to be found in *Smith's Leading Cases*, 13th ed. (1929), vol. II, pp. 46–56. I adhere to what I then said. All I would say is that nowadays some people seem to think that a contract is never discharged by a breach—no matter how fundamental—unless it is accepted by the other side. That is a great mistake. It is the result of the modern phraseology about 'repudiatory breach.' A repudiation by words only, saying that he will not perform a future obligation—an anticipatory breach—is, of course, a thing 'writ in water.' It is as nothing unless and until it is accepted. But a repudiatory breach is better described as a 'fundamental breach' or a 'breach going to the root of the contract.' Such a breach may well lead to the discharge of a contract without any need for acceptance. The classic instance is where a singer genuinely fell ill and could not attend the rehearsals. Her incapacity discharged the theatre from further performance, without any talk of acceptance. It would be just the same if she had not really been ill but had pretended to be ill and thus been guilty of a breach going to the root of the contract. Again the contract would be discharged without any talk of acceptance. That is clear from the illuminating judgment of Blackburn J in *Poussard* v *Spiers & Pond* [1876] 1 QBD 410, 414–415, which I have often quoted.

If we put anticipatory breach on one side, these actual breaches can be divided at common law into three categories. I will illustrate the position from some modern cases. First, in *Laws* v *London Chronicle (Indicator Newspapers) Ltd* [1959] 1 WLR 698, the managing director at a business meeting said to the lady representative: 'You stay where you are.' She did not do so but walked out of the room. Till then she had been a good employee. She was dismissed. Her conduct was a breach of her contract of employment, but it did not go to the root of the contract such as to justify her dismissal. The company were liable in damages for wrongful dismissal. Second, in *Pepper* v *Webb* [1969] 1 WLR 514, the lady of the house asked the head gardener to put some plants in the greenhouse. He said he was not going to do it. The master of the house went out and said to him: 'The job will only take half-an-hour. Why make all this fuss about it?' The head gardener said: 'I couldn't care less about your bloody greenhouse and your sodding garden.' It was a breach going to the root of the contract. It gave the master an option whether to dismiss him or not. He elected to dismiss him. It was justifiable. The master was not liable for wrongful dismissal. Third, but if the head gardener had just walked off and got another job, it would be a breach which discharged the contract of employment without any need for acceptance. If the head gardener had disliked his new job and came back after a fortnight, the master would have been entitled to say: 'You gave up your job here. I cannot have you back now.'

The statute

Under our modern legislation a new question arises. It arises under [ERA 1996, s. 94], re-enacting earlier sections going back to 1971. When an employee is dismissed for misconduct, we have to ask—and to answer—the question: who 'terminates' the contract? If the employer terminates it, it is taken to be unfair unless the employer proves that it was fair. But, if the employee terminates it by his own misconduct, he gets nothing.

Much difference of opinion has been evoked amongst the judges on that question under the Act. So much so that I feel it is desirable for this court to afford some guidance. I think it is best done by applying the common law principles which I have just stated. The cases fall into two groups.

The employee terminates it

The first group is when the misconduct of the employee is such that it is completely inconsistent with the continuance of the contract of employment. So much so that the ordinary member of the tribunal would say of him: 'He sacked himself.' In these cases it is the employee himself who terminates the contract. His misconduct itself is such as to evince an intention himself to bring the contract to an end. Such as when an employee leaves and gets another job, or when he absconds with money from the till, or goes off indefinitely without a word to his employer. If he comes back and asks for his job back, the employer can properly reply: 'I cannot have you back now.' There is no election in that case. The man dismisses himself. In the words of Shaw LJ in *Gunton v Richmond-upon-Thames London Borough Council* [1980] ICR 755, 763, there is a 'complete and intended withdrawal of his service by the employee.'

The employer terminates it

The second group is where the misconduct of the employee is bad enough to justify the employer at common law in dismissing him, but leaves it open to the employer whether to dismiss him for it or not. His misconduct is such as to show that he is not going to fulfil his duties as he ought to do: but nevertheless it is not such as to be entirely disruptive of the contract. He does not sack himself, but he is guilty of a breach which entitles the employer at common law to dismiss him. If the employer does elect to dismiss him, it is the employer who terminates the contract...

TEMPLEMAN LJ: I can see no reason why a contract of employment or services should be determined by repudiation and not by the acceptance of repudiation. The argument has little practical importance at common law. The only difference which would exist at common law between self-dismissal and accepted repudiation is that self-dismissal would determine the contract when the worker walked out or otherwise committed a repudiatory breach of the contract whereas accepted repudiation determines the contract when the employer expressly or impliedly gives notice to the worker that the employer accepts the repudiation and does not wish to affirm the contract. But, in practice, at common law self-dismissal and acceptance of repudiation in contracts of service are usually simultaneous both being implied rather than express where affirmation of the contract would be meaningless; in any event, they involve similar consequences in almost all cases. A difficulty, however, arises under the Act of 1978 if Mr Scrivener's argument of a special category of determination of a contract by self-dismissal is correct. When a worker commits a breach of contract, neither he nor the employer nor in the final analysis the industrial tribunal may be entirely clear whether the breach is repudiatory or not. Whatever the nature of the breach, the worker may seek expressly or impliedly to persuade the employer to affirm the contract and to allow the worker to continue in or resume his employment. If the employer does not allow the worker to continue or resume his employment, then if Mr Scrivener is right an industrial tribunal must first decide whether the worker's breach of contract is repudiatory or not. If the breach of contract is so fundamental as to be repudiatory of the contract, then the tribunal must decide whether the repudiatory act is of a special kind which amounts to self-dismissal. If these matters are decided in favour of the employer, then the tribunal is not authorised to consider whether in the circumstances the refusal of the employer to affirm the contract and to allow the worker to continue or resume employment is fair or unfair unless, despite the finding of self-dismissal, the worker is able to establish conduct on the part of the employer which converts self-dismissal into constructive dismissal. If the tribunal decide that the breach of contract by the worker was not repudiatory or if the tribunal decide that the repudiatory breach was not of the special kind which amounts to self-dismissal, then they must conclude that the contract was terminated by the employer and they must then consider whether the employer satisfies the onus of proving that the termination of the contract which amounts to dismissal was in fact fair dismissal.

These complications arise, and only arise, if there is grafted on to the old common law rule that a repudiated contract is only terminated by acceptance, an exception in the case of contracts of employment. In my view any such exception is contrary to principle, unsupported by authority binding on this court and undesirable in practice. If a worker walks out of his job and does not thereafter claim to be entitled to resume work, then he repudiates his contract and the employer accepts that repudiation by taking no action to affirm the contract. No question of unfair dismissal can arise unless the worker claims that he was constructively dismissed. If a worker walks out of his job or commits any other breach of contract, repudiatory or otherwise, but at any time claims that he is entitled to resume or to continue his work, then his contract of employment is only determined if the employer expressly or impliedly asserts and accepts repudiation on the part of the worker. Acceptance can take the form of formal writing or can take the form of refusing to allow the worker to resume or continue his work. Where the contract of employment is determined by the employer purporting to accept repudiation on the part of the worker, the tribunal must decide whether the worker has been unfairly dismissed.

In my judgment, the acceptance by an employer of repudiation by a worker who wishes to continue his employment notwithstanding his repudiatory conduct constitutes the determination of the contract of employment by the employer; the employer relying on the repudiatory conduct of the worker must satisfy the tribunal in the words of section 57(3) [now ERA 1996, s. 98(4)] that in the circumstances, having regard to equity and the substantial merits of the case, the employer acted reasonably in treating the repudiatory conduct as sufficient reason for accepting repudiation and thus determining the contract.

Rigby v Ferodo Ltd
[1988] ICR 29, House of Lords

The employee, a lathe operator with a 12-week notice entitlement, had a 5 per cent wage reduction imposed by his employers who were in financial difficulties. The trade union was approached but no decision was taken as to whether to accept the reduction; the only vote was against industrial action if the reduction was imposed. The pay cut was imposed on 18 September 1982. The employee continued to work and, in 1984, successfully sued for the return of the money he had lost since the imposition of the pay cut. The House of Lords upheld his claim. The employer had been guilty of a fundamental breach in reducing the wage and, since that breach had not been accepted by the employee, he was entitled to recover a sum representing his lost wages.

LORD OLIVER: The principal argument advanced on the appellant's behalf was to the following effect. It was not contended and could not, in the light of the trial judge's findings of fact, be contended that the appellant's repudiation of its contractual obligation to pay the agreed wages in full was ever expressly accepted by Mr Rigby. Equally it is accepted that, as a general rule, an unaccepted repudiation leaves the contractual obligations of the parties unaffected. It is, however, argued that contracts of employment form a special category of their own, constituting an exception to the general rule. The wrongful repudiation of the fundamental obligations of either party under such a contract, it is said, not only brings to an end the relationship of employer and employee (which, as a practical matter, cannot continue in the face of a refusal to perform or accept the services which the employee has agreed to perform) but also, of itself and by itself, terminates the contract of service forthwith without the necessity of any acceptance, express or implied, by the party not in default. Thus, it is argued, when the appellant's management implemented the reduction of Mr Rigby's wages without his agreement and against his will, his contract of employment with the appellant was terminated—wrongfully terminated, no doubt, but terminated—and could no longer be claimed by him to be subsisting. His sole remedy, therefore, was to sue for damages and the only damage suffered was the amount of the shortfall from the original contractual wage over the period of 12 weeks on the expiration of which the contract could have been lawfully terminated.

Mr Wingate-Saul QC, on behalf of the appellant, accepts that this argument is inconsistent with the number of reported decisions of the Court of Appeal—in particular *Gunton* v *Richmond-upon-Thames London Borough Council* [1980] ICR 755; *London Transport Executive* v *Clarke* [1981] ICR 355 and *Norwest Holst Group Administration Ltd* v *Harrison* [1985] ICR 668—but submits that those cases, in so far as they rested upon the proposition that an acceptance of a wrongful repudiation of a contract of employment is necessary to bring the contract to an end, were wrongly decided and that your Lordships should prefer the dissenting views of Shaw LJ in *Gunton's* case [1980] ICR 755 and of Lord Denning MR in *London Transport Executive* v *Clarke* [1981] ICR 355. In his dissenting judgment in *Gunton's* case, Shaw LJ expressed the view that the practical basis for according an election to the injured party has no reality in relation to a contract of service where the repudiation takes the form of an express and direct termination of the contract in contravention of its terms. The contrary (and majority) view is that, whilst from a practical point of view a wrongful dismissal puts an end to the status of the dismissed employee as an employee and confines him to a remedy in damages for breach of contract (so that there will normally be little difficulty in inferring an acceptance of the repudiation), there is no reason in principle why, if the employee clearly indicates that he does not accept the employer's breach as a termination of the contract, it should not remain on foot and enforceable so far as concerns obligations which do not of necessity depend on the existence of the relationship of master and servant. My Lords, there is much to be said for both views and the majority opinion in *Gunton's* case [1980] ICR 755 has not been without its critics. But although it seems that one reason at least why the Court of Appeal here thought it right to grant leave to appeal to your Lordships' House was to afford an opportunity for a consideration of the correctness or otherwise of that majority opinion, the instant case is not on any analysis one of wrongful dismissal but is concerned with a very different state of facts, including the actual and intended continuation of the relationship of employer and employee without interruption. Having regard to the fact that your Lordships have not found it necessary to call upon counsel for the respondent, it would not, in my view, be appropriate that your Lordships should decide a not unimportant point of law which, on the facts before your Lordships, is of academic interest only.

Whatever may be the position under a contract of service where the repudiation takes the form either of a walk-out by the employee or of a refusal by the employer any longer to regard the employee as his servant, I know of no principle of law that any breach which the innocent party is entitled to treat as repudiatory of the other party's obligations brings the contract to an end automatically. No authority has been cited for so broad a proposition and indeed Mr Wingate-Saul has not contended for it. What he has submitted is that where there is a combination of three factors, that is to say, (a) a breach of contract going to an essential term, (b) a desire in the party in breach either not to continue the contract or to continue it in a different form and (c) no practical option in the other party but to accept the breach, then the contract is automatically brought to an end. My Lords, for my part, I have found myself unable either to accept this formulation as a matter of law or to see why it should be so. I entirely fail to see how the continuance of the primary contractual obligation can be made to depend upon the subjective desire of the contract-breaker and I do not understand what is meant by the injured party having no alternative but to accept the breach. If this means that, if the contract-breaker persists, the injured party may have to put up with the fact that he will not be able to enforce the primary obligation of performance, that is, of course, true of every contract which is not susceptible of a decree of specific performance. If it means that he has no alternative to accepting the breach as a repudiation and thus terminating the contract, it begs the question. For my part, I can see no reason in law or logic why, leaving aside for the moment the extreme case of outright dismissal or walk-out, a contract of employment should be on any different footing from any other contract as regards the principle that 'an unaccepted repudiation is a thing writ in water and of no value to anybody': *per* Asquith LJ in *Howard* v *Pickford Tool Co. Ltd* [1951] 1 KB 417, 421.

NOTES

1. In *MacRuary* v *Washington Irvine Ltd*, IDS Brief 518, June 1994 (noted by Miller, K., 'Unilateral variation of terms: Rights and remedies' (1995) ILJ 162), the employer sought to withdraw a guaranteed entitlement to two hours' overtime per week. MacRuary continued working under protest at the change and claimed, successfully, that the change was an unlawful deduction of wages within the meaning of s. 7 of the Wages Act 1986 (now the ERA 1996, s. 27). Miller argues that cases like *Rigby* v *Ferodo* can be dealt with, as an alternative course of action, under the protection of wages provisions now contained in the ERA 1996, Pt II.

2. What action is necessary to amount to an acceptance of a repudiatory breach of contract? In *Gunton* v *London Borough of Richmond-upon-Thames* [1980] ICR 755, the Court of Appeal not only approved the elective theory of termination but also held (*per* Buckley LJ) that acceptance of a repudiatory breach will be 'readily inferred'. However, to infer acceptance 'readily' is to blur the distinction between the elective and automatic theories of termination. Both aspects of *Gunton* were doubted by all three members of the Court of Appeal in the decision of *Boyo* v *London Borough of Lambeth*.

Boyo v *London Borough of Lambeth*

[1995] IRLR 50, Court of Appeal

Boyo was employed by Lambeth as an accountant. His contract entitled him to four weeks' notice of termination unless he was guilty of gross misconduct, in which case he could be dismissed summarily. He was accused of offences of fraud (of which he was ultimately acquitted) and in August 1991 he was suspended on full pay. His bail conditions prevented him having any contact with his employers, and on 28 October he was charged with the separate offence of conspiracy to pervert the course of justice. On 29 October, Lambeth purported to terminate his contract of employment on the ground that it had been frustrated. Boyo rejected that termination and turned up for work on 3 November but was barred. He continued to insist that he was available for work. He issued unfair dismissal proceedings in late November 1991 and county court proceedings for wrongful dismissal in May 1992 after his acquittal of all criminal charges. At the county court hearing in December 1992, the employers conceded that the contract had not been frustrated; neither had Boyo been guilty of gross misconduct to warrant summary dismissal. The issue for the court, therefore, was when the contract ended so as to be able to calculate the amount of damages. The county court judge held:

(a) The letter of 29 October 1991 was an effective termination of the contract of employment.

(b) Boyo's refusal to accept such termination was 'contrary to reality' (i.e. supporting the automatic theory of termination).

(c) In any event, Boyo could not obtain salary for periods during which he did not work.

(d) He was entitled to damages covering one month's loss of notice plus five months, being the period he assessed for the employer to carry out proper disciplinary procedures.

Both parties appealed. The Court of Appeal held:

(a) But for *Gunton* it would have held that an unaccepted wrongful dismissal did bring the contract to an end.

(b) It could not accept that acceptance of repudiation should readily be inferred.

(c) It would not interfere with the damages awarded by the county court judge.

RALPH GIBSON LJ: There has long been an unresolved controversy, as is pointed out in vol. 16 of the fourth edition of *Halsbury's Laws*, 1992, at paragraph 303, as to whether (i) the contract of employment is an exception to normal contract law so that an employee wrongfully dismissed by his employer must accept that repudiation because, according to the 'unilateral' theory, the employee's only remedy in law becomes one of damages, and a repudiation of a contract of employment automatically terminates it; or (ii) contracts of employment are not formally exceptions to the normal rule that a repudiation of a contract is not effective unless and until the innocent party accepts that repudiation: see the cases there cited. The arguments and authorities have been considered in various cases including *Gunton* and *Dietman* v *London Borough of Brent* [1988] IRLR 299.

The matter was argued in *Rigby* v *Ferodo Ltd* [1987] IRLR 516, but it was held by the House of Lords that it was not, for the decision of that appeal, necessary to decide the question. Lord Oliver at paragraph 11 said:

> In his dissenting judgment in *Gunton*'s case, Shaw LJ expressed the view that the practical basis for according an election to the injured party has no reality in relation to a contract of service where the repudiation takes the form of an express and direct termination of the contract in contravention of its terms. The contrary (and majority) view is that, whilst from a practical point of view a wrongful dismissal puts an end to the status of the dismissed employee as an employee and confines him to a remedy in damages for breach of contract (so that there will normally be little difficulty in inferring an acceptance of the repudiation), there is no reason in principle why, if the employee clearly indicates that he does not accept the employer's breach as a termination of the contract, it should not remain on foot and enforceable so far as concerns obligations which do not of necessity depend on the existence of the relationship of master and servant... there is much to be said for both views...

The decision of this Court in *Gunton*'s case, however, was binding upon Judge James and is binding upon this Court in respect of matters of decision there set out. The facts of this case, as it seems to me, raise the question as to which of the two theories is correct...

It is next, therefore, necessary to determine what was decided by this court in *Gunton*'s case. The facts were that Mr Gunton was employed as a college registrar under a contract terminable by one month's notice. Regulations which prescribed a procedure for the dismissal of employees on disciplinary grounds formed part of his contract. On 14 January 1976 the defendant gave notice to terminate Mr Gunton's contract on 14 February and he was told he was not required to attend work. The reason for the dismissal was disciplinary but the procedure had not been fully followed. Mr Gunton brought in 1976 an action for a declaration that the purported termination of his contract was void and that he remained registrar. The judge at the trial in October 1978 declared that the notice was ineffective lawfully to determine the contract of employment and on Mr Gunton at trial electing to claim damages at common law, ordered an enquiry as to damages on the basis that Mr Gunton was entitled to remain in his employment until retirement, unless in the meantime liable to redundancy or dismissal under the procedure, and subject to the obligation of the plaintiff to mitigate his loss.

As I understand the effect of that order, Mr Gunton would have been entitled to recover either his salary, since he was willing to perform his obligations, or damages in the amount of his salary, subject to reduction for failure to mitigate if any, from the date of the notice on 14 January 1976, giving credit for any payment, down to the date of assessment of damages and, thereafter, such sum as represented his probable earnings, having regard to the assessed risks of redundancy, discharge on disciplinary grounds and, pursuant to the duty to mitigate, the amount of probable future earnings. That, in substance, is what the plaintiff claims in this action should have been awarded by the judge.

In *Gunton*'s case Shaw LJ held that Mr Gunton could not remain idle and demand his salary, because he had not earned it. If he claimed damages he must, by implication treat his contract as at an end because the court would not reinstate him by an order for specific performance. Mr Gunton had, since his dismissal, had other employments for short terms. That would constitute acceptance of the repudiation but that was not necessary: the wrongful dismissal in January 1976 brought the contract to a summary end. It did not matter for calculation of damages because, if the contract was brought to an end, as Shaw LJ held that it was, and if Mr Gunton suffered damage as a result of the disciplinary procedure not being followed, he would be entitled to recover that damage. He therefore concurred with the order proposed by Buckley LJ.

Buckley LJ approached the issue of damages as follows. The council's dismissal of Mr Gunton was wrongful but it was nevertheless a dismissal and de facto it brought his employment to an end. Having considered the previous decisions on the effect of a wrongful repudiation upon a contract of employment, Buckley LJ (p. 771) held that the doctrine of the need for acceptance of a repudiating act operated in the case of a contract for personal services as in the generality of contracts. Cases of wrongful dismissal, however, in breach of a contract of personal services have certain special features: they include the fact that a servant cannot sue in debt under the contract of remuneration in respect of any period after the wrongful dismissal because the right to receive remuneration and the obligation to render services are mutually interdependent. A wrongfully dismissed servant had, in the absence of special circumstances, no option but to accept the master's repudiation of the contract. Therefore, in the absence of special circumstances, the court should easily infer that the innocent party has accepted the guilty party's repudiation of the contract. Mr Gunton accepted repudiation at the trial if not earlier.

Lord Justice Buckley dealt with the damages in *Gunton*'s case as follows:

(a) If the master, who is entitled to dismiss on not less than three months' notice, purports to dismiss summarily, the dismissal is a nullity and the servant can recover as damages for breach of contract three months' remuneration and no more, subject to mitigation: i.e. for the three months following dismissal.

(b) But if the master were to dismiss the servant summarily and the servant did not accept the master's repudiation of the contract until the end of 10 weeks from the exclusion of the servant from his employment, then, if acceptance of repudiation is required in master and servant cases, the master is guilty of a breach of contract continuing from day to day for refusing to offer employment from the date of exclusion down to the date of acceptance and thereafter on the basis of wrongful repudiation.

(c) The servant could not claim damages under the second head in relation to a period of three months from the date of acceptance, as well as damages under the first head in relation to the 10-week period, because his cause of action would have arisen when wrongfully excluded from his employment. Subsequent acceptance of the repudiation would not create a new cause of action although it might affect the remedy. The question must be for how long the servant could have insisted at the date of commencement of the cause of action upon being continued in his employment.

(d) Therefore, Mr Gunton was entitled at 14 January 1976 when he was excluded from his employment, to insist upon a right not to be dismissed on disciplinary grounds until the disciplinary procedures were recommenced and carried out in due order but with reasonable expedition. He was thus entitled at 14 January to damages assessed upon the basis of a reasonable period from 14 January 1976 plus one month.

For my part, I have difficulty in accepting in full the validity of this reasoning. In *Sanders* v *Ernest Neale Ltd* [1974] IRLR 236, in one of the cases cited by Lord Justice Buckley in *Gunton*, Sir John Donaldson, president of the NIRC, referred to the reasoning of Sachs LJ and of Salmon LJ in the *Decro-Wall* case [1971] 1 WLR 361. He continued:

In essence it proceeds by the following stages.

(i) A servant cannot sue for wages if he has not rendered services, and the wrongful dismissal prevents him from rendering services.

(ii) This leaves him with a claim for damages as his only remedy.

(iii) Any claim for damages is subject to a duty to mitigate the loss and the only way to perform this duty is to accept the repudiation as terminating the contract of employment and seek other employment.

If there is any fault in this line of reasoning, it lies in point (i). Why should not the servant sue for wages if it is the act of the employer which has prevented his performing the condition precedent of rendering services? And if he can sue in debt for his wages, no duty to mitigate would arise and there would be no practical necessity to accept a wrongful dismissal as terminating the contract of employment, provided that the employer is solvent and the servant is sure that the dismissal was wrongful.

Further, if there is a requirement of law for acceptance by the servant of the repudiation by the master, I am unable to see why it is not a requirement for a real acceptance, that is to say a conscious acceptance intending to bring the contract to an end or the doing of some act which is inconsistent with continuation of the contract. If that is right, I do not understand how the courts would apply the notion of 'easily inferring that the innocent party has accepted... the repudiation'. Further, I do not understand why the taking of employment should automatically constitute acceptance. If I tell my employer, who has in breach of contract refused to let me do my work, that I do not accept his repudiation—and that I shall get another job but remain willing and able to do my work when sent for by him—why should I be treated as having accepted what I have not accepted? And should it make any difference that I know enough of the law to give such a notice to my repudiating employer?

To the majority of the court in *Gunton*'s case, however, it was clear that it would be contrary to the basic concepts of the law of contract, in the absence of special circumstances in which the court may prevent an employer from implementing a decision to dismiss, to require an employer who has de facto dismissed a servant in breach of contract, to pay damages on the basis that the employer's obligation to the servant continues after the end of that period of time by which under the terms of the contract the employer could lawfully have brought it to an end as from the date of the dismissal. That was also the opinion of Shaw LJ who agreed with that of Sir John Donaldson expressed in the case of *Sanders* v *Neale*. I agree with it also.

I also accept that principle must permit the continued existence, after a wrongful dismissal which brings the de facto relationship of master and servant to an end, of obligations contained in the contract which, in Lord Oliver's words in *Ferodo*, 'do not of necessity depend on the existence of the relationship of master and servant', such as the provision for disciplinary proceedings when held to be relevant to the assessment of damages, or to a term restricting the actions of the servant after termination of the contract such as was considered by Sir Robert Megarry VC in *Thomas Marshall (Exports) Ltd* v *Guinle* [1978] IRLR 174.

Subject to that qualification, if it were open to this Court to depart from the conclusion of the majority in *Gunton*, I would prefer the view expressed by Sir John Donaldson in *Sanders*'s case. It seems to me, however, that this Court is not free to depart from that decision with reference to any matter which was in that case a ground of decision. The grounds of decision include the reasoning stated by Buckley LJ which, as set out above, limited recovery by Mr Gunton to the reasonable time for disciplinary procedures plus one month from the date of wrongful exclusion.

[Staunton and Purchas LLJ gave concurring judgments.]

NOTE: The long-standing conflict between the 'automatic' and 'elective' theories of termination of employment contract has now been resolved by the Supreme Court in *Société Générale, London Branch* v *Geys* [2013] IRLR 122.

Société Générale (London Branch) v Geys

[2013] IRLR 122, Supreme Court

Mr Geys was employed by Société Générale as the Managing Director of its European Fixed Income Sales, Financial Institutions division. Société Générale purported to dismiss Mr Geys without cause but with immediate effect on 29 November 2007. They were not entitled to do this as Mr Geys' contract contained a three-month notice provision. Accordingly, the purported termination was a repudiatory breach of contract. On 18 December 2007, Société Générale sought to exercise a PILON (payment in lieu of notice) clause in its Staff Handbook by paying Mr Geys' notice pay into his bank account. However, they failed to inform Mr Geys that they had done this until they wrote to him on 4 January 2008.

The key question before the Court was when Mr Geys' contract terminated: 29 November 2007, 18 December 2007, or 6 January 2008 (the deemed date of receipt of Société Générale's letter of 4 January).

Société Générale's argument in favour of 29 November 2007 was that, in the case of a wrongful summary termination of an employment contract, it is not open to the employee to elect whether to accept the employer's breach (and bring the contract to an end) or to affirm the contract and keep it in existence: the contract comes to an end at the date of the wrongful termination. Their alternative argument, in favour of 18 December 2007, was that the payment of the notice pay into the employee's bank account is sufficient to exercise the PILON clause: there is no need to also notify the employee that the clause has been exercised. The significance for Société Générale of establishing a 2007 termination date, rather than 2008, was that it would save them almost €2 million because of the way in which the termination payment due to Mr Geys under his contract was calculated.

The Court rejected both of Société Générale's arguments and found that Mr Geys' contract terminated on 6 January 2008. They clarified and reaffirmed the existing law that in the case of a repudiatory breach of an employment contract, the contract continues in existence unless and until the innocent party elects to accept the breach. The Court pointed out that if an employer's repudiatory breach were to terminate the contract, it would make it much easier for the employer to orchestrate the termination of the employment for a time beneficial to it, for example shortly before the employee was due to receive a bonus or salary rise.

In relation to the exercise of the PILON clause, the Court held that for this to be effective the employee must be given clear and unambiguous notice that the clause has been exercised and informed of the date when the payment has been or is to be made. If the notice is given before the payment is made, the contract will terminate on the date of the payment. If it is given after the payment (as in Mr Geys' case), the contract terminates on the date of the notice. The notice need not be in writing (subject to any contrary provision in the contract) but it is clearly advisable that it should be. In reaching its conclusion on this issue, the Court highlighted the unfairness of a situation where employees would have to regularly check their bank accounts to see if they had been dismissed. The Court also drew attention to the potentially serious consequences of an employee's life and health insurance coming to an end on termination of his contract but without his being aware of this because he had not been notified that a PILON payment had been made.

LORD WILSON: In the light of the fact that a central incident of the automatic theory is that, upon automatic termination of the contract, the innocent party has a right to damages, the first question must be whether it matters that the contract is terminated forthwith upon repudiation or, instead, survives until some further, terminating, event? The answer is that sometimes it does matter. It depends on the terms of the contract. The date of termination fixes the end of some contractual obligations and, sometimes, the beginning of others. An increase in salary may depend on the survival of the contract until a particular date. The amount of a pension may be calculated by reference to the final salary paid throughout a completed year of service or to an aggregate of salaries, including the final completed year. An entitlement to holiday pay may similarly depend on the contract's survival to a particular date.

...

In proposing that the court should endorse the automatic theory, the Bank invites it to cause the law of England and Wales in relation to the contract of employment to set sail, unaccompanied, upon a journey for which I can discern no just purpose and can identify no final destination. I consider, on the contrary, that we should keep the contract of employment firmly within the harbour which the common law has solidly constructed for the entire fleet of contracts in order to protect the innocent party, as far as practicable, from the consequences of the other's breach.

NOTE: As Blackham observes, 'there is no indication that the decision in [*Geys*] will make it easier [for an employee who has refused to accept an employer's repudiation] to obtain an equitable remedy (such as an injunction) to keep a repudiated employment contract on foot' (Blackham, A., 'Uncertain junctures between employment and contract law'(2013) 72 *Cambridge Law Journal* 269. The judicial reluctance to grant specific performance of employment contracts is deep rooted.

In addition, the Supreme Court's decision raises issues concerned with the statutory right to claim unfair dismissal. As Rubenstein observes:

> *Geys* is a common law case, however, and none of the opinions in the Supreme Court considers the impact of the decision on statutory rights. Can an employee refuse to accept a repudiatory breach and thereby extend their service in order to reach the unfair dismissal qualifying period? This will have to be tested in the courts. The effective date of termination is a statutory construct dependent, where no notice was given, on 'the date when the contract of employment was terminated by the employer.' It is arguable that a contract can be 'terminated' by the employer on a particular date, even if that termination is not effective at common law because it requires the employee to bring the contract to an end by accepting the repudiatory breach. If *Geys* applies, the statutory language on the effective date where dismissal is without notice would apply only where summary dismissal is justified and therefore not in breach of contract (Rubenstein, M., 'Highlights' IRLR February 2013).

■ QUESTION

What choices does an employee have when faced with a repudiatory breach by his or her employer? See generally McColgan, A., 'Remedies for breach of employment contracts' (1992) ILJ 58; Ewing, K., 'Remedies for breach of the contract of employment' (1993) 52 *Cambridge Law Journal* 405.

(iii) An employee who accepts a breach of contract by his employer can nevertheless include that breach as part of conduct justifying later resignation

Lewis v Motorworld

[1986] ICR 157, Court of Appeal

In December 1981, the employer, in breach of the employment contract, demoted the applicant and reduced his pay. The employee accepted the breach and affirmed the contract but over the following eight months his employer persistently criticised him until finally, in August 1982, the applicant resigned and complained of unfair dismissal, relying on both the demotion and the constant criticism. The tribunal dismissed the claim holding that the applicant could not rely upon the demotion to justify his resignation because that breach had been accepted, and that the criticism thereafter was not so fundamental a breach as to entitle the applicant to claim that he had been constructively dismissed. The Court of Appeal allowed the employee's appeal, holding that a breach that had been affirmed by an employee could nevertheless form part of a course of conduct justifying resignation.

GLIDEWELL LJ: The principles to be found in the relevant authorities can, I believe, be summarised as follows.

(1) In order to prove that he has suffered constructive dismissal, an employee who leaves his employment must prove that he did so as the result of a breach of contract by his employer, which shows that the employer no longer intends to be bound by an essential term of the contract: see *Western Excavating (ECC) Ltd v Sharp* [1978] ICR 221.

(2) However, there are normally implied in a contract of employment mutual rights and obligations of trust and confidence. A breach of this implied term may justify the employee in leaving and claiming he has been constructively dismissed: see *Post Office v Roberts* [1980] IRLR 347 and *Woods v W.M. Car Services (Peterborough) Ltd* [1981] ICR 666, 670, *per* Browne-Wilkinson J.

(3) The breach of this implied obligation of trust and confidence may consist of a series of actions on the part of the employer which cumulatively amount to a breach of the term, though each individual incident may not do so. In particular in such a case the last action of the employer which leads to the employee leaving need not itself be a breach of contract; the question is, does the cumulative series of acts taken together amount to a breach of the implied term? (See *Woods v W.M. Car Services (Peterborough) Ltd* [1981] ICR 666.) This is the 'last straw' situation.

(4) The decision whether there has been a breach of contract by the employer so as to constitute constructive dismissal of the employee is one of mixed law and fact for the industrial tribunal. An appellate court, whether the Employment Appeal Tribunal or the Court of Appeal, may only overrule that decision if the industrial tribunal have misdirected themselves as to the relevant law or have made a finding of fact for which there is no supporting evidence or which no reasonable tribunal could make: see *Pedersen v Camden London Borough Council (Note)* [1981] ICR 674 and *Woods v W.M. Car Services (Peterborough) Ltd* [1982] ICR 693 both in the Court of Appeal, applying the test laid down in *Edwards v Bairstow* [1956] AC 14.

This case raises another issue of principle which, so far as I can ascertain, has not yet been considered by this court. If the employer is in breach of an express term of a contract of employment, of such seriousness that the employee would be justified in leaving and claiming constructive dismissal, but the employee does not leave and accepts the altered terms of employment; and if subsequently a series of actions by the employer might constitute together a breach of the implied obligation of trust and confidence; is the employee then entitled to treat the original action by the employer which was a breach of the express terms of the contract as a part—the start—of the series of actions which, taken together with the employer's other actions, might cumulatively amount to a breach of the implied terms? In my judgment the answer to this question is clearly 'yes.'...

NOTE: For a detailed discussion of this area, see Ewing, K. D., 'Remedies for breach of the contract of employment' (1993) 52 *Cambridge Law Journal* 405.

SECTION 2: TERMINATIONS WHICH MAY NOT AMOUNT TO DISMISSAL

A: Frustration

Morgan v *Manser*
[1947] 2 All ER 666, King's Bench Division

STREATFEILD J: If there is an event or change of circumstances which is so fundamental as to be regarded by the law as striking at the root of the contract as a whole, and as going beyond what was contemplated by the parties and such that to hold the parties to the contract would be to bind them to terms which they would not have made had they contemplated that event or those circumstances, then the contract is frustrated by that event immediately and irrespective of the volition or the intention of the parties, or their knowledge as to that particular event, and this even though they have continued for a time to treat the contract as still subsisting.

NOTE: Frustration automatically terminates a contract without the need for affirmation or acceptance by the innocent party. If frustration is established, there will be no dismissal and, therefore, no right to claim unfair dismissal or redundancy payments. For this reason the courts have shown a degree of reluctance about applying the doctrine of frustration fully to contracts of employment. (For a recent example of this judicial reticence, see *Gryf-Lowczowski* v *Hinchingbrooke Healthcare NHS Trust* [2006] IRLR 100, HC.)

The usual frustrating events in this area are sickness and imprisonment.

(i) Sickness

Notcutt v *Universal Equipment Co. (London) Ltd*
[1986] ICR 414, Court of Appeal

The applicant had begun working for the employer in 1957 under a contract which permitted termination on one week's notice and provided for no remuneration during periods of sickness. In 1983, he suffered a coronary attack, and by July 1984 it was clear that he would not be able to work again. Accordingly, he was given 12 weeks' notice of termination. He brought an action in the county court claiming 12 weeks' sick pay on the basis that he was absent from work during the period of notice. The Court of Appeal agreed his contract had ended due to frustration prior to the notice period by reason of his illness.

DILLON LJ: The arguments of Mr Allen for the employee were first, and generally, that the doctrine of frustration can have no application to a periodic contract of employment because there is no need for it—the contract can always be terminated by short or relatively short notice. And secondly that in the circumstances of the present case there was no frustration as absence for sickness, injury or incapacity was envisaged by the contract and also by paragraph 3 of Schedule 3 to the Act.

In *Harman* v *Flexible Lamps Ltd* [1980] IRLR 418 Bristow J commented, at p. 419:

In the employment field the concept of discharge by operation of law, that is frustration, is normally only in play where the contract of employment is for a long term which cannot be determined by notice. Where the contract is terminable by notice, there is really no need to consider the question of frustration and if it were the law that in circumstances such as are before us in this case an employer was in a position to say 'this contract has been frustrated', then that would be a very convenient way in which to avoid the provisions of the Employment Protection (Consolidation) Act. In our judgment, that is not the law in these sort of circumstances.

In the present case, the argument of frustration is of course unashamedly put forward to avoid the provisions of the Act; in that it has succeeded in the court below. Notwithstanding the views expressed by Bristow J however there have been several cases in the National Industrial Relations Court and the Employment Appeal Tribunal in which those courts have considered that a contract of employment which is terminable by relatively short notice is in law capable of being terminated, without notice, by frustration as a result of the illness of the employee, and those courts have endeavoured to list by way of guideline the factors of which account should be taken in considering whether a particular such contract has been so frustrated: see *Marshall v Harland & Wolff Ltd* [1972] ICR 101; *Egg Stores (Stamford Hill) Ltd v Leibovici* [1977] ICR 260 and *Hart v A.R. Marshall & Sons (Bulwell) Ltd* [1977] ICR 539. The judge in the present case was in his judgment endeavouring to apply the guidelines laid down in those cases to the facts of the present case.

In this court in *Hare v Murphy Brothers Ltd* [1974] ICR 603, 607, Lord Denning MR held that a contract of employment of a workman was frustrated when the man was sentenced to imprisonment for 12 months. In reaching that conclusion Lord Denning MR considered by way of analogy that if the man had been grievously injured in a road accident and incapacitated for eight months his contract of employment would be frustrated. However, though the man's contract was presumably determinable on short notice, no argument was founded on this; the discussion seems to have been over whether the contract was terminated by frustration or by repudiatory breach on the part of the man in committing the offence for which he was imprisoned.

For my part, as a periodic contract of employment determinable by short, or relatively short, notice may none the less be intended in many cases by both parties to last for many years and as the power of the employer to terminate the contract by notice is subject to the provisions for the protection of employees against unfair dismissal now in the Act of 1978 [now the ERA 1996], I can see no reason in principle why such a periodic contract of employment should not, in appropriate circumstances, be held to have been terminated without notice by frustration according to the accepted and long established doctrine of frustration in our law of contract. The mere fact that the contract can be terminated by the employer by relatively short notice cannot of itself render the doctrine of frustration inevitably inapplicable. Accordingly the words of Bristow J in *Harman v Flexible Lamps Ltd* [1980] IRLR 418, 419, cited earlier in this judgment, must be taken as no more than a warning that the court must look carefully at any submission that a periodic contract of employment has been discharged by frustration if that submission is put forward to avoid the provisions of the Act. If Bristow J intended to go further than that I cannot agree with him.

Williams v Watsons Luxury Coaches Ltd

[1990] IRLR 164, Employment Appeal Tribunal

WOOD J: A modern statement of the principles involved is to be found in *Paal Wilson & Co. A/S v Partenreederei Hannah Blumenthal* [1983] 1 AC 854, 909, where Lord Brandon of Oakbrook says:

> There are two essential factors which must be present in order to frustrate a contract. The first essential factor is that there must be some outside event or extraneous change of situation, not foreseen or provided for by the parties at the time of contracting, which either makes it impossible for the contract to be performed at all, or at least renders its performance something radically different from what the parties contemplated when they entered into it. The second essential factor is that the outside event or extraneous change of situation concerned, and the consequences of either in relation to the performance of the contract, must have occurred without either the fault or the default of either party to the contract.

In the field of employment law the doctrine has found its expression in respect of two types of events—imprisonment and illness. It is only the latter which is relevant for our present purposes. The four leading cases are *Marshall v Harland & Wolff Ltd* [1972] ICR 101; *Egg Stores (Stamford Hill) Ltd v Leibovici* [1977] ICR 260; *Hart v A.R. Marshall & Sons (Bulwell) Ltd* [1977] ICR 539 and *Notcutt v Universal Equipment Co. (London) Ltd* [1986] ICR 414.

A number of principles relevant to the application of the doctrine to contracts of employment can be derived from these decisions which, in any event, are rare occurrences in the realm of employment law.

First, that the court must guard against too easy an application of the doctrine, more especially when redundancy occurs and also when the true situation may be a dismissal by reason of disability. Secondly, that although it is not necessary to decide that frustration occurred on a particular date, nevertheless an attempt to decide the relevant date is far from a useless exercise as it may help to determine in the mind of the court whether it really is a true frustration situation. Thirdly, that there are a number of factors which may help to decide the issue as they may each point in one or other direction. These we take from the judgment of Phillips J in *Egg Stores (Stamford Hill) Ltd* v *Leibovici* [1977] ICR 260, 265:

> Among the matters to be taken into account in such a case in reaching a decision are these: (1) the length of the previous employment; (2) how long it had been expected that the employment would continue; (3) the nature of the job; (4) the nature, length and effect of the illness or disabling event; (5) the need of the employer for the work to be done, and the need for a replacement to do it; (6) the risk to the employer of acquiring obligations in respect of redundancy payments or compensation for unfair dismissal to the replacement employee; (7) whether wages have continued to be paid; (8) the acts and the statements of the employer in relation to the employment, including the dismissal of, or failure to dismiss, the employee; and (9) whether in all the circumstances a reasonable employer could be expected to wait any longer.

To these we would add the terms of the contract as to the provisions for sickness pay, if any, and also, a consideration of the prospects of recovery. Fourthly—see *F.C. Shepherd & Co. Ltd* v *Jerrom* [1986] ICR 802—the party alleging frustration should not be allowed to rely upon the frustrating event if that event was caused by that party—at least where it was caused by its fault.

(ii) Imprisonment

Shepherd & Co. Ltd v *Jerrom*
[1986] IRLR 358, Court of Appeal

The applicant had entered into a four-year apprenticeship when, after 21 months, he was sentenced to a minimum of six months in Borstal. On his release, his employers refused to take him back and he complained of unfair dismissal. The tribunal rejected the employer's argument that the contract had been frustrated by reason of the custodial sentence, but the Court of Appeal allowed the employer's appeal.

BALCOMBE LJ: The only case in the Court of Appeal in which the question has been considered is *Hare* v *Murphy Brothers* [1974] IRLR 342. That is not a very satisfactory decision: one side was not represented and did not appear, so the court heard argument from one side only. Lord Denning MR, held that a sentence of imprisonment did frustrate the contract of employment; Lord Justice Stephenson held that the sentence of imprisonment did terminate the employment, and it mattered not whether the termination was labelled a frustrating event, repudiatory conduct, a breach going to the root of the contract of employment, or impossibility of performance. Lord Justice Lawton did not deal with this question. In my judgment *Hare* v *Murphy Brothers* is not a decision which binds this Court to hold that a sentence of imprisonment is capable of frustrating a contract of employment. Nevertheless I find the reasoning of Lord Denning MR, highly persuasive. There are decisions of lower courts that a sentence of imprisonment is capable of frustrating a contract of employment—see *Harrington* v *Kent County Council* [1980] IRLR 353; *Chakki* v *United Yeast Co. Limited* [1982] ICR 140; to the contrary effect is *Norris* v *Southampton City Council* [1982] IRLR 141—but none of these decisions is binding upon us.

In *Universal Cargo Carriers Corporation* v *Citati* [1957] 2 QB 401, 436–8 Mr Justice Devlin (as he then was) considered the law relating to anticipatory breach of contract.

> The law on the right to rescind is succinctly stated by Lord Porter in *Heyman* v *Darwins Ltd* [1942] AC 356, 397... as follows:
> The three sets of circumstances giving rise to a discharge of contract are tabulated by Anson as: (1) renunciation by a party of his liabilities under it; (2) impossibility created by his own act... In the case of the first two, the renunciation may occur or impossibility be created either before or at the time for performance... the first two state the two modes of anticipatory breach... A renunciation can be made either by words or by conduct, provided it is clearly made. It is often put that the party renunciating must 'evince an intention' not to go on with the contract. The intention can be evinced either by words or by conduct. The test of whether an intention is sufficiently evinced by conduct is whether the party renunciating has acted in such a way as to lead a reasonable person to the conclusion that he does not intend to fulfil his part of the contract... Since a man must be both ready and willing to perform, a profession by words or conduct of inability is by itself enough to constitute renunciation. But unwillingness and inability are often difficult to disentangle, and is rarely necessary to make the attempt.

Inability often lies at the root of unwillingness to perform. Willingness in this context does not mean cheerfulness; it means simply an intent to perform. To say: 'I would like to but I cannot' negatives intent just as much as 'I will not'… If a man says 'I cannot perform,' he renounces his contract by that statement, and the cause of the inability is immaterial.

Mr Clark, appearing for the apprentice before us, submits that this principle enunciated by Mr Justice Devlin that impossibility of performance of contractual obligation created by the act of a party to the contract amounts to the renunciation (or repudiation) of the contract by that party is but the obverse of the coin, where the reverse is Lord Brandon's second factor in *Paal Wilson & Co. Partenreederei*. Accordingly he submits that… this cannot be a case of frustration: it must be a case of repudiation by the apprentice.

While I can see the logical attraction of that submission, and whatever may be the rule in the case of a commercial contract, I find difficulty in applying it to the case of a contract of employment and the imprisonment of the employee. What is the conduct of the employee by which he 'evinces an intention' not to go on with the contract? It cannot be the commission of the criminal offence, since in most cases it will not follow that he will necessarily suffer a sentence of imprisonment. What is the position between the commission of the offence and trial, while it remains uncertain whether the employee will be imprisoned, or will suffer some other punishment which will not necessarily prevent him from fulfilling his obligations under his contract of employment? What is the position of an employee who is remanded in custody pending trial: does this 'evince an intention' not to go on with the contract? For myself, I find it impossible to give a sensible answer to these questions. Further, I agree with Lord Denning's analysis of the position in *Hare* v *Murphy Brothers* (supra). In that case the National Industrial Relations Court had held that Mr Hare's sentence of imprisonment was not a frustrating event because it was brought about by his own act in committing the offence for which he was sentenced to imprisonment. It was, however, a breach by him of his contract of so serious a nature, bearing in mind the length of time during which he would be away from work and the importance of his position as foreman, that it went to the root and constituted a repudiation of his contract of employment. In criticising that decision Lord Denning MR, said:

> I cannot agree with that reasoning. In the first place, I do not think that Mr Hare was guilty of any breach of contract. Take the brawl in March 1971 when Mr Hare struck a blow by which he unlawfully wounded someone or other. That was quite unconnected with his employment. It was no breach by him of his contract of employment.
>
> Take next the sentence of imprisonment for 12 months in June 1971. That, too, was not a breach by him. If he had been given a suspended sentence or put on probation he would not be guilty of any breach of his contract of employment. Nor is it when he is sentenced to 12 months. That was the act of the court which sentenced him. It was no breach by him. But nevertheless—contrary to the Industrial Court—I think there was a frustrating event. The sentence of 12 months' imprisonment frustrated the contract of employment. I know that it was brought about by his own act, namely, the unlawful wounding. In that way it may be said to be 'self-induced'; but still it was a frustrating event.

In my judgment that analysis is entirely consistent with the realities of the situation.

I appreciate that mine may be a simplistic approach to a difficult jurisprudential problem, but I am conscious that employment law is today largely administered by industrial tribunals, often without the benefit of legal representation of some or all of the parties before them. In my view it is important that, if possible, the legal concepts relating to the existence and termination of a contract of employment should be readily comprehensible. If that approach involves a degree of inconsistency between contracts of employment and commercial contracts, then that is a price I am prepared to pay.

Accordingly, I answer question 2 above in the affirmative: a custodial sentence imposed upon an employee is capable of frustrating a contract of employment.

NOTE: While frustration arguments may well succeed in exceptional cases, the courts are generally reluctant to apply the doctrine. For recent illustrations, see *Four Seasons Healthcare Ltd* v *Maughan* [2005] IRLR 324, EAT and *Gryf-Lowczowski* v *Hinchingbrooke Healthcare NHS Trust* [2006] IRLR 100, HC. In *Williams* v *Watsons Luxury Coaches Ltd* (Section (i)), the EAT attributed this judicial caution to the view that the doctrine can do harm to good industrial relations, as it provides an easy escape from the obligations of investigation which should be carried out by a reasonable employer. It is therefore better for the employer to take dismissal action.

■ QUESTION

Should 'frustration' arguments have any part to play in the supposedly 'user-friendly' remedies of unfair dismissal or redundancy? (See Hepple, R., 'Restructuring employment rights' (1986) 15 ILJ 69; Collins, H., *Justice in Dismissal* (Oxford: Clarendon Press, 1992), pp. 44–5.)

B: Termination by mutual agreement

(i) Genuine mutual agreement

Birch and Humber v The University of Liverpool
[1985] IRLR 165, Court of Appeal

The applicants were members of the University's technical staff. In 1981, a Premature Retirement Compensation Scheme was introduced. It was made clear that the scheme was not a redundancy scheme and that any retirement pursuant to the scheme could only take place with the agreement of both the University and the employee. In 1982, the University announced that there was a need to cut back staff but expressed the hope that such could take place by way of early retirement rather than redundancy. The applicants applied for early retirement under the scheme and, it having been granted, thereafter applied to the tribunal on the grounds that they had been dismissed by reason of redundancy. The Court of Appeal agreed with the EAT finding that the applicants' employment ended not by a dismissal but by mutual agreement.

ACKNER LJ: The decision whether or not there has been a dismissal within the meaning of s. 83 [now ERA 1996, s. 136] has to be decided before one considers whether the result of that dismissal is to entitle the employee to make a claim for redundancy payments. The two are disassociated. Miss Cotton has shown us no authority for the proposition, which I find a strange one, that the mere fact that the requirement of the business for employees is expected to diminish, should make it in law not possible to have a determination of the contract by mutual consent. I put to her the simple example of an employer who envisages some time in the future, e.g. because of new technology, the need to slim down his workforce and makes an offer to those who are prepared to resign rather than to wait to volunteer for redundancy and supports that offer with a financial inducement which is far in excess of what is likely to be obtained under the redundancy legislation. It seems to me clear that in such a situation, assuming no question of any coercion of any kind, that if that offer is accepted there can be no question of there having been a dismissal...

Since the appellants' case is based on s. 83(2)(a) of the 1978 Act [now ERA 1996, s. 136(1)(a)], it may perhaps be worth making one observation as to the construction of the relevant wording of that subsection, which reads as follows:

s. 83(2)—An employee shall be treated as dismissed by his employer if, but only if—

(a) the contract under which he is employed by the employer is terminated by the employer, whether it is so terminated by notice or without notice...

In my opinion this subsection, on its true construction, is directed to the case where, on a proper analysis of the facts, the contract of employment is terminated by the employer alone. It is not apt to cover the case where, on such an analysis, the contract of employment has been terminated by the employee, or by the mutual, freely given, consent of the employer and the employee. In a case where it has been terminated by such mutual agreement, it may properly be said that the contract has been terminated by both the employer and the employee jointly, but it cannot, in my view, be said that it has been terminated by the employer alone.

(ii) The employer cannot impose the agreement

Igbo v Johnson Matthey Chemical Ltd
[1986] IRLR 215, Court of Appeal

Mrs Igbo wanted to take extended leave to visit her husband and children in Nigeria. The employers were prepared to grant such leave but only on the basis of Mrs Igbo agreeing that, should she not return by 28 September 1983, her contract would be automatically terminated. Mrs Igbo returned to the UK on 26 September but did not report for work on 28 September due to sickness. The employer treated her contract as ended in accordance with a letter signed by Mrs Igbo. The Court of Appeal held that she had been dismissed and, in so doing, overruled the decision on virtually identical facts in *British Leyland (UK) Ltd* v *Ashraf* [1978] IRLR 330, EAT.

PARKER LJ: Before proceeding to a consideration of the merits of the contention we should mention three matters. First there is no question of the respondents' seeking to behave improperly in granting leave on the terms here agreed. It is a common practice and designed to ensure that employees, particularly perhaps those going overseas, do not overstay their leave, a situation which occurs all too frequently. The respondents, in common with many employers, use the method here adopted to protect themselves from such occurrences. Secondly, there is no doubt that Mrs Igbo had the terms explained to her before she signed the copy of the letter of 18 August.

Thirdly, however, despite the above it must be recognised that the effect of the terms, if *Ashraf's* case is right, can be very harsh. An employee who had been employed for many years with an impeccable record might, for example, be knocked down by a car when within mere feet of the factory gate, which he was about to enter at the proper time. If he managed to crawl to the gate and was then promptly sent home by the employers in an ambulance his contract would not terminate. If, however, he could not move and was taken away by an ambulance without getting inside the gate, his contract would terminate. If he was able to report for work the next day and was turned away he would then be left without remedy either at common law or under the 1978 Act [now the ERA 1996]. No doubt it would be said that in such circumstances no employer would dream of turning him away, but this only serves to show that in substance he would, if turned away, be being dismissed. Furthermore, to say of an employee who failed to return to work in such circumstances that there was a consensual termination of the contract offends against commonsense. There would be nothing consensual about it. The employee's desire throughout would clearly have been that the contract should continue.

With this preliminary we turn to s. 140 of the 1978 Act [now the ERA 1996, s. 203]. It provides:

(1) Except as provided by the following provisions of this section, any provision in an agreement (whether a contract of employment or not) shall be void in so far as it purports—

    (a) to exclude or *limit* the operation of any provision of this Act; or

    (b) to preclude any person from presenting a complaint to, or bringing any proceedings under this Act before, an industrial tribunal.

It is common ground, and was established in *Joseph* v *Joseph* [1967] 1 Ch 78, that the words 'in so far as it purports to exclude or limit' mean 'in so far as it has the effect of excluding or limiting'. The appellant relies on subsection (1)(a) only. The question is, therefore, whether any provision in the Holiday Agreement has the effect of excluding or limiting the operation of any provision of the Act. It is indisputable that the Holiday Agreement (so far as it was valid) had the effect of varying the conditions of the appellant's contract of employment. She contends that the provision for automatic termination of the contract on failure to return to work has the effect of excluding or limiting the operation of ss. 54 and 55 of the Act [now the ERA 1996, ss. 94 and 95]…

It is clear that both before and after 18 August Mrs Igbo had the right conferred by s. 54(1) and thus that neither s. 54 nor s. 55 was 'excluded' by the Holiday Agreement. It is however equally clear that but for the provision for automatic termination she would had the respondents turned her off on 28 September have been dismissed within the meaning of s. 55. The termination provision therefore, it is said, had the effect of 'limiting the operation' of ss. 54 and 55. To this the respondents answer that it did nothing of the sort. Its effect was only to bring the contract to an end otherwise than in one of the four ways which, by subsections (2) and (3) of s. 55, alone constitute dismissal for the purposes of s. 54, namely by consensual agreement.

It is, we think, important to dispose at the outset of any idea that the termination of a contract of employment by agreement by itself prevents an employee being dismissed for the purposes of the 1978 Act. Every fixed term contract is terminated by consensual agreement on its expiry date, yet non-renewal constitutes dismissal under s. 55(2)(b). Every contract which is subject to termination on notice terminates by agreement if the employer gives proper notice, yet such termination constitutes dismissal under s. 55(2)(a). Hence, if on 18 August Mrs Igbo and the respondents had agreed that her contract should end on 28 September without more, she would have had a contract for a fixed term and non-renewal on that date would have constituted dismissal. Furthermore it is to be noted that, by virtue of s. 55(3), an employee under a valid notice, who gives notice to leave before the expiry of the notice is nevertheless taken to have been dismissed. This can, as it seems to us, only be due to the fact that the employee is in such circumstances treated by the Act as being not genuinely willing to leave. He will have departed voluntarily before he need have done but he will only have done so because he was under notice.

If the respondents' contention is correct, it must follow that the whole object of the Act can be easily defeated by the inclusion of a term in a contract of employment that if the employee is late for work on the first Monday in any month, or indeed on any day, no matter for what reason, the contract shall automatically terminate. Could it be said that such a provision did not limit the operation of ss. 54 and 55? In our judgment it could not. Such a provision would vitally limit the operation of s. 54(1), for the right not to be unfairly dismissed would become subject to the condition that the employee was on time for work on the first Monday in each month, or every day, as the case might be.

Hellyer Bros Ltd v Atkinson and Dickinson
[1994] IRLR 88, Court of Appeal

The applicants were crew members on fishing boats owned by their employers. It was customary to sign a crew agreement which lasted for several voyages, after which the employee would be asked to 'sign off' and sign a new agreement to cover the next series of fishing trips. Both applicants 'signed off' their previous voyages, Atkinson before and Dickinson after, having been told that their employers were decommissioning their ships. They both sought redundancy payments. The employer argued unsuccessfully that they had terminated their employment by mutual consent and, accordingly, had not been dismissed.

HENRY LJ: [The] findings by the Tribunal were of mixed law and fact, in this case predominantly fact. An appeal only lies from the Industrial Tribunal on questions of law. And here there was ample evidence to support the factual findings. So the employer's task in upsetting those findings is formidable.

They sought before the EAT and in this Court to do it in this way. First, they rely on the terms of the crew agreement:

The form and provisions of this agreement are approved by the Department of Trade & Industry under s. 1(3) of the Merchant Shipping Act 1970.

If the form and provisions of this agreement are amended or clauses are added without the prior approval of the Department it will not be regarded as approved under the said section of the Act.

...

Contractual clauses

(i) It is agreed that:...

(ii) After one voyage has been completed by a seaman under this agreement, either the seaman or the employer may give to the other notice (in writing or orally before a witness) to terminate the seaman's employment under this agreement, such notice to take effect at a port in the United Kingdom and to be given not less than 29 hours either before the vessel is due to arrive at that port, or before it is due to sail, if the employment is to terminate at the port where the vessel is when the notice is given...

(v) In relation to an individual seaman this agreement may be terminated:

(a) by mutual consent;

(b) by appropriate notice in accordance with the terms of this agreement;

(c) by loss or total unseaworthiness of the vessel.

Next, they point out that it is common ground between the parties that the Industrial Tribunal must have based their decision on subsection (a) of s. 83(2) of the 1978 Act [now the ERA 1996, s. 136(1)(a)]; namely, that the contracts of employment were terminated by the employer, whether by notice or without notice.

Here the employers did not give 24 hours' written notice in terminating the contract to the employees; and nor was any such notice given orally in the presence of a witness. So the employers refer to clause (v) (see above) and say that, of the three ways of terminating an agreement with an individual seaman there set out, this contract could only have been determined on grounds (a) or (b). It was not determined on ground (b) (the giving of appropriate notice in accordance with the terms of this agreement), as the employers had not given appropriate notice. Therefore, by a process of elimination, the termination of the agreement must in law have been under ground (a), by mutual consent (despite the Tribunal's emphatic finding that it was not). And if it was by mutual consent, then of course the employees were not dismissed by reason of redundancy.

That submission, advanced by Mr Pardoe QC on behalf of the employers, is in my view hopeless.

First, clause (v) does not list all the ways of terminating the contract; it only lists those 'clean break' terminations of the contract which leave neither party with any common law cause of action arising out of the contract.

The Industrial Tribunal on the evidence inevitably and rightly found that the service agreements were not determined by mutual consent. There is nothing in this contract which could require that truth to be ignored or reversed.

In these cases the effective notice of termination was the information that the vessel would not be sailing for a bit in Mr Atkinson's case, and not sailing at all in Mr Dickinson's case. Each such notice was given more than 24 hours before the vessels were to sail—as they were to be decommissioned. So the imperfection in each notice was simply as to form: it was not given in writing, and was not given in the presence of a witness. Had any seaman been pedantic enough to have objected to these formalities being ignored, doubtless the employers' representatives would immediately have put it in writing or repeated it once a witness had been found. But the normal seaman would act just as these men did—waive the formalities and accept the inevitable.

And that is what the EAT found: an implicit finding of waiver by the Industrial Tribunal. So it clearly was. But Mr Pardoe submits that as these crew agreements and as any variation of them required the approval of the DTI, so any waiver by an individual of formalities inserted for his protection in all cases requires the same approval before acquiring force in law; and absent that approval, any such waiver must be ignored. Such, he submits, is the proper construction of s. 1(3), and represents the intention of Parliament.

On the facts of this case such a submission is legalism gone mad. There are certain statutory protections which the law does not permit parties to contract out of, such protections usually being inserted to remedy the weak bargaining power of the protected party. But that is not this case. These seamen were faced with the inevitable. They sensibly and realistically did not insist on being told the bad news again, albeit more formally. The contractual requirements as to the formalities attendant on the giving of notice offered them no useful protection in the circumstances. This was a classic waiver in the sense of a voluntary forbearance to insist on pedantic performance of—in this case—a now irrelevant contractual formality. The suggestion that by some malign legal alchemy that forbearance turned the plain fact that they had been dismissed by their employer into a termination of their longstanding employment by mutual consent, depriving them of their redundancy payments, is in my view without any merit and fails.

...

Appeal dismissed with costs. Leave to appeal to the House of Lords refused.

NOTES

1. As a result of the Court of Appeal's decision, the Government announced that it would set up a fund to compensate trawlermen made redundant in the late 1970s and early 1980s, who were misled by local officials of the Department of Employment into believing that they failed to qualify for a redundancy payment. This is long overdue. It had been agreed, as long ago as 1983, that *ex gratia* payments should be made in cases where there was evidence of misdirection leading to a claim not being submitted in time and where the claim, had it been submitted in time, would have been valid. However, in *McLeod and others* v *Hellyer Bros Ltd* [1987] IRLR 232, the Court of Appeal held that most of the claims by trawlermen would fail because of lack of continuity of employment. The *Atkinson* decision changes that position and the Government will make payments, including interest, for the whole period since the men were dismissed.

   At common law, termination without dismissal also occurs on the death of an employee or on the death of an individual employer (the ERA 1996, s. 136(5) allows a redundancy claim by an employee in such circumstances).

   The contract may also be terminated by expiry of time if a fixed-term contract. This is discussed in Section 4.

   A contract will also be deemed terminated on dissolution of a partnership or on appointment of a receiver save that such events in the context of a transfer may, of course, be covered by the Transfer of Undertakings Regulations (see Chapter 9).

2. In *Sandhu* v *Jan de Rijk Transport Ltd* [2007] IRLR 519, CA, the employee was called to a meeting at which he was told at the outset that he was being dismissed. The rest of the meeting was then spent discussing severance terms, and agreement was reached. The employers contended that this led to a termination by mutual consent, rather than a dismissal, but the Court of Appeal failed to agree. According to the Court of Appeal, resignation implies some form of negotiation and discussion; it predicates a result on the part of the employee. Plainly, if the employee has the opportunity to take independent advice and then offers to resign, that fact would be powerful evidence pointing towards resignation rather than dismissal.

SECTION 3: CONSTRUCTIVE DISMISSAL

EMPLOYMENT RIGHTS ACT 1996

95. Circumstances in which an employee is dismissed

(1) For the purposes of this Part an employee is dismissed by his employer if (and, subject to subsection (2) and section 96, only if)—

...

(c) the employee terminates the contract under which he is employed (with or without notice) in circumstances in which he is entitled to terminate it without notice by reason of the employer's conduct.

A: Dismissal or resignation?

(i) Are the words or actions of resignation unambiguous?

Sovereign House Security Services Ltd v Savage
[1989] IRLR 115, Court of Appeal

Savage, a security officer, was told that he was to be suspended pending police investigations into the theft of money from the employer's offices. Savage told his immediate superior to pass on the fact that he was 'jacking it in'. The Court of Appeal agreed that the employer was entitled to treat these words as amounting to a resignation.

MAY LJ: In my opinion, generally speaking, where unambiguous words of resignation are used by an employee to the employer direct or by an intermediary, and are so understood by the employer, the proper conclusion of fact is that the employee has in truth resigned. In my view tribunals should not be astute to find otherwise. However, in some cases there may be something in the context of the exchange between the employer and the employee or, in the circumstances of the employee him or herself, to entitle the Tribunal of fact to conclude that notwithstanding the appearances there was no real resignation despite what it might appear to be at first sight.

We were referred in this connection to the earlier decision in this court of *Sothern v Franks Charlesly & Co* [1981] IRLR 278. In that case a partnership secretary to a firm of solicitors had in circumstances into which it is wholly unnecessary to go, said, 'I am resigning'. Both the Industrial Tribunal and the Employment Appeal Tribunal held that those words were ambiguous and that in consequence the employee had been dismissed. When the matter reached this court, it took a different view, concluded that the words were wholly unambiguous and that in the circumstances there had been a resignation and not a dismissal. Nevertheless in his judgment Fox LJ at para. 19 in the report said this:

As regards Mrs Sothern's intentions when she said, 'I am resigning', it seems to me that when the words used by a person are unambiguous words of resignation and so understood by her employers, the question of what a reasonable employer might have understood does not arise. The natural meaning of the words and the fact that the employer understood them to mean that the employee was resigning cannot be overridden by appeals to what a reasonable employer might have assumed. The non-disclosed intention of a person using language as to his intended meaning is not properly to be taken into account in determining what the true meaning is.

I turn to para. 21:

Secondly, this is not a case of an immature employee, or of a decision taken in the heat of the moment, or of an employee being jostled into a decision by the employers.

The learned Lord Justice was there contemplating the possibility to which I have referred, that if one is concerned with an immature employee or decisions taken in the heat of the moment, then what might otherwise appear to be a clear resignation, should not be so construed.

Dame Elizabeth Lane, in giving the second judgment of the court, agreed with the decision that there had been a resignation, but in the course of her judgment, referring to the words used, she said this:

Those were not idle words or words spoken under emotional stress which the employers knew or ought to have known were not meant to be taken seriously. Nor was it a case of employers anxious to be rid of an employee who seized upon her words and gave them a meaning which she did not intend. They were sorry to receive the resignation and said so.

So Dame Elizabeth Lane was again taking the same approach as Fox LJ: generally speaking a resignation is to be imputed, but there may be circumstances in which, notwithstanding what would appear at first sight, the circumstances are such that what occurred was a dismissal rather than a resignation.

(ii) Allowance for 'heat of the moment' utterances

Tanner v *Kean*
[1978] IRLR 160, Employment Appeal Tribunal

The employee had been loaned £275 so that he could buy his own vehicle, thereby making it unnecessary to use the employer's van outside work hours. Nevertheless Tanner continued to use the van for his own purposes. On discovering this the employer said 'What's my fucking van doing outside; you're a tight bastard. I've just lent you £275 to buy a car and you're too tight to put juice in it. That's it; you're finished with me.' The EAT agreed that these words should not have been treated by the employee as a dismissal.

PHILLIPS J: Turning to the appeal, the first thing to note is that there is only an appeal to us on a question of law. No doubt there are some words and acts which as a matter of law could be said only to constitute dismissal or resignation, or of which it could be said that they could not constitute dismissal or resignation. But in many cases they are in the middle territory where it is uncertain whether they do or not, and there it is necessary to look at all the circumstances of the case, in particular to see what was the intention with which the words were spoken.

In the present case the words are those set out in paragraph 1 of the Reasons: 'What's my fucking van doing outside; you're a tight bastard. I've just lent you £275 to buy a car and you are too tight to put juice in it. That's it; you're finished with me.' Part of the circumstances were that that was said in a country club to which Mr Tanner had taken the firm's van, and where he acted as a part-time doorman and had met Mr Kean, his employer. It seems to us—and although they do not say so, no doubt it seemed to the Tribunal—that those words, in all the circumstances of the case, were not as a matter of law in one category or the other; in other words, whether what was said constituted a dismissal depended on all the circumstances of the case. In our judgment the test which has to be applied in cases of this kind is along these lines. Were the words spoken those of dismissal, that is to say, were they intended to bring the contract of employment to an end? What was the employer's intention? In answering that a relevant, and perhaps the most important, question is how would a reasonable employee, in all circumstances, have understood what the employer intended by what he said and did? Then in most of these cases, and in this case, it becomes relevant to look at the later events following the utterance of the words and preceding the actual departure of the employee. Some care, it seems to us, is necessary in regard to later events, and it might be put, we think, like this: that later events, unless relied on as themselves constituting a dismissal, are only relevant to the extent that they throw light on the employer's intention; that is to say, we would stress, his intention at the time of the alleged dismissal. A word of caution is necessary because in considering later events it is necessary to remember that a dismissal or resignation, once it has taken effect, cannot be unilaterally withdrawn. Accordingly, as it seems to us, later events need to be scrutinised with some care in order to see whether they are genuinely explanatory of the acts alleged to constitute dismissal, or whether they reflect a change of mind. If they are in the former category they may be valuable as showing what was really intended.

NOTE: See also *Kwik-fit (GB) Ltd* v *Lineham* [1992] ICR 183.

B: The concept of constructive dismissal

Western Excavating (ECC) Ltd v *Sharp*
[1978] QB 761, Court of Appeal

An employee was suspended without pay for having taken time off without permission. He was, therefore, short of money and sought an advance against accrued holiday pay from his employer, which request was refused. He then asked for a loan which was also refused. Accordingly, he resigned in order to obtain his accrued holiday pay. The industrial tribunal held he was justified in terminating his contract because of the employer's behaviour. The Court of Appeal overturned the decision, Lord Denning giving the seminal judgment on the proper test to be applied in considering an averment of constructive dismissal.

LORD DENNING MR: [Lord Denning was referring to the definition of 'constructive dismissal' set out in the Trade Union and Labour Relations Act 1974. That same definition is now contained in ERA 1996, s. 95(1)(c).] The rival tests are as follows.

The contract test

On the one hand, it is said that the words of paragraph 5(2)(c) express a legal concept which is already well settled in the books on contract under the rubric 'discharge by breach.' If the employer is guilty of conduct which is a significant breach going to the root of the contract of employment, or which shows that the employer no longer intends to be bound by one or more of the essential terms of the contract, then the employee is entitled to treat himself as discharged from any further performance. If he does so, then he terminates the contract by reason of the employer's conduct. He is constructively dismissed. The employee is entitled in those circumstances to leave at the instant without giving any notice at all or, alternatively, he may give notice and say he is leaving at the end of the notice. But the conduct must in either case be sufficiently serious to entitle him to leave at once. Moreover, he must make up his mind soon after the conduct of which he complains: for, if he continues for any length of time without leaving, he will lose his right to treat himself as discharged. He will be regarded as having elected to affirm the contract.

The unreasonableness test

On the other hand, it is said that the words of paragraph 5(2)(c) do not express any settled legal concept. They introduce a new concept into contracts of employment. It is that the employer must act reasonably in his treatment of his employees. If he conducts himself or his affairs so unreasonably that the employee cannot fairly be expected to put up with it any longer, the employee is justified in leaving. He can go, with or without giving notice, and claim compensation for unfair dismissal.

The result

In my opinion, the contract test is the right test. My reasons are as follows. (i) The statute itself draws a distinction between 'dismissal' in paragraph 5(2)(c) and 'unfairness' in paragraph 6(8). If Parliament intended that same test to apply, it would have said so. (ii) 'Dismissal' in paragraph 5(2) goes back to 'dismissal' in the Redundancy Payments Act 1965. Its interpretation should not be influenced by paragraph 6(8) which was introduced first in 1971 in the Industrial Relations Act 1971. (iii) Paragraph 5(2)(c) uses words which have a legal connotation, especially the words 'entitled' and 'without notice.' If a non-legal connotation were intended, it would have added 'justified in leaving at once' or some such non-legal phrase. (iv) Paragraph 5(2)(a) and (c) deal with different situations. Paragraph 5(2)(a) deals with cases where the employer himself terminates the contract by dismissing the man with or without notice. That is, when the employer says to the man: 'You must go.' Paragraph 5(2)(c) deals with the cases where the employee himself terminates the contract by saying: 'I can't stand it any longer. I want my cards.' (v) The new test of 'unreasonable conduct' of the employer is too indefinite by far. It has led to acute difference of opinion between the members of tribunals. Often there are majority opinions. It has led to findings of 'constructive dismissal' on the most whimsical grounds. The Employment Appeal Tribunal tells us so. It is better to have the contract test of the common law. It is more certain: as it can well be understood by intelligent laymen under the direction of a legal chairman. (vi) I would adopt the reasoning of the considered judgment of the Employment Appeal Tribunal in *Wetherall (Bond St. W1) Ltd* v *Lynn* [1978] ICR 205, 211:

> Parliament might well have said, in relation to whether the employer's conduct had been reasonable having regard to equity and the substantial merits of the case, but it neither laid down that special statutory criterion or any other. So, in our judgment, the answer can only be, entitled according to law, and it is to the law of contract that you have to look.

(vii) The test of unreasonableness gives no effect to the words 'without notice.' They impose a legal test which no test of 'unreasonableness' can do.

Conclusion

The present case is a good illustration of a 'whimsical decision.' Applying the test of 'unreasonable conduct,' the industrial tribunal decided by a majority of two to one in favour of the employee. All three members of the Employment Appeal Tribunal would have decided in favour of the employers, but felt that it was a matter of fact on which they could not reverse the industrial tribunal. So counting heads, it was four to two in favour of the employers, but yet the case was decided against them—because of the test of 'unreasonable conduct.'

If the contract test had been applied, the result would have been plain. There was no dismissal, constructive or otherwise, by the employers. The employers were not in breach at all. Nor had they repudiated the contract at all. The employee left of his own accord without anything wrong done by the employers. His claim should have been rejected. The decision against the employers was most unjust to them. I would allow the appeal, accordingly.

LAWTON LJ: For the purpose of this judgment, I do not find it either necessary or advisable to express any opinion as to what principles of law operate to bring a contract of employment to an end by reason of an employer's conduct. Sensible persons have no difficulty in recognising such conduct when they hear about it. Persistent and unwanted amorous advances by an employer to a female member of his staff would, for example, clearly be such conduct; and for a chairman of an industrial tribunal in such a case to discuss with his lay members whether there had been a repudiation or a breach of a fundamental term by the employer would be for most lay members a waste of legal learning. There may occasionally be border-line cases which would require a chairman to analyse the legal principles applicable for the benefit of the lay members; but when such cases do occur he should try to do so in the kind of language which 19th century judges used when directing juries about the law applicable to contracts of employment, rather than the language which nowadays would be understood and appreciated by academic lawyers. I appreciate that the principles of law applicable to the termination by an employee of a contract of employment because of his employer's conduct are difficult to put concisely in the language judges use in court. Lay members of industrial tribunals, however, do not spend all their time in court and when out of court they may use, and certainly will hear, short words and terse phrases which describe clearly the kind of employer of whom an employee is entitled without notice to rid himself ...

NOTES

1. For an illustration of the contract test in relation to constructive dismissal, see *Judge* v *Crown Leisure Ltd* [2005] IRLR 823, CA. The Court of Appeal held that an employee was not entitled to rely on a promise made at a Christmas party that he would receive a future pay increase in order to bring his pay in line with a fellow employee. The court ruled that in order for there to be a legally binding and enforceable contractual commitment, there must be certainty as to the contractual commitment entered into, or, alternatively, facts from which certainty can be established. Otherwise, a promise amounts to nothing more than a statement of intention. A promise to achieve parity within two years might well be sufficiently certain to be capable of enforcement. However, a promise to achieve parity 'eventually' or 'in due course' is too vague ever to amount to a binding contractual commitment.

   In the present case, the employment tribunal had found that, although contrary to the employers' contention, a conversation had taken place during which the employers' commitment to bring the salaries of all those in the claimant's position roughly into line was reiterated, there had been no promise, as the claimant contended, to achieve parity within two years. It was the inevitable consequence of that finding that what was said was too vague and uncertain to amount to a binding contractual promise and that, therefore, the employers' failure to bring about parity within two years did not amount to a fundamental breach of contract which entitled the claimant to resign and claim unfair constructive dismissal.

2. In *Keegan* v *Newcastle United Football Co Ltd* [2010] IRLR 94, the Premier League Managers' Arbitration Tribunal found that the club was in breach of a term in Mr Keegan's contract as manager that he would have the final say as to transfer of players, and that this breach was fundamental, entitling Mr Keegan to resign.

3. At the time of the *Western Excavating (ECC) Ltd* v *Sharp* decision, many commentators took the view that the contractual test would unduly limit the scope of constructive dismissal. However, this has not occurred because of the development of an implied duty to maintain trust and confidence and a willingness, on occasion, to circumvent the strict contractual approach (see *Greenaway Harrison* v *Wiles* [1994] IRLR 380, EAT). As a result the distinction between the *Western Excavating (ECC) Ltd* v *Sharp* approach and the discredited 'reasonableness' test looks slim indeed, as is illustrated by looking at just some of the situations where the implied obligation has been held to be broken:

(a) failing to respond to an employee's complaint about the lack of adequate safety equipment (*British Aircraft Corporation Ltd* v *Austin* [1978] IRLR 332);

(b) undermining the authority of senior staff over subordinates (*Courtaulds Northern Textiles Ltd* v *Andrew* [1979] IRLR 84);

(c) failing to protect an employee from harassment from fellow employees (*Wigan Borough Council* v *Davies* [1979] IRLR 127);

(d) failing properly to investigate allegations of sexual harassment or treating the complaint with sufficient seriousness (*Bracebridge Engineering Ltd* v *Derby* [1990] IRLR 3, see Section C(i));

(e) foul language by employer (*Palmanor Ltd* v *Cedron* [1978] IRLR 303, see Section C(ii); *Horkulak* v *Cantor Fitzgerald International* [2003] IRLR 756, QBD; *Stanley Cole (Wainfleet) Ltd* v *Sheridan* [2003] IRLR 52, EAT);

(f) imposing a disciplinary penalty grossly out of proportion to the offence (*British Broadcasting Corporation* v *Beckett* [1983] IRLR 43);

(g) significantly reducing the employee's role without consultation (*McBride* v *Falkirk Football & Athletic Club* [2012] IRLR 22, EAT);

(h) a series of minor incidents of harassment over a period of time which cumulatively amount to repudiation: the so-called 'last straw' doctrine (*Woods* v *WM Car Services (Peterborough) Ltd* [1982] ICR 693, see the following extract). (In *L.B. of Waltham Forest* v *Omilaju* [2005] IRLR 35, the Court of Appeal held that in order to result in a breach of trust and confidence term, a last straw, which is not in itself a breach of contract, must be an act in a series of earlier acts which cumulatively amount to a breach of the implied term. According to Dyson LJ: 'The act does not have to be of the same character as the earlier acts. Its essential quality is that, when taken in conjunction with the earlier acts on which the employer relies, it amounts to the breach of the implied term of trust and confidence. It must contribute something to that breach, although what it adds may be relatively insignificant.');

(i) unlawful discrimination can amount to a repudiatory breach of contract, entitling an employee to claim constructive dismissal (*Shaw* v *CCL Ltd* [2008] IRLR 284). (The EAT held that a breach of the discrimination statutes can give rise to a claim of constructive dismissal, and did so in this case, in which the employer was found to have both directly and indirectly discriminated on grounds of sex in turning down the claimant's request to be allowed to work flexibly on returning from maternity leave.)

4. As we shall see, the test for whether an employer has acted reasonably in dismissing an employee is whether the employer's actions fell within the 'band of reasonable responses'. Does the band of reasonableness test apply when judging an employer's conduct for the purpose of determining whether an employee is entitled to resign and claim constructive dismissal? Two EAT decisions suggest that the test is applicable in such cases (see *Abbey National* v *Fairbrother* [2007] IRLR 320 EAT, and *Claridge* v *Daler Rowney* [2008] IRLR 672, EAT). However, in *Bournemouth University Higher Education Corporation* v *Buckland* [2009] IRLR 606, another division of the EAT rejected the contention that an employee can only show a fundamental breach of contract—and thus constructive dismissal—where the actions of the employer fall outside the band of reasonable responses open to the employer. It is submitted that the approach adopted in *Buckland* is the correct one and, indeed, the Court of Appeal in *Buckland* endorsed the EAT's view [2010] IRLR 445.

The Court of Appeal also held that once there has been a repudiatory breach, it is not open to the employer, by remedying it, to preclude the employee from accepting the breach as terminating the contract.

5. Whether the employer's behaviour is sufficient to justify the resignation is a question of fact for the tribunal; accordingly the appeal court should not lightly interfere with the decision of the tribunal on this question. This point was emphasised in the following case. This case also provides useful guidance on the scope of constructive dismissal.

Woods v WM Car Services (Peterborough) Ltd
[1981] ICR 666, Employment Appeal Tribunal

New owners of a business, having agreed to continue employment of employees on no less favourable terms than previously, asked the applicant to accept a lower wage and work longer hours. The applicant, having been told that if she did not accept the new terms she would be dismissed, left. The EAT refused to interfere with the tribunal's finding that she had not been constructively dismissed.

BROWNE-WILKINSON J: … In our view it is clearly established that there is implied in a contract of employment a term that the employers will not, without reasonable and proper cause, conduct themselves in a manner calculated or likely to destroy or seriously damage the relationship of trust and confidence between employer and employee… To constitute a breach of this implied term it is not necessary to show that the employer intended any repudiation of the contract: the tribunal's function is to look at the employer's conduct as a whole and determine whether it is such that its effect, judged reasonably and sensibly, is such that the employee cannot be expected to put up with it… The conduct of the parties has to be looked at as a whole and its cumulative impact assessed…

NOTES
1. Subsequently, the Court of Appeal dismissed the employee's appeal ([1982] ICR 693).
2. In *Baldwin* v *Brighton and Hove City Council* [2007] IRLR 332, the EAT held that the formulation of the implied term by Lord Steyn in *Malik* v *BCCI* [1997] IRLR 462 (see Section 5.A) as 'the employer shall not without reasonable and proper cause, conduct itself in a manner calculated *and* likely to destroy or seriously damage the relationship of trust and confidence between the employer and employee', on its literal wording, imposes a higher hurdle for a claimant than the disjunctive test set out by Browne-Wilkinson J in *Woods* v *WM Car Services (Peterborough) Ltd* that the 'employer shall not without reasonable and proper cause, conduct itself in a manner calculated *or* likely to destroy or seriously damage the relationship of confidence and trust between employer and employee'. On a literal reading, the phrase as formulated by Lord Steyn imports a two-fold conjunctive test: is the employer's conduct (a) calculated and (b) likely to destroy the trust and confidence in the employment relationship? The claimant must not only show that the employer's conduct was likely to destroy confidence but also that it was calculated (intended) by the employer to do so.
    On the basis, however, of the line of authority cited by Lord Steyn with apparent approval, his use of the word 'and' instead of 'or' in his formulation of the implied term should be regarded as an error of transcription. Lord Steyn cited the *Woods* formulation with apparent approval and it was clear from the remainder of his speech in *BCCI* that he intended to adopt the *Woods* formulation.
    Accordingly, in order to establish a breach of the implied term, it is sufficient for the claimant to show conduct by a respondent which, objectively considered, is likely to seriously undermine the necessary trust and confidence in the employment relationship. This approach was followed by the EAT in *Leeds Dental Team Ltd* v *Rose* [2014] IRLR 8, where it was stated: 'the test does not require a tribunal to make a factual finding as to what the actual intention of the employer was; the employer's subjective intention is irrelevant. If the employer acts in such a way, considered objectively, that his conduct is likely to destroy or seriously damage the relationship of trust and confidence, then he is taken to have the objective intention spoken of…'
3. *RDF Media Group* v *Clements* [2008] IRLR 207 is an important decision on the implied term of trust and confidence. The case concerned a television producer who signed a three-year restrictive covenant with a non-compete clause when the company of which he was a shareholder was sold to RDF. Some 16 months into the agreement, the producer gave notice of termination and indicated that he intended to take employment with a competitor, SMG. RDF placed him on garden leave and brought proceedings seeking an injunction to require Mr Clements to abide by his non-competition obligations for the remainder of the period. Mr Clements counterclaimed. He alleged that in a media briefing a director of the employers made remarks about him which were highly damaging to his reputation, and that he had been constructively dismissed. In the High Court, Bernard Livesey QC accepted that the remarks, 'whether they were true or not', constituted conduct beyond what was reasonable or proper, and amounted to a breach of the

trust and confidence term. However, he went on to find that, prior to the press briefing, the producer had extensive contacts with SMG and had transferred his loyalty to them in breach of the mutual obligation and/or the duty of loyalty and fidelity. On that basis, the judge held that an employee who is himself in repudiatory breach of a mutual obligation cannot rely on the employer's subsequent repudiatory breach so as to claim constructive dismissal. Consequently, it was the employee's own conduct that seriously damaged or destroyed the relationship. This applies even where the employer did not know of the employee's breach until later.

However, this was not the approach adopted by the EAT in *Atkinson* v *Community Gateway Association* [2014] IRLR 834. The claimant resigned from his post as director of resources in a housing association at a time when disciplinary proceedings against him were pending. Subsequently, he lodged a number of employment tribunal claims, including one for unfair constructive dismissal. The employment tribunal struck out the claim as having no reasonable prospect of success because, as a matter of law, the claimant was himself in fundamental breach of contract in that he had breached the employer's email system by sending overtly sexual messages to his lover in another housing association and by seeking to help her obtain a vacant position with the respondent. On appeal, the EAT reviewed the authorities and in particular the decision of the Court of Session in *Aberdeen City Council* v *McNeill (No. 2)* [2014] IRLR 113, which held that there was no basis as a matter of Scots law for holding that an employee could be debarred from bringing a constructive dismissal claim because of their prior conduct. According to EAT's decision in *Atkinson*, this embodies 'the correct principle in English law, namely that while a contract of employment subsists, the obligations which that contract imposes upon the parties continue to subsist'. Thus, the mutual obligations of trust and confidence 'are not suspended or put in abeyance because one party has broken that obligation. If one party commits a fundamental or repudiatory breach of that obligation and the other does not accept that breach as bringing the contract to an end, whether because he does not know about the breach or otherwise, the contract continues.'

It is submitted that the approach adopted in *Atkinson* is to be preferred. In *SG & R Valuation Service Co* v *Boudrais & Ors* [2008] EWHC 1340 QB, Cranston J stated: 'I would be concerned about situations where, if the employee was in repudiatory breach, the employer could take whatever repudiatory breach it wished and the employe[e] could not accept the employe[r]'s repudiation as bringing the employment relationship to an end. That could lead to some very undesirable scenarios in the employment relationship.' Of course, any subsequently discovered fundamental breach on the part of the employee can be taken into account in the assessment of compensation on the basis that, if the employer had known about it, the employee would have been fairly dismissed in any event.

C: Examples of conduct justifying resignation

(i) Assault

Bracebridge Engineering Ltd v Darby
[1990] IRLR 3, Employment Appeal Tribunal

Mrs Darby was physically manhandled into the works manager's office and indecently assaulted by the chargehand and the works manager. The next morning she complained to the general manager but, because the offenders denied everything, no action was taken. Mrs Darby resigned and complained of both sex discrimination and of unfair dismissal. Both applications succeeded and the EAT rejected the employer's appeal.

WOODS J: ... The second limb is the issue of constructive dismissal. The Tribunal dealt with it late in their decision after the findings of the fact about the enquiry. The enquiry was carried out by Miss Reynolds who has some 10 years' experience as the general manager. She saw the applicant, Mrs Darby, on two occasions. First of all on her own and later with the men involved. The Tribunal find that the enquiry was rather superficial. Their summary is to be found in paragraphs 27–29 of the decision. They deal with it in this way. They said:

The applicant goes on to complain of constructive dismissal and that that dismissal was unfair. What she is in effect saying is that following these incidents she made a complaint, but her allegations were not treated seriously and she felt compelled to terminate her employment. This brings us to the interview with Miss Reynolds. The first point is the extent of the applicant's complaint at the time. She complained of being carried by Mr Smith and Mr Daly to Mr Daly's office, and Miss Reynolds was told of the assault there by Mr Daly. The applicant believes that she also mentioned the further assault by Mr Smith in the office. We take the view that even if that were not so, Miss Reynolds did receive complaints of serious misconduct involving both men.

According to the company's own disciplinary procedure (which has been produced) Miss Reynolds ought to have been aware that such an allegation could have led to her suspending Mr Smith and Mr Daly and should in any event have led to a full investigation. The complaints were of assaults with sexual overtones which made them extremely serious. The view that we take is that the enquiry by Miss Reynolds was not an indepth enquiry following serious allegations. It may be that at the end of the day Miss Reynolds felt that in the circumstances she had done her best. We feel that she was too easily persuaded that there was insufficient evidence to substantiate the claims. Had there been a full investigation enquiries might have been made of Mrs Merritt and Tina to whom the applicant immediately complained. It would have been necessary to enquire whether the applicant had been guilty of misconduct in attempting to leave early. As it was Miss Reynolds accepted this to be so without any investigation and that Mr Smith was correct in speaking to the applicant.

We feel at the end of the day the applicant was entitled to say her allegations had not been treated as seriously as they ought. That on the other hand she was being reprimanded without the complaint against her being enquired into. She was entitled to take the view her allegations were being brushed aside.

Then they accept her evidence that at the end of the incident she was disgusted. They felt that she was entitled to be disgruntled and then they go on:

We feel taking into account the particular circumstances including the nature of the events, her long service to the respondents and the inadequacy of the enquiry she was justified in terminating her contract of employment. We find she left because of the conduct of the respondents within s. 55(2)(c) of the Act [now ERA 1996, s. 95(1)(c)]. For these reasons we find the applicant was constructively dismissed and that dismissal was unfair. We uphold her complaint.

They then assessed compensation.

Mr de Mello criticises the directions which the Tribunal gave itself on the issue of constructive dismissal. He points to the phrase referring to the conduct of the respondents and to s. 55(2)(c) of the 1978 Act [now ERA 1996, s. 95(1)(c)]. We hope we sufficiently summarise his argument in this way. He submits that the Tribunal have fallen into the trap which existed before the decision in the Court of Appeal in *Western Excavating* v *Sharp* [1978] IRLR 27 where the Court of Appeal dealt with the two arguments of constructive dismissal: one whether it was based on the reasonable attitude of the employer and the other where it was based on strictly contractual basis. It was resolved in that case that the proper basis was the contractual basis; one therefore needs to look to see what were the terms of the contract and what was the fundamental serious or important term of which there was a breach and which was of sufficient severity that the employee was entitled to say 'that indicates that I cannot properly continue under the terms of the contract', and to accept that repudiation which acceptance needed to be made within a reasonable time. We repeat that principle without looking in detail at the wording of Lord Denning in that case. The submission here is that the Tribunal failed to make the proper approach.

We were told that in fact *Western Excavating* was cited to the Tribunal and in any event it is well known that the learned chairman of this Tribunal is extremely experienced. It may be because in their Reasons they dealt at great length and necessary length with all the factual background and the details of the case that when they came to deal with constructive dismissal they dealt with it in paragraph 30 quite shortly right at the end of the judgment. Had the matter not been preceded by the sexual discrimination problems and the findings of fact, the reasoning might have been set out at greater length. Therefore, looking at these decisions as a whole, although the wording is capable of criticism we feel that the learned chairman, especially as *Western Excavating* was cited to him, in fact was well aware of the principles involved and did apply them. But lest there be any feeling that the matter has not been sufficiently investigated here on behalf of the company, it is right to say this: that the findings of fact were perfectly clear. If the Tribunal had directed itself *in extenso* in law then it would have asked itself whether on the facts as found by the Tribunal the term whereby the mutual obligation, trust, confidence and support and the obligation not to undermine the confidence of the female staff had been breached. In a case of this nature where sexual discrimination and investigation are concerned it is an extremely important one for the female staff.

The findings of fact were that this lady, Mrs Darby, had clearly been greatly upset and suffered shock and trauma as a result of this extremely unpleasant incident in the office of the chargehand. She made her complaint that it had not been treated with the seriousness and the gravity which it should. The Tribunal found on the facts that there had been a breach of that term. Thereafter the question would have been 'had it been accepted as repudiation?' and that followed a week later when Mrs Darby left. Thirdly, they decided it was a reasonable period of time in which she had to make up her mind. It seems again to those sitting with me with experience of situations such as this, that it was evidently reasonable that she should be allowed a week in which to decide about it, the more especially as she might have been waiting for the chairman, Mr Reynolds, to return and he did not return until just after she had left. In the circumstances, therefore, if properly directed we have no doubt that the only conclusion to which the Tribunal could have come on its finding of fact was that there had been a constructive dismissal.

(ii) Abuse

Palmanor Ltd v *Cedron*
[1978] IRLR 303, Employment Appeal Tribunal

The applicant was employed at a night club and, one night, after he had previously arranged to attend later than normal, he was wrongly accused by the night club manager of being late. The manager then became abusive, saying 'You are a big bastard, a big cunt, you are pig-headed, you think you are always right.' When Cedron objected, the manager responded 'I can talk to you any way I like, you big cunt' and 'If you leave me now, don't bother to collect your money, papers or anything else. I'll make sure you don't get a job anywhere in London.' Cedron resigned and his claim that he had been constructively dismissed by reason of this abuse was upheld by the EAT.

SLYNN J: We have considered anxiously the words used in the Decision of this Tribunal, because the Decision of the Court of Appeal in *Western Excavating (ECC) Ltd* v *Sharp* was not given until after the Tribunal had come to their determination. The Tribunal's words which to us appear to be important are that the various matters to which they referred 'rendered this conduct which entitled the applicant to treat himself as dismissed' under the paragraph of the Schedule. It can be said, as Mr Jarvis in his attractive and persuasive argument has said, that this is doing no more than asking the question, was this reasonable conduct? Mr Jarvis points to another reference in the Decision of the Industrial Tribunal where Mr Owide is said to have acted unreasonably. On the other hand it is clear from the judgment of Lord Denning MR that there may be cases where conduct is sufficiently serious to entitle an employee to leave at once. Certainly Lawton LJ gave instances of this kind of behaviour on the part of an employer which would be regarded as so intolerable that an employee could not be expected to put up with it. It seems to us that in a case of this kind the Tribunal is required to ask itself the question whether the conduct was so unreasonable, that it really went beyond the limits of the contract. We observe that in the course of the argument on behalf of the applicant, Mr Cedron, it was submitted that the treatment that the employee was accorded was a repudiation of the contract.

We consider here that the Tribunal has not been shown to have failed to ask itself the right question—that they have, reading their Decision as a whole, approached the matter in the right way and have considered whether the behaviour of Mr Owide was really so intolerable that Mr Cedron could not be expected to stay. It is to be observed that this is not simply a case, like some of the cases which have been cited to us, where merely abusive language was used. Mr Jarvis has cited a number of cases where foul language was used and yet that was held not to justify dismissal. We attach importance to the fact that what Mr Owide said, after Mr Cedron had sought to argue with him that he had no right to speak like that, was 'If you don't like it, you can go', and 'I can talk to you any way I like'; and then he added further abusive language. Moreover Mr Cedron, whose evidence was clearly accepted by the Tribunal, also contends that he was told by Mr Owide 'I'll make sure you don't get another job anywhere in London'. Before the Tribunal it was suggested that the words 'if you leave me now, don't bother to collect your money' indicated that Mr Owide did not intend there to be a dismissal or did not consider that Mr Cedron was in any way no longer part of his staff. But we think, taking the position as a whole, that the Tribunal here cannot be said to have erred in law. Moreover it seems to us that although it is quite right that in these cases Tribunals have to be careful not to attach too great importance to words used in the heat of the moment or in anger, as was stressed in the case of *Chesham Shipping Ltd* v *C.A. Rowe* [1977] IRLR 391, nonetheless there comes a time when the language is such that even if the person using it is in a state of anger, an employee cannot be expected to tolerate it. Accordingly we are of the view that the attack on the Decision that there had been an unfair dismissal, fails.

(iii) Enforcement of mobility clause

United Bank Ltd v *Akhtar*
[1989] IRLR 507, Employment Appeal Tribunal

The applicant had been employed at the employer's branch in Leeds since 1978. In 1987 he was asked, in accordance with a mobility clause in the contract, to move to its branch in Birmingham. He was given very short notice and offered no financial assistance with the move. He refused and claimed constructive dismissal. His claim succeeded before the tribunal, which held that there was an implied term that the mobility clause would be exercised by the employer in such a way as to make it feasible for the employee to comply with the requirement to move branches, i.e. by giving reasonable notice and offering financial assistance. The EAT dismissed the employer's appeal.

KNOX J: As regards the giving of relocation allowance or other allowances, it is of course plain that the bank has a discretion. It seems to us that there is a fallacy in the argument that an employee, by accepting employment on terms which include the grant of such a discretion to an employer, was thereby accepting that he would be under an obligation to move without any financial assistance at all, if the bank thought fit to require such a move.

What Mr Akhtar, by signing the contract, accepted was that there was conferred upon the bank a discretion. What Mr Akhtar did not, in our view, accept, was that the bank, in any particular circumstances, would not necessarily be under an obligation to exercise that discretion. It seems to us that there is a clear distinction between implying a term which negatives a provision which is expressly stated in the contract and implying a term which controls the exercise of a discretion which is expressly conferred in a contract. The first is, of course, impermissible. We were referred to authority for that proposition but authority is hardly needed for it. The second, in our judgment, is not impermissible because there may well be circumstances where discretions are conferred but, nevertheless, they are not unfettered discretions, which can be exercised in a capricious way.

The same acceptance of an implied obligation to cooperate and not to frustrate another party's attempt to perform a contract, would appear to point in the same direction because the facts, as found by the Industrial Tribunal, in our judgment, clearly indicate that the bank was acting or, rather, failing to act, in a manner which frustrated Mr Akhtar's attempts to perform the obligation which he accepted of removing his seat of activities on behalf of the bank from Leeds to Birmingham.

It, therefore, follows that the contract does, in our view, include as a necessary implication, first the requirement to give reasonable notice and, secondly, the requirement so to exercise the discretion to give relocation or other allowances in such a way as not to make performance of the employee's duties impossible.

We see no conflict between that conclusion and the well-established principles to which Mr Lynch drew our attention that terms can only be implied in contract at common law in clearly defined circumstances and according to well-established rules. The first to which we were referred was that no term can be implied which is contrary to or inconsistent with an express term and, upon this aspect of the matter, we have already expressed our view. There is no conflict between a limit on the way in which a discretion can be exercised, on the one hand, and the existence of the discretion on the other.

Secondly, we accept that it is now well-established that implications of a term in a contract, which the parties have reduced to writing, can only be made first to give business efficacy to their contracts; secondly, where the implication is to give effect to an obvious combined intention of the parties; and, thirdly, where it is a necessary addition to the expression of the particular relationship between the parties and an implication which completes their contractual arrangements. Reference was made to *Chitty on Contracts*, paragraph 847, which sums up this branch of the law by saying: 'The touchstone is always necessity and not merely reasonableness'.

Those arguments are aimed at the construction of the contract and the question whether or not an implication can be made in it.

The third principle, which is enunciated by Mr Justice Browne-Wilkinson's judgment, from which I read an extract, is of much wider import and is capable of applying to a series of actions by an employer, which individually can be justified as being within the four corners of the contract because we take it as inherent in what fell from Mr Justice Browne-Wilkinson that there may well be conduct which is either calculated or likely to

destroy or seriously damage the relationship of confidence and trust between employer and employee, which a literal interpretation of the written words of the contract might appear to justify, and it is in this sense that we consider that in the field of employment law it is proper to imply an over-riding obligation in the terms used by Mr Justice Browne-Wilkinson, which is independent of, and in addition to, the literal interpretation of the actions which are permitted to the employer under the terms of the contract. On that aspect of the matter, we have the Industrial Tribunal's finding that the situation here was that the bank's conduct, in which we include inactivity rather than activity, was such that if one looks at it reasonably and sensibly, it was such that the employee could not be expected to put up with it.

White v Reflecting Roadstuds Ltd
[1991] IRLR 331, Employment Appeal Tribunal

Mr White had for four years worked in the despatch department. He was then moved to the highly paid but more onerous mixing department, which move White disliked and asked to be changed. This request was refused and White's attendance at work declined to such extent that he was given a written warning; but the situation did not improve and others in the mixing department resented White's attitude. Accordingly, in October 1988 he was moved to the pressing department, which carried with it a dramatic drop in pay. White resigned a few months later and claimed constructive dismissal. White's contract included the right of the employer to move employees to different departments. The tribunal upheld the claim; following the decision in *United Bank Ltd* v *Akhtar*, it held that the mobility use was subject to implied terms that it would be exercised in a reasonable manner and not in such a way as would result in a reduction in pay. The EAT allowed the employer's appeal and, in so doing, limited the application of the *Akhtar* principle.

WOOD J [referring to *United Bank Ltd* v *Akhtar*]: This case must be examined with care. It is too broad an understanding of the words of Mr Justice Knox to say that the implied term was that the employer should act reasonably. We do not so understand him and indeed, so to find would fly in the face of authority of *Western Excavating* (supra) itself. It would be to reintroduce the reasonable test by the back door. The term found to be implied by Mr Justice Knox and those sitting with him was that an employer when dealing with a mobility clause in a contract of employment should not exercise his discretion in such a way as to prevent his employee from being able to carry out his part of the contract. That is a very different consideration.

■ QUESTION

Is the distinction between *United Bank Ltd* v *Akhtar* and *White* v *Reflecting Roadstuds Ltd* one of substance or merely one of semantics?

NOTES
1. A mobility clause may be unlawfully discriminatory within the meaning of the Sex Discrimination Act (SDA) 1975, s. 77. See *Meade-Hill and National Union of Civil Servants* v *British Council* [1995] IRLR 478, referred to at p. 262 (Chapter 5, Section 4.B(i)).
2. The tribunal will be slow to imply employee acceptance of a unilaterally imposed mobility clause.

Aparau v Iceland Frozen Foods
[1996] IRLR 119, Employment Appeal Tribunal

Following a takeover Aparau, who was employed as a cashier, was given new terms and conditions including a requirement that she may be required 'to move to a different location at any time'. She did not return the form indicating her consent to the change of terms but continued to work for a further 12 months before resigning when asked to work elsewhere. The EAT agreed that she had been constructively dismissed.

HICKS J: ... We deal then with those three ways in which the tribunal reached its conclusion.

As to the first, whether Mrs Aparau accepted the new terms which the respondents, Iceland Frozen Foods, sought to incorporate in the contract, we start from the position that Iceland Foods were not entitled unilaterally to alter the contract, nor indeed do they put their case on that basis. The question is whether there was a fresh contract, whether by way of the old or substitution for it. Clearly, in the traditional analysis of contract formation, the circulation by Iceland Frozen Foods of those terms was an offer Mrs Aparau could accept or reject. The mode of acceptance was in fact specified by Iceland Frozen Foods, the person making the offer, because, as I have said, the form contained in Clause 20 an express acceptance which the employee was invited to sign and return.

We therefore start from the position which is helpfully summarised in *Chitty on Contracts* 27th Edition, paragraph 2–042:

> An offer which requires the acceptance to be expressed or communicated in a certain way can generally be accepted only in that way.

Then at paragraph 2–045:

> Even if the prescribed method of acceptance is not complied with, the offeror would no doubt be bound if he had acquiesced in a different mode of acceptance and had so waived the stipulated mode.

At 2–047:

> An offeree who does nothing in response to an offer is not bound by its terms. This is so even though the offer provides that it can be accepted by silence.

At 2–050:

> The general rule that there can be no acceptance by silence does not mean that an acceptance always has to be given in so many words. An offer can be accepted by conduct; and this is never thought to give rise to any difficulty where the conduct takes the form of a positive act.

So much by way of background and really uncontroversial general principles.

The difficulty in the present case was of course that there was no positive act of acceptance, neither the prescribed act of signing and returning the duplicate form nor any other positive act in the sense of a change, because all that happened was that Mrs Aparau went on working at the same place and being paid exactly as before. The question is whether her doing so, and specifically in the terms of the industrial tribunal's judgment doing so for as long as 12 months, could of itself amount to an acceptance.

There is, in our view, a helpful passage on the application of the general principles to the particular circumstances of an employment contract in the case in this Appeal Tribunal of *Jones* v *Associated Tunnelling Co. Ltd* [1981] IRLR 477, and the relevant passage begins in paragraph 21 of the judgment, where the tribunal was dealing again, with a case where there had been varied terms issued by the employers but not signed by the employee who had simply continued working without outward change of circumstance. Dealing with the situation where an employer issues a statutory statement of terms of conditions of employment, the tribunal say this:

> ... the first of such statements to be issued is often compelling evidence of what terms have in fact been agreed.

That, I interpose, is not strictly applicable here, because it seems from the Industrial Tribunal's findings that the Bejam contract was not simply a statutory statement, but was in fact the contract. However, that does not affect what follows in the judgment in the *Jones* case, which continues:

> But where there are two or more statements which are not in identical terms, the later statement can only be evidence of an agreed variation of the original terms. Such variation may be either express or implied. If, as in the present case, there is no evidence of any oral discussion varying the original terms, the fact that a statement of terms and conditions containing different terms has been issued cannot be compelling evidence of an express oral variation. The most that can be said is that by continuing to work without objection after receiving such further statement, the employee may have impliedly agreed to the variation recorded in the second statement or be estopped from denying it.

In our view, to imply an agreement to vary or to raise an estoppel against the employee on the grounds that he has not objected to a false record by the employers of the terms actually agreed is a course which should be adopted with great caution. If the variation related to a matter which has immediate practical application (e.g. the rate of pay) and the employee continues to work without objection after effect has been given to the variation (e.g. his pay packet has been reduced) then obviously he may well be taken to have impliedly agreed. But where, as in the present case, the variation has no immediate practical effect the position is not the same. It is the view of both members of this tribunal with experience in industrial relations (with which the chairman, without such experience, agrees) that it is asking too much of the ordinary employee to require him either to object to an erroneous statement of his terms of employment having no immediate practical impact on him or to be taken to have assented to the variation. So to hold would involve an unrealistic view of the inclination and ability of the ordinary employee to read and fully understand such statements.

Even if he does read the statement and can understand it, it would be unrealistic of the law to require him to risk a confrontation with his employer on a matter which has no immediate practical impact on the employee. For those reasons, as at present advised, we would not be inclined to imply any assent to a variation from a mere failure by the employee to object to the unilateral alteration by the employer of the terms of employment contained in a statutory statement.

(iv) Removal of privileges

Dryden v Greater Glasgow Health Board

[1992] IRLR 469, Employment Appeal Tribunal

The applicant smoked 30 cigarettes a day and her job was such that she could not leave the premises during the day in order to partake of a cigarette. Until 1991, the employer set aside smoking places. These were withdrawn, and Dryden resigned and claimed constructive dismissal. The EAT agreed that the introduction of a 'no smoking' policy by the employer did not justify the resignation.

LORD COULSFIELD: ... We are not aware of any case concerned with the present situation, in which what is sought is to treat a change in the rules governing behaviour in the place of work which affects all employees as a repudiatory breach of an implied term in relation to one employee. There can, in our view, be no doubt that an employer is entitled to make rules for the conduct of employees in their place of work, as he is entitled to give lawful orders, within the scope of the contract; nor can there be any doubt, in our view, that once it has been held that there is no implied term in the contract which entitled the employee to facilities for smoking, a rule against smoking is, in itself, a lawful rule. The appellant's argument in the present case can only succeed if it is shown that the Industrial Tribunal erred in law. The suggested error is that the Industrial Tribunal failed to approach the question from the point of view of the specific circumstances of the appellant. The Industrial Tribunal did, however, have regard to the circumstances of the appellant, along with all the other circumstances of the case. What the appellant's argument really involves, therefore, is the submission that if an employer introduces a rule which applies to all employees generally, but one with which one employee is unable to comply, the employer must be held to repudiate the contract in relation to that employee. We do not think that any of the terms implied in *United Bank* v *Akhtar* supra or *Woods* supra, or the principles underlying them, go so far as to justify restricting the employer's ability to make and alter working rules to that extent. It may not be difficult to envisage an implied term to the effect that the employer will not change the rules of the workplace in a way which adversely affects an employee or group of employees without reasonable notice or without consultation or, perhaps, without some substantial reason. It is very much more difficult to envisage that, in the absence of a relevant particular term in the contract, it might be held that there was an implied term restricting the employer's right to change the working rules by reference to the views, or even the requirements, of each particular employee. In *Woods* [1982] IRLR 413 in the Court of Appeal Watkins LJ said at p. 416:

Employers must not, in my opinion, be put in a position where, through the wrongful refusal of their employees to accept change, they are prevented from introducing improved business methods in furtherance of seeking success for their enterprise.

The context of that observation was rather different from that of the present case, and Watkins LJ was concerned with a refusal to accept change rather than an inability to do so. Nevertheless, in our view, the same point does apply here, and it is necessary to exercise caution before holding that there are implied contract terms which restrict the employer's power to control what happens in the workplace by making, and altering from time to time, rules for the conduct of the work and the employees. It must also be borne in mind that the term held to be implied in *Woods* [1981] IRLR 347 at p. 349 was that:

... the employers will not, *without reasonable and proper cause*, conduct themselves in a manner calculated to destroy or seriously damage the relationship of confidence and trust...

Where a rule is introduced for a legitimate purpose, the fact that it bears hardly on a particular employee does not, in our view, in itself justify an inference that the employer has acted in such a way as to repudiate the contract with that employee. There may well be rules which are unwelcome to some employees but welcome to others, and a rule banning smoking might be an example of the kind. That being so, we cannot see that there is any justification for the appellant's argument that where the employer introduces a rule which is to apply generally but with which a particular employee cannot comply, it follows that there is repudiatory conduct on the part of the employer.

It has repeatedly been held that the question whether or not there has been repudiatory conduct is one of the particular facts. In the present case, the Industrial Tribunal has considered the whole facts and circumstances very fully, and, in our view, there is no reason to think that they have erred in their assessment of them or fallen into any error of law. It seems to us, indeed, that once the suggestion that there might be an implied term in the appellant's contract, to the effect that she would continue to enjoy some facilities for smoking during working hours, is out of the picture, the result at which the Industrial Tribunal arrived must be the correct one, in the circumstances of this case. The appeal must, therefore, be refused.

(v) Failure to provide or implement proper grievance procedures

W. A. Goold (Pearmak) Ltd v McConnell and another

[1995] IRLR 516, Employment Appeal Tribunal

McConnell was employed by Goold as a jewellery salesman and was paid both a salary and commission. In 1992, changes in selling methods resulted in a significant drop in his salary. There was no established procedure for dealing with McConnell's concerns and he had not been given a written statement of terms and conditions indicating how a grievance should be pursued. McConnell raised his concerns with the manager and an incoming new managing director, and attempted to see the chairman. Nothing was done and he resigned. The EAT agreed that his resignation was justified by the failure to implement a grievance procedure.

MORRISON J: ... It seems to us quite clear that the breach of contract identified by the industrial tribunal related to the way the employees' grievances were dealt with. Their process of reasoning was that Parliament requires employers to provide their employees with written particulars of their employment in compliance with the statutory requirements. Section 3(1) of the Employment Protection (Consolidation) Act 1978 (as amended) [now ERA 1996, s. 3(1)] provides that the written statement required under s.1 of the Act shall include a note specifying, by description or otherwise, to whom and in what manner the employee may apply if he is either dissatisfied with any disciplinary decision or has any other grievance, and an explanation of any further steps in the grievance procedure. It is clear therefore, that Parliament considered that good industrial relations requires employers to provide their employees with a method of dealing with grievances in a proper and timeous fashion. This is also consistent, of course, with the codes of practice. That being so, the industrial tribunal was entitled, in our judgment, to conclude that there was an implied term in the contract of employment that the employers would reasonably and promptly afford a reasonable opportunity to their employees to obtain redress of any grievance they may have. It was in our judgment rightly conceded at the industrial tribunal that such could be a breach of contract.

Further, it seems to us that the right to obtain redress against a grievance is fundamental for very obvious reasons. The working environment may well lead to employees experiencing difficulties, whether because of the physical conditions under which they are required to work, or because of a breakdown in human relationships, which can readily occur when people of different backgrounds and sensitivities are required to work together, often under pressure.

There may well be difficulties arising out of the way that authority and control is exercised—sometimes by people who themselves have insufficient experience and training to exercise such power wisely.

It is of course regrettable, in this case, that the employers have failed to comply with their statutory obligations, or to appreciate the need to provide a specific mechanism whereby a genuine sense of grievance can be ventilated and redressed. Instead, the employees in this case were fobbed off, and Mr Maloney plainly felt his authority was threatened by the employees' wish to speak to the chairman. The provision of a sensible grievance procedure would cost nothing and may well have avoided this litigation.

NOTES

1. Employees will lose the right to bring claims for constructive dismissal if there is a delay in resigning in the face of the employer's repudiation. The employee will be deemed to have affirmed the contract. To avoid this risk, employees should come to a speedy decision as to whether to resign, or, if they do continue to work for a period post-repudiation, make it clear that they do not accept the employer's conduct and are working under protest. In the latter case, the employee cannot continue to work under protest indefinitely and must make a decision whether to stay on or leave within a reasonable period.

In *Cockram* v *Air Products plc* [2014] IRLR 672, the claimant was employed as director of business information. His contract required him to give three months' notice of termination. He resigned promptly because of his treatment by his line manager and the way a grievance concerning this was handled. However, for his own financial reasons, his resignation letter gave seven months' notice of termination. This led to an employment judge striking out his constructive dismissal claim on grounds that the claimant had affirmed the contract. On appeal, it was argued that there is no limit on the length of notice which an employee can give for the purposes of s. 95(1)(c) and that conduct post-resignation cannot be treated as affirmation. However, the EAT dismissed the claimant's appeal, holding that it is possible for an employee to affirm their contract even after they have resigned because of a repudiatory breach. The EAT stated:

> Where an employee resigns on notice and despite doing so, his conduct is inconsistent with saying that he has not affirmed the contract, that conduct must be capable of consideration by a fact-finding tribunal. Where he gives notice in excess of the notice required by his contract, he is offering additional performance of the contract to that which is required by it. That additional performance may be consistent only with affirmation of the contract. It is a question of fact and degree whether in such circumstances his conduct is properly to be regarded as affirmation of the contract.

In *Weathersfield Ltd* v *Sargent* [1999] IRLR 94, the CA held that, as a matter of law, there is no absolute requirement on the employee to inform the employer that he is leaving because of the employer's repudiatory act. The test is one of causation, i.e. was the employer's conduct a causal factor in prompting the employee's resignation?

Moreover, the contractual breach by the employer does not have to be the primary or effective cause of the resignation. In *Wright* v *North Ayrshire Council* [2014] IRLR 4, the issue before the EAT was what, in determining a claim for constructive dismissal where more than one reason played a part in the employee's resignation, is the correct test of whether the contractual breach by the employer was 'the effective cause' of the employee's resignation? In this case, the employment tribunal found that the employer had committed breaches going to the root of the claimant's contract, but that the claimant also had caring responsibilities, and that it was these that were the effective cause of the resignation. Allowing the claimant's appeal, the EAT stated that the correct test is whether the repudiatory breach 'played a part in the resignation' and that 'where there is more than one reason why an employee leaves a job the correct approach is to examine whether any of them is a response to the breach, not to see which amongst them is the effective cause.'

2. A dismissed employee is not entitled to bring a common law claim for damages on the basis that the dismissal breached the implied term of mutual trust and confidence. Such a claim would circumvent the statutory unfair dismissal regime and falls within the so-called *Johnson* exclusion zone. In *Gebremariam* v *Ethiopian Airlines Enterprise* [2014] IRLR 354, the EAT held that the *Johnson* exclusion zone does not apply to an unfair constructive dismissal claim.

SECTION 4: FIXED-TERM, 'TASK', AND CONTINGENT CONTRACTS

EMPLOYMENT RIGHTS ACT 1996

95. Circumstances in which an employee is dismissed

(1) For the purposes of this Part an employee is dismissed by his employer if (and, subject to subsection (2) and section 96, only if)—

...

(b) he is employed under a limited-term contract and that contract terminates by virtue of the limiting event without being renewed under the same contract…

235. Other definitions

(2A) For the purposes of this Act a contract of employment is a 'limited-term contract' if—

(a) the employment under the contract is not intended to be permanent, and

(b) provision is accordingly made in the contract for it to terminate by virtue of a limiting event.

(2B) In this Act, 'limiting event', in relation to a contract of employment means—

(a) in the case of a contract for a fixed-term, the expiry of the term,

(b) in the case of a contract made in contemplation of the performance of a specific task, the performance of the task, and

(c) in the case of a contract which provides for its termination on the occurrence of an event (or the failure of an event to occur), the occurrence of the event (or the failure of the event to occur).

NOTES

1. Since its introduction, the statutory framework of unfair dismissal has regarded the expiry of a fixed-term contract as a dismissal. The protection offered to those on fixed-term contracts represented a limited recognition on the part of those who drafted the legislation that any other approach would invite employers to employ large sections of their workforce under such arrangements and so avoid liability for unfair dismissal and redundancy payments.

   However, this protection was limited for three reasons. First, a dismissal of an employee who comes to an end of a 'temporary' contract may, in the circumstances be held to be fair as 'some other substantial reason'. Second, s. 197 of the ERA 1996 stated that, where an employee was employed on a fixed term of a year or more, he or she could agree in writing to exclude any right to claim unfair dismissal and, if employed for two years, any right to redundancy payments also should the contract not be renewed at completion of its term. Finally, the courts drew a distinction between a fixed-term contract, deemed to be a dismissal under the legislation, and a contract for the completion of a particular task at the end of which there is no dismissal. A 'task' contract is discharged by performance of the particular task and cannot give rise to a dismissal—for example, a seafarer engaged for a particular voyage or a worker hired to paint a house (the leading cases on the definition of a fixed-term contract are: *BBC* v *Dixon* [1977] IRLR 337, CA; *Wiltshire County Council* v *NATFHE and Guy* [1980] IRLR 198, CA). In *Brown* v *Knowsley Borough Council* [1986] IRLR 102, EAT the distinction between a fixed-term contract and a contract to perform a particular task was extended to cover contracts terminable on the happening or non-happening of a future event. In that case, a further education college lecturer, having been previously employed under a number of fixed-term contracts, was then employed under a one-year temporary contract from 1 September 1983 which was expressed to last for only so long as sufficient funds were provided by the Manpower Services Commission (MSC) to support the course which she taught. On 3 August 1984, she was given written notice that, as MSC funds had ceased to be available, her employment would terminate on 31 August 1984. The applicant's claim for a redundancy payment was rejected by the employment tribunal and the EAT on the basis that there had been no dismissal and that her contract was terminable on the happening or non-happening of a future event—the withdrawal of MSC sponsorship.

   In *Fairness at Work* (Cmnd. 3968), May 1998, para. 3.13, the Government undertook to consider possible options for changing the law allowing employees with fixed-term contracts to waive their right to claim unfair dismissal and to receive statutory redundancy payments. Subsequently, s. 18(1) of the Employment Relations Act 1999 repealed parts of the ERA 1996, s. 197 which permitted agreements to exclude unfair dismissal claims in fixed-term contracts, and so such agreements are void. Finally, the possibility of agreeing a waiver of redundancy payments claims was closed down by the Fixed-Term Employees (Prevention of Less Favourable Treatment) Regulations 2002 (SI 2002/2034). Any redundancy waiver that is included in a fixed-term contract which is agreed, extended, or renewed after 1 October 2002 will be invalid.

   The regulations also amended the ERA 1996, s. 95 (extracted earlier) so as to create a broader protection than that previously offered to those employees on fixed-term contracts. As can be seen from the definition of the new concept of a 'limited-term' contract in the ERA 1996, s. 235, as amended, employees engaged on fixed-term, task and contingent contracts are now covered.

2. In *Allen* v *National Australia Group Europe Ltd* [2004] IRLR 847, the EAT had to construe the Fixed-Term Employees (Prevention of Less Favourable Treatment) Regulations 2002. The question

was whether a contract which is specified to terminate on a fixed date is a fixed-term contract for the purposes of the regulations, even if it contains a further provision allowing it to be terminated earlier by notice. The EAT ruled that the ability of the parties to bring the contract to an end at an earlier date does not make the contract anything other than one for a fixed term. The EAT held that what is envisaged by the regulations is a provision relating to the termination of the relationship 'in the normal course'. Provision for earlier notice does not destroy the original intention of such a contract that the parties would see through the fixed term, unless and until some event which was not in the normal course occurred. This interpretation is in line with the approach adopted by the Court of Appeal in *BBC* v *Dixon* in relation to the definition as it applied to unfair dismissal provisions.

SECTION 5: REMEDIES

A: Damages

As stated earlier, as long as reasonable notice is given, the common law permits termination of a contract of employment. Accordingly, it is only when the employer fails to give the required notice or wages in lieu of notice that the common law action of wrongful dismissal will lie. Even then, the damages will be limited to the monies properly due during the period of notice that should have been given together with monies to cover the period which, in the opinion of the court, would have elapsed for the employer to carry out proper dismissal procedures. See *Dietman* v *London Borough of Brent* [1987] IRLR 146 and *Boyo* v *London Borough of Lambeth* [1995] IRLR 50 (Section 1.B(ii)).

The limited nature of damages for wrongful dismissal was determined by the House of Lords in *Addis* v *Gramophone Co. Ltd* [1909] AC 488. For over a century, this judgment has been accepted as authority for the proposition that damages for wrongful dismissal cannot include compensation (i) for the manner of dismissal, i.e. for injured feelings; or (ii) for loss an employee might sustain from the fact that the dismissal itself makes it more difficult for him or her to obtain future employment. The rationale for this approach is that since the employer could, at any time, terminate the contract lawfully by giving notice or pay in lieu of notice, this is all that the employee has lost through being wrongfully dismissed.

As a result, the dismissed employee will find the remedies offered by an application to the tribunal under the ERA 1996 based on unfair dismissal more attractive than a wrongful dismissal claim. However, the common law action remains attractive to the fixed-term employee and, as we shall see, the employee who is seeking a remedy other than damages.

McMullen has argued ((1997) 26 ILJ 246, at p. 246) that:

> the twin rules [established in *Addis*] are clearly inconsistent with the modern view of the duties owed by employers to employees. As Lord Slynn observed in *Spring* v *Guardian Assurance* [1994] 3 All ER 129, the law today imposes 'far greater duties' on employers than in the past 'to care for the physical, financial and even psychological welfare of the employee'. But while courts in other jurisdictions have, from time to time, circumvented or even ignored *Addis* (see *Brown* v *Waterloo Regional Board of Commissioners of Police* (1982) 136 DLR (3d) 49; *Pilon* v *Peugeot Canada Ltd* (1980) 114 DLR (3d) 378; *Ogilvy and Mather (New Zealand)* v *Turner* [1996] 1 NZLR 641), UK courts have been bound by this antiquated House of Lords authority (see *Shove* v *Downs Surgical plc* [1984] ICR 532, 542; *Bliss* v *South East Thames Regional Health Authority* [1987] ICR 700).

Bliss v South East Thames Regional Health Authority
[1987] ICR 700, Court of Appeal

The plaintiff was employed as a consultant orthopaedic surgeon and had written a number of angry and offensive letters to a colleague with whom he was in dispute. The tone and content of these letters raised some doubt in the employer's mind about the plaintiff's ability to do his job.

The employer asked the plaintiff to undergo a psychiatric examination but this request was refused. The employer suspended the plaintiff in May 1980 and disciplinary proceedings were brought against him but these were discontinued in July 1981. Subsequently, the employer gave the plaintiff until August 1981 to return to work.

By solicitor's letter dated 25 September 1981, the plaintiff claimed that, by its conduct, the employer had repudiated the contract and that the plaintiff accepted the repudiation. The plaintiff brought an action for breach of contract, seeking damages for frustration and mental distress. The judge allowed the plaintiff the sum of £2,000 under this head. The employer's appeal against this award was allowed by the Court of Appeal.

DILLON LJ: It remains to consider the final point on the cross-appeal, viz. the validity of the judge's award of £2,000 with interest by way of general damages for frustration and mental distress. In making such an award, the judge considered that he was justified by the decision of Lawson J in *Cox* v *Philips Industries Ltd* [1976] ICR 138. With every respect to them, however, the views of Lawson J in that case and of the judge in the present case are on this point, in my judgment, wrong.

The general rule laid down by the House of Lords in *Addis* v *Gramophone Co. Ltd* [1909] AC 488 is that where damages fall to be assessed for breach of contract rather than in tort it is not permissible to award general damages for frustration, mental distress, injured feelings or annoyance occasioned by the breach. Modern thinking tends to be that the amount of damages recoverable for a wrong should be the same whether the cause of action is laid in contract or in tort. But in the *Addis* case Lord Loreburn regarded the rule that damages for injured feelings cannot be recovered in contract for wrongful dismissal as too inveterate to be altered, and Lord James of Hereford supported his concurrence in the speech of Lord Loreburn by reference to his own experience at the Bar.

There are exceptions now recognised where the contract which has been broken was itself a contract to provide peace of mind or freedom from distress: see *Jarvis* v *Swans Tours Ltd* [1973] QB 233 and *Heywood* v *Wellers* [1976] QB 446. Those decisions do not however cover this present case.

In *Cox* v *Philips Industries Ltd* [1976] ICR 138 Lawson J took the view that damages for distress, vexation and frustration, including consequent ill-health, could be recovered for breach of a contract of employment if it could be said to have been in the contemplation of the parties that the breach would cause such distress etc. For my part, I do not think that that general approach is open to this court unless and until the House of Lords has reconsidered its decision in the *Addis* case.

NOTE: In the next case, we see the House of Lords side-stepping the antiquated precedent of *Addis* on the basis that it was decided before the development of the implied term of trust and confidence. In doing so, the House of Lords established the general principle that damages are available where breach of the duty of trust and confidence makes it more difficult for an employee to obtain further employment.

Malik v BCCI SA (in liq.)
[1997] IRLR 462, House of Lords

Mr Malik and Mr Mahmud were formerly employed by the Bank of Credit and Commerce International (BCCI) for periods of 16 and 12 years respectively. Both were dismissed on grounds of redundancy by the provisional liquidators following the bank's collapse. Neither had since been able to obtain employment in the financial services sector.

Mr Malik and Mr Mahmud claimed 'stigma' damages for pecuniary loss allegedly caused by the bank's breach of an implied contractual obligation of trust and confidence. They maintained that their mere association with the bank at the moment of its liquidation and the alleged fraudulent practices which subsequently came to light put them at a disadvantage in the employment market, even though they were personally innocent of any wrongdoing. The liquidators rejected the claims.

The employees appealed against that decision. Mr Justice Evans-Lombe decided as a preliminary issue that the evidence failed to disclose a reasonable cause of action or a sustainable claim for damages. The Court of Appeal affirmed that decision, holding that, in reality, the damages claimed were for injury to the employees' previously existing reputations and therefore, in accordance with the general principles established in *Addis* v *Gramophone Co. Ltd* [1995] IRLR 375, they were not legally recoverable. Mr Malik and Mr Mahmud had their appeals allowed by the House of Lords.

LORD NICHOLLS OF BIRKENHEAD:... In the Court of Appeal and in your Lordships' House the parties were agreed that the contracts of employment of these two former employees each contained an implied term to the effect that the bank would not, without reasonable and proper cause, conduct itself in a manner likely to destroy or seriously damage the relationship of confidence and trust between employer and employee. Argument proceeded on this footing, and ranged round the type of conduct and other circumstances which could or could not constitute a breach of this implied term. The submissions embraced questions such as the following: whether the trust-destroying conduct must be directed at the employee, either individually or as part of a group; whether an employee must know of the employer's trust-destroying conduct while still employed; and whether the employee's trust must actually be undermined. Furthermore, and at the heart of this case, the submissions raised an important question on the damages recoverable for breach of the implied term, with particular reference to the decisions in *Addis* v *Gramophone Co. Ltd* [1909] AC 488 and *Withers* v *General Theatre Corporation Ltd* [1933] 2 KB 536.

A dishonest and corrupt business

These questions are best approached by focusing first on the particular conduct of which complaint is made. The bank operated its business dishonestly and corruptly. On the assumed facts, this was not a case where one or two individuals, however senior, were behaving dishonestly. Matters had gone beyond this. They had reached the point where the bank itself could properly be identified with the dishonesty. This was a dishonest business, a corrupt business.

It is against this background that the position of an innocent employee has to be considered. In my view, when an innocent employee of the bank learned the true nature of the bank's business, from whatever source, he was entitled to say: 'I wish to have nothing more to do with this organisation. I am not prepared to help this business, by working for it. I am leaving at once.' This is my intuitive response in the case of all innocent employees of the business, from the most senior to the most junior, from the most long-serving to the most recently joined. No one could be expected to have to continue to work with and for such a company against his wish.

This intuitive response is no more than a reflection of what goes without saying in any ordinary contract of employment, namely, that in agreeing to work for an employer the employee, whatever his status, cannot be taken to have agreed to work in furtherance of a dishonest business. This is as much true of a doorkeeper or cleaner as a senior executive or branch manager.

An implied obligation

Two points can be noted here. First, as a matter of legal analysis, the innocent employee's entitlement to leave at once must derive from the bank being in breach of a term of the contract of employment which the employee is entitled to treat as a repudiation by the bank of its contractual obligations. That is the source of his right to step away from the contract forthwith.

In other words, and this is the necessary corollary of the employee's right to leave at once, the bank was under an implied obligation to its employees not to conduct a dishonest or corrupt business. This implied obligation is no more than one particular aspect of the portmanteau, general obligation not to engage in conduct likely to undermine the trust and confidence required if the employment relationship is to continue in the manner the employment contract implicitly envisages.

Second, I do not accept the liquidators' submission that the conduct of which complaint is made must be targeted in some way at the employee or a group of employees. No doubt that will often be the position, perhaps usually so. But there is no reason in principle why this must always be so. The trust and confidence required in the employment relationship can be undermined by an employer, or indeed an employee, in many different ways. I can see no justification for the law giving the employee a remedy if the unjustified trust-destroying conduct occurs in some ways but refusing a remedy if it occurs in others. The conduct must, of course, impinge on the relationship in the sense that, looked at objectively, it is likely to destroy or seriously damage the degree of trust and confidence the employee is reasonably entitled to have in his employer. That requires one to look at all the circumstances.

Breach

The objective standard just mentioned provides the answer to the liquidators' submission that unless the employee's confidence is actually undermined there is no breach. A breach occurs when the proscribed conduct takes place: here, operating a dishonest and corrupt business. Proof of a subjective loss of confidence in the employer is not an essential element of the breach, although the time when the employee learns of the misconduct and his response to it may affect his remedy.

Remedies: (1) acceptance of breach as repudiation

The next step is to consider the consequences which flow from the bank being in breach of its obligation to its innocent employees by operating a corrupt banking business. The first remedy of an employee has already been noted. The employee may treat the bank's conduct as a repudiatory breach, entitling him to leave. He is not compelled to leave. He may choose to stay. The extent to which staying would be more than an election to remain, and would be a waiver of the breach for all purposes, depends on the circumstances.

I need say no more about waiver in the present case. The assumed facts do not state whether the appellants first learned of the corrupt nature of BCCI after their dismissal on 3 October 1991, or whether they acquired this knowledge earlier, in the interval of three months between the appointment of the provisional liquidators on 5 July 1991 and 3 October 1991. If anything should turn on this, the matter can be investigated further in due course.

In the nature of things, the remedy of treating the conduct as a repudiatory breach, entitling the employee to leave, can only avail an employee who learns of the facts while still employed. If he does not discover the facts while his employment is still continuing, perforce this remedy is not open to him. But this does not mean he has no remedy. In the ordinary course breach of a contractual term entitles the innocent party to damages.

Remedies: (2) damages

Can an employee recover damages for breach of the trust and confidence term when he first learns of the breach after he has left the employment? The answer to this question is inextricably bound up with the further question of what damages are recoverable for a breach of this term. In turn, the answer to this further question is inextricably linked with one aspect of the decision in *Addis* v *Gramophone Co. Ltd* [1909] AC 488.

At first sight, it seems almost a contradiction in terms that an employee can suffer recoverable loss if he first learns of the trust-destroying conduct after the employment contract has already ended for other reasons. But of the many forms which trust destroying conduct may take, some may have continuing adverse financial effects on an employee even after his employment has ceased. In such a case, the fact that the employee only learned of the employer's conduct after the employment had ended ought not, in principle, to be a bar to recovery. If it were otherwise, an employer who conceals a breach would be better placed than an employer who does not.

Premature termination losses

This proposition calls for elaboration. The starting point is to note that the purpose of the trust and confidence implied term is to facilitate the proper functioning of the contract. If the employer commits a breach of the term, and in consequence the contract comes to an end prematurely, the employee loses the benefits he should have received had the contract run its course until it expired or was duly terminated. In addition to financial benefits such as salary and commission and pension rights, the losses caused by the premature termination of the contract ('the premature termination losses') may include other promised benefits, for instance, a course of training, or publicity for an actor or pop star. Prima facie, and subject always to established principles of mitigation and so forth, the dismissed employee can recover damages to compensate him for these promised benefits lost to him in consequence of the premature termination of the contract.

It follows that premature termination losses cannot be attributable to a breach of the trust and confidence term if the contract is terminated for other reasons, for instance, for redundancy or if the employee leaves of his own volition. Since the trust-destroying conduct did not bring about the premature termination of the contract, ex hypothesi the employee did not sustain any loss of pay and so forth by reason of the breach of the trust and confidence term. That is the position in the present case.

Continuing financial losses

Exceptionally, however, the losses suffered by an employee as a result of a breach of the trust and confidence term may not consist of, or be confined to, loss of pay and other premature termination losses. Leaving aside injured feelings and anxiety, which are not the basis of the claim in the present case, an employee may find himself worse off financially than when he entered into the contract. The most obvious example is conduct, in breach of the trust and confidence term, which prejudicially affects an employee's future employment prospects. The conduct may diminish the employee's attractiveness to future employers.

The loss in the present case is of this character. BCCI promised, in an implied term, not to conduct a dishonest or corrupt business. The promised benefit was employment by an honest employer. This benefit did not materialise. Proof that Mr Mahmud and Mr Malik were handicapped in the labour market in consequence of BCCI's corruption may not be easy, but that is an assumed fact for the purpose of this preliminary issue.

There is here an important point of principle. Are financial losses of this character, which I shall call 'continuing financial losses', recoverable for breach of the trust and confidence term? This is the crucial point in the present appeals. In my view, if it was reasonably foreseeable that a particular type of loss of this character was a serious possibility, and loss of this type is sustained in consequence of a breach, then in principle damages in respect of the loss should be recoverable.

In the present case the agreed facts make no assumption, either way, about whether the appellants' handicap in the labour market was reasonably foreseeable by the bank. On this there must be scope for argument. I would not regard the absence of this necessary ingredient from the assumed facts as a sufficient reason for refusing to permit the former employees' claims to proceed further.

The contrary argument of principle is that since the purpose of the trust and confidence term is to preserve the employment relationship and to enable that relationship to prosper and continue, the losses recoverable for breach should be confined to those flowing from the premature termination of the relationship. Thus, a breach of the term should not be regarded as giving rise to recoverable losses beyond those I have described as premature termination losses. In this way, the measure of damages would be commensurate with, and not go beyond, the scope of the protection the trust and confidence term is intended to provide for the employee.

This is an unacceptably narrow evaluation of the trust and confidence term. Employers may be under no common law obligation, through the medium of an implied contractual term of general application, to take steps to improve their employees' future job prospects. But failure to improve is one thing, positively to damage is another. Employment, and job prospects, are matters of vital concern to most people. Jobs of all descriptions are less secure than formerly, people change jobs more frequently, and the job market is not always buoyant. Everyone knows this. An employment contract creates a close personal relationship, where there is often a disparity of power between the parties. Frequently the employee is vulnerable. Although the underlying purpose of the trust and confidence term is to protect the employment relationship, there can be nothing unfairly onerous or unreasonable in requiring an employer who breaches the trust and confidence term to be liable if he thereby causes continuing financial loss of a nature that was reasonably foreseeable. Employers must take care not to damage their employees' future employment prospects, by harsh and oppressive behaviour or by any other form of conduct which is unacceptable today as falling below the standards set by the implied trust and confidence term.

This approach brings one face to face with the decision in the wrongful dismissal case of *Addis* v *Gramophone Co. Ltd* [1909] AC 488. It does so, because the measure of damages recoverable for breach of the trust and confidence term cannot be decided without having some regard to a comparable question which arises regarding the measure of damages recoverable for wrongful dismissal. An employee may elect to treat a sufficiently serious breach of the trust and confidence term as discharging him from the contract and, hence, as a constructive dismissal. The damages in such a case ought, in principle, to be the same as they would be if the employer had expressly dismissed the employee. The employee should be no better off, or worse off, in the two situations. In principle, so far as the recoverability of continuing financial losses are concerned, there is no basis for distinguishing (a) wrongful dismissal following a breach of the trust and confidence term, (b) constructive dismissal following a breach of the trust and confidence term, and (c) a breach of the trust and confidence term which only becomes known after the contract has ended for other reasons. The present case is in the last category, but a principled answer cannot be given for cases in this category without considering the other two categories from which it is indistinguishable.

Addis v *Gramophone Co.*

Against this background I turn to the much-discussed case of *Addis* v *Gramophone Co. Ltd* [1909] AC 488. Mr Addis, it will be recalled, was wrongfully and contumeliously dismissed from his post as the defendant's manager in Calcutta. At trial he was awarded damages exceeding the amount of his salary for the period of notice to which he was entitled. The case is generally regarded as having decided, echoing the words of Lord Loreburn LC, at p. 491, that an employee cannot recover damages for the manner in which the wrongful dismissal took place, for injured feelings or for any loss he may sustain from the fact that his having been dismissed of itself makes it more difficult for him to obtain fresh employment. In particular, *Addis* is generally understood to have decided that any loss suffered by the adverse impact on the employee's chances of obtaining alternative employment is to be excluded from an assessment of damages for wrongful dismissal: see, for instance, *O'Laoire* v *Jackel International Ltd (No. 2)* [1991] IRLR 170, following earlier authorities; in Canada, the decision of the Supreme Court in *Vorvis* v *Insurance Corporation of British Columbia* [1989] 58 DLR (4th) 193, 205; and, in New Zealand, *Vivian* v *Coca-Cola Export Corporation* [1984] 2 NZLR 289, 292; *Whelan* v *Waitaki Meats Ltd* [1991] 2 NZLR 74, where Gallen J disagreed with the decision in *Addis*; and *Brandt* v *Nixdorf Computer Ltd* [1991] 3 NZLR 750.

For present purposes, I am not concerned with the exclusion of damages for injured feelings. The present case is concerned only with financial loss. The report of the facts in *Addis* is sketchy. Whether Mr Addis sought to prove that the manner of his dismissal caused him financial loss over and above his premature termination losses is not clear beyond a peradventure. If he did, it is surprising that their Lordships did not address this important feature more specifically. Instead there are references to injured feelings, the fact of dismissal of itself, aggravated damages, exemplary damages amounting to damages for defamation, damages being compensatory and not punitive, and the irrelevance of motive. The dissenting speech of Lord Collins was based on competence to award exemplary or vindictive damages.

However, Lord Loreburn's observations were framed in quite general terms, and he expressly disagreed with the suggestion of Lord Coleridge CJ in *Maw* v *Jones* [1890] 25 QBD 107, 108, to the effect that an assessment of damages might take into account the greater difficulty which an apprentice dismissed with a slur on his character might have in obtaining other employment. Similarly general observations were made by Lord James of Hereford, Lord Atkinson, Lord Gorell and Lord Shaw of Dunfermline.

In my view, these observations cannot be read as precluding the recovery of damages where the manner of dismissal involved a breach of the trust and confidence term and this caused financial loss. *Addis* v *Gramophone Co. Ltd* was decided in the days before this implied term was adumbrated. Now that this term exists and is normally implied in every contract of employment, damages for its breach should be assessed in accordance with ordinary contractual principles. This is as much true if the breach occurs before or in connection with dismissal as at any other time.

This approach would accord, in its result, with the approach adopted by courts and tribunals in unfair dismissal cases when exercising the statutory jurisdiction… to award an amount of compensation which the court or tribunal considers 'just and reasonable' in all the circumstances. Writing on a clean slate, the courts have interpreted this as enabling awards to include compensation in respect of the manner and circumstances of dismissal if these would give rise to a risk of financial loss by, for instance, making the employee less acceptable to potential employers see ss. 123 and 124 of the Employment Rights Act 1996 and *Norton Tool Co. Ltd* v *Tewson* [1972] IRLR 86.

I do not believe this approach gives rise to artificiality. On the contrary, the trust and confidence term is a useful tool, well established now in employment law. At common law damages are awarded to compensate for *wrongful* dismissal. Thus, loss which an employee would have suffered even if the dismissal had been after due notice is irrecoverable, because such loss does not derive from the wrongful element in the dismissal. Further, it is difficult to see how the mere fact of wrongful dismissal, rather than dismissal after due notice, could of itself handicap an employee in the labour market. All this is in line with *Addis*. But the manner and circumstances of the dismissal, as measured by the standards of conduct now identified in the implied trust and confidence term, may give rise to such a handicap. The law would be blemished if this were not recognised today. There now exists the separate cause of action whose absence Lord Shaw of Dunfermline noted with 'a certain regret': see *Addis* v *Gramophone Co. Ltd* [1909] AC 488, 504. The trust and confidence term has removed the cause for his regret.

…

Furthermore, the fact that the breach of contract injures the plaintiff's reputation in circumstances where no claim for defamation would lie is not, by itself, a reason for excluding from the damages recoverable for breach of contract compensation for financial loss which on ordinary principles would be recoverable. An award of damages for breach of contract has a different objective: compensation for financial loss suffered by a breach of contract, not compensation for injury to reputation.

Sometimes, in practice, the distinction between damage to reputation and financial loss can become blurred. Damage to the reputation of professional persons, or persons carrying on a business, frequently causes financial loss. Nonetheless, the distinction is fundamentally sound, and when awarding damages for breach of contract courts take care to confine the damages to their proper ambit: making good financial loss. In *Herbert Clayton and Jack Waller Ltd* v *Oliver* [1930] AC 209, 220, when considering an award of damages to an actor who should have been billed to appear at the London Hippodrome, Lord Buckmaster regarded loss of publicity rather than loss of reputation as the preferable expression. In *Aerial Advertising Co.* v *Batchelor's Peas Ltd (Manchester)* [1938] 2 All ER 788, 796–797, where aerial advertising ('Eat Batchelor's Peas') took place during Armistice Day services, Atkinson

J was careful to confine damages to the financial loss flowing from public boycotting of the defendant's goods and to exclude damages for loss of reputation. Lord Denning MR drew the same distinction in *GKN Centrax Gears Ltd* v *Matbro Ltd* [1976] 2 Lloyd's Rep 555, 573.

Breach of contract and existing reputation

The second submission concerning reputation was that the appellants' claims for damages to their existing reputations is barred by the decision of the Court of Appeal in *Withers* v *General Theatre Corporation Ltd* [1933] 2 KB 536.

There is an acute conflict between this decision and the earlier decision, also of the Court of Appeal, in *Marbe* v *George Edwardes (Daly's Theatre) Ltd* [1928] 1 KB 269. In *Marbe*, clear views were expressed that when assessing damages for loss flowing from a failure to provide promised publicity, the loss may include loss to existing reputation: see Bankes LJ at p. 281 and Atkin LJ at p. 288. In *Withers*, equally clear views were firmly stated to the contrary by all three members of the court: see Scrutton LJ at p. 547, Greer LJ at p. 554 and Romer LJ at p. 556. I have to say that, faced with the embarrassing necessity to choose, I prefer the views expressed in *Marbe*. They accord better with principle. Loss of promised publicity might cause an actor financial loss, for two reasons: first, through loss of opportunity to enhance his professional reputation and, secondly, his absence from the theatre scene might actually damage his existing professional reputation. If as a matter of fact an actor does suffer financial loss under both heads, and that is a question of evidence, I can see no reason why the law should deny recovery of damages in respect of the second head of loss.

Conclusion

For these reasons I would allow these appeals. The agreed set of assumed facts discloses a good cause of action. Unlike the courts below, this House is not bound by the observations in *Addis* v *Gramophone Co. Ltd* [1909] AC 488 regarding irrecoverability of loss flowing from the manner of dismissal, or by the decision in *Withers* v *General Theatre Corporation Ltd* [1933] 2 KB 536.

I add some cautionary footnotes, having in mind the assumed facts in the present case. First, when considering these appeals I have been particularly conscious of the potential difficulties which claims of this sort may present for liquidators. I am conscious that the outcome of the present appeals may be seen by some as opening the door to speculative claims, to the detriment of admitted creditors. Claims of handicap in the labour market, and the other ingredients of the cause of action now under consideration, may give rise to lengthy and costly investigations and, ultimately, litigation. If the claims eventually fail, liquidators may well be unable to recover their costs from the former employees. The expense of liquidations, and the time they often take, are matters already giving rise to concern. I am aware of the dangers here, but it could not be right to allow 'floodgates' arguments of this nature to stand in the way of claims which, as a matter of ordinary legal principle, are well founded. After all, if the former employee's claim is well founded in fact as well as in law, he himself is a creditor and ought to be admitted as such.

Secondly, one of the assumed facts in the present case is that the employer was conducting a dishonest and corrupt business. I would like to think this will rarely happen in practice. Thirdly, there are many circumstances in which an employee's reputation may suffer from his having been associated with an unsuccessful business, or an unsuccessful department within a business. In the ordinary way this will not found a claim of the nature made in the present case, even if the business or department was run with gross incompetence. A key feature in the present case is the assumed fact that the business was dishonest or corrupt. Finally, although the implied term that the business will not be conducted dishonestly is a term which avails all employees, proof of consequential handicap in the labour market may well be much more difficult for some classes of employees than others. An employer seeking to employ a messenger, for instance, might be wholly unconcerned by an applicant's former employment in a dishonest business, whereas he might take a different view if he were seeking a senior executive.

NOTE: *Malik* involved a claim for breach of contract rather than a dismissal and this distinction was seized upon by the House of Lords in the following case.

Johnson v *Unisys Ltd*

[2001] IRLR 279, House of Lords

Mr Johnson commenced employment with Unisys in 1971. At the end of 1985, he suffered from a psychological illness brought on by work-related stress. He was prescribed antidepressants by his doctor and had to take time off work. In January 1994, he was summarily dismissed for some alleged irregularity. His complaint of unfair dismissal was upheld by the employment tribunal. The tribunal found that the company had not given him a fair opportunity to defend himself and had not complied with its disciplinary procedure. He was awarded the maximum compensation then allowed under the statute, reduced by 25 per cent on the ground of his contributory fault. His total award was just under £11,700.

Some two years later, Mr Johnson commenced an action against the company in the county court for damages at common law, claiming alternatively for breach of contract or negligence. He alleged that his dismissal was in breach of various implied terms of his contract of employment including the implied term of trust and confidence. The alleged breach was said to lie in the fact that he was dismissed without a hearing and in breach of the company's disciplinary procedure.

Mr Johnson contended that in consequence of the manner and fact of his dismissal, he suffered a mental breakdown which affected his family life and made it impossible for him to find work. He became depressed, attempted suicide, started to drink heavily, and spent five months in a mental hospital.

Mr Johnson's claim was struck out on the ground that the facts disclosed no cause of action at common law. The Court of Appeal dismissed Mr Johnson's appeal ([1999] IRLR 90). According to Lord Woolf, with whom the other members of the court agreed, notwithstanding any indication to the contrary in *Malik v BCCI, Addis v Gramophone Co. Ltd* remains binding authority for the principle that damages for wrongful dismissal cannot include compensation for the employee's injured feelings, or for the loss the employee may sustain from the fact the dismissal makes it more difficult to get fresh employment. The views expressed by the House of Lords in *Malik* had merely distinguished *Addis's* case on the facts and had not departed from it. The Court of Appeal concluded, therefore, that since Mr Johnson's claim related to the manner of dismissal, *Addis* was fatal to his claim.

Mr Johnson's appeal to the House of Lords was dismissed.

LORD HOFFMANN: ... My Lords, the first question is whether the implied term of trust and confidence upon which Mr Johnson relies, and about which there is no real dispute, or any of the other implied terms, applies to a dismissal. At common law the contract of employment was regarded by the courts as a contract like any other. The parties were free to negotiate whatever terms they liked and no terms would be implied unless they satisfied the strict test of necessity applied to a commercial contract. Freedom of contract meant that the stronger party, usually the employer, was free to impose his terms on the weaker. But over the last 30 years or so, the nature of the contract of employment has been transformed. It has been recognised that a person's employment is usually one of the most important things in his or her life. It gives not only a livelihood but an occupation, an identity and a sense of self-esteem. The law has changed to recognise this social reality. Most of the changes have been made by Parliament. The Employment Rights Act 1996 consolidates numerous statutes which have conferred rights upon employees. European law has made a substantial contribution. And the common law has adapted itself to the new attitudes, proceeding sometimes by analogy with statutory rights.

The contribution of the common law to the employment revolution has been by the evolution of implied terms in the contract of employment. The most far-reaching is the implied term of trust and confidence. But there have been others. For example, in *W. A. Goold (Pearmak) Ltd v McConnell* [1995] IRLR 516, Morison J (sitting in the Employment Appeal Tribunal) said that it was an implied term of the contract of employment that an employer would reasonably and promptly afford employees an opportunity to obtain redress of grievances. He inferred such a term from what is now s. 3 of the Employment Rights Act 1996, which requires that an employee be provided with a written statement of the particulars of his employment, including a note of how he may apply if he has any grievances. So statute and common law have proceeded hand in hand.

The problem lies in extending or adapting any of these implied terms to dismissal. There are two reasons why dismissal presents special problems. The first is that any terms which the courts imply into a contract must be consistent with the express terms. Implied terms may supplement the express terms of the contract but cannot contradict them. Only Parliament may actually override what the parties have agreed. The second reason is that judges, in developing the law, must have regard to the policies expressed by Parliament in legislation. Employment law requires a balancing of the interests of employers and employees, with proper regard not only to the individual dignity and worth of the employees but also to the general economic interest. Subject to observance of fundamental human rights, the point at which this balance should be struck is a matter for democratic decision. The development of the common law by the judges plays a subsidiary role. Their traditional function is to adapt and modernise the common law. But such developments must be consistent with legislative policy as expressed in statutes. The courts may proceed in harmony with Parliament but there should be no discord.

My Lords, I shall consider first the problem posed by the express terms of the contract. In developing the implied term of trust and confidence and other similar terms applicable to the continuing employment relationship, the courts were advancing across open country. No express provision that BCCI would be entitled to conduct a fraudulent business, or that the employer in *W. A. Goold (Pearmak) Ltd* v *McConnell* would have no grievance procedure, stood in their way. But the employer's right to dismiss the employee is strongly defended by the terms of the contract. In the present case, Mr Johnson's contract provided:

If you decide to leave Unisys you are required to give the company four weeks' notice; equally, the company may terminate your employment on four weeks' notice... In the event of gross misconduct, the company may terminate your employment without notice.

...

My Lords, in the face of this express provision that Unisys was entitled to terminate Mr Johnson's employment on four weeks' notice without any reason, I think it is very difficult to imply a term that the company should not do so except for some good cause and after giving him a reasonable opportunity to demonstrate that no such cause existed.

On the other hand, I do not say that there is nothing which, consistently with such an express term, judicial creativity could do to provide a remedy in a case like this. In *Wallace* v *United Grain Growers Ltd* [1997] 152 DLR (4th) 1, 44–8, McLachlin J (in a minority judgment) said that the courts could imply an obligation to exercise the power of dismissal in good faith. That did not mean that the employer could not dismiss without cause. The contract entitled him to do so. But in so doing, he should be honest with the employee and refrain from untruthful, unfair or insensitive conduct. He should recognise, that an employee losing his or her job was exceptionally vulnerable and behave accordingly. For breach of this implied obligation, McLachlin J would have awarded the employee, who had been dismissed in brutal circumstances, damages for mental distress and loss of reputation and prestige.

My Lords, such an approach would in this country have to circumvent or overcome the obstacle of *Addis* v *Gramophone Co. Ltd* [1909] AC 488, in which it was decided that an employee cannot recover damages for injured feelings, mental distress or damage to his reputation, arising out of the manner of his dismissal. Speaking for myself, I think that, if this task was one which I felt called upon to perform, I would be able to do so. In *Malik* v *Bank of Credit and Commerce International SA* [1997] IRLR 462, 51 Lord Steyn said that the true ratio of *Addis's* case was that the damages were recoverable only for loss caused by a breach of contract, not for loss caused by the manner of its breach. As McLachlin J said in the passage I have quoted, the only loss caused by a wrongful dismissal flows from a failure to give proper notice or make payment in lieu. Therefore, if wrongful dismissal is the only cause of action, nothing can be recovered for mental distress or damage to reputation. On the other hand, if such damage is loss flowing from a breach of another implied term of the contract, *Addis's* case does not stand in the way. That is why in *Malik's* case itself, damages were recoverable for financial loss flowing from damage to reputation caused by a breach of the implied term of trust and confidence.

In this case, Mr Johnson says likewise that his psychiatric injury is a consequence of a breach of the implied term of trust and confidence, which required Unisys to treat him fairly in the procedures for dismissal. He says that implied term now fills the gap which Lord Shaw of Dunfermline perceived and regretted in *Addis's* case (at pp. 504–05) by creating a breach of contract additional to the dismissal itself.

It may be a matter of words, but I rather doubt whether the term of trust and confidence should be pressed so far. In the way it has always been formulated, it is concerned with preserving the continuing relationship which should subsist between employer and employee. So it does not seem altogether appropriate for use in connection with the way that relationship is terminated. If one is looking for an implied term, I think a more elegant solution is McLachlin J's implication of a separate term that the power of dismissal will be exercised fairly and in good faith. But the result would be the same as that for which Mr Johnson contends by invoking the implied term of trust and confidence. As I have said, I think it would be possible to reach such a conclusion without contradicting the express term that the employer is entitled to dismiss without cause.

I must, however, make it clear that, although in my opinion it would be jurisprudentially possible to imply a term which gave a remedy in this case, I do not think that even if the courts were free of legislative constraint (a point to which I shall return in a moment) it would necessarily be wise to do so. It is not simply an incremental step from the duty of trust and confidence implied in *Malik* v *Bank of Credit and Commerce International SA* [1997] IRLR 462. The close association between the acts alleged to be in breach of the implied term and the irremovable and lawful fact of dismissal give rise to special problems. So, in *Wallace* v *United Grain Growers Ltd* [1997] 152 DLR

(4th) 1, the majority rejected an implied duty to exercise the power of dismissal in good faith. Iacobucci J said, at p. 28, that such a step was better left to the legislature. It would be 'overly intrusive and inconsistent with established principles of employment law'.

Some of the potential problems can be illustrated by the facts of this case, in which Mr Johnson claims some £400,000 damages for the financial consequences of psychiatric damage. This form of damage notoriously gives rise at the best of times to extremely difficult questions of causation. But the difficulties are made greater when the expert witnesses are required to perform the task of distinguishing between the psychiatric consequences of the fact of dismissal (for which no damages are recoverable) and the unfair circumstances in which the dismissal took place, which constituted a breach of the implied term. The agreed statement of facts records that for the purposes of this appeal against a strike-out it is accepted that Mr Johnson's psychiatric illness was caused by 'the circumstances and the fact' of his dismissal. At a trial, however, it would be necessary to decide what was caused by what.

Another difficulty is the open-ended nature of liability. Mr Johnson's case is that Unisys had knowledge of his psychological fragility by reason of facts lodged in the corporate memory in 1985–87 and therefore should have foreseen when he was engaged that a failure to comply with proper disciplinary procedures on dismissal might result in injury which deprived him of the ability ever to work again. On general common law principles it seems to me that if the necessary term is implied and these facts are made out, the claim should succeed. It may be that such liability would be grossly disproportionate to the employer's degree of fault. It may be likely to inhibit the future engagement of psychologically fragile personnel. But the common law decides cases according to principle and cannot impose arbitrary limitations on liability because of the circumstances of the particular case. Only statute can lay down limiting rules based upon policy rather than principle. In this connection it is interesting to notice that although the majority in *Wallace* v *United Grain Growers Ltd* were unwilling to accept an implied term as to the manner of dismissal, they treated it as relevant to the period of notice which should reasonably have been given. McLachlin J said that this was illogical and so perhaps it is. But one can understand a desire to place some limit upon the employer's potential liability under this head.

It follows, my Lords, that if there was no relevant legislation in this area, I would regard the question of whether judges should develop the law by implying a suitable term into the contract of employment as finely balanced. But now I must consider the statutory background against which your Lordships are invited to create such a cause of action.

…

My Lords, this statutory system for dealing with unfair dismissals was set up by Parliament to deal with the recognised deficiencies of the law as it stood at the time of *Malloch* v *Aberdeen Corporation* [1971] 1 WLR 1581. The remedy adopted by Parliament was not to build upon the common law by creating a statutory implied term that the power of dismissal should be exercised fairly or in good faith, leaving the courts to give a remedy on general principles of contractual damages. Instead, it set up an entirely new system outside the ordinary courts, with tribunals staffed by a majority of lay members, applying new statutory concepts and offering statutory remedies. Many of the new rules, such as the exclusion of certain classes of employees and the limit on the amount of the compensatory award, were not based upon any principle which it would have been open to the courts to apply. They were based upon policy and represented an attempt to balance fairness to employees against the general economic interests of the community. And I should imagine that Parliament also had in mind the practical difficulties I have mentioned about causation and proportionality which would arise if the remedy was unlimited. So Parliament adopted the practical solution of giving the tribunals a very broad jurisdiction to award what they considered just and equitable but subject to a limit on the amount.

In my opinion, all the matters of which Mr Johnson complains in these proceedings were within the jurisdiction of the industrial tribunal. His most substantial complaint is of financial loss flowing from his psychiatric injury which he says was a consequence of the unfair manner of his dismissal. Such loss is a consequence of the dismissal which may form the subject-matter of a compensatory award. The only doubtful question is whether it would have been open to the tribunal to include a sum by way of compensation for his distress, damage to family life and similar matters. As the award, even reduced by 25 per cent, exceeded the statutory maximum and had to be reduced to £11,000, the point would have been academic. But perhaps I may be allowed a comment all the same. I know that in the early days of the National Industrial Relations Court it was laid down that only financial loss could be compensated: see *Norton Tool Co. Ltd* v *Tewson* [1972] IRLR 86; *Wellman Alloys Ltd* v *Russell* [1973] ICR 616. It was said that the word 'loss' can only mean financial loss. But I think that is too narrow a construction. The emphasis is upon the tribunal awarding such compensation as it thinks just and equitable. So I see no reason why in an appropriate case it should not include compensation for distress, humiliation, damage to reputation in the community or to family life.

Part X of the Employment Rights Act 1996 therefore gives a remedy for exactly the conduct of which Mr Johnson complains. But Parliament had restricted that remedy to a maximum of £11,000, whereas Mr Johnson wants to claim a good deal more. The question is whether the courts should develop the common law to give a parallel remedy which is not subject to any such limit.

My Lords, I do not think that it is a proper exercise of the judicial function of the House to take such a step. Judge Ansell, to whose unreserved judgment I would pay respectful tribute, went in my opinion to the heart of the matter when he said:

> there is not one hint in the authorities that the... tens of thousands of people that appear before the tribunals can have, as it were, a possible second bite in common law and I ask myself, if this is the situation, why on earth do we have this special statutory framework? What is the point of it if it can be circumvented in this way?... it would mean that effectively the statutory limit on compensation for unfair dismissal would disappear.

I can see no answer to these questions. For the judiciary to construct a general common law remedy for unfair circumstances attending dismissal would be to go contrary to the evident intention of Parliament that there should be such a remedy but that it should be limited in application and extent.

The same reason is in my opinion fatal to the claim based upon a duty of care. It is of course true that a duty of care can exist independently of the contractual relationship. But the grounds upon which I think it would be wrong to impose an implied contractual duty would make it equally wrong to achieve the same result by the imposition of a duty of care.

...

I would dismiss the appeal.

NOTES
1. This decision would seem to put a severe impediment in the way of the further development of implied terms relating to the manner of dismissal. *Malik* is still authority for the proposition that damages may be recovered against the employer for a breach of contract—as opposed to a dismissal—which damages an employee's reputation. This principle was reinforced by the House of Lords in *Mahmoud v Bank of Credit and Commerce International SA* [1988] AC 20. However, Lord Steyn did point out the difficulties facing an employee in claiming so-called 'stigma damages':
   > The principled position is as follows. Provided that a relevant breach of contract can be established, and the requirements of causation, remoteness and mitigation can be satisfied, there is no reason why in the field of employment law recovery of financial loss in respect of damage to reputation is necessarily excluded... Earlier, I drew attention to the fact that the implied obligation of trust and confidence only applies where there is no 'reasonable and proper cause' for the employer's conduct, and then only if the conduct is calculated to destroy and *seriously* damage the relationship of trust and confidence. That circumscribes the potential reach and scope of the implied obligation. Moreover, even if the employee can establish a breach of this obligation, it does not follow that he will be able to recover damages for injury to his employment prospects. The Law Commission has pointed out that loss of reputation is inherently difficult to prove: *Law Commission, Consultation Paper No. 132 on Aggravated, Exemplary and Restitutionary Damages*, p. 22, paragraph 2.15. It is, therefore, improbable that many employees would be able to prove 'stigma compensation'. The limiting principles of causation, remoteness and mitigation present formidable practical obstacles to such claims succeeding. But difficulties of proof cannot alter the legal principles which permit, in appropriate cases, such claims for financial loss caused by breach of contract being put forward for consideration.

   (For a practical example of the difficulties associated with a 'stigma damages' claim, see *Bank of Credit and Commerce International SA v Ali (No. 3)* [1999] IRLR 508.)
2. It was held by the Court of Appeal in *French v Barclays Bank plc* [1998] IRLR 652, that *Malik* had 'not cast doubt on the Court of Appeal decisions such as *Bliss* which restricted claims to damages for stress and anxiety flowing from a breach of contract to the exceptional category of case.' However, *Addis*, *Bliss*, and *French* were distinguished in the following case.

Gogay v *Hertfordshire County Council*
[2000] IRLR 703, Court of Appeal

Gogay worked in a Hertfordshire County Council children's home as a care assistant. She worked with a child with learning difficulties, who had been severely sexually abused by her parents and tended to act in a sexually provocative way. Gogay requested that she was not left alone with the child and was commended by the area manager for handling the situation professionally.

Subsequently, however, the child made comments which could have been construed as allegations of sexual abuse against Gogay. The council suspended her. An inquiry found no case to answer and reinstated Gogay but she was, by then, unable to work due to clinical depression, caused substantially by the suspension. She brought a claim against the council for damages and loss of earnings resulting from a breach of her contract of employment. The court found the council had, in suspending Gogay, breached the implied duty of trust and confidence between employer and employee.

The council appealed on two counts: first, that the suspension was not, in and of itself, a breach of the implied duty of trust and confidence; second, that even if there was a breach, there could not be an award of damages for injury, since this was a breach of contract claim, and damages for injury to feelings and/or mental distress cannot be awarded in those circumstances (following the principles set out in *Addis* v *Gramophone Ltd*).

The Court of Appeal dismissed the council's argument, holding that there had been a breach of the implied duty of trust and confidence. Furthermore, it said, there is 'all the difference in the world between hurt, upset and injury to feelings' and a 'recognised psychiatric illness'. Consequently, there was nothing to prevent the trial judge awarding damages for clinical depression and the losses arising from it; this case was distinguishable from *Addis* and other cases on hurt feelings.

LADY JUSTICE HALE:

The implied term of confidence and trust

...

Did the authority's conduct in this case amount to a breach of this implied term? The test is a severe one. The conduct must be such as to destroy or seriously damage the relationship. The conduct in this case was not only to suspend the claimant, but to do so by means of a letter which stated that 'the issue to be investigated is an allegation of sexual abuse made by a young person in our care'. Sexual abuse is a very serious matter, doing untold damage to those who suffer it. To be accused of it is also a serious matter. To be told by one's employer that one has been so accused is clearly calculated to seriously damage the relationship between employer and employee. The question is therefore whether there was 'reasonable and proper cause' to do this.

...

On analysis therefore, the actions of the local authority towards the claimant in this case were indeed in breach of its implied obligation not without reasonable and proper cause to act in a way which seriously damaged the relationship of confidence and trust between them. But in reaching this conclusion, I would not want local authorities to feel in any way inhibited in making inquiries which they feel appropriate to safeguard the children in their care. Nor should there be any doubt that if there is a conflict between the interests of a child in their care and the interests of an employee, the interests of the child should prevail. But the employee is entitled to something better than the 'knee-jerk' reaction which happened in this case.

Damages

Miss Sinclair [Counsel for the local authority] argues that, even if there were such a breach, the claimant would not be entitled to compensation for her depressive illness and resulting inability to do residential care work. There is clear authority for the proposition that general damages cannot be awarded for frustration, mental distress or injured feelings arising from an employer's breach of the implied term of confidence and trust: see *Bliss* v *South East Thames Regional Health Authority* [1985] IRLR 308, CA, holding that the principle laid down in *Addis* v *Gramophone Co. Ltd* [1909] AC 488 applied to this breach as it did to wrongful dismissal; and *French* v *Barclays Bank plc* [1998] IRLR 646, affirming that proposition despite other observations of the House of Lords in *Malik* v *BCCI* [1997] IRLR 462.

...

There is, however, a clear distinction between frustration, mental distress and injured feelings, on the one hand, and a recognised psychiatric illness on the other... The employer owes his employees duties both in contract and tort. In *Walker* v *Northumberland County Council* [1995] IRLR 35, at paragraph 74, Coleman J pointed out that 'the scope of the duty of care owed to an employee to take reasonable steps to provide a safe system of work is coextensive with the scope of the implied term as to the employee's safety in the contract of employment'. He awarded damages for a mental breakdown resulting from a breach of that duty. The duty in this case is owed purely in contract, rather than in tort, but there can be no more reason to distinguish between physical and psychiatric injury in this case than there is in the case of other breaches of an employer's duties.

In my judgment, that is correct. There is all the difference in the world between hurt, upset and injury to feelings, for which in general the law does not provide compensation whether in contract or (with certain well defined exceptions) in tort, and a recognised psychiatric illness... I would therefore hold such damages to be recoverable unless constrained by authority to the contrary.

...

Miss Sinclair understandably places great emphasis upon the decision of this court in *Johnson* v *Unisys* [1999] IRLR 90. The claimant claimed damages for a mental breakdown allegedly caused by his wrongful dismissal for gross misconduct. The Court of Appeal upheld the judge's decision to strike out the claim. Lord Woolf recognised that the *Malik* case 'does, however, mean that damages for loss of reputation can be recovered in a case where the damage to reputation is caused by a dismissal which is summary, unfair or without proper notice' (paragraph 24). Whatever may be the differences between the speeches of Lord Nicholls and Lord Steyn in *Malik*, that much is clear. If damages for damage to reputation can be recovered for wrongful dismissal, why cannot damages for psychiatric illness also be recovered? There would still be no breach of the general principle that damages for upset feelings cannot be recovered. It is difficult to discern from the report of *Johnson* that the distinction between hurt feelings and psychiatric injury was explored before court...

The case before us can be distinguished from *Johnson*. The complaint here relates to a suspension, which manifestly contemplates the continuation of the employment relationship. The clear import of *Malik* is that the ambit of *Addis* should be confined. There are in this case two differences from *Addis*; first, this was not a dismissal, and secondly, this was a psychiatric illness rather than hurt feelings. In my judgment, therefore, the judge was right to award damages for both financial loss and nonpecuniary damage resulting from the claimant's illness.

I recognise that this produces the strange result that, according to *Johnson*, the defendant authority would have done better had they dismissed rather than suspended the claimant. That simply reinforces my view that the sooner these matters are comprehensively resolved by higher authority or by Parliament, the better.

NOTES

1. The Court of Appeal points out that it does not inevitably follow that an employee should be suspended merely because there are reasonable grounds for an investigation. There are other options open to the employer, such as transfer. In this case, there was no reasonable and proper cause for the suspension and therefore a breach of the trust and confidence obligation. The decision in *Gogay* may be seen as a fetter on the exercise of a well-tried management tool, increasing the burden on employers to make difficult judgements about the mental fitness of their employees. Having said that, the facts in *Gogay* were unusual. (See also *Holladay* v *East Kent Hospitals and NHS Trust* [2003] EWCA Civ 1696.)

2. *Gogay* sits uneasily with *Johnson* v *Unisys* [2001] IRLR 279 (extracted earlier), where the employee failed to recover any damages for a mental breakdown caused by the manner of dismissal. As Hale LJ acknowledges, it means the council might have been better off if it had dismissed rather than suspended Gogay.

3. In *Johnson* v *Unisys*, the House of Lords held that the implied term of trust and confidence does not apply to the way the employment relationship is terminated. *King* v *University Court of the University of St Andrews* [2002] IRLR 252 raises the important issue of whether this means that the duty of trust and confidence does not apply to investigating disciplinary charges. The employee sought damages for breach of contract on the basis that, in breach of the trust and confidence term, he had not been given a proper opportunity to reply to the charges against him and was not allowed to cross-examine witnesses during the disciplinary hearing. The Outer House of the Court of Session interpreted *Johnson* as limiting the application of the trust and confidence term only once the decision to dismiss is taken. On that basis, the court held that the duty applies during the stage when an employer is investigating allegations against an employee and considering whether to dismiss him. 'For an employer to act in breach of that duty during an assessment which has the potential either to reinforce or to terminate the contract of employment would clearly be highly destructive of and damaging to the relationship between them' (*per* Lady Smith). Just as the plaintiff in *Gogay* was entitled to rely on the implied duty as subsisting during the period between the allegations being made against her and the outcome of the formal investigation which then ensued, so the pursuer in this case was entitled to rely on the implied duty of trust and confidence having subsisted while the investigation procedures were being carried out.

Edwards v *Chesterfield Royal Hospital NHS Foundation Trust*
[2012] IRLR 129, SC

In this case, the Supreme Court held, by a majority of four to three, that the *Johnson* approach of limiting damages at common law for breach of an *implied* term applied equally where the employer is in breach of an *express* term of the employment contract. As a consequence, damages based on procedural breaches are limited to what the employee would have earned during the time it would have taken for the correct disciplinary period to be carried out, together with the notice period, and not for damage to reputation and loss of future earnings.

LORD DYSON: ... if provisions about disciplinary procedure are incorporated as express terms into an employment contract, they are not ordinary contractual terms agreed by the parties in the usual way ... The question remains whether, if provisions about disciplinary procedure are incorporated into a contract of employment, they are intended to be actionable at common law giving rise to claims for damages in the ordinary courts. Parliament intended such provisions to apply to contracts of employment, inter alia, in order to protect employees from unfair dismissal and to enhance their right not to be unfairly dismissed. It has specified the consequences of a failure to comply with such provisions in unfair dismissal proceedings. It could not have intended that the inclusion of these provisions in a contract would also give rise to a common law claim for damages for all the reasons given by the House of Lords in *Johnson* v *Unisys Ltd* for not extending the implied term of trust and confidence to a claim for damages for unfair manner of dismissal. It is necessarily to be inferred from this statutory background that, unless they otherwise agree, the parties to an employment contract do not intend that a failure to comply with contractually binding disciplinary procedures will give rise to a common law claim for damages ...

BARONESS HALE [DISSENTING]: There is no reason at all to suppose that, in [introducing the statutory right to claim unfair dismissal], Parliament intended to cut down upon or reduce the remedies available to employees whose employers acted in breach of their contracts of employment. Quite the reverse. Parliament intended to create a new statutory remedy for unfair dismissal which would supplement whatever rights the employee already had under his contract of employment. Parliament did that because most employees had very few rights under their contracts of employment.

NOTE: However, where there has been a lapse in the disciplinary procedure, an employee may be able to seek an injunction to restrain his or her dismissal (see *West London Mental Health NHS Trust* v *Chhabra* [2014] IRLR 227, SC).

Eastwood and another v *Magnox Electric plc; McCabe* v *Cornwall County Council*
[2004] IRLR 733, House of Lords

The claimant employees in one case appealed against the dismissal of their psychiatric illness claims and the defendant employer in the other case appealed against the decision that the employee's claim for psychiatric illness should go to trial.

In the first case two employees (Eastwood and Williams) were dismissed by their employer after, they claimed, a campaign to demoralise and undermine them. Both pursued claims for unfair dismissal in the employment tribunal. The claims were settled. Both then commenced proceedings in the county court alleging negligence and breach of the implied term of mutual trust and confidence in their employment contracts and claiming damages for personal injuries in the form of psychiatric injuries caused by deliberate misconduct in the disciplinary processes used against them. The claims were dismissed by the judge and Court of Appeal on the basis that the common law implied term of trust and confidence could not be used in the area of unfair dismissal that included the operation of disciplinary machinery, applying *Johnson* v *Unisys Ltd* [2001] IRLR 279.

In the second case the employment tribunal found that the employee, a teacher (McCabe), had been unfairly dismissed after suspension and disciplinary proceedings.

McCabe (M) brought proceedings in the High Court alleging that he had sustained psychiatric illness by reason of the failure to investigate the allegations against him and to conduct the disciplinary proceedings properly. The judge struck out the claim relying on *Johnson* as extended in the case of *Eastwood*. The Court of Appeal allowed M's appeal on the basis that there should be a trial to determine where on the facts the line should be drawn between dismissal and conduct prior to that causing injury compensable in damages at common law. The House of Lords dismissed the employer's appeal in M's case and the appeals of Eastwood and Williams were allowed. In the case of all three the assumed facts constituted causes of action that accrued before the dismissals. They disclosed reasonable causes of action that should proceed to trial.

LORD NICHOLLS OF BIRKENHEAD: Identifying the boundary of the '*Johnson* exclusion area', as it has been called, is comparatively straightforward. The statutory code provides for remedies for infringement of the statutory right not to be *dismissed* unfairly. An employee's remedy for unfair dismissal, whether actual or constructive, is the remedy provided by statute. If before his dismissal, whether actual or constructive, an employee has acquired a cause of action at law, for breach of contract or otherwise, that cause of action remains unimpaired by his subsequent unfair dismissal and the statutory rights flowing therefrom. By definition, in law, such a cause of action exists independently of the dismissal.

In the ordinary course, suspension apart, an employer's failure to act fairly in the steps leading to dismissal does not of itself cause the employee financial loss. The loss arises when the employee is dismissed and it arises by reason of his dismissal. Then the resultant claim for loss falls squarely within the *Johnson* exclusion area.

Exceptionally, this is not so. Exceptionally, financial loss may flow directly from the employer's failure to act fairly when taking steps leading to the dismissal. Financial loss flowing from suspension is an instance. Another instance is cases such as those now before the House, when an employee suffers loss from psychiatric or other illness caused by his pre-dismissal unfair treatment. On such cases, the employee has a common law cause of action which precedes, and is independent of, his subsequent dismissal. In respect of his subsequent dismissal, he may of course present a claim to an employment tribunal. If he brings proceedings both in court and before a tribunal he cannot recover any overlapping heads of loss twice over.

If identifying the boundary between the common law rights and remedies and the statutory rights and remedies is relatively straightforward, the same cannot be said of the practical consequences of this unusual boundary. Particularly in cases concerning financial loss flowing from psychiatric illnesses, some of the practical consequences are far from straightforward or desirable. The first and most obvious drawback is that in such cases the division of remedial jurisdiction between an employment tribunal will lead to a duplication of proceedings. In practice there will be cases where the employment tribunal and the court each traverse much of the same ground in deciding the factual issues before them, with attendant waste of resources and costs.

Second, the existence of this boundary line means that in some cases a continuing course of conduct, typically a disciplinary process followed by dismissal, may have to be chopped artificially into separate pieces. In cases of constructive dismissal a distinction will have to be drawn between loss flowing from antecedent breaches of the trust and confidence term and loss flowing from the employee's acceptance of these breaches as a repudiation of the contract. The loss flowing from the impugned conduct taking place before actual and constructive dismissal lies outside the *Johnson* exclusion area; the loss flowing from the dismissal itself is within that area. In some cases this legalistic distinction may give rise to difficult questions of causation in cases such as those now before the House, where financial loss is claimed as a consequence of psychiatric illness said to have been brought on by the employer's conduct before the employee was dismissed. Judges and tribunals, faced with conflicting medical evidence, may have to decide whether the fact of the dismissal was really the last straw which proved too much for the employee, or whether the onset of the illness occurred even before he was dismissed.

The existence of this boundary line produces other strange results. For example, an employer may be better off dismissing an employee than suspending him. A statutory claim for unfair dismissal would be subject to the statutory cap; a common law claim for unfair suspension would not. The decision of the Court of Appeal in *Gogay* v *Hertfordshire County Council* [2000] IRLR 703 is an example of the latter. Likewise, the decision in *Johnson's* case means that an employee who is psychologically vulnerable is owed no duty of care in respect of his dismissal although, depending on the circumstances, he may be owed a duty of care in respect of his suspension. It goes without saying that an inter-relation between the common law and statute having these awkward and unfortunate consequences is not satisfactory. The difficulties arise principally because of the cap on the amount of compensatory awards for unfair dismissal. Although the cap was raised substantially in 1998, at times tribunals are still precluded from awarding full compensation for a dismissed employee's financial loss. So, understandably, employees and their legal advisers are seeking to side-step the statutory limit by identifying elements in the events preceding the dismissal, but leading up to the dismissal, which can be used as pegs on which to hang a common law claim for breach of an employer's implied contractual obligation to act fairly. This situation merits early attention by the government and the legislature.

NOTES

1. As a result of these decisions, we are left with the situation that when judging a psychiatric injury claim by an employee, courts and tribunals can take into account everything but the dismissal itself. This is a recipe for a 'field day' for the lawyers and psychiatrists in constructing tortuous arguments about what was the operative cause of the psychiatric injury (see *GAB Robins (UK) Ltd v Triggs* [2008] IRLR 317, CA).

2. Both Lord Nicholls and Lord Steyn recognised that the current legal position was unsatisfactory, pointing out the anomalies that will now flow from drawing this artificial boundary between disciplinary process and dismissal. According to Lord Nicholls, the situation merited urgent attention by the government and the legislature. This is unlikely to happen.

3. Lord Nicholls described the trust and confidence term as an 'implied obligation to act fairly'. This definition is wider than previous versions (see *White* v *Reflecting Roadstuds Ltd* [1991] IRLR 331, EAT—an extract appears at p. 360 (Section 3.C(iii)).

Harper v Virgin Net Ltd
[2004] IRLR 390, Court of Appeal

Under Sally Harper's contract of employment, she was entitled to three months' notice of termination. She was summarily dismissed 33 days short of the date when she would have completed the one-year period of employment qualifying her to bring a claim of unfair dismissal.

An employment tribunal found that Ms Harper had been wrongfully dismissed and awarded damages of £9,514.04 in respect of the net notice pay. The tribunal also awarded an additional sum representing the full award had she been given the requisite three months' contractual notice so as to have the necessary qualifying service to bring a claim of unfair dismissal. The tribunal held that she would have succeeded in such a claim because her dismissal was so clearly unfair.

The EAT allowed the employers' appeal against the award of damages for loss of the chance of recovering compensation for unfair dismissal. The EAT held that Ms Harper's claim was impermissible as a matter of law because it was an attempt to circumvent the statutory qualifying period. The EAT pointed out that the law has long provided that the effective date of termination is extended in a case of summary dismissal by the length of the statutory notice to which the employee was entitled but that Parliament had chosen not to extend the date by reference to the contractual notice period, where that is longer. The EAT also found that since Ms Harper's claim was directed exclusively on the decision to dismiss her summarily, it fell foul of the decision in *Johnson* v *Unisys* [2001] IRLR 279, HL that an applicant cannot recover, by way of damages for breach of contract of employment, loss flowing from the fact and manner of dismissal. The Court of Appeal dismissed Ms Harper's appeal.

BROOKE LJ: I do not consider it is open to the courts, through the machinery of an award of damages for wrongful dismissal, to rewrite Parliament's scheme and to place a financial burden on employers which Parliament decided not to impose on them. If [the] submissions on behalf of Ms Harper are well-founded, a wrongfully dismissed employee whose EDT pre-dates the end of his/her first year of employment (perhaps by a number of months) will have the benefit of a much longer limitation period and then making a claim for compensation for unfair dismissal. In Ms Harper's case, this claim cannot be based on the actual facts of her dismissal because by statute she has no right to claim compensation for unfair dismissal in respect of that dismissal. Instead, the court would have to speculate about the chances of her being unfairly dismissed on some later hypothetical occasion after her statutory right had accrued. This, in my judgment, would be a very unsatisfactory way of proceeding ...

NOTES

1. In *Horkulak* v *Cantor Fitzgerald International* [2004] IRLR 942, CA, the main issue before the Court of Appeal was whether the High Court judge was right to assess damages on the basis that had the claimant remained in employment, he would have received payments under a clause in his contract which provided that the company 'may in its discretion pay you an annual discretionary bonus'. The Court of Appeal held that a discretion provided for in a contract which is prima facie of an unlimited nature will be regarded as subject to an implied term that it will be exercised genuinely and rationally. That is presumed to be the reasonable expectation and therefore the common intention of the parties, even though they are likely to have conflicting interests and the provisions of the contract effectively place the resolution of that conflict in the hands of the party exercising that discretion. The principle in *Lavarack* v *Woods of Colchester* [1967] QB 278, CA, that damages for wrongful dismissal could not confer on an employee benefits under a bonus scheme which the contract did not oblige the employer to confer, even though the employee might reasonably have expected his or her employer to confer them in due course, provided no rule of thumb applicable to discretionary bonus cases. Nothing was said in *Lavarack* v *Woods* to suggest that, in respect of a claim for damages put upon the basis that the claimant would have received payments under a discretionary bonus scheme of which he or she was already a potential beneficiary, the court should assume that the employer's discretion would be exercised against him/her in a case where such a decision would be irrational or arbitrary or one which no reasonable employer would make. The broad principle that a defendant in an action for breach of contract is not liable for doing that which he is not bound to do will not be applicable 'willy-nilly' in a case where the employer is contractually obliged to exercise its discretion rationally and in good faith in awarding or withholding a benefit provided for under the contract of employment. Where the employer fails to do so, the employee is entitled to compensation in respect of such a failure.

2. In *Fraser* v *HLMAD Ltd* [2006] IRLR 687, the Court of Appeal held that claimants who bring wrongful dismissal claims in the employment tribunal, where the statutory limit of £25,000 applies, cannot recover or 'top-up' the excess damages in the High Court.

B: When will remedies other than damages be granted?

(i) Equitable remedies

The common law has been most reluctant to enforce contracts of employment remedies which require the contract to continue, i.e. injunction and specific performance. There are a number of reasons for this. First, damages are often adequate as a remedy, and it is a general rule of contract that where this is the case then the equitable remedies of injunction and specific performance should not be considered. Second, and perhaps most importantly, contracts of employment require mutual trust and confidence. This element would be missing if employer and employee were to continue a relationship of service against the will of one or the other. As Fry LJ said in *De Francesco* v *Barnum* (1890) 45 ChD 430, the courts 'are very unwilling to extend decisions the effect of which is to compel persons who are not desirous of maintaining personal relations with one another to continue those personal relations… I think the courts are bound to be jealous lest they should turn contracts of service into contracts of slavery.'

However, in recent years, the courts, prompted by the decision of the Court of Appeal in *Hill* v *C.A. Parsons & Co. Ltd* [1972] 1 Ch 305, have shown a greater willingness to grant these equitable remedies:

(a) where proper contractual procedures have not been complied with prior to dismissal; and

(b) where mutual trust and confidence remains between the parties.

Irani v *Southampton and South-West Hampshire Health Authority*
[1985] IRLR 203, Queen's Bench Division

A part-time ophthalmologist was dismissed after having quarrelled with his consultant, his employers considering, after an *ad hoc* inquiry, that the differences were irreconcilable and that they could not, therefore, continue to work together. However, the employers failed to carry out the disputes procedure laid down by the Whitley Council for the Health Services (the 'blue book' procedure), the conditions of which were incorporated into the contract of employment. Irani successfully sought an injunction preventing his dismissal until the proper disputes procedure had been adhered to.

WARNER J: I mentioned that Mr Clifford seeks to distinguish *Hill* v *C.A. Parsons & Co. Ltd* on the ground that it was a very exceptional case indeed. I find it helpful in that respect to refer to the judgment of Mr Justice Megarry (as he then was) in *Chappel* v *Times Newspapers Ltd* [1975] IRLR 90 where, he deals with the reasons why *Hill* v *Parsons* was such an exceptional case. He says this:

> There were three main grounds for this decision. First, there was still complete confidence between employer and employee. The defendant did not want to terminate the plaintiff's employment but he had been coerced by the union. Second, the Industrial Relations Act 1971 was expected to come into force shortly. It had been passed but the relevant parts had not been brought into operation. As soon as the Act was in force, one probable result would be that the closed shop would no longer be enforceable and that the plaintiff would be free to remain a member of the union of his choice. He would also obtain the rights conferred by the Act to compensation for unfair dismissal if he was then dismissed. Third, in the circumstances of the case, damages would not be an adequate remedy.

I will take those three reasons seriatim and, in relation to each, compare the situation here. First:

> complete confidence between employer and employee. The defendant did not want to terminate the plaintiff's employment but had been coerced by the union.

I have already mentioned the fact that the defendant authority here makes no complaint as to or criticism of Mr Irani's conduct or professional competence. Mr Clifford submitted at one time that the real distinction between this case and *Hill* v *C.A. Parsons & Co. Ltd* was that in *Hill* v *C.A. Parsons & Co. ltd* the employers positively wanted their employee back. There are passages in the report of *Hill* v *C.A. Parsons & Co. Ltd* which show, it seems to me, that that was not so. Lord Denning, at page 316 said:

> If ever there was a case where an injunction should be granted against the employers, this is the case. It is quite plain that the employers have done wrong. I know that the employers have been under pressure from a powerful trade union. That makes plain their conduct, but it does not excuse it. They have purported to terminate Mr Hill's employment by notice which is too short by far. They seek to take advantage of their own wrong by asserting that his services were terminated by their own 'say-so' at the date selected by them—to the grave prejudice of Mr Hill. They cannot be allowed to break the law in this way. It is, to my mind, a clear case for an injunction.

Lord Justice Sachs, at pages 320/321 said:

> For the defendants it was suggested that an order of the court, if made as claimed, would endanger industrial peace as between the defendant company and its employees.

Lord Justice Stamp, at page 323 said:

> On behalf of the defendant it is pointed out, and I think this is a more realistic approach, that it is not correct to say that the defendants are willing to employ the plaintiff but that the true position is that they would be willing to do so but for the fact that they have under pressure entered into an agreement with DATA requiring them to dismiss him and that this agreement cannot be broken without dire consequences. Unless therefore the court is prepared to infer, as I do not think it ought to do, that the defendants' opposition to the making of an order for specific performance is not genuine, it appears to me that the existence of the fears which dictated the dismissal is a strong ground for not making an exception to the general rule that the court will not order specific performance of a contract of employment.

I think the true position here is that the defendant authority would be willing to continue employing Mr Irani were it not for the fact that they are convinced that his and Mr Walker's continued employment are incompatible.

Mr Clifford more happily, I think, expressed the distinction between this case and the *Parsons* case in this way. He said that in the *Parsons* case the defendant fought the case because it was in fear of what the trade union might do if it did not, whereas here the defendant is fighting the case because it genuinely wants to be rid of Mr Irani. But, to revert to what I said earlier when I quoted from the judgment of Lord Justice Geoffrey Lane in the *Chappell* case, it remains the fact that the defendant authority has perfect faith in the honesty, integrity and loyalty of Mr Irani.

Turning to Mr Justice Megarry's second reason for the decision in the *Parsons* case, it seems to me that there is a comparable reason here. In the *Parsons* case, Mr Hill was seeking the protection of the Industrial Relations Act. Here Mr Irani is seeking the protection of section 33 of the blue book to which he is entitled if the circumstances are appropriate.

Thirdly, as Mr Harwood-Stevenson has pointed out, this is a case—and I anticipate now on what I shall have to say in a moment about some subsidiary submissions of Mr Clifford—where damages would not be an adequate remedy.

If I were to decline to grant the injunction sought by Mr Harwood-Stevenson, I would in effect be holding that, without doubt, an authority in the position of the defendant is entitled to snap its fingers at the rights of its employees under the blue book. Indeed, that is what Mr Clifford invites me to hold. He invites me to hold that, despite the existence in the blue book of sections 33 and 40, a health authority is entitled to dismiss a medical practitioner summarily and to say that, if and in so far as his rights under those sections are infringed, his remedy lies in damages only. If that is correct, it means that the same applies to clause 190 in the red book, as indeed in 1958 Mr Justice Barry held that it did. It means that for the price of damages—and the authorities show that damages at common law for wrongful dismissal are not generous—a health authority may, among other things, ignore the requirement at the end of clause 190 that:

> where the Secretary of State's decision cannot be given before the expiry of the notice given, such notice shall be extended for a month or longer period by the authority until the Secretary of State's decision is given.

The development of the law since the decision in [*Barber* v *Manchester Regional Hospital Board* [1958] 1 WLR 181] leads me to the conclusion that it is open to question whether that is right. If it is not right, nor can it be right, in my view, that, in the case of a more junior practitioner, the employing authority can ignore the rules in the blue book. For those reasons I reject Mr Clifford's primary submission.

In his subsidiary submissions, he took issue with Mr Harwood-Stevenson on the latter's grounds for saying that in this case damages would not be an adequate remedy. As to the point made by Mr Harwood-Stevenson on the basis of Mr Coley's evidence that, if dismissed by the defendant, Mr Irani will never again be able to secure employment in the National Health Service, Mr Clifford said that if, at the trial, Mr Irani could show that he was entitled to the benefit of section 33 and that, as a result of the action of the defendant authority, he never could again obtain employment within the National Health Service, damages could be assessed. Similarly, he said that if Mr Irani could show at the trial that he was indeed entitled to treat private patients in the Lymington Hospital and that, because of the action of the defendant authority, he had been deprived of that right, again damages could be assessed.

I do not myself find those submissions very convincing, any more than I find convincing Mr Clifford's further submission that Mr Irani ought to put to the test his ability to obtain employment elsewhere in the National Health Service. (Mr Clifford pointed out in that connection that Mr Irani also works in London.) Mr Clifford conceded however that, whatever might be the answers to those points, he had no answer, if he was wrong—as I have held—in his primary submission, to the point made by Mr Harwood-Stevenson that, if no injunction issued now, it was very possible that at the trial it would be too late for Mr Irani to rely on section 33 because he would by then have ceased to be an employee of the defendant authority.

I accordingly propose to grant the injunction sought by Mr Harwood-Stevenson.

Powell v Brent London Borough Council
[1988] ICR 176, Court of Appeal

The plaintiff had been 'promoted' from Senior Benefits Officer to Principal Benefits Officer after a competitive promotion procedure. However, one of the unsuccessful candidates complained of breaches of the council's equal opportunities policy in the selection procedures and it was decided to re-advertise the post. The plaintiff sought an injunction preventing the re-advertising of the post. Pending that application, she had been allowed to continue doing the work of a Principal Benefits Officer. The question arose as to whether an interlocutory injunction should be granted pending the hearing of the main action. The Court of Appeal held that it should.

NICHOLLS LJ: [I]f at the trial the court should decide, contrary to the council's contention, that the plaintiff was validly and effectually appointed as Principal Benefits Officer (Policy and Training), it seems to me that, as the evidence stands, this might be a case in which the court might decide that, if it were otherwise appropriate to grant an injunction, an injunction should be granted, there being no sufficient evidence of any lack of the necessary degree of confidence of the council in the plaintiff. I therefore think that, on the evidence now before the court, this is a case in which, exceptionally, if the plaintiff succeeded at the trial she might be confirmed in her post in the defendant council's organisation by grant of a suitably worded injunction.

If the plaintiff should so succeed but an interlocutory injunction is refused, an award of damages would not wholly recompense her. Making up the loss of salary would leave her uncompensated for her distress and embarrassment in having to resume her former job meanwhile and not having the opportunity to take up the more senior post at once. I do not find this uncompensatable loss weighty, but I find the equivalent loss in the case of the council even less compelling. The council offered to this court an undertaking, pending the trial or further order, not to re-advertise or fill the post of Principal Benefits Officer. So pending the trial the only 'loss' suffered by the council if an injunction is now granted but is discharged at the trial will be having to accept the plaintiff as Principal Benefits Officer against their will pending the trial. But, looking at the matter practically, the up to date position is that it is now some five months since the plaintiff assumed the role of Principal Benefits Officer, and there is no evidence from the council that it has become apparent, over this period, that, through lack of the particular abilities required for this post or clash of personalities or otherwise, the plaintiff is not able satisfactorily to discharge the office of Principal Benefits Officer in the council's organisation or that unsatisfactory consequences may ensue if, pending the trial, she continues to discharge the functions of her new post. This is so despite the absence of such evidence and the inferences that might be drawn from this having been mentioned specifically to Mr Newman on the first day of the hearing of this appeal.

NOTES

1. Most recently, in *Anderson v Pringle of Scotland Ltd* [1998] LRLR 64, the Scottish Court of Session granted an issue to restrain an employer from dismissing an employee in breach of the terms of a redundancy selection procedure. The important issue in the case was whether the trust and confidence requirement applied to redundancy selection. In the earlier case of *Alexander v Standard Telephones and Cables* [1990] ICR 291, the view was taken that it was axiomatic that an employer had less confidence in the employees it proposed to make redundant than in those it proposed to retain. In *Anderson*, Lord Prosser took a different approach and stated:

   > If there were any question of mistrust, the position would no doubt be very different; but at least on the material before me, I am not persuaded that there is a true analogy between the respondents' preference for other employees and the need for confidence which is inherent in the employer/employee relationship.

   This must surely be correct. Trust and confidence in an employee is not destroyed purely because of an economic downturn. The question for the court is whether the necessary trust and confidence to continue the employment relationship exists, so as to grant the injunction, not whether the employer has even more confidence in the workers it has not selected for redundancy.

2. In exceptional circumstances, equitable remedies may be granted even where mutual trust and confidence have been lost, so long as the court is satisfied that 'a workable situation' can prevail.

Wadcock v London Borough of Brent
[1990] IRLR 223, Queen's Bench Division

The plaintiff had been employed as a social worker since 1975. The employer reorganised the work so that social workers were appointed to one of three specialist teams. Wadcock refused to indicate his preference and was placed, against his wishes, in the special needs division. The plaintiff refused to work in the new team from the due date of 21 November, but on 7 December he did attach himself to the special needs team, although he remained uncooperative. On 8 December, he was dismissed with 12 weeks' notice. He sought an injunction preventing the dismissal pending trial of his application for a declaration that the council's demand that he work in the special needs division was unlawful. Despite Wadcock being prepared to work in that division until trial, the council rejected the proposal on the basis of the 'breakdown of confidence between the plaintiff and defendant'. The High Court granted the interlocutory injunction.

MERVYN DAVIES J: [I]t seems to me quite impossible to conclude that if an injunction is made in the terms sought in paragraph (2) in the notice of motion there will arise between the parties a 'workable situation' as that phrase is used above. On the other hand, there is no doubt that Mr Wadcock is a competent social worker and would be well able to work in special needs if he were minded to obey the orders of his team leader and other superiors. That he may have discussed his own position with some of his 'clients' is lamentable but perhaps understandable. As a separate point, I have in mind that Mr Wadcock may have been deprived of the protection of the disciplinary procedure.

In these circumstances I propose to make an Order embracing these provisions:

(a) On Mr Wadcock undertaking henceforth to work in accordance with the orders, instructions and wishes expressed orally or in writing by his team leader for the time being or by any other member of the Social Services Department having authority over him, Brent are to allow Mr Wadcock, pending trial, to work for them in special needs at the usual rate of pay;

(b) I will retain this matter pending trial and give leave to Brent to apply on two days' notice to revoke this Order should Mr Wadcock's undertaking be breached in any respect. If Mr Wadcock is not willing to give that undertaking unreservedly, there will be no order on the motion.

Robb v London Borough of Hammersmith and Fulham

[1991] IRLR 72, Queen's Bench Division

The plaintiff was employed by the defendant as its Director of Finance. The council had been involved in financial dealings which, in May 1990, had been declared illegal by the High Court. Accordingly, disciplinary procedures were invoked against Robb. Robb was asked to take leave with pay while preliminary investigations were undertaken. Negotiations then took place to achieve a mutually agreed termination of Robb's contract of employment and, as a result, the disciplinary procedures were discontinued. However, the negotiations broke down, and on 26 July 1990 Robb was summarily dismissed. He sought an injunction restraining the employers from dismissing him until all the proper contractual disciplinary procedures had been carried out. He did not wish to be reinstated but sought continuation of his suspension with pay until those procedures had been completed. The High Court granted his application.

MORLAND J: I now conclude as to why in my judgment, the plaintiff has established that he is entitled to the injunctive relief sought:

(1) The defendants are in admitted breach of contract in ending the paragraph 41 procedure and dismissing the plaintiff summarily without notice.

(2) Although damages would be an adequate remedy for the defendants' breach of contract in summarily dismissing the plaintiff and he would be entitled to damages representing not only loss of salary during the three-month notice and a time extended for the probable length of the paragraph 41 procedure to completion, damages would not be an adequate remedy for the manner of his unlawful dismissal and his deprivation of the paragraph 41 procedure.

(3) Without the injunction sought, the plaintiff has lost the opportunity of ventilating his case and justifying himself at the hearings and enquiries under the paragraph 41 procedure. The Industrial Tribunal is not a suitable alternative Tribunal for adjudicating on the capabilities of the plaintiff in such complex matters as interest swaps.

(4) The paragraph 41 procedure is workable now but could well become impracticable if delayed until the conclusion of the trial.

(5) Injunctive relief now restores the plaintiff to his position and entitlement to paragraph 41 procedure which the defendants unlawfully deprived him of in the last week of July.

In my judgment the balance of convenience requires me to give the relief sought, otherwise, to echo the words of Warner J in *Irani* v *Southampton and South-West Hampshire Health Authority* [1985] IRLR 203, the defendants would be 'snapping their fingers' at the legal rights of the plaintiff.

NOTE: In *West London Mental Health NHS Trust* v *Chhabra* [2014] IRLR 227, the Supreme Court over-ruled the Court of Appeal and granted an injunction preventing a disciplinary panel appointed by the employer from investigating a complaint against the claimant about breach of patient confidentiality as being a matter of gross misconduct under the terms of the Trust's disciplinary procedure. The claimant, a consultant forensic psychiatrist at Broadmoor Hospital, was allegedly seen on a train reading notes, discussing patients, and dictating mental health tribunal reports.

The claimant issued proceedings seeking an injunction to restrain the defendant from going ahead with disciplinary charges relating to breaches of patient confidentiality while criticisms of her were on foot in separate capability proceedings.

In the High Court, the judge held that the claimant had been entitled as a matter of contract to have the breach of confidentiality matter determined in a way which was not under a charge of gross misconduct for which she was dismissible. Further, the judge held that the defendant had erred in categorising the allegations as allegations of gross misconduct, and, accordingly, had not been entitled to enforce its rights of discipline in respect of that. Accordingly, the judge granted the injunction and declaration sought.

The Court of Appeal overturned this, holding that the employer was entitled to treat a breach of confidentiality as a potentially serious case of misconduct.

Delivering the Supreme Court's opinion, Lord Hodge accepted that the Trust was entitled to regard the allegations against the claimant as 'serious misconduct', and therefore to be dealt with under its conduct procedure. However, the Supreme Court held that the findings of the case investigator did not support a charge of 'gross misconduct'. The disciplinary policy referred to misconduct 'so serious as to potentially make any further relationship and trust between the Trust and the employee impossible.' Lord Hodge observed that 'this language describes conduct which could involve a repudiatory breach of contract' but there was no material in the case investigator's report 'to support the view that the breaches of confidentiality which she recorded... were wilful in the sense that they were deliberate breaches of that duty. In my view they were qualitatively different from a deliberate breach of confidentiality such as speaking to the media about a patient.' The Trust was also in breach of contract by allowing the case investigator's conclusions to be amended by an HR adviser. This was 'behaviour which the objective observer would not consider reasonable: Dr Chhabra had an implied contractual right to a fair process' and the involvement of the HR adviser 'undermined the fairness of the disciplinary process'. The Supreme Court granted an order restraining the employer from treating the confidentiality concerns as matters of gross misconduct and from pursuing any confidentiality concerns without first re-investigating.

Rubenstein draws a number of conclusions from the Supreme Court's decision.

> First, the Supreme Court has recognised an implied contractual right to a fair disciplinary process. Secondly, Chhabra confirms that it is open to an employee to use the courts to seek to restrain disciplinary proceedings being carried out in breach of contract, including breach of that implied contractual right and breach of an express procedure which forms part of the employee's contract. Although Lord Hodge acknowledges that 'as a general rule it is not appropriate for the courts to intervene to remedy minor irregularities in the course of disciplinary proceedings', it was appropriate to do so in a case such as this one where the irregularities were of 'a more serious nature'. Thirdly, the Supreme Court has drawn a line between 'serious' misconduct and 'gross' misconduct. Although an employer will have some discretion as to how it characterises particular forms of behaviour, and the sanctions attached to it, gross misconduct justifying dismissal is unlikely to extend to conduct which was not a wilful or deliberate breach of rule. ('Highlights' IRLR March 2014).
>
>> LORD HODGE: As a general rule it is not appropriate for the courts to intervene to remedy minor irregularities in the course of disciplinary proceedings between employer and employee—its role is not the 'micro-management' of such proceedings... Such intervention would produce unnecessary delay and expense. But in this case the irregularities... are of a more serious nature. I also bear in mind that any common law damages which [the claimant] might obtain if she were to succeed in a claim based on those irregularities after her employment were terminated might be very limited: *Edwards* v *Chesterfield Royal Hospital NHS Foundation Trust* [2012] IRLR 129 and *Geys* v *Société Générale (London Branch)* [2013] IRLR 122, paragraph 73, Lord Wilson.
>
> As can be seen from the above extract from Lord Hodge's judgment, in exercising its discretion to grant an injunction, the Court took into consideration the fact that any common law damages that Chhabra might obtain if she were to succeed in a claim based on the procedural irregularities after her employment were terminated would be very limited. Indeed, any common law redress would fail to adequately compensate an employee whose prospects of future employment, in the event of dismissal, would almost certainly be irrevocably damaged due to the nature of her profession. Her only remedy would be a claim for unfair dismissal, compensation for which is subject to a statutory cap (cf *Hendy* v *Ministry of Justice* [2014] IRLR 856, HC, ChD).

■ **QUESTION**

In the light of the trio of Supreme Court judgments in *Edwards, Geys,* and *Chhabra*, do you think that injunctive relief will be more readily available to employees in the case of breaches of binding disciplinary procedures or wrongful dismissals?

(ii) Public law remedies

Order 53 of the Rules of the Supreme Court 1981 (CPR, Sch. 1) sets out a judicial review procedure for dealing with complaints in the public law domain. It is a procedure designed to limit complaints about actions by administrative bodies. For example, complaints generally have to be brought within three months of the matter complained of and there is a two-stage procedure. An applicant first needs to apply for leave to seek judicial review and, having overcome that hurdle, to show at the full hearing that the administrative body has, in some way, acted in breach of the various rules of administrative law. While the leave procedure was designed as a hurdle intended to filter out unmeritorious claims, it has been seen and used as a cheap and speedy way of obtaining the views of a High Court judge on the merits of a claim. Many applications for 'leave' are paper applications made only in writing, i.e. application and affidavit in support showing grounds. Frequently the granting of leave is seen as sufficient support for the merits of a claim so as to persuade the respondent to seek to settle the matter without the need for, and avoiding the publicity of, a full hearing.

As regards contracts of employment, the most important administrative law principle is the requirement to act according to the rules of natural justice and fairness. Because of the import of this principle and the relatively inexpensive nature of the application for leave, those employed in the public domain have been tempted to seek judicial review of the termination of their contracts of employment. The courts, however, have attempted to close the door to such applications by reference to what is called the 'public law/private law divide' (see *O'Reilly* v *Mackman* [1983] 2 AC 237). Just because one is employed in the public domain has been held not to be a sufficient reason to justify a public law remedy. In most cases the complaint will be of breach of the employee's private contractual rights and the complainant is restricted to a private law action for breach of contract.

R v *East Berkshire Health Authority, ex p. Walsh*
[1984] IRLR 278, Court of Appeal

Mr Walsh was a senior nursing officer employed under a contract of service by the health authority. He was dismissed by a district nursing officer and applied for judicial review to quash the dismissal on the grounds that the district nursing officer had no power to dismiss him and there had been a breach of natural justice in the procedure which led up to his dismissal. The health authority, however, contended that judicial review was not the appropriate procedure by which to remedy his alleged grievance. The judge rejected the health authority's argument, but the Court of Appeal accepted it.

SIR JOHN DONALDSON MR: The ordinary employer is free to act in breach of his contracts of employment and if he does so his employee will acquire certain private law rights and remedies in damages for wrongful dismissal, an order for reinstatement or re-engagement and so on. Parliament can underpin the position of public authority employees by directly restricting the freedom of the public authority to dismiss, thus giving the employee 'public law' rights and at least making him a potential candidate for administrative law remedies. Alternatively, it can require the authority to contract with its employees on specified terms with a view to the employee acquiring 'private law' rights under the contract of employment. If the authority fails or refuses thus to create 'private law' rights for the employee, the employee will have 'public law' rights to compel compliance, the remedy being mandamus requiring the authority so to contract or a declaration that the employee had those rights. If, however, the authority gives the employee the required protection, a breach of that contract is not a matter of 'public law' and gives rise to no administrative law remedies.

NOTES

1. For a detailed review of the principles and authorities in this area, see *Roy* v *Kensington and Chelsea and Westminster Family Practitioner Committee* [1992] IRLR 233, HL; and *McLaren* v *Home Office* [1990] IRLR 338, CA.

2. A call for a reconsideration of the public law/private law divide has been made by Lord Lowry in *R* v *Secretary of State for Employment, ex p. EOC* [1994] IRLR 176, at p. 183:

> … I have never been entirely happy with the wide procedural restriction for which *O'Reilly* v *Mackman* [1983] 2 AC 237 is an authority, and I hope that that case will one day be the subject of your Lordships' further consideration.

FURTHER READING

Cabrelli, D., *Employment Law in Context: Text and materials* (Oxford: OUP, 2014), Ch. 15.

Honeyball S., *Honeyball and Bowers' Textbook on Employment Law*, 13th edn (Oxford: OUP, 2014), Ch. 4.

8

Unfair Dismissal

Royal Commission on Trade Unions and Employers' Associations
(Cmnd. 3623, 1968)

521. In the eye of the law employer and employee are free and equal parties to the contract of employment. Hence, either employer or employee has the right to bring the contract to an end in accordance with its terms. Thus, an employer is legally entitled to dismiss an employee whenever he wishes and for whatever reasons, provided only that he gives due notice. At common law he does not even have to reveal his reason, much less to justify it.

...

526. We share in full the belief that the present situation is unsatisfactory. In practice there is usually no comparison between the consequences for an employer if an employee terminates the contract of employment and those which will ensue for an employee if he is dismissed. In reality people build much of their lives around their jobs. Their incomes and prospects for the future are inevitably founded in the expectation that their jobs will continue. For workers in many situations dismissal is a disaster. For some workers it may make inevitable the breaking up of a community and the uprooting of homes and families. Others, and particularly older workers, may be faced with the greatest difficulty in getting work at all. The statutory provision for redundancy goes some way to recognise what is really at stake for an employee when his job is involved, but it is no less at stake if he is being dismissed for alleged incompetence or for misconduct than if he is being dismissed for redundancy. To this it is no answer that good employers will dismiss employees only if they have no alternative. Not all employers are good employers. Even if the employer's intentions are good, is it certain that his subordinate's intentions are always also good? And even when all concerned in management act in good faith, are they always necessarily right? Should their view of the case automatically prevail over the employee's?

...

528. From the point of view of industrial peace, it is also plain that the present situation leaves much to be desired. In 1964–66 some 276 unofficial strikes took place each year on average as a result of disputes about whether individuals should or should not be employed, suspended or dismissed. The committee on dismissals analysed stoppages—whether official or unofficial—arising out of dismissals *other than redundancies* over this period and found that there were on average 203 a year. It can be argued that the right to secure a speedy and impartial decision on the justification for a dismissal might have averted many of these stoppages, though some cases would no doubt still have occurred where workers were taking spontaneous action to try to prevent a dismissal being given effect.

529. For all these reasons we believe it urgently necessary for workers to be given better protection against unfair dismissal.

NOTES
1. In 1964, the Government announced its acceptance of International Labour Organization (ILO) Recommendation No. 119 (1963) on the termination of employment, which provides that an employer should not dismiss an employee without a valid reason and without the dismissed employee having a right to complain to an independent tribunal. This, together with the Royal Commission's proposals, led to the enactment of the first statutory provisions in the Industrial Relations Act 1971, which came into force on 28 February 1972. For a detailed analysis of the aims and origins of the legislation, see Collins, C., *Justice in Dismissal: The law of termination of employment* (Oxford: Clarendon Press, 1992), Ch. 1.
2. The Royal Commission's argument that the introduction of the right to claim unfair dismissal would reduce the industrial action over matters of discipline has not been sustained. Strikes over

non-redundancy dismissals, accounting on average for 10% of stoppages in 1964–6, still made up 9% of stoppages in 1982 (see Dickens et al., *Dismissed: A study of unfair dismissal and the industrial tribunal system* (Oxford: Blackwell, 1985), pp. 224–7).

3. Until relatively recently, the legislation governing unfair dismissal remained largely unaltered, the major amendments being concerned with the introduction of protection for those employees dismissed for non-union membership. The other significant change concerned the qualification period necessary to claim, which was raised from 26 weeks in 1979 to two years in 1985. Following the proposal contained in the Government's *Fairness at Work* White Paper (Cm. 3968, May 1998), the qualifying period was reduced to one year with effect from 1 June 1999 (Unfair Dismissal and Statement of Reasons for Dismissal (Variation of Qualifying Period) Order 1999) (SI 1999/1436)). With effect from 6 April 2012, the two-year qualifying period for unfair dismissal (and requests for a statement of reasons for dismissal) was restored (see the Unfair Dismissal and Statement of Reasons for Dismissal (Variation of Qualifying Period) Order 2012).

4. In 1978, an attempt was made to consolidate the legislation in the Employment Protection (Consolidation) Act. After 1978, a number of amendments were made via a succession of Employment Acts, the Sex Discrimination Act (SDA) 1986, the Trade Union Reform and Employment Rights Act (TURERA) 1993 and a number of pieces of subordinate legislation. As a result, a further consolidation statute was necessary in the form of the Employment Rights Act (ERA) 1996.

5. With the election of the Labour Government, further and more far-reaching changes to the unfair dismissal regime were introduced. The Employment Rights (Dispute Resolution) Act 1998 contains provisions to implement those aspects of the Green Paper, *Resolving Employment Rights Disputes: Options for reform* (Cm. 2707, 1994), which attracted wide support and required primary legislation. The most significant change under the Act is to grant ACAS powers to fund and provide an arbitration scheme for unfair dismissal claims. This is available as an alternative to an employment tribunal hearing and is voluntary on both sides. After some delay, the ACAS Arbitration Scheme came into force in England and Wales on 21 May 2001 (and was extended to Scotland from April 2004). The scheme got off to a sluggish start, with only 23 cases heard in its first full year of operation and an overall total of 60 up to 31 March 2008. The ACAS Annual Report states: 'While the number of cases received has not fulfilled expectations, the scheme provides a low cost, informal alternative to employment tribunals' (ACAS Annual Report and Accounts 2007–8, p. 35). Indeed, from its inception in 2001 until 2009, only 61 cases were lodged (*ACAS Annual Report 2008-09*).

   In *Fairness at Work*, the Government put forward a number of proposals aimed at strengthening the unfair dismissal remedy. These included:
   (a) abolishing the maximum limit on the compensatory award;
   (b) index-linking limits on the basic award, subject to a maximum rate;
   (c) prohibiting the use of waivers for unfair dismissal claims but continuing to allow them for redundancy payments;
   (d) creating a legal right for individuals to be accompanied by a fellow employee or trade union representative of their choice during grievance and disciplinary hearings;
   (e) reducing the qualifying period for claimants to one year.
   The Employment Relations Act 1999 and a ministerial order implemented these proposals with one exception. The ceiling on the compensation award was not completely removed but the maximum limit was raised from £12,000 to £50,000. This maximum is automatically indexed to retail prices and with effect from 6 April 2015 is £78,335.

   The Employment Relations Act 1999, s. 34 requires the Secretary of State to make orders to index link maximum monetary awards which employment tribunals can make by reference to the Retail Price Index for September, up or down, in each year. With effect from 6 April 2015, the maximum amount of a week's pay for calculating a redundancy payment or the basic or additional award of compensation for unfair dismissal or payments to employees in the event of employer insolvency is £475.

6. Finally, the Employment Act (EA) 2002 contained provisions which had the potential to make a significant impact on the statutory unfair dismissal regime. The statutory procedures set out in Sch. 2 to the Act required every employer to implement procedures to deal with disciplinary and dismissal issues, and employee grievances.

   The statutory dispute resolution procedures were set out in detail in the Employment Act 2002 (Dispute Resolution) Regulations 2004 (SI 2004/752). The purpose of the regulations was to encourage resolution of disputes between employers and employees internally, without recourse to an employment tribunal. The regulations contained dismissal and disciplinary procedures (DDPs) which the employer must follow, as a minimum, when contemplating dismissing an employee or taking 'relevant disciplinary action' against an employee. The regulations also contained procedures which an employee must follow if he or she wished to raise a grievance against their employer. Employees who failed to follow a set procedure could be barred from bringing a tribunal claim.

For the purposes of unfair dismissal, there was a standard three-stage procedure for dismissal/discipline and a modified two-stage procedure. The latter was only to be used in a small number of gross misconduct dismissals where it was reasonable for an employer to dismiss an employee summarily, i.e. without notice. The three-stage dismissal/disciplinary procedure is as follows:

- The employer is to set out in writing the employee's alleged misconduct. The employer must send a copy to the employee and invite him or her to attend a meeting to discuss the matter.
- The meeting is to take place before any action is taken. Following the meeting, the employee must be informed of the decision and any rights of appeal.
- The employee must inform the employer if he or she intends to appeal. The employee must then be invited to a further meeting and be informed of the decision.

An employer's failure to follow a statutory procedure was a potential ground for unfair dismissal in its own right, attracting a separate and minimum compensatory award of four weeks' pay, provided that the employee had the required one year's continuous service. But this was not to be the case if the employer had failed to take procedural steps outside the minimum framework of the relevant DDP and could show that the employee would have been dismissed even if the additional procedural steps had been followed (this was the controversial and so-called *Polkey-reversal* provision—see Section 2.C(iii)).

Failure on the part of an employer or employee to complete the steps set out in the statutory procedures could also affect the amount of compensation awarded by tribunals, not just in unfair dismissal claims but also in claims of unlawful discrimination, unlawful deduction from wages, breach of contract, and breach of working time or national minimum wage regulations. The EA 2002 contained provisions requiring employment tribunals to vary compensatory awards upwards or downwards for failures to use the statutory procedures before applications are made to employment tribunals. Unless there were exceptional circumstances, the variation would range between 10% and 50% of the award. However, in exceptional circumstances where a variation on that scale would be unjust or inequitable, tribunals could vary the award by less than 10% or decide to make no variation at all.

At a very early stage in the life of the new regulatory framework, it became clear that it was not achieving its policy objective of resolving disciplinary and grievance disputes internally. Indeed, tribunals were inundated with disputes over the precise interpretation of the regulations.

In December 2006 the Secretary of State commissioned Michael Gibbons, a member of the Better Regulation Task Force, to review the options for improving employment dispute resolution. The Gibbons Report was published on 21 March 2007 (*Better Dispute Resolution: A review of employment dispute resolution in Great Britain* (DTI, 2007)), alongside a DTI consultation document based on its proposals (*Success at Work: Resolving disputes in the workplace* (DTI, March 2007)). The consultation period closed in June 2007. Gibbons's main conclusion is that the statutory dispute resolution procedures have been counterproductive and that rather than encouraging early resolution of disputes, the procedures have fostered the use of formal processes to deal with issues which could have been settled on an informal basis. As a result, disputes escalate, leading to increasing demands on management time and unnecessary stress for employees. Consequently, the Review's 'headline recommendation' is the complete repeal of the statutory dispute resolution procedures as set out in the 2004 Dispute Resolution Regulations, to be replaced instead by a broader discretion for tribunals to take into consideration the reasonableness of parties' behaviour and the procedure when making awards and costs orders.

Gibbons stated in the Foreword to his Report:

> In conducting the Review, I was struck by the overwhelming consensus that the intentions of the 2004 Regulations were sound and that there had been a genuine attempt to keep them simple, and yet there is the same near unanimity that as formal legislation they have failed to produce the desired policy outcome. This is perhaps a classic case of good policy, but inappropriately inflexible and prescriptive regulation.
>
> There is a corollary to this. The key message from this Review is that inflexible, prescriptive legislation has been unsuccessful in this context and it follows that measures to be used in the future should be much simpler and more flexible—and therefore will offer rather less certainty and predictability in their operation. I trust that those parties who have so strongly opposed

the current regulations will as willingly accept the challenges that a different style of regulation will bring about. [p. 5]

The main impact of the EA 2008 is to repeal the statutory dismissal and grievance procedures contained in ss. 29–33 of and Schs. 2–4 to the EA 2002. It also repeals s. 98A of the ERA 1996 and revert to reliance on the pre-2004 *Polkey* v *A. E. Dayton Services Ltd* [1987] IRLR 503 line of cases. The Act seeks to achieve a 'beefing up' of the status of the ACAS code, consequently simplifying the procedure for employers. The tribunal will be able to award up to 25% more if an employer has unreasonably failed to comply with the ACAS Code of Practice (see Trade Union and Labour Relations (Consolidation) Act (TULR(C)A) 1992, s. 207A (extracted in Section 2.C(iii)).

7. The Coalition Government introduced four significant changes which affect the right to claim unfair dismissal:
   - a return to a two-year qualification period for unfair dismissal claims (w.e.f. 6 April 2012);
   - the introduction of fees for lodging tribunal claims (see Ch. 1 at p. 22);
   - employee shareholder status;
   - a decrease in the compensatory award.

8. *Employee Shareholder Status* The Growth and Infrastructure Act 2013, which received Royal Assent on 25 April 2013, introduces a new employee shareholder employment status under which an existing employee or new recruit can agree to trade certain statutory employment rights, including unfair dismissal and redundancy remedies, for shares in the company (s. 31; see now ERA 1996, s. 205A). During the then Bill's passage through Parliament, the House of Lords twice rejected the relevant clause but finally accepted it after the Government made a number of concessions, such as introducing requirements that an offer contains details of the rights being foregone and that the individual receives independent legal advice at the employer's expense.

   These concessions were in addition to earlier concessions, namely:
   - there is a seven-day 'cooling off' period, during which any acceptance of employee shareholder status will not be binding;
   - employers must provide a written statement with full details about the shares and the rights they carry;
   - any jobseeker who refuses an offer with employee shareholder status will not forfeit their social security benefits;
   - the first £2,000 of shares will not attract income tax;
   - Capital Gains Tax is not payable on the first £50,000 of any gain on disposal of the shares;
   - existing workers will be protected from detriment if they refuse to switch to an employee-shareholder contract—any dismissal will be automatically unfair.

   Employee shareholder status came into force on 1 September 2013.

9. *A Decrease in the Compensatory Award* The Enterprise and Regulatory Reform Act 2013 provides a power to vary the unfair dismissal compensation limit (currently £76,574) and the Government stated its intention that, from July 2013, unfair dismissal compensation will be limited to 52 weeks' pay or the existing £76, 574 limit, whichever is the lower for each claimant. The Unfair Dismissal (Variation of the Limit of Compensatory Award) Order 2013 brought this limit into force w.e.f. 29 July 2013.

W. Devis & Sons Ltd v Atkin

[1976] IRLR 16, Employment Appeal Tribunal

PHILLIPS J, President: The expression unfair dismissal is in no sense a common sense expression capable of being understood by the man in the street.

Cook v Thomas Linnell & Sons Ltd

[1977] ICR 770, Employment Appeal Tribunal

PHILLIPS J, President: It is important that the operation of the legislation in relation to unfair dismissal should not impede employers unreasonably in the efficient management of their business, which must be in the interests of all.

■ **QUESTION**

What impression do the above extracts convey regarding the operation of the law of unfair dismissal? Compare your view with the critique offered at the end of this chapter.

SECTION 2: ESTABLISHING UNFAIR DISMISSAL

We can analyse the law of unfair dismissal in four stages (see Figure 8.1).

STAGE ONE—Has a dismissal taken place?
STAGE TWO—Is the applicant qualified to make a claim?
STAGE THREE—Is the dismissal fair or unfair?
STAGE FOUR—What remedies are available?

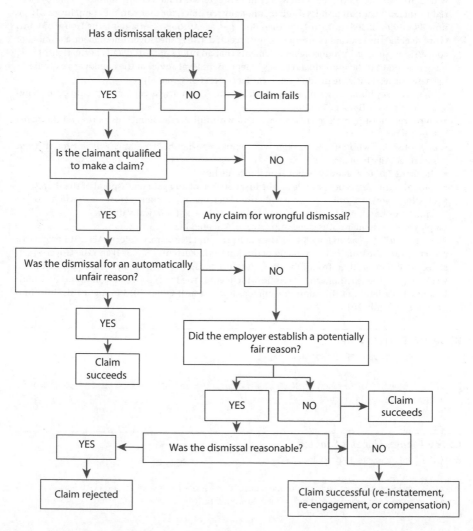

Figure 8.1 Unfair dismissal: a flowchart

A: Stage one: has a dismissal taken place?

EMPLOYMENT RIGHTS ACT 1996

95. Circumstances in which an employee is dismissed

(1) For the purposes of this Part an employee is dismissed by his employer if (and, subject to subsection (2) and section 96, only if)—

(a) the contract under which he is employed is terminated by the employer (whether with or without notice),

(b) he is employed under a limited-term contract and that contract terminates by virtue of the limiting event without being renewed under the same contract, or

(c) the employee terminates the contract under which he is employed (with or without notice) in circumstances in which he is entitled to terminate it without notice by reason of the employer's conduct.

(2) An employee shall be taken to be dismissed by his employer for the purposes of this Part if—

(a) the employer gives notice to the employee to terminate his contract of employment, and

(b) at a time within the period of that notice the employee gives notice to the employer to terminate the contract of employment on a date earlier than the date on which the employer's notice is due to expire;

and the reason for the dismissal is to be taken to be the reason for which the employer's notice is given.

NOTE: See Chapter 7 for a full discussion of the concept of dismissal.

B: Stage two: is the applicant qualified to make a claim?

The following employees generally are excluded from the right to claim unfair dismissal:

(a) workers who fail to satisfy the status of 'employee' (see Chapter 2);

(b) employees who have not worked for a continuous period of two years;

(c) share fishermen (the ERA 1996, s. 199);

(d) the police (the ERA 1996, s. 200); members of the armed forces (the ERA 1996, s. 192);

(e) Crown employees where the relevant minister has issued an excepting certificate on grounds of national security (see the ERA 1996, s. 193); *Council of Civil Service Unions* v *Minister for the Civil Service* [1985] ICR 14);

(f) workers who, at the time of their dismissal, are taking industrial action which has lasted more than 12 weeks, and there has been no selective dismissal or re-engagement of those taking the action—unofficial strikers may be selectively dismissed or re-engaged (TULR(C)A 1992, ss. 237, 238, 238A; see Chapter 11);

(g) those employees covered by a disciplinary procedure, voluntarily agreed between employers and an independent trade union, where the Secretary of State has designated it to apply instead of the statutory scheme—the designation will be granted only if the voluntary scheme is at least as beneficial to employees as statutory protection (the ERA 1996, s. 110);

(h) illegal contracts: a contract of employment to do an act which is unlawful is unenforceable—the position is different, however, if the contract is capable of being performed lawfully, and was initially intended to be so performed, but has in fact been performed by unlawful means; in this situation, the contract will be unenforceable only if the employee was a knowing and willing party to the illegality and stood to benefit (see *Hewcastle Catering Ltd* v *Ahmed and Elkamah* [1991] IRLR 473, CA; *Colen* v *Cebrian (UK) Ltd* [2004] IRLR 210, CA; *Enfield Technical Services Ltd* v *Payne* [2007] IRLR 840, EAT);

(i) where a settlement of the claim has been agreed with the involvement of an ACAS Conciliation Officer and the employee has agreed to withdraw his or her complaint (the ERA 1996, s. 203(2)(e))—where the employee enters into a valid compromise contract satisfying the conditions set out in s. 203(3); these include that the employee should have taken independent legal advice;

(j) employment where under the employee's contract of employment s/he ordinarily works outside Great Britain (ERA 1996, s. 196; see *Lawson* v *Serco Ltd* [2006] IRLR 289,HL; *Duncombe* v *Secretary of State for Children, Schools and Families* [2011] IRLR 840,SC; *Ravat* v *Halliburton Manufacturing & Services Ltd* [2012] ICR 389, SC);

(k) employee shareholders (ERA 1996, s. 205A(2)).

NOTE: It was the case before the introduction of the Employment Equality (Age) Regulations 2006 (SI 2006/1031) on 1 October 2006 that employees over the age of 65 or the 'normal retiring age' for employees were exempted from claiming unfair dismissal (ERA 1996, s. 109 (now repealed)). Following the introduction of the Regulations, the position changed and the upper age limit of 65 for claiming both unfair dismissal and redundancy payments was removed. However, the fairness of such 'retirement' dismissals was not to be determined in the ordinary way under s. 98(4), but under ERA 1996, ss. 98ZA–ZG.

Schedule 9, paragraph 8 of the Equality Act (EqA) 2010 provided 'It is not an age contravention to dismiss a relevant worker at or over the age of 65 if the reason for dismissal is retirement' (the so-called Default Retirement Age (DRA)).

What was a retirement dismissal? This was defined in ss. 98ZA–ZF of the ERA 1996, a highly complex set of provisions, but which in essence stated that if someone is 65 or over, and is retired, then it is a retirement dismissal. As long as the employer had given the employee six months' notice of his intention to retire the employee and informed the employee of his or her right to request working beyond retirement, the retirement dismissal would be fair. The employer was not even obliged to offer reasons for its rejection of the request. Only if the employer failed to follow this procedure, was there any chance of an employee mounting a successful unfair dismissal claim.

In relation to those employees who had a 'normal', generally held to be the contractual, retirement age (see *Nothman* v *Barnet London Borough Council* [1979] IRLR 35, HL) under the age of 65, there was—and still is—a requirement for the retirement to be objectively justified.

The Employment Equality (Repeal of Retirement Age Provisions) Regulations 2011 (SI 2011/1069), which came into force on 6 April 2011, introduced transitional arrangements for the removal of the DRA. The Regulations also repealed sections of the equalities legislation and ERA 1996 relating to retirement. As a result, as from 1 October 2011, compulsory retirements constitute age discrimination unless the employer can justify the dismissal as a proportionate means of achieving a legitimate aim (see EqA 2010, s. 13(2)). See Chapter 6, Section 5 for further detail on these changes.

(i) Claim in time

EMPLOYMENT RIGHTS ACT 1996

111. Complaints to industrial tribunal

...

(2) Subject to subsection (3), an industrial tribunal shall not consider a complaint under this section unless it is presented to the tribunal—

   (a) before the end of the period of three months beginning with the effective date of termination, or
   (b) within such further period as the tribunal considers reasonable in a case where it is satisfied that it was not reasonably practicable for the complaint to be presented before the end of that period of three months.

Palmer v Southend-on-Sea Borough Council
[1984] IRLR 119, Court of Appeal

Mr Palmer and Mr Saunders, both employed by the council for nearly 25 years, were charged with theft in the summer of 1980 and were suspended on half pay. In April

1981, the two men were convicted of theft in the Crown Court and were summarily dismissed by their employer on 8 April. The employees' appeal against dismissal was dismissed on 22 April and, on the following day, the council's chief executive wrote to the employees' trade union representative in the following terms:

... in the event of an appeal to a higher court against the Crown Court's decision being decided in favour of your members, [the Appeal's Committee] would (without any promise as to the outcome of such consideration) be prepared to look at the matter again.

On 19 February 1982, the Court of Appeal, Criminal Division, quashed the convictions and, on the same day, the employees' union official wrote to the council seeking their reinstatement. This request was refused on 1 April 1982 and, on 28 April 1982, Mr Palmer and Mr Saunders filed applications for unfair dismissal.

A preliminary hearing was held to determine whether or not it had been reasonably practicable for the complaints to have been presented within the three-month time limit set out in what is now the ERA 1996, s. 111(2). On behalf of the employees, it was argued that on a proper construction of the Chief Executive's letter of 23 April 1981, the council's domestic procedure had not been exhausted; that in the event of a successful appeal against conviction, they would have the right to ask for a review; and that it was a reasonable course of action not to make a complaint to an industrial tribunal and thus prejudice their domestic appeals before the Court of Appeal had announced its decision. This argument was rejected by the industrial tribunal and the employees' appeals were rejected by both the Employment Appeal Tribunal (EAT) and the Court of Appeal.

MAY LJ: ... In the end, most of the decided cases have been decisions on their own particular facts and must be regarded as such. However we think that one can say that to construe the words 'reasonably practicable' as the equivalent of 'reasonable' is to take a view too favourable to the employee. On the other hand 'reasonably practicable' means more than merely what is reasonably capable physically of being done different, for instance, from its construction in the context of the legislation relating to factories: compare *Marshal* v *Gotham* [1954] AC 360. In the context in which the words are used in the 1978 Consolidation Act, however ineptly as we think, they mean something between these two. Perhaps to read the word 'practicable' as the equivalent of 'feasible' as Sir John Brightman did in *Singh's* case and to ask colloquially and untrammelled by too much legal logic 'was it reasonably feasible to present the complaint to the Industrial Tribunal within the relevant three months?'—is the best approach to correct application of the relevant subsection.

What, however, is abundantly clear on all the authorities is that the answer to the relevant question is pre-eminently an issue of fact for the Industrial Tribunal and that it is seldom that an appeal from its decision will be. Dependent upon the circumstances of the particular case, an Industrial Tribunal may wish to consider the manner in which and reason for which the employee was dismissed, including the extent to which, if at all, the employer's conciliator appeals machinery has been used. It will no doubt investigate what was the substantial cause of the employee's failure to comply with the statutory time limit: whether he had been physically prevented from complying with the limitation period, for instance by illness or a postal strike or something similar. It may be relevant for the Industrial Tribunal to investigate whether at the time when he was dismissed, and if not then when thereafter, he knew that he had the right to complain that he had been unfairly dismissed, in some cases the Tribunal may have to consider whether there has been any misrepresentation about any relevant matter by the employer to the employee. It will frequently be necessary for it to know whether the employee was being advised at any material time and, if so, by whom of the extent of the advisors' knowledge of the facts of the employee's case; and of the nature of any advice which they may have given to him. In any event it will probably be relevant in most cases for the Industrial Tribunal to ask itself whether there has been any substantial fault on the part of the employee or his advisor which has led to the failure to comply with the statutory time limit. Any list of possible relevant considerations, however, cannot be exhaustive and, as we have stressed, at the end of the day the matter is one of fact for the Industrial Tribunal taking all the circumstances of the given case into account.

■ QUESTION

Do you agree with the approach adopted in this case? The now repealed dispute resolution procedures of the EA 2002 contained provisions to encourage the parties to exhaust internal remedies before resorting to an employment tribunal.

NOTE: In *Biggs* v *Somerset County Council* [1996] IRLR 203, Neill LJ said that while the phrase 'not reasonably practicable' might apply to a mistake of fact, it did not cover a mistake of law.

Machine Tool Industry Research Association v *Simpson*
[1988] IRLR 212, Court of Appeal

Ms Simpson was told and accepted that she was being dismissed for redundancy. Subsequently, however, she heard that another employee had been re-engaged, and that caused her to form the belief that the real reason for her dismissal may not have been redundancy.

She made a complaint of unfair dismissal but this was received by the industrial tribunal some three days outside the statutory three-month time limit. The industrial tribunal held that in the circumstances it had not been reasonably practicable for Ms Simpson to present her claim in time, that it was presented within a reasonable time thereafter and that they had jurisdiction to consider her complaint. The EAT and the Court of Appeal dismissed the employers' appeal against that decision.

PURCHAS LJ: Taken in the context of the whole of [s. 111] and applying the plain reading to the words of the section, for my part I see little difficulty in the view that fundamentally the exercise to be performed is a study of the subjective state of mind of the employee when, at a late stage, he or she decides that after all there is a case to bring before the industrial tribunal. There is no indication in the wording of the section that it is necessary for an applicant to be relieved of the strict time limit to establish, as facts, those facts which have caused a genuine frame of mind, and reasonably so caused it, to form a decision to present a complaint to the tribunal out of time.

So one turns to look to see how the subjective state of mind must be approached.

In my judgement, the submissions made by Mr Ouseley (amicus curiae) are correct. They not only reflect the ordinary meaning of the section, to which I have just referred, but are supported by such authority as is available to this court. Mr Ouseley submitted that the expression 'reasonably practicable' imports three stages, the proof of which rests on the applicant. The first proposition relevant to this case is that it was reasonable for the applicant not to be aware of the factual basis upon which she could bring an application to the tribunal during the currency of the three-month limitation period. Mr Ouseley argues with some force that if that is established it cannot be reasonably practicable to expect an applicant to bring a case based upon facts of which she is ignorant. Secondly, the applicant must establish that the knowledge which she gains has, in the circumstances, been reasonably been gained by her, and that knowledge is either crucial, fundamental or important—it matters not which particular epithet, if any, is applied—to her change of belief from one which she does not believe that she has grounds for an application, to a belief which she reasonably and genuinely holds, that she has a ground for making such an application. I am grateful to adopt the summary of that concept in the words that Mr Ouseley used, that it is an objective qualification of reasonableness, in the circumstances, to a subjective test of the applicant's state of mind.

The third ground, which Mr Ouseley accepts is really a restatement of the first two, is that the acquisition of this knowledge had to be crucial to the decision to bring the claim in any event.

NOTE: The above cases show that the time limit is rigorously applied. Such is the stringency of the approach that it has been held that an applicant may not use the excuse that his or her failure to claim was due to a mistake of a 'skilled adviser' such as a lawyer, trade union official, or Citizens' Advice Bureau worker (*Riley* v *Tesco Stores Ltd* [1980] IRLR 103).

However, in *Jean Sorelle Ltd* v *Rybak* [1991] IRLR 153, the EAT held that there is a clear factual difference between, on the one hand, advice obtained from someone who is asked, whether for a fee or not, to advise the applicant in the presentation of a claim against the employer and, on the other hand, advice obtained from an industrial tribunal employee. Therefore, the fact that Ms Rybak was given erroneous advice concerning the final date for presentation of her claim by an industrial tribunal clerk provided grounds to excuse her late claim.

In the next extract, we see the 'skilled adviser' test under even stronger attack.

London International College v *Sen*
[1993] IRLR 333, Court of Appeal

Dr Sen was given erroneous advice regarding the time limit from a solicitor, and then received the same advice from a member of staff of the Central Office of the Industrial Tribunals when he telephoned to check. As a result, he presented his claim one day late. Upholding a tribunal finding in favour of Dr Sen, the EAT held that there is no rule that taking the advice of a solicitor makes it reasonably practicable to comply with the time limit. The Court of Appeal dismissed the employer's appeal.

SIR THOMAS BINGHAM MR: Mr Pitt-Payne [Counsel for the appellant employer] drew our attention to two authorities in particular, the first of them *Dedman* v *British Building & Engineering Appliances Ltd* [1973] IRLR 379 and the second *Riley and another* v *Tesco Stores Ltd* [1980] IRLR 103 (CA). Those authorities, Mr Pitt-Payne contended, gave support to the principle for which he contended.

I would for my part accept that those authorities, and in particular the passages referred to, do lend support to the proposition for which Mr Pitt-Payne contended. When a prospective complainant consults a solicitor or a trade union official or similar adviser, the authorities do suggest that he can no longer say that it was not reasonably practicable for him to comply with the time limit even if the adviser advised wrongly.

I must, however, say that, for my part, I find the rationale of that principle very hard to understand. If the test is whether it was reasonably practicable or practically possible or reasonably feasible to present the complaint in time, it would seem to me irrelevant whether or not the complainant had consulted a solicitor. That would seem to me to be a possible approach to the language of the section but it is one which previous authority has firmly rejected and such authority has concentrated on the state of mind of the prospective complainant and the extent to which he understood his position. If, however, it is his state of mind and his understanding of his position which matters, it seems strange to me that a complainant who is misled by incorrect advice into misapprehending his rights is unable to rely on the escape clause provided in [s. 111(2)]. If the rationale is that he cannot rely on the escape clause because in such circumstances it is his adviser and not the employer who should compensate him, then there would appear, as the authorities suggest, to be a distinction between a solicitor who is prima facie liable for misleading advice and other sources of advice which are not, or may not be, liable for giving incorrect advice. In the second category I would put an employee of an Industrial Tribunal whose liability for incorrect advice is at best far from clear.

I do not for my part find it easy to apply these principles because, as I have indicated, I do not find it easy to understand them. I question, however, whether the earlier cases were really purporting to lay down a rule of law to govern what is essentially a question of fact, and I am not persuaded that the prospective complainant loses for all time his rights to rely on the escape clause in [s. 111(2)] absolutely once he consults a solicitor potentially liable for wrong advice if, as in the present case, he distrusts that advice and immediately proceeds to obtain further advice from a body such as an Industrial Tribunal which may not be so liable. That, in effect, was the decision both of the Industrial Tribunal and of the Employment Appeal Tribunal and I do not, for my part, feel able to say that they were wrong in law to reach the conclusion that they did.

NOTE: Where the applicant discovers new facts surrounding his or her dismissal, the relevant date for assessing the reasonableness of the applicant's belief in the existence of a cause of action is the date when he or she was considering making the complaint. Indeed, where two grounds of challenge subsequently come to light, the correct approach is to apply the 'reasonably practicable' test to each individually (see *Marley (UK) Ltd and another* v *Anderson* [1996] IRLR 163, CA).

(ii) 'The effective date of termination'

Establishing the date of termination will determine whether a claim is made in time, whether the applicant possessed the requisite continuity of employment at the date of dismissal, whether the retirement age exclusion is to operate in any particular case and, if the claim is successful, when to calculate compensation.

EMPLOYMENT RIGHTS ACT 1996

97. EFFECTIVE DATE OF TERMINATION

(1) Subject to the following provisions of this section, in this Part 'the effective date of termination'—

    (a) in relation to an employee whose contract of employment is terminated by notice, whether given by his employer or by the employee, means the date on which the notice expires,

    (b) in relation to an employee whose contract of employment is terminated without notice, means the date on which the termination takes effect, and

    (c) in relation to an employee who is employed under a limited-term contract which terminates by virtue of the limiting event without being renewed under the same contract, means the date on which the termination takes effect.

NOTES

1. Two useful cases in this area are *Robert Cort & Sons* v *Charman* [1981] IRLR 437 and *Stapp* v *The Shaftesbury Society* [1982] IRLR 326, which both uphold the view that the effective date of termination (EDT) is the actual date of termination regardless of whether the employment was lawfully or unlawfully terminated. So where, as in *Robert Cort & Sons* v *Charman*, an employee is immediately dismissed with wages in lieu of notice, the 'effective date of termination' is the actual date on which the employee is told of the dismissal and not the date on which notice would expire (see also *Batchelor* v *British Railways Board* [1987] IRLR 136).

2. Where the dismissed employee exercises a right of appeal, the question may arise as to whether the EDT becomes the date of the determination of the appeal, or the original date of dismissal still stands as the EDT.

    The leading case on this question is the Court of Appeal's decision in *J. Sainsbury Ltd* v *Savage* [1981] ICR 1, where it was held that if the dismissed employee invokes an internal appeal which is subsequently rejected, the EDT is the date of the original dismissal, unless the contract provides to the contrary. This approach was expressly approved by the House of Lords in the important case of *West Midlands Cooperative Society Ltd* v *Tipton* [1986] IRLR 112, which is discussed in more detail at p. 514 (Section C(v)).

3. Section 97(2) artificially extends the EDT, either where summary dismissal has occurred despite a period of statutory minimum notice under s. 86, or where the statutory notice required to be given is longer than the actual notice given. In either case, the ending of the s. 86 notice period is treated as the EDT.

    A question arises as to whether the s. 97(2) extension of the EDT will apply in the event of a dismissal for 'gross misconduct'. This is because s. 86(6) declares that the minimum notice entitlement under the section 'does not affect any right of either party... to treat the contract as terminable without notice by reason of the conduct of the other party.'

    The only authority on this point is *Lanton Leisure Ltd* v *White & Gibson* [1987] IRLR 119. In this case, the EAT ruled that an employer cannot avoid the effect of what is now s. 97(2) merely by dismissing summarily and labelling his reason for dismissal as gross misconduct. The EAT decided that, in such a case, 'it is first necessary to find out by means of an enquiry on the merits whether there was in fact such conduct which would enable an employer to terminate without notice.' Since the tribunal's decision on whether there has been conduct meriting summary dismissal will be virtually the same as whether the dismissal was fair or unfair, it would appear that in practice s. 86(6) does not prevent the operation of s. 97(2).

4. In *Fitzgerald* v *University of Kent* [2004] IRLR 300, the Court of Appeal held that the EDT is a statutory construct which is to be objectively determined, and cannot be fixed by agreement between employer and employee.

5. In *GISDA CYF* v *Barratt* [2010] IRLR 1073, SC, GISDA dismissed Mrs Barratt in a letter, delivered by recorded delivery and signed for by her son, on 30 November 2006. She was expecting the decision letter to arrive, but had to be away for a few days as her sister was giving birth. She did not open the letter and learn about the decision until 4 December. She presented an unfair dismissal claim on 2 March. If the effective date of termination was 30 November, her unfair dismissal claim was out of time. If it was 4 December, her unfair dismissal claim was presented within time.

    The Supreme Court held that the effective date of termination was 4 December, i.e. when she actually read the letter. It held that she should not be criticised for wanting the letter to remain at home unopened, instead of asking her son to read it to her, as its contents were private. As she neither knew of the decision until 4 December, nor had deliberately failed to open the letter or gone away to avoid reading it, then the effective date of termination would be the date she actually learned of the decision to dismiss. The Supreme Court stated that, on policy grounds, it was desirable to interpret the time limit legislation in a way favourable to the employee, and that strict contractual laws concerning termination of contracts should not displace the statutory framework.

Accordingly Mrs Barratt's claim was presented within time.

C: Stage three: is the dismissal fair or unfair?

(i) Potentially fair dismissals

EMPLOYMENT RIGHTS ACT 1996

98. General

(1) In determining for the purposes of this Part whether the dismissal of an employee is fair or unfair, it is for the employer to show—

    (a) the reason (or, if more than one, the principal reason) for the dismissal, and

    (b) that it is either a reason falling within subsection (2) or some other substantial reason of a kind such as to justify the dismissal of an employee holding the position which the employee held.

(2) A reason falls within this subsection if it—

    (a) relates to the capability or qualifications of the employee for performing work of the kind which he was employed by the employer to do,

    (b) relates to the conduct of the employee,

    (c) is that the employee was redundant, or

    (d) is that the employee could not continue to work in the position which he held without contravention (either on his part or on that of his employer) of a duty or restriction imposed by or under an enactment.

(3) In subsection (2)(a)—

    (a) 'capability', in relation to an employee, means his capability assessed by reference to skill, aptitude, health or any other physical or mental quality, and

    (b) 'qualifications', in relation to an employee, means any degree, diploma or other academic, technical or professional qualification relevant to the position which he held.

NOTES

1. This stage in the process of justifying the dismissal will generally not be difficult to satisfy since it does not involve any consideration of fairness. All that must be proved is the employer's subjective motivation for dismissal. As Cairns LJ put it in *Abernethy* v *Mott, Hay & Anderson* [1974] ICR 323: 'A reason for the dismissal of an employee is a set of facts known to the employer or beliefs held by him which cause him to dismiss the employee.' This subjective test was reiterated by the Court of Appeal in *Willow Oak Developments Ltd t/a Windsor Recruitment* v *Silverwood* [2006] IRLR 607. In this case, recruitment consultants were dismissed for refusing to sign a new restrictive covenant, with which they had been presented earlier in the day. An employment tribunal found that the proposed covenants were unlawful as being unreasonably wide and therefore, the dismissals could not be regarded as being for 'some other substantial reason'. Both the EAT and the Court of Appeal rejected this approach. According to Buxton LJ:

> The clue to this issue is that the question asked by s. 98(1) is whether the employer's reason is of a *kind* such as to justify dismissal. That language clearly indicates that the question is whether the reason falls within a *category* of reason that is not excluded by law as a ground for dismissal... If the reason is whimsical or capricious or dishonest... or is based on an inadmissible ground such as race or sex, then it will be excluded by s. 98(1). But if, as in our case, the category into which the reason falls—an employee's refusal to accept covenants proposed by the employer for the protection of his legitimate interests—is one that can in law form a ground for dismissal, then it is necessary to proceed to the second stage of considering whether the employer has, under s. 98(4)(a), acted reasonably or unreasonably in treating that reason as a sufficient reason for dismissing the employee.

2. In *Wilson* v *Post Office* [2000] IRLR 834, CA it was held that it is a question of legal analysis to determine under which part of s. 98 of the ERA 1996 a reason for dismissal falls. An error of 'characterisation' of the reason for dismissal is an error of law and thus can be corrected on appeal. In *Wilson*, the employer's notice of appearance stated that the reason for the dismissal was 'incapability by reason of unsatisfactory attendance record'. Because of the use of the word

'incapability', the employment tribunal treated the case as one relating to 'capability' within the meaning of s. 98(2)(a) and found that the employer had acted unreasonably in dismissing for ill health. This was an error because the correct reason for dismissing was that the employee's attendance record did not meet the requirements of the attendance procedure which had been agreed with the trade union. Even though the employee's ill health was the cause of his poor attendance record, it was not the reason for his dismissal. The Court of Appeal distinguished this kind of case from that in *Nelson* v *BBC*, where Roskill LJ said that once an employer has identified a particular reason, it cannot later claim that the dismissal was for a different reason. *Wilson* was not a case in which the employer had tried to change the nature of the case. 'It is simply a piece of nominalism and nothing more that causes it to appear that the basis upon which the employer is pursuing the matter has altered' (*per* Buxton LJ).

3. An employer will only be allowed to rely upon facts known at the time of the dismissal to establish the reason for the dismissal. Facts which come to light after the dismissal cannot be relied upon to justify the dismissal—though they may persuade a tribunal to reduce compensation: see the following case.

W. Devis & Sons Ltd v Atkins

[1977] AC 931, House of Lords

The employee was dismissed because of his refusal to comply with his employers' wishes. The employers subsequently discovered that the employee had been guilty of serious misconduct. At the hearing of the employee's unfair dismissal claim, the employers sought to adduce evidence of his misconduct to show that they had acted reasonably in the circumstances in dismissing the employee. Permission was refused. The House of Lords upheld the industrial tribunal's decision.

VISCOUNT DILHORNE: [The statutory provision to which Viscount Dilhorne refers is TULRA 1974, Sch. 1, para. 6(8). The corresponding provision is now ERA 1996, s. 98(4)]... Reverting now to paragraph 6(8) it is to be observed that the paragraph does not require the tribunal to consider whether the complainant in fact suffered any injustice by being dismissed. If it had, then I see no reason to suppose that evidence subsequently discovered of the complainant's misconduct would not have been relevant to that question and admissible. The onus is on the employer to show what the reason was (paragraph 6(1)) and that it was a reason falling within paragraph 6(2) or some other substantial reason of a kind such as to justify the dismissal of an employee holding the position which that employee held. In this case the employer's reason fell within paragraph 6(2) as it related to the conduct of the respondent.

Then paragraph 6(8) requires the determination of the question whether the dismissal was unfair 'having regard to the reason shown by the employer' to depend on whether in the circumstances the employer had acted 'reasonably in treating it as a sufficient reason for dismissing the employee.'

'It' must refer to the reason shown by the employer and to the reason for which the employee was dismissed. Without doing very great violence to the language I cannot construe this paragraph as enabling the tribunal to have regard to matters of which the employer was unaware at the time of dismissal and which therefore cannot have formed part of his reason or reasons for dismissing an employee.

Paragraph 6(8) appears to me to direct the tribunal to focus its attention on the conduct of the employer and not on whether the employee in fact suffered any injustice. If in the tribunal's view the employer has failed to satisfy it that he acted reasonably in treating the reason shown to be the reason for the dismissal as a sufficient reason for that dismissal, the conclusion will be that the dismissal was unfair...

In my opinion it is not the case that an employer can establish that a dismissal was fair by relying on matters of which he did not know at the time but which he ought reasonably to have known. The Schedule does not so provide. If, however, the reasons shown appear to have been a sufficient reason, it cannot, in my opinion, be said that the employer acted reasonably in treating it as such if he only did so in consequence of ignoring matters which he ought reasonably to have known and which would have shown that the reason was insufficient...

NOTES
1. The ERA 1996, s. 92, provides that an employee who is under notice or who has been dismissed has the right, on request to the employer, to be provided within 14 days with a written statement of reasons for the dismissal. The period of continuous employment necessary for ex-employees to exercise this right is two years (s. 92(2)). The significance of s. 92 is that a written statement

provided under the section is expressly made admissible in subsequent proceedings. Any basic inconsistency between the contents of the statement and the reason actually put forward before the tribunal could seriously undermine the employer's case.

If an employer unreasonably refuses to comply with the request or provides particulars which are 'inadequate or untrue', the employee may present a complaint to an employment tribunal, who may declare what it finds the reasons for dismissal are and also make an award of two weeks' wages to the employee (s. 93).

The statement provided by the employer must at least contain a simple statement of the essential reasons for the dismissal but no particular form is required. Indeed, it has been held that it is acceptable for a written statement to refer the employee to earlier correspondence which contains the reasons for dismissal, attaching a copy of that correspondence (*Kent County Council* v *Gilham and others* [1985] IRLR 16).

It does not matter whether the reason put forward by the employer is 'intrinsically a good, bad or indifferent one'; at this stage the tribunal is only concerned with identifying the genuine reason for the dismissal. So, in *Harvard Securities plc* v *Younghusband* [1990] IRLR 17, where the employers stated that they had dismissed the employee for divulging confidential information to a third party, whether the employers were correct in describing that information as 'confidential' was irrelevant to the identification of their reason for dismissal.

2. The ERA 1996, s. 107, sets out the position where there is pressure on an employer to dismiss.

EMPLOYMENT RIGHTS ACT 1996

107. Pressure on employer to dismiss unfairly

(1) This section applies where there falls to be determined for the purposes of this Part a question—

(a) as to the reason, or principal reason, for which an employee was dismissed,

(b) whether the reason or principal reason for which an employee was dismissed was a reason fulfilling the requirement of section 98(1)(b), or

(c) whether an employer acted reasonably in treating the reason or principal reason for which an employee was dismissed as a sufficient reason for dismissing him.

(2) In determining the question no account shall be taken of any pressure which by calling, organising, procuring or financing a strike or other industrial action, or threatening to do so, was exercised on the employer to dismiss the employee; and the question shall be determined as if no such pressure had been exercised.

Nevertheless, a trade union or union official who has exerted pressure to force the employer to dismiss a non-union member may be joined in subsequent unfair dismissal proceedings and be ordered to pay all or part of any compensation awarded (TULR(C) A 1992, s. 160).

(ii) Dismissals which are deemed to be unfair

Certain reasons for dismissal are regarded as automatically unfair. In these cases, there is no requirement to establish that the dismissal was reasonable/unreasonable under ERA 1996, s. 98(4). These include:

(a) *dismissal for trade union membership and activity, or because of refusal to join a trade union or particular trade union; selection for redundancy on grounds related to union membership or activities* (TULR(C)A 1992, ss. 152–3; see Chapter 10)

(b) *dismissal because of a conviction which is 'spent' under the terms of the Rehabilitation of Offenders Act 1974* (see s. 4(3)(b), p. 438 (Section (vi)(d)))

(c) *dismissal connected with the transfer of an undertaking unless there are 'economic, technical or organisational' reasons entailing changes in the workforce* (see the Transfer of Undertakings (Protection of Employment) Regulations 2006, reg. 7, and Chapter 9)

(d) *dismissal on the ground of redundancy if the circumstances constituting the redundancy also applied equally to one or more employees in the same undertaking who held posts similar to that held by the dismissed employee and they have not been dismissed and either*:

(i) the reason (or, if more than one, the principal reason) for selecting the employee was union-related (TULR(C)A 1992, s. 153);

(ii) the reason for the dismissal was because of pregnancy or childbirth (see point (p), or because the employee had been involved in raising or taking action on health and safety issues (see point (e)); asserted certain statutory rights (see point (g)); performed (or proposed to perform) any functions as a trustee of an occupational pension scheme (see point (h)); performed (or proposed to perform) the functions or activities of an employee representative for the purpose of consultation over redundancies or the transfer of an undertaking (see point (x); as a 'protected' or 'opted out' shop or betting worker refused to work on a Sunday (see point (i)); has been involved in working time cases (see point (f)); made a protected disclosure (see point (j)); asserted rights under National Minimum Wage Act (see point (g) note 43); had taken part in protected industrial action within the terms of TULR(C) A 1992, s. 238A(2) (see point (u); was or was proposing to be an employee representative within the terms of the Transnational Information and Consultation of Employees Regulations (see point (n)); or had sought to enforce rights under the Part-time Workers (Prevention of Less Favourable Treatment) Regulations 2000 (see point (l)) or under Fixed-term Employees (Prevention of Less Favourable Treatment) Regulations 2002 (see point (m)) (the ERA 1996, s. 105)

(e) *dismissal of employees in health and safety cases* (the ERA 1996, s. 100)

EMPLOYMENT RIGHTS ACT 1996

100. Health and safety cases

(1) An employee who is dismissed shall be regarded for the purposes of this Part as unfairly dismissed if the reason (or, if more than one, the principal reason) for the dismissal is that—

(a) having been designated by the employer to carry out activities in connection with preventing or reducing risks to health and safety at work, the employee carried out (or proposed to carry out) any such activities,

(b) being a representative of workers on matters of health and safety at work or member of a safety committee—

(i) in accordance with arrangements established under or by virtue of any enactment, or

(ii) by reason of being acknowledged as such by the employer,

the employee performed (or proposed to perform) any functions as such a representative or a member of such a committee,

(c) being an employee at a place where—

(i) there was no such representative or safety committee, or

(ii) there was such a representative or safety committee but it was not reasonably practicable for the employee to raise the matter by those means,

he brought to his employer's attention, by reasonable means, circumstances connected with his work which he reasonably believed were harmful or potentially harmful to health or safety,

(d) in circumstances of danger which the employee reasonably believed to be serious and imminent and which he could not reasonably have been expected to avert, he left (or proposed to leave) or (while the danger persisted) refused to return to his place of work or any dangerous part of his place of work, or

(e) in circumstances of danger which the employee reasonably believed to be serious and imminent, he took (or proposed to take) appropriate steps to protect himself or other persons from the danger.

(2) For the purposes of subsection (1)(e) whether steps which an employee took (or proposed to take) were appropriate is to be judged by reference to all the circumstances including, in particular, his knowledge and the facilities and advice available to him at the time.

(3) Where the reason (or, if more than one, the principal reason) for the dismissal of an employee is that specified in subsection (1)(e), he shall not be regarded as unfairly dismissed if the employer shows that it was (or would have been) so negligent for the employee to take the steps which he took (or proposed to take) that a reasonable employer might have dismissed him for taking (or proposing to take) them.

NOTE: This is part of a new set of employment protection rights introduced by TURERA 1993 in order to implement the EC Framework Directive on measures to encourage improvements in the safety and health of workers at work (89/391). A dismissal in any of the situations mentioned will be automatically unfair, except where the employer is able to establish a defence of 'negligence' by the employee. Selection for redundancy in any of those situations will be for an 'inadmissible' reason, and therefore automatically unfair (the ERA 1996, s. 105(3)). There are no qualifying hours of work or periods of service in order to enforce either of the dismissal protection rights (see *Oudahar* v *Esporta Group Ltd* [2011] IRLR 730, EAT where it was held that the employee's belief that there is a serious and imminent danger must be objectively reasonable and not fanciful, but so long as that is the case, the employee will be protected regardless of the employer's assessment of the level of risk).

By virtue of the ERA 1996, s. 44, such workers also have the right not to suffer any detriment short of dismissal.

The remedies are akin to those available in the case of victimisation relating to trade union membership (see Chapter 10). In the case of dismissal, employees will also be able to apply for 'interim relief' pending the full hearing of an employment tribunal complaint. There is a minimum basic award of £5,807 (w.e.f. 6 April 2015) where the dismissal is found to be unfair under s. 101(1)(a) and (b).

(f) *dismissal following disputes over working time*

EMPLOYMENT RIGHTS ACT 1996

101A. Working time cases

An employee who is dismissed shall be regarded for the purposes of this Part as unfairly dismissed if the reason (or, if more than one, the principal reason) for the dismissal is that the employee—

(a) refused (or proposed to refuse) to comply with a requirement which the employer imposed (or proposed to impose) in contravention of the Working Time Regulations 1998,

(b) refused (or proposed to refuse) to forgo a right conferred on him by those Regulations,

(c) failed to sign a workforce agreement for the purposes of those Regulations, or to enter into, or agree to vary or extend, any other agreement with his employer which is provided for in those Regulations, or

(d) being—

(i) a representative of members of the workforce for the purposes of Schedule 1 to those Regulations, or

(ii) a candidate in an election in which any person elected will, on being elected, be such a representative, performed (or proposed to perform) any functions or activities as such a representative or candidate.

NOTE: Although protection in the Working Time Regulations is given broadly to 'workers', the protection of this section is given to 'employees' in line with the remainder of unfair dismissal law.

Exercise of statutory rights under the regulations is also covered by s. 104(4)(d), as added, and protection is given against redundancy selection on those grounds (s. 105(4A)). The qualifying period does not apply, nor the upper age limit (ss. 108(3), 109(2)), and interim relief and a special award of compensation are available (ss. 118(3), 128(1)). Where there is a dismissal under s. 101A(d), there is a minimum basic award of £5,807 (w.e.f 6 April 2015).

For further discussion of the Working Time Regulations, see p. 115 *et seq.* (Chapter 3, Section 7.A(d)).

(g) *dismissal on the grounds of the assertion of a statutory right* (the ERA 1996, s. 104)

EMPLOYMENT RIGHTS ACT 1996

104. Assertion of statutory right

(1) An employee who is dismissed shall be regarded for the purposes of this Part as unfairly dismissed if the reason (or, if more than one, the principal reason) for the dismissal is that the employee—

(a) brought proceedings against the employer to enforce a right of his which is a relevant statutory right, or

(b) alleged that the employer had infringed a right of his which is a relevant statutory right.

(2) It is immaterial for the purposes of subsection (1)—

(a) whether or not the employee has the right, or

(b) whether or not the right has been infringed;

but, for that subsection to apply, the claim to the right and that it has been infringed must be made in good faith.

(3) It is sufficient for subsection (1) to apply that the employee, without specifying the right, made it reasonably clear to the employer what the right claimed to have been infringed was.

(4) The following are relevant statutory rights for the purposes of this section—

(a) any right conferred by this Act for which the remedy for its infringement is by way of a complaint or reference to an industrial tribunal,

(b) the right conferred by section 86 of this Act, and

(c) the rights conferred by sections 68, 86, 146, 168, 169 and 170 of the Trade Union and Labour Relations (Consolidation) Act 1992 (deductions from pay, union activities and time off)[, and

(d) the rights conferred by the Working Time Regulations 1998.]

NOTES

1. A welcome and long overdue amendment to the legislation achieved by TURERA 1993. Previously, only those who were involved in asserting rights against sex and race discrimination were offered any measure of protection against victimisation. The amendments introduced by TURERA 1993 also render selection for redundancy on the ground that the employee has asserted a relevant statutory right an inadmissible reason (see the ERA 1996, s. 105(7)). There is no qualifying period of employment for those victimised in the manner described by s. 104 (see the ERA 1996, s. 108(3)(g)).

2. *Mennell v Newell & Wright (Transport Contractors) Ltd* (1997) IRLR 519 was the first case to be considered by the Court of Appeal under this jurisdiction. The applicant was dismissed after having refused to accept new contractual arrangements, which included a clause permitting the employers to recover certain training costs by way of deduction from final salary on termination of employment. As he lacked the then normal requirement of two years' service for unfair dismissal, Mr Mennell claimed that there was a contravention of s. 104 because the deduction of wages without consent would be unlawful. The employment tribunal held that there was no actual infringement of any right relating to wages which could form the basis of a claim, and therefore no infringement of a relevant statutory right. The Court of Appeal, however, confirmed that there *can* be a claim based on dismissal for asserting a statutory right even where there was no showing that the relevant statutory right had been infringed by the employers.

It is sufficient if the employee has alleged that his employer infringed his statutory right and that the making of that allegation was the reason or the principal reason for his dismissal. The allegation need not be specific, provided that it has been made reasonably clear to the employer what right was claimed to have been infringed. The allegation need not be correct, either as to entitlement to the right or as to its infringement, provided that the claim was made in good faith (*per* Mummery LJ).

However, in the instant case, as the employee was unable to show that he had ever made an allegation that the employers were in breach of a statutory right, such an allegation could not have been the reason for his dismissal and his claim failed.

■ QUESTION

In practice, will it be easy to distinguish between a dismissal for refusing to accept a contractual change (as in *Mennell*) and dismissal for protesting that the proposed contractual change breaches a statutory right?

3. As can be seen in the *Mennell* case, a deduction from wages can amount to a breach of a statutory right. In *Elizabeth Claire Care Management Ltd v Francis* [2005] IRLR 858, it was held that this can extend to a situation where an employee is dismissed for complaining about the employer's failure to pay her salary on time. According to the EAT, the term 'deduction from wages' has a wide meaning. 'It would be strange if an employee could claim that there has been "a deduction from wages" … and that this had infringed a "relevant statutory right" when he was paid all but £1 of his wages but that he could not make such a claim if he was not paid *any* of his wages' (Silber J).

4. Section 25 of the National Minimum Wage Act 1998 inserts new ss. 104A and 105(7A) into the ERA 1996. They provide that employees who are dismissed or selected for redundancy will be regarded as unfairly dismissed if the sole or main reason for the dismissal or selection was that either:

(a) they asserted in good faith their right to the national minimum wage, their right of access to records or their right to recover the difference between what (if anything) they have been paid and the national minimum wage;

(b) as a result of such an assertion, their employer was prosecuted for an offence under the Act;

(c) they qualify, or will or might qualify for the national minimum wage or for a particular national minimum wage rate.

The normal qualifying period for unfair dismissal does not apply (s. 108(3)(gg)), nor does the upper age limit (s. 109(2)(gg)).

(h) *an employee who is a trustee of an occupational pension scheme established under a trust* Such an employee will be regarded as unfairly dismissed if the reason—or, if more than one, the principal reason—for the dismissal is that the employee performed, or proposed to perform, any of the functions of a trustee (the ERA 1996, s. 102)).

(i) *a 'protected' or 'opted out' shop or betting worker who is dismissed for refusing to work on a Sunday* This will be regarded as unfair dismissal—similarly, it will be unfair to dismiss a shop or betting worker because he or she gave, or proposed to give, an opting-out notice to the employer (the ERA 1996, s. 101). Broadly, a shop or betting worker is 'protected' if, before the commencement dates of the legislation which liberalised Sunday trading and betting, he or she was not required under the contract of employment to work on Sunday. A shop or betting worker who is contractually required to work on a Sunday may give three months' written notice of his or her intention to 'opt out' of Sunday working at the end of the notice period but not before (the ERA 1996, Pt IV).

(j) *dismissal for making a protected disclosure*

EMPLOYMENT RIGHTS ACT 1996

103A. Protected disclosure

An employee who is dismissed shall be regarded for the purposes of this Part as unfairly dismissed if the reason (or, if more than one, the principal reason) for the dismissal is that the employee made a protected disclosure.

NOTE: There is a minimum basic award of compensation of £5,807 (w.e.f. 6 April 2015).

Part IVA of the 1996 Act defines protected disclosures:

EMPLOYMENT RIGHTS ACT 1996

PART IVA PROTECTED DISCLOSURES

43A. Meaning of 'protected disclosure'

In this Act a 'protected disclosure' means a qualifying disclosure (as defined by section 43B) which is made by a worker in accordance with any of sections 43C to 43H.

43B. Disclosures qualifying for protection

(1) In this Part a 'qualifying disclosure' means any disclosure of information which, in the reasonable belief of the worker making the disclosure, is made in the public interest and tends to show one or more of the following—

(a) that a criminal offence has been committed, is being committed or is likely to be committed,

(b) that a person has failed, is failing or is likely to fail to comply with any legal obligation to which he is subject,

(c) that a miscarriage of justice has occurred, is occurring or is likely to occur,

(d) that the health or safety of any individual has been, is being or is likely to be endangered,

(e) that the environment has been, is being or is likely to be damaged, or

(f) that information tending to show any matter falling within any one of the preceding paragraphs has been, or is likely to be deliberately concealed.

(2) For the purposes of subsection (1), it is immaterial whether the relevant failure occurred, occurs or would occur in the United Kingdom or elsewhere, and whether the law applying to it is that of the United Kingdom or of any other country or territory.

(3) A disclosure of information is not a qualifying disclosure if the person making the disclosure commits an offence by making it.

(4) A disclosure of information in respect of which a claim to legal professional privilege (or, in Scotland, to confidentiality as between client and professional legal adviser) could be maintained in legal proceedings is not a qualifying disclosure if it is made by a person to whom the information had been disclosed in the course of obtaining legal advice.

(5) In this Part 'the relevant failure', in relation to a qualifying disclosure, means the matter falling within paragraphs (a) to (f) of subsection (1).

43C. Disclosure to employer or other responsible person

(1) A qualifying disclosure is made in accordance with this section if the worker makes the disclosure in good faith—

    (a) to his employer, or

    (b) where the worker reasonably believes that the relevant failure relates solely or mainly to—

        (i) the conduct of a person other than his employer, or

        (ii) any other matter for which a person other than his employer has legal responsibility

    (c) to that other person.

(2) A worker who, in accordance with a procedure whose use by him is authorised by his employer, makes a qualifying disclosure to a person other than his employer, is to be treated for the purposes of this Part as making the qualifying disclosure to his employer.

43D. Disclosure to legal adviser

A qualifying disclosure is made in accordance with this section if it is made in the course of obtaining legal advice.

43E. Disclosure to Minister of the Crown

A qualifying disclosure is made in accordance with this section if—

    (a) the worker's employer is—

        (i) an individual appointed under any enactment by a Minister of the Crown, or

        (ii) a body any of whose members are so appointed, and

    (b) the disclosure is made in good faith to a Minister of the Crown.

43F. Disclosure to prescribed person

(1) A qualifying disclosure is made in accordance with this section if the worker—

    (a) makes the disclosure in good faith to a person prescribed by an order made by the Secretary of State for the purposes of this section, and

    (b) reasonably believes—

        (i) that the relevant failure falls within any description of matters in respect of which that person is so prescribed, and

        (ii) that the information disclosed, and any allegation contained in it, are substantially true.

(2) An order prescribing persons for the purposes of this section may specify persons or descriptions of persons, and shall specify the descriptions of matters in respect of which each person, or persons of each description, is or are prescribed.

43G. Disclosure in other cases

(1) A qualifying disclosure is made in accordance with this section if—

    (a) [repealed]

    (b) he reasonably believes that the information disclosed, and any allegation contained in it, are substantially true,

    (c) he does not make the disclosure for purposes of personal gain,

    (d) any of the conditions in subsection (2) is met, and

    (e) in all the circumstances of the case, it is reasonable for him to make the disclosure.

(2) The conditions referred to in subsection (1)(d) are—

    (a) that, at the time he makes the disclosure, the worker reasonably believes that he will be subjected to a detriment by his employer if he makes a disclosure to his employer or in accordance with section 43F,

(b) that, in a case where no person is prescribed for the purposes of section 43F in relation to the relevant failure, the worker reasonably believes that it is likely that evidence relating to the relevant failure will be concealed or destroyed if he makes a disclosure to his employer, or

(c) that the worker has previously made a disclosure of substantially the same information—
   (i) to his employer, or
   (ii) in accordance with section 43F.

(3) In determining for the purposes of subsection (1)(e) whether it is reasonable for the worker to make the disclosure, regard shall be had, in particular, to—

(a) the identity of the person to whom the disclosure is made,

(b) the seriousness of the relevant failure,

(c) whether the relevant failure is continuing or is likely to occur in the future,

(d) whether the disclosure is made in breach of a duty of confidentiality owed by the employer to any other person,

(e) in a case falling within subsection (2)(c)(i) or (ii), any action which the employer or the person to whom the previous disclosure in accordance with section 43F was made has taken or might reasonably be expected to have taken as a result of the previous disclosure, and

(f) in a case falling within subsection (2)(c)(i), whether in making the disclosure to the employer the worker complied with any procedure whose use by him was authorised by the employer.

(4) For the purposes of this section a subsequent disclosure may be regarded as a disclosure of substantially the same information as that disclosed by a previous disclosure as mentioned in subsection (2)(c) even though the subsequent disclosure extends to information about action taken or not taken by any person as a result of the previous disclosure.

43H. Disclosure of exceptionally serious failure

(1) A qualifying disclosure is made in accordance with this section if—

(a) [repealed]

(b) he reasonably believes that the information disclosed, and any allegation contained in it, are substantially true,

(c) he does not make the disclosure for purposes of personal gain,

(d) the relevant failure is of an exceptionally serious nature, and

in all the circumstances of the case, it is reasonable for him to make the disclosure.

(2) In determining for the purposes of subsection (1)(e) whether it is reasonable for the worker to make the disclosure, regard shall be had, in particular, to the identity of the person to whom the disclosure is made.

43J. Contractual duties of confidentiality

(1) Any provision in an agreement to which this section applies is void in so far as it purports to preclude the worker from making a protected disclosure.

(2) This section applies to any agreement between a worker and his employer (whether a worker's contract or not), including an agreement to refrain from instituting or continuing any proceedings under this Act or any proceedings for breach of contract.

NOTES

1. As noted in Chapter 1, the Public Interest Disclosure Act 1998 began life as a private member's bill. Its aims are 'to protect individuals who make certain disclosures of information in the public interest; to allow such individuals to bring action in respect of victimisation; and for connected purposes.' Section 103A was incorporated within the ERA 1996 by s. 5 of the 1998 Act. No qualifying period of service is required and the normal age restrictions on claimants are lifted. Section 105(6A) of the ERA 1996 also makes it unfair to select employees for redundancy if the reason (or, if more than one, the principal reason) for which the employee was selected for dismissal was that he or she made a protected disclosure.

2. The Enterprise and Regulatory Reform Act 2013 revised the scope of whistle-blowing protection. Despite its title and the qualifications it imposes upon disclosures, the Public Interest Disclosure Act 1998 did not expressly require whistle-blowing to be in the public interest. As a result, many cases have involved individuals seeking to rely on the legislation to challenge alleged breaches of their own employment contracts (see *Parkins* v *Sodexho Ltd* [2002] IRLR 109, EAT). The Government perceived this to be contrary to the purpose of the legislation, and, as a result, the Act included an amendment to s. 43B(1) which requires disclosures to be in the public interest if they are to be protected. With a view to countering any deterrent effects of this change, disclosures will no longer need to be made in good faith, with motive only being relevant if or

when compensation comes to be assessed. These changes apply where a qualifying disclosure is made on or after 25 June 2013.

3. Section 127B of the ERA 1996 empowers the Secretary of State to make regulations determining how compensation for dismissal in breach of s. 103A or s. 105(6A) is to be calculated. By virtue of amendments to s. 128(1)(b) and s. 129(1), the interim relief remedy is extended to protected disclosure dismissals.

4. While only *employees* can claim unfair dismissal as a result of making a protected disclosure, the Act protects a much wider category of workers from suffering a detriment where such disclosures are made. Indeed, s. 43K(1) of the ERA 1996 seeks to include individuals who would not normally fit within the statutory definition of 'worker' set out in s. 230(3). The extended definition encompasses agency workers; certain workers who would not otherwise be covered because they are not obliged to carry out all of their duties personally; NHS practitioners such as GPs, dentists, opticians, and pharmacists; and certain work experience trainees.

5. The definition of 'detriment' makes it clear that it covers both actions and deliberate failures to act (the ERA 1996, s. 47B(1)). Examples of detriment might include dismissal, pay cuts, or failure to offer a pay rise or training opportunities (see *Ferguson* v *Abertawe Bro Morgannwg University Health Board* [2014] IRLR 14).

6. Compensation for suffering a detriment is normally unlimited. However, a limit is imposed on those workers who have suffered a detriment by having their employment terminated. In such a case, compensation must not exceed that which could be awarded to an employee making a claim for unfair dismissal under s. 103A (see the ERA 1996, s. 49(6)). The aim of this provision is to ensure that those who are not employees do not receive higher compensation than employees claiming unfair dismissal for making a protected disclosure. In any case, such an eventuality is much less likely with the increase in the compensatory award for unfair dismissal brought about by the Employment Relations Act 1999. (Compensation awards can include injury to feelings: see *Virgo Fidelis Senior School* v *Boyle* [2004] IRLR 268, EAT.)

7. For a detailed discussion of the Public Interest Disclosure Act 1998, see Lewis, D. (1998) 27 ILJ 325, who concludes:

> Whilst this legislation is to be welcomed for extending individual rights, its limitations in promoting a culture of openness must also be acknowledged First, it does not *oblige* employers either to have a policy on the reporting of concerns about impropriety, or a procedure for making disclosures. Secondly, there is nothing to prevent employers refusing to hire workers on the basis that they are known to have made a protected disclosure. Thirdly, the sheer complexity of the amendments to the ERA 1996 means that potential disclosers will need proper advice if they are to discharge the burdens that are imposed upon them. Unfortunately, advisers will also have to point out that if a reasonable belief turns out to be incorrect, defamation proceedings could be commenced against a worker who has made a protected disclosure! Where there has been sufficient publication, a discloser who failed to establish the truth of the allegations would have to rely on the defence of qualified privilege. In the author's opinion, it would have been useful if the Act had expressly provided that those who make a protected disclosure are entitled to rely on this defence.

For a discussion of the early cases, see Hobby, C., *Whistleblowing and the Public Interest Disclosure Act 1998* (London: Institute of Employment Rights, 2001). See also Lewis, D., 'Whistleblowing at work: On what principles should legislation be based' (2001) 30 ILJ 169–93 and Lewis, D., *A Survey of Whistleblowing/Confidential Reporting Procedures Used by Persons Prescribed under the Public Interest Disclosure Act 1998*, Centre for Legal Research Working Paper Series in Law (Paper 1) (London: Middlesex University, 2007).

8. In *Bolton School* v *Evans* [2007] IRLR 140, the Court of Appeal distinguished between victimisation on the grounds of the disclosure itself and other conduct, which is not protected. The Court of Appeal held that the term 'disclosure' should be given its ordinary meaning, and does not protect a course of conduct leading up to the disclosure. The employee was disciplined for breaking into the student computer system and not for informing the employer about the data security issues. Rubenstein comments:

> There can be little quarrel with the general principle that the whistleblowing protection does not provide a cloak for acts of misconduct. On the other hand, in order to attract protection at all, the employee must be able to show that they had a 'reasonable belief' that the information disclosed tended to show some form of wrongdoing by the employer, such as a breach of legal obligation. This places a prospective whistleblower in a 'Catch 22' situation: unless their belief is based on reasonable grounds, they will not be protected, but if establishing that their belief is reasonable entails a breach of one of the employer's rules, the employee is unlikely to be protected either. As the statute from which it derives makes clear, disclosure is often in the public

interest. Cases like *Bolton School* v *Evans* will have a chilling effect on potential whistleblowers. ['Highlights' [2007] IRLR 86]

9. The statutory protection given to whistleblowers continues to operate after the contract of employment has been terminated (*Woodward* v *Abbey National plc* [2006] IRLR 677, CA). The Court of Appeal's decision underlines that employers can be liable for subjecting a former employee to a detriment because he or she made a protected disclosure during their employment. The most common form of post-employment victimisation is in respect of the supply and content of references about the former employee to prospective new employers.The EAT's decision in *Onyango* v *Adrian Berkeley t/a Berkeley Solicitors* [2013] IRLR 338 makes it clear that s.47B also covers a detriment suffered as a result of making a protected disclosure *after* the employment relationship has ended.

10. In *Babula* v *Waltham Forest College* [2007] IRLR 346, the Court of Appeal held that, in order to bring a claim in respect of a protected disclosure, it is sufficient that the employee reasonably believes that the matters he or she relies upon amount to a criminal act, or found a legal obligation. The construction of s. 43B(1) set out in *Kraus* v *Penna plc* [2004] IRLR 260, EAT—that in order for a disclosure to be protected, the employee must be able to point to an actual legal obligation and 'if the employers are under no legal obligation, as a matter of law, a worker cannot claim the protection of this legislation by claiming that he reasonably believed they were'—was not a correct statement of the law and should not be followed. According to Wall LJ: 'To expect employees on the factory floor or in shops and offices to have a detailed knowledge of the criminal law sufficient to enable them to determine whether or not on particular facts which they reasonably believe to be true are capable, as a matter of law, of constituting a particular criminal offence seems to me to be both unrealistic and to work against the policy of the statute.'

11. In *Kuzel* v *Roche Products Ltd* [2007] IRLR 309, the EAT offered guidance on the burden of proof where it is alleged that there is dismissal on the grounds of a protected disclosure under s. 103A. In the view of the EAT, if an employee is otherwise qualified to claim unfair dismissal, the employee must raise a prima facie case by showing that there is a real issue as to whether the reason put forward by the employer was the real reason. If a prima facie case is established, the burden then shifts to the employer to disprove that the dismissal was on the grounds of a protected disclosure.

12. The disclosure need not be of wrongdoing on the part of the employer. In *Hibbins* v *Hester Way Neighbourhood Project* [2009] IRLR 198, the EAT observed that s. 43B(1) of the Act expressly refers to a 'qualifying disclosure' which tends to show that 'a person' has failed to comply with a legal obligation. This, the EAT held, 'expands the legislative grasp to include all legal persons without being limited to the employer. In other words, there is no limitation whatsoever on the people or the entities whose wrongdoings can be subject of qualified disclosures.' If the protection applied only to wrongdoing by the employer or a fellow employee, it would not apply where the wrongdoing by a client or customer of an employer comes to the attention of an employee. As the EAT points out, such an employee is 'vulnerable to retribution by an employer who fears losing the business of the client as a result of the employee's disclosure'.

13. The case law indicates that, in order to qualify as a protected disclosure, the employee must disclose factual information relating to the alleged wrongdoing; mere allegations or adverse opinion are not sufficient. In *Cavendish Munro Ltd* v *Geduld* [2010] IRLR 38, the example was given that if a nurse made a complaint that needles were being left unsafely on wards, that could constitute a protected disclosure; if, however, the nurse merely expressed the opinion that health and safety was not being taken seriously at the hospital, that would not be (see also *Millbank Financial Services Ltd* v *Crawford* [2014] IRLR 18, EAT).

14. The Small Business, Enterprise and Employment Act 2015, inserts a new s. 43FA into ERA 1996. Under existing legislation, there is no legal obligation on prescribed persons to take any action in relation to public interest disclosures they receive. The clause provides for the Secretary of State to require certain bodies listed on the Public Interest Disclosure (Prescribed Persons) Order 1999 to report annually on disclosures by workers. The clause makes provision to protect both the identity of the individual who has made the disclosure and the employer or organisation to which the disclosure relates.

(k) *dismissal for exercising the right to be accompanied or to accompany at a disciplinary or grievance hearing* (Employment Relations Act 1999, s. 12)

For further details see pp. 428–433 (Section C(iii)).

(l)   *dismissal for exercising rights under the Part-time Workers (Prevention of Less Favourable Treatment) Regulations 2000* (SI 2000/1551)

Part-time employees will be held to be unfairly dismissed (or selected for redundancy), regardless of length of service or age, if the reason, or the main reason, for the dismissal is that:

- they exercised or sought to enforce rights under the regulations, refused to forgo them or alleged that the employer had infringed them; requested a written statement; or that

- they gave evidence or information in connection with proceedings brought by an employee under the regulations; or that

- the employer believed that the employee intended to do any of these things.

(m) *dismissal for exercising rights under the Fixed-term Employees (Prevention of Less Favourable Treatment) Regulations 2002* (SI 2002/2034):

- Employees on fixed-term contracts will be held to be unfairly dismissed (or selected for redundancy), regardless of length of service or age, if the reason, or the main reason, for the dismissal is that:

- they exercised or sought to enforce rights under the regulations, refused to forgo them or alleged that the employer had infringed them; requested a written statement; or that

- they gave evidence or information in connection with proceedings brought by an employee under the regulations; or that

- they performed or proposed to perform any functions or activities as a representative of the workforce for the purpose of a workforce agreement under the regulations, or a candidate to become such a representative, or declined to sign such an agreement; or that

- the employer believed that the employee intended to do any of these things.

(n)   *dismissal relating to the Transnational Information and Consultation Regulations 1999* (SI 1999/3323) It is unfair to dismiss (or select for redundancy) an employee who is an information and consultation representative, a member of a special negotiating body or a European Works Council, or a candidate to be such a member or representative if the main reason for the dismissal was that they performed those functions or proposed to perform them. There is no qualifying period of service or age limit for employees making a complaint of unfair dismissal for these reasons.

(o)   *dismissal on the grounds of trade union recognition* It is unfair to dismiss (or to select for redundancy) an employee because they acted with a view to obtaining or preventing the recognition of a union(s) under Sch. A1 to the TULR(C)A 1992 or acted with a view to securing or preventing the ending under that schedule of bargaining arrangements. Employees can make an application to an employment tribunal if they consider that reason or principal reason related to one of those issues. There is no qualifying period of service or upper age limit for employees who wish to claim that they have been unfairly dismissed for these reasons.

(p)   *dismissal related to taking leave for family reasons*

EMPLOYMENT RIGHTS ACT 1996

99. Leave for family reasons

(1) An employee who is dismissed shall be regarded for the purposes of this Part as unfairly dismissed if—
    (a) the reason or principal reason for the dismissal is of a prescribed kind, or
    (b) the dismissal takes place in prescribed circumstances.

(2) In this section 'prescribed' means prescribed by regulations made by the Secretary of State.

(3) A reason or set of circumstances prescribed under this section must relate to—

    (a) pregnancy, childbirth or maternity,

    (b) ordinary, compulsory or additional maternity leave,

    (ba) ordinary or additional adoption leave,

    (c) parental leave,

    (ca) paternity leave, or

    (d) time off under s. 57(A);

and it may also relate to redundancy or other factors.

(4) A reason or set of circumstances prescribed under subsection (1) satisfies subsection (3) (c) or (d) if it relates to action which an employee—

    (a) takes,

    (b) agrees to take, or

    (c) refuses to take,

under or in respect of a collective or workforce agreement which deals with parental leave.

(5) [omitted]

NOTES

1. The detailed provisions on dismissal and other detriment are to be found in the Maternity and Parental Leave etc. Regulations 1999 (SI 1999/3312, regs. 19, 20).

2. There is no qualifying period of service or upper age limit for employees who wish to claim that they have been unfairly dismissed for the above reasons.

(q) *dismissal relating to the Tax Credits Act 2002* (the ERA 1996, s. 104B) The Tax Credits Act 2002 introduced working tax credit with effect from April 2003. Employees will be held to be unfairly dismissed (or selected for redundancy) if the reason, or the main reason, for the dismissal is:

- that they are entitled, or will or may be entitled, to working tax credit;

- that they took (or proposed to take) any action with a view to enforcing or otherwise securing a right conferred by regulation under the Tax Credits Act 2002;

- from the same date, that their employer was prosecuted or fined as a result of such action.

There is no qualifying period of service or upper age limit for employees who wish to complain that they have been dismissed for one of these reasons.

(r) *dismissal relating to making an application for flexible working arrangements* (the ERA 1996, s. 104C):

- Employees are protected from suffering a detriment or dismissal for making an application for flexible working arrangements under the right conferred by the ERA 1996, s. 80F. It is unlawful for an employer to dismiss an employee who has one year's continuous service if the reason or the main reason for the dismissal is that:

- they made an application to work flexibly under this right;

- their application to work flexibly has been granted;

- they have made or stated their intention to make an application to an employment tribunal in respect of their application to work flexibly.

(s) *dismissal of an employee for having refused to accept an offer by the employer for the employee to become an employee shareholder within the meaning of ERA 1996, s.205A (ERA 1996, s. 104G)*

(t) *dismissal of an employee related to the fact that s/he is include on a blacklist within the terms of reg. 3 of the Employment Relations Act 1999 (Blacklists) Regulations 2010 and either the employer has contravened reg. 3 in relation to that prohibited list, or the employer relies on information supplied by a person who contravenes that regulation in relation to that list, and knows or ought reasonably to know that the information relied on is supplied in contravention of that regulation (ERA 1996, s.104F)*

(u) *the reason for the dismissal was that the employee participated in official industrial action either during the first twelve weeks of that action or, if the employee has stopped taking part in in industrial action, after this period (TULR(C) 1992, s. 238A)*

(v) *dismissal where the employee has exercised his/her rights in relation to study or training leave under ERA 1996, ss. 63D, 63F,63I (ERA 1996,s. 104E)*

(w) *dismissal of an employee for having been summoned to undertake jury service, or because s/he was absent from work on that ground (ERA 1996, s. 98B)*

(x) *dismissal where the employee performed (or proposed to perform) the functions or activities of an employee representative for the purpose of consultation over redundancies or the transfer of an undertaking.*

(iii) Did the employer act reasonably?

EMPLOYMENT RIGHTS ACT 1996

98. General

...

(4) Where the employer has fulfilled the requirements of subsection (1), the determination of the question whether the dismissal is fair or unfair (having regard to the reason shown by the employer)—

  (a) depends on whether in the circumstances (including the size and administrative resources of the employer's undertaking) the employer acted reasonably or unreasonably in treating it as a sufficient reason for dismissing the employee, and

  (b) shall be determined in accordance with equity and the substantial merits of the case.

NOTE: Prior to 1980, the burden of proof in unfair dismissal claims at this stage was on the employer. The EA 1980 amended the test, primarily by removing the requirement that the employer *shall* satisfy the industrial tribunal as to the reasonableness of his action, and so rendered the burden of proof 'neutral'. A further amendment required tribunals to have regard to the size and administrative resources of the employer's undertaking in assessing the reasonableness of the dismissal. The specific reference to size and administrative resources is an encouragement to tribunals to be less exacting in their examination of the disciplinary standards and procedures of small employers.

Iceland Frozen Foods v *Jones*

[1982] IRLR 439, Employment Appeal Tribunal

BROWNE-WILKINSON J: Since the state of the present law can only be found by going through a number of different authorities, it may be convenient if we should summarise the present law. We consider that the authorities establish that in law the correct approach for the industrial tribunal to adopt in answering the question posed by [ERA 1996, s. 98(4)] is as follows:

  (1) the starting point should always be the words of [s. 98(4)] themselves;

  (2) in applying the section an industrial tribunal must consider the reasonableness of the employer's conduct, not simply whether they (the members of the industrial tribunal) consider the dismissal to be fair;

  (3) in judging the reasonableness of the employer's conduct an industrial tribunal must not substitute its decision as to what was the right course to adopt for that of the employer;

  (4) in many (though not all) cases where there is a band of reasonable responses to the employee's conduct within which one employer might reasonably take one view, another might quite reasonably take another;

  (5) the function of the industrial tribunal, as an industrial jury, is to determine whether in the particular circumstances of each case the decision to dismiss the employee fell within the band of reasonable responses which a reasonable employer might have adopted. If the dismissal falls within the band, the dismissal is fair; if the dismissal falls outside the band it is unfair.

NOTES
1. See also *British Leyland (UK) Ltd* v *Swift* [1981] IRLR 91, CA.
2. In *Orr* v *Milton Keynes Council* [2011] IRLR 317, the Court of Appeal held that whether a dismissal is fair must be judged solely on the basis of what the particular manager taking the decision knew or ought to have known when the decision was taken. The employer is not to be taken to know exculpatory facts which are known to the employee's manager but are withheld from the manager to whom the disciplinary decision has been delegated. Lord Justice Moore-Bick stated that the Act 'must be interpreted in a manner that makes it capable of practical application in the workplace… The very fact that in order to be reasonable a belief in the guilt of the employee must proceed on the basis of a reasonable investigation supports the conclusion that the employer may delegate that investigation and the subsequent decision on dismissal…' If that proposition is correct, the next question that arises is, 'whose knowledge or state of mind was for this purpose intended to count as the state of knowledge or state of mind of the employer?' According to the majority of the Court of Appeal (Sedley LJ dissenting), the answer will be 'the person who was deputed to carry out the employer's functions under s. 98.'

■ **QUESTION**

To what extent does the 'band of reasonable responses' test restrict managerial prerogative in the area of dismissal?

NOTE: In *Haddon* v *Van Den Bergh Foods Ltd* [1999] IRLR 672, the EAT held that the 'range of reasonable responses' test is an unhelpful gloss on the statute and should no longer be applied by employment tribunals. Instead, the test of fairness should be applied 'without embellishment, and without using mantras so favoured by lawyers in this field' (*per* Morrison J). In place of the authorities favouring the band of reasonableness test, the EAT advocates the approach adopted in *Gilham* v *Kent County Council (No. 2)* [1985] IRLR 18, CA. This latter decision emphasised that whether a dismissal was fair or unfair is a pure question of fact for the tribunal. Subsequently, the Court of Appeal restored the 'band of reasonable responses' test.

Post Office v Foley; HSBC Bank v Madden
[2000] IRLR 827, Court of Appeal

Mr Foley was employed by the Post Office as a postal worker, while Mr Madden was employed by Midland Bank plc (now HSBC) as a lending officer, until they were dismissed for reasons relating to their conduct. Each of them complained of unfair dismissal to an employment tribunal.

Mr Foley had been given permission to leave his shift early to deal with a domestic problem. About an hour later, an off-duty manager reported seeing him in a nearby pub. Mr Foley maintained that he had gone to the pub to call for a taxi and had left some time before the alleged sighting. The employers rejected that explanation and decided to dismiss him. That decision was upheld following an appeal which took the form of a rehearing.

The employment tribunal decided that Mr Foley had not been unfairly dismissed. The tribunal found that the decision to dismiss—though 'harsh'—was not unreasonable. The tribunal, 'mindful that we must not impose our decision upon that of a reasoned on-tlaw-spot management', concluded that dismissal for the alleged offence was within the range of reasonable responses. His appeal against that decision was allowed by the EAT on the ground that there had been no consideration as to what was the range of reasonable responses to the conduct in question.

The case was decided before *Haddon* v *Van Den Bergh Foods Ltd* [1999] IRLR 672, EAT, where the EAT held that the 'band of reasonable responses' test had led tribunals into applying what amounts to a 'perversity' test and should no longer be applied. The test of fairness in ERA, s. 98(4), the EAT said, should be applied without embellishment and, where appropriate, in applying that test, the tribunal should substitute its own decision for that of the employer. On the employer's appeal to the Court of Appeal, it was submitted for Mr Foley that if the tribunal had taken the approach in *Haddon*, it would have given effect to its express view that the decision was 'harsh' and would have concluded that the dismissal of Mr Foley, who had a clean disciplinary record, for an offence which was not gross misconduct was manifestly unfair.

Mr Madden was dismissed by the bank after internal investigations indicated that he had been involved in misappropriation and fraudulent use of three customer debit cards. An employment tribunal found that Mr Madden had been unfairly dismissed. The tribunal concluded that the whole tenor of the internal investigation was to point to Mr Madden as the likely culprit and that the investigator's conclusions had been accepted too readily and uncritically.

In dismissing the employer's appeal against that decision, the EAT suggested that all three elements of the test laid down in *British Home Stores Ltd* v *Burchell* [1978] IRLR 379, EAT—belief in the employee's guilt, reasonable grounds for that belief, and reasonable investigation—relate to establishing the reason for the dismissal and not to the question of reasonableness ([2000] IRLR 288). In a disputed misconduct case, said the EAT, an employment tribunal is free to substitute its own view for that of the employer in coming to a view on each of the three parts of the *Burchell* test. The EAT further held that a tribunal is also free to substitute its own views for those of the employer as to the reasonableness of the dismissal as a response to the reason shown for it.

The hearing of the two appeals before the Court of Appeal was expedited in view of the state of uncertainty following the EAT's decisions in *Haddon* and *Madden*. The employers' appeals in both cases were upheld.

MUMMERY LJ: In my judgment, the employment tribunals should continue to apply the law enacted in s. 98(1), (2) and (4) of the Employment Rights Act ('the 1996 Act'), giving to those provisions the same interpretation as was placed for many years by this court and the Employment Appeal Tribunal on the equivalent provision in s. 57(1), (2) and (3) of the Employment Protection (Consolidation) Act 1978 ('the 1978 Act').

This means that for all practical purposes:

(1) The band of reasonable responses' approach to the issue of the reasonableness or unreasonableness of a dismissal, as expounded by Browne-Wilkinson J in *Iceland Frozen Foods Ltd* v *Jones* [1982] IRLR 439 at 442–443 and as approved and applied by this court (see *Gilliam* v *Kent County Council (No. 2)* [1985] IRLR 18; *Neale* v *Hereford & Worcester Council* [1986] IRLR 168; *Campion* v *Hamworthy Engineering Ltd* [1987] ICR 966; and *Morgan* v *Electro* [1991] IRLR 89), remains binding on this court as well as on the employment tribunals and the Employment Appeal Tribunal. The disapproval of that approach in *Haddon* (see p. 676, 25–26) on the basis that (a) the expression was a 'mantra' which led employment tribunals into applying what amounts to a perversity test of reasonableness, instead of the statutory test of reasonableness as it stands, and that (b) it prevented members of employment tribunals from approaching the issue of reasonableness by reference to their own judgment of what they would have done had they been the employers, is an unwarranted departure from binding authority.

(2) The tripartite approach to (a) the reason for, and (b) the reasonableness or unreasonableness of, a dismissal for a reason relating to the conduct of the employee, as expounded by Arnold J in *British Home Stores Ltd* v *Burchell* [1978] IRLR 379 at 380 and 382, 20–21, and as approved and applied in *W Weddel & Co. Ltd* v *Tepper* [1980] IRLR 96, remains binding on this court, as well as on employment tribunals and the Employment Appeal Tribunal. Any departure from that approach indicated in *Madden* (for example, by suggesting that reasonable grounds for belief in the employee's misconduct and the carrying out of a reasonable investigation into the matter relate to establishing the reason for dismissal rather than to the reasonableness of the dismissal) is inconsistent with binding authority.

Unless and until the statutory provisions are differently interpreted by the House of Lords or are amended by an Act of Parliament, that is the law which should continue to be applied to claims of unfair dismissal... In this case the interpretation placed by the tribunals and courts, including this court, on the provisions of the 1978 Act in the cases of *Iceland Foods* and *Burchell* has not led Parliament to amend the relevant provisions, even though Parliament has from time to time made other amendments to the law of unfair dismissal, since those authoritative rulings on interpretation were first made. So those rulings, which have followed almost every day in almost every employment tribunal and on appeals for nearly 20 years, remain standing.

They should be applied to the two cases under appeal with the result that both appeals should be allowed and both claims for unfair dismissal fail...

Perversity point

It was made clear in *Iceland Foods* that the provisions of s. 57(3) of the 1978 Act (which were re-enacted in s. 98(4) of the 1996 Act) did not require 'such a high degree of unreasonableness to be shown that nothing short of a perverse decision to dismiss can be held to be unfair within the section'. The tribunals were advised to follow the formulation of the band of reasonable responses approach instead.

If an employment tribunal in any particular case misinterprets or misapplies that approach, so as to amount to a requirement of a perverse decision to dismiss, that would be an error of law with which an appellate body could interfere.

The range of reasonable responses approach does not, however, become one of perversity nor is it rendered 'unhelpful' by the fact that there may be extremes and that (as observed in *Haddon* at p. 676, 26) 'dismissal is the ultimate sanction'. Further, that approach is not in practice required in every case. There will be cases in which there is no band or range to consider. If, for example, an employee, without good cause, deliberately sets fire to his employer's factory and it is burnt to the ground, dismissal is the only reasonable response. If an employee is dismissed for politely saying 'Good morning' to his line manager, that would be an unreasonable response. But in between those extreme cases, there will be cases where there is room for reasonable disagreement among reasonable employers as to whether dismissal for the particular misconduct is a reasonable or an unreasonable response. In those cases it is helpful for the tribunal to consider 'the range of reasonable responses'.

Substitution point

It was also made clear in *Iceland Foods* at p. 442, 24–25 that the members of the tribunal must not simply consider whether they personally think that the dismissal is fair and they must not substitute their decision as to what was the right course to adopt for that of the employer. Their proper function is to determine whether the decision to dismiss the employee fell within the band of reasonable responses 'which a reasonable employer might have adopted'.

In one sense it is true that, if the application of that approach leads the members of the tribunal to conclude that the dismissal was unfair, they are in effect substituting their judgement for that of the employer. But that process must always be conducted by reference to the objective standards of the hypothetical reasonable employer which are imported by the statutory references to 'reasonably or unreasonably' and not by reference to their own subjective views of what they would in fact have done as an employer in the same circumstances. In other words, although the members of the tribunal can substitute their *decision* for that of the employer, that decision must not be reached by a process of substituting *themselves* for the employer and forming an opinion of what they would have done had they been the employer, which they were not.

NOTE: Commenting on this case, Rubenstein has identified 'the practical difficulties of drawing a meaningful distinction between the range of reasonable responses and a test of perversity. Parliament did not say that no dismissal is to be held unfair unless the decision to dismiss was perverse. Yet applying the test of perversity, in this context, would mean that a dismissal would be fair unless no reasonable employer would have dismissed, so what is the difference between that and the range of reasonable responses?' ('Highlights' [2000] IRLR 501).

The ambiguities surrounding the 'band of reasonable responses' test and the scope of an employment tribunal's discretion in applying it are well illustrated by the next case.

Bowater v North West London Hospitals NHS Trust

[2011] IRLR 331, Court of Appeal

The claimant was a senior staff nurse employed by Northwest London Hospitals NHS Trust. On 11 July 2006, she was leaving the hospital at the end of her 12-hour shift when she went to the aid of her colleagues who were seeking to restrain and pacify a patient on a trolley who was having an epileptic fit. The patient was extremely strong, and his fit was causing him to be violent towards the nursing team and the doctor who was trying to give him an injection to calm him down before he injured himself or inflicted injury on the nursing team. To do that, the nursing team had to remove the patient's trousers and underwear so that the doctor could administer an injection into the patient's buttocks. Although a hospital gown was placed over the patient, this was soon disturbed by his erratic movements. The injection had no effect on the patient.

The doctor sought to give the patient a second injection. He thought that by attempting to restrain the patient, the nursing team might be exacerbating his hostile behaviour. He told everyone to release the patient. When they did so, the patient tried to climb off the trolley, and in the process turned over from lying in a prone position to lying in a supine position, thereby exposing his private parts to full view by the team. At that time, the claimant was trying to hold on to the patient's ankles. She had climbed on to the end of the trolley and was sitting astride the patient's ankles. When the patient turned over, he managed to kick the claimant between her legs, lifting her up so that she then landed astride the patient's naked genitals. That allowed sufficient time to the doctor to administer the second injection which caused the patient's hostile behaviour to subside. While straddling the patient, the claimant had said 'It's been a few months since I have been in this position with a man underneath me'. At no time during the incident was the patient capable of understanding what was going on or what had been said. No relative of the patient or member of the public was present at the time.

Six weeks later disciplinary proceedings were brought against the claimant. The disciplinary tribunal held that she was guilty of gross misconduct in two respects: first, the method of restraint employed had been inappropriate and unacceptable; and second, the remark she had made had been unprofessional. She was summarily dismissed. Prior to the incident, her record had been clean. The internal appeal tribunal affirmed the decision. The claimant brought unfair dismissal proceedings.

The employment tribunal (by a majority) upheld the claimant's complaint. It held that the decision to dismiss her had fallen outside the band of reasonable responses which a reasonable employer could adopt. The tribunal considered that the primary responsibility for the failure to restrain the patient lay partially with the employer in failing to have in place a proper restraint policy; partially with the doctor in requiring the nursing team to restrain the patient on a trolley rather than on the floor; and finally with the nurse in charge of the nursing team, who had not made any criticism when the claimant had got onto the trolley to assist. The tribunal considered that the comment, in the circumstances, was not sufficient in itself to deprive a nurse of her career, and a decision to the contrary could not possibly be within the band of reasonable responses. It found that no reasonable employer would have failed to take into account the mitigating circumstances that (i) the claimant had not been trained in restraint processes; (ii) she had volunteered to help, having finished a 12-hour shift; (iii) the comment had been made at the end of a very stressful experience, working on the front line of a crisis situation; (iv) the comment was directed at the claimant, not specifically at the patient; (v) at worst the comment could be described as lewd, but a large proportion of the population would have considered it to be merely humorous; (vi) although it had been made in an area that was open to the public, no member of the public had in fact been present; and (vii) the claimant had had a clean disciplinary record.

The EAT reversed the tribunal's decision. It accepted that in the circumstances the inappropriateness of the restraint would not justify dismissal when the employer had not adopted a procedure. It based its decision on the comment made by the claimant, which it considered was not only inappropriate, but was a sexual innuendo involving sexual relations with a patient. It considered that the tribunal had wrongly substituted its own opinion of what would have been reasonable. It gave as an example of that the tribunal's comment that a large proportion of the population would have regarded the remark as humorous. The EAT considered that to be an irrelevant factor and found that the tribunal had failed to apply the correct test, namely to consider how a reasonable NHS trust would have treated the comment, and whether the decision to dismiss was outside the band of reasonable responses. The claimant appealed.

The Court of Appeal allowed the appeal and restored the order of the employment tribunal.

LORD JUSTICE STANLEY BURNTON: In my view, the EAT was overcritical and wrong in its criticism… of the ET's decision. … The appellant's conduct was rightly made the subject of disciplinary action. It is right that the ET, the EAT and this court should respect the opinions of the experienced professionals who decided that summary dismissal was appropriate. However, having done so, it was for the ET to decide whether their views represented a reasonable response to the appellant's conduct. It did so. In agreement with the majority of the ET, I consider that summary dismissal was wholly unreasonable in the circumstances of this case.

LORD JUSTICE LONGMORE: I agree with Stanley Burnton LJ that dismissal of the appellant for her lewd comment was outside the range of reasonable responses open to a reasonable employer in the circumstances of the case. The EAT decided that the ET had substituted its own judgment for that of the judgment to which the employer had come. But the employer cannot be the final arbiter of its own conduct in dismissing an employee. It is for the ET to make its judgment always bearing in mind that the test is whether dismissal is within the range of reasonable options open to a reasonable employer. The ET made it more than plain that that was the test which they were applying. … The EAT apparently did not believe that the ET decision were being true to their word, but there is just no evidence of that.

…

It is important that, in cases of this kind, the EAT pays proper respect to the decision of the ET. It is the ET to whom Parliament has entrusted the responsibility of making what are, no doubt sometimes, difficult and borderline decisions in relation to the fairness of dismissal. An appeal to the EAT only lies on a point of law and it goes without saying that the EAT must not, under the guise of a charge of perversity, substitute its own judgment for that of the ET.

NOTE: See *Fuller* v *London Borough of Brent* [2011] IRLR 414, CA; *Tayeh* v *Barchester Healthcare Ltd* [2013] IRLR 387, CA to similar effect.

Sainsbury's Supermarkets Ltd v *Hitt*
[2003] IRLR 23, Court of Appeal

In this case, the Court of Appeal held that the range of reasonable responses test applies to the question of whether the employer's investigation into suspected misconduct was reasonable in the circumstances—the third element of the *British Home Stores* v *Burchell* test. The EAT, below, had held that the band of reasonableness test applies to whether the employer had reasonable grounds for believing that the employee was guilty but does not apply to the question as to whether there was an adequate investigation.

According to MUMMERY LJ: The employment tribunal were understandably faced with a confusing state of the law as between, on the one hand, the long established approach laid down by Arnold J in the Employment Appeal Tribunal in *Burchell* and, on the other hand, the more recent decisions of the Employment Appeal Tribunal in *Haddon* and *Madden*. I had hoped that that confusion would have been removed by the subsequent decision of the Court of Appeal on the appeal in *Madden*, and that it had been made clear in the judgments that it was necessary to apply the objective standards of the reasonable employers to *all* aspects of the question whether the employee had been fairly and reasonably dismissed. Unfortunately, it appears that the law has not been made as clear as it should have been, since experienced members of the Employment Appeal Tribunal have [sic] in this case interpreted what was said in Madden, in relation to the objective standards of reasonableness and the range of reasonable responses test, as not applying to the question whether an investigation into the alleged or suspected misconduct was reasonable in the circumstances of the case.

In my judgment, the Employment Appeal Tribunal have not correctly interpreted the impact of the decision of the Court of Appeal in *Madden*. The range of reasonable responses test (or to put it another way, the need to apply the objective standards of the reasonable employer) applies as much to the question whether the investigation into the suspected misconduct was reasonable in all the circumstances of the case as it does to the reasonableness of the decision to dismiss for the conduct reason.

NOTES
1. This decision provides a solid underpinning to managerial prerogative in dismissals for misconduct. As Rubenstein observes:

A reasonable investigation in a misconduct case has been held to include making appropriate inquiries before making the decision to dismiss and giving the employee a fair opportunity of explaining. The effect of *Hitt* is to hold that tribunals should not find that a dismissal is unfair merely because the employer failed to adhere to these components of a fair investigation. It is only where dismissal without, for example, affording the employee an opportunity of explaining can be said to be outside the range of reasonable responses that the dismissal should be found to be unfair. The problem with this standard is that it is difficult to reconcile with the principle laid down by the House of Lords' decision in *Polkey* that 'in a case of failure to give an opportunity to explain, except in the rare case where a reasonable employer could properly take the view on the facts known to him at the time of dismissal that no explanation or mitigation could alter his decision to dismiss, an industrial tribunal would be likely to hold that the lack of "equity" inherent in the failure would render the dismissal unfair.' Thus, in effect, *Polkey* means that a dismissal without an opportunity to explain is unfair unless a reasonable employer could take the view that no explanation was necessary, whereas *Hitt* appears to mean that a dismissal without an opportunity to explain is fair unless no reasonable employer could take the view that no explanation was necessary. ['Highlights' [2003] IRLR 1]

2. The following case examines the substantive merits of the decision to dismiss.

Proctor v *British Gypsum Ltd*

[1992] IRLR 7, Employment Appeal Tribunal

Mr Proctor, an acting foreman, was dismissed for assaulting a fellow employee who was under his supervision. Fighting was specified in the employer's disciplinary rules as gross misconduct which 'may result in dismissal'. Mr Proctor claimed unfair dismissal, arguing that his dismissal was inconsistent with the penalty imposed in the past and that, therefore, the normal disciplinary result for fighting was not dismissal. The majority of the tribunal concluded that the employers had considered each incident on its merits and that the decision to dismiss was reasonable in all the circumstances of the case. Mr Proctor's appeal was dismissed by the EAT.

WOOD J (President): There are three cases to which we were referred and which are the three principal cases relevant to this issue. The first is *The Post Office* v *Fennell* [1981] IRLR 221. This case establishes that it is open to an Industrial Tribunal to classify as unfair a dismissal which demonstrates inconsistency on the part of the employer even though in any and every respect the employer's actions have been reasonable. It also stresses as indicated in the judgment of Lord Justice Brandon that it was for the Industrial Tribunal to say what weight they attach to the evidence and that inconsistency was essentially a question of fact for the Industrial Tribunal.

The second case is *Hadjioannou* v *Coral Casinos Ltd* [1981] IRLR 352. The facts of that case are not particularly material but its importance is in the guidance given by this Court presided over by Mr Justice Waterhouse in paras. 24, 25 and 26:

24. In resisting the appeal, counsel for the respondents, Mr Tabachnik, has submitted that an argument by a dismissed employee based upon disparity can only be relevant in limited circumstances. He suggests that, in broad terms, there are only three sets of circumstances in which such an argument may be relevant to a decision by an Industrial Tribunal under [s. 98 of the Act of 1996]. Firstly, it may be relevant if there is evidence that certain categories of conduct will be either overlooked, or at least will not be dealt with by the sanction of dismissal. Secondly, there may be cases in which evidence about decisions made in relation to other cases supports an inference that the purported reason stated by the employers is not the real or genuine reason for a dismissal. Mr Tabachnik illustrates that situation by the argument advanced in the present case on behalf of the appellant, that the general manager was determined to get rid of him and merely used the evidence about the incidents with customers as an occasion or excuse for dismissing him. If that had been the case, the Industrial Tribunal would have reached a different conclusion on the appellant's complaint but they considered the submissions about it and rejected them. Thirdly, Mr Tabachnik concedes that evidence as to decisions made by an employer in truly parallel circumstances may be sufficient to support an argument, in a particular case, that it was not reasonable on the part of the employer to visit the employee's conduct with the penalty of dismissal and that some lesser penalty would have been appropriate in the circumstances.

25. We accept that analysis by counsel for the respondents of the potential relevance of arguments based on disparity. We should add, however, as counsel has urged upon us, that Industrial Tribunals would be wise to scrutinise arguments based upon disparity with particular care. It is only in the limited

circumstances that we have indicated that the argument is likely to be relevant and there will not be many cases in which the evidence supports the proposition that there are other cases which are truly similar, or sufficiently similar, to afford an adequate basis for the argument. The danger of the argument is that a Tribunal may be led away from a proper consideration of the issues raised by [s. 98(4) of the Act of 1996]. The emphasis in that section is upon the particular circumstances of the individual employee's case. It would be most regrettable if Tribunals or employers were to be encouraged to adopt rules of thumb, or codes, for dealing with industrial relations problems and, in particular, issues arising when dismissal is being considered. It is of the highest importance that flexibility should be retained, and we hope that nothing that we say in the course of our judgment will encourage employers or Tribunals to think that a tariff approach to industrial misconduct is appropriate. One has only to consider for a moment the dangers of the tariff approach in other spheres of the law to realise how inappropriate it would be to import it into this particular legislation.

26. At the end of the argument, we have not been persuaded that the evidence in this case established any inconsistency of treatment by the respondents of employees in relation to breaches of the socialising rule. It was open to the Industrial Tribunal to take the view that inconsistency had not been established and this part of the appeal is based on an issue of fact rather than one involving a question of law. For that reason we are unable to uphold the appeal on the ground of disparity.

Finally, we would refer to the recent decision in this Court of *Cain* v *Leeds Western Health Authority* [1990] IRLR 168 (Sir David Croom-Johnson, T.S. Batho and R.J. Lewis). Mr Batho is a member of the present Court. In that case Mr Cain was a hospital laundry worker and was summarily dismissed by the health authority on the ground of gross misconduct for fighting with a fellow employee. He complained to an Industrial Tribunal of unfair dismissal. The Tribunal considered the cases of two other employees which had not resulted in dismissal for gross misconduct put forward as comparable, but rejected consideration of those two further cases on the ground that they had occurred seven years earlier at different hospitals. The reason for rejecting those comparables was that the other cases had been dealt with by different personnel on behalf of the authority and could not necessarily be said to be therefore comparable with the present case in assessing inconsistency. This Court held that an employer must act consistently between all employees and it was no answer that the decision in the other cases had been taken by different servants or agents of the employer. This was held to amount to material misdirection.

As in so many aspects of industrial relations a reasoned and reasonable balance must be sought. This is emphasised in *Hadjioannou*. Before reaching a decision to dismiss an employer should consider truly comparable cases of which he knew or ought reasonably to have known. The information may be forthcoming at the initial stage or on appeal. If the employee or those representing him know of other such incidents it will no doubt be in his best interests that they should be identified or at least drawn to the attention of the employer. If necessary an adjournment can be taken for further investigation. A small concern may not keep any records of dismissal; a large employer may do so as a matter of sound administration. We do not suggest any obligation so to do. Unless the personnel manager has been in post for a substantial period it may be reasonable to make enquiry of others, as did Mr Scott in the present case.

Industrial situations within a unit or on a site may change from time to time as may physical conditions. There may be an increase in dishonesty, fighting or absenteeism. Thus, it may not be reasonable to look back more than a few years.

These may be some but by no means all the factors which may be relevant to the approach of this employer in these circumstances. The question will always be one of fairness.

Whatever the relevant factors, the overriding principles must be that each case must be considered on its own facts and with freedom to consider mitigating aspects. The dangers of a tariff and of untrue comparability are only too obvious. Not every case of leniency should be considered to be a deviation from declared policy.

For the reasons we have given, this appeal is dismissed. Leave to appeal.

NOTES
1. See also *London Borough of Harrow* v *Cunningham* [1996] IRLR 356, EAT.
2. In reaching a decision as to the reasonableness of a decision to dismiss, it is appropriate for a tribunal to take into account an employee's length of service and previous disciplinary record (see *Strouthos* v *London Underground Ltd* [2004] IRLR 636, CA).
3. The more serious the consequences of dismissal for the employee, the more careful an investigation is required. Thus in *Salford NHS Trust* v *Roldan* [2010] EWCA Civ 522, a careful investigation was necessary because the consequence of dismissal was that the employee would be deported (see also *Crawford* v *Suffolk Mental Health Partnership NHS Trust* [2012] EWCA Civ 138, where the automatic suspension of an employee pending a disciplinary investigation was held not to be a reasonable response on the part of the employer).
4. With regard to disciplinary matters, employers should practise procedural fairness.

TRADE UNION AND LABOUR RELATIONS (CONSOLIDATION) ACT 1992

207. Effect of failure to comply with Code

(1) A failure on the part of any person to observe any provision of a Code of Practice issued under this Chapter shall not of itself render him liable to any proceedings.

(2) In any proceedings before an industrial tribunal or the Central Arbitration Committee any Code of Practice issued under this Chapter by ACAS shall be admissible in evidence, and any provision of the Code which appears to the tribunal or Committee to be relevant to any question arising in the proceedings shall be taken into account in determining that question.

207A Effect of failure to comply with Code: adjustment of awards

(1) This section applies to proceedings before an employment tribunal relating to a claim by an employee under any of the jurisdictions listed in Schedule A2.

(2) If, in the case of proceedings to which this section applies, it appears to the employment tribunal that—

(a) the claim to which the proceedings relate concerns a matter to which a relevant Code of Practice applies,

(b) the employer has failed to comply with that Code in relation to that matter, and

(c) that failure was unreasonable,

the employment tribunal may, if it considers it just and equitable in all the circumstances to do so, increase any award it makes to the employee by no more than 25%.

(3) If, in the case of proceedings to which this section applies, it appears to the employment tribunal that—

(a) the claim to which the proceedings relate concerns a matter to which a relevant Code of Practice applies,

(b) the employee has failed to comply with that Code in relation to that matter, and

(c) that failure was unreasonable,

the employment tribunal may, if it considers it just and equitable in all the circumstances to do so, reduce any award it makes to the employee by no more than 25%.

(4) In subsections (2) and (3), 'relevant Code of Practice' means a Code of Practice issued under this Chapter which relates exclusively or primarily to procedure for the resolution of disputes.

(5) Where an award falls to be adjusted under this section and under section 38 of the Employment Act 2002, the adjustment under this section shall be made before the adjustment under that section.

NOTES

1. The concept of procedural fairness is not expressly articulated in the legislation, but its development was influenced by the Code of Practice which was introduced to accompany the legislation. The Code was originally issued by ACAS under the EPA 1975, s. 6, and was brought into effect on 20 June 1977 (by SI 1977/867). A revised version of the Code, issued under TULR(C)A 1992, came into effect on 4 September 2000. ACAS updated its Code of Practice to take account of the new statutory procedures set out in the EA 2002. The revised Code came into effect on 1 October 2004 at the same time as the regulations giving effect to the new dispute resolution procedures. Following the abolition of the short-lived dispute resolution procedures by the EA 2008, ACAS produced a revised Code of Practice on disciplinary and grievance procedures, operative from 6 April 2009. Section 207A allows employment tribunals to increase or reduce awards to employers/employees by up to 25% to the extent that they are adjudged to have unreasonably failed to comply with the Code.

2. To accompany the new Code, ACAS published a new non-statutory guide: *Discipline and Grievances at Work* (2009). Although the guide has no statutory force, given that it concisely summarises the views of the leading cases on what constitutes good disciplinary practice, it is well worthy of careful study and may well be influential in employment tribunal determinations.

3. A revised Code of Practice came into force on 11 March 2015. The revisions relate to the sections of the Code dealing with the right to be accompanied at a disciplinary or grievance hearing.

ACAS Code of Practice 1 on Disciplinary and Grievance Procedures

(2015): in force with effect from 11 March 2015

1. ... The Code does not apply to redundancy dismissals or the non renewal of fixed term contracts on their expiry.

2. Fairness and transparency are promoted by developing and using rules and procedures for handling disciplinary and grievance situations. These should be set down in writing, be specific and clear. Employees and, where appropriate, their representatives should be involved in the development of rules and procedures. It is also important to help employees and managers understand what the rules and procedures are, where they can be found and how they are to be used.

3. Where some form of formal action is needed, what action is reasonable or justified will depend on all the circumstances of the particular case. Employment tribunals will take the size and resources of an employer into account when deciding on relevant cases and it may sometimes not be practicable for all employers to take all of the steps set out in this Code.

4. That said, whenever a disciplinary or grievance process is being followed it is important to deal with issues fairly. There are a number of elements to this:

- Employers and employees should raise and deal with issues promptly and should not unreasonably delay meetings, decisions or confirmation of those decisions.
- Employers and employees should act consistently.
- Employers should carry out any necessary investigations, to establish the facts of the case.
- Employers should inform employees of the basis of the problem and give them an opportunity to put their case in response before any decisions are made.
- Employers should allow employees to be accompanied at any formal disciplinary or grievance meeting.
- Employers should allow an employee to appeal against any formal decision made.

Keys to handling disciplinary issues in the workplace

Establish the facts of each case

5. It is important to carry out necessary investigations of potential disciplinary matters without unreasonable delay to establish the facts of the case. In some cases this will require the holding of an investigatory meeting with the employee before proceeding to any disciplinary hearing. In others, the investigatory stage will be the collation of evidence by the employer for use at any disciplinary hearing.

6. In misconduct cases, where practicable, different people should carry out the investigation and disciplinary hearing.

7. If there is an investigatory meeting this should not by itself result in any disciplinary action. Although there is no statutory right for an employee to be accompanied at a formal investigatory meeting, such a right may be allowed under an employer's own procedure.

8. In cases where a period of suspension with pay is considered necessary, this period should be as brief as possible, should be kept under review and it should be made clear that this suspension is not considered a disciplinary action.

Inform the employee of the problem

9. If it is decided that there is a disciplinary case to answer, the employee should be notified of this in writing. This notification should contain sufficient information about the alleged misconduct or poor performance and its possible consequences to enable the employee to prepare to answer the case at a disciplinary meeting. It would normally be appropriate to provide copies of any written evidence, which may include any witness statements, with the notification.

10. The notification should also give details of the time and venue for the disciplinary meeting and advise the employee of their right to be accompanied at the meeting.

Hold a meeting with the employee to discuss the problem

11. The meeting should be held without unreasonable delay whilst allowing the employee reasonable time to prepare their case.

12. Employers and employees (and their companions) should make every effort to attend the meeting. At the meeting the employer should explain the complaint against the employee and go through the evidence that has been gathered. The employee should be allowed to set out their case and answer any allegations that have been made. The employee should also be given a reasonable opportunity to ask questions, present evidence and call relevant witnesses. They should also be given an opportunity to raise points about any information provided by witnesses. Where an employer or employee intends to call relevant witnesses they should give advance notice that they intend to do this.

Allow the employee to be accompanied at the meeting

13. Workers have a statutory right to be accompanied by a companion where the disciplinary meeting could result in:
- a formal warning being issued; or
- the taking of some other disciplinary action; or
- the confirmation of a warning or some other disciplinary action (appeal hearings).

14. The statutory right is to be accompanied by a fellow worker, a trade union representative, or an official employed by the trade union. A trade union representative who is not an employed official must have been certified by their union as being competent to accompany a worker. Employers must agree to a request to be accompanied by any companion from one of these categories. Workers may also alter their choice of companion if they wish. As a matter of good practice, in making their choice workers should bear in mind the practicalities of the arrangements. For instance, a worker may choose to be accompanied by a companion who is suitable, willing, and available on site rather than someone from a geographically remote location.

15. To exercise the statutory right to be accompanied, workers must make a reasonable request. What is reasonable will depend on the circumstances of each individual case. A request to be accompanied does not have to be in writing or within a certain time frame. However, a worker should provide enough time for the employer to deal with the companion's attendance at the meeting. Workers should also consider how they make their request so that it clearly understood, for instance by letting the employer know in advance the name of the companion where possible and whether they are a fellow worker or trade union official or representative.

16. If a worker's chosen companion will not be available at the time proposed for the hearing by the employer, the employer must postpone the hearing to a time proposed by the worker provided that the alternative time is both reasonable and not more than five working days after the date originally proposed.

17. The companion should be allowed to address the hearing to put and sum up the worker's case, respond on behalf of the worker to any views expressed at the meeting, and confer with the worker during the hearing. The companion does not, however, have the right to answer questions on the worker's behalf, address the hearing if the worker does not wish it or prevent the employer from explaining their case.

Decide on appropriate action

18. After the meeting decide whether or not disciplinary or any other action is justified and inform the employee accordingly in writing.

19. Where misconduct is confirmed or the employee is found to be performing unsatisfactorily it is usual to give the employee a written warning. A further act of misconduct or failure to improve performance within a set period would normally result in a final written warning.

20. If an employee's first misconduct or unsatisfactory performance is sufficiently serious, it may be appropriate to move directly to a final written warning. This might occur where the employee's actions have had, or are liable to have, a serious or harmful impact on the organisation.

21. A first or final written warning should set out the nature of the misconduct or poor performance and the change in behaviour or improvement in performance required (with timescale). The employee should be told how long the warning will remain current. The employee should be informed of the consequences of further misconduct, or failure to improve performance, within the set period following a final warning. For instance that it may result in dismissal or some other contractual penalty such as demotion or loss of seniority.

22. A decision to dismiss should only be taken by a manager who has the authority to do so. The employee should be informed as soon as possible of the reasons for the dismissal, the date on which the employment contract will end, the appropriate period of notice and their right of appeal.

23. Some acts, termed gross misconduct, are so serious in themselves or have such serious consequences that they may call for dismissal without notice for a first offence. But a fair disciplinary process should always be followed, before dismissing for gross misconduct.

24. Disciplinary rules should give examples of acts which the employer regards as acts of gross misconduct. These may vary according to the nature of the organisation and what it does, but might include things such as theft or fraud, physical violence, gross negligence or serious insubordination.

25. Where an employee is persistently unable or unwilling to attend a disciplinary meeting without good cause the employer should make a decision on the evidence available.

Provide employees with an opportunity to appeal

26. Where an employee feels that disciplinary action taken against them is wrong or unjust they should appeal against the decision. Appeals should be heard without unreasonable delay and ideally at an agreed time and place. Employees should let employers know the grounds for their appeal in writing.

27. The appeal should be dealt with impartially and wherever possible, by a manager who has not previously been involved in the case.

28. Workers have a statutory right to be accompanied at appeal hearings.

29. Employees should be informed in writing of the results of the appeal hearing as soon as possible.

NOTE: The latest version of the Code (para. 21) repeats the advice of earlier versions that 'the employee should be told how long the warning will remain current'. The guide offers the view that in relation to a first formal written warning it should be disregarded for disciplinary purposes after a specified period (e.g. six months). In relation to a final written warning, the guide advises that such a warning should normally remain current for a specified period, e.g. 12 months. In *Diosynth Ltd* v *Thomson* [2006] IRLR 284, the Scottish Court of Session, Inner House, underlined that it is not reasonable for an employer to rely on a lapsed warning to justify a subsequent dismissal. This was *not* the view taken by the Court of Appeal in *Airbus UK Ltd* v *Webb* [2008] IRLR 309, where it was held that there is nothing in the wide wording of s. 98(4) that laid down a rule that the employee's previous misconduct must be ignored by the employer—even if the time-limited warning has lapsed.

Auguste Noel Ltd v *Curtis*
[1990] IRLR 326, Employment Appeal Tribunal

Mr Curtis, a 'multi-drop' driver, was dismissed on 18 March 1988 for an act of misconduct involving mishandling company property. In deciding to dismiss him for that offence, the employer took into account two previous written warnings, one dated 16 October 1987 concerning his relationship with other employees, and the other dated 25 February 1988 which referred to unsatisfactory documentation and absenteeism. The EAT held that the tribunal had been wrong to find that the dismissal for mishandling company property was unfair because, in deciding to dismiss for that reason, the employer had taken into account two final written warnings for different offences.

WOOD J: [I]t can very rarely be said, if ever, that warnings are irrelevant to the consideration of an employer who is considering dismissal. The mere fact that the conduct was of a different kind on those occasions when warnings were given does not seem to us to render them irrelevant. It is essentially a matter of balance, of doing what is fair and reasonable in the circumstances and the employer is entitled to consider the existence of warnings. He is entitled to look at the substance of the complaint on each of those occasions, how many warnings there have been, the dates and the periods of time between those warnings and indeed all the circumstances of the case.

NOTES
1. Given the relative lack of authority on the point and the fact that advice in the ACAS Code and the advisory handbook seems to affirm the basis that warnings are being given for the same reason, it may be that employers are still best advised to keep warnings for different offences separate. Of course, there may come a point when the cumulative effect of a number of warnings on different matters provides reasonable grounds to dismiss on the ground of generally unacceptable behaviour (see Smith, I.T. and Baker, A., *Smith and Wood's Employment Law*, 10th edn (Oxford: OUP, 2010), p. 425).
2. Written warnings underlying a dismissal can only be reviewed by a tribunal if allegedly issued in bad faith or 'manifestly inappropriate'. In *Davies* v *Sandwell Metropolitan Borough Council* [2013] IRLR 374, a teacher was given a warning for misconduct. She appealed against the warning, but the appeal was adjourned and never re-arranged. Subsequently, there was another act of alleged misconduct, and the claimant was dismissed. It was accepted that she would not have been dismissed if she had not received a prior final written warning. Lord Justice Mummery stated: 'it is not the function of the ET to re-open the final warning and rule on an issue raised by the claimant as to whether the final warning should, or should not, have been issued and whether it was a legally valid warning or a "nullity". The function of the ET is to apply the objective statutory test of reasonableness to determine whether the final warning was a circumstance, which a reasonable employer could reasonably take into account in the decision to dismiss the claimant for subsequent misconduct.' However, 'it is relevant for the ET to consider whether | the final warning was issued in good faith, whether there were prima facie grounds for following the final warning procedure and whether it was manifestly inappropriate to issue the warning.' In this case, it was clear that the final warning was properly taken into account by the employer in dismissing the claimant.
3. The ACAS Guide also covers cases of gross misconduct.

Discipline and Grievances at Work: The ACAS Guide (2009)

Dismissal without notice

Employers should give all employees a clear indication of the type of misconduct which, in the light of the requirements of the employer's business, will warrant dismissal without the normal period of notice or pay in lieu of notice. So far as possible the types of offences which fall into this category of 'gross misconduct' should be clearly specified in the rules, although such a list cannot normally be exhaustive.

What is gross misconduct?

Gross misconduct is generally seen as misconduct serious enough to overturn the contract between the employer and the employee thus justifying summary dismissal. Acts which constitute gross misconduct must be very serious and are best determined by organisations in the light of their own particular circumstances. However, examples of gross misconduct might include:

- theft or fraud
- physical violence or bullying
- deliberate and serious damage to property
- serious misuse of an organisation's property or name
- deliberately accessing internet sites containing pornographic, offensive or obscene material
- serious insubordination
- unlawful discrimination or harassment
- bringing the organisation into serious disrepute
- serious incapability at work brought on by alcohol or illegal drugs
- causing loss, damage or injury through serious negligence
- a serious breach of health and safety rules
- a serious breach of confidence.

If an employer considers an employee guilty of gross misconduct and thus liable for summary dismissal, it is still important to follow a fair procedure as for any other disciplinary offence. This will include establishing the facts of the case before taking any action, holding a meeting with the employee and allowing the employee the right of appeal. It should be made clear to the employee that dismissal is a possibility. A short period of suspension with full pay to help establish the facts or to allow tempers to cool may be helpful. However, such a period of suspension should only be imposed after careful consideration and should be kept under review. It should be made clear to the employee that the suspension is not a disciplinary action and does not involve any prejudgement.

NOTE: The ERA 1996, s. 3(1)(a), requires that the written statement of terms of employment must include 'any disciplinary rules applicable to the employee'. However, the EA 1989 removed the statutory requirement to provide a note of disciplinary rules and appeals procedures where the number of employees of the employer and any associated employer is fewer than 20 (see now the ERA 1996, s. 3(3)). This amendment was yet a further example of the then Conservative Government's policy of deregulation in the name of encouraging the growth of small businesses. However, given that a factor which will be influential in many dismissal cases is whether the employer adequately brought the existence of a particular disciplinary rule to the attention of an employee, small employers were well advised not to take advantage of this exemption. The 'fewer than 20' threshold was hard to justify and the EA 2002 removed the exemption.

Ladbroke Racing v *Arnott*
[1983] IRLR 154, Court of Session

The applicants were employed in a betting shop. The employer's disciplinary rules specifically provided that employees were not permitted to place bets or to allow other staff to do so. Two of the applicants had placed such bets, one for her brother on one occasion and the other occasionally for old-age pensioners, and the third, the office manager, had condoned these actions. All three employees were dismissed and an industrial tribunal found the dismissals to be unfair. This decision was upheld by the EAT and the Court of Session.

LORD DUNPARK: It was the appellants who failed to appreciate that paragraph 6(8) [see now ERA 1996, s. 98(4)] required them to have regard to all the circumstances of the case against each employee if they were to satisfy the industrial tribunal that their dismissals were fair. If the appellants' attitude is that any breach, however minor, of the rule, which carries the penalty of immediate dismissal, warrants immediate dismissal, then they cannot meet the standard set by paragraph 6(8). As there was no positive evidence in this case that the appellants' reason for dismissal was based upon factors other than breach of the rule *per se*, they could not comply with the provisions of paragraph 6(8), which the Appeal Tribunal correctly describes as 'over-riding provisions'. That means that they are superimposed on the rule which carries the penalty of instant dismissal, so that the appellants could not satisfy these provisions by imposing that penalty without regard to any facts or circumstances other than the breach *per se*.

Ulsterbus v *Henderson*

[1989] IRLR 253, Northern Ireland Court of Appeal

Mr Henderson was dismissed from his job as a bus conductor following a complaint that he had failed to give tickets in return for payment of fares. An industrial tribunal upheld his complaint of unfair dismissal. One of the grounds for this finding was the fact that it had not been made clear in the company's disciplinary procedure that offences of this nature would attract the sanction of dismissal.

The Northern Ireland Court of Appeal allowed the employer's appeal and quashed the industrial tribunal's decision.

O'DONNELL LJ: There may be circumstances in which it would be unreasonable for an employer to dismiss an employee for a minor misdemeanour without warning that dismissal might result from such an act. The failure to give tickets in return for payment was a most serious offence and was likely to lead to dismissal; such a result would be obvious to any employee.

Dairy Produce Packers Ltd v *Beverstock*

[1981] IRLR 265, Employment Appeal Tribunal

Mr Beverstock worked as a delivery man. He was dismissed for drinking at a public house in working time. Mr Beverstock claimed unfair dismissal and adduced evidence of three other employees who had been found drunk at work or had arrived late smelling of drink: all had been warned but none dismissed. The employer argued that Mr Beverstock's offence was more serious because he worked away from the factory and how he conducted himself had to be based on trust.

LORD MACDONALD: ... [A] reasonable employer may require to impose different standards with regard to the question of alcohol dependent upon a number of factors, such as the nature of his business, the extent to which other personnel may be put at risk and the effect which conduct of this nature may have on public opinion. Where it is considered necessary to have specific penalties attached to the use of alcohol in a particular enterprise then it is proper, as the industrial tribunal have pointed out, that this should be clearly laid down and made a term of the contract of employment.

In the present case there is no such clear term contained in the contract of employment: it was argued on behalf of the appellants that the view which a reasonable employer would take would be that in the circumstances of the present case the offence of drinking during working hours outside the factory was more serious than similar drinking within the factory premises.

... In our opinion this is an argument which seeks to add yet another category of offence relating to alcohol and certainly if it had been the intention of the appellants that such a distinction fell to be made they should have had this clearly spelt out in the contracts of employment which they entered into with the employers.

■ **QUESTION**

Is it possible to rationalise the approaches adopted in the *Henderson* and *Beverstock* cases?

NOTES

1. While it is clear that the employer does not need to list every offence which could lead to dismissal, the offences which are listed will be taken as an indication of the character and class of offence which the employer views as gross misconduct. Therefore, a dismissal for an offence of a less serious class or of an entirely different character than those set out in the disciplinary rules is likely to be regarded as unfair (see *Dietman* v *London Borough of Brent* [1988] IRLR 299, CA).

2. For an interesting application of the rules relating to gross misconduct, see *Denco* v *Joinson* [1991] IRLR 63, where an employee's unauthorised access to a computer warranted summary dismissal. The employee's motive was held to be irrelevant (an extract from the judgment in this case is included at p. 329 (Chapter 7, Section 1.B(i)).

(iv) Hearings

See paragraphs 11–12 of the Code of Practice (Section (iii)).

NOTES

1. In *Ulsterbus* v *Henderson* (Section (iii)), an industrial tribunal upheld Mr Henderson's complaint of unfair dismissal. One of the grounds for this finding was that, at the formal disciplinary proceedings which led to his dismissal, Mr Henderson was not provided with the opportunity to question the passengers who had made the complaint. The Northern Ireland Court of Appeal allowed the employer's appeal and quashed the industrial tribunal's decision. O'Donnell LJ said:

    > What the tribunal appears to be suggesting is that in certain circumstances it is incumbent on a reasonable employer to carry out a quasi-judicial investigation with a confrontation of witnesses, and cross-examination of witnesses. While some employers might consider this to be necessary or desirable, to suggest as the tribunal did, that an employer who failed to do it in a case such as this was acting unreasonably… is in my view unsupportable.

2. It is a general principle that a person who holds an inquiry must be seen to be impartial, that justice must not only be done but be seen to be done, and that if a reasonable observer with full knowledge of the facts would conclude that the hearing might not be impartial that is enough. An illustration of an application of these principles is to be found in the decision of the EAT in *Moyes* v *Hylton Castle Working Men's Social Club and Institute* [1986] IRLR 483, where two witnesses to an alleged act of sexual harassment by a club steward towards a barmaid also were members of the committee which dismissed the steward. The EAT held the dismissal to be unfair on the ground that it was a breach of natural justice for an apparently biased committee to decide the disciplinary matter. While the general rule is that if a person has been a witness he or she should not conduct the inquiry, the EAT did identify certain exceptions, e.g. the one-man firm.

EMPLOYMENT RELATIONS ACT 1999

DISCIPLINARY AND GRIEVANCE HEARINGS

10. Right to be accompanied

(1) This section applies where a worker—
   (a) is required or invited by his employer to attend a disciplinary or grievance hearing, and
   (b) reasonably requests to be accompanied at the hearing.

(2) *[repealed]*

(2A) Where this section applies, the employer must permit the worker to be accompanied at the hearing by one companion who—
   (a) is chosen by the worker; and
   (b) is within subsection (3).

(2B) The employer must permit the worker's companion to—
   (a) address the hearing in order to do any or all of the following—
      (i) put the worker's case;
      (ii) sum up that case;
      (iii) respond on the worker's behalf to any view expressed at the hearing;
   (b) confer with the worker during the hearing.

(2C) Subsection (2B) does not require the employer to permit the worker's companion to—
   (a) answer questions on behalf of the worker;
   (b) address the hearing if the worker indicates at it that he does not wish his companion to do so; or

(c) use the powers conferred by that subsection in a way that prevents the employer from explaining his case or prevents any other person at the hearing from making his contribution to it.

(3) A person is within this subsection if he is—

(a) employed by a trade union of which he is an official within the meaning of sections 1 and 119 of the Trade Union and Labour Relations (Consolidation) Act 1992,

(b) an official of a trade union (within that meaning) whom the union has reasonably certified in writing as having experience of, or as having received training in, acting as a worker's companion at disciplinary or grievance hearings, or

(c) another of the employer's workers.

(4) If—

(a) a worker has a right under this section to be accompanied at a hearing,

(b) his chosen companion will not be available at the time proposed for the hearing by the employer, and

(c) the worker proposes an alternative time which satisfies subsection (5), the employer must postpone the hearing to the time proposed by the worker.

(5) An alternative time must—

(a) be reasonable, and

(b) fall before the end of the period of five working days beginning with the first working day after the day proposed by the employer.

(6) An employer shall permit a worker to take time off during working hours for the purpose of accompanying another of the employer's workers in accordance with a request under subsection (1)(b).

(7) Sections 168(3) and (4), 169 and 171 to 173 of the Trade Union and Labour Relations (Consolidation) Act 1992 (time off for carrying out trade union duties) shall apply in relation to subsection (6) above as they apply in relation to section 168(1) of that Act.

11. Complaint to employment tribunal

(1) A worker may present a complaint to an employment tribunal that his employer has failed, or threatened to fail, to comply with section 10(2A), (2B) or (4).

(2) A tribunal shall not consider a complaint under this section in relation to a failure or threat unless the complaint is presented—

(a) before the end of the period of three months beginning with the date of the failure or threat, or

(b) within such further period as the tribunal considers reasonable in a case where it is satisfied that it was not reasonably practicable for the complaint to be presented before the end of that period of three months.

(3) Where a tribunal finds that a complaint under this section is well-founded it shall order the employer to pay compensation to the worker of an amount not exceeding two weeks' pay.

(4) Chapter II of Part XIV of the Employment Rights Act 1996 (calculation of a week's pay) shall apply for the purposes of subsection (3); and in applying that Chapter the calculation date shall be taken to be—

(a) in the case of a claim which is made in the course of a claim for unfair dismissal, the date on which the employer's notice of dismissal was given or, if there was no notice, the effective date of termination, and

(b) in any other case, the date on which the relevant hearing took place (or was to have taken place).

(5) The limit in section 227(1) of the Employment Rights Act 1996 (maximum amount of week's pay) shall apply for the purposes of subsection (3) above.

(6) [repealed].

12. Detriment and dismissal

(1) A worker has the right not to be subjected to any detriment by any act, or any deliberate failure to act, by his employer done on the ground that he—

(a) exercised or sought to exercise the right under section 10(2A), (2B) or (4), or

(b) accompanied or sought to accompany another worker (whether of the same employer or not) pursuant to a request under that section.

(2) Section 48 of the Employment Rights Act 1996 shall apply in relation to contraventions of subsection (1) above as it applies in relation to contraventions of certain sections of that Act.

(3) A worker who is dismissed shall be regarded for the purposes of Part X of the Employment Rights Act 1996 as unfairly dismissed if the reason (or, if more than one, the principal reason) for the dismissal is that he—

(a) exercised or sought to exercise the right under section 10(2A), (2B) or (4), or

(b) accompanied or sought to accompany another worker (whether of the same employer or not) pursuant to a request under that section.

(4) Sections 108 and 109 of that Act (qualifying period of employment and upper age limit) shall not apply in relation to subsection (3) above.

(5) Sections 128 to 132 of that Act (interim relief) shall apply in relation to dismissal for the reason specified in subsection (3)(a) or (b) above as they apply in relation to dismissal for a reason specified in section 128(1)(b) of that Act.

(6) In the application of Chapter II of Part X of that Act in relation to subsection (3) above, a reference to an employee shall be taken as a reference to a worker.

13. Interpretation

(1) In sections 10 to 12 and this section 'worker' means an individual who is—

  (a) a worker within the meaning of section 230(3) of the Employment Rights Act 1996,

  (b) an agency worker,

  (c) a home worker,

  (d) a person in Crown employment within the meaning of section 191 of that Act, other than a member of the naval, military, air or reserve forces of the Crown, or

  (e) employed as a relevant member of the House of Lords staff or the House of Commons staff within the meaning of section 194(6) or 195(5) of that Act.

(2) In subsection (1) 'agency worker' means an individual who—

  (a) is supplied by a person ('the agent') to do work for another ('the principal') by arrangement between the agent and the principal,

  (b) is not a party to a worker's contract, within the meaning of section 230(3) of that Act, relating to that work, and

  (c) is not a party to a contract relating to that work under which he undertakes to do the work for another party to the contract whose status is, by virtue of the contract, that of a client or customer of any professional or business undertaking carried on by the individual;

and, for the purposes of sections 10 to 12, both the agent and the principal are employers of an agency worker.

(3) In subsection (1) 'home worker' means an individual who—

  (a) contracts with a person, for the purposes of the person's business, for the execution of work to be done in a place not under the person's control or management, and

  (b) is not a party to a contract relating to that work under which the work is to be executed for another party to the contract whose status is, by virtue of the contract, that of a client or customer of any professional or business undertaking carried on by the individual;

and, for the purposes of sections 10 to 12, the person mentioned in paragraph (a) is the home worker's employer.

(4) For the purposes of section 10 a disciplinary hearing is a hearing which could result in—

  (a) the administration of a formal warning to a worker by his employer,

  (b) the taking of some other action in respect of a worker by his employer, or

  (c) the confirmation of a warning issued or some other action taken.

(5) For the purposes of section 10 a grievance hearing is a hearing which concerns the performance of a duty by an employer in relation to a worker.

(6) For the purposes of section 10(5)(b) in its application to a part of Great Britain a working day is a day other than—

  (a) a Saturday or a Sunday,

  (b) Christmas Day or Good Friday, or

  (c) a day which is a bank holiday under the Banking and Financial Dealings Act 1971 in that part of Great Britain.

NOTES

1. The purpose of s. 10 is to create a statutory right for a worker to be accompanied by a fellow employee or trade union official of his or her choice. The 1999 Act does not place a duty on trade union officials or fellow employees to perform the role as the accompanying individual.

2. A revised Code of Practice came into force on 11 March 2015. The revisions solely relate to the sections of the Code dealing with the right to be accompanied at a disciplinary or grievance hearing. In the unrevised Code, ACAS stated that it would not normally be reasonable to insist on being accompanied by a companion who would have to come from a remote geographical location if someone suitable and willing was available on site, or whose presence would prejudice the hearing (paras 15, 36).

   However, in *Toal* v *GB Oils Ltd* [2013] IRLR 696, the EAT held that if a worker has been invited to a disciplinary or grievance hearing then, provided they have made a reasonable request to be accompanied at the hearing, they have the right to choose whoever they like as a companion—so long as the companion is from one of the categories set out in s. 10, i.e. a fellow worker, a person employed by a trade union, or a trade union representative who has been certified in writing as having experience of, or having been trained in, acting as a worker's companion at disciplinary or grievance hearings. The revised Code brings its guidance in line with the interpretation of s. 10 in *Toal*.

In terms of the reasonableness of the request to be accompanied, the revised Code states that the request does not have to be in writing but that, for example, a worker should 'provide enough time for the employer to deal with the companion's attendance at the meeting' and let the employer 'know in advance the name of the companion where possible and whether they are a fellow worker or trade union official or on representative'.

For the avoidance of doubt, the Code now also makes it clear that its guidance that 'a worker may choose to be accompanied by a companion who is suitable, willing and available on site rather than someone from a geographically remote location' is a matter of good practice only and not a legal requirement (see new paras 14–16).

3. Section 13(4) and (5) defines 'disciplinary' and 'grievance' hearings for the purposes of s. 10. A grievance hearing is defined as a hearing which 'concerns the performance of a duty by the employer in relation to a worker'. According to the explanatory notes produced by the Department of Trade and Industry to accompany the legislation, this means a legal duty, i.e. statutory, contractual, or common law. The purpose of the subsection is to seek to ensure that workers do not have the right to be accompanied at hearings where trivial or minor complaints are dealt with.

4. In respect of disciplinary hearings, the right to be accompanied is triggered by a hearing which 'could result in—(a) the administration of a formal warning to a worker by his employer, (b) the taking of some other action in respect of a worker by his employer' (the ERA 1996, s. 13(4)). In *London Underground Ltd* v *Ferenc-Batchelor* [2003] IRLR 252, EAT, the issue was whether employees called to a hearing under the employees' disciplinary procedure were entitled to be accompanied at a hearing which could result in an 'informal oral warning'. The EAT held that a disciplinary warning becomes a 'formal warning' in terms of the statutory right if it becomes part of the employee's disciplinary record. In the instant case, London Underground's procedures provided that an 'informal oral warning' would be confirmed in writing, would have a formal timescale for continuation attached to it, would be part of the disciplinary record of the employee and would be taken into account in the event of a similar offence. According to the EAT, that made it a formal warning.

The issue in *Heathmill Multimedia Asp Ltd* v *Jones* [2003] IRLR 856, EAT, was whether a meeting to inform an employee that he is to be dismissed on the grounds of redundancy falls within the definition and is a meeting at which the employee has the right to be accompanied. The EAT holds that the phrase 'the taking of some other action' must be interpreted as the taking of some other *disciplinary* action in respect of a worker and that where the purpose of the meeting is simply to inform an employee that he is to be dismissed for redundancy, that is not a 'disciplinary hearing'.

5. Both the statutory provisions and the Code are silent regarding the situations in which the worker may ask to be legally represented. At present, the case law on this indicates that an employer is not obliged to afford legal representation, and s. 10's silence on the matter would appear to give this unsatisfactory position implicit statutory support. *Sharma* v *British Gas Corporation*, EAT 495/82, 27 July 1983, is one example of where it was held that there is no requirement to afford legal representation. However, there are a number of possible situations where this might well be essential, particularly where the worker is due to be involved in criminal and civil proceedings, where he or she may have wider concerns (commercial, intellectual property, etc.) to protect in addition to his or her job or where dismissal would prevent them from working in their chosen profession. Indeed, the latter scenario received the consideration of the Court of Appeal in *Kulkarni* v *Milton Keynes Hospital NHS Foundation Trust* [2009] IRLR 829. In this case, the Court of Appeal held that, *under the terms of his contract*, a doctor was entitled to be legally represented at an internal disciplinary hearing. However, Lady Justice Smith also offered some more general comments on when the right to a fair hearing guaranteed by Article 6 of the ECHR might require the right to legal representation. Considering the case law of the ECHR, she stated that Article 6 is not engaged in the case of ordinary disciplinary proceedings, 'where all that could be at stake was the loss of a specific job', but that it is engaged 'where the effect of the proceedings could be far more serious and could… deprive the employee of the right to practice his or her profession.' That covers a case where an NHS doctor faces charges which are of such gravity that, if proved,

he will be effectively barred from employment in the NHS and, by extension, would also apply to a wide range of other professions which are subject to professional regulation. However, a more restrictive approach was adopted by the Supreme Court in the next case.

R (on the application of G) v *Governors of X School and Y City Council*
[2011] IRLR 756, Supreme Court

The claimant, a teaching assistant, was charged with kissing a 15-year-old male student on a work experience placement at the school. His request to have his solicitors represent him at a disciplinary hearing by the school governors was turned down. He was told he could only be represented by his trade union representative or work colleague. In the event, he was summarily dismissed and, as a result, the matter was reported to the Independent Safeguarding Authority (ISA), which maintains a list of those to be barred from working with children. The Administrative Court held that, on the facts of the case, the claimant had a right to legal representation for the purposes of the internal disciplinary proceedings and ordered the allegations to be heard by a committee at which he was to be allowed legal representation. The Court of Appeal dismissed the school's appeal. Both courts held that there was a sufficient connection between the internal disciplinary hearing, in which the claimant's civil rights were not being explicitly determined, and the ISA proceedings in which they were being explicitly determined. The Supreme Court overturned the Court of Appeal's decision and allowed the school's appeal.

LORD DYSON: In deciding whether Article 6(1) applies, the European Court of Human Rights takes into account a number of factors including (i) whether the decision in the first proceedings is capable of being dispositive of the determination of civil rights in the second proceedings, or at least of causing irreversible prejudice, in effect, by partially determining the outcome of the second proceedings; (iii) whether the object of the two proceedings is the same; and (iv) whether there are any policy reasons for holding that Article 6(1) should not apply in the first proceedings.

In the light of that, the 'substantial influence or effect' test set out above, although not explicitly approved by the European Court of Human Rights, is a useful formulation. It captures the idea of the outcome of the first proceedings being capable of playing a major part in the civil rights determination in the second proceedings. That is what fairness requires. Anything less would be 'excessively formalist' and would give too much weight to the fact that the two sets of proceedings are, as a matter of form, separate. The focus should be on the substance of the matter. The court should always keep in mind the importance of ensuring that the guarantees afforded by Article 6(1) are not illusory. It is clearly established that, where a decision in the first proceedings is dispositive of the second proceedings, Article 6(1) applies in both proceedings. That is what the right to a fair hearing in the second proceedings requires. Fairness requires the same where the decision in the first proceedings, although not strictly determinative, is likely to have a major influence on the outcome in the second proceedings. As a matter of substance, there is not much difference between an outcome of the first proceedings which is major influence on the second proceedings, and an outcome which is dispositive. In each case, the civil right of the person concerned is greatly affected by what occurs in the first proceedings. If there is to be a difference in the application of Article 6(1) between the two cases, it needs to be justified. There may be policy reasons based on the nature of the body charged with the second proceedings which justify a different approach. But without such policy reasons, it is difficult to see why Article 6(1) should not apply in both cases. No such policy reasons have been identified in the present case.

The Court of Appeal had therefore applied the correct test in the present case. However, it had erred in the application of that test. It was clear that the ISA was required to make its own findings of fact and bring its own independent judgment to bear as to their seriousness and significance before deciding whether it was appropriate to place the person on the barred list. Although the ISA did not operate a procedure for oral hearings with cross-examination, there was nothing to prevent it from doing so, and nothing to sanction it either. In any event, there would be very few cases where the lack of an oral hearing (with examination and cross-examination of witnesses) would make it unduly difficult for the ISA to make findings of fact applying its own judgment to the material. It was only in very few cases that a decision-making body was faced with a conflict of evidence which it resolved solely or even primarily on the basis of the demeanour shown by the witnesses. The lack of an oral hearing did not prevent the ISA from making its own findings of fact. There was no reason to believe that, contrary to its statutory duty and guidance, the ISA would be unable to form its own view of the facts independently of the view formed by the school authorities and governors. The school's disciplinary panel reached its conclusions as part of an inquiry into a question that was different from that which was addressed by the ISA. The ISA case workers knew that they were required to form their own opinion on the gravity and significance of the facts and on whether it was appropriate to include the referred person in the barred list. There was no reason to suppose that the ISA would be influenced profoundly or at all by the school's opinion of how the primary facts should be viewed.

It followed that the disciplinary proceedings did not have a substantial influence or effect on the barred list procedure. Article 6(1) did not, therefore, apply to the disciplinary proceedings.

NOTES

1. Section 10(2) states that the companion is permitted to address the hearing and to confer with the worker during the hearing, but he or she is not permitted to answer questions on behalf of the worker.

2. Section 11 provides that a complaint may be made to a tribunal that an employer has failed, or has *threatened* to fail, to comply with the right to accompaniment. An award not exceeding two weeks' pay may be ordered. In *Toal v GB Oils Ltd* [2013] IRLR 696, the EAT stated: 'Parliament has… provided that when a tribunal finds a complaint well-founded "it shall order the employer to pay compensation". That suggests to us that the tribunal does not have a right to order that no compensation should be payable. Accordingly, in a case in which it is satisfied that no loss or detriment has been suffered by an employee, the tribunal may feel constrained (and in our view should feel constrained) to make an order of nominal compensation only, either in the traditional sum now replacing 40 shillings—£2—or in some small sum of that order.'

3. Section 12 provides that the worker has the right not to be subject to any detriment by any act, or failure to act by his employer, on the grounds that he or she sought to exercise the right to be accompanied or sought to accompany a worker in accordance with s. 10. It expressly provides that accompanying workers have these rights whether or not they share the same employer as the worker seeking accompaniment. An employer will not, however, be required to pay his employee for time taken off to accompany another employer's worker.

   By virtue of s. 12(3), where the reason for a dismissal is the exercising of rights under s. 10, or the fact that a person has accompanied another in accordance with that section, the dismissal will be automatically unfair. Subsection (4) provides that rights under the section are not subject to any age limit or qualifying period. Subsection (5) extends the availability of interim relief, provided for by ss. 128–32 of the ERA 1996, to dismissals for seeking the right to be accompanied.

4. For the purposes of these new rights, a 'worker' is defined in s. 13 in wider terms than just an 'employee'. It extends to 'worker' as already defined in the ERA 1996, s. 230(3) (contracts of employment and other contracts whereby the person undertakes personal services or work), and also to agency and home workers (as defined by s. 13(2), (3)) and Crown servants, among others.

(v) Appeals

Discipline and Grievances at Work: The ACAS Guide
(2009)

Provide employees with an opportunity to appeal

The opportunity to appeal against a disciplinary decision is essential to natural justice, and appeals may be raised by employees on any number of grounds, for instance new evidence, undue severity or inconsistency of the penalty. The appeal may either be a review of the disciplinary sanction or a re-hearing depending on the grounds of the appeal.

An appeal must never be used as an opportunity to punish the employee for appealing the original decision, and it should not result in any increase in penalty as this may deter individuals from appealing.

What should an appeals procedure contain?

It should:

- specify a time-limit within which the appeal should be lodged (five working days is commonly felt appropriate although this may be extended in particular circumstances)

- provide for appeals to be dealt with speedily, particularly those involving suspension or dismissal
- wherever possible provide for the appeal to be heard by someone senior in authority to the person who took the disciplinary decision and, if possible, someone who was not involved in the original meeting or decision
- spell out what action may be taken by those hearing the appeal
- set out the right to be accompanied at any appeal meeting
- provide that the employee, or a companion if the employee so wishes, has an opportunity to comment on any new evidence arising during the appeal before any decision is taken.

Small organisations

In small organisations, even if there is no more senior manager available, another manager should, if possible, hear the appeal. If this is not possible consider whether the owner or, in the case of a charity, the board of trustees, should hear the appeal. Whoever hears the appeal should consider it as impartially as possible.

NOTE: Under s. 127A of the ERA 1996, if a dismissal was found to be unfair, a tribunal had the power to make a supplementary award of up to two weeks' pay where the employer prevented the employee from appealing against dismissal under the employer's procedure. Conversely, where the employee did not utilise the employer's appeal procedure the tribunal had the power to reduce any award by up to two weeks' pay. The aim of the section was to encourage recourse to internal appeals against dismissal. The EA 2002 contained provisions to enable tribunals to vary compensatory awards by up to 50% where the employer or the applicant has failed to use the minimum statutory internal procedures the EA 2002 (s. 31). These provisions in effect replaced s. 127A, which was repealed. With the repeal of the provisions relating to statutory dispute resolution by the EA 2008, tribunals will still have the discretion under what is now TULRA(C)A 1992, s. 207A to increase compensation where the right of appeal has been denied.

West Midlands Cooperative Society v *Tipton*
[1986] IRLR 112, House of Lords

Mr Tipton was summarily dismissed by his employers on the grounds of his poor attendance record. He was not permitted to exercise his contractual right to appeal against the dismissal.

An industrial tribunal found the dismissal to be unfair. On appeal to the EAT, the employers argued that in determining the fairness of the dismissal the industrial tribunal should not have taken into account their refusal to permit an appeal. This argument was based on an interpretation of the decision of the House of Lords in *W. Devis & Sons Ltd* v *Atkins* [1977] IRLR 314, where it was held that in assessing fairness a tribunal cannot have regard to matters of which the employer was unaware at the time of the dismissal. This argument was rejected by the EAT but succeeded before the Court of Appeal. The House of Lords restored the decision of the EAT that the dismissal was unfair.

LORD BRIDGE OF HARWICH: The linchpin of the argument for the respondents is the decision of this House in *W Devis & Sons Ltd* v *Atkins* [1977] IRLR 314...

Under [s. 98 of the 1996 Act] there are three questions which must be answered in determining whether a dismissal was fair or unfair:

(1) What was the reason (or principal reason) for the dismissal?

(2) Was *that* reason a reason falling within subsection (2) of [s. 98] or some other substantial reason of a kind such as to justify the dismissal of an employee holding the position which that employee held?

(3) Did the employer act reasonably or unreasonably in treating *that* reason as a sufficient reason for dismissing the employee?

As to question (1), Cairns LJ said in *Abernethy* v *Mott. Hay & Anderson* [1974] IRLR 213 at p. 215, in a passage approved by Viscount Dilhorne in the case of *Devis:*

A reason for the dismissal of an employee is a set of facts known to the employer, or it may be of beliefs held by him, which cause him to dismiss the employee. If at the time of his dismissal the employer gives a reason for it, that is no doubt evidence, at any rate as against him, as to the real reason, but it does not necessarily constitute the real reason. He may knowingly give a reason different from the real reason out of kindness…

The reason shown by the employer in answer to question (1) may, therefore, be aptly termed the real reason. Once the real reason is established the answer to question (2) will depend on the application of the statutory criteria to that reason. Then comes the crucial question (3): did the employer act reasonably or unreasonably in treating the real reason as a sufficient reason for dismissing the employee? Conduct of the employee unrelated to the real reason for dismissal obviously cannot affect the answer to this question. This, and no more than this, is what the case of *Devis* decided. But I can see nothing in the language of the statute to exclude from consideration in answering question (3) 'in accordance with equity and the substantial merits of the case' evidence relevant to show the strength or weakness of the real reason for dismissal which the employer had the opportunity to consider in the course of an appeal heard pursuant to a disciplinary procedure which complies with the statutory code of practice. The apparent injustice of excluding, in relation to this question, misconduct of the employee which is irrelevant to the real reason for dismissal is mitigated, as I have earlier pointed out, by the provisions relating to compensation in such a case. But there is nothing to mitigate the injustice to an employee which would result if he were unable to complain that his employer, though acting reasonably on the facts known to him when he summarily dismissed the employee, acted quite unreasonably in maintaining his decision to dismiss in the face of mitigating circumstances established in the course of the domestic appeal procedure which a reasonable employer would have treated as sufficient to excuse the employee's offence on which the employer's real reason for the dismissal depended. Adopting the analysis which found favour in *J Sainsbury Ltd v Savage* [1980] IRLR 109, if the domestic appeal succeeds the employee is reinstated with retrospective effect; if it fails the summary dismissal takes effect from the original date. Thus, in so far as the original dismissal and the decision on the domestic appeal are governed by the same consideration, so, the real reason for dismissal, there is no reason to treat the effective date of termination as a watershed which separates the one process from the other. Both the original and the appellate decision by the employer, in any case where the contract of employment provides for an appeal, and the right of appeal is invoked by the employee, are necessary elements in the overall process of terminating the contract of employment. To separate them and to consider only one half of the process in determining whether the employer acted reasonably or unreasonably in treating his real reason for dismissal as sufficient is to introduce an unnecessary artificiality into proceedings on a claim of unfair dismissal calculated to defeat, rather than accord, with the 'equity and substantial merits of case' and for which the language of the statute affords no warrant.

This is the conclusion I should reach as a matter of construction, taking due account of the decision in the case of *Devis*, if there were no other authority to guide me. But the conclusion is powerfully reinforced by the series of decisions of the Employment Appeal Tribunal, to which I have earlier referred, with which it is in full accord. The relevant cases are *Rank Xerox (UK) Ltd v Goodchild* [1979] IRLR 185; *Quantrill v Eastern Counties Omnibus Co. Ltd* (unreported), 30.6.80; *National Heart and Chest Hospitals Board of Governors v Nambiar* [1981] IRLR 196; *Sillifant v Powell Duffryn Timber Ltd* [1983] IRLR 91; and *Greenall Whitley plc v Carr* [1985] IRLR 289…

> … A dismissal is unfair if the employer unreasonably treats his real reason as a sufficient reason to dismiss the employee, either when he makes his original decision to dismiss or when he maintains that decision at the conclusion of an internal appeal. By the same token, a dismissal may be held to be unfair when the employer has refused to entertain an appeal to which the employee was contractually entitled and thereby denied to the employee the opportunity of showing that, in all the circumstances, the employer's real reason for dismissing him could not reasonably be treated as sufficient. There may, of course, be cases where, on the undisputed facts, the dismissal was inevitable, as for example where a trusted employee, before dismissal, was charged with, and pleaded guilty to, a serious offence of dishonesty committed in the course of his employment. In such a case the employer could reasonably refuse to entertain a domestic appeal on the ground that it could not affect the outcome. It has never been suggested, however, that this was such a case.

NOTES

1. In *Parkinson v March Consulting Ltd* [1997] IRLR 308, CA, it was held that where dismissal is with notice it may be necessary for a tribunal to consider fairness in the circumstances at the time of giving notice *and* when the notice expires. This could result in factors or evidence arising during the notice period becoming relevant to the eventual decision. This approach was subsequently endorsed by the Court of Appeal's decision in *Alboni v Ind Coope Retail Ltd* [1998] IRLR 131.

   Ms Alboni and her former partner were employed under a joint contract of employment as manager and manageress of a public house. The contract contained an express term that, 'your employment is inextricably bound to that of your partner, therefore if the employment of either of you terminates, [that of] the other person will terminate automatically.' When Ms

Alboni's partner resigned, she was given eight weeks' notice. The vacancy was advertised, and she put a proposal to the respondents that she should remain as sole manager which they promised to consider. Although this proposal eventually came to nothing, the tribunal took into account the employers' readiness to consider any application from Ms Alboni to manage the pub single-handed in their finding that her dismissal was fair. This approach was found to be an error of law by the EAT because a tribunal is not allowed to consider 'events which had post-dated the dismissal'. However, the Court of Appeal restored the decision of the industrial tribunal. After referring to the decision in *Parkinson*, Simon Brown LJ stated:

> I do not find the majority decision in that case altogether easy to follow, and it occurs to me it may in future give rise to difficulties of application. For present purposes, however, it seems to make it entirely clear that the industrial tribunal in the present case were not merely entitled, but were bound to have regard to events between notice and dismissal, both for s. 98(1) purposes and also, indeed to my mind *a fortiori*, for s. 98(4) purposes.

■ QUESTION

The principle established by the Court of Appeal in *Alboni* and *Parkinson* has been criticised by Michael Rubenstein, editor of the IRLR, on the basis that 'it will serve as an incentive to employers to dismiss first and ask questions later' ('Highlights' [1998] IRLR 107). Do you share his concern?

2. In *Roberts* v *West Coast Trains Ltd* [2004] IRLR 788, CA, the employee was dismissed for gross misconduct, but exercised his right to appeal under the contractual disciplinary procedure. Before the date of the appeal hearing, he lodged an unfair dismissal claim. Subsequently, his appeal was partially successful in that the sanction of dismissal was reduced to a demotion, one of the alternative penalties provided for under the procedure. The employee contended that he was not debarred from continuing to pursue his unfair dismissal claim because he was dismissed at the time he lodged his employment tribunal application. The Court of Appeal, upholding the decisions of the EAT and employment tribunal below, held that the claim could not be heard. According to the Court of Appeal, there was no dismissal at law because the effect of the decision on appeal was to revive retrospectively the contract of employment terminated by the earlier decision to dismiss, so as to treat the employee as if he had never been dismissed. As the contractual procedure allowed the employers to demote, there was no termination of the previous contract. The employee was not in a position where he could choose to accept or reject the demotion.

3. In *Taylor* v *OCS Group Ltd* [2006] IRLR 613, the Court of Appeal held that there is no rule of law that only a rehearing is capable of curing earlier defects in a disciplinary procedure. Properly understood, the EAT in *Whitbread & Co.* v *Mills* [1988] IRLR 501 was not saying that the question of whether the defects of a first hearing had been cured at a second hearing depended on whether the second hearing could be categorised as a rehearing or review. What matters is not whether the internal appeal was technically a rehearing or review, but whether the disciplinary process as a whole was fair.

Sartor v *P&O European Ferries (Felixstowe) Ltd*
[1992] IRLR 273, Court of Appeal

Miss Sartor was employed as a stewardess on one of the respondent's ships. Her employers decided to institute disciplinary proceedings against her following reports from customs officers that a catering-size pack of tea bags had been seen in her car when leaving the docks.

At that time, Miss Sartor was on a week's leave and she was telephoned and told not to report for duty at the end of her leave period but to attend a disciplinary hearing. She was given no information about the reason for the hearing.

At the disciplinary hearing before the ship's master it was decided to dismiss Miss Sartor and she appealed against that decision. Her appeal was heard by the deputy personnel manager and the catering and purchasing manager, who, after rehearing all the evidence and giving Miss Sartor an opportunity to state her case, decided to affirm the dismissal. Her claim for unfair dismissal was dismissed by the industrial tribunal, the EAT, and the Court of Appeal.

RALPH GIBSON LJ: [T]he appellant ought to have been told the terms of the charge against her before the hearing before the captain. Nevertheless, the appeal was by way of rehearing and there was on that occasion no significant defect in the proceedings. Any defects in what had gone on before were cured by the opportunity to appeal.

NOTE: The following cases demonstrate the courts' renewed emphasis on procedural rectitude.

Polkey v *A. E. Dayton Services*
[1987] IRLR 503, House of Lords

Polkey was one of four van drivers employed by the respondent company. As part of a reorganisation, it was decided to replace the four van drivers with two van salesmen and a sales representative. Only one of the four van drivers was considered suitable for transfer to the new duties and accordingly the other three were made redundant.

The first that Mr Polkey knew of the position was when he was called into the office of the branch manager and told that he was being made redundant. He was immediately driven home by one of the drivers, who was himself dismissed on his return.

Mr Polkey's claim of unfair dismissal was rejected by the industrial tribunal and his appeals were dismissed by the EAT and the Court of Appeal. The Court of Appeal endorsed the principles set out in *British Labour Pump Co. Ltd* v *Byrne* [1979] IRLR 94, and approved by the Court of Appeal in *Wass* v *Binns* [1982] ICR 347, and held that Mr Polkey's dismissal was not unfair, despite the employer's failure to consult with him, because such consultation would not have made any difference to the result. The House of Lords allowed Mr Polkey's appeal and remitted the case to a new industrial tribunal.

LORD MACKAY OF CLASHFERN: This appeal raises an important question in the law of unfair dismissal. Where an industrial tribunal has found that the reason for an applicant's dismissal was a reason of a kind such as could justify the dismissal and has found that there has been a failure to consult or warn the applicant in accordance with the code of practice, should the tribunal consider whether, if the employee had been consulted or warned before dismissal was decided upon, he would nevertheless have been dismissed? The answer depends upon the application to this situation of [what is now ERA 1996 s. 98(4)].

... [T]he subject matter for the tribunal's consideration is the employer's action in treating the reason as a sufficient reason for dismissing the employee. It is that action and that action only that the tribunal is required to characterise as reasonable or unreasonable. That leaves no scope for the tribunal considering whether, if the employer had acted differently, he might have dismissed the employee. It is what the employer did that is to be judged, not what he might have done. On the other hand, in judging whether what the employer did was reasonable it is right to consider what a reasonable employer would have had in mind at the time he decided to dismiss as the consequence of not consulting or not warning.

If the employer could reasonably have concluded in the light of the circumstances known to him at the time of dismissal that consultation or warning would be utterly useless he might well act reasonably even if he did not observe the provisions of the code. Failure to observe the requirement of the code relating to consultation or warning will not necessarily render a dismissal unfair. Whether in any particular case it did so is a matter for the industrial tribunal to consider in the light of the circumstances known to the employer at the time he dismissed the employee.

I turn to consider how these views accord with the decided cases. Very early in the history of this legislation and its statutory predecessors Sir John Donaldson in *Earl* v *Slater & Wheeler (Airlyne) Ltd* [1972] IRLR 115 said:

With respect to the tribunal, we think that it erred in holding that an unfair procedure which led to no injustice is incapable of rendering unfair a dismissal which would otherwise be fair. The question in every case is whether the employer acted reasonably or unreasonably in treating the reason as sufficient for dismissing the employee and it has to be answered with reference to the circumstances known to the employer at the moment of dismissal. If an employer thinks that his accountant may be taking the firm's money, but has no real grounds for so thinking and dismisses him for this reason, he acts wholly unreasonably and commits the unfair industrial practice of unfair dismissal, notwithstanding that it is later proved that the accountant had in fact been guilty of embezzlement. Proof of the embezzlement affects the amount of the compensation, but not the issue of fair or unfair dismissal.

...

This approach to the legislation was endorsed in this House in *W. Devis & Sons Ltd* v *Atkins* [1977] IRLR 314. Viscount Dilhorne, in a speech with which the other members of the House sitting in the appeal agreed, said of the statutory predecessor of s. 57(3) [see now ERA 1996, s. 98(4)], at p. 317:

> It [para. 6(8) of Schedule 1 to the Trade Union and Labour Relations Act 1971] appears to me to direct the Tribunal to focus its attention on the conduct of the employer and not on whether the employee in fact suffered any injustice.

After quoting, with approval, the principal part of the passage I have already cited from Sir John Donaldson in *Earl* v *Slater & Wheeler (Airlyne) Ltd* and after referring to the statutory provision then entitling the Tribunal to take the code into account Viscount Dilhorne said, at p. 318:

> It does not follow that non-compliance with the code necessarily renders a dismissal unfair, but I agree with the view expressed by Sir John Donaldson in *Earl* v *Slater & Wheeler (Airlyne) Ltd* [1972] IRLR 115 that a failure to follow a procedure prescribed in the code may lead to the conclusion that a dismissal was unfair, which, if that procedure had been followed, would have been held to have been fair.
>
> So far, the current of decision is entirely in accordance with the views I have expressed, but the Tribunal in the present case were bound by a stream of authority applying the so-called *British Labour Pump* principle *(British Labour Pump Co. Ltd* v *Byrne* [1979] IRLR 94).

Browne-Wilkinson J in *Sillifant* v *Powell Duffryn Timber Ltd* [1983] IRLR 91 thus described the principle, at p. 92:

> Even if, judged in the light of the circumstances known at the time of dismissal, the employer's decision was not reasonable because of some failure to follow a fair procedure yet the dismissal can be held fair if, on the facts proved before the Industrial Tribunal, the Industrial Tribunal comes to the conclusion that the employer could reasonably have decided to dismiss if he had followed a fair procedure.

It is because one of its statements is contained in *British Labour Pump Co. Ltd* v *Byrne* that it has been called the *British Labour Pump* principle although it did not originate in that decision. In *Sillifant's case* the Employment Appeal Tribunal were urged to hold that the principle was unsound and not to give effect to it. After referring to the cases which introduced this principle, namely *Charles Letts & Co. Ltd* v *Howard* [1976] IRLR 248, a decision relating only to compensation, *Lowndes* v *Specialist Heavy Engineering Ltd* [1976] IRLR 246, *British United Shoe Machinery Co. Ltd* v *Clarke* [1977] IRLR 297 and the *British Labour Pump* case itself, Browne-Wilkinson J continued at p. 97:

> Apart therefore from recent Court of Appeal authority and the *Lowndes* case, the *British Labour Pump* principle appears to have become established in practice without it being appreciated that it represented a fundamental departure from both basic principle and the earlier decisions. If we felt able to do so we would hold that it is wrong in principle and undesirable in its practical effect. It introduces just that confusion which *Devis* v *Atkins* was concerned to avoid between the fairness of the dismissal (which depends solely upon the reasonableness of the employer's conduct) and the compensation payable to the employee (which takes into account the conduct of the employee whether known to the employer or not). In our judgment, apart from the authority to which we are about to refer, the correct approach to such a case would be as follows. The only test of the fairness of a dismissal is the reasonableness of the employer's decision to dismiss judged at the time at which the dismissal takes effect. An Industrial Tribunal is not bound to hold that *any* procedural failure by the employer renders the dismissal unfair: it is one of the factors to be weighed by the Industrial Tribunal in deciding whether or not the dismissal was reasonable within s. 57(3) [see now ERA 1996, s. 98(4)]. The weight to be attached to such procedural failure should depend upon the circumstances known to the employer at the time of dismissal, not on the actual consequence of such failure. Thus in the case of a failure to give an opportunity to explain, except in the rare case where a reasonable employer could properly take the view on the facts known to him at the time of dismissal that no explanation or mitigation could alter his decision to dismiss, an Industrial Tribunal would be likely to hold that the lack of 'equity' inherent in the failure would render the dismissal unfair. But there may be cases where the offence is so heinous and the facts so manifestly clear that a reasonable employer could, on the facts known to him at the time of dismissal, take the view that whatever explanation the employee advanced it would make no difference: see the example referred to by Lawton LJ in *Bailey* v *BP Oil (Kent Refinery) Ltd* [1980] IRLR 287. Where, in the circumstances known at the time of dismissal, it was not reasonable for the employer to dismiss without giving an opportunity to explain the facts subsequently discovered or proved before the Industrial Tribunal show that the

dismissal was in fact merited, compensation would be reduced to nil. Such an approach ensures that an employee who could have been fairly dismissed does not get compensation but would prevent the suggestion of 'double standards' inherent in the *British Labour Pump* principle. An employee dismissed for suspected dishonesty who is in fact innocent has no redress: if the employer acted fairly in dismissing him on the facts and in the circumstances known to him at the time of dismissal the employee's innocence is irrelevant. Why should an employer be entitled to a finding that he acted fairly when, on the facts known and in the circumstances existing at the time of dismissal, his actions were unfair but which facts subsequently coming to light show did not cause any injustice? The choice in dealing with [s. 98(4)] is between looking at the reasonableness of the employer or justice to the employee. *Devis* v *Atkins* shows that the correct test is the reasonableness of the employer; the *British Labour Pump* principle confuses the two approaches.

I gratefully adopt that analysis. The Employment Appeal Tribunal, however, went on to hold that they were bound by the decision of the Court of Appeal in *W & J Wass* v *Binns* [1982] IRLR 283 which held that the *British Labour Pump* principle is good law…

[The] reasons given by the Court of Appeal in the present case for supporting the *British Labour Pump* principle involve an impermissible reliance upon matters not known to the employers before the dismissal and a confusion between unreasonable conduct in reaching the conclusion to dismiss, which is a necessary ingredient of an unfair dismissal, and injustice to the employee which is not a necessary ingredient of an unfair dismissal, although its absence will be important in relation to a compensatory award.

It follows that I do not agree with the decision of the Court of Appeal in the present case and this appeal should be allowed, the *British Labour Pump* principle and all decisions supporting it are inconsistent with the relevant statutory provision and should be overruled, and, in particular, the decision of the Court of Appeal in *W & J Wass Ltd* v *Binns* [1982] IRLR 283 should be overruled.

LORD BRIDGE OF HARWICH: Employers contesting a claim of unfair dismissal will commonly advance as their reason for dismissal one of the reasons specifically recognised as valid by s. 57(2)(a), (b) and (c) of the Employment Protection (Consolidation) Act 1978 [see now ERA 1996, s. 98(2)(a), (b) and (c)]. These, put shortly, are: (a) that the employee could not do his job properly; (b) that he had been guilty of misconduct; (c) that he was redundant. But an employer having prima facie grounds to dismiss for one of these reasons will in the great majority of cases not act reasonably in treating the reason as a sufficient reason for dismissal unless and until he has taken the steps, conveniently classified in most of the authorities as 'procedural', which are necessary in the circumstances of the case to justify that course of action. Thus, in the case of incapacity, the employer will normally not act reasonably unless he gives the employee fair warning and an opportunity to mend his ways and show that he can do the job; in the case of misconduct, the employer will normally not act reasonably unless he investigates the complaint of misconduct fully and fairly and hears whatever the employee wishes to say in his defence or in explanation or mitigation; in the case of redundancy, the employer will normally not act reasonably unless he warns and consults any employees affected or their representative, adopts a fair basis on which to select for redundancy and takes such steps as may be reasonable to avoid or minimise redundancy by redeployment within his own organisation. If an employer has failed to take the appropriate procedural steps in any particular case, the one question the Industrial Tribunal is *not* permitted to ask in applying the test of reasonableness posed by [s. 98(4)] is the hypothetical question whether it would have made any difference to the outcome if the appropriate procedural steps had been taken. On the true construction of [s. 98(4)] this question is simply irrelevant. It is quite a different matter if the Tribunal is able to conclude that the employer himself, at the time of the dismissal, acted reasonably in taking the view that, in the exceptional circumstances of the particular case, the procedural steps normally appropriate would have been futile, could not have altered the decision to dismiss and therefore could be dispensed with. In such a case the test of reasonableness under [s. 98(4)] may be satisfied.

My Lords, I think these conclusions are fully justified by the cogent reasoning of Browne-Wilkinson J in *Sillifant* v *Powell Duffryn Timber Ltd* [1983] IRLR 91 to which my noble and learned friend the Lord Chancellor has already drawn attention.

If it is held that taking the appropriate steps which the employer failed to take before dismissing the employee would not have affected the outcome, this will often lead to the result that the employee, though unfairly dismissed, will recover no compensation, or, in the case of redundancy, no compensation in excess of his redundancy payment. Thus in *Earl* v *Slater & Wheeler (Airlyne) Ltd* [1972] IRLR 115 the employee was held to have been unfairly dismissed, but nevertheless lost his appeal to the Industrial Relations Court because his misconduct disentitled him to any award of compensation, which was at that time the only effective remedy. But in spite of this the application of the so-called *British Labour Pump* principle (*British Labour Pump Co. Ltd* v *Byrne* [1979] IRLR 94) tends to distort the operation of the employment protection legislation in two important ways. First, as was pointed out by Browne-Wilkinson J in *Sillifant's case*, if the Industrial Tribunal, in considering whether the employer who has omitted to take the appropriate procedural steps acted reasonably or unreasonably in treating his reason as a sufficient reason for dismissal, poses for itself the hypothetical question whether the result would have been any different if the appropriate procedural steps had been taken, it can only answer that question on a balance of probabilities. Accordingly, applying the *British Labour Pump* principle, if the answer is that it probably would have made no difference, the employee's unfair dismissal claim fails. But if the likely effect of taking the appropriate procedural steps is only considered, as it should be, at the stage of assessing compensation, the position is quite different. In that situation, as Browne-Wilkinson J puts it in *Sillifant's* case, at p. 96:

> There is no need for an 'all or nothing' decision. If the Industrial Tribunal thinks there is a doubt whether or not the employee would have been dismissed, this element can be reflected by reducing the normal amount of compensation by a percentage representing the chance that the employee would still have lost his employment.

The second consideration is perhaps of particular importance in redundancy cases. As an Industrial Tribunal may conclude, as in the instant case, that the appropriate procedural steps would not have avoided the employee's dismissal as redundant. But if, as your Lordships now hold, that conclusion does not defeat his claim of unfair dismissal, the Industrial Tribunal, apart from any question of compensation, will also have to consider whether to make any order under s. 69 of the Act of 1978 [see now ERA 1996, s. 113]. It is noteworthy that an Industrial Tribunal may, if it thinks fit, make an order for re-engagement under that section and in so doing exercise a very wide discretion as to the terms of the order. In a case where an Industrial Tribunal held that dismissal on the ground of redundancy would have been inevitable at the time when it took place, even if the appropriate procedural steps had been taken, I do not, as at present advised, think this would necessarily preclude a discretionary order for re-engagement on suitable terms, if the altered circumstances considered by the Tribunal at the date of the hearing were thought to justify it.

For these reasons and for those given by my noble and learned friend the Lord Chancellor I would allow the appeal and remit the case to be heard by another Industrial Tribunal.

NOTES
1. It has been argued that there is a significant practical difference between asking whether at the time of the dismissal the employer had reasonable grounds for believing that a fair procedure would have been 'utterly useless' (the new test) and asking whether, in retrospect, it would have made any difference to the outcome (the old test). As a result it is likely that failure to follow a fair procedure may well lead to a finding of unfair dismissal in a much increased proportion of cases.

    In *Duffy* v *Yeomans and Partners Ltd* [1994] IRLR 642, CA, it was held that *Polkey* does not require that the employer must have consciously taken a decision not to consult with the employee. According to Balcombe LJ, it is sufficient that, judged objectively, the employer does what a reasonable employer might do. The danger inherent in this objective text is that it resembles the 'did it make any difference?' test that *Polkey* rejected.

2. Even post-*Polkey*, the courts and tribunals have still shown a propensity to forgive minor procedural lapses, provided that in the overall context of the case they did not result in unfairness: see *Eclipse Blinds Ltd* v *Wright* [1992] IRLR 133 (set out at p. 445 (Section (vi)(b)), *Westminster City Council* v *Cabaj* [1996] IRLR 399, CA, and the next case.

Fuller v Lloyds Bank plc
[1991] IRLR 337, Employment Appeal Tribunal

Mr Fuller was dismissed following an incident which occurred in a public house on Christmas Eve, when a fellow employee received severe facial injuries from a glass held by Mr Fuller. During the course of the employer's disciplinary proceedings, statements were taken from a number of witnesses. Those statements formed the basis of the employer's decision to dismiss Mr Fuller. However, they were never disclosed to Mr Fuller or his union representative.

Mr Fuller's complaint of unfair dismissal was rejected by the industrial tribunal and his appeal against that decision was dismissed by the EAT.

KNOX J: That it is desirable in the normal state of affairs for the material upon which a disciplinary investigation is founded and on which any penalties may be based on the person who is being disciplined, to be available to that person is something with which we heartily agree. It has frequently been emphasised, in this Tribunal and elsewhere, that this is a matter which should, in the normal course of events, be shown to a person in Mr Fuller's shoes.

We were referred specifically to two recent decisions in the EAT, *Linfood Cash & Carry Ltd* v *Thomson* [1989] IRLR 235 and *Louies* v *Coventry Hood & Seating Co. Ltd* [1990] IRLR 324 in both of which sentiments in that regard were uttered by Mr Justice Wood.

In the former, the *Linfood Cash & Carry Ltd* case at p. 237, 20 there are set out 10 paragraphs of general guidance prefaced by a statement that: 'Every case must depend upon its own facts, and circumstances may vary widely.' They are prefaced also with the hope that what are described as 'comments' may prove to be of assistance. The first of those 'comments' reads as follows:

> The information given by the informant should be reduced into writing in one or more statements. Initially these statements should be taken without regard to the fact that in those cases where anonymity is to be preserved, it may subsequently prove to be necessary to omit or erase certain parts of the statements before submission to others, in order to prevent identification

and paragraph 7:

> The written statement of the informant—if necessary with omissions to avoid identification—should be made available to the employee and his representatives.

...

The other decision of late, the *Louies* case, contains a passage at p. 326, 11, where Mr Justice Wood said this:

> It does seem to me that it must be a very rare case indeed for the procedures to be fair where statements which have been given in writing by witnesses and upon which in essence the employer is going to rely almost entirely—and that is this case—that an employee should not have a sight of them or that he should not be told very clearly exactly what is in them or possibly have them read to him.

...

The appeal before us is based on two alternative grounds.

The first is that there is an error of law involved in the Industrial Tribunal's approach in this matter. That approach was that whereas the Industrial Tribunal identified, in the passages which I have already read, the failure by the bank to provide material to Mr Fuller and his representatives, which should properly have been provided, that nevertheless was not conclusive and the dismissal was not, in the circumstances, unfair.

Having set out the well-known passage which originally derives from *Byrne* v *Kinematograph Renters Society Ltd* [1958] 1 WLR 762, a decision of Mr Justice Harman, and which was adopted by the Privy Council in the *University of Ceylon* v *Fernando* [1960] 1 WLR 225, the Industrial Tribunal considered that the three requirements identified in that citation of authority had in fact been supplied in this case.

Those requirements are, and I quote the passage in question:

> What then are the requirements of natural justice in a case of this kind? First, I think that the person accused should know the nature of the accusation made; second, that he should be given an opportunity to state his case; and, third, of course, that the Tribunal should act in good faith.

Mr Justice Harman said: 'I do not myself think that there really is anything more.'

In that context the Industrial Tribunal said this:

> There is no dispute that the respondents did tell the applicant the nature of the case which was made against him and indeed they set out a charge in formal terms. What they did not set out was the evidence, the material on which they were proposing to reach their decision.

They then set out certain reasons why, in this case, the material was not supplied, to which I will return later on the second branch of the appellant's argument.

They went on to express their conclusion on this aspect of the matter in the following terms:

> We have come to the conclusion that in the particular circumstances of this case failure to provide the witness statements did not go outside the band of reasonable procedures which should have been carried out. The allegation in essence was a simple one and the applicant knew exactly what was being alleged. Indeed he knew the identity of many of the witnesses and had received witness statements produced by the police for the criminal prosecution. The police witness statements produced before us maintain the same essential allegations as are contained in the witness statements.

It was submitted to us in answer to the predictable claim on behalf of the bank, that that was a finding of fact, that Mr Fuller knew exactly what was being alleged against him, that there was a fundamental error in principle in the Industrial Tribunal's approach in this sense, that the Industrial Tribunal had found that there was a certain policy of not disclosing witness statements and that it had been in pursuance of that policy that the non-disclosure of those statements had ensued.

It argued that the process of reasoning of the Industrial Tribunal in finding that that failure did not go outside the band of reasonable procedures which should have been carried out, carried in it the same fatal flaw as was identified in the well-known decision of the House of Lords in *Polkey* v *A. E. Dayton Services* [1987] IRLR 503 and that on analysis the Industrial Tribunal was saying that although the procedure was defective, Mr Fuller would, in any event, have been properly found guilty of the conduct with which he was charged and that in those circumstances the dismissal was not unfair.

If that analysis was correct we would certainly accept that the dismissal would have been shown to be unfair. But we are not satisfied that the analysis is an accurate one.

In our judgment where one has a procedural defect, which we entirely accept there was in this case, and whether that procedural defect is based on a policy adopted for good, bad or indifferent reasons, the question for investigation by an Industrial Tribunal does not alter simply because the defect was a matter of policy. There remain essentially the requirements that have been, over the years, many times identified and were stated in *British Home Stores Ltd* v *Burchell* [1978] IRLR 379 to which the Industrial Tribunal had regard.

The third essential element for present purposes in that investigation is, did the employer 'operate a reasonable procedure which entitles them to say they acted reasonably in dismissing the applicant.' I quote what the Industrial Tribunal said on this score. It could be translated into terms of unfairness, did the employer's procedure constitute a fair process.

That will always remain an essential matter for investigation and this case is no exception to that.

The actual defect has, however, to be analysed in the context of what has occurred, and it may be that that analysis will produce the conclusion that there was a defect of such seriousness that the procedure was not fair. In that event there will have been necessarily an unfair dismissal, although there may well be a conclusion that the compensation has to be severely limited because of the potential justification for the decision that the employer took albeit in an unfair way.

What will not be a relevant subject of enquiry, in our view, is the motivation of the employer in adopting the policy which led to the procedural defect. That has to be judged by its fruits rather than by the reason for its adoption.

The other possibility is that the procedural defect does not produce a procedure which is in itself unfair, but it may nevertheless be that the results taken overall are unfair, and there again, the conclusion that the Industrial Tribunal will reach will be that the dismissal cannot in those circumstances be upheld as anything other than unfair.

But here again, the motivation of the employer in adopting the original defective procedure is in our view nothing to do with that conclusion, which is an objective one in all the circumstances of the case.

In this case the Industrial Tribunal has undoubtedly seen the defect and has identified it quite accurately. It has nevertheless come to what we regard as a dual conclusion.

First of all, it concluded that the defect was not such as to render the procedure intrinsically unfair so as to require the dismissal not to stand as fair.

Secondly, the Industrial Tribunal came, as we see it, to the conclusion that overall the process whereby Mr Fuller was dismissed was not unfair.

(vi) Some common disciplinary issues

(a) Sub-standard work

Alidair Ltd v Taylor
[1978] IRLR 82, Court of Appeal

A summary of the facts appears at p. 444 (later in this section).

LORD DENNING MR: Wherever a man is dismissed for incapacity or incompetence it is sufficient that the employer honestly believes on reasonable grounds that the man is incapable or incompetent. It is not necessary for the employer to prove that he is in fact incapable or incompetent.

Cook v Thomas Linnell & Sons Ltd
[1977] IRLR 132, Employment Appeal Tribunal

Mr Cook was employed as manager of one of the respondents' 'non-food' depots from 1966 to 1974. He was then promoted to manager of a food depot in Norwich although he had no previous experience of that side of the business. In May 1976 he was dismissed on grounds of poor performance. The industrial tribunal and EAT found the dismissal to be fair.

PHILLIPS J: A central theme in Mr Tabachnik's submission [on behalf of Mr Cook] was that although there was plenty of contemporary evidence to show that the employers had lost confidence in the ability of Mr Cook as a manager there was no hard factual evidence of a particular kind to support that judgment. Criticism and exhortation, he submitted, however strong, do not by themselves provide evidence of incapacity. It amounts to no more than an assertion of an opinion. It seems to us that this goes too far, although we accept that there is something in the point. When responsible employers have genuinely come to the conclusion over a reasonable period of time that a manager is incompetent we think that it is some evidence that he is incompetent. When one is dealing with routine operations which may be more precisely assessed there is no real problem. It is more difficult when one is dealing with such imponderables as the quality of management, which in the last resort can only be judged by those competent in the field. In such cases as this there may be two extremes. At one extreme is the case where it can be demonstrated, perhaps by some calamitous performance, that the manager is incompetent. The other extreme is the case where no more can be said than that in the opinion of the employer the manager is incompetent, that opinion being expressed for the first time before his dismissal. In between will be cases such as the present where it can be established that throughout the period of employment concerned the employers had progressively growing doubts about the ability of the manager to perform his tasks satisfactorily. If that can be shown, it is in our judgment some evidence of his incapacity. It will then be necessary to look to see whether there is any other supporting evidence.

NOTE: The ACAS Guide, 'Discipline and grievances at work' (2009) offers the following guidance on how alleged poor performance cases should be approached:

Resolve discipline issues informally
Cases of… unsatisfactory performance are usually best dealt with informally. A quiet word is often all that is required to improve an employee's… performance. In some cases additional training, coaching and advice may be what is needed. An informal approach may be particularly helpful in small firms, where problems can be resolved quickly and confidentially. There will be situations where matters are more serious or where an informal approach has been tried but is not working. If informal action does not bring about an improvement, or the… unsatisfactory performance is considered too serious to be classed as minor, employers should provide employees with a clear signal of their dissatisfaction by taking formal action.

Imposing the disciplinary penalty
First formal action—unsatisfactory performance

In cases of unsatisfactory performance an employee should be given an 'improvement note', setting out:
- the performance problem
- the improvement that is required
- the timescale for achieving this improvement
- a review date and
- any support, including any training, that the employer will provide to assist the employee.

The employee should be informed that the note represents the first stage of a formal procedure and is equivalent to a first written warning and that failure to improve could lead to a final written warning and, ultimately, dismissal. A copy of the note should be kept and used as the basis for monitoring and reviewing performance over a specified period (eg, six months).

If an employee's unsatisfactory performance—or its continuance—is sufficiently serious, for example because it is having, or is likely to have, a serious harmful effect on the organisation, it may be justifiable to move directly to a final written warning.

Final written warning

If the employee has a current warning about… performance then further… unsatisfactory performance may warrant a final written warning… Such a warning should normally remain current for a specified period, for example, 12 months, and contain a statement that further… unsatisfactory performance may lead to dismissal.

Alidair Ltd v Taylor
[1978] IRLR 82, Court of Appeal

A commercial pilot made a faulty landing while flying 77 passengers in reasonable weather conditions. No one was hurt but the aircraft sustained considerable damage. He was dismissed following an inquiry into the incident. His claim of unfair dismissal was rejected by the industrial tribunal, EAT, and Court of Appeal.

LORD DENNING MR: There are activities in which the degree of professional skill which must be required is so high, and the potential consequences of the smallest departure from that high standard are so serious, that one failure to perform in accordance with those standards is enough to justify the dismissal. The passenger carrying airline pilot, the scientist operating the nuclear reactor, the chemist in charge of research into the possible effects of, for example, thalidomide, the driver of the Manchester to London express, the driver of an articulated lorry full of sulphuric acid, are all in situations in which one failure to maintain the proper standard of professional skill can bring about a major disaster.

(b) Long-term sickness absence
In cases of exceptionally severe and incapacitating illness where it is highly unlikely that the employee will ever be fit to return to work, the contract may be regarded as frustrated and therefore terminated by operation of law other than dismissal. The rules governing the doctrine of frustration and its relationship to long-term sickness absence and imprisonment were discussed at p. 342 (Chapter 7, Section 2.A).

Given that the frustration doctrine offers employers a convenient way in which to avoid the unfair dismissal provisions, the courts are generally reluctant to apply it to contracts which are terminable by notice. Therefore, in less drastic cases of long-term sickness absence, a body of case law has developed on the question of the fairness of a dismissal in such circumstances.

Spencer v Paragon Wallpapers Ltd
[1976] IRLR 373, Employment Appeal Tribunal

PHILLIPS J: There is no doubt that the industrial tribunal directed their minds to the correct question in this case… They took into account the nature of the illness, the likely length of the continuing absence, the need for the employers to have done the work which the employee was engaged to do… The basic question which has to be determined in every case is whether, in all the circumstances, the employer can be expected to wait any longer and, if so, how much longer? Every case will be different, depending on the circumstances.

East Lindsey District Council v Daubney
[1977] IRLR 181, Employment Appeal Tribunal

PHILLIPS J: Unless there are wholly exceptional circumstances before an employee is dismissed on the grounds of ill-health it is necessary that he should be consulted and the matter discussed with him, and that in one way or another steps should be taken by the employer to discover the true medical position. We do not propose to lay down detailed principles to be applied in such cases, for what will be necessary in one case may not be appropriate in another. But if in every case employers take such steps as are sensible according to the circumstances to consult the employee and to discuss the matter with him, and to inform themselves upon the true medical position, it will be found in practice that all that is necessary has been done. Discussions and consultation will often bring to light facts and circumstances of which the employers were unaware, and which will throw new light on the problem. Or the employee may wish to seek medical advice on his own account, which, brought to the notice of the employers' medical advisers, will cause them to change their opinion. There are many possibilities. Only one thing is certain, and that is that if the employee is not consulted, and given an opportunity to state his case, an injustice may be done.

NOTE: The need for consultation with the employee was stressed in *Spencer* and strongly affirmed by the EAT's decision in *Daubney*. On the other hand, consultation has not always been required by industrial tribunals. In *Taylorplan Catering (Scotland) Ltd* v *McInally* [1980] IRLR 53, it was suggested that where a tribunal finds that the circumstances were such that a consultation would have made no difference to the result, lack of consultation could be justified. In this case, the EAT was of the view that the guidelines in *British Labour Pump* could be applied in cases involving ill health. With the rejection of those guidelines by the House of Lords in *Polkey* it is likely that consultation will be required in the vast majority of cases. However, minor or understandable breaches of procedure in ill-health dismissals may be excused: see *A. Links & Co. Ltd* v *Rose* [1991] IRLR 353 and the next case.

Eclipse Blinds v Wright
[1992] IRLR 133, Court of Session, Inner House

Mrs Wright, a registered disabled person, had been employed by the appellant company since 1978. She was regarded as an excellent employee but, from 1985, her health deteriorated and her rate of sickness absence increased. At the end of 1987, she became a part-time worker and her attendance showed some improvement.

However, in March 1989, Mrs Wright became ill and was off work for some time. In May, she submitted a sick note for a further 13 weeks. She told the personnel officer that she thought her health was improving. She gave permission for her GP to be contacted in order to obtain his view as to her ability to return to work after 13 weeks. The GP's prognosis was not good and he could not see any possibility of her returning to work in the near future.

In the light of the GP's report, the company reluctantly decided that they would have to dismiss Mrs Wright and employ a permanent replacement. The director who took the decision decided against interviewing Mrs Wright. He was concerned that she did not appear to appreciate the seriousness of her condition and thought that her health was improving. He therefore decided to write to her, rather than running the risk of an interview where it might be difficult to avoid disclosing information about Mrs Wright's health of which she was unaware.

An industrial tribunal held that, in the circumstances, Mrs Wright's dismissal was not rendered unfair by the employer's failure to consult. The EAT, in allowing an appeal against that decision, considered that a sensitive consultation should have been carried out and a failure to consult was not justified. The Court of Session, Inner House, allowed the employer's appeal.

LORD ALLANBRIDGE: It is true that Lord McDonald in *Taylorplan Catering (Scotland) Ltd* v *McInally* [1980] IRLR 53 referred to what is expected in the normal case as regards the necessity for consultation, whereas Mr Justice Phillips referred to 'wholly exceptional circumstances' in several of the English cases in 1977. However, in our opinion these two approaches to the question of whether or not a consultation should have been held are not inconsistent with each other. One is the converse of the other, as if a case is wholly exceptional it is not normal. This was the view reached by this Court in the case of *A Links & Company Ltd* v *Rose* [1991] IRLR 353, but it is fair to note that, as stated at p. 12, there was no dispute in that case as to the duty of an employer who is considering dismissing an employee on the grounds of ill health, so the alleged inconsistency was not argued. In that case this Court held that it would require to go to a fresh Industrial Tribunal to decide *inter alia* whether consultation was appropriate in the circumstances because there had been no consideration given to that matter at the original hearing.

However, in the case of *A Links & Company Ltd*, it was also held by this Court, at p. 355, 6, that an Industrial Tribunal in approaching the question as to whether the employer acted fairly or unfairly must determine, as a matter of fact and judgment, what consultation, if any, was necessary or desirable in the known circumstances of the particular case. We are quite satisfied that that is the correct approach. We stress that it is a matter of fact to be determined by the Industrial Tribunal. This is also the approach suggested by Lord President Emslie at p. 238, para. 14 in *Leonard* v *Fergus & Haynes Civil Engineering Ltd* [1979] IRLR 235, CS. Furthermore, the Lord Chancellor in a somewhat different case did stress that the matters of consultation or warning were matters for an Industrial Tribunal to consider in the light of the circumstances known to the employer at the time he dismissed the employee (see *Polkey* v *A. E. Dayton Services* [1987] IRLR 503] at p. 504. para. 5).

In this case it was quite clear from the agreed facts that the Industrial Tribunal did consider all the necessary and relevant facts. This was a case that the Industrial Tribunal decided was not normal and was exceptional as regards the question of consulting with the applicant. They accepted in terms, at p. 4H of their decision, that in normal circumstances the employers would have been expected to consult with the applicant before telling her she was to be dismissed. However, they decided, as stated at p. 5A–B, that Mr McNeil had a genuine concern to avoid giving the applicant information with regard to her health of which she did not appear to be aware and therefore concluded that his decision could not be said, in all the circumstances, to be so unreasonable as to render the dismissal unfair. This was a judgment which the Industrial Tribunal was entitled to make on the facts and it was therefore not open to the Employment Appeal Tribunal to displace that judgment on fact by its own view or judgment. No error in law by the Industrial Tribunal had occurred.

In this situation we allow the appeal, reverse the Appeal Tribunal and restore the decision of the Industrial Tribunal.

NOTE: In *BS* v *Dundee City Council* [2014] IRLR 131, the Inner House of Court of Session, reviewed the early ill health authorities of *Spencer* v *Paragon Wallpapers Ltd* and *Daubney* v *East Lindsey District Council* and addressed the relevance of length of service to a decision to dismiss.

Lord Drummond Young stated:

> Three important themes emerge from the decisions in *Spencer* and *Daubney*. First, in a case where an employee has been absent from work for some time owing to sickness, it is essential to consider the question of whether the employer can be expected to wait longer. Secondly, there is a need to consult the employee and take his views into account. We would emphasise, however, that this is a factor that can operate both for and against dismissal. If the employee states that he is anxious to return to work as soon as he can and hopes that he will be able to do so in the near future, that operates in his favour; if, on the other hand he states that he is no better and does not know when he can return to work, that is a significant factor operating against him. Thirdly, there is a need to take steps to discover the employee's medical condition and his likely prognosis, but this merely requires the obtaining of proper medical advice; it does not require the employer to pursue detailed medical examination; all that the employer requires to do is to ensure that the correct question is asked and answered.
>
> . . .
>
> In misconduct cases length of service will often be relevant, because if the employee has worked for a long time without misconduct that may be a strong indication that either he is unlikely to have done anything seriously wrong or what he has done can be treated as a temporary aberration: *O'Brien* v *Boots Pure Drug Co* [1973] IRLR 261; *Johnson Matthey Metals Ltd* v *Harding* [1978] IRLR 248. In cases involving dismissal on the ground of ill health, the relevance of length of service is not quite so clear cut. In an appropriate case, however, it may show that the employee in question is a good and willing worker with a good attendance record, someone who would do his utmost to get back to work as soon as he could. The critical question in every case is whether the length of the employee's service, and the manner in which he worked during that period, yields inferences that indicate that the employee is likely to return to work as soon as he can.

Discipline and Grievances at Work: The ACAS Guide
(2009)

How should longer-term absence through ill health be handled?

Where absence is due to medically certificated illness, the issue becomes one of capability rather than conduct. Employers need to take a more sympathetic and considerate approach, particularly if the employee is disabled and where reasonable adjustments at the workplace might enable them to return to work. There are certain steps an employer should take when considering the problem of long-term absence:

- employee and employer should keep in regular contact with each other
- the employee must be kept fully informed if there is any risk to employment

- if the employer wishes to contact the employee's doctor, he or she must notify the employee in writing that they intend to make such an application and they must secure the employee's consent in writing. The employer must inform the individual that he or she has:
    - the right to withhold consent to the application being made
    - the right to state that he or she wishes to have access to the report. (The Access to Medical Reports Act 1988 also gives the individual the right to have access to the medical practitioner's report for up to six months after it was supplied)
    - rights concerning access to the report before (and/or after) it is supplied
    - the right to withhold consent to the report being supplied to the employer
    - the right to request amendments to the report
- where the employee states that he or she wishes to have access to the report, the employer must let the GP know this when making the application and at the same time let the employee know that the report has been requested
- the letter of enquiry reproduced in Appendix 3—Sample letters, and approved by the British Medical Association, may be used, and the employee's permission to the enquiry should be attached to the letter
- the employee must contact the GP within 21 days of the date of application to make arrangement to see the report. Otherwise the rights under the 1988 Act will be lost
- if the employee considers the report to be incorrect or misleading, the employee may make a written request to the GP to make appropriate amendments
- if the GP refuses, the employee has the right to ask the GP to attach a statement to the report reflecting the employee's view on any matters of disagreement
- the employee may withhold consent to the report being supplied to the employer
- on the basis of the GP's report the employer should consider whether alternative work is available
- the employer is not expected to create a special job for the employee concerned, nor to be a medical expert, but to take action on the basis of the medical evidence
- where there is a reasonable doubt about the nature of the illness or injury, the employee should be asked if he or she would agree to be examined by a doctor to be appointed by the organisation
- where an employee refuses to cooperate in providing medical evidence, or to undergo an independent medical examination, the employee should be told in writing that a decision will be taken on the basis of the information available and that it could result in dismissal
- where the employee is allergic to a product used in the workplace the employer should consider remedial action or a transfer to alternative work
- where the employee's job can no longer be held open, and no suitable alternative work is available, the employee should be informed of the likelihood of dismissal
- where dismissal action is taken the employee should be given the period of notice to which he or she is entitled by statute or contract and informed of any right of appeal.

Where an employee has been on long-term sick absence and there is little likelihood of he or she becoming fit enough to return, it may be argued that the contract of employment has been terminated through 'frustration'. However, the doctrine of frustration should not be relied on since the courts are generally reluctant to apply it where a procedure exists for termination of the contract. It is therefore better for the employer to take dismissal action after following proper procedures.

Specific health problems

Consideration should be given to introducing measures to help employees, regardless of status or seniority, who are suffering from alcohol or drug abuse, or from stress. The aim should be to identify employees affected and encourage them to seek help and treatment…

Employers should consider whether it is appropriate to treat the problem as a medical rather than a disciplinary matter.

There is sometimes workforce pressure to dismiss an employee because of a medical condition, or even threats of industrial action. If such an employee is dismissed, then he or she may be able to claim unfair dismissal before an employment tribunal, or breach of contract. Also, the Disability Discrimination Act 1995 makes it unlawful for an employer of any size to treat a disabled person less favourably for a reason relating to their disability, without a justifiable reason. Employers are required to make a reasonable adjustment to working conditions or the workplace where that would help to accommodate a particular disabled person.

NOTES

1. In *McAdie* v *Royal Bank of Scotland plc* [2007] IRLR 895, the Court of Appeal held that the fact that an employer had caused the employee's incapacity (in this case, a stress-related illness), however culpably, cannot preclude it forever from effecting a fair dismissal. If it were otherwise,

employers would in such circumstances be obliged to retain on their books indefinitely employees who were incapable of any useful work. Employees who have been injured as a result of a breach of duty by their employers are entitled to compensation in the ordinary courts, which in an appropriate case will include compensation for lost earnings and lost capacity. However, tribunals must resist the temptation of being led by sympathy for the employee into granting by way of compensation for unfair dismissal what is, in truth, an award of compensation for injury.

2. In *First West Yorkshire Ltd* v *Haigh* [2008] IRLR 182, the issue before the EAT was 'where an employee's pension scheme contains provisions entitling the employee to an ill health pension on grounds of permanent incapacity, is a tribunal entitled to expect the employer to give consideration to retirement on ill health grounds before dismissing the employee?' The employers maintained that the issue is whether a dismissal is within the band of reasonable responses, and entitlement to retirement on ill health grounds is a distinct matter. But the EAT adopted the view that 'fairness requires the reasonable employer to give proper consideration to an ill health retirement scheme before he dismisses for long-term sickness. According to the EAT:

> As a general rule, when an employee is absent through ill health in the long term, an employer will be expected, prior to dismissing the employee, to take reasonable steps to consult him, to ascertain by means of appropriate medical evidence the nature and prognosis for his condition, and to consider alternative employment... Where, however, an employer provides an enhanced pension on retirement through ill health, it seems to us that an employer will also be expected to take reasonable steps to ascertain whether the employee is entitled to the benefit of ill health retirement.

As Judge Richardson put it, 'if an employer could proceed to dismiss a sick employee who might be entitled to an enhanced retirement pension without considering that question, substantial injustice might occur.'

3. A Government-commissioned report by Dame Carol Black and David Frost in 2011 led to a comprehensive review of sickness absence in the UK. A number of issues were identified, including that, after four weeks' absence, many employee slip into long-term absence but that early interventions were highly effective in reversing this trend.

In response to these findings, the Government set up a new service, 'Fit for Work' (FfW), to provide free occupational health advice and support for employees, employers, and GPs. The main features of the scheme are as follows:

- The responsibility GPs currently have to assess their patients' long-term capability for work will be passed to a new occupational health service—the FfW scheme.
- There are two websites: Fit for Work—England and Wales and Fit for Work—Scotland.
- FfW is a state-funded, assessment service for any employee who is off work for four weeks or more ill or injured.
- A referral to FfW should be made after four weeks' continuous absence, this being the point when the Government considers it's likely that a longer-term absence will occur with the increased risk that an employee will move on to claiming state benefits.
- GPs will need an employee's consent to make a referral. In some circumstances, employers will be able to make a referral themselves.
- The service aims to signpost relevant interventions that might return the employee to the workplace more quickly.
- FfW will make an assessment and produce a return-to-work plan. Some of the findings of FfW can be used by both employers and employees to make adjustments in the workplace that might lead to a shortened absence. Alternatively, the assessment process might result in the employee being given early signposting to medical treatments.
- The service will be a telephone/web-based assessment tool for the majority of users.
- Relief, capped at an annual expenditure of £500 per employee, is available (w.e.f. 1 January 2015) to help employers fund the recommended medical treatments of staff.
- The helpline became operational in December 2014 and a gradual roll out of the assessment service is expected between January and May 2015.

Employers need to appreciate that there might be consequences if the return-to-work plan is not acted upon. Cooperation with FfW is entirely voluntary but there may be legal implications relating to unfair dismissal and disability discrimination where the recommendations have not been put in place.

...

(c) Persistent absenteeism

While long-term absence is treated as a matter of incapability, it is clear that persistent absenteeism should be regarded as a matter of misconduct and can be dealt with under the ordinary disciplinary procedure (see *International Sports Ltd* v *Thomson* [1980] IRLR 340; *Rolls Royce* v *Walpole* [1980] IRLR 343).

The following extract from the ACAS Guide provides a checklist of what the courts and tribunals expect from employers in handling cases of frequent and persistent short-term absence.

Discipline and Grievances at Work: The ACAS Guide
(2009)

How should frequent and persistent short-term absence be handled?

- unexpected absences should be investigated promptly and the employee asked for an explanation at a return-to-work interview
- if there are no acceptable reasons then the employer may wish to treat the matter as a conduct issue and deal with it under the disciplinary procedure
- where there is no medical certificate to support frequent short-term, self-certified, absences then the employee should be asked to see a doctor to establish whether treatment is necessary and whether the underlying reason for the absence is work-related. If no medical support is forthcoming the employer should consider whether to take action under the disciplinary procedure
- if the absence could be disability related the employer should consider what reasonable adjustments could be made in the workplace to help the employee (this might be something as simple as an adequate, ergonomic chair, or a power-assisted piece of equipment. Reasonable adjustment also means redeployment to a different type of work if necessary
- if the absence is because of temporary problems relating to dependants, the employee may be entitled to have time off under the provisions of the Employment Rights Act 1996 relating to time off for dependants
- if the absence is because the employee has difficulty managing both work and home responsibilities then the employer should give serious consideration to more flexible ways of working. Employees who are parents of children aged 16 and under (disabled children under 18) and carers of adults have the right to request flexible working arrangements—including job-sharing, part-time working, flexi-time, working from home/teleworking and school time contracts—and employers must have a good business reason for rejecting any application
- in all cases the employee should be told what improvement in attendance is expected and warned of the likely consequences if this does not happen
- if there is no improvement, the employee's length of service, performance, the likelihood of a change in attendance, the availability of suitable alternative work where appropriate, and the effect of past and future absences on the organisation should all be taken into account in deciding appropriate action. In order to show both the employee concerned, and other employees, that absence is regarded as a serious matter and may result in dismissal, it is very important that persistent absence is dealt with promptly, firmly and consistently.

An examination of records will identify those employees who are frequently absent and may show an absence pattern.

(d) Dishonesty and other criminal offences

ACAS Code of Practice 1, *Disciplinary and Grievance Procedures in Employment*
(2015)

31. If an employee is charged with, or convicted of a criminal offence this is not normally in itself reason for disciplinary action. Consideration needs to be given to what effect the charge or conviction has on the employee's suitability to do the job and their relationship with their employer, work colleagues and customers.

Discipline and Grievances at Work: The ACAS Guide
(2009)

Where it is thought the conduct warrants disciplinary action the following guidance should be borne in mind:
- the employer should investigate the facts as far as possible, come to a view about them and consider whether the conduct is sufficiently serious to warrant instituting the disciplinary procedure
- where the conduct requires prompt attention the employer need not await the outcome of the prosecution before taking fair and reasonable action
- where the police are called in they should not be asked to conduct any investigation on behalf of the employer, nor should they be present at any meeting or disciplinary meeting.

In some cases the nature of the alleged offence may not justify disciplinary action—for example, off-duty conduct which has no bearing on employment—but the employee may not be available for work because he or she is in custody or on remand. In these cases employers should decide whether, in the light of the needs of the organisation, the employee's job can be held open.

Where a criminal conviction leads, for example, to the loss of a licence so that continued employment in a particular job would be illegal, employers should consider whether alternative work is appropriate and available.

Where an employee, charged with or convicted of a criminal offence, refuses or is unable to cooperate with the employer's disciplinary investigations and proceedings, this should not deter an employer from taking action. The employee should be advised in writing that unless further information is provided, a disciplinary decision will be taken on the basis of the information available and could result in dismissal.

Where there is little likelihood of an employee returning to employment, it may be argued that the contract of employment has been terminated through 'frustration'. However, the doctrine is normally accepted by the courts only where the frustrating event renders all performance of the employment contract clearly impossible. It is normally better for the employer to take disciplinary action.

An employee who has been charged with, or convicted of, a criminal offence may become unacceptable to colleagues, resulting in workforce pressure to dismiss and threats of industrial action. Employers should bear in mind that they may have to justify the reasonableness of any decision to dismiss and that an employment tribunal will ignore threats of, and actual industrial action when determining the fairness of a decision (Section 107, Employment Rights Act 1996). They should consider all relevant factors, not just disruption to production, before reaching a reasonable decision.

NOTES

1. There may be cases where the period of absence on remand is lengthy and the employer may be held to be justified, in the interests of the business, in seeking a permanent replacement (see *Kingston* v *British Railways Board* [1984] IRLR 146, CA). Indeed, as recognised by the ACAS Guide, a lengthy period in custody on remand or a sentence of imprisonment on conviction may result in a finding that the employment contract has been 'frustrated'.

2. An employee may be fairly dismissed where he or she conceals from his or her employer a criminal conviction imposed before the employment began and which is not a 'spent' conviction under the Rehabilitation of Offenders Act 1974. Whether or not a conviction is spent and the individual is a 'rehabilitated person' under the Act depends upon the severity of the sentence and the time which has elapsed since it was imposed. A sentence of life imprisonment or a sentence exceeding 30 months are never spent. There is a sliding scale for the periods of time for the conviction to become spent, from six months for an absolute discharge, five years for a fine, seven years for a period of imprisonment under six months, up to ten years where there is a sentence of six months to two and a half years.

3. In *Securicor Guarding Ltd* v *R* [1994] IRLR 633, the EAT gave its explicit support to the principles set out in what is now paragraph 30 of the Code. The applicant, who worked as a security guard on the premises of an important customer, was charged with sex offences against children. He was dismissed even though he denied the charges to the employers; a collective agreement provided for suspension on full pay where investigations into misconduct could not be completed; and the employers never contacted the customer concerned to discuss the matter. Upholding the finding of unfair dismissal, the EAT stated: 'It does appear to us that it would be a very remarkable thing if it could be said that wherever an employee is in a sensitive position the mere fact that he has been charged with an offence will justify an employer not in suspending him; not in taking him away from a sensitive position; but in dismissing him.'

REHABILITATION OF OFFENDERS ACT 1974

4. Effect of rehabilitation

(3) Subject to the provisions of any order made under subsection (4) below—

...

(b) a conviction which has become spent or any circumstances ancillary thereto, or any failure to disclose a spent conviction or any such circumstances, shall not be a proper ground for dismissing or excluding a person from any office, profession, occupation or employment, or for prejudicing him in any way in any occupation or employment.

NOTES

1. See *Property Guards Ltd* v *Taylor and Kershaw* [1982] IRLR 175.
2. The scope of this provision is limited by subsequent regulations made under s. 4(4) which exclude certain professions and employments from the Act. Exempted groups include: medical practitioners, lawyers, accountants, veterinary surgeons, dentists, nurses, opticians, pharmaceutical chemists, judicial appointments, justices' clerks, probation officers, those employed by local authorities in connection with the provision of social services, and those offices and employments concerned with the provisions of services, schooling, training, etc. to persons under the age of 18 where the holder will have access to young persons (or employment on premises used for providing such services) (see the Rehabilitation of Offenders Act 1974 (Exceptions) Order 1975 (SI 1975/1023) as amended by the Rehabilitation of Offenders Act 1974 (Exceptions) (Amendment) Orders 1986 (SI 1986/1249 and SI 1986/ 2268) and 2002 (SI 2002/441)).
3. An employer, when recruiting to an exempted occupation, should inform candidates in writing that spent convictions must be disclosed. If a person is then employed having failed to disclose a conviction, the employer may be held to have acted fairly if it dismisses on subsequent discovery of the conviction (see *Torr* v *British Railways Board* [1977] ICR 785).

(e) Suspected dishonesty within employment

BHS v Burchell

[1978] IRLR 379, Employment Appeal Tribunal

The employer successfully appealed to the EAT against a finding by an industrial tribunal that Ms Burchell's dismissal for suspected dishonesty was unfair.

ARNOLD J: What the tribunal have to decide every time is, broadly expressed, whether the employer who discharged the employee on the ground of the misconduct in question (usually, though not necessarily, dishonest conduct) entertained a reasonable suspicion amounting to a belief in the guilt of the employee of that misconduct at that time. That is really stating shortly and compendiously what is in fact more than one element. First of all, there must be established by the employer the fact of that belief; that the employer did believe it. Secondly, that the employer had in his mind reasonable grounds upon which to sustain that belief. And thirdly, we think, that the employer, at the stage at which he formed that belief on those grounds, at any rate at the final stage at which he formed that belief on those grounds, had carried out as much investigation into the matter as was reasonable in all the circumstances of the case. It is the employer who manages to discharge the onus of demonstrating those three matters, we think, who must not be examined further. It is not relevant, as we think, that the tribunal would themselves have shared that view in those circumstances. It is not relevant, as we think, for the tribunal to examine the quality of the material which the employer had before him, for instance to see whether it was the sort of material, objectively considered, which would lead to a certain conclusion on the balance of probabilities, or whether it was the sort of material which would lead to the same conclusion only upon the basis of being 'sure' as it is now said more normally in a criminal context, or, to use the more old-fashioned term, such as to put the matter 'beyond reasonable doubt'. The test, and the test all the way through, is reasonableness; and certainly, as it seems to us, a conclusion on the balance of probabilities will in any surmisable circumstance be a reasonable conclusion.

NOTES

1. The *BHS* v *Burchell* approach was subsequently approved by the Court of Appeal in *W. Weddel & Co. Ltd* v *Tepper* [1980] IRLR 96, CA.

2. In *Boys and Girls Welfare Society* v *McDonald* [1996] IRLR 129, the EAT warned industrial tribunals against an unduly mechanistic application of the *Burchell* guidelines. The EAT stated that *Burchell* was decided before the amendment to the Employment Protection (Consolidation) Act 1978, s. 57(3), which established a neutral burden of proof. Therefore, a simplistic application of the *Burchell* test in each and every case involving dismissal on grounds of conduct raises a danger of the tribunal falling into error by placing the onus on the employer to satisfy it as to reasonableness. Nor is *Burchell* to be understood as saying that an employer who fails one or more of the three tests is, without more, guilty of unfair dismissal. The tribunal must ask itself whether dismissal fell within the range of reasonable responses.
3. In *S.S. for Justice* v *Mansfield* [2010] UKEAT/0539/09/RN, the EAT held that where an employee facing disciplinary charges is at the same time being investigated by the police, the employer has a wide discretion on whether to continue or postpone the disciplinary hearing.

■ **QUESTION**

What if the criminal court subsequently acquits a person dismissed for suspected dishonesty?

Monie v Coral Racing Ltd
[1980] IRLR 96, Court of Appeal

The appellant worked for the respondent company as an area manager with control over 19 betting shops, and only he and his assistant knew the combination for the safe in the area headquarters. While Mr Monie was on holiday, his assistant discovered that £1,750 was missing from the safe. There were no indications that either the premises or the safe had been forcibly entered, and the respondents' security officer concluded that one or other or both were guilty. Both were dismissed. Monie appealed to the managing director, who accepted that Monie had not been dishonest but that his admitted laxity in security matters justified dismissal in any event.

A tribunal found the dismissal fair on the basis of the employers' reasonable suspicion of dishonesty. The EAT held that suspicion was not sufficient to establish a sufficient reason for dismissal and that there were no grounds in this case for a reasonable belief in dishonesty; but that the dismissal was fair on the basis of Monie's laxity. Monie's appeal to the Court of Appeal was rejected. One of the issues for the Court of Appeal was whether it was fair to dismiss for suspected dishonesty in the particular circumstances of the case.

STEPHENSON LJ: To treat belief in the guilt of the particular employee as applicable to a situation in which an employer finds himself reasonably believing in the guilt of one or more of two employees but unable in fairness to decide which of them is guilty is to pervert a valuable guideline to interpreting and applying the statute in a way which turns justice into an inflexible rule which constrains tribunals to decide cases contrary to justice and equity and to the letter and spirit of the statute.

SIR DAVID CAIRNS: There has been much discussion as to whether a man can be fairly dismissed by reason of a reasonable suspicion of dishonesty or whether actual belief that he had been dishonest is necessary... This court has... given its approval to a type of test which requires something more than reasonable suspicion. This derived from a passage in the judgment of Arnold J in *British Home Stores* v *Burchell*...

While guidelines such as those provided by Arnold J are helpful each case must in the end depend on its own facts. There is a great deal of difference between a case where only one man is under suspicion on the ground of some evidence of greater or less weight and a case where it is virtually certain that a serious theft has been committed by one or both of two men and it is impossible to tell which.

DUNN LJ: I agree with my Lords that in a situation of this kind, where there is a reasonable suspicion that one of two or possibly both employees must have acted dishonestly it is not necessary for the employer to believe that either of them acted dishonestly.

NOTE: This principle concerning 'blanket' dismissals has subsequently been extended by the EAT to cases of conduct or capability not involving dishonesty: see *Whitbread & Co.* v *Thomas* [1988]

IRLR 43. According to this case, an employer who cannot identify which member of a group was responsible for an act can fairly dismiss the whole group, even where it is probable that not all were guilty of the act, *provided three conditions are satisfied*:

(a) The act in question must be such that, if committed by an identified individual, it would justify dismissal of that individual.

(b) The tribunal must be satisfied that the act was committed by one or more of the group, all of whom can be shown to be individually capable of having committed the act complained of.

(c) The tribunal must be satisfied that there has been a proper investigation by the employer to identify the person or persons responsible for the act.

(See also *Parr* v *Whitbread plc* [1990] IRLR 39, EAT.)

Frames Snooker Centre v *Boyce*

[1992] IRLR 472, Employment Appeal Tribunal

Burglaries at the employers' premises led to the view that they must have been an 'inside job'. Police suspicions focused on the three managers, but they could not narrow their suspicions further and made no arrests. After a further burglary, the employers decided on dismissal, but only dismissed two of the three, the third manager being the daughter of the owners, in whose honesty the employers had confidence. One of the two dismissed claimed unfair dismissal, on the ground that it was unfair to dismiss only two of the three. The industrial tribunal found the dismissal unfair, but this view was overturned on appeal.

HAGUE J: As a general rule, if the circumstances of the members of the group in relation to the relevant offences are similar, it is likely to be unreasonable for the employer to dismiss one or more members of the group and not others, and those dismissed will thus succeed in a claim for unfair dismissal. But if the employer is able to show that he had solid and sensible grounds (which do not have to be related to the relevant offence) for differentiating between members of the group and not dismissing one or more of them, that will not of itself render the dismissal of the remainder unfair.

D: Stage four: what remedies are available?

EMPLOYMENT RIGHTS ACT 1996

112. The remedies: orders and compensation

(1) This section applies where, on a complaint under section 111, an employment tribunal finds that the grounds of the complaint are well-founded.

(2) The tribunal shall—

(a) explain to the complainant what orders may be made under section 113 and in what circumstances they may be made, and

(b) ask him whether he wishes the tribunal to make such an order.

(3) If the complainant expresses such a wish, the tribunal may make an order under section 113.

(4) If no order is made under section 113, the tribunal shall make an award of compensation for unfair dismissal (calculated in accordance with sections 118 to 127) to be paid by the employer to the employee.

NOTE: Although reinstatement and re-engagement orders are regarded as primary remedies by the statute, in practice compensation is the normal remedy for unfair dismissal, such orders being made by tribunals in around 0.3% only of successful cases. As a result, the re-employment of dismissed workers has been described as 'the lost remedy' (see Dickens et al., *Dismissed* (Oxford: Blackwell, 1985)).

There may be many reasons for the level of re-engagement/reinstatement orders. By the time the tribunal hearing is held—normally three to four months after the dismissal—the applicant may have found another job. Even if this is not the case, the passage of time and the adversarial nature of the proceedings may result in the relationship between the parties breaking down so severely that it would be unrealistic to expect them to resume a normal working relationship (see Lewis, P.,

'An analysis of why legislation has failed to provide employment protection for unfairly dismissed employees' (1981) 19 *British Journal of Industrial Relations* 316–26).

(i) Reinstatement and re-engagement

EMPLOYMENT RIGHTS ACT 1996

113. The orders

An order under this section may be—
- (a) an order for reinstatement (in accordance with section 114), or
- (b) an order for re-engagement (in accordance with section 115), as the tribunal may decide.

114. Order for reinstatement

(1) An order for reinstatement is an order that the employer shall treat the complainant in all respects as if he had not been dismissed.

(2) On making an order for reinstatement the tribunal shall specify—
- (a) any amount payable by the employer in respect of any benefit which the complainant might reasonably be expected to have had but for the dismissal (including arrears of pay) for the period between the date of termination of employment and the date of reinstatement,
- (b) any rights and privileges (including seniority and pension rights) which must be restored to the employee, and
- (c) the date by which the order must be complied with.

(3) If the complainant would have benefited from an improvement in his terms and conditions of employment had he not been dismissed, an order for reinstatement shall require him to be treated as if he had benefited from that improvement from the date on which he would have done so but for being dismissed.

(4) In calculating for the purposes of subsection (2)(a) any amount payable by the employer, the tribunal shall take into account, so as to reduce the employer's liability, any sums received by the complainant in respect of the period between the date of termination of employment and the date of reinstatement by way of—
- (a) wages in lieu of notice or ex gratia payments paid by the employer, or
- (b) remuneration paid in respect of employment with another employer, and such other benefits as the tribunal thinks appropriate in the circumstances.

115. Order for re-engagement

(1) An order for re-engagement is an order, on such terms as the tribunal may decide, that the complainant be engaged by the employer, or by a successor of the employer or by an associated employer, in employment comparable to that from which he was dismissed or other suitable employment.

(2) On making an order for re-engagement the tribunal shall specify the terms on which re-engagement is to take place, including—
- (a) the identity of the employer,
- (b) the nature of the employment,
- (c) the remuneration for the employment,
- (d) any amount payable by the employer in respect of any benefit which the complainant might reasonably be expected to have had but for the dismissal (including arrears of pay) for the period between the date of termination of employment and the date of re-engagement,
- (e) any rights and privileges (including seniority and pension rights) which must be restored to the employee, and
- (f) the date by which the order must be complied with.

(3) In calculating for the purposes of subsection (2)(d) any amount payable by the employer, the tribunal shall take into account, so as to reduce the employer's liability, any sums received by the complainant in respect of the period between the date of termination of employment and the date of re-engagement by way of—
- (a) wages in lieu of notice or ex gratia payments paid by the employer, or
- (b) remuneration paid in respect of employment with another employer, and such other benefits as the tribunal thinks appropriate in the circumstances.

116. Choice of order and its terms

(1) In exercising its discretion under section 113 the tribunal shall first consider whether to make an order for reinstatement and in so doing shall take into account—
- (a) whether the complainant wishes to be reinstated,
- (b) whether it is practicable for the employer to comply with an order for reinstatement, and

(c) where the complainant caused or contributed to some extent to the dismissal, whether it would be just to order his reinstatement.

(2) If the tribunal decides not to make an order for reinstatement it shall then consider whether to make an order for re-engagement and, if so, on what terms.

(3) In so doing the tribunal shall take into account—

(a) any wish expressed by the complainant as to the nature of the order to be made,

(b) whether it is practicable for the employer (or a successor or an associated employer) to comply with an order for re-engagement, and

(c) where the complainant caused or contributed to some extent to the dismissal, whether it would be just to order his re-engagement and (if so) on what terms.

(4) Except in a case where the tribunal takes into account contributory fault under subsection (3)(c) it shall, if it orders re-engagement, do so on terms which are, so far as is reasonably practicable, as favourable as an order for reinstatement.

(5) Where in any case an employer has engaged a permanent replacement for a dismissed employee, the tribunal shall not take that fact into account in determining, for the purposes of subsection (1)(b) or (3)(b), whether it is practicable to comply with an order for reinstatement or re-engagement.

(6) Subsection (5) does not apply where the employer shows—

(a) that it was not practicable for him to arrange for the dismissed employee's work to be done without engaging a permanent replacement, or

(b) that—

(i) he engaged the replacement after the lapse of a reasonable period, without having heard from the dismissed employee that he wished to be reinstated or re-engaged, and

(ii) when the employer engaged the replacement it was no longer reasonable for him to arrange for the dismissed employee's work to be done except by a permanent replacement.

117. Enforcement of order and compensation

(1) An employment tribunal shall make an award of compensation, to be paid by the employer to the employee, if—

(a) an order under section 113 is made and the complainant is reinstated or re-engaged, but

(b) the terms of the order are not fully complied with.

(2) Subject to section 124, the amount of the compensation shall be such as the tribunal thinks fit having regard to the loss sustained by the complainant in consequence of the failure to comply fully with the terms of the order.

(2A) There shall be deducted from any award under subsection (1) the amount of any award made under section 112(5) at the time of the order under section 113.

(3) Subject to subsections (1) and (2), if an order under section 113 is made but the complainant is not reinstated or re-engaged in accordance with the order, the tribunal shall make—

(a) an award of compensation for unfair dismissal (calculated in accordance with sections 118 to 126), and

(b) except where this paragraph does not apply, an additional award of compensation of an amount not less than twenty-six nor more than fifty-two weeks' pay, to be paid by the employer to the employee.

(4) Subsection (3)(b) does not apply where—

(a) the employer satisfies the tribunal that it was not practicable to comply with the order,

(b) [deleted by Employment Relations Act 1999, s. 33]

(5), (6) [deleted by ERA 1999]

(7) Where in any case an employer has engaged a permanent replacement for a dismissed employee, the tribunal shall not take that fact into account in determining for the purposes of subsection (4)(a) whether it was practicable to comply with the order for reinstatement or re-engagement unless the employer shows that it was not practicable for him to arrange for the dismissed employee's work to be done without engaging a permanent replacement.

(8) Where in any case an industrial tribunal finds that the complainant has unreasonably prevented an order under section 113 from being complied with, in making an award of compensation for unfair dismissal it shall take that conduct into account as a failure on the part of the complainant to mitigate his loss.

124. Limit of compensatory award etc.

(1) The amount of—

(a) any compensation awarded to a person under section 117(1) and (2), or

(b) a compensatory award to a person calculated in accordance with section 123,

shall not exceed the amount specified in subsection (1ZA)..

(1ZA) The amount specified in this subsection is the lower of—

(a) £78,335 [w.e.f. 6 April 2015]
(b) 52 multiplied by a week's pay of the person concerned.

(1A) Subsection (1) shall not apply to compensation awarded, or a compensatory award made, to a person in case where he is regarded as unfairly dismissed by virtue of section 100, 103A, 105(3) or 105(6A).

(2) [deleted by ERA 1999, s. 36]

(3) In the case of compensation awarded to a person under section 117(1) and (2), the limit imposed by this section may be exceeded to the extent necessary to enable the award fully to reflect the amount specified as payable under section 114(2)(a) or section 115(2)(d).

(4) Where—
(a) a compensatory award is an award under paragraph (a) of subsection (3) of section 117, and
(b) an additional award falls to be made under paragraph (b) of that subsection,

the limit imposed by this section on the compensatory award may be exceeded to the extent necessary to enable the aggregate of the compensatory and additional awards fully to reflect the amount specified as payable under section 114(2)(a) or section 115(2)(d).

NOTES

1. The provisions which now appear as the ERA 1996, s. 124(3)–(4) were originally inserted by TURERA 1993, s. 30. These changes and other changes made in the compensation provisions (see Section (ii)) are designed to tackle the weaknesses graphically illustrated in *O'Laoire* v *Jackel International Ltd* [1990] IRLR 70. An employment tribunal, as part of an order for reinstatement, specified that the complainant should receive a sum totalling £27,833 gross representing back-pay between the date of the dismissal and the date of reinstatement. The employers refused to comply with the order and the complainant was awarded compensation of £12,185 (including an additional award) which was the maximum which at that time could be awarded given the statutory limit on unfair dismissal compensation awards. His actual losses, as found by the tribunal, exceeded £100,000. The complainant then sought to enforce in the county court the provisions relating to back-pay set out in the reinstatement order. The Court of Appeal held that such an action was not available to the complainant. A reinstatement order is wholly unenforceable. If such an order is not complied with, whether wholly or in part, the complainant's only remedy is to apply to the employment tribunal for compensation. The monetary provisions of a reinstatement order do not create a cause of action enforceable through the county courts.

   Noting the injustice of the position in the case of higher paid employees, the Master of the Rolls expressed the view that the present maximum level of compensation for unfair dismissal could positively discourage employers from complying with an order for reinstatement. He felt the time had arrived for a fundamental review of the compensation limits.

2. In the more frequent situation of a total failure to comply with the order, the tribunal will award compensation using the normal rules of computation plus an 'additional award' (see the ERA 1996, s. 117).

3. It is a defence to the granting of the additional award if the employer can show that it was not practicable to comply with the order. Impracticability is therefore a possible defence at two stages in the process of tribunal decision-making. The following circumstances have been held to render a reinstatement/re-engagement impracticable.
   (a) where it would inevitably lead to industrial unrest (*Coleman* v *Magnet Joinery Ltd* [1974] IRLR 343);
   (b) where there is no suitable vacancy; a re-engagement order does not place a duty on the employer to search for and find work for the dismissed employee irrespective of existing vacancies (*Freemans plc* v *Flynn* [1984] IRLR 486);
   (c) where the employee believes himself or herself to be a victim of conspiracy by the employers, or he or she is not likely to be a satisfactory employee in any circumstances if reinstated or re-engaged (*Nothman* v *Barnet London Borough Council (No. 2)* [1980] IRLR 65);
   (d) where there must exist a close personal relationship, reinstatement can only be appropriate in exceptional circumstances, and to enforce it upon a reluctant employer is not a course which an employment tribunal should pursue unless persuaded by powerful evidence that it would succeed (*obiter* from *Enessy Co. SA t/a The Tulchan Estate* v *Minoprio and Minoprio* [1978] IRLR 489).

(ii) Compensation

EMPLOYMENT RIGHTS ACT 1996

118. General

(1) Where a tribunal makes an award of compensation for unfair dismissal under section 112(4) or 117(3)(a) the award shall consist of—

    (a) a basic award (calculated in accordance with sections 119 to 122 and 126), and

    (b) a compensatory award (calculated in accordance with sections 123, 124, 126 and 127).

(2)–(4) [repealed].

119. Basic award

(1) Subject to the provisions of this section, sections 120 to 122 and section 126, the amount of the basic award shall be calculated by—

    (a) determining the period, ending with the effective date of termination, during which the employee has been continuously employed,

    (b) reckoning backwards from the end of that period the number of years of employment falling within that period, and

    (c) allowing the appropriate amount for each of those years of employment.

(2) In subsection (1)(c) 'the appropriate amount' means—

    (a) one and a half weeks' pay for a year of employment in which the employee was not below the age of forty-one,

    (b) one week's pay for a year of employment (not within paragraph (a)) in which he was not below the age of twenty-two, and

    (c) half a week's pay for a year of employment not within paragraph (a) or (b).

(3) Where twenty years of employment have been reckoned under subsection (1), no account shall be taken under that subsection of any year of employment earlier than those twenty years.

NOTES

1. The number of years' service that can be taken into account is subject to a maximum of 20 years (s. 119(3)). A week's pay is calculated in accordance with the ERA 1996, ss. 220–9 and is based on gross pay. The maximum allowable for a week's pay is currently £475 (w.e.f. 6 April 2015). Therefore, in general, the maximum payment under this head of calculation in 2015–16 is £475 × 20 × 1½ = £14,250.

 Various payments and employment tribunal awards under TULR(C)A 1992 and the ERA 1996 are subject to minimum and/or maximum limits. Prior to the passage of the Employment Relations Act 1999, some of these limits were required to be reviewed each calendar year (for example, the limit on a week's pay used in calculating statutory redundancy payments and the basic and additional awards which may be made on a finding of unfair dismissal). Other awards and payments were not required to be reviewed annually but could be increased at the Secretary of State's discretion (for example, the compensatory award in unfair dismissal cases). Section 34 of the Employment Relations Act 1999 now provides that limits on these payments and awards will instead be index-linked.

 Section 34(1) sets out the awards and payments to be index-linked. Section 34(2) provides that the limits on these payments and awards will be linked to percentage changes in the retail prices index, using the September index in each year as the reference point.

2. The basic award used to be subject to a minimum award of two weeks' pay but this was abolished by the EA 1980. Therefore, given the operation of the deduction provisions set out in the following case extracts, it is possible for a tribunal to reduce the basic award to nil. However, there are two situations where a minimum award is still maintained:

    (a) Where the industrial tribunal finds that the reason or principal reason for the dismissal was redundancy but:

      (i) the employee refused or left suitable alternative employment, or

      (ii) the employee's contract was renewed or he or she was re-engaged within four weeks,

    the employee will be entitled to a basic award of two weeks' pay (the ERA 1996, s. 121). This is despite the fact that he or she would not be considered to be dismissed for the purposes of claiming statutory redundancy payments.

    (b) Where the dismissal is regarded as 'automatically unfair' because, for example, it is related to membership/non-membership of a trade union or union activity under TULR(C)A 1992,

s. 152 or s. 153 or health and safety cases under the ERA 1996, s. 100, the basic award (before any reduction for reasons set out later) is £5,807 as at 6 April 2015 and is subject to annual review (the ERA 1996, s. 120(1)). Where the employee is regarded as unfairly dismissed by virtue of section 104F (blacklists), the amount of the basic award shall be not be less than £5,000 (ERA, 1996, s.120(1C).

3. Prior to the coming into force of Employment Equality (Age) Regulations 2006 (SI 2006/1031) w.e.f. 1 October 2006, if the claimant was 64 years of age, entitlement went down one-twelfth for each whole month which had elapsed between the complainant's 64th birthday and the effective date of termination. For example, an employee aged 64 years and six months would have his or her basic award reduced by six-twelfths (half). Fortunately, the regulations abolished this rampantly ageist provision.

4. Where the applicant has received a redundancy payment, whether under the statutory or a private scheme, the basic award will be reduced by the amount of that payment (the ERA 1996, s. 122(4)(a)).

5. Where the employee has unreasonably refused an offer of reinstatement by the employer, the basic award will be reduced by an amount which the tribunal considers just and equitable (the ERA 1996, s. 122(1)).

6. Where the employer makes an *ex gratia* payment which is specifically intended to cover any liability to compensation, if large enough this may also be set off against any entitlement to a compensatory award (see *Chelsea Football & Athletic Club* v *Heath* [1981] IRLR 73).

7. Where the tribunal considers that any conduct of the complainant before the dismissal (or, where the dismissal was with notice, before the notice was given) was such that it would be just and equitable to do so, it may reduce the basic award (the ERA 1996, s. 122(2)).

8. The ERA 1996, s. 123, provides for the calculation of any compensatory award made under s. 118 of the Act.

EMPLOYMENT RIGHTS ACT 1996

123. Compensatory award

(1) Subject to the provisions of this section and sections 124 and 126, the amount of the compensatory award shall be such amount as the tribunal considers just and equitable in all the circumstances having regard to the loss sustained by the complainant in consequence of the dismissal in so far as that loss is attributable to action taken by the employer.

(2) The loss referred to in subsection (1) shall be taken to include—

   (a) any expenses reasonably incurred by the complainant in consequence of the dismissal, and

   (b) subject to subsection (3), loss of any benefit which he might reasonably be expected to have had but for the dismissal.

(3) The loss referred to in subsection (1) shall be taken to include in respect of any loss of—

   (a) any entitlement or potential entitlement to a payment on account of dismissal by reason of redundancy (whether in pursuance of Part XI or otherwise), or

   (b) any expectation of such a payment,

only the loss referable to the amount (if any) by which the amount of that payment would have exceeded the amount of a basic award (apart from any reduction under section 122) in respect of the same dismissal.

NOTE: The aim of the compensatory award is to reimburse the employee for any financial loss experienced; it is not to punish the employer for poor personnel practices (see *Clarkson International Tools Ltd* v *Short* [1973] IRLR 90). It follows, therefore, that if the employee has in fact suffered no loss then he or she should not receive a compensatory award. We have already discussed the decision of the House of Lords in *Polkey* v *A. E. Dayton Services Ltd* [1987] IRLR 503, where it was held that a dismissal could not be held to be substantively fair merely because with hindsight a procedural lapse would not have made any difference to the outcome. However, the reasoning of their Lordships in that case fully accepts the position that if failures in procedure would not have prevented the dismissal taking place then this should be reflected in the level of the compensatory award.

Rao v Civil Aviation Authority
[1994] IRLR 240, Court of Appeal

Mr Rao had a long record of poor attendance, for which he received a warning. After a medical showed no definite cause, he was dismissed. This was held to be procedurally unfair by the industrial tribunal. It decided against reinstatement and awarded compensation based on the following considerations:

(a) both basic and compensatory awards were to be reduced for contributory fault;

(b) to the reduced figure for the compensatory award there should then be a further reduction of 80% on account of their finding that had the employers followed a fair procedure, there was only a 20% chance of Mr Rao's employment continuing.

Mr Rao appealed against this decision arguing that the tribunal had adopted too strict a test in deciding whether re-employment was practicable. In addition, he alleged that by reducing the compensatory award because of the employee's conduct and then reducing it further on account that he would still have been dismissed even if the correct procedure had been followed, the tribunal had imposed a double penalty. Both the EAT and the Court of Appeal dismissed Mr Rao's appeal.

SIR THOMAS BINGHAM MR: It is argued by Mr Rao, who appears in this appeal in person, that a further deduction is not justified and that any appropriate deduction is to be made under [what is now ERA 1996 s. 123(1)]. Against that Mr McManus, representing the Authority, argues that a further deduction is permissible if warranted in the judgment of the Tribunal on the facts. In support of that he points both to the practice of the Employment Appeal Tribunal and more significantly to the fact that there are these two subsections in [what is now s. 123], one of which, subsection (1), is clearly directed primarily to the issue of loss and the second to the question of a reduction of the compensatory award to the extent considered just and equitable having regard to the employee's conduct and the extent to which it caused or contributed to any action of the employer.

For my part I consider that it is permissible in principle for a deduction to be made under both [s. 123(1)] and [s. 123(6)], and I would think the section curiously drafted if indeed both those subsections were directed to the same thing. It would, however, seem to me appropriate that those making this calculation should first of all assess what is the amount of the loss which the employee has sustained under subsection (1), and thereafter, and in the light of that finding, make their decision as to the extent to which the employee caused or contributed to the dismissal and on the question of what reduction it would be fair and equitable to make having regard to that finding. It does therefore seem to me that the 80% deduction should be considered first, and the contributory just and equitable finding should follow.

One asks, therefore, whether the Tribunal said anything different. To my mind it is extremely doubtful whether the Tribunal had anything different in mind, in particular because they did in fact specify the 80% deduction as one that they thought appropriate but did not specify any percentage in relation to the [s. 123(6)] deduction. It therefore seems to me that, whether as a result of science or the way that they set about it, they did exactly what the section indicates. Insofar as their statement of principle may suggest anything different, I think that may very well be because they were addressing themselves to the calculation of the basic award under [what is now ERA 1996 s. 122(2)] as well, and in that case there is no equivalent of [s. 123(1)]. Be that as it may, it seems to me plain that the next task of the Tribunal, when the matter eventually returns, is for them to consider what percentage deduction should be made from the basic award under [s. 122(2)] and what deduction, if any, should be made from the compensatory award under [s. 123(6)]. I say 'if any' because the fact that an 80% deduction has been made may very well in many cases, if not in this case, have a very significant bearing on what further deduction may fall to be made. That is, however, a question for the Tribunal, and to my mind there is no real room for doubt as to the manner in which they should or indeed propose to set about it. I therefore would dismiss the appeal and the matter will then go back to the Tribunal for the final assessment of the compensation. Mr Rao, who has argued his own case with skill and moderation, has pleaded that in view of the lapse of time that there has already been, it is desirable that the final decision before the Industrial Tribunal should be as early as possible. I am for my part extremely sympathetic to that desire on his part, and I would content myself with observing that the delay does not in any sense appear to be one that could be laid at the door of the Tribunal. Nonetheless, I hope the matter can be finally resolved as soon as possible.

Red Bank Manufacturing Co. Ltd v Meadows
[1992] IRLR 209, Employment Appeal Tribunal

Mr Meadows was made redundant after 32 years' employment with the company. An industrial tribunal found the dismissal unfair because the employers had failed to consult with the employee before dismissing him. In assessing the amount of compensation to be awarded, the tribunal based its calculation on the difference between Mr Meadows's actual earnings since dismissal and what he would have received in the job from which he was dismissed.

The employers appealed against the sum awarded on the following grounds. First, even if a fair procedure had been followed, no job would have been offered to Mr Meadows and therefore compensation should be nil or, at the very least, reduced by a percentage. Second, since Mr Meadows's old job had been extinguished by redundancy, his loss of earnings could at best have been the difference between his actual earnings in his new job and what he would have earned in any job he might have been offered by the appellants. The EAT accepted this as the correct approach and remitted the case to the industrial tribunal for further consideration as to the appropriate award.

> TUCKER J: [I]t seems to us that since the decision in *Polkey* it is necessary for a tribunal when calculating the amount to be awarded for compensation to ask itself this two-stage question: If the proper procedure had been followed, and if consultation had taken place, would it have resulted in an offer of employment? This was the question to which the tribunal did address themselves in the earlier hearing, and to which they gave the answer that it might have done so. What the tribunal failed to do, and what in our view they should have done, was to go on to consider first what that employment would have been, and second what wage would have been paid in respect of it.

NOTE: In *Scope* v *Thornett* [2007] IRLR 155, the Court of Appeal held that the tribunal's task, when deciding what compensation is just and equitable for future loss of earnings, will almost inevitably involve a consideration of uncertainties. Any assessment of a future loss is by way of prediction and inevitably involves a speculative element. The tribunal's statutory duty to assess what is just and equitable by way of compensatory award may involve making predictions on evidence they have heard, and tribunals cannot be allowed to opt out of that because their task is a difficult one and may involve speculation. Although there may be cases in which evidence is so sparse that a tribunal should approach the question on the basis that loss of earnings in the employment would have continued indefinitely, where there is evidence that it may not have been so, that evidence must be taken into account.

Norton Tool Co. v Tewson

[1972] IRLR 86, National Industrial Relations Court

(One of the earliest unfair dismissal cases, but a case which still provides valuable guidance to employment tribunals in approaching the compensatory award.)

> SIR JOHN DONALDSON P: [T]he passage in the tribunal's reasons dealing with compensation is short:
>
>> With regard to the [employee's] loss of wages, he was paid 64p per hour for a 40 hour week, which works out at a weekly wage of £25.60. He was out of work for four weeks, so that he has lost four weeks' wages. In addition, we are entitled to take into account the circumstances of his dismissal; the fact that it was abrupt, that a sacking without notice involves a degree of stigma and that furthermore the [employee] had 11 years' service with the employers and he had lost the benefit of that.
>
> ... the amount to be awarded is that which is just and equitable in all the circumstances, having regard to the loss sustained by the complainant. 'Loss' in the context of section 116 [of the Industrial Relations Act 1971, and the precursor of ERA 1996, s. 123(1)] does not include injury to pride or feelings. In its natural meaning the word is not to be so construed, and that this meaning is intended seems to us to be clear from the elaboration contained in s. 116(2) [see now ERA 1996, s. 123(2)]. The discretionary element is introduced by the words 'having regard to the loss'. This does not mean that the court or tribunal can have regard to other matters, but rather that the amount of compensation is not precisely and arithmetically related to the proved loss...
>
> But it is a corollary of the discretion conferred upon the tribunals that it is their duty to set out their reasoning in sufficient detail to show the principles upon which they have proceeded... Were it otherwise, the parties would in effect be deprived of their right of appeal on questions of law. No great elaboration is required and the task should not constitute a burden. Indeed, the need to give reasons may well assist in the process of properly making the discretionary assessment of damages.

In the present case the tribunal has not made entirely clear the principles upon which it has acted and to that extent it has erred in law…

In these circumstances, and in the light of the request of the parties to which we have already referred, we shall substitute our own award. In our judgement the employee is entitled to compensation in the sum of £375. This sum we regard just and equitable in all the circumstances having regard to the loss sustained by him. That loss falls to be considered under the following heads.

(a) Immediate loss of wages

The Contracts of Employment Act 1963, as amended by the Act of 1971, entitles a worker with more than ten years' continuous employment to not less than six weeks' notice to terminate his employment. [NB: an employee who had Mr Tewson's length of service would now be entitled to at least 12 weeks' notice (ERA 1996, s. 86).] Good industrial relations practice requires the employer either to give this notice or pay six weeks' wages in lieu. The employee was given neither. In an action for damages for wrongful, as opposed to unfair, dismissal he could have claimed that six weeks' wages, but would have had to give credit for anything which he earned or could have earned during the notice period. In the event he would have had to give credit for what he earned in the last two weeks, thus reducing his claim to about four weeks' wages. But if he had been paid the wages in lieu of notice at the time of his dismissal, he would not have to make any repayment upon obtaining further employment during the notice period. In the context of compensation for unfair dismissal we think that it is appropriate and in accordance with the intentions of Parliament that we should treat the employee as having suffered a loss in so far as he receives less than he would have received in accordance with good industrial practice. Accordingly, no deduction has been made for his earnings during the notice period.

We have no information as to whether the £25.60 per week is a gross or a take-home figure. The relevant figure is the take-home pay since this and not the gross pay is what he should have received from his employer.

(b) Manner of dismissal

As the employee secured employment within four weeks of his dismissal and we have taken full account of his loss during this period, we need only consider whether the manner and circumstances of his dismissal could give rise to any financial loss at a later stage by, for example, making him less acceptable to potential employers or exceptionally liable to selection for dismissal. There is no evidence of any such disability and accordingly our assessment of the compensation takes no account of the manner of his dismissal. This took place during a heated exchange of words between him and one of the directors.

(c) Future loss of wages

There is no evidence to suggest that the employee's present employment is any less secure than his former employment, and we have therefore taken no account of possible future losses due to short-time working, lay-off or unemployment, apart from loss of his rights in respect of redundancy and unfair dismissal which are considered separately below.

(d) Loss of protection in respect of unfair dismissal or dismissal by reason of redundancy

These losses may be more serious. So long as the employee remained in the employ of the employers he was entitled to protection in respect of unfair dismissal. He will acquire no such rights against his new employers until he has worked for them for at least two years… Accordingly, if he is unfairly dismissed during this period, his remedy will be limited to claiming damages for wrongful dismissal, which are unlikely to exceed six weeks' wages and may be less. Furthermore, upon obtaining further employment he will be faced with starting a fresh two-year period. This process could be repeated indefinitely, so that he was never again protected in respect of unfair dismissal. Whilst it is impossible for us to quantify this loss, which must be much affected by local conditions, we think that we shall do the employee no injustice if we include £20 in our assessment on account of it.

NOTES

1. Immediate loss of wages represents loss of net earnings from the date of dismissal until the date of the hearing. It may include sums covering overtime payments and tips which may not be counted under the narrower rules governing a 'week's pay' for the purpose of the basic award. Furthermore, for the purpose of calculating immediate loss of wages, there is no limit on the amount of the weekly wage as there is when the basic award is calculated.

   The tribunal will take account of wages paid in lieu of notice and earnings in other employments and set these payments off against the compensation otherwise payable under this head. The one exception to this principle of deduction is where the employee receives earnings from a new employment during what should have been his or her notice period with the former employer: in this case the amount earned will not normally be deducted from compensation (see *Babcock FATA Ltd* v *Addison* [1987] IRLR 173, CA). A contrary view was taken by the EAT in *Hardy* v *Polk (Leeds) Ltd* [2004] IRLR 420, applying *Cerberus Software Ltd* v *Rowley* [2001] IRLR 160, CA. However, in *Burco* v *Langley* [2007] IRLR 145, the Court of Appeal restored the principle set out in *Norton Tool Co. Ltd* v *Tewson* [1972] IRLR 86, NIRC that, in calculating an unfairly dismissed employee's compensation, an employee who is dismissed without a full payment of lieu of notice does not have to give credit for the sums earned from other employers during the notice period. This principle is an exception to the general rule that an employee should be compensated only for loss actually suffered and was expressly based on a precept of good industrial practice: the employer should either give notice or pay the appropriate wages in lieu, and should not be in a better position if they failed to comply with that practice than if they did.

In *Stuart Peters Ltd* v *Bell* [2009] IRLR 941, the Court of Appeal had to decide whether this principle also applies in a case of constructive dismissal, and whether the earnings during what would have been the notice period of an employee who resigns should be offset against their unfair dismissal compensation. The Court of Appeal overruled the EAT and held that the *Norton* principle does not extend to a case of constructive dismissal, even though this produces inconsistency in terms of the compensation that may be awarded to those constructively dismissed and those whose contracts are terminated by the employer. Lord Justice Elias maintained that the same considerations as to what is good industrial relations practice do not apply to a case of alleged constructive dismissal. It is not 'a general practice, let alone good practice, for the employer to make a payment in lieu of notice at the point when an employee resigns in response to an alleged repudiatory breach.'

2. Loss of fringe benefits such as company car, private healthcare, low-interest loan or subsidised accommodation will also be taken into account in assessing compensation for both past and future loss. The ERA 1996, s. 123(2)(a), makes specific reference to the inclusion of 'any expenses reasonably incurred by the complainant in consequence of the dismissal'. This might include the expenses incurred in looking for alternative employment but does not include the legal costs involved in bringing the unfair dismissal action.

3. Where the complainant is still without a job at the date of the hearing, or has taken a job which is at a lower wage, the tribunal will have to embark on a highly speculative exercise of forecasting the future losses which she will, or she is likely to, sustain, including wages, pensions and other fringe benefits. Given that assessment of future loss can only be an approximation, and the fact that the statute gives a wide discretion to the tribunal, an award will not be overturned on appeal unless clearly misguided.

4. Loss of non-transferable pension rights on dismissal can be substantial. In *Copson* v *Eversure Accessories Ltd* [1974] IRLR 247, two types of loss were identified: (a) loss of the pension earned up to the date of dismissal, e.g. 15 years' service towards a pension of £X in 20 years' time at the age of 65; and (b) the individual's loss of future opportunity to improve on his or her pension position, i.e. the opportunity of improving his or her position until the time at which the pension becomes payable. Given the complexities and uncertainties surrounding loss of pension rights, a document was drawn up in 1980 by the Government Actuary's Department for the guidance of industrial tribunals. In 1991, this document was replaced by a new set of guidelines prepared by a committee of industrial tribunal chairs in consultation with the Actuary's Department—*Industrial Tribunals: Compensation for loss of pension rights* (HMSO, 1991). The booklet gives general guidance on several aspects of pension loss with specific advice on the three main heads of loss: loss of pension rights from the date of the dismissal to the date of hearing; loss of future rights; and loss of enhancement of accrued rights. The authors emphasise that they are only offering guidelines and that it is always open to the parties to present their own actuarial assessments. Nevertheless, in this area of uncertainty the booklet will undoubtedly be very influential.

5. Where the employee is dismissed, he or she will have 'to start from scratch' in terms of building the necessary periods of continuous employment required to claim unfair dismissal and redundancy payment rights in the future. As a result, the tribunal will normally award a nominal sum as compensation for the loss of this protection. In *S. H. Muffett Ltd* v *Head* [1986] IRLR 488, the appropriate figure was assessed to be normally £100. It is to be assumed that inflationary forces will have raised this figure.

6. In *Norton Tool*, it was held that, as is the case with the common law action for wrongful dismissal, no account will be taken of injury to feelings in assessing the compensatory award. However,

there may be the exceptional case where the manner of the dismissal has had a tangible effect on the complainant's future employment prospects (e.g. by damaging his or her reputation in the trade or industry) and in such a case compensation may be claimed under this head (see *Vaughan v Weighpack Ltd* [1974] IRLR 105).

7. Deductions may be made from the compensatory award under ERA 1996, s. 123.

The next case finds the House of Lords approving *Norton Tool.*

Dunnachie v Kingston upon Hull City Council

[2004] IRLR 727, House of Lords

The appellant local authority appealed against a decision holding that the respondent (D) was entitled to an award for injury to feelings following a successful claim for unfair dismissal. D resigned from the local authority's employment and commenced proceedings for constructive dismissal. He was successful at the employment tribunal (the tribunal). His award for compensation under the ERA 1996, s. 123(1) included an award for injury to feelings. The tribunal held that it was entitled to make such an award on the basis of Lord Hoffmann's observations in *Johnson v Unisys Ltd* [2001] UKHL 13, [2003] 1 AC 518. The EAT allowed the local authority's appeal. It held that Lord Hoffmann's comments in *Johnson* were *obiter. Norton Tool Co. Ltd v Tewson* [1972] ICR 501 remained good law and showed that compensation could not be recovered for injury to feelings under s. 123(1). D successfully appealed to the Court of Appeal. Although the Court of Appeal agreed that Lord Hoffmann's comments in *Johnson* were *obiter*, it allowed D's appeal by a different route. It held that *Norton Tool* was wrongly decided and that a proper construction of s. 123(1) allowed an award for injury to feelings, as it required compensation to be what was just and equitable having regard to the loss. That meant that aside from compensating for the loss itself, the tribunal could also make an award for injury to feelings if justice and equity required it.

The House of Lords held (Lord Steyn giving the leading judgment): (1) Lord Hoffmann's comments in *Johnson* were *obiter dictum*; (2) the word 'loss' in s. 123(1) excluded non-economic loss such as for injury to feelings. The decision in *Norton Tool* was still good law. The view of the Court of Appeal in the instant case was wrong. It was clear from *Norton Tool* that the phrase 'just and equitable' was designed to give the tribunal a degree of flexibility as claims before it were often presented in person without detailed articulation of every item of loss. The phrase did not control the scope of the word 'loss'.

LORD STEYN: It can readily be accepted that the words 'loss' in varying contexts may have wider and narrower meanings. But that proposition is of no legal interest. The question before the House is the meaning of the word 'loss' in s. 116(1) of the 1971 statute. If properly construed, it was restricted to economic loss; the re-enactment of the statutory formula in 1996 must bear the same meaning... Nothing that happened since 1971 which could justify giving the statutory formula a meaning it did not originally bear.

NOTE: Michael Rubenstein states:

> Lord Steyn places great emphasis on what the drafter meant in 1971 when the original words were enacted... Lord Steyn's approach takes little account of changes to employment law since the legislation was drafted. In 1971, when the language of unfair dismissal compensation was adopted, there was no discrimination legislation, damages for psychiatric injury were unknown, and the implied term of trust and confidence had yet to be developed. Dismissal is a distressing experience, and there is no doubt that the House of Lords' decision in *Dunnachie* will save employers a great deal of money. Yet if an employee suffers emotional distress as a result of an arbitrary dismissal, does it really make sense from the standpoint of a coherent system of employment law that this injury should only be compensatable if the dismissal is tainted by discrimination of one form or another? For so long as this is the case, it should come as no surprise if dismissed employees take every opportunity to claim both unfair dismissal and unlawful discrimination. ['Highlights' [2004] IRLR 669].

EMPLOYMENT RIGHTS ACT 1996

123. Compensatory award

(6) Where the tribunal finds that the dismissal was to any extent caused or contributed to by any action of the complainant, it shall reduce the amount of the compensatory award by such proportion as it considers just and equitable having regard to that finding.

NOTES

1. Normally, the same percentage deduction will apply to both basic and compensatory awards (*RSPCA* v *Cruden* [1986] IRLR 83).
2. If the employee is found to have contributed to the dismissal, the award of compensation may be reduced by as much as 100% (*W. Devis & Sons Ltd* v *Atkins* [1977] IRLR 314, HL).
3. In *Nelson* v *British Broadcasting Corporation (No. 2)* [1979] IRLR 346, the Court of Appeal emphasised that while there must be a finding that there was conduct on the part of the employee in connection with the dismissal which was culpable or blameworthy:

   > [it] does not necessarily have to involve conduct amounting to a breach of contract or a tort. It... also includes conduct which while not amounting to a breach of contract or a tort is nevertheless perverse or foolish or bloody minded. It may also include conduct which though not meriting any of those more pejorative epithets, is nevertheless unacceptable in the circumstances.

4. It is easy to envisage the rules on contributory fault operating in cases of misconduct, but can they also apply in cases of dismissal for incapability? Conflicting answers have been given to this question. In *Kraft Foods Ltd* v *Fox* [1977] IRLR 431, it was held that where employees are doing their best and their best is not good enough, it would be wrong to reduce compensation on the basis of contributory fault. However, in *Moncur* v *International Paint Co. Ltd* [1978] IRLR 223, it was doubted whether an act or failing which is attributable to a defect of character or personality of the claimant, and which is not within his or her control to alter, can never be material when deciding the contributory fault. This approach has now received the approval of the EAT in *Finnie* v *Top Hat Frozen Foods Ltd* [1985] IRLR 365. While there is some doubt, therefore, about whether contributory fault is applicable in every type of incapability dismissal, it is clear that the principle of contribution *will* apply where the so-called incapability was due to the employee's laziness, negligence or idleness (see *Sutton & Gates (Luton) Ltd* v *Boxall* [1978] IRLR 486).

   In *Slaughter* v *C. Brewer & Sons Ltd* [1990] IRLR 426, the EAT stated that, while ill-health will rarely justify a deduction for contributory fault, it may justify a reduction under the general just and equitable ground in ERA 1996, s. 123(1), where it is clear that the employee is incapable of doing the job.
5. Section 123(4) of the 1996 Act further requires the claimant to mitigate his or her loss.

EMPLOYMENT RIGHTS ACT 1996

123. Compensatory award

(4) In ascertaining the loss referred to in subsection (1) the tribunal shall apply the same rule concerning the duty of a person to mitigate his loss as applies to damages recoverable under the common law of England and Wales or (as the case may be) Scotland.

NOTES

1. A complainant must make reasonable attempts to obtain alternative employment. Unreasonable refusal of an offer of reinstatement by the same employer may amount to a failure to mitigate (*Sweetlove* v *Redbridge and Waltham Forest Area Health Authority* [1979] IRLR 195).
2. In *Aon Training Ltd* v *Dore* [2005] IRLR 891, the Court of Appeal laid down the correct approach to mitigation of loss where a dismissed employee subsequently starts his own business. If the ET is satisfied that mitigation in that way was reasonable in the circumstances, the conventional way to assess compensation under the ERA requires the tribunal first to calculate what sum represents loss of remuneration. It should consider the costs incurred in mitigating loss and such a sum, if reasonably incurred, should be added to the loss. From that sum should be deducted the earnings from the new business.
3. There is an unresolved conflict as to whether a failure to invoke a right of appeal amounts to a failure to take reasonable steps to mitigate loss allowing the employment tribunal to reduce

compensation accordingly. See *Hoover Ltd* v *Forde* [1980] ICR 239 which favours this approach and the decision of the Scottish EAT in *William Muir (Bond 9) Ltd* v *Lamb* [1985] IRLR 95 which came out strongly against it. More recently, *Lamb* was followed by the EAT in *Lock* v *Connell Estate Agents* [1994] IRLR 444.

4. Where the employer is able to establish that the complainant has failed to mitigate loss, this can result in reduction of the compensatory reward.

5. Any *ex gratia* payment made by the employer will be deducted from the compensatory award. The ERA 1996, s. 124(5)(a), makes it clear that the amount of the *ex gratia* payment must be taken into account *before* the statutory maximum is applied (see *McCarthy* v *British Insulated Callendars Cables* [1985] IRLR 94).

   Similarly, the statutory maximum will only be imposed after the deduction of the percentage determined for contributory fault. On this basis, it is still possible for complainants to receive a maximum compensatory award despite being held to have contributed to their own dismissal. There is a conflict of authority as to whether payments made by the employer to the complainant should be deducted before or after deductions for contributory fault (*Clement-Clarke International Ltd* v *Manley* [1979] ICR 74; cf. *UBAF Bank Ltd* v *Davis* [1978] IRLR 442).

6. In calculating compensation for unfair dismissal, employment tribunals no longer deduct sums—as they did prior to 1977—in respect of unemployment benefit (now Jobseeker's Allowance) or income support which the complainant may have received. Under the Employment Protection (Recoupment of Jobseeker's Allowance and Income Support) Regulations 1996 (SI 1996/2349), the tribunal, when making an award of compensation, must identify the 'prescribed element' of the award. This element represents the amount of the compensatory award which is attributable to the loss of earnings between date of termination and the end of the tribunal proceedings. This part of the award must then be withheld from the complainant by the former employer. The Department for Business, Innovation and Skills will then serve on the employer a recoupment notice which requires the employer to pay back to them from the 'prescribed element' an amount representing any social security benefits which have been paid to the employee. Once this has been done, the balance of the 'prescribed element' must be paid by the employer to the successful complainant. The Recoupment Regulations only apply where jobseeker's allowance or income support was actually claimed during the period.

   In assessing future loss, the tribunal also does not have to take into account the possibility of the receipt of future benefits by the complainant. Where compensation is based on unemployment for X weeks, for example, then the complainant is disqualified from receipt of benefit during this period.

■ QUESTION

What do the statistics set out in Table 8.1 (Section 3.A(i)) tell us about:

(a) success rates;

(b) frequency of reinstatement or re-engagement;

(c) typical compensation levels?

SECTION 3: **THE LAW OF UNFAIR DISMISSAL: A CRITIQUE**

Critics of this legislation (see Collins, H., 'Capitalist discipline and corporatist law' (1982) 11 ILJ 78, at p. 170; see also Denham, D. J., 'Unfair dismissal law and the legitimation of managerial control' (1990) 41 *Capital & Class* 83) argue that the law has been unsuccessful as an effective control upon managerial prerogative in relation to dismissals and that, far from acting as a constraint on power, the law actually legitimates managerial control. An explanation for the weakness of the law lies in the attitude of the appeal court judges to the legislation. The judges are not happy with the unfair dismissal provisions because they are perceived to be 'corporatist', in that they overstep the boundary between matters which are suitable for State intervention and those which are not. The judges feel unhappy about meddling in affairs they have always thought should be left to individuals to resolve. Consequently, the courts and tribunals are unwilling to substitute their own standards of fairness for management opinion and instead have the tendency to endorse the ordinary practices of employers. Once this occurs it is inevitable that the concept of fairness will tend to favour managerial control. Evidence of this approach can be seen in the next section.

A: The concept of the reasonable employer

Earlier in the chapter we saw that in assessing reasonableness, the question is what the reasonable employer would have done in the circumstances and not what the employment tribunal would have thought. In this sense, the courts do not set the norms of behaviour but merely reflect existing managerial standards. A notorious example of this approach can be seen in *Saunders v Scottish National Camps Association Ltd*.

Saunders v Scottish National Camps Association Ltd
[1980] IRLR 174, Employment Appeal Tribunal

The employee was a maintenance handyman at a children's camp. He was dismissed on the ground of being a homosexual. A psychiatrist gave evidence before the tribunal that, having examined Saunders, he considered that he represented no danger to young people and, further, that heterosexuals were as likely as homosexuals to represent such a danger. The dismissal was held to be fair because a considerable proportion of employers would take the view that the employment of a homosexual should be restricted, particularly when required to work in close proximity to children. Mr Saunders' appeal was rejected by the EAT.

LORD McDONALD: It was argued on behalf of the appellant that the tribunal had made illegitimate and misinformed use of their knowledge and experience of how a reasonable employer would react. They had assumed, it was argued, in the teeth of the evidence that homosexuals created a special risk to the young. This does less than justice to their finding which is that a considerable proportion of employers would take the view that the employment of a homosexual should be restricted, particularly when required to work in proximity and contact with children. Whether that view is scientifically sound may be open to question but there was clear evidence from the psychiatrist that it exists as a fact. That evidence the tribunal were entitled to accept and it appears to have coincided with their own knowledge and experience.

(i) Overriding contractual rights

One of the most controversial areas of unfair dismissal has concerned the correct approach to the situation where the employer wishes to reorganise the business in such a way that changes result in the employees' terms and conditions of employment. These changes may not fall within the legal concept of redundancy because the work that the employee does is not diminished (see *Johnson v Nottinghamshire Combined Police Authority* [1974] IRLR 20; *Lesney Products Ltd v Nolan* [1977] IRLR 77). The test of fairness is not inevitably controlled by the content of the contract of employment. As a result, the courts and tribunals have been prepared to hold as fair dismissals where the employee has refused to agree to a change in terms and conditions of employment in line with the employer's perception of business efficacy. Dismissals for refusal to agree to unilateral changes in job content, pay, location, and hours of work have been held to be for 'some other substantial reason' and fair (see, for example, *Ellis v Brighton Cooperative Society* [1976] IRLR 419).

Hollister v National Union of Farmers
[1979] IRLR 238, Court of Appeal

Hollister was employed by the National Union of Farmers as a group secretary in Cornwall. In 1976, the union decided to reorganise its insurance business in Cornwall, and this resulted in radical changes in the terms and conditions of the Cornish group secretaries. These changes were negotiated at head office level without consultation with the group secretaries affected. Mr Hollister refused to accept the new contract and was dismissed.

An industrial tribunal found that there was 'some other substantial reason' for the dismissal and that the employers had acted reasonably. The EAT allowed Mr Hollister's appeal on the ground that there had been insufficient consultation. The Court of Appeal restored the decision of the tribunal.

LORD DENNING MR: The question which is being discussed in this case is whether the reorganisation of the business, which the National Farmers' Union felt they had to undertake in 1976, coupled with Mr Hollister's refusal to accept the new agreement, was a substantial reason of such a kind as to justify the dismissal of the employee. Upon that there have only been one or two cases. One we were particularly referred to was the case of *Ellis* v *Brighton Cooperative Society Ltd* [1976] IRLR 419, where it was recognised by the Court that reorganisation of business may on occasion be a sufficient reason justifying the dismissal of an employee. They went on to say:

Where there has been a properly consulted-upon reorganisation which, if it is not done, is going to bring the whole business to a standstill, a failure to go along with the new arrangements may well—it is not bound to but it may well—constitute 'some other substantial reason'.

Certainly, I think, everybody would agree with that. But in the present case Mr Justice Arnold expanded it a little where there was some sound, good business reason for the reorganisation. I must say I see no reason to differ from Mr Justice Arnold's view on that. It must depend on all the circumstances whether the reorganisation was such that the only sensible thing to do was to terminate the employee's contract unless he would agree to a new arrangement. It seems to me that paragraph may well be satisfied, and indeed was satisfied in this case, having regard to the commercial necessity of the arrangements being made and the termination of the relationship with the Cornish Mutual, and the setting up of a new relationship via the National Farmers' Union Mutual Insurance Ltd. On that rearrangement being made, it was absolutely essential for new contracts to be made with the existing group secretaries: and the only way to deal with it was to terminate the agreements and offer them reasonable new ones. It seems to me that would be, and was, a substantial reason of a kind sufficient to justify this kind of dismissal.

NOTES
1. The tribunal will expect the employer to lead evidence to show why it was felt to be necessary to impose the changes (*Banerjee* v *City and East London AHA* [1979] IRLR 147), and it is also material for the tribunal to know whether the company was making profits or losses (*Ladbroke Courage Holidays Ltd* v *Asten* [1981] IRLR 59).

   On the other hand, the courts and tribunals have not imposed particularly strict criteria when judging the 'substantiality' of the decision to reorganise. In *Ellis* (mentioned earlier in this section) it was suggested that the test was whether, if the changes were not implemented, the whole business would be brought to a standstill. A much less stringent test was formulated by Lord Denning in *Hollister* where he felt that the principle should extend to situations 'where there was some sound, good business reason for the reorganisation'. In subsequent cases, the EAT has been prepared to dilute the test even further; in one case requiring only that the changes were considered as 'matters of importance' or to have 'discernible advantages to the organisation' (*Banerjee* (Section 2.C(iii))) and in another demanding that the reorganisation be 'beneficial' (*Bowater Containers Ltd* v *McCormack* [1980] IRLR 50).

2. Surveys of the case law on reorganisation or 'business efficacy' tend to show the adoption of a strong conception of managerial prerogative by the courts and tribunals (see Painter, 'Any other substantial reason: A managerial prerogative?' (1981) *New Law Journal* 131). *Hollister*—where the Court of Appeal held that consultation is only one of the factors to be taken into account when judging reasonableness and lack of it would not necessarily render a dismissal unfair—should

be reassessed following the decision of the House of Lords in *Polkey* v *A. E. Dayton Services Ltd*. Having said that, there is no clear guidance on the form the consultation should take. In *Ellis* v *Brighton Cooperative Society Ltd*, the EAT were satisfied that the requirement of consultation had been fulfilled by union agreement to the scheme even though Ellis, as a non-union member, had little chance in participating in the scheme. In *Martin* v *Automobile Proprietary Ltd* [1979] IRLR 64, on the other hand, there are suggestions that non-union members should expect to be individually consulted.

3. In *Garside and Laycock Ltd* v *Booth* [2011] IRLR 735, EAT, the company was undergoing trading difficulties and decided to ask its employees to accept a 5% reduction in pay. Management held a number of meetings with all staff to explain the company's financial situation and asked them to vote on accepting the pay cut to avoid possible redundancies. The company asked its employees to accept a majority vote of 51% or more and said that abstentions would be counted as votes in favour. A substantial majority of the employees voted in favour; there were several abstentions and four votes against. Ultimately, however, the claimant was the only employee who persisted in refusing to accept the pay cut and the company sought to impose it upon him. The claimant, who had worked at the company for seven years, then had meetings with management, who offered him a new contract that would have given him the option of either accepting the new terms and conditions on offer to all staff or to maintain his conditions save as to pay, with the possibility of bonuses. He refused this offer and was dismissed. During his internal appeal hearing, he also rejected a further offer to review his pay levels after six months.

The claimant brought employment tribunal proceedings against the company alleging unfair dismissal. Section 98(1) of the ERA 1996, so far as material, provides that, in determining whether the dismissal of an employee was unfair, it was for the employer to give reasons which either fell in certain categories described in subsection (2) or for 'some other substantial reason'. It was common ground that the claimant did not fall within any of the categories in subsection (2). Section 98(4), so far as material, provides that, where the employer has fulfilled the requirements of subsection (1), the determination of the question of whether the dismissal was fair or unfair depends on whether the employer had '(a)... acted reasonably or unreasonably' in treating its reason as a sufficient reason for dismissing the employee and would be determined '(b)... in accordance with equity and the substantial merits of the case'. The employment tribunal decided that the company had established 'some other substantial reason'.

The tribunal then turned to consider the s. 98(4) question of whether in the circumstances it was reasonable for the company to dismiss for that reason. It placed reliance on what it considered to be the approach taken by the EAT in *Catamaran Ltd* v *Williams* [1994] IRLR 386, EAT, considering whether the company had been in a situation so 'desperate' that the only way of saving the business had been to impose reductions in pay and conditions and whether the pay cut had been imposed for 'arbitrary' reasons. It decided that there had been no suggestion that the company would have been unable to save the business unless the pay cut had been accepted and that the company could not have been said to have been 'desperate'. It also decided that the company's attempt to impose the pay cut had not been arbitrary, but had 'lacked cogency'. The tribunal sought to balance the relative advantages and disadvantages of the reduction in pay and the imposition of the new terms and conditions, deciding that it had been reasonable for the claimant to reject the pay cut. It considered the consultation to have been a 'poor attempt', rendered less effective as the employees were required to sign the voting paper and because abstentions were treated as 'yes' votes, and found that the company had closed its mind to any other option than imposing a pay cut. It noted that the company had not replaced the claimant and was using outside contractors to perform the work he had done. It concluded that the dismissal had been unfair. The company appealed.

The EAT allowed the appeal and remitted the case to a different employment tribunal for rehearing.

The EAT held that the employment tribunal had erred in law. *Catamaran* does not establish the proposition that a dismissal for refusing to accept a pay cut is only fair where the employer is in a situation so desperate that the only method of saving the business is to impose a pay cut. That principle was in fact rejected by the EAT in that case and is plainly and obviously wrong.

Furthermore, the focus of the tribunal, under s. 98(4) should be on the reasonableness of the employer's decision, not on the reasonableness of what the employee has done. It may be that the employer's decision, in order to be reasonable, will take into account whether the employee himself regards that reason as reasonable, but that is very different from saying that the decision depends on what the employee thinks reasonable.

In the present case, the tribunal had therefore misread *Catamaran* and had erred in focusing on what had been reasonable for the claimant to do. Moreover, the tribunal's reasoning was incorrect and opaque in rejecting the company's approach due to a perceived lack of cogency. There was nothing lacking in cogency about a business facing trading difficulties which sought to reduce its costs, and nothing inherently unreasonable in seeking to ensure that all members of the workforce were on the same pay scales and that one man did not stand out by being paid more purely by rejecting a pay cut that all his colleagues had accepted. Given these errors made by the tribunal, the EAT had no hesitation in concluding that the appeal would be allowed and the case would be remitted to a differently constituted employment tribunal for rehearing.

Mr Justice Langstaff observed:

> On the s. 98(4) question as to whether it was reasonable or unreasonable for the employer to dismiss, an employment tribunal must look at the circumstances as identified by s. 98(4)(a), but it also has to determine the question 'in accordance with equity'. The word may have a particular force in circumstances where, for instance, an employer proposes cuts in the wages

Table 8.1 Employment Tribunal Statistics (GB) 1 April 2013 to 31 March 2014

(a) All unfair dismissal jurisdictions disposed of at a hearing

	No.	Percentage of unfair dismissal cases proceeding to hearing	Percentage of all unfair dismissal cases disposed of
Cases dismissed			
At preliminary hearing	1,032	11.3	2.8
Unsuccessful at hearing	4,221	46.3	11.3
All cases dismissed	5,253	57.7	14.0
Cases upheld			
Reinstatement or re-engagement	13	0.1	0.0
Remedy left to parties	329	3.6	0.9
Compensation	1,884	20.7	5.0
All cases upheld	3,858	42.3	10.3
All cases proceeding to a hearing	9,111	100	24.3

(b) Compensation awarded by tribunals—cases with unfair dismissal jurisdictions

Sum	No.	%	Sum	No.	%
£500	143	8	£10,000–£12,499	119	6
£500–£999	113	6	£12,500–£14,999	80	4
£1,000–£1,999	221	12	£15,000–£19,999	107	6
£2,000–£2,999	161	9	£20,000–£29,999	114	6
£3,000–£3,999	154	8	£30,000–£39,999	39	2
£4,000–£4,999	139	7	£40,000–£49,999	26	1
£5,000–£5,999	107	6	£50,000+	52	3
£6,000–£6,999	111	6	All	1,884	100
£7,000–£7,999	75	4	Maximum award	£3,402,245	
£8,000–£8,999	69	4	Median award	£5,016	
£9,000–£9,999	54	3	Average(mean) award	£11,813	

Source: Tribunal statistics quarterly: April to June 2014, Ministry of Justice, September 2014 (https://www.gov.uk/government/statistics/tribunal-statistics-quarterly-april-to-June-2014)

of the workforce. It may be highly relevant to a decision as to fairness for a tribunal to consider upon whom of the workforce those cuts would fall. There may be situations in which management proposes a cut to the pay of those who are not in management, but retains the pay of those who are in management as it has always been. A tribunal would have to consider whether equity, with its implied sense of fair dealing in order to meet a combined challenge of reduced trading profits, would be served by dismissals of those refuseniks not in management in such a case. Similarly, reasonableness will depend much upon the procedural aspects of a decision. That often requires a close focus upon the nature of those proceedings and how appropriate they were. It might involve issues as to the extent to which the workforce were or were not persuaded by reasons which were not good and proper reasons for adopting a common approach in favour of cuts, when otherwise they might not have done so. It may also be relevant to consider other cost-saving measures which the employer might have taken.

(ii) The dilution of procedural fairness

An additional criticism of the approach of the judges was their increasing willingness to put less emphasis on the need to follow a fair procedure. Since the *Polkey* decision, however, it may well be that flouting procedures will result in a finding of unfair dismissal in a much larger number of cases. But employees in such cases may find that they have achieved a Pyrrhic victory, because the tribunal may reduce their compensation to nil if it is found that they were in any way at fault for their dismissal (see *Rao* v *Civil Aviation Authority* [1992] IRLR 203 and *Red Bank Manufacturing Co. Ltd* v *Meadows* [1992] IRLR 209, at pp. 458 and 459 respectively).

(iii) Conclusion

These illustrations tend to confirm the view that the judges are most reluctant to trespass too far into the area of managerial prerogative. If they do intervene it has been to regulate the procedure by which the decision to dismiss is effected rather than to question the substance of the decision.

Bob Hepple, 'The fall and rise of unfair dismissal' in W. McCarthy (ed.),
Legal Intervention in Industrial Relations: Gains and losses
(Oxford: Blackwell, 1992), p. 95

The question therefore becomes: how can one create *universalized* security of employment, at a reasonable level, for individuals while retaining economic flexibility? In my view, the key lies in the development of democratic participation. The first principle is universality, that is, the coverage of the *whole* employed workforce within the scope of unfair dismissal law. The second principle is that of representative institutions to control dismissals. In the British context, this might be achieved by building trade unions into the procedures for handling all types of dismissal, and by facilitating a speedy non-legalistic system of enforcement through an inspectorate with powers to reinstate workers subject to an appeal to a tribunal. The present two-stage approach to the determination of unfairness could be replaced by a broad concept of 'just cause' under which the substantive interests of management and the employee would be equally considered. But unfair dismissal law itself cannot operate in a vacuum. There is little point in developing this particular human rights guarantee in the employment relationship unless there are also macro-economic policies directed towards the growth of employment and welfare.

Cabrelli, D., *Employment Law in Context: Text and Materials*
(Oxford: OUP, 2014) p. 688

Even if an employee is able to satisfy the relevant [qualification] criteria and succeeds with an unfair dismissal claim, our examination of the range of remedies available has demonstrated how they offer no more than a modest degree of financial protection to employers. This is demonstrated by the low level of median and average compensatory awards for unfair dismissal. The way in which the effectiveness of the reinstatement and re-engagement remedies have been marginalized through an incremental process of judicial interpretation can be conceptualized as a clear rejection of the notions of job property or job security on the part of the judiciary. In fact, the position of the courts is symptomatic of an approach which is primarily concerned with the *employer's* property and common law rights.

FURTHER READING

Cabrelli, D., *Employment Law in Context: Text and materials* (Oxford: OUP, 2014), Chs. 16, 17.

Honeyball S., *Honeyball and Bowers' Textbook on Employment Law,* 13th edn (Oxford: OUP, 2014), Chs. 8, 9.

9

Redundancy

Professor Cyril Grunfeld, *Law of Redundancy*
3rd edn (London: Sweet & Maxwell, 1989), pp. 2–3

The original Act's purpose was to mitigate the resistance of individual employees (and their unions) to the extensive changes which have accompanied and will continue to accompany the response of British industry, commerce and finance to the searching demands of world trade and competition…In pursuing the 'policy that unnecessary workmen should not be retained in any industry but should be released so as to be free to take employment elsewhere' (*Hawkins* v *Thomas Foreman and Sons Ltd* [1967] ITR 59, at p. 61), the new legislation tempered the wind of industrial and commercial change to the redundant employee by providing an additional pecuniary cushion against the ancient hardship of loss of employment. The principal end of the Act was the national economic one of facilitating higher standards of efficiency and effectiveness in industry and commerce; the means used are of a social character, an extension on a selective basis of the social security system dealing with employment.

By the early 1960s, industrial innovation highlighted overmanning in almost all industries. The Government's response was the introduction, in 1965, of the Redundancy Payments Act (now repealed, but the main provisions of which are now to be found in the Employment Rights Act (ERA) 1996). The 1965 Act is regarded as the first attempt to set up a specific and discrete body of employment law. Hitherto, employment legislation sought to do nothing more than tinker with existing common law principles of contract law which were of general application. For the first time, the Act gave positive rights to employees by recognising the concept of a proprietary right in a job, the loss of which merited compensation.

The sum awardable pursuant to the statutory scheme is calculated in exactly the same way as for a basic award for unfair dismissal (see Chapter 8), although many employers have, in conjunction with the unions, negotiated and agreed upon their own more generous schemes. The entitlement to a redundancy payment arises irrespective of whether or not the employee gains immediate alternative employment with another employer. Generally, it is to be hoped that the employer will make the payment voluntarily, thereby avoiding the necessity for an application to the employment tribunal for enforcement. If the employer is unable to make the payment, e.g. by reason of insolvency, then a government fund is available to satisfy a claim to a redundancy payment. This was originally known as the Redundancy Fund but is now encompassed in the National Insurance Fund. Until the Employment Act 1989, some employers were also able to apply to this Fund for a rebate against redundancy payments made. When this allowance ended, in 1989, it had been restricted to a 35% rebate for those employing fewer than ten.

The Redundancy Payment Act 1965 was passed some six years before the introduction of the right not to be unfairly dismissed. Prior to 1971, dismissed employees sought to bring themselves within the provisions of the 1965 Act in order to claim their redundancy payment. Today, however, it is the employer who is rather more anxious to argue that the dismissal was due to redundancy. The affected employee would rather claim that he or she was unfairly dismissed simply because of the greater financial award available, having regard to the fact that with unfair dismissal a compensatory award may be made in addition to the basic award.

Lloyd v *Brassey*
[1969] 2 QB 98, Court of Appeal

LORD DENNING MR: ...As this is one of our first cases on the Redundancy Payments Act 1965, it is as well to remind ourselves of the policy of this legislation. As I read the Act, a worker of long standing is now recognised as having an accrued right in his job; and his rights gain in value with the years. So much so that if the job is shut down he is entitled to compensation for loss of the job—just as a director gets compensation for loss of office. The director gets a golden handshake. The worker gets a redundancy payment. It is not unemployment pay. I repeat 'not'. Even if he gets another job straightaway, he nevertheless is entitled to a full redundancy payment. It is, in a real sense, compensation for long service. No man gets it unless he has been employed for at least two years by the employer; and then the amount of it depends solely upon his age and length of service...

NOTES
1. For a discussion of the policy objectives underlying the Redundancy Payments Act 1965, see Davies, P. and Freedland, M., *Labour Law Text and Materials*, 2nd edn (London: Weidenfeld and Nicholson, 1984), pp. 394–6; Fryer, M., 'The myths of the Redundancy Payments Act' (1973) 2 ILJ 1. The latter takes a more critical perspective on the policy objectives of the legislation than that adopted by Professor Cyril Grunfeld in the extract which introduced this chapter.
2. See p. 583 et seq. for discussion of the law relating to unfair selection for redundancy on grounds related to union membership or activities.

■ QUESTION
In times of high unemployment, can the award of a sum equal to the basic award be regarded as adequate compensation for the loss of the right to keep a job?

SECTION 2: WHO QUALIFIES FOR A REDUNDANCY PAYMENT?

In order to qualify for a redundancy payment the applicant must show that:

(a) he or she is a qualifying employee; and

(b) he or she has been dismissed; and

(c) redundancy was the reason for the dismissal (the ERA 1996, s. 135).

A: Employees who do not qualify

In order to be entitled to a redundancy payment, an applicant must first ensure that he or she does not fall foul of the list of excluded persons contained in the ERA 1996, the main ones being:

(a) those with less than two years' continuous employment (s. 155);

(b) share fishermen, employees of foreign governments and Crown servants (see ss. 199(2), 159 and 160);

(c) those refusing suitable alternative employment with the same or an associated employer (s. 141(2)) (see Section C);

(d) those subject to an agreement made between an employer's organisation and a trade union pursuant to which an application for exemption from the Act has been granted by ministerial order (s. 157);

(e) those dismissed for misconduct (see s. 140 in the following extract);

(f) prima facie, those who have failed to make a claim for payment in writing to their employers or to an employment tribunal within six months of the 'relevant date' of termination. However, if an employee submits a claim within a further six-month period, the tribunal has discretion to make an award (s. 164(1) and (2)).

B: Dismissal

The definition of dismissal for redundancy purposes (s. 136) is the same as that for unfair dismissal (s. 95, see p. 395 (Chapter 8, Section 2.A)).

(i) Dismissal for misconduct

EMPLOYMENT RIGHTS ACT 1996

140. Summary dismissal

(1) Subject to subsections (2) and (3), an employee is not entitled to a redundancy payment by reason of dismissal where his employer, being entitled to terminate his contract of employment without notice by reason of the employee's conduct, terminates it either—

(a) without notice,

(b) by giving shorter notice than that which, in the absence of conduct entitling the employer to terminate the contract without notice, the employer would be required to give to terminate the contract, or

(c) by giving notice which includes, or is accompanied by, a statement in writing that the employer would, by reason of the employee's conduct, be entitled to terminate the contract without notice.

NOTES

1. This is a somewhat puzzling provision. After all, if an employee is dismissed for misconduct then that would be the principal reason for the dismissal and not redundancy. There is no clear decision on what this provision is intended to achieve. In *Sanders v Ernest A. Neale Ltd* [1974] ICR 565 (in the following extract), however, it was suggested that what is now s. 140 will exclude a claim where the employee is dismissed for redundancy but in circumstances where the employer could have dismissed for cause.

2. Because most forms of industrial action are viewed as breaches of contract, workers engaged in this form of activity may fall foul of this provision.

3. The exceptions to the operation of s. 140(1), i.e. s. 140(2)–(3), are referred to in the note following the next case.

Sanders v *Ernest Neale*

[1974] 3 All ER 327, National Industrial Relations Court

Two employees were dismissed by reason of redundancy and other members of the workforce went on strike in protest. They were dismissed and the factory eventually closed down. The dismissed strikers then claimed redundancy payments but their claims were rejected since their dismissal was by reason of misconduct (i.e. the strike) and not redundancy.

DONALDSON P: ... We should like to take this opportunity of exorcising the ghost of 'self-induced redundancy'. It can certainly occur, but as such it has no legal significance. Interruption of service due to industrial action can cause customers to look to competitors or to turn to substitute materials or services. This can lead to a diminution in the requirements of the business for employees to carry out work of a particular kind and to workers being dismissed. But the mere fact that the employees' action created the redundancy situation does not disentitle them to a redundancy payment. The entitlement depends on the words of the statute and there is no room for any general consideration of whether it is equitable that the employee should receive a payment.

The first issue in a redundancy claim is whether the applicant was dismissed by the employer. What constitutes such a dismissal is set out in s. 3 of the Redundancy Payments Act 1965 and it is for the employee to prove the dismissal if it is not admitted. The second issue is whether the employee has been dismissed by reason of redundancy. Here it is for the employer to prove either that there was no redundancy situation or that the dismissal was neither wholly nor mainly attributable to that situation (see the presumption set out in s. 9(2) of the 1965 Act). He may, of course, prove both. What is a redundancy situation is defined by s. 1(2) of the 1965 Act, but it should be remembered that the mere fact that the employer proposes a change in the terms and conditions of employment and is unable to carry on his business on the existing terms does not of itself prove that a redundancy situation exists (see *Chapman* v *Goonvean* [1973] ICR 310 and *Johnson* v *Nottinghamshire Combined Police Authority* [1974] ICR 170). If the employer fails or does not attempt to prove the absence of a redundancy situation, he can still try to show that the dismissal was wholly or mainly attributable to some other cause.

In the present appeals there was indeed a redundancy situation, but the tribunal found that it in no way caused the dismissals. The converse was true. It was the dismissals which caused the redundancy. The appellants were dismissed because they persistently refused to work normally. Their claim fails not because the redundancy was self-induced, but because it did not cause their dismissal.

NOTE: The disentitlement imposed by the ERA 1996, s. 140(1), is subject to two significant exceptions:
(a) If the dismissal for gross misconduct takes place when the employee is already under the 'obligatory period' of notice for redundancy, the employee may apply to the employment tribunal which can award all or part of the redundancy payment (s. 140(3)). (The obligatory period is defined by s. 136(4) and is the period of notice which by statute or the contract the employer is obliged to give in order lawfully to terminate the contract.) In *Lignacite Products Ltd* v *Krollman* [1979] IRLR 22, an employee, having been given notice of redundancy, was thereafter caught stealing and summarily dismissed. The EAT agreed that it was right to reduce his redundancy award by 40 per cent.
(b) If the misconduct takes the form of participation in a strike during the 'obligatory period' of notice, then any dismissal for that form of 'misconduct' will not operate to disqualify the payment claim (s. 140(2)). Protection will be lost, however, where an employee who is already on strike is then dismissed for reasons which might amount to redundancy. (See *Simmons* v *Hoover Ltd* [1977] QB 284.)

(ii) Dismissal—the onus of proof

The onus of proof is upon the applicant to show that he or she was dismissed.

Morton Sundour Fabrics Ltd v *Shaw*
[1966] ITR 327, Queen's Bench Division

A foreman was warned he would be made redundant in the near future. The foreman immediately secured alternative employment, gave his employer one month's notice and claimed redundancy. It was held that he was not entitled to a redundancy payment because the warning did not amount to a dismissal.

WIDGERY J: As a matter of law an employer cannot dismiss his employee by saying: 'I intend to dispense with your services at some time in the coming months'. In order to terminate the contract of employment the notice must either specify the date or contain material from which that date is positively ascertainable. It is, I think, evident from what the tribunal has found that nothing which the employers in this case said to Mr Shaw in the early days of March could possibly be interpreted as specifying a date upon which he was to go, or as giving material upon which such a date might be ascertained. It was on its face not inappropriately described by Mr Henry in his argument to us as a warning of what was to come. If that is the true position, then nothing done by the employers at the beginning of March operated to terminate the contract of employment, and it would follow that the actual terminating event was the notice given by Mr Shaw later that month and not any action taken by the employers. That is a result achieved by applying the strict principles of law to this case, as in my judgment they clearly must be applied.

■ QUESTION

To what extent does the approach evidenced in this case advance the policies supposedly underlying the redundancy payments scheme?

Burton Allton & Johnson v Peck

[1975] ICR 193, Queen's Bench Division

An employee was told by his employer that it would be in his own interests to accept redundancy. He thereupon volunteered for redundancy. It was held, nevertheless, that he had been dismissed.

GRIFFITHS J: It must be appreciated that it is to be hoped that in the large majority of cases where a man is made redundant, it will be effected after discussions and where both parties are in agreement that that is the best course to take. In any large organisation one expects to find that there are consultations between management and unions to thrash out the whole redundancy situation, that the employees are then brought into the discussions and that the first to be made redundant are those who volunteer for it. One also hopes that before they are made redundant very serious attempts will have been made to have other employment ready for them. But the fact that all that is done does not prevent the dismissal, when it comes, being a dismissal within the terms of section 3(1)(a) of the Act of 1965 [now ERA 1996, s. 136]...

Mr Brown also relied on a decision of the Divisional Court in *Hempel* v *Parrish* (1968) 3 ITR 240, but the facts there were very different. Mr Parrish ran a small one man business as a painter and decorator, Mr Hempel was a friend of his, and the two men had worked together, although in law with the relationship of master and servant, for many years. Times became difficult and they both decided that they would temporarily go and work for another firm until, it was hoped, business would pick up and Mr Parrish would be able to resume again his own business. In that case the Divisional Court refused to reverse the decision of the industrial tribunal, which had held that there had been no dismissal under those circumstances. That is a very different case from the present one, and it is interesting to observe that even in that case Lord Parker CJ only agreed with some reluctance but did so, recognising that it was a question of fact and that it was impossible to say there was no evidence upon which the tribunal could have come to its finding.

The fact that the employee agreed to this redundancy is no ground for holding that it was not a dismissal within the meaning of section 3(1)(a) of the Act of 1965.

NOTE: Compare this case to *Birch* v *University of Liverpool* [1985] IRLR 165, CA (an extract appears at p. 346 (Chapter 7, Section 2.B(i))).

C: When is the dismissal by reason of redundancy?

(i) The statutory presumption

EMPLOYMENT RIGHTS ACT 1996

163. References to industrial tribunals

(1) Any question arising under this Part as to—
  (a) the right of an employee to a redundancy payment, or
  (b) the amount of a redundancy payment,
shall be referred to and determined by an industrial tribunal.

(2) For the purposes of any such reference, an employee who has been dismissed by his employer shall, unless the contrary is proved, be presumed to have been so dismissed by reason of redundancy.

(ii) The statutory definition

The ERA 1996, s. 139(1) defines a dismissal due to redundancy:

EMPLOYMENT RIGHTS ACT 1996

39. Redundancy

(1) For the purposes of this Act an employee who is dismissed shall be taken to be dismissed by reason of redundancy if the dismissal is wholly or mainly attributable to—

    (a) the fact that his employer has ceased, or intends to cease—

        (i) to carry on the business for the purposes of which the employee was employed by him, or

        (ii) to carry on that business in the place where the employee was so employed, or

    (b) the fact that the requirements of that business—

        (i) for employees to carry out work of a particular kind, or

        (ii) for employees to carry out work of a particular kind in the place where the employee was so employed by the employer,

    (c) have ceased or diminished or are expected to cease or diminish.

(2) For the purposes of subsection (1), the business of the employer together with the business or businesses of his associated employers shall be treated as one (unless either of the conditions specified in paragraphs (a) and (b) of that subsection would be satisfied without so treating them).

NOTE: In the following case the court was asked to investigate an allegation by the applicant employees that the closure of the business was motivated by malice rather than economics, the employer being fed up with alleged bad industrial relations at the plant.

Moon v *Homeworthy Furniture (Northern) Ltd*

[1977] ICR 177, Employment Appeal Tribunal

KILNER BROWN J: After the evidence of Mr Bullard was given, the chairman of the industrial tribunal with acute cogency asked Mr Stephenson whether or not he accepted that there was a cessation of work and therefore a closure. With integrity and common sense Mr Stephenson conceded the point. Technically, therefore, a redundancy situation was proved up to the hilt. But Mr Stephenson hung on to his proposition that if the reason of redundancy was relied on it ought to be open to challenge the declaration of redundancy on its merits. In the view of this appeal tribunal the argument then rails. There was a long discussion as to the meaning of paragraph 6(8) of Schedule [now ERA 1996, s. 95] and whether or not in the circumstances a reasonable exercise of judgment or assessment of the situation required to make a dismissal fair extended also to the decision to close down the factory. In other words, did the guidelines as to fairness of dismissal entitle the employees to challenge the creation of a redundancy? This brought the industrial tribunal back to realities and Mr Stephenson was asked what evidence he had other than evidence which sought to challenge the validity of the decision to close down. As he had none the tribunal ruled that as this was evidence he could not call he was bereft of any ammunition and his case must go by default.

Notwithstanding the care and the ability with which Mr Stephenson put his case, we are unable to criticise the way in which the chairman handled the matter or to find fault with his reasoning. However we would prefer to put the matter on a much broader and, in our view, more important basis.

The employees were and are seeking to use the industrial tribunal and the Employment Appeal Tribunal as a platform for the ventilation of an industrial dispute. This appeal tribunal is unanimously of the opinion that if that is what this matter is all about then it must be stifled at birth, for it was this imaginary ogre which brought about the demise of the National Industrial Relations Court. The Act of 1974 has taken away all powers of the courts to investigate the rights and wrongs of industrial disputes and we cannot tolerate any attempt by anybody to go behind the limits imposed on industrial tribunals.

NOTES

1. This unwillingness to question the need for the redundancies is a further example of a general reluctance on the part of the courts and tribunals to restrain managerial prerogative. For other examples of this reluctance, see Chapter 8.

2. The question of the dismissal being made because of the employer ceasing to carry on the business in 'the place' where the employee was employed was considered in the next case.

United Kingdom Atomic Energy Authority v *Claydon*

[1974] ICR 128, National Industrial Relations Court

Claydon was employed as a draughtsman under a contract which expressly permitted the employer to require its employees to work at any of its establishments in Great Britain or overseas. Claydon had worked since 1964 at the employer's Suffolk plant. In 1971, he was asked to move to its Aldermaston premises. He refused and was dismissed. He claimed, unsuccessfully, that the dismissal was for redundancy.

DONALDSON J: The problems which arose in this case would have been avoided if the employers had exercised their right to require the employee to transfer to Aldermaston. We appreciate that they refrained from doing so with the best of intentions. They were satisfied that the employee was unwilling to transfer and did not wish to be or appear oppressive or abrasive. We think that they made a mistake. If the contract of employment enables an employer to transfer an employee from a place where there is no work to some other place where there is work, the employer should first seek to persuade the employee to transfer voluntarily. If this is unsuccessful, he should require the employee to transfer. This should be clear and may have to be formal, but need not be in the least abrasive. It should spell out the consequences of failing to comply in order that the employee shall be in a position to make up his mind with full knowledge of all the relevant factors.

In the present case, for example, the employers could have written to the employee saying, 'We appreciate that you are reluctant to transfer from Orfordness to Aldermaston. Nevertheless we are faced with the problem that we need your services at Aldermaston and will have no work for you to do at Orfordness. As you will no doubt remember, your appointment in the service of the employers was on terms that the employers reserved the right to require any member of their staff to work at any of their establishments. A copy of the relevant conditions is enclosed. In the circumstances the employers find themselves obliged to require you to work at Aldermaston on and from September 1, 1971. It is for you to decide and let us know whether you are willing to comply with this formal requirement, but it is only fair that we should make it clear that if you are unwilling to do so the employers will be forced to terminate your employment upon the grounds that you have thereby broken your contract. In such an event you would not be entitled to a redundancy payment.'

Many men and women are employed under contracts of employment which provide for transfers over a wide area. If work is short in one place but available elsewhere within the area, there will be no redundancy situation and the employer can dismiss without being liable to make any redundancy payment. If, however, he does so without offering to transfer the employee to a place where work is available, he will risk being liable to pay compensation for unfair dismissal. That does not, of course, arise on the facts of this case, but employers should heed this warning.

NOTES

1. As was seen in Chapter 3, even if the contract is silent as to mobility, such a clause may be implied (see *Jones* v *Associated Tunnelling Co. Ltd* [1981] IRLR 477, p. 97, note 2 (Chapter 3, Section 1)). In *O'Brien* v *Associated Fire Alarms Ltd* [1968] 1 WLR 1916, an expectation that employees should move from Liverpool to Barrow-in-Furness some 120 miles away was held to be something that could not be implied into the contract and amounted, therefore, to a dismissal for redundancy.

2. This conventional approach evidenced by *Claydon* was challenged by the EAT in *Bass Leisure Ltd* v *Thomas* [1994] IRLR 104. In this decision, the EAT ruled that 'the place' where an employee was employed for redundancy payment purposes does not extend to any place where he or she could be contractually required to work. According to the EAT, 'the place where an employee was employed for the purposes of [what is now the ERA 1996, s. 139(1)(a) and (b)] is to be established by a factual inquiry, taking into account the employee's fixed or changing places of work and any contractual terms which go to evidence or define the place of employment and its extent, but not those (if any) which make provision for the employee to be transferred to another'.

3. The EAT's reasoning in *Bass Leisure* received the approval of the Court of Appeal in the following case.

High Table Ltd v *Horst*
[1997] IRLR 513, Court of Appeal

Mrs Horst was employed as a silver-service waitress by the appellant company, which provided catering services for companies and firms in the City of London and elsewhere. Her letter of appointment specified that she was appointed as waitress to one particular client, Hill Samuel, and she worked there from July 1988 until her dismissal.

The appellants' staff handbook, which formed part of the employees' terms of employment, provided that, 'Your place of work is as stated in your letter of appointment, which acts as part of your terms and conditions. However, given the nature of our business, it is sometimes necessary to transfer staff on a temporary or permanent basis to another location. Whenever possible, this will be within reasonable travelling distance of your existing place of work.'

At the beginning of 1993, cuts in Hill Samuel's catering budget necessitated a reorganisation of services provided by the appellants which resulted in the need for fewer waitresses working longer hours. Consequently, Mrs Horst and the two other applicants were dismissed as redundant. The employees presented complaints for unfair dismissal. The industrial tribunal rejected the claims, holding that the employees had been dismissed for redundancy and that, in all the circumstances, the dismissals were fair. On appeal, the Employment Appeal Tribunal (EAT) decided that the industrial tribunal had facts before it which raised the question as to whether there was any redundancy at all but had failed to consider the matter. The EAT allowed the appeal on that ground and remitted the case for re-hearing.

The main issue on appeal to the Court of Appeal was whether what is now the ERA 1996, s. 139(1)(a)–(b) imposes a contractual test or a primary factual test in order to determine 'the place where the employee was so employed'.

PETER GIBSON LJ [referring to the EAT's reasoning in *Bass Leisure Ltd* v *Thomas*]: I am in broad agreement with this interpretation of the statutory language. The question it poses—where was the employee employed by the employer for the purposes of the business?—is one to be answered primarily by a consideration of the factual circumstances which obtained until the dismissal. If an employee has worked in only one location under his contract of employment for the purposes of the employer's business, it defies common sense to widen the extent of the place where he was so employed, merely because of the existence of a mobility clause. Of course, the refusal by the employee to obey a lawful requirement under the contract of employment for the employee to move may constitute a valid reason for dismissal, but the issues of dismissal, redundancy and reasonableness in the actions of an employer should be kept distinct. It would be unfortunate if the law were to encourage the inclusion of mobility clauses in contracts of employment to defeat genuine redundancy claims. Parliament has recognised the importance of the employee's right to a redundancy payment. If the work of the employee for his employer has involved a change of location, as would be the case where the nature of the work required the employee to go from place to place, then the contract of employment may be helpful to determine the extent of the place where the employee was employed. But it cannot be right to let the contract be the sole determinant, regardless of where the employee actually worked for the employer. The question what was the place of employment is one that can safely be left to the good sense of the industrial tribunal.

In my judgment, a remission on the first issue is not justified. It is plain that for all of the employees the place where they were employed by the employers was Hill Samuel and that there was a redundancy situation there which caused the employees to be dismissed.

NOTES
1. One point about the reasoning in the judgment is worth special mention, as it emphasises indirectly the often topsy-turvy nature of a redundancy claim. The court argues that the factual test is necessary to protect Parliament's intention that the importance of an employee's redundancy rights should be recognised, and to ensure that those rights are not to be negated by unscrupulous use by employers of mobility clauses. Put in those terms, the judgment sounds

pro-employee. However, the reverse may be the case. On the facts here (waitresses being made redundant by their service company employer when the client no longer wanted their work, with the employer then making no attempt to redeploy them), as is so often the case it was the *employers* who wanted it to be redundancy (as the simplest and cheapest option); the employees wanted it *not* to be redundancy in order to open up the prospect of a finding of unfair dismissal. This can be seen from the actual outcome of the case—the court upheld the employer's appeal and restored the original tribunal's decision that the employees *had* been dismissed for redundancy.

This decision in effect will often make it easier to establish a redundancy, and allow the employer the best of both worlds with a mobility clause—if there is one in the contract and the employee refuses an order to move pursuant to it, there could well be a fair dismissal; if, however, the employer does *not* activate it when work ceases or diminishes in the existing locality, the employer can still rely on a redundancy in spite of the clause. The court in fact recognised this paradox, but said that 'issues of dismissal, redundancy and reasonableness in the actions of an employer should be kept distinct' (*Harvey on Industrial Relations and Employment Law*, Bulletin No. 229, August 1997, p. 3).

2. The emphasis in the ERA 1996, s. 139(1)(b), is on the cessation of or diminution in the need for employees to do work of a particular kind, thereby creating a surplus of labour. It is important to appreciate that the crucial element is the excess of labour rather than the diminution in work—the amount of work may remain the same but reorganisation may lead to the need for fewer employees to do it.

McCrea v *Cullen & Davison Ltd*

[1988] IRLR 30, Northern Ireland Court of Appeal

Mr McCrea was employed as manager of the appellant company, which was experiencing financial difficulties. When Mr McCrea had to go into hospital, his work was taken over by Mr Bailey, the company's managing director. Mr Bailey realised that carrying out Mr McCrea's work in addition to his own was both practical and efficient. Accordingly, Mr McCrea was dismissed and given a redundancy payment.

His complaint of unfair dismissal was upheld by an industrial tribunal. According to the tribunal, Mr McCrea was not redundant because the amount of management work had not diminished. Rather, he had been dismissed for 'some other substantial reason' and in the circumstances his dismissal was unfair. The Northern Ireland Court of Appeal allowed the employer's appeal.

(NB: The definition of redundancy set out in s. 11(2)(b) of the Contracts of Employment and Redundancy Payments Act (Northern Ireland) 1965 is identical to that contained in the ERA 1996, s. 139(1)(b).)

GIBSON LJ [referring to s. 11(2)(b)]: The most obvious situation for the application of this provision is where the volume of work of a particular employer or in some department of the work of an employer has fallen off or been totally lost. In such a case some or all of the employees engaged in that work are surplus to the requirements of the business and so are redundant. It has been expressly found by the Tribunal that 'there was no evidence of any diminution either in the amount of work or in the type of work carried on' by the company. In this case the separate job of manager has disappeared, but that is not a determining consideration. If a manager is dismissed and another person employed to do his work whether he is given a lesser title such as supervisor, or given a lesser salary, or the converse, there has been no redundancy. The question to be considered is not does the business require a manager but does the business require the work of management carried out by the applicant to be performed by him or another doing the same work and only that work?

The Act was passed at a time when it was generally recognised that if British industry was to recover its competitive position in world markets the widespread practice of overmanning had to be reduced, and the provision of redundancy payments for those who were to lose their jobs in consequence was designed to make the implementation of the policy more acceptable to the trade unions. So it was immediately recognised that the Act applied to a second class of case where there has been no reduction in the volume of work of any particular kind but the requirement of the employer for as many persons to do the work has been reduced because of improved mechanisation, automation or other technical advance. The present case does not fall into that category.

A further situation in which the requirement of a business for fewer employees to do a particular kind of work may arise although there has been no reduction in the volume of work or production is where there has been a reorganisation of the workforce or a reallocation of functions between them disclosing a position of overmanning. It is this situation which at one time appeared to cause a divergence of opinion as to whether any employee dismissed in consequence of such a reorganisation could be said to be redundant within the meaning of the section. Certain portions of the judgments, and particularly those of Lord Denning MR, in *Johnson* v *Nottinghamshire Combined Police Authority* [1974] IRLR 20 and *Lesney Products & Co. Ltd* v *Nolan* [1977] IRLR 77 were by other judges regarded as indicating that if as a result of more efficient organisation or disposition of employees one who was dismissed in consequence could not be said to have been redundant. However, reconsideration of the context in which the observations were made clearly indicates that no such general proposition was intended. As Phillips J pointed out in *Robinson* v *British Island Airways Ltd* [1977] IRLR 477 at p. 478.7:

> Reorganisation may or may not end in redundancy: it all depends on the nature and effect of the reorganisation.

The point is well made in the following quotation from the judgment of Cumming-Bruce J in *Delanair Ltd* v *Mead* [1976] IRLR 340 at p. 342.9:

> It is submitted by Mr Irvine on behalf of the employers that the Industrial Tribunal have applied the wrong test and have confused the diminution of work of a particular kind with the diminution of the requirement of the business for employees to carry out such work. It is clear that those two concepts differ in important respects, because the volume of work may remain the same though the requirement of the business for employees to carry it out has diminished. There are two obvious examples: (1) when a new machine is introduced which enables the same volume of work to be carried out by fewer men; (2) where there is overmanning such that on reorganisation of duties or terms and conditions of work the same volume of work is carried out by a slimmed down workforce. Mr Irvine submits that this case illustrates a third example, namely where for reasons of economy the employers introduce a new structure of management and supervision, and so reallocate duties that the same volume of work is carried out without the requirement of a foreman supervisor to organise and oversee its performance. That such reallocation of duties may give rise to dismissal by reason of redundancy is illustrated by *Sutton* v *Revlon Ltd* [1973] IRLR 173 and *Scarth* v *Economic Forestry Ltd* [1973] ICR 322. As Griffiths J said at p. 325 of the latter case: 'The fallacy is to equate the requirement to achieve an end with the requirement of the business to have employees in order to achieve the end'.

Sir Denys Buckley also emphasised the point in *Murphy* v *Epsom College* [1984] IRLR 271 at p. 276.37 as follows:

> Every case of reorganisation must, I think, depend intimately on its particular facts. In each case it must be for the Industrial Tribunal to decide whether the reorganisation and reallocation of functions within the staff is such as to change the particular kind of work which a particular employee, or successive employees, is or are required to carry out, and whether such change has had any, and if so what, effect on the employer's requirement for employees to carry out a particular kind of work.

S. 11(2)(b) when applied to the facts of this case may be reduced to the proposition that an employee is dismissed by reason of redundancy if the dismissal is attributed to the fact that the requirements of the business for employees to carry out the work of management has diminished. It will be seen that what the section is directed towards is not a diminution in the work of management but a diminution in the requirement of the company for employees to do the work of management. Though the work of management remains to be done the applicant will be redundant if the company has so organised its affairs that the work is done by fewer employees. So the question resolves itself into one of fact, namely, is Mr Bailey merely doing the work formerly done by the applicant, in which case there is no redundancy but the replacement of one employee by another to do the work of the other, or has he undertaken the work of the applicant additionally to his own, in which case there has been a reduction in the number of employees required to do the work and the applicant's dismissal is attributable to redundancy.

NOTE: In *Shawkat* v *Nottingham City Hospital NHS Trust (No. 2)* [2001] IRLR 555, the Court of Appeal held that the mere fact of a reorganisation of the business, as a result of which the employer requires one or more employees to do a different job from which he or she was previously doing, is not conclusive of redundancy. The tribunal must go on to decide whether that change had any effect, and if so what, on the employer's requirements for employees to carry out work of a particular kind. It does not necessarily follow from the fact that a new post is different in kind from the previous post or posts that the requirements of the employer's business for employees to carry out work of a particular kind must have diminished. Nor does the fact that an employee of one skill was replaced by an employee of a different skill compel the conclusion that the requirements for work of a particular kind have ceased or diminished. That is always a question of fact for the tribunal to decide.

In Shawkat's case, a tribunal was entitled to find that dismissal of a thoracic surgeon, following a reorganisation as a result of which he was asked to carry out cardiac surgery in addition to thoracic surgery, was not by reason of redundancy. The requirements for employees to carry out thoracic surgery had not diminished even though the reorganisation changed the work which the employees in the thoracic department, including the applicant, were required to carry out.

■ QUESTION

In s. 139(1)(b) of the 1996 Act, is 'work of a particular kind' the work which the employee actually performs (the 'factual test'), or is it the work which the employee could be obliged to do under the contract of employment (the 'contract test')?

The authors of *Smith and Wood* supply the answer:

It was the latter [the contract test] that eventually gained ground [see *Cowen* v *Haden Ltd* [1983] ICR 1, CA; and *Pink* v *White & Co. Ltd* [1985] IRLR 489], based on two decidedly ambiguous Court of Appeal decisions [*Nelson* v *BBC* [1977] IRLR 148, CA; and *Nelson* v *BBC (No. 2)* [1979] IRLR 346, CA], which could have the effect of making it more difficult to establish redundancy where the contractual obligations were drafted to include a level of flexibility. However, on this point we have seen a major change of approach. This began with the judgment of Judge Clark in *Safeway Stores plc* v *Burrell* [1997] IRLR 200 [Smith, I. T. and Baker, A., *Smith & Wood's Employment Law*, 10th edn (Oxford: OUP, 2010), p. 499].

Safeway Stores plc v *Burrell*
[1997] IRLR 200, Employment Appeal Tribunal

Mr Burrell, a petrol station manager, was told that there would be a reorganisation of the management structure and that the post of 'petrol station manager' would disappear. It would be replaced by a new post of petrol filling station controller (at a lower salary). Existing post-holders could apply for the posts, although as there were fewer posts than managers there would be redundancies. Mr Burrell declined the invitation to apply and brought a complaint of unfair dismissal. He argued that the new job was essentially the same as the old one so that there was no 'redundancy' situation. The employer contended that it was a genuine redundancy, or, alternatively, that there was justification for the dismissal on the basis of 'some other substantial reason', namely, a reorganisation. The majority of the industrial tribunal upheld his claim. Many of the jobs he had actually done (the 'function' test) were still required, albeit by someone with a different job title. The tribunal chairman (in the minority) looked at what Mr Burrell's contract required (the 'contract' test) and concluded that the job he was *employed* to do 'no longer existed'. The EAT allowed the appeal and remitted the case for reconsideration by another industrial tribunal.

JUDGE PETER CLARK: ...Free of authority, we understand the statutory framework of s. 81(2)(b) to involve a three-stage process:

(1) was the employee dismissed? If so,

(2) had the requirements of the employer's business for employees to carry out work of a particular kind ceased or diminished, or were they expected to cease or diminish? If so,

(3) was the dismissal of the employee (the applicant before the industrial tribunal) caused wholly or mainly by the state of affairs identified at stage 2 above?

The position is, however, not free of authority. Far from it. It is therefore to those authorities, with the assistance of counsel, which we must now turn.

...

The correct approach

Like the appeal tribunal in *Cowen* v *Haden Carrier*, we started by looking at the statute and construing the words free of authority. Similarly, we have looked at the authorities. Unlike that tribunal, we return to our original approach and conclude first that it was correct, and secondly that no binding authority causes us to abandon that position. We would summarise it as follows:

(1) There may be a number of underlying causes leading to a true redundancy situation; our stage 2. There may be a need for economies; a reorganisation in the interests of efficiency; a reduction in production requirements; unilateral changes in the employees' terms and conditions of employment. None of these factors are themselves determinative of the stage 2 question. The only question to be asked is: was there a diminution/cessation in the employer's requirement for *employees* to carry out work of a particular kind, or an expectation of such cessation/diminution in the future [redundancy]? At this stage it is irrelevant to consider the terms of the applicant employee's contract of employment. That will only be relevant, if at all, at stage 3 (assuming that there is a dismissal).

(2) At stage 3 the tribunal is concerned with causation. Was the dismissal attributable wholly or mainly to the redundancy? Thus–

(a) Even if a redundancy situation arises, as in *Nelson*, if that does not cause the dismissal, the employee has not been dismissed by reason of redundancy. In *Nelson* the employee was directed to transfer to another job as provided for in his contract. He refused to do so. That was why he was dismissed.

(b) If the requirement for employees to perform the work of a transport clerk and transport manager diminishes, so that one employee can do both jobs, the dismissed employee is dismissed by reason of redundancy. See *Carry All Motors Ltd* v *Pennington* [1980] IRLR 455, EAT. The same explanation applies, on the facts, to the eventual decision in *Robinson* v *British Island Airways* [1977] IRLR 477, EAT. In *Cowen* v *Haden Carrier* the requirement for employees to do the work of a divisional contracts surveyor ceased. The postholder was dismissed. That was a dismissal by reason of redundancy.

(c) Conversely, if the requirement for employees to do work of a particular kind remains the same, there can be no dismissal by reason of redundancy, notwithstanding any unilateral variation to their contracts of employment. See *Chapman, Lesney* and *Johnson* v *Nottinghamshire Combined Police Authority* [1974] ICR 170.

(d) The contract versus function test debate is predicated on a misreading of both the statute and the cases of *Nelson* and *Cowen* v *Haden Carrier*. Save for the limited circumstances arising from *Nelson* where an employee is redeployed under the terms of his contract of employment and refuses to move, and this causes his dismissal, the applicant/employee's terms and conditions of employment are irrelevant to the questions raised by the statute.

(e) This explains the concept of 'bumped redundancies'. Take this example: an employee is employed to work as a fork-lift truck driver, delivering materials to six production machines on the shop floor. Each machine has its own operator. The employer decides that it needs to run only five machines and that one machine operator must go. That is a stage 2 redundancy situation. Selection for dismissal is done on the LIFO principle within the department. The fork-lift truck driver has the least service. Accordingly, one machine operator is transferred to driving the truck; the short-service truck driver is dismissed. Is he dismissed by reason of redundancy? The answer is yes. Although under both the contract and function tests he is employed as a fork-lift driver, and there is no diminution in the requirement for fork-lift drivers, nevertheless there is a diminution in the requirement for employees to carry out the operators' work and that has caused the employee's dismissal. See, for example, *W Gimbert & Sons Ltd* v *Spurett* [1967] 2 ITR 308; *Elliott Turbomachinery* v *Bates* [1981] ICR 218. In our judgment, the principle of 'bumped' redundancies is statutorily correct, and further demonstrates the flaw in the 'contract test' adumbrated in *Pink*.

(f) Our approach is also consistent with the decision of the Court of Appeal in *Murphy* v *Epsom College* [1984] IRLR 271. There, the applicant was one of two plumbers employed by a school. His work consisted mainly of general plumbing work. The employers decided to employ a heating technician to maintain their improved heating system. They then decided to dismiss one of the two plumbers and selected the employee for dismissal. The Court of Appeal upheld the majority view of the industrial tribunal that the reason for dismissal was redundancy. The employer originally had two plumbers; now it only required one. The employee was dismissed by reason of redundancy.

The instant case

In our judgment, the tribunal fell into error in the following respects:

(1) The majority failed to apply the correct statutory test in finding that the applicant's dismissal was not by reason of redundancy. It failed to ask itself whether there was a stage 2 redundancy situation, looking at the overall requirement of the employer for employees to carry out work of a particular kind, and then to consider whether that redundancy situation caused the applicant's admitted dismissal.

(2) The majority failed to consider whether Safeway had, in the alternative, established some other substantial reason for dismissal.

(3) It follows that the tribunal made no finding as to whether or not the employer acted reasonably in treating the true reason for dismissal as a sufficient reason.

The appeal is allowed.

NOTES

1. The reasoning in *Safeway* was not followed by the EAT in *Church* v *West Lancashire NHS Trust* [1998] IRLR 4, EAT. The employer decided to restructure the department in which Mr Church worked. One post was abolished and all the employees were invited to apply for the remaining posts on a competitive basis. A 'bumping' situation was thereby created which meant that displaced employees replaced those whose jobs were not directly affected by the reorganisation. On that basis, Mr Church was 'bumped' and selected for redundancy, even though his job remained the same and was filled by another employee who otherwise would have been dismissed. Mr Church alleged that, in the circumstances, his dismissal was not by reason of redundancy and was unfair.

   The industrial tribunal, relying on a line of authority endorsing the notion of 'bumped' redundancies, in particular the decision of the Divisional Court in *W. Gimbert & Sons Ltd* v *Spurett* [1967] 2 ITR 308, HC and that of the EAT in *Elliott Turbo Machinery Ltd* v *Bates* [1981] ICR 218, concluded that the reason for Mr Church's dismissal was redundancy, that he had been fairly selected and properly consulted, and that his dismissal was fair.

   Subsequent to the tribunal's decision in *Church*, the EAT concluded in *Safeway Stores Ltd* v *Burrell* that the work of a particular kind referred to in s. 139 did not need to be the work of the dismissed employee. Thus, if the requirements for employees to do A's work had diminished, and A replaced B, whose work was different and for which the requirements for employees had not diminished, then B was dismissed by reason of redundancy. The EAT allowed the employer's appeal.

2. *Church* makes two main criticisms of *Safeway*. First is that *Safeway* is wrong if and so far as it maintains that the contract of employment is irrelevant in determining whether the business needed fewer employees to even out work of a particular kind. *Church* states that 'the proper test is neither contractual nor functional but a sensible blend of the two'. This view was shared by the EAT in the more recent case of *Shawkat* v *Nottingham City Hospital* [1999] IRLR 340. The second criticism is that the proper meaning of 'work of a particular kind' is that it is 'work of a particular kind which the *relevant employee* was employed to do'. It follows from *Church* that a 'bumped' dismissal is not within the statutory definition of redundancy. If the reasoning in *Church* is correct:

   > the practical consequence will be to undermine many redundancy selection procedures, especially the more sophisticated seniority-based systems. It will also bring an extra element of uncertainty into redundancy situations. Before deciding to dismiss one employee rather than another for an economic reason, a judgment will have to be made as to whether the work of two employees is sufficiently similar so as to amount to the same 'work of a particular kind'. If it is not, even though the employees may have transferable skills and be subject to a flexibility agreement, the ensuing dismissal would not be on grounds of redundancy, the employee would not be entitled to a statutory redundancy payment, and the employer might have to defend an unfair dismissal claim. Thus, this decision enhances the value of contractual severance terms which will apply to regardless of whether the statutory definition of redundancy is satisfied. [Michael Rubenstein, 'Highlights' [1998] IRLR 1]

3. The *Safeway/Church* controversy has now been resolved by the House of Lords, in the next case.

Murray and another v *Foyle Meats*

[1999] IRLR 56, House of Lords

The applicants were employed as meat plant operatives. They normally worked in the slaughter hall, but under their contracts of employment they could be required to work elsewhere in the factory and occasionally had done so. Employees who worked in other parts of the factory, such as the boning hall or the loading bay, were also engaged as meat plant operatives on similar terms.

In 1995, a decline in the business prompted a reorganisation in the slaughter hall which resulted in the need to reduce the number of skilled slaughterers. Following consultation with the trade union on the criteria for selection, the applicants were dismissed as redundant. They complained that their dismissals were unfair.

The employers submitted that the applicants' dismissals were wholly attributable to the fact that the requirements of the business for employees to carry out work of a particular kind, namely, on the slaughtering line, had diminished and therefore fell within the statutory definition of redundancy.

A Northern Ireland employment tribunal accepted the employers' submission and dismissed the applicants' claims. On appeal to the House of Lords, it was submitted for the applicants that 'requirements for employees to carry out work of a particular kind' means 'requirements for employees contractually engaged to carry out work of a particular kind'. Since the employers chose to engage all their employees on similar terms, no distinction could be made between those who worked in the slaughter hall and those who worked elsewhere in the factory, and it was wrong to select for redundancy solely from those who normally worked in the slaughter hall.

The House of Lords dismissed the appeal.

LORD IRVINE OF LAIRG LC: My Lords, the language of para. (b) is in my view simplicity itself. It asks two questions of fact. The first is whether one or other of various states of economic affairs exists. In this case, the relevant one is whether the requirements of the business for employees to carry out work of a particular kind have diminished. The second question is whether the dismissal is attributable, wholly or mainly, to that state of affairs. This is a question of causation. In the present case, the tribunal found as a fact that the requirements of the business for employees to work in the slaughter hall had diminished. Secondly, they found that that state of affairs had led to the appellants being dismissed. That, in my opinion, is the end of the matter.

This conclusion is in accordance with the analysis of the statutory provisions by Judge Peter Clark in *Safeway Stores plc v Burrell* IRLR 200 and I need to say no more than that I entirely agree with his admirably clear reasoning and conclusions. But I should, out of respect for the submissions of Mr Declan Morgan QC for the appellants, say something about the earlier cases which may have encouraged a belief that the statute had a different meaning.

In *Nelson v British Broadcasting Corporation* [1977] IRLR 148, Mr Nelson was employed by the BBC under a contract which required him to perform any duties to which he might be assigned. In fact he worked for the General Overseas Service broadcasting to the Caribbean. In 1974 the BBC reduced its services to the Caribbean, as a result of which Mr Nelson's services in that capacity were no longer required. When he refused alternative employment, he was dismissed on grounds of redundancy. The industrial tribunal concluded that he had been dismissed for redundancy, apparently on the grounds that a term could be implied into Mr Nelson's contract of employment that he should carry out work on Caribbean programmes. The Court of Appeal rightly rejected the implication of such a term. But they went on to hold that Mr Nelson was therefore not redundant. This was wrong. Whatever the terms of Mr Nelson's contract, it was open to the tribunal to find that he had been dismissed because the BBC's requirements for work on Caribbean programmes had diminished. This was a question of fact.

The basis for the fallacy is to be found in the judgment of Brandon LJ in *Nelson v British Broadcasting Corporation (No. 2)* [1979] IRLR 346, when Mr Nelson's case came again before the Court of Appeal. He said (at p. 353) that Mr Nelson had been right in law in maintaining that 'because the work which he was employed to do continued to exist, he was not redundant.' In saying this Brandon LJ appears to have meant that because Mr Nelson was employed to do any work to which he might be assigned with the BBC and because the BBC was still carrying on business, he could not be redundant. In my opinion this cannot be right. The fact was that the BBC's requirements for employees in the General Overseas Service in general and for Caribbean broadcasts in particular had diminished. It must therefore have been open to the tribunal to decide that Mr Nelson's dismissal was attributable to that state of affairs. Of course, the BBC did not necessarily have to respond in that way. They could, for example, have transferred Mr Nelson to broadcasts which were still being maintained at full strength (say, to West Africa) in the place of a less experienced employee and made the latter redundant instead. In that case, it would have been open to the tribunal to find that the other employee had been dismissed on account of redundancy. (Compare *Safeway Stores plc v Burrell* [1997] IRLR 200 at p. 207.) In each case, the factual question of whether the dismissal was 'attributable' to the statutory state of affairs is one for the tribunal.

The judgments in the two *Nelson* cases have caused understandable difficulty for industrial tribunals. They have been treated as authority for what has been called the 'contract test', which requires consideration of whether there was a diminution in the kind of work for which, according to the terms of his contract the employee had been engaged. I give one example. In *Pink v White* [1985] IRLR 489, Mr Pink was engaged to work in a shoe factory as a 'making and finishing room operative.' In practice, he did more specialised work as sole layer/pre-sole fitter. Because of a reduction in demand, the employer's requirements for making and finishing room operatives in general diminished, but their need for sole layers and pre-sole fitters remained the same.

Nevertheless, they selected Mr Pink for redundancy, apparently because he had been absent for lengthy periods and the employer had had to train someone else to do his work while he was away. The argument before the Employment Appeal Tribunal turned on whether the 'contract test' ought to be applied (i.e., did the company need less employees of the kind specified in Mr Pink's contract), in which case he was redundant, or the 'function test' (did it need less employees to do the kind of work he was actually doing), in which case he was not. It held that it was bound by *Nelson* v *British Broadcasting Corporation* [1977] IRLR 148 to apply the contract test and held that Mr Pink was redundant. I have no doubt that on its facts the case was rightly decided, but both the contract test and the function test miss the point. The key word in the statute is 'attributable' and there is no reason in law why the dismissal of an employee should not be attributable to a diminution in the employer's need for employees irrespective of the terms of his contract or the function which he performed. Of course the dismissal of an employee who could perfectly well have been redeployed or who was doing work unaffected by the fall in demand may require some explanation to establish the necessary causal connection. But this is a question of fact, not law.

For these reasons, I would dismiss the appeal.

NOTE: This decision, it is hoped, has laid to rest the debate as to whether the 'function' or 'contract' test should be applied in redundancy cases. According to the Lord Chancellor, both tests 'miss the point' and a broad-brush approach should be adopted which focuses on causation. As a result a dismissal must now be regarded as by reason of redundancy wherever it is attributable to redundancy. This approach would also appear to encompass 'bumping' within the statutory definition of redundancy.

■ QUESTIONS

1. If the Lord Chancellor's reasoning in *Murray* is correct, why did Parliament include the phrase 'work of a particular kind' in the statutory definition of redundancy?

2. If in the process of reorganisation, an employer substantially changes the contractual terms and conditions relating to the existing job, has there been a cessation of the 'particular kind of work'? The following two cases provide the answer.

Lesney Products Ltd v *Nolan*
[1977] ICR 235, Court of Appeal

The employees were machine maintenance setters who worked in a toy factory where a three-shift system of day, evening and night work was in operation. To cut operating costs the night shift was ended for both the direct workers and the setters. The latter, instead of working a day shift with long overtime and a night shift, were asked to work a double-day shift on alternate weeks. Among other things this reduced their opportunities to earn overtime pay, which was not fully recompensed despite payment of a shift premium. Some of the setters were sacked for refusing to accept the changes, and a number of them argued that the changes amounted to a 'redundancy'. The claims were dismissed by the Court of Appeal.

LORD DENNING MR: Now the matter comes before this court. It must say that it is a difficult case. The relevant principles were stated by this court in *Johnson* v *Nottinghamshire Combined Police Authority* [1974] ICR 170, 176:

It is settled by those cases that an employer is entitled to reorganise his business so as to improve its efficiency and, in so doing, to propose to his staff a change in the terms and conditions of their employment: and to dispense with their services if they do not agree. Such a change does not automatically give the staff a right to redundancy payments. It only does so if the change in the terms and conditions is due to a redundancy situation.

While I adhere to what I there said, I think the phrase 'a redundancy situation' may be misleading. It is shorthand: and it is better always to check it by the statutory words. The dismissal must be attributable to 'the fact that the requirements of that business for employees to carry out work of a particular kind…have ceased or diminished,' etc.

In applying that principle, it is important that nothing should be done to impair the ability of employers to reorganise their work force and their times and conditions of work so as to improve efficiency. They may reorganise it so as to reduce overtime and thus to save themselves money, but that does not give the man a right to redundancy payment. Overtime might be reduced, for instance, by taking on more men: but that would not give the existing staff a right to redundancy payments. Also when overtime is reduced by a reorganisation of working hours, that does not give rise to a right to redundancy payment, so long as the work to be done is the same.

Chapman v Coonvean and Rostowrack China Clay Co. Ltd
[1973] ICR 310, Court of Appeal

The employers provided free transport for their employees who lived 30 miles away. This concession was withdrawn on economic grounds. Some employees resigned and claimed redundancy. It was argued for the employees (following *Dutton* v *C. H. Bailey Ltd* [1968] 2 Lloyd's Rep 122) that the proper approach to their claim was to determine whether in all the circumstances the requirements of the business would have ceased or diminished if the employees had been retained by the company on the old terms. The Court of Appeal, overruling *Dutton's* case, rejected this argument.

LORD DENNING MR: Although the seven men were 'dismissed,' the question is whether they were dismissed 'by reason of redundancy.' This depends on section 1(2) of the Act [now ERA 1996, s. 139(1)(b)]...Taking those words as they stand, this case is not one of dismissal for redundancy. The requirements of the business—for the work of these seven men—continued just the same as before. After they stopped work, the firm had to take on seven other men to replace them and to do the work that they had been doing. The requirements for work of that kind in that place had not ceased or diminished, nor were they expected to do so. So it would seem that the case does not come within the statute.

Vaux and Associated Breweries Ltd v Ward
[1969] 7 KIR 308, Queen's Bench Division

A traditional hotel and public house was modernised and the employer wanted to introduce younger and more glamorous bar staff. Accordingly, Ward, an employee of some 17 years, was dismissed. It was held that the dismissal was not for redundancy.

LORD PARKER CJ: When the matter came before the Divisional Court, the court took the view that the mere fact that an employee was dismissed because a younger employee was preferred was not of itself a dismissal by reason of redundancy, but that something more would be necessary; the further question had to be answered, namely, whether the particular kind of work on which the barmaid had been engaged had ceased or was likely to cease or diminish or, put more shortly, as I said in giving judgment, 'Was the work that the barmaid in the altered premises was going to do work of a different kind to what a barmaid in the unaltered premises had been doing?'

When the matter went back to the tribunal, further evidence was called, in particular the evidence of a Mr Embleton as to the exact nature of the work expected of the barmaid, both before and after certain alterations had been effected to the premises. In the latest decision, the tribunal unhesitatingly said that the work was in no way different. In paragraph 4 of their reasons it was stated:

> The tribunal were of opinion that the work to be carried out by a barmaid after Mrs Ward was dismissed was not different from that which she had carried out. She was engaged in serving behind the bar, either directly to customers or to waitresses to take to customers. Occasionally, if the waitress was not present, Mrs Ward would carry drinks to customers in the buffet. 70 per cent of the drinks dispensed were beer...The present barmaid serves behind the bar, only occasionally going in front of the bar to serve customers.

That finding was followed by this:

> The tribunal reaffirms the findings of fact contained in paragraphs 10 and 11 of the previous reasons. In particular, it reaffirms the opinion expressed in the last sentence of paragraph 11. Its opinion is (and was at the first hearing) that the manager wanted younger staff because they would be physically more attractive than the existing staff, and more likely to attract new customers. The reason was not that the work had changed and could be done more efficiently by younger staff.

I confess that having regard to the history of this matter, and in view of that finding, I should have thought there could only be one answer, namely that the present appellants had discharged the burden upon them, and it had been shown that the dismissal of Mrs Ward was not by reason of redundancy.

North Riding Garages Ltd v Butterwick
[1967] 2 QB 56, Queen's Bench Division

The applicant had been employed at a garage in Whitby for some 30 years, rising to the position of workshop manager in charge of the repairs shop. In view of the comparative smallness of the staff he was expected to spend part of his time performing the mechanics' work on the vehicles. New owners required him to undertake more of a managerial role, including the paperwork. He was not able to undertake this new role particularly well and eight months later was dismissed. He claimed that a new sort of employee was now needed to do his job so that the requirements for the work that he had done for some 30 years had diminished. The Court of Appeal rejected this argument.

WIDGERY J: It is we think, important to observe that a claim under [s. 139(1)(b)] is conditional upon a change in the requirements of the business. If the requirement of the business for employees to carry out work of a particular kind increases or remains constant no redundancy payment can be claimed by an employee, in work of that kind, whose dismissal is attributable to personal deficiencies which prevent him from satisfying his employer. The very fact of dismissal shows that the employee's services are no longer required by his employer and that he may, in a popular sense, be said to have become redundant, but if the dismissal was attributable to age, physical disability or inability to meet his employer's standards he was not dismissed on account of redundancy within the meaning of the Act. For the purpose of this Act an employee who remains in the same kind of work is expected to adapt himself to new methods and techniques and cannot complain if his employer insists on higher standards of efficiency than those previously required; but if new methods alter the nature of the work required to be done it may follow that no requirement remains for employees to do work of the particular kind which has been superseded and that they are truly redundant. Thus, if a motor manufacturer decides to use plastics instead of wood in the bodywork of his cars and dismisses his woodworkers, they may well be entitled to redundancy payments on the footing that their dismissal is attributable to a cessation of the requirement of the business for employees to carry out work of a particular kind, namely, woodworking.

If one looks at the primary facts disclosed by the evidence in this case it is difficult to see what is the particular kind of work in which a requirement for employees has ceased or diminished. The vehicle workshop remained, as did the requirement for a workshop manager, and we do not understand the tribunal to have found that the volume of repair work had diminished to such an extent as to make the respondent's dismissal wholly or mainly attributable to that fact. The only possible conclusion which appears to us to have been open to the tribunal on the evidence was that the respondent was dismissed because he could not do his job in accordance with the new methods and new standards required by the appellants.

NOTE: The court in this case largely ignored the question of when demands for greater efficiency reach the point that the nature of the job changes. Critics of this decision have argued that there is not one single class of workshop manager and that the applicant, who had done nothing but manage a small workshop, had strong grounds to claim that he was engaged in an entirely different job rather than being inefficient in the old one.

Hindle v *Percival Boats Ltd*

[1969] 1 WLR 174, Court of Appeal

The applicant's forte was in building traditional wooden boats, but increasingly the modern demand was for fibre-glass-constructed vessels. Hindle was too slow when it came to fibre-glass models and he was dismissed for being 'too good and too slow'. He was not replaced but his work was carried on by other members of the workforce. His claim for a redundancy payment was rejected.

SACHS LJ: I would add that provided the requirements of the business referred to in [s. 139(1)(b)] remain constant it does not matter whether the slowness of employee which leads to the failure to 'pay for his keep' stems from the onset of years, from some physical cause, or from over-great addiction to what is sometimes termed perfectionism. Unfortunately for such addicts, perfectionism can produce a form of inefficiency in many walks of life—not merely in a workshop—however much one may praise the look of the product.

The onus placed on the employer by section [163(2)] of the Act is simply to show (using the standard test of balance of probabilities applicable where the facts are largely within the knowledge of a party against whom a claim is made) that the dismissal of the employee was not attributable to redundancy. There are cases, as where the tribunal find in favour of the employer on the first condition precedent, when it is not necessary to inquire further into the precise ground on which the employee was dismissed. But in any event once the tribunal is satisfied that the ground put forward by the employer is genuine and is the one to which the dismissal is mainly attributable the onus is discharged—and it ceases to be in point that the ground was unwise or based on a mistaken view of facts, though such matters may well be relevant for consideration by the tribunal when assessing the truth of the employer's evidence.

The above conclusions are all consistent with my view, differing unfortunately in some respects from those just stated by my Lord, that compensation is provided by the Act for one, but one only, of life's changes of fortune as between employee and employer: that is, dismissal on account of redundancy within the meaning of the Act. It thus neither purports to nor does provide for other changes of fortune, such as ill-health or a deterioration in the employer's views of the capabilities of the employee. Similarly it does not provide for the case where an employer wishes to see if someone else can do the job better: it could indeed be industrially unfortunate if it puts a brake on employers seeking to get the best man for any given job. Nor does it provide for any case where an employer simply wishes not to continue to employ a particular employee...so long as the requirements of the business for employees of a particular kind remain the same the Act does not provide for changes consequential upon a reorganisation: (see *North Riding Garages Ltd* v *Butterwick* [1967] 2 QB 56). In short, it does not provide security of employment in the accepted sense of that phrase.

■ QUESTIONS

1. In the light of the above decisions, to what extent, if at all, do you consider the legal concept of 'redundancy' equates with the public understanding of what constitutes a redundancy situation?

2. Consider the proposition that the law on redundancy favours the employer rather than the employee. The view of one commentator is as follows:

Not only are the courts prepared to enlarge managerial discretion under employment contracts at the expense of reducing the chance for a redundancy payment; they are also prepared to give a strict reading to the nature of 'work' in the statutory definition. [Anderman, S. D., *Labour Law: Management decisions and workers' rights*, 2nd edn (London: Butterworths, 1993), p. 162]

NOTE: For a decision which adopts a narrower approach to 'kind of work', see *Murphy* v *Epsom College* [1984] IRLR 271, CA. In that case, the college's heating system was modernised, and Mr Murphy, one of the college's two existing plumbers, stated that he was not technically qualified to maintain it. He was dismissed and replaced by a 'heating engineer'. Mr Murphy was unsuccessful in his claim for unfair dismissal. The Court of Appeal upheld the tribunal's decision that the employee was redundant since the college's requirement for plumbers—as opposed to 'heating engineers'—was reduced from two to one.

SECTION 3: OFFERS OF SUITABLE ALTERNATIVE EMPLOYMENT

When we considered employees who were disqualified from applying for a redundancy payment, we included those who had refused offers of suitable alternative employment. This is covered by the ERA 1996, s. 141, which reads as follows:

EMPLOYMENT RIGHTS ACT 1996

141. Renewal of contract or re-engagement

(1) This section applies where an offer (whether in writing or not) is made to an employee before the end of his employment—

    (a) to renew his contract of employment, or

    (b) to re-engage him under a new contract of employment,

with renewal or re-engagement to take effect either immediately on, or after an interval of not more than four weeks after, the end of his employment.

(2) Where subsection (3) is satisfied, the employee is not entitled to a redundancy payment if he unreasonably refuses the offer.

(3) This subsection is satisfied where—

    (a) the provisions of the contract as renewed, or of the new contract, as to—

        (i)   the capacity and place in which the employee would be employed, and

        (ii) the other terms and conditions of his employment,

    would not differ from the corresponding provisions of the previous contract, or

    (b) those provisions of the contract as renewed, or of the new contract, would differ from the corresponding provisions of the previous contract but the offer constitutes an offer of suitable employment in relation to the employee.

(4) The employee is not entitled to a redundancy payment if—

    (a) his contract of employment is renewed, or he is re-engaged under a new contract of employment, in pursuance of the offer,

    (b) the provisions of the contract as renewed or new contract as to the capacity or place in which he is employed or the other terms and conditions of his employment differ (wholly or in part) from the corresponding provisions of the previous contract,

    (c) the employment is suitable in relation to him, and

    (d) during the trial period he unreasonably terminates the contract or unreasonably gives notice to terminate it and it is in consequence terminated.

NOTE: Two questions therefore fall to be considered: (a) is the offer of alternative employment suitable; and (b) if so, is the refusal by the employee to take it up unreasonable? (These two questions do to differing degrees overlap—see the comments of Neill LJ in *Spencer* v *Gloucestershire County Council* [19185] IRLR 393, below at p. 494 (Section B).)

A: Suitable alternative employment?

(i) The general duty

Vokes* v *Bear

[1974] ICR 1, National Industrial Relations Court

The applicant was dismissed without any prior warning, with no time off given to find other work and with no attempt made to find alternative employment for him in any of the 299 other companies forming part of the employer's group of companies. The failure to make any attempt to find alternative employment meant that although there was a redundancy situation, the dismissal was unfair.

SIR HUGH GRIFFITHS: Having decided that the employee was dismissed by reason of redundancy the tribunal then turned to consider whether nevertheless his dismissal was unfair by virtue of the provisions of section 24(6) of the Industrial Relations Act 1971 [now ERA 1996, s. 98(4)]. The tribunal held that it was unfair because no attempt whatever had been made to see if the employee could have been fitted into some other position in the group before he was dismissed. The evidence showed that the Tilling Group consisted of some 300 companies and there was evidence that at least one of those companies was advertising for persons to fill senior management positions shortly after the employee's dismissal. The Tilling Group apparently had no centralised machinery for providing services to all the companies in the group and it was argued before the tribunal and before this court that in all the circumstances it would have been impracticable to have made any inquiries within the group to see if there was another position that the employee might fill. The tribunal would have none of this argument. They said:

> We do not think that such inquiries were impracticable. We think that some inquiries should have been made to see whether it was possible to help someone like [the employee] whose services had proved satisfactory to his employers in every respect. We think the [employers'] failure to consider the question of finding some other position for the [employee] in the group made the dismissal unfair.

We find ourselves in full agreement with the way in which the tribunal expressed themselves. It would have been the simplest of matters to have circulated an inquiry through the group to see if any assistance could be given to the employee in the very difficult circumstances in which he would shortly find himself.

...

These employers made no offer of help to the employee before they dismissed him, nor did they allow him any time off to seek work. As the employee reasonably complained: 'It's more difficult to find employment if you have been summarily dismissed than if you are seeking a new job while still in employment.' In so far as it is argued that this paragraph is not meant to apply to managers, we would answer, how is a company to expect its managers to comply with the provision if it treats them as it did the employee? He was literally put out on the pavement at a moment's notice in circumstances which appear to us to have lacked any humanitarian approach on the part of the employers.

But, with whatever indignation we may regard the behaviour of his employers, the question still remains whether the dismissal was fair or unfair within the meaning of section 24(6) of the Act of 1971 [now ERA 1996, s. 98(4)] ...

Mr Irvine submits that the only 'circumstances' that the tribunal are entitled to take into account are circumstances which relate to or surround the employer's grounds for dismissal and that, as he put it, the tribunal are not entitled to take into account an employer's failure to mitigate the consequences of an otherwise fair dismissal.

It is not altogether easy to see what particular meaning should attach to the words 'in the circumstances,' for if these words were omitted from the subsection it would hardly seem to alter its meaning. Suppose the subsection read: 'the determination of the question whether the dismissal was fair or unfair, having regard to the reason shown by the employer, shall depend on whether he acted reasonably or unreasonably in treating it as a sufficient reason for dismissing the employee.' How is the tribunal to determine whether the employer's action was reasonable or unreasonable unless it considers 'the circumstances' in which it was taken? It cannot decide this matter in the air.

We are unable to accept the submission that 'the circumstances' are limited to those directly affecting the ground of dismissal, in the sense submitted by Mr Irvine. 'The circumstances' embrace all relevant matters that should weigh with a good employer when deciding at a given moment in time whether or not he should dismiss his employee. The subsection is focusing the tribunal's attention upon 'the dismissal,' that is, the dismissal on March 2. The question they have to ask themselves is whether on March 2 the employers were acting reasonably in treating redundancy as a sufficient reason for dismissing the employee on that date. The tribunal are entitled to take into account all the circumstances affecting both the employers and the employee at the time of the dismissal. In the present case, no doubt the time would have come when the employers would have to dismiss the employee for redundancy for the good of the company as a whole, but the tribunal were fully entitled to take the view that that moment had not yet arrived by March 2. The employers had not yet done that which in all fairness and reason they should do, namely, to make the obvious attempt to see if the employee could be placed somewhere else within this large group.

The position is somewhat analogous to the case of a warning. An employer may have good grounds for thinking that a man is not capable of doing his job properly, but in the general run of cases it will not be reasonable for him to regard that lack of capability as a sufficient reason for dismissing him until he is given a warning so that the man has the chance to show if he can do better. So in this case there was a redundancy situation but there was no compelling reason why the axe should fall until the employers had done their best to help the employee ...

NOTE: In *Samsung Electronics v Monte-D'Cruz* [2012] UKEAT 0039, the EAT held that, when after reorganisation, a redundant employee is invited to apply for a newly created role, the employer can appoint the best person for the job even if the decision involves a degree of subjectivity.

(ii) What is meant by suitable?

Taylor v *Kent County Council*
[1969] 2 QB 560, Queen's Bench Division

The applicant lost his post as headmaster due to the amalgamation of two schools. He was offered the post of a mobile teacher (at the same salary as he had received as headmaster), forming one of a pool who would serve for short periods at different schools, during which period of service he would be under the control of that particular school's headmaster. He refused the offer. Did he thereby lose his entitlement to a redundancy payment? The Divisional Court held that the offer of alternative employment was not suitable and Taylor was entitled to refuse it.

LORD PARKER CJ: ... The tribunal in their decision said:

The suitability of the alternative offer must be considered in all the surrounding circumstances not just one—to wit: status. Taking into account not only the applicant's age, qualifications, experience, loss of status, but also the protection afforded by his contract',—pausing there, that means that his salary as headmaster is going to continue pursuant to section Q of the Burnham award—'and not forgetting the unfortunate showing at the interview, we have come to the conclusion that in all the circumstances the offer of appointment to the mobile pool was one of suitable employment in relation to the applicant. Of course another headmastership would have been more suitable, but his employers were not in a position to make a written offer of such a post. However, the fact that the offer that was made was less suitable, does not necessarily make it unsuitable.

Let me say at once, suitability is almost entirely a matter of degree and fact for the tribunal, and not a matter with which this court would wish to or could interfere, unless it was plain that they had misdirected themselves in some way in law, or had taken into consideration matters which were not relevant for the purpose. It is to be observed that so far as age was concerned, so far as qualifications were concerned, so far as experience was concerned, they negative the suitability of this offer, because he is going to be put into a position where he has to go where he is told at any time for short periods, to any place, and be put under a headmaster and assigned duties by him.

The only matter which can be put against that as making this offer suitable is the guarantee of salary under Scale Q. One would think, speaking for myself, that for a headmaster of this experience, he would think an offer which, while guaranteeing him the same salary, reduced his status, was quite unsuitable. To go to quite a different sphere of activity, a director under a service agreement of a company is offered on dismissal a job as a navvy, and it is said: but we will guarantee you the same salary as you have been getting. I should have thought such an offer was plainly unsuitable. Here one wonders whether one of the matters which affected the tribunal was this reference to the words 'Not forgetting the unfortunate showing at the interview.' That is a reference to when he was interviewed, not by the Kent County Council, but by the governors of the school with a view to taking on the headmastership of the new school. One really wonders what the relevance of that was unless it be that the tribunal felt from what they had heard that he was not up to a headmastership at all. But at once one says to oneself: if that was in their mind, it was not evidence upon which they could properly act, having regard to the fact that this man had given satisfaction for some ten years, and if he was not up to his job he could have been dismissed for that reason, and no question of redundancy would have arisen.

But for my part I feel that the tribunal have here misdirected themselves in law as to the meaning of 'suitable employment.' I accept, of course, that suitable employment is as is said: suitable employment in relation to the employee in question. But it does seem to me here that by the words 'suitable employment,' suitability means employment which is substantially equivalent to the employment which has ceased. Section 2(3) [now ERA 1996, s. 141(3)(a)] which I read at the beginning is dealing with the case where the fundamental terms are the same, and then no offer in writing is needed, but when they differ, then it has to be put in writing and must be suitable. I for my part think that what is meant by 'suitable' in relation to the employee means conditions of employment which are reasonably equivalent to those under the previous employment, not the same, because then subsection (2) [now ERA 1996, s. 141(3)(b)] would apply, but it does not seem to me that by 'suitable employment' is meant employment of an entirely different nature, but in respect of which the salary is going to be the same. Looked at in that way, it seems to me that there could be only one answer in this case, and that is that this man was being asked to do something utterly different; as I have said, just as if a director under a service agreement with a company was being asked to do a workman's job, albeit at the same salary.

(iii) The relevance of a salary reduction

The mere fact that the alternative post offers less salary or denies the opportunity to earn overtime (as to the latter see *Sheppard* v *National Coal Board* [1966] 1 KIR 101) does not, by itself, make the offer of alternative employment unsuitable.

Hindes v *Supersine Ltd*
[1979] ICR 517, Employment Appeal Tribunal

The employee was offered a post at another factory but at a reduced salary. He agreed to try the new job but left after a few days, stating that the smell of paint made him ill. The industrial tribunal dismissed his redundancy application holding that, since he had indicated that the reduction in salary would have been acceptable had he liked his new job, he had accepted that the alternative employment was suitable. The EAT allowed the employee's appeal.

TALBOT J: Therefore, there is stated there a clear way of looking at this: is the employment offered substantially equivalent to the employment which has ceased? It is plain that so far as pay is concerned the new job offered to the employee was not substantially equivalent to the job that had come to an end. Had the matter rested there, then quite clearly (as, indeed, the industrial tribunal rightly said) that would have been the end of the matter on the question of suitability, because the job offered to the employee would have been unsuitable.

Mrs Gill, as we would understand her, would be seen to be saying that there ought not to have been taken into account the fact that, had he liked the new job, he would not have regarded the drop in pay as of importance. That is certainly a matter personal to him; but it would be our view that had the employee disregarded, without any conditions, the change in pay, then what would otherwise have been an unsuitable job, because of the drop in pay, could have been found to be suitable. But, it is plain from the facts of this case that the employee's preparedness to accept the drop in pay was conditional upon his liking the new job in all other respects. The facts also clearly show (because, from the words we have quoted, it is clear that the industrial tribunal accepted what the employee told them) that he did not like the new job and could not tolerate it for the reasons which he stated. Therefore, in those circumstances, the matter goes back to be considered on the question of suitability, namely, whether the drop in pay rendered the job unsuitable. The employee was only prepared to accept the drop in pay if he tolerated the job, and, as he did not tolerate the job, then he is not prepared to accept the drop in pay. In our view the industrial tribunal failed to look at this question in the way that they should have looked at it. It is not a matter of us expressing our view; we are saying that they have omitted to take into consideration that which should have been very much to the forefront of their consideration, namely, that the employee's acceptance of the job was conditional upon his being able to tolerate and like it in other respects. They therefore omitted to consider the vital matter of evidence and in that respect they are in error.

(iv) Reduction of level of skill, etc. required

A reduction in the level of expertise and skill required by the new post being offered may make it unsuitable.

Standard Telephones v *Yates*
[1981] IRLR 21, Employment Appeal Tribunal

The applicant had been employed for ten years as a card wirer, a job demanding both skill and experience. She was offered the alternative post of assembly line operator, which she refused. The EAT agreed that the offer of alternative employment was not suitable.

BRISTOW J: Now Mr Moss, who has put the company's case with admirable clarity and persistence, says that [the tribunal] went wrong in law in that they applied the wrong test in deciding whether the offer was suitable or not and, in support of his submission, he relied on the decision of the Queen's Bench Division at Court in the case of *Taylor* v *Kent County Council* [1969] 2 QB 560. Mr Moss submits that there Lord Parker CJ laid down as a matter of law that what suitable employment in the predecessor of s. 5(b) [now ERA, s. 141(3)(b)] means is 'employment which is substantially equivalent to the employment which has ceased'. Now no doubt if an Industrial Tribunal finds that the employment offered is employment substantially equivalent to the employment which has ceased, it will find that the offer is an offer of suitable employment but we point out that the words used in the statute where the law is to be found are not an offer of employment which is substantially equivalent to the employment which has ceased but an offer of suitable employment. Whether it is any easier for an Industrial Tribunal which has put upon it by Parliament the duty to make the value judgment whether the offer is of suitable employment will find it any more difficult to do that than to find whether the employment is substantially equivalent to the employment which has ceased, it is perhaps difficult to say. It is merely putting the same problem in other words. But in our judgment, if the Industrial Tribunal, having considered the evidence, comes to the conclusion, in its wisdom as an industrial jury, that the offer is one of suitable employment, the fact that it does not use the words of any gloss which has been put upon the requirements of the statute by the courts, does not mean that it has gone wrong in law. It will only go wrong in law if, having done what the statute requires it to do and considered whether the offer constitutes an offer of suitable employment, it is found that there was no evidence on which it could have come to the conclusion to which it did come; or that it took into consideration something which it should not have done; or left out of consideration something which it should have considered; or that its conclusion is so wildly out of line that it must have misdirected itself and so gone wrong in law—that being the form of error of law which is usually referred to as a 'perverse decision' in this jurisdiction.

Now in our judgment, there was evidence before this Tribunal on which they could find, as they did find, that the offer made was not an offer of suitable employment and what they said was:

> First of all the employment was not suitable work. Certainly it was suitable in that the applicant was quite capable of doing it, but it was not work which employed the skills which she had been using for 10 years. Had it been explained to her as Mr Bridges explained it in evidence, namely that she would very quickly find herself in a wiring occupation, then the assembly work might have been suitable alternative employment as a short term measure.

Their conclusion was, having heard the evidence, that her potential, which she was entitled to expect to have the opportunity to use, was greater than the potential required in the boxing department. As we have said, on the evidence before them, it seems to us that it was open to them to come to such a conclusion—whether or not we would have come to it is neither here nor there and it certainly is not a conclusion which could be stigmatised as perverse.

B: The reasonableness of a refusal

In assessing the reasonableness or otherwise of the employee's refusal to take up an offer of alternative employment, subjective considerations are taken into account, e.g. the travelling involved and its effect on domestic life, loss of friends, and the effect on children's education if a house move is required.

Spencer v *Gloucestershire County Council*
[1985] IRLR 393, Court of Appeal

The employees were school cleaners who, as a cost-cutting exercise, were asked to accept fewer hours. They refused on the basis that they felt they could not do the job properly in the reduced working time. The EAT considered the refusal unreasonable since the employer took the view that whatever could be done within the shorter hours would be acceptable. The Court of Appeal allowed the appeal and, in so doing, made some observations on the overlap between the two questions of suitability of the offer and reasonableness of the refusal.

NEILL LJ: Speaking for myself, it seems to me that it only leads to confusion if one tries to draw too rigid a distinction between suitability of employment and the circumstances which may lead an employee reasonably or, in some cases, unreasonably to refuse to accept a particular offer. Some factors may be common to both aspects of the case. It may be that a factor may reflect both on the suitability of the work for the particular employee and also be something which the employee can take into account when he comes to judge whether he can properly accept the employer's offer. I would deprecate trying to draw too rigid a distinction and say that some particular factors must fall exclusively under one heading and other factors under the other heading. The Industrial Tribunal clearly must look at the two separate points—in other words, whether the employment is suitable in relation to the employee and, secondly, whether or not the employee has unreasonably refused to accept the offer...

Returning to the facts of this case, it seems to me that it cannot be right to say as a general proposition that it is not a good reason for an employee to refuse to do work because he considers that the work he is being asked to do does not come up to a standard which he himself wishes to observe. It all depends on the facts of the case. There may well be cases where an employee wishes to apply a wholly unreasonable standard to the work, and say, 'I am only prepared to work to that standard'. But it seems to me that this is eminently a matter for the Industrial Tribunal to evaluate in the particular circumstances. In paragraph 11 the Industrial Tribunal set out the factors which they had in mind. It is clear from the way they expressed themselves in their reasons that they had a substantial amount of evidence from the applicants as to why they (the applicants) thought that the job could not be done satisfactorily in the way in which the employer suggested. In those circumstances, it seems to me, it was for the Industrial Tribunal to decide on the facts then before them whether or not each individual employee had unreasonably refused the offer of employment. With all respect to the Employment Appeal Tribunal, it does not seem to me to be a case where they were entitled to overturn the decision of the Industrial Tribunal.

Paton Calvert & Co. Ltd v Westerside

[1979] IRLR 108, Employment Appeal Tribunal

The employee had been sent a redundancy notice, but the employer wrote again to his employees indicating that because of a recently acquired government grant the company was able to continue trading. As a result the employer was able to offer continuing employment on the same terms. Westerside, who was aged 61 and sceptical about the future viability of the company, refused and claimed redundancy having, in the meantime, secured alternative employment elsewhere. The EAT held that the refusal of the offer was reasonable.

SLYNN J: ...So, adding these three factors together; his age, the new job and also at least the possibility that the company would not necessarily survive, [the tribunal] held that he had not unreasonably refused the offer.

It is contended before us by Mr Leveson, to whom we are indebted for his research and for a very careful and concise argument, that they were wrong. He submits that here the onus was on Mr Westerside to show that he had not unreasonably refused the offer. He says that in a number of cases the particular matters which are here relied on have been held not to be sufficient for the purposes of deciding that a refusal was reasonable.

In the first place he refers us to the case of *Pilkington* v *Pickstone* [1966] ITR 364. There the [Manchester Industrial Tribunal] stressed that the matters which are relevant for the purposes of reasonableness must either be such matters as can be considered as arising between the employer and the employee or in relation to the special circumstances affecting an employee personally. He says here these are not matters of that kind. They are not matters which go to the employer/employee relationship.

He then goes on to say that in the case of *McNulty* v *T Bridges and Company* [1966] 1 ITR 367 the fact that a man has accepted another job does not necessarily make it reasonable for him to refuse an offer or does not mean that he has not unreasonably accepted the new offer from his company. He also says that the fact that an industry may be contracting and that futures were not assured is not of itself a ground for refusing a new offer reasonably, and he refers us to the case of *James and Jones* v *The National Coal Board* [[1969] ITR 70].

He also stressed that in the case of *Morganite Crucible Limited* v *Street* [[1972] ICR 110], John Donaldson stressed that as long as the new employment which is offered is regular employment then it does not matter that it is of a shorter rather than a longer duration. The Court, further, in that case, did recognise that there can be exceptions to that as a general rule.

Now, it is, of course, as Mr Leveson has stressed to us, important to consider the 1965 Act against the Employment Protection Act of 1975, and we desire to say nothing which would in any way impede the desire of employers and union representatives and the Secretary of State to seek to avoid redundancies which may appear to be likely. It is clearly of great importance that discussions should take place so that if possible redundancy notices should be withdrawn and that employees should continue in their employment. But Parliament has clearly provided that if the employee does not unreasonably refuse an offer of further employment he may still be entitled to a redundancy payment.

We follow what has been said that these individual reasons may not in themselves be sufficient to justify as reasonable a refusal of a further offer of employment. We consider, however, that the various factors which are relied upon here are capable of being special circumstances affecting Mr Westerside personally, and, indeed, that the future viability of the company is something which falls into the alternative category of a matter arising between the employer and the employee as referred to in *Pilkington* v *Pickstone*. Moreover, we consider that it is possible for a man's age and for the apparent viability of the company to be capable of creating exceptional cases within the general rule defined in *Morganite Crucible Limited* v *Street*.

We have been referred to a more recent Industrial Tribunal case, *Thomas Wragg & Sons Limited* v *Wood* [[1976] ICR 313]. There the employee was given notice and he obtained other work only one day before the expiry of the 90-day notice. He was given an offer of alternative employment. He was a man of 56. He was a man who feared for future redundancies in the construction industry and the Tribunal there were prepared to accept that the fears of future redundancy were not in themselves necessarily sufficient to justify a refusal to accept a new offer, nor necessarily in itself was the lateness of the offer of new employment. But they paid regard to the fact that the employee in the case had with diligence obtained another employment, and they said that if all those factors were put together, as it was right to put them together, then the Industrial Tribunal had been entitled to conclude that the employee had not unreasonably refused a further offer of employment.

These cases are not always easy, but we are satisfied in the present case that the combination of Mr Westerside's age with the uncertainty as to the future of his employment with the company, which is indicated in the letter of 15 December, coupled with the fact that he had obtained another job thereby avoiding the possibility of his being unemployed in the future, were sufficient to make it not unreasonable for him to refuse that offer. In our view the factors which exist in this case and which have been relied upon by the Tribunal are sufficient to entitle him to say that he was not unreasonable in refusing the offer.

NOTE: While the courts have high regard to the motives of the employee, the approach is not entirely subjective, as the next case illustrates.

Fuller v *Stephanie Bowman (Sales) Ltd*
[1977] IRLR 87, Industrial Tribunal

The applicant refused to move with her employers from a West End address to one in Soho, where the new business premises were above a sex shop. Her refusal was held to be unreasonable by the industrial tribunal.

N. F. STOGDEN (Chairman): The applicant said in evidence that she had the strongest objection to money for sex, and she would not work over a sex shop. That could be a valid objection. Personal factors must be taken into consideration. The test is not the attitude of the reasonable woman but reasonable objections of this applicant: *Universal Fisher Engineering Ltd* v *Stratton* (1971) 7 ITR 66, NIRC. Mere fads and fancies are not enough. Apart from that the test is as stated in such cases as *Kerr* v *National Coal Board* [1970] ITR 48. Whether the refusal of an offer is reasonable is a question of fact for the Tribunal.

The Tribunal, which included a lady member, therefore, decided to view both premises. The Chairman especially was well aware that working over a sex shop could be a reasonable objection in some circumstances. People have just as much right to hold strong views about sex as they do about politics or religion. Of course, for those who disapprove of modern sexual laxity, Mayfair is nearly as bad as Soho, Piccadilly Circus, Shaftesbury Avenue, the Charing Cross Road and that area generally. For those who are shocked there are as many pictures outside cinemas and some theatres as there are in sex shop windows. The only advantage for Mayfair is that in many parts the activities are not so obvious. The Tribunal found that the entrance to the upper part of Berwick Street premises was at the side of the sex shop and no part of it. No prostitutes used the other floors. These were respectively a company office and a tailor. The work in the premises had been reasonably well done and no exception could be taken to anything except the sex shop. Berwick Street has a large street market at the south end, but that was a good 300 yards away. The street has numerous shops and business premises. Most of them have nothing to do with sex. There are few prostitutes' bells. We saw none very close to the premises. Finally the applicant was 53 at the time. She was not likely to be mistaken for a prostitute. The street in daytime is full of shoppers and those going to and from the market. It is certainly not one of the worst streets in Soho.

On the facts the Tribunal considered that the dislike of the sex shop was not enough to make the refusal of the offer reasonable, especially as there had been no attempts by the applicant to look into the letter of 18 June. Had the applicant's views on sex been so strong that she refused to work anywhere in the West End that might have been different.

NOTES

1. In *Devon Primary Care Trust* v *Readman* [2013] IRLR 878, CA, the claimant, a nurse, was placed at risk of redundancy and offered three alternative posts by her employer. One of the posts, a Hospital Matron position, was correctly found by the employment tribunal to amount to suitable alternative employment under s. 141(3) of the ERA 1996. Mrs Readman refused this post on the ground that, having worked in community nursing since 1985, she had no desire to return to a hospital setting. In the circumstances, she was denied a redundancy payment by her employer, relying on s. 141 of the ERA 1996. The employment tribunal similarly refused Mrs Readman a redundancy payment on the ground that her refusal had been unreasonable. In reaching this conclusion, the tribunal asked itself, in effect, whether a reasonable employee would have accepted the employer's offer and concluded that they would have done.

   Overturning the decision on appeal, the EAT held that the tribunal had fallen into error by applying a wholly objective test to the question of reasonableness. The proper question for a tribunal, when considering whether a refusal of suitable alternative employment is unreasonable, is whether her decision 'to refuse the [alternative] job for the reasons she gave and viewed from her point of view was within the band of reasonable responses which were open to her.'

   The EAT therefore allowed the appeal and substituted a finding that Mrs Readman was entitled to receive a redundancy payment.

   The CA allowed the Trust's appeal on the basis that the EAT had applied the wrong test and remitted the case to an employment tribunal.

   The CA stated that it was not helpful to import into the s. 141 analysis the reasonable responses test used in unfair dismissal cases. In unfair dismissal cases the tribunal has to make a judgment on the evidence as to whether a decision to dismiss fell within the reasonable band of responses which a reasonable employer might have adopted. That is different from the test under s. 141, which, as stated in *Everest (Executors)* v *Cox* [1980] ICR 415, EAT, involves a judgment as to whether an employee has unreasonably refused an offer, '[l]ooking at it from her point of view on the basis of the facts as they appeared or ought reasonably have appeared to her at the time the decision had to be made.' A specific judgment needs to be made, not a judgment on whether the decision fell within a reasonable band of responses which a reasonable employee might have made. The task under s. 141(2)(b) is that stated in *Cox*, whether this particular employee in this particular situation acted reasonably in refusing the offer of employment is a clear test and has been applied by tribunals for 30 years. See also *Bird* v *Stoke-on-Trent Primary Care Trust* [2011] ALL ER (D) 142 (Aug.), EAT.

2. The offer of alternative employment must be made before the existing contract is due to end, and the new contract must start within four weeks of the ending of the old one.

3. The ERA 1996, s. 138, allows the employee and employer a four-week trial period before either finally commits themselves to the new contract. If the employer dismisses within the four-week period the employee will be treated as dismissed for redundancy under the old job. If the employee resigns within the four-week period, he or she will be treated as entitled to a redundancy payment under his or her old job if he or she can show that the new employment was unsuitable, etc. In *Turvey* v *C. W. Cheyney & Son Ltd* [1979] IRLR 105 it was suggested that the reasonable common law period for accepting the employer's repudiation of contract was to be added on to the statutory trial period. This view was rejected in *Optical Express Ltd* v *Williams* [2007] IRLR 936, EAT. According to Burton J: 'We are entirely satisfied that this tribunal was not entitled in law to conclude that a right to a statutory redundancy payment survived, notwithstanding the operation of, but non-compliance with, the statutory procedure... [w]here, as here, there is an express offer and an express acceptance of a s. 138 contract of re-engagement for a trial period, it appears to us that it is impossible to suggest that the common law trial period runs alongside.' In other words, if a statutory trial period is operating, the employee must give notice of termination within the trial period in order to put himself or herself in the position of qualifying for a redundancy payment.

SECTION 4: LAY-OFF AND SHORT-TIME WORKING

EMPLOYMENT RIGHTS ACT 1996

LAY-OFF AND SHORT-TIME

147. Meaning of 'lay-off' and 'short-time'

(1) For the purposes of this Part an employee shall be taken to be laid off for a week if—

   (a) he is employed under a contract on terms and conditions such that his remuneration under the contract depends on his being provided by the employer with work of the kind which he is employed to do, but

   (b) he is not entitled to any remuneration under the contract in respect of the week because the employer does not provide such work for him.

(2) For the purposes of this Part an employee shall be taken to be kept on short-time for a week if by reason of a diminution in the work provided for the employee by his employer (being work of a kind which under his contract the employee is employed to do) the employee's remuneration for the week is less than half a week's pay.

148. Eligibility by reason of lay-off or short-time

(1) Subject to the following provisions of this Part, for the purposes of this Part an employee is eligible for a redundancy payment by reason of being laid off or kept on short-time if—

   (a) he gives notice in writing to his employer indicating (in whatever terms) his intention to claim a redundancy payment in respect of lay-off or short-time (referred to in this Part as 'notice of intention to claim'), and

   (b) before the service of the notice he has been laid off or kept on short-time in circumstances in which subsection (2) applies.

(2) This subsection applies if the employee has been laid off or kept on short-time—

   (a) for four or more consecutive weeks of which the last before the service of the notice ended on, or not more than four weeks before, the date of service of the notice, or

   (b) for a series of six or more weeks (of which not more than three were consecutive) within a period of thirteen weeks, where the last week of the series before the service of the notice ended on, or not more than four weeks before, the date of service of the notice.

EXCLUSIONS

149. Counter-notices

Where an employee gives to his employer notice of intention to claim but—

   (a) the employer gives to the employee, within seven days after the service of that notice, notice in writing (referred to in this Part as a 'counter-notice') that he will contest any liability to pay to the employee a redundancy payment in pursuance of the Employee's notice, and

   (b) the employer does not withdraw the counter-notice by a subsequent notice in writing,

   the employee is not entitled to a redundancy payment in pursuance of his notice of intention to claim except in accordance with a decision of an industrial tribunal.

150. Resignation

(1) An employee is not entitled to a redundancy payment by reason of being laid off or kept on short-time unless he terminates his contract of employment by giving such period of notice as is required for the purposes of this section before the end of the relevant period.

(2) The period of notice required for the purposes of this section—

   (a) where the employee is required by his contract of employment to give more than one week's notice to terminate the contract, is the minimum period which he is required to give, and

   (b) otherwise, is one week.

(3) In subsection (1) 'the relevant period'—

   (a) if the employer does not give a counter-notice within seven days after the service of the notice of intention to claim, is three weeks after the end of those seven days,

   (b) if the employer gives a counter-notice within that period of seven days but withdraws it by a subsequent notice in writing, is three weeks after the service of the notice of withdrawal, and

   (c) if—

(i) the employer gives a counter-notice within that period of seven days, and does not so withdraw it, and

(ii) a question as to the right of the employee to a redundancy payment in pursuance of the notice of intention to claim is referred to an industrial tribunal, is three weeks after the tribunal has notified to the employee its decision on that reference.

(4) For the purposes of subsection (3)(c) no account shall be taken of—

(a) any appeal against the decision of the tribunal, or

(b) any proceedings or decision in consequence of any such appeal.

151. Dismissal

(1) An employee is not entitled to a redundancy payment by reason of being laid off or kept on short-time if he is dismissed by his employer.

(2) Subsection (1) does not prejudice any right of the employee to a redundancy payment in respect of the dismissal.

152. Likelihood of full employment

(1) An employee is not entitled to a redundancy payment in pursuance of a notice of intention to claim if—

(a) on the date of service of the notice it was reasonably to be expected that the employee (if he continued to be employed by the same employer) would, not later than four weeks after that date, enter on a period of employment of not less than thirteen weeks during which he would not be laid off or kept on short-time for any week, and

(b) the employer gives a counter-notice to the employee within seven days after the service of the notice of intention to claim.

(2) Subsection (1) does not apply where the employee—

(a) continues or has continued, during the next four weeks after the date of service of the notice of intention to claim, to be employed by the same employer, and

(b) is or has been laid off or kept on short-time for each of those weeks.

NOTE: An employer is not entitled to lay off an employee unless there is an express or implied power to do so in the contract. If the employer does not possess this power, any lay-off will amount to a constructive dismissal (see *Jewell* v *Neptune Concrete Ltd* [1975] IRLR 147). Where the employer does possess the contractual authority to lay off, the above provisions seek to offer employees a degree of protection.

SECTION 5: TRANSFER OF UNDERTAKINGS

A: Introduction

What happens to the contracts of employment of the workforce when a business is sold? The original common law position was set out in the following case.

Nokes v *Doncaster Amalgamated Collieries Ltd*
[1940] AC 1014, House of Lords

The House of Lords had to decide whether, when an order was made under the then companies legislation for the amalgamation of two companies, the contracts of employment were transferred as well as the assets. By a majority (Lord Romer dissenting) it refused to so hold.

LORD ATKIN: When one regards the remarkable legal consequences of the construction adopted by the courts below one is driven to ask what the reasons may be supposed to be that brought about this revolution in the law, and that led to one class of person, companies under the Companies Act, being able to shake off the restrictions which bind ordinary persons, though only when they are minded to transfer their business to another and probably a larger company. Before 1928 no such privilege existed. Amalgamations, a vague term, were possible: companies could dispose of their undertaking to other companies. But it was necessary to invoke the machinery of a winding up: assets would be transferred by conveyances to which the liquidator was party: assignments had to be negotiated: and dissolution of the company could not take place until after the winding up had been completed. But all such sales of undertaking were subject to the ordinary law, and had of course to respect the rights of third parties. Nothing was transferable by a company that was not transferable by an individual: and in particular no one suggested that contracts of service could be transferred. On the contrary, a winding-up order or resolution operated as a discharge of existing servants, resulting in the right to claim damages for wrongful dismissal. It is true that the transferee company would ordinarily offer to employ the former servants of the transferor company: and an unreasonable refusal to accept such offer would mitigate or perhaps get rid of any damages. But the servant was left with his inalienable right to choose whether he would serve a new master or not.

NOTES
1. The rule in *Nokes* was explicable on the basis of freedom of contract. This 'freedom', however, could work against the employee, because a person to whom the business was transferred was under no obligation to offer to employ existing employees working in the transferred business. If no such offer was forthcoming, the employee's only claim was against his or her former—often insolvent—employer. The Employment Protection (Consolidation) Act (EPCA) 1978, s. 94, modified the common law position and offered protection to the former employer by barring the right of an employee to claim redundancy if, on the change of ownership, he or she refused an offer of alternative employment with the new employer on the same or similar terms. Where the employee accepted the offer of re-engagement by the transferee employer, statutory continuity was and is now preserved by the ERA 1996, s. 218(2) (see Section B(i)).
2. The Acquired Rights Directive (EC/77/187) set out to change the position and to offer a greater measure of protection to employees caught up in business transfers. Under pressure from the European Commission and with great reluctance, the Government purported to implement the directive through the Transfer of Undertakings (Protection of Employment) Regulations 1981. The history of judicial interpretation of these regulations since 1981 has been one of increasingly pushing back the frontiers of their application to meet the objectives of the EC directive. The Government has been forced on a number of occasions to amend the regulations accordingly. The Acquired Rights Directive was revised in 1998 and a consolidated version produced in 2001 (see the Acquired Rights Directive (2001/23/EC). Although the first consultation on reforming UK domestic law to accommodate the changes was published in 2001, it was not until 2006 that the new Transfer of Undertakings (Protection of Employment) (TUPE) Regulations came into force. These completely replace the 1981 Regulations and apply to all transfers taking place from 6 April 2006.

   The main changes introduced in the 2006 Regulations are:
   - a widening of the scope of the regulations to cover cases where services are outsourced, insourced or assigned by a client to a new contractor (described as 'service provision changes');
   - a new duty on the old transferor employer to supply information about the transferring employees to the new transferee employer (by providing what is described as 'employee liability information');
   - special provisions making it easier for insolvent businesses to be transferred to a new employer;
   - provisions which clarify the ability of employers and employees to agree to vary contracts of employment in circumstances where a relevant transfer occurs;
   - provisions which clarify the circumstances under which it is unfair for employers to dismiss employees for reasons connected with a relevant transfer.

   The Regulations were amended by the Collective Redundancies and Transfer of Undertakings (Protection of Employment) (Amendment) Regulations 2014 (SI 2014/14) which came into force on 31 January 2014.

B: The Transfer of Undertakings (Protection of Employment) Regulations 2006

The main effect of the regulations is that on a business transfer:

(a) the contracts of employment together with employment rights are automatically transferred to the new owner, thereby completely changing the common law position (reg. 4) and making the EPCA 1978, s. 94 redundant (hence its eventual and long overdue repeal by the Trade Union Reform and Employment Rights Act (TURERA) 1993);

(b) dismissal connected with the sale of a business may be automatically unfair (reg. 7);

(c) duties to inform and consult with employee representatives arise (regs. 13–16).

The House of Lords has made it clear in a number of cases that the regulations will be applied having regard to a purposive interpretation of the EC directive. Any ambiguity in the regulations will be resolved by recourse to the directive and European Court interpretations thereof. Indeed, as will be seen, the regulations have been amended where European Court decisions have thrown up any inconsistency between the directive and the regulations.

The European Court of Justice has held that the contract is automatically transferred to the new owner only if the employee so consents (see *Katsikas* v *Konstantinidis* [1993] IRLR 179 at p. 528 (Section B(iii)).

(i) The scope of the regulations

TRANSFER OF UNDERTAKINGS (PROTECTION OF EMPLOYMENT) REGULATIONS 2006 (SI 2006/246) (as amended)

3 A relevant transfer

(1) These Regulations apply to—

  (a) a transfer of an undertaking, business or part of an undertaking or business situated immediately before the transfer in the United Kingdom to another person where there is a transfer of an economic entity which retains its identity;

  (b) a service provision change, that is a situation in which—

    (i) activities cease to be carried out by a person ('a client') on his own behalf and are carried out instead by another person on the client's behalf ('a contractor');

    (ii) activities cease to be carried out by a contractor on a client's behalf (whether or not those activities had previously been carried out by the client on his own behalf) and are carried out instead by another person ('a subsequent contractor') on the client's behalf; or

    (iii) activities cease to be carried out by a contractor or a subsequent contractor on a client's behalf (whether or not those activities had previously been carried out by the client on his own behalf) and are carried out instead by the client on his own behalf,

  (c) and in which the conditions set out in paragraph (3) are satisfied.

(2) In this regulation 'economic entity' means an organised grouping of resources which has the objective of pursuing an economic activity, whether or not that activity is central or ancillary.

(2A) References in paragraph (1)(b) to activities being carried out instead by another person (including the client) are to activities which are fundamentally the same as the activities carried out by the person who has ceased to carry them out.

(3) The conditions referred to in paragraph (1)(b) are that—

  (a) immediately before the service provision change—

    (i) there is an organised grouping of employees situated in Great Britain which has as its principal purpose the carrying out of the activities concerned on behalf of the client;

    (ii) the client intends that the activities will, following the service provision change, be carried out by the transferee other than in connection with a single specific event or task of short-term duration; and

  (b) the activities concerned do not consist wholly or mainly of the supply of goods for the client's use.

(4) Subject to paragraph (1), these Regulations apply to—

  (a) public and private undertakings engaged in economic activities whether or not they are operating for gain;

  (b) a transfer or service provision change howsoever effected notwithstanding—

(i) that the transfer of an undertaking, business or part of an undertaking or business is governed or effected by the law of a country or territory outside the United Kingdom or that the service provision change is governed or effected by the law of a country or territory outside Great Britain;

(ii) that the employment of persons employed in the undertaking, business or part transferred or, in the case of a service provision change, persons employed in the organised grouping of employees, is governed by any such law;

(c) a transfer of an undertaking, business or part of an undertaking or business (which may also be a service provision change) where persons employed in the undertaking, business or part transferred ordinarily work outside the United Kingdom.

(5) An administrative reorganisation of public administrative authorities or the transfer of administrative functions between public administrative authorities is not a relevant transfer.

(6) A relevant transfer—

(a) may be effected by a series of two or more transactions; and

(b) may take place whether or not any property is transferred to the transferee by the transferor.

(7) Where, in consequence (whether directly or indirectly) of the transfer of an undertaking, business or part of an undertaking or business which was situated immediately before the transfer in the United Kingdom, a ship within the meaning of the Merchant Shipping Act 1995 registered in the United Kingdom ceases to be so registered, these Regulations shall not affect the right conferred by section 29 of that Act (right of seamen to be discharged when ship ceases to be registered in the United Kingdom) on a seaman employed in the ship.

NOTES

1. Under the regulations and the directive, there 'must be a transfer of an economic entity which retains its identity'. The *economic entity* concept was defined by the ECJ in *Spijkers* v *Gebroeders Benedik Abattor CV* [1986] 2 CMLR 296:

> [T]he decisive criterion for establishing the existence of a transfer within the meaning of the directive is whether the entity in question retains its identity.
>
> Consequently, it cannot be said that there is a transfer of an enterprise, business or part of a business on the sole ground that its assets have been sold. On the contrary, in a case like the present, it is necessary to determine whether what has been sold is an economic entity which is still in existence, and this will be apparent from the fact that its operation is actually being continued or has been taken over by the new employer, with the same economic or similar activities.
>
> To decide whether these conditions are fulfilled, it is necessary to take account of all the factual circumstances of the transaction in question, including the type of undertaking or business in question, the transfer or otherwise of tangible assets such as buildings and stocks, the value of intangible assets at the date of transfer, whether the majority of the staff are taken over by the new employer, the transfer or otherwise of the circle of customers and the degree of similarity between activities before and after the transfer and the duration of any interruption of those activities. It should be made clear, however, that each of these factors is only a part of the overall assessment which is required and therefore they cannot be examined independently of each other.
>
> ... [I]t is necessary to consider whether, having regard to all the facts characterising the transaction, the business was disposed of as a going concern, as would be indicated inter alia by the fact that its operation was actually continued or resumed by the new employer, with the same or similar activities...

2. Regulation 3(5) states that: 'An administrative reorganisation of public administrative authorities or the transfer of administrative functions between public administrative authorities is not a relevant transfer.' *Scattolon* v *Ministero dell'Istruzione, dell'Università e della Ricerca* [2011] IRLR 1020 was an Italian reference to the Court of Justice of the European Union (CJEU) arising out of the transfer of school cleaners from employment by local authorities to employment by national government. The Italian Government questioned whether this amounted to a transfer of an undertaking for the purposes of the European directive. In finding that there was a relevant transfer, the CJEU held that the exclusion from the scope of the directive in respect of the reorganisation of public administration is limited to cases where the transfer concerns 'activities which fall within the exercise of public powers'. It stated that there would be no justification for creating a wider exception.

3. The original definition of 'undertaking' excluded non-commercial undertakings. TURERA 1993, s. 33(2) introduced an amendment in order to bring the regulations into line with the directive as interpreted by the European Court of Justice (ECJ) in the *Redmond* case in the following extract (see now reg. 3(4)(a)).

4. Neither the regulations nor the directive apply to transfers by way of share sales. This is because both regulations and directive refer specifically to a change of employer. In 1974, the original proposal for the Acquired Rights Directive encompassed share transfer cases, but following negotiations its scope was narrowed. Share transfer was and remains one of the most frequent mechanisms for takeovers in the UK, and although there is no change in legal personality of the employer, it may have as serious consequences for employees as a business transfer carried through by other means. This is underlined by *Brookes* v *Borough Care Services* [1998] IRLR 636, EAT. In this case, a transfer had been arranged of certain care homes, on the basis that there would be a transfer under the regulations, but that the transferees would renegotiate terms and conditions with the staff concerned. When the legality of the agreed variation of terms and conditions was called into question by *Wilson* v *St Helens BC* (see p. (Section B(iii))), it was agreed to seek to avoid the regulations by rearranging matters so as to effect the transfer by the transferee acquiring shares in the transferor instead. In spite of the fact that this device had been adopted to avoid liability, the EAT refused to lift the corporate veil.

The House of Lords Select Committee on the European Communities, with the support of the trade unions and despite opposition from the CBI, recommended that takeovers by share transfer should be brought within the scope of the directive (HL 38, Session 1995–6, paras. 34–8). However, the Government did not support the Select Committee's proposal and the EU Commission did not propose extending the scope of the law to cover share transfers in any of its draft of the amending directive.

However, in *Millam* v *The Print Factory (London) 1991 Ltd* [2007] IRLR 526, the Court of Appeal took the view that the mere fact that there has been a transfer of shares does not prevent a finding that there has been a TUPE transfer. According to Buxton LJ: 'the question is whether as a matter of fact the business in which the claimant is employed has been transferred from company to another', and that 'the legal structure is of course important, but it cannot be conclusive in deciding the issue of whether, within that legal structure, control of the business has been transferred as a matter of fact.'

As Rubenstein states: 'This case suggests, therefore, that on appropriate facts, even if there is share transfer, the employees of the company acquired can be regarded as transferring to the purchaser under a TUPE transfer if the purchaser assumes subsequently effective control of the company. With respect, merely stating that proposition reveals its deficiencies. TUPE imposes rights and obligations which operate before and at the time of the transfer. Whether there is a TUPE transfer should not be dependent upon how decisions are taken in the weeks and months following the transaction' ('Highlights' [2007] IRLR 467).

Dr Sophie Redmond Stichting v Bartol
[1992] IRLR 366, European Court of Justice

The applicant ran a foundation in Holland which gave assistance to drug addicts. It was originally funded by grants from the local authority, which also provided premises. As from January 1991, those grants were given instead to the Sigma Foundation. The lease of the Redmond building was transferred to Sigma, and Sigma were content to keep on some of the Redmond employees but not all. If the directive applied, then Sigma were bound to take on all the Redmond employees. In accordance with Dutch law, Redmond applied for permission to terminate the contracts of those employees not required by Sigma. Whether that could happen was referred by the national court to the ECJ, which held that transactions arising out of subsidies to foundations or associations whose services were not remunerated (i.e. non-commercial undertakings) *were* covered by the directive.

On the concept of 'legal transfer'

It should be recalled that in its judgment of 7 February 1985, *Abels* (135/83, Rep. p. 469, points 11–13), the Court held that the scope of the provision of the Directive at issue cannot be appraised solely on the basis of a textual interpretation because of the differences between the various language versions of that provision and because of the divergencies between the national legislation defining the concept of a contractual transfer.

In consequence the Court gave a sufficiently broad interpretation to that concept to give effect to the purpose of the Directive, which is to ensure that the rights of employees are protected in the event of a transfer of their undertaking, and held that that Directive was applicable wherever, in the context of contractual relations, there is a change in the legal or natural person who is responsible for carrying on the business and who incurs the obligations of an employer towards employees of the undertaking (see most recently the judgment of 15 June 1988, *Bork International* [1989] IRLR 41, 13.

In particular, the Court has held that the scope of the Directive covers the leasing of an establishment followed by the rescinding of that lease and the taking over of the operation by the owner herself (judgment of 17 December 1987, *Ny Molle Kro*, 287/86, [1989] IRLR 37 ECJ, the leasing of a restaurant followed by the rescinding of that lease and the conclusion of a new lease with a new lessee (judgment of 10 February 1988, *Daddy's Dance Hall*, 324/86, [1988] IRLR 315 ECJ) and finally the transfer of a bar-discotheque by means of a lease-purchase agreement and the restoration of the undertaking to its owner as the result of a judicial decision (judgment of 5 May 1988, *Berg*, 144/87 and 145/87 [1989] IRLR 447 ECJ).

As is stressed in the judgment of 15 June 1988 (*Bork*, cited above, point 14), where a lessee who is also the employer ceases to be the employer and a third party becomes the employer thereafter under a contract of sale concluded with the owner, the resulting transaction may fall within the scope of the Directive as defined in Article 1(1) thereof. The fact that in such a case the transfer is effected in two stages, in as much as the undertaking is first returned from the lessee to the owner and the latter then transfers it to the new owner, does not prevent the Directive from applying.

As described in the Order for reference, the transaction to which the preliminary questions put by the Kantonrechter of Groningen relate is governed by comparable reasoning. This is in fact a situation in which a local authority which finances, by a subsidy, the activities of a foundation engaged in providing assistance to drug dependants, decides to terminate this subsidy, as a result of which the activities of that foundation are terminated, in order to switch the subsidy to another foundation pursuing the same activities.

It is true that the judge making the reference asks, in his sixth question, whether the fact that the decision to make the switch is taken unilaterally by the public body, and does not result from an agreement concluded by it with the body subsidised, prevents the Directive from applying in this case.

This question must be answered in the negative.

On the one hand, there is a unilateral decision just as much where an owner decides to change a new lessee as when a public body alters its policy on subsidies. In this respect, the nature of the subsidy, which is granted by a unilateral act accompanied by certain conditions in some Member States, and by subsidy agreements in others, cannot be taken into account. In all cases, the change of the beneficiary of the subsidy takes place in the context of a contractual relationship within the meaning of the Directive and of the case law (judgments of 5 May 1988, *Berg*, cited above, point 19; and of 15 June 1988, *Bork*, cited above, points 13 and 14). Furthermore, although the Redmond foundation disputes in its observations submitted to the Court that agreements had been concluded, the Kantonrechter expressly states in the grounds of its Order that 'the plaintiff, just as much as the Sigma foundation, has declared itself ready to collaborate actively on the "transfer" of the clients/patients of the plaintiff to the Sigma foundation, to which end a working group for the "incorporation of the activities of the Redmond foundation into the Sigma foundation" has, furthermore, been set up.'

On the other hand, as is stressed, moreover, by the Commission in its observations, the fact that, in the present case, the transaction arises out of the grant of subsidies to foundations or associations whose services are not remunerated, does not exclude this transaction from the scope of the Directive. In fact, this Directive, as has been noted, has the object of guaranteeing the rights of employees, and it applies to all employees who are covered by protection against dismissal, even if it be limited, under national law…

NOTES

1. There must be a transfer of the 'business'. A distinction has been drawn between a sale of the whole business as opposed to a sale of all or part of its assets. Such a distinction had already been drawn for the purposes of deciding the extent of an applicant's continuity of employment under the 1996 Act generally. Those cases are, therefore, applicable here.

2. Article 3(1) of the directive stipulates that not only the transferor's rights and obligations 'arising from a contract of employment' shall transfer, but also those 'from an employment relationship'. In this sense Article 3(1) is wider than reg. 4, which appears to limit the effect of the transfer to rights and duties under or in connection with 'a contract of employment'. This raises the question of whether statutory rights are covered and demonstrates the need to retain the statutory provision set out next.

EMPLOYMENT RIGHTS ACT 1996

218. Change of employer

(1) Subject to the provisions of this section, this Chapter relates only to employment by the one employer.

(2) If a trade or business, or an undertaking (whether or not established by or under an Act), is transferred from one person to another—

    (a) the period of employment of an employee in the trade or business or undertaking at the time of the transfer counts as a period of employment with the transferee, and

    (b) the transfer does not break the continuity of the period of employment.

NOTE: In *Astley* v *Celtec Ltd* [2002] IRLR 629, the Court of Appeal held that the wording of the EC Acquired Rights Directive is sufficiently wide in its terms to embrace a transfer of an undertaking which takes place over a period, and does not imply that the transfer must take place at a moment in time. Once it is accepted that a business can be transferred over a period of time, the establishment of the period of time during which the transfer takes place is a task for the tribunal of fact.

In this case, civil servants employed by the Department of Employment were seconded for three years to a Training and Enterprise Council (TEC) when, in September 1990, the TEC took over the Department's training and enterprise role. In mid-1993, they opted to become employees of the TEC. In 1998, a redundancy situation arose, and the question arose as to whether the applicants could count their previous employment with the Department of Employment. This depended on when the TUPE transfer took place. If it took place over a number of years via a series of transactions and was not complete until each of the secondees from the civil service transferred to become employees of the TEC, then the applicants were employed by the transferor at the time of the transfer. This was the view taken by the employment tribunal, the Court of Appeal and the Advocate-General. However, if there was a precise date for the transfer to have taken place—September 1990, according to the EAT—then they did not transfer their employment to the TEC and remained Department of Employment employees for a further three years post-transfer. The ECJ ruling is in line with the EAT's analysis: that continuity of employment was not preserved when the civil servants transferred to the TEC (*Celtec* v *Astley and others*, C–478/03 [2005] IRLR 647). In a somewhat surprising and, no doubt, purposive judgment, the House of Lords ([2006] IRLR 635) held that the continuity of the claimants was preserved by virtue of the EC Business Transfers Directive despite the fact that they did not resign from the civil service until three years after the date of the transfer. The House of Lords held that the general rule is that contracts of employment of workers assigned to the undertaking transferred are automatically transferred from the transferor to the transferee on the date of the transfer. The sole exception to that rule is that it is open to an employee whose contract of employment would otherwise be transferred automatically from the transferor to the transferee on the date of the transfer of his own free will to withdraw from this arrangement by declining to enter the employment of the transferee. Application of that rule depends on the employee being in a position to choose whether or not to enter the employment of the transferee after the date of transfer, and on the employee in fact exercising that choice by deciding of his own free will not to do so.

In the instant case, the sole reservation to the general rule did not apply. The claimants were in a position on or after the date of transfer to choose of their own free will not to work for the transferees, but they did not make that choice. They continued to do the same work after the transfer of the undertaking, albeit that they believed that they remained in the employment of the transferors. That led inevitably to the conclusion that their contracts of employment were transferred automatically to the transferees with continuity on the date of transfer.

Melon v Hector Powe Ltd
[1981] ICR 43, House of Lords

Hector Powe had factories in both England and Scotland. In 1977, Hector Powe decided to sell the Scottish factory to Executex. The sale included the assignment of the factory lease, plant and machinery, and the taking over of work in progress by the purchaser. There was also a clause requiring the purchaser to take on the employees of the factory on similar terms. The employees were taken on by the purchaser but brought a claim for redundancy payments against Hector Powe, their former employer. The House of Lords held that their claim should succeed.

LORD ELWYN JONES: ... The following finding by the industrial tribunal seems to me to be of some significance in considering the question before us:

It is fair to say, therefore, that the factory at Blantyre before the take-over by Executex, was employed solely in providing garments for sale by the [appellants] and their associated company [Willerby]. After the take-over, however, a different situation prevailed at Blantyre. Executex made garments of a different quality from those made by Hector Powe Ltd. They are in business to manufacture garments on a CMT ['cut, make and trim'] basis for whatever customers they can attract.

Counsel for the appellants argued that there were no factors which could have been taken to show that this was a mere sale of assets. I cannot agree. One such factor was the difference between the business of the appellants and that of Executex which I have already mentioned and which the industrial tribunal said had impressed them. Another was the absence of any transfer to Executex of the right to use the appellants' name or of any general transfer of assets and liabilities. There was ample material upon which the industrial tribunal was entitled to take the view they did that the Blantyre factory was not transferred to Executex as a going concern. No doubt it was open to the tribunal to have taken the opposite view, but that is nothing to the point.

The appeal must, therefore, fail, unless it can be shown that the industrial tribunal made some error of law in reaching their decision. They are said to have erred by applying the wrong test in asking themselves whether this was a transfer of a going concern. I do not agree. It seems to me that the essential distinction between the transfer of a business, or part of a business, and a transfer of physical assets, is that in the former case the business is transferred as a going concern 'so that the business remains the same business but in different hands'—if I may quote from Lord Denning MR in *Lloyd* v *Brassey* [1969] 2 QB 98, 103 in a passage quoted by the industrial tribunal—whereas in the latter case the assets are transferred to the new owner to be used in whatever business he chooses. Individual employees may continue to do the same work in the same environment and they may not appreciate that they are working in a different business, but that may be the true position on consideration of the whole circumstances.

NOTE: See also *Woodhouse* v *Peter Brotherhood Ltd* [1972] ICR 186, CA.

(ii) Contracting-out of services

(a) *The position prior to the 2006 Regulations*
Considerable uncertainty surrounded the question of the extent to which the contracting-out of services was covered by the Acquired Rights Directive and the Transfer of Undertakings (Protection of Employment) Regulations 1981.

Rask and Christensen v ISS Kantineservice A/S
[1993] IRLR 133, European Court of Justice

Rask and Christensen were employed in Philips's factory in Denmark as canteen assistants. Philips decided to contract out the running of the canteen to the defendants, ISS, who agreed to offer employment on the same pay to Philips canteen employees. The plaintiffs complained that the date of their monthly salary payment was altered and also that they no longer received shoe and laundry allowances. On announcing that she would not accept the movement of her payment day, Rask was dismissed and claimed unfair dismissal by ISS. The question for the ECJ was whether the contracting-out of a service for employees amounted to a transfer of an undertaking within the meaning of the directive. The ECJ found that there was a transfer.

The defendant in the main proceedings is of the opinion that, on the contrary, an agreement such as that described by the judge making the reference does not constitute a 'transfer of an undertaking' within the meaning of the Directive, unless one is to give to the Directive an excessively broad scope. It maintains, on the one hand, that an agreement of this type does not effect any transfer within the meaning intended by the Directive since it does not confer on the other contracting party either full and entire responsibility for the provision of the services, particularly insofar as the customers and the fixing of prices is concerned, nor ownership of the assets necessary for the provision of these services. It maintains, on the other hand, that an agreement such as this relates to services which cannot be called 'an undertaking' within the meaning of the Directive, taking into account the fact that they are ancillary to the activity of the transferor.

According to the case law of the Court (see the judgment of 5 May 1988, *Berg*, 144/87 and 145/87 [1989] IRLR 447 paragraph 18), the Directive is applicable in any case where, following a legal transfer or merger, there is a change in the legal or natural person who is responsible for carrying on the business and who by virtue of that fact incurs the obligation of an employer vis à vis the employees of the undertaking, regardless of whether or not ownership of the undertaking is transferred.

Under Article 1(1), the protection provided by the Directive applies, in particular, where the transfer only concerns a business or part of a business, that is to say a part of an undertaking. It therefore concerns the employees assigned to that part of the undertaking since, as the Court held in its judgment of 7 February 1985, *Botzen* (186/83, Rep. p. 519, point 15), the employment relationship is essentially characterised by the link existing between the employee and the part of the undertaking to which he is assigned to carry out his duties.

Thus, where the owner of an undertaking entrusts, by means of an agreement, the responsibility for providing a service to his undertaking, such as a canteen, to the owner of another undertaking who assumes, by reason of it, the obligations of an employer vis à vis the employees who are engaged in the provisions of that service, the resulting transaction is capable of falling within the scope of the Directive as defined in Article 1(1). The fact that, in such a case, the activity transferred is only an ancillary activity of the transferor undertaking not necessarily related to its objects cannot have the effect of excluding that transaction from the scope of the Directive. Similarly, the fact that the agreement between the transferor and the transferee relates to the provision of services provided exclusively for the benefit of the transferor in return for a fee, the form of which is fixed by the agreement, does not prevent the Directive from applying either.

It is for the national judge to assess whether all the factual circumstances as described in his Order for Reference are characteristic of a 'transfer of an undertaking' within the meaning of the Directive. That is why, as a point of information, he should be reminded that he must take into account the following considerations (see, most recently, the judgment of 19 May 1992, *Redmond*, C-29/91 [1992] IRLR 366 at p. 369 paragraphs 23 and 24).

On the one hand, the decisive criterion for establishing whether there is a transfer within the meaning of the Directive is whether the business retains its identity, as would be indicated, in particular, by the fact that its operation was either continued or resumed.

On the other hand, in order to determine whether those conditions are fulfilled, it is necessary to consider all the factual circumstances characterising the transaction in question, including the type of undertaking or business concerned, whether the business's tangible assets, such as buildings and movable property, are transferred, the value of its intangible assets at the time of the transfer, whether or not the majority of its employees are taken over by the new employer, whether or not its customers are transferred and the degree of similarity between the activities carried on before and after the transfer and the period, if any, for which those activities are suspended. It should be noted, however, that all those circumstances are merely single factors in the overall assessment which must be made and cannot therefore be considered in isolation.

NOTE: In *Kenny* v *South Manchester College* [1993] IRLR 265, Queen's Bench Division, prior to April 1993, the Home Office honoured its obligation to provide education in prisons by using teaching staff supplied by the local education authority. From April 1993, those educational services were to be put out for competitive tender to further education colleges now trading as private corporations. The plaintiff had been employed by Cheshire County Council as a lecturer at a young offenders' institution, but the contract to do such work was won by the defendant, South Manchester College. The plaintiff successfully sought a declaration to the effect that his contract would automatically transfer from the county council to the South Manchester College by virtue of the directive.

Kenny was approved and supported by the Court of Appeal when applying the regulations in the following case.

Dines and others v Initial Health Care Services and another
[1994] IRLR 336, Court of Appeal

Twelve cleaners were originally employed by Initial Health Care Services to provide cleaning services at a hospital pursuant to a contract gained by Initial from the Area Health Authority. This contract expired on 30 April 1991 and, with effect from 1 May 1991, was awarded to Pall Mall Services (the second respondent). Having failed to obtain the contract, Initial dismissed their 12 employees on the grounds of redundancy. The employees commenced work with Pall Mall at the same hospital as from 1 May 1991 but at a lower rate of pay. They argued successfully before the Appeal Court that this was a transfer within the Transfer of Undertakings Regulations and, therefore, that Pall Mall were obliged to take over the contract of employment from Initial on exactly the same terms as to salary.

NEILL LJ: ...I have come to the conclusion that the approach of the Industrial Tribunal indicated by the penultimate sentence in paragraph 10 amounts to a misdirection. I should repeat this passage:

> However, when one company enters into competition with a number of other companies to obtain a contract, as happened in this case, and a different company wins the contract from the company that was previously providing the services, then this is a cessation of the business of the first contractors on the hospital premises and the commencement of a new business by [Pall Mall] when they are awarded the contract.

The European cases demonstrate that the fact that another company takes over the provision of certain services as a result of competitive tendering does not mean that the first business or undertaking necessarily comes to an end. Moreover, as was pointed out in the decision in *Daddy's Dance Hall* [1988] IRLR 315 and elsewhere, a transfer may take place in two phases.

I have given careful consideration to whether this passage in paragraph 10 can be interpreted as merely a decision on the facts and no more. It seems to me, however, that with the words 'when one company enters into competition with a number of other companies to obtain a contract, as happened in this case ...' the Industrial Tribunal was in effect applying a general proposition to the facts of the case. In my judgment the general proposition does not accord with the approach of the European Court.

In these circumstances, I would be disposed to allow the appeal because this misdirection was of fundamental importance.

In some cases this would mean that the matter would have to go back to be reheard by another Industrial Tribunal to reach a conclusion on the particular facts. In the present case, however, there is the special feature that the facts were not in dispute before the Industrial Tribunal and therefore it seems to me that this Court is in as good a position as was the Industrial Tribunal to reach a conclusion. It is true that we do not know what type of equipment was used for the cleaning of the hospital, and it may be that some changes in cleaning methods were introduced by Pall Mall when they took over. Hospital cleaning, however, though of the utmost importance, is not an operation which lends itself to the employment of many different techniques. The cleaning services were to be carried out by (mainly) the same staff on the same premises and for the same authority.

I consider that on the agreed facts there was a transfer of an undertaking for the purpose of the 1981 Regulations. It took place in two phases—(a) the handing back by Initial to the authority on 30 April of the cleaning services at the hospital; and (b) the grant or handing over by the authority to Pall Mall on 1 May of the cleaning services which were operated as from that date by essentially the same labour force.

NOTES

1. Following *Dines*, cases have extended the meaning of a 'relevant transfer'. In *Betts v Brintel Helicopters and KLM* [1996] IRLR 45, Brintel had, until 1995, exclusive rights to service Shell's helicopter requirements for all their North Sea oil rigs. In 1995, Shell decided to split the contract between Brintel and KLM, and 66 Brintel employees were left without jobs. Betts and six others claimed, successfully, that they were now employed by KLM. The High Court held that there had been a transfer of the 'activity' from Brintel to KLM even though there was no transfer of employees or assets. However, the Court of Appeal ([1997] IRLR 361) subsequently decided that because no employees were transferred, nor any tangible assets, there was no relevant transfer. Thus the employees working for the contractor who lost the contract received no protection from the Transfer Regulations.

   In *Porter v Queens Medical Centre* [1993] IRLR 486, a transfer of paediatric and neo-natal services from two district health authorities to an NHS trust was held to be a relevant transfer.

2. In *Schmidt*, Case C–392/92 [1994] IRLR 302, the ECJ held that the contracting-out of cleaning involving one person amounted to a protected transfer under the directive. This case provides a literal interpretation and suggests that the transfer of an entity which retains its economic identity could be found in circumstances in which no assets, tangible or intangible, were transferred, but simply the performance of an identifiable business function.

   In *Rynda (UK) Ltd.* v *Rhijnsburger* [2015] EWCA Civ. 75, the CA held that a commercial manager, solely responsible for managing a group of Dutch properties for a client, was an 'organised grouping of workers' for the pupeses of reg. 3(3)(a)(i) of the TUPE Regulations. Although she worked alone, she was effectively a one-person department and the employer had deliberately allocated to her the Dutch properties. The fact that she had, in the past, assumed some responsibilities for other properties did not undermine this, as she had always devoted the majority of her time to the Dutch properties, and so the 'principal purpose' test was satisfied.

A case that appeared possibly to be bucking this trend towards a very wide interpretation of what is a relevant transfer is:

Rygaard v *Strø Mølle Akustik A/S*
[1996] IRLR 51, European Court of Justice

Rygaard had been employed by Pedersen, a firm of carpenters in Denmark. Pedersen had a contract to build a canteen for SAS. SAS agreed to let Pedersen give the responsibility for completing part of the canteen to the respondents. On 1 February 1992, Pedersen told Rygaard that they intended winding up their company and that his employment would end in three months' time. In the meantime Rygaard was told to work with the respondents on the completion of the canteen, which he did until he was dismissed by them in May 1992. Had there been a relevant transfer so that Rygaard could bring wrongful dismissal proceedings against the respondents? The ECJ held that there was *not* a relevant transfer.

DECISION: ...

Is Council Directive 77/187/EEC applicable when contractor B, pursuant to an agreement with contractor A, continues part of building works began by contractor A, and

(i) an agreement is made between contractor A and contractor B under which some of contractor A's workers are to continue working for contractor B and contractor B is to take over materials on the building site in order to complete the contracted work; and

(ii) after the taking over, there is a period in which contractor A and contractor B are both working on the building works at the same time?

Does it make any difference that the agreement on the completion of the works is entered into between the awarder of the main building contract and contractor B with contractor A's consent?

By its question the national court is essentially asking whether the taking over, with a view to completing, with the consent of the awarder of the main building contract, works started by another undertaking, of two apprentices and an employee, together with the materials assigned to those works, constitutes a transfer of an undertaking business or part of a business, within the meaning of Article 1(1) of the Directive.

According to the Court's case law, it is clear from the scheme of the Directive and from the terms of Article 1(1) thereof that the Directive is intended to ensure continuity of employment relationships existing within a business, irrespective of any change of ownership. It follows that the decisive criterion for establishing whether there is a transfer for the purposes of the Directive is whether the business in question retains its identity (see, in particular, the judgment in case 24/85 *Spijkers* v *Benedik* [1986] ECR 1119, paragraph 11).

According to that same judgment in order to ascertain whether that criterion is satisfied, it is necessary to consider whether the operation of the entity in question is actually continued or resumed by the new employer, with the same or similar economic activities (*Spijkers* v *Benedik*, paragraph 12).

It is then necessary to consider all the facts characterising the transaction in question, including the type of undertaking or business concerned, whether or not tangible assets, such as buildings and moveable property, are transferred, the value of the intangible assets at the time of the transfer, whether or not most of the personnel are taken over by the new employer, whether or not customers are transferred and the degree of similarity between the activities carried on before and after the transfer and the period of any suspension of those activities. All those circumstances are, however, only individual factors in the overall assessment to be made and they cannot therefore be considered in isolation (*Spijkers* v *Benedik*, paragraph 13).

Mr Rygaard considers that those conditions are satisfied in the present case. He observes that the works taken over by Strø Mølle are the same as those which had been entrusted to Svend Pedersen A/S and that the duration of the works cannot be decisive in determining whether a transfer of an undertaking, within the meaning of the Directive, has taken place, just as the scale of the activity transferred was not held to be decisive in *Schmidt* v *Spar-und Leihkasse des früheren Ämter Bordesholm, Kiel und Cronshagen*, C–392/92 [1994] IRLR 302.

That argument cannot be accepted.

The authorities cited above presuppose that the transfer relates to a stable economic entity whose activity is not limited to performing one specific works contract.

That is not the case of an undertaking which transfers to another undertaking one of its building works with a view to the completion of that work. Such a transfer could come within the terms of the Directive only if it included the transfer of a body of assets enabling the activities or certain activities of the transferor undertaking to be carried on in a stable way.

That is not so where, as in the case now referred, the transferor undertaking merely makes available to the new contractor certain workers and material for carrying out the works in question.

The reply to the question submitted must therefore be that the taking over—with a view to completing, with the consent of the awarder of the main building contract, works started by another undertaking—of two apprentices and an employee, together with the materials assigned to those works, does not constitute a transfer of an undertaking, business or part of a business, within the meaning of Article 1(1) of the Directive.

NOTE: That the approach in *Rygaard* was to be limited was made clear in *BSG Services* v *Tuck* [1996] IRLR 134, in which Tuck and 13 others were employed by Mid-Bedfordshire District Council as housing maintenance personnel. On 12 February 1993, the council terminated Tuck's employment (effective 15 May 1993), and on 14 May 1993 it concluded a contract with BSG whereby the latter was to provide the housing maintenance services. BSG intended to use self-employed contractors and did not employ Tuck or any of the other applicants. The EAT agreed that there had been a transfer to BSG and that they were liable to Tuck for unfair dismissal.

Mummery J held that *Rygaard* did not alter the general approach in *Dines* and that the *Rygaard* principle is limited to 'activities under a short-term one-off contract'.

The following ECJ case endorses the view that *Rygaard* is of limited application:

Merckx and Neuhuys v Ford Motor Co. Belgium

[1996] IRLR 467, European Court of Justice

Merckx and Neuhuys were employed as car salesmen by Anfo Motors, a Ford dealership in which Ford was the principal shareholder (and who took over defence of the action when Anfo went into liquidation). In 1987 Anfo decided to end the dealership and Ford transferred it to Novarobel—an independent dealer—as from November 1987. No tangible assets were transferred to Novarobel, but Anfo recommended its services to its old customers. Although three-quarters of Anfo's staff were dismissed, the applicants' jobs were to be transferred to Novarobel. The applicants refused to transfer to Novarobel because they were concerned that their level of remuneration would be reduced. They brought proceedings against Anfo (now Ford) claiming breach of contract. The ECJ held that there was a transfer of the undertaking to Novarobel even though there was no contractual link between the two dealers, no tangible assets passed between them, and the dealership was carried on by Novarobel under a different name, from different premises, and with different facilities. The applicants' objection to transfer meant that Anfo (Ford) had terminated their contract pursuant to Article 4(2) of the directive (see *Katsikas'* case in Section (iii)).

DECISION: …In order to determine whether that condition is met, it is necessary to consider all the facts characterising the transaction in question, including the type of undertaking or business, whether or not the business's tangible assets, such as buildings and movable property, are transferred, the value of its intangible assets at the time of the transfer, whether or not the majority of its employees is taken over by the new employer, whether or not its customers are transferred and the degree of similarity between the activities carried on before and after the transfer and the period, if any, for which those activities were suspended. It should be noted, however, that all those circumstances are merely single factors in the overall assessment which must be made and cannot therefore be considered in isolation (judgment in case C–29/91 *Redmond Stichting*, cited above, paragraph 24).

In the light of those principles, the Court notes that in the situation with which the main proceedings are concerned Ford, the main shareholder in Anfo Motors, transferred to Novarobel the dealership for the sale of vehicles in the territory covered by Anfo Motors and so transferred the economic risk associated with that business to an undertaking outside its own group of companies, that Novarobel carried on the activity performed by Anfo Motors, without interruption, in the same sector and subject to similar conditions, that it took on part of its staff and that it was recommended to customers in order to ensure continuity in the operation of the dealership.

All those factors, taken as a whole, support the view that the transfer of the dealership in the circumstances of the main proceedings is capable of falling within the scope of the Directive. It must be ascertained, however, whether certain factors relied on by Mr Merckx and Mr Neuhuys may rebut that finding.

First, Mr Merckx and Mr Neuhuys claimed that in the circumstances at issue in the main proceedings there had been neither a transfer of the company's tangible or intangible assets nor at least partial preservation of the undertaking's structure and organisation. Moreover, the municipalities of the Brussels conurbation in which Novarobel has its principal place of business are different from those in which Anfo Motors carried on its business.

Those circumstances are not such as to prevent the application of the Directive, since, having regard to the nature of the activity pursued, the transfer of tangible assets is not conclusive of whether the entity in question retains its economic identity (see to that effect the judgment in case C–392/92 *Schmidt v Spar- und Leihkasse der früheren Ämter Bordesholm, Kiel und Cronshagen* [1994] IRLR 302, paragraph 16). The purpose of an exclusive dealership for the sale of motor vehicles of a particular make in a certain sector remains the same even if it is carried on under a different name, from different premises and with different facilities. It is also irrelevant that the principal place of business is situated in a different area of the same conurbation, provided that the contract territory remains the same.

Secondly, Mr Merckx and Mr Neuhuys claimed that there could not be a transfer for the purposes of the Directive when an undertaking definitively ceased trading and was put into liquidation, as was the case with Anfo Motors. In such circumstances, the economic entity had ceased to exist and could not retain its identity.

In that regard, if the Directive's aim of protecting workers is not to be undermined, its application cannot be excluded merely because the transferor discontinues its activities when the transfer is made and is then put into liquidation. If the business of that undertaking is carried on by another undertaking, those facts tend to confirm, rather, that there has been a transfer for the purposes of the Directive.

Thirdly, Mr Merckx and Mr Neuhuys claimed that the fact that the majority of the staff had been dismissed upon the transfer of the dealership indicated that the Directive did not apply.

Article 4(1) of the Directive provides that the transfer of an undertaking, business or part of the business does not in itself constitute grounds for dismissal. However, that provision is not to stand in the way of dismissals that may take place for economic, technical or organisational reasons entailing changes in the workforce.

Accordingly, the fact that the majority of the staff was dismissed when the transfer took place is not sufficient to preclude the application of the Directive. The dismissals might have taken place for economic, technical or organisational reasons, in compliance with Article 4(1), cited above. In any event, failure to comply with that provision could not affect the existence of a transfer for the purposes of the Directive.

Finally, Mr Merckx and Mr Neuhuys claimed that, even if there had in fact been a transfer for the purposes of the Directive, it was not the result of a legal transfer as required by Article 1 thereof. That concept necessarily required the existence of a contractual link between the transferor and the transferee. There was no such link in the present case.

On account of the differences between the language versions of the Directive and the divergences between the laws of the Member States with regard to the concept of legal transfer, the Court has given that concept a sufficiently flexible interpretation in keeping with the objective of the Directive, which is to safeguard employees in the event of a transfer of their undertaking, and has held that the Directive is applicable wherever, in the context of contractual relations, there is a change in the natural or legal person who is responsible for carrying on the business and who incurs the obligations of an employer towards employees of the undertaking (see, inter alia, the judgment in *Redmond Stichting*, cited above, at paragraphs 10 and 11).

The Court has therefore held that the Directive applies to the termination of a lease of a restaurant followed by the conclusion of a new management contract with another operator (case 324/86 *Foreningen af Arbejdsledere i Danmark v Daddy's Dance Hall* [1988] IRLR 315), the termination of a lease followed by a sale by the owner (case 101/87 *Bork P International A/S v Foreningen af Arbejdsledere i Danmark* [1989] IRLR 41), and also a situation in which a public authority ceases to grant subsidies to a legal person, thereby bringing about the full and definitive termination of its activities in order to transfer them to another legal person with a similar aim (*Redmond Stichting*, cited above).

It is clear from that case law that, for the Directive to apply, it is not necessary for there to be a direct contractual relationship between the transferor and the transferee. Consequently, where a motor vehicle dealership concluded with one undertaking is terminated and a new dealership is awarded to another undertaking pursuing the same activities, the transfer of undertaking is the result of a legal transfer for the purposes of the Directive, as interpreted by the Court.

Furthermore, it is clear from the documents before the Court that the circumstances of the actions brought before the national court are that Ford, the principal shareholder of Anfo Motors, concluded an 'agreement and guarantee' with Novarobel, by which it undertook, inter alia, to bear the expenses relating to certain payments for breach of contract, unlawful dismissal or redundancy which might be payable by Novarobel to members of the staff previously employed by Anfo Motors. That fact confirms that there was a legal transfer within the meaning of the Directive.

Consequently, the answer to the first part of the question as reformulated above must be that Article 1(1) of the Directive must be interpreted as applying where an undertaking holding a motor vehicle dealership for a particular territory discontinues its activities and the dealership is then transferred to another undertaking which takes on part of the staff and is recommended to customers, without any transfer of assets.

The employee's power to prevent the transfer of his contract or the employment relationship

As regards the second part of the question as reformulated above, the Court held in case 105/84 *Foreningen af Arbejdsledere i Danmark* v *Danmols Inventar* [1985] ECR 2639, paragraph 16, that the protection which the Directive is intended to guarantee is redundant where the person concerned decides of his own accord not to continue the employment relationship with the new employer after the transfer.

It also follows from the judgment in joined cases C–132/91, C–138/91 and C–139/91 *Katsikas and others* v *Konstantinidis* [1993] IRLR 179, paragraphs 21 and 32, that, whilst the Directive allows the employee to remain in the employ of his new employer on the same conditions as were agreed with the transferor, it cannot be interpreted as obliging the employee to continue his employment relationship with the transferee. Such an obligation would jeopardise the fundamental rights of the employee who must be free to choose his employer and cannot be obliged to work for an employer whom he has not freely chosen.

It follows that, in the event of the employee deciding of his own accord not to continue with the contract of employment or employment relationship with the transferee, it is for the Member States to determine what the fate of the contract of employment or employment relationship should be. The Member States may provide, in particular, that in such a case the contract of employment or employment relationship must be regarded as terminated either by the employee or by the employer. They may also provide that the contract or employment relationship should be maintained with the transferor (judgment in *Katsikas and others*, cited above, paragraphs 35 and 36).

Mr Merckx and Mr Neuhuys claimed, moreover, that in the case in point Novarobel refused to guarantee to maintain their level of remuneration, which was calculated by reference, in particular, to the turnover achieved.

In the light of that submission, it should be noted that Article 4(2) provides that if the contract of employment or the employment relationship is terminated because the transfer within the meaning of Article 1(1) involves a substantial change in working conditions to the detriment of the employee, the employer is to be regarded as having been responsible for termination.

A change in the level of remuneration awarded to an employee is a substantial change in working conditions within the meaning of that provision, even where the remuneration depends in particular on the turnover achieved. Where the contract of employment or the employment relationship is terminated because the transfer involves such a change, the employer must be regarded as having been responsible for the termination.

Consequently, the answer to the second part of the question as reformulated must be that Article 3(1) of the Directive does not preclude an employee employed by the transferor at the date of the transfer of an undertaking from objecting to the transfer to the transferee of the contract of employment or the employment relationship. In such a case, it is for the Member States to determine what the fate of the contract of employment or employment relationship with the transferor should be. However, where the contract of employment or the employment relationship is terminated on account of a change in the level of remuneration awarded to the employee, Article 4(2) of the Directive requires the Member States to provide that the employer is to be regarded as having been responsible for the termination.

NOTES
1. The 2006 Regulations now specifically exclude short-term 'one off' contracts (see reg. 3(3)(a)(ii)).
2. *Tenco Service Industries SA* v *Imzilyen* [2002] IRLR 214, ECJ was a case involving a change of cleaning contractors at Volkswagen plants in Belgium. The key question before the ECJ was whether there can be a transfer even though there is no contractual link between the two contractors. The ECJ confirmed that 'the absence of a contractual link between the transferor and transferee cannot preclude a transfer within the meaning of the Directive' because a transfer 'can be effected in two successive contracts', i.e. between the principal and the outgoing contractor and the principal and the incoming contractor. According to the ECJ, it is sufficient for a transaction to be 'part of a web of contractual relations'.

Süzen v *Zehnacker Gebaudereinigung GmbH Krankenhausservice*
Case C–13/95 [1997] IRLR 255, European Court of Justice

Zehnacker had a contract to clean a private church-run secondary school in Bonn-Bad-Godesberg. The school terminated the cleaning contract with effect from 30 June 1994 and contracted out its cleaning to Lefarth instead. Mrs Süzen was employed by Zehnacker and, together with seven other cleaners at the school, was dismissed when the employers lost the contract. She claimed that this dismissal was invalid, relying upon Directive 77/187/EEC. The Arbeitsgericht (Labour Court) of Bonn referred the following questions to the European Court of Justice for a preliminary ruling:

1. On the basis of the judgments of the Court of Justice of 14 April 1994 in Case C–92/92 *Schmidt* and 19 May 1992 in Case C–29/91 *Redmond Stichting,* is Directive 77/187/EEC applicable if an undertaking terminates a contract with an outside undertaking in order then to transfer it to another outside undertaking?

2. Is there a legal transfer within the meaning of the directive in the case of the operation described in Question 1 even if no tangible or intangible business assets are transferred?

Advocate-General La Pergola, whose Opinion was delivered on 15 October 1996, gave the following suggested reply:

In the absence of other factors which might affect the situation, the termination of a cleaning contract with one undertaking and the subsequent award of the same contract to another does not fall within the scope of Directive 77/187/CEE.

DECISION: …In *Schmidt*, cited above, the Court held that that provision must be interpreted as covering a situation, such as that outlined in the order for reference, in which an undertaking entrusts by contract to another undertaking the responsibility for carrying out cleaning operations which it previously performed itself, even though, prior to the transfer, such work was carried out by a single employee. Earlier, in *Redmond Stichting*, cited above, the Court took the view in particular that the term 'legal transfer' covers a situation in which a public authority decides to terminate the subsidy paid to one legal person, as a result of which the activities of that legal person are fully and definitively terminated, and to transfer it to another legal person with a similar aim.

By its two questions, which it is appropriate to consider together, the national court asks whether the Directive also applies to a situation in which a person who had entrusted the cleaning of his premises to a first undertaking terminates his contract with the latter and, for the performance of similar work, enters into a new contract with a second undertaking without any concomitant transfer of tangible or intangible business assets from one undertaking to the other.

The aim of the Directive is to ensure continuity of employment relationships within a business, irrespective of any change of ownership. The decisive criterion for establishing the existence of a transfer within the meaning of the Directive is whether the entity in question retains its identity, as indicated inter alia by the fact that its operation is actually continued or resumed (case 24/85 *Spijkers* [1986] ECR 1119,…and, most recently, joined cases C–171/94 and C–172/94 *Merckx and Neuhuys* [1996] IRLR 467…see also the advisory opinion of the Court of the European Free Trade Association of 19 December 1996 in case E-2/96 *Ulstein and Røiseng*, not yet reported…).

Whilst the lack of any contractual link between the transferor and the transferee or, as in this case, between the two undertakings successively entrusted with the cleaning of a school, may point to the absence of a transfer within the meaning of the Directive, it is certainly not conclusive.

As has been held—most recently in *Merckx and Neuhuys*…—the Directive is applicable wherever, in the context of contractual relations, there is a change in the natural or legal person who is responsible for carrying on the business and who incurs the obligations of an employer towards employees of the undertaking. Thus, there is no need, in order for the Directive to be applicable, for there to be any direct contractual relationship between the transferor and the transferee: the transfer may also take place in two stages, through the intermediary of a third party such as the owner or the person putting up the capital.

For the Directive to be applicable, however, the transfer must relate to a stable economic entity whose activity is not limited to performing one specific works contract (case C–48/94 *Rygaard* [1996] IRLR 51. ...The term entity thus refers to an organised grouping of persons and assets facilitating the exercise of an economic activity which pursues a specific objective.

In order to determine whether the conditions for the transfer of an entity are met, it is necessary to consider all the facts characterising the transaction in question, including in particular the type of undertaking or business, whether or not its tangible assets, such as buildings and moveable property, are transferred, the value of its intangible assets at the time of the transfer, whether or not the majority of its employees are taken over by the new employer, whether or not its customers are transferred, the degree of similarity between the activities carried on before and after the transfer, and the period, if any, for which those activities were suspended. However, all those circumstances are merely single factors in the overall assessment which must be made and cannot therefore be considered in isolation (see, in particular, *Spijkers* and *Redmond Stichting* ...).

As observed by most of the parties who commented on this point, the mere fact that the service provided by the old and the new awardees of a contract is similar does not therefore support the conclusion that an economic entity has been transferred. An entity cannot be reduced to the activity entrusted to it. Its identity also emerges from other factors, such as its workforce, its management staff, the way in which its work is organised, its operating methods or indeed, where appropriate, the operational resources available to it.

The mere loss of a service contract to a competitor cannot therefore by itself indicate the existence of a transfer within the meaning of the Directive. In those circumstances, the service undertaking previously entrusted with the contract does not, on losing a customer, thereby cease fully to exist, and a business or part of a business belonging to it cannot be considered to have been transferred to the new awardee of the contract.

It must also be noted that, although the transfer of assets is one of the criteria to be taken into account by the national court in deciding whether an undertaking has in fact been transferred, the absence of such assets does not necessarily preclude the existence of such a transfer (*Schmidt* and *Merckx*, cited above).

As pointed out [above], the national court, in assessing the facts characterising the transaction in question, must take into account among other things the type of undertaking or business concerned. It follows that the degree of importance to be attached to each criterion for determining whether or not there has been a transfer within the meaning of the Directive will necessarily vary according to the activity carried on, or indeed the production or operating methods employed in the relevant undertaking, business or part of a business. Where in particular an economic entity is able, in certain sectors, to function without any significant tangible or intangible assets, the maintenance of its identity following the transaction affecting it cannot, logically, depend on the transfer or such assets.

The United Kingdom Government and the Commission have argued that, for the entity previously entrusted with a service contract to have been the subject of a transfer within the meaning of the Directive, it may be sufficient in certain circumstances for the new awardee of the contract to have voluntarily taken over the majority of the employees specially assigned by his predecessor to the performance of the contract.

In that regard, it should be borne in mind that the factual circumstances to be taken into account in determining whether the conditions for a transfer are met include in particular, in addition to the degree of similarity of the activity carried on before and after the transfer and the type of undertaking or business concerned, the question whether or not the majority of the employees were taken over by the new employer (*Spijkers*, cited above, para. 13).

Since in certain labour-intensive sectors a group of workers engaged in a joint activity on a permanent basis may constitute an economic entity, it must be recognised that such an entity is capable of maintaining its identity after it has been transferred where the new employer does not merely pursue the activity in question but also takes over a major part, in terms of their numbers and skills, of the employees specially assigned by his predecessor to that task. In those circumstances, as stated in paragraph 21 of *Rygaard*, cited above, the new employer takes over a body of assets enabling him to carry on the activities or certain activities of the transferor undertaking on a regular basis.

It is for the national court to establish, in the light of the foregoing interpretative guidance, whether a transfer has occurred in this case.

The answer to the questions from the national court must therefore be that Article 1(1) of the Directive is to be interpreted as meaning that the Directive does not apply to a situation in which a person who had entrusted the cleaning of his premises to a first undertaking terminates his contract with the latter and, for the performance of similar work, enters into a new contract with a second undertaking, if there is no concomitant transfer from one undertaking to the other of significant tangible or intangible assets or taking over by the new employer of a major part of the workforce, in terms of their numbers and skills, assigned to his predecessor to the performance of the contract.

NOTE: According to the ECJ in *Süzen*, an activity does not, in itself, constitute a stable economic entity. Consequently, the ECJ stated, the mere fact that a similar activity is carried on before and after the change of contractors does not mean that there is a transfer of the undertaking. In the case of a labour-intensive undertaking with no significant assets (e.g. contract cleaning) the *Süzen* approach will mean that there will generally be no transfer unless the new contractor takes on the majority of the old contractor's staff (for an example of the UK courts adopting the *Süzen* approach, see *Betts* v *Brintel Helicopters Ltd and KLM ERA Helicopters (UK) Ltd* [1997] IRLR 361).

Süzen is a decision where the court did not attempt to reconcile its decision with the reasoning in *Schmidt*, failed to have regard to the principle of employment protection which underpins the Acquired Rights Directive, and opened up a possible evasion strategy for transferee employers. The decision would appear to leave the contractor with the choice as to whether to be bound by the 1981 Regulations by taking on the majority of the existing staff. Where the existing workforce are unskilled and easily replaceable there is no incentive to assume responsibilities towards them. The workforce are relegated to the status of mere assets. As a result, the weakest members of the labour market—the unskilled—are disenfranchised from the protection of the acquired rights legislation.

More recently, however, in *Francisco Hernandez Vidal SA* v *Gomez Perez and others* [1999] IRLR 132; *Sanchez Hidalgo and others* v *Asociacion De Servicios ASEH and Sociedad Cooperativa Minerva* [1999] IRLR 136, we see a possible softening of the *Süzen* approach, though with no clarity in this regard. The focus in these rulings is on whether 'an economic entity' has been transferred, as opposed to whether a 'major part of the workforce' has been taken over, as in *Süzen*. This approach seems to lay emphasis on what the undertaking looked like pre-transfer rather than post-transfer, and as a result reduces the possibility that a transferee can evade the 1981 Regulations by refusing to engage the employees in the undertaking transferred. In respect of the provision of services, the ECJ holds that 'an organised grouping of wage earners who are specifically and permanently assigned to a common task may, in the absence of other factors of production, amount to an economic entity.'

It is frustrating that these recent rulings do not provide clear guidance. In both decisions, the ECJ adopts word-for-word the tests approved in *Süzen*, an approach cynically characterised by Rubenstein as 'jurisprudence by word processor' ([1999] IRLR 73). Both *Gomez* and *Sanchez* slavishly adopt the *Süzen* test:

> In order to determine/consider whether the conditions for a transfer of an entity are met, it is necessary to consider all the facts characterising the transaction in question, including in particular the type of undertaking or business, whether or not its tangible assets, such as buildings and movable property, are transferred, the value of its intangible assets at the time of the transfer, *whether or not the majority of its employees are taken over by the new employer*, whether or not its customers are transferred on before and after the transfer, and the period, if any, for which those activities were suspended. However, all those circumstances are merely single factors in the overall assessment which must be made and therefore cannot be considered in isolation. [[1999] IRLR 139 at para. 29; *cf.* [1997] IRLR 259 at para. 14]

It is suggested that a possible route through this confusion would be to adopt the purposive approach adopted by Morrison J in *ECM (Vehicle Delivery Service) Ltd* v *Cox and others* [1998] IRLR 416, where he concluded that it would not be proper for a transferee to be able to control the extent of its obligations by refusing to comply with them in the first place. As Morrison J stated: 'The issue as to whether employees should have been taken on cannot be determined by asking whether they were taken on' (p. 419, at para. 24). This approach focuses attention on the motive for refusing to take on the existing workforce, so as to decide whether the motivation was the avoidance of the regulations or some other reason. Even then, there will be difficult questions of proof in establishing the true motive. The Court of Appeal has now endorsed Morrison J's approach (see the following extract).

According to Paul Davies, the reasoning in *Süzen* comes very close to the Commission's original proposal which sought to distinguish the mere transfer of an activity from the transfer of an undertaking. Furthermore, it would appear, as Davies argues, 'that the Council has set its seal of approval on what the Court of Justice has done so far in interpreting the scope of the Directive, and has left further consideration of this "hot potato" in the hands of the court' (Davies (1998) 27 JLJ 365, at p. 366; see also Davies (1996) 25 ILJ 193).

In 1998, Directive 98/50/EEC amending the Acquired Rights Directive (77/187/EEC) was adopted. Unfortunately, its definition of the scope of the amended directive is of little assistance in clarifying matters. Article 1(b) states that there is a transfer 'where there is an economic entity which retains its identity'. This is merely a repetition of the standard test adopted by the ECJ and which has produced such contradictory outcomes. Article 1(b) goes on to define an entity as 'an organised grouping of resources which has the objective of pursuing an economic activity, whether or not that activity is central or ancillary.' This part of the definition is very similar to the formula adopted by the ECJ's decision in *Süzen*. (For a commentary on the amended directive, see Davies (1998) 27 ILJ 365.)

ECM (Vehicle Delivery Service) Ltd v Cox and others
[1999] IRLR 559, Court of Appeal

The applicants were employed by Axial Ltd as drivers and yardmen. Axial had a contract with VAG Ltd to deliver Audi and Volkswagen cars imported into the UK through the port of Grimsby.

VAG decided that the delivery contract should be changed in a number of ways and Axial lost the contract to ECM. When ECM was appointed, the site from which the work was carried out was changed, a different system of delivery was introduced and the arrangements for administering the contract were altered.

ECM did not offer employment to any of the employees who had worked on the contract prior to the change of contractor. The employment tribunal found as a fact that this was because the employees were claiming through their trade union representative that the Transfer of Undertakings Regulations 1981 applied and were threatening an action for unfair dismissal if they were not employed by ECM.

In the event, the employees successfully brought unfair dismissal complaints against ECM. The employment tribunal found that there was a relevant transfer to ECM within the meaning of the 1981 Regulations. Subsequent to the tribunal's decision, the ECJ handed down its decision in the *Süzen* case. It was argued on behalf of the employers on appeal that, in the light of *Süzen*, the tribunal had erred in equating the transfer of a service contract with the transfer of an undertaking, and that all that had been transferred in this particular case was a particular activity. On behalf of the applicants, it was argued that *Süzen* does not deal with a situation in which an employer decides not to take on employees in an attempt to avoid the operation of the regulations.

The EAT dismissed the employers' appeal, finding that the tribunal's decision that there was a transfer of an economic entity which retained its identity was not inconsistent with *Süzen* or with the decision of the Court of Appeal in *Betts* v *Brintel Helicopters Ltd* [1997] IRLR 361, CA. According to the EAT, when properly understood, there is no conflict with the decision of the European Court in *Schmidt*. There is an economic entity, as distinct from a mere activity, where the employees concerned are dedicated to a particular contract and their employment is contingent upon the continued existence of the service contract. In contrast, there is no transfer of a business where the loss of a customer does not of itself result in dedicated and identified staff losing their employment. The EAT further held that there is nothing in *Süzen* which requires an interpretation of the regulations which would allow a transferee to cause the regulations to be disapplied by refusing to take on the workforce.

On appeal to the Court of Appeal, it was argued that there is no transfer of an undertaking where the only continuing feature is the nature of the activity and all that continues is the service itself. The Court of Appeal dismissed the appeal.

MUMMERY LJ: ...In my judgment, this appeal fails on the ground that there is no error of law in the decision of the employment tribunal. In reaching its conclusion that the 1981 Regulations applied, the employment tribunal had regard to all those factors which were held by the European Court of Justice in *Spijkers* to be relevant to the determination of the issue whether there was a transfer of an undertaking. The employment tribunal considered the factors on each side. They noted the differences in the way that ECM carried out the VAG contract, but pointed out that the customers were essentially the same and that the work that was going on was essentially the same i.e. cars were unloaded at Grimsby, were put onto transporters and were driven to VAG dealers. The result was the same. The employment tribunal were entitled to conclude that, even though ECM did not take on any Axial staff, the identity of the economic entity in the hands of Axial was still retained in the hands of ECM after the loss of the VAG contract. This justified the finding of a transfer.

The employment tribunal applied the correct test, as laid down by the European court in *Spijkers* and followed in other cases, such as *Schmidt* [1994] IRLR 302. Although the *Süzen* decision has been described as involving a shift of emphasis or a clarification of the law, nothing was said in *Süzen* which casts doubts on the correctness of the interpretation of the Directive in the earlier decisions cited to and applied by the employment tribunal in the extended reasons.

In my judgment, it is clear that, but for the argument about the scope and effect of the later decision in *Süzen*, there would be no possible ground of appeal in this case. ECM's case has to be that *Süzen* makes all the difference. It does not in this case. The importance of *Süzen* had, I think, been overstated. The ruling in *Süzen* should be seen in its proper context.

(1) The Court of Justice has not overruled its previous interpretative rulings in cases such as *Spijkers* and *Schmidt*. This is clear not only from the citation of those cases in the judgment in *Süzen*, but also from their continued prominence in the reasoning of the Court of Justice in its post-*Süzen* decision in *Sánchez Hidalgo* [1999] IRLR 136.

(2) It is still the case that it is for the national court to make the 'necessary factual appraisal' in order to decide whether there is a transfer in the light of the criteria laid down by the Court of Justice.

(3) It is still the case that those criteria involve consideration of 'all the facts characterising the transaction in question', as identified in *Spijkers* at paragraph 13 of the judgment of the Court of Justice, in order to determine whether the undertaking has continued and retained its identity in different hands. The employment tribunal carried out a full factual appraisal, applied the correct criteria and concluded that, despite changes in the organisation of the operation for the delivery of cars under the VAG contract, there was a continuation in the hands of ECM of the existence of the discrete economic entity previously carried on by Axial.

(4) The importance of *Süzen* is that the Court of Justice identified limits to the application of the Directive. On the one hand, it affirmed that:

    (a) 'The decisive criterion for establishing the existence of a transfer within the meaning of the Directive is whether the entity in question retains its identity, as indicated inter alia by the fact that its operation is actually continued...' (paragraph 10);

    (b) a direct contractual link or relationship between the transferor and the transferee is not conclusive against a transfer (paragraphs 12 and 13);

    (c) consideration of all the facts characterising the transaction in question is necessary (paragraph 14).

(5) On the other hand, it set limits by indicating that:

    (a) '...the mere fact that the service provided by the old and the new awardees of a contract is similar does not therefore support the conclusion that an economic entity has been transferred.'

Other factors are important—the workforce, the management staff, its operating methods and its operational resources (paragraph 15):

    (a) 'The mere loss of a service contract to a competitor cannot therefore by itself indicate the existence of a transfer within the meaning of the Directive...In those circumstances, the service undertaking previously entrusted with the contract does not, on losing a customer, thereby cease fully to exist, and a business or part of a business belonging to it cannot be considered to have been transferred to the new awardee of the contract' (paragraph 16);

    (b) The question whether the majority of the employees are taken over by the new employer to enable him to carry on the activities of the undertaking on a regular basis is a factual circumstance to be taken into account, as well as the similarity of the pre- and post-transfer activities and the type of undertaking concerned e.g. in labour-intensive sectors (paragraphs 20 and 21).

(6) This case is unaffected by the limits indicated in *Süzen*. It is not a case (like *Süzen*) of the loss of a contract with one customer being asserted to amount to a transfer of an undertaking. It is not a case like *Betts* of the loss of a contract for one location being asserted to be a transfer of an undertaking. It is not a

case of a transfer depending merely on a comparison of the similarity of the activities of Axial and ECM after the loss of the VAG contract by Axial. The transfer was established by the employment tribunal looking at all the relevant facts and concluding that this undertaking was based on the VAG contract and that it continued in different hands, even though no employees of Axial were appointed by ECM. The tribunal was entitled to have regard, as a relevant circumstance, to the reason why those employees were not appointed by ECM. The Court of Justice has not decided in *Süzen* or in any other case that this is an irrelevant circumstance or that the failure of the transferee to appoint any of the former employees of the transferor points conclusively against a transfer.

I would dismiss this appeal.

NOTE: 'Lord Justice Mummery's interpretation may or may not be an accurate reflection of what the European Court intended, but it will be widely welcomed regardless. The Court of Appeal's decision in *ECM* amounts to a dispensation to employment tribunals to determine whether there has been a transfer of undertaking on the basis of all the facts, using the shopping list set out in *Spijkers* and reiterated most recently in *Sanchez Hidalgo*. From a practical standpoint, *ECM* means that a transferee cannot necessarily avoid a TUPE transfer by refusing to take on an existing workforce' (Rubenstein, 'Highlights' [1999] IRLR 506). However, the next case shows the ECJ adopting an even narrower approach to the definition of transfer than was taken in *Süzen*.

Oy Liikenne Ab v *Liskojärvi and another*
Case C–172/99 [2001] IRLR 171, European Court of Justice

Following a tender procedure, the Greater Helsinki Joint Board ('the YTV') awarded the contract for the operation of seven local bus routes, previously operated by Hakunilan Liikenne ('HL'), to Liikenne. HL dismissed 45 drivers, 33 of whom—i.e. all those who applied—were re-engaged by Liikenne. They were re-engaged, however, on less favourable terms and conditions than those that applied at HL. When Liikenne replaced HL, no vehicles or other significant assets connected with the operation of the bus routes were transferred.

Two of the HL drivers taken on by Liikenne claimed in the Finnish courts that there had been a transfer of an undertaking within the meaning of Article 1(1) of the directive, and that they were accordingly entitled to continue to enjoy their previous (i.e. HL) terms and conditions by virtue of Article 3. The court of first instance and the initial appeal court ruled in the drivers' favour. A further appeal court, however, referred the question of the applicability of Article 1(1) to the ECJ for a preliminary ruling.

EXTRACT FROM THE JUDGMENT: …In view of the possible application of Directive 77/187 to a situation such as that before the national court, that court should…be given the criteria necessary to enable it to assess whether there was a transfer within the meaning of Article 1(1) of that Directive in the present case. The national court observes in this respect that the takeover of the bus routes was not based on a contract between the old and new contractors and no significant assets were transferred between them.

The test for establishing the existence of a transfer within the meaning of Directive 77/187 is whether the entity in question retains its identity, as indicated inter alia by the fact that its operation is actually continued or resumed (case 24/85 *Spijkers* [1986] ECR 1119, paragraphs 11 and 12, and case C–234/98 *Allen and others* [2000] IRLR 119, paragraph 23).

While the absence of any contractual link between the transferor and the transferee or, as in this case, between the two undertakings successively entrusted with the operation of bus routes may point to the absence of a transfer within the meaning of Directive 77/187, it is certainly not conclusive (case C–13195 *Süzen* [1997] IRLR 255, paragraph 11).

Directive 77/187 is applicable wherever, in the context of contractual relations, there is a change in the natural or legal person responsible for carrying on the business and entering into the obligations of an employer towards employees of the undertaking. Thus there is no need, in order for that Directive to be applicable, for there to be any direct contractual relationship between the transferor and the transferee: the transfer may take place in two stages, through the intermediary of a third party such as the owner or the person putting up the capital (see, inter alia, joined cases C–171/94 and C–172/94 *Merckx and Neuhuys* [1996] IRLR 467, paragraphs 28–30, and *Süzen*, paragraph 12).

Directive 77/187 can therefore apply where there is no direct contractual link between two undertakings successively awarded a contract, following procedures for the award of public service contracts in accordance with Directive 92/50, for a non-maritime public transport service, such as the operation of scheduled local bus routes, by a legal person governed by public law.

For Directive 77/187 to be applicable, however, the transfer must relate to a stable economic entity whose activity is not limited to performing one specific works contract (case C–48/94 *Rygaard* [1996] IRLR 51, paragraph 20). The term 'entity' thus refers to an organised grouping of persons and assets facilitating the exercise of an economic activity which pursues a specific objective (*Süzen*, paragraph 13).

It is for the national court to establish if necessary, in the light of the guiding factors set out above, whether the operation of the bus routes at issue in the main proceedings was organised as an economic entity within Hakunilan Liikenne before being entrusted to Liikenne.

However, to determine whether the conditions for the transfer of an economic entity are satisfied, it is also necessary to consider all the factual circumstances characterising the transaction in question, including in particular the type of undertaking or business involved, whether or not its tangible assets such as buildings and movable property are transferred, the value of its intangible assets at the time of the transfer, whether or not the core of its employees are taken over by the new employer, whether or not its customers are transferred, the degree of similarity between the activities carried on before and after the transfer, and the period, if any, for which those activities were suspended. These are, however, merely single factors in the overall assessment which must be made, and cannot therefore be considered in isolation (see, in particular, *Spijkers*, paragraph 13, and *Süzen*, paragraph 14).

So the mere fact that the service provided by the old and the new contractors is similar does not justify the conclusion that there has been a transfer of an economic entity between the two undertakings. Such an entity cannot be reduced to the activity entrusted to it. Its identity also emerges from other factors, such as its workforce, its management staff, the way in which its work is organised, its operating methods or indeed, where appropriate, the operational resources available to it (*Süzen*, paragraph 15, *Sánchez Hidalgo*, paragraph 30, and *Allen*, paragraph 27; see also joined cases C–127/96, C–229/96 and C–74/97 *Hernández Vidal and others* [1999] IRLR 132, paragraph 30).

As pointed out in paragraph 32 above, the national court, in assessing the facts characterising the transaction in question, must take into account among other things the type of undertaking or business concerned. It follows that the degree of importance to be attached to the various criteria for determining whether or not there has been a transfer within the meaning of the Directive will necessarily vary according to the activity carried on, and indeed the production or operating methods employed in the relevant undertaking, business or part of a business (*Süzen*, paragraph 18, *Hernández Vidal*, paragraph 31, and *Sánchez Hidalgo*, paragraph 31).

On this point, the Commission submits, referring to *Süzen*, that the absence of a transfer of assets between the old and new holders of the contract for bus transport is of no importance, whereas the fact that the new contractor took on an essential part of the employees of the old contractor is decisive.

The Court has indeed held that an economic entity may, in certain sectors, be able to function without any significant tangible or intangible assets, so that the maintenance of the identity of such an entity following the transaction affecting it cannot logically depend on the transfer of such assets (*Süzen*, paragraph *18, Hernández Vidal*, paragraph 31, and *Sánchez Hidalgo*, paragraph 31).

The Court thus held that, since in certain sectors in which activities are based essentially on manpower a group of workers engaged in a joint activity on a permanent basis may constitute an economic entity, it must be recognised that such an entity is capable of maintaining its identity after it has been transferred where the new employer does not merely pursue the activity in question but also takes over a major part, in terms of their numbers and skills, of the employees specially assigned by his predecessor to that task. In those circumstances, the new employer takes over an organised body of assets enabling him to carry on the activities or certain activities of the transferor undertaking on a regular basis (*Süzen*, paragraph 21, *Hernández Vidal*, paragraph 32, and *Sánchez Hidalgo*, paragraph 32).

However, bus transport cannot be regarded as an activity based essentially on manpower, as it requires substantial plant and equipment (see, reaching the same conclusion with respect to driveage work in mines, *Allen*, paragraph 30). The fact that the tangible assets used for operating the bus routes were not transferred from the old to the new contractor therefore constitutes a circumstance to be taken into account.

At the hearing, the representative of the defendants in the main proceedings emphasised the economic value of the contract between the contracting authority YTV and Liikenne, and submitted that this was a significant intangible asset. That value cannot be denied; but in the context of an award which is to be renewed, the value of such an intangible asset in principle falls to nil on the expiry of the old contract, since the award is necessarily thrown open again.

If an award procedure such as that at issue in the main proceedings provides for the new contractor to take over the existing contracts with customers, or if the majority of the customers may be regarded as captive, then it should nevertheless be considered that there is a transfer of customers.

However, in a sector such as scheduled public transport by bus, where the tangible assets contribute significantly to the performance of the activity, the absence of a transfer to a significant extent from the old to the new contractor of such assets, which are necessary for the proper functioning of the entity, must lead to the conclusion that the entity does not retain its identity.

Consequently, in a situation such as that in the main proceedings, Directive 77/187 does not apply in the absence of a transfer of significant tangible assets from the old to the new contractor.

The second answer to be given to the national court must therefore be that Article 1(1) of Directive 77/187 is to be interpreted as meaning that:

— that Directive may apply where there is no direct contractual link between two undertakings which are successively awarded, following procedures for the award of public service contracts conducted in accordance with Directive 92/50, a nonmaritime public transport service—such as the operation of scheduled local bus routes—by a legal person governed by public law;

— in a situation such as that in the main proceedings, Directive 77/187 does not apply where there is no transfer of significant tangible assets between those two undertakings.

NOTES

1. Paul Davies has summed up the implications of the decision in *Oy Liikenne Ab* as follows:

> It seems that where the assets of the business consist almost entirely of employees, the most important question in relation to 'identity' is whether the employees go across. (See Joined Cases C–127/96 and 74/97, and *Vidal* [1998] ECR I-8179, para 32.) This might be referred to as 'labour only' contracting-out of services. Where, however, the business requires significant assets as well as employees, the crucial factor is the transfer of those assets and where the employees end up is not important for the answer to the transfer question. There is one rider to this distinction between activities 'based essentially on manpower' and those where assets play a significant part in the provision of the service. If the necessary assets are retained in the hands of the client and provided in turn to the various contractors who provide the service, it seems that, for the purposes of the above distinction, the contracted out activity is one 'based essentially on manpower'. (See Case C–234/98 *Allen* [2000] ICR 436, judgment at para. 30.)
>
> There is one identifiable benefit from this narrowing of the definition of transfer. Under the analysis whereby the two criteria identified in *Süzen* were equally effective in bringing about a transfer, the new employer was under a perverse incentive not to offer employment to the former employer's workers for fear that this would trigger liabilities under the Directive...Where assets are a significant part of the business in question...the ECJ's latest decision makes it clear that the new employer who takes over no assets may freely make offers of employment to the employees of the former employer, without triggering the Directive's liabilities...
>
> However, what the latest decision of the ECJ fails to do is to address the argument that the distinction between activities based essentially on manpower and those needing assets is arbitrary in policy terms. In fact, in this case the Court affirms *Süzen* and shows no hankering after a return to *Schmidt*. In contracting out of services the impact of the Directive has become, if not voluntary, at least highly contingent upon the structuring of the commercial deal by which the contracting- out, contracting in or reassignment of the contract is effected. Where assets are an essential part of the business, the application of the Directive can be avoided by not transferring the assets; where the business is 'based essentially on manpower', it can be avoided, it seems, by the new employer not offering jobs to the to the former employer's workforce. It is true that in some cases the new employer may be unable to follow such a course of action, for example, where the former employer's assets or workforce are highly special-ised and cannot be easily replaced by going into the market. However, this response simply highlights the arbitrary impact of the Directive. It is precisely workers who are not skilled and who might be thought to be most in need of the protection of the law (such as cleaners) whom the new employer is most likely to be able to replace by going into the labour market and thereby avoid the application of the Directive (in the case of 'activities based essentially on manpower'). [Davies, P., 'Transfers—the UK will have to make up its own mind' (2001) 30 ILJ 231, at pp. 233–4.]

Davies goes on to argue that the British legislature now has the power to solve this particu-lar threat to effective employment protection legislation. In relation to transfers, s. 38 of the Employment Relations Act 1999 expands the Government's powers of secondary legislation under the European Communities Act 1972 so as to cover cases 'other than those to which the Community obligation applies'. This power has already been used in the public sector to over-come the *Henke* decision (Case C–298/94 [1996] ECR I–4989). See the Transfer of Undertakings

(Protection of Employment) (Rent Officer Service) Regulations 1999 (SI 1999/2511). In addition the directive allows the introduction of national laws which are more favourable to employees than those the directive requires (Article 7). Indeed, the government 'grasped the nettle' of going beyond the requirements of EU Law and applying TUPE 2006 to a change of service provision as well as a transfer of undertaking (see the following extract).

2. The *Oy Liikenne* decision raises the further possibility that recent attempts by the UK judiciary to restrict the effect of the ECJ's ruling in *Süzen*, particularly in relation to its apparent emphasis on the need in labour-intensive sectors for the transfer of a majority of the putative transferor's workforce, may prove to have failed. However, the Court of Appeal in *ADI (UK) Ltd* v *Willer and others* [2001] IRLR 542 showed a staunch loyalty to the *ECM* principle. In *ADI*, the court ruled that if an economic entity is labour-intensive such that, applying *Süzen*, there is no transfer if the workforce is not taken on but would be if they were, then there is a duty on an employment tribunal to consider why the workers did not transfer. If it is established that the reason or principal reason for this was to avoid the application of TUPE, then the tribunal is obliged to treat the case as if the workers had transferred. According to Dyson LJ, this approach did not conflict with ECJ case law because none of the ECJ cases have dealt directly with the point at issue in *ECM*: avoidance strategies.

3. This reluctance to 'toe the *Süzen* line' is again in evidence in the most recent decision of the Court of Appeal.

RCO Support Services v Unison
[2002] IRLR 401, Court of Appeal

The Court of Appeal upheld a finding that TUPE applied when there was a change in hospitals providing inpatient care within the same NHS trust area, and new contractors took over the provision of cleaning and catering. The Court of Appeal held that there can be a TUPE transfer even where there is no transfer of significant assets and none of the relevant employees was taken on by the new employer.

MUMMERY LJ: I agree that it has become clear from *Süzen* and later judgments that the Court of Justice now interprets the Directive as setting limits to its application in contracting out cases which were not expressly identified in *Spijkers* [1986] ECR 1119, or in *Schmidt* and other earlier judgments of the Court of Justice. In particular, the mere fact that the putative transferee carries on the same activities or supplies the same services as the putative transferor had done does by itself support the conclusion that an entity retains its identity. It is not correct to treat that single circumstance as determinative in favour of a transfer. Indeed, there may be no scope for the application of the Directive in a case where, although the same labour-intensive activities are continued or the same services are supplied by a new contractor, none of the workforce has been taken on.

I am, however, unable to accept RCO's submissions that the limits on the application of the Directive set in *Süzen* mean that, as a matter of Community law, there can never be a transfer of an undertaking in a contracting out case if neither assets nor workforce are transferred; that the only legally permissible conclusion on the facts of this case was that, as none of the workforce were taken on by RCO, no transfer could have taken place; and that the employment tribunal must have erred in law in concluding that there were in fact transfers within the meaning of TUPE.

I do not read *Süzen* as singling out, to the exclusion of all other circumstances, the particular circumstance of none of the workforce being taken on and treating that as determinative of the transfer issue in every case. That interpretation of the Directive would run counter to what is described in RCO's submissions as the 'multifactorial approach' to the retention of identity test in *Spijkers*.

Whether or not the majority of employees are taken on by the new employer is only one of all the facts, which must be considered by the national court in making an overall assessment of the facts characterising the transaction. Single factors must not be considered in isolation.

NOTES

1. The court also held that in determining whether there was a transfer of undertaking, in accordance with the decision of the Court of Appeal in *ECM (Vehicle Delivery) Service* v *Cox* [1999] IRLR 559, the employment tribunal was entitled to have regard, as a relevant circumstance, to the reason why the employees were not taken on by the new employer. The *Süzen* decision, as stated by the majority of the Court of Appeal in *ADI (UK)* v *Willer* [2001] IRLR 542, does not require the

national court to exclude from its consideration of all the facts characterising the transaction the circumstances of the decision by the putative transferee not to take on the workforce.

The fact that none of the workforce is taken on is relevant to, but not necessarily conclusive of, the issue of retention of identity. As it is a relevant factor, it is necessary for the employment tribunal to assess its significance by considering the context in which the decision was made. This exercise involves an objective consideration and assessment of all the facts, including the circumstances of the decision not to take on the workforce rather than a matter of the subjective motive of the putative transferee to avoid application of the directive and TUPE.

In the present case, the employment tribunal was entitled to take into account as relevant evidence pointing to, rather than away from, the retention of the identity of the cleaning and catering undertakings, the willingness of the first appellants to take on the workforce cleaners if they first resigned from their previous employment and accepted re-employment on its terms and conditions, in preference to automatic employment on the terms and conditions applicable as a result of a TUPE transfer.

2. In *Astle* v *Cheshire County Council* [2005] IRLR 12, the EAT set out guidance for applying the *ECM* principle that the transferee's motives are a relevant factor to be taken into account in deciding whether a TUPE transfer has occurred.

According to Burton J, if the reason or principal reason that the transferee did not take on the transferor's workforce is to avoid the application of TUPE, then it is a relevant factor to be taken into account in applying the multifactorial approach set out by the ECJ in the *Spijkers* case and may be decisive. This will depend on asking the question whether there would have been a TUPE transfer if the workforce had been taken on, or by considering what would have happened 'but for' the adoption of a TUPE avoidance policy.

In the instant case, the council took back architectural services from a contractor and arranged for the work to be done by a panel of self-employed consultants. This was termed a 'market economy' approach.

The EAT held that the employment tribunal did not misdirect itself or reach a perverse conclusion when it found that the principal reason for entering into a new structure, which had no need for an employed workforce, was not to thwart TUPE but to implement a market economy as the best method of delivering architectural services. The situation was not one in which the structure the council put in place had no commercial or economic justification.

3. In *P&O Trans European Ltd* v *Initial Transport Services Ltd* [2003] IRLR 128, the EAT gave a narrow interpretation to *Oy Liikenne*. *P&O* was a case of an asset-reliant business (fuel transport) where the putative transferee did not purchase the transferor's vehicles. Upholding a finding that there was nevertheless a TUPE transfer, the EAT reinforced the 'multifactorial' approach and stated that the ECJ in *Oy Liikenne* 'was not laying down a principle that in all cases of asset-intensive industries the absence of a transfer, to a significant extent, of such assets would always lead to the conclusion that no transfer had taken place.' In the view of Nelson J: 'The relative significance of assets in relation to manpower and how each contributes to the performance of a particular activity will vary according to the facts of the particular case.'

4. The distinction between 'asset-reliant' businesses and 'labour-intensive' businesses is underlined by the ECJ in the following case.

Abler and others v Sodexho MM Catering Gesellschaft mbH
[2004] IRLR 168, European Court of Justice

Sodexho MM Catering Gesellschaft mbH (Sodexho), a catering company, had been awarded the contract to provide catering services at a hospital in Vienna. It was the contractor's responsibility to draw up menus; purchase, store, produce, portion and transport meals to various hospital departments; serve meals in the dining room; wash the crockery; and clean the premises used. However, the premises themselves, as well as water, energy, and equipment, were provided by the management authority for the hospital.

Mr Abler and 21 other catering workers had worked for Sanre catering company, which had provided the same hospital catering services before Sodexho's successful tender for the contract, Sanrest's contract having been terminated. Sodexho took over the premises and equipment. However, it refused to take on any of the catering staff.

The employees brought an action against Sodexho, seeking a declaration that their employment continued with Sodexho following the transfer of the catering contract from Sanrest. Sodexho argued that their failure to take on any of Sanrest's employees meant that there could not be a transfer within the meaning of the directive. This was on the basis of the existing ECJ case law to the effect that, where functions based essentially on manpower are concerned, these will only be the subject of a business transfer where the new employer carries on the function and retains a major part, in terms of their number and skills, of the employees assigned to that function (e.g. *Süzen*).

JUDGMENT OF THE ECJ: [*Sodexho*] bases its argument on the judgments in which the Court of Justice has held that in certain sectors in which activities are based essentially on manpower a group of workers engaged in a joint activity on a permanent basis may constitute an economic entity. According to that case-law, such an entity is thus capable of maintaining its entity after it has been transferred where the new employer does not merely purchase the activity in question but also takes over a major part, in terms of their numbers and skills, of the employees specially assigned by his predecessor to that task (see inter alia *Süzen*, paragraph 21, and joined cases C–173/96 and C–247/96 *Hidalgo and others* [1999] IRLR 136, paragraph 32).

In order to determine whether the conditions for the transfer of an organised economic entity are met, it is necessary to consider all the facts characterising the transaction in question, including in particular the type of undertaking or business, whether or not its tangible assets, such as buildings and movable property, are transferred, the value of its intangible assets at the time of the transfer, whether or not the majority of its employees are taken over by the new employer, whether or not its customers are transferred, the degree of similarity between the activities carried on before and after the transfer, and the period, if any, for which those activities were suspended (see *Spijkers*,…paragraph 13, and *Süzen*, paragraph 14).

However, all those circumstances are merely single factors in the overall assessment which must be made and cannot therefore be considered in isolation (see inter alia *Spijkers*, paragraph 13, and *Süzen*, paragraph 14).

The national court, in assessing the facts characterising the transaction in question, must take into account the type of business or undertaking concerned. It follows that the degree of importance to be attached to each criterion for determining whether or not there has been a transfer within the meaning of Directive 77/187 will necessarily vary according to the activity carried on, or indeed the production or operation methods employed in the relevant undertaking, business or part of a business (*Süzen*, paragraph 18, and *Hidalgo*…paragraph 31).

Catering cannot be regarded as an activity based on manpower since it requires a significant amount of equipment. In the main proceedings, as the Commission points out, the tangible assets needed for the activity in question—namely, the premises, water and energy and small and large equipment (inter alia the appliances needed for preparing meals and the dishwashers)—were taken over by Sodexho. Moreover, a defining feature of the situation at issue in the main proceedings is the express and fundamental obligation to prepare meals in the hospital kitchen and thus to take over those tangible assets. The transfer of the premises and the equipment provided by the hospital, which is indispensable for the preparation and distribution of meals to hospital patients and staff is sufficient, in the circumstances, to make this a transfer of an economic entity. It is moreover clear that, given their captive status, the new contractor necessarily took on most of the customers of its predecessor.

It follows that the failure of the new contractor to take over, in terms of numbers and skills, an essential part of the staff which its predecessor employed to perform the same activity is not sufficient to preclude the existence of a transfer of an entity which retains its identity within the meaning of Directive 77/187 in a sector such as catering, where the activity is based essentially on equipment. As the United Kingdom and Commission rightly point out, any other conclusion would run counter to the principal objective of Directive 77/187, which is to ensure continuity, even against the wishes of the transferee, of the employment contracts of the employees of the transferor.

…

Finally, Sodexho contends that the fact that the management authority remains the owner of the premises and equipment necessary for the performance of the activity precludes a mere change in the contractor from being regarded as a transfer of an economic entity.

However, it is clear from the wording of Article 1 of Directive 77/187 that it is applicable whenever, in the context of contractual relations, there is a change in the legal or natural person who is responsible for carrying on the business and who by virtue of that fact incurs the obligations of an employer vis-à-vis the employees of the undertaking, regardless of whether or not the ownership of the tangible assets is transferred (case 287/86 *Landsorganisationen i Danmark for Tjenerforbundet i Danmark* v *Ny Molle Kro* [1989] IRLR 37, paragraph 12, and case C–209/91 *Watson Rask and Christensen* [1993] IRLR 133, paragraph 15).

The fact that the tangible assets taken over by the new contractor did not belong to its predecessor but were provided by the contracting authority cannot therefore preclude the existence of a transfer within the meaning of Directive 77/187.

NOTE: It can be argued there is now a clear distinction at ECJ level between 'asset-reliant' businesses and 'labour-intensive' businesses. For there to be a transfer in the case of an 'asset-reliant' business, the key assets must be transferred, and for there to be a transfer of a 'labour-intensive' activity, labour must be transferred. Catering services, perhaps somewhat surprisingly, are regarded as asset-intensive. After *Abler*, Rubenstein questions whether the dichotomy between asset and labour-intensive is that clear cut:

> At first impression, . . . this decision draws a bright line between asset-reliant and labour-intensive businesses. The difficulty is that it is by no means clear at the moment which businesses will fall on which side of this line. Veteran readers of this column will recall the problem I posed some years ago as to TUPE and the garden contractors at my home in leafy Surrey. We provide the contractor with some rather expensive equipment like a sit-on mower and they send in a small team to cut the lawn, trim the hedges and undertake other gardening jobs. The analysis of whether TUPE could apply if we changed the garden contractors for this modest economic entity seems to have varied over the years. After *Abler*, it is once more uncertain. ['Highlights' [2004] IRLR 93]

The question of the significance of asset transfer in transfer of undertakings cases has continued to occupy the minds of both the Court of Appeal and the ECJ (see *Balfour Beatty Power Networks Ltd* v *Wilcox* [2007] IRLR 63, CA and *Guney-Gorres* v *Security Aviation* [2006] IRLR 305, ECJ).

(iii) Contracting-out

(a) The changes made by the 2006 Regulations

As can be seen, under the unrevised TUPE regulations, it was very difficult to predict whether the regulations would encompass a change in service provider. The 2006 Regulations seek to clarify the position and to provide an 'extended definition' in such cases. According to McMullen: 'The Government's rationale for the extended definition is to reduce uncertainty in the law, to insulate the parties to service provision changeovers from the effects of ECJ jurisprudence and to create a level playing field, so that a contractor's bid for services is based on its commercial merits, rather on differing views of the employment rights of employees' (McMullen, J., 'An analysis of the Transfer of Undertakings (Protection of Employment) Regulations 2006' (2006) 35 ILJ 113, p. 120). The term 'service provision change' describes situations where a contract to provide a client (public or private sector) with a business service: (a) is awarded to a contractor; (b) relate to a new contract on subsequent retendering; or (c) ended with the bringing 'in house' of the service activities in question (see reg. 3). These changes mean that, generally, TUPE will apply on a change in service provider, thus avoiding the narrow reasoning applied by the ECJ in *Süzen*.

The impact of the regulatory change can be seen in *Metropolitan Resources Ltd* v *Churchill Dulwich Ltd* [2009] IRLR 700, EAT. The case involved a change in the contractor providing accommodation for asylum seekers. The crucial issue was whether the 'multifactorial' approach to whether there has been a TUPE transfer, which continues to apply in a standard TUPE transfer (see *Cheeseman* v *Brewer Contracts Ltd* [2001] IRLR 144, EAT), also applies to a service provision change. The EAT held that this was not the case. The EAT set out the three situations covered by the service provision change definition in reg. 3(1)(b): outsourcing, in-sourcing and change in the provision of activities or services carried out on behalf of a client between one contractor and another. 'The introduction of reg. 3(1)(b) enables a transfer to be established in any of those three situations if the activities previously carried out by client or contractor have ceased to be so carried out and, instead, are carried out by a contractor or a new contractor or by the client.' The EAT went on to hold that:

the circumstances in which service provision change is established are…comprehensively and clearly set out in reg. 3(1)(b) itself and reg. 3(3): if there was, immediately before the change relied upon, an organised grouping of employees which had as its principal purpose the carrying out of the activities in question, the client intends that those activities will be carried out by the alleged transferee, other than in connection with a single specific event or a task of short-term duration, and the activities do not consist totally or mainly of the supply of goods for the client's use, and if those activities cease to be carried out by the alleged transferor and are carried out instead by the alleged transferee, a relevant transfer exists. In contrast to the words used to define transfer in TUPE 1981 the new provisions appear to be straightforward; and their application to an individual case is, in my judgment, essentially one of fact.

Consequently, the EAT determined that 'there is no need for a judicially prescribed multi-factorial approach…In a case in which reg. 3(1)(b) is relied upon, the employment tribunal should ask itself simply whether, on the facts, one of the three situations set out in reg. 3(1)(b) existed and whether the conditions set out in reg. 3(3) are satisfied.' The EAT emphasised that when comparing the activities of the alleged transferor and transferee, detailed differences will be inevitable. It cannot have been intended that the concept of service provision change should not apply because of 'some minor difference'. Instead, 'a commonsense and pragmatic approach is required': the tribunal 'needs to ask itself whether the activities carried on by the alleged transferee are fundamentally or essentially the same as those carried out by the alleged transferor'. This test was applied by the EAT in *Enterprise Management Services Ltd* v *Connect-up Ltd* [2012] IRLR 190 and approved by Elias LJ in the Court of Appeal in *Hunter* v *McCarrick* [2013] ICR 235. The test has now been incorporated into the TUPE Regulations via reg. 3(2A).

The authors of *Smith & Wood's Employment Law* observe that there are grounds for hoping that the provisions in the 2006 Regulations on contracting-out cases might constitute a 'year-zero' approach, i.e. 'to treat them as entirely novel and not to construe them by reference to the (dreadful) previous case law' (Smith, I. and Baker, A., *Smith & Wood's Employment Law*, 10th edn (Oxford: OUP, 2010) p. 561). *Metropolitan Resources Ltd* v *Churchill Dulwich Ltd* offers us some hope in this regard.

Smith and Wood's point is underlined by a recent decision by the CJEU. In *CLECE SA* v *Valor* [2011] IRLR 251, the Court held that the Transfer of Undertakings Directive (2001/23) does not apply to a situation in which a municipal authority which had contracted out the cleaning of its premises to a private company decided to terminate its contract with that company and to undertake those cleaning services itself, by hiring new agency staff for that purpose. There was no significant transfer of assets. According to the CJEU, the local authority was free to do this because there was no transfer of an economic entity that retained its identity in that a significant number of the employees of the transferor had not been retained. So whether the Transfer of Undertakings Directive applied so as to transfer the contracts of employees of the old employer depended on whether the new employer took on the 'majority' of the employees of the old employer: 'the identity of an economic entity…which is essentially based on manpower, cannot be retained if the majority of its employees are not taken on by the alleged transferee.' As Rubenstein states: 'This is exactly the circular reasoning, leaving the rights of the transferor's employees in the hands of the putative transferee, that led to TUPE 2006, and reg. 3(1)(b), which separately covers service provision changes, such as in this case, not covered by the Directive as it has been interpreted by the CJEU' ('Highlights' [2011] IRLR 193).

Moreover, if the Coalition Government's consultative proposal to remove the specific inclusion of 'service provision change' from TUPE had been brought into force, we would have returned to the complexity created by *Süzen* and related European case law (see 'Flexible, effective, fair: Promoting economic growth through a strong and efficient labour market', Department for Business Innovation and Skills, October 2011).

THE TRANSFER OF EMPLOYMENT (PROTECTION OF EMPLOYMENT) REGULATIONS 2006 (SI 2006/246)

4 Effect of relevant transfer on contracts of employment

(1) Except where objection is made under paragraph (7), a relevant transfer shall not operate so as to terminate the contract of employment of any person employed by the transferor and assigned to the organised grouping of resources or employees that is subject to the relevant transfer, which would otherwise be terminated by the transfer, but any such contract shall have effect after the transfer as if originally made between the person so employed and the transferee.

(2) Without prejudice to paragraph (1), but subject to paragraph (6), and regulations 8 and 15(9), on the completion of a relevant transfer—

(a) all the transferor's rights, powers, duties and liabilities under or in connection with any such contract shall be transferred by virtue of this regulation to the transferee; and

(b) any act or omission before the transfer is completed, of or in relation to the transferor in respect of that contract or a person assigned to that organised grouping of resources or employees, shall be deemed to have been an act or omission of or in relation to the transferee.

(3) Any reference in paragraph (1) to a person employed by the transferor and assigned to the organised grouping of resources or employees that is subject to a relevant transfer, is a reference to a person so employed immediately before the transfer, or who would have been so employed if he had not been dismissed in the circumstances described in regulation 7(1), including, where the transfer is effected by a series of two or more transactions, a person so employed and assigned or who would have been so employed and assigned immediately before any of those transactions.

(4) Subject to regulation 9, in respect of a contract of employment that is, or will be, transferred by paragraph (1), any purported variation of the contract shall be void if the sole or principal reason for the variation is—

(a) the transfer itself; or

(b) a reason connected with the transfer that is not an economic, technical or organisational reason entailing changes in the workforce.

(5) Paragraph (4) does not prevent a variation of the contract of employment if -

(a) the sole or principal reason for the variation is an economic, technical, or organisational reason entailing changes in the workforce, provided that the employer and employee agree that variation; or

(b) the terms of that contract permit the employer to make such a variation.

(5A) in paragraph (5), the expression 'changes in the workforce' includes a change to the place where employees are employed by the employer to carry on the business of the employer or to carry out work of a particular kind for the employer (and the reference to such a place has the same meaning as in section 139 of the 19996 Act).

(5B) Paragraph (4) does not apply in respect of a variation of the contract of employment in so far as it varies a term or condition incorporated from a collective agreement, provided that-

(a) the variation of the contract takes effect on a date more than one year after the date of the transfer; and

(b) following that variation, the rights and obligations in the employee's contract, when considered together, are no less favourable to the employee than those which applied immediately before the variation.

(5C) Paragraphs (5) and (5B) do not affect any rule of law as to whether a contract of em ployment is effectively varied.

(6) Paragraph (2) shall not transfer or otherwise affect the liability of any person to be prosecuted for, convicted of and sentenced for any offence.

(7) Paragraphs (1) and (2) shall not operate to transfer the contract of employment and the rights, powers, duties and liabilities under or in connection with it of an employee who informs the transferor or the transferee that he objects to becoming employed by the transferee.

(8) Subject to paragraphs (9) and (11), where an employee so objects, the relevant transfer shall operate so as to terminate his contract of employment with the transferor but he shall not be treated, for any purpose, as having been dismissed by the transferor.

(9) Subject to regulation 9, where a relevant transfer involves or would involve a substantial change in working conditions to the material detriment of a person whose contract of employment is or would be transferred under paragraph (1), such an employee may treat the contract of employment as having been terminated, and the employee shall be treated for any purpose as having been dismissed by the employer.

(10) No damages shall be payable by an employer as a result of a dismissal falling within paragraph (9) in respect of any failure by the employer to pay wages to an employee in respect of a notice period which the employee has failed to work.

(11) Paragraphs (1), (7), (8) and (9) are without prejudice to any right of an employee arising apart from these Regulations to terminate his contract of employment without notice in acceptance of a repudiatory breach of contract by his employer.

NOTES
1. In *DJM International* v *Nicholas* [1996] ICR 214, it was held that what is now reg. 4(2)(b) had the effect of passing liability to the transferee for an allegation of sex discrimination based on the fact that prior to the transfer the applicant had been moved from full-time to part-time employment.
2. The principal effect of the regulations is that the common law position has been abolished.
3. Some terms which are tailored to the identity of the transferor—such as share option schemes, restrictive covenants and mobility clauses—may not be interpreted in the same way in relation to the transferee (*Tapere* v *South London and Maudsley NHS Trust* [2009] IRLR 972, EAT).

Premier Motors (Medway) Ltd v *Total Oil Great Britain Ltd*
[1984] 1 WLR 377, Employment Appeal Tribunal

The employer sold the business but the purchaser had no wish to run the business or employ its former employees. Accordingly, while the sale was completed on 1 June 1982 the vendors continued to run the business as licensees of the purchasers until 30 June when the purchasers appointed a caretaker for the premises and the applicants' employment was terminated. The Court of Appeal held that the effect of the regulations was that on 1 June 1982 the purchasers became the employers of the applicants and, accordingly, it was they who were obliged to meet their redundancy payments.

BROWNE-WILKINSON LJ: ... In our judgment in the ordinary case the effect of the Regulations is that, if a business is transferred, the employees are automatically transferred with it irrespective of the wishes of the transferee or of the employees. The contract is automatically continued by operation of the Regulations even if the transferee has no wish to continue the employment. In consequence, the employees' contractual and statutory rights become enforceable against the transferee, not the transferor. When, as in the present case, the transferee makes it clear that he will not continue to employ the employees, in our judgment he repudiates the continuing contract and thereby constructively dismisses the employee. The employee is dismissed because of redundancy and becomes entitled to a redundancy payment from the transferee. A transferee of a business who does not wish to take over the employees of that business will even so be liable to the employees for the redundancy payments. To protect himself, the transferee must agree with the transferor either that the transferor will dismiss the employee before the transfer or will indemnify the transferee against redundancy payments and other employment liabilities.

That being in our judgment the clear effect of the Regulations in a case where the transferee is himself going to carry on the business, does it make any difference that the transferee (the purchasers) are not themselves going to carry on the business but are immediately assigning or licensing to a third party (Mr Lawrence) the right to run the business? In our judgment it is impossible to treat such a case differently from the ordinary case without running contrary to the scheme of the Regulations, i.e. the automatic transfer of employment...

Morris Angel Ltd v *Hollande*
[1993] IRLR 169, Court of Appeal

Hollande was employed as group managing director of a company called Altolight and all its subsidiaries. His contract contained a restraint of trade clause (clause 15(1)) barring him for one year after leaving the company's employment from soliciting the customers of the company and its subsidiaries. The company was purchased by the plaintiffs and, following completion of the sale agreement, Mr Hollande was dismissed. The plaintiffs subsequently sought to enforce the restraint of trade clause. The question which arose was whether, in the light of what is now reg. 4(1) of the regulations, the plaintiffs were entitled to enforce the restriction in relation to those who had done business with Altolight or its subsidiaries during the relevant year, or whether the effect of reg. 4(1) was that, following the transfer of the undertaking, the restriction had to be read as relating to those who had done business with the plaintiffs in that period. Allowing the plaintiffs' appeal, the Court of Appeal adopted the former interpretation.

DILLON LJ: The key words in regulation [4(1)] are the words: '[the contract] shall have effect after the transfer as if originally made between the person so employed and the transferee.' It does have in a sense retrospective effect. Turner J considered that the service agreement was therefore to be read ab initio as if made between the plaintiffs rather than the company and Mr Hollande. Clause 15(1) was therefore to be read as an agreement by Mr Hollande not in the relevant year to solicit or undertake business for persons who in the previous year—on the facts of this case the year to 29 April 1992—had done business with the plaintiffs, not the persons who in that year had done business with the company or its subsidiaries—the group. It followed that, as Mr Hollande was not seeking to do business with persons who in the previous year had done business with the plaintiffs, but only with the persons who had done business with the company, there was no covenant available to the plaintiffs under which injunctive relief could be granted. Turner J said:

It does not seem to me that the plaintiffs have come within measurable distance of being able to assert a valid right which they can enforce under the provisions of clause 15(1) or (2) of the contract of employment.

The difficulty about that approach to my mind is that it turns the obligation on the employee under clause 15(1) into a quite different and possibly much wider obligation than the obligation which bound him before the transfer, that is to say an obligation not to do business, etc. with the persons who had done business in the relevant year with the plaintiffs, not the company. Such an obligation was not remotely in contemplation when the service agreement was entered into and I can see no reason why the regulation should have sought to change the burden on the employee. As Lord Templeman pointed out, the object was that the benefit and burden should devolve on the new employer. That would mean in the present context that the transferee should be able to enforce the same restriction.

The more reasonable construction is in my judgment that the words '[the contract] shall have effect' are to be read as referring to the transferee as the owner of the undertaking transferred or in respect of the undertaking transferred. The effect therefore is that clause 15(1) can be enforced by the plaintiffs if Mr Hollande within the year after 29 April 1992 does business with persons who in the previous year had done business with the undertaking transferred of which the plaintiffs are deemed as a result of the transfer retrospectively to have been the owner. The plaintiffs are thus given locus standi to enforce the restriction.

I therefore respectfully differ from Turner J on the construction point and I would hold so far as that point is concerned that regulation [4(1)] entitles the plaintiffs to enforce clause 15(1) as against Mr Hollande if he solicits or does business with those who have done business with the company in the previous year...

NOTES

1. In *Allan and others* v *Stirling District Council* [1994] IRLR 208 the EAT sitting in Scotland held that what is now reg. 4(2) does not release the transferor from its liabilities, e.g. for unfair dismissal, that it would otherwise have to bear had there been no transfer of an undertaking.

    Does this pedantic interpretation of reg. 4(2) accord with the spirit of the Transfer of Undertakings Regulations?

2. The contract is transferred only if the employee consents.

Katsikas v *Konstantinidis*
[1993] IRLR 179, European Court of Justice

The plaintiff was employed as a cook in the defendant's restaurant in Germany. The restaurant was sold to a Mr Mitossis, but the plaintiff had such a dislike of the purchaser that he refused to work for him and was dismissed by the defendant. The plaintiff brought a claim against his original employer, Konstantinidis, who argued that the responsible person was, by virtue of the directive, the new owner, Mitossis. The ECJ held that the directive did not preclude an employee objecting to the automatic transfer of his contract. To oblige the employee to work for the new owner would be a breach of his fundamental rights. However, the ECJ also held that it was for Member States to decide what would be the effect of an employee's objection to the transfer of his contract of employment. The directive does not oblige Member States to provide that the contract of employment or employment relationship be continued where an employee freely decides not to continue employment with the transferee. The fate of the contract of employment or the employment relationship in such cases is for Member States to determine.

In fact, if the Directive, which is intended to achieve only partial harmonisation of the subject-matter (see judgment of *Daddy's Dance Hall* [1988] IRLR 315), allows an employee to remain in employment with a new employer on the same conditions as those agreed with the transferor it cannot be interpreted as obliging the employee to continue his employment relationship with the transferee.

Such an obligation would undermine the fundamental rights of the employee who must be free to choose his employer and cannot be obliged to work for an employer that he has not freely chosen.

It follows from that that the provisions of Article 3(1) of the Directive do not prevent an employee from objecting to the transfer of his contract of employment or of his employment relationship and, thus, from not benefiting from the protection provided to him by the Directive.

Nevertheless, as the Court has held (in its judgment in *Berg and Busschers* [1989] IRLR 447), the purpose of the Directive is not to ensure that the contract of employment or the employment relationship with the transferor is continued where the undertaking's employees do not wish to remain in the transferee's employ.

It follows from that that the Directive does not oblige Member States to provide that the contract of employment or employment relationship be continued with the transferor in a case where an employee freely decides not to continue the contract of employment or the employment relationship with the transferee. In such cases, it is for the Member States to determine the fate of the contract of employment or of the employment relationship.

The Member States may, in particular, provide that in this case, the contract of employment or the employment relationship may be considered as terminated either on the initiative of the employee or on the initiative of the employer. They may also provide that the contract of employment or the employment relationship be continued with the transferor.

NOTES

1. As a result of the decision in *Katsikas*, the Government hurriedly introduced an amendment to the regulations via s. 33(4) of TURERA 1993. The amendments are now represented by reg. 4(7)–(8) of the 2006 Regulations (see earlier extract in this section). Regulation 4(7) provides that the automatic transfer principle shall not apply in the case 'of an employee who informs the transferor or transferee that he objects to becoming employed by the transferee'.

   The consequences of such an objection are by reg. 4(8) stated to be that the transfer operates 'to terminate his contract of employment with the transferor but he shall not be treated, for any purpose, as having been dismissed by the transferor.'

   The cumulative effect of these strange provisions is that, although the worker has a theoretical right to refuse to transfer, if that right is exercised, he or she has no rights against either transferee or transferor in terms of unfair dismissal or redundancy payments. However, there are two exceptions to this rather hopeless position from the employee's point of view. First, reg. 4(9)–(10) introduces a new right to complain of unfair constructive dismissal where the transfer involves a substantial change in working conditions which are to the material detriment of the employee but falls short of constituting a repudiatory breach of the contract. Regulation 4(9) overturns the decision of the Court of Appeal in *Rossiter* v *Pendragon plc* [2002] IRLR 248 where it was held that an employee can only be claimed to have been constructively dismissed under the TUPE Regulations by reason of a substantial change in his working conditions if the employer's actions amounted to a repudiatory contractual breach. The second exception is contained in reg. 4(11) and expressly retains the employee's right to claim constructive dismissal by terminating the contract without notice in response to a repudiatory breach of contract by the employer.

2. In *Photostation Copiers* v *Okuda* [1995] IRLR 11, the EAT held that an employee cannot consent to a transfer if he does not know about it; accordingly, in such a situation he continued to be employed by the transferor.

3. The 1981 Regulations appeared to indicate that the purchaser of a business took on its employees only if they were employed by the transferor 'immediately before' the transfer. This wording was interpreted very strictly in *Secretary of State for Employment* v *Spence* [1987] 1 QB 179, where

the Court of Appeal held that the 1981 Regulations applied only to employees employed by the transferor at the very moment of transfer. In other words, a business purchaser could not be made liable for dismissals carried out by the vendor before transfer.

In the light of the decision in *Spence*, it was possible for a transferee to make it a condition of purchase that the vendor should dismiss all or some of its employees prior to the transfer date, i.e. that the vendor takes on the responsibility of meeting any redundancy payments. Indeed, an insolvent or near insolvent vendor may not object too much to such a proposal because the likelihood would be that such payments would be met by the State Fund.

This major gap in the protection offered by the regulations was closed as a result of the following case and subsequent amendment to the regulations.

Litster v Forth Dry Dock Engineering Ltd
[1989] IRLR 161, House of Lords

The employer went into liquidation in September 1983, and at 3.30 p.m. on 6 February 1984 the 12 applicant employees were summarily dismissed. Later that day, the assets of the business were purchased and the purchaser engaged some of the former employees but not the applicants. The House of Lords held that in the case of an unfair dismissal the words 'immediately before the transfer' must be read as if there were inserted after the words 'or would have been so employed if he had not been unfairly dismissed within the circumstances described in regulation 8(1).' Accordingly the purchaser of the business was held liable to compensate the applicants.

References in this extract are to the Articles of the Acquired Rights Directive (77/187/EEC) and the TUPE Regulations (1981).

LORD OLIVER: ...It is, I think, now clear that under Article 4 of the Directive, as construed by the European Court of Justice, a dismissal effected before the transfer and solely because of the transfer of the business is, in effect, prohibited and is, for the purpose of considering the application of Article 3(1), required to be treated as ineffective. The question is whether the Regulations are so framed as to be capable of being construed in conformity with that interpretation of the Directive.

...Having regard to the manifest purpose of the Regulations, I do not, for my part, feel inhibited from making such an implication in the instant case. The provision in regulation 8(1) that a dismissal by reason of a transfer is to be treated as an unfair dismissal, is merely a different way of saying that the transfer is not to 'constitute a ground for dismissal' as contemplated by Article 4 of the Directive and there is no good reason for denying to it the same effect as that attributed to that Article. In effect this involves reading regulation 5(3) as if there were inserted after the words 'immediately before the transfer' the words 'or would have been so employed if he had not been unfairly dismissed in the circumstances described in regulation 8(1).' For my part, I would make such an implication which is entirely consistent with the general scheme of the Regulations and which is necessary if they are effectively to fulfil the purpose for which they were made of giving effect to the provisions of the Directive.

NOTES
1. Regulation 4(3) of the 2006 Regulations gives statutory effect to the decision of the House of Lords in *Litster*.
2. In addition to arguing that the particular transfer is not covered by the 1981 Regulations, two other possibilities exist where a transferee employer is seeking to avoid inheriting the terms and conditions enjoyed by the transferor's workforce. The first is for the transferee to dismiss and then offer to re-engage on new terms and conditions. This will render the transferee liable to unfair dismissal claims and can hardly be held up as good industrial relations practice. The other possibility is for the transferee to seek to negotiate an agreed variation of terms and conditions with the workforce or their representatives. The legal implications of both approaches were considered by the House of Lords in the following cases.

Wilson and others v St Helens Borough Council; British Fuels Ltd v Meade and Baxendale
[1988] IRLR 706, House of Lords

In the *British Fuels* case, Mr Baxendale was employed from 1977, and Mr Meade from 1978, by National Fuels Distributors, a subsidiary of the British Coal Corporation. On

20 August 1992, they were given notice that they were to be dismissed by reason of redundancy, effective from 28 August. They received wages in lieu of notice, statutory and enhanced redundancy pay.

On the same day that they received notice of dismissal, British Fuels Ltd, another subsidiary of the British Coal Corporation, offered them employment with effect from 1 September 1992 on terms that were less favourable than those they had enjoyed with National Fuels Distributors. They accepted the offers of employment and started work for British Fuels Ltd on 1 September. On the same day National Fuels was merged with British Fuels.

Both men sought a declaration from an employment tribunal under what is now s. 11 of the ERA 1996. It was contended that their dismissals were ineffective as a matter of European law. Therefore, it followed that they had transferred to British Fuels on the terms and conditions they had enjoyed with National Fuels Distributors. The claims were rejected and their appeal was dismissed by the EAT. The Court of Appeal decided in the applicants' favour, but gave leave to appeal to the House of Lords.

In the other case, Wilson and his colleagues were employed by Lancashire County Council at Red Bank Controlled Community Home. In 1990, Lancashire gave notice to the home's trustees that, because of funding problems, it would cease to manage the school after 30 September 1992. St Helens Borough Council agreed to take over the control of the home on 1 October 1992, on condition that the running of the school would involve no charge on its own resources. Prior to the transfer, there were negotiations between the transferor and the recognised union, NASUWT. It was agreed that staff at the home would be reduced from 162 to 72, that those transferring to St Helens would be appointed to new posts with different job descriptions and that those not transferring would be redeployed by Lancashire. It was assumed that the transfer of the management of the home to St Helens was not covered by the 1981 Regulations.

The 72 employees were offered employment by St Helens on terms which were different from those on which they had previously been employed. They were sent letters by Lancashire terminating their employment. After the transfer, nine of the employees, including Mr Wilson, made complaints under the Wages Act, claiming that they were being paid less than they were contractually entitled to when working for Lancashire County Council, and that the difference was an unlawful deduction from their wages which they should be paid. The industrial tribunal dismissed the applications on the grounds that there had been an effective variation in the employees' terms of employment when they agreed new terms following transfer. The EAT, however, held that if the operative reason for an agreed variation in an employee's terms and conditions is the transfer of an undertaking, the variation is ineffective and the terms of the original contract of employment remain in force. The EAT relied on the decision of the ECJ in *Foreningen af Arbejdsledere i Danmark* v *Daddy's Dance Hall* [1988] IRLR 315, where it was held that:

> An employee cannot waive the rights conferred upon him by the mandatory provisions of Directive 77/187/EEC even if the disadvantages resulting from his waiver are offset by such benefits, that taking the matter as a whole, he is not placed in a worse position.

The Court of Appeal allowed the employer's appeal, holding that a dismissal because of a transfer of an undertaking is prohibited and a legal nullity unless the dismissal is for an economic, technical or organisational (ETO) reason entailing changes in the workforce. In the *Wilson* case, the industrial tribunal was entitled to find that there was an ETO reason for the variation in the terms and conditions of employment which occurred on the transfer, and that the termination of the employees' contracts was not simply due to the transfer. The employees' appeal was dismissed by the House of Lords.

LORD SLYNN OF HADLEY: …Two issues are broadly common to the two appeals. The first is whether, on the transfer the employees were entitled to retain the benefit of their previous terms and conditions. The first issue in effect raises the question as to whether the dismissals or purported dismissals by the previous employers took effect or whether they were nullities. Put another way, the question is whether the dismissed employee can compel the transferee to employ him or whether he is given the right to enforce as against the transferee such remedies under national law as he could have enforced against the transferor. The second is whether, if despite dismissal they were entitled to retain the benefit of their previous terms, the employees either by initially agreeing terms with their new employers, or by continuing to work for the new employers or (in the case of Mr Meade and Mr Baxendale by accepting the statement of terms and conditions subsequently) varied any entitlement to the previous terms and conditions.

…

[His Lordship considered the following European authorities: *Wendelboe* v *LJ Music APS*, C–19/83 [1985] ECR 457; *Arbejdsledere i Danmark* v *A/S Danmols Inventar ('Mikkelsen's case')*, C–105/84 [1985] ECR 2639; *Katsikas* v *Konstantinidis and others*, C–139/91 [1993] IRLR 179; *D'Urso and others* v *Ercole Marelli Elettromeccanica Generale and others*, C–262/89 [1992] IRLR 136; *Rask* v *ISS Kantineservice A/S*, C–209/91 [1983] IRLR 133; *Jules Dethier Equipement SA* v *Dassy and Sovram*, C–319/94 [1998] IRLR 266. Commenting on the contention that the purported dismissals were a nullity—the first issue—he stated:]

In my opinion, the overriding emphasis in the European Court's judgments is that the existing rights of employees are to be safeguarded if there is a transfer. That means no more and no less than that the employee can look to the transferee to perform those obligations which the employee could have enforced against the transferor. The employer, be he transferor or transferee, cannot use the transfer as a justification for dismissal, but if he does dismiss it is a question for national law as to what those rights are. As I have already said, in English law there would as a general rule be no order for specific performance. The claim would be for damages for wrongful dismissal or for statutory rights including, it is true, reinstatement or re-engagement where applicable. It may be in other countries that an order for specific performance could be obtained under the appropriate domestic law and that on this approach different results would be achieved in different Member States. That I do not find surprising or shocking. The Directive is to 'approximate' the laws of the Member States. Its purpose is to 'safeguard' rights on a transfer. The 'rights' of an employee must depend on national rules of the law of contract or of legislation. There is no Community law of contract common to Member States, nor is there a common system or remedies. The object and purpose of the Directive is to ensure in all Member States that on a transfer an employee has against the transferee the rights and remedies which he would have had against the original employer. To that extent it reduces the differences which may exist in the event of a change of employers as to the enforcement by employees of existing rights. They must all provide for enforcement against the transferee of rights existing against the transferor at the time of transfer. It seems to me that the Court has clearly recognised that the precise rights to be transferred depend on national law. But neither the Regulations nor the Directive nor the jurisprudence of the Court create a Community law right to continue in employment which does not exist under national law.

It is said that this is not an adequate remedy because some employees do not have statutory rights—e.g. those in the United Kingdom who have not been employed for a qualifying period—but that is inherent in the differences which exist in the laws of the Member States and seems to me to derive from the wording and limited purpose of the Directive.

Thus, where there is a transfer of an undertaking and the transferee actually takes on the employee the contract of employment is automatically transferred so that, in the absence of a permissible variation, the terms of the initial contract go with the employee, who, though he may refuse to go, cannot as a matter of public policy waive the rights which the Directive and the Regulations confer on him. Where the transferee does not take on the employees who are dismissed on transfer the dismissal is not a nullity, though the contractual rights formerly available against the transferor remain intact against the transferee. For the latter purpose, an employee dismissed prior to the transfer contrary to Article 4(1), i.e. on the basis of the transfer, is to be treated as still in the employment of the transferor at the date of transfer so as to satisfy the rule in *Wendelboe* as consistently followed, e.g. in *Ny Mølle Kro*.

…

Accordingly, it is not strictly necessary to deal with the second issue which has been raised as to whether variation of the terms of employment could lawfully be agreed between the parties. Since the matter has been fully argued, particularly in the case of *Wilson*, I express my opinion on the point.

The second issue

…

The question as to whether and in what situations, where there has been a transfer and employees have accepted the dismissal, claimed compensation based on it and worked for a long period after the transfer, there can be a valid variation by conduct is not an easy one. I do not accept the argument that the variation is only invalid if it is agreed on or as a part of the transfer itself. The variation may still be due to the transfer and for no other reason even if it comes later. However, it seems that there must, or at least may, come a time when the link with the transfer is broken or can be treated as no longer effective. If the appeal turned on this question I would find it necessary to refer a question to the European Court under Article 177 of the Treaty both in the case of Mr Meade and in the case of Mr Baxendale. Since in my view the dismissal was effective, so that no question of variation falls to be considered, it is not necessary for your Lordships to decide the matter or to refer a question to the European Court.

...

It seems to me clear, as Miss Booth QC contended, that the industrial tribunal in *Wilson*'s case found on the evidence before it, and the Court of Appeal accepted, that the home could not continue unless there were radical organisational changes which would reduce the cost of running the school. LCC could not or would not continue to carry the existing costs. St Helens could not take over the running of the school with those costs and without organisational changes and reduced costs. Those changes were for an economic or organisational reason and entailed a change in the workforce since the number of employees at the school was considerably reduced, whether or not the 'ETO' defence can strictly be relied on in the present circumstances. The staff had the option of staying with LCC or going to St Helens on the new terms to give effect to these economic and organisational reasons. In the circumstances, the industrial tribunal and the Court of Appeal were entitled to find that the transfer of the undertaking did not constitute the reason for the variation. It was a variation of the terms of employment 'to the same extent as it could have been with regard to the transferor' (*Daddy's Dance Hall*, paragraph 17). That seems to me to be sufficient on the facts to determine the appeal in *Wilson*'s case. But I add that, although on a transfer, the employees' rights previously existing against the transferor are enforceable against the transferee and cannot be amended by the transfer itself, it does not follow there cannot be a variation of the terms of the contract for reasons which are not due to the transfer either on or after the transfer of the undertaking. It may be difficult to decide whether the variation is due to the transfer or attributable to some separate cause. If, however, the variation is not due to the transfer it can, in my opinion, on the basis of the authorities to which I have referred, validly be made.

Conclusion

In the result, however, I would allow the appeal of British Fuels Ltd in both Mr Baxendale's and Mr Meade's cases and I would dismiss the appeal of Mr Wilson and others against St Helens Borough Council.

NOTES

1. Following the judgments in *Wilson* and *Meade*, employers who wish to vary terms and conditions after a transfer through voluntary agreement are still left uncertain whether such a change will be effective. On the other hand, employers involved in a transfer can change terms and conditions of employment by dismissing employees with full contractual notice and offering new contracts on the revised terms. However, such a dismissal will be held to be automatically unfair in most cases. The reason for this is that it was held in *Berriman* v *Delabole Slate Ltd* [1985] IRLR 305 that it is not usually possible to establish an ETO reason where the change does not directly entail a reduction in the workforce.

   Nevertheless, an employer might decide, following a cost–benefit analysis, that the cost savings achieved through changes in conditions outweigh the costs of any unfair dismissal compensation. This may be a less frequent conclusion in future now that the Employment Relations Act 1999 raised substantially the upper limit on unfair dismissal compensation from £12,000 to £50,000 (and from then on index-linked to the annual rate of inflation—currently £78,335 (w.e.f. 6 April 2015). In any event, it may well be that most good employers eschew this 'fire and rehire' strategy, regarding it as a throwback to 'macho management' approaches that gained currency during the 1980s.

   In this context then, it is disappointing that good employers who seek to agree changes in terms and conditions of employment with their workforce will find that any agreed variation is invalid if the change is prompted by the transfer. Of course, what underlies the 'no waiver' principle are the difficulties in determining whether or not a particular agreement is truly based on the consent of the workers affected (consequently, see reg. 18 in the following extract). This certainly may be a legitimate concern where employees do not have recourse to trade union representation, but less so where a trade union is recognised and there are established collective bargaining arrangements. There is a contradiction between the 'no waiver' principle and the consultation requirements laid down by the 1981 Regulations and the Acquired Rights Directive.

There is little point in engaging in consultation with employee representatives about the consequences of a transfer if an agreement to vary terms and conditions, which is the outcome of the consultative process, is null and void. Moreover, as Rubenstein, commenting on the EAT stage in *Wilson*, observes: 'The decision also creates the paradox that a transferee needing to reduce costs is protected by TUPE if it dismisses employees on the grounds of redundancy, but is precluded from offering to save jobs if costs can be reduced by varying contractual terms' ('Highlights' [1996] IRLR 317).

This contradiction is further underlined when certain of the amendments to the Acquired Rights Directive are examined. The directive, as amended, allows Member States options to limit or restrict its operation in relation to transfers by insolvent transferors. Article 4a(2) permits a transferor which is insolvent to agree with transferees and representatives of its employees alterations to the employees' terms and conditions of employment 'designed to safeguard employment opportunities by ensuring the survival of the undertaking'. This provision represents a modification of the principle of the compulsory transfer of employment on the employees' existing terms and conditions where there is collective agreement: a modification firmly rejected by both the British and European courts (see *Foreningen af Arbejdsledere i Danmark* v *Daddy's Dance Hall A/S* (Case 324/86 [1988] IRLR 315, ECJ; *Rask* v *ISS Kantineservice A/S* [1993] IRLR 133, ECJ; *Crédit Suisse First Boston (Europe) Ltd* v *Lister* [1998] IRLR 700, CA; *Martin* v *South Bank University* [2004] IRLR 74, ECJ).

2. In the light of the confused legal position, regs. 4(4), (5), (5A), (5B), and (5C) of the 2006 Regulations (as amended by the 2014 Regulations) seek to add some clarification. The effect of these provisions are set out in the following guidance produced by the Department for Business Innovation and Skills *[authors' notes and comments in parenthesis and italics]*.

Changes to terms and conditions

The Regulations ensure that employees are not penalised when they are transferred by being placed on inferior terms and conditions. So, not only are their pre-existing terms and conditions transferred across on the first day of their employment with the new employer, but employees may not validly waive their acquired rights. The Regulations therefore impose limitations on the ability of the new employer and employee to agree a variation to terms and conditions thereafter.

The position for cases to which the amendments made by the 2014 Regulations apply

The general rule is that contracts cannot be varied if the sole or principal reason for the variation is the transfer. If there is such a purported variation, the Regulations render those changes void. This is so even if the employer and employee agreed the variation and it would have been a valid variation had there not been a transfer.

The same restrictions apply to the transferor where he contemplates changing terms and conditions of those employees who will transfer to the new employer in anticipation of the transfer occurring *[reg 4(4)]*. However, the employer may vary terms and conditions in any of the following circumstances:

A. When the reason for variation is unrelated to the transfer. In this case, the sole or principal reason for the variation will not be the transfer and therefore the restriction in the TUPE Regulations does not apply.

B. When the sole or principal reason for variation is 'an economic, technical or organisational reason entailing changes in the workforce', provided that the employer and employee agree that variation... *[reg 4(5)(a)]*

C. When the terms of the employment contract permit the employer to make such a variation *[e.g. pursuant to a 'mobility' or 'flexibility' clause]*. However, employees cannot waive their rights under the Regulations. So if an employer seeks to agree a term giving the employer power to make variations in future, if the sole or principal reason for agreeing that power is the transfer, this will be caught by the general restriction on variations of contract and be void. *[reg. 4(5)(b)]*

D. When the contract of employment incorporates terms and conditions from a collective agreement, those terms and conditions may be varied in limited circumstances even though the sole or principal reason for the variation is the transfer. They may be varied from the date which is more than a year after the date of the transfer provided that after that variation, overall, the employee's contract is no less favourable to the employee than it was immediately before the variation *[reg. 4(5B)]*. This means that the employer could seek to agree effective variations to terms and conditions incorporated from a collective agreement, which may result in those particular terms being less favourable to the employee, provided that the employee gets some other more favourable terms, so that overall, the employee is in a no less favourable position after the variation compared to immediately before it. It is only the terms incorporated from a collective agreement which the employer can seek to make less favourable under this exception, although the employer could agree to new individual terms which are entirely beneficial to the employee to offset the less favourable changes. Changes to other terms are not within this exception and the general rule that they cannot be varied if the sole or principal reason is the transfer continues to apply. If the test that overall the changes are no less favourable is not satisfied, then the purported variation is void.

E. When changes are entirely positive from the employee's perspective. The underlying purpose of the Regulations is to ensure that employees are not penalised when a transfer takes place. Changes to terms and conditions agreed by the parties which are entirely positive are not prevented by the Regulations. *[There is no express provision in the Regulations to justify this statement. The logic of Wilson would suggest that a transferring employee would be denied the benefits of a post-transfer modification which was entirely positive. However, the statement is supported by the Court of Appeal decision in Power v Regent Security Services Ltd [2008] ICR 442).]*

F. In certain insolvency situations *[see reg. 9]*

Apart from the exception for insolvency situations, the general rules as to whether a contract of employment is effectively varied continue to apply. Nothing in TUPE gives the employer any ability to impose variations to contracts. For example, if the employer is seeking to rely upon a term of the contract which purports to give it a power to vary a particular provision (such as a mobility clause), the employer will only be able validly to vary the contract in a particular way if such variation would be given effect by the law in the absence of a TUPE transfer. Any ambiguity in the meaning of such a term is generally resolved in favour of the employee and other terms of the contract may also limit what the employer can do under it.

These exceptions do not affect the operation of regulation 4(9) of the TUPE Regulations, which is concerned with the situation where a transfer involves a substantial change in working conditions to the material detriment of an employee who is transferring…So if an employer sought to vary contracts in reliance upon a term of the contract giving it the power to vary something, an employee might be entitled to treat the contract as having been terminated (*Employment Rights on the Transfer of Undertaking: A guide to the 2006 Regulations (as amended by the Collective Redundancies and Transfer of Undertakings (Protection of Employment) (Amendment) Regulations 2014) for employees, employers and representatives*, Department for Business Innovation and Skills, January 2014).

3. As can be seen from the above extract, reg. 4(5B) states where a term of the employment contract is derived from a collective agreement and the contractual variation:
   (a) takes effect more than one year after the date of the transfer; and
   (b) results in a contract which is overall no less favourable to the employee,
   the variation will be valid.

   For transfers which took place *before* the 2014 Amendment Regulations came into force (31 January 2014), the meaning of the TUPE Regulations was reliant on the outcome of EU litigation which was finally resolved in 2013.

   In *Werhof* v *Freeway Traffic Systems Gmb & Co KG* [2006] IRLR 400, the ECJ decided that the Acquired Rights Directive did not intend a transferee employer to be bound by any collective agreement other than one in force at the time of the transfer. In other words, those liabilities arising from a collective agreement incorporated into a contract of employment, which transfer under TUPE, will cease when the collective agreement is terminated, expires or is replaced by a new collective agreement (the so-called 'static' approach). The competing view is that the transferee is obliged to observe new negotiated terms and conditions so long as that term remains in the employees' contracts of employment (the so-called 'dynamic' approach).

   In *Parkwood Leisure Ltd* v *Alemo-Herron* [2013] 744, the CJEU finally resolved the question on whether *Werhof* prevents UK courts from giving TUPE a dynamic interpretation. The EAT, in this case, had held that the judgment in *Werhof*, which was as to the scope of the directive, did not prevent domestic law providing for wider rights. The Court of Appeal reversed the EAT's decision, holding that reg. 5 of TUPE simply implemented Article 3(1) and did not provide for wider rights. The Supreme Court has referred the case to the CJEU requesting guidance on whether Article 3(1) precludes national courts from giving a dynamic interpretation to reg. 5 of TUPE in a case such as *Parkwood Leisure*.

   The CJEU held that Article 3(1) 'must be interpreted as precluding a Member State from providing, in the event of a transfer of undertaking, that dynamic clauses referring to collective agreements negotiated and adopted after the date of transfer are enforceable against the transferee, where the transferee does not have the possibility of participating in the negotiation process of such collective agreements concluded after the date of the transfer'.

4. The EAT's decision in *Solectron Scotland Ltd* v *Roper* [2004] IRLR 4 deals with the question whether it is possible to use a compromise agreement in order to harmonise the terms of the transferred employees with those of the new employer. The EAT holds that case law establishes that an

employer cannot, after a transfer, vary the terms of an employee's contract if that variation is solely by reason of the transfer. However, the EAT goes on to rule that, in the instant case, the compromise agreement did not arise solely or even mainly by reason of the transfer. Its effect was solely to compromise a financial claim that the employee had on the termination of contract, i.e. the enhanced redundancy terms the employees brought with them following a TUPE transfer. The employer was not purporting to vary the contract but merely to compromise a dispute as to its value. There was no change in the terms and conditions for the future by reason of the fact that the contract had come to an end. Accordingly, the policy underlying the directive, *Daddy's Dance Hall*, and related cases, was not infringed by permitting compromise agreements of this kind.

TRANSFER OF UNDERTAKINGS (PROTECTION OF EMPLOYMENT) REGULATIONS 2006 (SI 2006/246) (as amended)

7 Dismissal of employee because of relevant transfer

(1) Where before or after a relevant transfer, any employee of the transferor or transferee is dismissed, that employee shall be treated for the purposes of Part 10 of the 1996 Act (unfair dismissal) as unfairly dismissed if the sole or principal reason for his dismissal is the transfer.

(2) This paragraph applies where the sole or principal reason for the dismissal is an economic, technical or organisational reason entailing changes in the workforce of either the transferor or the transferee before or after a relevant transfer.

(3) Where paragraph (2) applies—

(a) paragraph (1) shall not apply;

(b) without prejudice to the application of section 98(4) of the 1996 Act (test of fair dismissal), for the purposes of sections 98(1) and 135 of that Act (reason for dismissal)—

(i) the dismissal is regarded as having been for redundancy where section 98(2)(c) of that Act applies; or

(ii) in any other case, the dismissal is regarded as having been for a substantial reason of a kind such as to justify the dismissal of an employee holding the position which that employee held.

(3A) In paragraph (2), the expression 'changes in the workforce' includes a change to the place where employees are employed by the employer to carry on the business of the employer or to carry out work of a particular kind for the employer (and the reference to such a place has the same meaning as in section 139 of the 1996 Act.

(4) The provisions of this regulation apply irrespective of whether the employee in question is assigned to the organised grouping of resources or employees that is, or will be, transferred.

(5) Paragraph (1) shall not apply in relation to the dismissal of any employee which was required by reason of the application of section 5 of the Aliens Restriction (Amendment) Act 1919 to his employment.

(6) Paragraph (1) shall not apply in relation to a dismissal of an employee if the application of section 94 of the 1996 Act to the dismissal of the employee is excluded by or under any provision of the 1996 Act, the 1996 Tribunals Act or the 1992 Act.

NOTES

1. Regulation 7 provides that a dismissal of an employee of the transferor or transferee where the sole or principal reason is the transfer of the business is automatically unfair unless it is for an 'economic, technical, or organisational reason entailing changes in the workforce' (the 'ETO' defence). By virtue of reg. 7(3)(ii), such dismissals are deemed to be for a substantial reason for the purpose of the ERA 1996, s. 98(1), and are fair provided they pass the statutory test of reasonableness. If the employer does successfully establish the ETO defence, an employee can claim a redundancy payment if redundancy was the reason for the transfer dismissal (*Gorictree Ltd* v *Jenkinson* [1984] IRLR 391; s.7(3)(i)).

2. The scope of the ETO defence was considered by the Court of Appeal in *Berriman* v *Delabole Slate Ltd* [1985] IRLR 305. The court held that in order to come within what is now reg. 7(2), the employer must show that a plan to achieve changes in the workforce, not just a possible consequence of the plan. So where an employee resigned following a transfer because the transferee employer proposed to remove his guaranteed weekly wage so as to bring his pay into line with the transferee's existing workforce, the reason behind the plan was to produce uniform terms and conditions and was not in any way to reduce the numbers in the workforce.

In *Hazel* v *The Manchester College* [2014] IRLR 392, CA, the claimants were dismissed after they refused to agree to new terms of employment, including a reduction in pay, that were offered as part of a large-scale attempt to harmonise terms and conditions following a TUPE transfer. It was argued on behalf of the employers that an ETO reason applied because the dismissals were part of an overall rationalisation that included workforce changes in the form of redundancies, but the Court of Appeal did not agree and upheld the findings below that the dismissals were unfair. Lord Justice Underhill stated that 'the proposed harmonisation of terms was in a general sense related to the proposal for redundancies... But the fact that there was a relationship of that kind has no bearing on the statutory question of what was "the sole or principal reason for" the claimants' dismissals.'

3. A contrasting case is *Crawford* v *Swinton Insurance Brokers Ltd* [1990] IRLR 42. Prior to transfer of the business, Mrs Crawford was a clerk typist working mainly from home. After the transfer, she was offered other work with the changed function of selling insurance. She refused and claimed she had been constructively and unfairly dismissed. The EAT held that if, as a result of an organisational change on a relevant transfer, a workforce is engaged in a different occupation or function, there is a change of workforce for the purpose of what is now reg. 7(2) and any dismissal is potentially fair.

4. It has been held that where a prospective purchaser insists on the prior dismissal of existing employees, this is not an 'economic reason' within the meaning of reg. 7(2) so that a dismissal in such circumstances will be unfair (*Wheeler* v *Patel* [1987] ICR 631). However, *Wheeler* was distinguished by the Court of Appeal in *Whitehouse* v *Chas A. Blachford & Sons Ltd* [1999] IRLR 492. In this case, the transferees were the successful bidders for a contract, but this was made conditional upon a cost reduction to be achieved by making one of the 13 technicians redundant. The man selected, Mr Whitehouse, complained that his dismissal was in breach of the 1981 Regulations and thus unfair. The Court of Appeal, in dismissing his appeal, held that it was open to the employment tribunal to conclude that the transfer was not the reason for the appellant's dismissal and that the dismissal was for an economic or organisational reason. The court could not accept the argument on behalf of the appellant that there was no difference between a dismissal to secure the sale of a business—as in *Wheeler*—and a dismissal which was in order to get a contract. The demand for services under the contract was for one less technician, and the position would have been the same if the previous employers had been awarded the contract. In those circumstances, the transfer of the undertaking was the occasion for the reduction in the requirements for the services of the technicians, but it was not the cause or reason for that reduction. The reduction was directly connected with the provision of the services and with the conduct of any business which provided them. That was in no way analogous to the position of the vendor of a business who dismisses employees solely for the purpose of achieving the best price for the business. In *Hynd* v *Armstrong* [2007] IRLR 338, the Court of Session, Inner House, confirmed that a transferor employer cannot rely on the tranferee's reason for dismissal in order to establish an ETO defence. In *Hynd*, a pre-transfer dismissal of a solicitor because the transferees did not require him was held to be automatically unfair. The Court of Session held that it was 'reasonably clear' that the EU Transfers Directive did not 'permit dismissal in such circumstances'. A transferor can only rely on a reason of its own.

5. In *Spaceright Europe Ltd* v *Baillavoine* [2012] IRLR 111, CA, Lord Justice Mummery said that: 'For an ETO reason to be available there must be an intention to change the workforce and to continue to conduct the business, as distinct from the purpose of selling it. It is not available in the case of dismissing an employee to enable the administrators to make the business of the company a more attractive proposition to prospective transferees of a going concern.' This dictum was distinguished in *Crystal Palace FC Ltd* v *Kavanagh* [2014] IRLR 139. The CA held that dismissals by an administrator in order to reduce the wage bill so as to keep the business afloat were for an ETO reason entailing changes in the workforce. Although the administrator had a longer-term objective of securing the sale of the business, that was a separate reason from the administrator's shorter-term objective. As a result, the dismissals were not automatically unfair and liability did not pass to the new owner of the business.

6. The amendments made by the 2014 Regulations added a further situation covered by the phrase 'entailing changes in the workforce'. As a result, a change to the place where employees are employed on the business of the employer, or to carry out work of a particular kind for the employer now constitutes an ETO reason (s. 7(3A)).

TRANSFER OF UNDERTAKINGS (PROTECTION OF EMPLOYMENT) REGULATIONS 2006 (SI 2006/246) (as amended)

10 Pensions

(1) Regulations 4 and 5 shall not apply—

  (a) to so much of a contract of employment or collective agreement as relates to an occupational pension scheme within the meaning of the Pension Schemes Act 1993; or

  (b) to any rights, powers, duties or liabilities under or in connection with any such contract or subsisting by virtue of any such agreement and relating to such a scheme or otherwise arising in connection with that person's employment and relating to such a scheme.

(2) For the purposes of paragraphs (1) and (3), any provisions of an occupational pension scheme which do not relate to benefits for old age, invalidity or survivors shall not be treated as being part of the scheme.

(3) An employee whose contract of employment is transferred in the circumstances described in regulation 4(1) shall not be entitled to bring a claim against the transferor for—

  (a) breach of contract; or

  (b) constructive unfair dismissal under section 95(1)(c) of the 1996 Act,

arising out of a loss or reduction in his rights under an occupational pension scheme in consequence of the transfer, save insofar as the alleged breach of contract or dismissal (as the case may be) occurred prior to the date on which these Regulations took effect.

18 Restriction on contracting out

Section 203 of the 1996 Act (restrictions on contracting out) shall apply in relation to these Regulations as if they were contained in that Act, save for that section shall not apply in so far as these Regulations provide for an agreement (whether a contract of employment or not) to exclude or limit the operation of these Regulations.

NOTES

1. Regulation 10 excludes transfer of 'so much of a contract of employment or collective agreement as relates to an occupational pension scheme'. The question in *Beckmann* v *Dynamco Whicheloe Macfarlane Ltd* [2002] IRLR 578 was whether this exclusion covered the rights of a former NHS employee under the superannuation provisions of the NHS Whitley Agreement to enhanced benefits in the event of premature retirement on the grounds of redundancy, or whether the right to an early retirement pension and lump sum compensation became an inherited liability of the private sector transferee employer. The ECJ adopted a narrow interpretation of the exclusion, stating:

   > Early retirement benefits and benefits intended to enhance the conditions of such retirement, paid in the event of dismissal to employees who have reached a certain age, such as the benefits at issue in the main proceedings, are not old-age, invalidity, or survivors' benefits... [I]t is only benefits paid from the time when an employee reaches the end of his normal working life as laid down by the general structure of the pension scheme in question... that can be classified as old-age benefits, even if they are calculated by reference to the rules for calculating normal pension for benefits.

   This is an important decision in that it means that many private sector employers who have taken on public sector employees via TUPE transfers may be liable to honour public sector redundancy schemes if they make such workers redundant.

2. More recently, the *Beckmann* approach was followed by the ECJ in *Martin* v *South Bank University* [2004] IRLR 74. In that case, the Court also dealt with the question whether the directive precludes the transferee offering and an employee agreeing, less favourable terms and conditions (in this case less favourable early-retirement terms). The ECJ, following the principle established in *Daddy's Dance Hall* [1988] IRLR 315, ECJ, held that Article 3 of the Business Transfers Directive precludes the transferee from offering the employees of a transferred entity less favourable terms than those offered to them by the transferor in respect of early retirement, and those employees from accepting those terms, where those terms are merely brought into line with the terms offered to the transferee's other employees at the time of the transfer. The ECJ stated that, although the directive does not preclude an agreement between an employee and the new employer to alter the employment relationship, the transfer of the undertaking itself may never constitute the reason for that alteration. In the present case, the alteration of the employment relationship was connected to the transfer and invalid.

3. The exclusion of the transfer of occupational pension rights under reg. 10 has been ameliorated to an extent by the Pensions Act 2004, ss. 257–8 and the Transfer of Employment (Pension

Protection) Regulations 2005 (SI 2005/649). The regulations came into force with effect from 6 April 2005. In brief summary, the effects of these provisions are:
- if the previous employer provided a pension scheme, then the transferee employer must provide some sort of occupational pension scheme for employees who were members (or eligible for membership) of the transferor employer's scheme;
- the new pension scheme does not have to be the same as the arrangement provided by the transferor employer, but does have to be of a certain minimum standard assessed partly by taking into account the scheme provided by the previous employer.

4. What is now reg. 7(6) was introduced by the Collective Redundancies and Transfer of Undertakings (Protection of Employment) (Amendment) Regulations 1995 to reverse the decision in *Milligan v Securicor Cleaning Ltd* [1995] IRLR 288 to the effect that an employee did *not* need to have two years' continuous employment to claim unfair dismissal on a transfer pursuant to what is now reg. 7. The effect of the decision was that someone dismissed after one week's employment because of a transfer could claim unfair dismissal, whereas the employee of 23 months' duration dismissed in a non-transfer situation could not! The decision has been overruled by the High Court in *R v Secretary of State for Trade and Industry, ex p. Unison* [1996] IRLR 438.

5. The fundamental principle of the regulations is that the existing terms and conditions of employment of the transferring employees automatically transfer with them along with the business. The only exception is reg. 10, i.e. rights and benefits under occupational pension schemes. The EC Business Transfers Directive specifically excludes only 'old age, invalidity or survivor's benefits'. In practice, some pension schemes contain other benefits of employment which are not strictly related to old age. TURERA 1993, s. 33, introduced what is now reg. 10(2), making clear that only old-age, invalidity or survivor's benefits under an occupational pension scheme fall under the reg. 10 exception.

TRANSFER OF UNDERTAKINGS (PROTECTION OF EMPLOYMENT) REGULATIONS 1981 (SI 2006/246)

6 Effect of relevant transfer on trade union recognition

(1) This regulation applies where after a relevant transfer the transferred organised grouping of resources or employees maintains an identity distinct from the remainder of the transferee's undertaking.

(2) Where before such a transfer an independent trade union is recognised to any extent by the transferor in respect of employees of any description who in consequence of the transfer become employees of the transferee, then, after the transfer—
   (a) the trade union shall be deemed to have been recognised by the transferee to the same extent in respect of employees of that description so employed; and
   (b) any agreement for recognition may be varied or rescinded accordingly.

13 Duty to inform and consult representatives

(1) In this regulation and regulations 13A, 14 and 15 references to affected employees, in relation to a relevant transfer, are to any employees of the transferor or the transferee (whether or not assigned to the organised grouping of resources or employees that is the subject of a relevant transfer) who may be affected by the transfer or may be affected by measures taken in connection with it; and references to the employer shall be construed accordingly.

(2) Long enough before a relevant transfer to enable the employer of any affected employees to consult the appropriate representatives of any affected employees, the employer shall inform those representatives of—
   (a) the fact that the transfer is to take place, the date or proposed date of the transfer and the reasons for it;
   (b) the legal, economic and social implications of the transfer for any affected employees;
   (c) the measures which he envisages he will, in connection with the transfer, take in relation to any affected employees or, if he envisages that no measures will be so taken, that fact; and
   (d) if the employer is the transferor, the measures, in connection with the transfer, which he envisages the transferee will take in relation to any affected employees who will become employees of the transferee after the transfer by virtue of regulation 4 or, if he envisages that no measures will be so taken, that fact.

(2A) Where the information is to be supplied under paragraph (2) by an employer-
   (a) this must include suitable information relating to the use of agency workers (if any) by that employer; and
   (b) 'suitable information relating to the use of agency workers' means—

(i) the number of agency workers working temporarily for and under the supervision and direction of the employer;

(ii) the parts of the employer's undertaking in which those agency workers are working; and

(iii) the type of work those agency workers are carrying out.

(3) For the purposes of this regulation the appropriate representatives of any affected employees are—

(a) if the employees are of a description in respect of which an independent trade union is recognised by their employer, representatives of the trade union; or

(b) in any other case, whichever of the following employee representatives the employer chooses—

(i) employee representatives appointed or elected by the affected employees otherwise than for the purposes of this regulation, who (having regard to the purposes for, and the method by which they were appointed or elected) have authority from those employees to receive information and to be consulted about the transfer on their behalf;

(ii) employee representatives elected by any affected employees, for the purposes of this regulation, in an election satisfying the requirements of regulation 14(1).

(4) The transferee shall give the transferor such information at such a time as will enable the transferor to perform the duty imposed on him by virtue of paragraph (2)(d).

(5) The information which is to be given to the appropriate representatives shall be given to each of them by being delivered to them, or sent by post to an address notified by them to the employer, or (in the case of representatives of a trade union) sent by post to the trade union at the address of its head or main office.

(6) An employer of an affected employee who envisages that he will take measures in relation to an affected employee, in connection with the relevant transfer, shall consult the appropriate representatives of that employee with a view to seeking their agreement to the intended measures.

(7) In the course of those consultations the employer shall—

(a) consider any representations made by the appropriate representatives; and

(b) reply to those representations and, if he rejects any of those representations, state his reasons.

(8) The employer shall allow the appropriate representatives access to any affected employees and shall afford to those representatives such accommodation and other facilities as may be appropriate.

(9) If in any case there are special circumstances which render it not reasonably practicable for an employer to perform a duty imposed on him by any of paragraphs (2) to (7), he shall take all such steps towards performing that duty as are reasonably practicable in the circumstances.

(10) Where—

(a) the employer has invited any of the affected employee to elect employee representatives; and

(b) the invitation was issued long enough before the time when the employer is required to give information under paragraph (2) to allow them to elect representatives by that time,

the employer shall be treated as complying with the requirements of this regulation in relation to those employees if he complies with those requirements as soon as is reasonably practicable after the election of the representatives.

(11) If, after the employer has invited any affected employees to elect representatives, they fail to do so within a reasonable time, he shall give to any affected employees the information set out in paragraph (2).

(12) The duties imposed on an employer by this regulation shall apply irrespective of whether the decision resulting in the relevant transfer is taken by the employer or a person controlling the employer.

13A Micro-business's duty to inform and consult where no appropriate representatives

(1) This regulation applies if, at the time when the employer is required to give information under regulation 13(2)—

(a) the employer employs fewer than 10 employees;

(b) there are no appropriate representatives within the meaning of regulation 13(3); and

(c) the employer has not invited any of the affected employees to elect employee representatives.

(2) The employer may comply with regulation 13 by performing any duty which relates to appropriate representatives as if each of the affected employees were an appropriate representative.

14 Election of employee representatives

(1) The requirements for the election of employee representatives under regulation 13(3) are that—

(a) the employer shall make such arrangements as are reasonably practicable to ensure that the election is fair;

(b) the employer shall determine the number of representatives to be elected so that there are sufficient representatives to represent the interests of all affected employees having regard to the number and classes of those employees;

(c) the employer shall determine whether the affected employees should be represented either by representatives of all the affected employees or by representatives of particular classes of those employees;

(d) before the election the employer shall determine the term of office as employee representatives so that it is of sufficient length to enable information to be given and consultations under regulation 13 to be completed;

(e) the candidates for election as employee representatives are affected employees on the date of the election;

(f) no affected employee is unreasonably excluded from standing for election;

(g) all affected employees on the date of the election are entitled to vote for employee representatives;

(h) the employees entitled to vote may vote for as many candidates as there are representatives to be elected to represent them or, if there are to be representatives for particular classes of employees, may vote for as many candidates as there are representatives to be elected to represent their particular class of employee;

(i) the election is conducted so as to secure that—

(i) so far as is reasonably practicable, those voting do so in secret; and

(ii) the votes given at the election are accurately counted.

(2) Where, after an election of employee representatives satisfying the requirements of paragraph (1) has been held, one of those elected ceases to act as an employee representative and as a result any affected employees are no longer represented, those employees shall elect another representative by an election satisfying the requirements of paragraph (1)(a), (e), (f) and (i).

15 Failure to inform or consult

(1) Where an employer has failed to comply with a requirement of regulation 13 or regulation 14, a complaint may be presented to an employment tribunal on that ground—

(a) in the case of a failure relating to the election of employee representatives, by any of his employees who are affected employees;

(b) in the case of any other failure relating to employee representatives, by any of the employee representatives to whom the failure related;

(c) in the case of failure relating to representatives of a trade union, by the trade union; and

(d) in any other case, by any of his employees who are affected employees.

(2) If on a complaint under paragraph (1) a question arises whether or not it was reasonably practicable for an employer to perform a particular duty or as to what steps he took towards performing it, it shall be for him to show—

(a) that there were special circumstances which rendered it not reasonably practicable for him to perform the duty; and

(b) that he took all such steps towards its performance as were reasonably practicable in those circumstances.

(3) If on a complaint under paragraph (1) a question arises as to whether or not an employee representative was an appropriate representative for the purposes of regulation 13, it shall be for the employer to show that the employee representative had the necessary authority to represent the affected employees.

(3A) If on a complaint under paragraph (1) a question arises as to whether or not regulation 13A applied, it is for the employer to show that the conditions in sub-paragraphs (a) and (b) of regulation 13A(1) applied at the time referred to in regulation 13A(1).

(4) On a complaint under paragraph (1)(a) it shall be for the employer to show that the requirements in regulation 14 have been satisfied.

(5) On a complaint against a transferor that he had failed to perform the duty imposed upon him by virtue of regulation 13(2)(d) or, so far as relating thereto, regulation 13(9), he may not show that it was not reasonably practicable for him to perform the duty in question for the reason that the transferee had failed to give him the requisite information at the requisite time in accordance with regulation 13(4) unless he gives the transferee notice of his intention to show that fact; and the giving of the notice shall make the transferee a party to the proceedings.

(6) In relation to any complaint under paragraph (1), a failure on the part of a person controlling (directly or indirectly) the employer to provide information to the employer shall not constitute special circumstances rendering it not reasonably practicable for the employer to comply with such a requirement.

(7) Where the tribunal finds a complaint against a transferee under paragraph (1) well-founded it shall make a declaration to that effect and may order the transferee to pay appropriate compensation to such descriptions of affected employees as may be specified in the award.

(8) Where the tribunal finds a complaint against a transferor under paragraph (1) well-founded it shall make a declaration to that effect and may—

    (a) order the transferor, subject to paragraph (9), to pay appropriate compensation to such descriptions of affected employees as may be specified in the award; or

    (b) if the complaint is that the transferor did not perform the duty mentioned in paragraph (5) and the transferor (after giving due notice) shows the facts so mentioned, order the transferee to pay appropriate compensation to such descriptions of affected employees as may be specified in the award.

(9) The transferee shall be jointly and severally liable with the transferor in respect of compensation payable under sub-paragraph (8)(a) or paragraph (11).

(10) An employee may present a complaint to an employment tribunal on the ground that he is an employee of a description to which an order under paragraph (7) or (8) relates and that—

    (a) in respect of an order under paragraph (7), the transferee has failed, wholly or in part, to pay him compensation in pursuance of the order;

    (b) in respect of an order under paragraph (8), the transferor or transferee, as applicable, has failed, wholly or in part, to pay him compensation in pursuance of the order.

(11) Where the tribunal finds a complaint under paragraph (10) well-founded it shall order the transferor or transferee as applicable to pay the complainant the amount of compensation which it finds is due to him.

(12) An employment tribunal shall not consider a complaint under paragraph (1) or (10) unless it is presented to the tribunal before the end of the period of three months beginning with—

    (a) in respect of a complaint under paragraph (1), the date on which the relevant transfer is completed; or

    (b) in respect of a complaint under paragraph (10), the date of the tribunal's order under paragraph (7) or (8),

or within such further period as the tribunal considers reasonable in a case where it is satisfied that it was not reasonably practicable for the complaint to be presented before the end of the period of three months.

  ...

16 Failure to inform or consult: supplemental

(1) Section 205(1) of the 1996 Act (complaint to be sole remedy for breach of relevant rights) and section 18 of the 1996 Tribunals Act (conciliation) shall apply to the rights conferred by regulation 15 and to proceedings under this regulation as they apply to the rights conferred by those Acts and the employment tribunal proceedings mentioned in those Acts.

(2) An appeal shall lie and shall lie only to the Employment Appeal Tribunal on a question of law arising from any decision of, or arising in any proceedings before, an employment tribunal under or by virtue of these Regulations; and section 11(1) of the Tribunals and Inquiries Act 1992 (appeals from certain tribunals to the High Court) shall not apply in relation to any such proceedings.

(3) 'Appropriate compensation' in regulation 15 means such sum not exceeding thirteen weeks' pay for the employee in question as the tribunal considers just and equitable having regard to the seriousness of the failure of the employer to comply with his duty.

(4) Sections 220 to 228 of the 1996 Act shall apply for calculating the amount of a week's pay for any employee for the purposes of paragraph (3) and, for the purposes of that calculation, the calculation date shall be—

    (a) in the case of an employee who is dismissed by reason of redundancy (within the meaning of sections 139 and 155 of the 1996 Act) the date which is the calculation date for the purposes of any entitlement of his to a redundancy payment (within the meaning of those sections) or which would be that calculation date if he were so entitled;

    (b) in the case of an employee who is dismissed for any other reason, the effective date of termination (within the meaning of sections 95(1) and (2) and 97 of the 1996 Act) of his contract of employment;

    (c) in any other case, the date of the relevant transfer.

NOTES

1. The regulations originally required the employer to consult with representatives of any independent union recognised by him to any extent for the purposes of collective bargaining in respect of employees who might be affected by the transfer. However, following the ECJ decision in *EC Commission* v *United Kingdom of Great Britain and Northern Ireland*, C–373/92 [1994] IRLR 142, the duty to consult was extended to cover employee representatives. The ECJ held that the regulations did not comply with the Acquired Rights Directive because they did not provide for a mechanism for consultation where there was no recognised trade union. As a

result the Collective Redundancies and Transfer of Undertakings (Protection of Employment) (Amendment) Regulations 1995 (SI 1995/2587) amended the regulations.

2. Controversially, those regulations allowed the employer to elect to consult non-union employee representatives even in situations where there was a recognised union. Early in 1998, the Government launched a consultation exercise on possible further amendments to the legislation governing consultation on collective redundancies and transfers of undertakings. The Collective Redundancies and Transfer of Undertakings (Protection of Employment) (Amendment) Regulations 1999 (SI 1999/1925) were the result of that process. Under the amended regulations, there is now a requirement for employers to consult and/or inform an independent trade union where it is recognised for collective bargaining purposes in respect of any of the affected employees. It is irrelevant whether those employees are union members, provided they belong to a class, grade or 'description' of employees in respect of which the union is recognised.

3. Where no union is recognised in relation to any of the affected employees, *and* where affected employees are not covered by the scope of union recognition, the employer may choose whether to consult or inform existing employee representatives who have the appropriate authority, or employee representatives elected specifically for the purposes of consultation and receiving information. Regulation 13(11) provides: 'If, after the employer has invited affected employees to elect representatives, they fail to do so within a reasonable time, he shall give to each affected employee the information.' In *Howard* v *Millrise Ltd* [2005] IRLR 84, the EAT held that the employee was entitled to compensation because the employers failed to invite an election of representatives or, in default of such election, give information to the applicant himself.

4. The Commission was also critical of the UK's failure to provide effective sanctions in the case of failure to inform and consult. As a result, TURERA 1993 raised the maximum compensation payable for a breach of this requirement from two weeks' pay to four weeks' pay. The 1999 Regulations further raised the maximum to 13 weeks' pay (see now TUPE Regulations 2006, reg. 16(3)). Also, the regulation, which allowed protective awards under Trade Union and Labour Relations (Consolidation) Act (TULR(C)A) 1992, ss. 189–90 and wages in lieu payable in respect of the protected period to be offset against compensation for failure to inform or consult, was removed by TURERA 1993, s. 33(7).

5. In *Sweetin* v *Coral Racing* [2006] IRLR 252, the EAT held that awards of compensation for an employer's failure to consult as required by TUPE should be assessed in the same way as protective awards in respect of failure to consult in advance of redundancies. This means that employment tribunals should follow the guidance set out by the Court of Appeal in the redundancy case of *Susie Radin Ltd* v *GMB* [2004] IRLR 400, CA (see Section 6.B) that such awards are intended to be punitive and have a deterrent effect.

6. In *Royal Mail Group Ltd* v *Communication Workers Union* [2009] IRLR 1046, the Court of Appeal held that an employer was not in breach of its information duty where it failed to provide information to the union on the transfer's legal implications for employees because it had received incorrect legal advice that the transaction would not be a TUPE transfer.

7. See also *Cable Realisations Ltd* v *GMB Northern* [2010] IRLR 42, EAT.

8. TULR(C)A 1992, ss. 198A and 198B enable a transferee to engage in 'pre-transfer' consultation over collective redundancies with representatives of the transferor's workforce who may be affected by the redundancies.

TRANSFER OF UNDERTAKINGS (PROTECTION OF EMPLOYMENT) REGULATIONS 2006 (SI 2006/246)

8 Insolvency

(1) If at the time of a relevant transfer the transferor is subject to relevant insolvency proceedings paragraphs (2) to (6) apply.

(2) In this regulation 'relevant employee' means an employee of the transferor—

(a) whose contract of employment transfers to the transferee by virtue of the operation of these Regulations; or

(b) whose employment with the transferor is terminated before the time of the relevant transfer in the circumstances described in regulation 7(1).

(3) The relevant statutory scheme specified in paragraph (4)(b) (including that sub-paragraph as applied by paragraph 5 of Schedule 1) shall apply in the case of a relevant employee irrespective of the fact that the qualifying requirement that the employee's employment has been terminated is not met and for those

purposes the date of the transfer shall be treated as the date of the termination and the transferor shall be treated as the employer.

(4) In this regulation the 'relevant statutory schemes' are—

(a) Chapter VI of Part XI of the 1996 Act;

(b) Part XII of the 1996 Act.

(5) Regulation 4 shall not operate to transfer liability for the sums payable to the relevant employee under the relevant statutory schemes.

(6) In this regulation 'relevant insolvency proceedings' means insolvency proceedings which have been opened in relation to the transferor not with a view to the liquidation of the assets of the transferor and which are under the supervision of an insolvency practitioner.

(7) Regulations 4 and 7 do not apply to any relevant transfer where the transferor is the subject of bankruptcy proceedings or any analogous insolvency proceedings which have been instituted with a view to the liquidation of the assets of the transferor and are under the supervision of an insolvency practitioner.

NOTE: In *Secretary of State for Trade and Industry* v *Slater* [2007] IRLR 928, the EA T held that, given there were no insolvency proceedings instituted before the business was transferred, the Insolvency Fund was not liable for debts owed to the claimants.

9 Variations of contract where transferors are subject to relevant insolvency proceedings

(1) If at the time of a relevant transfer the transferor is subject to relevant insolvency proceedings these Regulations shall not prevent the transferor or transferee (or an insolvency practitioner) and appropriate representatives of assigned employees agreeing to permitted variations.

(2) For the purposes of this regulation 'appropriate representatives' are—

(a) if the employees are of a description in respect of which an independent trade union is recognised by their employer, representatives of the trade union; or

(b) in any other case, whichever of the following employee representatives the employer chooses—

(i) employee representatives appointed or elected by the assigned employees (whether they make the appointment or election alone or with others) otherwise than for the purposes of this regulation, who (having regard to the purposes for, and the method by which they were appointed or elected) have authority from those employees to agree permitted variations to contracts of employment on their behalf;

(ii) employee representatives elected by assigned employees (whether they make the appointment or election alone or with others) for these particular purposes, in an election satisfying requirements identical to those contained in regulation 14 except those in regulation 14(1)(d).

(3) An individual may be an appropriate representative for the purposes of both this regulation and regulation 13 provided that where the representative is not a trade union representative he is either elected by or has authority from assigned employees (within the meaning of this regulation) and affected employees (as described in regulation 13(1)).

(4) In section 168 of the 1992 Act (time off for carrying out trade union duties) in subsection (1), after paragraph (c) there is inserted—

', or

(d) negotiations with a view to entering into an agreement under regulation 9 of the Transfer of Undertakings (Protection of Employment) Regulations 2006 that applies to employees of the employer, or

(e) the performance on behalf of employees of the employer of functions related to or connected with the making of an agreement under that regulation.'

(5) Where assigned employees are represented by non-trade union representatives—

(a) the agreement recording a permitted variation must be in writing and signed by each of the representatives who have made it or, where that is not reasonably practicable, by a duly authorised agent of that representative; and

(b) the employer must, before the agreement is made available for signature, provide all employees to whom it is intended to apply on the date on which it is to come into effect with copies of the text of the agreement and such guidance as those employees might reasonably require in order to understand it fully.

(6) A permitted variation shall take effect as a term or condition of the assigned employee's contract of employment in place, where relevant, of any term or condition which it varies.

(7) In this regulation—

'assigned employees' means those employees assigned to the organised grouping of resources or employees that is the subject of a relevant transfer;

'permitted variation' is a variation to the contract of employment of an assigned employee where—
- (a) the sole or principal reason for it is the transfer itself or a reason connected with the transfer that is not an economic, technical or organisational reason entailing changes in the workforce; and
- (b) it is designed to safeguard employment opportunities by ensuring the survival of the undertaking, business or part of the undertaking or business that is the subject of the relevant transfer;
— 'relevant insolvency proceedings' has the meaning given to the expression by regulation 8(6).

NOTE: Article 5(1) of the revised Directive(2001/23/EC) provides:

> Unless the Member States provide otherwise, Articles 3 and 4 [automatic transfer principle and protection from dismissal] shall not apply to any transfer where the transferor is the subject of bankruptcy proceedings or any analogous proceedings which have been instituted with a view to the liquidation of the assets of the transferor and are under the supervision of a competent public authority (which may be an insolvency practitioner authorised by a competent public authority.

Article 5(2) applies where insolvency proceedings have been opened in relation to a transferor (whether or not proceedings have been instituted with a view to the liquidation of the assets of the transferor) and under the supervision of a competent public authority, including an authorised insolvency practitioner. The Article gives Member States two options in such situations:
- to provide that certain of the transferor's pre-existing debts to employees should not pass to the transferee;
- to provide that employers and employee representatives may agree changes to terms and conditions of employment by reason of the transfer itself, provided that this is in accordance with current law and practice and with a view to ensuring the survival of the business and thereby preserving jobs.

According to the DTI: 'The underlying aim of these options is to allow Member States to promote the sale of insolvent businesses as going concerns and to promote the "rescue culture"' (Explanatory Memorandum to the Transfer of Undertakings (Protection of Employment) Regulations 2006, DTI, 2006).

The regulations adopt both of the options offered by the revised directive. Regulation 8 prevents the operation of reg. 4 to transfer liability for unpaid debts owed to transferring employees provided these are sums reimbursable by the Secretary of State under the 'relevant statutory schemes'. The latter are defined as:
- Chapter VI of Pt XI of the ERA 1996, i.e. the statutory redundancy scheme; and
- Part XII of the ERA 1996, i.e. the insolvency payments provisions.

The liability for any other debts owed by the insolvent transferor to relevant employees—i.e. debts that either fall outside the categories payable under the relevant statutory schemes or exceed the upper limits on payments under these provisions—will still pass to the transferee.

Where the transfer is one of the types of insolvency proceedings defined in Article 5.2 of the directive, the 2006 Regulations permit the transferor or transferee (or an insolvency practitioner) to agree 'permitted variations' to terms and conditions with appropriate representatives of the employees. 'Permitted variation' means a variation that would normally be unlawful under the regulations (i.e. because the sole or principal reason for it is the transfer itself or a reason connected with the transfer which is not an ETO reason) and is designed to safeguard employment opportunities by ensuring the survival of the undertaking or part of the undertaking subject to the relevant transfer.

11 Notification of Employee Liability Information

(1) The transferor shall notify to the transferee the employee liability information of any person employed by him who is assigned to the organised grouping of resources or employees that is the subject of a relevant transfer—
- (a) in writing; or
- (b) by making it available to him in a readily accessible form.

(2) In this regulation and in regulation 12 'employee liability information' means—
- (a) the identity and age of the employee;
- (b) those particulars of employment that an employer is obliged to give to an employee pursuant to section 1 of the 1996 Act;
- (c) information of any—
  - (i) disciplinary procedure taken against an employee;
  - (ii) grievance procedure taken by an employee,

within the previous two years, in circumstances where a Code of Practice issued under Part IV of the Trade Union and Labour Relations (Consolidation) Act 1992 which relates exclusively or primarily to the resolution of disputes applies;

(d) information of any court or tribunal case, claim or action—

(i) brought by an employee against the transferor, within the previous two years;

(ii) that the transferor has reasonable grounds to believe that an employee may bring against the transferee, arising out of the employee's employment with the transferor; and

(e) information of any collective agreement which will have effect after the transfer, in its application in relation to the employee, pursuant to regulation 5(a).

(3) Employee liability information shall contain information as at a specified date not more than fourteen days before the date on which the information is notified to the transferee.

(4) The duty to provide employee liability information in paragraph (1) shall include a duty to provide employee liability information of any person who would have been employed by the transferor and assigned to the organised grouping of resources or employees that is the subject of a relevant transfer immediately before the transfer if he had not been dismissed in the circumstances described in regulation 7(1), including, where the transfer is effected by a series of two or more transactions, a person so employed and assigned or who would have been so employed and assigned immediately before any of those transactions.

(5) Following notification of the employee liability information in accordance with this regulation, the transferor shall notify the transferee in writing of any change in the employee liability information.

(6) A notification under this regulation shall be given not less than 28 days before the relevant transfer or, if special circumstances make this not reasonably practicable, as soon as reasonably practicable thereafter.

(7) A notification under this regulation may be given—

(a) in more than one instalment;

(b) indirectly, through a third party.

12 Remedy for failure to notify employee liability information

(1) On or after a relevant transfer, the transferee may present a complaint to an employment tribunal that the transferor has failed to comply with any provision of regulation 11.

(2) An employment tribunal shall not consider a complaint under this regulation unless it is presented—

(a) before the end of the period of three months beginning with the date of the relevant transfer;

(b) within such further period as the tribunal considers reasonable in a case where it is satisfied that it was not reasonably practicable for the complaint to be presented before the end of that period of three months.

. . .

(3) Where an employment tribunal finds a complaint under paragraph (1) well-founded, the tribunal—

(a) shall make a declaration to that effect; and

(b) may make an award of compensation to be paid by the transferor to the transferee.

(4) The amount of the compensation shall be such as the tribunal considers just and equitable in all the circumstances, subject to paragraph (5), having particular regard to—

(a) any loss sustained by the transferee which is attributable to the matters complained of; and

(b) the terms of any contract between the transferor and the transferee relating to the transfer under which the transferor may be liable to pay any sum to the transferee in respect of a failure to notify the transferee of employee liability information.

(5) Subject to paragraph (6), the amount of compensation awarded under paragraph (3) shall be not less than £500 per employee in respect of whom the transferor has failed to comply with a provision of regulation 11, unless the tribunal considers it just and equitable, in all the circumstances, to award a lesser sum.

(6) In ascertaining the loss referred to in paragraph (4)(a) the tribunal shall apply the same rule concerning the duty of a person to mitigate his loss as applies to any damages recoverable under the common law of England and Wales, Northern Ireland or Scotland, as applicable.

(7) Section 18A to 18C of the 1996 Tribunals Act (conciliation) shall apply to the right conferred by this regulation and to proceedings under this regulation as it applies to the rights conferred by that Act and the employment tribunal proceedings mentioned in that Act.

NOTE: Article 3(2) of the revised directive gave Member States a new option to introduce provisions requiring the transferor to notify the transferee of the rights and obligations in relation to employees that will be transferred, so far as those rights and obligations are or ought to be known to the transferor at the time of the transfer. This has been adopted by reg. 11.

The minimum period for the supply of the liability information was increased from 14 to 28 days by the 2014 Regulations.

Where the notification requirement is breached, the transferee will be able to present a complaint to an employment tribunal. If the complaint is upheld, the tribunal will make a declaration to that effect and to make an award of compensation for any loss which cannot be mitigated. The amount of compensation must not be less than £500 per employee involved, unless the tribunal considers that it would just and equitable to award a smaller sum. The original draft regulations had provided for a penalty not exceeding £75,000 but following the consultation process, this was replaced by a loss-based model.

SECTION 6: UNFAIR REDUNDANCY DISMISSALS

A: Automatically unfair redundancy dismissals

The effect of TULRCA 1992, s. 153 and ERA 1996, s. 105 is that a dismissal on the ground of redundancy will be automatically unfair if the circumstances constituting the redundancy also applied equally to one or more employees in the same undertaking who held posts similar to that held by the dismissed employee and they have not been dismissed and either:

(i) the reason (or, if more than one, the principal reason) for selecting the employee was union-related (TULR(C)A 1992, s. 153);

(ii) because the employee had been involved in raising or taking action on health and safety issues; asserted certain statutory rights; performed (or proposed to perform) any functions as a trustee of an occupational pension scheme; performed (or proposed to perform) the functions or activities of an employee representative for the purpose of consultation over redundancies or the transfer of an undertaking; as a 'protected' or 'opted out' shop or betting worker refused to work on a Sunday; has been involved in working time cases; made a protected disclosure; asserted rights under National Minimum Wage Act; had taken part in protected industrial action within the terms of TULR(C)A 1992, s. 238A(2); was or was proposing to be an employee representative within the terms of the Transnational Information and Consultation of Employees Regulations had sought to enforce rights under the Part-time Workers (Prevention of Less Favourable Treatment) Regulations 2000 or under Fixed-term Employees (Prevention of Less Favourable Treatment) Regulations 2002 (ERA 1996, s. 105).

NOTES

1. Special rules apply in the case of a redundancy which is connected with family reasons as defined by ERA 1996, s. 99, the Maternity Pay and Parental Leave Regulations 1999 (MPLR), reg. 20; and the Paternity and Adoption Leave Regulations 2002 (PAL), reg. 29). First, a dismissal will be automatically unfair if the employee is made redundant and it is shown that s/he was selected for redundancy in preference to other comparable employees for one of the prescribed family reasons. Second, where a redundancy situation arises during the employee's ordinary or additional maternity or adoption leave which makes it impracticable for the employer to continue to employ her under her original contract of employment, the employee is entitled to be offered suitable alternative employment with her employer (or with a successor, or an associated employer) where there is a suitable available vacancy (MPLR 1999, reg. 10; PAL Regulations 2002, reg. 23). If the employer has a suitable vacancy available, but makes the employee redundant during ordinary or additional maternity or adoption leave without first offering it to her, the redundancy dismissal will be unfair (MPLR 1999, reg. 20(1)(b); PAL Regulations 2002, reg. 29(1)(b); see also *Sefton Borough Council* v *Wainwright* [2014] UKEAT 0168_14_1310. If the employee unreasonably refuses the offer of suitable alternative employment, she will lose her entitlement to a redundancy payment (MPLR 1999, reg. 20(7); PAL Regulations 2002, reg. 29(5)).

2. There is no qualifying period for dismissals contrary to ERA 1996, ss. 99, 105 (ERA 1996, s.108(3) (b), (h)).

3. Under what was the EPCA 1978, s. 59(1)(b), it was automatically unfair to select an employee for redundancy in contravention of a customary arrangement or agreed procedure relating to redundancy and where there were no special reasons justifying departure. This provision was repealed by the Deregulation and Contracting Out Act 1994. Research has shown that the influence of such agreed procedures has declined in recent years, and recent case law had taken a rather generous approach to the scope of the 'special reasons' defence (see *Rolls Royce Motor Cars Ltd* v *Price* [1993] IRLR 203, EAT).

4. For discussion of unfair redundancy selection on trade union grounds, now contained in TULR(C)A 1992, s. 153, see Chapter 10, Section E.

B: Generally unfair redundancy dismissals under ERA 1996, s. 98(4)

Polkey v *A. E. Dayton Services Ltd*
[1988] AC 344, House of Lords

LORD BRIDGE: [I]n the case of redundancy, the employer will normally not act reasonably unless he warns and consults any employees affected or their representatives, adopts a fair basis on which to select for redundancy and takes such steps as may be reasonable to avoid or minimise redundancy by redeployment within his own organisation.

NOTE: See the full discussion of *Polkey* at p. 437 (Chapter 8, Section 2.C(v)). *Polkey* approved the guidelines as regards proper procedures laid down by the EAT in the following case.

Williams v *Compair Maxam Ltd*
[1982] ICR 157, Employment Appeal Tribunal

BROWNE-WILKINSON J: [T]here is a generally accepted view in industrial relations that, in cases where the employees are represented by an independent union recognised by the employer, reasonable employers will seek to act in accordance with the following principles:

1. The employer will seek to give as much warning as possible of impending redundancies so as to enable the union and employees who may be affected to take early steps to inform themselves of the relevant facts consider possible alternative solutions and, if necessary, find alternative employment in the undertaking or elsewhere.

2. The employer will consult the union as to the best means by which the desired management result can be achieved fairly and with as little hardship to the employees as possible. In particular, the employer will seek to agree with the union the criteria to be applied in selecting the employee to be made redundant. When a selection has been made, the employer will consider with the union whether the selection has been made in accordance with those criteria.

3. Whether or not an agreement as to the criteria to be adopted has been agreed with the union, the employer will seek to establish criteria for selection which so far as possible do not depend solely upon the opinions of the person making the selection but can be objectively checked against such things as attendance record, efficiency at the job, experience, length of service.

4. The employer will seek to ensure that the selection is made fairly in accordance with these criteria and will consider any representations union may make as to such selection.

5. The employer will seek to see whether instead of dismissing an employee he could offer him alternative employment.

The lay members stress that not all these factors are present in every case since circumstances may prevent one or more of them being given effect to. But the lay members would expect these principles to be departed from only where some good reason is shown to justify such departure. The basic approach is that, in the unfortunate circumstances that necessarily attend redundancies, as much as is reasonably possible should be done to mitigate the impact on the work force and to satisfy them that the selection has been made fairly and not on the basis of personal whim.

That these are the broad principles currently adopted by reasonable employers is supported both by the practice of the industrial tribunals and to an extent by statute ...

NOTES
1. In Scotland, it has been suggested that the *Williams* v *Compair Maxam* guidelines are more suitable for the larger concerns, particularly the unionised ones. See *Meikle* v *McPhail (Charleston Arms)* [1983] IRLR 351 and *Simpson* v *Findlater* [1983] IRLR 401.
2. Where the employer failed to consult because on a previous occasion the workforce indicated that they would rather have just been told they were going to be made redundant, the dismissal 'for redundancy' was, nevertheless, held to be unfair. See *Ferguson* v *Prestwick Circuits Ltd* [1992] IRLR 266.
3. ACAS has published an advisory booklet entitled *Redundancy Handling* (Advisory Booklet No. 12) which provides a useful checklist for employers when considering pre-redundancy procedures.

SECTION 7: CONSULTATION WITH THE TRADE UNION

Consultation requirements with the relevant trade union are contained in EEC Redundancy Consultation Directive (1975/129) and were given statutory effect originally by the Employment Protection Act 1975. The provisions are now contained in TULR(C)A 1992, ss. 188–98, which was amended by TURERA 1993 in order to bring the legislation into line with the new requirements introduced by Directive 1992/56. The significant amendment was the addition of s. 188(2), which changed what, previously, was merely an obligation to consult and listen to representations to a requirement that employers negotiate with the union and try, thereby, to reach an agreement about such things as ways of avoiding dismissals, reducing the numbers involved, and mitigating the consequences of dismissals.

This moved consultation closer to negotiation. Previously, the question of the decision to make redundancies had generally been non-negotiable and trade unions had been restricted to seeking to limit the numbers of employees who were to lose their jobs. Agreement does not have to be achieved, but the employer will have to show that there was a serious attempt to reach a consensus on these issues.

The original statutory provision (the Employment Protection Act 1975, ss. 99–107) required the employer to consult with representatives of any independent recognised union recognised by him/her to any extent for the purposes of collective bargaining in respect of employees who might be affected by the transfer. However, following the ECJ decision in *EC Commission* v *United Kingdom of Great Britain and Northern Ireland*, Case C–383/92 [1994] IRLR 142, the duty to consult was extended to cover employee representatives. As a result, the Collective Redundancies and Transfer of Undertakings (Protection of Employment) (Amendment) Regulations 1995 (SI 1995/2587) amended TULR(C)A 1992, s. 188. Controversially, those regulations allowed the employer to elect to consult non-union employee representatives even in situations where there was a recognised union. Early in 1998, the Government launched a consultation exercise on possible further amendments to the legislation governing consultation on collective redundancies and transfers of undertakings. The Collective Redundancies and Transfer of Undertakings (Protection of Employment) (Amendment) Regulations 1999 (SI 1999/1925) are the result of that process. The main—and most controversial—difference from the original proposals is that the obligation to consult and provide information will continue to apply only where an employer 'is proposing to dismiss as redundant 20 or more employees at one establishment within a period of

90 days or less'. More positively, under the amended regulations, there is now a requirement for employers to consult and/or inform an independent trade union where it is recognised for collective bargaining purposes in respect of any of the affected employees. It is irrelevant whether those employees are union members, provided they belong to a class, grade or 'description' of employees in respect of which the union is recognised.

Where no union is recognised in relation to any of the affected employees, the employer may choose whether to consult and inform existing employee representatives who have the appropriate authority, or employee representatives elected specifically for the purposes of consultation and receiving information. If the employers opt for the latter, the 1999 Regulations introduce detailed statutory requirements for the election of employee representatives (TULR(C)A 1992, s. 188A). If, after the employer invites affected employees to elect representatives, they fail to do so within a reasonable time, it must give to each affected employee the information set out in s. 188(4).

Employers have to consult 'all the persons who are appropriate representatives of any of the employees *who may be affected by the proposed dismissals or may be affected by measures taken in connection with those dismissals*' (emphasis added). Clearly, the employees most directly affected are those whom it is proposed to dismiss. However, the employer will now have to analyse any possible consequential impact (direct or indirect) on the workforce that remains.

Minimum periods of consultation are laid down by s. 188(1), (1A) 'where an employer is proposing to dismiss as redundant 20 or more employees at one establishment within a period of 90 days or less'. The consultation must begin in good time, and in any event 45 days before the first dismissal takes effect if the employer is proposing to dismiss 100 or more employees. This period was reduced from 90 days by the Trade Union and Labour Relations (Consolidation) Act (Amendment) order 2013 (SI 2013/763). Thirty days must be allowed for this process where between 20 and 99 are to be dismissed.

Failure to adopt proper consultation procedures may lead to a sum of damages (a 'protective award') being awarded in respect of each dismissed employee. The protective award is within the tribunal's discretion. The maximum duration of the protected period under a protective award that may be ordered by a tribunal in respect of employees who have been dismissed is now 90 days in all cases (TULR(C)A 1992, s. 189(4), as amended by the Collective Redundancies and Transfer of Undertakings (Protection of Employment) Regulations 1999). Consequently, the maximum 30-day period, which previously applied to 20 to 99 redundancies, is abolished.

Previously, express protection against detrimental treatment or dismissal in the context of the redundancy and transfers consultation and information procedures (other than in respect of the protection afforded to those taking part in trade union action activities) was limited to employee representatives and candidates for election as such representatives. Protection is extended by the 1999 Regulations to those who 'participated' in an election of employee representatives (see new s. 47(1A) of the ERA 1996) or who 'took part' in such an election (see the new s. 103(2) of the ERA 1996).

TRADE UNION AND LABOUR RELATIONS (CONSOLIDATION) ACT 1992

188. Duty of employer to consult representatives

(1) Where an employer is proposing to dismiss as redundant 20 or more employees at one establishment within a period of 90 days or less, the employer shall consult about the dismissals all the persons who are appropriate representatives of any of the employees who may be affected by the proposed dismissals or may be affected by measures taken in connection with those dismissals.

(1A) The consultation shall begin in good time and in any event—

    (a) where the employer is proposing to dismiss 100 or more employees as mentioned in subsection (1), at least 45 days, and

    (b) otherwise, at least 30 days,

before the first of the dismissals takes effect.

(1B) For the purposes of this section the appropriate representatives of any affected employees are—

    (a) if the employees are of a description in respect of which an independent trade union is recognised by their employer, representatives of the trade union, or

    (b) in any other case, whichever of the following employee representatives the employer chooses—

        (i) employee representatives appointed or elected by the affected employees otherwise than for the purposes of this section, who (having regard to the purposes for and the method by which they were appointed or elected) have authority from those employees to receive information and to be consulted about the proposed dismissals on their behalf;

        (ii) employee representatives elected by the affected employees, for the purposes of this section, in an election satisfying the requirements of section 188A(1).

(2) The consultation shall include consultation about ways of—

    (a) avoiding the dismissals,

    (b) reducing the numbers of employees to be dismissed, and

    (c) mitigating the consequences of the dismissals,

and shall be undertaken by the employer with a view to reaching agreement with the appropriate representatives.

(3) In determining how many employees an employer is proposing to dismiss as redundant no account shall be taken of employees in respect of whose proposed dismissals consultation has already begun.

(4) For the purposes of the consultation the employer shall disclose in writing to the appropriate representatives—

    (a) the reasons for his proposals,

    (b) the numbers and descriptions of employees whom it is proposed to dismiss as redundant,

    (c) the total number of employees of any such description employed by the employer at the establishment in question,

    (d) the proposed method of selecting the employees who may be dismissed,

    (e) the proposed method of carrying out the dismissals, with due regard to any agreed procedure, including the period over which the dismissals are to take effect.

    (f) the proposed method of calculating the amount of any redundancy payments to be made (otherwise than in compliance with an obligation imposed by or by virtue of any enactment) to employees who may be dismissed.

(5) That information shall be given to each of the appropriate representatives by being delivered to them or sent by post to an address notified by them to the employer, or (in the case of representatives of a trade union) sent by post to the union at the address of its head or main office.

(5A) The employer shall allow the appropriate representatives access to the affected employees and shall afford to those representatives such accommodation and other facilities as may be appropriate.

…

(7) If in any case there are special circumstances which render it not reasonably practicable for the employer to comply with a requirement of subsection (1A), (2) or (4), the employer shall take all such steps towards compliance with that requirement as are reasonably practicable in those circumstances. Where the decision leading to the proposed dismissals is that of a person controlling the employer (directly or indirectly), a failure on the part of that person to provide information to the employer shall not constitute special circumstances rendering it not reasonably practicable for the employer to comply with such a requirement.

(7A) Where—

    (a) the employer has invited any of the affected employees to elect employee representatives, and

    (b) the invitation was issued long enough before the time when the consultation is required by subsection (1A)(a) or (b) to begin to allow them to elect representatives by that time,

    the employer shall be treated as complying with the requirements of this section in relation to those employees if he complies with those requirements as soon as is reasonably practicable after the election of the representatives.

(7B) If, after the employer has invited affected employees to elect representatives, the affected employees fail to do so within a reasonable time, he shall give to each affected employee the information set out in subsection (4).

(8) This section does not confer any rights on a trade union, a representative or an employee except as provided by sections 189 to 192 below.

188A. Election of employee representatives

(1) The requirements for the election of employee representatives under section 188(1B)(b)(ii) are that—

    (a) the employer shall make such arrangements as are reasonably practical to ensure that the election is fair;

(b) the employer shall determine the number of representatives to be elected so that there are sufficient representatives to represent the interests of all the affected employees having regard to the number and classes of those employees;

(c) the employer shall determine whether the affected employees should be represented either by representatives of all the affected employees or by representatives of particular classes of those employees;

(d) before the election the employer shall determine the term of office as employee representatives so that it is of sufficient length to enable information to be given and consultations under section 188 to be completed;

(e) the candidates for election as employee representatives are affected employees on the date of the election;

(f) no affected employee is unreasonably excluded from standing for election;

(g) all affected employees on the date of the election are entitled to vote for employee representatives;

(h) the employees entitled to vote may vote for as many candidates as there are representatives to be elected to represent them or, if there are to be representatives for particular classes of employees, may vote for as many candidates as there are representatives to be elected to represent their particular class of employee;

(i) the election is conducted so as to secure that—

(i) so far as is reasonably practicable, those voting do so in secret, and

(ii) the votes given at the election are accurately counted.

(2) Where, after an election of employee representatives satisfying the requirements of subsection (1) has been held, one of those elected ceases to act as an employee representative and any of those employees are no longer represented, they shall elect another representative by an election satisfying the requirements of subsection (1)(a), (e), (f) and (i).

NOTES

1. Under s. 188, the obligation to inform and consult arises where the employer is 'proposing to dismiss'. This phrase suggests that there must be something more definite than the contemplation of the possibility of redundancies: see, e.g., *APAC* v *Kirvin Ltd* [1978] IRLR 318 (company in financial difficulties and looking for a buyer, did not 'propose' any redundancies until last prospective purchaser had disappeared); *Hough and Apex* v *Leyland Daf Ltd* [1991] IRLR 194 ('matters should have reached a stage where a specific proposal has been formulated and that this is a later stage than the diagnosis of a problem and the appreciation that at least one way of dealing with it would be by declaring redundancies'). Section 188(1) is designed to implement Council Directive 75/129/EEC, and Article 2 of that directive requires consultation 'where an employer is *contemplating* collective redundancies'. It is arguable that the obligation under Article 2 could arise at an earlier stage than that of a definite *proposal* of redundancies. Indeed, in *R* v *Coal Corporation, ex p. Vardy* [1993] IRLR 104, HC, Glidewell LJ expressed the view that s. 188 failed fully to implement the directive:

> I say this because in the Directive consultation is to begin as soon as an employer contemplates redundancies, whereas under the Act it only needs to begin when he proposes to dismiss as redundant an employee. The verb 'proposes' in its ordinary usage relates to a state of mind which is much more certain and further along the decision-making process than the verb 'contemplate'; in other words, the Directive envisages consultation at an early stage when the employer is first envisaging the possibility that he may have to make employees redundant. Section 188 applies when he has decided that, whether because he has to close a plant or for some other reason, it is his intention, however reluctant, to make employees redundant.

(Cf. *Griffin* v *South West Water Services Ltd* [1995] IRLR 15, HC.)

The crucial point in *MSF* v *Refuge Assurance plc* [2002] IRLR 324, EAT, which arose out of a merger of Refuge Assurance and United Friendly Insurance, was whether there was a difference between the EU and UK trigger points for consultation and, if so, whether the UK domestic legislation can be interpreted to match the requirements of the directive. The EAT held that there is a difference in the domestic and EU trigger points and that it is not possible to interpret the UK legislation to accord with the EU directive's requirements. In the view of Lindsay J, 'contemplation' means 'having a view' and relates to a relatively early stage in the decision-making process, whereas 'proposing' relates to a state of mind which is much more certain.

The EAT held that it would be distorting the words of s. 188(1) 'is proposing to dismiss' to make it akin to the directive's 'is contemplating'. The EAT, adopting the view of Glidewell LJ in *R* v

British Coal Corporation, ex p. Vardy, held that 'proposes' relates to a state of mind which is much more certain and further along the decision-making process than 'contemplates'. The most fitting dictionary definition of the word 'propose' is 'to lay before another or others as something which one offers to do or wishes to be done', a stage later than 'contemplation', the ordinary meaning of which is 'having a view, taking into account as a contingency', reflecting an early stage in the decision-making process.

In the view of the EAT in *MSF*, the employment tribunal had correctly held that the words 'proposing to dismiss' in s. 188(1) mean that the employer has reached a stage where he has proposals to make, as distinct from a plan having been formulated at management level which may have the likely consequence of redundancies at some time in the future. The tribunal had correctly applied its conclusions to the facts and was entitled to find that consultations with the union about all the proposed redundancies had begun within the statutory timescale. The EAT held that it was not possible to interpret the UK legislation to accord with the EU directive's requirements and, since the Union was not in a position to seek direct enforcement of the directive (i.e. not representing employees of an emanation of the State), its appeal was dismissed.

In *Akavan Erityisalojen Keskusliitto AEK ry* v *Fujitsu Siemens Computers Oy* [2009] IRLR 944, the ECJ purported to offer guidance on the timing of consultation. However, it is fair to say that the 'guidance' generates more heat than light. The Court viewed the obligation to consult as commencing when there is an 'intention' on the part of the employer to make collective redundancies. In other words, when a business decision has been taken that compels the employer to contemplate or plan for collective redundancies. There is no obligation to consult 'where a decision deemed likely to lead to collective redundancies is merely contemplated and where, accordingly, such collective redundancies are only a probability'. It is recognised that a premature triggering of the consultation obligation could lead to results contrary to the purpose of the directive; restricting the flexibility available to employers when restructuring, creating heavier administrative burdens and causing unnecessary uncertainty for workers about the safety of their jobs. On the other hand, 'a consultation which began when a decision making such collective redundancies necessary had already been taken could not usefully involve any examination of conceivable alternatives with the aim of avoiding them.'

In the view of the ECJ:

> [I]n order for such participation to be effective, it must take place at a moment when the subject-matter of the negotiations is liable to be sufficiently specific; that moment cannot be other than that at which it is apparent that the employer intends to make collective redundancies or, at least, that he already foresees the possibility of doing so as a consequence of the measures planned. It is only at that moment that the employer can be considered to be required to begin consultations. Prior to that moment, workers' representatives cannot properly participate in decision-making concerning the employment of the workforce and genuine alternatives to collective redundancies; consequently, consultations would not be useful.

As Rubenstein observes: 'The ECJ's interpretation of the Directive's requirements in this respect appears closer to the UK criterion of a "proposal" than may have been understood before, although there still appears to be a gap between "proposing" and "contemplating" ' ('Highlights' [2009] IRLR 881).

2. Section 188(1) requires 'the employer' to consult with appropriate representatives where it 'is proposing to dismiss as redundant 20 or more employees *at one establishment* within a period of 90 days or less'. Surprisingly, the terms 'employer' and 'at one establishment' are not defined in either TULR(C)A or the Collective Redundancies Directive. How these terms are interpreted will affect the minimum amount of time for consultation which is dependent on the number persons to be made redundant at the 'establishment in question. For example, where an employer operates at several locations, if each location is a separate 'establishment' and there are fewer than 20 proposed redundancies at each, the threshold set by s. 188(1) will not be crossed even if the *overall* number of proposed redundancies is high.

In *Rockfon A/S* v *Specialarbejderforbundet i Danmark* [1996] IRLR 168, the ECJ stated 'that the term "establishment" appearing in article 1(1)(a) of the [Collective Redundancies Directive] must be undertood as meaning, depending on the circumstances, the unit to which the workers made redundant are assigned to carry out their duties. It is not essential, in order for concerns, in particulartthere to be an "establishment", for the unit in question to be endowed with a management which can independently effect collective redundancies.'

This guidance was further elaborated upon by the ECJ in *Athinaiki Charttoposia AE* v *Panagiotidis* [2007] IRLR 234, where the Court stated that:

> for the purposes of the application of the [Collective Redundancies Directive], an 'establishment', in the context of an undertaking, may consist of a distinct entity, having a certain degree of permanence and stability, which is assigned to perform one or more given tasks and which has a workforce, technical means and a certain organisational structure allowing for the accomplishment of those tasks. Given that the objective pursued by the [Collective Redundancies Directive] concerns in particular, the socio-economic effects which collective redundancies may have in a given local context and social environment, the entity in question need not have any legal autonomy, nor need it have economic, financial, administrative or technological autonomy, in order to be regarded as an 'establishment'. It is, moreover, in this spirit that the Court has held that it is not essential, in order for there to be an 'establishment', for the unit in question to be endowed with a management which can independently effect collective redundancies...Nor must there be a geographical separation from the other units and facilities of the undertaking.

In *Barratt Developments (Bradford) Ltd* v *UCATT* [1977] IRLR 403, the EAT held that what constitutes an 'establishment' is a question for the employment tribunal as an 'industrial jury' to decide. Consequently, it upheld the tribunal's decision that 14 house-building sites in Lancashire, administered from headquarters near Bradford, in fact constituted one establishment.

Further confusion was caused by the EAT's decision in *USDAW* v *Ethel Austin Ltd (In Administration)* [2013] IRLR 686.

When Woolworths (and Ethel Austin) became insolvent, there was collective consultation. Each store was treated as 'one establishment', as has been accepted practice in the UK for many years. As a result, there was only collective consultation at the bigger stores, i.e. those with more than 20 employees.

The EAT held that in order to comply with the requirements of the Directive, the obligation to inform and consult is triggered whenever an employer proposes to dismiss as redundant 20 or more employees within a 90-day period, regardless of whether the employees work at the same or separate establishments.

The EAT reached its decision based on the following reasoning. The EU Collective Redundancies Directive provided two options for Member States to frame how the consultation duty is triggered. The UK, according to Hansard and other contemporaneous publications, intended to adopt the second of these two options when implementing the Directive into UK law. This second option requires the duty to be triggered when 'over a period of 90 days, at least 20, whatever the number of workers in the establishments in question' may be dismissed. However, s. 188 limits the obligation to where there are 20 or more dismissals *at one establishment*. The EAT was of the view that the clear parliamentary intention was to implement the Directive correctly and the introduction of the 'at one establishment' wording was potentially a drafting error and did not reflect the express intention of Parliament to limit the protection of s. 188. When interpreting UK legislation compatibly with EU law obligations, the EAT took the view that legal principles permit 'additional words to be put in. They could be taken out; they can be moved around' (according to *Marleasing SA* v *La Comercial Internacional de Alimentación SA*). According to the EAT, the correct interpretation of this option is that the obligation to consult arises when 20 or more are to be dismissed *irrespective of where they work*. As a court must construe UK law so that it complies with EU law, the EAT decided that the words 'at one establishment' should therefore be deleted from s. 188.

The result of the decision was that all the employees from the smaller stores (1,210 employees at Ethel Austin, and 3,233 at Woolworths) became entitled to a protective award.On appeal, however, the Court of Appeal asked the CJEU whether the EU Collective Redundancies Directive 98/59 require that the numbers of employees dismissed across an employer's various establishments be aggregated to see if the thresholds for protection are met?

The Advocate General answered this in the negative (see *USDAW; Wilson* v *WW Realisation 1 Ltd, in liquidation; Ethel Austin Ltd; Secretary of State for Business, Innovation and Skills* (2015) Case C–80/14).

The Court of Appeal asked the CJEU whether the phrase in the Directive *'at least 20'* dismissals referred to dismissals over the employer's establishments, or the number in each establishment, and if it did refer to each establishment, what was meant by *'establishment'*?

The Advocate General noted (para. 61):

> that directive does not require—nor does it preclude—aggregating the number of dismissals in all the employer's establishments for the purposes of verifying whether the thresholds set in Article 1(1)(a) are met...

and noted that

> It is for the Member States to decide, where appropriate, to increase the level of protection...provided that, on every occasion...it would be more favourable to the workers made redundant...

The Advocate General recommended answering that the meaning of *'establishment'* in the Directive was the same under Article 1 (1) (a) (i) and (ii) and 'that concept denotes the unit to which the workers made redundant are assigned to carry out their duties, which it is for the national court to determine'.

Subsequently, the ECJ concurred with this opinion (Case C-80/14, 30/4/15).

3. *Middlesbrough Borough Council* v *TGWU* [2002] IRLR 332, EAT, concerned the scope of the duty to consult in advance of redundancies. Section 188(2) of TULR(C)A requires that redundancy consultation, which must be undertaken with a view to reaching agreement with appropriate union representatives, 'shall include consultation about ways of (a) avoiding the dismissals, (b) reducing the numbers of employees to be dismissed, and (c) mitigating the consequences of the dismissals'. In this case, the employment tribunal held that although the employers had genuinely consulted with the recognised unions over redundancy selection and redundancy arrangements, they were in breach of the statutory requirement because they had already taken a decision before starting consultations that there would need to be compulsory redundancies.

Upholding the tribunal's finding, the EAT held that the three elements of consultation required by s. 188(2) are disjunctive. Thus, an employer may genuinely consult with employee representatives about ways of reducing the number of employees to be dismissed and mitigating the consequences of the dismissals, without genuinely consulting as to the principle of whether to declare redundancies at all. As a result, there is a statutory duty on the employer to genuinely consult with employee representatives, with a view to reaching agreement, about ways of avoiding dismissals. According to Clark J:

> It is not open to an employer, for this purpose, to argue, as would be open to him in defending a complaint of unfair dismissal by the individual employee, that consultation would, in the circumstances, be futile or utterly useless.

4. According to recent case law, the consultation obligations require employers to consult in advance with employee representatives *over the reasons for proposing the redundancies*, and not just over ways in which the consequences of the redundancies can be mitigated (see *UK Coal Mining Ltd* v *National Union of Mineworkers (Northumberland Area)* [2008] IRLR 4, EAT). In the view of the EAT, the legislation now requires employers to consult about ways of 'avoiding the dismissals'. On that basis, the EAT took the view that 'the obligation to consult over avoiding the proposed redundancies inevitably involves engaging with the reasons for the dismissals, and that in turn requires consultation over the reasons for the closure.' As Rubenstein observes:

> Although on its facts and on its language, the case concerned a closure, the reasoning would seem to apply to all mass redundancies. Given that consultation should take place before a firm decision has been reached, and must be 'with a view to reaching agreement', this judgment is likely to have significant ramifications for both the timing and the substance of redundancy consultation. By requiring consultation over the business reasons for the employer's decision, the EAT takes us an important step closer to European consultation practice. ['Highlights' [2008] IRLR 1]

See also *United States of America* v *Nolan* [2009] IRLR 923, EAT, where the contention that *UK Coal* applies only to commercial decisions and not to decisions which involve public policy was rejected.

5. The EAT in the *Middlesbrough Borough Council* case did hold that the employment tribunal below had erred in interpreting the reference in s. 188(1A) to consultation beginning at least '90 days before the first of dismissals takes effect' as meaning 90 days before notice of dismissal is issued rather than when that notice expires. According to the EAT, the passing observation of Phillips J in *National Union of Teachers* v *Avon County Council* [1978] IRLR 55, EAT that, in the context of the redundancy consultation provisions, 'dismiss' refers to the giving of notice and not its expiry, was not correct. Just as it is relevant in a redundancy unfair dismissal complaint for an employment tribunal to look at consultation which took place after notice was given but before expiry of that notice, so for the purposes of s. 188, consultation may continue up to the expiry of the notice and the minimum 90-day period is to be counted back from the expiry date (notwithstanding that error of law, however, the employment tribunal's finding that the employers had not genuinely consulted with the unions as to ways of avoiding dismissals was 'plainly and unarguably right' and the employer's appeal was dismissed).

6. However, in *Junk* v *Kuhnel*, Case C–188/03 [2005] IRLR 310, the ECJ held that a 'redundancy' within the meaning of the Collective Redundancies Directive (1998/59) means the declaration by an employer of its intention to terminate the contract of employment rather than the actual cessation of the employment relationship upon expiry of the period of notice. Therefore, the consultation process with employee representatives must take place before employees are given notice of dismissal.

It would appear that UK legislation, which lays down that consultations in advance of large-scale redundancies must begin at least 90 days before the first of the dismissals takes effect, is not consistent with EU law.

7. In Leicestershire County Council v Unison [2005] IRLR 920, EAT, as a result of a job evaluation exercise, council officials wanted to vary the terms and conditions of two groups of employees by dismissing them and re-engaging them on new contracts. This proposal was put to a committee of councillors and approved. An employment tribunal found that the council was in breach of its consultation obligations and this decision was upheld by the EAT.

MCMULLEN J: We consider that effect must be given to the construction of the Directive which aims to avoid dismissal for redundancy and which requires there to be consultation at a stage before decisions on dismissal for redundancy are made. There is no straining of the language of s. 188 in order to give effect to this purpose by construing 'proposing to dismiss' as 'proposing to give notice of dismissal'. We would therefore follow *Junk* v *Kuhnel*, C–188/03 [2005] IRLR 310 ECJ, seek to apply it and uphold the tribunal's judgment as correct.

Note that the EAT decision focuses on when redundancy consultation must begin. It is not authority for the proposition that notice of dismissal cannot be given until the full period allowed for consultation under UK law has elapsed.

8. Where the redundancy consultation involves the same employer and the same prospective redundancies, s. 188 does not require a fresh round of consultation. The reference in s. 188 to a period of 90 days does not mean that, if the process of consultation extends beyond that period, the statute requires that it must restart. The 90-day period fixes the start of the consultation period. It does not determine when it finishes (Vauxhall Motors Ltd v TGWU [2006] IRLR 674, EAT).

9. In *University of Stirling* v *University & College Union* [2011] UKEAT/001/11/BI), the EAT decided, controversially, that the collective consultation obligations in s. 188 were not engaged upon the expiry of some fixed-term contracts. The non-renewal of a fixed-term contract may or may not be a redundancy dismissal. It will depend on the reasons the employer had for not renewing that contract. If one of the reasons for non-renewal is individual to that employee (and in this case the employee had accepted that their employment would come to an end at a defined point), then that non-renewal does not count for collective redundancy purposes. Where the non-renewal is not personal (e.g. the shutting of a department or where it is brought to an end early), the non-renewal may amount to a redundancy if the reasons are not personal to the employee.

The Trade Union and Labour Relations (Consolidation) Act (Amendment)) Order 2013 (SI 2013/763), para. (4) amends s. 282 to exclude the expiry of fixed term contracts from the provisions dealing with collective redundancies in the 1992 Act. The expiry of a fixed term contract will not be excluded from the provisions dealing with collective redundancies if the employer is proposing to dismiss the employee as redundant (as defined in s. 195) and the dismissal will take effect before the point at which it was agreed in the contract that it would expire. This point could be on the expiry of a specific period of time. Alternatively, it could be on the completion of a particular task such as a research project or on the occurrence (or non-occurrence) of an event such as external funding for a particular role coming to an end.

10. Section 188(7) permits a failure to consult where there are 'special circumstances which render it not reasonably practicable for the employer to comply'. In *Middlesbrough Borough Council* v *TGWU*, the EAT also held that it could not be accepted that the council's relatively long-standing financial difficulties amounted to 'special circumstances' within the meaning of s. 188(7) which rendered it not reasonably practicable for the council to consult with the unions within the statutory timescale about ways of avoiding the redundancies. In the view of Clark J:

[W]e cannot conceive of circumstances in which the employer has sufficient time to consult and does genuinely consult on matters detailed in subsection (2)(b) and (c), but enters into sham or no consultation on the matter identified in subsection (2)(a) which could be said to be special, rendering it not reasonably practicable to enter into genuine consultation on that matter.

Clarkes of Hove Ltd v *Bakers' Union*
[1978] ICR 1077, Court of Appeal

The employers had been in financial difficulty for some time. On 24 October 1976, all hope of a financial rescue package disappeared and they dismissed all 368 employees and ceased trading. The union complained about the failure to consult. The Court of Appeal held that insolvency was not a 'special circumstance' (in the absence of any special cause for the insolvency) so that consultation should have taken place.

GEOFFREY LANE LJ: [I]t seems to me that the way in which the phrase was interpreted by the industrial tribunal is correct. What they said, in effect, was this, that insolvency is, on its own, neither here nor there. It may be a special circumstance; it may not be a special circumstance. It will depend entirely on the cause of the insolvency whether the circumstances can be described as special or not. If, for example, sudden disaster strikes a company, making it necessary to close the concern, then plainly that would be a matter which was capable of being a special circumstance; and that is so whether the disaster is physical or financial. If the insolvency, however, were merely due to a gradual run-down of the company, as it was in this case, then those are facts on which the industrial tribunal can come to the conclusion that the circumstances were not special. In other words, to be special the event must be something out of the ordinary, something uncommon; and that is the meaning of the word 'special' in the context of this Act.

NOTES
1. The EC Commission, when amending the Collective Redundancies Directive, took the view that in cases of multinational corporations, the decision to make redundancies at a particular plant is often made by the parent company. It was felt that the directive should be amended in order to stop employers using their foreign parent companies as an excuse for their failure to consult. TURERA 1993 included an amendment to TULR(C)A 1992, s. 188(7), in order to comply with the amended directive. As a result, the 'special circumstances' defence will not apply where the failure arose because a person controlling the employer did not provide the employer with the necessary information.

   The ECJ's judgment in *Akavan Erityisalojen Keskusliitto AEK ry* v *Fujitsu Siemens Computers Oy* [2009] IRLR 944 is in a similar vein. The case concerned the closure of the company's production plant in Finland. The claimants (certain Finnish trade unions) contended that the parent company of the respondents had decided upon this before carrying out the consultation procedure, and one of the issues before the ECJ was whether the redundancy consultation obligation is only imposed on the actual employer, or whether it extends to decisions made by a parent company. The ECJ held that in a case of a group of undertakings, it is for the employer of the employees in question to hold the consultations and this obligation is not dependent on the subsidiary employer being able to supply all the necessary information to employee representatives. Information can be provided during the course of the consultation.

2. Failure to adopt proper consultation procedures with the trade union may lead to a sum of damages (a 'protective award') being awarded to the union on behalf of the employee(s). The protective award is within the tribunal's discretion, subject to a maximum of 90 days' pay.

3. Prior to the passage of TURERA 1993, TULR(C)A 1992, s. 190(3) allowed the employer to offset any payment of wages or wages in lieu of notice against the protective award. In *Vosper Thorneycroft (UK) Ltd* v *TGWU* [1988] ICR 270, the EAT held that this meant that the gross amount of such a payment was to be deducted, not just the net amount (so that where the employer had paid 13 weeks' wages in lieu of notice, this extinguished the 90-day protective award completely). In such cases, the penalty for failure to comply with s. 188 was non-existent. An amendment, introduced by TURERA 1993, s. 34(3), repeals TULR(C)A 1992, s. 190(3) and removes the right to offset pay in lieu of notice against liability for a protective award.

4. In *Susie Radin Ltd* v *GMB* [2004] IRLR 400, it was argued that a protective award covering the maximum period of 90 days after a failure to consult at all over a factory closure was inappropriate because there was a finding of fact that consultation would have been futile. The Court of Appeal held that the futility of consultation is not relevant to the making of a protective award. The purpose of the award is to provide a sanction for breach by the employer of the consultation obligations. In *Amicus* v *GBS Tooling Ltd (in administration)* [2005] IRLR 683, the EAT held that the guidelines laid down by the Court of Appeal in *Susie Radin Ltd* make it clear that in deciding the

length of a protected period, an employment tribunal has a wide discretion to do what is just and equitable in all the circumstances and, in exercising that wide discretion, is obliged to consider the seriousness of the employer's breach and any mitigating circumstances put before it.

FURTHER READING

Cabrelli, D., *Employment Law in Context: Text and materials* (Oxford: OUP, 2014), Chs. 18, 19.

Honeyball S., *Honeyball and Bowers' Textbook on Employment Law*, 13th edn (Oxford: OUP, 2014), Chs. 6, 9.

10

Trade Unions and their Members

SECTION 1: **THE TRADE UNION**

A: The legal definition

TRADE UNION AND LABOUR RELATIONS (CONSOLIDATION) ACT 1992

1. Meaning of 'trade union'

In this Act a 'trade union' means an organisation (whether temporary or permanent)—

(a) which consists wholly or mainly of workers of one or more descriptions and whose principal purposes include the regulation of relations between workers of that description or those descriptions and employers or employers' associations; or

(b) which consists wholly or mainly of—

    (i) constituent or affiliated organisations which fulfil the conditions in paragraph (a) (or themselves consist wholly or mainly of constituent or affiliated organisations which fulfil those conditions) or,

    (ii) representatives of such constituent or affiliated organisations, and whose principal purposes include the regulation of relations between workers and employers' associations, or the regulation of relations between its constituent or affiliated organisations.

Midland Cold Storage Ltd v *Turner*

[1972] ICR 773, National Industrial Relations Court

The plaintiffs sought to prevent a joint shop stewards committee from taking industrial action. The action was brought to restrain the commission of certain 'unfair industrial practices' created by the Industrial Relations Act 1971. It was necessary to establish that the committee was an 'organisation of workers', a term defined by s. 61 of the Act in substantially the same words as in s. 1 (extracted earlier).

SIR JOHN DONALDSON: ...It follows that, if Midland are to obtain an order against the committee, they must satisfy us that (a) it is an organisation; (b) consists wholly or mainly of workers; (c) its principal objects include the regulation of relations between workers of that description and employers.

We have no doubt at all that the committee exists and has great influence in the London docks. We have no evidence as to its composition, other than the fact that it has a chairman and secretary, and that, as we infer from its name and our general knowledge of organisation in the docks, it is composed wholly or mainly of trade union shop stewards. It is not recognised by employers, although they are well aware of its existence and may take account of its activities. Furthermore, there is no evidence that it seeks recognition by employers as a bargaining agent for any bargaining unit or as a representative body for or of any union or unions. It is proved to be an influential pressure group. Our general knowledge of the industry tells us that its activities are to some extent coordinated with those of other shop stewards' committees in other docks by a national shop stewards' committee, but that those other committees may have different compositions and functions. If we have to be able to point to evidence to confirm what as members of an industrial court we ought to know and do know, it was provided at a late stage in the hearing by the production of a printed leaflet, purporting to be issued by the committee, referring to support from the national committee. Its most apparent activity seems to consist of the recommending, the taking or abandonment of industrial action in the London docks and organising any such action which may be decided upon. Thereafter it does not seem to enter into negotiations with the employers, but leaves this task to the established union machinery.

Against this background, we are satisfied that prima facie the committee is an organisation and that it consists wholly or mainly of workers as defined in the Act of 1971. However, we are not satisfied that there is a prima facie case for holding that its principal objects include the regulation of relations between workers of that description (namely registered dock workers) and employers. No body whose principal objects included such regulation could fail at least to seek recognition from employers and of such an attempt we have no evidence. Accordingly, we are unable to make any order against the committee as such.

NOTES

1. Before 1971, the Registrar of Friendly Societies had the responsibility of maintaining a register of trade unions and most unions complied because there were tax advantages. The Industrial Relations Act 1971 introduced the office of Registrar of Trade Unions and made registration the precondition to any benefits to be gained under the Act. Since it also involved many interventions in the internal affairs of unions and control of the rule book, only a few registered. Any union that did register was expelled from the TUC.

   The Trade Union and Labour Relations Act (TULRA) 1974 reverted to the substance of the pre-1971 approach and the law is now set out in the Trade Union and Labour Relations (Consolidation) Act (TULR(C)A) 1992, ss. 2, 3 and 4. By s. 2, the Certification Officer is charged with the duty of keeping a voluntary list of trade unions and employers' associations. The Certification Officer grants a listing if he is satisfied that the organisation comes within the appropriate definition.

   Inclusion on the list is evidence that the organisation is a trade union. Unions on the list receive tax relief in respect of sums paid as 'provident benefits' (Income and Corporation Taxes Act 1988, s. 467) and listing is a precondition for the grant of a certificate from the Certification Officer that the union is 'independent'. Such status is an important attribute in relation to the following rights of unions, officials, and members: to take part in trade union activities; to gain information for collective bargaining; to secure consultation over redundancies; to insist on time off for union duties and activities; and to appoint health and safety representatives.

2. In *Atkinosun v The Certification Officer* [2013] IRLR 937, the EAT held that the question whether the regulation of employment relations is one of the principal purposes of the organisation is a question of fact, rather than those simply stated in the rulebook. The focus is on the collective nature of the organisation. Consequently, if a body's purpose is to represent individual employees in grievance or disciplinary proceedings, it will not qualify as a trade union.

3. On 31 March 2014 there were 162 'listed' unions compared with 165 'listed' on 31 March 2013 and less than 12% of the all-time highest total of 1,384 in 1920 (*Annual Report of the Certification Officer 2013–14*). Around 6.5 million employees were members of trade unions in 2013. The level of overall membership was broadly unchanged from 2012, with a reduction of only 6,000 over the year (a 0.1% decline) but well below the peak of 13.3 million (55.8% of the workforce) in 1979.

   The number of UK employees increased between 2012 and 2013. As a result, the membership rate (density) fell slightly to 25.6% in 2013, from 26% in 2012. This is the lowest rate of union membership density recorded between 19995 and 2013. Over this period, the proportion of employees who were trade union members in the UK has decreased by around 7 percentage points from 32.4% in 1995.

   Union membership density in the private sector was 14.4% in 2013. In the public sector density stood at 55.4%.

   Female employees are more likely to be trade union members. The proportion of female employees who were in a trade union was around 28% in 2013, compared with 23% of male employees.

   Trade union members are increasingly older employees. Over the 18 years to 2013, the proportion of employees who belonged to a trade union fell in all age groups except those aged over 65. About 37% of trade union member employees were over 50 in 2013, but only 27% of all employees are in this age group.

   Employees in professional occupations are more likely to be trade union members than employees in other occupations. Employees in professional occupations account for 37% of all union members, but only 21% of all employees worked in this sector.

   A higher proportion of UK-born employees are in a trade union compared with non-UK born employees. About 27% of UK-born employees were in a trade union, compared with 18% of non-UK born employees.

The decline in union density has been particularly marked among male employees, manual employees, and those in production industries, all areas which traditionally recorded high union-membership density levels and which once formed the core of trade union membership. By comparison, union density has fallen less slowly among female employees, those working part time, and non-manual employees.

In 2013, only 29.5% of employees were covered by collective bargaining. However, collective bargaining coverage is not even across the economy. In the public sector, 68.8% of employees were covered by collective bargaining, compared with only 16.6% in the private sector (*Trade Union Membership 2013: Statistical Bulletin,* Department of Business Innovation and Skills, May 2014).

Union density is highest in the Scandinavian countries of Sweden (70.8%), Finland (70.3%), and Denmark (69.1%), and lowest in Hungary (16.9%), the USA (11.6%), and France (7.8%). Where countries were ranked in descending order by union density, out of 30 countries, the UK was ranked as number 12 (see Barratt, C., *Trade Union Membership 2008*, BERR, April 2009)

4. The Transparency of Lobbying, Non-party Campaigning and Trade Union Administration Act 2014 (Part 3) amends TULR(C)A's existing s. 24 which requires trade unions to maintain an accurate and up-to-date register of members—so far as reasonably practicable.

- In particular, the Act will require unions to send, annually, to the Certification Officer (CO) a membership audit certificate.
- Where the trade union has up to 10,000 members, it may self-certify that it has complied with its section 24 duties.
- Larger unions must appoint a qualified independent person (an 'Assurer') to certify that the trade union's system for compiling and maintaining the register are satisfactory for the purposes of complying with section 24.
- The Act also contains new related investigatory and enforcement powers for the CO.
- Trade unions lobbied against the new audit duty, voicing concerns over extra cost and red tape, as well as data protection and privacy issues surrounding the disclosure of membership data to assurers and potentially the CO. There were some suggestions of a challenge based on human rights law.
- There is clearly an overlap between the TULR(C)A duty to maintain an accurate register of members and the strike ballot and notice duties which require a degree of accuracy over identifying those members affected by a potential strike. However, it should be remembered that these duties are not absolute and provide for a margin of error by the trade unions, for example, applying a reasonableness test.
- The Act received Royal Assent on 30 January 2014 and the new obligations on trade unions came into force on 6 April 2015.

B: Certificate of independence

Employers who wish to prevent trade unions recruiting their workforce may engage in two forms of 'peaceful competition'. They may ensure that the terms and conditions of their workforce are better than the negotiated rates, or they can encourage the formation of a staff association, which does not pose an effective challenge to management's power. Such organisations are termed 'sweetheart unions'. The certificate of independence is the means by which the law seeks to ensure that such groupings do not receive the rights accorded to independent trade unions.

TRADE UNION AND LABOUR RELATIONS (CONSOLIDATION) ACT 1992

5. Meaning of 'independent trade union'

In this Act an 'independent trade union' means a trade union which—

(a) is not under the domination or control of an employer or group of employers or of one or more employers' associations, and

(b) is not liable to interference by an employer or any such group or association (arising out of the provision of financial or material support or by any other means whatsoever) tending towards such control;

...

Squibb UK Staff Association v *Certification Officer*

[1980] IRLR 431, Court of Appeal

The staff association was refused a certificate of independence. While accepting that the organisation was not under the domination or control of the employer, the Certification Officer took the view that it was 'liable to interference' because it was dependent on the employer for facilities and in a weak financial position. The association successfully appealed to the EAT which took the view that interference had to be 'likely' or 'not unlikely'. The Court of Appeal upheld the Certification Officer's decision.

LORD DENNING MR: One has to envisage the possibility that there may be a difference of opinion in the future between the employers and the staff association. It does not matter whether it is likely or not—it may be completely unlikely—but one has to envisage the possibility of a difference of opinion…But when it arises, the questions have to be asked. What is the strength of the employers? What pressures could they bring to bear against the staff association? What facilities could they withdraw?…

The employers could take away the four facilities which the Certification Officer mentioned in his reasons. They could take away the facility of time for meetings. They could take away the facility of free use of office accommodation, and so forth. Those are pressures which the employers could bring to bear on their side. On the other side, this association is rather weak. It has a narrow membership base. It has small financial resources. Weighing the two sides, one against the other, the Certification Officer came to the conclusion that the association was liable to interference in this way: the association was so weak that it was vulnerable, in that it was exposed to the risk of interference tending towards control by the employers.

The Employment Appeal Tribunal reversed the Certification Officer. It seems to me that it misdirected itself. It concentrated too much on the 'likelihood of interference' whereas it should have had regard to the 'vulnerability to interference'. I would therefore allow the appeal and restore the decision of the Certification Officer.

Blue Circle Staff Association v *Certification Officer*

[1977] IRLR 20, Employment Appeal Tribunal

CUMMING-BRUCE J: In response to a question from the tribunal the Certification Officer described his approach. He stated that he had found no nice clear yardstick which could be laid against each case, but that it was a case of looking at the factors and doing a balancing act. He then indicated certain criteria which he found useful. In view of the novelty and importance of the subject matter we set out the criteria as the witness described them, though we do not think it would give a fair impression of his evidence if we suggested that he presented them either as comprehensive, or of similar weight in any two cases.

1. *Finance*: If there is any evidence that a union is getting a direct subsidy from an employer, it is immediately ruled out.

2. *Other Assistance*: The Certification Officer's inspectors see what material support, such as free premises, time off work for officials, or office facilities a union is getting from an employer, and attempt to cost them out.

3. *Employer Interference*: If a union is very small, and weak, and gets a good deal of help, then on the face of it its independence must be in danger and liable to interference.

4. *History*: The recent history of a union, important in the case of the Blue Circle Staff Association which before February 1976 was dominated by the employers, is considered. It was not unusual for a staff association to start as a 'creature of management and grow into something independent'. The staff association had started on this road but still had a way to travel.

5. *Rules*: The applicant union's rule book is scrutinised to see if the employer can interfere with, or control it, and if there are any restrictions on membership. If a union is run by people near the top of a company it could be detrimental to the rank and file members.

6. *Single Company Unions*: While they were not debarred from getting certificates, because such a rule could exclude unions like those of the miners and railwaymen, they were more liable to employer interference. Broadly based multi-company unions were more difficult to influence.

7. *Organisation*: The Certification Officer's inspectors then examine the applicant union in detail, its size and recruiting ability, whether it is run by competent and experienced officers, the state of its finance, and its branch and committee structure. Again, if the union was run by senior men in a company, employer interference was a greater risk.

8. *Attitude*: Once the other factors had been assessed, inspectors looked for a 'robust attitude in negotiation' as a sign of genuine independence, backed up by a good negotiating record...

NOTES

1. In coming to his decision, the Certification Officer is free to make such inquiries as he thinks fit and 'shall take into account any relevant information submitted to him by any person'. If an applicant union is refused a certificate, an appeal on fact or law lies to the Employment Appeal Tribunal (EAT). The right to appeal in TULR(C)A 1992, s. 9(2), is so worded that no other competing union can appeal against the Certification Officer's decision to grant a certificate (*General and Municipal Workers' Union* v *Certification Officer* [1977] ICR 183).

2. An application of the provisions relating to independence can be seen in *Government Communications Staff Federation* v *Certification Officer* [1992] IRLR 260, EAT. Following the Government's decision to ban trade unions at GCHQ, the GC Staff Association was formed. Its application for a certificate of independence was opposed by the TUC and the Council of Civil Service Unions, and was rejected by the Certification Officer. Its appeal to the EAT was dismissed. Wood P held that it was 'liable to interference by an employer' because:
   (a) it was a condition of service that staff were not allowed to be members of other unions, and any attempt to affiliate with another union would probably result in derecognition;
   (b) approval or recognition could be withdrawn at any time by the employer on the ground of national security.

C: The legal status of a trade union

TRADE UNION AND LABOUR RELATIONS (CONSOLIDATION) ACT 1992

10. Quasi-corporate status of trade unions

(1) A trade union is not a body corporate but—
   (a) it is capable of making contracts;
   (b) it is capable of suing and being sued in its own name, whether in proceedings relating to property or founded on contract or tort or any other cause of action; and
   (c) proceedings for an offence alleged to have been committed by it or on its behalf may be brought against it in its own name.

(2)–(3) [*omitted*].

NOTE: A trade union has a strange status in law. A trade union is not a body corporate, i.e. a separate legal entity, existing independently of its members. It is an unincorporated association and its property must rest in the hands of trustees. When unions first received recognition under law, they were allowed, but not obliged, to register under the Trade Union Act 1871.

Whether they were registered or not, unions remained unincorporated associations, and it was therefore assumed that it was impossible to sue them in their own name.

The notorious House of Lords decision in *Taff Vale Railway Co.* v *Amalgamated Society of Railway Servants* [1901] AC 426 held that a trade union registered under the 1871 Act could be sued in tort, registered unions having a rather peculiar quasi-corporate status. The later House of Lords decision in *Bonsor* v *Musicians Union* [1956] AC 104 confirmed this position.

The Industrial Relations Act 1971 then incorporated registered trade unions.

TULRA 1974 essentially restored the pre-1971 position, except that no distinction is now drawn between listed and non-listed trade unions and their status was put on the more satisfactory legal footing, now set out in TULR(C)A 1992, s. 10.

There are, however, some residual consequences of unincorporated status. For example, a trade union does not have the necessary legal personality to suffer injury to its reputation and cannot sue for libel (*EETPU* v *Times Newspapers* [1980] 1 All ER 1097).

D: Restraint of trade

TRADE UNION AND LABOUR RELATIONS (CONSOLIDATION) ACT 1992

11. Exclusion of common law rules as to restraint of trade

(1) The purposes of a trade union are not, by reason only that they are in restraint of trade, unlawful so as—

    (a) to make any member of the trade union liable to criminal proceedings for conspiracy or otherwise, or

    (b) to make any agreement or trust void or voidable.

(2) No rule of a trade union is unlawful or unenforceable by reason only that it is in restraint of trade.

NOTE: The immunity contained in s. 11 is fundamental if unions are to operate lawfully. Where a union is empowered to take strike action or to impose various other forms of pressure on an employer, at common law these would be regarded as restraints of trade. Consequently, a union would be perceived to be an organisation pursuing purposes in a manner contrary to public policy, and as such would be unable to enforce its rules or protect its funds.

The vulnerability of the unions to the doctrine of restraint of trade was vividly illustrated in *Hornby* v *Close* (1867) LR 2 QB 153. The United Order of Boilermakers, which had registered under the Friendly Societies Act 1855, wanted the help of the courts to prosecute an official who had embezzled its funds. It was refused. Blackburn J said: 'I do not say the objects of this society are criminal. I do not say they are not. But I am clearly of the opinion that the rules referred to are illegal in the sense that they cannot be enforced.'

Consequently, it was recognised by the framers of the Trade Union Act 1871 that if unions were to be made lawful they would need to be granted immunity from this doctrine. TULR(C)A 1992, s. 11, retains this immunity but expands it slightly to cover rules in addition to purposes.

This extension of the immunity to rules was necessary because of the restrictive interpretation placed on 'purposes' by the Court of Appeal in *Edwards* v *SOGAT* [1971] 3 All ER 689. The plaintiff was expelled from the defendant trade union of which he had been classed a temporary member. His expulsion was carried out under r. 18(4)(h) of the union rules which provided for automatic termination of membership for arrears of subscription. The defendant conceded that expulsion for this reason was unlawful because it was based on a misunderstanding about payment of the plaintiff's dues. However, the union argued that his damages should be nominal, since he could have been validly expelled under another rule, r. 18(4)(j), which it was argued gave the union an unfettered right to terminate the membership of temporary members. Sachs LJ rejected this argument and found such an all-empowering rule an unreasonable restraint of trade on the basis that it could not be said that a rule that enabled such 'capricious and despotic action' was proper to the purposes of any trade union.

This approach is now no longer possible given the extended s. 11. However, the reasoning adopted by another judge in the case, Lord Denning, was based on general public policy and a 'right to work' not tied to the doctrine of restraint of trade: if this approach is correct, then s. 11 would not offer immunity in such circumstances.

E: Political funds and objects

The Trade Union Act 1913 was enacted in order to restore the right of unions to spend money on political objects following the decision of the House of Lords in *Amalgamated Society of Railway Servants* v *Osborne* [1910] AC 87, which held that it was unlawful for a union to impose on its members a compulsory levy for the purposes of creating a parliamentary fund to promote Labour MPs. However, while the Act allowed trade unions the right to maintain a political fund, it imposed a series of restrictive conditions on their ability to incur expenditure in respect of certain specified political objects. The union was required to ballot its members in order to approve the adoption of political objects, payments in furtherance of such objects had to be made out of a separate political fund and individual members were allowed to 'contract out' and were safeguarded against discrimination arising from their failure to contribute to the fund.

The two major changes introduced into this system by the Trade Union Act 1984 related to the introduction of periodic ballots to test continued support for the political objects of the union and a new definition of 'political objects'. The law is now contained in TULR(C)A 1992.

The 1992 Act provides that trade unions which maintain political funds must ballot their members at least every ten years to determine the continued operation of such funds. The Act stipulates rules regarding the conduct of political fund ballots which have to be approved by the Certification Officer. Most notably, the ballot must be a fully postal ballot, the papers being sent out and returned by post. (The other ballot requirements are listed in the section on 'Union Elections and Ballots' at p. 624 *et seq*. (Section 4.E(vi))).

The second major change concerns the enlarged definition of those objects of expenditure which must be met out of the political fund.

TRADE UNION AND LABOUR RELATIONS (CONSOLIDATION) ACT 1992

72. Political objects to which restriction applies

(1) The political objects to which this Chapter applies are the expenditure of money—
  (a) on any contribution to the funds of, or on the payment of expenses incurred directly or indirectly by, a political party;
  (b) on the provision of any service or property for use by or on behalf of any political party;
  (c) in connection with the registration of electors, the candidature of any person, the selection of any candidate or the holding of any ballot by the union in connection with any election to a political office;
  (d) on the maintenance of any holder of a political office;
  (e) on the holding of any conference or meeting by or on behalf of a political party or of any other meeting the main purpose of which is the transaction of business in connection with a political party;
  (f) on the production, publication or distribution of any literature, document, film, sound recording or advertisement the main purpose of which is to persuade people to vote for a political party or candidate or to persuade them not to vote for a political party or candidate.

Paul and Frazer v National and Local Government Officers' Association
[1987] IRLR 413, Chancery Division

Mr Paul and Mr Frazer, both members of NALGO, brought an action against the union in respect of a large-scale publicity campaign which it was conducting during the build-up to the local and general elections. The campaign, 'Make People Matter', focused on government policy in the public sector and was part of a wider TUC initiative which designated 1987 as 'Public Services Year'.

The complaints related to leaflets and posters which, it was alleged, were intended to persuade people to vote against the Conservative Party and, as such, were illegal by reason of s. 3(3) of the Trade Union Act 1913 as amended by the Trade Union Act 1984 (now TULR(C)A 1992, s. 72(1)). The union conceded that if the expenditure on the literature in question did fall within what is now TULR(C)A 1992, s. 72(1), then it was unlawful as being *ultra vires* the union, since the union did not, at that time, have a political fund within the meaning of the Act.

The High Court, Chancery Division, declared that the literature was contrary to the relevant provision, that it was *ultra vires* and granted an injunction in the terms sought.

THE VICE CHANCELLOR: ...I will now turn to consider the literature which is complained of in this case, the effect of which I have sought to summarise. I have no doubt whatsoever that one purpose of the literature, particularly the leaflets, is to persuade people not to vote for the Conservative Party. The burden of the literature is to criticise the record of the Conservative Government which is said to be the run-down of the public services. That censure on the Conservative Government is confined to the Conservative Government. Though Mr Monks, the Union's Deputy Publicity Officer, said, as I am sure is the case, that NALGO have been complaining of government cut-backs since before 1979, it is notable that in no place in the literature is any reference made to any cut-backs earlier than 1979. Each leaflet refers to the Conservative Government only and each leaflet refers to its policies and the implementation of its policies unfavourably. It does not refer to any other government critically or unfavourably, and it contains nothing critical of any other party. What is more, it takes matters of policy which are known to be Conservative Party policy, such as privatisation, and decries them.

The leaflets then go on, having given that one-sided view of the effect of the Conservative policy and its non-coincidence with NALGO policy, to invite the electorate to think and then to vote. Every one of the leaflets complained of expressly invites the member receiving the leaflet to vote. The inference to my mind from the leaflet itself is really overwhelming. It says that the Government's policies since 1979 are bad, you have to think about it, and having thought about it you have to vote. The only rational message to be drawn from that is, 'If you accept the message of the leaflet vote against the Conservatives'.

Each leaflet contains the disclaimer, saying we are not inviting you to vote this way or that. I think where a message is as clear as this one a disclaimer of that kind is no more effective to avoid liability than is a disclaimer where in a libel case it is said that nobody in this book bears any resemblance to anybody in real life. It is not effective to escape liability once one looks at the purpose of the document as a whole. Therefore I have no doubt that one purpose of the literature was to persuade people to vote against the Conservative Party.

…

To sum up, in my judgment what we have here is literature which gives one side of the political argument. It attributes a bad record to the Conservative Party (admittedly indirectly by calling it the Government). That literature is then timed to be published at the time of an election. The same literature invites people to vote, taking into account that one-sided version of the issues involved. In those circumstances it seems to me impossible to say that the main purpose was not to influence the voting. While I have no explanation as to how the reference to voting crept in the fact is that it did. In those circumstances in my judgment the expenditure was unlawful as being in breach of s. 3 of the 1913 Act [now TULR(C)A 1992, s. 72].

…

Finally I would like to say that nothing in this judgment should be taken as suggesting that a publicity campaign organised by a union at times other than an election and therefore at a time when neither directly nor indirectly can the union be inviting anybody to exercise a vote at the time, is unlawful, merely because it expresses disapproval of the Government's policy. Unions, like anybody else, are entitled to disapprove of government policy and to say so. The vice in this case to my mind is that they have linked this disapproval in a biased way with an invitation to vote at the time of an election.

NOTES

1. Publicity campaigns against privatisation or trade union legislation, for example, will need a thorough vetting if they are to be financed from the general fund. It is important to bear in mind that these changes affect all unions, whether they possess a political fund or not, since they limit the ways in which general funds can be spent.

2. Sections 89–91 of the 1992 Act deal with the case of a union which has a political fund but which fails to renew its resolution, either by failing to get a majority in favour of renewal or by failing to call a ballot within a ten-year period. In such situations, the trade union must ensure that the collection of contributions to the political fund is discontinued 'as soon as is reasonably practicable'. Any contributions which are received after a political resolution has lapsed may be paid into any of its other funds, subject to the individual member's right to claim a refund.

   Where a union has held a ballot but fails to secure a majority for renewal, the union is allowed a period of six months during which it may continue to spend on political objects. Unions which fail to call a ballot within the ten-year period are penalised by not being allowed this 'breathing space'. Trade unions which do not run down their political funds in such situations may transfer the money into their non-political funds. Alternatively, the political fund may be frozen until such time as the union can secure a majority in favour of renewal in a subsequent ballot.

   Any member who claims that a union has failed to comply with the political fund ballot rules may apply to the High Court (Court of Session in Scotland) or the Certification Officer for a declaration to that effect. The High Court or Certification Officer may, in addition, make an enforcement order specifying the steps the union must take and the time scale within which they must be taken. The court order may be enforced by any individual who was a member both at the time the original order was made and when enforcement proceedings are commenced. The right of enforcement is, therefore, not confined to the original litigant.

F: Contracting out of the political levy and the check-off

TRADE UNION AND LABOUR RELATIONS (CONSOLIDATION) ACT 1992

DUTIES OF EMPLOYER WHO DEDUCTS UNION CONTRIBUTIONS

86. Certificate of exemption or objection to contributing to political fund

(1) If a member of a trade union which has a political fund certifies in writing to his employer that, or to the effect that—

    (a) he is exempt from the obligation to contribute to the fund, or

    (b) he has, in accordance with section 84, notified the union in writing of his objection to contributing to the fund, the employer shall ensure that no amount representing a contribution to the political fund is deducted by him from emoluments payable to the member.

(2) The employer's duty under subsection (1) applies from the first day, following the giving of the certificate, on which it is reasonably practicable for him to comply with that subsection, until the certificate is withdrawn.

(3) An employer may not refuse to deduct any union dues from emoluments payable to a person who has given a certificate under this section if he continues to deduct union dues from emoluments payable to other members of the union, unless his refusal is not attributable to the giving of the certificate or otherwise connected with the duty imposed by subsection (1).

87. Application to court in respect of employer's failure

(1) A person who claims his employer has failed to comply with section 86 in deducting or refusing to deduct any amount from emoluments payable to him may apply to the county court or, in Scotland, the sheriff court.

(2) If the court is satisfied that there has been such a failure it shall make a declaration to that effect.

(3) The court may, if it considers it appropriate to do so in order to prevent a repetition of the failure, make an order requiring the employer to take, within a specified time, the steps specified in the order in relation to emoluments payable by him to the applicant.

(4) Where in proceedings arising out of section 86(3) (refusal to deduct union dues) the question arises whether the employer's refusal to deduct an amount was attributable to the certificate having been given or was otherwise connected with the duty under section 86(1), it is for the employer to satisfy the court that it was not.

NOTE: Employers are often unwilling to deduct different amounts from employees' wages, according to whether or not they pay the political levy. As a result, unions adopted the practice of periodically refunding to exempt members such amounts deducted by their employer as represent the political levy. This practice, held to be lawful by the EAT in *Reeves* v *TGWU* [1980] ICR 728, is now outlawed by s. 86(3) of the 1992 Act. Employers are now faced with the choice between the administrative burden of operating a check-off system which deducts variable amounts from pay, depending on whether the employee does or does not contribute to the political fund, or completely abandoning the check-off system.

G: Deduction of trade union membership subscriptions

TRADE UNION AND LABOUR RELATIONS (CONSOLIDATION) ACT 1992

68. Right not to suffer deduction of unauthorised or excessive subscriptions

(1) Where arrangements ('subscription deduction arrangements') exist between the employer of a worker and a trade union relating to the making from workers' wages of deductions representing payments to the union in respect of the workers' membership of the union ('subscription deductions'), the employer shall ensure—

    (a) that no subscription deduction is made from wages payable to the worker on any day ('the relevant day') unless it is an authorised deduction, and

    (b) that the amount of any subscription deduction which is so made does not exceed the permitted amount.

(2) For the purposes of subsection (1)(a) a subscription deduction is an authorised deduction in relation to the relevant day if—

(a) a document containing the worker's authorisation of the making from his wages of subscription deductions has been signed and dated by the worker, and

(b) the authorisation is current on that day.

(3) For the purposes of subsection (2)(b) an authorisation is current on the relevant day if that day falls within the period of three years beginning with the day on which the worker signs and dates the document containing the authorisation and subsection (4) does not apply.

(4) This subsection applies if a document containing the worker's withdrawal of the authorisation has been received by the employer in time for it to be reasonably practicable for him to secure that no subscription deduction is made from wages payable to the worker on the relevant day.

(5) For the purposes of subsection (1)(b) the permitted amount in relation to the relevant day is—

(a) the amount of the subscription deduction which falls to be made from wages payable to the worker on that day in accordance with the subscription deduction arrangements, or

(b) if there is a relevant increase in the amount of subscription deductions and appropriate notice has not been given by the employer to the worker at least one month before that day, the amount referred to in paragraph (a) less the amount of the increase.

(6) So much of the increase referred to in subsection (5)(b) is relevant as is not attributable solely to an increase in the wages payable on the relevant day.

(7) In subsection (5)(b) 'appropriate notice' means, subject to subsection (8) below, notice in writing stating—

(a) the amount of the increase and the increased amount of the subscription deductions, and

(b) that the worker may at any time withdraw his authorisation of the making of subscription deductions by giving notice in writing to the employer.

(8) Where the relevant increase is attributable to an increase in any percentage by reference to which the worker's subscription deductions are calculated, subsection (7) above shall have effect with the substitution, in paragraph (a), for the reference to the amount of the increase and the increased amount of the deductions of a reference to the percentage before and the percentage after the increase.

(9) A worker's authorisation of the making of subscription deductions from his wages shall not give rise to any obligation on the part of the employer to the worker to maintain or continue to maintain subscription deduction arrangements.

(10) Where arrangements, whether included in subscription deduction arrangements or not, exist between the parties to subscription deduction arrangements for the making from workers' wages of deductions representing payments to the union which are additional to subscription deductions, the amount of the deductions representing such additional payments shall be treated for the purposes of this section (where they would otherwise not be so treated) as part of the subscription deductions.

(11) In this section and section 68A 'employer', 'wages' and 'worker' have the same meanings as in Part I of the Wages Act 1986.

NOTES

1. Under the unamended TULR(C)A 1992, s. 68, union members already had the right to require their employers to stop deducting union subscriptions if they ceased to be members of the union. But in its Green Paper, *Industrial Relations in the 1990s*, the Conservative Government expressed concern that existing union members were having their union subscriptions deducted in pursuance of collective agreements made between employers and trade unions, without the express approval of individual members. This, it said, had led to cases of deductions being made from the pay of employees who might not want this arrangement, but whose only recourse would be to terminate their union membership. Similarly, the Government pointed to an instance where a strike 'levy' had been added to the subscriptions, with employers effectively collecting this 'strike pay' for the union. The amendments made by the Trade Union and Employment Rights Act (TURERA) 1993 to TULR(C)A 1992, s. 62, were designed to rectify these perceived deficiencies.

2. If a worker suffers a deduction in breach of the new s. 68, he or she may complain to an employment tribunal (ET). If the complaint is upheld the tribunal will make a declaration and order the employer to refund the amount of the unauthorised deduction.

SECTION 2: FREEDOM OF ASSOCIATION

A: International standards

INTERNATIONAL LABOUR ORGANISATION CONVENTION NO. 87 (1948) FREEDOM OF ASSOCIATION AND PROTECTION OF THE RIGHT TO ORGANISE

PART 1 FREEDOM OF ASSOCIATION

Article 1

Each Member of the International Labour Organisation for which this Convention is in force undertakes to give effect to the following provisions.

Article 2

Workers and employers, without distinction whatsoever, shall have the right to establish and, subject only to the rules of the organisation concerned, to join organisations of their own choosing without previous authorisation.

Article 3

1. Workers' and employers' organisations shall have the right to draw up their constitutions and rules, to elect their representatives in full freedom, to organise their administration and activities and to formulate their programmes.

2. The public authorities shall refrain from any interference which would restrict this right or impede the lawful exercise thereof.

Article 4

Workers' and employers' organisations shall not be liable to be dissolved or suspended by administrative authority...

INTERNATIONAL LABOUR ORGANISATION CONVENTION (NO. 98) (1949) CONCERNING THE APPLICATION OF THE PRINCIPLES OF THE RIGHT TO ORGANISE AND BARGAIN COLLECTIVELY

Article 1

1. Workers shall enjoy adequate protection against acts of anti-union discrimination in respect of their employment.

2. Such protection shall apply more particularly in respect of acts calculated to:
   (a) make the employment of a worker subject to a condition that he shall not join a union or shall relinquish trade union membership;
   (b) cause the dismissal of or otherwise prejudice a worker by reason of union membership or because of participation in union activities outside working hours or, with the consent of the employer, within working hours.

NOTE: Given the free market philosophy of the previous Conservative Governments, it is perhaps not surprising that the UK has been found to be in breach of International Labour Organization (ILO) Conventions which this country had ratified. The banning of union membership at Government Communications Headquarters in 1984 was found by the ILO's Committee on Freedom of Association to be in breach of Convention No. 87 (extracted earlier). The second of the three major complaints to the ILO related to the Teachers' Pay and Conditions Act 1987, which effectively abolished collective bargaining for teachers. This time the Government was held to be in breach of Convention No. 98 which provides, amongst other things, 'that machinery appropriate to national conditions shall be taken, where necessary, to encourage and promote the full development and utilisation of machinery for voluntary negotiation between employers or employer's organisations and workers' organisations with a view to the regulation of terms and conditions of employment by means of collective agreements.'

In 1988 a complaint to the ILO was made by the TUC and the NUM relating to various aspects of the Conservative Government's employment legislation. The Committee of Experts concluded that UK labour law had fallen below the acceptable standards set by Convention No. 87 on no fewer than six different grounds (ILO Committee of Experts, Observation 1989 on Convention No. 87). These were as follows:

(a) The GCHQ dismissals of those who refused to relinquish trade union membership—the Committee of Experts, like the Committee on Freedom of Association before them, found that the Government's action was in breach of Article 2 of Convention No. 87.

(b) The Committee of Experts were of the view that the Employment Act (EA) 1988, s. 3 (now TULR(C)A 1992, s. 64) was in conflict with Article 3 of Convention No. 87. The particular concern revolved around the fact that s. 3 made it unlawful for trade unions to discipline members who refuse to participate in industrial action. In the view of the Committee, Article 3 requires that 'union members should be permitted, when drawing up their constitutions and rules, to determine whether or not it should be possible to discipline members who refuse to participate in lawful strikes and other industrial action.' They concluded that s. 3 should be amended accordingly.

(c) The Committee found that s. 8 of the EA 1988 (now TULR(C)A 1992, s. 15), which made it unlawful for the property of any trade union to be applied so as to indemnify any individual against any criminal sanction or contempt of court, was in breach of Article 3 of Convention No. 87 and should be amended. The statutory provision was held to be an infringement of the right of unions to draw up their constitutions or rules and to organise their administration and activities free of interference by the public authorities, and a denial of the right to utilise their funds as they wish for normal and lawful trade union purposes.

(d) The Committee expressed the view that the narrowing of the definition of a trade dispute in 1992 and restrictions on secondary action introduced in s. 17 of the EA 1980 unduly restricted workers' legitimate right to strike in protection of their own economic and social interests, as guaranteed by Articles 3, 8, and 10 of the Convention.

(e) The Committee considered that it was inconsistent with the right to strike as guaranteed by Articles 3, 8, and 10 of the Convention for an employer to be permitted to refuse to reinstate some or all of its employees at the conclusion of a strike, lock-out, or other industrial action without those employees having the right to challenge the fairness of that dismissal before an independent court or tribunal. This was exactly the freedom given to employers under the Employment Protection (Consolidation) Act (EPCA) 1978 (now TULR(C)A 1992, s. 238).

(f) Lastly, the Committee expressed its concern at the volume and complexity of legislative change since 1980: 'Whilst it is true that most of the legislative measures under consideration are not incompatible with the requirements of the Convention, there is a point at which the cumulative effect of legislative changes which are themselves consistent with the principles of freedom of association may nevertheless by virtue of their complexity and extent, constitute an incursion upon the rights guaranteed by the Convention.' The complexity and uncertainty of the law may inhibit industrial action. Concern was also expressed that by giving so much emphasis to individual 'rights', the Government had demonstrated lesser concern for the 'rights' of individual trade unionists. The Committee considered that a more positive statement of these rights would be 'of advantage'.

The Conservative Government did nothing to meet any of the ILO's concerns. Indeed, as we have seen, since the ILO observation was published in 1989, the Conservative Administration introduced yet more legislation, which further weakened job protection for strikers and almost completely outlawed sympathy action. In terms of the complexity of the legislation, the Government made a very limited response by consolidating collective labour law and all the changes made during the 1980s and 1990s into one statute, TULR(C)A 1992. Even then, the new provisions contained in TURERA 1993 further complicated matters.

The response (or lack of it) by the Conservative Government to the ILO's findings exposes the lack of effective sanctions to deal with those who violate ILO standards.

EUROPEAN CONVENTION FOR THE PROTECTION OF HUMAN RIGHTS AND FUNDAMENTAL FREEDOMS 1950

Article 11

1. Everyone has the right to freedom of peaceful assembly and to freedom of association with others, including the right to form and join trade unions for the protection of his interests.

2. No restrictions shall be placed on the exercise of these rights other than such as are prescribed by law and are necessary in a democratic society in the interests of national security or public safety, for the prevention of disorder or crime, for the protection of health or morals or for the protection of the rights and freedoms

of others. This Article shall not prevent the imposition of lawful restrictions on the exercise of these rights by members of the armed forces, of the police or of the administration of the State.

NOTES

1. Sheldon Leader has observed:

   Like most instruments guaranteeing basic rights, the Convention gives with one hand what it then qualifies with another. It provides certain potential rights to trade unionists, as well as to dissident members of trade unions under Article 11(1), while also allowing the state to limit their exercise under Article 11(2) if doing so can be shown, *inter alia*, to protect other competing rights and if it can also be shown that such a limitation is 'necessary in a democratic society'.

   ['The European Convention on Human Rights, the Employment Act (EA) 1988 and the right to refuse to strike' (1991) 20 ILJ 39.]

2. The application to the European Commission by the Council of Civil Service Unions, alleging a breach of Article 11 as a result of the ban on union membership at GCHQ, was rejected. The GCHQ workers were involved in the administration of the State and therefore excluded (App. No. 11603 *Council of Civil Service Unions* v *United Kingdom* (1987) 10 EHRR 269). An early action taken by the Labour Government elected in May 1997 was to restore the right of staff at GCHQ to belong to trade unions.

3. In *Young, James and Webster* v *United Kingdom* [1981] IRLR 408, three non-unionists were dismissed by British Rail in 1976 as a result of the signing of a union membership only (closed shop) agreement with the three rail unions. The European Court of Human Rights held by a majority of 18:3 that Article 11 was contravened by UK law which permitted the closed shop at that time, because employees could be dismissed if they refused to join. Those in the minority dissented on the basis of clear evidence from the *travaux préparatoires* that it was intended by those who drafted the Convention that the closed shop should be unaffected because of lack of consensus between States on the issue. The majority, while refusing to decide whether Article 11 guarantees an implied 'negative right' to dissociate as strong as the positive right set out in its text, held that on the facts there was a breach of the Article. This was because the applicants' choice as regards the unions which they could join of their own volition was restricted. Consequently, '[a]n individual does not enjoy the right to freedom of association if in reality the freedom of action or choice which remains available to him is either non-existent or so reduced as to be of no practical value.' However, six judges who concurred with the majority would have gone further and held that Article 11 contained a correlative 'negative right'. More recently, the European Court of Human Rights, claiming that the Convention is a 'living instrument which must be interpreted in the light of present-day conditions', has determined that Article 11 does include a negative right, at least to a limited extent (*Sigurjonsson* v *Iceland* (1993) 16 EHRR 462).

4. In the course of an analysis of the implications for labour law of the incorporation of the European Convention on Human Rights (ECHR) into domestic law by the Human Rights Act 1998, Ewing observes:

   Although perhaps the most obviously applicable provision for labour law, the contribution of article 11 to date has been disappointing, failing to deliver any meaningful protection for trade union activities, while being used as an instrument for undermining trade union security.
   [Ewing, K. D., 'The Human Rights Act and labour law' (1998) 27 ILJ 275, at p. 279.]

5. On a more optimistic level, the decision of the Court in three joined applications led by *Wilson and the NUJ* v *United Kingdom* [2002] IRLR 566 is the first time the Court has upheld a claim relating to trade union rights under Article 11 (cf. *Unison* v *United Kingdom* [2002] IRLR 497).

6. In *Ministry of Justice* v *Prison Officers' Association* [2008] IRLR 380, QBD, it was held that Article 11 confers no express right to strike. Even if it does, it is clear that Article 11(2) affords considerable latitude to a contracting State to regulate the circumstances in which the right may be removed, e.g. in relation to those carrying out essential public duties such as prison officers.

7. Departing from earlier case law, the ECtHR has now held that the right of freedom of association under Article 11 includes the right to participate in collective bargaining and to enter into collective agreements (*Demir and Baykara* v *Turkey* [2009] IRLR 766 (ECtHR)).

8. In *RMT* v *UK* [2014] IRLR 467, the ECtHR upheld the UK's ban on secondary action. It was decided that the ban did not strike at the very substance of the trade union's right to freedom of association under Article 11. The Court was also of the view that Member States must be allowed a margin of appreciation as how to maintain an appropriate balance between the interests of labour and those of management.

B: Refusal of employment on grounds of trade union membership

TRADE UNION AND LABOUR RELATIONS (CONSOLIDATION) ACT 1992

137. Refusal of employment on grounds related to union membership

(1) It is unlawful to refuse a person employment—

   (a) because he is, or is not, a member of a trade union, or

   (b) because he is unwilling to accept a requirement—

      (i) to take steps to become or cease to be, or to remain or not to become, a member of a trade union, or

      (ii) to make payments or suffer deductions in the event of his not being a member of a trade union.

(2) A person who is thus unlawfully refused employment has a right of complaint to an industrial tribunal.

(3) Where an advertisement is published which indicates, or might reasonably be understood as indicating—

   (a) that employment to which the advertisement relates is open only to a person who is, or is not, a member of a trade union, or

   (b) that any such requirement as is mentioned in subsection (1)(b) will be imposed in relation to employment to which the advertisement relates,

a person who does not satisfy that condition or, as the case may be, is unwilling to accept that requirement, and who seeks and is refused employment to which the advertisement relates, shall be conclusively presumed to have been refused employment for that reason.

(4) Where there is an arrangement or practice under which employment is offered only to persons put forward or approved by a trade union, and the trade union puts forward or approves only persons who are members of the union, a person who is not a member of the union and who is refused employment in pursuance of the arrangement or practice shall be taken to have been refused employment because he is not a member of the trade union.

(5) A person shall be taken to be refused employment if he seeks employment of any description with a person and that person—

   (a) refuses or deliberately omits to entertain and process his application or enquiry, or

   (b) causes him to withdraw or cease to pursue his application or enquiry, or

   (c) refuses or deliberately omits to offer him employment of that description, or

   (d) makes him an offer of such employment the terms of which are such as no reasonable employer who wished to fill the post would offer and which is not accepted, or

   (e) makes him an offer of such employment but withdraws it or causes him not to accept it.

(6) Where a person is offered employment on terms which include a requirement that he is, or is not, a member of a trade union, or any such requirement as is mentioned in subsection (1)(b), and he does not accept the offer because he does not satisfy or, as the case may be, is unwilling to accept that requirement, he shall be treated as having been refused employment for that reason.

(7) Where a person may not be considered for appointment or election to an office in a trade union unless he is a member of the union, or of a particular branch or section of the union or of one of a number of particular branches or sections of the union, nothing in this section applies to anything done for the purpose of securing compliance with that condition although as holder of the office he would be employed by the union.

For this purpose an 'office' means any position—

   (a) by virtue of which the holder is an official of the union, or

   (b) to which Chapter IV of Part I applies (duty to hold elections).

(8) The provisions of this section apply in relation to an employment agency acting, or purporting to act, on behalf of an employer as in relation to an employer.

NOTES

1. The EA 1988 finally removed all legal protection accorded to the operation of the post-entry closed shop. These provisions did not affect the pre-entry closed shop, i.e. a requirement to be a union member *before* being considered for the job. This gap was closed by the EA 1990, and the relevant provisions are now contained in ss. 137–43 of TULR(C)A 1992.

2. Complaints of breach of these provisions may be made to an ET, which may make a declaration, order the employer to pay compensation (up to the limit of the compensatory award for unfair dismissal), and/or recommend that the respondent take remedial action.

C: Detriment on grounds related to union membership or activities

TRADE UNION AND LABOUR RELATIONS (CONSOLIDATION) ACT 1992

146. Detriment on grounds related to union membership or activities

(1) A worker has the right not to be subjected to any detriment as an individual by any act, or any deliberate failure to act, by his employer if the act or failure takes place for the sole or main purpose of—

(a) preventing or deterring him from being or seeking to become a member of an independent trade union, or penalising him for doing so,

(b) preventing or deterring him from taking part in the activities of an independent trade union at an appropriate time, or penalising him for doing so,

(ba) preventing or deterring him from making use of trade union services at an appropriate time, or penalising him for doing so, or

(c) compelling him to be or become a member of any trade union or of a particular trade union or of one of a number of particular trade unions.

(2) In subsection (1) 'an appropriate time' means—

(a) a time outside the [worker's] working hours, or

(b) a time within his working hours at which, in accordance with arrangements agreed with or consent given by his employer, it is permissible for him to take part in the activities of a trade union or (as the case may be) make use of trade union services;

and for this purpose 'working hours', in relation to [a worker], means any time when, in accordance with his contract of employment [(or other contract personally to do work or perform services)], he is required to be at work.

(2A) In this section—

(a) 'trade union services' means services made available to the worker by an independent trade union by virtue of his membership of the union, and

(b) references to a worker's 'making use' of trade union services include his consenting to the raising of a matter on his behalf by an independent trade union of which he is a member.

(2B) If an independent trade union of which a worker is a member raises a matter on his behalf (with or without his consent), penalising the worker for that is to be treated as penalising him as mentioned in subsection (1)(ba).

(2C) A worker also has the right not to be subjected to any detriment as an individual by any act, or any deliberate failure to act, by his employer if the act or failure takes place because of the worker's failure to accept an offer made in contravention of section 145A or 145B.

(2D) For the purposes of subsection (2C), not conferring a benefit that, if the offer had been accepted by the worker, would have been conferred on him under the resulting agreement shall be taken to be subjecting him to a detriment as an individual (and to be a deliberate failure to act).

(3) A worker also has the right not to [be subjected to any detriment as an individual by any act, or any deliberate failure to act, by his employer if the act or failure takes place] for [the sole or main purpose] of enforcing a requirement (whether or not imposed by [a contract of employment] or in writing) that, in the event of his not being a member of any trade union or of a particular trade union or of one of a number of particular trade unions, he must make one or more payments.

(4) For the purposes of subsection (3) any deduction made by an employer from the remuneration payable to [a worker] in respect of his employment shall, if it is attributable to his not being a member of any trade union or of a particular trade union or of one of a number of particular trade unions, be treated [as a detriment to which he has been subjected as an individual by an act of his employer taking place] for [the sole or main purpose] of enforcing a requirement of a kind mentioned in that subsection.

(5) [A worker or former worker] may present a complaint to an [employment tribunal] on the ground that [he has been subjected to a detriment] by his employer in contravention of this section.

(5A) This section does not apply where—

(a) the worker is an employee; and

(b) the detriment in question amounts to dismissal.

NOTE: Prior to the amendments introduced by the Employment Relations Act 1999, the law was held to protect employees against *positive* acts to prevent or deter trade union membership but not against *omissions* on the same grounds. So, for example, the giving of 'sweetener payments' to employees who agreed to give up collective bargaining did not constitute 'action' against those who refused through an omission to give them the same payments. Further amendments introduced by the EA 2004 made it unlawful for employers to subject a worker to any detriment for making use of 'trade union services' (see s. 146(1)(ba), (2A)(a) extracted earlier). These were the key issues before the House of Lords in the next case—a case which eventually was heard by the European Court of Human Rights and which prompted the above amendments.

Wilson and the NUJ v United Kingdom; Palmer, Wyeth and National Union of Rail, Maritime and Transport Workers; Doolan and others v United Kingdom
[2002] IRLR 566, European Court of Human Rights

Mr Wilson was a journalist on the *Daily Mail*. He was a member of the NUJ and father of the chapel. In 1989 the employers gave notice that they were terminating the current collective agreement, withdrawing recognition from the union and instituting a system of personal contracts. Only those journalists who entered into the new contracts were given a 4.5% pay increase. Mr Wilson refused to sign and so did not get the increase. His complaint to the industrial tribunal was successful but the EAT upheld the employers' appeal. The EAT found that the employers' purpose in offering the financial incentive was not to deter employees from remaining members of the union but to end collective bargaining. In any event, that could not be said to deter employees from union membership or penalise them because of their membership since those who signed the new contracts were free to remain union members.

Mr Palmer was a manual worker employed by Associated British Ports. Such workers were members of the National Union of Rail, Maritime and Transport Workers which, at the relevant time, was recognised by the employers for collective bargaining purposes. In February 1991 all manual workers were sent a letter setting out the terms on which personal contracts would be offered, including substantially higher basic pay and increased overtime rates. In return, the employees were required to relinquish trade union representation by their union, and collectively agreed terms would no longer apply to them. Mr Palmer was one of a small percentage of workers who refused to accept personal contracts. The company continued to negotiate with the union in respect of this group of workers but the pay settlement agreed for them for 1991 was significantly lower than for those manual workers who had agreed personal contracts and agreed to relinquish union representation.

Mr Doolan and seven other applicants were employed by Associated British Ports at the Bute Docks in Cardiff. They were also members of the RMT, which was the recognised union. In 1991, the employees were offered personal contracts with pay increases if they relinquished all rights to trade union recognition and representation and agreed that annual pay increases and other terms and conditions would no longer be negotiated with the union on their behalf. The applicants refused to sign. Employees holding the same positions as the applicants who accepted personal contracts received a pay rise which was approximately 8–9% greater than that awarded to the applicants. In 1992 the employers gave notice that they were terminating the collective agreement and derecognising the trade union for all purposes.

Mr Palmer and the others complained that the employers had taken action against them short of dismissal on grounds of their union membership in contravention of what is now TULR(C)A 1992, s. 146. The employers argued that their purpose in offering preferential terms for those who entered into personal contracts was not to prevent or deter employees from continuing to be members but to achieve greater flexibility. They underlined that there was nothing in the personal contract preventing the employee from remaining a trade union member. The industrial tribunal upheld the employees' complaints. While accepting that the employers honestly believed that their purpose was to create greater flexibility, 'the reality is that their purpose was to penalise those who would not forgo union representation by not conferring on them the benefits bestowed upon those who were prepared to do so with the objective of achieving greater flexibility.'

The EAT allowed the employers' appeal. According to Wood P, the industrial tribunal had confused their 'purpose' in conferring benefits on those who entered into personal contracts with the 'means' of achieving that purpose and the intermediate or collateral results which might be caused in achieving it. Flexibility was the purpose and ending union representation was the means of achieving it.

Both employee appeals were upheld by the Court of Appeal. According to the Court of Appeal, the right of an employee under the EPCA 1978, s. 23(1)(a) (now TULR(C)A 1992, s. 146(1)(a)) was not only a right to union membership itself. Dillon LJ, giving the leading judgment, approved the decision in *Discount Confectionery Ltd* v *Armitage* [1990] IRLR I5, EAT, that there is no genuine distinction between membership of the union and making use of the essential services of the union.

On appeal to the House of Lords, a new point of law was taken which had not been available to the courts below, namely whether the word 'action' in s. 23(1)(a) (now TULR(C)A 1992, s. 146(1)(a)) might properly be construed as including an 'omission'. Section 153(1) of the EPCA 1978 provided that: 'In this Act…except so far as the context otherwise requires—"act" and "action" each includes omission and references to doing an act or taking action shall be construed accordingly' (see now TULR(C)A 1992, s. 298).

On the authority of the decision in *National Coal Board* v *Ridgway* [1987] ICR 641, CA, the courts below were bound to accept that the application of s. 23(1)(a) had the effect that, if an employer conferred a benefit on employee A which he withheld from employee B, the omission to confer the benefit on B may amount to 'action (short of dismissal) taken against' B for one of the purposes prohibited by s. 23(1), irrespective of whether B had any reasonable expectation of receiving that benefit.

The House of Lords upheld the employers' appeals [1995] IRLR 258. The Law Lords held by a 3:2 majority that the employee's right 'not to have action…taken against him' cannot possibly be construed as including an 'omission to act'. This is despite the statutory definition of 'act' and 'action' which provides that 'in this Act…except so far as the context otherwise requires "act" and "action" each includes omission and references to doing an act and taking action shall be construed accordingly.' On the law as it stood following *Wilson*, it would be difficult to conceive of an action short of dismissal which would be covered by this interpretation of the statutory provision. The amendments to s. 146 by the Employment Relations Act 1999, Sch. 2, remove this spurious distinction between 'acts' and 'omissions'.

All five Law Lords allowed the employers' appeals on another ground, the 'membership issue'. This concerned whether the reference in s. 146(1)(a) to preventing or deterring 'membership' of a trade union (or penalising for it) can be read as including an attack on the *functions or advantages* of trade union membership, in particular being covered by collective bargaining arrangements. In the instant case, the employer was not *overtly* trying to get employees to give up membership *per se*. Lord Lloyd focused on the 'purpose' to be established under s. 146. His Lordship took the view that s. 146 was not to be stretched to safeguard indirectly a union's interest in being recognised. At least three Law Lords came down against the general principle thought to have been established in *Discount Tobacco Ltd* v *Armitage* [1990] IRLR 15, EAT, that there is no distinction between union membership and making use of union services.

Subsequent to the Court of Appeal's decision in *Wilson and Palmer*, the Government controversially sought to overturn its effects by introducing an amendment to what was then the Trade Union Reform and Employment Rights Bill when it was in the House of Lords (Hansard HL 24 May 1993, cols. 12–67). Section 13 of TURERA 1993 introduced the amendment now contained in TULR(C)A 1992, s. 148(3). Section 13 provided that there shall be no infringement of the right under s. 146(1) where 'the employer's purpose was to further a change in his relationship with all or any class of his employees', unless the employer's action was action which no reasonable employer would take.

Section 13 was criticised by the Committee of Independent Experts set up under the European Social Charter and by the ILO's Committee on Freedom of Association. The Committee of Experts found that s. 13 was in breach of Article 5 of the Social Charter since it 'permits employers to take certain measures such as awarding preferential remuneration to employees in order to persuade them to relinquish trade union activities and collective bargaining.' The ILO's Committee on Freedom of Association called on the UK Government to take steps to amend the section 'so that it ensures workers' organisations adequate protection from acts of interference on the part of the employer and so that it does not result in fact in the discouragement of collective bargaining.'

The applicants appealed to the European Court of Human Rights complaining that the law applicable in the UK failed to secure their rights under Article 11 of the ECHR. The applicants submitted that the right to union membership 'for the protection of his interests' under Article 11 necessarily involved the right of every employee (1) to be represented by his or her union in negotiations with the employer, and (2) not to be discriminated against for choosing to exercise the right to be represented. The right of union membership is inherent in the right of union representation but the decision of the House of Lords had made it plain that this was not recognised in UK law.

On behalf of the UK Government, it was contended that there is no inherent right in Article 11 to collective bargaining or individual union members to receive identical benefits to those agreed between an employer and other employees who declined to be represented by a union. Under domestic law at the relevant time, trade unions had the freedom to take action to protect their members' interests, and where a particular union was not recognised by an employer, it was open to it to take steps, including strike action, to persuade the employer to recognise it for the purposes of collective bargaining.

The European Court of Human Rights held that there was a violation of Article 11 and awarded each individual applicant €7,730 for non-pecuniary damage and jointly to the union applicants €122,250 for costs and expenses.

JUDGMENT: …

The time of the events complained

The Court recalls that Article 11 paragraph 1 presents trade union freedom as one form of a special aspect of freedom of association (see the *National Union of Belgian Police* v *Belgium* judgment of 27 October 1975, Series A no. 19, paragraph 38, and the *Swedish Engine Drivers Union* judgment of 6 February 1976, Series A no. 20 paragraph 39). The words 'for the protection of his interests' in Article 11 Paragraph 1 are not redundant, and the Convention safeguards freedom to protect the occupational interests of trade union members by trade union action, the conduct and development of which the Contracting States must both permit and make possible. A trade union must be free to strive for the protection of its members' interests, and the individual members have a right, in order to protect their interests, that the trade union should be heard (see the above-mentioned *Belgian Police* judgment, paragraphs 39–40, and the above-mentioned *Swedish Engine Drivers* judgment, paragraphs 40–41). Article 11 does not, however, secure any particular treatment of trade unions or their members and leaves each State a free choice of the means to be used to secure the right to be heard (see the above-mentioned *Belgian Police* judgment, paragraphs 38–39, and the above-mentioned *Swedish Engine Drivers* judgment, paragraphs 39–40).

The Court notes that, at the time of the events complained of by the applicants, United Kingdom law provided for a wholly voluntary system of collective bargaining, with no legal obligation on employers to recognise trade unions for the purpose of collective bargaining. There was, therefore, no remedy in law by which the applicants could prevent the employers in the present case from de-recognising the unions and refusing to renew the collective bargaining agreements…

However, the Court has consistently held that, although collective bargaining may be one of the ways by which trade unions may be enabled to protect their members' interests, it is not indispensable for the effective enjoyment of trade union freedom. Compulsory collective bargaining would impose on employers an obligation to conduct negotiations with trade unions. The Court has not yet been prepared to hold that the freedom of a trade union to make its voice heard extends to imposing on an employer an obligation to recognise a trade union. The union and its members must however be free, in one way or another, to seek to persuade the employer to listen to what it has to say on behalf of its members. In view of the sensitive character of the social and political issues involved in achieving a proper balance between the competing interests and the wide degree of divergence between the domestic systems in this field, Contracting States enjoy a wide margin of appreciation as to how trade union freedom may be secured (see the *Swedish Engine Drivers* judgment, paragraph 39, the *Gustafsson* judgment, para. 45 and *Schettini and others* v *Italy* (dec.), no. 29529/95, 9 November 2000).

The Court observes that there were other measures available to the applicant unions by which they could further their members' interests. In particular, domestic law conferred protection on a trade union which called for or supported strike action 'in contemplation or furtherance of a trade dispute'…The grant of the right to strike, while it may be subject to regulation, represents one of the most important of the means by which the State may secure a trade union's freedom to protects its members' occupational interests (see *Schmidt and Dahlstrom* v *Sweden* judgment 6 February 1976, Series A no. 21, paragraph 36 and…*Unison* v *the United Kingdom* (dec. no. 53574/99) [2002] IRLR 497). Against this background, the Court does consider that the absence under United Kingdom law of an obligation on employers to enter into collective bargaining gave rise, in itself, to a violation of Article 11 of the Convention.

The Court agrees with the Government that the essence of a voluntary system of collective bargaining is that it must be possible for a trade union which is not recognised by an employer to take steps including, if necessary, organising industrial action, with a view to persuading the employer to enter into collective bargaining with it on those issues which the union believes are important for its members' interests. Furthermore, it is of the essence of the right to join a trade union for the protection of their interests that employees should be free to instruct or permit the union to make representations to their employer or to take action in support of their interests on their behalf. If workers are prevented from so doing, their freedom to belong to a trade union, for the protection of their interests becomes illusory. It is the role of the State to ensure that trade union members are not prevented or restrained from using their union to represent them in attempts to regulate their relations with their employers.

In the present case, it was open to the employers to seek to pre-empt any protest on the part of the unions or their members against the imposition of limits on voluntary collective bargaining, by offering those employees who acquiesced in the termination of collective bargaining substantial pay rises, which were not provided to those who refused to sign contracts accepting the end of union representation. The corollary of this was that United Kingdom law permitted employers to treat less favourably employees who were not prepared to renounce a freedom that was an essential feature of trade union membership. Such conduct constituted a disincentive or restraint on the use by employees of union membership to protect their interests. However, as the House of Lords judgment made clear, domestic law did not prohibit the employer from offering an inducement to employees who relinquished the right to union representation, even if the aim and outcome of the exercise was to bring an end to collective bargaining and thus substantially to reduce the authority of the union, as long as the employer did not act with the purpose of preventing or deterring the individual employee simply from being a member of a trade union.

Under United Kingdom law at the relevant time it was, therefore possible for an employer effectively to undermine or frustrate a trade union's ability to strive for the protection of its members' interests. The Court notes that this aspect of domestic law has been the subject of criticism by Social Charter's Committee of Independent Experts and the ILO's Committee of Independent Experts…It considers that, by permitting employers to use financial incentives to induce employees to surrender important union rights, the respondent State failed to secure the enjoyment of the rights under Article 11 of the Convention. This failure amounted to a violation of Article 11, as regards both the applicant unions and the individual applicants.

NOTE: Set out below is the provision which attracted the criticism of the European Court of Justice in *Wilson and Palmer.*

TRADE UNION AND LABOUR RELATIONS (CONSOLIDATION) ACT 1992 (PRIOR TO AMENDMENT BY THE EMPLOYMENT RIGHTS ACT 2004)

148. Consideration of complaint

(3) In determining what was the purpose for which [the employer acted or failed to act] in a case where—

    (a) there is evidence that the employer's purpose was to further a change in his relationship with all or any class of his employees, and

> (b) there is also evidence that his purpose was one falling within section 146,
> the tribunal shall regard the purpose mentioned in paragraph (a) (and not the purpose mentioned in paragraph (b)) as the purpose for which the employer [acted or failed to act, unless it considers that no reasonable employer would act or fail to act in the way concerned] having regard to the purpose mentioned in paragraph (a).

NOTES

1. The words in square brackets represent the consequential amendments following the amendment of s. 146 by the Employment Relations Act 1999. But that was as far as the amendments went and it was still lawful for employers to offer inducements to employees to sign personal contracts if the purpose is to dismantle collective bargaining arrangements. However, the Employment Relations Act 2004 did contain measures to implement the European Court of Human Rights decision in *Wilson and Palmer* and which seek to ensure that union members have clear rights to use their union's services and cannot be bribed by employers to relinquish essential union rights by 'sweeteners'.

   Section 29 of the 2004 Act inserted new ss. 145A–F into TULR(C)A 1992.

   Section 145A: Section 145A(1) gives a worker the right not to have an offer made to him by his employer where the employer's sole or main purpose is to induce the worker to do or not do certain things. These are (1) not to be or seek to become a member of an independent trade union, (2) not to take part in the activities of an independent trade union at 'an appropriate time', (3) not to make use of the services of a trade union at an 'appropriate time', and (4) to be or become a member of a trade union.

   Subsection (2) defines the term 'appropriate time' for the purposes of the rights under this section as outside the worker's working hours, or during them at a time when, in accordance with arrangements agreed with the employer or consent given by the employer, it is permissible for him or her to do so.

   Section 145B: This section provides a new right to a worker who is a member of an independent trade union recognised by his employer not to have an offer made to him or her by the employer if acceptance of the offer would result in his or her employment terms no longer being determined by collective bargaining ('the prohibited result'), and the employer's sole or main purpose in making the offer was to achieve that result (this was the very point in issue in *Wilson and Palmer*).

   Section 145C: This section imposes the usual general three-month time limit on bringing a complaint relating to the infringement of these new rights. The time starts to run on the day the offer was made or, where the offer is part of a series of similar offers, the date when the last offer was made.

   Section 145D: This section deals with how tribunals are to deal with complaints under ss. 145A and 145B. In particular, subss. (1)–(2) provide that on a complaint under s. 145A or 145B it shall be for the employer to show what his sole or main purpose in making the offer was.

   Section 145E: Subsections (1)–(2) have the effect that if the tribunal finds a complaint to be well founded it is to make a declaration to that effect and make an award to be paid by the employer to the worker in respect of the offer complained of. Subsection (3) has the effect that the award to be paid to the worker is a fixed sum of £3,800 (with effect from 6th April 2015) but that award can be subject to a reduction or increase under the provisions of the EA 2002.

2. An employee who suffers victimisation on trade union grounds may complain to an ET within three months of the act of victimisation. Where the alleged victimisation is part of a series of similar actions, the complaint must be presented within three months of the last of those actions (TULR(C)A 1992, s. 147(2) as amended). The following convoluted wording now determines the time limits in dealing with an omission to act (new s. 147(3), inserted by Employment Relations Act 1999, Sch. 2):

   > . . . in the absence of evidence establishing the contrary an employer shall be taken to decide on a failure to act—
   > (a) when he does an act inconsistent with doing the failed act, or
   > (b) if he has done no such inconsistent act, when the period expires within which he might reasonably have been expected to do the failed act if it was to be done.

   If the complaint is well founded, the tribunal must make a declaration to that effect, and it may make an award of compensation which 'shall be such as the tribunal considers just and equitable in all the circumstances having regard to the infringement complained of and to any loss sustained by the complainant which is attributable to the action which infringed his right' (s. 149(1)–(2)).

3. In *Brassington* v *Cauldon Wholesale* [1978] IRLR 479, the EAT stated that 'compensation for the employee, not a fine on the employer, however tactfully wrapped up, is the basis for the award'. The complainants were awarded compensation to cover their expenses in going to tribunal and non-pecuniary losses such as 'the stress engendered by such a situation' and the frustration of a 'deep and sincere wish to join a union'. The availability of compensation for non-pecuniary loss was doubted by May LJ in *Ridgway and Fairbrother* v *National Coal Board* [1987] IRLR 80, though Nicholls and Bingham LJJ expressed no view on the matter.

4. The tribunal may reduce the amount of any compensatory award if the action complained of was to any extent caused or contributed to by the complainant (TULR(C)A 1992, s. 149(6)). In determining compensation, no account is to be taken of any pressure exercised on the employer by the threat or use of industrial action. But the employer or employee may apply to have the union or other third party joined as a party to the proceedings. The compensation award may be made wholly or partly against the party so joined (TULR(C)A 1992, s. 150).

D: Dismissal on grounds related to union membership or activities

TRADE UNION AND LABOUR RELATIONS (CONSOLIDATION) ACT 1992

152 Dismissal of employee on grounds related to union membership or activities

(1) For purposes of Part X of the Employment Rights Act 1996 (unfair dismissal) the dismissal of an employee shall be regarded as unfair if the reason for it (or, if more than one, the principal reason) was that the employee—

(a) was, or proposed to become, a member of an independent trade union,

(b) had taken part, or proposed to take part, in the activities of an independent trade union at an appropriate time,

(ba) had made use, or proposed to make use, of trade union services at an appropriate time,

(bb) had failed to accept an offer made in contravention of section 145A or 145B, or

(c) was not a member of any trade union, or of a particular trade union, or of one of a number of particular trade unions, or had refused, or proposed to refuse, to become or remain a member.

(2) In subsection (1) 'an appropriate time' means—

(a) a time outside the employee's working hours, or

(b) a time within his working hours at which, in accordance with arrangements agreed with or consent given by his employer, it is permissible for him to take part in the activities of a trade union [or (as the case may be) make use of trade union services];

and for this purpose 'working hours', in relation to an employee, means any time when, in accordance with his contract of employment, he is required to be at work.

(2A) In this section—

(a) 'trade union services' means services made available to the employee by an independent trade union by virtue of his membership of the union, and

(b) references to an employee's 'making use' of trade union services include his consenting to the raising of a matter on his behalf by an independent trade union of which he is a member.

(2B) Where the reason or one of the reasons for the dismissal was that an independent trade union (with or without the employee's consent) raised a matter on behalf of the employee as one of its members, the reason shall be treated as falling within subsection (1)(ba).

(3) Where the reason, or one of the reasons, for the dismissal was—

(a) the employee's refusal, or proposed refusal, to comply with a requirement (whether or not imposed by his contract of employment or in writing) that, in the event of his not being a member of any trade union, or of a particular trade union, or of one of a number of particular trade unions, he must make one or more payments, or

(b) his objection, or proposed objection (however expressed) to the operation of a provision (whether or not forming part of his contract of employment or in writing) under which, in the event mentioned in paragraph (a), his employer is entitled to deduct one or more sums from the remuneration payable to him in respect of his employment,

the reason shall be treated as falling within subsection (1)(c).

(4) References in this section to being, becoming or ceasing to remain a member of a trade union include references to being, becoming or ceasing to remain a member of a particular branch or section of that union or of one of a number of particular branches or sections of that trade union.

(5) References in this section—

(a) to taking part in the activities of a trade union, and

(b) to services made available by a trade union by virtue of membership of the union, shall be construed in accordance with subsection (4).

NOTES

1. Where a dismissal is unfair by virtue of s. 152(1), there is a minimum basic award of £5,807 (w.e.f. 6 April 2015).

2. The following two cases provide contrasting examples of judicial approaches to trade union membership discrimination. In *Therm-a-Stor Ltd* v *Atkins* [1983] IRLR 78, CA, a large majority of the shop-floor workforce applied to join the union. The company's response to the union's claim for recognition was to dismiss 20 employees. The selection was left to chargehands and, although there was no evidence that the selections were made on the basis of union membership, all those selected for dismissal were union members. The Court of Appeal held that the dismissals fell outside the section because they were in response to the union's claim for recognition and *not* because of any of the dismissed individuals' union membership or activities. For a more liberal approach see *Discount Tobacco & Confectionery Ltd* v *Armitage* [1990] IRLR 15, where it was held that the protection from dismissal in TULR(C)A 1992, s. 152(1)(a) on the grounds of union membership should extend beyond the mere status of union membership and apply to dismissal for making use of the essential services of the union (in that case, seeking union assistance in obtaining a s. 1 statement from the employer). The position has now been clarified by amendments introduced by the Employment Rights Act (ERA) 2004 which adopt the *Armitage* approach (see s. 152(1)(ba)).

3. Most cases arising under s. 152 involve the question of whether the dismissal was for taking part in the activities of a trade union at an appropriate time. The scope of the trade union activities protected by s. 152(1)(b) has been viewed restrictively by the courts. It has been held that the personal activities of a union member are not the activities of a trade union within the meaning of s. 152. For example, in *Chant* v *Aquaboats Ltd* [1978] 1 All ER 102, a union member who organised a petition complaining about safety standards was held not to be engaged in trade union activity, notwithstanding the fact that a union official had vetted the petition before it was presented. The EAT stated that 'The mere fact that one or two of the employees making representations happen to be trade unionists, and the mere fact that the spokesman of the men happens to be a trade unionist does not make such representations a trade union activity.' (Note that Mr Chant would now be able to seek protection under the ERA 1996, s. 44, which makes it unlawful to victimise employees for raising concerns about safety.)

The courts and tribunals have tended to require that the activity is connected with the institutional aspects of trade unions, such as taking part in trade union meetings, distributing union material, recruiting a fellow employee or consulting a trade union official.

4. For trade union activity to be protected it must take place at 'an appropriate time'. This is defined as not only occasions 'outside the employee's working hours' but also time 'within working hours at which, in accordance with arrangements agreed with, or consent given by his employer, it is permissible for him to take part in those activities' (TULR(C)A 1992, s. 152(2)). Working hours means hours when, in accordance with his contract, the employee is required to be at work. It has been held that 'periods when in accordance with his contract the worker is on his employer's premises but not actually working' are outside 'working hours' (*per* Lord Reid in *Post Office* v *UPW* [1974] IRLR 22). Consequently, the view has been taken that a paid meal break is not a time within working hours so as to require the employer's consent to take part in trade union activities (*Zucker* v *Astrid Jewels Ltd* [1978] IRLR 385).

Where the activities take place within working hours, there must be consent by the employer. Consent may be express or implied. In *Zucker*, for example, the employee alleged that he had been dismissed for discussing trade union matters while working on a machine, and encouraging union recruitment during meal breaks. The EAT held that such conduct could constitute trade union activities at an appropriate time, for the employees were permitted to converse during working hours, and consequently they had an implied right to discuss trade union matters. However, in *Marley Tile Co. Ltd* v *Shaw* [1980] IRLR 25, the Court of Appeal was not prepared to imply the employer's consent from his silence in response to the announcement of an unaccredited shop steward that he would be calling a meeting during working hours.

In *Bass Taverns* v *Burgess* [1995] IRLR 596, CA, a shop steward was demoted and constructively dismissed for criticising the employers during a presentation on the union at an induction course for new managers. An industrial tribunal found that because the employee had abused the privilege given to him by the employers, the dismissal could not be on the grounds of trade union activities. This finding was overruled by the Court of Appeal which rejected the view that there was an implied limitation on the employers' consent to the meeting being used as a recruitment forum such that the recruiter would say nothing to criticise or undermine the company. There was, therefore, no 'abuse of privilege'. According to Balcombe LJ, 'a consent to recruit must include a consent to underline the services which the union can provide. That may reasonably involve a submission to prospective members that in some respects the union will provide a service which the company does not.' One possible limitation expressed in the case is that the section might cease to apply if the employee conducting the recruitment indulged in malicious, untruthful or irrelevant invective.

5. In *Drew* v *St Edmundsbury BC* [1980] IRLR 88, it was held that taking part in industrial action does not constitute taking part in the activities of an independent trade union within the meaning of s. 152 and, as we shall see in Chapter 11, a dismissal for that reason may not be challenged at all if it comes within TULR(C)A 1992, ss. 237–8.

6. In *Birmingham City District Council* v *Beyer* [1977] IRLR 211, the EAT took the view that s. 152 applies only to trade union activities which take place after employment with a particular employer has commenced and 'could not conceivably refer to activities before the employment began'. Subsequently, the EA 1990 made it unlawful to refuse a person employment because he or she is, or is not, a member of a trade union (see now TULR(C)A 1992, s. 137). However, it may be argued that the provision will still not prevent an employer from excluding a candidate on the grounds of past 'activities', or because he or she is regarded as a 'troublemaker'. This sort of victimisation may now be caught by s. 152 as a result of the decision of the Court of Appeal in the next case.

Fitzpatrick v *British Railways Board*

[1991] IRLR 376, Court of Appeal

When Ms Fitzpatrick obtained a job with British Railways Board, she deliberately failed to provide full details of her previous employment or to disclose her former participation in trade union activities. She joined the National Union of Railwaymen and engaged in some recruiting activity, attended some meetings and intended seeking an official position in the union.

Subsequently, her employers came across a newspaper article in which Ms Fitzpatrick was referred to as a union activist with links with ultra-left groups. After some investigation, they decided to dismiss her.

Ms Fitzpatrick claimed that she had been dismissed on grounds of trade union activities and that her dismissal was therefore unfair under what is now TULR(C)A 1992, s. 152(1)(b). The employers argued that she was dismissed because she had obtained the job by deceit. An industrial tribunal found that the reason for Ms Fitzpatrick's dismissal was her previous union activities and her reputation as a militant. By a majority, however, the tribunal held that she was not dismissed for trade union activities within the meaning of s. 152(1)(b). Following the decision in *Birmingham District Council* v *Beyer* [1977] IRLR 211, the EAT concluded that, as far as proposed trade union activities are concerned, in order to fall within s. 152(1)(b) there must be 'some cogent and identifiable act and not some possible trouble in the future'.

The Court of Appeal allowed Ms Fitzpatrick's appeal and substituted a finding that she had been unfairly dismissed.

WOOLF LJ: In this case British Rail purported to dismiss the appellant on the basis of her deceit in concealing her previous trade union activities. If the Industrial Tribunal had accepted that it was her deceit which caused them to dismiss her, or if that was the primary reason for her dismissal, then the situation is that she would not have been able to bring herself within the language of s. 152(1)(b). However, as already indicated, all three members of the Industrial Tribunal accepted that it was not the deceit which was the operative cause for her dismissal.

What the majority concluded was, and I read here from paragraph 27 of the decision:

> It was the [appellant's] previous trade union (and possibly her political) activities, which gave her a reputation for being a disruptive force; and that was the prime reason for her dismissal.

That paragraph, in my judgment, discloses a failure on the part of the Industrial Tribunal to answer the critical question. The fact that the appellant had a reputation with regard to trade union activities was, as Miss Booth in her argument made clear, only relevant to British Rail in so far as it would have an effect on what she did while she was employed by them. Miss Booth submits, clearly with justification, that British Rail did not suggest and would not in fact seek to dismiss the appellant merely in order to punish her for her previous trade union activities. Miss Booth submits that what the Industrial Tribunal failed to do was to identify why it was that because of her previous trade union, and possibly political, activities British Rail decided to dismiss the appellant. If the Tribunal had asked the question the answer would have been obvious. It would be that they would fear a repetition of the same conduct while employed by them.

The reason that the majority of the Industrial Tribunal did not address the critical question is probably because of their understanding of the *Beyer* decision. They say, having examined that decision, that so far as proposed activities are concerned it must, and I quote: 'involve some cogent and identifiable act and not some possible trouble in the future'. In other words the Industrial Tribunal are saying that in order to comply with the provisions of s. 152(1)(b) there must have been some activity on the part of the employee to which they took exception, which was not a mere possibility but something which was sufficiently precise to be identifiable in her present employment.

In my judgment, to adopt this approach is to read into the language of s. 152(1)(b) a restriction which Parliament has not identified. To limit the language, in the way which the Industrial Tribunal did, would prevent the actual reason for the dismissal in a case such as this from being considered by the Industrial Tribunal. As long as the reason which motivated the employer falls within the words 'activities that the employee...proposed to take part in', there is no reason to limit the language. The purpose of the subsection, in so far as (b) is concerned, is to protect those who engage in trade union activities and I can see no reason why that should not apply irrespective of whether the precise activities can be identified.

If an employer, having learnt of an employee's previous trade union activities, decides that he wishes to dismiss that employee, that is likely to be a situation where almost inevitably the employer is dismissing the employee because he feels that the employee will indulge in industrial activities of a trade union nature in his current employment. There is no reason for a rational and reasonable employer to object to the previous activities of an employee except in so far as they will impinge upon the employee's current employment.

■ QUESTION

If British Rail had discovered Ms Fitzpatrick's union activism before she was appointed and refused to employ her, would she have had a remedy?

NOTE: The answer to the question posed above is that an employee who was refused employment on the grounds of his or her trade union activities did not have a remedy. It was hoped that the Labour Government would remedy this omission. In *Fairness at Work*, the Government had proposed to close this loophole and also to prohibit the blacklisting of trade unionists (para. 4.25). The Employment Relations Act 1999 fails to close the loophole, but offered the prospect of making trade unionist blacklisting unlawful:

3. Blacklists

(1) The Secretary of State may make regulations prohibiting the compilation of lists which—
   (a) contain details of members of trade unions or persons who have taken part in the activities of trade unions, and
   (b) are compiled with a view to being used by employers or employment agencies for the purposes of discrimination in relation to recruitment or in relation to the treatment of workers.

(2) The Secretary of State may make regulations prohibiting—
   (a) the use of lists to which subsection (1) applies;
   (b) the sale or supply of lists to which subsection (1) applies.

In 2003, the Government consulted on draft regulations but did not implement them as there was no evidence that blacklisting occurred. However, in 2009, the Government introduced a consultation on a set of revised regulations, prompted by evidence uncovered by the Information Commissioner which indicated that blacklisting was occurring in parts of the construction industry.

The Employment Relations Act 1999 (Blacklists) Regulations 2010 (SI 2010/493) give trade union members and activists rights where organisations collect information on them to enable employers or employment agencies to discriminate against them in relation to recruitment or their treatment.

Regulation 3, makes it unlawful to compile, use, sell or supply a 'prohibited list' (blacklist).

Regulations 5 and 6 make it unlawful for employers and employment agencies to rely on such information if they know or ought reasonably to know that it is supplied in contravention of the regulations.

The Regulations give the trade union member a right to complain to an employment tribunal if refused employment, dismissed, or subjected to any other detriment because of inclusion on a prohibited list. In the case of dismissal, this will constitute an automatically unfair reason under ERA 1996, s. 104F. Where there is a refusal of employment under Regs. 5 or 6 or the individual has suffered a detriment under reg. 9, the ET's award of compensation (which can include injury to feelings) shall not be less than £5,000.

An alternative remedy for contravention of reg. 3 is provided under reg. 13. An application may be made to the High Court for breach of statutory duty.The court has the discretion to award damages (which may include compensation for injured feelings) and/or make such order as it sees fit for the purpose of restraining or preventing the defendant from contravening reg. 3.

E: Selection for redundancy on grounds related to union membership or activities

TRADE UNION AND LABOUR RELATIONS (CONSOLIDATION) ACT 1992

153. Selection for redundancy on grounds related to union membership or activities

Where the reason or principal reason for the dismissal of an employee was that he was redundant, but it is shown—

(a) that the circumstances constituting the redundancy applied equally to one or more other employees in the same undertaking who held positions similar to that held by him and who have not been dismissed by the employer, and

(b) that the reason (or, if more than one, the principal reason) why he was selected for dismissal was one of those specified in section 152(1), the dismissal shall be regarded as unfair for the purposes of Part V of the Employment Protection (Consolidation) Act 1978 (unfair dismissal).

NOTES

1. Under TURERA 1993, complaints of unfair redundancy selection on trade union grounds are no longer subject to a qualifying period of service (see Sch. 7, para. 1, which amends TULR(C) A 1992, s. 154). This removes a clear inconsistency in the law, where protection against trade union-related dismissals under s. 152(1) applies to all employees but protection against selection for redundancy for trade union-related reasons previously was limited to those with two years' service.

2. By virtue of amendments introduced by the EA 1982, the amount of compensation to be awarded to employees who are unfairly dismissed (or selected for redundancy) on grounds of trade union membership and activities or non-membership was much higher than for other types of dismissal because a 'special award' was made in addition to the basic and compensatory elements. Where a complaint under s. 153 is successful, there is a minimum basic award (£5,807 w.e.f. 6 April 2015).

   With the raising of the compensation award limit to £75,000 and above, there is less need for the 'special award' in trade union cases. Consequently, s. 33 of the Employment Relations Act 1999 simplifies arrangements by replacing special awards with additional awards.

3. Either the employer or the applicant may request that a trade union or other party be joined in the proceedings where they have exerted or threatened to exert industrial pressure on the employer to dismiss. If the tribunal finds the complaint of third party pressure well founded, the tribunal has the power to order the trade union or other party to pay any or all of the compensation awarded.

4. An employee who alleges that he or she has been dismissed for union/non-union membership or trade union activities can apply to the tribunal for an order for interim relief (TULR(C)A 1992, s. 161).

The order for interim relief is intended to preserve the status quo until full hearing of cases which by their very nature can be extremely damaging to the industrial relations in any organisation. Where relief is granted it will result in either the reinstatement/re-engagement of the employee pending full hearing or, in some cases, a suspension of the employee on continued terms and conditions (TULR(C)A 1992, ss. 161–6).

Recently, these provisions have been extended to dismissals of health and safety representatives, employee trustees of occupational pension schemes, and employee representatives for the purposes of consultation over redundancies and business transfers (see ERA 1996, s. 128).

SECTION 3: TRADE UNIONS AND COLLECTIVE BARGAINING

TRADE UNION AND LABOUR RELATIONS (CONSOLIDATION) Act 1992

179. Collective agreements and collective bargaining

(1) In this Act 'collective agreement' means any agreement or arrangement made by or on behalf of one or more trade unions and one or more employers or employers' associations and relating to one or more of the matters specified below; and 'collective bargaining' means negotiations relating to or connected with one or more of those matters.

(2) The matters referred to above are—

(a) terms and conditions of employment, or the physical conditions in which any workers are required to work;

(b) engagement or non-engagement, or termination or suspension of employment or the duties of employment, of one or more workers;

(c) allocation of work or the duties of employment between workers or groups of workers;

(d) matters of discipline;

(e) a worker's membership or non-membership of a trade union;

(f) facilities for officials of trade unions; and

(g) machinery for negotiation or consultation, and other procedures, relating to any of the above matters, including the recognition by employers or employers' associations of the right of a trade union to represent workers in such negotiation or consultation or in the carrying out of such procedures.

(3) In this Act 'recognition', in relation to a trade union, means the recognition of the union by an employer, or two or more associated employers, to any extent, for the purpose of collective bargaining; and 'recognised' and other related expressions shall be construed accordingly.

NOTE: Recognition of a trade union means that the employer has given the trade union negotiating rights over certain issues. In other words, in these areas changes are made as a result of bilateral agreement rather than unilateral decision-making on the part of the employer. Between 1980 and 1999 there was no legal right to recognition. The Industrial Relations Act 1971 provided such a right but the TUC refused to take advantage of the provisions as part of a campaign of general opposition to the legislation. The Employment Protection Act 1975 also allowed for a statutory recognition procedure, but the machinery was so complex that employers were able to challenge ACAS determinations via a series of legal loopholes (see *Grunwick Processing Laboratories* v *Advisory, Conciliation and Arbitration Service* [1978] AC 655). This provided the new Conservative Government with the rationale to abandon the statutory right altogether by the EA 1980.

A: The statutory recognition procedure

There has been a substantial decline in union recognition in Britain—from 66% of workplaces of 25 or more employees in 1984, to 53% of workplaces in 1990, and to 45% in 1997–8. In that last year, of the 10.1 million employees in workplaces with union recognition, 8.1 million were covered by collective bargaining. This represents a mere 36% of all employees, compared to the peak coverage of 85% recorded in 1979 (see Cully, M., et al., *The 1998 Workplace Employee Relations Survey: First findings* (London: Department of Trade and Industry, 1998)). As we have seen, by 2013, the proportion of workers covered by collective bargaining had declined even further to 29.8% (*Trade Union Membership 2013: Statistical Bulletin,* Department of Business Innovation and Skills, May 2014).

The most significant collective labour law reform proposed in the *Fairness at Work* White Paper was the reintroduction of a legally backed procedure by which trade unions can seek recognition by employers which refuse to agree to collective bargaining on a voluntary basis. The Employment Relations Act 1999 contains provisions that substantially implement the scheme detailed in the White Paper.

(i) Request for recognition

Section 1 of the 1999 Act inserts a new Sch. A1 into TULR(C)A 1992. Paragraph 1 provides that a trade union (or trade unions) may make a request for recognition in accordance with Pt I of the schedule. Paragraph 2 sets out the definitions, in particular that of a 'bargaining unit':

TRADE UNION AND LABOUR RELATIONS (CONSOLIDATION) ACT 1992

SCHEDULE A1 COLLECTIVE BARGAINING: RECOGNITION

PART I RECOGNITION

2....(2) References to the bargaining unit are to the group of workers concerned (or the groups taken together).

(3) References to the proposed bargaining unit are to the bargaining unit proposed in the request for recognition.

[Paragraph 3 offers a narrower definition of 'collective bargaining' than that employed in other parts of the 1992 Act:]

3.—(1) This paragraph applies for the purpose of this part of this Schedule.

(2) The meaning of collective bargaining given by section 178(1) shall not apply.

(3) References to collective bargaining are to negotiations relating to pay, hours and holidays; but this has effect subject to sub-paragraph (4).

(4) If the parties agree matters as the subject of collective bargaining, references to collective bargaining are to negotiations relating to the agreed matters; and this is the case whether the agreement is made before or after the time when the CAC issues a declaration, or the parties agree, that the union is (or unions are) entitled to conduct collective bargaining on behalf of the bargaining unit.

NOTE: In *UNIFI* v *Union Bank of Nigeria plc* [2001] IRLR 712, following a Central Arbitration Committee (CAC) declaration of recognition, the parties agreed on all the matters that would be covered in negotiations with the union, except on whether the obligation to negotiate on 'pay' included an obligation to negotiate on matters relating to pensions. The employers contended that the limited definition of collective bargaining in the statutory recognition provisions, as opposed to the wider definition in TULR(C)A, s. 178 indicated that the word 'pay' should have a minimalist meaning and one that did not include pensions. However, the CAC panel, following a detailed review of the case law, other legislation and the debates when the recognition went through Parliament, decided that the obligation to negotiate on 'pay' included all matters relating to the levels or amounts of the employer's contributions to the defined contribution group personal pension money purchase scheme. These are seen, from an industrial standpoint, as an 'integral and important part of a worker's pay'. This view was supported by the case law, where 'pay', the term Parliament had chosen to use in the statutory recognition scheme, has been given a wider meaning than 'wages' or 'remuneration'.

4. —(1) The union or unions seeking recognition must make a request of recognition to the employer.

...

5. The request is not valid unless it is received by the employer.

6. The request is not valid unless the union (or each of the unions) has a certificate under section 6 that it is independent.

7. —(1) The request is not valid unless the employer, taken with any associated employer or employers, employs—

(a) at least 21 workers on the day the employer receives the request, or

(b) an average of at least 21 workers in the 13 weeks ending with that day.

NOTES

1. Associated employers are counted as long as they are registered in the UK. It is worth emphasising that the term 'worker' is used rather than the narrower term, 'employee'. Any request for recognition will also be invalid unless it is in writing, identifies the union or unions and the bargaining unit, and states that it is made under the schedule (Sch. A1, para. 8).

   After an application has been received, the employer has only ten working days ('the first period') in which to respond. There are four possible responses:

   (a) *The employer agrees the bargaining unit and the union is recognised* (Sch. A1, para. 10(1)). The effect is that recognition is voluntary and not legally enforceable.

   (b) *The employer does not accept the request but is willing to negotiate* (Sch. A1, para. 10(2)). There is then a period of negotiations lasting up to 20 days, starting with the day after that on which the first period ends ('the second period'). If the parties agree, this period may be extended. The employer and the union(s) may request ACAS to assist in conducting the negotiations (Sch. A1, para. 10(5)).

   (c) *The employer rejects the application or fails to respond.* The union may apply to the CAC to decide one or more of the following:

   (i) whether the proposed bargaining unit is appropriate or some other bargaining unit is appropriate;

   (ii) whether the union has (or unions have) the support of a majority of the workers constituting the appropriate bargaining unit (Sch. A1, para. 11(2)).

   (d) *The employer negotiates in the second period but no agreement is reached.* The union(s) may apply to the CAC to determine the appropriateness of the proposed bargaining unit and whether the union has (or unions have) the support of the majority of the workers constituting the proposed bargaining unit. However, the CAC will not consider an application if the union has rejected or failed to respond to an employer's proposal to involve ACAS in the negotiations within ten working days of the employer agreeing to negotiate (Sch. A1, para. 12).

   If a union applies to the CAC under para. 11 or 12, before the application may proceed the CAC must be satisfied that it is valid and admissible.

   Paragraph 14 applies if two or more applications are received by the CAC and the bargaining units proposed or agreed in respect of the applications overlap, i.e. at least one worker is a member of all the bargaining units. In this situation, each application is subject to the '10 per cent' test to determine whether at least 10% of the bargaining unit are union members. If only one application passes the test, it may proceed; if both pass or neither passes, neither application will be successful.

   Paragraph 15 requires any application under para. 11 or 12 to be valid in terms of paras. 5–9, and admissible in terms of paras. 33–42. The CAC has ten working days (or longer, if it notifies the union and the employer of its reason for extending the period) in which to decide whether the application is valid and admissible. In order to be admissible, an application must:

   (i) be made in such form and be supported by such documents as the CAC specifies (Sch. A1, para. 33);

   (ii) be copied to the employer, together with any supporting documents (Sch. A1, para. 34);

   (iii) not cover any workers in respect of whom the union is already recognised, unless that union has no certificate of independence, was previously recognised in respect of the same (or substantially the same) bargaining unit, and ceased to be recognised within three years prior to the application (Sch. A1, para. 35);

   (iv) satisfy the CAC that at least 10% of the proposed bargaining unit are members of the union and 'a majority of the workers constituting the bargaining unit would be likely to favour recognition of the union (or unions) as entitled to conduct collective bargaining on behalf of the bargaining unit' (Sch. A1, para. 36);

   (v) (in the case of an application made by more than one union) show that the unions 'will co-operate with each other in a manner likely to maintain stable and effective collective bargaining' and, if the employer wishes, conduct single-table collective bargaining (Sch. A1, para. 37);

(vi)   not cover any workers in respect of whom the CAC has already an application, i.e. the bargaining unit must not overlap with another unit in respect of which the CAC has accepted an application (Sch. A1, para. 38);

(vii) not be substantially the same as an application which the CAC accepted within the previous three years (Sch. A1, para. 39);

(viii) not be made within three years of a declaration by the CAC that the union was (or the same group of unions were) not entitled to be recognised in respect of the same (or substantially the same) bargaining unit as in the current application (Sch. A1, para. 40).

2. In *R (on the application of the National Union of Journalists)* v *Central Arbitration Committee* [2006] IRLR 53, the Court of Appeal upheld the CAC's view that it had no power to accept a statutory claim for recognition by the NUJ relating to the Mirror Group of Newspapers because the employees had already entered into a recognition agreement with another union in respect of the workers concerned. Paragraph 35 of Sch. A1 to TULR(C)A prevents the CAC from accepting an application for recognition if there is already 'in force a collective agreement under which a union is ... recognised as entitled to conduct collective bargaining on behalf of any of the workers within the relevant bargaining unit.' The Court of Appeal also held that the right to freedom of association and to join trade unions under Article 11 of the ECHR does not extend to a right of a union to be recognised for the purposes of collective bargaining.

(ii) Appropriate bargaining unit

TRADE UNION AND LABOUR RELATIONS (CONSOLIDATION) ACT 1992

SCHEDULE A1 COLLECTIVE BARGAINING: RECOGNITION

PART I RECOGNITION

Appropriate bargaining unit

18.—(1) If the CAC accepts an application under paragraph 11(2) or 12(2) it must try to help the parties to reach within the appropriate period an agreement as to what the appropriate bargaining unit is.

...

NOTES

1. The 'appropriate period' is 20 working days starting with the day after that on which the CAC gives notice of acceptance of the application, or such longer period as the CAC may specify with reason (Sch. A1, para. 18(2)). If negotiations with the CAC's assistance fail, the CAC must decide the appropriate bargaining unit within ten working days of the end of the appropriate period, or such longer period as the CAC may specify with reasons (Sch. A1, para. 19(1)–(2)).

2. Section 2 of the Employment Relations Act 2004 amends para. 18 in the schedule, and gives the CAC power to end the appropriate period early if it concludes that there is no reasonable prospect of the parties reaching such an agreement. This means that the CAC will be free to move on to the next stage of the procedure. Section 3 inserts a new para. 18A into the schedule which requires the employer, within five working days, to supply the union and the CAC with a list of categories of worker in the unions proposed bargaining unit, their workplaces and the number of workers at each workplace.

19....(3) In deciding the appropriate bargaining unit the CAC must take these matters into account—

(a) the need for the unit to be compatible with effective management;

(b) the matters listed in sub-paragraph (4), so far as they do not conflict with that need.

(4) The matters are—

(a) the views of the employer and of the union (or unions);

(b) existing national and local bargaining arrangements;

(c) the desirability of avoiding small fragmented bargaining units within an undertaking;

(d) the characteristics of the workers falling within the proposed bargaining unit and of any other employees of the employer whom the CAC considers relevant;

(e) the location of workers.

...

(5) The CAC must give notice of its decision to the parties.

NOTES
1. Section 4 of the Employment Relations Act 2004 amends para. 19 of the schedule to add to the list the matters that the CAC must take into account when making such a determination. The CAC must, in future, take into account any view the employer has about any other bargaining unit that it considers would be appropriate. This will supersede the Court of Appeal's decision in *R v CAC and another, ex p. Kwikfit* [2003] IRLR 395. In *Kwikfit*, the Court of Appeal considered that, because there was no formal provision in the schedule for the employer to make an alternative proposal, the CAC had to consider the union's proposal only and, if it found that appropriate, it did not need to look any further.
2. Under the previous law, it was only when the CAC had decided that it was necessary to hold a ballot for the workers to be asked whether they want the union to conduct collective bargaining on their behalf that, under para. 26 of the schedule, the employer became obliged to give the union reasonable access to the workers, and to give their names and home addresses to the person conducting the ballot, so that he or she may send onto them information received from the union.

Section 5 of the Employment Relations Act 2004 inserts new paras. 19C–F into the schedule to make provision for the union to have access to the workers much earlier. Under new para. 19C, once the initial application for union recognition is made to the CAC, the union may apply to the CAC for the appointment of a suitable independent person to handle communications between the union and the relevant workers during the 'initial period' (i.e. until the CAC makes its decision either to determine the bargaining unit itself or to allow a ballot to be held). The employer will be required under new para. 19D to give this information as to names and home addresses of workers.

Under new para. 19F, if the CAC is satisfied that the employer is not carrying out its duty in this regard, it may first make a 'remedial order' requiring the employer to take specific steps to remedy its failure. If the employer fails to comply with a remedial order and an appropriate bargaining unit has already been established, the CAC will have the power, without more, to issue a declaration that the union is recognised on behalf of the workers in that unit. If the CAC subsequently decides to hold a ballot, the employer need not supply the same information again but must inform the person appointed to conduct the ballot if any person has joined or ceased to be in the unit.

(iii) Recognition ballots

NOTES
1. Once the bargaining unit is agreed or determined by the CAC, the CAC must be 'satisfied that a majority of the workers constituting the bargaining unit are members of the union (or unions)' (Sch. A1, para. 22). If this condition is met, then the CAC must issue a declaration that the union is recognised 'as entitled to conduct collective bargaining on behalf of workers constituting the bargaining unit' (para. 22(2)) unless any of the following conditions apply:
    (a) the CAC is satisfied that a ballot should be held in the interests of good industrial relations;
    (b) a significant number of the union members within the bargaining unit inform the CAC that they do not want the union (or unions) to conduct collective bargaining on their behalf;
    (c) membership evidence is produced which leaves the CAC to conclude that there are doubts whether a significant number of union members within the bargaining unit want the union (or unions) to conduct collective bargaining on their behalf (para. 22(4)).
In such cases, the CAC must hold a ballot. This is the only significant amendment to the White Paper proposals and represents a dilution of the principle of 'automacity'. Lord McCarthy has questioned the justification for this dilution:

> Where are those workers who join unions, pay subscriptions and do not want representation? Who knows of a firm where recognition can only be expected to be good for future relations if it is preceded by a ballot? Perhaps these last minute caveats are best explained as concessions to the more ignorant sections of employer opinion, by negotiators who took them to be largely irrelevant? [*Fairness at Work and Trade Union Recognition: Past comparisons and future problems* (London: The Institute of Employment Rights, 1999), at p. 38]

If the CAC is not satisfied that a majority of the workers constituting the bargaining unit are members of the union (or unions), it 'must give notice to the parties that it intends to arrange for the holding of a secret ballot in which the workers constituting the bargaining unit are asked whether they want the union (or unions) to conduct collective bargaining on their behalf' (Sch. A1, para. 23(2)).

Paragraph 25 of Sch. A1 sets out the requirements for the conduct of recognition ballots. They must be supervised by a qualified independent person appointed by the CAC. The ballot must be held within 20 working days starting with the day after that on which the qualified independent person is appointed, unless the time limit is extended by the CAC. The ballot may be conducted at the workplace or by post, or by a combination of the two, at the discretion of the CAC. In exercising its discretion, the CAC must take into account: the likelihood of the ballot being affected by unfairness and malpractice if it were conducted at the workplace(s); costs and practicality; and any such other matters as the CAC considers appropriate. Paragraph 25(9) requires the CAC to inform the employer and union of the arrangements for the ballot as soon as reasonably practicable. The costs of the ballot are to be shared equally by the employer and the union (Sch. A1, para. 28).

As soon as the employer is informed of the holding of the ballot, it must comply with three duties, which are:

(a) to cooperate generally in connection with the ballot, with the union and the person appointed to conduct it;

(b) to give the union reasonable access to the workers constituting the bargaining unit to allow them to inform the workers of the object of the ballot and to seek their support and their opinions;

(c) to do the following:

  (i) to give the CAC within a period of ten working days the names and home addresses of the workers constituting the bargaining unit;

  (ii) to give the CAC as soon as is reasonably practicable the name and address of any worker who joins the unit thereafter;

  (iii) to inform the CAC as soon as is reasonably practicable of any worker who ceases to be within the unit (Sch. A1, para. 26(1)–(4)).

The second and third duties are not to prejudice the generality of the first duty to cooperate. The union also has the right to ask the independent person to distribute materials to workers in the unit at their home addresses. This is to be at the union's expense (Sch. A1, para. 26(6)(7)).

2. Section 7 of the Employment Relations Act 2004 amends para. 24 of the schedule to give more flexibility over the decision whether or not to hold a ballot. The CAC now has a new power, on the joint application of the union and the employer, to extend the ten-day 'notification period'. This is the period within which the union, or the union and the employer jointly, may inform the CAC that they do not want a ballot to be held. In these circumstances, the CAC cannot hold a ballot.

Section 8(1) of the Employment Relations Act 2004 amends para. 25 of the schedule to modify the requirement that the ballot be conducted either at the workplace or by post, to allow workers, who would not otherwise be entitled to do so, to request the right to a postal vote if they are absent and thus unable to vote at the workplace.

3. The Employment Relations Act 2004 brought into effect measures to tackle the intimidation of workers during recognition and derecognition ballots by introducing rules which define improper campaigning activity by employers and unions, and by clarifying what constitutes the 'reasonable access' that unions should have in relation to workers in the bargaining unit (see the ERA 2004, ss. 10 and 13 and the Code of Practice on Access and Unfair Industrial Practices During Recognition and Derecognition Ballots (which took effect from 1 October 2005)).

TRADE UNION AND LABOUR RELATIONS (CONSOLIDATION) ACT 1992

SCHEDULE A1 COLLECTIVE BARGAINING: RECOGNITION

PART I RECOGNITION

Union recognition

27.—(1) If the CAC is satisfied that the employer has failed to fulfil any of the three duties imposed by paragraph 26, and the ballot has not been held, the CAC may order the employer—

  (a) to take such steps to remedy the failure as the CAC considers reasonable and specifies in the order, and

  (b) to do so within such period as the CAC considers reasonable and specifies in the order.

(2) If the CAC is satisfied that the employer has failed to comply with an order under sub-paragraph (1), and the ballot has not been held, the CAC may issue a declaration that the union is (or unions are) recognised as entitled to conduct collective bargaining on behalf of the bargaining unit.

(3) If the CAC issues a declaration under sub-paragraph (2) it shall take steps to cancel the holding of the ballot; and if the ballot is held it shall have no effect.

28. [omitted]

29.—(1) As soon as is reasonably practicable after the CAC is informed of the result of the ballot by the person conducting it, the CAC must act under this paragraph.

(2) The CAC must inform the employer and the union (or unions) of the result of the ballot.

(3) If the result is that the union is (or unions are) supported by—

(a) a majority of the workers voting, and

(b) at least 40% of the workers constituting the bargaining unit, the CAC must issue a declaration that the union is (or unions are) recognised as entitled to conduct collective bargaining on behalf of the bargaining unit.

(4) If the result is otherwise the CAC must issue a declaration that the union is (or unions are) not entitled to be so recognised.

(5) The Secretary of State may by order amend sub-paragraph (3) so as to specify a different degree of support; and different provision may be made for different circumstances.

NOTES

1. In drafting the new statutory redundancy procedure, the Government has attempted to learn from the failure of previous recognition legislation (ss. 11–16 of the Employment Protection Act 1975). The earlier legal framework's weaknesses were vividly exposed by the Grunwick dispute in the 1970s. In this case, a strike by a minority of the workers resulted in their dismissal. The sacked strikers joined a union which then made a statutory recognition claim to ACAS. George Ward, the Grunwick proprietor, refused ACAS access to the non-striking employees in the workplace. Consequently, ACAS could survey only those employees they could reach—mainly the strikers. Unsurprisingly, the workers surveyed were overwhelmingly in favour of recognition and ACAS reported accordingly.

   The House of Lords held that ACAS had acted *ultra vires*. Their Lordships held that s. 12 of the 1975 Act, which had allowed ACAS to make only 'such inquiries as it thinks fit', must be presumed to involve an interest in the views of all workers affected. Although ACAS was not obliged to ascertain the opinion of each and every worker, it could not make a recommendation while being in ignorance of the views of the majority of the workforce or of conflicting opinions held by any significant group. The House of Lords saw no grounds for it to refuse Grunwick the discretionary remedy of a declaration. In their Lordships' view, the company had done nothing wrong, because an employer was under no legal obligation to cooperate with ACAS in its inquiries and consultation in a recognition issue (*ACAS v Grunwick Processing Laboratories Ltd* [1978] IRLR 38, HL).

2. The three duties on employers to cooperate in the ballot (Sch. A1, para. 26) would have certainly been more effective in a case such as *Grunwick*.

3. It remains to be seen whether the CAC will be any less vulnerable to legal challenges by way of judicial review than ACAS. However, Sch. A1 seeks to avoid this by requiring the CAC to operate according to closely defined criteria as opposed to exercising wide discretion.

   In *Fullerton Computer Industries Ltd* v *Central Arbitration Committee* [2001] IRLR 752, we see the first attempt by an employer to challenge a CAC decision by way of judicial review. This case concerned a CAC panel's decision to order an employer to recognise the Iron and Steel Trades Confederation without a ballot, having established that 51.3% of the bargaining unit were members. The Act provides that if the CAC is satisfied that there is a majority of union members in the bargaining unit, it must award recognition unless one of three qualifying conditions are met:

   > (a) the CAC is satisfied that a ballot should be held in the interests of good industrial relations; (b) a significant number of union members within the bargaining unit inform the CAC that they do not want the union to conduct collective bargaining on their behalf; (c) membership evidence is produced which leads the CAC to conclude that there are doubts whether a significant number within the bargaining unit want the union to conduct collective bargaining on their behalf.

   Although the CAC is not obliged to give reasons for its decisions, in this case, it did so. The panel explained that, although the union membership majority was slender, to require a ballot to be held on that ground alone 'would impose, in effect, a threshold for recognition without a ballot, higher than that stipulated by the legislators'. Dismissing the employer's application for judicial review, the Scottish Court of Session held that where reasons for a decision are not required but are nonetheless given, the decision will only be set aside if the reasons given disclose that the panel has exercised its discretion in an irrational or flawed way. The following extract from Lord Johnston's judgment explains the non-interventionist stance of the court:

> If I were to hold otherwise, I would be substituting my view for that of the industrial jury and I consider that to be wholly inappropriate. At the end of the day the decision with regard to the applicability of the exception lies in the discretion of the panel and it has not been demonstrated to me that they exercised that discretion in any irrational or flawed way, even if there is room for more than one view.

4. The new legislation seeks to avoid the involvement of the CAC in inter-union recognition disputes. Under the current regime, there is no procedure for the CAC to determine which union is most representative of the workforce and the emphasis is on voluntary agreement (see para. 35 of Sch. A1 to the TULR(C)A 1992 and *National Union of Journalists* v *Central Arbitration Committee* [2006] IRLR 53, CA).

(iv) Consequences of recognition

Paragraph 30 of Sch. A1 sets out the consequences of recognition. There is first a period of 30 days, or longer as agreed between the parties ('the negotiation period'), for the parties to agree 'a method by which they will conduct collective bargaining'. If the employer and union are still unable to agree after the 'negotiation period', either party may request the CAC to assist them and there is then a 20-day period, or longer if all agree ('the agreement period'), when the CAC 'must try to help the parties' reach agreement (Sch. A1, para. 31(2)).

TRADE UNION AND LABOUR RELATIONS (CONSOLIDATION) ACT 1992

SCHEDULE A1 COLLECTIVE BARGAINING: RECOGNITION

PART I RECOGNITION

Consequences of recognition

31....(3) If at the end of the agreement period the parties have not made such an agreement the CAC must specify to the parties the method by which they are to conduct collective bargaining.

(4) Any method specified under sub-paragraph (3) is to have effect as if it were contained in a legally enforceable contract made by the parties.

(5) But if the parties agree in writing—

    (a) that sub-paragraph (4) shall not apply, or shall not apply to particular parts of the method specified by the CAC, or

    (b) to vary or replace the method specified by the CAC,

    (c) the written agreement shall have effect as a legally enforceable contract made by the parties.

(6) Specific performance shall be the only remedy available for breach of anything which is a legally enforceable contract by virtue of this paragraph.

(7) If at any time before a specification is made under sub-paragraph (3) the parties jointly apply to the CAC requesting it to stop taking steps under this paragraph, the CAC must comply with the request.

NOTES

1. The only remedy available for breach of anything which is a legally enforceable contract is 'specific performance'—i.e. a positive injunction. Of course, breach of an order for specific performance could be contempt of court. It is this enforcement mechanism which has been the subject of most criticism by commentators on the new statutory recognition procedure. Bob Simpson argues: 'It strains credibility beyond breaking point to suppose that the High Court would readily order specific performance, a discretionary remedy, let alone that a striking reversal of the 1980s experience would turn the tables on employers which refused to comply with a court order to observe a DPA [Default Procedure Agreement] by subjecting them to sanctions for contempt' ((1998) 27 ILJ 245, at p. 246).

Other critics point to the weakness inherent in an imposed procedure and the absence of sub-stantive sanctions. Drawing on the experience in other countries, particularly that of the United States, Lord McCarthy argues that:

> reliance on a procedural model affords a recalcitrant management with considerable oppor-tunities for delay and prevarication. They remain free to accept the form of recognition while denying the substance...[T]he remedies need to be supplemented by some form of claims procedure. The simplest way would be to provide for legally binding arbitration to be activated by the CAC on proof of persistent employer prevarication and non-observance. [*Fairness at Work and Trade Union Recognition: Past comparisons and future problems* (London: The Institute of Employment Rights, 1999), at p. 4]

Indeed, under the previous statutory recognition regime contained in ss. 11–16 of the Employment Protection Act 1975, a recalcitrant employer could be subject to compulsory arbitration before the CAC and the latter award 'improved terms and conditions' which were incorporated into the individual worker's contract and enforced in the ordinary courts (for an example of another avoidance strategy, see *R* v *CAB and MGN Ltd* [2006] IRLR 53, CA).

2. Part II of Sch. A1 to the 1992 Act is expressed to be concerned with what would be an obvious loophole in the provisions, where the employer agrees voluntarily to negotiate when the union makes an application under this schedule, but either the parties have not agreed a method to conduct collective bargaining or have agreed a method 'but have failed to carry out the agree-ment' (Sch. A1, para. 59(1)). The CAC must try to help the parties reach agreement, but in the absence of agreement, the CAC must specify the method which again becomes a legally enforce-able contract as if made by the parties.

This part of Sch. A1 is drafted widely enough not only to close the loophole mentioned above, but could also cover all current recognition agreements. Further, applications to the CAC to specify a method can be made by unions or employers.

■ **QUESTION**

If a union calls its members out on industrial action in breach of an agreed dispute pro-cedure agreement, does that fall within the criterion that 'the parties have agreed such a method but have failed to carry out the agreement'?

The question will be whether the failure must be *ab initio*, or can it be at any time during the course of the agreement. If the latter analysis is correct, how is the system of the CAC specifying the method for collective bargaining which is legally enforceable, to be reconciled with s. 180 of the 1992 Act, which provides strict criteria for anything in a collective agreement which restricts the right of workers to strike or take part in other industrial action?

(v) Changes affecting the bargaining unit

TRADE UNION AND LABOUR RELATIONS (CONSOLIDATION) ACT 1992

SCHEDULE A1 COLLECTIVE BARGAINING: RECOGNITION

PART III CHANGES AFFECTING THE BARGAINING UNIT

...

Either party believes unit no longer appropriate

66.—(1) This paragraph applies if the employer believes or the union believes (or unions believe) that the original unit is no longer an appropriate bargaining unit.

(2) The employer or union (or unions) may apply to the CAC to make a decision as to what is an appropriate bargaining unit.

67.—(1) An application under paragraph 66 is not admissible unless the CAC decides that it is likely that the original unit is no longer appropriate by reason of any of the matters specified in sub-paragraph (2).

(2) The matters are—

    (a) a change in the organisation or structure of the business carried on by the employer;

    (b) a change in the activities pursued by the employer in the course of the business carried on by him;

    (c) a substantial change in the number of workers employed in the original unit.

NOTE: Paragraph 69 gives ten working days in which the employer and union may attempt to agree a new bargaining unit. If they do so, the CAC must declare the union recognised for the new unit, and the method of collective bargaining for the original unit shall apply to the new unit, with any modifications the CAC deems it necessary to make. If the union and employer fail to agree, para. 70 gives the CAC ten working days in which to decide:

(a) whether the original unit is appropriate, using the same criteria as in para. 67(2) in the extract;
(b) if the original unit is not appropriate, what other unit (if any) is appropriate.

70.—(4) In deciding what other bargaining unit is or units are appropriate the CAC must take these matters into account—
    (a) the need for the unit or units to be compatible with effective management;
    (b) the matters listed in sub-paragraph (5), so far as they do not conflict with that need.
(5) The matters are—
    (a) the views of the employer and of the union (or unions);
    (b) existing national and local bargaining arrangements;
    (c) the desirability of avoiding small fragmented bargaining units within an undertaking;
    (d) the characteristics of workers falling within the original unit and of any other employees of the employer whom the CAC considers relevant;
    (e) the location of the workers.
(6) If the CAC decides that two or more bargaining units are appropriate its decision must be such that no worker falls within more than one of them.

NOTES
1. It is possible for the CAC to decide that no unit is appropriate, in which case the union will be derecognised.
2. If the CAC decides a new appropriate bargaining unit, it must also determine whether the difference between the new unit and the original unit is such that support for recognition needs to be reassessed. If support does not have to be reassessed because the changes are relatively minor, the CAC must declare the union recognised for the new unit. If support needs to be assessed then tests mirror those in Pt I: the CAC has to decide whether the union has 10% membership in the new unit and whether recognition is likely to have majority support. If these tests are not satisfied, the union ceases to be recognised. If the tests are passed, automatic recognition may be granted to unions with over 50% membership of the bargaining unit, or a ballot may be held (Sch. A1, paras. 85–9).

(vi) Statutory derecognition

Application for derecognition under the statutory procedure set out in Pt IV of Sch. A1 applies only where a declaration of recognition has been made under Pt I or III, or where the union has had a collective bargaining method specified by the CAC under Pt II. Part IV does not apply if a voluntary recognised union is derecognised, and there is nothing to prevent an employer derecognising a union if it currently voluntarily recognises that union. Applications for derecognition may not take place until three or more years after the CAC's original decision. The procedure is very similar to the procedure for statutory recognition.

Paragraph 99 of Sch. A1 provides that if the employer employs an average of fewer than 21 workers he may, at the end of the period of three years, give notice to the union of the fact and state that the existing bargaining arrangements will not apply from the given date which is to be at least 35 working days starting with the day after the union is notified. The union may appeal to the CAC that the employer's notice is inadmissible and/or on the question whether the employer has fewer than 21 workers. The CAC has ten working days to reach a decision. It may extend this period by giving notice and reasons to the parties.

Paragraphs 104–11 set out the procedures to be followed in circumstances where the employer still has more than 21 workers but applies for derecognition on the basis that three years have passed and the majority of the workers support derecognition. The CAC must not proceed with the application for derecognition unless it decides that:

(a) at least 10% of the workers constituting the bargaining unit favour an end of the bargaining arrangements; and

(b) a majority of the workers constituting the bargaining unit would be likely to favour an end of the bargaining arrangements (Sch. A1, para. 110(1)).

Paragraph 112 of Sch. A1 provides that it is not only the employer but also a worker or workers within the bargaining unit who may make an application, after three years have passed, for the bargaining arrangement to end.

Paragraph 116 requires the CAC to help the employer, union and worker with a view either to the employer and union agreeing to end the bargaining arrangements, or the worker withdrawing the application in the 20 days after the application is accepted. If an agreement is reached or the application is withdrawn, the CAC will take no further action. Otherwise, it must hold a ballot.

Paragraph 117 lays down the procedure for ballots on derecognition. They mirror the procedure on recognition, except that there is no provision for automatic derecognition if over 50% of the workers are no longer union members.

Paragraph 121 sets out the threshold that must be satisfied in the ballot. It is the same as for recognition, namely that the proposition that bargaining arrangements should be ended is supported by a majority of the workers voting and at least 40% of the workers constituting the bargaining unit.

Part V of Sch. A1 provides for a different procedure for derecognition in circumstances where the CAC has issued a declaration that a union is 'automatically' recognised as entitled to conduct collective bargaining on behalf of the bargaining unit (i.e. without a ballot). Again, applications for derecognition will be accepted only three or more years after recognition. An application 'is not admissible unless the CAC is satisfied that fewer than half of the workers constituting the bargaining unit are members of the union (or unions)' (Sch. A1, para. 131(1)). If the CAC is satisfied, a ballot of the workers in the bargaining unit will conducted.

Part VI of Sch. A1 provides that workers will be able to apply to the CAC for derecognition of a union which does not have a certificate of independence and which has been voluntarily recognised by an employer. This is the only exception to the principle that, if the CAC did not declare recognition or prescribe collective bargaining procedures, the statutory derecognition procedure does not apply. An additional difference is that, in the case of applications to derecognise non-independent unions, there is no three-year time bar. The CAC must not proceed with an application unless it decides that at least 10% of the bargaining unit favour an end to collective bargaining arrangements and the majority of the bargaining unit are likely to do so.

(vii) Worker protection

Part VIII of Sch. A1 sets out provisions protecting workers from action short of dismissal on grounds relating to recognition or derecognition of the union. Under Sch. A1, para. 156(2), the grounds are that:

(a) the worker acted with a view to obtaining or preventing recognition of a union (or unions) by the employer under Sch. A1;

(b) the worker indicated that he supported or did not support recognition of a union (or unions) by the employer under Sch. A1;

(c) the worker acted with a view to securing or preventing the ending under Sch. A1 of bargaining arrangements;

(d) the worker indicated that he supported or did not support the ending under Sch. A1 of bargaining arrangements;

(e) the worker influenced or sought to influence the way in which votes were to be cast by other workers in a ballot arranged under Sch. A1;

(f) the worker influenced or sought to influence other workers to vote or to abstain from voting in such a ballot;

(g) the worker voted in such a ballot;

(h) the worker proposed to do, failed to do, or proposed to decline to do, any of the things referred to in paras (a) to (g).

Under para. 156(3), a ground does not fall within sub-para. (2) if it constitutes an unreasonable act or omission by the worker.

The normal time limit of three months for applications to ETs applies, and compensation is to be assessed in the same way as for other claims of detriment as found in s. 146 of the 1992 Act and Pt V of the 1996 Act.

Paragraph 161 of Sch. A1 provides that an employee's dismissal is unfair if the reason for dismissal relates to recognition or derecognition as listed. Paragraph 162 makes similar provision in respect of selection for redundancy.

Paragraph 164 provides that dismissal as a result of an employee acting or failing to act for or against recognition or derecognition of the union is unfair even if the employee has not completed the qualifying period for unfair dismissal or has passed the normal upper age limit for dismissal protection (see ss. 108–9 of the 1996 Act).

(viii) Training

Section 5 of the Employment Relations Act 1999 inserts new ss. 70B and 70C into Pt I of TULR(C)A 1992. If a union is recognised under procedures set out in Sch. A1 and the methods for the conduct of collective bargaining have been specified by the CAC, the employer must invite representatives of the union to consult on the employer's policy on training and to consult on the employer's plan for training in the next six months.

The duty applies only in respect of workers within the bargaining unit and the first meeting must be held within six months of the CAC imposing a method of collective bargaining, with periodic meetings every six months or earlier thereafter. The employers are obliged to give the union information which is in line with good industrial relations practice to provide and which would impede the union in participating in a meeting if it did not have. The information must be provided at least two weeks before the meeting, and thereafter the union has four weeks in which to make written representations on training matters discussed at the meeting of which the employer must take account.

New s. 70C allows the union to complain to an ET that the employer has failed to fulfil its s. 70B obligations. This could, for example, consist of a failure to convene meetings or to provide sufficient information to the union prior to a meeting. If the tribunal upholds the complaint, which must be made within three months of the failure, then it may award compensation to each member of the bargaining unit to a maximum of two weeks' pay.

(ix) The significance of recognition for statutory rights

A number of important statutory rights are conferred upon an 'independent' trade union if it has been recognised by the employer. These include:

(a) the right for its members and officials to take time off work (TULR(C)A 1992, ss. 168 and 170);

(b) the right to information from the employer for the purposes of collective bargaining (TULR(C)A 1992, s. 181);

(c) the right to consultation over impending redundancies (TULR(C)A 1992, s. 188);

(d) the right to information and consultation in connection with a transfer of an undertaking (Transfer of Undertakings (Protection of Employment) Regulations 1981 (SI 1981/1794));

(e) the right to information and consultation under the Health and Safety at Work etc. Act 1974 (Safety Representatives and Safety Committees Regulations 1977 (SI 1977/500); Management of Health and Safety at Work Regulations 1992 (SI 1992/2051));

(f) rights to information and consultation on occupational pension schemes (Pension Schemes Act 1993, s. 11(5); the Occupational Pension Schemes (Contracting-out) Regulations 1996 (SI 1996/1172); the Pension Schemes Act 1993, s. 113; the Occupational Pension Schemes (Disclosure of Information) Regulations 1996 (SI 1996/1655), as amended).

National Union of Gold, Silver Allied and Trades v *Albury Brothers Ltd*
[1978] IRLR 504, Court of Appeal

Eight of the company's 55 employees joined the union, and two days later the union's district secretary wrote to the company requesting a meeting to discuss rates of pay. A meeting was held at which the wages of one employee were discussed but no agreement was concluded. Soon after, four employees were dismissed on the grounds of redundancy without prior consultation with the union. The union alleged that the lack of consultation constituted a breach of what is now TULR(C)A 1992, s. 181.

LORD DENNING MR: A recognition issue is a most important matter for industry; and therefore an employer is not to be held to have recognised a trade union unless the evidence is clear. Sometimes there is an actual agreement of recognition. Sometimes there is an implied agreement of recognition. But at all events there must be something sufficiently clear and distinct by conduct or otherwise so that one can say, 'They have mutually recognised one another, the trade union and the employers, for the purposes of collective bargaining'.

Then one comes to this particular case. Were those few letters and the one meeting recognition of the trade union? It is agreed by Mr Sedley [counsel for the union] that if the employers had simply banged the door and told the union representative to go off, that would not be recognition. Is it recognition when [he] goes along with the letter in his hand and is ready to discuss wages? It seems to me that that is not sufficient. Nor is it sufficient if he starts discussing the wages of one particular man...There must be something a great deal more than that.

NOTE: See also *USDAW* v *Sketchley* [1981] IRLR 291, where the EAT re-emphasised that the statutory test for recognition required there to be an express or implicit acceptance of the union's role in negotiation over terms and conditions. An agreement to consult is not an agreement to negotiate and does not amount to recognition for the purposes of collective bargaining.

Compare *Joshua Wilson and Brothers Ltd* v *USDAW* [1978] IRLR 120, where although the employer had at no stage *expressly* agreed to recognise the union, the EAT was prepared to infer it from the facts that the employer allowed a shop steward to put up a notice publicising a pay increase agreed by the Joint Industrial Council whose agreements were observed by the employer; the shop steward had been allowed to collect union dues on the premises; and there had been some consultation over changed allocation of duties with the shop steward and with the union's area organiser over discipline and security.

■ QUESTION

Do you think that the *Joshua Wilson* case was correctly decided? Was there recognition *for the purpose of collective bargaining*?

B: Effects of provisions restricting the right to take industrial action

TRADE UNION AND LABOUR RELATIONS (CONSOLIDATION) ACT 1992

180. Effects of provisions restricting right to take industrial action

(1) Any terms of a collective agreement which prohibit or restrict the right of workers to engage in a strike or other industrial action, or have the effect of prohibiting or restricting that right, shall not form part of any contract between a worker and the person for whom he works unless the following conditions are met.

(2) The conditions are that the collective agreement—

    (a) is in writing,

    (b) contains a provision expressly stating that those terms shall or may be incorporated in such a contract,

    (c) is reasonably accessible at his place of work to the worker to whom it applies and is available for him to consult during working hours, and

    (d) is one where each trade union which is a party to the agreement is an independent trade union; and that the contract with the worker expressly or impliedly incorporates those terms in the contract.

(3) The above provisions have effect notwithstanding anything in section 179 and notwithstanding any provision to the contrary in any agreement (including a collective agreement or a contract with any worker).

C: Disclosure of information for the purposes of collective bargaining

TRADE UNION AND LABOUR RELATIONS (CONSOLIDATION) ACT 1992

181. General duty of employers to disclose information

(1) An employer who recognises an independent trade union shall, for the purposes of all stages of collective bargaining about matters, and in relation to descriptions of workers, in respect of which the union is recognised by him, disclose to representatives of the union, on request, the information required by this section.

In this section and sections 182 to 185 'representative', in relation to a trade union, means an official or other person authorised by the union to carry on such collective bargaining.

(2) The information to be disclosed is all information relating to the employer's undertaking which is in his possession, or that of an associated employer, and is information—

    (a) without which the trade union representatives would be to a material extent impeded in carrying on collective bargaining with him, and

    (b) which it would be in accordance with good industrial relations practice that he should disclose to them for the purposes of collective bargaining.

(3) A request by trade union representatives for information under this section shall, if the employer so requests, be in writing or be confirmed in writing.

(4) In determining what would be in accordance with good industrial relations practice, regard shall be had to the relevant provisions of any Code of Practice issued by ACAS, but not so as to exclude any other evidence of what that practice is.

(5) Information which an employer is required by virtue of this section to disclose to trade union representatives shall, if they so request, be disclosed or confirmed in writing.

182. Restrictions on general duty

(1) An employer is not required by section 181 to disclose information—

    (a) the disclosure of which would be against the interests of national security, or

    (b) which he could not disclose without contravening a prohibition imposed by or under an enactment, or

(c) which has been communicated to him in confidence, or which he has otherwise obtained in consequence of the confidence reposed in him by another person, or

(d) which relates specifically to an individual (unless that individual has consented to its being disclosed), or

(e) the disclosure of which would cause substantial injury to his undertaking for reasons other than its effect on collective bargaining, or

(f) obtained by him for the purpose of bringing, prosecuting or defending any legal proceedings.

In formulating the provisions of any Code of Practice relating to the disclosure of information, ACAS shall have regard to the provisions of this subsection.

(2) In the performance of his duty under section 181 an employer is not required—

(a) to produce, or allow inspection of, any document (other than a document prepared for the purpose of conveying or confirming the information) or to make a copy of or extracts from any document, or

(b) to compile or assemble any information where the compilation or assembly would involve an amount of work or expenditure out of reasonable proportion to the value of the information in the conduct of collective bargaining.

NOTES

1. This right is one of the few statutory props to collective bargaining to have survived the 1980s. But the right is limited in a number of ways. First, it becomes operative only where the union is 'recognised' by the employer and, secondly, it applies only in relation to those matters for which the union is recognised for collective bargaining. Consequently, a union that has achieved 'partial recognition' will not be able to claim information relating to matters outside the sphere of that partial recognition. So, in *R v CAC, ex p. BTP Tioxide Ltd* [1992] IRLR 60, the trade union had secured recognition to bargain in respect of certain terms and conditions but had no negotiating rights over the operation of a particular job evaluation scheme. As a result, the Divisional Court held that the CAC had exceeded its jurisdiction in requiring the employer to disclose to the union information relating to the scheme.

   The provision is unlikely to provide an impetus for the extension of union participation into areas of business decision-making traditionally outside the scope of collective bargaining, for example investment strategy. This is because disclosure can only be for the purposes of collective bargaining and that is restrictively defined by TULR(C)A 1992, s. 178.

2. ACAS has produced a Code of Practice, *Disclosure of Information to Trade Unions for Collective Bargaining Purposes* (ACAS Code No. 2, 1977; revised code brought into effect on 5 February 1998 by SI 1998/45), which seeks to provide guidance on the kind of information which should be disclosed. In addition, the Code recommends that:

   > Employers and trade unions should endeavour to arrive at a joint understanding on how the provisions on the disclosure of information can be implemented most effectively. They should consider what information is likely to be required, what is available, and what could readily be made available. Consideration should also be given to the form in which the information will be presented and to whom. In particular, the parties should endeavour to reach an understanding on what information could most appropriately be provided on a regular basis. [Para. 22]

3. If a trade union is of the view that the employer has failed to comply with the disclosure provisions, it may complain to the CAC. The CAC may refer the complaint to ACAS for conciliation. If there is no such referral or conciliation fails, the CAC may proceed to hear and determine the claim. Where the claim is upheld, the CAC will specify the information which should have been disclosed and set a deadline for its disclosure (TULR(C)A 1992, s. 183).

   If the employer fails to supply the information within the set timescale, the union may present a further complaint to the CAC and claim changes in those parts of the individual contract in respect of which the union is recognised. The right to present a claim expires if the employer discloses the required information before the CAC has made an award on the claim (TULR(C)A 1992, ss. 184–5).

   Bowers and Honeyball offer the following observations on the effectiveness of the disclosure provisions:

   > The policy appears to be that if the union does not have information to achieve meaningful collective bargaining, the CAC will arbitrate the bargaining for it. The employer may render the whole remedial process meaningless, however, if he complies with the statute even at the last minute. The stages may move like a tortoise and the remedy will be effective only long

after collective bargaining for the year has been completed. The CAC itself has commented that this remedy, 'is unlikely to be attractive to either party except in very special cases'. This partly explains why less use has been made of the provisions thus far than was originally anticipated. Another explanation suggests that many employers are volunteering to provide the necessary information. [Bowers, J. and Honeyball, S., *Textbook on Labour Law*, 5th edn (London: Blackstone Press, 1998), p. 381]

4. Given the widespread dismantlement of the statutory props to collective bargaining since 1979, why have the disclosure provisions been retained? Anderman offers the following rationalisation:

> One reason why the legislation was retained since 1979 is that it is not simply an advantage for trade unions in the bargaining process. It is also useful to prompt employers to present information in such a way as to produce more realistic demands by trade unions by convincing them to take into greater account the economic problems of the firm.

Indeed, the Act specifically provides that employers do not have to provide original documents, or even copies of original documents, but are entitled to prepare information in a special form to be disclosed to trade unions. This entitlement is a virtual invitation to the sophisticated presentation. [Anderman, S. D., *Labour Law: Management decisions and workers' rights*, 3rd edn (London: Butterworths, 1998), at p. 321]

5. As we have seen, between 1980 and the introduction of the statutory recognition procedure by the Employment Relations Act 1999, UK law did not attempt to force an employer to recognise and bargain with a trade union. It does impose a general duty on the employer to *provide information* to a recognised trade union for the purposes of collective bargaining (see previous extract). Moreover, in certain specified situations the law goes further and requires the employer to *consult* with a recognised trade union or other employee representatives, i.e. redundancy, transfer of undertakings, health and safety, and some pension schemes. But UK law offers no *general* right to consultation on matters of strategic importance to the future of the undertaking. As Anderman observes:

> The characteristic feature of the rights of employee representatives in relation to redundancies is that even when they amount to influence over the employer's decision, their focus is upon the effects of specific investment decisions by employers. They offer little guarantee that such consultations can take place in the context of the ongoing investment decisions taken at higher levels of management. [*Labour Law: Management decisions and workers' rights*, 3rd edn (London: Butterworths, 1998), at p. 330]

Since the 1970s, there have been several EU social policy initiatives which have aimed to provide employee representatives with information and consultation rights in respect of the wider strategic decisions of management. All failed to attract the requisite unanimous support in the Council of Ministers as a result of vetoes by the then Conservative Government. However, in September 1994, the other Member States, utilising the Maastricht protocol, adopted the European Works Council Directive (94/45/EC). It became operative two years later, on 22 September 1996. The Commission felt that the legislation was necessary in order to bridge the gap between increasingly transnational corporate decision making and domestic information and consultation rights.

The directive initially covered all EC Member States (with the exception of the UK) plus Norway, Iceland and Liechtenstein. Even though technically the directive did not apply to the UK:

> [I]n practice, right from the start, it affected hundreds of UK companies and thousands of UK employees. UK multinationals which operated in two or more of the other seventeen countries were obliged to observe the directive in respect of their overseas employees at least; and most of those multinationals which were caught by the directive (whether based in the UK or not), being obliged to establish transnational consultative machinery for their overseas employees, decided that it was convenient to incorporate their UK employees in that process too. [*Harvey on Industrial Relations and Employment Law*, vol. 2, N/932, para. 1253.01]

With the election of the new Labour Government in 1997, the UK agreed to sign up to the directive. As a result, the directive was re-adopted by the unanimous agreement of Member States under Article 94 (ex 100) on 15 December 1997. The UK had to give effect to the directive by December 1999.

The directive requires large enterprises operating in the European Economic Area to inform and consult workers either by establishing a European Works Council, or by another appropriate procedure. All organisations with more than 1,000 employees in the participating States and at least 150 workers in each of two or more of these countries are covered by the directive. A copy of the DTI's guidance note on the directive and the UK's regulations which seek to implement it follows:

Guidance Note
(Employment Rights Directorate, DTI, December 1999)

TRANSNATIONAL INFORMATION AND CONSULTATION OF EMPLOYEES REGULATIONS 1999 IMPLEMENT THE EUROPEAN WORKS COUNCIL DIRECTIVE IN THE UK

Background

1. The European Works Councils (EWC) Directive sets out requirements for informing and consulting employees at the European level, in undertakings (which may include partnerships or other forms of organisation as well as companies) or groups with at least 1,000 employees across the Member States and at least 150 employees in each of two or more of those Member States. It was adopted by the other EU Member States on 22 September 1994, under Article 2(2) of the Agreement on Social Policy (the 'Social Chapter') and was later extended to cover the rest of the European Economic Area (Norway, Liechtenstein and Iceland). The deadline for national implementation in these Member States was 22 September 1996. The original Directive was extended to cover the UK by Directive 97/74/EC in December 1997. Implementation of the second Directive will mean that employees in the UK must be included in present and future EWC agreements. In many cases UK employees in both UK-based and non-UK undertakings had already been voluntarily included in EWC arrangements concluded by undertakings subject to the original Directive.

The UK Regulations

2. The Directive is implemented in the UK by the Transnational Information and Consultation of Employees Regulations 1999 which were laid before Parliament on 14 December 1999 and came into force on 15 January 2000. They set out the procedures for negotiating a European Works Council agreement (or other European-level information and consultation procedure), the enforcement mechanisms, provisions on confidential information, transitional provisions and exemptions, and statutory protections for employees.

3. An EWC agreement will normally result from negotiations between management and the employees. The process is triggered either on management's own initiative or after a written request from at least 100 employees or their representatives in two or more Member States (no obligation exists if no request is received). The employees are to be represented in the negotiations by a 'special negotiating body' (SNB) which consists of representatives of employees from all the EEA Member States in which the undertaking has operations. The number of representatives for each Member State is determined by a formula in the legislation in the State where the undertaking's central management is located (or representative agent where the central management is outside the EEA). The UK Regulations prescribe one representative from each of the EEA countries in which the undertaking operates plus additional ones where 25% or more, 50% or more and 75% or more of the European workforce is located in a Member State, up to a total maximum of four. The way in which the SNB members are selected is determined by the legislation of the Member State where they are employed. UK members are to be selected by a ballot of the UK workforce unless there exists a consultative committee whose members were elected by a ballot of all the UK employees and which performs an information and consultation function on their behalf. Where such a consultative committee does exist, it may appoint from within its members the UK representatives on the SNB.

4. The Regulations are largely concerned with the initial establishment of the SNB: the subsequent negotiations and the details of the EWC agreements are for the most part left for agreement between the parties concerned.

5. If management refuses to negotiate within 6 months of receiving a request for an EWC, or if the parties fail to conclude an agreement on transnational information and consultation procedures within 3 years, an EWC must be set up in accordance with the 'statutory model' set out in the Schedule to the Regulations. This sets out requirements concerning the size, establishment and operation of a European Works Council. In particular, the Schedule lists topics on which the European Works Council has the right to be informed and consulted (e.g. the economic and financial situation of the business; its likely development; probable employment trends; the introduction of new working methods; and substantial organisational changes).

6. Enforcement will be through the CAC and EAT in Great Britain and the Industrial Court in Northern Ireland (the Regulations apply on a UK-wide basis). In general, the CAC will hear disputes as to whether an undertaking is subject to the Directive and about the procedures leading to the establishment of an EWC. The EAT will hear disputes about the operation of an EWC or its non-establishment. The EAT will also hear appeals on points of law from the CAC and will be able to impose civil financial penalties up to £75,000 where management acts in breach of its main obligations. Both the CAC and EAT may refer cases to ACAS if conciliation is considered useful.

7. The Regulations provide that management may withhold information, or require the EWC to hold it in confidence, where 'according to objective criteria it would seriously harm the functioning of the undertaking or be prejudicial to it' if it were revealed. EWC members can appeal to the CAC if they believe the management is withholding information or imposing confidentiality beyond what is permitted in the Regulations, and the CAC would then make a ruling on a case by case basis.

8. The employees and SNB/EWC members will be given statutory protections when asserting their rights or performing duties under the Regulations. Employment Tribunals will hear any claims relating to victimisation or unfair dismissal.

9. The Regulations do not apply to undertakings which have already concluded voluntary agreements providing for the transnational information and consultation of the employees, and which cover the entire workforce in the EEA. Such agreements have to have been concluded by 22 September 1996 or 15 December 1999, depending on whether the undertaking was subject to the original Directive or not. Undertakings which consider they have a valid voluntary agreement but which receive a request to establish an EWC, may apply to the CAC for a declaration that the Regulations do not apply to them. The Regulations also contain exceptions in respect of certain merchant navy crew members.

10. The Regulations contain transitional provisions in respect of those UK based undertakings which have started negotiations under the law of another Member State before the entry into force of the UK Regulations. In such cases the negotiations will become subject to the UK Regulations but will continue on the same timetable. UK representatives will have to be elected if the UK employees are under-represented on the SNB compared with the formula for the allocation of seats. Where a UK-based undertaking has concluded an EWC agreement in another Member State before the entry into force of the UK Regulations, it may be made subject to the UK Regulations with the consent of the parties to the agreement.

NOTES

1. Directive 2002/14/EC established a general framework for informing and consulting employees in the EC. Adopted in February 2002, the directive requires Member States to introduce new legislation requiring all undertakings with at least 50 employees to inform and consult employee representatives on a range of key business, employment and restructuring issues, e.g. the business's economic situation, employment prospects, decisions likely to lead to substantial changes in work organisation or contractual relations, including redundancies and transfers. The UK had three years to commence the implementation of the directive (i.e. with effect from April 2005). In the first instance, it applies to businesses with 150 or more employees (6 April 2005). In April 2007, it applied to businesses with 100 or more employees and after a further one year (i.e. April 2008) to ones with 50 or more employees. Businesses with 50 or more employees account for about 1% of all businesses in the UK, and about 75% of UK employees.

   Information and consultation has to take place at an appropriate time and at the relevant level of management. Normally it will be done via employee representatives, defined according to national law and practice. The representatives, having received the appropriate information, may meet the employer, present their opinion and receive a reasoned response.

   Employers and employees may agree procedures which are different to those set out in the directive, and may meet their obligations by means of existing agreements on information and consultation (see *Stewart* v *Moray Council* [2006] IRLR 168, EAT). Member States are left to determine the practical arrangements for the exercise of the right, and the enforcement measures.

   Employers may withhold information the disclosure of which would seriously harm the company or be prejudicial to it, or they may require that it be kept confidential by the employee representatives to whom it is disclosed.

2. The directive was transposed into UK law by the Information and Consultation of Employees Regulations 2004 (SI 2004/3426). The consultation arrangements are triggered by 10% of the workforce in the undertaking submitting a written 'employee request' for an information and consultation system (reg. 7(1),(2)). The request will normally be made to the employer but can also be addressed to the CAC if confidentiality is an issue (reg. 7(4)–(6)). If a valid 'employee request' is made, there are three possible outcomes under the regulations:
   - the employer must proceed to negotiate an information and consultation system;
   - the employer may resist having to do so on the basis of pre-existing agreements;
   - neither of the above applies and the employer becomes bound by the 'standard information and consultation provisions' as laid down in the regulations.

   Where there is no satisfactory pre-existing agreement and the employer fails to meet its obligations under the regulations, the penalties are relatively harsh. In *Amicus* v *Macmillan Publishers Ltd* [2007] IRLR 885, the EAT held that a failure to hold a ballot of employees to elect information and consultation representatives was worthy of a fine of £55,000.

D: Time off for trade union duties and activities

TRADE UNION AND LABOUR RELATIONS (CONSOLIDATION) ACT 1992

168. Time off for carrying out trade union duties

(1) An employer shall permit an employee of his who is an official of an independent trade union recognised by the employer to take time off during his working hours for the purpose of carrying out any duties of his, as such an official, concerned with—

(a) negotiations with the employer related to or connected with matters falling within section 178(2) (collective bargaining) in relation to which the trade union is recognised by the employer, or

(b) the performance on behalf of employees of the employer of functions related to or connected with matters falling within that provision which the employer has agreed may be so performed by the trade union.

(2) He shall also permit such an employee to take time off during his working hours for the purpose of undergoing training in aspects of industrial relations—

(a) relevant to the carrying out of such duties as are mentioned in subsection (1), and

(b) approved by the Trades Union Congress or by the independent trade union of which he is an official.

(3) The amount of time off which an employee is to be permitted to take under this section and the purposes for which, the occasions on which and any conditions subject to which time off may be so taken are those that are reasonable in all the circumstances having regard to any relevant provisions of a Code of Practice issued by ACAS.

(4) An employee may present a complaint to an industrial tribunal that his employer has failed to permit him to take time off as required by this section.

170. Time off for trade union activities

(1) An employer shall permit an employee of his who is a member of an independent trade union recognised by the employer in respect of that description of employee to take time off during his working hours for the purpose of taking part in—

(a) any activities of the union, and

(b) any activities in relation to which the employee is acting as a representative of the union.

(2) The right conferred by subsection (1) does not extend to activities which themselves consist of industrial action, whether or not in contemplation or furtherance of a trade dispute.

(3) The amount of time off which an employee is to be permitted to take under this section and the purposes for which, the occasions on which and any conditions subject to which time off may be so taken are those that are reasonable in all the circumstances having regard to any relevant provisions of a Code of Practice issued by ACAS.

(4) An employee may present a complaint to an industrial tribunal that his employer has failed to permit him to take time off as required by this section.

NOTES

1. First introduced during the 1970s as part of a general policy to encourage and extend collective bargaining, the rights to paid time off for trade union duties and training and unpaid time off for union members to participate in union activities, were significantly restricted by the Conservative Government through amendments introduced by the EA 1989. In particular, it restricted the range of issues for which paid time off for trade union duties can be claimed to those covered by recognition agreements between employers and trade unions. Under the old definition, officials could seek time off for any of their duties concerned with industrial relations in general. Additionally, union duties must relate to the official's own employer and cannot extend, as was previously the case, to negotiations with an associated employer.

   Paid time off for training is now similarly limited to duties relating to matters in respect of which the union is recognised by the employer.

   The statutory provisions are supplemented by the ACAS Code of Practice, *Time Off For Trade Union Duties and Activities*, which has been twice revised—in 1991 and 1998—in order to reflect the amendments to the statutory provisions.

   There is no minimum period of continuous employment required in order to qualify for these rights. However, in order to claim, and in common with most other employment protection rights, the employee currently must work 16 hours or more per week, or have worked for five years on a normal working week of at least eight hours.

2. There is also a right under the Health and Safety at Work etc. Act 1974 for safety representatives to claim paid time off in order to fulfil their functions and a right to unpaid leave from certain kinds of public duties (the ERA 1996, s. 50).

ACAS Code of Practice No. 3, *Time Off For Trade Union Duties and Activities*
(as revised and brought into effect on 1 January 2010)

12. Subject to the recognition or other agreement, trade union representatives should be allowed to take reasonable time off for duties concerned with negotiations or, where their employer has agreed, for duties concerned with other functions related to or connected with the subject of collective bargaining.

13. The subjects connected with collective bargaining may include one or more of the following:

(a) **terms and conditions of employment, or the physical conditions in which workers are required to work. Examples could include:**
- pay
- hours of work
- holidays and holiday pay
- sick pay arrangements
- pensions
- learning and training
- equality and diversity
- notice periods
- the working environment
- operation of digital equipment and other machinery;

(b) **engagement or non-engagement, or termination or suspension of employment or the duties of employment, of one or more workers. Examples could include:**
- recruitment and selection policies
- human resource planning
- redundancy and dismissal arrangements;

(c) **allocation of work or the duties of employment as between workers or groups of workers.** Examples could include:
- job grading
- job evaluation
- job descriptions
- flexible working practices
- work-life balance;

(d) **matters of discipline**. Examples could include:
- disciplinary procedures
- arrangements for representing or accompanying employees at internal interviews
- arrangements for appearing on behalf of trade union members, or as witnesses, before agreed outside appeal bodies or employment tribunals;

(e) **trade union membership or non-membership**. Examples could include:
- representational arrangements
- any union involvement in the induction of new workers;

(f) **facilities for trade union representatives**. Examples could include any agreed arrangements for the provision of:
- accommodation
- equipment
- names of new workers to the union;

(g) **machinery for negotiation or consultation and other procedures**. Examples could include arrangements for:
- collective bargaining at the employer and/or multi-employer level
- grievance procedures
- joint consultation
- communicating with members
- communicating with other trade union representatives and union full-time officers also concerned with collective bargaining with the employer.

14. The duties of all representatives of a recognised trade union must be connected with or related to negotiations or the performance of functions both in time and subject matter. Reasonable time off may be sought, for example, to:
- prepare for negotiations, including attending relevant meetings
- inform members of progress and outcomes

- prepare for meetings with the employer about matters for which the trade union has only representational rights.

What are examples of trade union activities?

37. The activities of a trade union member can be, for example:

- attending workplace meetings to discuss and vote on the outcome of negotiations with the employer. Where relevant, and with the employer's agreement, this can include attending such workplace meetings at the employer's neighbouring locations.
- meeting full-time officers to discuss issues relevant to the workplace
- voting in union elections
- having access to services provided by a Union Learning representative.

38. Where the member is acting as a representative of a recognised union activities can be, for example, taking part in:

- branch, area or regional meetings of the union where the business of the union is under discussion
- meetings of official policy making bodies such as the executive committee or annual conference
- meetings with full-time officers to discuss issues relevant to the workplace.

39. There is no right to time off for trade union activities which themselves consist of industrial action.

NOTES

1. The Code (para. 14 in the extract) suggests that time off may be sought for preparation for negotiations and informing members as to their progress and outcome. This would accord with the approach of the Court of Appeal in interpreting the scope of the unamended provision (see *Adlington* v *British Bakeries (Northern) Limited* [1989] IRLR 218, CA).
2. In *Luce* v *London Borough of Bexley* [1990] IRLR 422, the EAT held that whether the trade union activity concerned fell within the scope of the provision was a matter of fact and degree:

   > Although we do not consider that the phrase should be understood too restrictively, we are satisfied that it cannot have been the intention of Parliament to have included any activity of whatever nature.
   >   The whole context of the phrase is within the ambit of the employment relationship between that employee and that employer and that trade union. ... Thus it seems to us in a broad sense the activity should be one which is linked to that employment relationship, i.e. between that employer, that employee and that trade union.

   The EAT went on to hold that an industrial tribunal had been entitled to find that teachers were not entitled to time off to lobby Parliament against the Education Reform Bill.
3. For a critical analysis of the revised Code, see Wynn, M. and Pitt, G., 'The Revised ACAS Code of Practice on time off for trade union duties and activities: another missed opportunity' (2010) 39 ILJ 209.

Hairsine v *Kingston-upon-Hull City Council*

[1992] IRLR 211, Employment Appeal Tribunal

Mr Hairsine was a shop steward. In April 1989, he was given permission by his employers to attend a union training course taking place on 12 consecutive Thursdays, beginning on 13 April. He was given day release with pay for attendance at all sessions of the course when he would normally be at work.

Mr Hairsine worked a 39-hour week on a shift basis. On 13 April he was rostered to work the shift between 3.00 p.m. and 11.00 p.m. On that day, he attended the first session of his union course between 9.00 a.m. and 4.00 p.m. He attended work at 4.40 p.m. and stayed until 7.00 p.m. He then went home. The employers contended that he was not entitled to be paid for the entire shift because he had not worked between 7.00 p.m. and 11.00 p.m.

Mr Hairsine argued that, under what is now TULR(C)A 1992, s. 168, he was entitled to be paid for the hours during which he attended the course, whether or not he attended for work in the evening. An industrial tribunal dismissed his claim.

On appeal to the EAT, Mr Hairsine submitted that hours allowed as time off under s. 168 are in substitution for the equivalent number of hours which the employee was contractually liable to work on that day, i.e. they are in lieu of working hours. Therefore, as his course had lasted for the equivalent of an eight-hour shift, he was entitled to be paid for those hours. His attendance at work in the evening was purely voluntary. The EAT dismissed his appeal.

WOOD J (President): 'Time off' is effectively defined within s. 27(1) [now TULR(C)A 1992, s. 168(1)] as time 'during the employee's working hours for the purpose of enabling him…' to attend the course. Two conditions must be satisfied therefore. The first is that it must be part of his 'working hours', and secondly, that it must be permitted by the employer for the purpose of 'enabling him to attend' the course. If it fails either condition it is not 'time off' for which an employee is entitled to be paid. We emphasise again that the reasonableness of the terms of the permission are a matter for the Industrial Tribunal if there is any dispute.

This view of the true meaning of 'time off' in s. 27(1) is in our judgment supported by the wording of s. 32(1) [now TULR(C)A 1992, s. 173(1)]. If 'working hours' were intended only to be those hours which he was contracted to work during any given day, then the phrasing of s. 32(1) could have been quite different. The phrase is that time when 'he is required to be *at work*'. It seems to us clear therefore that 'time off' means 'those hours when he would normally have been *at work* and which it was reasonable that he should be allowed to take off in order *to enable him* to attend a course (trade union activities)'.

Looked at in this way the present practice as it is understood by the industrial members to have existed for many years can be allowed to continue.

Let us apply that to some of the examples given already. In each of the examples given arrangements would be sought to be made by agreement that the trade union activity should take place outside those hours during which the employee should be at work. It may be possible to change the working hours so as to minimise interruption with production or service. It may also be possible to change the shifts. However, it may also be necessary, for instance in the case of night duty, to grant 'time off' for the whole of a nightshift in order that the employee should be allowed some sleep, that is if he were on permanent duty and not merely on shifts. It might also be reasonable to allow some 'time off', perhaps one or two hours, from the end of a day's work if there was a substantial distance to travel. All these are matters for negotiation and for a reasonable approach from both sides. In the event of disagreement on what is reasonable to be permitted, the decision is one for the Industrial Tribunal. If an employee shop steward is going to need 'time off' to enable him to attend, then of course he must be paid for that time off.

Turning to the facts of the present case, it seems to us that it was made abundantly clear in the practice operated by the respondents under their policy on the provision of time off for trade union duties and activities that the applicant, Mr Hairsine, was going to be required to attend the evening shift after he had attended his course. There might possibly have been an argument that he should be allowed to arrive late for the evening shift as travel might have been difficult and he had clearly made special arrangements, but that is a minor detail. The case presented to the Tribunal was not an allegation that the terms of the permission were unreasonable, although Ms Smith takes the view that it should have been so presented, nor was that the way in which it was presented to us. The case presented to us is that all hours of a trade union course for which permission has been given are substituted for an equivalent number of hours for which the employee would have been at work and therefore not only is the employee automatically entitled to take the equivalent hours out of his work time but he is entitled to be paid for so doing. It seems to us in the present case that the Tribunal were entirely correct in reaching the conclusion that the hours between 7 p.m. and 11 p.m. on his evening shift were not hours for which permission had been granted for 'time off' in order to 'enable him' to attend the morning course. Those hours were not 'time off' within the meaning of the statute and were not therefore hours for which he was entitled to be paid.

As we have already emphasised, one of our members is of the view that the terms of the permission granted were not reasonable. The majority, however, point out that this was not the issue raised before the Industrial Tribunal, nor indeed before this Court. The tone of the decision of the Industrial Tribunal does not indicate that it would have viewed the permission granted in this way, and indeed if it had thought that the issue should have been argued, there was nothing to prevent the Tribunal amending the application and allowing the issue of reasonableness to be raised. That issue would essentially be one for the Tribunal to decide.

We are therefore unable to discern any error of law in the decision of this Industrial Tribunal and this appeal must be dismissed. Leave to appeal.

■ QUESTION

Do you think it was 'reasonable' of the employers to have expected Mr Hairsine to attend any part of his evening shift after attending the training course between 9.00 a.m. to 4.00 p.m.?

ACAS Code of Practice No. 2, *Time Off For Trade Union Duties and Activities*
(1977) (as revised)

25. **The amount and frequency of time off should be reasonable in all the circumstances**. Although the statutory provisions apply to all employers without exception as to size and type of business or service, trade unions should be aware of the wide variety of difficulties and operational requirements to be taken into account when seeking or agreeing arrangements for time off, for example:
   - the size of the organisation and the number of workers
   - the production process
   - the need to maintain a service to the public
   - the need for safety and security at all times.

26. Employers in turn should have in mind the difficulties for trade union officials and members in ensuring representation and communications with, for example:
   - shift workers
   - part-time workers
   - those employed at dispersed locations
   - workers with particular domestic commitments.

27. For time off arrangements to work satisfactorily trade unions should:
   - ensure that officials are aware of their role, responsibilities and functions
   - inform management, in writing, as soon as possible of appointments or resignations of officials
   - ensure that officials receive any appropriate written credentials promptly.

28. Employers should consider making available to officials the facilities necessary for them to perform their duties efficiently and communicate effectively with their members, fellow lay officials and full-time officers. Where resources permit the facilities could include:
   - accommodation for meetings
   - access to a telephone and other office equipment
   - the use of notice boards
   - where the volume of the official's work justifies it, the use of dedicated office space.

NOTES

1. In *Wignall* v *British Gas Corporation* [1984] IRLR 493, a NALGO official employed as a meter reader for British Gas had already been granted 12 weeks' leave for union business when he requested a further ten days' leave in order to edit a union magazine. The EAT upheld the industrial tribunal's decision that it was reasonable for the employers to refuse the further request.

2. In *Ryford Ltd* v *Drinkwater* [1996] IRLR 16, the EAT held that before an employee can establish a right to compensation under s. 168(4) on the ground that his employer 'has failed to permit him to take time off', he must establish, on the balance of probabilities, that the request for time off was made, that it came to the notice of the employer's appropriate representative, and that they either refused it, ignored it, or failed to respond to it. Section 168 plainly requires that the employer should know of the request before he can 'fail to permit' time off. The concept of permission must import knowledge of a request for permission.

3. An employee who claims that his or her employer has either failed to permit time off or has failed to pay the whole or part of any amount due under the statutory provisions may complain to an ET. Where a tribunal upholds a complaint that time off has been *refused* by the employer, it must make a declaration to that effect and may make an award of compensation which it 'considers just and equitable in all the circumstances having regard to the employer's default . . . and to any loss sustained by the employee' (TULR(C)A 1992, s. 172(2)). If the complaint is of the failure to pay the employee in whole or in part for time off which has been permitted under the Act, the tribunal must order the employer to pay the amount which it finds to be due.

SECTION 4: TRADE UNIONS AND THEIR MEMBERS

The past three decades or so have witnessed an increasing tendency to subject internal union affairs to legal regulation. Although the Donovan Commission (1968), para. 622 found 'it unlikely that abuse of power by trade unions is widespread', it still recommended that the Chief Registrar of Trade Unions be given a supervisory role over the content of union rules and that an independent review body should be created to deal with arbitrary exclusion and expulsions. Section 65 of the Industrial Relations Act 1971 laid down a number of 'guiding principles' for trade union rules which forbid, *inter alia*, arbitrary or unreasonable exclusions from membership and unfair or unreasonable disciplinary action. In the 1980s, we witnessed considerable statutory intervention in this field. Moreover, judicial intervention via the common law has also played a major role in the trend towards intervention in internal union affairs.

A: The residual importance of the common law

Statutory protection for individuals has increased markedly since 1980, with the enactment of the right not to be unreasonably excluded or expelled from union membership where there is a closed shop in operation (the EA 1980, s. 4) and the right not to be disciplined for certain listed reasons (the EA 1988, s. 3). TURERA 1993 introduced yet more restrictions on trade union freedoms within this sphere by enlarging the scope of unjustifiable discipline and enacting a general right not to be excluded and expelled from a trade union unless for a statutory 'permitted reason'. Nevertheless, an examination of the common law on admission, discipline and expulsion is relevant, 'first, because common law actions may still have a considerable impact (as was seen particularly in the miners' strike of 1984–85) and secondly, because the statutory provisions for the most part build upon the common law foundation rather than replacing it' (Smith, I. T. and Thomas, G. H., *Smith and Woods' Industrial Law*, 8th edn (London: Butterworths, 2003), p. 700). Additionally, an analysis of the common law provides context and meaning to the form which has been adopted for statutory intervention.

(i) The union rule book and the courts
The starting point for judicial involvement has traditionally been the contract of membership. The professed function of the law in this area is to strike a balance between the conflicting notions of union autonomy on the one hand and the rights of the individual member on the other.

In readily intervening to protect the individual, it may be that—as with strike law—the courts have shown little understanding of the needs for collective solidarity within trade unions.

(ii) Admission to a union at common law

Faramus v Film Artistes Association
[1964] 1 All ER 25, House of Lords

Rule 4(2) of the defendant association provided that 'No person who has been convicted in a court of law of a criminal offence (other than a motoring offence not punishable by imprisonment) shall be eligible for, or retain membership of the association.' When he signed the application forms for membership, the appellant denied that he had been convicted of any offence, though he had twice been convicted of minor offences in Jersey several years earlier. After he had been in the union for eight years, his previous convictions were discovered and the union claimed that he was not, and had never been, a member. He sought a declaration that he was a member and an injunction restraining the union from excluding him from membership.

LORD EVERSHED: Like the majority of the Court of Appeal, I am unable to see any ground on which it could be seriously submitted that the rule could be disregarded by the court because of the vagueness of its terms or because its application in certain circumstances might not only be difficult of ascertainment but productive of embarrassment in the conduct of the respondent union's business. Nor can it, as I think, be suggested that to a rule of this kind there can be applied any principle of natural justice. The case is in no sense analogous to the case of rules applicable to someone whose contract of membership is being terminated, where it may well be that for their validity the rules must make provision to enable such a person at any rate to have a proper opportunity to put his case. In the circumstances, therefore, the only ground on which the applicant can, as I think, succeed is if he were able to establish that the terms of this rule operated as unreasonable restraint of trade and that the rule was not saved by s. 3 of the Trade Union Act 1871 ...

I ... accept unequivocally the view taken by the majority of the Court of Appeal, and say that if the contract constituted by the rules in this case be or contain (at any rate so far as this sub-rule is concerned) an unreasonable restraint of trade, none the less the rules (and sub-r. (2) of r. 4 in particular) are validated by the section. I add only that it is unreal and impossible, as I think, to sever this particular sub-rule from the rules as a whole and to treat it therefore as something quite distinct not only from the other rules but also from the purposes of the union to which, of course, it is essentially addressed ...

NOTE: The absence of a contractual relationship between the union and the applicant for membership has made it difficult for the courts to find a theoretical basis for review in exclusion cases. The concept of the 'right to work', however, has provided the most radical alternative means of attack for the judges. This was a development carried out almost single-handedly by Lord Denning. Although first discussed in 1952 (*Lee* v *Showmen's Guild* [1952] 2 QB 329, CA), it was used for the first time in the next case.

Nagle v *Feilden*
[1966] 2 QB 633, Court of Appeal

The stewards of the Jockey Club refused Mrs Nagle a licence to train racehorses in pursuance of their unwritten policy of refusing a licence to a woman. Mrs Nagle sued for an injunction and a declaration that the practice was against public policy, but her statement of claim was struck out as disclosing no cause of action. She appealed against this decision. The Court of Appeal granted an interlocutory injunction on the basis that she had an arguable case.

LORD DENNING: The common law of England has for centuries recognised that a man has a right to work at his trade or profession without being unjustly excluded from it. He is not to be shut out from it at the whim of those having the governance of it. If they make a rule which enables them to reject his application arbitrarily or capriciously, not reasonably, that rule is bad. It is against public policy. The court will not give effect to it.

NOTE: The interlocutory injunction enabled the parties to reach a settlement. Hence the case did not come to court for final judgment. The next case constituted the most radical application of the 'right to work' doctrine.

Edwards v *SOGAT*
[1971] Ch 354, Court of Appeal

(The facts of this case are set out at p. 564 (Section 1.D).)

LORD DENNING MR: I do not think the defendant union, or any other trade union, can give itself by its rules an unfettered discretion to expel a man or to withdraw his membership. The reason lies in the man's right to work. This is now fully recognised by law. It is a right which is of especial importance when a trade union operates a 'closed shop' or '100 per cent membership', for that means that no man can become employed or remain in employment with a firm unless he is a member of the union. If his union card is withdrawn, he has to leave the employment. He is deprived of his livelihood. The courts of this country will not allow so great a power to be exercised arbitrarily or capriciously or with unfair discrimination, neither in the making of rules, nor in the enforcement of them.

NOTE: Prima facie the *Nagle* v *Feilden* doctrine would seem equally applicable to those unions operating a closed shop. However, there is a fundamental difficulty. It is not clear that the concept of the 'right to work' is anything more than the doctrine of restraint of trade reinterpreted from the standpoint of the individual. Whenever a union by its rules or policies arbitrarily or unreasonably restrains trade, it necessarily arbitrarily or unreasonably interferes with the right to work. This point is addressed in neither *Nagle* nor *Edwards*.

(iii) Discipline and expulsion at common law

Lee v *Showmen's Guild of Great Britain*
[1952] 2 QB 329, Court of Appeal

The plaintiff was charged with 'unfair competition' under a union rule. An area committee of the union fined him for breaking the rule. Failure to pay the fine was, under the rules, to result in expulsion. The plaintiff did not pay the fine and was expelled. He sought an injunction to prevent the union from enforcing his expulsion. The Court of Appeal granted the injunction.

DENNING LJ: Although the jurisdiction of a domestic tribunal is founded on contract, express or implied, nevertheless the parties are not free to make any contract they like. There are important limitations imposed by public policy. The tribunal must, for instance, observe the principles of natural justice. They must give the man notice of the charge and a reasonable opportunity of meeting it. Any stipulation to the contrary would be invalid. They cannot stipulate for a power to condemn a man unheard...

Another limitation arises out of the well-known principle that parties cannot by contract oust the ordinary courts of their jurisdiction: see *Scott* v *Avery* (1865) 5 HL Cas 845 at 846 per Alderson B and Cranworth LC. They can, of course, agree to leave questions of law, as well as questions of fact, to the decision of the domestic tribunal. They can, indeed, make the tribunal the final arbiter on questions of fact, but they cannot make it the final arbiter on questions of law. They cannot prevent its decisions being examined by the courts. If parties should seek, by agreement, to take the law out of the hands of the courts and into the hands of a private tribunal, without any recourse at all to the courts in case of error of law, then the agreement is to that extent contrary to public policy and void...

...[T]he question whether the committee has acted within its jurisdiction depends, in my opinion, on whether the facts adduced before them were reasonably capable of being held to be a breach of the rules. If they were, then the proper inference is that the committee correctly construed the rules and have acted within their jurisdiction. If, however, the facts were not reasonably capable of being held to be a breach and yet the committee held them to be a breach, then the only inference is that the committee have misconstrued the rules and exceeded their jurisdiction.

Esterman v *NALGO*
[1974] ICR 625, Chancery Division

The trade union, NALGO, and the local authorities were involved in a pay dispute. NALGO held a ballot on the question of selective strike action but achieved only 49% of the vote in favour. Subsequently the union had instructed its members not to assist in administering local elections. Esterman defied this instruction and, in consequence, was to be disciplined by the union on the basis that she was guilty of conduct rendering her unfit for membership.

The relevant rule read:

> Any member who disregards any regulation issued by the branch, or is guilty of conduct which, in the opinion of the executive committee, renders him unfit for membership, shall be liable to expulsion.

Esterman sought and obtained an injunction against the union to restrain it from taking disciplinary action against her.

> TEMPLEMAN J: In my judgment, when the national executive council take the serious step of interfering with the right of a member to volunteer to take work of any description outside his normal employment, the national executive are only entitled to one hundred per cent and implicit obedience to that order if it is clear that they have been given power to issue the order and if it is clear that they are not abusing that power. If a member disobeys an order of the national executive council which does not satisfy those tests, then it seems to me that he cannot be found guilty on that account of conduct which renders him unfit to be a member of NALGO…
>
> On this application, I have listened to very long and very learned argument on the interesting question of whether, on the true construction of the rules and also on the construction of the procedure for strike action, the national executive council had power to issue the order dated 8 April 1974 [i.e. the instruction to members not to assist in the local elections]. It is sufficient for present purposes that not only am I in some doubt now as to the answer to that question, but also that every member of NALGO who received the order could not have been clear as to whether there was power to issue that particular order…
>
> As at present advised, I emphatically reject the submission that it was the duty of every member blindly to obey the orders of the national executive council in the prevailing circumstances and that he could only disobey the order if he were prepared to take the risk of being expelled from NALGO. I also reject the submission that a member who disobeyed the particular order given by the national executive not to assist returning officers showed prima facie that he was unfit to be a member of NALGO. An Act of Parliament carries penalties for its breach, but it is a fallacy to assume that every democratically elected body is entitled to obedience to every order on pain of being found guilty of being unfit to be a member of an association. It must depend on the order and it must depend on the circumstances and, in my judgement, if implicit obedience is to be exacted, those who issue the order must make quite sure that they have the power, that no reasonable man could be in doubt that they have the power and that they are making a proper exercise of the power, and that no reasonable man could conscientiously say to himself that 'this is an order which I have no duty to obey'. In the present case, it was not so clear.

NOTES

1. The *Lee* and *Esterman* cases are important because they emphasise that the courts' jurisdiction between unions and members is based on contract; that questions of interpretation are reserved to the courts, and they indicate the way in which the courts will control general 'blanket' disciplinary provisions. *Esterman's* case shows that the mere fact that the provision is in subjective terms—'in the opinion of the disciplinary body'—is unlikely to make a difference to the willingness of the courts to intervene.
2. 'The power of a union to discipline a member depends upon the express terms of the rulebook. A power to discipline or expel will not be implied' (*Harvey on Industrial Relations and Employment Law*, vol. II, para. M 2652). However, in *McVitae v Unison* [1996] IRLR 33, ChD, Harrison J felt that this proposition was too broadly stated:

> In my view, the court can imply such a disciplinary power, although the court's power to do so is one which should be exercised with care and only where there are compelling circumstances to justify it. The reason why the court should be slow to imply a disciplinary power is that it is penal and could include serious consequences affecting the reputation and livelihood of the union member.

> In the instant case, it was held that the circumstances of the case warranted implying such a term. The plaintiffs were former NALGO members against whom disciplinary proceedings had been initiated, but no hearing held, when NALGO merged into Unison and ceased to exist. Charges were brought under the Unison rules but the plaintiffs brought proceedings on the ground that there was no express rule allowing Unison to take disciplinary action in respect of conduct prior to the union's inception. Harrison J rejected this argument and stated:

I cannot conceive that it was intended that there should be a complete amnesty for pre-inception conduct. There is certainly no evidence of such an intention and common sense suggests that it would not have been intended. It offends against common sense that a member who has, for instance, done something dishonest before amalgamation which contravenes both the rules of his former union and the rules of Unison should escape penalty simply because of the amalgamation. As a responsible union, Unison would be just as intent on ensuring that such conduct was disciplined as would have been the former union. It is not in the interests of Unison that they should be unable to regulate their membership or the holding of office in such circumstances. In my judgment, it would have been the expectation of members in such circumstances that the union should be able to take disciplinary action. If they had been asked about it, they would have said that it was so obvious that it must have been intended to form part of the agreement between Unison and its members.

(iv) Natural justice

Annamunthodo v Oilfield Workers' Trade Union
[1961] 3 All ER 621, Privy Council

The appellant had publicly alleged that the president general of the respondent union had embezzled union funds. The appellant was charged in writing with four specific offences under a named union rule. The maximum penalty for each of the offences was a fine. The initial hearing attended by the appellant was adjourned and he did not attend the remainder of the hearing. He was subsequently informed that he had been convicted on all four charges but had been expelled under a blanket rule with which he had not been charged. The order for expulsion was set aside by the Privy Council.

LORD DENNING: …Counsel for the respondent union sought to treat the specific formulation of *charges* as immaterial. The substance of the matter lay, he said, in the *facts* alleged in the letter as to the meetings which the appellant had attended and the allegations he had made. Their Lordships cannot accede to this view. If a domestic tribunal formulates specific charges, which lead only to a fine, it cannot without notice resort to other charges, which lead to far more severe penalties.

White v Kuzych
[1951] AC 585, Privy Council

VISCOUNT SIMON: Whatever the correct details may be, their Lordships are bound to conclude that there was, before and after the trial, strong and widespread resentment felt against the respondent by many in the union and that Clark, among others, formed and expressed adverse views about him. If the so-called 'trial' and the general meeting which followed had to be conducted by persons previously free from all bias and prejudice, this condition was certainly not fulfilled. It would, indeed, be an error to demand from those who took part the strict impartiality of mind with which a judge should approach and decide an issue between two litigants—that 'icy impartiality of a Rhadamanthus' which Bowen LJ in *Jackson v Barry Rly Co.* [1893] 1 Ch 248 thought could not be expected of an engineer-arbitrator—or to regard as disqualified from acting any member who had held or expressed the view that the 'closed shop' principle was essential to the policy and purpose of the union. What those who considered the charges against the respondent and decided whether he was guilty ought to bring to their task was a will to reach an honest conclusion after hearing what was argued on either side and a resolve not to make their minds up beforehand on his personal guilt, however firmly they held their conviction as to union policy and however strongly they had shared in previous adverse criticism of the respondent's conduct.

Roebuck v NUM (Yorkshire Area) (No. 2)
[1978] ICR 676, Chancery Division

The union area president (Arthur Scargill), acting on behalf of the union, had successfully sued a newspaper for libel. In the action two union members had given evidence for the newspaper. At the instigation of Mr Scargill, the area executive resolved to charge those members with conduct detrimental to the interests of the union. The executive found the charges proved and this was confirmed by the area council which had originally referred the matter to the executive. Mr Scargill was president of both bodies and participated in their proceedings, questioning the plaintiffs and taking part in their deliberations. However, he did not vote on the resolution to suspend one of the plaintiffs from office as branch chairman and declare the other ineligible for office in the union for two years. The plaintiffs obtained an injunction to prevent the implementation of the decisions.

TEMPLEMAN J: Mr Roebuck and Mr O'Brien were entitled to be tried by a tribunal whose chairman did not appear to have a special reason for bias, conscious or unconscious, against them. True it is that all members of the executive committee and the area council, in common with all members of a domestic tribunal where the interests of their organisation are at stake, have a general inclination to defend the union and its officers against attack from any source; this fact, every trade unionist and every member of a domestic organisation knows and accepts.

But Mr Scargill had a special position, which clearly disqualified him from taking part in the critical meetings of the executive committee and the area committee which he did take...Whether he recognised the fact or not, Mr Scargill must inevitably have appeared to be biased against Mr Roebuck and Mr O'Brien. The appearance of bias was inevitable; the exercise of bias, conscious or unconscious, was probable. I am content to rest my judgement on the ground that it was manifestly unfair to Mr Roebuck and Mr O'Brien that Mr Scargill should have acted as chairman, and should have played the part which he admits to have played at the relevant meetings of the executive committee and the area council.

(v) Excluding the jurisdiction of the court at common law

A union rule which seeks to bar the member from pursuing legal redress is void and unenforceable as against public policy (see *Lee* v *Showmen's Guild* [1952] 2 QB 329, extracted in Section (iii)). Less clear-cut is the validity of a rule that the union's internal disciplinary procedures must be exhausted before a member can apply to the court. The courts recognise that there are many advantages to internal resolution of the dispute.

Leigh v *NUR*

[1970] Ch 326, Chancery Division

GOFF J: [W]here there is an express provision in the rules that the plaintiff must first exhaust his domestic remedies, the court is not absolutely bound by that because its jurisdiction cannot be ousted, but the plaintiff will have to show cause why it should interfere with the contractual position...

...[In] the absence of such a provision the court can readily, or at all events more readily, grant relief without prior recourse to the domestic remedies, but may require the plaintiff to resort first to those remedies.

NOTE: Exhaustion of internal procedures would not be required where the domestic proceedings were irretrievably biased or involved a serious point of law, or where fraud is at issue or internal procedures would involve excessive delay.

In *Esterman* v *NALGO* (Section (iii)) the court went further to hold that a plaintiff may bring an action to stop *impending* disciplinary action if he or she can show that there is no lawful basis for them.

The EA 1988, s. 2, provided a new right for union members not to be denied access to the court to pursue a grievance against their union. The relevant provisions are now to be found in TULR(C)A 1992.

TRADE UNION AND LABOUR RELATIONS (CONSOLIDATION) ACT 1992

63. Right not to be denied access to the courts

(2) Notwithstanding anything in the rules of the union or in the practice of any court, if a member or former member of the union begins proceedings in a court with respect to a matter to which this section applies, then if—

> (a) he has previously made a valid application to the union for the matter to be submitted for determination or conciliation in accordance with the union's rules, and
>
> (b) the court proceedings are begun after the end of the period of six months beginning with the day on which the union received the application,
>
> the rules requiring or allowing the matter to be so submitted, and the fact that any relevant steps remain to be taken under the rules, shall be regarded for all purposes as irrelevant to any question whether the court proceedings should be dismissed, stayed or sisted, or adjourned.

NOTE: However, TULR(C)A 1992, s. 63(6) states that this six-month rule is without prejudice to any rule of law by which a court could ignore any such union rule already, so the principles discussed in *Leigh* v *NUR* (extracted earlier) are still relevant.

B: Refusals to admit and expulsions in the interests of inter-union relations

The TUC has drawn up a set of *Principles Governing Relations Between Unions*—the so-called 'Bridlington Principles'. They require every affiliated union to ask all applicants for membership if they are or have recently been a union member. The new union must then ask the old union whether the member has resigned, has any subscription arrears, is 'under discipline or penalty' or if there are any other reasons why he or she should not be accepted. If the old union objects, the dispute may be resolved by the TUC Disputes Committee. Most affiliated unions have a provision in their rule books providing for the automatic termination of membership, following a period of notice, in order to comply with the decision of the Disputes Committee. The courts have upheld the validity of such rules, provided that the power is exercised following a *valid* decision of the Disputes Committee itself (see *Rothwell* v *APEX* [1975] IRLR 375).

In *Cheall* v *APEX* [1983] 2 AC 180, the House of Lords held that an individual trade unionist had no right to be heard by the TUC Disputes Committee before it made its determination. Furthermore, there was 'no existing rule of public policy that would prevent trade unions from entering into arrangements with one another which they consider to be in the interests of their members in promoting order in industrial relations and enhancing their members' bargaining power with their employers.'

In their 1991 Green Paper, *Industrial Relations in the 1990s* (Cm. 1602), the Government expressed the view that the law should be amended so as to guarantee freedom of choice where more than one trade union can genuinely claim to be able to represent an employee's interests. In the Government's opinion, a union should not be obliged to accept someone into membership if it does not represent employees of a similar skill or occupation. Nor should it be obliged to accept an applicant who has been an unsatisfactory member of another union because, for example, he has a record of refusing to pay his subscriptions. However, a union should not be at liberty to refuse to accept an individual into membership simply because he was previously a member of another union which claims sole recruitment rights in a particular company or sector. Section 14 of TURERA 1993 was designed to implement these views (see now TULR(C)A 1992, s. 17).

The remedy for an infringement of this right is by way of a complaint to an ET for a declaration and compensation. The remedies operate in a very similar way to those which apply to unreasonable exclusion or expulsion from a trade union, and to unjustifiable discipline by a trade union (see the following section).

C: Statutory controls over admissions and expulsions

(i) Pre-1980 law

As we have seen, the Donovan Commission suggested that a review body should be created to hear complaints concerning arbitrary exclusions or expulsions. No such body was ever created by statute, although the Industrial Relations Act 1971, s. 65 did contain provisions prohibiting arbitrary or unreasonable discrimination against applicants as members. A similar provision contained in TULRA 1974, s. 5, was repealed by TULR(C)A 1976. In response, the TUC established its own Independent Review Committee (IRC) in April 1976 to provide a voluntary forum for hearing cases alleging unreasonable exclusion or expulsion from unions operating a closed shop.

The IRC's awards were not legally binding but the affiliates agreed to be bound by them. The remedy was a recommendation that a union admit or readmit the complainant into membership; the IRC had no authority to award compensation. The major weakness was that an IRC recommendation could not be enforced against employers, i.e. even if the union reinstated a worker there was nothing to force the employer to take an employee back if he or she had been dismissed, though of course there is now the unfair dismissal remedy in such cases.

Once the Government introduced legislation covering the area of admissions and expulsions in unions operating the closed shop, the voluntary machinery, in the words of the TUC, 'faded away'.

(ii) The Employment Acts 1980–90

The Conservative Government was not satisfied with the TUC's self-regulation and enacted the EA 1980, s. 4. This reverted the position to broadly that of the period of the Industrial Relations Act 1971, except s. 4 applied *only* where the employer operated a union membership agreement. The EA 1988 introduced more general provisions on unjustifiable discipline by trade unions, which apply in all cases whether inside or outside closed shops (see Section D). Finally, as we saw earlier in this chapter, closed shops experienced yet a further legal onslaught as a result of the EA 1990, which made it unlawful to refuse a person employment because he or she is or does not wish to become a union member. (See now TULR(C)A 1992, s. 137.)

(iii) Statutory 'permitted' reasons

Prior to the passage of TURERA 1993, an individual seeking a job where a 'closed shop'— or 'Union Membership Agreement'—operated had a right (a) not to have his or her membership application unreasonably refused; and (b) not to be unreasonably expelled from the union (TULR(C)A 1992, ss. 174–7). TURERA 1993 replaced these provisions with new ss. 174–7, which provide a general right for workers not to be excluded or expelled from any union unless the exclusion or expulsion is for a statutory 'permitted' reason. Section 174 was amended by the Employment Relations Act 2004 ('the 2004 Act'). The section was further amended by the EA 2008 in response to the European Court of Human Rights' ruling in *ASLEF* v *UK* [2007] IRLR 361 (extracted later in this section).

TRADE UNION AND LABOUR RELATIONS (CONSOLIDATION) ACT 1992

PART III RIGHTS IN RELATION TO UNION MEMBERSHIP AND ACTIVITIES

Right to membership of trade union

174. Right not to be excluded or expelled from union.

(1) An individual shall not be excluded or expelled from a trade union unless the exclusion or expulsion is permitted by this section.

(2) The exclusion or expulsion of an individual from a trade union is permitted by this section if (and only if)—

  (a) he does not satisfy, or no longer satisfies, an enforceable membership requirement contained in the rules of the union,

  (b) he does not qualify, or no longer qualifies, for membership of the union by reason of the union operating only in a particular part or particular parts of Great Britain,

  (c) in the case of a union whose purpose is the regulation of relations between its members and one particular employer or a number of particular employers who are associated, he is not, or is no longer, employed by that employer or one of those employers, or

  (d) the exclusion or expulsion is entirely attributable to conduct of his (other than excluded conduct) and the conduct to which it is wholly or mainly attributable is not protected conduct.

(3) A requirement in relation to membership of a union is 'enforceable' for the purposes of subsection (2)(a) if it restricts membership solely by reference to one or more of the following criteria—

  (a) employment in a specified trade, industry or profession,

  (b) occupational description (including grade, level or category of appointment), and

  (c) possession of specified trade, industrial or professional qualifications or work experience.

(4) For the purposes of subsection (2)(d) 'excluded conduct', in relation to an individual, means—

  (a) conduct which consists in his being or ceasing to be, or having been or ceased to be, a member of another trade union,

  (b) conduct which consists in his being or ceasing to be, or having been or ceased to be, employed by a particular employer or at a particular place, or

  (c) conduct to which section 65 (conduct for which an individual may not be disciplined by a union) applies or would apply if the references in that section to the trade union which is relevant for the purposes of that section were references to any trade union.

(4A) For the purposes of subsection (2)(d) 'protected conduct' is conduct which consists in the individual's being or ceasing to be, or having been or ceased to be, a member of a political party.

(4B) Conduct which consists of activities undertaken by an individual as a member of a political party is not conduct falling within subsection (4A).

(4C) Conduct which consists in an individual's being or having been a member of a political party is not conduct falling within subsection (4A) if membership of that political party is contrary to—

  (a) a rule of the trade union, or

  (b) an objective of the trade union.

(4D) For the purposes of subsection (4C)(b) in the case of conduct consisting in an individual's being a member of a political party, an objective is to be disregarded—

  (a) in relation to an exclusion, if it is not reasonably practicable for the objective to be ascertained by a person working in the same trade, industry or profession as the individual;

  (b) in relation to an expulsion, if it is not reasonably practicable for the objective to be ascertained by a member of the union.

(4E) For the purposes of subsection (4C)(b) in the case of conduct consisting in an individual's having been a member of a political party, an objective is to be disregarded—

  (a) in relation to an exclusion, if at the time of the conduct it was not reasonably practicable for the objective to be ascertained by a person working in the same trade, industry or profession as the individual;

  (b) in relation to an expulsion, if at the time of the conduct it was not reasonably practicable for the objective to be ascertained by a member of the union.

(4F) Where the exclusion or expulsion of an individual from a trade union is wholly or mainly attributable to conduct which consists of an individual's being or having been a member of a political party but which by virtue of subsection (4C) is not conduct falling within subsection (4A), the exclusion or expulsion is not permitted by virtue of subsection (2)(d) if any one or more of the conditions in subsection (4G) apply.

(4G) Those conditions are—

  (a) the decision to exclude or expel is taken otherwise than in accordance with the union's rules;

  (b) the decision to exclude or expel is taken unfairly;

  (c) the individual would lose his livelihood or suffer other exceptional hardship by reason of not being, or ceasing to be, a member of the union.

(4H) For the purposes of subsection (4G)(b) a decision to exclude or expel an individual is taken unfairly if (and only if)—

  (a) before the decision is taken the individual is not given—

    (i) notice of the proposal to exclude or expel him and the reasons for that proposal, and

    (ii) a fair opportunity to make representations in respect of that proposal, or

  (b) representations made by the individual in respect of that proposal are not considered fairly.

(5) An individual who claims that he has been excluded or expelled from a trade union in contravention of this section may present a complaint to an employment tribunal.

NOTES

1. Section 174 is designed to generally ensure that any individual who wishes to join or remain a member of a trade union has the right to do so. The union may exclude or expel that person only for one of a number of permitted reasons. Those reasons are set out in s. 174(2)(a)–(d). One of them is that the person's 'conduct' is unacceptable (see s. 174(2)(d)). However, the section sets out the following three categories of conduct, jointly classified as 'excluded conduct', for which it is always unlawful for a union to expel or exclude a person, even where such conduct was a minor reason among several reasons for the union's decision to exclude or expel:
   • current or former membership of a trade union;
   • current or former employment;
   • conduct for which disciplinary action taken against an individual would be regarded as unjustifiable under section 65 of the 1992 Act.
   Section 65 provides protection against disciplinary action by the union for three categories of conduct: first, where the conduct relates to a failure to support industrial action; second, where the conduct relates to the making of an assertion that the union had breached its rules or statute, and the person making that assertion did so in good faith (i.e. not knowing that the assertion was false); and third, for certain other types of conduct such as refusing to allow subscriptions to be deducted direct from pay.
   Section 174 also establishes a further category of conduct called 'protected conduct', which is essentially current or former membership of a political party. However, s. 174(4)(B) explicitly states that the activities a person undertakes as a member of a political party do not constitute 'protected conduct'. It is unlawful for a union to exclude or expel a person wholly or mainly on the grounds of that person's 'protected conduct'. The net effect of these provisions is to provide some scope for a union lawfully to expel or exclude its members on the basis of their political activities, such as standing for political office or campaigning on behalf of a political party.
   Prior to the Employment Relations Act 2004, when s. 174 was significantly amended, the law made no explicit distinction between 'political party membership' and 'political party activities'. Also, the previous law did not include membership of a political party in the definition of 'conduct' for which it was lawful for a union to expel or exclude a person. Consequently, prior to the passage of the 2004 Act, the ability of a union to act against political extremists was less clear and more constrained than now.
   The remedies are complex. A person who has obtained a declaration from a tribunal that he or she was unreasonably excluded or expelled may claim compensation. The applicant must wait for at least four weeks after the date of the declaration (to give the union an opportunity to admit or readmit), but then has up to six months after the date of the declaration to present a claim for compensation. The maximum compensation is 30 times the maximum amount of a week's pay allowable in computing the basic award for unfair dismissal cases, plus the maximum compensatory award for the time being in force in respect of unfair dismissal (TULR(C)A 1992, s. 176(4)(6)). There is a minimum award (£8,868 with effect from 1 April 2015) where the union refuses to admit or readmit. However, the minimum award does not apply in cases where the exclusion or expulsion was unlawful because it was mainly attributable to 'protected conduct' and where conduct contrary to a rule or objective of the trade union was a subsidiary reason for the union's decision to expel or exclude. This exception award was introduced in the 2004 Act, and was designed to ensure that political extremists had limited financial incentive to make a complaint to a tribunal where their political activities were contrary to the stated position of the trade union. Prior to the 2004 Act, the minimum award of compensation applied to all cases where the exclusion or expulsion was based on political party membership.
   Where the ET finds that the exclusion or expulsion complained of was to any extent caused or contributed to by the action of the applicant, it shall reduce the amount of compensation by such proportion as it considers just and equitable in the circumstances (TULR(C)A 1992, s. 176(5); see *Howard* v *NGA* [1985] ICR 101, EAT).

2. In *NACODS* v *Gluchowski* [1996] IRLR 252, EAT, the applicant was suspended from membership of the union as a result of complaints relating to his business activities. He challenged this under TULR(C)A 1992, s. 174 as being an unlawful exclusion or expulsion from the union and his claim was upheld by the industrial tribunal. However, on appeal, the EAT held that the tribunal

had erred in holding that the applicant's suspension from the appellant union amounted to 'exclusion'. In reaching that decision, the tribunal had erred in concluding that 'exclusion' must include exclusion from the benefits of membership and the ability to make use of any of its privileges.

According to the EAT, 'exclusion' from a trade union in s. 174(1) refers to a refusal to admit into membership, not to suspension of the privileges of membership. That interpretation was supported by the distinction between trade union membership and enjoyment of the benefits of union membership which was drawn in some of the speeches in the House of Lords in *Associated Newspapers* v *Wilson* and *Associated British Ports* v *Palmer* [1995] IRLR 258, HL. The tribunal's concern that a narrow definition of exclusion would mean that a trade union could impose a permanent suspension and argue that an individual had neither been excluded nor expelled, was misplaced since that kind of situation could lead to a remedy by other routes.

3. Despite the greater freedom provided by the 2004 Act for unions to exclude or expel political activists, the political membership protection provision contained in s. 174 has been successfully challenged in the European Court of Human Rights. This led to further amendments to s. 174 by the EA 2008.

Associated Society of Locomotive Engineers & Firemen (ASLEF) v *United Kingdom*
[2007] IRLR 361, European Court of Human Rights

The applicant trade union had about 18,000 members. There was no 'closed shop' and railway workers were free to join ASLEF or other unions or not join a union at all. One of ASLEF's objects was to:

promote and develop and enact positive policies in regard to equality of treatment in our industries and ASLEF regardless of sex, sexual orientation, marital status, religion, creed, colour, race or ethnic origin.

In 1978 its governing body resolved to campaign to 'expose the obnoxious policies of political parties such as the National Front'.

Mr Lee, a member of the British National Party (BNP), joined ASLEF in February 2002 and two months later stood as a BNP candidate in local elections. An ASLEF officer subsequently informed the General Secretary that Mr Lee was a BNP activist. His report included an article which Mr Lee had written for the BNP magazine and a fax from Bexley Council for Racial Equality stating that he had seriously harassed Anti-Nazi League pamphleteers. On 19 April 2002, ASLEF's Executive Committee voted unanimously to expel Mr Lee, stating that his membership of the BNP was incompatible with membership of the union.

After the ASLEF Appeals Committee had rejected his appeal, Mr Lee successfully challenged his expulsion in an ET on the basis of s. 174 of TULR(C)A 1992. ASLEF appealed to the EAT, which in March 2004 quashed the decision and remitted it to a second ET. The EAT held that a union could expel a member on the ground of his or her conduct as long as that conduct was not the fact of being a member of a political party. A second ET again upheld Mr Lee's complaint because his expulsion was 'primarily because of his membership of the BNP'. ASLEF did not appeal against that decision and had to readmit Mr Lee in breach of its own rules.

Relying on Article 11 of the Convention, the union complained that it had been prevented from expelling one of its members due to his membership of the BNP, a political party which advocated views inimical to its own.

The European Court of Human Rights held unanimously:

(1) that the application was admissible;

(2) that there had been a violation of Article 11;

(3) that the respondent State was to pay the applicant €53,900 in respect of costs and expenses.

JUDGMENT:

The Court's assessment

General principles

The essential object of Art. 11 is to protect the individual against arbitrary interference by public authorities with the exercise of the rights protected. The right to form and join trade unions is a special aspect of freedom of association which also protects, first and foremost, against state action. The State may not interfere with the forming and joining of trade unions except on the basis of the conditions set forth in Art. 11(2). The right to form trade unions involves, for example, the right of trade unions to draw up their own rules and to administer their own affairs. Such trade union rights are explicitly recognised in Arts. 3 and 5 of ILO Convention No. 87, the provisions of which have been taken into account by the Convention organs in previous cases. Prima facie trade unions enjoy the freedom to set up their own rules concerning conditions of membership, including administrative formalities and payment of fees, as well as other more substantive criteria, such as the profession or trade exercised by the would-be member.

As an employee or worker should be free to join, or not join a trade union without being sanctioned or subject to disincentives, so should the trade union be equally free to choose its members. Article 11 cannot be interpreted as imposing an obligation on associations or organisations to admit whosoever wishes to join. Where associations are formed by people, who, espousing particular values or ideals, intend to pursue common goals, it would run counter to the very effectiveness of the freedom at stake if they had no control over their membership. By way of example, it is uncontroversial that religious bodies and political parties can generally regulate their membership to include only those who share their beliefs and ideals. Similarly, the right to join a union 'for the protection of his interests' cannot be interpreted as conferring a general right to join the union of one's choice irrespective of the rules of the union: in the exercise of their rights under Art. 11(1) unions must remain free to decide, in accordance with union rules, questions concerning admission to and expulsion from the union.

This basic premise holds good where the association or trade union is a private and independent body, and is not, for example, through receipt of public funds or through the fulfilment of public duties imposed upon it, acting in a wider context, such as assisting the State in securing the enjoyment of rights and freedoms, where other considerations may well come into play.

Accordingly, where the State does intervene in internal trade union matters, such intervention must comply with the requirements of Art. 11(2), namely be 'prescribed by law' and 'necessary in a democratic society' for one or more of the permitted aims. In this context, the following should be noted.

First, 'necessary' in this context does not have the flexibility of such expressions as 'useful' or 'desirable'.

Secondly, pluralism, tolerance and broadmindedness are hallmarks of a 'democratic society'. Although individual interests must on occasion be subordinated to those of a group, democracy does not simply mean that the views of a majority must always prevail: a balance must be achieved which ensures the fair and proper treatment of minorities and avoids any abuse of a dominant position. For the individual right to join a union to be effective, the State must nonetheless protect the individual against any abuse of a dominant position by trade unions. Such abuse might occur, for example, where exclusion or expulsion from a trade union was not in accordance with union rules or where the rules were wholly unreasonable or arbitrary or where the consequences of exclusion or expulsion resulted in exceptional hardship.

Thirdly, any restriction imposed on a Convention right must be proportionate to the legitimate aim pursued.

Fourthly, where there is a conflict between differing Convention rights, the State must find a fair and proper balance.

Finally, in striking a fair balance between the competing interests, the State enjoys a certain margin of appreciation in determining the steps to be taken to ensure compliance with the Convention. However, since this is not an area of general policy, on which opinions within a democratic society may reasonably differ widely and in which the role of the domestic policy-maker should be given special weight, the margin of appreciation will play only a limited role.

Application in the present case

The question that arises in the present case concerns the extent to which the State may intervene to protect the trade union member, Mr Lee, against measures taken against him by his union, the applicant.

It is accepted by the parties in this case that s. 174 had the effect in this case of prohibiting the applicant from expelling Mr Lee as it barred unions from such action where it was motivated, at least in part, by membership of a political party. This constituted an interference with the applicant's freedom of association under the first paragraph of Art. 11 which requires to be justified in the terms set out above.

In the context of the case, lawfulness is not an issue. Nor is it disputed that the measure had the aim of protecting the rights of individuals, such as Mr Lee, to exercise their various political rights and freedoms without undue hindrance. The crucial question is whether the State has struck the right balance between Mr Lee's rights and those of the applicant trade union.

Taking due consideration of the Government's argument as to the importance of safeguarding fundamental individual rights, the Court is not persuaded however that the measure of expulsion impinged in any significant way on Mr Lee's exercise of freedom of expression or his lawful political activities. Nor is it apparent that Mr Lee suffered any particular detriment, save loss of membership itself in the union. As there was no closed-shop agreement for example, there was no apparent prejudice suffered by the applicant in terms of his livelihood or in his conditions of employment. The Court has taken account of the fact that membership of a trade union is often regarded, in particular due to the trade union movement's historical background, as a fundamental safeguard for workers against employers' abuse and it has some sympathy with the notion that any worker should be able to join a trade union. However, as pointed by the applicant, ASLEF represents all workers in the collective bargaining context and there is nothing to suggest in the present case that Mr Lee is at any individual risk of, or is unprotected from, any arbitrary or unlawful action by his employer. Of more weight in the balance is the applicant's right to choose its members. Historically, trade unions in the United Kingdom, and elsewhere in Europe, were, and though perhaps to a lesser extent today are, commonly affiliated to political parties or movements, particularly those on the left. They are not bodies solely devoted to politically-neutral aspects of the well-being of their members, but are often ideological, with strongly held views on social and political issues. There was no hint in the domestic proceedings that the applicant erred in its conclusion that Mr Lee's political values and ideals clashed, fundamentally, with its own. There is no indication that the applicant had any public duty or role conferred on it, or has taken the advantage of state funding, such that it may reasonably be required to take on members to fulfil any other wider purposes.

As regards the Government's assertion that domestic law would have permitted the expulsion of Mr Lee if the applicant had restricted its grounds to conduct not related to his membership of the BNP, the Court would note that the Employment Tribunal found that the applicant's objections to Mr Lee were primarily based on his membership of the BNP. It does not find it reasonable to expect the applicant to have used the pretext of relying purely on Mr Lee's conduct which was largely carried out by him as a member of, and reflected his adherence to the aims of, the BNP.

Accordingly, in the absence of any identifiable hardship suffered by Mr Lee or any abusive and unreasonable conduct by the applicant, the Court concludes that the balance has not been properly struck and that the case falls outside any acceptable margin of appreciation.

There has, accordingly, been a violation of Art. 11 of the Convention.

NOTES

1. Following the judgment, the Government issued a consultation document, 'ECHR Judgment in *ASLEF* v *UK* case—Implications for Trade Union Law', DTI, May 2007. There were two main options to amend s. 174 which the UK Government asked respondents to consider:

> Option (A)—Section 174 should be amended to ensure there is no explicit reference to a special category of conduct relating to political party membership or activities. This change would in effect position political party membership and activities under the general heading of 'conduct' (which was the situation before the Trade Union Reform and Employment Rights Act 1993 was implemented). Where such political party membership or activities were 'unacceptable' to the trade union, it would therefore be lawful for the union to expel or exclude on those grounds.
>
> Option (B)—The special category of conduct relating to political party membership and activities should be retained but the rights not to be excluded or expelled for such conduct should be significantly amended. The amendment would refer to the limited conditions under which it would remain unlawful for the trade union to exclude or expel an individual on the grounds of their political party membership or activities. Those conditions would specify that the union's decision would be unlawful unless the political party membership or activity concerned was incompatible with a rule or objective of the union, and the decision to exclude or expel was taken in accordance with union rules or established procedures.

Option A would significantly simplify the wording of s. 174. It would provide trade unions with much greater autonomy in deciding their membership. However, there would be no special safeguards against possible abuse. Such safeguards may not be necessary in any event: there is no evidence that trade unions would make use of this greater freedom by expelling members or activists of mainstream political parties. Also, if a trade union acted outside its rules when expelling a member, then that person could seek legal redress by bringing a breach of rule claim before the courts.

In contrast, Option B would specify particular safeguards against potential abuse. Those safeguards are based on the reasoning of the Court which noted the need for the trade union to avoid arbitrary behaviour and to act transparently in accordance with its rules. Many union rule books now refer to racist, xenophobic or extremist political behaviour as unacceptable to the union. So, little adaptation by those trade unions would be needed in order to comply with this option.

Where a trade union was required to amend its rule book, then members and potential members should gain because they would be properly informed of the potential consequences of their political actions. Option B might, however, create grey areas and give scope for legal action to arise about the precise meaning of a union's rules or objectives.

The EA 2008 amended s. 174 so as to implement the 'Option (B)' solution (see subss. (4C)–(4H).

2. Several other statutes are relevant to this area. The Sex Discrimination Act 1975, Race Relations Act 1976 and Disability Discrimination Act 1995 make it unlawful to discriminate on grounds of sex, race or disability against an applicant for trade union membership. The TULR(C)A 1992, s. 82(c), states that where the union operates a political fund, it must not make contribution to the fund a condition of admission or discriminate against a non-contributor. Union rule books are required to contain a rule to this effect. Lastly, as we see in the next section, the EA 1988 imposed a general prohibition on unjustifiable discipline of trade union members. The law is now set out in TULR(C)A 1992, ss. 64–7, as amended by TURERA 1993, s. 16.

D: Unjustifiable discipline

TRADE UNION AND LABOUR RELATIONS (CONSOLIDATION) ACT 1992

64. Right not to be unjustifiably disciplined

(1) An individual who is or has been a member of a trade union has the right not to be unjustifiably disciplined by the union.

(2) For this purpose an individual is 'disciplined' by a trade union if a determination is made, or purportedly made, under the rules of the union or by an official of the union or a number of persons including an official that—

(a) he should be expelled from the union or a branch or section of the union,

(b) he should pay a sum to the union, to a branch or section of the union or to any other person;

(c) sums tendered by him in respect of an obligation to pay subscriptions or other sums to the union, or to a branch or section of the union, should be treated as unpaid or paid for a different purpose,

(d) he should be deprived to any extent of, or of access to, any benefits, services or facilities which would otherwise be provided or made available to him by virtue of his membership of the union, or a branch or section of the union,

(e) another trade union, or a branch or section of it, should be encouraged or advised not to accept him as a member, or

(f) he should be subjected to some other detriment; and whether an individual is 'unjustifiably disciplined' shall be determined in accordance with section 65.

(3) Where a determination made in infringement of an individual's right under this section requires the payment of a sum or the performance of an obligation, no person is entitled in any proceedings to rely on that determination for the purpose of recovering the sum or enforcing the obligation.

(4) Subject to that, the remedies for infringement of the right conferred by this section are as provided by sections 66 and 67, and not otherwise.

(5) The right not to be unjustifiably disciplined is in addition to (and not in substitution for) any right which exists apart from this section; and nothing in this section or sections 65 to 67 affects any remedy for infringement of any such right.

65. Meaning of 'unjustifiably disciplined'

(1) An individual is unjustifiably disciplined by a trade union if the actual or supposed conduct which constitutes the reason, or one of the reasons, for disciplining him is—

(a) conduct to which this section applies, or

(b) something which is believed by the union to amount to such conduct; but subject to subsection (6) (cases of bad faith in relation to assertion of wrongdoing).

(2) This section applies to conduct which consists in—

(a) failing to participate in or support a strike or other industrial action (whether by members of the union or by others), or indicating opposition to or a lack of support for such action;

(b) failing to contravene, for a purpose connected with such a strike or other industrial action, a requirement imposed on him by or under a contract of employment;

(c) asserting (whether by bringing proceedings or otherwise) that the union, any official or representative of it or a trustee of its property has contravened, or is proposing to contravene, a requirement which is, or is thought to be, imposed by or under the rules of the union or any other agreement or by or under any enactment (whenever passed) or any rule of law;

(d) encouraging or assisting a person—

(i) to perform an obligation imposed on him by a contract of employment, or

(ii) to make or attempt to vindicate any such assertion as is mentioned in paragraph (c); or

(e) contravening a requirement imposed by or in consequence of a determination which infringes the individual's or another individual's right not to be unjustifiably disciplined,

(f) failing to agree, or withdrawing agreement, to the making from his wages (in accordance with arrangements between his employer and the union) of deductions representing payments to the union in respect of his membership,

(g) resigning or proposing to resign from the union or from another union, becoming or proposing to become a member of another union, refusing to become a member of another union, or being a member of another union,

(h) working with, or proposing to work with, individuals who are not members of the union or who are or are not members of another union,

(i) working for, or proposing to work for, an employer who employs or who has employed individuals who are not members of the union or who are or are not members of another union, or

(j) requiring the union to do an act which the union is, by any provision of this Act, required to do on the requisition of a member.

(3) This section applies to conduct which involves the Commissioner for the Rights of Trade Union Members or the Certification Officer being consulted or asked to provide advice or assistance with respect to any matter whatever, or which involves any person being consulted or asked to provide advice or assistance with respect to a matter which forms, or might form, the subject-matter of any such assertion as is mentioned in subsection (2)(c) above.

(4) This section also applies to conduct which consists in proposing to engage in, or doing anything preparatory or incidental to, conduct falling within subsection (2) or (3).

(5) This section does not apply to an act, omission or statement comprised in conduct falling within subsection (2), (3) or (4) above if it is shown that the act, omission or statement is one in respect of which individuals would be disciplined by the union irrespective of whether their acts, omissions or statements were in connection with conduct within subsection (2) or (3) above.

(6) An individual is not unjustifiably disciplined if it is shown—

(a) that the reason for disciplining him, or one of them, is that he made such an assertion as is mentioned in subsection (2)(c), or encouraged or assisted another person to make or attempt to vindicate such an assertion,

(b) that the assertion was false, and

(c) that he made the assertion, or encouraged or assisted another person to make or attempt to vindicate it, in the belief that it was false or otherwise in bad faith, and that there was no other reason for disciplining him or that the only other reasons were reasons in respect of which he does not fall to be treated as unjustifiably disciplined.

(7) In this section—

'conduct' includes statements, acts and omissions;

'contract of employment', in relation to an individual, includes any agreement between that individual and a person for whom he works or normally works; and

'representative', in relation to a union, means a person acting or purporting to act—

(a) in his capacity as a member of the union, or

(b) on the instructions or advice of a person acting or purporting to act in that capacity or in the capacity of an official of the union.

'require' (on the part of an individual) includes request or apply for, and 'requisition' shall be construed accordingly.

'wages' shall be construed in accordance with the definitions of 'contract of employment', 'employer' and related expressions.

(8) Where a person holds any office or employment under the Crown on terms which do not constitute a contract of employment between him and the Crown, those terms shall nevertheless be deemed to constitute such a contract for the purposes of this section.

NOTES

1. One of the specified grounds where discipline is unjustifiable is where the reason is that a member failed to 'participate in or support a strike or other industrial action' or indicated 'opposition to' such action. The phrase 'other industrial action' is not defined in the Act, but some guidance was offered by the EAT in *Fire Brigades Union* v *Knowles* [1996] IRLR 337. In this case, two full-time fire-fighters were disciplined by their union when, in contravention of union policy, they accepted additional employment as retained (part-time) fire-fighters. The EAT held that the union's policy did not constitute 'other industrial action'. According to Keene LJ:

> Not every action which involves pressure on an employer together with some effect on that employer's freedom of action will constitute 'other industrial action'. There must be some action directed against the employer with the object of obtaining some advantage for the employees...In the present case, the industrial tribunal appears to have accepted that the ban on combining full-time and retained duties was imposed for safety reasons. There is no suggestion that it was imposed in order to enhance the union's bargaining position when the time came for negotiations on wages or conditions. It seems that there was no ulterior industrial objective to the restriction contained in the union's policy.

Do you agree with this reasoning? Surely, a dispute relating to health and safety issues would fall within the statutory definition of trade dispute for the purpose of establishing tortious liability? (See TULR(C)A 1992, s. 244, discussed at p. 657 (Chapter 11, Section 3.B(i).) The decision in *Knowles* was subsequently upheld by the Court of Appeal (see [1996] IRLR 617).

2. This is a controversial set of provisions, widely regarded by critics as a 'scab's charter'. A union is prohibited from disciplining a member for not taking part in industrial action notwithstanding that a majority of that member's fellow workers voted in favour of the action in a properly held ballot. As such, TULR(C)A 1992, s. 64 is understandably seen by the union movement as an attack on the fundamental concepts of union solidarity and collectivism.

Ewan McKendrick has argued:

> By prohibiting the exercise of disciplinary sanctions by unions, [section 64] stacks all the disciplinary powers on the side of the employer. In sum [section 64] is an objectionable intervention in union affairs, it is a possible violation of our international obligations and it elevates the individual interest of a union member to a point where it unacceptably undermines the collective strength of the union and represents an unwarranted intrusion into internal union affairs. ['The rights of trade union members—Part I of the Employment Act 1988' (1988) 17 ILJ 141, at pp. 149, 150]

3. TURERA 1993, s. 16 extended the list of conduct for which it is unjustifiable for a trade union to discipline a member (see TULR(C)A 1992, s. 65(2)(f)–(j) in the previous extract).

4. A claim must be made to the ET within three months of the imposition of the disciplinary sanction. There is power to extend the period if the tribunal is satisfied:

   (a) that it was not reasonably practicable for the complaint to have been presented within the three-month limit; and

   (b) that any delay in making the complaint is wholly or partly attributable to any reasonable attempt to appeal internally against the determination to which the complaint relates.

Where the tribunal finds that the complainant has been unjustifiably disciplined, it will make a declaration to that effect. The complainant may then make a further application to the tribunal for compensation, not earlier than four weeks but not later than six months after the date of the initial declaration.

What happens next depends on the trade union's response. If the union has revoked its disciplinary decision and taken all necessary steps to put that decision into effect, the further application is to the ET.

The amount of compensation to be awarded will be such as is considered to be just and equitable in all the circumstances of the case, subject to the usual rules relating to mitigation of loss and contributory fault.

On application to the ET, the maximum award is 30 times a week's pay, together with the maximum compensatory award currently available. If at the time of the application, the union has not revoked its decision or reversed anything done pursuant to it, a minimum sum of £8,868 (w.e.f. 6th April 2015) will be awarded.

E: Trade union democracy

(i) Rule book as contract and constitution

At common law, the government and administration of a union must be carried out in accordance with the terms of the contract of membership which are contained primarily in the rule book. A failure to do this will normally constitute a breach of contract, and the courts may well declare it *ultra vires* (beyond the powers of) the union.

The potential for challenging the action taken by a union in breach of its rules was repeatedly illustrated in the cases raised by working miners against various areas of the NUM during the miners' strike of 1984–5. In these cases, the judges relied on a strict construction of the NUM's rule book to establish the requirement for conducting ballots before authorising industrial action. In *Taylor* v *NUM (Derbyshire Area) (No. 1)* [1984] IRLR 440, it was held that the local area was required by its rules to obtain 55% support in a ballot for strike action before such action could be official, and in *Taylor* v *NUM (Yorkshire Area)* [1984] IRLR 445, it was held that an area ballot held some two and a half years previously was too remote to be capable of justifying a lawful call for strike action under the rules. In both cases the judges accepted that the strike in reality constituted national action, which was also unlawful in the absence of a national ballot.

Once the strike was declared in breach of the rules, injunctions were granted preventing the issuing of instructions to the membership not to work, or to cross picket lines (*Taylor* v *NUM (Derbyshire Area) (No. 1)*). A second consequence of the holding that the action was beyond the rules was that the use of union funds to support the strike could be restrained. In *Taylor* v *NUM (Derbyshire Area) (No. 3)* [1985] IRLR 99, the judge held that it was *ultra vires* for the union to authorise expenditure on strike action which had been called in breach of the area's rules. Further, the officials who had misapplied union monies in this way were in breach of the fiduciary duty which they owed to the members, and could be personally liable for such unauthorised expenditure. The miners' cases demonstrated the readiness of the judges to issue interlocutory injunctions to restrain the alleged unlawful behaviour and, as we shall see, the potential for using 'scab' workers to mount legal challenges against a striking union was not lost on the Government when it framed the EA 1988. (For a penetrating analysis of the litigation during the miners' strike, see Ewing, K. D., 'The strike, the courts and the rule-books' (1985) 14 ILJ 160–75.)

(ii) Union accounts

TULR(C)A 1992 imposes a duty on a trade union to send to the Certification Officer annual financial returns (s. 32). Failure either to submit a return or maintain proper accounting controls is a criminal offence (s. 45(1)). It is also an offence to falsify accounts (s. 45(4)).

(iii) Members' right of access to trade union's accounts

A union is under a duty to maintain proper accounting records and make them for inspection for any member (ss. 28–30).

Prior to 1988, an ordinary member did not possess a statutory right to inspect the union's accounts, though he or she might be given that right under the rule book. If there is such a right under a rule, then the member also has the right to be accompanied by an accountant or other agent (see *Norey* v *Keep* [1909] 1 Ch 561 and *Taylor* v *NUM (Derbyshire Area)* [1985] IRLR 65).

The first *statutory* provision giving rights of access to union records, whether or not there is an express rule, was provided by the EA 1988. The relevant provisions are now contained in TULR(C)A 1992, s. 30.

Where it is claimed that a union has failed to comply with a request, within 28 days, the member may apply to the court for an order requiring inspection, etc. It is also a criminal offence to fail to keep accounting records available for inspection (TULR(C)A 1992, s. 31).

(iv) Indemnification by unions of officials

It is unlawful for property of a trade union to be applied towards the payment for an individual of a penalty which has or may be imposed on him for an offence or for contempt of court (s. 15).

(v) Control of union trustees

Section 16 provides a union member with a remedy against a union's trustees for unlawful use of the union's property.

(vi) Union elections and ballots

Imposition of balloting requirements was a central feature of the Conservative Government's industrial relations policy, although views on the efficacy of ballots varied over time. The Donovan Commission rejected compulsory *strike* ballots on the ground that the North American experience showed that they are seen as 'tests of solidarity' and nearly always favour industrial action.

The Industrial Relations Act 1971 contained compulsory balloting procedures, but they were employed on only one occasion, during the railwaymen's dispute of 1972, when the subsequent vote resulted 5 to 1 in favour of strike action.

In 1979 the Conservative Government again tried to encourage trade union ballots, providing subsidies from public funds under the EA 1980. The Trade Union Act 1984 went further and required ballots before industrial action, for the principal executive committee and on retaining the political fund. The EA 1988 refined and modified these requirements and also introduced the office of Commissioner for the Rights of Trade Union Members (see the General Notes at the end of this section).

Most TUC unions at first refused to accept government funds as part of their overall policy of non-cooperation with the Government's employment legislation. The exceptions were the Electrical, Electronic, Telecommunications and Plumbing Union and the AUEW, who were threatened with TUC discipline for doing so. This policy was subsequently reviewed and the decision whether or not to claim was left to individual unions. By the late 1980s many unions were claiming under the 1980 Act. In 1991, 78 unions made applications in respect of 716 ballots; the Certification Officer made payments during that year of £4 million. This contrasts with applications in respect of 30 ballots and payments amounting to £72,498 in 1984.

At the end of 1992, the then Employment Secretary, Gillian Shephard, announced plans to phase the scheme out over the next three years. In her view 'the scheme now operates largely as a public subsidy for ballots which unions are required to carry out to meet their obligations under the law' (Hansard HC 10 December 1992, cols. 797–8). The scheme ceased to operate from 1 April 1996 (see the Funds for Trade Union Ballots (Revocation) Regulations 1993 (SI 1993/233)).

Executive elections are covered by TULR(C)A 1992, Ch. IV.

TRADE UNION AND LABOUR RELATIONS (CONSOLIDATION) ACT 1992

CHAPTER IV ELECTIONS FOR CERTAIN POSITIONS

DUTY TO HOLD ELECTIONS

46. Duty to hold elections for certain positions

(1) A trade union shall secure—

(a) that every person who holds a position in the union to which this Chapter applies does so by virtue of having been elected to it at an election satisfying the requirements of this Chapter, and

(b) that no person continues to hold such a position for more than five years without being re-elected at such an election.

(2) The positions to which this Chapter applies (subject as mentioned below) are—

(a) member of the executive,

(b) any position by virtue of which a person is a member of the executive,

(c) president, and

(d) general secretary;

and the requirements referred to above are those set out in sections 47 to 52 below.

(3) In this Chapter 'member of the executive' includes any person who, under the rules or practice of the union, may attend and speak at some or all of the meetings of the executive, otherwise than for the purpose of providing the committee with factual information or with technical or professional advice with respect to matters taken into account by the executive in carrying out its functions.

(4) This Chapter does not apply to the position of president or general secretary if the holder of that position—

(a) is not, in respect of that position, either a voting member of the executive or an employee of the union,

(b) holds that position for a period which under the rules of the union cannot end more than 13 months after he took it up, and

(c) has not held either position at any time in the period of twelve months ending with the day before he took up that position.

(5) A 'voting member of the executive' means a person entitled in his own right to attend meetings of the executive and to vote on matters on which votes are taken by the executive (whether or not he is entitled to attend all such meetings or to vote on all such matters or in all circumstances).

(6) The provisions of this Chapter apply notwithstanding anything in the rules or practice of the union; and the terms and conditions on which a person is employed by the union shall be disregarded in so far as they would prevent the union from complying with the provisions of this Chapter.

NOTES

1. By the Trade Union Act 1984, every *voting* member of the principal executive committee of a trade union had to be elected every five years by all members of the union. The Act overrode anything provided in the rule book of the union, and the union could face an enforcement order in the High Court. The Act also overrode any provision to the contrary in a contract of employment of any executive committee member relating to the tenure.

   The 1984 Act related only to a voting member of the executive. But, in certain unions, the president or general secretary do not have a vote. Even if they had a vote, there was nothing to stop the union changing its rules by constitutional means—to remove the right to vote and therefore avoid the application of the Act. Indeed, such a rule change was carried out by the NUM in 1985 to remove their president's vote. This was seen by the Government to be a weakness in its legislative framework and the law was considerably tightened by what Smith and Wood describe as the 'We'll get Scargill this time' amendments in the EA 1988. (See Smith, I. T. and Thomas, G. H., *Smith and Wood's Industrial Law*, 9th edn (Oxford: OUP, 2008), p. 680.)

2. The Trade Union Act 1984 stipulated a postal ballot as the norm but went on to allow a trade union to opt for a semi or full workplace ballot if the union was satisfied that there were no reasonable grounds to believe that this would not result in a free election as required by the Act. The 1987 Green Paper, however, pointed to 'concern over...the non-postal ballot held in 1984 for the election of the Transport and General Workers Union's General Secretary and more recent Civil and Public Services Association elections for General Secretary', as a 'justification for examining

this issue more closely'. In the Government's view, postal ballots offered less scope for manipulation in the context of executive elections and political fund ballots. This is despite the fact that the most infamous example of union election malpractice, the *ETU* case, involved a postal ballot. The EA 1988 ensured that such ballots were to be held by postal voting only. Ballot papers must now both be sent out and returned by post.

3. TULR(C)A 1992, s. 48 obliges trade unions to provide every election candidate with an opportunity of preparing an election address and to secure that, so far as reasonably practicable, copies of every election address are distributed to each of the members entitled to vote in the election (s. 48).

TRADE UNION AND LABOUR RELATIONS (CONSOLIDATION) ACT (1992)

50. Entitlement to vote

(1) Subject to the provisions of this section, entitlement to vote shall be accorded equally to all members of the trade union.

(2) The rules of the union may exclude entitlement to vote in the case of all members belonging to one of the following classes, or to a class falling within one of the following—

    (a) members who are not in employment;

    (b) members who are in arrears in respect of any subscription or contribution due to the union;

    (c) members who are apprentices, trainees or students or new members of the union.

(3) The rules of the union may restrict entitlement to vote to members who fall within—

    (a) a class determined by reference to a trade or occupation,

    (b) a class determined by reference to a geographical area, or

    (c) a class which is by virtue of the rules of the union treated as a separate section within the union,

or to members who fall within a class determined by reference to any combination of the factors mentioned in paragraphs (a), (b) and (c).

The reference in paragraph (c) to a section of a trade union includes a part of the union which is itself a trade union.

(4) Entitlement may not be restricted in accordance with subsection (3) if the effect is that any member of the union is denied entitlement to vote at all elections held for the purposes of this Chapter otherwise than by virtue of belonging to a class excluded in accordance with subsection (2).

51. Voting

(1) The method of voting must be by the marking of a voting paper by the person voting.

(2) Each voting paper must—

    (a) state the name of the independent scrutineer and clearly specify the address to which, and the date by which, it is to be returned,

    (b) be given one of a series of consecutive whole numbers every one of which is used in giving a different number in that series to each voting paper printed or otherwise produced for the purposes of the election, and

    (c) be marked with its number.

(3) Every person who is entitled to vote at the election must—

    (a) be allowed to vote without interference from, or constraint imposed by, the union or any of its members, officials or employees, and

    (b) so far as is reasonably practicable, be enabled to do so without incurring any direct cost to himself.

(4) So far as is reasonably practicable, every person who is entitled to vote at the election must—

    (a) have sent to him by post, at his home address or another address which he has requested the trade union in writing to treat as his postal address, a voting paper which either lists the candidates at the election or is accompanied by a separate list of those candidates; and

    (b) be given a convenient opportunity to vote by post.

(5) The ballot shall be conducted so as to secure that—

    (a) so far as is reasonably practicable, those voting do so in secret, and

    (b) the votes given at the election are fairly and accurately counted.

For the purposes of paragraph (b) an inaccuracy in counting shall be disregarded if it is accidental and on a scale which could not affect the result of the election.

(6) The ballot shall be so conducted as to secure that the result of the election is determined solely by counting the number of votes cast directly for each candidate.

(7) Nothing in subsection (6) shall be taken to prevent the system of voting used for the election being the single transferable vote, that is, a vote capable of being given so as to indicate the voter's order of preference for the candidates and of being transferred to the next choice—
    (a) when it is not required to give a prior choice the necessary quota of votes, or
    (b) when, owing to the deficiency in the number of votes given for a prior choice, that choice is eliminated from the list of candidates.

NOTES

1. Under TULR(C)A 1992, s. 49, both political fund and principal executive committee ballots must be independently scrutinised. TURERA 1993 extended this requirement to industrial action ballots and a failure to subject the ballot to independent scrutiny will render any subsequent industrial action unlawful.
2. The scrutineer must satisfy conditions set down in an Order made by the Secretary of State (TULR(C)A 1992, s. 49(2)). Under this Order, the following may be scrutineers:
   (a) solicitors or accountants qualified to be an auditor;
   (b) the Electoral Reform Society, the Industrial Society or Unity Security Services Ltd (Trade Union Ballots and Elections (Independent Scrutineers Qualifications) Order 1988 (SI 1988/2117)).
3. The scrutineer's report shall state, *inter alia*, whether the scrutineer is satisfied that there are no reasonable grounds for believing that there was any contravention of a requirement imposed by or under any enactment in relation to the election (s. 52(2)). A trade union is under an obligation to notify its membership of the contents of the report within three months of receiving it (s. 52(4)).

GENERAL NOTES ON THE ELECTION REQUIREMENTS

1. Enforcement of the requirements set out in TULR(C)A 1992, Ch. IV may be sought by way of an application to the Certification Officer or the High Court for a declaration.

   In complaints concerning improperly held elections, the complainant must have been a member both at the date of the election *and* when the application is made to the court. If the complaint is that the election has *not* been held, the complainant must be a member on the date of the application. Action must be taken within one year from the default.

   The court or the Certification Officer has the power to make an enforcement order. Such an order will require the union to hold an election, to take such other steps to remedy the declared failure within a specified time or to abstain from certain acts in the future. Failure to comply with the order amounts to a contempt of court (TULR(C)A 1992, ss. 54–6).
2. Part II of the Trade Union Act 1984 withdrew certain of the immunities contained in TULRA 1974, s. 13, in respect of industrial action not approved by a ballot. So, under the original formulation, it was the employers who were seen to be the potential plaintiffs: it did *not* provide a cause of action to trade union members themselves.

   At common law the member's rights are very restricted. The member may apply to the High Court for an interim mandatory injunction requiring the union to hold a ballot in accordance with its rules, but such an action requires that there is a positive obligation under union rules to hold a ballot and, even in such a case, an interim injunction may be refused because it is a 'very exceptional form of relief' (see *Taylor* v *NUM (Yorkshire Area)* [1984] IRLR 445). The Green Paper, *Trade Unions and Their Members*, pointed out (para. 2.5) that in the miners' strike (1984–5) there were 19 common law actions brought against the NUM under the rule book for failing to hold a ballot.

   The EA 1988 changed the position in line with the proposals contained in the Green Paper and provided a cause of action to members themselves. The complex rules surrounding ballots before industrial action are discussed in detail in Chapter 11.
3. The EA 1988 created the office of the Commissioner for the Rights of Trade Union Members (CRTUM). The Commissioner's main functions were to provide assistance to individuals taking or contemplating certain legal proceedings against unions or union officials. From its inception, the CRTUM assisted, on average, ten applications a year. The Employment Relations Act 1999, s. 28, implements the Government's proposals in Chapter 4 of *Fairness at Work* to abolish the office. The Act gives new powers to the Certification Officer (CO) to hear complaints involving most aspects of the law where CRTUM was previously empowered to provide assistance. Section 29 gives effect to Sch. 6, which amends the statutory powers of the Certification Officer as set out in the 1992 Act. The overall effect is to widen the scope for trade union members to

make complaints to the CO of alleged breaches of trade union law or trade union rules, thereby enlarging the CO's role as an alternative to the courts as a means to resolve disputes. The Act achieves this by giving the CO order-making powers in areas of trade union law where he previously made only declarations, and by extending his powers to make declarations and orders into areas where previously he had no competence to hear complaints and issue orders.

FURTHER READING

Honeyball S., *Honeyball and Bowers' Textbook on Employment Law*, 13th edn (Oxford: OUP, 2014), Chs. 13–14.

Moore, S., McKay, S., and Veale, S., *Statutory Recognition and Employment Relations: The impact of trade union recognition* (Basingstoke: Palgrave MacMillan, 2013)

11

Industrial Conflict (1)

Scrutton LJ addressing the University of Cambridge Law Society
18 November 1920 (1 Cambridge Law Journal, p. 8)

The habits you are trained in, the people with whom you mix, lead to your having a certain class of ideas of such a nature that, when you have to deal with other ideas, you do not give as sound and accurate judgements as you would wish. This is one of the great difficulties at present with Labour. Labour says 'Where are your impartial judges? They all move in the same circle as the employers, and they are all educated and nursed in the same ideas as the employers. How can a labour man or a trade unionist get impartial justice?' It is very difficult sometimes to be sure that you have put yourself into a thoroughly impartial position between two disputants, one of your own class and one not of your class.

Maurice Kay LJ, Metrobus Ltd v Unite the Union
[2009] IRLR 851, Court of Appeal

In this country, the right to strike has never been much more than a slogan or a legal metaphor. Such a right has not been bestowed by statute. What has happened is that since the Trade Disputes Act 1906, legislation has provided limited immunities from liability in tort. At times the immunities have been widened, at other times they have been narrowed. Outside the scope of the immunities, the rigour of the common law applies in the form of a breach of contract on the part of the strikers and the economic torts as regards the organisers and their union.

Lord Wedderburn, 'Industrial relations and the courts'
(1980) 9 ILJ 65

In strict juridical terms, there does not exist in Britain any 'right' to organise or any 'right' to strike. The law still provides no more than a 'liberty' to associate in trade unions and certain 'liberties' of action by which trade unions can carry on industrial struggle. Statutory provisions protect trade unions or workers' strikes and other industrial action from illegalities which would otherwise be imposed upon them by the law, largely by the common law created by judicial decisions. When he goes into court in 1980 to defend himself, the trade union official believes he is defending his 'rights'; but he finds that judges see his statutory protections as some form of 'privilege'. Such an attitude on the part of the judiciary at once becomes the source of tension, even hostility, between British trade unions and the ordinary courts.

■ QUESTION

The last extract was written in 1980. In the light of developments over the past two decades or so, referred to in Chapter 1, would it not be more relevant to focus on the tension which now exists between the trade union movement and Parliament?

NOTES

1. The perceived problems with the immunities approach as a means of protecting the freedom to strike have produced calls from a number of quarters for the enactment of a positive right to strike, perhaps adjudicated by a specialised labour court (see Ewing, K. D., 'The right to strike' (1986) 15 ILJ 143; Ewing, K. D., *A Bill of Rights for Britain* (London: Institute of Employment Rights, 1990); Lord Wedderburn, *The Worker and the Law*, 3rd edn (Harmondsworth: Penguin, 1986), Ch. 10; Welch, R., *The Right to Strike: A trade union view* (London: Institute of Employment Rights, 1991)).

   The problem with a right to strike, perhaps enshrined in a Bill of Rights along with other protections for workers and their trade unions, is that it will still be up to courts to interpret the scope of such a right. In a number of writings, Lord Wedderburn has advanced the argument that the question of rights *versus* immunities is not of practical relevance, the major issue being the type of forum and procedure for the adjudication of industrial disputes. He advocates the establishment of a system of autonomous labour courts staffed by lay experts in industrial relations and lawyers of both genders and drawn from differing ethnic and class backgrounds (see Lord Wedderburn, 'The new politics of labour law: Immunities or positive rights?' in *Employment Rights in Britain and Europe* (London: Lawrence and Wishart, 1991), Ch. 4; see also Ewing, K. D., *Working Life: A new perspective on labour law* (London: Institute of Employment Rights, 1996), Ch. 8).

2. In 2013, 443,600 working days were lost due to labour disputes, up from 248,000 in 2012. Also there were more workers involved, with 395,400 involved in stoppages, compared with 236,800 a year before. However, there were fewer stoppages overall: 114 in 2013 compared to 131 in 2012.

   The number of stoppages is also slightly lower than the average from the 2000s (144), but considerably down on the 1990s when the average number of stoppages was 266.

   The number of workers involved in labour disputes in 2013 is lower than the average number per year in the 2000s (402,100) and 1980s (1,040,300). However, it is much higher than the average in the 1990s (201,600).

   The 2013 total for working days lost per year is lower than the average for the 2000s and earlier decades when industrial action was much more common. Looking at the past 20 years compared with the previous 20 years shows that the average number of working days lost has decreased considerably from 7.8 million days in the period 1973–1992 to 615,700 days in the period 1993–2012 (*Labour Disputes-Annual Report 2013*, Office for National Statistics, 17 July 2014).

SECTION 2: SANCTIONS AGAINST INDIVIDUAL STRIKERS

TRADE UNION AND LABOUR RELATIONS (CONSOLIDATION) ACT 1992

237. Dismissal of those taking part in unofficial industrial action

(1) An employee has no right to complain of unfair dismissal if at the time of dismissal he was taking part in an unofficial strike or other unofficial industrial action.

(1A) Subsection (1) does not apply to the dismissal of the employee if it is shown that the reason (or, if more than one, the principal reason) for the dismissal or, in a redundancy case, for selecting the employee for dismissal was one of those specified in section 99(1) to (3), 100 or 103 of the Employment Rights Act 1996 (dismissal in maternity, health and safety and employee representative cases).

In this subsection 'redundancy case' has the meaning given in section 105(9) of that Act.

(2) A strike or other industrial action is unofficial in relation to an employee unless—

   (a) he is a member of a trade union and the action is authorised or endorsed by that union, or

   (b) he is not a member of a trade union but there are among those taking part in the industrial action members of a trade union by which the action has been authorised or endorsed.

Provided that, a strike or other industrial action shall not be regarded as unofficial if none of those taking part in it are members of a trade union.

(3) The provisions of section 20(2) apply for the purpose of determining whether industrial action is to be taken to have been authorised or endorsed by a trade union.

(4) The question whether industrial action is to be so taken in any case shall be determined by reference to the facts as at the time of dismissal.

Provided that, where an act is repudiated as mentioned in section 21, industrial action shall not thereby be treated as unofficial before the end of the next working day after the day on which the repudiation takes place.

(5) In this section the 'time of dismissal' means—

    (a) where the employee's contract of employment is terminated by notice, when the notice is given,

    (b) where the employee's contract of employment is terminated without notice, when the termination takes effect, and

    (c) where the employee is employed under a contract for a fixed term which expires without being renewed under the same contract, when that term expires;

and a 'working day' means any day which is not a Saturday or Sunday, Christmas Day, Good Friday or a bank holiday under the Banking and Financial Dealings Act 1971.

(6) For the purposes of this section membership of a trade union for purposes unconnected with the employment in question shall be disregarded; but an employee who was a member of a trade union when he began to take part in industrial action shall continue to be treated as a member for the purpose of determining whether that action is unofficial in relation to him or another notwithstanding that he may in fact have ceased to be a member.

238. Dismissals in connection with other industrial action

(1) This section applies in relation to an employee who has a right to complain of unfair dismissal (the 'complainant') and who claims to have been unfairly dismissed, where at the date of the dismissal—

    (a) the employer was conducting or instituting a lock-out, or

    (b) the complainant was taking part in a strike or other industrial action.

(2) In such a case an industrial tribunal shall not determine whether the dismissal was fair or unfair unless it is shown—

    (a) that one or more relevant employees of the same employer have not been dismissed, or

    (b) that a relevant employee has before the expiry of the period of three months beginning with the date of his dismissal been offered re-engagement and that the complainant has not been offered re-engagement.

(2A) Subsection (2) does not apply to the dismissal of the employee if it is shown that the reason (or, if more than one, the principal reason) for the dismissal or, in a redundancy case, for selecting the employee for dismissal was one of those specified in section 99(1) to (3), 100 or 103 of the Employment Rights Act 1996 (dismissal in maternity, health and safety and employee representative cases).

In this subsection 'redundancy case' has the meaning given in section 105(9) of that Act.

(2B) Subsection (2) does not apply in relation to an employee who is regarded as unfairly dismissed by virtue of section 238A below.

(3) For this purpose 'relevant employees' means—

    (a) in relation to a lock-out, employees who were directly interested in the dispute in contemplation or furtherance of which the lock-out occurred, and

    (b) in relation to a strike or other industrial action, those employees at the establishment of the employer at or from which the complainant works who at the date of his dismissal were taking part in the action.

Nothing in section 237 (dismissal of those taking part in unofficial industrial action) affects the question who are relevant employees for the purposes of this section.

(4) An offer of re-engagement means an offer (made either by the original employer or by a successor of that employer or an associated employer) to re-engage an employee, either in the job which he held immediately before the date of dismissal or in a different job which would be reasonably suitable in his case.

(5) In this section 'date of dismissal' means—

    (a) where the employee's contract of employment was terminated by notice, the date on which the employer's notice was given, and

    (b) in any other case, the effective date of termination.

238A. Participation in official industrial action

(1) For the purposes of this section an employee takes protected industrial action if he commits an act which, or a series of acts each of which, he is induced to commit by an act which by virtue of section 219 is not actionable in tort.

(2) An employee who is dismissed shall be regarded for the purposes of Part X of the Employment Rights Act 1996 (unfair dismissal) as unfairly dismissed if—

    (a) the reason (or, if more than one, the principal reason) for the dismissal is that the employee took protected industrial action, and

    (b) subsection (3), (4) or (5) applies to the dismissal.

(3) This subsection applies to a dismissal if [the date of dismissal is] within the [protected] period.

(4) This subsection applies to a dismissal if—

    (a) the date of dismissal is] after the end of that period, and

    (b) the employee had stopped taking protected industrial action before the end of that period.

(5) This subsection applies to a dismissal if—

    (a) [the date of dismissal is] after the end of that period,

    (b) the employee had not stopped taking protected industrial action before the end of that period, and

    (c) the employer had not taken such procedural steps as would have been reasonable for the purposes of resolving the dispute to which the protected industrial action relates.

(6) In determining whether an employer has taken those steps regard shall be had, in particular, to—

    (a) whether the employer or a union had complied with procedures established by any applicable collective or other agreement;

    (b) whether the employer or a union offered or agreed to commence or resume negotiations after the start of the protected industrial action;

    (c) whether the employer or a union unreasonably refused, after the start of the protected industrial action, a request that conciliation services be used;

    (d) whether the employer or a union unreasonably refused, after the start of the protected industrial action, a request that mediation services be used in relation to procedures to be adopted for the purposes of resolving the dispute.

(7) In determining whether an employer has taken those steps no regard shall be had to the merits of the dispute.

[(7A) For the purposes of this section 'the protected period', in relation to the dismissal of an employee, is the sum of the basic period and any extension period in relation to that employee.

(7B) The basic period is twelve weeks beginning with the first day of protected industrial action.

(7C) An extension period in relation to an employee is a period equal to the number of days falling on or after the first day of protected industrial action (but before the protected period ends) during the whole or any part of which the employer is locked out by the employer.

(7D) In subsections (7B) and (7C), the 'first day of protected industrial action' means the day on which the employee starts to take protected industrial action (even if on that day he is locked out by his employer)].

(8) For the purposes of this section no account shall be taken of the repudiation of any act by a trade union as mentioned in section 21 in relation to anything which occurs before the end of the next working day (within the meaning of section 237) after the day on which the repudiation takes place.

[(9) In this section 'date of dismissal' has the meaning given by section 238(5).

239. Supplementary provisions relating to unfair dismissal

(1) Sections 237 to 238A (loss of unfair dismissal protection in connection with industrial action) shall be construed as one with Part X of the Employment Rights Act 1996 (unfair dismissal); but sections 108 and 109 of that Act (qualifying period and age limit) shall not apply in relation to section 238A of this Act.

(2) In relation to a complaint to which section 238 or 238A applies, section 111(2) of that Act (time limit for complaint) does not apply, but an industrial tribunal shall not consider the complaint unless it is presented to the tribunal—

    (a) before the end of the period of six months beginning with the date of the complainant's dismissal (as defined by section 238(5)), or

    (b) where the tribunal is satisfied that it was not reasonably practicable for the complaint to be presented before the end of that period, within such further period as the tribunal considers reasonable.

(3) Where it is shown that the condition referred to in section 238(2)(b) is fulfilled (discriminatory re-engagement), the references in—

    (a) sections 98 to 106 of the Employment Rights Act 1996, and

    (b) sections 152 and 153 of this Act,

to the reason or principal reason for which the complainant was dismissed shall be read as references to the reason or principal reason he has not been offered re-engagement.

(4) In relation to a complaint under section 111 of the 1996 Act (unfair dismissal: complaint to employment tribunal) that a dismissal was unfair by virtue of section 238A of this Act—

    (a) no order shall be made under section 113 of the 1996 Act (reinstatement or re-engagement) until after the conclusion of protected industrial action by any employee in relation to the relevant dispute,

    (b) regulations under section 7 of the Employment Tribunals Act 1996 may make provision about the adjournment and renewal of applications (including provision requiring adjournment in specified circumstances), and

    (c) regulations under section 9 of that Act may require a pre-hearing review to be carried out in specified circumstances.

NOTES

1. It is interesting to note that what is now the Trade Union and Labour Relations (Consolidation) Act (TULR(C)A) 1992, s. 238, although substantially strengthened by the Conservative Government in 1982 and 1990, owes its origins to the previous Labour Government. The policy underlying it is that the courts and tribunals are not appropriate places in which to decide the rights and wrongs of industrial disputes. As such, the provision is very much in line with the earlier abstentionist tradition in British industrial relations.

2. The fact that the employer had until 1999 the legal freedom to sack those taking industrial action, even if the action had been sanctioned by a properly conducted ballot, may have come as a surprise to many trade unionists. Indeed, research conducted by Roger Welch in 1987 established that almost 45% of his sample of active trade unionists believed that employers could not dismiss strikers. This figure increased to 70% if the industrial action involved was short of a strike, such as an overtime ban (*The Right To Strike: A trade union view* (London: Institute of Employment Rights, 1991)). This misconception is entirely understandable. After all, how can we talk of a right or freedom to strike unless it is possible for workers to withdraw their labour, in whole or in part, without fearing lawful dismissal? The existence of this legal prop to managerial prerogative will come as no surprise to the News International printers and the P&O seafarers who, during the 1980s, fell victim to its use in defeating strikes.

3. The Employment Act (EA) 1990 tightened the law even further. No employee can complain of unfair dismissal if at the time of the dismissal he or she was taking part in *unofficial industrial action*. In such a situation the employer may selectively dismiss or re-engage any participating employee without risking unfair dismissal liability (see now TULR(C)A 1992, s. 237, in the previous extract).

4. In Chapter 4 of *Fairness at Work*, the Government proposed to extend the protection against dismissal to workers taking *official* industrial action in certain circumstances. In proposing the new rights the Government said it believed that 'in general employees dismissed for taking part in lawfully organised official industrial action should have the right to complain of unfair dismissal to a tribunal' (para. 4.22). It then invited views on the tests which should be applied to determine whether dismissals in such circumstances are fair. Subsequently, s. 16 of and Sch. 5 to the Employment Relations Act 1999 introduced a new s. 238A into TULR(C)A 1992.

   From a trade unionist perspective, the end result is rather disappointing, with only a limited protection against dismissal being extended to those engaged in industrial action. The protection covers only lawfully organised official industrial action and *generally* lasted only for the first eight weeks of the employee's involvement. By virtue of amendments introduced by the Employment Relations Act 2004, the 'protected period' is now 12 weeks and 'locked-out' days are disregarded when determining the length of this period. Given the massive complexity of the law relating to industrial action, it will rarely be the case that workers can be certain that the action they are taking is lawful. If it is found to be unlawful, or their involvement in the dispute extends beyond eight weeks, they risk dismissal without redress unless they can establish selective dismissal/re-engagement within the terms of s. 238. Where the dispute is unofficial, the employee has no protection against dismissal unless it is shown that the reason or principal reason for dismissal or selection for dismissal was one of those specified in ss. 99(1)–(3), 100, 101A(d) or 103 of the Employment Rights Act (ERA) 1996 (dismissal in maternity, health and safety, and employee representative cases) or s. 103A (making a protected disclosure).

   The changes introduced by the 1999 Act still fail to guarantee an effective right to strike and are unlikely to satisfy International Labour Organization Standards.

5. The new rights under s. 238A are not dependent on length of service, so that all employees are covered immediately from the start of their employment. Section 239 is extended to take into account the new provisions and to link them to the ERA 1996, Part X unfair dismissal procedures. Consequential changes are also made to the selective redundancy procedures in s. 105 to take into account the new rights.

Faust v Power Packing Casemakers Ltd
[1983] IRLR 117, Court of Appeal

Three employees refused to work overtime because of a dispute over wages. The industrial tribunal had found their dismissals unfair on the ground that there was no contractual obligation to work overtime.

On appeal to the EAT, the employers argued that the industrial tribunal did not have jurisdiction to consider the complaints since the employees were dismissed for taking part 'in other industrial action' within the meaning of what is now TULR(C)A 1992, s. 238. This argument was accepted by both the Employment Appeal Tribunal (EAT) and the Court of Appeal.

STEPHENSON LJ: Mr Jones submits that to give these words the extended (and what, contrary to his first submission, I have held to be the natural) meaning which they bear if not confined to breaches of contract, would do injustice and defeat the purpose and object of [s. 238] and its predecessor in the Act of 1975, namely, to deprive an employee of his right to complain to an Industrial Tribunal of unfair dismissal if, and only if, he has been guilty of misconduct or has broken the terms of his contract. If Mr Jones' gloss—for such, contrary to his submission, it clearly is—upon the language of the section is rejected, unscrupulous employers will be allowed, so he submits, to dismiss unfairly and unjustly those who take legitimate industrial action, without any fear of the circumstances being investigated by the statutory Tribunals, or of having to pay compensation or reinstate those unfairly dismissed employees. He calls attention to an obvious misunderstanding by the Appeal Tribunal of the effect of their interpretation of [s. 238]. At p. 6 of the judgment of Mr Justice May he said this:

> In our view, the phrase 'other industrial action' in s. 62 of the 1978 Act [now TULR(C)A 1992, s. 238] does not necessarily have to be conduct in breach of contract on the part of the employee and we are, for present purposes, only concerned with the employee. We do not propose to define the phrase 'other industrial action' in s. 62. As we have already said there is no definition in the relevant section in the Act nor in the definition section, and we think that the decision whether or not something was 'other industrial action' within s. 62 can and should be left to the good sense of Industrial Tribunals. They are locally situated. They know the local employment position. They know, for instance, the area's industries. They know what conditions are in the area. They no doubt know, in some cases at any rate, the parties involved. They will be able to ascertain all the relevant facts. They will be able to make findings about what perhaps may be one of the most important aspects of such a case, namely the motives actuating both sides, that is to say, both employer and employee in the dispute concerned. Having considered these and all other matters which they think pertinent and relevant they will be able to decide whether or not the employees were taking 'other industrial action' within [s. 238] and were dismissed in consequence. When one stresses, as we do, that Industrial Tribunals should, in considering this part of the relevant legislation, look at not merely the actions but also the motives of both sides of the dispute, employer and employee, we feel quite happy that this judgment will not provide the licence for many uncompensated dismissals, which Mr Jones suggested would follow our decision.

Now with all that I respectfully agree, except with the statement that Tribunals will be able to ascertain all the relevant facts, including the motives actuating *the employer* and the question whether or not the employees were dismissed in consequence of their industrial action. For once an Industrial Tribunal, in the exercise of its good sense, decides that an employee was, at the date of his dismissal, taking part in industrial action, whether in breach of his contract or not, with the object of applying pressure on his employer or of disrupting his business, the Tribunal must refuse to entertain the complaint or to go into the questions of the employers' motive or reasons for dismissing. And this is a result which requires plain language. If there was any ambiguity in the words of the section, I would reject the Appeal Tribunal's construction of the phrase, their refusal to define it and their leaving its application to the good sense of Industrial Tribunals.

Mr Carr concedes that the criticisms of this part of Mr Justice May's judgment are well founded, but counters the potential injustice relied on by Mr Jones by submitting that the purpose and object of the section is to avoid courts of law and Tribunals being required to investigate the rights and wrongs, or to adjudicate on the merits, of trade disputes in the context of unfair dismissal applications. He referred us to what Lord Scarman said in *NWL Ltd* v *Woods* [1979] IRLR 478 about the policy of the Act of 1974 to exclude trade disputes from judicial review by the courts and to substitute an advisory, conciliation and arbitration process; and he pointed out that such disputes are often complex and to give the determination of them to Industrial Tribunals would defeat the legislative aim of providing cheap and speedy hearings of unfair dismissal complaints by such Tribunals. These considerations must, he submitted, have outweighed with the legislature the potential injustice created by the statutory ban imposed not only on determining complaints by strikers or those engaged in industrial action by [s. 238(1)(b)], but imposed by [s. 238(1)(a)] on determining complaints by employees locked-out by employers at the date of dismissal.

I feel the force of these submissions, but no certainty as to the intention of the legislature in enacting this provision.

In threading my way from sections and subsections to schedules and paragraphs, and from schedule back to section, I may have lost the way, or the thread, or sight of Parliament's aim and object, even if Parliament itself did not. But of this I have no doubt, that as there is no compelling reason why the words of the provision should not be given their natural and ordinary meaning, and good reason why they should not now be defined as once they were, we ought to give them that meaning and apply them, as the Appeal Tribunal did, to the undisputed facts of the case in favour of the respondents.

I would accordingly affirm their decision and dismiss this appeal.

NOTE: As will be seen later in the chapter, most forms of industrial action involve a breach of contract. A strike, whether or not notice is given, amounts to a fundamental breach of contract entitling the employer to dismiss at common law (see *Simmons* v *Hoover Ltd* [1976] IRLR 266; *Boxfoldia Ltd* v *NGA (1982)* [1988] IRLR 383). Most other forms of industrial action short of a strike also amount to contractual breaches. If workers 'boycott' (refuse to carry out) certain work then they are in breach for refusing to comply with a reasonable order. A 'go-slow' or 'work to rule' probably breaks an implied term not to frustrate the commercial objectives of the business (*Secretary of State for Employment* v *ASLEF (No. 2)* [1972] 2 QB 455, p. 107). An overtime ban will also certainly amount to breach of contract if the employer is entitled under the contract to demand overtime, but not if overtime is voluntary on the part of the employee. The previous case goes even further in the sense that, even on the rare occasion that the industrial action does not amount to a breach of contract, the workers involved will not be protected under the law of unfair dismissal.

The following case is concerned with the question of whether there was a selective dismissal as defined by TULR(C)A 1992, s. 238(2)(a).

P&O European Ferries (Dover) Ltd v *Byrne*
[1989] IRLR 254, Court of Appeal

More than 1,000 P&O employees who were dismissed by the employers while on strike claimed that they had been unfairly dismissed. Mr Byrne's case was the first to come before an industrial tribunal. Mr Byrne alleged that one 'relevant employee' had not been dismissed at the relevant time. The employers applied for an order requiring disclosure of the identity of the employee not dismissed on the ground that it was essential for them to know that information. The industrial tribunal dismissed the employers' application on two grounds: (i) that if the time at which it has to be shown that one or more relevant employees had not been dismissed for the purpose of the Employment Protection (Consolidation) Act (EPCA) 1978, s. 62(2)(a) (now TULR(C)A 1992, s. 238(2)(a)) is the conclusion of the tribunal hearing, disclosure would enable the employers to defeat Mr Byrne's claim by dismissing the employee forthwith; (ii) the order for particulars would enable the employers to defeat the claims of the other 1,024 employees whose complaints had yet to be heard. The EAT upheld the tribunal's view but the employers' appeal to the Court of Appeal was successful.

MAY LJ: ... The issue which arises on the proper construction of [s. 238] is at what point in time was the Industrial Tribunal required to look, to see whether there had or had not been discrimination, to decide whether or not they had jurisdiction to determine the applications for compensation for unfair dismissal started by Mr Byrne and by his 1,024 fellow employees.

Insofar as the reasons which the Industrial Tribunal gave and in which they were supported by the Employment Appeal Tribunal for not ordering particulars is concerned, I respectfully disagree with both Tribunals. It was, I think, an improper exercise of the discretion of the Tribunals below not to order such particulars on the ground that to do so would enable the employers to put matters right, if one relevant employee had got through the net and was not dismissed at the time when the remaining 1,025 employees were dismissed. It is true that a party to litigation is not entitled to particulars solely for the purpose of ascertaining the names of his opponent's witnesses. But a party is entitled to particulars to enable him to know what case he has to meet, even though giving those particulars will identify one or more of the potential witnesses on behalf of the other party...

The particular parts of [s. 238(2)(a)] which require careful consideration are, first, the word 'determine' in the earlier part of the subsection, and in the next line the words 'unless it is shown'. The use of the word 'determine' is in my judgment arguably ambiguous. One speaks of a determination in the litigious context both of the final decision of the issues in that litigation and also of the actual hearing itself. In one sense a court determines by a trial from the time that the case is called on until the time when the court gives its ultimate decision. But there is no such ambiguity in the words 'unless it is shown'. Those words necessarily direct one's attention to the conclusion of the relevant hearing before the Industrial Tribunal and in my opinion require one to conclude that on its proper construction the material point in time is when the Industrial Tribunal either determines the substantive hearing which involves determining the jurisdiction point as well, or alternatively determines the jurisdiction point on a preliminary hearing prior to going on, or not going on, as the case may be, with the substantive hearing for compensation.

That in my judgment is the clear and plain meaning of the statutory provision and although we were pressed on the one side not to and on the other side to insert words into the subsection and also to adopt what was said to be a purposive construction of [s. 238(2)(a)], to lead us to adopt a construction which looked to the start of the hearing rather than its conclusion as the material time, Mr Supperstone, who has said everything that could be said on behalf of the respondent employee with skill and cogency was in the end, as I think, almost bound to accept that the meaning of the statutory phrase was clear. When pressed to detail the respects in which he suggested that one should give the phrase a narrow rather than a wider construction, as he suggested at one point was the correct approach, he very properly and realistically found himself unable to do so.

I should just mention that Mr Supperstone also pointed to this potential difficulty if the construction for which he contended was not to be accepted and that is that in the circumstances the unknown Mr 'X' is put in an invidious position. If he is called to give evidence to the effect that he was on strike but not dismissed, he would clearly know that the consequence would be that he would in fact immediately be dismissed so as to preclude the continuing existence of any discrimination under the provisions of [s. 238(2)(a)]. But this cannot affect what in my view is the clear and literal meaning of the subsection.

For my part I do not think that much more need be said on this appeal, although that is in no way intended to be disrespectful to the interesting arguments which counsel on both sides have addressed to the court. In my judgment the Industrial Tribunal, and the Employment Appeal Tribunal following them, erred in directing themselves that it was a legitimate reason for refusing to order particulars which the employers had to have in order to meet the case made against them, that to do so might prejudice not only Mr Byrne's claim but also perhaps the claim of the other 1,024 people and indeed might have a deleterious effect on the continued employment prospects of the unknown Mr 'X'. The allegation had been made against the employers that there had been discrimination in that Mr 'X' had not been dismissed and they were entitled to know who he was so that they could meet that case. They were entitled to know that at that stage in the litigation, particularly having regard to the proper construction of [s. 238(2)(a)] which requires one to look to the end of the decision of the relevant determination by the Industrial Tribunal and not the start.

In those circumstances I would allow this appeal and, subject to hearing further from counsel if necessary, make an order directing that the relevant particulars be given by the employee respondent to the employer appellant.

■ QUESTION

Given the amount of power already ceded to employers by TULR(C)A 1992, s. 239, do you agree with the approach adopted in this case?

Coates and Venables v Modern Methods and Materials Ltd
[1982] IRLR 318, Court of Appeal

In February 1980, weeks of unrest among the employer's workforce came to a head. One of their three factories had been closed and some employees had been transferred. Management called for volunteers for further transfers but none were forthcoming. On Tuesday 12 February, the workforce met outside the factory gate and nearly all remained there refusing to work.

Mrs Leith, an employee of some seven years' standing, had a history of back trouble. On 11 February she had hurt her back and made an appointment to see her doctor. However, she turned up at the factory on 12 February expecting to work. She did not go in because, she said, those employees who had gone in had been abused by fellow workers and she did not herself wish to suffer that abuse. She stayed at the gate for about one hour and then went home. Mrs Leith then saw her doctor who gave her a note certifying her inability to work. She remained absent until 25 April when she returned to work.

The employers dismissed the applicants when they were taking part in the strike. The applicants contended that Mrs Leith was a 'relevant employee' who had taken part in the strike but had not been dismissed. The industrial tribunal held that Mrs Leith was a 'relevant employee' but this view was rejected by the EAT. The Court of Appeal (Eveleigh LJ dissenting) allowed the appeal of Mrs Coates and Mrs Venables.

STEPHENSON LJ: I have found this a difficult case. It ought to be easy to decide what 'taking part in a strike' means and whether on proved or accepted facts a particular employee was or was not taking part in a strike. The industrial tribunal seem to have found it easy, because they unanimously decided that Mrs Leith was taking part, and on an application for review the chairman thought the weight of the evidence showed that she was taking part and a review had no reasonable prospect of success. I know that the construction of a statute is a question of law; but the meaning of ordinary words is not, and the meaning of 'taking part in a strike' seems to me to be just the sort of question which an industrial jury is best fitted to decide. No member of either tribunal has spelt out its meaning, perhaps because it was thought unwise or impossible to attempt a paraphrase of plain words. But I should be very reluctant to assume that any of them attributed to the words an unnatural meaning which they were incapable of bearing in their context, or to differ from their conclusion that Mrs Leith took part in the strike. Only the plainest error in law would enable me to differ from them on such a finding, particularly when the majority of the appeal tribunal, whose decision convicts them of such error, appear themselves to be influenced by an erroneous conception of their power to interfere with the industrial tribunal's decision.

On the other hand, I think that on the evidence without argument and reflection I should have taken the view which Mrs Leith's employers appear to have taken that she was not on strike or striking or taking part in the strike. That view takes into account her state of mind, her intention, her motive, her wishes. Some support for doing that is to be found in what Talbot J said in giving the judgment of the appeal tribunal in *McCormick* v *Horsepower Ltd* [1980] ICR 278 at 283 about Mr Brazier not being motivated by fear in refusing to cross the picket line and withdrawing his labour to aid the strikers; and also in what Lawton LJ in the passage I have quoted from his judgment in the Court of Appeal in the same case said obiter about giving help generally and about Mr Brazier not being shown to have had a common purpose with the striking boilermakers. Furthermore, it seems hard on an employer who takes the trouble to investigate an employee's motives and reasons for stopping work to be told, 'You were wrong to accept what she told you; you ought to have dismissed her and so prevented two other strikers from complaining to the industrial tribunal of unfair dismissal.'

On the other side it is said that it would be intolerable to impose on employers the burden, which these employers undertook with one employee, of looking into the mind of every employee withholding his or her labour before deciding whether to dismiss, in order to see if each had some reason for stopping work unconnected with the object of the strike.

I have come to the conclusion that participation in a strike must be judged by what the employee does and not by what he thinks or why he does it. If he stops work when his workmates come out on strike and does not say or do anything to make plain his disagreement, or which could amount to a refusal to join them, he takes part in their strike. The line between unwilling participation and not taking part may be difficult to draw, but those who stay away from work with the strikers without protest for whatever reason are to be regarded as having crossed that line to take part in the strike. In the field of industrial action those who are not openly against it are presumably for it.

This seems to be the thinking behind the industrial tribunal's decision. If the words in question are capable of bearing that meaning, they are capable of being applied to Mrs Leith's actions on the morning of 12 February 1980, though her time outside the factory gates with the strikers was short and her reason for not entering the factory was accepted. In my judgment a reasonable tribunal could give that meaning to the statutory words and could apply them to Mrs Leith. The industrial tribunal did not, therefore, go wrong in law and it was the majority of the appeal tribunal who did.

I would accordingly allow the appeal, set aside the decision of the Employment Appeal Tribunal and restore the decision of the industrial tribunal.

NOTE: In *Sehmi* v *Gate Gourmet London Ltd* [2009] IRLR 807, EAT, a number of employees stopped work and gathered in the staff canteen to protest about the hiring of seasonal staff. When they refused to disperse despite warnings from management, they were dismissed. On behalf of the employees it was argued that mere physical presence at the gathering was insufficient to amount to participation in unofficial industrial action. However, the EAT held that 'unauthorised and unexplained absence from work at a time when industrial action is in progress will constitute participation'. Mr Justice Underhill stated: 'the deliberate choice of most of the employees to go to the canteen when they should have been working and of all of them to remain there when asked to leave plainly rendered them participants.'

Bigham and Keogh v GKN Kwikform Ltd
[1992] IRLR 4, Employment Appeal Tribunal

Mr Keogh was employed as a scaffolder on the employers' site in Greenford, Middlesex. Mr Bigham was a foreman on that site. The site was operated from the employers' Hammersmith depot. Following the employers' proposal to transfer Mr Bigham because of dissatisfaction with his work, the scaffolders went on strike in protest. Those on strike, including Mr Bigham and Mr Keogh, were dismissed as a result.

Less than three months later, Mr Bigham successfully applied for employment at the company's Luton office. On his application form, he stated that he worked for the company previously in Hammersmith, but did not disclose his earlier dismissal from the Greenford site. When Mr Bigham was taken on, the wages clerk at Luton was on holiday. On his return, he realised that Mr Bigham had been previously dismissed and Mr Bigham was immediately dismissed again.

The industrial tribunal accepted that Mr Bigham was not being fraudulent in failing to disclose that he had been dismissed at Greenford but held that:

> The re-engagement was effected by a mistake and that it would never have been done had the wages clerk been present and not on holiday. It was not therefore an effective re-engagement for the purpose of permitting these tribunals to assume jurisdiction; if we were to find otherwise it would permit the unscrupulous employee… dismissed by a large national organisation simply by some means or other to obtain employment at a distant branch of his company and thereby prevent the operation of the otherwise clear provisions of [s. 238] of the Act.

The EAT allowed Mr Keogh's appeal and remitted the case to the industrial tribunal.

> SIR DAVID CROOM-JOHNSON: Large scaffolding firms with decentralised offices and sites and with a large turnover of labour may have difficulties. Taking on Bigham in a hurry, if that is what happened, was a risk and is a risk which employers of that kind who organise their businesses in that way have to run unless they take steps to avoid it.
>
> We have come to the conclusion that on the submissions which have been put before us and the facts as they were established, that GKN must be said to have had constructive knowledge of what went on at Greenford with Bigham. The employer in each case was the same. It was GKN and they had more than one office but they had records relating to them. Mr Bigham, who was acquitted of any intent to defraud, had revealed on the form that he had worked previously for GKN, although he did not say when, and he told them that he had done so at Hammersmith, that is to say through the Hammersmith office including of course the site at Greenford. All that was required on the part of the wages clerk who was engaging him was to pick up the telephone and to telephone through to Hammersmith and ask what they knew about Mr Bigham. If he had done so, he would have been told straight away. 'Oh yes, he is somebody we had to dismiss less than three months ago because he took part in an unofficial strike,' and in those circumstances one can safely assume that the offer of re-engagement which was made at Luton on that day would never have been made. Unfortunately, the enquiry was not made and nothing was done until the full-time wages clerk, who knew all about Mr Bigham's history, returned to work after his holiday.
>
> In the circumstances therefore, on the facts of the present case, and even accepting as we do the construction of [s. 238] as advanced by Mr Moon, we have come to the conclusion that the offer of re-engagement which was made was one which was within the section and accordingly, Mr Bigham having received an offer of re-engagement within the period, Mr Keogh is entitled to say that the Industrial Tribunal had jurisdiction given to it (otherwise than by [s. 238]), which is an excepting section, and accordingly this appeal by Mr Keogh should be allowed.

NOTES

1. Those sacked while engaging in industrial action may also find that they have jeopardised any right to claim redundancy payments (see the ERA 1996, s. 140).
2. Given that virtually all forms of industrial action constitute a breach of contract, an alternative sanction available to the employer is to make deductions from the wages of those employees engaged in the action (see *Ticehurst and Thompson* v *British Telecommunications* [1992] IRLR 219, CA (Section 3.A(i))).

SECTION 3: LEGAL ACTION AGAINST THE TRADE UNION AND STRIKE ORGANISERS

In trying to make sense of the law relating to industrial action it is important that a structured approach is adopted. The following three-stage framework of analysis was developed by Brightman LJ in *Marina Shipping Ltd* v *Laughton* [1982] QB 1127, and was subsequently employed by Lord Diplock in *Merkur Island Shipping* v *Laughton* [1983] 2 All ER 189:

— STAGE ONE: Does the industrial action give rise to civil liability at common law?

— STAGE TWO: If so, is there an immunity from liability provided by what was s. 13 of the Trade Union and Labour Relations Act (TULRA) 1974 (now TULR(C)A 1992, s. 219)?

— STAGE THREE: If so, has that immunity now been removed by virtue of the changes introduced by the Employment Acts 1980–90, the Trade Union Act 1984 and the Trade Union Reform and Employment Rights Act (TURERA) 1993?

A: Stage one: civil liabilities for industrial action

(i) Industrial action and the contract of employment

Ticehurst and Thompson **v** *British Telecommunications*
[1992] IRLR 219, Court of Appeal

Mrs Ticehurst, a BT manager, participated in a withdrawal of cooperation organised by her union. The action included working strictly to conditioned hours and refusing to undertake new, temporary advancement. Her employers asked her to sign a document undertaking 'to work normally in accordance with the terms of my contract with BT from now on'. When she refused to sign, she was asked to leave the premises and was not paid for the day in question. The same thing occurred on all subsequent working days up to the date when the pay dispute was settled.

At first instance, Mrs Ticehurst's claim for wages due for the relevant period was upheld on the grounds that Mrs Ticehurst was ready and willing to work normally but was not permitted to do so. The Court of Appeal allowed the employer's appeal.

RALPH GIBSON LJ: The implied term upon which BT relies was described in [*Secretary of State for Employment* v *ASLEF (No. 2)* [1972] 2 QB 455]. Although that case arose under the provisions of the Industrial Relations Act 1971, an essential issue was whether the conduct in question constituted a breach of contract according to ordinary common law principles. In April 1972 instructions to union members to work 'strictly to rule' had caused much dislocation of rail services. After resumption of normal working the unions, on the failure of further negotiations, instructed their members to resume 'work to rule'. This Court, dismissing an appeal from the NIRC, held that obedience to instructions to 'work to rule' constituted breach of contract…

The analysis which I respectfully find most apt to define the relevant duties of Mrs Ticehurst under her contract of employment as a manager employed by BT, is that stated by Buckley LJ, namely 'an implied term to serve the employer faithfully within the requirements of the contract'. It is, I think, consistent with the judgments of Lord Denning and Roskill LJ. It was not suggested that there is any express term in the contract of employment of Mrs Ticehurst, or anything else in the general circumstances of this case, which would make it wrong to imply such a term into her contract. It is, in my judgment, necessary to imply such a term in the case of a manager who is given charge of the work of other employees and who therefore must necessarily be trusted to exercise her judgment and discretion in giving instructions to others and in supervising their work. Such a discretion, if the contract is to work properly, must be exercised faithfully in the interests of the employers.

Next, it seems to me clear that participation by Mrs Ticehurst in the concerted action of withdrawal of goodwill, as it was devised and carried out by STE and the members, would constitute a breach of that term if Mrs Ticehurst was intending to continue to participate in it. For example, a manager who intends, when opportunity offers, to consider how much choice she has in performing any task within those listed by STE and then to choose that which would cause the most inconvenience to her employers, is intending, in my judgment, to break her obligation to serve her employers faithfully. Similarly, the doing of the other acts listed in paragraphs 8, 10 and 11 of the statement of the facts above, not from a genuine intention or interest but so as to cause disruption, would be a breach of that obligation. In addition to those acts by Mrs Ticehurst herself, she was intending after 12 April (if she was intending to continue in the action of the withdrawal of goodwill) to continue, as a committee member of the Stone branch of STE, to advise and encourage other members of STE at Stone to carry on that action by herself distributing STE documents and by being available to answer questions of members by telephone. Her name and telephone number were included in documents distributed by the Stone branch committee for that purpose.

I do not accept the submission of Mr Elias that there can be no breach of the implied term for faithful service unless the intended disruption of BT's undertaking was achieved by the action taken, whether to the extent of rendering the business unmanageable or to some other level of disruption. The term is breached, in my judgment, when the employee does an act, or omits to do an act, which it would be within her contract and the discretion allowed to her not to do, or to do, as the case may be, and the employee so acts or omits to do the act, not in honest exercise of choice or discretion for the faithful performance of her work but in order to disrupt the employer's business or to cause the most inconvenience that can be caused. We need not consider the position which would arise if the ill-intentioned course of conduct is shown to have had no significant consequences adverse to the employer and to be incapable of causing any such adverse consequences in future. This action by way of withdrawal of goodwill did have adverse consequences (see paragraph 28 of the facts above) and the fact that STE was asserting that the effect of the action was greater than that in fact achieved does not cause the conduct not to have been a breach of contract.

If on her return to work Mrs Ticehurst was evincing an intention to continue to participate in the action of withdrawal of goodwill, BT was in my judgment entitled on that ground, and without terminating the contract of employment, to refuse to let her remain at work…

NOTES

1. See also *Miles* v *Wakefield Metropolitan District Council* [1987] IRLR 193 and *Wiluszynski* v *Tower Hamlets London Borough Council* [1989] IRLR 259: extracts from these cases appear at pp. 134–136 (Chapter 3, Section 8.A(i)). For a more recent illustration, see *Spackman* v *London Metropolitan University* [2007] IRLR 744.

2. The editors of *Harvey on Industrial Relations and Employment Law* (London: Butterworths) believe that the *Ticehurst* case raises several profoundly important questions (vol. 2, N/1410).

    (a) Is the duty not to be disruptive confined to managerial, supervisory, or professional positions, or is it of general application? The editors of *Harvey* take the view that the general tenor of the judgment suggests the latter.

    (b) Does the unlawfulness lie in the intent rather than the effect? The logic of the judgment would suggest that conduct which is intended to disrupt, but which fails to have that effect, is nevertheless a breach of contract.

    (c) If bloody-mindedness on the part of the worker is a breach of contract, is bloody-mindedness on the part of the employer also a breach of contract? See *Woods* v *WM Car Services (Peterborough) Ltd* [1982] IRLR 413, CA, and *United Bank Ltd* v *Akhtar* [1989] IRLR 507.

    (d) If industrial action is in principle a breach of contract by the workers, are the circumstances relevant in which it takes place? Should we treat workers any differently who are reactively taking industrial action in the face of provocation by their employer as against those who are aggressively pursuing a claim? The editors of *Harvey* think that this is unlikely because the courts would be most reluctant to get involved in the rights and wrongs of a particular dispute, but point out an inconsistency with this approach:

> The courts cannot say whether industrial action is justified, whatever the circumstances; but they can say that an individual who participates in that very same industrial action is unjustified, whatever the circumstances. Heads the employer wins; tails the worker loses.

(ii) The economic torts: inducement of breach of contract

Lumley v Gye
(1853) 2 E & B 216, Queen's Bench Division

The plaintiff, manager of the Queen's Theatre, had a contract with Joanna Wagner, an opera singer, under which she agreed to perform at his theatre for three months and not to sing anywhere else during that time. The plaintiff sued the defendant for wrongfully inducing the breach of Miss Wagner's contract by persuading her to sing at Her Majesty's Theatre instead.

CROMPTON J: Whatever may have been the origin or foundation of the law as to enticing servants, and whether it be, as contended by the plaintiff, an instance and branch of a wider rule, or whether it be, as contended by the defendant, an anomaly and an exception from the general rule of law on such subjects, it must now be considered clear law that a person who wrongfully and maliciously, or which is the same thing, with notice, interrupts the relation subsisting between master and servant by procuring the servant to depart from the master's service, or by harbouring and keeping him as a servant after he has quitted it and during the time stipulated for as the period of service, whereby the master is injured, commits a wrongful act for which he is responsible at law.

NOTE: Inducement to breach of contract is the main economic tort and derives from the decision in this case. Since, as we have seen, virtually all industrial action involves a breach of contract, you can readily appreciate that anyone who calls on workers to take industrial action commits the tort. The inducement may take one of two forms: direct (as in *Lumley* v *Gye* itself) and indirect.

Indirect inducement occurs where the unlawful means (e.g. a breach of employment contracts) are used to render performance of the commercial contract by one of the parties impossible.

D.C. Thomson & Co. Ltd v Deakin
[1952] 2 All ER 361, Court of Appeal

D. C. Thomson operated a non-union shop and dismissed a worker who joined the printing union, NATSOPA. A boycott was organised and lorry drivers employed at Bowaters, the company which supplied D. C. Thomson with paper, told Bowaters that they might not be prepared to deliver paper to Thomson. Bowaters never ordered the men to deliver the paper but did inform D. C. Thomson that they would not be able to deliver paper under contract. D. C. Thomson sought an interlocutory injunction against officials of the various unions concerned to restrain them from procuring any breach by Bowaters of their contract with D. C. Thomson.

SIR RAYMOND EVERSHED: It was suggested in the course of argument... that the tort must still be properly confined to such direct intervention, that is, to cases where the intervener or persuader uses by personal intervention persuasion on the mind of one of the parties to the contract so as to procure that party to break it.

I am unable to agree that any such limitation is logical, rational or part of law... [I]t seems to me that the intervener, assuming in all cases that he knows of the contract and acts with the aim and object of procuring its breach to the damage of B, one of the contracting parties, will be liable not only (1) if he directly intervenes by persuading A to break it, but also (2) if he intervenes by the commission of some act wrongful in itself so as to prevent A from in fact performing his contract; and also (3) if he persuades a third party, for example, a servant of

A, to do an act in itself wrongful or not legitimate (as committing a breach of a contract of service with A) so as to render, as was intended, impossible A's performance of his contract with B.

JENKINS LJ: ... I see no distinction in principle for the present purpose between persuading a man to break his contract with another, preventing him by physical restraint from performing it, making his performance of it impossible by taking away or damaging his tools or machinery, and making his performance of it impossible by depriving him, in breach of their contracts, of the services of his employees. All these are wrongful acts, and if done with knowledge of and intention to bring about a breach of a contract to which the person directly wronged is a party, and, if in fact producing that result, I fail to see why they should not all alike fall within the sphere of actionable interference with contractual relations delimited by Lords MacNaghten and Lindley in *Quinn* v *Leathem* [1901] AC 495.

But, while admitting this form of actionable interference in principle, I would hold it strictly confined to cases where it is clearly shown, first, that the person charged with actionable interference knew of the existence of the contract and intended to procure its breach; secondly, that the person so charged did definitely and unequivocally persuade, induce or procure the employees concerned to break their contracts of employment with the intent I have mentioned; thirdly, that the employees so persuaded, induced or procured did in fact break their contracts of employment; and, fourth, that breach of the contract forming the alleged subject of interference ensued as a necessary consequence of the breaches by the employees concerned of their contracts of employment.

NOTES
1. The court held that the union officials had not directly procured a breach of contract by the suppliers, nor had they intentionally intervened by unlawful means as there had been no breach of contract by the suppliers' employees.
2. The necessary elements of this tort are as follows:
   (a) *Knowledge of the contract* ('that the person charged with actionable interference knew of the existence of the contract and intended to procure its breach').

Emerald Construction Co. Ltd v *Lowthian*
[1966] 1 All ER 1013, Court of Appeal

A trade union sought to bring about the termination of a 'labour-only' subcontract by industrial action. The union officers knew of the existence of the subcontract but did not know its precise terms until after the industrial action commenced. The action continued after they knew of the precise terms of the subcontract, under which the main contractor had the right to terminate if the plaintiff subcontractor did not maintain reasonable progress. The plaintiff sought an interlocutory injunction to stop the defendant union officials from doing anything to procure termination by the main contractors of the subcontract. The defendants argued unsuccessfully that they had not committed any tort as they did not know the terms of the contract; in particular, they did not know the grounds upon which it could be terminated.

LORD DENNING MR: ... If the officers of the trade union, knowing of the contract, deliberately sought to procure a breach of it they would do wrong: see *Lumley* v *Gye*. Even if they did not know of the actual terms of the contract, but had the means of knowledge—which they deliberately disregarded—that would be enough. Like the man who turns a blind eye. So here, if the officers deliberately sought to get his contract terminated, heedless of its terms, regardless whether it was terminated by breach or not, they would do wrong. For it is unlawful for a third person to procure a breach of a contract knowingly, or recklessly, indifferent whether it is a breach or not.

However, the view that wilful blindness as to whether the contract can be lawfully terminated or not will not be sufficient to constitute the tort, as was rejected by the House of Lords in *OBG Ltd* v *Allan* [2007] IRLR 608 (see later in this section).
(b) *Intention to cause its breach* ('that the person so charged did definitely and unequivocally persuade, induce or procure the employees concerned to break their contracts of employment with... intent'). Compare the following extracts:

D. C. Thomson & Co. Ltd v Deakin
[1952] 2 All ER 361, Court of Appeal

JENKINS LJ: … It is now well settled that, apart from conspiracy to injure, no actionable wrong is committed by a person who, by acts not in themselves unlawful prevents another person from obtaining goods or services necessary for the purposes of his business, or who induces others so to prevent that person by any lawful means. It follows in my view, that (again apart from conspiracy to injure) there is nothing unlawful, under the law as enunciated in *Allen* v *Flood* [[1898] AC 1], and subsequent cases, in general appeals to others to prevent a given person from obtaining goods or services, for that is a purpose capable of being lawfully carried out, and there can, therefore, be nothing unlawful in advocating it, unless unlawful means are advocated. The result of such advocacy may well be that unlawful means are adopted by some to achieve the purpose advocated, but that is not to say that a person who advocates the object without advocating the means is to be taken to have advocated recourse to unlawful means. If by reference to the form of actionable interference with contractual rights now propounded, general exhortations issued in the course of a trade dispute, such as 'Stop supplies to X', 'Refuse to handle X's goods', 'Treat X as "black"', and the like, were regarded as amounting to actionable interference, because persons reached by such exhortations might respond to them by breaking their contracts of employment and thereby causing breaches of contracts between their employers and other persons, and because the person issuing such exhortations must be taken constructively to have known that the employers concerned must have contracts of some kind or other with other persons, and that his exhortations (general as they were) might lead to breaches of those contracts through breaches of contracts of employment committed by persons moved by his exhortations, then the proposition must be accepted that it is an actionable wrong to advocate objects which can be achieved by lawful means because they can also be achieved by unlawful means, and to that proposition I decline to subscribe.

Torquay Hotel Co. Ltd v Cousins
[1969] 2 Ch 106, Court of Appeal

The facts of this case are set out at p. 644 later in this section.

WINN LJ: … It was one of [counsel for the defendants'] main submissions that mere advice, warning or information cannot amount to tortious procurement of breach of contract. Whilst granting *arguendi causa* that a communication which went no further would, in general, not, in the absence of circumstances giving a particular significance, amount to a threat or intimidation, I am unable to understand why it may not amount to an inducement. In the ordinary meaning of language it would surely be said that a father who told his daughter that her fiancé had been convicted of indecent exposure, had thereby induced her, with or without justification, by truth or by slander, to break her engagement. A man who writes to his mother-in-law telling her that the central heating in his house has broken down may thereby induce her to cancel an intended visit…

The extracts from *Emerald Construction* and *Torquay Hotel* evidence the ways in which the courts widened the scope of the tort of inducing breach during the 1960s—a decade in which there was a moral panic concerning the British 'strike problem'.

The traditional view is that the defendant must directly intend to injure the claimant. However, in *Falconer* v *ASLEF and NUR* [1986] IRLR 331, the tort of inducement to breach of contract was held to be established where the unions had held a one-day rail strike, thereby inconveniencing the plaintiff's travel arrangements. The unions' argument that it was their intention to harm British Rail, not the plaintiff, was rejected as 'both naive and divorced from reality'. The unions did not appeal against this county court decision because, if it had been upheld, liability under the tort would have been broadened considerably. Subsequently, however, in *Barretts & Baird (Wholesale) Ltd* v *IPCS* [1987] IRLR 3, Henry J stated that to make an individual striker liable in tort to any third party damaged by that strike, the test must be that the striker's *predominant purpose* must be injury to the claimant.

(c) *Unlawful means* ('that the employees so persuaded, induced or procured did in fact break their contracts of employment').

D. C. Thomson & Co. Ltd v Deakin
[1952] 2 All ER 361, Court of Appeal

SIR RAYMOND EVERSHED: I need only add that on the evidence there was no breach of contract by any workman, since Bowaters, for reasons which, I doubt not were prudent, took the line that they would not order any man to load or to deliver paper for the plaintiffs.

(d) *Causing actual breach* ('that breach of the contract forming the alleged subject of interference ensued as a necessary consequence of the breaches by the employees concerned of their contracts of employment').

D. C. Thomson & Co. Ltd v Deakin
[1952] 2 All ER 361, Court of Appeal

JENKINS LJ: Finally, not every breach of a contract of employment with a trading or manufacturing concern by an employee engaged in services required for the performance of a contract between his employer and some other person carries with it as a necessary consequence… the breach of the last mentioned contract. For instance, A induces B, C's lorry driver, to refuse, in breach of his contract of employment, to carry goods which C is under contract to deliver to D, and does so with a view to causing the breach of C's contract with D. C could if he chose, engage some other lorry, or arrange alternative means of transport, but does not do so. He fails to deliver the goods, telling D he is prevented from doing so by B's breach of contract. In such circumstances, there has been no direct invasion by A of C's contract with D, and, although A has committed an actionable wrong against C, designed to bring about the breach of C's contract with D, and a breach has in fact occurred, it cannot be said that the breach has in fact been caused by A's wrongful act, and therefore D cannot, in my view, establish as against A an actionable interference with his rights under his contract with C.

Torquay Hotel Co. Ltd v Cousins
[1969] 2 Ch 106, Court of Appeal

As a result of picketing of the Imperial Hotel, drivers for the hotel's oil suppliers refused to deliver oil to the hotel. The officials of the union claimed that they had not committed the tort of inducing a breach of the contract to supply as there was in the contract between the hotel and the suppliers an exemption clause exempting the suppliers from liability to deliver.

RUSSELL LJ: It was argued that the exception clause had the effect that Esso could not be in breach of its supply contract if failure to do so was due to labour disputes. In my view, the exception clause means what it says and no more; it *assumes* a failure to fulfil a term of the contract—i.e., a breach of contract—and excludes liability—i.e., in damages—for that breach in stated circumstances. It is an exception from liability for non-performance rather than an exception for obligation to perform.

WINN LJ: [T]he argument of counsel for the defendants that clause 10 of the written contract between Esso and the Imperial Hotel for a year's supply would have operated to prevent a failure or failures to deliver ordered instalments of fuel thereunder from being a breach does not seem to be sound. As I construe the clause it affords only an immunity against any claim for damages; it could not bar a right to treat the contract as repudiated by continuing breach…

DENNING LJ: … I have always understood that if one person deliberately interferes with the trade or business of another, and does so by unlawful means, that is, by an act which he is not at liberty to commit, then he is acting unlawfully, even though he does not procure or induce any actual breach of contract.

■ QUESTION
In what sense is Lord Denning's perception of the scope of liability much wider than that of his fellow Lord Justices?

NOTES
1. Justification provides a defence to inducement to breach of contract, but it has been raised successfully in only one case involving industrial action. In *Brimelow* v *Casson* [1924] 1 Ch 302, the defence succeeded where chorus girls were called upon to strike in protest at low wages which in many cases had driven them to prostitution. Apart from this exceptional case, the courts have not been prepared to accept as justification the fact the inducement proceeds from a desire by union officials to protect their members' interests (see *South Wales Miners' Federation* v *Glamorgan Coal Co.* [1905] AC 205).
2. The constituent elements of the tort of inducing breach of contract were restated by the House of Lords in *OBG Ltd* v *Allan* [2007] IRLR 608.

OBG Ltd v Allan; Douglas and others v Hello! Ltd; Mainstream Properties Ltd v Young and others

[2007] IRLR 608, House of Lords

LORD HOFFMANN:

(1) These three appeals are principally concerned with claims in tort for economic loss caused by intentional acts

(a) In *OBG Ltd* v *Allan* the defendants were receivers purportedly appointed under a floating charge which is admitted to have been invalid. Acting in good faith, they took control of the claimant company's assets and undertaking. The claimant says that this was not only a trespass to its land and a conversion of its chattels but also the tort of unlawful interference with its contractual relations. It claims that the defendants are liable in damages for the value of the assets and undertaking, including the value of the contractual claims, as at the date of their appointment. Alternatively, it says the defendants are liable for the same damages in conversion.

(b) In *Douglas* v *Hello! Ltd,* the magazine OK! contracted for the exclusive right to publish photographs of a celebrity wedding at which all other photography would be forbidden. The rival magazine Hello! published photographs which it knew to have been surreptitiously taken by an unauthorised photographer pretending to be a waiter or guest. OK! says that this was interference by unlawful means with its contractual or business relations or a breach of its equitable right to confidentiality in photographic images of the wedding.

(c) In *Mainstream Properties Ltd* v *Young* two employees of a property company, in breach of their contracts, diverted a development opportunity to a joint venture in which they were interested. The defendant, knowing of their duties but wrongly thinking that they would not be in breach, facilitated the acquisition by providing finance. The company says that he is liable for the tort of wrongfully inducing breach of contract…

Inducing breach of contract: elements of the *Lumley* v *Gye* tort

To be liable for inducing breach of contract, you must know that you are inducing a breach of contract. It is not enough that you know that you are procuring an act which, as a matter of law or construction of the contract, is a breach. You must actually realise that it will have this effect. Nor does it matter that you ought reasonably to have done so. This proposition is most strikingly illustrated by the decision of this House in *British Industrial Plastics Ltd* v *Ferguson* [1940] 1 All ER 479, in which the claimant's former employee offered the defendant information about one of the claimant's secret processes which he, as an employee, had invented. The defendant knew that the employee had a contractual obligation not to reveal trade secrets but held the eccentric opinion that if the process was patentable, it would be the exclusive property of the employee. He took the information in the honest belief that the employee would not be in breach of contract. In the Court of Appeal McKinnon LJ observed tartly that in accepting this evidence the judge had 'vindicated [his] honesty… at the expense of his intelligence' but he and the House of Lords agreed that he could not be held liable for inducing a breach of contract.

The question of what counts as knowledge for the purposes of liability for inducing a breach of contract has also been the subject of a consistent line of decisions. In *Emerald Construction Co Ltd* v *Lowthian* [1966] 1 WLR 691, union officials threatened a building contractor with a strike unless he terminated a sub-contract for the supply of labour. The defendants obviously knew that there was a contract—they wanted it terminated—but the court found that they did not know its terms and, in particular, how soon it could be terminated. Lord Denning MR said:

> Even if they did not know the actual terms of the contract, but had the means of knowledge—which they deliberately disregarded—that would be enough. Like the man who turns a blind eye. So here, if the officers deliberately sought to get this contract terminated, heedless of its terms, regardless whether

> it was terminated by breach or not, they would do wrong. For it is unlawful for a third person to procure a breach of contract knowingly, or recklessly, indifferent whether it is a breach or not.
>
> This statement of the law has since been followed in many cases and, so far as I am aware, has not given rise to any difficulty...
>
> The next question is what counts as an intention to procure a breach of contract. It is necessary for this purpose to distinguish between ends, means and consequences. If someone knowingly causes a breach of contract, it does not normally matter that it is the means by which he intends to achieve some further end or even that he would rather have been able to achieve that end without causing a breach. Mr Gye would very likely have preferred to be able to obtain Miss Wagner's services without her having to break her contract. But that did not matter. Again, people seldom knowingly cause loss by unlawful means out of simple disinterested malice. It is usually to achieve the further end of securing an economic advantage to themselves. As I said earlier, the Dunlop employees who took off the tyres in *GWK Ltd* v *Dunlop Rubber Co Ltd* (1926) 42 TLR 326 intended to advance the interests of the Dunlop company.
>
> On the other hand, if the breach of contract is neither an end in itself nor a means to an end, but merely a foreseeable consequence, then in my opinion it cannot for this purpose be said to have been intended. That, I think, is what judges and writers mean when they say that the claimant must have been 'targeted' or 'aimed at'...
>
> Finally, what counts as a breach of contract? In *Torquay Hotel Co Ltd* v *Cousins* [1969] 2 Ch 106, 138, Lord Denning said that there could be liability for preventing or hindering performance of the contract on the same principle as liability for procuring a breach. This dictum was approved by Lord Diplock in *Merkur Island Shipping Corporation* [1983] 2 AC 570, 607–608. One could therefore have liability for interference with contractual relations even though the contracting party committed no breach. But these remarks were made in the context of the unified theory which treated procuring a breach as part of the same tort as causing loss by unlawful means. If the torts are to be separated, then I think that one cannot be liable for inducing a breach unless there has been a breach. No secondary liability without primary liability. Cases in which interference with contractual relations have been treated as coming within the *Lumley* v *Gye* tort (like *Dimbleby & Sons* v *National Union of Journalists* [1984] IRLR 67 and 161) are really cases of causing loss by unlawful means...

NOTE: Following *OBG*, the fundamentals for the tort of inducing breach of contract are:
(a) knowledge that the action will bring about a breach of contract;
(b) an intention to bring about that breach;
(c) an actual breach of contract.

(iii) The economic torts: interference with contract, trade, or business

In contrast to the well-established tort of inducement to breach of contract, this tort is of more recent vintage. In several cases, Lord Denning MR expressed his view that 'if one party interferes with the trade or business of another, and does so by unlawful means, then he is acting unlawfully, even though he does not procure or induce any actual breach of contract' (*Daily Mirror Newspapers* v *Gardner* [1968] 2 All ER 163; see also the earlier extract from *Torquay Hotels Co. Ltd* v *Cousins*). Therefore, it will be unlawful to interfere with a contract short of breach, for example by preventing performance in cases where the contract contains a *force majeure* clause, exempting a party in breach from liability to pay damages (but see the extract from *OBG Ltd* v *Allan* [2007] IRLR 608 (later in this section)).

More recently, it would appear that this head of liability is even broader in scope, encompassing any intentional use of unlawful means aimed at interfering with the claimant's trade or business.

Merkur Island Shipping Corporation v Laughton
[1983] 2 All ER 189, House of Lords

The plaintiffs were the registered owners of a cargo vessel sailing under a flag of convenience and manned by an Asian crew who were paid below the rates approved by the International Transport Workers Federation (the ITF). The ship was time chartered to charterers, who had in turn sub-chartered it. Both the charter and sub-charter required the captain, acting on behalf of the owners, to 'prosecute his voyages with the utmost despatch' and required the charterers or sub-charterers to provide and pay for towage into and out of berths when the ship docked. Under the terms of the time charter, hire was not payable to the shipowners in the event of time being lost because of a labour dispute.

The ship docked at Liverpool in order to load, and when it was ready to sail the sub-charterers arranged for a tug company, with whom they had a running contract, to move the ship out of dock. The ITF decided to black the ship because of the low rates of pay to the crew and persuaded the tugmen employed by the tug company to refuse to operate tugs assigned to move the ship, with the result that it was prevented from leaving port. The tugmen's refusal to take the vessel out was a breach of their contracts of employment with the tug company.

The plaintiff shipowners applied for, and were granted, an interlocutory injunction requiring the ITF to lift the blacking. The defendants appealed against the injunction, contending, *inter alia*, that the part of the shipowners' writ relating to unlawful interference with the charter contract disclosed no cause of action at common law. The Court of Appeal dismissed the appeal and the defendants unsuccessfully appealed to the House of Lords.

LORD DIPLOCK: The common law tort relied on by the shipowners under head (1) of the writ is the tort of interfering by unlawful means with the performance of a contract. The contract of which the performance was interfered with was the charter; the form the interference took was by immobilising the ship in Liverpool to prevent the captain from performing the contractual obligation of the shipowners under cl 8 of the charter to 'prosecute his voyages with the utmost despatch'. The unlawful means by which the interference was effected was by procuring the tugmen and the lockmen to break their contracts of employment by refusing to carry out the operations on the part of the tugowners and the port authorities that were necessary to enable the ship to leave the dock.

The reason why the shipowners relied on interference with the performance of the charter rather than procuring a breach of it was the presence in the charter of cll 51 and 60 which were in the following terms:

Clause 51. Blockade/Boycott. In the event of loss of time due to boycott of the vessel in any port or place by shore labour or others, or arising from Government restrictions by reason of the vessel's flag, or arising from the terms and conditions on which the members of the crew are employed, or by reason of the trading of this vessel, payment of hire shall cease for time thereby lost.

Clause 60. Cancellation. Should the vessel be prevented from work for the reasons as outlined in Clauses 49/50/51 and 52 for more than ten days, Charterers shall have the option of cancelling this contract.

My Lords, your Lordships have had the dubious benefit during the course of the argument in this appeal of having been referred once more to many of those cases, spanning more than a century, that were the subject of analysis in the judgment of Jenkins LJ in *D.C. Thomson & Co. Ltd* v *Deakin* [1952] 2 All ER 361, [1952] Ch 646 and led to his statement of the law as to what are the essential elements in the tort of actionable interference with contractual rights by blacking that is cited by Sir John Donaldson MR and, at rather greater length, by O'Connor LJ in their judgments in the instant case. That statement has, for 30 years now, been regarded as authoritative, and for my part, I do not think that any benefit is gained by raking over once again the previous decisions. The elements of the tort as stated by Jenkins LJ were ([1952] 2 All ER 361 at 379–380, [1952] Ch 646 at 697):

... first, that the person charged with actionable interference knew of the existence of the contract and intended to procure its breach; secondly, that the person so charged did definitely and unequivocally persuade, induce or procure the employees concerned to break their contracts of employment with the intent I have mentioned; thirdly, that the employees so persuaded, induced or procured did in fact break their contracts of employment; and, fourthly, that breach of the contract forming the alleged subject of interference ensued as a necessary consequence of the breaches by the employees concerned of their contracts of employment.

D.C. Thomson & Co. Ltd v *Deakin* was a case in which the only interference with contractual rights relied on was procuring a *breach* by a third party of a contract between that third party and the plaintiff. That is why in the passage that I have picked out for citation Jenkins LJ restricts himself to that form of actionable interference with contractual rights which consists of procuring an actual breach of the contract that formed the subject matter of interference; but it is evident from the passages in his judgment which precede the passage I have cited and are themselves set out in the judgment of O'Connor LJ that Jenkins LJ, though using the expression 'breach', was not intending to confine the tort of actionable interference with contractual rights to the procuring of such non-performance of primary obligations under a contract as would necessarily give rise to secondary obligations to make monetary compensation by way of damages. All prevention of due performance of a primary obligation under a contract was intended to be included even though no secondary obligation to make monetary compensation thereupon came into existence, because the secondary obligation was excluded by some force majeure clause.

If there were any doubt about this matter, it was resolved in 1969 by the judgments of the Court of Appeal in *Torquay Hotel Co. Ltd* v *Cousins* [1969] 1 All ER 522, [1969] 2 Ch 106. That was a case in which the contract the performance of which was interfered with was one for the delivery of fuel. It contained a force majeure clause excusing the seller from liability for non-delivery if delayed, hindered or prevented by, inter alia, labour disputes. Lord Denning MR stated the principle thus ([1969] 1 All ER 522 at 530, [1969] 2 Ch 106 at 138):

> … there must be *interference* in the execution of a contract. The interference is not confined to the procurement of a *breach* of contract. It extends to a case where a third person *prevents* or *hinders* one party from performing his contract, even though it be not a breach. (Lord Denning's emphasis.)

Parliamentary recognition that the tort of actionable interference with contractual rights is as broad as Lord Denning MR stated in the passage I have just quoted is, in my view, to be found in s. 13(1) of the 1974 Act itself, which refers to inducement not only 'to break a contract', but also 'to interfere with its performance', and treats them as being *pari materia* [see now TULR(C)A 1992, s. 219(1)].

So I turn to the four elements of the tort of actionable interference with contractual rights as Jenkins LJ stated them, but substituting 'interference with performance' for 'breach', except in relation to the breaking by employees of their own contracts of employment where such breach has as its necessary consequence the interference with the performance of the contract concerned.

The first requirement is actually twofold: (1) knowledge of the existence of the contract concerned and (2) intention to interfere with its performance.

As respect knowledge, the ITF had been given an actual copy of the charter on 19 July 1980, three days after the blacking started but two days before the application to Parker J was made. Quite apart from this, however, there can hardly be anyone better informed than the ITF as to the terms of the sort of contracts under which ships are employed, particularly those flying flags of convenience. I agree with what was said by Sir John Donaldson MR on the question of the ITF's knowledge ([1983] 1 All ER 334 at 349, [1983] 2 WLR 45 at 63):

> Whatever the precise degree of knowledge of the defendants at any particular time, faced with a laden ship which, as they well knew, was about to leave port, the defendants must in my judgment be deemed to have known of the almost certain existence of contracts of carriage to which the shipowners were parties. The wholly exceptional case would be that of a ship carrying the owner's own goods. Whether that contract or those contracts consisted of a time charter, a voyage charter or one or more bill of lading contracts or some or all of such contracts would have been immaterial to the defendants. Prima facie their intention was to immobilise the ship and in so doing to interfere with the performance by the owners of their contract or contracts of carriage; immobilising a laden ship which had no contractual obligation to move would have been a pointless exercise, since it would have brought no pressure to bear on the owners.

The last sentence of this citation deals also with intention. It was the shipowners on whom the ITF wanted to bring pressure to bear, because it was they who were employing seamen at rates of pay lower than those it was the policy of the ITF to enforce. The only way in which income could be derived by the shipowners from the ownership of their ship was by entering into contracts with third parties for the carriage of goods under which a primary obligation of the shipowners would be to prosecute the contract voyages with the utmost dispatch, and their earnings from their ship would be diminished by its immobilisation in port. Diminishing their earnings under the contract of carriage was the only way in which pressure could be brought to bear on the shipowners.

…

OBG Ltd v Allan; Douglas and others v Hello! Ltd; Mainstream Properties Ltd v Young and others

[2007] IRLR 608, House of Lords

LORD HOFFMANN: In my opinion, and subject to one qualification, acts against a third party count as unlawful means only if they are actionable by that third party. The qualification is that they will also be unlawful means if the only reason why they are not actionable is because the third party has suffered no loss. In the case of intimidation, for example, the threat will usually give rise to no cause of action by the third party because he will have suffered no loss. If he submits to the threat, then, as the defendant intended, the claimant will have suffered loss instead. It is nevertheless unlawful means. But the threat must be to do something which would have been actionable if the third party had suffered loss. Likewise, in *National Phonograph Co Ltd* v *Edison-Bell Consolidated Phonograph Co Ltd* [1908] 1 Ch 335 the defendant intentionally caused loss to the claimant by fraudulently inducing a third party to act to the claimant's detriment. The fraud was unlawful means because it would have been actionable if the third party had suffered any loss, even though in the event it was the claimant who suffered. In this respect, procuring the actions of a third party by fraud (dolus) is obviously very similar to procuring them by intimidation (metus).

Lonrho plc v *Fayed* [1990] 2 QB 479 was arguably within the same principle as the *National Phonograph Co* case. The claimant said that the defendant had intentionally caused it loss by making fraudulent statements to the directors of the company which owned Harrods, and to the Secretary of State for Trade and Industry, which induced the directors to accept his bid for Harrods and the Secretary of State not to refer the bid to the Monopolies Commission. The defendant was thereby able to gain control of Harrods to the detriment of the claimant, who wanted to buy it instead. In the Court of Appeal, Dillon LJ referred to the *National Phonograph* case as authority for rejecting an argument that the means used to cause loss to the plaintiff could not be unlawful because neither the directors nor the Secretary of State had suffered any loss. That seems to me correct. The allegations were of fraudulent representations made to third parties, which would have been actionable by them if they had suffered loss, but which were intended to induce the third parties to act in a way which caused loss to the claimant. The Court of Appeal therefore refused to strike out the claim as unarguable and their decision was upheld by the House of Lords.

Unlawful means therefore consists of acts intended to cause loss to the claimant by interfering with the freedom of a third party in a way which is unlawful as against that third party and which is intended to cause loss to the claimant. It does not in my opinion include acts which may be unlawful against a third party but which do not affect his freedom to deal with the claimant.

Thus in *RCA Corporation* v *Pollard* [1983] Ch 135 the claimant had the exclusive right to exploit records made by Elvis Presley. The defendant was selling bootleg records made at Elvis Presley concerts without his consent. This was an infringement of section 1 of the Dramatic and Musical Performers' Protection Act 1958, which made bootlegging a criminal offence and, being enacted for the protection of performers, would have given Elvis Presley a cause of action: see Lord Diplock in *Lonrho Ltd* v *Shell Petroleum Co Ltd (No 2)* [1982] AC 173, 187. The Court of Appeal held that the infringement of the Act did not give RCA a cause of action. The defendant was not interfering with the liberty of the Presley estate to perform the exclusive recording contract which, as Oliver LJ noted was 'no more than an undertaking that he will not give consent to a recording by anyone else'. Nor did it prevent the Presley estate from doing any other act affecting the plaintiffs. The bootlegger's conduct, said Oliver LJ:

> merely potentially reduces the profits which [the claimants] make as the result of the performance by Mr Presley's executors of their contractual obligations…

Lonrho Ltd v *Shell Petroleum Co Ltd (No 2)* [1982] AC 173 was an attempt to found a cause of action simply on the fact that the conduct alleged to have caused loss was contrary to law. The defendant's conduct was alleged to be a criminal offence but not actionable by anyone. In this respect it was unlike *RCA* v *Pollard* and *Isaac Oren* v *Red Box Toy Factory Ltd*, in which it could at least be said that the conduct was a wrong against someone in contractual relations with the claimant. Lonrho owned and operated a refinery in Rhodesia supplied by a pipeline from the port of Beira. When Rhodesia declared independence in 1965, the UK imposed sanctions which made it unlawful for anyone to supply the country with oil. As a result, the refinery and pipeline stood idle until the independence regime came to an end. Lonrho alleged that Shell had prolonged the regime by unlawfully supplying Rhodesia with oil through other routes and thereby caused it loss. The House of Lords decided that the alleged illegality gave rise to no cause of action on which Lonrho could rely. Again, there was no allegation that Shell had intended to cause loss to Lonrho, but I cannot see how that would have made any difference. Shell did not interfere with any third party's dealings with Lonrho and even if it had done so, its acts were not wrongful in the sense of being actionable by such third party…

■ **QUESTION**

Does it now follow that the decision in *Torquay Hotel* v *Cousins* [1969] 2 Ch 106, CA—where the Court of Appeal held that it was tortious knowingly to interfere with the performance of a contract, even though not causing a breach—was wrongly decided?

NOTE: The remaining issue in relation to establishing liability for the tort of causing loss by unlawful means is the matter of intention. According to Lord Hoffmann in *OBG Ltd*:

> In the *Lumley* v *Gye* tort, there must be an intention to procure a breach of contract. In the unlawful means tort, there must be an intention to cause loss. The ends which must have been intended are different. *South Wales Miners' Federation* v *Glamorgan Coal Co Ltd* [1905] AC 239 shows that one may intend to procure a breach of contract without intending to cause loss. Likewise, one may intend to cause loss without intending to procure a breach of contract. But the concept of intention is in both cases the same. In both cases it is necessary to distinguish between ends, means and consequences. One intends to cause loss even though it is the means by which one achieved the end of enriching oneself. On the other hand, one is not liable for loss which is neither a desired end nor a means of attaining it but merely a foreseeable consequence of one's actions.

The master of the *Othello* in *Tarleton* v *M'Gawley* may have had nothing against the other trader. If he had gone off to make his fortune in other waters, he would have wished him well. He simply wanted a monopoly of the local trade for himself. But he nevertheless intended to cause him loss. This, I think, is all that Woolf LJ was intending to say in a passage in *Lonrho plc* v *Fayed* [1990] 2 QB 479, 494, which has proved controversial:

> Albeit that he may have no desire to bring about that consequence in order to achieve what he regards as his ultimate ends, from the point of view of the plaintiff, whatever the motive of the defendant, the damage which he suffers will be the same.

On the other hand, I think that Henry J was right in *Barretts & Baird (Wholesale) Ltd* v *Institution of Professional Civil Servants* [1987] IRLR 3 when he decided a strike by civil servants in the Ministry of Agriculture in support of a pay claim was not intended to cause damage to an abattoir which was unable to obtain the certificates necessary for exporting meat and claiming subsidies. The damage to the abattoir was neither the purpose of the strike nor the means of achieving that purpose, which was to put pressure on the government...

(iv) Intimidation

The tort of intimidation may take the form of compelling a person by threats of unlawful action to do some act which causes him loss; or of intimidating other persons, by threats of unlawful action, with the intention and effect of causing loss to a third party. Prior to 1964, it was assumed that the tort was confined to threats of physical violence, but in that year the House of Lords held that threats to break a contract were encompassed by the tort.

Rookes v *Barnard*
[1964] AC 1129, House of Lords

BOAC and the draughtsmen's union (AESD) operated an informal closed shop arrangement. The plaintiff was a draughtsman employed by BOAC, and in 1955 he resigned from the union. Officials of the union threatened BOAC that, unless they dismissed the plaintiff, union members would go on strike. Rookes was given notice and his contract of employment was lawfully terminated. He sued the union officials alleging, *inter alia*, intimidation.

LORD DEVLIN: ... It is not, of course, disputed that if the act threatened is a crime, the threat is unlawful. But otherwise is it enough to say that the act threatened is actionable as a breach of contract or must it be actionable as a tort? My Lords, I see no good grounds for the latter limitation... The essence of the offence is coercion. It cannot be said that every form of coercion is wrong. A dividing line must be drawn and the natural line runs between what is lawful and unlawful as against the party threatened...

I find therefore nothing to differentiate a threat of a breach of contract from a threat of physical violence or any other illegal threat. The nature of the threat is immaterial... All that matters to the plaintiff is that, metaphorically speaking, a club has been used. It does not matter to the plaintiff what the club is made of—whether it is a physical club or an economic club, a tortious club or an otherwise illegal club. If an intermediate party is improperly coerced, it does not matter to the plaintiff how he is coerced.

I think, therefore, that at common law there is a tort of intimidation and that on the facts of this case each of the respondents has committed it, both individually (since the jury has found that each took an overt and active part) and in combination with others.

(v) Conspiracy

This tort may take two forms:

(a) conspiracy to commit an unlawful act (a conspiracy to commit a crime or tort is clearly included in this category);

(b) conspiracy to injure by lawful means ('simple conspiracy').

Quinn v Leathem

[1901] AC 495, House of Lords

The plaintiff, a flesher, employed non-union men. The defendants told the plaintiff and one of his best customers, a butcher, that unless he dismissed the non-unionists, they would be subject to industrial action. As a result, the plaintiff lost his customer and the plaintiff sued for conspiracy to injure.

LORD LINDLEY: Black lists are real instruments of coercion, as every man whose name is on one soon discovers to his cost. A combination not to work is one thing, and is lawful. A combination to prevent others from working by annoying them if they do is a very different thing, and is prima facie unlawful. Again, not to work oneself is lawful so long as one keeps off the poor-rates, but to order men not to work when they are willing to work is another thing. A threat to call men out given by a trade union official to an employer of men belonging to the union and willing to work with him is a form of coercion, intimidation and molestation, or annoyance to them and to him very difficult to resist, and, to say the least, requiring justification. None was offered in this case.

NOTE: This form of conspiracy which was developed in *Quinn* v *Leathem* is most dangerous, because it makes it unlawful when two or more persons do something which would have been quite lawful if performed by an individual. A conspiracy to injure is simply an agreement to cause deliberate loss to another without justification. The motive or purpose of the defendants is important. If the predominant purpose is to injure the claimant, the conspiracy is actionable. If, on the other hand, the principal aim is to achieve a legitimate goal, the action is not unlawful, even if in so doing the claimant suffers injury. While it took the courts some time to accept trade union objectives as legitimate, later decisions adopted a more liberal stance, as the next extract illustrates.

Crofter Hand-Woven Harris Tweed Co. v Veitch

[1942] AC 435, House of Lords

The millowners on the Island of Lewis refused to enter into a closed shop agreement with the union or grant a pay increase because of competition from the plaintiffs' mills which imported cheap spun yarn from the mainland. The defendant trade union officials instructed their members who were dockers at Stornoway not to handle yarn destined for the plaintiffs. There was no breach of employment contracts by the dockers. The plaintiffs sued the defendants for conspiracy to injure.

LORD WRIGHT: As the claim is for a tort, it is necessary to ascertain what constitutes the tort alleged. It cannot be merely that the appellants' right to freedom in conducting their trade has been interfered with. That right is not an absolute or unconditional right. It is only a particular aspect of the citizen's right to personal freedom, and like other aspects of that right is qualified by various legal limitations, either by statute or common law. Such limitations are inevitable in organised societies where the rights of individuals may clash. In commercial affairs each trader's rights are qualified by the rights of others to compete. Where the rights of labour are concerned, the rights of the employer are conditioned by the rights of the men to give or withhold their services. The right of workmen to strike is an essential element in the principle of collective bargaining…

It is thus clear that employers of workmen or those who like the appellants depend in part on the services of workmen, have in the conduct of their affairs to reckon with this freedom of the men and to realise that the exercise of the men's rights may involve some limitation on their own freedom in the management of their business. Such interference with a person's business, so long as the limitations enforced by law are not contravened, involves no legal wrong against the person. In the present case the respondents are sued for imposing the 'embargo', which corresponds to calling the men out on strike. The dockers were free to obey or not obey the call to refuse to handle the appellants' goods. In refusing to handle the goods they did not commit any breach of contract with anyone; they were merely exercising their own rights. But there might be circumstances which rendered the action wrongful. The men might be called out in breach of their contracts with their employer, and that would be clearly a wrongful act against the employer, an interference with his contractual right, for which damages could be claimed not only as against the contract breaker, but against the person who counselled or procured or advised the breach.…

But in *Allen* v *Flood* [1898] AC 1, this House was considering a case of an individual actor, where the element of combination was absent. In that case, it was held, the motive of the defendant is immaterial. Damage done intentionally and even malevolently to another, thus, it was held, gives no cause of action so long as no legal right of the other is infringed.… Thus, for the purposes of the present case we reach the position that apart from combination no wrong would have been committed. There was no coercion of the dockers. There were no threats to them. They were legally free to choose the alternative course which they preferred…

… The appellants must establish that they have been damnified by a conspiracy to injure, that is, that there was a wilful and concerted intention to injure without just cause, and consequent damage…

I have attempted to state principles so generally accepted as to pass into the realm of what has been called jurisprudence, at least in English law, which has for better or worse adopted the test of self-interest or selfishness as being capable of justifying the deliberate doing of lawful acts which inflict harm, so long as the means employed are not wrongful. The common law in England might have adopted a different criterion and one more consistent with the standpoint of a man who refuses to benefit himself at the cost of harming another. But we live in a competitive and acquisitive society, and the English common law may have felt that it was beyond its power to fix any but the crudest distinctions and metes and bounds which divide the rightful from the wrongful use of the actor's own freedom, leaving the precise application in any particular case to the jury or the judge of fact. If further principles of regulation or control are to be introduced, that is a matter for the legislature…

… The respondents had no quarrel with the yarn importers. Their sole object, the courts below have held, was to promote their union's interests by promoting the interest of the industry on which the men's wages depended. On these findings, with which I agree, it could not be said that their combination was without sufficient justification. Nor would this conclusion be vitiated, even though their motives may have been mixed, so long as the real or predominant object, if they had more than one object, was not wrongful. Nor is the objection tenable that the respondents' real or predominant object was to secure the employers' help to get 100 per cent membership of the union among the textile workers. Cases of mixed motives or, as I should prefer to say, of the presence of more than one object are not uncommon. If so, it is for the jury or judge of fact to decide which is the predominant object, as it may be assumed the jury did in *Quinn's* case, when they decided on the basis that the object of the combiners was vindictive punishment, not their own practical advantage…

NOTES

1. The courts have also held combinations to be justified where their purpose was to force an employer to lift a colour bar in a club (*Scala Ballroom (Wolverhampton) Ltd* v *Ratcliffe* [1958] 3 All ER 220, CA) and to enforce a 'closed shop' agreement (*Reynolds* v *Shipping Federation* [1924] 1 Ch 28).

2. Until the decision of the House of Lords in *Lonrho plc* v *Fayed* [1992] 1 AC 1129, it was assumed that both forms of conspiracy required the claimant to show that the predominant purpose of the conspirators was to injure the claimant. In *Fayed*, it was emphasised that, for the purposes of conspiracy to commit an unlawful act, it was merely sufficient to show that the conspirators acted with intent to injure the claimant.

(vi) Inducement of breach of statutory duty

Meade v *Haringey LBC*
[1979] 2 All ER 1016, Court of Appeal

School caretakers and ancillary staff threatened to close schools in support of a wage claim. In response, the defendant local authority instructed all headmasters in the area to close the schools and to advise parents not to send their children to school. Parents complained that the local authority was in breach of a statutory duty to make schools available for full-time education. The parents sought a mandatory injunction. By the time the case reached the Court of Appeal, the industrial action had been called off and all the schools were open. While the injunction was refused, the court held that there had been a prima facie breach of statutory duty.

LORD DENNING MR: Now comes the great question in this case: had the borough council any just cause or excuse for closing the schools as they did? On the evidence as it stands, the borough council were acting under the influence of the trade unions and indeed in combination with them. And the trade unions and their secretaries were, as I see it, acting quite unlawfully. They were calling on the local education authority to break their statutory duty, to close the schools instead of keeping them open as they should have done. Now s. 13 of the Trade Union and Labour Relations Act 1974 as amended gives them immunity if they induce a person to break a contract. But it gives them no immunity if they induce a local authority to break its statutory duty. The law is well-established that a public authority cannot enter into any contract or take any action incompatible with the due exercise of its statutory powers or the discharge of its statutory duties: see *Birkdale District Electric Supply Co. Ltd* v *Southport Corpn* [1926] AC 355 at 364 by Lord Birkenhead. It cannot effectively contract not to exercise its statutory powers or to abdicate its statutory duties: see *Staines Urban District Council's Agreement, Triggs* v *Staines Urban District Council* [1968] 2 All ER 1 at by Cross J. It seems to me that if the local education authority closed the schools, at the behest of the trade unions, or in agreement with them, they were acting unlawfully. The trade unions had no right whatever to ask the borough council to close the schools. The borough council had no business whatever to agree to it. Instead they should have kept the schools open, and risked the consequences of the dispute escalating. Or they should have moved the court for an injunction to restrain the leaders of the trade unions from interfering with the due opening of the schools. I am confident that the people at large would have supported such a move and expect the trade union leaders to obey it, and they would have obeyed it.

(vii) Economic duress

Dimskal Shipping Co. SA v *International Transport Workers' Federation*
[1992] IRLR 78, House of Lords

The plaintiffs, a Panamanian company, owned the 'Evia Luck', a ship registered in Panama, managed from Greece and crewed by Greeks and Filipinos.

When the ship berthed in Sweden, representatives of the Swedish affiliates of the ITF threatened that the ship would be blacked unless ITF employment contracts were entered into with the crew.

As a result of the threats, the plaintiffs orally agreed to pay a sum of US$103,463 to the ITF at its London headquarters, representing all the crew's backdated wages calculated in accordance with ITF wage scales. This sum was paid. In addition, the plaintiffs agreed to pay ITF entrance and membership fees and to make a contribution to the ITF welfare fund. The plaintiffs also agreed to lodge a bank performance guarantee of $200,000 and to provide deeds of undertaking to the effect that they would not institute proceedings against Filipino crew members, that they would enter into an ITF special agreement, that they would provide all crew members with ITF employment contracts, that they would sign a document declaring that they were complying voluntarily with ITF's demands and that they would provide letters of indemnity for all crew members.

Following a delay in execution of the required documents, the ship was blacked. As a result, the plaintiffs complied with ITF demands and signed the required documents. The plaintiffs also signed a letter of undertaking which included the following clause: 'This undertaking shall be legally enforceable within the meaning of s. 18 of the Trade Union and Labour Relations Act 1974 [now TULR(C)A 1992, s. 179], and be subject to English Law and the jurisdiction of the English courts.' The ship was then allowed to sail.

The plaintiffs sought restitution of the sums totalling US$111,743 which had been paid to the ITF on the ground that the payments had been made pursuant to contracts void for duress.

The Court of Appeal, overruling the decision of Phillips J, held that whether the economic pressure was legitimate was to be answered by reference to English law. The House of Lords, by a majority, dismissed the ITF's appeal.

LORD GOFF OF CHIEVELEY: The starting-point for the consideration of this question is the decision of your Lordships' House in *Universe Sentinel, The* [1982] IRLR 200, and in particular the speech in that case of Lord Diplock, who delivered the leading speech for the majority. For present purposes, the most relevant passage in Lord Diplock's speech is to be found at pp. 205–206, in which he considered the effect upon economic duress, as a basis for obtaining restitution, of the immunity then conferred by the Trade Union and Labour Relations Act 1974 [see now the Trade Union and Labour Relations (Consolidation) Act 1992]. The pressure in that case took the form of blacking the plaintiff's ship, at the instigation of the ITF, while she was lying at Milford Haven. The Act (in this respect no longer in force at the time of the events in the present case) conferred an immunity against an action in tort in respect of pressure of the type there exerted by the ITF. It did not expressly provide for any immunity in respect of an action in restitution. However, Lord Diplock said, at p. 205, 28:

> The use of economic duress to induce another person to part with property or money is not a tort per se; the form that the duress takes may or may not be tortious. The remedy to which economic duress gives rise is not an action for damages but an action for restitution of property or money exacted under such duress and the avoidance of any contract that had been induced by it; but where the particular form taken by the economic duress used is itself a tort, the restitutional remedy for money had and received by the defendant to the plaintiff's use is one which the plaintiff is entitled to pursue as an alternative remedy to an action for damages in tort.
>
> In extending into the field of industrial relations the common law concept of economic duress and the right to a restitutionary remedy for it which is currently in process of development by judicial decisions, this House would not, in my view, be exercising the restraint that is appropriate to such a process if it were so to develop the concept that, by the simple expedient of 'waiving the tort', a restitutionary remedy for money had and received is made enforceable in cases in which Parliament has, over so long a period of years, manifested its preference for a public policy that a particular kind of tortious act should be legitimised in the sense that I am using that expression.
>
> It is only in this indirect way that the provisions of the Trade Union and Labour Relations Act 1974 are relevant to the duress point. The immunities from liability in tort provided by ss. 13 and 14 [see now TULR(C)A 1992, s. 219] are not directly applicable to the shipowners' cause of action for money had and received. Nevertheless, these sections, together with the definition of trade dispute in s. 29 [now TULR(C) A 1992, s. 244], afford an indication, which your Lordships should respect, of where public policy requires that the line should be drawn between what kind of commercial pressure by a trade union upon an employer in the field of industrial relations ought to be treated as legitimised despite the fact that the will of the employer is thereby coerced, and what kind of commercial pressure in that field does amount to economic duress that entitles the employer victim to restitutionary remedies.

It is not necessary for present purposes to explore the basis of this decision. It appears to bear some affinity to the principle underlying those cases in which the courts have given effect to the inferred purpose of the legislature by holding a person entitled to sue for damages for breach of a statutory duty, though no such right of suit has been expressly created by the statute imposing the duty. It is enough to state that, by parity of reasoning, not only may an action of restitution be rejected as inconsistent with the policy of a statute such as that under consideration in *The Universe Sentinel*, [1982] IRLR 200, but in my opinion a claim that a contract is voidable for duress by reason of pressure legitimised by such a statute may likewise be rejected on the same ground.

It is against the background of that decision that the problem in the present case falls to be considered…

■ QUESTION

Would it be true to say that here is an inverse relationship between the scope of economic duress and the statutory trade dispute immunities?

(viii) EU cross-border industrial action

Recently, the tension between the rights of trade unions to take industrial action to protect their members' interests on the one hand and, on the other, the directly enforceable employers' economic freedoms of establishment and to provide services set out in Articles 43 and 49 of the EU Treaty, has come to the fore. The European Court of Justice (ECJ) has had to decide where the balance between social rights and competition rights should be struck.

International Transport Workers' Federation v *Viking Line ABP* [2008] IRLR 143 related to industrial action taken by FSU, the Finnish affiliate of the London-based ITF, to stop the employers from reflagging a ferry from Finland to Estonia, and staffing it with a cheaper Estonian crew. The ECJ characterised the right of establishment as 'a fundamental freedom', which is horizontally binding. It is capable of conferring rights on a private employer which may be relied on against a trade union. The ECJ held that the right to strike does not fall outside the scope of regulation by EU competition rules. In effect, this means that trade union activity is potentially reviewable by the courts under EU law and, if it infringes the rights of employers, the courts may examine the reasons for the industrial action to see whether they conform to the principles of proportionality. On the other hand, the ECJ also held, for the first time, that 'the right to take collective action, including the right to strike, must... be recognised as a fundamental right which forms an integral part of the general principles of Community law', even though it is not mentioned as such in the Treaty. Moreover, the right to strike 'in principle justifies a restriction of one of the fundamental freedoms guaranteed by the Treaty'. This is because the 'protection of workers' is an overriding reason of public interest. But not all collective action can be so characterised. Whether the industrial action is proportionate to achieve the protective aim is for the national court to decide. Previewing the outcome of *Viking* and *Laval* in the Industrial Law Journal, Lord Wedderburn writes: ' "Proportionate" to what? The national economy? The employers' wage policies? The poverty of union members?' The ECJ in *Viking* answers this by saying that the collective action must not 'go beyond what is necessary to achieve the objective pursued', such as protecting jobs or conditions of employment that have been jeopardised. In this case, that means 'whether, under the national rules and collective agreement law applicable to that action, FSU did not have other means at its disposal which were less restrictive of freedom of establishment in order to bring to a successful conclusion the collective negotiations entered into with Viking, and... whether that trade union had exhausted those means before initiating such action.' In a case where transnational competition rights are threatened, therefore, it will be up to the judges to decide whether the union has 'exhausted' other means before taking industrial action.

Laval un Partneri Ltd v *Svenska Byggnadsarbetareförbundet* [2008] IRLR 160 involved a boycott by Swedish building unions of sites manned by workers posted from Latvia who were paid lower wages than that provided for under the Swedish collective agreement for the building sector. The ECJ held that 'the right to take collective action for the protection of the workers of the host state against possible social dumping may constitute an overriding reason of public interest... which, in principle, justifies a restriction of one of the fundamental freedoms guaranteed by the Treaty', the freedom to provide services. However, in this particular case, the Court ruled that the industrial action could not be regarded as justified by the public interest of protecting workers because the Posted Workers Directive does not impose an obligation on foreign service providers to go beyond mandatory minimum standards in the host State and the union was attempting to force the Latvian employer to provide more favourable pay and conditions than that which had to be observed in Sweden by Swedish employers, where there is no statutory minimum wage. (See also *Ruffert* v *Land Niedersachsen*, C–346/06 [2008] IRLR 467, ECJ).

The Lindsey Oil Refinery dispute in the early spring and summer of 2009 raised issues about the posting of European Union workers to the UK to fulfil a contract on a multi-employer construction site at a time of high levels of unemployment in the UK construction industry and deepening recession. According to press reports, the dispute was resolved only with an agreement to hire at least 100 'British' workers at the site. This raises questions as to the compatibility of the deal with Community law (see Barnard, C., ' "British jobs for British workers": The Lindsey Oil Refinery dispute and the future of local labour clauses in an integrated EU market' (2009) 38 ILJ 245).

B: Stage two: the immunities

TRADE UNION AND LABOUR RELATIONS (CONSOLIDATION) ACT 1992

219. Protection from certain tort liabilities

(1) An act done by a person in contemplation or furtherance of a trade dispute is not actionable in tort on the ground only—

    (a) that it induces another person to break a contract or interferes or induces another person to interfere with its performance, or

    (b) that it consists in his threatening that a contract (whether one to which he is a party or not) will be broken or its performance interfered with, or that he will induce another person to break a contract or interfere with its performance.

(2) An agreement or combination by two or more persons to do or procure the doing of an act in contemplation or furtherance of a trade dispute is not actionable in tort if the act is one which if done without any such agreement or combination would not be actionable in tort.

NOTES
1. Under the Trade Disputes Act 1906, the immunity for inducements to breach in contemplation or furtherance of a trade dispute extended only to contracts of employment. This allowed the courts in the 1960s to find ways of holding trade unionists liable for inducing breaches of commercial contracts (see *J. T. Stratford & Sons Ltd* v *Lindley* [1965] AC 269).

    In the mid-1970s, immunity was extended to cover the breach of 'any' contract. The relevant provision states that an act done by a person in contemplation or furtherance of a trade dispute shall not be actionable in tort on the ground only 'that it induces another person to break a contract or interferes or induces any other person to interfere with its performance' (now TULR(C)A 1992, s. 219(1)(a)).

    As we shall see, however, it is important to view this immunity in the context of subsequent legislative developments. Section 219(1)(a) provides a prima facie immunity, but this immunity may be lost in certain instances, i.e. by taking unlawful secondary action, engaging in secondary picketing, enforcing trade union membership, or taking 'official' industrial action without first having called a secret ballot (s. 219(3)–(4)).

2. TULR(C)A 1992, s. 219(1)(a), provides an immunity against the tort of interference with contract. It does not, however, offer any explicit protection against the wider 'genus' tort of interference with trade or business by unlawful means. As a result it is of crucial importance to discover whether an act which is immune by virtue of s. 219 (inducement to breach of contract, for example) may nonetheless constitute the 'unlawful means' for the tort of interference with trade or business. Before the passage of the EA 1980, TULRA 1974, s. 13(3) (as amended) had stated that, 'for the avoidance of doubt', acts already given immunity could not found the unlawful-means element of other torts. When the 1980 statute repealed s. 13(3), the legal position became confused. However, it would appear that the correct view is that the repeal of s. 13(3) has not changed the position. According to the House of Lords in *Hadmor Productions Ltd* v *Hamilton* [1982] IRLR 102, s. 13(3) merely confirmed what was obvious anyway from s. 13(1), i.e. inducement is 'not actionable'. So if the unlawful means are immune, then no liability in tort can arise.

3. TULR(C)A 1992, s. 219(2), now provides the immunity against simple conspiracy originally contained in the Trade Disputes Act 1906.

(i) The trade dispute immunity

TRADE UNION AND LABOUR RELATIONS (CONSOLIDATION) ACT 1992

244. Meaning of 'trade dispute' in Part V

(1) In this Part a 'trade dispute' means a dispute between workers and their employer which relates wholly or mainly to one or more of the following—

    (a) terms and conditions of employment, or the physical conditions in which any workers are required to work;

    (b) engagement or non-engagement, or termination or suspension of employment or the duties of employment, of one or more workers;

    (c) allocation of work or the duties of employment between workers or groups of workers;

    (d) matters of discipline;

    (e) a worker's membership or non-membership of a trade union;

    (f) facilities for officials of trade unions; and

    (g) machinery for negotiation or consultation, and other procedures, relating to any of the above matters, including recognition by employers or employers' associations of the right of a trade union to represent workers in such negotiation or consultation or in the carrying out of such procedures.

(2) …

(3) There is a trade dispute even though it relates to matters occurring outside the United Kingdom, so long as the person or persons whose actions in the Kingdom are said to be in contemplation or furtherance of a trade dispute relating to matters occurring outside the United Kingdom are likely to be affected in respect of one or more of the matters specified in subsection (1) by the outcome of the dispute.

(4) An act, threat or demand done or made by one person or organisation against another which, if resisted, would have led to a trade dispute with that other, shall be treated as being done or made in contemplation of a trade dispute with that other, notwithstanding that because that other submits to the act or threat or accedes to the demand no dispute arises.

(5) In this section—

'employment' includes any relationship whereby one person personally does work or performs services for another; and 'worker', in relation to a dispute with an employer, means—

    (a) a worker employed by that employer; or

    (b) a person who has ceased to be so employed if his employment was terminated in connection with the dispute or if the termination of his employment was one of the circumstances giving rise to the dispute.

245. Crown employees and contracts

Where a person holds any office or employment under the Crown on terms which do not constitute a contract of employment between that person and the Crown, those terms shall nevertheless be deemed to constitute such a contract for the purposes of—

    (a) the law relating to liability in tort of a person who commits an act which—

        (i) induces another person to break a contract, interferes with the performance of that contract or induces another person to interfere with its performance, or

        (ii) consists in a threat that a contract will be broken or its performance interfered with, or that any person will be induced to break or interfere with its performance, and

    (b) the provisions of this or any other Act which refer (whether in relation to contracts generally or only in relation to contracts of employment) to such an act.

NOTE: The scope of the 'golden formula' was amended by the EA 1982 and significantly narrowed in the following ways:

1. A trade dispute must now be 'between workers and *their* employer' (emphasis added), not between 'employers and workers', which was the previous position. Furthermore, in repealing what was s. 29(4) of TULRA 1974, the 1982 Act no longer allowed trade unions and employers' associations to be regarded as parties to a trade dispute in their own right. Under the law as it stood before the 1982 Act, it was possible for there to be a 'trade dispute' between a trade union and an employer, even though none of the employer's workforce was involved in the dispute. In *NWL* v *Woods* [1979] IRLR 478, for example, the House of Lords held that there was a trade

dispute between the owners of a 'flag of convenience' ship and the International Transport Workers' Federation, although there was evidence that the crew did not support the union's action. As a result of the 1982 amendment, the ITF's action would not now be protected within the contemplation or furtherance of a trade dispute (ICFTD) formula. (See now TULR(C)A 1992, s. 244(1), (5).)

2. Disputes between 'workers and workers' are now omitted from the 'trade dispute' definition. While this means that disputes not involving an employer are unlawful, in practice it is rare for an employer not to be party to inter-union disputes. A demarcation dispute between unions will usually involve a dispute with an employer regarding terms and conditions of employment.

3. Since 1982, disputes relating to matters occurring outside the UK have been excluded from the immunity, unless the UK workers taking action in furtherance of the dispute are likely to be affected by its outcome in terms of the matters listed in s. 244 (see TULR(C)A 1992, s. 244(3)). This means that solidarity action taken by British workers in order to advertise the plight of workers in other countries will be unlawful. In any event, this sort of solidarity action would probably be regarded as a political rather than a trade dispute (*BBC* v *Hearn* [1977] IRLR 269).

4. A trade dispute must now relate 'wholly or mainly' to terms and conditions of employment and the other matters listed as legitimate in TULRA(C)A 1992, s. 244. Under the law existing prior to the 1982 Act, the dispute merely had to be 'connected' with such matters. The amended phrase marked a return to the form of words used under the Industrial Relations Act 1971 and was inserted to overrule another aspect of the decision of the House of Lords in *NWL* v *Woods* (in point (a)). In this case it was argued that the predominant purpose behind the 'blacking' of the 'Nawala' was the ITF's campaign against 'flags of convenience' shipping, and little to do with a trade dispute. The House of Lords did not agree, stating that as long as there was a genuine connection between the dispute and the subjects listed in the 1974 Act, it did not matter that other issues were predominant. The amendment wrought by the 1982 Act means that a mere connection with the matters specified in s. 244 will no longer suffice. So a dispute which is held to be predominantly a trade dispute will fall outside the trade dispute formula. In many instances it will be extremely difficult to decide which is the predominant element in the dispute, and this can be illustrated by the case set out below, the first case to deal with the issue.

Mercury Communications Ltd v Scott-Garner
[1983] IRLR 494, Court of Appeal

Mercury had been granted a government licence to run a private telecommunications system. The Post Office Engineers Union (POEU) objected to the government's policy of 'liberalisation' and ultimate 'privatisation' of the industry. The union instructed its members employed by British Telecom (BT) to refuse to connect Mercury's telecommunication system to the BT network. The Court of Appeal reversed the trial judge's finding that there was a trade dispute and granted an injunction to prevent the union continuing its instruction.

MAY LJ: ...

I think that from the union's own documents which are before us this has been and is in substantial degree a political and ideological campaign seeking to maintain the concept of public monopoly against private competition. I have no doubt that those who strenuously contend for the continuation of the monopoly in the postal and telecommunication fields honestly and fervently believe that this is in the best interests of the jobs and conditions of service of those working in the industry. It does not however follow that industrial action taken to further that campaign amounts to a dispute which is wholly or mainly about fears of redundancies if that monopoly is not maintained. Doing the best I can, I have come to the conclusion that it is unlikely that the defendants in this case will succeed in satisfying a court at trial that the dispute between BT and its employees over the blacking of Mercury and its shareholders was a trade dispute within the relevant legislation as now enacted... [I]n the present case the real dispute, as I think, is not between BT and the union but between the union and the government. The industrial action is no doubt being used as a bargaining counter in the dispute between the union and the government...

■ **QUESTION**

In the light of the reasoning in this case, to what extent do you think that the following questions posed by Otto Kahn-Freund are apposite?

Is not every major industrial problem a problem of governmental economic policy? Is it not true that, not only in publicly owned industries, governmental decisions on wages policies—whether statutory or not—on credits and subsidies, on the distribution of industry and on housing and town planning, and on a thousand other things, affect the terms and conditions of employment as much as the decisions of individual firms? [Davies, P. and Freedland, N., *Labour and the Law*, 3rd edn (London: Sweet & Maxwell, 1983), p. 317]

London Borough of Wandsworth v National Association of Schoolmasters/Union of Women Teachers

[1983] IRLR 344, Court of Appeal

The Education Reform Act 1988 contains provisions for a national curriculum, defining the core and foundation subjects and the key stages in a pupil's assessment. Under the Act, the Secretary of State could lay down attainment targets, programmes of studies and assessment arrangements. The first statutory assessment tests were planned to take place in June 1993 for pupils in key stage 3.

Under the Schoolteachers Pay and Conditions Act 1991, conditions relating to remuneration, professional duties and working time are prescribed by the Secretary of State. Since 1990, the union had been campaigning for a maximum limit to the working hours of teachers. In February 1993, the union balloted its members on the following question: 'In order to protest against the excessive workload and unreasonable imposition made upon teachers, as a consequence of the national curriculum and testing, are you willing to take action, short of strike action?' An 88% majority voted in favour of industrial action and the union instructed its members to boycott 'all the unreasonable and unnecessary elements of assessment connected with the national curriculum'.

The plaintiffs brought an action to restrain the union from continuing to issue the instruction and to call off the boycott. They contended that the union was inducing breaches of contracts of employment which the teachers had with the plaintiffs and that the union could not rely on TULR(C)A 1992, s. 219, because the dispute was not a 'trade dispute' within the meaning of s. 244.

Mantill J dismissed the application and the plaintiffs' appeal was dismissed by the Court of Appeal.

NEILL LJ: It is for the union to establish that they are protected from liability in tort by the provisions of the 1992 Act. By s. 219 it is provided:

An act done by a person in contemplation or furtherance of a trade dispute is not actionable in tort on the ground only:

(a) that it induces another person to break a contract or interferes or induces another person to interfere with its performance…

It is accepted on behalf of the union that their members who are schoolteachers are contractually obliged to carry out assessments and tests in accordance with the national curriculum. It is further accepted that unless protected by s. 219 the union is liable in tort by inducing its members to break their contracts of employment by the instructions it gave in relation to the boycott of certain parts of the test. The union asserts, however, that a trade dispute exists between the union and a minister of the crown so as to attract immunity in accordance with s. 219 and s. 244. It is necessary to set out the relevant provisions of s. 244 of the 1992 Act. The section provides:

(1) In this part a 'trade dispute' means a dispute between workers and their employer which relates wholly or mainly to one or more of the following:

(a) terms and conditions of employment…

(2) A dispute between a minister of the crown and any workers shall notwithstanding that he is not the employer of those workers be treated as a dispute between those workers and their employer if the dispute relates to matters which:

(a) . . .

(b) cannot be settled without him exercising the power conferred on him by or under an enactment.

The primary case for the union is that there is a trade dispute within the meaning of s. 244(2)(b) between the union and the Secretary of State because there is a dispute which relates wholly or mainly to the terms and conditions of employment of its members and that the dispute cannot be settled without the Secretary of State exercising the power conferred on him by or under either the 1991 Act or the 1988 Act. It is said that the dispute relates to the statutory conditions of employment defined in s. 1(2) of the 1991 Act and that the principal way in which the Secretary of State could settle the dispute would be by limiting the working time prescribed in the 1992 Document or by modifying the professional duties imposed on schoolteachers in the 1992 Document.

On behalf of the council, on the other hand, it was submitted that on a proper analysis of the dispute and of the evidence relating to it, it was apparent that the dispute was not wholly or mainly a dispute relating to terms and conditions of employment but was primarily or substantially concerned with the objections and reservations which members of the union had about the procedures which were to be used for the assessments and tests associated with the national curriculum. It is not a dispute about working time but a dispute about the content of the work which the national curriculum required schoolteachers to undertake.

. . .

We have come to a clear conclusion in this case. We have not set out all the relevant documents but we have had an opportunity to read them and study them. It seems to us to be quite clear that looking at the history since 1990 there has been increasing concern expressed by the union on behalf of its members with regard to working time. This concern came to a head as the date for the key stage 3 testing approached. It is quite clear that members of the union have criticisms to make about the national curriculum on educational grounds. This was recognised by Mr de Gruchy in paragraph 3 of his affidavit, but he added: 'Of most concern to the union in relation to its members is the excessive and unnecessary workload that the national curriculum imposes on teachers.'

That statement, which remains uncontradicted, is to be read in the context as referring primarily to the extra time which teachers have to work. Furthermore, we attach considerable importance to the wording of the question posed in the ballot paper. It is to be remembered that the ballot was authorised by the union Executive at the meeting on 5 February 1993.

In our judgment the dispute does mainly relate to the terms and conditions of employment of the union's members and is a trade dispute within the meaning of s. 244 of the 1992 Act. We consider that the judge reached the correct decision on these facts and we would dismiss the appeal.

Order that the appeal be dismissed with costs. Leave to appeal to the House of Lords refused.

NOTE: See also *Westminster City Council* v *Unison* [2001] IRLR 524, CA: an extract is included at p. 670 (Section C(iv)).

P v *National Association of Schoolmasters/Union of Women Teachers*
[2003] IRLR 307, House of Lords

The main point in issue in this case was whether the union's action in instructing its 35 members employed as teachers at a school not to comply with a headmaster's instruction to teach a disruptive pupil was a 'trade dispute'. Having balloted its members at the school, there was unanimous support for action short of a strike and a vote of 25 to 1 in favour of strike action. The union gave notice that as from 1 December 2000, its members would not comply with the instruction to teach the pupil.

From that date, the pupil was not taught by his normal teachers in the classroom, except for maths and drama, where the teachers were not members of the union. Instead, he sat on his own with a supply teacher and got on with work which was set by his usual teacher.

Proceedings were issued on the pupil's behalf against the union, relying principally on TULR(C)A 1992, s. 235A. This section provides that an individual who makes a claim that a union has done an unlawful act to induce industrial action, the effect of which is to adversely affect the provision of services to him, may apply to the High Court for an order under that section.

Mr Justice Morrison in the High Court dismissed the claim.

The claimant's appeal against that decision was dismissed by the Court of Appeal [2001] IRLR 532.

> I agree with [Morrison J's] view that the reality is that 'the working conditions of teachers were in dispute as were the instruction they were given' and that thus the dispute related to the terms and conditions of the teachers… [I]t would be totally anomalous to recognise a dispute between the teachers and their employer about the physical state of their classroom as a trade dispute, but not to recognise as a trade dispute, a dispute about their working conditions in the sense of the overtime they were directed to do, the number of pupils they were expected to teach, and the reasonableness or otherwise of a direction as to whom they were expected to teach.

The House of Lords dismissed the claimant's appeal.

> LORD HOFFMANN: In my opinion, this was plainly a dispute over terms and conditions of employment, which I regard as a composite phrase chosen to avoid arguments over whether something should properly be described as a 'term' or 'condition' of employment. It is sufficient that it should be one or the other. Furthermore, the use of such a composite expression shows that it was intended to be given a broad meaning: see Roskill LJ in *British Broadcasting Corporation* v *Hearn* [1977] IRLR 273, 276.
>
> In the present case, it seems to me that the dispute was about the contractual obligation of the teachers to teach P. It could be characterised as a dispute over whether there was such a contractual obligation: the union, as we have seen, contended that the head teacher's direction was unreasonable. Alternatively, it could be characterised as a dispute over whether there should be such a contractual obligation. It does not seem to me profitable to try to analyse it one way or another. The dispute arose because the head teacher said that the teachers were obliged to teach P and they said that they were not willing to do so. That seems to me a dispute which does not merely 'relate to' but is about their terms and conditions of employment.

NOTE: The judgment of the House of Lords adopts a broad interpretation of the trade dispute definition, holding that a dispute about the reasonableness of an instruction from an employer can be regarded as a dispute about 'terms and conditions of employment'. This would appear to be the case even where the order itself is lawful.

University College London Hospital NHS Trust v *Unison*
[1999] IRLR 31, Court of Appeal

University College London Hospital NHS Trust (UCLH) was, at all material times, in the business of providing hospital services at a group of hospitals, including University College Hospital in London. It employed over 5,000 staff, most of whom (particularly the non-clinical and nursing staff) were members of Unison.

In 1998, UCLH intended and was negotiating to transfer a part or parts of its business to a transferee consortium of private companies under the Private Finance Initiative whereby the private companies would, pursuant to the contracts to be negotiated, first erect and then run for UCLH a new hospital for a period of, in the first instance, 30 years.

Unison were opposed in principle to this method of financing the new hospital, regarding it as a form of privatisation. The union sought to persuade the trust to enter into a contractual arrangement with the consortium, under which the consortium, and its associates, subcontractors, and successors, would agree to guarantee for 30 years that it would observe equivalent terms and conditions to those of the trust, not just for staff transferring over but for new employees as well.

When the trust refused to agree to include this in the contract with the consortium, Unison gave notice of a ballot in relation to a trade dispute. This was described as relating to: 'The failure of the trust to agree that TUPE protection should be written into the Hospital New Build PFI Project, for the duration of the contract.' The ballot demonstrated an overwhelming majority in favour of strike action.

The trust applied to the High Court for an interlocutory injunction restraining the strike. Mr Justice Timothy Walker granted the injunction on grounds that it was unlikely that the union would succeed at trial of the action in establishing immunity for the strike action. He held that the definition of a 'trade dispute' in s. 244 of TULR(C) A 1992 was unlikely to be satisfied.

The judge took the view that the dispute was not about terms and conditions of employment, but about the terms and conditions of contracts yet to be entered into between the plaintiff employer and the new employers who were to take over the provision of services at the hospital. He considered that the reference in the ballot paper to 'future employees' did not fall within the definition of 'worker' in s. 244(5) because 'the Act does not protect a dispute involving workers yet to be engaged'. He also held that the court was likely to find that the dispute related mainly to the union's political objective of opposing the private finance initiative as a matter of policy. The Court of Appeal dismissed the appeal. Leave to appeal to the House of Lords was refused.

> LORD WOOLF MR: … As I have already indicated, there can be two strands to a policy. A union can have a policy of opposing a particular course of action root and branch which is seeking to achieve a political objective. At the same time it could have a more limited objective, namely to alleviate the adverse consequences which it anticipates could flow from the more general policy. That more limited objective can be the reason for taking strike action. That more limited policy can comply with the requirements of s. 244.
>
> I therefore turn to consider whether the more limited policy and objective of the union in this case falls within the requirements of s. 244. In doing so, I note that the statutory categories of permitted purposes must be the predominant purpose. The dispute must relate wholly or mainly to those purposes. If it relates to them, that is not sufficient to fulfil the statutory requirement.
>
> Together with the objectives of obtaining a guarantee for existing employees, the union is seeking to secure the same guarantee for employees who have never been employed by the trust. As the 30-year period for which the guarantee is at present being sought progresses, there is bound to be a situation which will arise where the great majority of the employees will never have been employed by the trust. I cannot see how it is possible to apply the language of s. 244(1)(a) and (5) in a way which covers the terms and conditions of employment of employees of a third party who have never been employed by the employer who is to be the subject of the strike action.
>
> This in itself is fatal to the case which the defendants advance on this appeal.
>
> …
>
> Accordingly, this appeal must be dismissed.

NOTE: As a result of this decision, industrial action may not be called for by trade unions unless the dispute is with an existing employer and in relation to existing terms and conditions. A strike call over future terms and conditions with an unidentified future employer will be held to be an unlawful inducement to breach of contract. Moreover, any worker who took industrial action in such a situation would risk dismissal without redress.

The decision represents a significant constraint on the ability of trade unions to put pressure on a transferor employer to insert terms in the transfer agreement which provide better protection than employees would have under the Transfer of Undertakings (Protection of Employment) Regulations 1981, for example ensuring comparable occupational pension rights. Surely, it should be legitimate for workers to attempt to persuade their existing employer to make arrangements in respect of their terms and conditions when working for a new employer. As Rubenstein observes: 'After all, the commercial transfer will be replete with terms protecting the interests of the transferor once the transfer has taken place. Why shouldn't the law allow pressure for these to include terms protecting the interests of the transferor's employees?' (Rubenstein, M., 'Highlights' [1999] IRLR 2).

Unison v UK

[2002] IRLR 497, European Court of Human Rights

Unison made an application to the European Court of Human Rights alleging that its right to strike had been subjected to unjustified restriction contrary to Article 11 of the European Convention. It claimed that the effect of the Court of Appeal's decision (in the previous extract) was that there can never be statutory protection (and hence freedom) for industrial action proposed or taken in contemplation or furtherance of a trade dispute in which the union and workers seek the protection of terms and conditions of employment after the transfer of a business or part of a business from an existing to a new employer.

Article 11 of the Convention provides:

1. Everyone has the right to freedom of peaceful assembly and to freedom of association with others, including the right to form and join trade unions for the protection of his interests.

2. No restrictions shall be placed on the exercise of these rights other than such as are prescribed by law and are necessary in a democratic society for the prevention of disorder and crime, for the protection of health or morals or for the protection of the rights and freedoms of others. This Article shall not prevent the imposition of lawful restrictions on the exercise of these rights by members of the armed forces, of the police or the administration of the State.

The European Court of Human Rights HELD: …

As regards the argument that the applicant's interests in protecting its members must weigh more heavily than the UCLH's economic interest, the Court considers that the impact of the restriction on the applicant's ability to take strike action has not been shown to place its members at any real or immediate risk of detriment or of being left defenceless against future attempts to downgrade pay or conditions. When, and if, its members are transferred, it may continue to act on their behalf as a recognised trade union and negotiate with the new employer in ongoing collective bargaining machinery. What it cannot claim under the Convention is a requirement that an employer enter into, or remain in, any particular collective bargaining arrangement or accede to its requests on behalf of its members. The Court therefore does not find that the respondent State has exceeded the margin of appreciation accorded to it in regulating trade union action.

(ii) In contemplation or furtherance of a trade dispute

Express Newspapers Ltd v *McShane*
[1980] AC 672, House of Lords

In the course of a dispute with provincial newspapers, the National Union of Journalists (NUJ) called on journalists employed by the Press Association (who were still supplying vital copy to the newspapers) to strike. When this call was not fully supported, the NUJ called on its members on the National Newspapers to refuse to handle any copy from the Press Association. This action was restrained by the Court of Appeal on the ground that it was not reasonably capable of achieving the objective of the trade dispute. The House of Lords, by a majority, allowed the union's appeal:

LORD DIPLOCK: My Lords, during the past two years there has been a series of judgments in the Court of Appeal given upon applications for interlocutory injunctions against trade union officials. These have the effect of imposing on the expression 'an act done by a person in contemplation or furtherance of a trade dispute' for which immunity from civil actions for specified kinds of torts is conferred by s. 13(1) of the Trade Union and Labour Relations Act, 1974 (as now amended), an interpretation restrictive of what, in common with the majority of your Lordships, I believe to be its plain and unambiguous meaning. The terms in which the limitations upon the ambit of the expression have been stated are not identical in the various judgments, but at the root of all of them there appears to lie an assumption that Parliament cannot really have intended to give so wide an immunity from the common law of tort as the words of ss. 13 and 29 would, on the face of them, appear to grant to everyone who engages in any form of what is popularly known as industrial action.

My Lords, I do not think that this is a legitimate assumption on which to approach the construction of the Act, notwithstanding that the training and traditions of anyone whose life has been spent in the practice of the law and the administration of justice in the courts must make such an assumption instinctively attractive to him. But the manifest policy of the Act was to strengthen the role of recognised trade unions in collective bargaining, so far as possible to confine the bargaining function to them, and, as my noble and learned friend Lord Scarman recently pointed out in *The Nawala (NWL) Ltd, The* v *Woods and another* [1979] 1 WLR 1294, to exclude trade disputes from judicial review by the courts. Parliament, as it was constituted when the Act and the subsequent amendments to it were passed, may well have felt so confident that trade unions could be relied upon always to act 'responsibly' in trade disputes that any need for legal sanctions against their failure to do so could be obviated.

This being so, it does not seem to me that it is a legitimate approach to the construction of the sections that deal with trade disputes, to assume that Parliament did *not* intend to give to trade unions and their officers a wide discretion to exercise their own judgment as to the steps which should be taken in an endeavour to help the workers' side in any trade dispute to achieve its objectives. And if their plain and ordinary meaning is given to the words 'An act done by a person in contemplation or furtherance of a trade dispute,' this, as it seems to me, is what s. 13 does. In the light of the express reference to the 'person' by whom the act is done and the association of 'furtherance' with 'contemplation' (which cannot refer to anything but the state of mind of the doer of the act) it is, in my view, clear that 'in furtherance' too can only refer to the state of mind of the person who does the act, and means: with the purpose of helping one of the parties to a trade dispute to achieve their objectives in it.

Given the existence of a trade dispute (the test of which, though broad, is nevertheless objective, see *The Nawala*), this makes the test of whether an act was done 'in furtherance of' it a purely subjective one. If the party who does the act honestly thinks at the time he does it that it may help one of the parties to the trade dispute to achieve their objectives and does it for that reason, he is protected by the section. I say 'may' rather than 'will' help, for it is in the nature of industrial action that success in achieving its objectives cannot be confidently predicted. Also there is nothing in the section that requires that there should be any proportionality between on the one hand the extent to which the act is likely to, or be capable of, increasing the 'industrial muscle' of one side to the dispute, and on the other hand the damage caused to the victim of the act which, but for the section, would have been tortious. The doer of the act may know full well that it cannot have more than a minor effect in bringing the trade dispute to the successful outcome that he favours, but nevertheless is bound to cause disastrous loss to the victim, who may be a stranger to the dispute and with no interest in its outcome. The act is none the less entitled to immunity under the section.

It is, I think, these consequences of applying the subjective test that, not surprisingly, have tended to stick in judicial gorges: that so great damage may be caused to innocent and disinterested third parties in order to obtain for one of the parties to a trade dispute tactical advantages which in the court's own view are highly speculative and, if obtained, could be no more than minor. This has led the Court of Appeal to seek to add some objective element to the subjective test of the *bona fide* purpose of the person who did the act.

… A test, suggested by Lord Denning in the instant case, is that the act done must have some 'practical' effect in bringing pressure to bear upon the opposite side to the dispute; acts done to assist the morale of the party to the dispute whose cause is favoured are not protected. [Alternatively] there is the test favoured by Lawton and Brandon LJJ, in the instant case: the act done must, in the view of the court, be reasonably capable of achieving the objective of the trade dispute.

My Lords, these tests though differently expressed, have the effect of enabling the court to substitute its own opinion for the *bona fide* opinion held by the trade union or its officers, as to whether action proposed to be taken or continued for the purpose of helping one side or bringing pressure to bear upon the other side to a trade dispute is likely to have the desired effect. Granted *bona fides* on the part of the trade union or its officer this is to convert the test from a purely subjective to a purely objective test and for the reasons I have given I do not think the wording of the section permits of this. The belief of the doer of the act that it will help the side he favours in the dispute must be honest; it need not be wise, nor need it take account of the damage it will cause to innocent and disinterested third parties. Upon an application for an interlocutory injunction the evidence may show positively by admission or by inference from the facts before the court that the act was not done to further an existing trade dispute but for some ulterior purpose such as revenge for previous conduct. Again, the facts in evidence before the court may be such as will justify the conclusion that no reasonable person versed in industrial relations could possibly have thought that the act was capable of helping one side in a trade dispute to achieve its objectives. But too this goes to honesty of purpose alone not to the reasonableness of the act, or its expediency…

… The withdrawal of PA copy from the provincial newspapers would be a crucial factor in strengthening the bargaining position of the striking journalists, but in view of PA's attitude this could only be achieved by forcing it to close down or at any rate to reduce its services drastically, by withdrawing journalistic labour from it. PA was not an NUJ closed shop and for economic reasons even the NUJ members on its staff were not likely to be enthusiastic at the prospect of being called out on strike. For my part I see no reason for doubting the honesty of the belief held by Mr McShane and Mr Dennis [another NUJ official], that the response of their members to the strike-call at PA might well be less numerous and less enduring if they knew that fellow members of their union on the national newspapers were continuing to make use of copy produced by those whom they would regard as 'blacklegs' at PA.

I would allow this appeal.

NOTES
1. See also *Duport Steels Ltd* v *Sirs* [1980] 1 All ER 529, HL.
2. It was, however, the approach of the Court of Appeal, and Lord Denning in particular, which most closely accorded with the newly elected Conservative Government's perspective on industrial relations. As a result, the EA 1980 included provisions which aimed to control, *inter alia*, 'secondary action' and, to use the words of one government spokesman, to 'return the law to Denning'. This legislation commenced the new legislative policy of stripping away the immunities.

C: Stage three: removal of the immunities

The scope of the immunities was restricted by the legislation of the 1980s: the Employment Acts 1980–90, the Trade Union Act 1984, and TURERA 1993. In this section we examine the restriction of secondary action; the provisions removing immunity in respect of actions aimed at enforcing the closed shop or trade union recognition on an employer; the loss of immunity for unlawful picketing; the requirements for secret ballots before industrial action; and industrial action taken in support of dismissed 'unofficial strikers'.

(i) Statutory control of secondary action

TRADE UNION AND LABOUR RELATIONS (CONSOLIDATION) ACT 1992

224. Secondary action

(1) An act is not protected if one of the facts relied on for the purpose of establishing liability is that there has been secondary action which is not lawful picketing.

(2) There is secondary action in relation to a trade dispute when, and only when, a person—

(a) induces another to break a contract of employment or interferes or induces another to interfere with its performance, or

(b) threatens that a contract of employment under which he or another is employed will be broken or its performance interfered with, or that he will induce another to break a contract of employment or interfere with its performance, and the employer under the contract of employment is not the employer party to the dispute.

(3) Lawful picketing means acts done in the course of such attendance as is declared lawful by section 220 (peaceful picketing)—

(a) by a worker employed (or, in the case of a worker not in employment, last employed) by the employer party to the dispute, or

(b) by a trade union official whose attendance is lawful by virtue of subsection (1)(b) of that section.

(4) For the purposes of this section an employer shall not be treated as party to a dispute between another employer and workers of that employer; and where more than one employer is in dispute with his workers, the dispute between each employer and his workers shall be treated as a separate dispute.

NOTES
1. Section 17 of the EA 1980 removed the protection provided by TULRA 1974, s. 13(1) (as amended) against liability for interfering with commercial contracts by secondary action unless the action satisfied conditions which enabled it to pass through one of three 'gateways to legality', the most important of which being the so-called 'first customer/first supplier' gateway. This permitted secondary action to be lawfully organised if it involved employees of persons who were in direct contractual relations with the employer involved in the primary dispute. The second gateway extended the 'first customer/first supplier' rule to cover cases where the supply which was disrupted was between the secondary employer and an employer 'associated' with the primary employer. This gateway applied only where the supplies which were disrupted were in substitution for the goods which but for the dispute would have been supplied by or to the primary employer. The third gateway maintained immunity where the secondary action was a consequence of lawful picketing.

While the policy behind the EA 1980, s. 17 is straightforward, its drafting was massively complex. Lord Denning described it as 'the most tortuous section I have ever come across' (*Hadmor*

Productions v *Hamilton* [1981] IRLR 210). Indeed, the complexity of the section was one of the reasons put forward for its repeal by the EA 1990, s. 4. The aim of s. 4 of the 1990 Act was that only direct disputes between an employer and its workers should attract immunity under what is now TULR(C)A 1992, s. 219. The only exception was to be secondary action arising out of lawful picketing—the only 'gateway to legality' to be retained from the repealed s. 17 of the 1980 Act.

2. The TULR(C)A 1992, s. 224(4) seeks to limit any attempt to extend the notion of the primary employer. The subsection states that an employer is not to be regarded as party to a dispute between another employer and its workers. This would appear to confirm the thinking of the House of Lords in *Dimbleby & Sons Ltd* v *National Union of Journalists* [1984] ICR 386, that an employer, even though associated with the employer involved in the primary dispute, was not to be regarded as party to that dispute.

(ii) Unlawful picketing

Actions such as picketing a place other than your own place of work will not attract immunity under s. 219 (see TULR(C)A 1992, s. 219(3) and the following chapter).

(iii) Enforcing union membership

TRADE UNION AND LABOUR RELATIONS (CONSOLIDATION) ACT 1992

222. Action to enforce trade union membership

(1) An act is not protected if the reason, or one of the reasons, for which it is done is the fact or belief that a particular employer—

    (a) is employing, has employed or might employ a person who is not a member of a trade union, or

    (b) is failing, has failed or might fail to discriminate against such a person.

(2) For the purposes of subsection (1)(b) an employer discriminates against a person if, but only if, he ensures that his conduct in relation to—

    (a) persons, or persons of any description, employed by him, or who apply to be, or are, considered by him for employment, or

    (b) the provision of employment for such persons is different, in some or all cases, according to whether or not they are members of a trade union, and is more favourable to those who are.

(3) An act is not protected if it constitutes, or is one of a number of acts which together constitute, an inducement or attempted inducement of a person—

    (a) to incorporate in a contract to which that person is a party, or a proposed contract to which he intends to be a party, a term or condition which is or would be void by virtue of section 144 (union membership requirement in contract for goods or services), or

    (b) to contravene section 145 (refusal to deal with person on grounds relating to union membership).

(4) References in this section to an employer employing a person are to a person acting in the capacity of the person for whom a worker works or normally works.

(5) References in this section to not being a member of a trade union are to not being a member of any trade union, of a particular trade union or of one of a number of particular trade unions.

Any such reference includes a reference to not being a member of a particular branch or section of a trade union or of one of a number of particular branches or sections of a trade union.

NOTE: We have already referred to the fact that the EA 1988 put further curbs on the closed shop. Section 10 removed the immunities contained in TULRA 1974, s. 13 (as amended) from primary industrial action where the reason, or one of the reasons, for the action is that the employer is employing, has employed or might employ a person who is not a member of a trade union or that the employer is failing, has failed or might fail to discriminate against such a person. As we saw in our chapter on unfair dismissal, s. 11 made it unfair for an employer to dismiss or to take action short of dismissal against an employee on the ground of the employee's non-membership of a union or a particular union. In both the situations covered by ss. 10–11, the fact that the closed shop has been approved in a ballot is an irrelevancy. (See now TULR(C)A 1992, s. 222.)

Section 14 of the EA 1982 withdrew the immunity where the reason for the industrial action is to compel another employer to 'recognise, negotiate or consult' with one or more trade unions, or to force the employer to discriminate in contract or tendering on the ground of union membership or non-membership in the contracting or tendering concern. (See now TULR(C)A 1992, s. 225.)

(iv) Secret ballots before industrial action

See TULR(C)A 1992, ss. 226–35.

Official industrial action will only attract the immunity offered by TULR(C)A 1992, s. 219, if the majority of union members likely to be called upon to take industrial action have supported that action in a properly conducted ballot. As we have already seen, the requirements for a lawful ballot and the ways in which a union can be held to be vicariously responsible for industrial action saw considerable additions and modifications as a result of the Employment Acts 1988 and 1990. Yet further requirements were added by TURERA 1993. To supplement these requirements, the Department of Employment issued a Code of Practice on Trade Union Ballots on Industrial Action. Originally issued in 1990, it was revised in 1991 and 1995. The current Code of Practice on Industrial Action Ballots and Notices came into effect on 1 October 2005. Breach of the Code does not of itself give rise to civil or criminal liability, but any court or tribunal must, where it is relevant, take it into account as evidence of good industrial relations practice (TULR(C)A 1992, s. 207).

The ballot and notice requirements are set out in TULR(C)A 1992, ss. 226–35B. The provisions are complex. The Government invited suggestions in *Fairness at Work* to clarify and simplify the law in this area. A large number of responses were received, especially from trade unions and legal bodies. The Employment Relations Act 1999, s. 4 gives effect to Sch. 3, which, drawing on some of the suggestions, amends the law in certain respects.

TRADE UNION AND LABOUR RELATIONS (CONSOLIDATION) ACT 1992

226. Requirement of ballot before action by trade union

(1) An act done by a trade union to induce a person to take part, or continue to take part, in industrial action

   (a) is not protected unless the industrial action has the support of a ballot, and

   (b) where section 226A falls to be complied with in relation to the person's employer, is not protected as respects the employer unless the trade union has complied with section 226A in relation to him.

In this section 'the relevant time', in relation to an act by a trade union to induce a person to take part, or continue to take part, in industrial action, means the time at which proceedings are commenced in respect of the act.

(2) Industrial action shall be regarded as having the support of a ballot only if—

   (a) the union has held a ballot in respect of the action—

      (i) in relation to which the requirements of section 226B so far as applicable before and during the holding of the ballot were satisfied,

      (ii) in relation to which the requirements of sections 227 to 231 were satisfied, and

      (iii) in which the majority voting in the ballot answered 'Yes' to the question applicable in accordance with section 229(2) to industrial action of the kind to which the act of inducement relates;

   (b) such of the requirements of the following sections as have fallen to be satisfied at the relevant time have been satisfied, namely—

      (i) section 226B so far as applicable after the holding of the ballot, and

      (ii) section 231B;

   (bb) section 232A does not prevent the industrial action from being regarded as having the support of the ballot; and

   (c) the requirements of section 233 (calling of industrial action with support of ballot) are satisfied.

Any reference in this subsection to a requirement of a provision which is disapplied or modified by section 232 has effect subject to that section.

(3) Where separate workplace ballots are held by virtue of section 228(1)—

   (a) industrial action shall be regarded as having the support of a ballot if the conditions specified in subsection (2) are satisfied, and

   (b) the trade union shall be taken to have complied with the requirements relating to a ballot imposed by section 226A if those requirements are complied with, in relation to the ballot for the place of work of the person induced to take part, or continue to take part, in the industrial action.

(3A) If the requirements of section 231A fall to be satisfied in relation to an employer, as respects that employer industrial action shall not be regarded as having the support of a ballot unless those requirements are satisfied in relation to that employer.

(4) For the purposes of this section an inducement, in relation to a person, includes an inducement which is or would be ineffective, whether because of his unwillingness to be influenced by it or for any other reason.

NOTE: Section 231A of the 1992 Act requires unions to inform employers about the result of an industrial action ballot which involves their employees. In cases where a union ballots its members employed by different employers, the union must supply the information to each of the employers concerned. Under the previous law, a failure to inform some, but not all, of the employers could make it unlawful for the union to induce any of its balloted members to take action. Paragraph 2(3) of Sch. 3 to the 1999 Act changes the law by making it lawful in these circumstances for a union to call on its members to take action where they are employed by an employer who was informed of the result. It will remain unlawful, however, for a union to induce its members to take action if their employer was not informed of the result.

TRADE UNION AND LABOUR RELATIONS (CONSOLIDATION) ACT 1992

226A. Notice of ballot and sample voting paper for employers

(1) The trade union must take such steps as are reasonably necessary to ensure that—
   (a) not later than the seventh day before the opening day of the ballot, the notice specified in subsection (2), and
   (b) not later than the third day before the opening day of the ballot, the sample voting paper specified in subsection (3),
is received by every person who it is reasonable for the union to believe (at the latest time when steps could be taken to comply with paragraph (a)) will be the employer of persons who will be entitled to vote in the ballot.

(2) The notice referred to in paragraph (a) of subsection (1) is a notice in writing—
   (a) stating that the union intends to hold the ballot,
   (b) specifying the date which the union reasonably believes will be the opening day of the ballot, and
   (c) containing—
       (i) the lists mentioned in subsection (2A) and the figures mentioned in subsection (2B), together with an explanation of how those figures were arrived at, or
       (ii) where some or all of the employees concerned are employees from whose wages the employer makes deductions representing payments to the union, either those lists and figures and that explanation or the information mentioned in subsection (2C).

(2A) The lists are—
   (a) a list of the categories of employee to which the employee concerned belong, and
   (b) a list of the workplaces at which the employees concerned work.

(2B) The figures are—
   (a) the total number of employees concerned,
   (b) the number of employees concerned in each of the categories in the list mentioned in subsection (2A)(a), and
   (c) the number of employees concerned who work at each workplace in the list mentioned in subsection (2A)(b).

(2C) The information referred to in subsection (2)(c)(ii) is such information as will enable the employer readily to deduce—
   (a) the total number of employees concerned,
   (b) the categories of employee to which the employees concerned belong and the number of employees concerned in each of those categories, and
   (c) the workplaces at which the employees concerned work and the number of them who work at each of those workplaces.

...

(2G) Nothing in this section requires a union to supply an employer with the names of the employees concerned.

(3) The sample voting paper referred to in paragraph (b) of subsection (1) is—
   (a) a sample of the form of voting paper which is to be sent to the employees who it is reasonable for the trade union to believe (at the time when the steps to comply with paragraph (a) of that subsection are taken) will be entitled to vote in the ballot, or

(b) where they are not all to be sent the same form of voting paper, a sample of each form of voting paper which is to be sent to any of them.

(3A) These rules apply for the purposes of paragraph (c) of subsection (2)—

(a) if the union possesses information as to the number, category or work-place of the employees concerned, a notice must contain that information (at least);

(b) if a notice does not name any employees, that fact shall not be a ground for holding that it does not comply with paragraph (c) of subsection (2).

(3B) In subsection (3) references to employees are to employees of the employer concerned.

(4) In this section references to the opening day of the ballot are references to the first day when a voting paper is sent to any person entitled to vote in the ballot.

(5) This section, in its application to a ballot in which merchant seamen to whom section 230(2A) applies are entitled to vote, shall have effect with the substitution in subsection (3), for references to the voting paper which is to be sent to the employees, of references to the voting paper which is to be sent or otherwise provided to them.

NOTES

1. If a trade union decides to call on its members to take or continue industrial action, it has no immunity from legal liability unless it holds a properly conducted secret ballot in advance of the proposed action. Unions are required under the 1992 Act to give to the employers concerned advance notice in writing both of the ballot and of any official industrial action which may result. The ballot notice must describe, so that their employer can readily ascertain them, the employees who it is reasonable for the union to believe will be entitled to vote. Likewise, the notice of official industrial action must describe, so that their employer can readily ascertain them, the employees the union intends should take part in the action. The law had been interpreted by the courts (most notably, in the case *Blackpool and the Fylde College* v *National Association of Teachers in Further and Higher Education* [1994] ICR 648, CA, and [1994] ICR 982, HL) as requiring the union in certain circumstances to give to the employer the names of those employees which it is balloting or calling upon to take industrial action. The 1999 Act amends the 1992 Act so as to ensure that unions are never required by the law to disclose the names of their members to employers in these circumstances.

   Paragraph 3 of Sch. 3 to the 1999 Act deals with the provisions of the 1992 Act which provide for a notice to be issued in advance of the ballot. It amends s. 226A(2) to redefine the purpose for which the notice is required as being to enable the employer to make plans to deal with the consequences of any industrial action and to provide information to those employees who are being balloted. Paragraph 3(3) inserts a new s. 226A(3A), which sets out the type of information which is to be included in the notice in order to satisfy the new s. 226A(2). It has the effect that a union is required to provide only information in its possession and that it is not required to name the employees concerned. Section 234A of the 1992 Act, which provides for a notice to be issued in advance of official industrial action, is amended in similar terms.

   EDF Energy Powerlink Ltd v *National Union of Rail Maritime and Transport Workers* [2010] IRLR 114 concerned a ballot notification in respect of craft workers employed in three of EDF's installations that supply electrical power to the London Underground system. The employers categorised the various functions carried out as 'fitters, jointers, test room inspectors, day testers, shift testers or OBLI fitters'. There were a number of unions recognised at the different sites and no check-off system, so the employers claimed they were unable to determine which of its employees belonged to which union. The union's notification said it would be balloting members employed in the category of 'engineer/technician'. The employers took the view that this did not sufficiently enable them to identify the category of members to be balloted, but the union argued that it did not have more detailed job descriptions on its database and that it was not obliged to use the same description of job categories as the employer. Granting an injunction restraining the union from calling a strike based on the notification, Mr Justice Blake held that the employer was entitled to be provided with information as to who was being balloted by particular trade. The fact that the union did not record the information in this way was not decisive, since it was accepted that it was possible for the union to contact the shop stewards at the workplace to find out the particular function in which employees were engaged. This is a narrow construction of the statutory provisions.

2. Section 226A(1) of the 1992 Act provides that a union proposing to conduct an industrial action ballot must ensure that a sample voting paper is received by every person who it is reasonable for the union to believe will be the employer of a person or persons who will be entitled to vote

in the ballot. The sample voting paper must be received not later than the third day before the opening of the ballot. Section 226A(3) has the effect that where more than one employer is involved and different forms of voting paper are used, samples of all the different forms of the voting paper must be sent to every employer.

Paragraph 3(3) of Sch. 3 to the 1999 Act inserts a new s. 226A(3B), which amends the requirement on unions so that they must ensure only that each employer receives the sample voting paper (or papers, where more than one form exists) which is to be sent to persons employed by that employer. In other words, unions are no longer required to ensure that an employer receives sample forms which are to be sent only to the employees of other employers.

■ QUESTION

Is the amended obligation to supply information any less onerous than its predecessor?

NOTE:　The case below would suggest that the information requirement regarding those employees to be balloted or called on to take industrial action is slightly less stringent than before. Note how Pill LJ distinguishes the decision in *RMT* v *London Underground Ltd* [2001] IRLR 228, CA, where a narrower approach to the information requirements was taken.

Westminster City Council v *Unison*
[2001] IRLR 524, Court of Appeal

The union proposed industrial action in response to the council's plan to privatise its housing assessment and advice unit, with the consequence that employees in the unit would cease to be council employees. The High Court held that this was a dispute about the public policy issue of privatisation itself, essentially a political strike, rather than about terms and conditions of employment. Therefore, it did not fall within the 'trade dispute' definition.

The second issue in the case concerned the information to be supplied to the employer by the union as to those to be balloted and called upon to take industrial action. The union's strike notice to the employers identified the employees entitled to vote in the ballot as 'all of those who pay their subscriptions via the deduction of contributions at source system. They work in the advice and assessment office at Harrow Road and can be described as A&A workers. I believe that there are 45 in total who will be balloted.' The High Court upheld the employer's contention that the notice did not satisfy TULR(C) A 1992, s. 226A because it had failed to identify the 'category' of workers concerned.

The Court of Appeal allowed the union's appeal on both counts.

LORD JUSTICE PILL: …

In my judgment, on the evidence which was before the judge, the judge has, with respect, so disregarded parts of it that this court is entitled to reassess the position and make up its own mind as to whether the dispute is a trade dispute. What the judge did was not only to draw an inference contrary to assertions by witnesses, such as the assertion of Mr Kent [a rehousing officer in the unit and Unison member] that he had no doubts that this dispute concerned the issue of the identity of the employer, but also contemporaneous documents before the court.

I do not doubt that a judge, even on occasions when witnesses have not been required for cross-examination, can in all the circumstances disregard or disbelieve evidence and draw inferences to the contrary. If that is done, reasoning however is required and in this case there are not only assertions but substantial contemporaneous documentary evidence of the importance attached to the change in employer such that, if the judge was to disbelieve and draw the inference which he did, fuller reasoning was required.

In my judgment, the learned judge has not approached the evidence comprehensively in this case and I am unable to accept the conclusion he reached. It is not simply a question of attaching weight to the evidence. His approach has disregarded entirely important parts of it. I understand the difficulties in which any tribunal is placed when having to decide an issue such as the present one. However, I reject the suggestion that this was in substance a high-minded dispute about public policy and conflicts of interest masquerading as a dispute about terms of employment.

...

The second issue relates to the alleged failure of Unison to comply with the requirements of s. 226A of the Act when organising their ballot....

Mr Bear [counsel for the employers] relies upon the recent decision of this Court in the *National Union of Rail, Maritime & Transport Workers* v *London Underground Ltd and others* [2001] IRLR 228. The situation in that case was, in my judgment, very different from the present case. The facts are set out at paragraphs 4 and 5 of the judgment of Robert Walker LJ, with whom the other members of the court agreed.

> 4. According to the affidavit sworn since the hearing by Mr Andrew Bindon, LUL's head of employment relations and partnership, the approximate numbers of employees employed by the six claimant companies are 11,200, 2,000, 1,600, 1,800, 60 and 200 respectively, making a total of a little under 17,000, of whom a little over 40 per cent are RMT members. The employees, including RMT members, are spread between a large number of different workplaces and between several different categories of work. Mr Bindon has deposed that:

RMT has members in a variety of different categories of our workforce, e.g. stations and revenue control, train staff, signal operations, and administrative, technical and operational managers. Additionally, LUL has over 40 different workplaces for station staff, over 20 different train depots, as well as separate locations for signalling operations.

> 5. LUL has what is known as check-off arrangement with ASLEF, under which LUL will make a direct deduction from the salary of an employee who is a member of ASLEF and who wishes his union dues to be collected in this way. That means that LUL has up-to-date information about ASLEF members and their workplaces and work categories. There has been no check-off arrangement with RMT since 1995 and so, as Mr Bindon has deposed, LUL is not able to identify the number, category and workplace of its employees who are RMT members. There is a high turnover of staff in station grades.

It was in that context that Robert Walker LJ, in his conclusions, made the statements to which the Court has been referred. Paragraph 47:

> If the amendments are approached in that way it becomes clear that the judge was right to interpret 'information as to number, category or workplace of the employee concerned' in such a way as to provide the employers with information which was useful to them. The usefulness of the information is seriously reduced if an employer is simply told '5,000 employees, all grades, all workplaces' without the additional information which could be conveyed by a grid or spreadsheet, with different categories (as appropriate) listed at the side and different workplaces listed at the top, and the appropriate numbers filled in.

The differences between the facts are plain from those references. What Mr Bear relies on is the statement of Robert Walker at paragraph 48 that 'the union is obliged to include it [that is the information], as an irreducible statutory minimum, in the notice'.

Robert Walker LJ considered the background to the amendments to s. 226A which changed the amount of information to be supplied but stated in paragraph 46:

> But there was not a significant change in the legislative policy or in the purpose for which information was to be given to the employer. The change was a change of means, not of objective, in order to meet the concerns of those members of a union who objected to being included in a list of names.

The legislative purpose was 'to enable an employer to know which part or parts of its workforce were being invited to take industrial action' (paragraph 45). The word 'category' was not defined by Robert Walker LJ in the *London Underground* case nor was it necessary for him to do so. Equally it is not necessary for this court to attempt comprehensive definition.

In my judgment, it is clear that the requirement was met upon the facts of the case and that the requirement as to 'category' was sufficiently met in the information provided. The number of staff involved was only 45. They were identified as A&A workers. The relevant staff are said to be those in the assessment and advice unit. While not identified by name, information was provided by reference to the DOCAS system, by which individual identities could easily be ascertained by the employers. It is not suggested that different professions or trades are involved within the A&A unit.

[Mr Bear submits] a distinction should have been drawn between managers and other staff and that the requirement as to category was not met in the absence of such a distinction. It is also submitted that the various sub-units of the unit should have been identified to meet the requirement as to category. I do not accept those submissions. In my judgment, the requirement as to category was sufficiently met in the notice.

NOTES

1. Section 22 of the Employment Relations Act 2004 amended s. 226A of the 1992 Act (TULR(C)A) by inserting new subss. (2A)–(2H), and deleting old subss. (3)–(3B). The effect is to require the trade union to supply the employer with more specific information as to the numbers and categories of employees concerned and their workplace.

2. In *EDF Energy Powerlink Ltd* v *National Union of Rail Maritime and Transport Workers* [2010] IRLR 114, failure to be sufficiently specific with regard to the precise categories of craft workers it would be balloting—'engineer/technician'—was unlawful where the employers categorised the various jobs as 'fitters, jointers, test room inspectors, day testers, shift testers or OBLI fitters'. However, in *National Union of Rail, Maritime and Transport Union* v *Serco Ltd; The Associated Society of Locomotive Engineers and Firemen* v *London and Birmingham Railway Ltd* [2011] EWCA Civ 226, the Court of Appeal took a less prescriptive approach.

   The case involved two separate transport strikes, involving London Midland Railway and London Docklands Railway, both of which were halted by employer injunctions granted by the High Court in December 2010 and January 2011 respectively. Aslef and RMT, the two unions involved, were successful in their appeals against the injunctions on the following grounds:

   • whilst sending ballot papers to two members who were not entitled to vote (where over 600 were balloted) breached TULR(C)A 1992, the statute provided a defence (s. 232). This defence permits small accidental failures in relation to entitlement to vote and the conduct of the ballot to be disregarded. The Court of Appeal held that to take advantage of this accidental failures defence, the failure must be unintentional, but it did not also have to be unavoidable. In other words, just because the union could have taken steps which avoided the error, like keeping better records, this did not mean by itself that it was deprived of the accidental failure defence because of human errors and failings;

   • in addition to the specific accidental failure defence (in the previous point) in TULR(C)A 1992, the unions argued successfully that a general principle of law permits other 'trifling' errors in the ballot and employer notifications to be ignored and should not form a basis for invalidating the whole process;

   • the court departed from previous High Court case law by deciding that, when complying with TULR(C)A 1992 rules about notifying the employer about the numbers, categories and workplaces of the employees involved in the dispute (in the ballot notice), it must provide those figures which are as accurate as reasonably practicable in the light of information it possesses at the time. The court stated that these were 'important limiting words' which need to be given weight when considering a union's obligation. As such, the trade union had complied in the circumstances. Importantly, by focusing on the information actually in the hands of the union, the court rejected the notion that trade unions have a duty to keep proper records, or collect further information, specifically in order to comply with the balloting and notice rules under TULR(C)A 1992. However, this does not mean that trade unions escape any obligation in this respect; as the court pointed out, it must still supply the employer with information as accurately as it reasonably can, for example collate and obtain relevant documents from union officers and analyse the information;

   • the Court of Appeal decided that a trade union's duty to provide an explanation of the figures (about employee numbers, workplaces, and categories) contained in the strike and ballot notices is not an onerous duty. Again, this runs contrary to recent High Court case law and means that the repeated use of a formulaic or generic explanation, as is often the case, can suffice. In reaching this decision, the Court of Appeal approved the analysis of what is required under paragraph 16 of the Industrial Action Code of Practice.

   The judgment will help avoid some of the complex obstacles put in place for unions balloting on industrial action by earlier High Court decisions, probably making interim injunctions less achievable.

TRADE UNION AND LABOUR RELATIONS (CONSOLIDATION) ACT 1992

226B. Appointment of scrutineer

(1) The trade union shall, before the ballot in respect of the industrial action is held, appoint a qualified person ('the scrutineer') whose terms of appointment shall require him to carry out in relation to the ballot the functions of—

(a) taking such steps as appear to him to be appropriate for the purpose of enabling him to make a report to the trade union (see section 231B); and

(b) making the report as soon as reasonably practicable after the date of the ballot and, in any event, not later than the end of the period of four weeks beginning with that date.

(2) A person is a qualified person in relation to a ballot if—

(a) he satisfies such conditions as may be specified for the purposes of this section by order of the Secretary of State or is himself so specified; and

(b) the trade union has no grounds for believing either that he will carry out the functions conferred on him under subsection (1) otherwise than competently or that his independence in relation to the union, or in relation to the ballot, might reasonably be called into question.

An order under paragraph (a) shall be made by statutory instrument which shall be subject to annulment in pursuance of a resolution of either House of Parliament.

(3) The trade union shall ensure that the scrutineer duly carries out the functions conferred on him under subsection (1) and that there is no interference with the carrying out of those functions from the union or any of its members, officials or employees.

(4) The trade union shall comply with all reasonable requests made by the scrutineer for the purposes of, or in connection with, the carrying out of those functions.

226C. Exclusion for small ballots

Nothing in section 226B, section 229(1A)(a) or section 231B shall impose a requirement on a trade union unless—

(a) the number of members entitled to vote in the ballot, or

(b) where separate workplace ballots are held in accordance with section 228(1), the aggregate of the number of members entitled to vote in each of them, exceeds 50.

NOTES

1. Provided that those entitled to vote are accorded the opportunity, a simple majority of those voting is all that is required: there is no requirement for an *absolute* majority of those voting in the ballot (s. 226(2)(a)(iii); see *West Midlands Trowel Ltd* v *TGWU* [1994] IRLR 578, CA). However, it is possible that a low turnout may provide evidential support for a claim by the employer or a member that the ballot is invalid because certain members have been denied their entitlement to vote, or that the union has not taken reasonably practicable steps to ensure that those entitled to vote have an opportunity to do so (ss. 227(1) and 230(1)–(2); and see *British Railways Board* v *NUR* [1989] IRLR 349—an extract appears at p. 679 later in this section).

2. As a result of the changes introduced by the Employment Relations Act 1999 to the law of industrial action ballots, a revised Code of Practice on Industrial Action Ballots and notice to employers came into effect on 18 September 2000.

3. Section 227(1) of the 1992 Act provides that entitlement to vote in an industrial action ballot must be accorded equally to all union members who it is reasonable at the time of the ballot for the union to believe will be induced to take part in the industrial action. No other members are entitled to vote. As unamended, s. 227(2) provided that these requirements were not satisfied if 'any person' who was a member at the time of the ballot and who was denied an entitlement to vote was subsequently induced by the union to take part in the action.

   The effect of these provisions was that unions were free to induce new members who joined the union after the ballot to take industrial action. However, they could not induce any members to take action if they were members at the time of the ballot but were denied an entitlement to vote. This included cases where members changed their job after the ballot and became employed within the group of workers which the union was proposing should take industrial action.

   Paragraph 4 of Sch. 3 to the 1999 Act repeals s. 227(2). Paragraph 6 inserts a new s. 232A into the 1992 Act, which defines circumstances where a union which induces a member to take industrial action who was denied an entitlement to vote in the ballot loses its protection from liability in tort. The effect of the new section is to maintain that protection for unions which induce members to take action where they were not balloted unless it was reasonable at the time of the ballot for the union to believe that they would be induced to take part. These provisions should enable unions to induce members who changed job after the ballot to take action. Paragraph 2(2) makes a consequential change to s. 226 of the 1992 Act, which defines the circumstances where industrial action can be regarded as having the support of a ballot.

4. Under TULR(C)A 1992, s. 228, separate ballots are generally required for each workplace.

TRADE UNION AND LABOUR RELATIONS (CONSOLIDATION) ACT 1992

228. Separate workplace ballots

(1) Subject to subsection (2), this section applies if the members entitled to vote in a ballot by virtue of section 227 do not all have the same workplace.

(2) This section does not apply if the union reasonably believes that all those members have the same workplace.

(3) Subject to section 228A, a separate ballot shall be held for each workplace; and entitlement to vote in each ballot shall be accorded equally to, and restricted to, members of the union who—

(a) are entitled to vote by virtue of section 227, and

(b) have that workplace.

(4) In this section and section 228A 'workplace' in relation to a person who is employed means—

(a) if the person works at or from a single set of premises, those premises, and

(b) in any other case, the premises with which the person's employment has the closest connection.

228A. Separate workplaces: single and aggregate ballots

(1) Where section 228(3) would require separate ballots to be held for each workplace, a ballot may be held in place of some or all of the separate ballots if one of subsections (2) to (4) is satisfied in relation to it.

(2) This subsection is satisfied in relation to a ballot if the workplace of each member entitled to vote in the ballot is the workplace of at least one member of the union who is affected by the dispute.

(3) This subsection is satisfied in relation to a ballot if entitlement to vote is accorded to, and limited to, all the members of the union who—

(a) according to the union's reasonable belief have an occupation of a particular kind or have any of a number of particular kinds of occupation, and

(b) are employed by a particular employer, or by any of a number of particular employers, with whom the union is in dispute.

(4) This subsection is satisfied in relation to a ballot if entitlement to vote is accorded to, and limited to, all the members of the union who are employed by a particular employer, or by any of a number of particular employers, with whom the union is in dispute.

(5) For the purposes of subsection (2) the following are members of the union affected by a dispute—

(a) if the dispute relates (wholly or partly) to a decision which the union reasonably believes the employer has made or will make concerning a matter specified in subsection (1)(a), (b) or (c) of section 244 (meaning of 'trade dispute'), members whom the decision directly affects,

(b) if the dispute relates (wholly or partly) to a matter specified in subsection (1)(d) of that section, members whom the matter directly affects,

(c) if the dispute relates (wholly or partly) to a matter specified in subsection (1)(e) of that section, persons whose membership or non-membership is in dispute,

(d) if the dispute relates (wholly or partly) to a matter specified in subsection (1)(f) of that section, officials of the union who have used or would use the facilities concerned in the dispute.

NOTES

1. As originally enacted, the Trade Union Act 1984 required a single ballot of all those who were expected to take part in the industrial action. This position was, however, changed by the EA 1988 and a union intending to organise industrial action generally must organise separate ballots for each place of work. Industrial action may not be lawfully taken at a particular workplace unless a majority of members have voted in favour of the action at that workplace.

2. The TULR(C)A 1992, s. 228A, provides certain exceptions to the requirement of separate ballots.

University of Central England v NALGO

[1993] IRLR 81, Queen's Bench Division

LATHAM J: In these two actions applications are made for injunctions on behalf of two of the new universities against the National and Local Government Officers' Association, restraining that association from holding industrial action without the support of a ballot, complying with ss. 10 and 11 of the Trade Union Act 1984. The particular industrial action against which the applications are directed is a one-day strike on 20 August this year, hence the urgency of the application today, although it is right to say that the union intends there to be, according to its present plans, further industrial action thereafter.

The background, very shortly, is this. As I have indicated, the two plaintiffs are now two of the new universities who used to be polytechnics and were members of the employers' association known as the Polytechnic and College Employers' Forum, which has for a number of years now negotiated with the National and Local Government Officers' Association, amongst others, the terms and conditions of their employees. It is said that the arrangements which were made for the collective bargaining were not such as to underpin the bargaining structure with any contractual entitlements as between employees and employers by reason of the parties' membership of the negotiating body. But I do not think that matters for the purposes of today.

The fact is that in practice—it is plain from the evidence before me that this is essentially accepted—the employing authorities complied with the recommendations which were negotiated in that forum, subject only to there being variations on occasions of the time of implementation. I am prepared to accept that it may well be that the plaintiffs to these actions consider that they are not, as I have already indicated, bound to comply with that, but I do not believe for the purposes of this application that the issue depends on whether they were so bound or not. The fact is that the expectation certainly of the defendants would reasonably be that the recommendations would be accepted.

The position today is that negotiations have in fact taken place for the 1992/93 pay year, and those negotiations ended on 3 July 1992. The consequence was that the employers' representatives offered a pay increase of 4.3%, which has been rejected by the unions. The defendants have held a ballot, but that ballot was held of all their members affected by these negotiations in all the former polytechnics and colleges covered by the negotiating forum. The consequence of that ballot was that there was a majority in favour of strike action of 3,630 to 3,004 on a 59% turnout.

The two plaintiffs are aggrieved by that decision for two reasons. One is that they consider that their own employees, who are members of the defendant union, were not themselves in favour of strike action; and that may or may not be factually correct. It certainly of itself has no legal significance. Their second grievance is that the ballot which was carried out was not a lawful ballot for the purposes of justifying, or to be more exact protecting, the defendants in relation to their strike call. The plaintiffs assert that, for the purposes of ss. 10 and 11 of the 1984 Act, the ballot had to be a ballot of each individual employer and it was not open to the defendants to protect their position by way of what one might loosely call the nationwide ballot.

...

... I am quite satisfied that, provided the defendants can show that it was reasonable for them to believe, and they did believe, that there was some common factor relating to the terms or conditions of employment in respect of which the industrial action is called for, they are entitled to hold a ballot of all their members affected by that factor, whether they are employed by the same employer or not. I am comforted to note that the Code of Practice which was published together with the Act, although there is no doubt that it is to some extent deficient, generally speaking can only have meaning if the construction which I have considered to be the appropriate construction of ss. 10 and 11 is that which was indeed intended by Parliament.

It follows that I refuse the applications for injunctions in these two actions. I am very grateful to both parties for their arguments.

NOTE: The method of voting in a ballot, and the content of the voting paper are specified by TULR(C)A 1992, s. 229, as amended.

229. Voting paper

(1) The method of voting in a ballot must be by the marking of a voting paper by the person voting.

(1A) Each voting paper must—

    (a) state the name of the independent scrutineer,

    (b) clearly specify the address to which, and the date by which, it is to be returned,

    (c) be given one of a series of consecutive whole numbers every one of which is used in giving a different number in that series to each voting paper printed or otherwise produced for the purposes of the ballot, and

    (d) be marked with its number.

This subsection, in its application to a ballot in which merchant seamen to whom section 230(2A) applies are entitled to vote, shall have effect with the substitution, for the reference to the address to which the voting paper is to be returned, of a reference to the ship to which the seamen belong.

(2) The voting paper must contain at least one of the following questions—

    (a) a question (however framed) which requires the person answering it to say, by answering 'Yes' or 'No', whether he is prepared to take part or, as the case may be, to continue to take part in a strike;

> (b) a question (however framed) which requires the person answering it to say, by answering 'Yes' or 'No', whether he is prepared to take part or, as the case may be, to continue to take part in industrial action short of a strike.
>
> (2A) For the purposes of subsection (2) an overtime ban and a call-out ban constitute industrial action short of a strike.
>
> (3) The voting paper must specify who, in the event of a vote in favour of industrial action, is authorised for the purposes of section 233 to call upon members to take part or continue to take part in the industrial action.
>
> The person or description of persons so specified need not be authorised under the rules of the union but must be within section 20(2) (persons for whose acts the union is taken to be responsible).
>
> (4) The following statement must (without being qualified or commented upon by anything else on the voting paper) appear on every voting paper—
>
> > 'If you take part in a strike or other industrial action, you may be in breach of your contract of employment. However, if you are dismissed for taking part in strike or other industrial action which is called officially and is otherwise lawful, the dismissal will be unfair if it takes place fewer than eight weeks after you started taking part in the action, and depending on the circumstances may be unfair if it takes place later.'

NOTES

1. Section 229(2) of the 1992 Act provides that the voting paper in an industrial action ballot must contain either or both of two questions asking whether the voter is prepared to take part in a 'strike' or in 'industrial action short of a strike'. In some cases it has been unclear whether overtime bans and call-out bans were strikes or industrial action short of a strike, and court action has ensued. In *Connex South Eastern Ltd* v *National Union of Rail Maritime and Transport Workers* [1999] IRLR 249, the Court of Appeal held that the definition of 'strike' encompasses any refusal by employees to work for periods of time for which they are employed to work, provided it is 'concerted', in the sense of being mutually planned. It was not restricted to stoppages of all work, but also includes stoppages of particular days and particular hours. Therefore, both an overtime ban and a ban on rest-day working would fall within the definition as they entail employees not working when they otherwise would have worked. Paragraph 6(2) of Sch. 3 to the 1999 Act reverses this decision and clarifies the status of call-out bans by defining both these forms of industrial action as 'industrial action short of a strike' for the purposes of s. 229(2).

2. Section 229(4) of the 1992 Act required the following statement to appear on all ballot voting papers: 'If you take part in a strike or other industrial action, you may be in breach of your contract of employment.' Paragraph 6(3) of Sch. 3 to the 1999 Act amends this statement by adding words which describe the main features of the new protections against the unfair dismissal of workers taking industrial action contained in Sch. 5 to the 1999 Act.

Post Office v Union of Communication Workers

[1990] IRLR 143, Court of Appeal

In late 1987, the Post Office began to formulate a policy to convert a large number of post offices to 'agency status', leading to the closure of Crown Office counters. The Union of Communication Workers (UCW) was opposed to the policy, and in August 1988 it decided to ballot its members who were postal officers or postal assistants on whether they were 'willing to take industrial action up to and including strike action in support of the UCW decision to oppose all aspects of the Post Office board's decision to close up to 750 Crown Office counters.'

The union received 51% support for the question it put in the ballot and between October and December called a series of selective 24-hour strikes. This culminated in a national one-day strike on 12 December.

Between January and April 1989, no industrial action was taken but the union mounted a public relations campaign in opposition to the policy. Closures of offices commenced in April 1989, and in May the union's assistant general secretary told the union's annual conference that the industrial action would continue. In September there was a one-day strike in Harrow, and there was a half-day strike in Aldridge in October.

In January 1990, the union called a 24-hour strike in London South-East. The Post Office applied for an interlocutory injunction, maintaining both that the wording of the ballot question had been defective and that the result of the ballot in August 1988 no longer legitimised industrial action. The application was refused by Turner J, but the Court of Appeal allowed the employers' appeal.

LORD DONALDSON MR: Prior to the passing of the Trade Union Act 1984, trade unions which, in furtherance or contemplation of an industrial dispute, took industrial action which induced a breach of the contracts of employment of its members were protected from claims for damages or injunctive relief by s. 13 of the Trade Union and Labour Relations Act 1974. The 1984 Act introduced the further requirement that this protection only subsisted if the action was supported by a ballot. This was achieved by s. 10 subsections (1) and (3) which were (and are) in the following terms:

Industrial action authorised or endorsed by trade union without support of a ballot.

10. (1) Nothing in s. 13 of the 1974 Act shall prevent an act done by a trade union without the support of a ballot from being actionable in tort (whether or not against the trade union) on the ground that it induced a person to break his contract of employment or to interfere with its performance.

...

(3) For the purposes of subsection (1) above, an act shall be taken as having been done with the support of a ballot if, but only if—
(a) the trade union has held a ballot in respect of the strike or other industrial action in the course of which the breach of interference referred to in subsection (1) above occurred;
(b) the majority of those voting in the ballot have answered 'Yes' to the appropriate question;
(c) the first authorisation or endorsement of any relevant act, and in the case of an authorisation the relevant act itself, took place after the date of the ballot and before the expiry of the period of four weeks beginning with that date; and
(d) s. 11 of this Act has been satisfied in relation to the ballot.

This section was followed by subsection (4), which has since been amended by the Employment Act 1988. This, in its unamended form, provided that:
(4) In subsection (3)(b) above 'appropriate question' means—
(a) where the industrial action mentioned in subsection (3)(a) above is, or includes, a strike, the question referred to in subsection (4)(a) of s. 11; and
(b) in any other case, that referred to in subsection (4)(b) of that section.

The key word here was the word 'includes'. As in the present case the union was seeking support for industrial action which *included* strike action, although it also extended to industrial action short of a strike, it may not unreasonably have thought that it was required to base the question which it put to its members in the ballot on s. 11(4)(a). Paragraphs (a) and (b) of s. 11(4) were in the following terms:
(a) a question (however framed) which requires the voter to say, by answering 'Yes' or 'No', whether he is prepared to take part, or as the case may be to continue to take part, in a strike involving him in a breach of his contract of employment;
(b) a question (however framed) which requires the voter to say, by answering 'Yes' or 'No', whether he is prepared to take part, or as the case may be to continue to take part in industrial action falling short of a strike but involving him in a breach of his contract of employment.

I am not entirely sure that the question as framed by the union would have passed muster under the unamended Act but the union could certainly have been forgiven for thinking that it would. This may indeed have been the position when the question was framed. Most unfortunately, from the point of view of the union, the 1988 amendment of the 1984 Act took effect on 26 July 1988, only a few days before the ballot was held. We have therefore to consider whether the 1984 Act as amended, and in particular the slightly amended s. 11, was satisfied in relation to the ballot which took place in the following month. The amendments were of crucial importance.

The first relevant amendment consisted of replacing s. 10(4), which I have already set out, with a new subsection and adding a new subsection (4A). These read:
(4) Subject to subsection (4A) below, in this section and s. 11 of this Act references to the appropriate question are references to whichever of the questions set out in subsection (4) of s. 11 of this Act is applicable to the strike or other industrial action.
(4A) Where both the questions mentioned in subsection (4) above are applicable in relation to any industrial action, an act inducing a breach or interference such as is mentioned in subsection (1) above shall be treated as an act for the purposes of which the requirement of para. (b) of subsection (3) above is satisfied if but only if that

paragraph (or, as the case may be, that paragraph as it has effect by virtue of subsection (3A) above) is satisfied in relation to the question applicable to that part of the action in the course of which the breach or interference occurred.

The questions set out in s. 11(4) were amended so that they read:

(4) The voting paper must contain at least one of the following questions—

    (a) a question (however framed) which requires the person answering it to say, by answering 'Yes' or 'No', whether he is prepared to take part or, as the case may be, to continue to take part in a strike;

    (b) a question (however framed) which requires the person answering it to say, by answering 'Yes' or 'No', whether he is prepared to take part or, as the case may be, to continue to take part in action short of a strike.

The combined effect of these amendments, read with the unamended subsection (3)(b) was to require that the majority of those voting should have answered 'Yes' to the strike question set out in s. 11(4)(a) if the union was calling for a strike and should have answered 'Yes' to the question set out in 11(4)(b) if the union was going to call for industrial action short of a strike. If, as was the case here, the union contemplated both types of action, it had to secure a 'Yes' vote in response to both questions. No longer was it even arguable that a majority 'Yes' vote for strike action would authorise industrial action falling short of a strike upon the grounds that the greater included the less.

If an Act of Parliament is unambiguous, as this one now is at least in this respect, the policy underlying it may not be directly relevant. However, it is reasonably clear that Parliament took account of the fact that some union members who might be prepared to take action short of a strike might not be prepared to take strike action or vice versa and it considered that the union should be required to respect their wishes.

The single question, as framed by the union—'are you willing to take industrial action up to and including strike action?'—does not permit its members to make this distinction. In effect, they have to say 'Yes' or 'No' to both the questions set out in s. 11(4) and this is contrary to the requirements of the amended Act, which clearly contemplate that, where both questions are asked, the members should be in a position to answer 'Yes' to one and 'No' to the other.

It follows from the fact that the majority of those voting in the ballot answered 'Yes' to an inappropriate and not to the appropriate question (s. 10(3)(b)) that the action of the union in calling for strikes was not in law an act done with the support of a ballot. As a result, the union is unable to rely upon s. 13 of the Trade Union and Labour Relations Act 1974 as a defence to the Post Office's complaint.

NOTES

1. In this case, the court also took the view that the second strike campaign constituted new and disconnected industrial action which needed the support of a fresh ballot.

   The question the court has to ask itself is whether the average reasonable trade union member, looking at the matter shortly after the interruption in the industrial action would say to himself, 'the industrial action has now come to an end', even if he might also say, 'the union may want us to come out again if the dispute continues' (*per* Lord Donaldson MR at p. 147).

   In *Monsanto plc v Transport and General Workers' Union* [1986] IRLR 406, CA, the union took industrial action following a ballot. The action was suspended for two weeks in order to allow for negotiations to take place. When the talks broke down, the industrial action was resumed more than four weeks after the date of the ballot. The Court of Appeal held that a fresh ballot was not necessary when there was a resumption of lawful industrial action, temporarily suspended in order to try to reach a settlement of the dispute.

2. Conduct of the ballot is now laid down by TULR(C)A 1992, ss. 227 and 230.

TRADE UNION AND LABOUR RELATIONS (CONSOLIDATION) ACT 1992

227. Entitlement to vote in ballot

(1) Entitlement to vote must be accorded equally to all the members of the trade union who it is reasonable at the time of the ballot for the union to believe will be induced by the union to take part or, as the case may be, to continue to take part in the industrial action in question, and to no others.

(2) [*repealed*].

NOTE: Two recent first instance cases have adopted a broad interpretation of this provision. In *United Closures and Plastics (the petitioner)* [2012] IRLR 29, the Court of Session held that it was lawful for the union to ballot all the members it intended to call out on strike and not just those affected by the changes introduced by the employer which were the subject of the dispute.

In *London Underground Ltd* v *ASLEF* [2012] IRLR 196, it was held in the High Court that a ballot is not restricted to those who will actually take the industrial action in question (i.e. withdraw their labour in breach of contract) but extends to those who will be invited to participate in it (e.g. by joining picket lines on a day when they are not rostered to work).

230. Conduct of ballot

(1) Every person who is entitled to vote in the ballot must—
    (a) be allowed to vote without interference from, or constraint imposed by, the union or any of its members, officials or employees, and
    (b) so far as is reasonably practicable, be enabled to do so without incurring any direct cost to himself.

(2) Except as regards persons falling within subsection (2A), so far as is reasonably practicable, every person who is entitled to vote in the ballot must—
    (a) have a voting paper sent to him by post at his home address or any other address which he has requested the trade union in writing to treat as his postal address; and
    (b) be given a convenient opportunity to vote by post.

(2A) Subsection (2B) applies to a merchant seaman if the trade union reasonably believes that—
    (a) he will be employed in a ship either at sea or at a place outside Great Britain at some time in the period during which votes may be cast, and
    (b) it will be convenient for him to receive a voting paper and to vote while on the ship or while at a place where the ship is rather than in accordance with subsection (2).

(2B) Where this subsection applies to a merchant seaman he shall, if it is reasonably practicable—
    (a) have a voting paper made available to him while on the ship or while at a place where the ship is, and
    (b) be given an opportunity to vote while on the ship or while at a place where the ship is.

(2C) In subsections (2A) and (2B) 'merchant seaman' means a person whose employment, or the greater part of it, is carried out on board sea-going ships.

(3) [*repealed*]

(4) A ballot shall be conducted so as to secure that—
    (a) so far as is reasonably practicable, those voting do so in secret, and
    (b) the votes given in the ballot are fairly and accurately counted.
For the purposes of paragraph (b) an inaccuracy in counting shall be disregarded if it is accidental and on a scale which could not affect the result of the ballot.

British Railways Board v NUR
[1989] IRLR 349, Court of Appeal

In a dispute with BR over pay and proposed changes to collective bargaining arrangements, the NUR balloted some 70,000 of its members on support for a series of 24-hour strikes. A total of 63,719 ballot papers were issued and 51,628 returned in a ballot which involved the distribution and return of papers by a variety of methods. BR's challenge to the validity of the ballot rested on evidence that some 200 members never had an opportunity to vote and the fact that some 6,000 members did not receive a ballot paper.

The employers appealed against the decision of Vinelott J dismissing an application for an interlocutory injunction. The Court of Appeal dismissed the appeal.

LORD DONALDSON MR: [T]he question which then arises is: Is there sufficient evidence to justify us in either holding or considering it likely that it would be held hereafter that there was a failure 'so far as reasonably practicable' to provide all the members entitled to vote with an opportunity of voting? I am bound to say that I do not think there is. It seems inevitable where you have a balloting operation of this size conducted in an industrial context that there will be a few people whose names ought to be on a list but which are not on a list, perhaps because they have changed jobs: there will be a few people who have not notified changes of address or whose ballot papers, if sent by post, may go astray; there will be a number of things which inevitably will go wrong. Indeed, if the situation had been that the NUR claimed to produce evidence that every one of the entitled members had received a ballot paper and returned it, I think that the Court would have been justified in looking very carefully at that evidence to see whether something had not been fiddled. It just does not happen like that in real life, and that, of course, was recognised by Parliament when it used the words 'so far as reasonably practicable'.

Under the balloting system which was adopted and which, as I say, has not been criticised by the Electoral Reform Society, the giving of the ballot papers to the members was decentralised to branch secretaries and others, the intention being that, where you had a group of people, perhaps 100 men, perhaps smaller units, gathering at one place, the ballot papers would be made available at that place. However, it was recognised that that would not cover all the NUR members because some of them work in very isolated conditions—signalmen, for instance. Others may be on leave so that they are not attending at British Rail premises at all during the period. The union and its officials went to great lengths on a decentralised basis to try and find out who those people were and to make alternative arrangements. To give an example, in one instance, and there were probably more, a branch secretary went up the line visiting signalmen, giving them their ballot papers and leaving ballot papers for the succeeding shift. In other cases where it was thought that there would be difficulty in members returning their completed ballot papers these were left at an appropriate place together with an envelope so that it could be posted back. In other cases ballot papers were posted to members, again containing an envelope which enabled the completed ballot paper to be posted back.

For my part, I cannot see that, against that background, there is any evidence at present available that so far as was reasonably practicable, every person who was entitled to vote did not have an opportunity of voting, subject always to what the lawyers describe as 'de minimis'—in other words, trifling errors which should not be allowed to form a basis for invalidating the ballot.

NOTE: Bob Simpson observes ((1989)18 ILJ 236):

> If the NUR had lost the *British Rail* case it would have been demonstrably impossible for trade unions to satisfy the requirement of ss. 10 and 11 [now TULR(C)A 1992, ss. 227 and 230] in ballots involving large numbers of workers. But the case still points up the existence of an avenue for challenge to ballots through labour injunction proceedings because of the imprecise nature of the obligations imposed.

In order to provide greater scope for such errors to be disregarded, provided they are accidental and on a scale which is unlikely to affect the outcome of a ballot, the Employment Relations Act 1999, Sch. 3, para. 9 introduces a new s. 232B into the 1992 Act, defining where failures to meet the requirements of s. 227(1) and parts of s. 230 can be disregarded.

TRADE UNION AND LABOUR RELATIONS (CONSOLIDATION) ACT 1992

232A. Inducement of member denied entitlement to vote

Industrial action shall not be regarded as having the support of a ballot if the following conditions apply in the case of any person—

(a) he was a member of the trade union at the time when the ballot was held,

(b) it was reasonable at that time for the trade union to believe he would be induced to take part or, as the case may be, to continue to take part in the industrial action,

(c) he was not accorded entitlement to vote in the ballot, and

(d) he was induced by the trade union to take part or, as the case may be, to continue to take part in the industrial action.

232B. Small accidental failures to be disregarded

(1) If—

(a) in relation to a ballot there is a failure (or there are failures) to comply with a provision mentioned in subsection (2) or with more than one of those provisions, and

(b) the failure is accidental and on a scale which is unlikely to affect the result of the ballot or, as the case may be, the failures are accidental and taken together are on a scale which is unlikely to affect the result of the ballot,

the failure (or failures) shall be disregarded for all purposes (including, in particular, those of section 232A(c)).

(2) The provisions are section 227(1), section 230(2) and section 230(2B).

NOTE: See *P* v *National Association of Schoolmasters' Union of Women Teachers* [2001] IRLR 532, CA, where an inadvertent error which resulted in two out of the 35 ballot constituents not receiving ballot papers was excused.

London Underground Ltd v National Union of Rail, Maritime and Transport Workers
[1995] IRLR 636, Court of Appeal

In furtherance of a trade dispute with London Underground over pay and conditions, the National Union of Rail, Maritime and Transport Workers (RMT) decided to ballot its members on industrial action. The ballot resulted in a vote in favour of industrial action. When the union informed the employer of the result of the ballot and, pursuant to s. 234A, served notice of its intention to call for industrial action on various dates, the list of members who were to be asked to take part in the action included 692 new members who had joined the union since the date of the ballot and, therefore, had not voted in the ballot or been included in the s. 226A notice.

The employer applied to the High Court for injunctive relief. The High Court granted an injunction restraining the union from inducing employees of London Underground who became members of the union after the date of the ballot to break their contracts of employment.

The Court of Appeal allowed the RMT's appeal.

MILLETT LJ: ...

The appeal: the 692

The question here is whether a trade union, without losing its immunity from suit, can call on a significant number of members to take part in industrial action who have joined the union since the date of the ballot and who have therefore not had an opportunity to vote in the ballot. A subsidiary question is whether it makes any difference that the new members have not joined the union by natural accretion during a long dispute, but have been actively recruited in order to make the industrial action more effective. The plaintiff insists that those who have been balloted represent the constituency of those who can be called on to take part in the action. If more than a de minimis number of members who have not been balloted are called upon to take part in industrial action, it is submitted that the action does not have the support of a ballot and the immunity is lost. It does not matter that the members in question joined the union after the ballot and so could not have been balloted. The union must take care to confine its call to take part in industrial action to those of its members who were balloted.

It is to be observed that the statutory immunity is conferred by s. 219 in wide and general terms. It is not limited to trade unions and their members, but extends to *any person* who induces *another person* to commit a breach of contract. The withdrawal of immunity for want of a ballot, however, is in more limited terms. It is withdrawn only in respect of acts done *by a trade union*, and only in respect of acts to induce a person *to take part or continue to take part in industrial action*.

The question turns on the meaning of the critical words in s. 226:

(1) An act done by a trade union to induce a person to take part, or continue to take part, in industrial action—
    (a) is not protected unless the industrial action has the support of a ballot...

The judge rightly concentrated on these words. He said:

> The key to all this lies in s. 226(1), which provides that, for a trade union to be protected in respect of inducement to a person to take part in industrial action—which I read as meaning 'by the particular person induced'—must have the support of the ballot. The question is whether it can fairly be said that a particular industrial action *by a particular person* does have the support of a ballot [my emphasis].

With respect, this is not only an unwarranted gloss on the words of the section but is syntactically incorrect and flies in the face of the plain meaning of the statutory language. What must have the support of a ballot is 'the industrial action', that is to say, the industrial action referred to in the preceding line. That is not industrial action by a particular person (assuming for the moment that that is capable of being an accurate expression), but the industrial action *in which a particular person has been induced to take part*. If the opening words of s. 226(1) are fully expanded, they read as follows:

(1) An act done by a trade union to induce a person to take part, or continue to take part, in industrial action—
    (a) is not protected unless the industrial action in which he has been induced to take part, or continue to take part, has the support of a ballot.

Industrial action is collective action. An individual does not take collective action; he takes part in it. Those who take part in it will normally be in breach of their contracts of employment. By inducing them to take part in it the union would be liable for the tort of inducing a breach of contract but for the immunity conferred by s. 219. That immunity is withdrawn by the combined effect of s. 219(4) and s. 226(1) if the industrial action does not have the support of a ballot. But the participation of a particular individual in collective industrial action and the industrial action itself are two different things. It is the industrial action which must have the support of a ballot, not the participation of those who have been induced to take part in it.

This construction of the section is supported by the text of other provisions to be found in this part of the Act. Every person taking part in the ballot, for example, must be asked whether he is prepared to take part, or continue to take part, in industrial action (s. 229(2)). If a majority of those who vote in the ballot answer 'Yes', and the other requirements of the Act are satisfied, then 'the industrial action shall be regarded as having the support of a ballot' (s. 226(2)). The industrial action which is to be regarded as having the support of a ballot is not the industrial action of any particular individual, nor is it the action of those who voted 'Yes'. Even those who voted 'No,' but were outvoted, may be called upon to take part in the industrial action without the union losing its immunity. It is the industrial action in which a majority of those voting in the ballot have declared themselves prepared to take part. The collective action is treated as distinct from the participation of the individuals who are prepared to take part in it.

There is nothing in the very detailed requirements which Parliament has laid down for the conduct of the ballot which compels the union to restrict its call for industrial action to those of its members who were members at the date of the ballot and were given the opportunity to take part in it. Parliament must be taken to have appreciated that there would be constant changes in the membership of a large union, and that by normal accretion alone significant numbers of new members might join the union between the date of the ballot notice given to the employer under s. 226A and the holding of the ballot, and between the holding of the ballot and the taking of industrial action. In the case of a lengthy dispute, the numbers in the latter case could be very large indeed.

But all this is expressly catered for. Section 226A requires the union to notify the employer of those of his employees who it is reasonably for the union to believe *at the time when it takes steps to give them notice* will be entitled to take part in the ballot. When the ballot is held s. 227(1) requires the union to ballot all those *of its members* who it is reasonable *at the time of the ballot* for the union to believe will be called upon to take part in the industrial action proposed and no others. If new members have joined since the service of the s. 226A notice, they *must* be included in the ballot. There is nothing in s. 227 which precludes the union from calling on them to take part in the industrial action. Non-members *must not* be included in the ballot.

If the union intends to call out signalmen but not train drivers, the signalmen *must* be balloted; the train drivers *must not*. The object is to prevent the union from distorting the result of the ballot by including militant members whom it does not intend to call upon to take part in industrial action. This is reinforced by subsection (2) which prevents the union from confining the ballot to militant members whom it does intend to call out and then changing its mind and calling out other less militant members. If it changes its mind and decides to extend the industrial action to members *who were members of the union at the time when the ballot was held* but who were not balloted, then it must hold a fresh ballot. But there is nothing in the section to preclude the union from including in the industrial action new members who were not balloted (and who could not lawfully be included in the ballot) because they were not members of the union at the time when the ballot was held.

What may have been a contrary view of what is now s. 227 was expressed by Lord Donaldson of Lymington MR in *Post Office* v *Union of Communication Workers* [1990] IRLR 143 at p. 147, 37. He said:

> The union clearly cannot identify and ballot those of its members who are not employees of the employer at the time of the ballot, but who will, in the event, join the workforce at a later date. It would seem to follow that any call for industrial action following a ballot should expressly be limited to those who were employed by the employer, and given an opportunity of voting at the time of the ballot. For the avoidance of doubt, let me say at once that I am not concerned, I do not think that any court would be concerned, at small changes in the workforce but, de minimis apart, this point may repay consideration.

Lord Donaldson appears to have been considering changes to the *workforce*, not to the membership of the union. The persons he appears to have had in mind are persons who *were* members of the union at the time of the ballot (and who should have been balloted) but who were not then employed by the employer. However, neither s. 227 nor its predecessor contain any reference at all to the employer. It is possible, therefore, that Lord Donaldson was intending to refer to changes in union membership rather than in the workforce. Whether this be so or not, his reasoning, if correct, would have even greater force in relation to persons who have become members of the union after the date of the ballot since, as I have already pointed out, the union is not only unable to identify them but is precluded from balloting them by the terms of the section itself.

Lord Donaldson's remarks were obiter and did not receive the support of the other members of the court. They are worthy of respect but are not binding upon us. I am satisfied that in relation to changes in union membership they are unsustainable. The conclusion at which he arrived does not follow from the section; indeed, the section points in the opposite direction. The union is required to ballot those, *and only those, of its members* who *at the time of the ballot* it is reasonable to believe will be called upon to take part in the industrial action. It cannot identify future members, but even if it could it must not ballot them, since the ballot is confined to persons who were members at the time of the ballot. If the section had been intended to preclude the union from calling out persons who were not balloted because they became members of the union after the ballot, subsection (2) would not have been confined to persons who were members of the union at the time of the ballot. In my view, the section makes it clear that a trade union does *not* lose its immunity if it induces members to take part in industrial action, so long as those persons were not members when the ballot was held…

The judge thought that there would be strange consequences if the union were permitted, without losing its statutory indemnity, to induce persons to break their contracts of employment who could not and did not fall within the constituency of those balloted. A small union, he pointed out, could hold a ballot of its own members and then set about inducing all the employees of a much larger constituency who had never been balloted to break their contracts of employment.

So it could; but with respect to the judge, there is nothing in the slightest strange in that. There has never been any identity between the constituency of those to be balloted and the constituency of those whom in contemplation or furtherance of a trade dispute the union may with impunity induce to break their contracts. As I have already pointed out, the immunity is in wide terms. It extends to anyone whom the union induces to break his contract; it is not confined to members. To this extent the immunity is commensurate with the tort. A union may in contemplation or furtherance of a trade dispute with impunity induce non-members to break their contracts.

This was plainly the law before 1984. In my view it is still the law. The immunities conferred by ss. 219 and 220 are still in the widest terms. Sections 226–235, which introduce the balloting requirements, are concerned exclusively with the relationship between a union and its members and are intended for the protection of members. Non-members have no right to be consulted before a union calls on its members to take industrial action; indeed, as we have seen, the union must not include them in the ballot. But there is nothing in ss. 226–235 to limit the union's right to seek to persuade non-members to support it by abstaining from work.

The language of the statute is striking. The immunity is from liability 'for inducing another person to break a contract' (s. 219) or from 'peacefully persuading any person… to abstain from working' (s. 220). These expressions are equally applicable to members and non-members. Immunity is withdrawn, however, in narrower circumstances. In describing them, the draftsman has carefully eschewed the use of the expression 'induce a person to break his contract'. Instead, he has throughout used the expression 'induce a person to take part in industrial action'. As a matter of ordinary language, no doubt, a non-member who stops work in support of his colleagues can be said to be taking part in their industrial action. But I am inclined to think that this is not the way in which the expression is used in ss. 226–235. The industrial action there referred to is collective action by members of the union which has called the action with the support of a ballot of its members, a majority of whom have declared that they are prepared to take part in the action. The action must be called by a person specified in that behalf on the ballot paper. There are numerous indications which support the view that the draftsman is drawing a sharp distinction between the act of a union in calling on its own members to take part in industrial action and its acts in calling upon non-members for support by breaking their contracts of employment. The distinction would also help to make sense of an otherwise difficult and perhaps unworkable s. 234A. As, however, we have heard no argument on this section, I prefer to express no view on this.

If inducing non-members to support industrial action by withdrawing their labour is to be distinguished from inducing members to take part in the industrial action called by the union, then it is an activity which attracts immunity under ss. 219 and 220 but falls outside the withdrawal of the immunity in s. 226(1). But even if the premise is not right, I think that the same conclusion is nevertheless correct. It would be astonishing if a right which was first conferred by Parliament in 1906, which has been enjoyed by trade unions ever since and which is today recognised as encompassing a fundamental human right, should have been removed by Parliament by enacting a series of provisions intended to strengthen industrial democracy and governing the relations between a union and its own members.

I conclude, therefore, that there is nothing in ss. 226–235 which curtails a union's long-accepted right to induce non-members to support the industrial action called by the union by breaking their own contracts of employment. But if this is so, then there is no reason to deny the same right in respect of non-members who have subsequently joined the union. There is simply no objection to a small union, which has the support of a ballot of its own members, seeking to attract support from non-members.

The judge may also have been influenced by the fact that the union has obtained a large influx of new members by an active recruiting campaign. I am unable to see what objection there can be to such activity. A union is plainly free to campaign actively for new members before it holds the ballot in the hope that such members will support industrial action. If they become members before the ballot, they *must* be balloted, even though their views may affect the result of the ballot. I am unable to see why activity which is unobjectionable before the ballot is objectionable after it.

I would allow the appeal.

NOTES

1. This is an important decision which addresses hitherto unresolved questions relating to the balloting requirements and holds that newly recruited members can take part in strike action without the need for a further ballot to be held. Note that the Court of Appeal disagrees with the *obiter* statement of Lord Donaldson in *Post Office* v *Union of Communication Workers* [1990] IRLR 143, CA that, *de minimis* apart, 'any call for action for industrial action following a ballot should expressly be limited to those who were employed by the employer, and given an opportunity to vote at the time of the ballot.'

2. In *British Airways* v *Unite the Union* [2010] IRLR 423, the High Court granted an interim injunction restraining the union from proceeding with a strike that it called prior to Christmas 2009. The judge upheld a claim that Unite erroneously balloted several hundred of its members who it knew would not be involved in the proposed strike action because they would have taken voluntary redundancy at the time the strike was called. It was held that it would have been 'practicable and reasonable' for the union to instruct its members not to vote if they were leaving employment.

London Borough of Newham v National and Local Government Officers Association

[1993] IRLR 83, Court of Appeal

A dispute arose between NALGO and the London Borough of Newham over redundancies which occurred at the end of 1991. Those made redundant included three officers in the poll tax section of the finance department. On 7 January 1992, a majority of the officers in that section went out on strike in protest at those redundancies. A ballot in accordance with the statutory requirements was not held until the strike had commenced. On 11 May, strike action was taken by officers in the rent and benefits department, and this was followed on 22 June by a strike of officers in the central grant unit. Both these stoppages had been authorised by a ballot.

The poll tax officers returned to work on 22 June, following a threat by the borough to dismiss them if they remained on strike. As a consequence of this threat the union's national emergency committee met on 18 June and agreed to a 'massive escalation' of industrial action. On the following day, the union's general secretary wrote to the leader of the council informing him of this decision and expressing the wish that a settlement could be reached in order to prevent the escalation. At the same time, the union wrote to all its members employed by the council informing them that there would be a branch-wide ballot on indefinite strike action. The letter stated that the national emergency committee had agreed to fund publicity and organise speakers from the national executive committee 'to help publicise the issues involved and the importance of a "Yes" vote in the ballot. It is envisaged that the ballot will take a month to carry out... Therefore, it is vital that all members of Newham NALGO become involved in the campaign and that we send a clear and unambiguous message to our employers: "Reinstate our sacked colleagues, and hands off our union".'

The ballot paper posed the single question to members: 'Are you prepared to be instructed to take indefinite strike action, on strike pay equivalent to full take-home pay in opposition to compulsory redundancies in the poll tax section and the council's threat to sack workers?' The ballot resulted in a majority in favour of the strike, and on 3 August a general strike began of all NALGO members employed by the council.

In the course of subsequent negotiations, the council offered to re-employ the three redundant poll tax officers and a commitment not to take action against individuals involved in industrial action 'that is authorised or endorsed by their trade union'. However, the union became dissatisfied with the terms of the offer of re-employment and the strike action continued.

The employers sought an injunction alleging that the union had contravened what is now TULR(C)A 1992, s. 233(3)(a). This provision requires that: 'There must have been no call by the trade union to take part or continue to take part in industrial action to which the ballot relates, or any authorisation or endorsement by the union of any such industrial action, before the date of the ballot.' The High Court granted an injunction restraining the strike action. The court found, first, that 'it seems clearly arguable' that there had been a call for, or endorsement of, industrial action by the union on a matter to which the indefinite strike ballot related, and that the union had decided on a course of action and were promoting it before the ballot.

However, the judge rejected the employers' alternative submission that the dispute to which the ballot related had already been resolved. The union appealed to the Court of Appeal on the first question, and the employers cross-appealed on the second point.

WOOLF LJ: On the first argument of the borough the answer to this issue depends upon ascertaining the effect of the two documents of 19 June when considered in the context in which they were written. Is it, at least, arguable on the documents read in their context, that the union was calling on its members to take part or to continue to take part or authorising or endorsing the members taking part or continuing to take part in industrial action to which the ballot relates so as to contravene the condition set out in s. 7(3) of the 1990 Act? Here I differ from the conclusion of the judge. Read in their context, it is clear to me that while the union were demonstrating that they wanted industrial action to be extended to other members in addition to those who were already on strike, they were not then calling on them to strike or authorising or endorsing their striking but communicating the decision of the union to authorise a ballot of all their members with a view to more extensive industrial action being taken and indicating the manner in which the ballot was going to be carried out. In other words, so far as those employees who were not already on strike was concerned, the effect of the documents in this context was to indicate that the union were intending to comply with the conditions in s. 7(3) of the 1990 Act and will not contravene those conditions. While the documents made it clear that the union was not adopting a neutral stance, not surprisingly the legislation does not make such an unreal requirement of the union. The union, as long as it complies with the legislation, is perfectly entitled to be partisan.

The Court of Appeal allowed the union's appeal.

NOTE: TULR(C)A 1992, ss. 231–231B set out the requirements to be met following a ballot.

TRADE UNION AND LABOUR RELATIONS (CONSOLIDATION) ACT 1992

231. Information as to result of ballot

As soon as is reasonably practicable after the holding of the ballot, the trade union shall take such steps as are reasonably necessary to ensure that all persons entitled to vote in the ballot are informed of the number of—
  (a) votes cast in the ballot,
  (b) individuals answering 'Yes' to the question, or as the case may be, to each question,
  (c) individuals answering 'No' to the question, or, as the case may be, to each question, and
  (d) spoiled voting papers.

231A. Employers to be informed of ballot result

(1) As soon as reasonably practicable after the holding of the ballot, the trade union shall take such steps as are reasonably necessary to ensure that every relevant employer is informed of the matters mentioned in section 231.

(2) In subsection (1) 'relevant employer' means a person who it is reasonable for the trade union to believe (at the time when the steps are taken) was at the time of the ballot the employer of any persons entitled to vote.

231B. Scrutineer's report

(1) The scrutineer's report on the ballot shall state whether the scrutineer is satisfied—
  (a) that there are no reasonable grounds for believing that there was any contravention of a requirement imposed by or under any enactment in relation to the ballot,
  (b) that the arrangements made with respect to the production, storage, distribution, return or other handling of the voting papers used in the ballot, and the arrangements for the counting of the votes, included all such security arrangements as were reasonably practicable for the purpose of minimising the risk that any unfairness or malpractice might occur, and
  (c) that he has been able to carry out the functions conferred on him under section 226B(1) without any interference from the trade union or any of its members, officials or employees;

and if he is not satisfied as to any of those matters, the report shall give particulars of his reason for not being satisfied as to that matter.

(2) If at any time within six months from the date of the ballot—

(a) any person entitled to vote in the ballot, or

(b) the employer of any such person,

requests a copy of the scrutineer's report, the trade union must, as soon as practicable, provide him with one either free of charge or on payment of such reasonable fee as may be specified by the trade union.

NOTES

1. In *Metrobus Ltd* v *Unite the Union* [2009] EWCA Civ 829, the Court of Appeal held that a two-day delay in informing the employer of the result of a ballot was in breach of s. 231A(1).

2. In *British Airways plc* v *Unite the Union* [2010] 1 All ER (D) 189 (May), the Court of Appeal discharged the interim injunction restraining Unite from taking industrial action on the basis that, whilst every possible means of communicating the results of the strike ballot had not been used by the union, the information supplied and the means of communication actually used had been sufficient to inform its members of the result within s. 231. The union had posted the results on two of its websites, posted the results on union notice boards and physically distributed the results at Heathrow and Gatwick airports.

3. Section 234 of the 1992 Act covers the timing of the industrial action.

TRADE UNION AND LABOUR RELATIONS (CONSOLIDATION) ACT 1992

234. Period after which ballot ceases to be effective

(1) Subject to the following provisions, a ballot ceases to be effective for the purposes of section 233(3)(b) in relation to industrial action by members of a trade union at the end of the period, beginning with the date of the ballot—

(a) of four weeks, or

(b) of such longer duration not exceeding eight weeks as is agreed between the union and the members' employer.

(2) Where for the whole or part of that period the calling or organising of industrial action is prohibited—

(a) by virtue of a court order which subsequently lapses or is discharged, recalled or set aside, or

(b) by virtue of an undertaking given to a court by any person from which he is subsequently released or by which he ceases to be bound,

the trade union may apply to the court for an order that the period during which the prohibition had effect shall not count towards the period referred to in subsection (1).

(3) The application must be made forthwith upon the prohibition ceasing to have effect—

(a) to the court by virtue of whose decision it ceases to have effect, or

(b) where an order lapses or an undertaking ceases to bind without any such decision, to the court by which the order was made or to which the undertaking was given;

and no application may be made after the end of the period of eight weeks beginning with the date of the ballot.

(4) The court shall not make an order if it appears to the court—

(a) that the result of the ballot no longer represents the views of the union members concerned, or

(b) that an event is likely to occur as a result of which those members would vote against industrial action if another ballot were to be held.

(5) No appeal lies from the decision of the court to make or refuse an order under this section.

(6) The period between the making of an application under this section and its determination does not count towards the period referred to in subsection (1).

But a ballot shall not by virtue of this subsection (together with any order of the court) be regarded as effective for the purposes of section 233(3)(b) after the end of the period of twelve weeks beginning with the date of the ballot.

NOTES

1. The normal rule is that the action must be called within four weeks, beginning with the date of the ballot (s. 234(1)(a)). However, the 1989 docks dispute and the litigation surrounding it showed the harsh effect of this time limit where the union was prevented from calling industrial action during the four-week period because of an injunction. The TGWU succeeded in getting the injunction lifted but then had to re-ballot because it was outside the four-week limit. Under

s. 234(2), a union may now apply for an extension of time to allow for the period during which it was prohibited from calling the action.

2. A case which illustrates the major complexities in this area is *RJB Mining (UK) Ltd* v *NUM* [1995] IRLR 556, CA. A ballot for industrial action closed at 10.00 a.m. on 16 May 1985, with a majority in favour of a series of one-day strikes. On 6 June, the union gave the employers written notice that 24-hour action would take place at the commencement of the day shift on 13 June, to the end of the night shift on the morning of 14 June, with more stoppages to follow.

   Under the unamended TULR(C)A 1992, s. 234, 'a ballot cease[d] to be effective... at the end of the period of four weeks beginning with the date of the ballot.' In this case, the union was initially wrongly advised that the four weeks did not start running until the time during the day the ballot closed and that, therefore, so long as the industrial action was called to commence before 10.00 a.m. on 13 June, it was within the time limit. The employers contended that the ballot of Tuesday 16 May ceased to be effective at midnight on Monday 12 June and the action called by the union to commence on 13 June fell outside that period. They applied for, and were granted, an interlocutory injunction restraining the union from calling the proposed strikes.

   On appeal, the union contended that the day shift of 13 June commenced at midnight on 12–13 June, that midnight is included in both days, and that, therefore, the ballot was still effective in respect of a strike called for the commencement of the day shift on 13 June. This argument was rejected by the Court of Appeal, holding that the four-week period ends at the stroke of midnight on the last day of the fourth week. In the words of Butler-Sloss LJ:

   > No part of a day can be both Monday and Tuesday... As a matter of legal precedent, midnight finishes one day and starts another, but conceptually they are different days and must remain so, otherwise we should be in cloud-cuckoo land.

   (Given the nit-picking complexity of these provisions, there are those of us who were under the distinct impression that we had already arrived!)

3. The Employment Relations Act 1999, Sch. 3, para. 10 amends s. 234(1) of the 1992 Act so that the four-week period may be extended by up to a maximum of four more weeks if both the union and the employer agree to the extension. The purpose of the amendment is to avoid circumstances where a union feels obliged to organise industrial action within the four-week period before a ballot becomes ineffective, even though the parties might be able to reach a settlement through further negotiation.

TRADE UNION AND LABOUR RELATIONS (CONSOLIDATION) ACT 1992

233. Calling of industrial action with support of ballot

(1) Industrial action shall not be regarded as having the support of a ballot unless it is called by a specified person and the conditions specified below are satisfied.

(2) A 'specified person' means a person specified or of a description specified in the voting paper for the ballot in accordance with section 229(3).

(3) The conditions are that—

(a) there must have been no call by the trade union to take part or continue to take part in industrial action to which the ballot relates, or any authorisation or endorsement by the union of any such industrial action, before the date of the ballot;

(b) there must be a call for industrial action by a specified person, and industrial action to which it relates must take place, before the ballot ceases to be effective in accordance with section 234.

(4) For the purposes of this section a call shall be taken to have been made by a trade union if it was authorised or endorsed by the union; and the provisions of section 20(2) to (4) apply for the purpose of determining whether a call, or industrial action, is to be taken to have been so authorised or endorsed.

NOTES

1. The courts have taken a realistic view of the requirement that the 'call for industrial action' must be by a 'specified person' and have held it to include the case where the specified person authorises a subordinate (e.g. regional or local officials) to call for industrial action if a final 'make or break' negotiation fails (*Tank and Drums Ltd* v *Transport and General Workers' Union* [1991] IRLR 372, CA).

2. In the Green Paper, *Industrial Relations in the 1990s*, the Government proposed that, once a ballot produced a majority in favour of (or continuing with) industrial action, a union should be required to give the employer seven days' written notice of any industrial action to which the

ballot related. The notice would have to identify which workers were to be called upon to take industrial action, and on what specific date the industrial action would begin. Where a union proposed to call for intermittent action, such as a series of one-day strikes, it would be required to give at least seven days' notice of each day or other separate period of industrial action. Moreover, if the union suspended or withdrew its support for the action, further notice would be required before any subsequent call to resume the action.

TURERA 1993 enshrined these proposals in TULR(C)A 1992, s. 234A.

TRADE UNION AND LABOUR RELATIONS (CONSOLIDATION) ACT 1992

234A. Notice to employers of industrial action

(1) An act done by a trade union to induce a person to take part, or continue to take part, in industrial action is not protected as respects his employer unless the union has taken or takes such steps as are reasonably necessary to ensure that the employer receives within the appropriate period a relevant notice covering the act.

(2) Subsection (1) imposes a requirement in the case of an employer only if it is reasonable for the union to believe, at the latest time when steps could be taken to ensure that he receives such a notice, that he is the employer of persons who will be or have been induced to take part, or continue to take part, in the industrial action.

(3) For the purposes of this section a relevant notice is a notice in writing which—

    (a) [contains—

        (i) the lists mentioned in subsection (3A) and the figures mentioned in subsection (3B), together with an explanation of how those figures were arrived at, or

        (ii) where some or all of the affected employees are employees from whose wages the employer makes deductions representing payments to the union, either those lists and figures and that explanation or the information mentioned in subsection (3C), and]

    (b) states whether industrial action is intended to be continuous or discontinuous and specifies—

        (i) where it is to be continuous, the intended date for any of the affected employees to begin to take part in the action,

        (ii) where it is to be discontinuous, the intended dates for any of the affected employees to take part in the action.

[(3A) The lists referred to in subsection (3)(a) are—

    (a) a list of the categories of employees to which the protected employees belong, and

    (b) a list of the workplaces at which the affected employees work.

(3B) The figures referred to in subsection (3)(a) are—

    (a) the total number of the affected employees,

    (b) the number of the affected employees in each of the categories in the list mentioned in subsection (3A)(a), and

    (c) the number of the affected employees who work at each workplace in the list mentioned in subsection (3A)(b).

(3C) The information referred to in subsection (3)(a)(ii) is such information as will enable the employer readily to deduce—

    (a) the total number of the affected employees,

    (b) the categories of employee to which the affected employees belong and the number of the affected employees in each of those categories, and

    (c) the workplaces at which the affected employees work and the number of them who work at each of those workplaces.

(3D) The lists and figures supplied under this section, or the information mentioned in subsection (3C) that is so supplied, must be as accurate as is reasonably practicable in the light of the information in the possession of the union at the time when it complies with subsection (1).

(3E) For the purposes of subsection (3D) information is in the possession of the union if it is held, for union purposes—

    (a) in a document, whether in electronic form or any other form, and

    (b) in the possession or under the control of an officer or employee of the union.

(3F) Nothing in this section requires a union to supply an employer with the names of the affected employees].

(4) For the purposes of subsection (1) the appropriate period is the period—

    (a) beginning with the day when the union satisfies the requirement of section 231A in relation to the ballot in respect of the industrial action, and

    (b) ending with the seventh day before the day, or before the first of the days, specified in the relevant notice.

(5) For the purposes of subsection (1) a relevant notice covers an act done by the union if the person induced is one of the affected employees and—

(a) where he is induced to take part or continue to take part in industrial action which the union intends to be continuous, if—

(i) the notice states that the union intends the industrial action to be continuous, and

(ii) there is no participation by him in the industrial action before the date specified in the notice in consequence of any inducement by the union not covered by a relevant notice; and

(b) where he is induced to take part or continue to take part in industrial action which the union intends to be discontinuous, if there is no participation by him in the industrial action on a day not so specified in consequence of any inducement by the union not covered by a relevant notice.

(5A) [*repealed*]

[(5B) In subsection (5)—

(a) a 'notified category of employee' means—

(i) a category of employee that is listed in the notice, or

(ii) where the notice contains the information mentioned in subsection (3C), a category of employee that the employer (at the time he receives the notice) can readily deduce from the notice is a category of employee to which some or all of the affected employees belong, and

(b) a 'notified workplace' means—

(i) a workplace that is listed in the notice, or

(ii) where the notice contains the information mentioned in subsection (3C), a workplace that the employer (at the time he receives the notice) can readily deduce from the notice is the workplace at which some or all of the affected employees work.

(5C) In this section references to the 'affected employees' are references to those employees of the employer who the union reasonably believes will be induced by the union, or have been so induced, to take part or continue to take part in industrial action.

(5D) For the purposes of this section, the workplace at which an employee works is—

(a) in relation to an employee who works at or from a single set of premises, those premises, and

(b) in relation to any other employee, the premises with which his employment has the closest connection].

(6) For the purposes of this section—

(a) a union intends industrial action to be discontinuous if it intends it to take place only on some days on which there is an opportunity to take the action, and

(b) a union intends industrial action to be continuous if it intends it to be not so restricted.

(7) Subject to subsections (7A) and (7B), where—

(a) continuous industrial action which has been authorised or endorsed by a union ceases to be so authorised or endorsed, and

(b) the industrial action has at a later date again been authorised or endorsed by the union (whether as continuous or discontinuous action),

no relevant notice covering acts done to induce persons to take part in the earlier action shall operate to cover acts done to induce persons to take part in the action authorised or endorsed at the later date and this section shall apply in relation to an act to induce a person to take part, or continue to take part, in the industrial action after that date as if the references in subsection (3)(b)(i) to the industrial action were to the industrial action taking place after that date.

(7A) Subsection (7) shall not apply where industrial action ceases to be authorised or endorsed in order to enable the union to comply with a court order or an undertaking given to a court.

(7B) Subsection (7) shall not apply where—

(a) a union agrees with an employer, before industrial action ceases to be authorised or endorsed, that it will cease to be authorised or endorsed with effect from a date specified in the agreement ('the suspension date') and that it may again be authorised or endorsed with effect from a date not earlier than a date specified in the agreement ('the resumption date'),

(b) the action ceases to be authorised or endorsed with effect from the suspension date, and

(c) the action is again authorised or endorsed with effect from a date which is not earlier than the resumption date or such later date as may be agreed between the union and the employer.

(8) The requirement imposed on a trade union by subsection (1) shall be treated as having been complied with if the steps were taken by other relevant persons or committees whose acts were authorised or endorsed by the union and references to the belief or intention of the union in subsection (2) or, as the case may be, subsections (3), (5) and (6) shall be construed as references to the belief or the intention of the person or committee taking the steps.

(9) The provisions of section 20(2) to (4) apply for the purpose of determining for the purposes of subsection (1) who are relevant persons or committees and whether the trade union is to be taken to have authorised or endorsed the steps the person or committee took and for the purposes of subsections (7) to (7B) whether the trade union is to be taken to have authorised or endorsed the industrial action.

NOTES

1. Section 234A of the 1992 Act provides for a trade union to send a notice to a person's employer informing him that the union intends to call upon all or some of his employees to take industrial action. The notice must be received at least seven days in advance of the commencement of the action.

   The notice must specify if action is continuous or discontinuous. Section 234A(7) deals with the position where continuous industrial action which has been authorised or endorsed by the union ceases to be so authorised or endorsed and is later authorised and endorsed again. It has the effect that the notice issued before the action ceased to be authorised or endorsed does not usually cover any action pursuant to the later authorisation or endorsement. This arrangement discourages unions from suspending industrial action to negotiate a settlement of the dispute because, if the negotiations fail, action cannot resume promptly because a fresh notice has to be issued at least seven days in advance.

   The Employment Relations Act 1999, Sch. 3, para. 11(5) inserts new subs. (7B) into s. 234A, which defines the circumstances where, following a specified period in which the industrial action has been suspended by joint agreement between the union and the employer, the action can be resumed without the need to issue a fresh notice. The specified period of the suspension can be extended by joint agreement.
2. The Employment Relations Act 2004 amended s. 234A. The effect is to require the trade union to supply the employer with more specific information as to the numbers and categories of employees concerned and their workplaces.
3. TULR(C)A 1992, s. 62, provides the member's statutory right to prevent unballoted action.

TRADE UNION AND LABOUR RELATIONS (CONSOLIDATION) ACT 1992

62. Right to a ballot before industrial action

(1) A member of a trade union who claims that members of the union, including himself, are likely to be or have been induced by the union to take part or to continue to take part in industrial action which does not have the support of a ballot may apply to the court for an order under this section.

(2) For this purpose industrial action shall be regarded as having the support of a ballot only if—

    (a) the union has held a ballot in respect of the action—

        (i) in relation to which the requirements of section 226B so far as practicable before and during the holding of the ballot were satisfied,

        (ii) in relation to which the requirements of sections 227–231 were satisfied, and

        (iii) in which the majority voting in the ballot answered 'Yes' to the question applicable in accordance with section 229(2) to industrial action of the kind which the applicant has been or is likely to take part in;

    (b) such of the requirements of the following sections as have fallen to be satisfied at the relevant time have been satisfied, namely—

        (i) section 226B so far as applicable after the holding of the ballot, and

        (ii) section 231(B);

    (bb) section 232A does not prevent the industrial action from being regarded as having the support of the ballot; and

    (c) the requirements of section 233 (calling for industrial action with support of ballot) are satisfied.

Any reference in this subsection to a requirement of a provision which is disapplied or modified by section 232 has effect subject to that section.

(3) Where on an application under this section the court is satisfied that the claim is well-founded, it shall make such order as it considers appropriate for requiring the union to take steps for ensuring—

    (a) that there is no, or no further, inducement of members of the union to take part or to continue to take part in the industrial action to which the application relates, and

    (b) that no member engages in conduct after the making of the order by virtue of having been induced before the making of the order to take part or continue to take part in the action.

(4) Without prejudice to any other power of the court, the court may on an application under this section grant such interlocutory relief (in Scotland, such interim order) as it considers appropriate.

(5) For the purposes of this section an act shall be taken to be done by a trade union if it is authorised or endorsed by the union; and the provisions of section 20(2) to (4) apply for the purpose of determining whether an act is to be taken to be so authorised or endorsed.

Those provisions also apply in relation to proceedings for failure to comply with an order under this section as they apply in relation to the original proceedings.

(6) In this section—

'inducement' includes an inducement which is or would be ineffective, whether because of the member's unwillingness to be influenced by it or for any other reason; and

'industrial action' means a strike or other industrial action by persons employed under contracts of employment.

(7) Where a person holds any office or employment under the Crown on terms which do not constitute a contract of employment between that person and the Crown, those terms shall nevertheless be deemed to constitute such a contract for the purposes of this section.

(8) References in this section to a contract of employment include any contract under which one person personally does work or performs services for another; and related expressions shall be construed accordingly.

(9) Nothing in this section shall be construed as requiring a trade union to hold separate ballots for the purposes of this section and sections 226 to 234 (requirement of ballot before action by trade union).

NOTES

1. While the failure to hold a ballot will result in the loss of immunities, the EA 1988 created the additional legal consequence set out in this extract.
2. The precise scope of the phrase 'industrial action' is unclear, but interpretation of that phrase under what is now TULR(C)A 1992, s. 238 (dealing with the dismissal of those taking part in a strike or other industrial action) would suggest it encompasses action which does not necessarily involve a breach of contract (see *Power Packing Casemakers* v *Faust* [1983] QB 471). The practical significance of this is not lost on the editors of *Harvey on Industrial Relations and Employment Law*:

> One purpose of balloting members over industrial action is to preserve the union's statutory immunity from a suit in tort brought by a plaintiff *employer*. The tort concerned will be or involve the tort of inducing a person to *break* a contract; and there is no need for any tort immunity. Therefore, for the purposes of the 1984 Act, the union does not need to ballot the members unless there is going to be a *breach* of contract. However under the 1988 Act, a member of the union can ask the court to restrain unballoted industrial action whether that industrial action involves breaches of contract or not. Ergo, the union, to be safe, needs to ballot *all* industrial action, whether or not there is going to be any breach of the member's contracts of employment. [IV[1131]]

(v) Industrial action in support of dismissed 'unofficial strikers'

TRADE UNION AND LABOUR RELATIONS (CONSOLIDATION) ACT 1992

223. Action taken because of dismissal for taking unofficial action

An act is not protected if the reason, or one of the reasons, for doing it is the fact or belief that an employer has dismissed one or more employees in circumstances such that by virtue of section 237 (dismissal in connection with unofficial action) they have no right to complain of unfair dismissal.

NOTE: Earlier in this chapter we described how the EA 1990 removed the limited unfair dismissal protection to 'unofficial' strikers (see now TULR(C)A 1992, s. 237). In order to strengthen the employer's position in such a situation, the 1990 Act removed the statutory immunity from any industrial action taken in protest against such dismissals (now TULR(C)A 1992, s. 223).

FURTHER READING

Honeyball S., *Honeyball and Bowers' Textbook on Employment Law*, 13th edn (Oxford: OUP, 2014), Ch. 15.

12

Industrial Conflict (2)

A: The freedom to picket

As with strike action, English law provides no right to picket. Instead it offers an extremely limited immunity from civil and criminal liability.

TRADE UNION AND LABOUR RELATIONS (CONSOLIDATION) ACT 1992

220. Peaceful picketing

(1) It is lawful for a person in contemplation or furtherance of a trade dispute to attend—
　(a) at or near his own place of work; or
　(b) if he is an official of a trade union, at or near the place of work of a member of that union whom he is accompanying and whom he represents,
for the purpose only of communicating information or peacefully persuading any person to work or abstain from working.

(2) If a person works or normally works—
　(a) otherwise than at any one place, or
　(b) at a place the location of which is such that attendance there for a purpose mentioned in subsection (1) is impracticable,
his place of work for the purposes of that subsection shall be any premises of his employer from which he works or from which his work is administered.

(3) In the case of a worker not in employment where—
　(a) his last employment was terminated in connection with a trade dispute, or
　(b) the termination of his employment was one of the circumstances giving rise to a trade dispute,
in relation to that trade dispute his former place of work shall be treated for the purpose of subsection (1) as being his place of work.

(4) A person who is an official of a trade union by virtue only of having been elected or appointed to be a representative of some of the members of the union shall be regarded for the purposes of subsection (1) as representing only those members; but otherwise an official of a union shall be regarded for those purposes as representing all its members.

NOTE: Picketing will receive the protection of the immunities only if the pickets are attending at or near their own workplace. So-called 'secondary picketing' was rendered unlawful by the amendments made by the Employment Act (EA) 1980.

There is no statutory definition of 'place of work'. However, the Code of Practice on Picketing, published in 1980 to accompany the amendments to the statute and revised in 1992, offers the following guidance:

> The law does not enable a picket to attend lawfully at an entrance to, or exit from any place of work other than his own. This applies even, for example, if those working at the other place of work are employed by the same employer, or are covered by the same collective bargaining arrangements as the picket. [Para. 18]

Rayware Ltd v TGWU
[1989] IRLR 134, Court of Appeal

Pickets assembled on the public highway at an entrance to an industrial estate which included the factory unit where they worked. They were actually ¾ mile from their factory unit, but this was the nearest practicable point to picket without committing a trespass.

At first instance, Judge Nance awarded the employers an injunction on the ground that the picketing was not 'at' or 'near' their premises. The Court of Appeal allowed the union's appeal.

MAY LJ: In my judgement the phrase 'at or near' in section 15(1) of the 1974 Act [now the Trade Union and Labour Relations (Consolidation) Act (TULR(C)A) 1992, s. 220(1)] must be considered in a geographical sense. We must bear in mind the intent and purpose of the legislation with which one is dealing. We are dealing with a statutory provision giving the right to picket. The context is the conduct of industrial relations in a dispute situation: a situation in which perhaps common sense has a greater part to play than in many others. The mere fact that the plaintiffs are on a private trading estate and that other concerns also lease properties on that estate is not in my view of itself sufficient to prevent the nearest point where pickets can lawfully stand from being at or near the plaintiffs' premises.

I do not accept, as I have already indicated the view of Judge Nance that Parliament intended that the picketing should be at a point where those in the factory would be informed or know of it by sight or sound that picketing was taking place.

In the end it is solely a question of fact and degree in each case, and I make no apologies for saying for the third time, perhaps a good dose of common sense.

NOURSE LJ: The words 'at or near', not being terms of art, must be construed with due regard for the purpose of the provision in which they are found. No experience of unlawful picketing, however grave, can obscure the clear purpose of section 15, which, broadly speaking, is to confer on an employee or group of employees a liberty to exert peaceful persuasion over fellow employees. It is not consistent with that purpose to construe the section so as to make it impracticable, in the conditions which many industrial and commercial developments are now found to exist, for many groups of employees to maintain pickets at all. That would be the result of the learned judge's decision, if it is held to be correct, is not in doubt…

Accordingly, adopting the view of Byles J [in *Guardians of the Society of Keelman on the River Tyne* v *Davison* (1864) 16 CBNS 612 at p. 622], that the word 'near' is not a restraining but an expanding word, to be extended so far as to give effect to the intention of the legislature, I think that on the facts of this case, as I have stated them, the plaintiff's employees have been attending near their own place of work within the meaning of section 15. For this purpose I assume, without deciding, that their place of work is limited to the plaintiff's premises and does not include the service road. If this conclusion establishes a precedent for other comparable industrial and commercial developments, we should not flinch from that result in an area of the law where it is especially desirable that rights and duties should be certain.

NOTE: The legislation restricts a dismissed employee to picketing 'his former place of work'. The impact of this restriction was clearly seen in *News Group Newspapers Ltd* v *SOGAT '82* [1986] IRLR 337, where the dismissed employees' work had been transferred from Gray's Inn Road and Bouverie Street to Wapping. Picketing by the dismissed employees at the Wapping plant was unlawful. According to Stuart-Smith J, 'place' refers to geographical location, and a place where an employee has never worked cannot become one where he does. (Other aspects of this case are presented later in the chapter.)

B: Civil liabilities for picketing

(i) The economic torts

TRADE UNION AND LABOUR RELATIONS (CONSOLIDATION) ACT 1992

219. Protection from certain tort liabilities

(3) Nothing in subsections (1) and (2) prevents an act done in the course of picketing from being actionable in tort unless it is done in the course of attendance declared lawful by section 220 (peaceful picketing).

(ii) Private nuisance

Private nuisance is an unlawful interference with an individual's use or enjoyment of his or her land. Unreasonable interference with that right by, for example, blocking an access route to the employer's property, may give rise to a cause of action. So, even though the pickets stand outside the employer's premises they may be liable for the tort of private nuisance.

Picketing which exceeds the bounds of peacefully obtaining or communicating information may involve liability for private nuisance. However, there is still doubt whether peaceful picketing *itself* amounts to a nuisance when not protected by the trade dispute immunity.

Lyons v *Wilkins*
[1899] 1 Ch 255, Court of Appeal

There was a peaceful picket of two men in connection with a strike at Lyons. A picket was also posted at the home of one of Lyons outworkers. No violence, intimidation or threat was alleged. The employers sought an interlocutory injunction to restrain what they alleged was a wrongful watching and besetting of property under the Conspiracy and Protection of Property Act 1875, s. 7 (now TULR(C)A 1992, s. 241).

LORD LINDLEY MR: The truth is that to watch or beset a man's house with a view to compel him to do or not to do what is lawful for him not to do or do is wrongful and without lawful authority unless some reasonable justification for it is consistent with the evidence. Such conduct seriously interferes with the ordinary comfort of human existence and ordinary enjoyment of the house beset and such conduct would support an action on the case for a nuisance at common law… Proof that the nuisance was 'peaceably to persuade other people' would afford no defence to such an action. Persons may be peaceably persuaded provided the method employed is not a nuisance to other people.

Ward Lock & Co. v *Operative Printers' Assistants' Society*
(1906) 22 TLR 327, Court of Appeal

Members of the union picketed the plaintiffs' printing works with the aim of persuading the employees to join the union so as to create a 'closed shop'. There was no evidence of violence, obstruction or common law nuisance and the pickets were found not to have induced the employees to breach their contracts of employment.

MOULTON LJ: … I am therefore of the opinion that in support of the plaintiffs' claim with regard to picketing, it must be shown that the defendants or one of them were guilty of a wrongful act, i.e., that the picketing constituted an interference with the plaintiffs' action wrongful at common law, or, as I think it may accurately be phrased, were guilty of a common law nuisance… I wish to add, that, in my opinion there is throughout a complete absence of anything in the nature of picketing or besetting which could constitute a nuisance.

Hubbard v *Pitt*

[1975] ICR 308, Court of Appeal

A tenants' association had mounted a weekly picket of between six to eight people outside the offices of an Islington firm of estate agents. The association was opposed to the practices of the estate agents and the property developers whom they represented. The pickets stood in line with placards and handed out leaflets to passers-by. They did not obstruct the highway and behaved in a peaceful manner. The employers sought and obtained an interlocutory injunction. The defendants appealed from this decision.

LORD DENNING MR: Picketing is not a nuisance in itself. Nor is it a nuisance for a group of people to attend at or near the plaintiff's premises in order to obtain or communicate information or in order to peacefully persuade. It does not become a nuisance unless it is associated with obstruction, violence, intimidation, molestation or threats.

NOTES

1. The majority of the Court of Appeal, on the other hand, merely affirmed the exercise of the High Court judge's discretion to grant an interlocutory injunction to the plaintiffs whose premises were being picketed, and had little to say on the substantive issue. However, Orr LJ did feel that the defendants' intentions and states of mind formed what he called 'a crucial question' in this matter, and he was satisfied that in this case the pickets intended to interfere with the plaintiffs' business.

   This sort of reasoning was applied subsequently in *Mersey Dock & Harbour Co. Ltd* v *Verrinder* [1982] IRLR 152, where the High Court held that the picketing of the entrances to container terminals at Mersey Docks amounted to private nuisance despite the fact that the picketing was carried out in an entirely peaceful manner by a small group of pickets. On the basis of this approach, it would appear that, if the intention of the pickets is to achieve more than the mere communication of information and actually to interfere with the picketed employer's business, the picket will be tortious.

   As can be seen, the conflict between the *Lyons* and the *Ward Lock* approaches is unresolved, though the weight of academic opinion favours the *Ward Lock* approach (see, for example, Lewis, R. (ed.), *Labour Law in Britain* (Oxford: Blackwell, 1986), at p. 199; Davies, P. and Freedland, M., *Labour Law Text, Cases and Materials*, 2nd edn (London: Weidenfeld and Nicolson, 1984), at p. 852).

2. *Thomas* v *NUM (South Wales Area)* [1985] IRLR 136, CD, was a case arising out of the protracted miners' strike of 1984–5. A group of working miners obtained injunctions restraining the area union from organising mass picketing at the collieries where they worked.

   Two important points arise from the decision. First, private nuisance is concerned with interference with the use of or enjoyment of land in which the claimant has an interest. In this case, a species of the tort was held to extend to interference with the right to use the highway.

   > A daily congregation on average of 50 to 70 men hurling abuse and in circumstances that require a police presence and require the working miners to be conveyed in vehicles do not in my view leave any real room for argument. The working miners have the right to go to work. Neither they or any other working man should be required, in order to exercise that right, to tolerate the situation I have described. Accordingly in my judgment the colliery gates picketing is tortious at the suit of the plaintiff or plaintiffs who work at the collieries in question.

   Second, the terms of the injunction granted by the court restricted picketing at the collieries to peacefully communicating and obtaining information and in numbers not exceeding six. This number is not a purely arbitrary figure; it comes from the Code of Practice on Picketing, which at para. 51 advises that 'pickets and their organisers should ensure that in general the number of pickets does not exceed six at any entrance to a workplace; frequently a smaller number will be appropriate.' The judge was using the guidance in the Code to fix the parameters of lawful picketing. If this view is correct, then any picketing numbering more than six will lose the immunity offered by s. 220 and will be tortious (see also *News Group Newspapers Ltd* v *SOGAT '82* [1986] IRLR 337, QBD).

3. In *Gate Gourmet London Ltd* v *Transport and General Workers Union* [2005] IRLR 881, Fulford J held that the incorporation of the European Convention on Human Rights into UK law arguably has

created a 'right to picket' to the extent that the right of peaceful assembly is guaranteed by Article 11 of the Convention. Moreover, Article 10 contains the right to freedom of expression. When considering granting relief that would infringe such rights, the court has an obligation to give 'due weight' to the importance of those rights. In the instant case, however, given the evidence that pickets had intimidated employees attempting to go to work by threatening or abusing them, the judge issued an order limiting the number of pickets to six and restraining them from approaching employees en route to and from their place of work. 'I have balanced the curtailment of the rights of those gathered at [the] sites... against what I perceive to be necessary in a democratic society for the prevention of crime.'

Although no ballot had preceded the industrial action, the injunction was issued against the union. Evidence that various union officials had been present at the pickets meant that there was a clear arguable case that the union fully appreciated and understood the types of unlawful activity which were being routinely perpetrated. It was arguable, given their probable knowledge as to what was occurring, that specific officials could be said to have authorised the unlawful and tortuous acts and that those officials who attended the site in reality constituted a group who were organising or coordinating industrial action. As the union had not repudiated the unlawful activity, it was right that the injunction should be directed at the union.

The injunction was granted against not only the union and certain named defendants, but also against unnamed defendants. Fulford J stated:

> I readily appreciate an injunction in such unspecific terms is unusual, but the courts undoubtedly have the power to make an order of this kind if the circumstances make it necessary. The court must particularly ensure the group of unknown persons is sufficiently clear to mean that those who are included and those who are not can be readily identified. I have no doubt that this is the position here: persons unknown in this case refers only to people engaging in unlawful picketing and/or otherwise assaulting, threatening, intimidating, harassing, molesting or otherwise abusing the employees of Gate Gourmet or its associated companies.

(iii) Trespass

In *Larkin* v *Belfast Harbour Commissioners* [1908] 2 IR 214, strikers picketed on the quayside which was the property of the harbour authority. It was held that the statute (Trade Disputes Act 1906, s. 2) did not authorise a trespass on private property.

In *British Airports Authority* v *Ashton* [1983] IRLR 287, a picket line was established within the parameter of Heathrow Airport, the property of BAA. It was held that TULRA 1974 did not authorise a picket line on private property. Mann J thought it would be 'astonishing' if Parliament had intended to imply a right to attend on land against the will of the landowner.

C: Criminal liability for picketing

While it is important to grasp the range of possible civil liabilities which may attach to certain types of picketing, it is the criminal law which is of the greatest practical significance in terms of control of the activity. This can clearly be seen from the employment of the criminal law during the miners' strike, where over 11,000 charges were brought in connection with incidents arising out of the dispute. These ranged in gravity from the serious offences of riot and unlawful assembly to the less serious charges of obstruction of the highway. Additional criminal offences which may be relevant to the conduct of picketing have been created by the Public Order Act 1986.

(i) Obstructing a police officer in the execution of his duty

---

Piddington v Bates

[1960] 1 WLR 162, Divisional Court

As a result of a telephone call for assistance, the police went to the picketed premises of Free Press Ltd. At the request of the police, the number of pickets at a factory was limited to two at the front entrance and two at the rear. Piddington went to join the picket at the rear entrance, but the police told him repeatedly that two were enough. Piddington pushed gently past the police officer and was gently arrested. There had been no obstruction of the highway, no disorder, nor any violence or threats of violence by the pickets. Piddington was convicted of obstructing a police officer in the execution of his duty.

LORD PARKER CJ: ... It seems to me that the law is reasonably plain. First, the mere statement by a constable that he did anticipate that there might be a breach of the peace is clearly not enough. There must exist proved facts from which a constable could reasonably anticipate such a breach. Secondly, it is not enough that his contemplation is that there is a remote possibility; there must be a real possibility of a breach of the peace. Accordingly, in every case, it becomes a question of whether, on the particular facts, it can be said that there were reasonable grounds on which a constable charged with this duty reasonably anticipated that a breach of the peace might occur.

As I have said, every case must depend upon its exact facts, and the matter which influences me in this case is the matter of numbers. It is, I think, perfectly clear from the wording of the case, although it is not expressly so found, that the police knew that in these small works there were only eight people working. They found two vehicles arriving, with 18 people milling about the street, trying to form pickets at the doors. On that ground alone, coupled with the telephone call which, I should have thought, intimated some sense of urgency and apprehension, the police were fully entitled to think as reasonable men that there was a real danger of something more than mere picketing to collect or impart information or peaceably to persuade. I think that in those circumstances the prosecutor had reasonable grounds for anticipating that a breach of the peace was a real possibility. It may be, and I think this is the real criticism, that it can be said: Well, to say that only two pickets should be allowed is purely arbitrary; why two? Why not three? Where do you draw the line? I think that a police officer charged with the duty of preserving the Queen's peace must be left to take such steps as on the evidence before him he thinks are proper. I am far from saying that there should be any rule that only two pickets should be allowed at any particular door. There, one gets into an arbitrary area, but so far as this case is concerned I cannot see that there was anything wrong in the action of the prosecutor.

■ **QUESTION**

While there must be an objective apprehension that a breach of the peace is a real as opposed to a remote possibility, do you think it likely that a court would reject a police officer's assessment of the situation?

NOTE: The Code of Practice on Picketing makes it clear that the recommended number of six pickets does not affect in any way the discretion of the police to limit the number of people on any one picket line (para. 51).

Moss v McLachlan
[1985] IRLR 76, Queen's Bench Division

Striking miners from other parts of the country travelled to Nottinghamshire in order to picket the pits which were still working. Four of the striking miners were stopped by a police cordon at a junction within one and a half miles of a working colliery. When the miners refused to accept a police instruction to turn back, they were arrested and convicted of wilfully obstructing a police officer in the execution of his duty. Their appeal was rejected.

SKINNER J: ... If a constable reasonably apprehends, on reasonable grounds, that a breach of the peace may be committed, he is not only entitled but is under a duty to take reasonable steps to prevent that breach occurring...

The possibility of a breach must be real to justify any preventative action. The imminence or immediacy of the threat to the peace determines what action is reasonable. If the police feared that a convoy of cars travelling towards a working coal field bearing banners and broadcasting, by sight or sound, hostility or threats towards working miners, might cause a violent episode, they would be justified in halting the convoy to enquire into its destination and purpose. If, on stopping the vehicles, the police were satisfied that there was a real possibility of the occupants causing a breach of the peace one-and-a-half miles away, a journey of less than five minutes by car, then in our judgement it would be their duty to prevent the convoy from proceeding further and they have the power to do so.

NOTES

1. For a detailed commentary on this case, see Morris (1985) 14 ILJ 109.
2. Under the Police and Criminal Evidence Act 1984, s. 4, police officers may also operate 'road checks' for purposes which include ascertaining whether a vehicle is carrying a person intending to commit an offence which a senior officer has reasonable grounds to believe is likely to lead to serious public disorder.

(ii) Obstruction of the highway

The offence of obstruction of the highway is contained in the Highways Act 1980, s. 137.

Tynan v Balmer

[1966] 2 All ER 133, Divisional Court

Tynan, a union official, was in charge of a group of 40 pickets assembled on an access road to a factory which formed part of the highway. He had organised the pickets into a continually moving circle. A constable ordered the defendant to stop the moving circle, and when he refused he was arrested and charged with wilfully obstructing the constable in the execution of his duty. He was convicted and appealed.

WIDGERY J: … In my judgement, the proper way to approach this question, and it is a way which may well have commended itself to the recorder also, is to ask whether the conduct of the pickets would have been a nuisance at common law as an unreasonable user of the highway. It seems, in my judgement, that it clearly would have been so regarded. One leaves aside for the moment any facilities enjoyed by those acting in furtherance of a trade dispute, and if one imagines these pickets as carrying banners advertising some patent medicine or advocating some political reform, it seems to me that their conduct in sealing off a part of the highway by this moving circle would have been an unreasonable user of the highway…

In my judgement, therefore, if one ignores section 2 of the Trade Disputes Act 1906, for the moment and considers the position at common law, this action would have been an unreasonable user of the highway, admittedly a nuisance, and a police officer would have been fully entitled to take action to move the pickets on.

… But what in my view one must do is to look carefully at section 2 and see exactly what it authorises. It authorises in its simplest terms a person to attend at or near one of the places described if he does so merely for the purpose of peacefully obtaining or communicating information or of peacefully persuading any person to work or abstain from working.

The recorder has found as a fact that the pickets in this case were not attending merely for the purposes described in the section. He has found as a fact that their object at any rate in part was to seal off the highway and to cause vehicles approaching the premises to stop. In my judgement that finding of fact is quite enough to require this court to say that as a matter of law the recorder's judgment in this case should be upheld.

Broome v Director of Public Prosecutions

[1974] IRLR 26, House of Lords

Broome was picketing a building site. He stood with a poster in front of a lorry trying to enter a factory. Broome was requested by a police officer to move, and on his refusal was arrested and charged with wilfully obstructing the highway. Throughout the whole incident there were no angry words or violent actions and the whole episode lasted only nine minutes. The House of Lords dismissed his appeal against conviction.

LORD REID: … I see no ground for implying any right to require the person whom it is sought to persuade to submit to any kind of constraint or restriction on his personal freedom. One is familiar with persons at the side of a road signalling to a driver requesting him to stop. It is then for the driver to decide whether he will stop or not. That, in my view, a picket is entitled to do. If the driver stops, the picket can talk to him but only for so long as the driver is willing to listen.

That must be so because if the picket had the statutory right to stop or to detain the driver that must necessarily imply that the Act had imposed on those passing along the road a statutory duty to stop or to remain for longer than they chose to stay. So far as my recollection goes it would be unique for Parliament to impose such a duty otherwise than by express words, and even if one envisages the possibility of such a duty being imposed by implication the need for it would have to be crystal clear. Here I can see no need at all for any such implication.

Without the protection of the section merely inviting a driver to stop and then, if he is willing to stop and listen, proceeding to try and persuade him not to go on, would in many cases be either an offence or a tort or both, particularly if more than a very few pickets were acting together. I see no reason to hold that the section confers any other right.

■ QUESTIONS

1. In the modern context, can it be said that there is an effective right to picket when pickets are not allowed to 'flag down' motor vehicles?

2. What difficulties would be encountered in drafting a provision providing a right for pickets to stop vehicles?

NOTE: The Labour Government did seek to amend the law in 1975 by 'declaring' that pickets had the right to seek to persuade people to stop for the purpose of exercising their rights of persuasion, whether the person sought to be stopped was in a vehicle or not. The amendment was defeated by the unlikely alliance of the Conservative Opposition and left-wing MPs. The latter thought that the provision did not go far enough because it did not authorise obstruction of the highway and so would not have helped a picket in Broome's situation.

In essence, the effective right to picket is wholly dependent on whether the police exercise their discretion to require vehicles to stop in order to allow the pickets to speak with the drivers.

(iii) Public nuisance

This offence derives from the common law and is committed where members of the public are obstructed in the exercise of rights which are common to all Her Majesty's subjects, including the right of free passage along the public highway. As with the more frequently charged offence under the Highways Act 1980, it is necessary for the prosecution to prove unreasonable use.

Where an individual suffers special damage, over and above that suffered by the rest of the public, an action in tort for public nuisance may also be brought.

(iv) Intimidation or annoyance by violence and otherwise

TRADE UNION AND LABOUR RELATIONS (CONSOLIDATION) ACT 1992

241. Intimidation or annoyance by violence or otherwise

(1) A person commits an offence who, with a view to compelling another person to abstain from doing or to do any act which that person has a legal right to do or abstain from doing, wrongfully and without legal authority—

(a) uses violence to or intimidates that person or his wife or children or injures his property,

(b) persistently follow that person about from place to place,

(c) hides any tools, clothes or other property owned or used by that person or deprives him or hinders him in the use thereof,

(d) watches or besets the house or other place where that person resides, works, carries on business or happens to be, or the approach to any such house or place, or

(e) follows that person with two or more other persons in a disorderly manner in or through any street or road.

NOTES

1. These offences first appeared in the Conspiracy and Protection of Property Act 1875, s. 7. Until relatively recently, it was assumed that this quaintly worded Victorian provision was only of historical interest and virtually obsolete in practical terms. During the miners' strike of 1984–5, however, at least 643 charges were brought under what is now TULR(C)A 1992, s. 241, mainly to deal with 'watching and besetting' working miners' homes. In the view of the Government, the section had demonstrated its continued efficacy in the circumstances of the strike and should not only be retained but strengthened (see *Review of Public Order Law* (Cmnd 9510), May 1985). Consequently, the Public Order Act 1986 increased the maximum penalty of three months' imprisonment and a £100 fine to six months' imprisonment and/or a fine (currently £5,000). The Act also made breach of what is now s. 241 an arrestable offence (see now TULR(C)A 1992, s. 241(2) and (3)).

2. Of the five offences listed in s. 241, watching or besetting is the one which is most likely to arise out of the course of picketing. In *Ward Lock & Co. Ltd* v *Operative Printers' Assistants' Society* (1906) 22 TLR 327, it was said that the Conspiracy and Protection of Property Act 1875, s. 7, 'legalises nothing, and renders nothing wrongful that was not so before' (*per* Fletcher Moulton LJ). So the watching or besetting must be of such a nature as to amount in itself to a tortious activity before it can give rise to liability under s. 241. If peaceful picketing is not tortious, then it cannot amount to a criminal watching or besetting either.

3. One final point on this section concerns the question whether mass picketing amounts to intimidation. In *Thomas* v *NUM (South Wales Area)* (Section (ii)), Scott J was of the view that not only was mass picketing a common law nuisance but it also amounted to intimidation under what is now s. 241, even where there was no physical obstruction of those going to work.

(v) The Public Order Act 1986

In putting forward the proposals which were later largely translated into the provisions of the Public Order Act 1986, the White Paper of 1985 stated:

The rights of peaceful protest and assembly are amongst our fundamental freedoms: they are numbered among the touchstones which distinguish a free society from a totalitarian one. Throughout the review the Government has been concerned to regulate those freedoms to the minimum extent necessary to preserve order and protect the rights of others. [*Review of Public Order Law* (Cmnd 9510), May 1985]

A number of commentators, however, have expressed a general concern that the provisions contained in the 1986 Act impose a dangerous restriction on the civil liberties of assembly and protest and, particularly in the light of events during the 1984–5 miners' strike, make it increasingly more difficult for the police to be seen to maintain a position of neutrality in the policing of industrial disputes (see Lewis, R. (ed.), *Labour Law in Britain* (Oxford: Blackwell, 1986), pp. 216–19; Lord Wedderburn, *The Worker and The Law*, 3rd edn (Harmondsworth: Penguin, 1986), pp. 550–3).

Part I of the Public Order Act 1986 contains five statutory offences which may have a relevance in the context of picketing. Sections 1–3 of the Act contain the offences of riot, violent disorder, and affray, and replace the common law offences of riot, rout, unlawful assembly, and affray whose ambit was confused and uncertain. Sections 4 and 5 contain the more minor offences of causing fear or provocation of violence and causing harassment, alarm or distress. Section 154 of the Criminal Justice and Public Order Act 1994 inserted s. 4A in the Public Order Act 1986 and creates the more serious offence of causing *intentional* harassment, alarm or distress.

Part II of the 1986 Act imposes controls over the conduct of marches or processions and static assemblies. Section 11 imposes a national requirement for organisers of 'public processions' normally to give at least six clear days' notice of their intention to the police. The notice must specify the date of the procession, its proposed starting time and route and the name and address of one of the organisers.

Picketing, by definition, is a static assembly outside the entrance of a workplace. However, protest marches are now a relatively frequent feature of larger industrial disputes, e.g. the protest marches held in support of the striking miners in 1984–5 and the marches, culminating in a mass picket outside the Wapping plant of News International, during 1986 in protest at the dismissal of some 5,500 print workers (see *News Group Newspapers Ltd* v *SOGAT '82* [1986] IRLR 337). In future such marches will have to comply with the terms of s. 11, though it should be noted that the notice requirement does not apply to processions 'commonly and customarily held', e.g. by trade unionists on May Day.

Section 12 enables the *most senior police officer present* to impose conditions, including route and timing, on processions when the officer reasonably believes that they may result in serious public disorder, serious damage to property or serious disruption to the life of the community, or where the purpose of the organisers is to intimidate others. Where a march or procession is *intended* to be held, 'the senior police officer' with the power to impose conditions is the chief officer of police.

The power to ban marches for up to three months under the Public Order Act 1986 on the ground of reasonable belief that it will result in 'serious public disorder' is retained. The major change is that the 1986 Act makes it an offence to participate in a banned march, punishable with a maximum fine, in addition to organising or inciting others to participate in one.

The Act provides the police for the first time ever with a clear *statutory* power to impose conditions which prescribe the location, and maximum duration of 'public assemblies' (defined as assemblies of 20 or more people in a 'public place' which is wholly or partly open to the air). As with processions, the most senior officer present will be able to impose such conditions where he or she reasonably believes that an assembly may result in serious disorder, serious damage to property, serious disruption of the life of the community or the 'intimidation of others with a view to compelling them not to do an act they have a right to do, or to do an act they have a right not to do'. This provision has the clearest relevance for pickets and provides a potent additional weapon of control for the police. As the White Paper observed, 'at Grunwick's or Warrington, for example, the police could have imposed conditions limiting the numbers of demonstrators, or moving the demonstration in support of the pickets further away from the factory' (para. 5.7).

Where conditions are imposed *in advance* of the assembly, then they may only be imposed by the chief officer of police, or his deputy or assistant. The organisers of a static assembly who fail to abide by the conditions, or those who incite disobedience, face a maximum penalty of three months' imprisonment and/or a fine. The participants in such an assembly risk a fine.

See also the Criminal Justice and Public Order Act 1994, s. 68, which creates the offence of aggravated trespass, and s. 70, which empowers chief police officers to seek an order from the district council prohibiting the holding of trespassory assemblies in the district for a specified period.

SECTION 2: INDUSTRIAL ACTION: CIVIL REMEDIES AND ENFORCEMENT

Currently, if a trade union organises industrial action which is unlawful, it can be restrained by an injunction from the courts on an application from the employer involved in the dispute, or any other party whose contractual rights have been infringed. Union members also have the right to restrain industrial action if they are, or are likely to be, induced to participate in industrial action which does not have the support of a ballot. The Trade Union Reform and Employment Rights Act (TURERA) 1993 extends the right of action to members of the public who suffer, or are likely to suffer, disruption from unlawful industrial action (see p. 706 (Section 2.D)).

A: An 'act done by a trade union'

The individuals organising unlawful industrial action will be personally liable. Prior to 1982, trade unions themselves enjoyed a wide immunity from actions in tort. This position was radically changed by the EA 1982, which made unions liable in tort, made them vicariously liable for the unlawful actions of their officials and which set out a scale of maximum damages depending on the size of the union. As a result, it is crucial to be able to identify an 'act done by a trade union'.

TRADE UNION AND LABOUR RELATIONS (CONSOLIDATION) ACT 1992

20. Liability of trade union in certain proceedings in tort

(1) Where proceedings in tort are brought against a trade union—
  (a) on the ground that an act—
    (i) induces another person to break a contract or interferes or induces another person to interfere with its performance, or
    (ii) consists in threatening that a contract (whether one to which the union is a party or not) will be broken or its performance interfered with, or that the union will induce another person to break a contract or interfere with its performance, or
  (b) in respect of an agreement or combination by two or more persons to do or to procure the doing of an act which, if it were done without any such agreement or combination, would be actionable in tort on such a ground,
  then, for the purpose of determining in those proceedings whether the union is liable in respect of the act in question, that act shall be taken to have been done by the union if, but only if, it is to be taken to have been authorised or endorsed by the trade union in accordance with the following provisions.
(2) An act shall be taken to have been authorised or endorsed by a trade union if it was done, or was authorised or endorsed—
  (a) by any person empowered by the rules to do, authorise or endorse acts of the kind in question, or
  (b) by the principal executive committee or the president or general secretary, or
  (c) by any other committee of the union or any other official of the union (whether employed by it or not).
(3) For the purposes of paragraph (c) of subsection (2)—
  (a) any group of persons constituted in accordance with the rules of the union is a committee of the union; and
  (b) an act shall be taken to have been done, authorised or endorsed by an official if it was done, authorised or endorsed by, or by any member of, any group of persons of which he was at the material time a member, the purposes of which included organising or co-ordinating industrial action.

NOTES

1. By virtue of amendments originally introduced by the EA 1990, the scope of union liability was further extended. What is now TULR(C)A 1992, s. 20(2)(c) means that a shop steward could render a union liable where he or she authorises or endorses action without a ballot. Moreover, by virtue of s. 20(3)(b), it is sufficient that such an official is a member of a group, the purpose of which includes organising or coordinating industrial action, and that *any member of that group* has authorised or endorsed the action. The insidious nature of this provision was highlighted by Lord Wedderburn during the House of Lords debates on the Bill that became the EA 1990:

   under this Bill the union is at risk from an act of an unknown person, some mysterious stranger acting unilaterally after the gathering of an unknown, shadowy group to which the official, at a material time, at some point entered and became, for a few moments, a member. [Hansard HL 23 July 1990, col. 1272]

2. A union may repudiate the purported authorisation or endorsement by the third group, i.e. other committees and officials, but can *never* repudiate the actions of the principal executive committee, president, general secretary or those acting under the rules. The requirements for an effective repudiation are far more stringent and complicated as a result of changes introduced by the 1990 Act.

TRADE UNION AND LABOUR RELATIONS (CONSOLIDATION) ACT 1992

21. Repudiation by union of certain acts

(1) An act shall not be taken to have been authorised or endorsed by a trade union by virtue only of paragraph (c) of section 20(2) if it was repudiated by the executive, president or general secretary as soon as reasonably practicable after coming to the knowledge of any of them.

(2) Where an act is repudiated—

(a) written notice of the repudiation must be given to the committee or official in question, without delay, and

(b) the union must do its best to give individual written notice of the fact and date of repudiation, without delay—

(i) to every member of the union who the union has reason to believe is taking part, or might otherwise take part, in industrial action as a result of the act, and

(ii) to the employer of every such member.

(3) The notice given to members in accordance with paragraph (b)(i) of subsection (2) must contain the following statement—

'Your union has repudiated the call (or calls) for industrial action to which this notice relates and will give no support to unofficial industrial action taken in response to it (or them). If you are dismissed while taking unofficial industrial action, you will have no right to complain of unfair dismissal.'

(4) If subsection (2) or (3) is not complied with, the repudiation shall be treated as ineffective.

(5) An act shall not be treated as repudiated if at any time after the union concerned purported to repudiate it the executive, president or general secretary has behaved in a manner which is inconsistent with the purported repudiation.

(6) The executive, president or general secretary shall be treated as so behaving if, on a request made to any of them within three months of the purported repudiation by a person who—

(a) is a party to a commercial contract whose performance has been or may be interfered with as a result of the act in question, and

(b) has not been given written notice by the union of the repudiation, it is not forthwith confirmed in writing that the act has been repudiated.

(7) In this section 'commercial contract' means any contract other than—

(a) a contract of employment, or

(b) any other contract under which a person agrees personally to do work or perform services for another.

B: Injunctions

An injunction is an order either requiring the defendant to cease a particular course of action (a negative injunction) or, in its mandatory form, an order requiring the defendant to do something. The most frequent form of order in industrial disputes is the interim injunction requiring the organisers to call off the industrial action pending full trial of the action. Employers who succeed at this stage rarely proceed to full trial: they have achieved their aim of halting the action. They know the suspension of the industrial action, although theoretically on a temporary basis, will defeat the strike in practical terms because the impetus will be lost. Given the crucial effect the obtaining of injunctive relief will have on the outcome of a dispute, the principles on which the court's discretion is based are of great importance.

TRADE UNION AND LABOUR RELATIONS (CONSOLIDATION) ACT 1992

221. Restrictions on grant of injunctions and interdicts

(1) Where—

(a) an application for an injunction is made to a court in the absence of the party against whom it is sought or any representative of his, and

(b) he claims, or in the opinion of the court would be likely to claim, that he acted in contemplation or furtherance of a trade dispute,

the court shall not grant the injunction or interdict unless satisfied that all steps which in the circumstances were reasonable have been taken with a view to securing that notice of the application and an opportunity of being heard with respect to the application have been given to him.

(2) Where—

(a) an application for an interlocutory injunction is made to a court pending the trial of an action, and

(b) the party against whom it is sought claims that he acted in contemplation or furtherance of a trade dispute,

the court shall in exercising its discretion whether or not to grant the injunction, have regard to the likelihood of that party's succeeding at the trial of the action in establishing any matter which would afford a defence to the action under section 219 (protection from certain tort liabilities) or section 220 (peaceful picketing).

NOTES

1. In *NWL* v *Woods* [1979] 3 All ER 614, Lord Diplock was of the view that the provision was intended as a reminder to judges that, in exercising their discretion, they should consider a number of 'practical realities', particularly the fact that the interlocutory injunction stage generally disposes of the whole action. However, in *Dimbleby & Sons Ltd* v *NUJ* [1984] ICR 386, his Lordship revised his view of the practical realities, given that in the interim period the EA 1982 had made it possible to pursue actions for damages against trade unions themselves and therefore it was wrong to assume that the matter would be disposed of at the interlocutory stage. Lord Diplock appears to suggest that this should make a judge more willing to grant an interim injunction. But surely this factor should weigh the balance of convenience *against* the grant of an injunction, given that the employer is now able to recover damages and costs at full trial from a solvent defendant.

2. There are suggestions in several cases (*NWL Ltd* v *Woods*; *Express Newspapers Ltd* v *McShane* [1980] AC 672; and *Duport Steels Ltd* v *Sirs* [1980] ICR 161) that the courts have a residual discretion to grant an injunction. Consequently, in cases where a strike posed serious consequences to the employer, a third party or the general public, what is now TULR(C)A 1992, s. 221(2) might be overridden. This possibility is of much less practical importance since the 1980s, given the considerable narrowing of the scope of the immunities which has taken place (for a detailed discussion of this highly complex area see Wedderburn, *The Worker and the Law*, pp. 681–717).

Mercury Communications Ltd v *Scott-Garner*

[1983] IRLR 494, Court of Appeal

The facts of this case are set out at p. 658 (Chapter 11, Section 3.B(i)).

SIR JOHN DONALDSON: … Proceeding by the appropriate stages, the questions and my answers are as follows:

(i) **Q.** Has Mercury shown that there is a serious issue to be tried?
A. Yes.

(ii) **Q.** Has Mercury shown that it has a real prospect of succeeding in its claim for a permanent injunction at the trial?
A. Yes.

(iii) **Q.** If Mercury succeeded, would it be adequately compensated by damages for the loss which it suffered as a result of the union being free to continue to take industrial action pending the trial?
A. No. Mercury is in a relatively frail condition as a newcomer to the field and has very large sums of money invested in the project. New customers cannot be attracted, whilst industrial action is threatened

and the losses will vastly exceed the maximum liability which can be imposed upon the union, namely £250,000 [see now TULR(C)A 1992, s. 22].

(iv) **Q.** If the union were to succeed at the trial in establishing its defence under [TULR(C)A 1992, s. 219], would it be adequately compensated by an award under the cross- undertaking?
A. Yes. The union would suffer no loss since, on this hypothesis, the dispute is wholly or mainly about redundancy and there is no suggestion that a temporary cessation in the industrial action would cause or hasten the redundancy.

(v) **Q.** Where does the balance of convenience lie?
A. It lies in protecting Mercury pending the trial of the action.

■ QUESTION

Do you agree with the reasoning of Sir John Donaldson in determining the balance of convenience? Have the commercial interests of the company been given a disproportionate weighting relative to the less tangible and unquantifiable interests of the union members?

C: Damages

TRADE UNION AND LABOUR RELATIONS (CONSOLIDATION) ACT 1992

22. Limit on damages awarded against trade unions in actions in tort

(1) This section applies to any proceedings in tort brought against a trade union, except—
   (a) proceedings for personal injury as a result of negligence, nuisance or breach of duty;
   (b) proceedings for breach of duty in connection with the ownership, occupation, possession, control or use of property;
   (c) proceedings brought by virtue of Part I of the Consumer Protection Act 1987 (product liability).

(2) In any proceedings in tort to which this section applies the amount which may be awarded against the union by way of damages shall not exceed the following limit—

Number of members of union	Maximum award of damages
Less than 5,000	£10,000
5,000 or more but less than 25,000	£50,000
25,000 or more but less than 100,000	£125,000
100,000 or more	£250,000

NOTE: These limits apply in 'any proceedings in tort brought against a trade union'. The effect of this phrase is that where a union is sued by various claimants (e.g. the employer in dispute, customers, suppliers, etc.) for the damages caused to them by the unlawful action, then the maximum will be applied to them separately. In this way, a large union, such as the T&GWU, could find it will be liable to pay well over the £250,000 in damages arising from any one dispute. You should also note these maximums do not apply in respect of the size of any fine imposed for contempt of court where there is a failure to comply with the terms of the injunction. Nor do the limits on damages include the legal costs the defendant union may have to pay. Hepple and Fredman cite the example of the *Stockport Messenger* action in 1983 against the National Graphical Association, as a result of which the union lost one-tenth of its assets.

> The damages against the union were assessed at £131,000 plus interest (which included aggravated and exemplary damages in relation to proved losses). When this was added to the £675,000 fines for contempt of court for non-compliance with an injunction, and legal costs of sequestration, it was estimated in December 1985 that the union had lost over £1 million. [*Labour Law and Industrial Relations in Great Britain*, 2nd edn (Alphen aan den Rijn: Kluwer, 1992), p. 212; see also *Messenger Newspapers Group Ltd* v *National Graphical Association (1982)* [1984] ICR 345.]

D: The citizen and the control of industrial action

TRADE UNION AND LABOUR RELATIONS (CONSOLIDATION) ACT 1992

235A. Industrial action affecting supply of goods or services to an individual

(1) Where an individual claims that—

    (a) any trade union or other person has done, or is likely to do, an unlawful act to induce any person to take part, or to continue to take part, in industrial action, and

    (b) an effect, or a likely effect, of the industrial action is or will be to—

        (i) prevent or delay the supply of goods or services, or

        (ii) reduce the quality of goods or services supplied,

to the individual making the claim, he may apply to the High Court or the Court of Session for an order under this section.

(2) For the purposes of this section an act to induce any person to take part, or to continue to take part, in industrial action is unlawful—

    (a) if it is actionable in tort by any one or more persons, or

    (b) (where it is or would be the act of a trade union) if it could form the basis of an application by a member under section 62.

(3) In determining whether an individual may make an application under this section it is immaterial whether or not the individual is entitled to be supplied with the goods or services in question.

(4) Where on an application under this section the court is satisfied that the claim is well-founded, it shall make such order as it considers appropriate for requiring the person by whom the act of inducement has been, or is likely to be, done to take steps for ensuring—

    (a) that no, or no further, act is done by him to induce any persons to take part or to continue to take part in the industrial action, and

    (b) that no person engages in conduct after the making of the order by virtue of having been induced by him before the making of the order to take part or continue to take part in the industrial action.

(5) Without prejudice to any other power of the court, the court may on an application under this section grant such interlocutory relief (in Scotland, such interim order) as it considers appropriate.

(6) For the purposes of this section an act of inducement shall be taken to be done by a trade union if it is authorised or endorsed by the union; and the provisions of section 20(2) to (4) apply for the purposes of determining whether such an act is to be taken to be so authorised or endorsed.

Those provisions also apply in relation to proceedings for failure to comply with an order under this section as they apply in relation to the original proceedings.

NOTES

1. The Green Paper *Industrial Relations in the 1990s*, while not proposing an outright ban on strikes in the public services, did advocate further legal constraints. It proposed that customers of public services within the scope of the so-called Citizen's Charter should have the right to bring proceedings to prevent or restrain the unlawful organisation of industrial action in, or affecting, any such service.

   While the Green Paper concerned itself solely with industrial action in the public services, TURERA 1993 extended the right to cover *all* industrial action, whether it takes place in the public sector or the private sector. Moreover, unlike the Green Paper, the Act does not make the exercise of the right conditional on the fact that no employer or union member had sought to challenge the legality of the industrial action in the courts.

2. The 1993 Act also created a new Commissioner for Protection against Unlawful Industrial Action, who would have the power, on application, to grant assistance for proceedings against a trade union under the right in TULR(C)A 1992, s. 235A. In 1996–7 only two formal applications for assistance were received. Of these, one was granted assistance. In addition, the Commissioner's office issued 1,027 information sheets, 233 guides and 369 reports at a cost to the taxpayer of £91,388. The office was abolished by the Employment Relations Act 1999, s. 28.

■ QUESTION

Why do you think the Conservative Government deemed it appropriate for individuals who wish to sue trade unions to be provided with legal assistance?

E: Workers whose right lawfully to withdraw their labour is wholly or partly restricted

(i) The armed forces

INCITEMENT TO DISAFFECTION ACT 1934

1. Penalty on persons endeavouring to seduce members of His Majesty's forces from their duty or allegiance

If any person maliciously and advisedly endeavours to seduce any member of His Majesty's forces from his duty or allegiance to His Majesty, he shall be guilty of an offence under this Act.

NOTE: Those taking the industrial action can be charged with desertion or mutiny.

(ii) The police

POLICE ACT 1996

91. Causing disaffection

(1) Any person who causes, or attempts to cause, or does any act calculated to cause disaffection amongst the members of any police force, or induces or attempts to induce, or does any act calculated to induce, any member of a police force to withhold his services, shall be guilty of an offence and liable—

    (a) on summary conviction, to imprisonment for a term not exceeding six months or to a fine not exceeding the statutory maximum, or to both;

    (b) on conviction of indictment, to imprisonment for a term not exceeding two years or to a fine or to both.

(2) This section applies to special constables appointed for a police area as it applies to members of a police force.

NOTE: Following an abortive strike in 1919, it was made a criminal offence to take any actions likely to cause disaffection or breach of discipline by members of the police force. This law is now contained in the Police Act 1996, s. 91. This statute also forbids police officers the right to join a trade union, though if they are already union members when they enlist, permission may be granted to retain that membership. The police may join the Police Federation, but that is not a trade union as such and is not affiliated to the TUC.

(iii) Prison officers

As a result of the Criminal Justice and Public Order Act 1994, s. 127, it is unlawful to induce a prison officer to take industrial action. As in other, similar, torts, it is the inducement that is unlawful: actually withholding services or committing breaches of discipline will not be within the section. The tort created by this section is only actionable by the Home Secretary. He or she is entitled to apply for an injunction to present an apprehended breach of duty without the need to show that he would suffer any actual loss or damage.

(iv) Communications workers

POST OFFICE ACT 1953

58. Opening or delaying of postal packets by officers of the Post Office

(1) If any person engaged in the business of the Post Office, contrary to his duty, opens, or procures or suffers to be opened, any postal packet in the course of transmission by post, or wilfully detains or delays, or procures or suffers to be detained or delayed, any such postal packet, he shall be guilty of a misdemeanour and be liable to imprisonment for a term not exceeding two years or to a fine, or to both.

NOTE: See also the Telecommunications Act 1984, ss. 44–5, which created similar offences in relation to telecommunications. The 1984 Act also created a new civil liability of inducing a breach of the licensed operator's duty to operate the telecommunications system or to interfere with the performance of that duty. Liability is established when the action is taken wholly or *partly* to achieve such a result (s. 18(5)–(7)). Industrial action by telecommunication workers could clearly fall foul of this form of liability and, in this context, it will be irrelevant that they are acting in contemplation or furtherance of a trade dispute.

(v) Merchant seafarers

The Merchant Shipping Acts create a variety of criminal offences which could be used against those who organise or take part in industrial action *while the ship is at sea*, e.g. in breach of duty endangering a ship, life or limb (Merchant Shipping Act 1995, s. 58); concerted disobedience and neglect of duty (s. 59).

(vi) Aliens

The Aliens Restriction (Amendment) Act 1919, s. 3(2), makes it a crime punishable by three months' imprisonment for an alien to promote industrial unrest unless engaged bona fide in the industry for at least two years. This piece of xenophobic legislation owes its place on the statute book to the panic which followed the Russian Revolution and the fear that foreign agitators were plotting a similar insurrection in Britain.

(vii) Endangering life

TRADE UNION AND LABOUR RELATIONS (CONSOLIDATION) ACT 1992

240. Breach of contract involving injury to persons or property

(1) A person commits an offence who wilfully and maliciously breaks a contract of service or hiring, knowing or having reasonable cause to believe that the probable consequence of his so doing, either alone or in combination with others, will be—

    (a) to endanger human life or cause serious bodily injury, or

    (b) to expose valuable property, whether real or personal, to destruction or serious injury.

(2) Subsection (1) applies equally whether the offence is committed from malice conceived against the person endangered or injured or, as the case may be, the owner of the property destroyed or injured, or otherwise.

(3) A person guilty of an offence under this section is liable on summary conviction to imprisonment for a term not exceeding three months or to a fine not exceeding level 2 on the standard scale or both.

(4) This section does not apply to seamen.

NOTE: Originally enacted as the Conspiracy and Protection of Property Act 1875, s. 5, this offence might be relevant to a wide range of occupations engaged in industrial action, e.g. hospital workers, firemen, dustmen, etc., but there is no record of this mid-Victorian provision ever being used.

F: Emergency powers

In the event of a national emergency, the Government possesses extremely wide powers to intervene in an industrial dispute. Under the Emergency Powers Acts of 1920 and 1964, the Government may proclaim a state of emergency and make regulations where there have occurred 'events of such a nature as to be calculated, by interfering with the supply and distribution of food, water or light, or with the means of locomotion, to deprive the community, or any substantial portion of the community, of the essentials of life.' The proclamation must be renewed after one month and Parliament must approve the regulations made by the Government.

While the Act gives almost unlimited power to the Government to make regulations, it cannot make it an offence to take part in a strike or to persuade others to do so, and it cannot introduce military or industrial conscription.

An emergency has been proclaimed 12 times since 1920 (including the seamen's strike in 1966, the docks strike in 1972, the miners' strike in 1972 and the coal and electricity shortages in 1973).

In addition, the Government has the power to call in the armed forces to be used on 'urgent work of national importance', and this power may be exercised without any proclamation or consultation with Parliament (see the Defence (Armed Forces) Regulations 1939, now made permanent by the Emergency Powers Act 1964, s. 2).

More recently, the legislation which privatised the electricity and water industries provides ministers with wide powers to issue confidential directions to the relevant operators for purposes which include 'mitigating the effects of any civil emergency which may occur'. The Secretary of State must lay a copy of every direction he or she gives before Parliament unless he or she 'is of the opinion that disclosure of the direction is against the interests of national security' or, in the case of electricity supply, he or she considers that it would be against the commercial interests of any person (Electricity Act 1989, s. 96; Water Act 1989, s. 170). (The Telecommunication Act 1984, s. 94, provides powers of direction.)

On the assumption that industrial action could come within the definition of a 'civil emergency', Gillian Morris has observed:

In the event of industrial action taking place the powers to regulate supplies which previously would have required approval under the Emergency Powers Act 1920 may now be exercised without the need for parliamentary involvement. At the same time as privatising these services, therefore, the Government has increased considerably its scope for taking measures on a wholly unaccountable basis to counter the impact of industrial action. ['Industrial action in essential services' (1991) 20 ILJ 89, at p. 82]

INDEX

References such as '178–9' indicate (not necessarily continuous) discussion of a topic across a range of pages. Wherever possible in the case of topics with many references, these have either been divided into sub-topics or only the most significant discussions of the topic are listed. Because the entire work is about 'employment law' the use of this term (and certain others which occur constantly throughout the book) as an entry point has been restricted. Information will be found under the corresponding detailed topics.

Revision & study guides from the **No.1** legal education publisher

When you're aiming high, reach for credible, high quality revision and study guides that will help you consolidate knowledge, focus your revision, and maximise your potential.

Oxford's **Concentrate** series

When you're serious about success

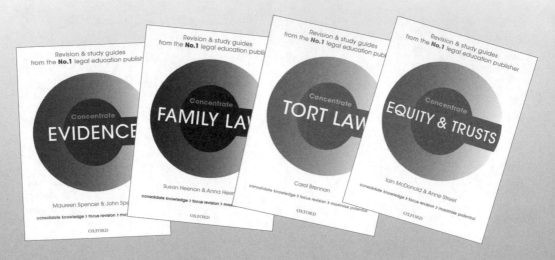

Oxford's **Q&A** series

Don't just answer the question: nail it